Goodheart-Willcox
automotive encyclopedia

fundamental principles, operation, construction, service, repair

WILLIAM K. TOBOLDT

LARRY JOHNSON

STEVEN W. OLIVE

South Holland, Illinois

THE GOODHEART-WILLCOX COMPANY, INC.

Publishers

WILLIAM K. TOBOLDT

Author of Diesel, Fundamentals, Service, Repair; Fix Your Ford, Fix Your Chevrolet; Auto Body Repairing and Repainting. Member, Society of Automotive Engineers. Associate Member, Automotive Engine Rebuilders Association. Associate Member, Association of Diesel Specialists.

LARRY JOHNSON

Author of Fix Your Volkswagen. Certified General Automobile Mechanic by National Institute for Automotive Service Excellence. Affiliate Member, Society of Automotive Engineers.

STEVEN W. OLIVE

State champion in the Illinois Plymouth Troubleshooting contest; Certified mechanic by the National Institute for Automotive Service Excellence; Associates degree in Automotive Technology from Southern Illinois University at Carbondale; Bachelor of Science degree in Occupational Education from Southern Illinois University at Carbondale; Masters of Education (Phi Delta Kappa) from the University of Illinois at Champaign-Urbana; Affiliate Member of the Society of Automotive Engineers.

Copyright 1989

by

THE GOODHEART-WILLCOX COMPANY, INC.

Previous Editions Copyright 1983, 1981, 1979, 1977, 1972, 1970, 1968

Library of Congress Catalog Card Number 89-11244
International Standard Book Number 0-87006-691-9

23456789-89-43210

Library of Congress Cataloging in Publication Data

Main entry under title:

Goodheart-Willcox automotive encyclopedia.

Includes index.
1. Automobiles. 2. Automobiles — Maintenance and repair. I. Toboldt, William King,
II. Johnson, Larry, III. Olive, Steven W.
IV. Title: Automotive encyclopedia.
TL205.G66 1989 629'.2'222 89-11244
ISBN 0-87006-691-9

The following figures are ''reproduced with permission of the Howard W. Sams and Co., the publisher, Indianapolis, Understanding Automotive Electronics by William B. Ribbens, ©1988.''

Figures: 29-44, 29-45, 29-46, 29-48, 29-51, 29-54, 29-55, 29-56, 29-57, 29-64, 29-66, 29-67, 29-72.

INTRODUCTION

The automotive service field offers many career opportunities for anyone who is mechanically inclined and has the educational background. This background must include a thorough knowledge of automotive fundamentals and extensive hands-on training in service and repair work.

AUTOMOTIVE ENCYCLOPEDIA is a book of fundamentals. It covers passenger car construction, principles of operation, and basic service procedures. This is the foundation on which a sound, thorough knowlege of auto mechanics is based. Once these fundamentals are learned, know-how through experience will enable you to diagnose trouble and perform needed repairs.

AUTOMOTIVE ENCYCLOPEDIA also explores the many sciences involved in vehicle operation: the fundamentals of electricity, electronics, computers, hydraulics, pneumatics, internal combustion, power transmission, steering and suspension geometry. Basic information on hand tools, fasteners, measuring instruments, meters, analyzers, and service equipment is also included.

In-depth coverage is devoted to engine fundamentals and service, emission controls, transmissions and transaxles, front wheel drive, four wheel drive, and anti-lock braking. Special emphasis is given to theory and diagnosis of computerized ignition/fuel systems. It is essential that you have a complete understanding of computers since every system and component on the car will eventually be monitored by the computer.

The final chapter in AUTOMOTIVE ENCYCLOPEDIA explains how to make full use of car manufacturers' service manuals. This information is especially helpful with respect to recommended service procedures, obtaining specifications, and trouble codes of computerized systems.

William K. Toboldt

Larry Johnson

Steven W. Olive

TABLE OF CONTENTS

Learn about anti-lock brake systems (ABS) in Chapter 52.   (Buick)

Learn how a speedometer works in Chapter 57. (GM Hughes Electronics)

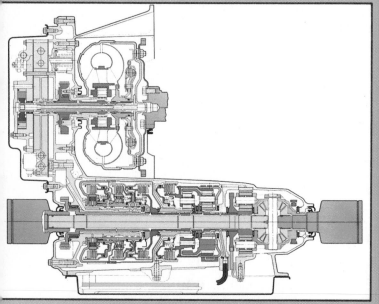

Learn about automatic transmissions and transaxles in Chapters 41, 42, and 43.

Learn about fuel injection in Chapter 26.   (Chevrolet)

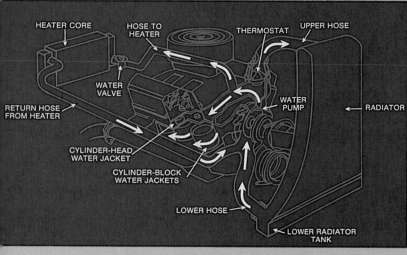

Learn more about engine cooling systems in Chapter 17.   (Everco)

Learn about turbocharging in Chapter 20.   (Pontiac)

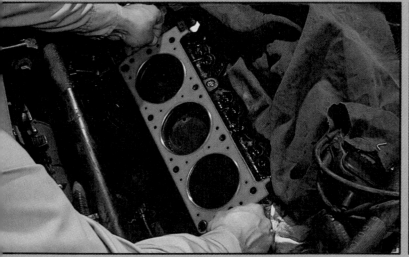

Learn about engines and engine repairs in Chapters 6 through 16.   (Fel-Pro, Inc.)

Learn about computerized tune-up and troubleshooting equipment in Chapters 35 and 36.   (Buick)*

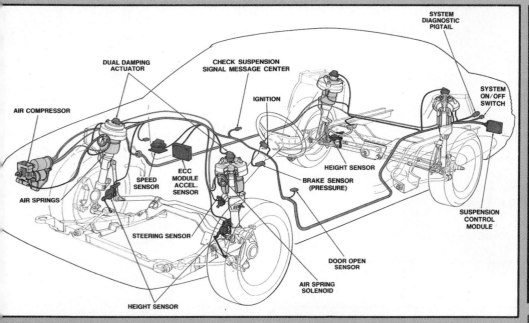

Learn about computerized suspension systems in Chapter 47.   (Ford)

Learn how to spray paint in Chapter 59.
(PPG/Ditzler)

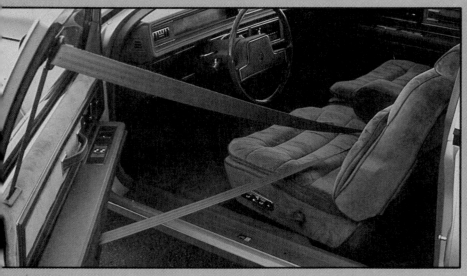

Learn about built-in safety systems in Chapter 54.

Learn about distributorless ignition systems in Chapter 29.   (Buick)

7

HEADLIGHTS OR HIGH BEAM	PARKING LIGHTS	TURN SIGNALS	HAZARD WARNING FLASHER	BRAKE
WINDSHIELD WASHER	WINDSHIELD WIPER	WINDSHIELD DEFROSTER	REAR WINDOW WIPER/WASHER	REAR WINDOW DEFOGGER
VENTILATION FAN	LIGHTER	DOOR LOCK/UNLOCK	TRUNK/HATCHBACK RELEASE	HOOD RELEASE
RADIO SELECTOR	RADIO VOLUME	SPEAKER BALANCE	FUEL	ENGINE COOLANT TEMPERATURE
FASTEN SEAT BELTS	CHOKE	ENGINE OIL PRESSURE	FUSE	BATTERY CHARGING SYSTEM
CAUTION: POSSIBLE INJURY	PROTECT EYES BY SHIELDING	CAUSTIC BATTERY ACID COULD CAUSE BURNS	AVOID SPARKS OR FLAME	SPARK OR FLAME COULD EXPLODE BATTERY

International symbols.   (Cadillac)

Chapter 1

AUTOMOTIVE TOOLS

After studying this chapter, you will be able to:
● Identify the various automotive tools.
● Describe the purpose of each tool.
● Use each tool safely.
● Select the right tool for the job.

TOOLS

Tools play an important part in any automotive service operation. Every repair job requires the use of at least one hand tool to remove, disassemble or adjust parts and replace units.

It follows naturally that anyone studying to be an auto mechanic should be thoroughly familiar with tools that will be used on the job. In addition, the beginning mechanic must learn the correct methods of using tools, not only to perform the work as quickly as possible, but also to complete the job with maximum accuracy and safety.

Cars have become increasingly complex, and a greater variety of hand tools is needed to service them. Without this "kit" of tools, an auto technician could not find employment. The kit represents a large investment, but experienced mechanics realize that good quality hand tools help them turn out precision jobs quickly and safely. When a mechanic's tool kit is complete, it will include the right tool for every job, Fig. 1-1.

Tool care is important, too. Apprentice mechanics soon learn that time will be saved if they take good care of their hand tools. This includes cleaning after use and returning the tools to their proper place in the kit to avoid future loss of time looking for a particular tool.

WRENCHES

One of the most important and most-used tools in a mechanic's kit is the open-end wrench, Fig. 1-2 and Fig. 1-3. These tools are used for loosening or tightening bolts and nuts.

Wrench size is determined by the width of the opening, and both English and metric sizes are available. A standard set of open-end wrenches in the English system usually ranges from 3/8 in. up to and including 1 in., increasing by 1/16 in. steps.

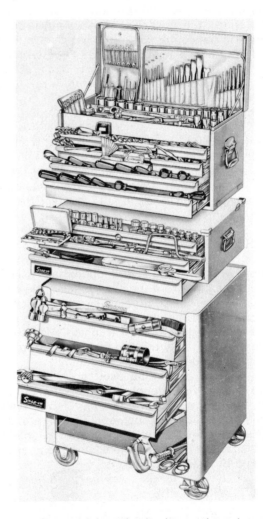

Fig. 1-1. Successful mechanics have a large investment in tools.

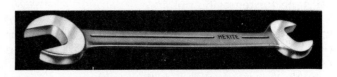

Fig. 1-2. An open-end wrench.

9

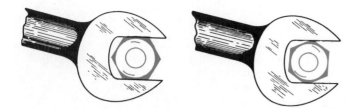

Fig. 1-3. Left. Select the wrench that fits the nut snugly. Right. If the wrench is too big, the nut will become rounded.

Fig. 1-4. Box wrench that is offset 15 degrees. The offset provides clearance for the mechanics knuckles.

Fig. 1-5. Flare nut wrench is designed for working on line fittings.

In the SI metric system, a typical set of open-end wrenches range in size from 7 millimeters (mm) to 10 millimeters (mm). Larger and smaller sizes are available in both English and metric wrenches, but usually on an individual wrench basis rather than part of a set.

To permit the open-end wrench to turn a nut in a restricted space, the open end of the wrench is designed at an angle to the center line of the handle. Usually this is 15 deg. By first placing one side of the wrench up, then the other, it is possible to turn the nut a few degrees at a time in each position until the nut is removed.

Wrenches are also made with openings at an angle of 22 1/2 deg., 30 deg., 60 deg., and 90 deg. to the handle.

While the smallest opening of a standard wrench set is usually 3/8 in., smaller wrenches known as "miniature," are also available. Such wrenches are needed for work on ignition systems and electrical connections. Openings range in size in 1/32 in. steps from 3/16 in. to 15/32 in.

Fig. 1-6. Crowfoot wrench must be used with an extension.

BOX WRENCHES

Box type wrenches, Fig. 1-4, reduce the possibility of the wrench slipping from the nut. Usually, the box is a double hexagon. The 12 grooves engage the corners of the nut and permit moving the wrench through an arc of as little as 30 deg. before repositioning. Also, the walls of the box are relatively thin, so less space surrounding the nut is required.

A box wrench cannot be used on tubing fittings. However, a box type wrench with a section cut away, Fig. 1-5, and a crowfoot wrench, Fig. 1-6 is available.

A combination box and open-end wrench is shown in Fig. 1-7. Both ends of this wrench are designed to fit the same size nut. This is a general purpose wrench and is preferred by many technicians.

Fig. 1-7. Combination wrench has a box wrench at one end and an open-end wrench at the other.

RATCHET WRENCHES

Ratchet wrenches, Fig. 1-8, like the box wrench, completely surround the nut to be tightened or loosened. In that way, there is little chance of the wrench slipping from the nut. With assorted handles they greatly reduce the time for removing nuts.

Usually, the ratchet wrench used in automotive work usually has either 12 or 6 grooves to engage the corners of the nut. Socket wrenches come in sizes from approximately 3/16 in. to 1 5/8 in.

Sockets manufactured with six grooves or eight grooves give added protection against slippage. The

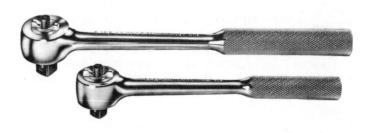

Fig. 1-8. A ratchet speeds the process of removing nuts and bolts.

drive opening of the socket (opening in which wrench handle is placed) is 1/4 in., 3/8 in., 1/2 in., or 3/4 in. square. This is known as the "drive." In addition, one manufacturer has a socket wrench with 7/16 in. drive, which is designed to take the place of both the 3/8 in. and 1/2 in. drive socket sets.

Mechanics usually have a set of 1/4 in., 3/8 in., and 1/2 in. drive ratchet wrenches in their kits. The 1/4 in. square drive socket set usually includes sockets ranging in size from 3/16 in. to 9/16. The 3/8 in. square drive socket set has sockets from 1/4 in. to 1 in. The 1/2 in. square drive socket set is designed for use on nuts ranging in size from 3/8 in. to 1 1/2 in.

In addition to sockets of standard depth, extra deep sockets are also available. Deep sockets are used primarily for removing spark plugs, sending units, etc., Fig. 1-9.

Ratchet wrenches used in automotive service work have detachable handles of various types. These handles have various purposes. Some are designed to give increased leverage, others to facilitate reaching areas which are normally obstructed, Fig. 1-10. Still others are designed to speed the removal and installation of nuts.

Fig. 1-11 illustrates a socket speed handle which as the name implies is designed to run the nut on or off the bolt rapidly.

Various types of accessory wrench handles are shown in Fig. 1-12. A socket sliding handle, A, makes it possible to slide the handle back and forth without detaching it from the nut. A flex handle, B, provides greater leverage and, in addition, the angle of the handle in relation to the nut can be changed.

A ratchet handle is shown at C in Fig. 1-12. This is a very important tool since the handle can be swung back and forth to tighten or loosen the nut without detaching the handle from the socket or the socket from the nut. A socket and short extension is shown at D, while a longer extension is shown at E. Extensions permit reaching down into enclosed areas.

Inside the head of the ratchet handle is a pawl which fits into one of the ratchet teeth. Pulling on the handle in one direction, the pawl holds and the socket turns. Moving the handle in the opposite direction, the pawl ratchets over the teeth, permitting the handle to be backed up without moving the socket.

Since the teeth of the ratchet are relatively fine, the ratchet handle can be swung through a very small angle or arc in order to get a new grip. By using a ratchet wrench, it is not necessary to disengage the socket from the nut until it is removed.

If it is not possible to get a direct pull when wrenching off a nut, a univeral joint is available for use between the handle and the socket. Also available are popular size socket wrenches complete with universal joints. See Fig. 1-13. Note that these are six point sockets. Universal sockets also come in eight point and 12 point sets.

Fig. 1-9. Left. Conventional length sockets. Right. Deep well sockets are used for removing spark plugs.

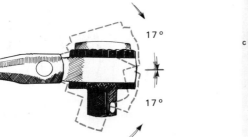

Fig. 1-10. Some ratchets have a flex-head. This allows the ratchet to reach spots that a normal ratchet cannot. (Central Tools)

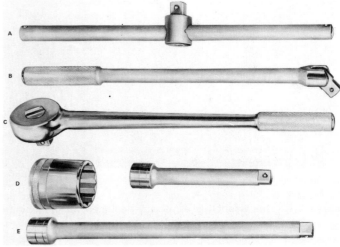

Fig. 1-12. A—Sliding T handle. B—Breaker bar. C—Ratchet. D—Socket. E—Extension.

Fig. 1-11. A speed wrench.

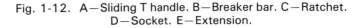

Fig. 1-13. A set of swivel sockets is useful in removing bolts in hard to reach places.

SPECIAL WRENCHES

Many wrenches are designed to do one specific job. Fig. 1-14 illustrates a wrench used to loosen and tighten bleeder screws on hydraulic brake systems.

TORQUE WRENCHES

Often, a nut must be tightened to a specified amount (torque). If overtightened, the mating parts may be distorted and leakage (oil, coolant, compression, etc.) may occur. Cylinder head bolts and engine bearing nuts and bolts especially need to be "torqued." When tightening these fasteners, a torque wrench must be used. See Fig. 1-15.

Torque wrenches indicate torque tightness in foot pounds, inch pounds or newton meters. To change foot pounds to newton meters, multiply by 1.355. When using a torque wrench, clean and oil the threads of the fasteners so that no additional friction will be present. Torque wrenches are used with special, heavy-duty sockets.

PLIERS

There are many different types of pliers used in automotive work. One most commonly used is the 6 in. combination slip-joint pliers, Fig. 1-16. The slip-joint permits the jaws to be opened wider at the hinge for gripping larger diameters.

Diagonal cutting pliers, Fig. 1-17, are needed not only for cutting wire but are also used for removing cotter pins.

Long nose pliers, Fig. 1-18, either the flat nose or duck bill type, are needed frequently in recovering a washer or a nut which has dropped into an inaccessible place. They are also used to aid in positioning small parts.

The interlocking joint gripping pliers, Fig. 1-19, is a variation of the slip-joint pliers in that it is adjustable. The opening of the pliers can be adjusted to several different sizes by means of a dog which engages any one of the circular channels. In that way, the jaws of the pliers remain approximately parallel regardless of the size of the opening.

Fig. 1-16. Slip-joint pliers.

Fig. 1-17. Diagonal cutting pliers are used to cut wire and to pull cotter pins.

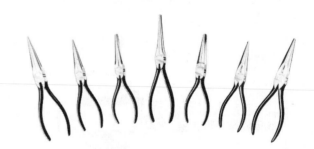

Fig. 1-18. An assortment of long and needle nose pliers.

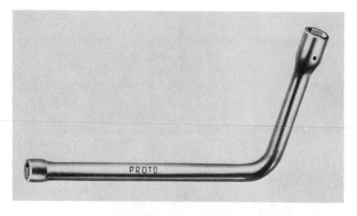

Fig. 1-14. This wrench is especially designed for loosening brake bleeder screws.

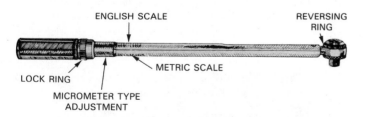

Fig. 1-15. A "click" type torque wrench. An audible "click" is heard when the pre-set torque has been reached. Note that one side of the wrench has a metric scale, while the other side is English. (Central Tools)

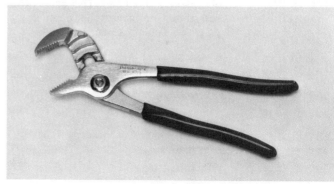

Fig. 1-19. Interlocking adjustable joint pliers.

One of the most versatile tools in the mechanic's kit is the vise-grip, or locking pliers, Fig. 1-20. When locked in position on a part, it will grip it firmly even though the area contacted by the jaws of the pliers is extremely small. It has an infinite number of uses, ranging from holding two parts together while they are being worked on, to gripping the end of a broken stud and turning it out of its threaded hole.

Snap ring pliers, Fig. 1-21, are important tools in every repair kit. They are used to remove snap rings from various parts, such as hydraulic valve lifters, transmission shafts, and bearings.

BRAKE PLIERS

Special pliers designed to assist in the removal and installation of brake shoes and brake shoe springs are also available. See Fig. 1-22.

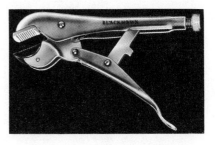

Fig. 1-20. Locking pliers.

Fig. 1-21. External snap ring pliers.

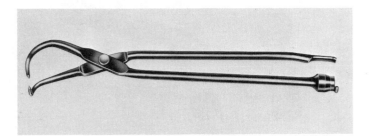

Fig. 1-22. Brake pliers are necessary in performing a brake job.

STUD REMOVERS

When it becomes necessary to remove and replace the stud, the preferred method is to use a stud remover, Fig. 1-23. These tools are designed with a 3/8 in. or 1/2 in. drive, so they can be used with a ratchet wrench.

SCREWDRIVERS

There are many different types of screwdrivers and each type has many different sizes. The size of a screwdriver is determined by the size of the bit (tip). The standard blade type screwdriver, Fig. 1-24, is determined by the width and thickness of the blade. The Phillips screwdriver, Fig. 1-25, comes in sizes #0 (the smallest), #1, #2 which is the most common size, #3, and #4 (the largest). The posi-drive screwdriver, Fig. 1-26, is similar to the Phillips screwdriver, but provides a tighter, positive fit. This prevents the head of the screw (where the bit is inserted into the head of the screw) from being rounded. The clutch driver, Fig. 1-27, is sometimes referred to as a figure eight or butterfly driver. The Torx head screw, Fig. 1-28, is used in many areas of the car.

Fig. 1-23. Stud remover is used with a ratchet.

Fig. 1-24. A blade type screwdriver must fit the slot.

Fig. 1-25. A Phillips screw head.

Fig. 1-26. A posi-drive head provides a positive grip.

It is rapidly replacing Phillips-type screws. The Torx driver comes in sizes T15 (the smallest), T20, T25, and T27 (the largest). The magnetic screwdriver, Fig. 1-29, is extremely useful when working on the dash of the car.

SETSCREW WRENCHES

The Allen wrench, Fig. 1-30, is hex shaped and comes in sizes .028 in. to 3/4 in. The speed hex wrench, Fig. 1-31, has a ball at one end of the hex wrench. The ball allows the wrench to swivel.

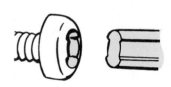

Fig. 1-27. A clutch screw head.

Fig. 1-28. A Torx screw head.

Fig. 1-29. This magnetic screwdriver has interchangeable bits. Each bit is magnetized. (S-K Tools)

Fig. 1-30. An Allen wrench is used on hex socket heads. (Deere & Co.)

HAMMERS

Automotive mechanics require hammers of various types and sizes. The most important is the ball peen hammer, Fig. 1-32. The flat portion of the head used for most hammering is called the face. The other end is the peen. When the peen is ball-shaped, it is known as a ball peen, which is used primarily for riveting work.

Ball peen hammers usually are classed according to the weight of the head without the handle. A good hammer set for automotive work would include 4 oz., 1 lb. and 3 lb. hammers. A small hammer is very handy for light work.

If there is any danger of damaging the surface or work, a "soft" hammer, Fig. 1-33, should be used. These special hammers have faces of rawhide, plastics, brass or lead.

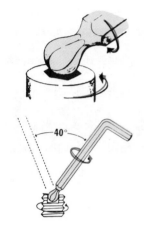

Fig. 1-31. A speed hex wrench can swivel in tight spots. (Lisle Co.)

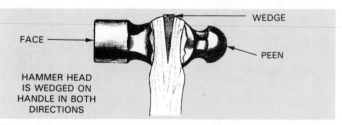

Fig. 1-32. Wood or steel wedges hold hammer head in place.

Fig. 1-33. A soft face hammer prevents marring the work surface.

Also available are "dinging" hammers and other peening and shrinking hammers of various sizes and shapes for straightening sheet metal on automobile bodies.

The hammer should be gripped close to the end of the handle, Fig. 1-34. In this way a heavier blow can be struck with less effort. Be careful not to strike the work with the edge of the hammer face, Fig. 1-35. The full face of the hammer should contact the head of the chisel or other work.

The end of the hammer handle should not be used for bumping purposes, as this will quickly split and ruin the handle. Neither should hammer handles be used as levers.

The hammer handle should always be tight on the head. Never work with a hammer with a loose head. This is dangerous as the head may fly off when the hammer is swung and cause an injury.

The eye or hole in the head of the hammer is made with a slight taper in both directions from the center. After the handle is tapered to fit the eye, it is inserted in the head. A steel wedge is then driven into the end of the handle, Fig. 1-32. This expands the taper in the eye and in that way the handle is wedged in both directions. If the wedge starts to come out, it should be driven in again until it is tight and the handle is secure in the head of the hammer.

CHISELS

Cold chisels, Fig. 1-36, are used for cutting metal, to cut the heads from rivets, chip metal, and to split nuts which have become rusted and cannot be loosened by means of a wrench.

The cape chisel, Fig. 1-36, has a narrow cutting edge. It is used primarily for cutting keyways and narrow grooves.

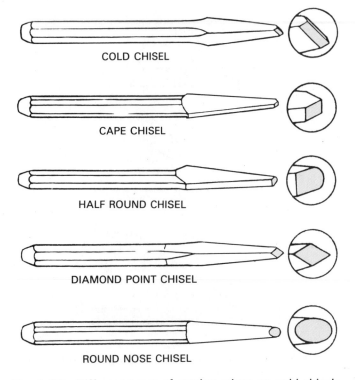

COLD CHISEL

CAPE CHISEL

HALF ROUND CHISEL

DIAMOND POINT CHISEL

ROUND NOSE CHISEL

Fig. 1-36. Different types of cutting edges on cold chisels.

In most cases, auto mechanics will use the cold, or flat chisel, and the sizes most frequently used are 3/8 in., 1/2 in., and 3/4 in.

A rivet buster, Fig. 1-37, is a special form of chisel designed specifically for cutting the heads from rivets. It differs from the conventional cold chisel in that only one side of the cutting edge is ground.

When using a chisel, a right-handed person would hold the tool in his left hand and wield the hammer with his right. The chisel should be held rather loosely with fingers curled around the chisel about one inch from the head of the chisel.

When chipping metal, the depth of the cut is controlled by the angle of the chisel, Fig. 1-38. Deeper cuts are taken as the angle of the chisel approaches the vertical. When chipping, the mechanic should keep his eye on the cutting edge, not on the head of the chisel.

Fig. 1-34. Grip the hammer near the end of the handle.

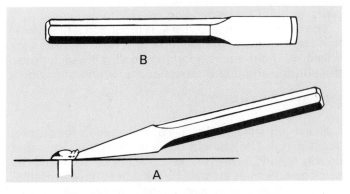

Fig. 1-37. A rivet buster shears the head off of rivets.

Fig. 1-35. Avoid striking the work with the edge of the hammer.

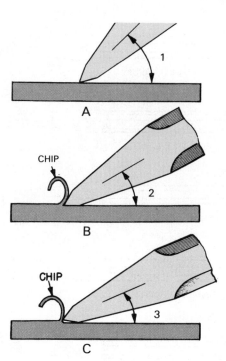

Fig. 1-38. Depth of cut is controlled by angle of chisel.

Goggles should be worn when chipping and grinding, and take precautions so that chips will not strike anyone who is nearby. Never use a chisel on which the head has been mushroomed, as in Fig. 1-39. When struck with a hammer, portions of the mushroom will fly off at high velocity and cause severe injuries. The mushroomed end of the chisel should be ground smooth, as in Fig. 1-40.

When sharpening a cold chisel, Fig. 1-41, the two ground surfaces should form an angle of 60 deg. Rivet busters are ground on one surface only at an angle of approximately 30 deg. See Fig. 1-37.

Many different types of punches, Fig. 1-42, are required in automotive work. The starting punch is designed to punch out rivets after the heads have been cut off. These punches are also used to start driving out straight or tapered pins, Fig. 1-43. After the pin has been driven partly from the hole, the starting punch can no longer be used because of its taper. A pin punch is then used to complete the job of punching out the pin. Pin punches should not be used to start such work because a hard blow on the punch would bend the slender shank.

A lining-up punch has a long taper. It is used to shift parts to bring corresponding holes into alignment.

The center punch, Fig. 1-44, is ground to a fine point. It is used to mark the location of a hole that is to be drilled. Without such a mark, the drill will wander over the surface and drill the hole at the wrong position.

METAL SHEARS

Heavy tin shears, Fig. 1-45, are needed for cutting sheet metal. The straight blade shear is the type most usually needed, however, the curved blade shear and the scroll pivoter snips are also convenient to have available. The curved blade shears are used for making curved cuts, and the scroll pivoter snips follow an irregular line easily.

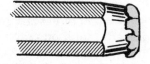

Fig. 1-39. After striking the end of a chisel repeatedly, the end become mushroomed.

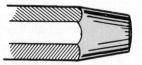

Fig. 1-40. The mushroomed end should be dressed with an electric grinder to prevent tiny pieces of metal from flying off when the hammer strikes this end.

Fig. 1-41. Sharpening the cutting edge of a chisel on an electric grinder.

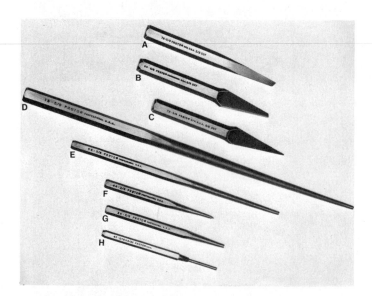

Fig. 1-42. A—Diamond point chisel. B—Cape chisel. C—Round nose chisel. D—Aligning punch. E—Short aligning punch. F—Center punch. G—Starting punch. H—Pin punch.

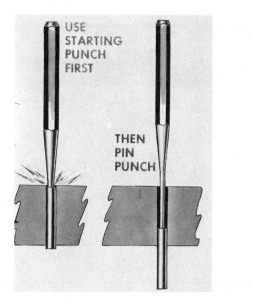

Fig. 1-43. Use starting punch, and then knock out with a pin punch.

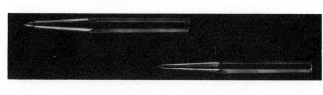

Fig. 1-44. Center punches.

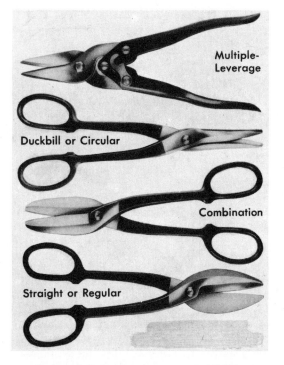

Fig. 1-45. Different types of shears.

ELECTRIC DRILLS

Electric drills, Fig. 1-46, come in several sizes and are a major, labor-saving piece of equipment. They are a must in every mechanic's tool kit, and many mechanics have both a 1/4 in. size and a 1/2 in. size electric drill.

Some drills are provided with special speed controls. This feature is of value because some materials are more easily drilled at slow speeds, while others require a faster speed. For example, soft metals require a faster speed than extremely hard metals. Also, some drills are reversible whereby the drill bit can be backed out if it is necessary.

POWER WRENCHES

Power wrenches (often called impact tools), Fig. 1-47, are designed for loosening and tightening nuts, quickly. Their use results not only in a considerable saving of time, but also a noticeable reduction in fatigue on the part of the mechanic. Designed for use with heavy-duty socket wrenches, both electrical and pneumatic types are available.

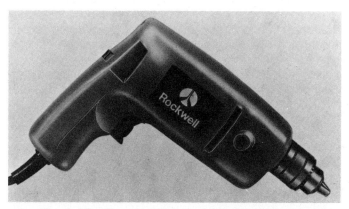

Fig. 1-46. Electric drill is an indispensable tool.

Fig. 1-47. A pneumatic impact tool.

As an example of the time that can be saved by using a power wrench, a valve job on an automotive engine required 4 hr. 20 min. when conventional hand tools were used. When the same job was done with the aid of a power wrench, only 3 hr. 14 min. were required.

FILES

Files are hardened steel hand tools designed to remove metal. They are also used for smoothing metal surfaces and for polishing.

The cutting edges of a file are diagonal rows of parallel teeth. There are more than 20 different types of files with sizes ranging from 3 to 18 in. A file with a single row of parallel teeth is called a single-cut file, Fig. 1-48. Files which have a row of teeth crossing another row in a crisscross pattern are known as double-cut, Fig. 1-48.

Files are graded according to the spacing of the teeth. The terms used to indicate the coarseness or fineness of a file are bastard, second-cut, and smooth. The file may also be either a single-cut or double-cut. The terms coarse and dead-smooth are also used in some classifications. The names of the different parts of a file are shown in Fig. 1-49.

There are many different shapes in which files are available, Fig. 1-50. The mill file is single-cut, tapering in thickness and width for one-third of its length. It is used primarily for fine work and is available with either square or round edges or with one safe edge (without teeth).

A double-cut file, tapering in thickness and width, is known as a flat file. It is used when a faster cut is desired. The hand file is single-cut and similar in shape to a flat file, with parallel sides and a slight taper in thickness. It has square edges, one of which is a safe edge. For rough filing, the bastard file is used.

The round file is tapered and usually single-cut. In larger sizes, it is also available in double-cut. For enlarging large holes, a round 12 in. bastard file is usually used. If the hole is of small diameter, a round 6 in. file, usually known as a rat-tail is used. Untapered round files are also available. The principal use of round files is to enlarge circular openings and file concave surfaces.

The half-round file is a double-cut file, tapering in thickness and width, with one flat and one oval side. It is used mainly for rough filing on concave surfaces.

The triangular file is useful for filing small notches, square or cornered holes. In addition, it can be used for recutting damaged threads on bolts.

As previously pointed out, files with coarse teeth are used when it is desired to remove a lot of metal as quickly as possible. Files with fine teeth remove less metal, but produce a smoother surface. In addition, the type of metal must be considered when selecting a file.

When filing cast iron, first use a bastard file, then use a second-cut file for finishing. On soft steel, a second-cut file is used first, and a smooth-cut for finishing. On hard steel, start with a smooth-cut and finish with a dead-smooth file.

On soft metals, such as brass or bronze, use a bastard-cut first, then a second-cut. On aluminum, babbitt or lead, a Vixen-cut file, Fig. 1-51, similar to those used by automotive body repairmen is preferred. If that type

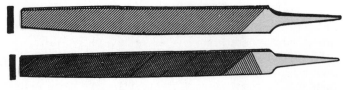

Fig. 1-48. A single-cut or mill file is shown above. A double-cut file is shown below.

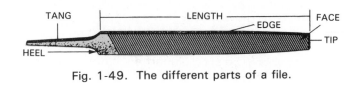

Fig. 1-49. The different parts of a file.

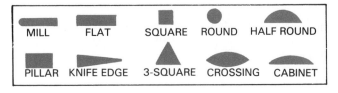

Fig. 1-50. Sectional view of different files.

Fig. 1-51. A Vixen-cut file is used to shape soft metals and body filler.

Fig. 1-52. Soft caps can be easily added and removed from a vise. These prevent marring of soft materials.

file is not available, a bastard file may be used.

Never use a file without a handle since the pointed tang may be driven into the palm of your hand, inflicting a bad wound. Whenever possible, clamp the work in the jaws of a vise. If the work is soft metal, cover the jaws of the vise with soft caps so that the work will not be marked or otherwise damaged, Fig. 1-52.

Another precaution regarding files is that they should never be used as levers. Files are brittle and will quickly break if hammered on or used as levers.

File teeth are designed to cut only when the tool is pushed forward. So the preferred method of filing is to raise the file from the work before drawing it back to start the next stroke.

Only enough pressure should be applied to the file to keep it cutting. Excessive pressure only results in increased effort being required to move the file forward.

The correct way to hold a file is shown in Fig. 1-53.

If you are a right-handed mechanic, grasp the file handle in your right hand. The other end of the file is held in your left hand with the fingers curled over the end. Your feet should be spread apart and your body should lean slightly forward so that your left shoulder will tend to be over the work. In order that a flat surface is filed, the forward movement of the file must be perfectly horizontal. Any rocking of the file will result in a convex surface. However, when filing a round surface, the file should be rocked as shown in Fig. 1-54.

File teeth will tend to become clogged, particularly when soft metals are being filed. As a result such material between the file teeth will tend to scratch the surface being filed. This can be overcome to a degree by first rubbing chalk on the file. To clean the teeth of a file, the teeth should be brushed with a file card or other wire bristled brush.

Files should be hung on a rack when not in use, as placing them in a drawer with other tools will quickly dull the teeth.

RETRIEVING TOOLS

Special tools have been designed to retrieve objects that have been dropped and are in difficult places to reach. A magnetic tool of this type is shown in Fig. 1-55. The magnet is attached to a handle by means of a universal joint, making the tool more flexible. Gripper-type retrieving tools are designed to grip the object.

SOLDERING

Soldering is a method of joining two metals together. On automotive body repair work, solder is used to fill dents to form a smooth surface. Another major use of soldering is in connecting electric wires to instruments and other electrical equipment. This keeps the wires from becoming loose or disconnected as the result of vibration.

Solder is an alloy of varying proportions of lead and tin having a melting point below 800°F. This is know as "soft solder." "Hard solders" (with silver, copper, or nickel bases) have melting points above 800°F., but also below that of the base metal.

The process of soldering consists of first cleaning the surfaces to be soldered. Then the joint is heated and a flux is applied. Flux is a chemical that keeps oxides from forming, thereby permitting the solder to adhere to the surfaces. After the flux is applied, the solder is melted into the joint, Fig. 1-56. This can be done by means of a soldering copper or the flame of a torch.

Soldering coppers, Fig. 1-57, often called soldering irons, are used mostly for soldering small pieces and when there is danger of an open flame damaging nearby parts. Made of copper, the tips of these tools must be given a coating of solder before they are used. Known as tinning, the process is to first file the tip of the copper so that it is clean and smooth. Then heat it, dip it in flux and apply solder.

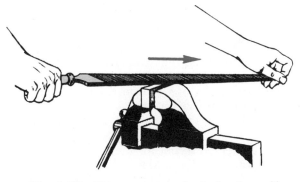

Fig. 1-53. The correct method of using a file.

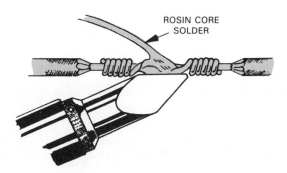

MAGNET

Fig. 1-55. A magnetic retrieving tool.

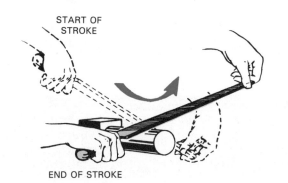

START OF STROKE

END OF STROKE

Fig. 1-54. When filing round objects, the file should be rocked.

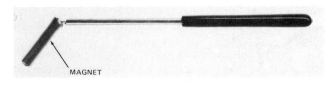

ROSIN CORE SOLDER

Fig. 1-56. Soldering a splice in an electric wire.

Fig. 1-57. A modern electric soldering gun.

Some mechanics prefer to melt the solder on the surface of a building brick, then rub the tip of the copper on the solder. Another method is to use a block of sal ammoniac.

After the iron has been tinned, take care that it is not overheated. That would burn the copper, and would be necessary to re-tin.

On some soldering jobs, it is desirable to first tin the surfaces to be joined, then solder them together. That process is usually followed on larger areas where a strong joint is to be made. It is also used when solder is to be applied to sheet iron. Soldering irons with electric heating elements may be used, Fig. 1-57.

There are many different types of fluxes available. Select the type best suited for the metals to be joined. For electrical connections, a rosin type flux is recommended. An acid type is used when soldering sheet iron.

HACKSAWS

Hacksaws are used to cut metal. As shown in Fig. 1-58, the detachable cutting blade is mounted in a metal frame. Different length frames are available, and some frames are made adjustable so that various size blades can be used. The usual lengths of hacksaw blades are 8, 10, and 12 in. The 10 and 12 in. sizes are most frequently used. For power-driven hacksaws, blades of 12, 14, 17, 18, 21, 24, and 30 in. lengths are available.

Hacksaw blades are made of high grade tool steel, hardened and tempered. There are two types, the all-hard and the flexible. All-hard blades are hardened throughout, while only the teeth of flexible blades are hardened.

The blades are provided with holes at both ends for installation on the pins on the frame. To adjust the tension of the blade, and also to secure it tightly to the frame, the position of one of the pins is adjustable. This adjustment is made by either a wing nut or by turning the handle.

The "set" in a saw refers to the amount the teeth are pushed out in opposite directions from the sides of the blade. The teeth of all hacksaw blades are set to provide clearance for the blade. The usual types of set are alternate, raker, and undulated. In addition, there is a double alternate set.

Blades for hand-operated hacksaws come with 14, 18, 24, and 32 teeth per inch. It is important that the teeth per inch be considered when selecting a hacksaw blade for a particular job, Fig. 1-59. Also, thought must be given to whether the all-hard or flexible blade is more suitable for a particular job.

In general, an all-hard blade is considered best for sawing brass, cast iron, steel, and other stock of heavy cross section. For cutting hollow shapes, and metals of light section such as channel iron, tubing tin, copper, aluminum, or babbitt, a flexible blade is preferable.

The most effective cutting speed is about one stroke per second. When the material is nearly cut through, the pressure on the blade should be reduced to prevent the teeth from catching. When cutting thin stock, it is advisable to clamp it between two pieces of wood or soft metal, then saw through all three pieces. This will prevent the saw from sticking, and also prevent possible damage to the work.

A hole saw is advisable for cutting round holes in metal. Driven by an electric drill, the hole saw is used for drilling large diameter holes in instrument panels and fire walls for the installation of instruments and other accessories. It is provided with a centering or pilot drill for starting and centering the cut.

Hacksaw blade manufacturers recommend that 14-tooth saws be used for cutting soft steel, brass, cast iron and stock of heavy cross section. For cutting drill rod, light angles, high speed steel, tool steel and small solids, 18-tooth blades are recommended. Use 24-tooth blades for cutting brass tubing, heavy BX cable, iron pipe, metal conduit and drill rod. For cutting thin tubing, sheet metal, light BX cable, channels, etc., 32-tooth blades are suggested.

After selecting the correct blade for the material, place it on the pins of the hacksaw frame with the teeth pointing toward the front of the frame. The blade is then stretched tightly in the frame.

If an accurate cut is to be made, it is advisable to mark the stock with a scriber, and nick the work with a file. The nick will make it easier for the saw to start cutting and also insure accuracy. Make sure the work is held securely in a vise, with the line to be cut as close to the vise jaws as possible. Use sufficient pressure on the saw when starting the cut, so that the saw teeth immediately begin to bite into the metal. The hacksaw blade should be held vertically and moved forward with a light steady stroke. At the end of the stroke, relieve the pressure and draw the saw straight back. See Fig. 1-60.

Fig. 1-58. Three different types of hacksaws.

14 TEETH PER INCH

FOR LARGE SECTIONS
OF MILD MATERIAL

18 TEETH PER INCH

FOR LARGE SECTIONS
OF TOUGH STEEL

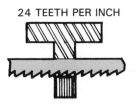

24 TEETH PER INCH

FOR ANGLE IRON, HEAVY
PIPE, BRASS, COPPER

32 TEETH PER INCH

FOR THIN TUBING

KEEP AT LEAST TWO TEETH CUTTING
TO AVOID THIS

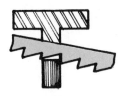

Fig. 1-59. The type of metal to be cut determines the type of hacksaw blade.

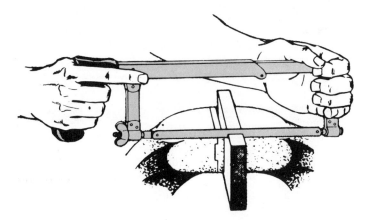

Fig. 1-60. The correct method of using a hacksaw.

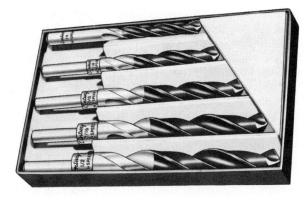

Fig. 1-61. A set of twist drills that all have a 1/4'' shank.

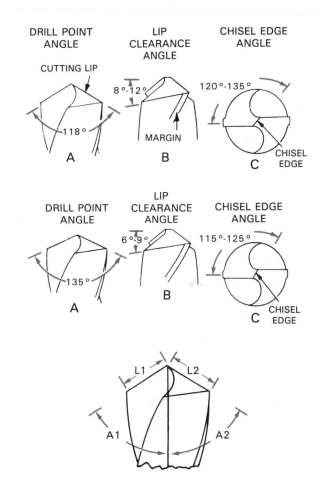

Fig. 1-62. The angles of a twist drill.

TWIST DRILLS

The tool used to do the actual cutting is known as a twist drill, Fig. 1-61. A twist drill has two cutting edges and is made of either carbon steel or high speed steel. However, the former quickly becomes dull and, if heated excessively, will lose its hardness. High speed steel will retain its temper when red hot, so twist drills of that material are preferred. The straight shank drill is generally used in automotive shops.

SHARPENING DRILLS

Before a drill is used, it should be correctly ground and sharpened. Unless the drill is in good condition, it may cut slowly, drill an oversize hole or possibly break.

A correctly sharpened drill will have:
1. Equal and correctly sized drill point angles.
2. Equal length cutting lips.
3. Correct clearance behind the cutting lips.
4. Correct chisel edge angle.

All four are equally important, Fig. 1-62.

For general drilling, the angles shown in the upper part of Fig. 1-62 are used. If very hard and tough materials are to be drilled, the angles shown in the center of the illustration are used. The lower portion of the illustration shows what is meant by the two halves (A-1 and A-2) of the drill point angle, as well as the two equal-length cutting lips (L-1 and L-2).

Lip clearance behind the cutting lip of the margin is determined by inspection. The cutting edge, or lip is measured by a gauge, Fig. 1-63. The lip clearance angle may be within certain limits, as shown in Fig. 1-62, but must be the same on both sides of the drill.

The margin, shown at the top of Fig. 1-62, is the narrow strip which extends practically the full diameter of the drill for the entire length of the flutes. The portion back of the margin is slightly less in diameter and is termed body clearance.

Both lips of a twist drill must be the same length. For most materials, the lips should be ground to an angle of 59 deg. If the cutting edges are ground at different angles, and the point is in the center, only one lip will cut. The angle of 59 deg. for the lip is correct when the drill is to be used on aluminum, steel, and cast iron. For brass and copper the angle should be 50 deg.; while 45 deg. is preferred for Bakelite, plastic, wood, or fiber.

The heel of the drill (surface of point back of cutting lips) should be at an angle of 12 to 15 deg., as shown in Fig. 1-62. Incorrect grinding of the lip clearance will result in drilling holes larger than the diameter of the drill, drill breakage and slow cutting.

The rake angle of the drill is the angle of the flutes in relation to the axis. A 22 to 30 deg. rake angle is built into the drill by the manufacturer.

Drills should be placed in a grinding jig or attachment for sharpening. This will insure accuracy. When sharpening a drill, it is held as shown in Fig. 1-64. Position "A" is a top view of the first step in grinding the drill. The axis of the drill should make an angle of about 59 deg. (half the drill-point angle) with the face of the grinding wheel. The cutting lip should be horizontal.

The actual grinding of the drill point consists of three definite motions of the shank of the drill while the point is held lightly against the grinding wheel. The three motions are:
1. To the left.
2. Clockwise rotation.
3. Downward.

Fig. 1-64 shows the motion to the left in three views as the angle between the face of the grinding wheel and the drill decreases from about 59 deg. to 50 deg. In Fig. 1-64, clockwise rotation is indicated by the advance of the rotation arrows in A, B, and C. Rotation is also illustrated by the change in position of the cutting lip as well as the tang.

REAMERS

If you want to finish a hole with a particularly smooth surface or to an exact diameter, a reamer, Fig. 1-65, should be used. The hole is first drilled to a diameter slightly smaller than the desired finished size, then finished with the reamer.

A reamer consists of three parts: body, shank, and cut-

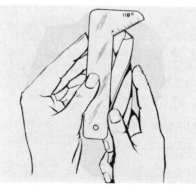

Fig. 1-63. A special gauge used to determine the angle of the cutting edge of a twist drill.

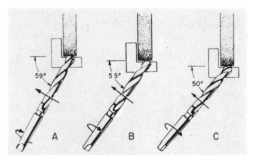

Fig. 1-64. The angle of the drill bit is increased while sharpening.

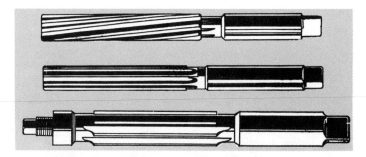

Fig. 1-65. Top. Spiral flute reamer. Middle. Straight flute reamer. Bottom. Adjustable reamer.

ting blades. The reamer can be rotated by means of a suitable wrench or handle; or it can be power driven. When power driven, the speed is approximately 50 rpm.

The blades of a reamer are made of steel, which is hardened to such an extent that it is extremely brittle. Therefore, reamers must be handled carefully and should be stored in a wooden rack with a separate division for each reamer.

When reaming a hole, turn the reamer in the cutting direction only. Remove very little metal at a time since reaming is a finishing operation. Reamers are not designed to make heavy cuts; usually .002 in. is the limit of metal to be removed. Maintain a steady, even rotation of the reamer to reduce "chattering."

Fig. 1-65 shows two solid reamers — a straight flute and a spiral flute — along with an adjustable reamer. The spiral flute type is more expensive than the straight flute reamer. Its advantage is less tendency toward chattering.

Solid reamers are available in standard sizes and also can be obtained in size variations of .001 in. for special work. Adjustable reamers give more flexibility, but care must be taken when adjusting the size of the reamer to be sure it is correctly set. A micrometer should be used for this purpose.

Adjustable reamers are usually available in standard sizes from 1/4 in. to 1 in. by 32nds. They are designed to allow the blades to expand 1/32 in. For example, a 1/4 in. adjustable reamer will cover hole sizes ranging from 1/4 in. to 9/32 in.

TAPS AND DIES

Taps, Fig. 1-66, and dies, Fig. 1-67, are thread-cutting tools. A tap is used to cut internal threads on nuts, while a die cuts external threads on bolts and studs.

There is special terminology used when discussing threads, bolts, and nuts, Fig. 1-68. To avoid confusion, it is essential that mechanics know these terms.

The major diameter, also known as the outside diameter, is the largest diameter of the thread. The minor diameter is the diameter taken at the base of the thread.

The pitch of the thread is the distance from a point on one screw thread to a corresponding point on the next thread, measured parallel to the axis, Fig. 1-68. You can calculate the pitch (fine threads are hard to measure) by dividing one inch by the number of threads per inch.

If you want to drill and tap a hole, you have to drill the hole to the correct diameter for the particular tap. This is called a tap drill. Thread size, thread series, and tap drill required are given in Fig. 1-69.

If you want to drill a hole through which a bolt is to be inserted, the drill is known as a clearance or body drill.

Taps and dies are marked according to the type and diameter thread they will cut. For example, an 8-32 is designed to cut 32 threads per inch on No. 8 stock.

When tapping a hole with a tap or cutting a thread with a die, considerable care is required. When using a tap or die, reverse the direction the tool is turned to free the tool of chips and also recut the threads. Forcing the tool will result in tool breakage, ruined parts and poor threads.

When threading steel parts, a lubricant such as lard oil should be used. Kerosene is preferred for use with aluminum. No lubricant is required for threading brass or cast iron.

FABRICATING TUBING

Tubing is used extensively in automobiles, trucks, and tractors for oil, fuel, and brake lines. Great care must be exercised in fitting tubing for specific jobs. Carelessness in fabrication, or in selecting the wrong type of material or fittings, may result in an accident and harm to the occupants of the vehicle.

Soft copper tubing is usually considered satisfactory for gasoline lines. It should never be used for hydraulic brake lines, however, since it is not strong enough to withstand the pressures developed in the brake system.

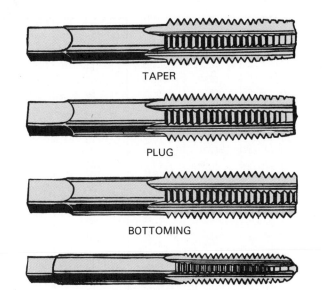

TAPER

PLUG

BOTTOMING

MACHINE SCREW

Fig. 1-66. Four different types of taps.

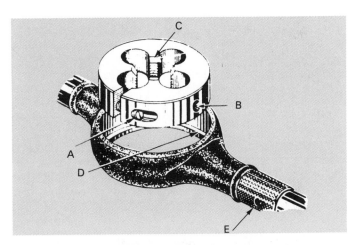

Fig. 1-67. Parts of a die, which is used for cutting external threads. A—Adjusting screw. B—Drive hole. C—Cutting edge. D—Shoulder. E—Handle.

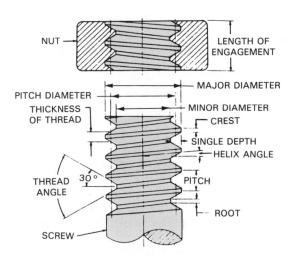

Fig. 1-68. Nomenclature of screw threads.

Nominal size	Thr'd series	Major diameter, inches	Root diameter, inches	Tap drill to produce approx. 75% full thread	Decimal equivalent of tap drill
0–80	N. F.	.0600	.0438	$\frac{3}{64}$	.0469
1–64	N. C.	.0730	.0527	53	.0595
72	N. F.	.0730	.0550	53	.0595
2–56	N. C.	.0860	.0628	50	.0700
64	N. F.	.0860	.0657	50	.0700
3–48	N. C.	.0990	.0719	47	.0785
56	N. F.	.0990	.0758	45	.0820
4–40	N. C.	.1120	.0795	43	.0890
48	N. F.	.1120	.0849	42	.0935
5–40	N. C.	.1250	.0925	38	.1015
44	N. F.	.1250	.0955	37	.1040
6–32	N. C.	.1380	.0974	36	.1065
40	N. F.	.1380	.1055	33	.1130
8–32	N. C.	.1640	.1234	29	.1360
36	N. F.	.1640	.1279	29	.1360
10–24	N. C.	.1900	.1359	25	.1495
32	N. F.	.1900	.1494	21	.1590
12–24	N. C.	.2160	.1619	16	.1770
28	N. F.	.2160	.1696	14	.1820
¼–20	N. C.	.2500	.1850	7	.2010
28	N. F.	.2500	.2036	3	.2130
$\frac{5}{16}$–18	N. C.	.3125	.2403	F	.2570
24	N. F.	.3125	.2584	I	.2720
⅜–16	N. C.	.3750	.2938	$\frac{5}{16}$	.3125
24	N. F.	.3750	.3209	Q	.3320
$\frac{7}{16}$–14	N. C.	.4375	.3447	U	.3680
20	N. F.	.4375	.3726	$\frac{25}{64}$	.3906
½–13	N. C.	.5000	.4001	$\frac{27}{64}$	.4219
20	N. F.	.5000	.4351	$\frac{29}{64}$	.4531
$\frac{9}{16}$–12	N. C.	.5625	.4542	$\frac{31}{64}$	.4844
18	N. F.	.5625	.4903	$\frac{33}{64}$	.5156
⅝–11	N. C.	.6250	.5069	$\frac{17}{32}$	.5312
18	N. F.	.6250	.5528	$\frac{37}{64}$	.5781
¾–10	N. C.	.7500	.6201	$\frac{21}{32}$	.6562
16	N. F.	.7500	.6688	$\frac{11}{16}$	.6875
⅞–9	N. C.	.8750	.7307	$\frac{49}{64}$	.7656
14	N. F.	.8750	.7822	$\frac{13}{16}$	.8125
1–8	N. C.	1.0000	8376	⅞	.8750
14	N. F.	1.0000	9072	$\frac{15}{16}$	.9375

Fig. 1-69. Tap chart shows the size of hole for a specific tap size.

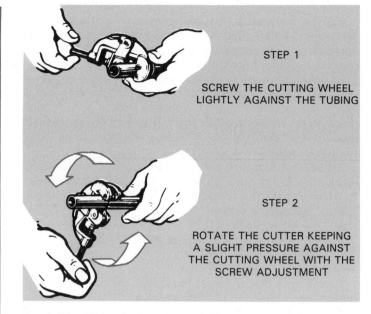

STEP 1

SCREW THE CUTTING WHEEL LIGHTLY AGAINST THE TUBING

STEP 2

ROTATE THE CUTTER KEEPING A SLIGHT PRESSURE AGAINST THE CUTTING WHEEL WITH THE SCREW ADJUSTMENT

Fig. 1-70. The procedure for cutting tubing. Increase the pressure of the cut until the tube has been cut through.

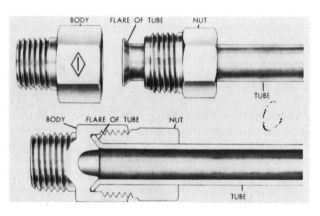

Fig. 1-71. An inverted flare fitting. (Imperial-Eastman)

Only special tubing designed for hydraulic brake lines should be used. This tubing is made of seamless steel.

When making a line of tubing, first select the size and material of which the line is to be made. Then unroll the tubing and cut off the desired amount.

The correct way to unroll the tubing is to place the coil of tubing on the workbench in a vertical position. Then hold the end of the tubing against the surface of the bench with one hand and unroll the coil slowly with the other hand. Never try to uncoil tubing by drawing it out sideways from the coil in a spiral. This will form a twist in the tubing and any attempt to straighten the tubing will work-harden it and create weak spots.

When cutting tubing, only special tubing cutters should be used, Fig. 1-70. It is imperative the tubing must be cut smoothly and at right angles to its center line. Unless the tubing is cut correctly, it will be impossible to make a leakproof joint.

The tube cutting tool shown in Fig. 1-70 will make a clean cut, square with the sides of the tubing. In addition, there is little possibility of filings getting into the tubing and subsequently causing trouble in the system. To use a tubing cutter, position the cutting wheel until it contacts the surface lightly. Swing the tool completely around the tubing, then readjust the cutting wheel. Repeat this procedure until the cut is completed.

After the tubing has been cut to the desired length, the ends should be reamed or deburred. One method is to use the reamer provided on one end of the tubing cutter. When reaming tubing, hold the end of the tubing pointed down, so metal chips will not drop into the tubing.

One type of reaming tool is an "inner and outer" reamer. This is a cylindrically shaped tool that reams both the inside and outside edges of the tubing. With the burrs removed, the tubing is ready for one of the several types of flared or flareless fittings available. The type of fitting used is dependent on the type of service and material which the tubing is to carry, Fig. 1-65.

The inverted flare fitting, Fig. 1-71, is widely used as original equipment on cars. It can be used for tubing of soft copper, aluminum, thin-walled steel, and other thin-walled metal tubing.

When the tubing is to carry liquids or gases, the SAE flare fitting, Fig. 1-72, is used. The tubing can be copper, brass, aluminum, or brazed steel (Bundy or GM). The flare fitting also can be used with plastic tubing.

Compression fittings, Fig. 1-73, are used with gasoline, grease, vacuum, and air lines. Copper, aluminum, brass, and brazed steel tubing can be used with this type of fitting.

Air brake fittings, Fig. 1-74, are used with copper, aluminum, and thin-walled steel tubing on Bendix-Westinghouse and other air brake systems.

For low and medium pressure work, the threaded sleeve fitting, Fig. 1-75, is employed. It can be used with almost all types of tubing.

The flexible hose coupling, Fig. 1-76, can be used wherever flexible hose is installed. It will carry gasoline, oil, water, cutting oil, diesel oil, and many hydraulic fluids.

Where vibration and minor tube movement is encountered, flex fittings are installed. Fig. 1-77 shows the details of this type of fitting.

When lines carry relatively high pressure and are subject to minor vibration, high duty fittings such as illustrated in Fig. 1-78 are used. In addition to brazed steel tubing, these fittings are used with copper, aluminum, and steel tubing. However, copper tubing should never be used to make brake lines. Brake lines should be made from seamless steel tubing.

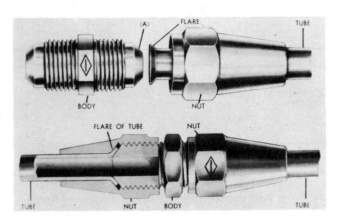

Fig. 1-72. Flare fitting used to connect lines when liquids or a gas are used.

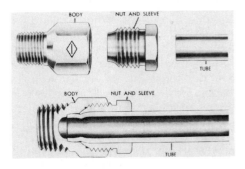

Fig. 1-75. A threaded sleeve fitting.

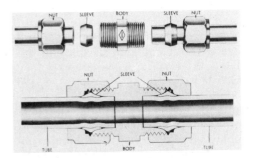

Fig. 1-73. Compression fittings are used to join lines together when the ends of the line are not flared. They should never be used on brake lines. (Imperial-Eastman)

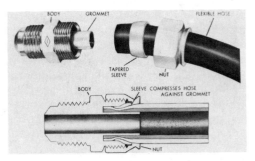

Fig. 1-76. A coupling that is used on flexible brake hoses. (Imperial-Eastman)

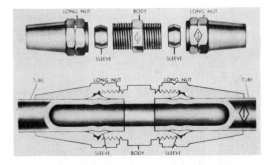

Fig. 1-74. Fitting used with air brakes. (Imperial-Eastman)

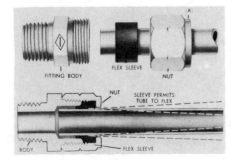

Fig. 1-77. This fitting is used where there are minor vibrations.

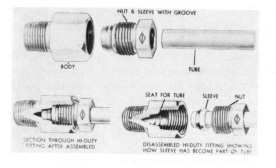

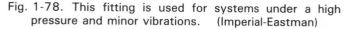

Fig. 1-78. This fitting is used for systems under a high pressure and minor vibrations. (Imperial-Eastman)

FLARING

There are several different types of flaring tools available. One type consists of a flaring bar and screw feed flaring yoke, Fig. 1-79. When making a flare with a tool of this type, place the tubing in the flaring bar with the end slightly protruding above the face of the bar. Firmly clamp the tubing in the bar, so pressure of the flaring cone will not force the tubing through the bar.

Before slipping the yoke over the bar to start flaring, place a little oil on the cone or spreader. Take particular care if the flared connection is to be used on units subject to vibration. Do not work the tubing any more than is necessary. Working will tend to make the metal hard and brittle, so it is more subject to breakage.

On tubes flared too short, the full clamping area of the fitting is not used. Consequently, the joint may leak or suffer early failure. Tubing flared too long will stick and jam on the threads during assembly. Flares that are not straight usually result if the tubing was cut on an angle.

Brazed steel tubing, such as used for hydraulic brake lines, must be double flared. If only single flared, it will invariably crack or split, Fig. 1-80. Double flaring is similar to single flaring except that an additional operation is introduced. To make a double flare with the tool shown in Fig. 1-81, two operations are involved. In the first operation, the tubing is belled through the use of an adapter. In the second operation, the adapter is

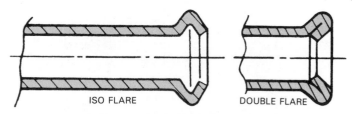

Fig. 1-80a. A—Single flare tends to split. B—Double flare is stronger and resists splitting. (Cadillac)

ISO FLARE   DOUBLE FLARE

Fig. 1-80b. Some manufacturer's use an (ISO) or bubble flare. (Ford)

removed and the flaring cone screwed down. This folds the tubing down on itself and forms an accurate 45 deg. dougle flare without cracking or splitting the tubing.

BENDING

It is frequently necessary to bend tubing. This should be done only with a special tube bender, and only soft temper tubing should be bent. On smaller size tubing, a simple outside bending coil spring generally is satisfactory. This bender is slipped over the outside of the tubing and prevents the tubing from kinking when it is bent. When using a spring-type tube bender, remember that the tubing must be bent somewhat further than required, then backed up to the desired angle. This loosens the spring tension in the bender and it can be easily removed.

Fig. 1-79. A flaring tool is needed to create a flare at the end of a tube.

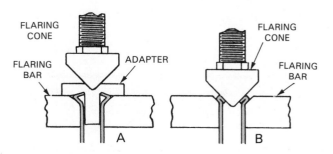

Fig. 1-81. Using a flaring tool to make a double flare in tubing.

On larger sizes of tubing, or where precise and uniform bends are required, the use of a lever-type or gear-type bender, Fig. 1-82, should be used. These benders can be slipped on the tubing at the exact point the bend is desired. They are particularly advantageous when the tubing has been partly connected, or is located in hard-to-get-at places.

Bulk tubing is sold in coils. When removing a piece of copper tubing from a coil, first place the coil on the bench. Hold down the free end of the tubing, then roll the coil of tubing along the bench until the desired length is obtained. In this way, kinking of the tubing will be avoided.

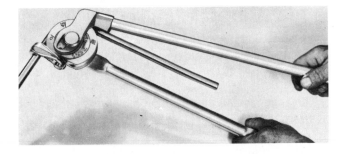

Fig. 1-82. Sometimes a tubing bender is used to provide smooth rounded curves.

CLEANING TOOLS

Cleaning parts is a basic requirement of all automotive service work. Having clean parts not only speeds the work, but also aids greatly in locating flaws and wear. A number of essential cleaning tools are illustrated in Figs. 1-83 and 1-84.

Tools such as scrapers and putty knives are hand tools, while certain brushes are designed for hand use and others are power driven. When using power driven wire brushes, goggles should be worn for safety's sake.

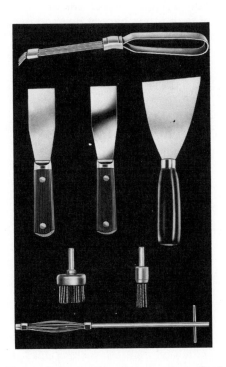

Fig.1-83. Top to bottom. A carbon scraper. Gasket scraper of various widths. Wire brushes used with electric drill to remove gasket material. A valve guide cleaner.

Chapter 1—REVIEW QUESTIONS

Write answers on a separate sheet paper. Do not write in this book.

1. The size of open-end wrenches increases in:
   a. 1/16 in. steps.
   b. 1/32 in. steps.
   c. 1/8 in. steps.
   d. 1/4 in. steps.
2. What is the main reason for using a box type wrench?
3. List the three standard size drives for socket wrenches.
4. Why are torque wrenches needed?
5. A Torx screwdriver is similar to a Phillips screwdriver. True or False?
6. Interlocking joint gripping pliers are designed to:
   a. Lock channels.
   b. Have adjustable openings of different sizes and, at the same time, the jaws remain parallel.
7. The end of a Phillips-type screwdriver is:
   a. A flat blade.
   b. Pointed end with four grooves.
   c. Fluted end.
8. A setscrew wrench has:
   a. Four sides.
   b. Six sides.
   c. Eight sides.
9. The rounded end of a machinists hammer is known as the _____.
10. A cape chisel is used to cut:
    a. Narrow grooves.
    b. Rivet heads.
    c. Tool steel.
11. When using a chisel, it should be held:
    a. Tightly in the hand.
    b. With a pair of slip-joint pliers.
    c. Loosely in the hand.

Fig. 1-84. Wire brushes used with electric drills.

12. A magnetic screwdriver has interchangeable bits. True or False?
13. A file with one row of teeth crossing the other is called:
    a. A crisscross file.
    b. A double-cut file.
    c. A Vixen-cut file.
14. A file with a single row of parallel teeth is called a _____.
15. When filing soft steel, which type file should be used first?
    a. A bastard file.
    b. A smooth-cut file.
    c. A second-cut file.
16. Solder is an alloy of:
    a. Lead and tin.
    b. Lead and zinc.
    c. Tin and zinc.
    d. Lead and cadmium.
17. Hacksaw blades are made of:
    a. High grade tool steel.
    b. Chilled cast iron.
    c. Carbaloy.
18. List the usual lengths of blades used in manually operated hacksaws.
19. Which saw blade is recommended to cut soft steel, cast iron and stock of heavy cross section?
    a. 16 tooth.
    b. 32 tooth.
    c. 24 tooth.
    d. 14 tooth.
20. What is the usual cutting lip angle on a twist drill?
21. A tap is used to cut external threads. True or False?
22. After cutting a piece of tubing, why should it be reamed?
    a. To increase it size.
    b. To restore it to its original size.
    c. To remove any burrs from the cut edge.
    d. To true the cut edge.
23. A box-type wrench is used to tighten nuts on brass fittings on tubing. True or False?
24. The SAE flare fitting cannot be used to carry gases. True or False?

Chapter 2

AUTOMOTIVE SAFETY

Caution: Brake and clutch linings are made of asbestos. The dust of these items is a carcinogen, which means it causes cancer. Always wear a respirator when working on brake and clutch linings.

After studying this chapter, you will be able to:
- Describe what a clean shop should look like and why.
- State what type of eye protection should be worn for a specific job.
- Cite fire preventive measures.
- List the precautions when raising a car off the floor.
- List the safety measures when using oxyacetylene.
- Demonstrate how to dress safely when in the shop.

SAFETY

Safety is everyone's responsibility, and it is concerned with all areas where people live and work. Even the U.S. Government is in the act with far-reaching safety regulations for the business world.

All of which makes your school shop the ideal place to:
1. Study safety regulations.
2. Learn to set up a safe shop.
3. Establish safe working conditions.
4. Make safety a part of every service procedure.

To be specific, the Occupational Safety and Health Administration (OSHA), which is a branch of the Department of LABOR, was formed to lay down guidelines for all types of businesses to insure they are operated under conditions of maximum safety and health. Now, every auto repair shop and service station is under the watchful eyes of OSHA to be sure the shop or station is operated under specific safe working conditions prescribed by the Government.

Most of the safety regulations set forth have already been put into practice by the careful shop or station owner. But, under the conditions of the Act, which went into effect in April, 1971, inspections will be made to be sure that its rules are being followed.

Before discussing any of the provisions of the Act, it is important to know that it provides that any employee (or representative thereof) who believes that a violation of job safety or health standard exists may request an inspection by sending a signed statement to the Department of Labor. While the employer may receive a copy of the complaint, the names of the complainants need not be furnished.

The safety inspectors may enter, without delay and at any reasonable time, any establishment covered by the Act to inspect the premises and all pertinent conditions, structures, machines, apparatus, devices, equipment and materials therein, and to question privately any employer, owner, operator, agent, or employee.

Where an investigation reveals a violation, the employer is issued a written citation describing the nature of the violation. All citations shall fix a reasonable time for abatement of the violation.

Willful or repeated violations of the Act's requirements by employers may incur very substantial fines for each particular violation. Citations issued for serious violations incur mandatory penalties. Any employer who fails to correct a violation for which a citation has been issued within the prescribed time period may be penalized by a substantial fine for each day that the violation persists.

A willful violation by an employer which results in the death of an employee is punishable by a large fine or imprisonment up to six months. A second conviction doubles these penalties.

Every employer must keep occupational injury and illness records of employees in the establishment at which the employees usually report for work. The records must be kept up to date and available to governmental representatives. And, the employer must post a summary of all occupational injuries and illnesses at the conclusion of the calendar year.

The law also requires that employees must be informed of job safety and health provisions. A poster is provided which must be posted in a prominent place in the establishment which the employees report for work.

Some of the safety and health items set forth in the Act include basic points, such as clean floors free of grease, oil, and dirt, Fig. 2-1. Washrooms must be kept clean and sanitary. Paint spray booths must be ventilated and meet specific requirements. Buildings must be designed with a sufficient number of exits, and aisles must not be obstructed.

Personal protective equipment for eyes, face, head and extremities as well as protective respiratory devices, shields, and barriers must be provided, Fig. 2-2. The employer is responsible for employee-owned equipment.

Equipment must be in good condition and provided with any safety guards, Fig. 2-3, and safety devices that may be necessary. Management is responsible for the safe operation of welding and cutting equipment. Electric wiring and equipment must meet underwriters' specifications and be in good condition, Fig. 2-4. No smoking signs must be prominently displayed, Fig. 2-5, and all combustible liquids must be kept in specified containers and limited as to the quantity that is permissible within the building, Fig. 2-6.

Fig. 2-1. A clean shop does not have tools lying on the floor, along with oil and grease, so that technicians do not have to worry about slipping and falling on or over something as they work. A shop should look like this before, during, and after working hours.

Fig. 2-3. Grinding wheel must have guards in place.
(Winona Van Norman)

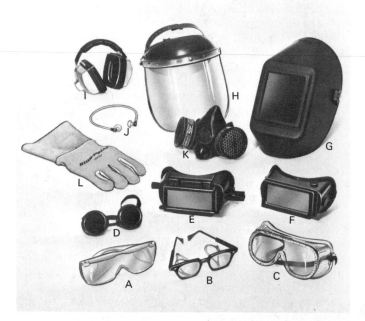

Fig. 2-2. Safety items: A, B, and C—Safety glasses. D, E, and F—Gas welding goggles. G—Arc welding helmet. H—Shield. I and J—Hearing protection. K—Respirator. L—Welding glove.
(Snap-on)

USE THE CORRECT PLUG!

SAFETY GROUND PIN

MAKE CERTAIN THAT THE TOOLS YOU USE HAVE A SAFETY PLUG AND CORD WITH INTEGRAL GROUNDING CONDUCTOR.

GROUNDING BLADE

Fig. 2-4. Electrical connections must be grounded.

NO SMOKING!

Fig. 2-5. No smoking signs must be displayed and followed.

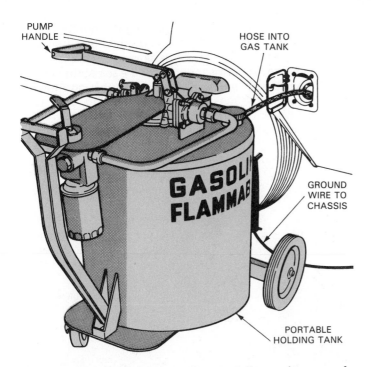

Fig. 2-6. Removing and storing gasoline using a safe procedure. (Chrysler)

Fig. 2-7. Class B fire extinguishers are for liquid and grease fires. Class C fire extinguishers are for electrical fires.

These are some of the major points set forth in the OSHA act. However, auto shop and service station operators should not limit their safety and health program to the regulations of the OSHA. There are many conditions not covered by the Act that should be followed and enforced by every owner.

FIRE PREVENTION

Because the many combustibles, such as gasoline, lacquer thinner, and certain cleaning fluids used in automobile repair shops, special precautions are needed to prevent fire. Fuel, thinner and other combustibles should always be kept in closed containers designed for the purpose, Fig. 2-6.

Smoking and unshielded flames should never be permitted. No Smoking signs, Fig. 2-5, should be prominently displayed.

All shops should be provided with an ample number of fire extinguishers. Everyone should be familiar with their location and use, Fig. 2-7. Remember, water cannot be used to extinguish a gasoline or grease fire. Use carbon tetrachloride, foam or, if nothing else is available, sand will help smother it.

As a further protection against fire, oil and paint rags should be kept in suitable containers, Fig. 2-8. Care must be exercised so that spontaneous combustion does not occur.

BATTERY SAFETY

Special safety precautions are necessary when working on automotive electrical circuits. Unless the battery is needed for making tests of the circuit, it should be disconnected. This precaution will eliminate the possibili-

Fig. 2-8. Always place oily rags in a sealed container.

ty of any short circuits and possibility of fire or damage to the circuit.

Most important, a flame should not be used to observe the level of the electrolyte in the battery. Acid fumes are highly explosive. When it becomes necessary to note the electrolyte level, a flashlight should be used.

VENTILATION

One of the most important safety precautions to be followed in an auto shop is proper ventilation. If it is necessary to operate an engine for more than a few seconds, the car should be driven outside. A large portion of exhaust fumes consist of carbon monoxide, which is a deadly poison. In small quantities, it produces drowsiness and headaches. In large quantities, death results.

Many shops are provided with special conduits which are connected to the tailpipe of the automobile, Fig. 2-9. These conduits conduct the exhaust gases out-of-doors, eliminating the danger from carbon monoxide poisoning.

JACKS AND LIFTS

If lifts are not available, and it is necessary to keep the car raised, the car should be placed on stands, Fig. 2-10. In that way, there will be no chance of the car falling as the result of a faulty jack. In addition, such practice frees the jack for work on other vehicles.

Whenever placing a car on the lift, refer to the service manual for positioning the car on the lift, Fig. 2-11. If the car is not positioned on the lift correctly, it could fall. Always raise the car a few inches off the ground, and then shake the car to make sure it is on the lift squarely prior to fully raising the car.

TOOL SAFETY

There are many safety precautions related to the use of tools:

Files should never be used without a handle, since there is always the danger of running the pointed tang into the palm of the hand. Neither should files be used as pry bars, nor should they be hammered. Files are made with hard temper. Consequently, they are quite brittle. When hammered, small pieces may fly off and cause severe wounds or loss of eyesight.

Fig. 2-10. Make sure that car is supported by a jackstand before working on a car. The seals on a hydraulic floor jack could give out at any time without warning.

Fig. 2-9. When an engine must be left running for testing, the doors to the shop must remain open. If weather does not permit, a ventilation system must be hooked to the car's exhaust system.

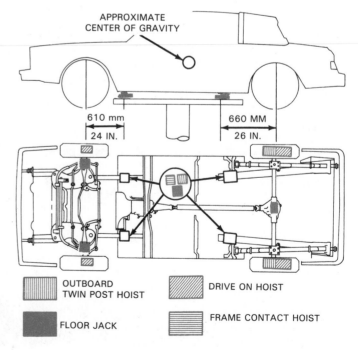

APPROXIMATE CENTER OF GRAVITY

610 mm
24 IN.

660 MM
26 IN.

OUTBOARD TWIN POST HOIST

DRIVE ON HOIST

FLOOR JACK

FRAME CONTACT HOIST

Fig. 2-11. Typical points that should be supported when working on a car. (Chrysler)

Hardened surfaces, such as the face of an anvil, should not be struck with a hammer as bits of steel may fly off and cause damage. Further, in connection with hammers and sledges, care must always be exercised that the head is always securely attached to the handle. Loose hammer and sledge heads may fly off when the tool is used. Anyone standing in the way will be struck and severely injured.

When the head of a chisel becomes mushroomed, it should be discarded, or reground to remove the mushroomed edges. This will prevent bits of steel from flying off and causing damage.

Whenever grinding is done, the mechanic should wear a shield to protect the eyes, Fig. 2-12. The grinding wheel should always be provided with a protecting guard to protect the technician from flying objects.

When using a wrench, pull on the handle rather than pushing on it. Should the wrench slip, there will be less danger of skinning your knuckles. When the jaws of a wrench become worn or sprung, discard the wrench.

Compressed air is an important "tool" in every shop. The air gun should not be pointed at anyone. The high pressure can blow dirt particles at such high speed that they will puncture the skin and/or get into the eyes.

DRESS SAFELY

Use care when working around any machinery, engine or motor that there is a chance of loose clothing being caught and entangled in rotating parts. For that reason, it is advisable to tuck neckties within the shirt. If long sleeves are being worn, these should be buttoned at the cuff or rolled-up past the elbows. Caps without brims are considered safer than those with brims, because of the possibility of the protruding brim being caught in some rotating part. Also, wear a sturdy pair of shoes or boots, preferably steel toes, to protect your feet.

OXYACETYLENE SAFETY

In regard to safety precautions when using oxygen and acetylene for welding, there are many points to observe. Never allow oil or grease to contact oxygen under pressure. Do not lubricate welding and cutting apparatus. Never use oxygen as a substitute for compressed air, as a source of pressure, or for ventilation. Before starting to weld or cut, make sure that flame, sparks, hot slag, or hot metal will not be likely to start a fire. Always wear welding gloves and goggles when working with a lighted torch.

Be sure to keep a clear space between the cylinders and the work, because you may find it necessary to reach and adjust the regulators quickly. Do not risk hand burns by lighting the torch with a match. Use a friction type lighter, Fig. 2-13; it is safer and easier. Never use acetylene pressure higher than 15 psi. Never release acetylene where it might cause a fire or an explosion. Always check equipment before starting to work. Never braze, weld, or use acetylene flame on gasoline or other fuel tanks. Oxygen and acetylene tanks should always be in a special carrier or chained to a post to prevent falling.

Fig. 2-12. Shield not only protects the eyes, but the entire face.

Fig. 2-13. Never use a match or cigarette lighter to ignite torches. Use only a friction type lighter.

GRINDING PRECAUTIONS

Grinding operations are an important part of an automotive mechanics job, and several safety precautions must be followed when using grinders of any type.

Before mounting a grinding wheel, make sure it is the type recommended for that particular operation. Also check the soundness of the wheel by tapping it with a handle of a screwdriver or similar tool. A ringing sound should be heard when the wheel is tapped in this manner. If not, the wheel is defective and should not be used. It is probably cracked and would burst when rotated at grinding speed.

The wheel should fit the spindle snugly, and the compressible washers (known as blotters) should be large enough to extend beyond the wheel flanges. After mounting, bring the grinding wheel up to speed slowly, if possible, and do not stand in the rotational plane of the wheel. In case of failure, the flying parts will cause severe injury. Always be sure that the wheel is provided with a proper guard as protection against breakage.

After completing the grinding operation, let the wheel rotate for several minutes in order to throw off excess coolant. If this is not done, coolant will remain in the lower portion of the wheel where it could cause a severe unbalance condition and consequent danger of bursting when put into operation.

Remember:
1. Always wear goggles when doing a grinding operation, Fig. 2-12.
2. Keep the tool rest as close to the wheel as possible.
3. When doing precision grinding, such as crankshaft journals, use a light feed.
4. Do not strike a grinding wheel while it is rotating.

Chapter 2—REVIEW QUESTIONS

Write all answers on a separate sheet of paper. Do not write in this book.
1. Why study OSHA (Occupational Safety and Health Administration) safety regulations?
   a. Regulations affect all businesses.
   b. Regulations give employee a voice in maintaining safe working conditions.
   c. All of above.
   d. None of above.
2. Under OSHA, employers are responsible for employee-owned equipment. True or False?
3. Why are running and practical jokes prohibited in shops?
4. Why should a mask be worn while working on a clutch or brakes?
5. Batteries should always remain connected in the circuit while working on the electrical system. True or False?
6. What happens when a file is used as a pry bar?
   a. It bends.
   b. It breaks.
7. Which of the following is correct?
   a. Carbon monoxide is used in welding.
   b. Carbon monoxide is a deadly poison.
   c. Carbon monoxide is used to inflate tires on race cars.
8. Why is it dangerous to stand in the plane of a rotating part?
9. Oxygen fittings on welding equipment should be well lubricated with mineral oil. True or False?
10. When using a grinding wheel, position the tool rest 1 in. from the wheel. Yes or No?

Chapter 3

FASTENERS, GASKETS, AND SEALS

After studying this chapter, you will be able to:
- List the different types of fasteners.
- Determine which fastener is appropriate for a specific job.
- State how to select and measure a bolt.
- Describe the different methods of repairing threads.
- Select the appropriate seal for a specific job.
- List and describe the different lubricants and sealers along with the use of each.
- Demonstrate the steps in preparing a new gasket for installation.

FASTENERS

There are many different devices used for fastening one part to another in the modern automobile. These devices range from the familiar bolt and nut to adhesives. You should know the difference between them, and be able to identify the various types of fastening devices.

THREADED FASTENERS

There are several factors involved in describing bolts, cap screws, machine screws, Fig. 3-1, sheet metal screws, and other fasteners. Full information is needed when ordering replacement parts. You need to know the length, type of head, number of threads per unit length, and whether measurements are in inches or millimeters.

Basically, a bolt is an externally threaded fastener, Fig. 3-2. A screw is also an externally threaded fastener.

A cap screw is usually torqued with a wrench, Fig. 3-3, while a machine screw is torqued with a screwdriver. The machine screw is smaller in diameter than the cap screw.

The diameter of a cap screw usually is measured in fractions of an inch, while the diameter of a machine screw is given in nominal size by number (such as No. 8, No. 10, etc.) or by a fraction or decimal equivalent. Common types of machine screws are shown in Fig. 3-1.

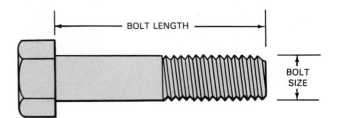

Fig. 3-2. A bolt has a hex head and external threads.
(Deere & Co.)

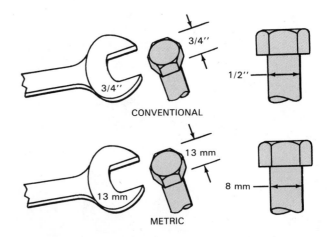

Fig. 3-3. The bolt diameters are 1/2 in. and 8 mm respectively. However, the size of the hex, or wrench size, is 3/4 in. and 13 mm respectively.

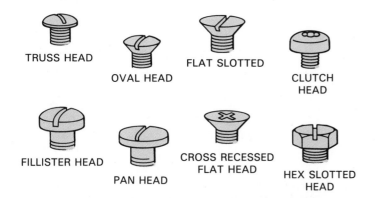

Fig. 3-1. Different types of machine screw heads.

35

A stud, Fig. 3-4, has both ends threaded. One end is screwed into a threaded hole. A part to be assembled is placed in position on the stud, then a nut is placed on the exposed end of the stud. When tightened, the parts are held together, Fig. 3-4.

Various types of nuts are illustrated in Fig. 3-5. The automotive field uses nuts of the hexagonal type. The castellated nut is tightened on a bolt or threaded shaft. Then a cotter key is inserted through the castles of the nut and through a hole in the bolt.

A wing nut, Fig. 3-5, is installed finger tight. It is used in places where the nut must be removed frequently, and where torque is not necessary. Cap nuts are decorative nuts used in such places where the conventional nut would be unsightly.

SELF-LOCKING NUTS

There are several types of self-locking nuts. The type shown in Fig. 3-6 has a composition plug which, when forced against the threads, prevents the nut from turning.

PALNUTS AND LOCK WASHERS

The palnut is a locking device, Fig. 3-7, stamped from thin sheet steel and designed to bind against the threads of the bolts when installed. The palnut is turned down to make firm contact with the regular nut, then it is given an additional one-half turn. The regular nut must be torqued to a specified amount before the palnut is installed.

Lock washers are designed to prevent nuts from coming loose. These washers are provided in several different forms, Fig. 3-8. A conventional flat washer, also shown in Fig. 3-8, is used under the nut to prevent galling of the surface contacted.

Fig. 3-6. A self-locking nut has a composition plug, which is forced against the threads to prevent the nut from turning. (Deere & Co.)

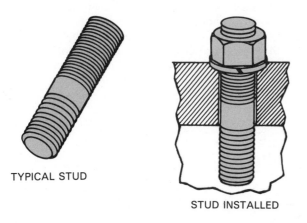

TYPICAL STUD

STUD INSTALLED

Fig. 3-4. A stud has threads at each end and has no head. (Deere & Co.)

Fig. 3-7. Palnuts are made of sheet metal and have inner prongs that engage the threads of a bolt to prevent nut from turning.

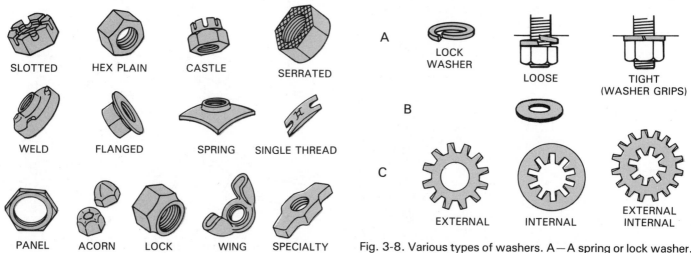

SLOTTED   HEX PLAIN   CASTLE   SERRATED

WELD   FLANGED   SPRING   SINGLE THREAD

PANEL   ACORN   LOCK   WING   SPECIALTY

Fig. 3-5. Different types of nuts.

A   LOCK WASHER   LOOSE   TIGHT (WASHER GRIPS)

B

C   EXTERNAL   INTERNAL   EXTERNAL INTERNAL

Fig. 3-8. Various types of washers. A—A spring or lock washer. B—A typical flat washer. C—Tooth type lock washers grip the metal. (Deere & Co.)

SHEET METAL SCREWS

A special and popular type of fastening device is the familiar sheet metal screw, or self-tapping screw, Fig. 3-9. Because of its fluted or tapered point, it cuts its own threads as it is screwed into the sheet metal. Sheet metal screws are used extensively in holding two metal parts together, Fig. 3-10. First, a hole is punched or drilled into the sheet metal, then the screw is turned into the hole.

KEYS AND PINS

Keys and pins are used to secure bolts, gears, and pulleys.

Keys used in automotive design include the Woodruff key, square key, and gib-head key, Fig. 3-11. The key fits into a slot, known as a keyway, which is cut into both the shaft and the mating part, Fig. 3-11. By design, the key extends into both the shaft and the mating part and rotate as one.

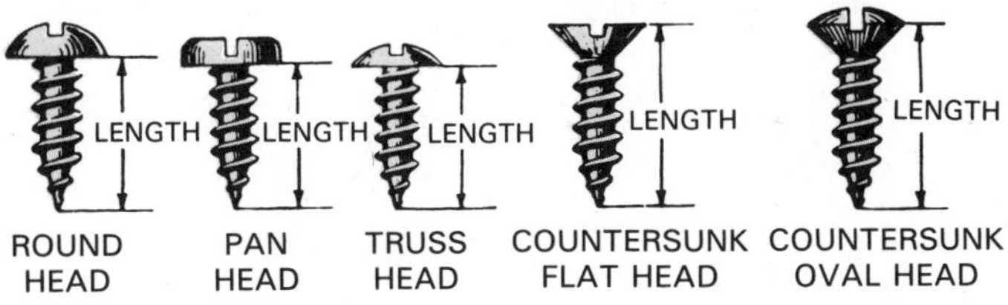

Fig. 3-9. Types of sheet metal screws.

Fig. 3-10. Different methods of using sheet metal screws.

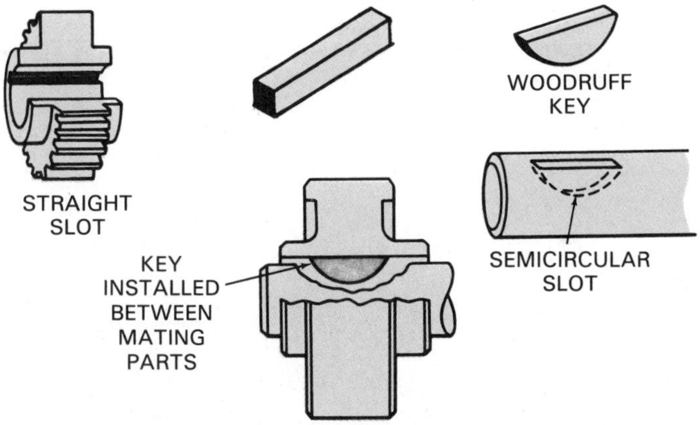

Fig. 3-11. Woodruff key is placed in semicircular slot. Slot on the inner diameter of gear slides over key and mates the two together. (Deere & Co.)

The cotter key, also known as a cotter pin, Fig. 3-12, is used with a castellated nut to prevent it from becoming loose. The cotter key is inserted through the castle of the nut and a hole in the bolt. The ends are then bent back and surplus ends are cut off. In addition to preventing nuts from coming loose, cotter keys are used with clevis pins and in the ends of control rods of the type, for example, used from the accelerator pedal to the carburetor throttle lever.

Dowel pins and taper pins, Fig. 3-13, are used to secure one part to another, such as a shaft and a gear. A hole is drilled through the two parts, and then the dowel or taper pin is driven into place.

SNAP RINGS

Snap rings, Fig. 3-14, are employed to prevent endwise movement of cylindrical parts and shafts. There are both internal and external snap rings. An internal type snap ring is used in a groove cut in a housing. An external snap ring is designed to fit in a groove cut on the outside of a cylindrical space, such as a shaft. They are used extensively in manual shift and automatic transmissions; also in hydraulic valve lifters.

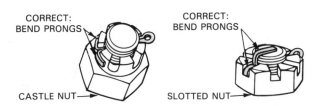

Fig. 3-12. The cotter key prevents the nut from coming loose.

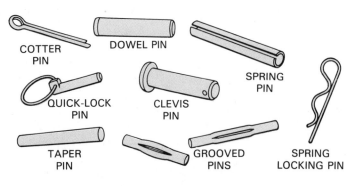

Fig. 3-13. Pins come in different shapes and sizes.
(Deere & Co.)

Fig. 3-14. Snap rings require the use of snap ring pliers.

SETSCREWS

Setscrews are designed to lock and position parts. For example, a pulley frequently is secured to a shaft by means of a setscrew. Setscrews are hardened and have different types of heads and ends; flat, pointed, or rounded.

In order to prevent the pulley from slipping, the shaft is usually spotted or slightly counterbored to take the point of the setscrew.

MEASURING THREADS

The Unified Thread Series is now the basic American standard for fastening types of screw threads. Most commonly used types are Unified Coarse (UNC) and Unified Fine (UNF).

Details and terminology of threads were discussed in Chapter 1.

In order to measure the number of threads per inch, or pitch if metric, a special gauge, Fig. 3-15, should be used.

REPAIRING THREADS

When internal or external threads are stripped, often they can be repaired by means of a tap or die, Fig. 3-16A.

If the threads are severely damaged, other repair techniques can be used. One method is to drill out the thread and tap the hole to the next larger size.

However, in some cases, this presents a problem. If a cylinder head bolt hole in the block was stripped, it would necessitate drilling out the head to accommodate the larger size stud. This could result in breaking through, into the water jacket.

One method provides a patented coil of wire. First, the stripped threads are drilled out of the hole, Fig. 3-16B. Next, it is tapped, Fig. 3-16C. Then, the coil is inserted, Fig. 3-16D and E, restoring the threaded hole to its original condition, Fig. 3-17.

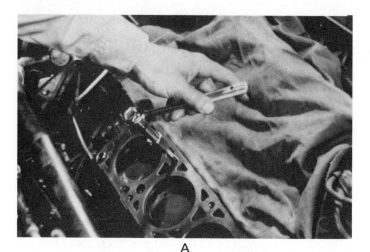

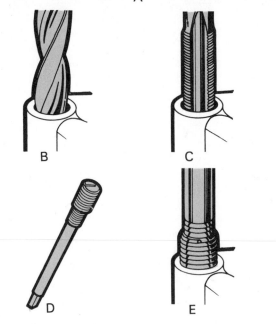

Fig. 3-16. Different methods of thread repairs. A—Using a tap to repair threads in the engine block. (Fel-Pro, Inc.) B—Drill out the hole. C—Tap hole. D—Install insert on mandrel. E—Screw insert into tapped hole. (Oldsmobile)

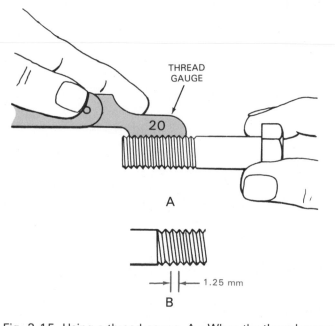

Fig. 3-15. Using a thread gauge. A—When the thread gauge seats squarely on the threads, look at the number stamped on the gauge. This number indicates the number of teeth per inch. B—Pitch is the distance between the two crests. (Deere & Co.)

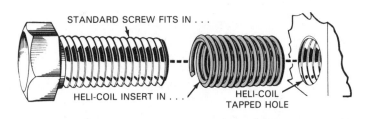

Fig. 3-17. Helical insert restores worn threads to original diameter.

RIVETS

A rivet is a metal pin with a head at one end. It is designed to fasten two parts together. A blind or pop riveter is a tool designed to install rivets when only one side of the parts to be riveted can be reached. They are available in hand-operated types, Fig. 3-18. Rivets used in a hand-operated blind riveter are shown in Fig. 3-19.

To install a blind rivet, drill a hole through both parts to be joined. Place the long stem of the rivet in the head of the tool, insert the short end in the hole in the parts. Squeeze the handle repeatedly to set the rivet and snap off its end.

REPLACING BOLTS AND NUTS

Frequently, it is necessary to replace bolts and nuts when servicing an automobile. When replacing them, be sure the new bolt and nut are equal in strength to the old ones which are being replaced.

The accompanying charts, Fig. 3-20 to 3-23, show markings on bolt heads and nuts which indicate strength, bolt torque, and how to read the dimensions of a bolt.

| GRADE 2 | GRADE 5 | GRADE 7 | GRADE 8 |
| (GM 260—M) | (GM 280—M) | (GM 290—M) | (GM 300—M) |

CUSTOMARY (INCH) BOLTS—IDENTIFICATION MARKS CORRESPOND TO BOLT STRENGTH—INCREASING NUMBERS REPRESENT INCREASING STRENGTH.

METRIC BOLTS—IDENTIFICATION CLASS NUMBERS CORRESPOND TO BOLT STRENGTH—INCREASING NUMBERS REPRESENT INCREASING STRENGTH.

Fig. 3-20. Strength of bolts is indicated on top of the hex. (Cadillac)

BOLT TORQUE				
	GRADE 5		**GRADE 8**	
Size	In. Lbs. Ft. Lbs.	Newton meters	In. Lbs. Ft. Lbs.	Newton meters
1/4-20	95 In. Lbs.	11	125 In. Lbs.	14
1/4-28	95 In. Lbs.	11	150 In. Lbs.	17
5/16-17	200 In. Lbs.	23	270 In. Lbs.	31
5/16-24	20 Ft. Lbs.	27	25 Ft. Lbs.	34
3/8-16	30 Ft. Lbs.	41	40 Ft. Lbs.	54
3/8-24	35 Ft. Lbs.	48	45 Ft. Lbs.	61
7/16-14	50 Ft. Lbs.	68	65 Ft. Lbs.	88
7/16-20	55 Ft. Lbs.	75	70 Ft. Lbs.	95
1/2-13	75 Ft. Lbs.	102	100 Ft. Lbs.	136
1/2-20	85 Ft. Lbs.	115	110 Ft. Lbs.	149
9/16-12	105 Ft. Lbs.	142	135 Ft. Lbs.	183
9/16-18	150 Ft. Lbs.	156	150 Ft. Lbs.	203
5/8-11	115 Ft. Lbs.	203	195 Ft. Lbs.	264
5/8-18	160 Ft. Lbs.	217	210 Ft. Lbs.	285
3/4-16	175 Ft. Lbs.	237	225 Ft. Lbs.	305

Fig. 3-21. The greater the grade, diameter of the bolt, and the number of teeth per inch, the greater the torque that can be applied to bolt. (Chrysler)

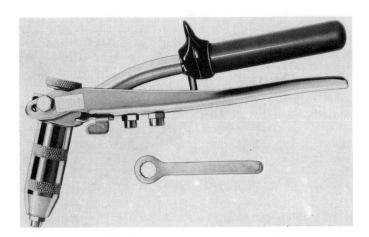

Fig. 3-18. A pop riveter installs blind rivets.

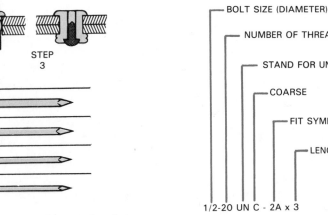

Fig. 3-19. 1—Rivet is placed into hole. 2—Handle of riveter is squeezed and rivet starts to compress. 3—Rivet is compressed and holds the two pieces of material together.

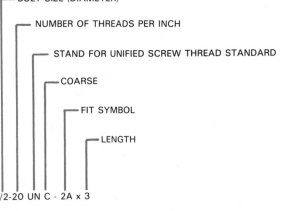

BOLT SIZE (DIAMETER)

NUMBER OF THREADS PER INCH

STAND FOR UNIFIED SCREW THREAD STANDARD

COARSE

FIT SYMBOL

LENGTH

1/2-20 UN C - 2A x 3

Fig. 3-22. Deciphering the markings for a SAE bolt. (Deere & Co.)

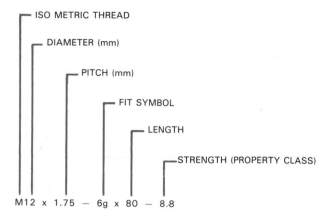

Fig. 3-23. Deciphering the marking for a metric bolt.
(Deere & Co.)

REMOVING BROKEN BOLTS

Every so often a bolt will break off during removal or installation. If this happens, the broken portion remaining must be removed. This is usually accomplished with an "E-Z out." The E-Z out, which has many spirals, is tapped into the broken bolt after a hole has been drilled at the top center of the broken bolt. This hole should be drilled at 1/2 the diameter of the bolt. The spirals on the E-Z out cause the E-Z out to be wedged into the bolt. Then a wrench or socket is applied to the hex head of the E-Z out. The broken bolt and E-Z out are backed out together. See Fig. 3-24.

LIQUID THREADLOCK

To prevent nuts, bolts, and screws from loosening due to vibration, a liquid threadlock can be applied to the threaded fastener, Fig. 3-25. This prevents the threaded fastener from vibrating loose, but allows easy removal of the threaded fastener should disassembly be required.

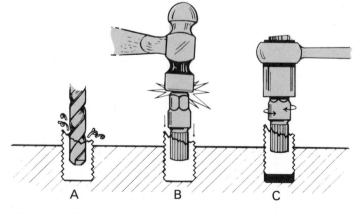

Fig. 3-24. Removing a broken bolt. A—Drill a hole in the center of broken bolt. Drill size should be approximately 1/2 the diameter of broken bolt. B—Using a hammer, tap in the E-Z out in previously drilled hole of broken bolt. C—Using a wrench or ratchet, twist the E-Z out. This will bring the broken bolt out along with the E-Z out. (Lisle Co.)

Fig. 3-25. Liquid threadlock prevents threaded fasteners from vibrating loose.

The liquid threadlock is applied to the entire threaded portion of the fastener, and is then torqued to specifications. To remove a threaded fastener that has liquid threadlock applied, after any length of time, just use a normal socket and ratchet, wrench, or screwdriver for removal.

ANTI-SEIZE LUBRICANT

Bolts, and any metal that is exposed to a continuous heat, can be "cold welded" together. To prevent this, an anti-seize lubricant should be applied to the bolt threads or connecting metal, Fig. 3-26. This is especially true of the threads on an oxygen sensor. If anti-seize lubricant is not placed on the threads, the removal will be impossible after a period of driving time. Use of anti-seize lubricant is not limited to the threads of an oxygen sensor. It can be used on exhaust manifold bolts, as well as any bolt on the exhaust system including exhaust pipe connections. Remember, this is a lubricant and not a sealer.

ROOM TEMPERATURE VULCANIZING (RTV)

RTV is also referred to as silicone sealer, Fig. 3-27. RTV can be used in place of SOME preformed gaskets, Fig. 3-28. RTV is clear in color in its pure form.

Fig. 3-26. Anti-seize lubricant is applied to the threads of fasteners, as well as connections of metal pipes that are exposed to continuous heat.

Fig. 3-27. Silicone sealer can be used in place of conventional pre-formed gaskets for many areas that require a paper, rubber, or cork gasket.

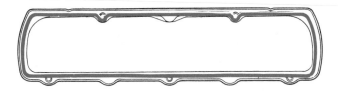

Fig. 3-28. A typical RTV bead pattern used as a valve cover gasket. Bead diameter should be approximately 1/4 in. (Oldsmobile)

Sometimes a dye is added to make the sealer black, red, orange, blue, or copper colored. RTV is either an acid or an amine base. The RTV that is of the acidic formula, when heated, causes vapors to be formed that can interfere with the operation of the oxygen sensor in the exhaust manifold. RTV can be used in place of paper, cork, or rubber gaskets. However, RTV CANNOT be used:

1. In place of an intake manifold gasket.
2. In place of a head gasket.
3. On carburetors.
4. On automatic transmissions.

To prevent any oil leaks, a dab of RTV should be placed on the rear main bearing cap, Fig. 3-29A. Also, where two gaskets, or a gasket and a seal meet, Fig. 3-29B.

Some cylinder head bolts extend through a water jacket. In those cases, the threads of the head bolt must be coated with RTV or a suitable sealer, Fig. 3-29C. If this is not done, coolant will seep past the head bolt threads and into the crankcase.

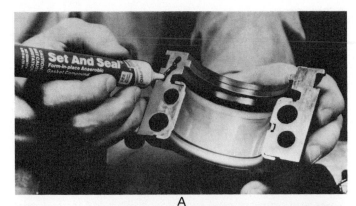

A

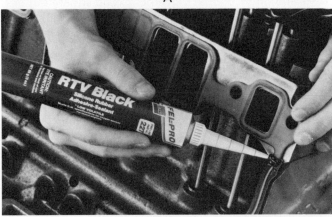

B

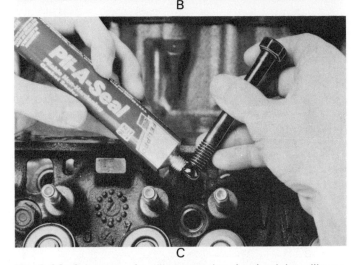

C

Fig. 3-29. Other uses for silicone sealer. A—Applying silicone sealer, or equivalent to rear main bearing cap to prevent oil leakage. B—Whenever two gasket ends meet, a dab of silicone sealer should be added at this point to prevent oil leakage. C—Always apply a sealer to threads of a cylinder head bolt that extends into a water jacket, or coolant will seep past threads. (Fel-Pro, Inc.)

SEALS

The purpose of any seal is to prevent a liquid from going where it is not wanted. A rear axle shaft seal prevents rear axle oil from contaminating the brake linings. The valve seal prevents oil from entering the combustion chamber through the valve guides. If a seal leaks there is a reason. The seal may be installed backwards, the vent may be plugged causing the seals to be blown out, or it may simply be old age of the seal. Or, it may not even be the seals fault. The bushing or bearing may be

so badly worn that it cannot control the oil flow, as the seal cannot handle the additional flow of oil. An example is when the rear axle bearing is worn, which may or may not be making noises, and the flow of oil to the seal is increased. The seal cannot handle a flood of oil, so some of the oil gets past the seal, although the seal is good. Seals are usually made of synthetic rubber, while some are made of nylon, Teflon, or steel.

O-RINGS

O-rings are round and made of Neoprene. O-rings are fitted into a groove, which holds them in place. O-rings are used where there is no rotational or axial movement of any kind, Fig. 3-30. The O-ring is usually used where a connection is made with a hose or tube fitting.

SQUARE CUT SEALS

Square cut seals are round, however the cross section is square, Fig. 3-31. The square cut seal is made of Neoprene and is used where there is slight axial movement and no rotational movement. The square cut seal is used in the clutch packs of automatic transmissions and disc brake calipers.

SEALING RINGS

Sealing rings are round, but like the square cut seal, the cross section is square. The sealing rings are either made of Teflon or steel. The Teflon sealing ring, Fig. 3-32A, is distinguished by an angle cut. While the Teflon seal can conform to irregularities, the disadvantage is that metal particles can become embedded in the sealing side reducing its effectiveness as a seal. The steel sealing ring is distinguished by the ends that are hooked together, Fig. 3-32B. Sealing rings are used where there is axial and rotational movement.

SHAFT SEALS

Shaft or lip seals, Fig. 3-33A, are usually made of Neoprene. Shaft seals are used against a shaft that rotates, Fig. 3-33B. The shaft seal prevents the oil or lubricant from leaking out while the shaft turns and prevents dirt from entering into the lubricant. If the seal is doing its job, the seal can actually cut a groove into the metal shaft, as there is no lubrication at this point, Fig. 3-34. This will only happen on high mileage vehicles. When this happens, the shaft must be reconditioned or replaced, as the oil will work its way under the seal at the groove.

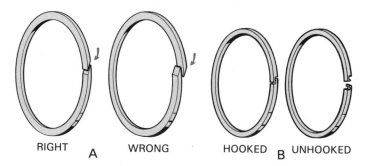

Fig. 3-32. Different types of sealing rings. A—Teflon sealing rings have an angle cut. B—Metal sealing rings have an interlocking feature. (Oldsmobile)

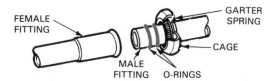

Fig. 3-30. O-rings are used where there is no axial or rotational movement. (Ford)

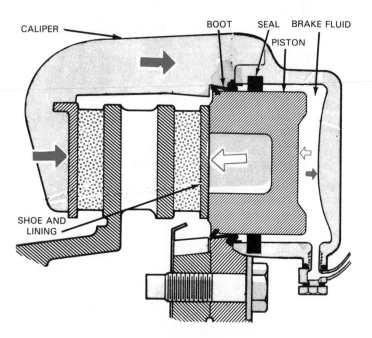

Fig. 3-31. A square cut seal is used where there is only axial movement, like a disc brake caliper. (Chrysler)

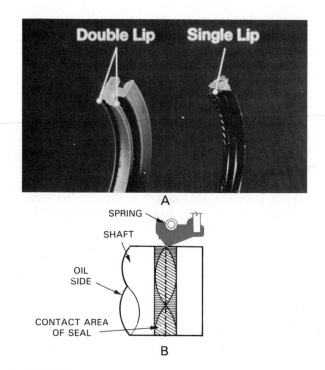

Fig. 3-33. Shaft type seals. A—Double lip seal prevents dirt from tearing inner lip seal. (Fel-Pro, Inc.) B—Shaft or lip seal is used where there is rotational movement. (C-R Industries)

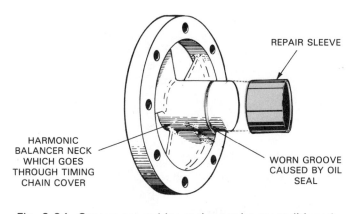

Fig. 3-34. Groove caused by seal must be reconditioned.

Fig. 3-36. Overtightening of this valve cover gasket caused the gasket to bulge out. Look up torque specifications and use a torque wrench.

VALVE SEALS

Valve seals are usually made of Nitrile, Polacrylate, or Viton. These seals are a synthetic rubber. However, Nitrile can only resist temperatures up to 250°F. The Viton seal, which is more expensive, can withstand temperatures up to 450°F. Since four cylinder engines run hotter, the Viton material must be used, or the seal will become brittle and crack, Fig. 3-35. However, Polacrylate is the most common as it can resist temperatures up to 350°F, and is not as expensive as Viton.

GASKETS

A gasket compensates for small irregularities between the two flat metal surfaces. This prevents oil and coolant from leaking. Also, in the case of a cylinder head gasket, the combustion pressure is kept in the cylinder. The most common cause for gasket failure is overtightening of the bolts that hold gasket between the metal surfaces, Fig. 3-36. To prevent overtightening of the gaskets, some manufacturers of gaskets incorporate a metal washer in

the bolt hole of the gasket. This metal washer limits the amount of torque that can be applied. Some auto manufacturers dimple the flange of the sheet metal that is bolted in place. Fig. 3-37. This has the same effect as a washer placed in the bolt hole of the gasket. Some gaskets must be installed in a specific manner, Fig. 3-38, while other gaskets do not. If there are no markings on the gasket, it can be installed any which way.

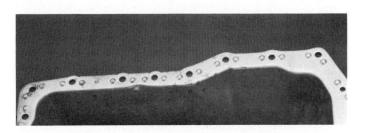
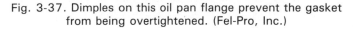

Fig. 3-37. Dimples on this oil pan flange prevent the gasket from being overtightened. (Fel-Pro, Inc.)

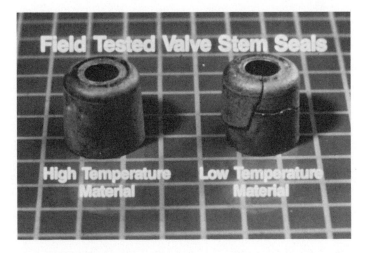

Fig. 3-35. Most all valve stem seals look the same when they are new. If high quality is not selected, early failure will result. (Fel-Pro, Inc.)

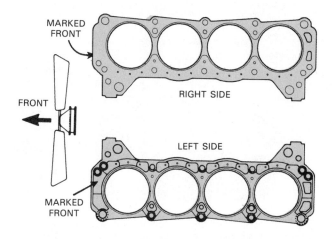

Fig. 3-38. Some gaskets must be installed in a specific manner.

MOLDED RUBBER GASKETS

Molded rubber gaskets prevent even minor oil leaks. Some of these gaskets are slightly smaller, which means that they must be stretched to fit the cover. Molded rubber gaskets are a one piece unit which eliminates any chance of leakage, Fig. 3-39. However, this type of gasket can only be used with flanges that can accommodate this type of gasket.

GASKET PREPARATION

Before installing a gasket, scrape both mating surfaces down to the bare metal, Fig. 3-40. All old gasket material must be removed. Check the mating surfaces for warpage, Fig. 3-41. If the surface of the cylinder head is warped more than .006 of an inch, the head must be shaved, Fig. 3-42. If more than .030 in. must be removed from a head, the remaining head on a V-type engine and intake manifold will have to be resurfaced, or the bolt holes and passages will not align, Fig. 3-43. If the oil pan or valve cover gasket flanges are not true, the surface must be straightened before installing the gasket, Fig. 3-44. A gasket can only compensate for small irregularities between the flat mating surfaces.

Fig. 3-41. After cleaning the mating surfaces to bare metal, the surface must be checked for warpage. Place a feeler gauge between head and straightedge. (Fel-Pro, Inc.)

Fig. 3-42. If the cylinder head is warped .006 of an inch or more, the head must be machined.

Fig. 3-39. Left. A molded rubber one piece oil pan gasket prevents oil leakage. Right. Conventional oil pan gasket has many places where oil can leak past. Silicone sealer must be used with this type of gasket. (Fel-Pro, Inc.)

Fig. 3-40. Before installing any new gasket, the mating surfaces must be removed of all old gasket material. Only bare metal must be left showing.

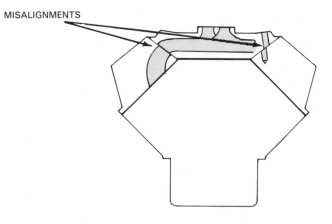

Fig. 3-43. If more than .030 of an inch must be removed from a cylinder head, the remaining cylinder head on a V-type engine and intake manifold must also be resurfaced. If this is not done, the bolt holes and intake passages will not align. (Fel-Pro, Inc.)

Fig. 3-44. If valve cover or oil pan flanges are not flat, they must also be trued.

Chapter 3—REVIEW QUESTIONS

Write your answers on a separate sheet of paper. Do not write in this book.

1. What is the major difference between a machine screw and a bolt?
2. A stud has threads on one end. True or False?
3. The largest diameter on a screw is known as:
   a. Pitch diameter.
   b. Major diameter.
   c. Minor diameter.
4. Most bolts have what shape head?
   a. Square head.
   b. Octagonal head.
   c. Hexagonal head.
   d. Round head.
5. What type of nut is used with a cotter key?
6. Name two methods used to keep nuts from working loose on a bolt.
7. Which can take more torque, a 7/16 in. diameter bolt, Grade 5, with 14 teeth per inch, or a 3/8 in. diameter bolt, Grade 8, with 24 teeth per inch?
8. A _____ is screwed down on another nut to keep it from getting loose.
9. When using a sheet metal screw, it is first necessary to tap the hole. True or False?
10. Silicone sealer can be used in place of a head gasket. True or False?
11. Stripped threads can:
    a. Not be repaired.
    b. Be repaired with tap or die.
    c. Be repaired with a helical insert.
    d. Either b or c.
12. A square cut seal is used where there is:
    a. No axial or rotational movement.
    b. Axial movement.
    c. Rotational movement.
    d. Both rotational and axial movement.
13. Anti-seize lubricant should be used on the threads of an oxygen sensor. True or False?
14. RTV should be applied to the threads of cylinder head bolts that extend into the water jacket. True or False?
15. Prior to installing a new gasket, the mating surfaces must be:
    a. Cleaned of all old gasket material.
    b. Checked for warpage.
    c. If warped, straightened or surfaced.
    d. All of the above.

Chapter 4

MEASURING INSTRUMENTS

After studying this chapter, you will be able to:
- List the different types of measuring instruments.
- Explain how to read a micrometer.
- Demonstrate how to read a Vernier caliper.
- State the purpose of telescoping gauges.

MICROMETERS

A micrometer is an instrument designed for linear measurement with accuracy of .001 in. or better. Micrometers are available to measure in either the metric or English system. The inside micrometer, Fig. 4-1, is used for measuring the distance between two parallel surfaces, and for measuring the inside diameter of cylinders.

The outside micrometer, Figs. 4-2 and 4-3, is designed to measure the outside diameter of cylindrical forms and the thickness of materials. Its spindle is attached to the thimble on the inside, at the point of adjustment. Often, a friction stop is provided. The part of the spindle concealed within the sleeve and thimble is threaded to fit a nut in the frame. The frame is stationary.

When the micrometer thimble is revolved by the thumb and finger, the spindle revolves with it and moves through the nut in the frame, moving toward or away from the anvil. The distance or measurement of the opening between the anvil and the spindle is indicated by the line and figures on the sleeve and the thimble. See Fig. 4-4.

Fig. 4-1. Measuring the inner diameter with an inside micrometer.

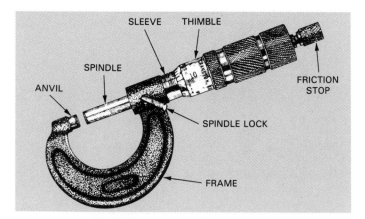

Fig. 4-2. Nomenclature of a conventional micrometer. (Central Tools)

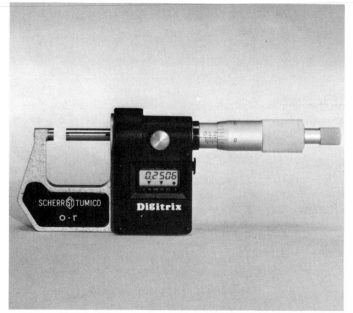

Fig. 4-3. A digital micrometer directly reads the measurement; no math is involved to obtain measurement.

46

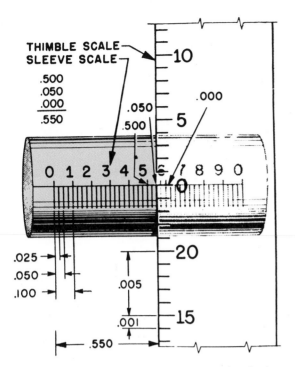

THIMBLE SCALE
SLEEVE SCALE

.500
.050
.000
.550

.050
.500

.000

0 1 2 3 4 5 6 7 8 9 0

10

5

0

.025
.050
.100

.005

.001

.550

20

15

Fig. 4-4. Micrometer readings on a conventional micrometer. The reading is 0.550 in.

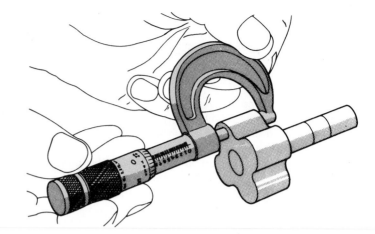

Fig. 4-5. Measuring with a micrometer.

READING A MICROMETER

When the micrometer is closed, the bevelled end of the thimble aligns with 0 on the sleeve. The 0 mark on the thimble is aligned with the horizontal line on the sleeve.

Opening the micrometer by revolving the thimble one full revolution will make the 0 line of the thimble align with the horizontal line of the sleeve. The distance between the anvil and spindle is now .025 in.

The bevelled edge of the thimble is marked in 25 divisions. Rotating the thimble from one of these divisions to the next moves the spindle .001 in.

To read the micrometer, multiply the number of vertical divisions that are visible on the sleeve by 25. Then add the number of divisions on the bevel of the thimble from 0 to the line which aligns with the horizontal line on the sleeve. The closeup view of a micrometer's sleeve and thimble, Fig. 4-4, shows a reading of .550 in.

Fig. 4-5 shows the correct method of holding a micrometer. The thimble is turned until the spindle and anvil just touch the object.

When using a micrometer, take care not to turn the thimble too tight. This will distort the frame and result in inaccurate readings. Only gentle pressure is used.

Telescoping gauges, Fig. 4-6, are available for measuring the diameter of small holes. After adjusting the gauge in the hole so that it fits snugly, the gauge is removed and measured with a micrometer.

The small hole gauge shown in Fig. 4-7 is used in the automotive machine shop for measuring the diameter of valve guide bores. The small hole gauge is inserted in the bore and expanded until it fills the diameter. Then it is withdrawn, and its width is measured with a micrometer.

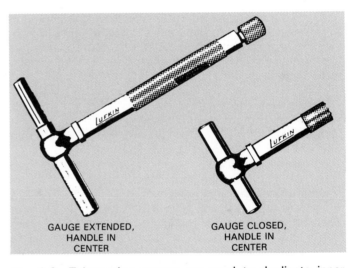

GAUGE EXTENDED,
HANDLE IN
CENTER

GAUGE CLOSED,
HANDLE IN
CENTER

Fig. 4-6. Telescoping gauges are used to duplicate inner dimensions. A micrometer is then used to measure the gauge.

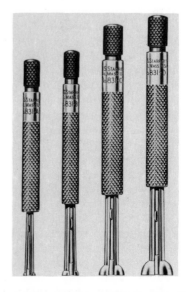

Fig. 4-7. Small hole gauges duplicate the size of hole. A micrometer then measures the gauge.

METRIC MICROMETERS

Metric micrometers are used in the same manner as the English type previously described, except that graduations are in metric units. Readings are obtained as follows:

Since the pitch of the spindle screw in metric micrometers is 0.5 millimeters (mm), one complete revolution of the thimble advances the spindle toward or away from the anvil exactly 0.5 mm.

The longitudinal line on the sleeve is graduated from 0 to 25 mm, and each millimeter is subdivided in 0.5 mm. Therefore, it requires two revolutions of the thimble to advance the spindle a distance equal to 1 mm.

The beveled edge of the thimble is graduated in 50 divisions, every fifth line being numbered from 0 to 50. Since a complete revolution of the thimble advances the spindle 0.5 mm, each graduation on the thimble is equal to 1/50 of 0.5 mm or 0.01 mm. Two graduations equal 0.02 mm, etc.

To read a metric micrometer, add the total reading in millimeters visible on the sleeve to the reading in hundredths of a millimeter indicated by the graduation on the thimble which aligns with the longitudinal line on the sleeve.

Example: Refer to Fig. 4-8:
The ''5'' mm graduation is visible,
  representing 5   mm
There is one additional 0.5 mm line visible,
  representing . . . . 0.5 mm
Line ''28'' on the thimble aligns with the
  longitudinal line on the sleeve, each line
  representing .01 mm . .28 x .01 mm = 0.28 mm
The metric micrometer reading is . . . . . . 5.78 mm

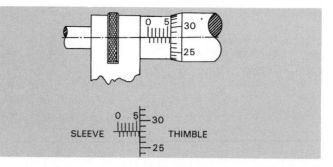

Fig. 4-8. A metric micrometer scale. Reading is 5.78 mm. (L.S. Starret Co.)

VERNIER CALIPER

The Vernier caliper is a measuring device capable of measuring to within one-thousandths of an inch (.001). It can measure both internal and external diameters, and some are provided with both metric and English scales. Fig. 4-9 shows a Vernier caliper.

The main bar of a Vernier caliper is graduated in increments of .025 in. Every fourth division, which represents one-tenth of an inch, is numbered, Fig. 4-10. The Vernier plate has a space divided into twenty-five divisions, numbered 0, 5, 10, 15, 20, and 25. These twenty-five divisions on the Vernier occupy the same space as the twenty-four divisions on the bar. The difference between the width of one of the twenty-five spaces on the Vernier and one of the twenty-four spaces on the bar is 1/1000 of an inch.

If the caliper is set so that 0 line on Vernier aligns with 0 line on bar, the line to the right of 0 on Vernier will differ from line to the right of 0 on bar by .001 in.; the second line by .002 in., etc. The difference will continue to increase .001 in. for each division until line 25 on Vernier aligns with line 24 on bar.

To read the tool, note how many inches, .100 and .025 from the 0 mark on the bar. Then note the number of divisions on the Vernier from the 0 to a line which aligns exactly with a line on the bar. For example: In Fig.

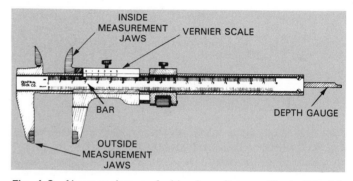

Fig. 4-9. Nonmenclature of a Vernier caliper. (Central Tools)

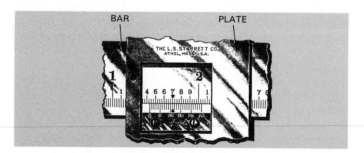

Fig. 4-10. Reading on Vernier caliper is 1.436 in.

4-10, the Vernier has moved to the right one and four-tenths and one-fortieth inches (1.425), as shown on the bar. Also, the eleventh line on the Vernier aligns with a line indicated by the star on the bar. Eleven-thousandths of an inch are added to the reading on the bar, and the total reading is 1.436 in.

DIAL GAUGES

Dial gauges, Fig. 4-11, are used extensively for measuring the backlash of gears and the end play of shafts, Fig. 4-12. This is particularly important to the adjustment of the rear axle pinion and ring gear. In addition, dial gauges can be used to determine out-of-roundness of a bore.

Movement of the needle of the gauge will show the variation in measurement. Dial gauges are calibrated to read in .001 in.

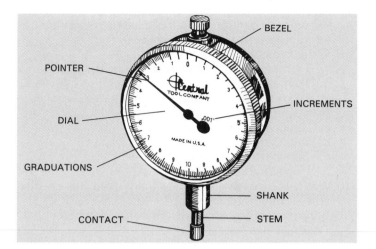

Fig. 4-11. Nomenclature of a dial gauge. (Central Tools)

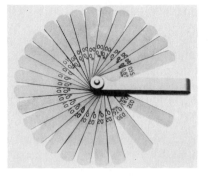

Fig. 4-13. Feeler gauge has markings in both English and metric. (Auto-Test)

THICKNESS GAUGE

The thickness gauge, or feeler gauge, is used for measuring the distance between two surfaces that are only a few thousandths of an inch apart. A feeler gauge consists of an assortment of steel strips of graduated thickness. Each blade of the gauge is marked with its thickness in thousandths of an inch, and/or in millimeters. This eliminates any unnecessary conversions.

Because of the increasing number of imported cars in the U.S. with service specifications given in millimeters, thickness gauges are not available with each blade marked in fractions of an inch and fractions of a millimeter, Fig. 4-13.

USING A FEELER GAUGE

To use a feeler gauge, insert a blade in the space to be measured. If the gauge blade is a snug fit, that space is equal to the blade thickness in thousandths of an inch. Feeler gauges are used extensively for measuring valve clearance, and the gap of spark plugs.

When a feeler gauge is used to measure the clearance between a piston and cylinder wall, the force required

to withdraw it is measured by a spring balance. See Fig. 4-14.

In addition to flat blade feeler gauges, thickness gauges having different diameter wire "feelers" are available, Fig. 4-15. Wire gauges are recommended for measuring plug gaps.

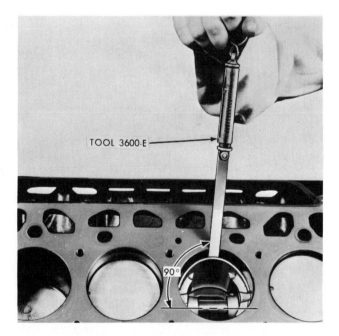

Fig. 4-14. Feeler gauge is attached to spring scale to check clearance between piston and cylinder.

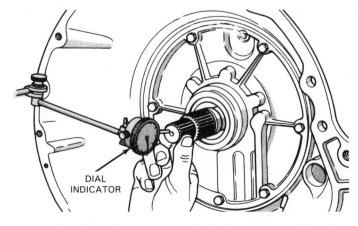

Fig. 4-12. Checking end play with dial indicator. (Chrysler)

Fig. 4-15. Wire type feeler gauge is used for measuring gap on spark plugs.

Chapter 4—REVIEW QUESTIONS

Write your answers on a separate sheet of paper. Do not write in this book.

1. For what purpose are inside micrometers frequently used in automotive service work?
2. When the thimble of a micrometer is turned one division of the thimble, how far has the spindle moved?
   a. .025 in.   c. .001 in.
   b. .0025 in.   d. .005 in.
3. When the thimble of a metric micrometer is turned one division as indicated by the lines on the beveled edge of the thimble, how far has the spindle moved?
   a. 5.0 mm   c. .05 mm   e. .1 mm
   b. .5 mm   d. .25 mm   f. .01 mm
4. For what two purposes is a dial gauge frequently used in automotive service work?
5. A thickness gauge is used:
   a. To measure the thickness of sheet metal.
   b. To measure the diameter of car engine cylinders.
   c. To measure the space between two surfaces.
6. A telescoping gauge is used to:
   a. Duplicate outside dimensions.
   b. Duplicate the thickness of an object.
   c. Duplicate inner dimensions.
   d. Duplicate itself.
7. What is the small hole gauge used for in the automotive machine shop?
8. A Vernier caliper can measure inside diameters only. True or False?

Chapter 5

METERS, TESTERS, AND ANALYZERS

After studying this chapter, you will be able to:
- List the basic instruments used for electrical systems testing.
- Describe the D'Arsonval meter movement.
- Tell the way in which voltmeter and ammeter leads must be hooked up to an electrical circuit.
- State tests that are possible with a battery fast charger/tester.
- Name and describe a broad range of engine analyzers.

There is one particular demonstration of automotive know-how that makes an engine service technician stand out as an expert. It is the abilty to systematically test, evaluate, and correct performance problems in all five major engine systems: starting, charging, fuel distribution, compression, and ignition.

The expert technician, however, performs as an expert with the help of a full range of reliably accurate meters, testers, and analyzers. For electrical systems testing, basic instruments include the AMMETER for measuring the current in amperes, the VOLTMETER for measuring the voltage or pressure, and the OHMMETER for testing resistance.

The technician also makes regular use of a battery-starter tester, alternator-regulator tester, battery charger, multimeter, infrared exhaust analyzer, digital engine systems analyzer, and on-board computer tester. For internal engine troubleshooting, support comes from a compression tester, vacuum gauge, and cylinder leakage tester.

D'ARSONVAL METER DESIGN

Basically, two types of meters are used in automotive service work: pointer and digital readout types. These sensitive instruments are designed to measure and indicate electrical values.

A POINTER TYPE METER has a calibrated dial (face with marked values) and a pointer that indicates the value of the electrical unit under test. DIGITAL READOUT METERS "spell" the value of the unit under test. This type of meter is especially well suited for use in computerized engine systems analyzers, on-board computer testers, and exhaust emissions analyzers.

Most pointer type meters (ammeters, voltmeters, and ohmmeters) used in the automotive service field are of the moving coil type. See Figs. 5-1 and 5-2. These instruments consist of a horseshoe-shaped or hoop-shaped permanent magnet and a movable coil. In addition, a damping spring (similar to hairspring of a watch) is attached to the pointer of the meter. The damping spring is used to prevent the pointer from going full scale too quickly when current is applied and removed.

This long established meter design is known as the D'ARSONVAL MOVEMENT. Usually, the D'Arsonval movement is "jeweled" to cut down on friction to insure the accuracy of its readings. Therefore, a D'Arsonval meter is reliably accurate — and sensitive. For this reason, it must be handled with utmost care. Any shock to the meter could damage the movement and ruin the meter.

In this same meter care area: When using any pointer type meter with multiple ranges, always start by adjusting the range selector switch to the highest range. Then reduce the switch setting until the meter is able to "read" the electrical value. Otherwise, a low range setting could result in "pegging the meter," which happens when the pointer swings hard against the high end of the meter scale.

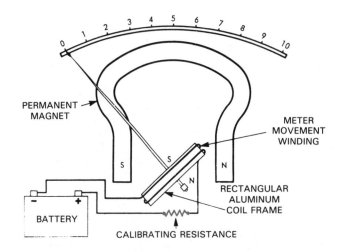

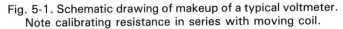

Fig. 5-1. Schematic drawing of makeup of a typical voltmeter. Note calibrating resistance in series with moving coil.

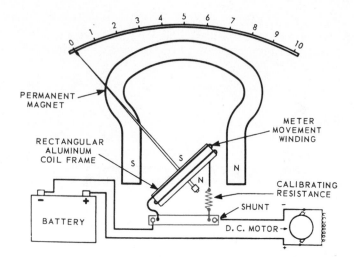

Fig. 5-2. Note that ammeter has a heavy resistance (shunt) connected across moving coil and another resistance connected in series with moving coil.

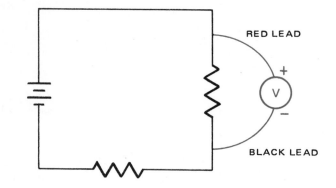

Fig. 5-3. Schematic shows how to hook up a voltmeter across circuit. Always connect test leads so that voltmeter is in parallel to circuit.

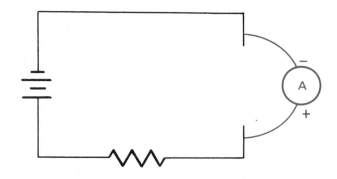

Fig. 5-4. Schematic shows how to hook up ammeter in series with circuit: open circuit; connect meter test leads; read meter.

AMMETER/VOLTMETER OPERATION

The basic design of an ammeter and a voltmeter is the same. However, as shown in Fig. 5-2, the ammeter is provided with a heavy SHUNT (alternate path for current) of low resistance connected across the movable coil. Another resistance is connected in series with one end of the shunt and the coil. This resistance is used for calibrating the instrument.

The voltmeter does not have a resistance shunted across the coil, but it does have the calibrating resistance in series with the movable coil. See Fig. 5-1. When hooking up voltmeter leads, always connect them in parallel to, or across, the terminals of the device or circuit, Fig. 5-3. On the other hand, always connect ammeter leads in series with the circuit, Fig. 5-4.

When the circuit to be tested is closed, current flowing through the movable coil of the ammeter or voltmeter reacts with the magnetic field, causing the coil to rotate against the tension of the damping spring. Relative movement of the coil is directly proportional to the current flowing through it. A pointer attached to the coil moves across a calibrated scale on the meter face to indicate the amount of current or voltage flowing through the coil.

A single voltmeter can be designed to cover different ranges of voltage (0-2, 0-20, etc.). This is done by varying the resistance in series with the movable coil. A separate resistance is provided for each range of the instrument. The resistance value — and the voltage range — is changed by means of a switch located on the instrument.

Ammeters also can be designed to cover different ranges of current (0-10, 0-100, etc.) by providing different shunts. When working with an ammeter, be sure to use the leads provided by the meter manufacturer. Leads having a different resistance will seriously affect the accuracy of the instrument.

A generally accepted standard for the maximum resistance of an ammeter is a 0.1 volt drop across the ammeter terminals of the connected ammeter leads with

10 amps flowing in the circuit. Therefore, the resistance would be .01 ohm.

In general, ammeters and voltmeters used for automotive service work should have an accuracy of one percent of full scale deflection. In addition, these instruments should be compensated for changes in temperature.

OHMMETERS

The ohmmeter is designed to measure resistance of an electric circuit or unit in ohms. A typical automotive application is testing the resistance type of high tension wiring. Another use is testing continuity (unbroken path for current flow).

Generally, the ohmmeter utilizes a D'Arsonval movement. In addition, it has a calibrated resistance, a variable resistance, and a self-contained dry cell. See Fig. 5-5. All ohmmeters need dry cells to serve as the voltage supply needed to force current through the circuit or unit being tested. *The power must be OFF in the circuit under test.*

The leads used to connect the ohmmeter to the circuit are of special low resistance. Since they are used for calibrating the instrument, these same leads must be used when measuring the resistance of a circuit. To calibrate the ohmmeter, it is necessary to "zero the meter." This is done by joining the two instrument leads together to establish zero resistance. Then, the variable

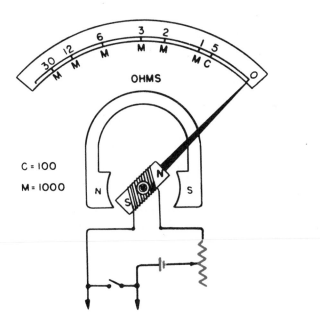

OHMS

C = 100

M = 1000

Fig. 5-5. Schematic drawing of makeup of a typical ohmmeter. Note dry cell and adjustable resistance.

resistance is adjusted to bring the pointer to the zero mark on the calibrated dial.

To measure resistance, simply connect the leads from the ohmmeter (or contact the probes) to the terminals of the unit to be tested. Then read the resistance in ohms on the dial of the meter. Most ohmmeters used in automotive service work have two ranges: 0-500 ohms and 0-50,000 ohms (50 kilohms).

MULTIMETERS

Compact digital multimeters are available that combine voltmeter, ohmmeter, and milliammeter in one instrument. The multimeter shown in Fig. 5-6 features

a push button switch that permits either manual or automatic ranging. A digital display provides a readout of test results. A continuity buzzer and diode function test are also featured.

TACHOMETERS

The TACHOMETER is designed to indicate the speed of a rotating part in revolutions per minute (rpm). For automotive use, the tachometer is "made" for measuring the speed of the engine.

Modern tachometers usually consist of a jeweled D'Arsonval movement, zero adjuster, and solid state, Zener diode-stabilized circuitry. Low and high ranges are generally provided. Low, for example, could be 0-1200 rpm; high range could be 0-6000 rpm.

In a typical engine speed test, connect one lead of the tachometer to the primary terminal of the distributor. Connect the other lead to ground. Set the control for low range to test curb idle and fast idle. Set the control for high range to make tests at speeds above 1200 rpm.

DWELL METERS

Often a dwell meter is contained in the same case as a tachometer. Usually, these are hand-held units called "tach-dwell meters." The DWELL METER is used mainly for measuring the angle through which the ignition distributor shaft turns while the breaker points are closed. This is known as point dwell or cam angle.

The vehicle manufacturer specifies what the cam angle should be for different engine applications. Since the cam angle relates to opening and closing of the breaker points, adjusting the point gap also adjusts the cam angle. After making the point gap setting, it can be checked for accuracy (and readjusted if necessary) by hooking up the dwell meter and measuring the cam angle.

BATTERY/STARTER TESTERS

Battery testing equipment ranges from the hydrometer to a voltmeter for making open circuit voltage tests to a multi-purpose unit that combines voltmeter, ammeter, and load control. See Figs. 5-7 and 5-8. Housed in a

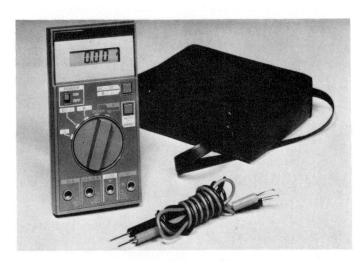

Fig. 5-6. Digital multimeter has five voltage ranges, starting at 0-0.2 volts. Current ranges are 0-200 milliamps and 10 amps ac and dc. Five resistance ranges start at 0-200 ohms and go to 20 megohms. (Accurate Instruments)

Fig. 5-7. Starting and charging systems tester shows amps and volts in digital display. It has an automatic return load control knob and a ripple indicator that reveals alternator defects. (Snap-on Tools)

single, portable cabinet, some of these combination units make it possible to test batteries, starters, alternators, voltage regulators, and related circuitry.

The tester shown in Fig. 5-7 has a 0-750 amp current range, zero amps control, and LED (light emitting diode) displays. It also has a "ripple" indicator that analyzes the quality of an alternator's dc output. Tests that can be performed by this combination unit include: battery load, starter current load, cranking voltage and engine cranking speed, diode-stator condition, alternator current output, and voltage regulator operation.

The tester shown in Fig. 5-8 is designed to test all recognized battery ratings, including cold cranking performance and ampere hours. It has a compensation adjustment for battery temperatures from 0-125 °F (−18-52 °C). A color-coded scale shows condition of battery, cables, alternator, and regulator.

BATTERY FAST CHARGERS

BATTERY FAST CHARGERS have become more automatic and foolproof. Most have alternator protection to guard against reverse hookup. One line of fast chargers uses a LED indicator that shows "green" for correct connection or "red" for reverse connection.

Charging rate output selection is provided on fast chargers. Some also have an electric timer with 120 minute "hold" position for slow charging. Maximum charging rates are in the 60-100 amp range; cranking power, 200-300 amps. See Fig. 5-9.

One step up from the fast charger is the FAST CHARGER/TESTER. In addition to alternator protection and slow charge timer, the charger/tester provides a "start charge" for completely discharged batteries. It also has a thermal overload device and battery type selector (conventional or maintenance-free). A battery rating control compensates for capacity of the battery in cold cranking amps or ampere hours.

As a tester, the battery fast charger/tester can analyze battery condition, state of charge, and battery operating performance. It also checks the charging system, starter, cables, and will reveal short circuits in the electrical system.

EXHAUST GAS ANALYZERS

With so much emphasis on exhaust emission control, service technicians need suitable test equipment to verify (through various modes of engine operation) whether or not the engine is emitting excessive amounts of air pollutants. INFRARED EXHAUST GAS ANALYZERS are most commonly used to detect the amounts of hydrocarbons (HC) and carbon monoxide (CO) in the exhaust gas. See Fig. 5-10.

Fig. 5-9. Battery fast charger has silicon rectifier to change ac input to dc output. Heavy duty unit has a six-position charge rate selector, 0-100 amp ammeter scale, and a dead battery activator. (Christie Electric Corp.)

Fig. 5-8. Portable battery tester also checks condition of alternator, regulator, and primary circuit cables. Tester has a built-in discharge load comparable to car's starter current draw. (Christie Electric Corp.)

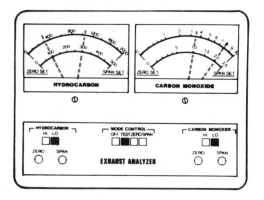

Fig. 5-10. Diagram of a typical infrared exhaust analyzer. Dashed lines show normal range of readings on low scale of HC and CO meters.

Infrared Block Diagram

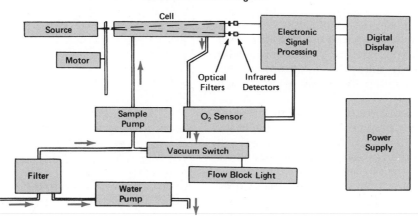

Fig. 5-11. Infrared exhaust analyzer block diagram traces flow of exhaust gas sample through cell where sample absorbs infrared energy from source. Digital display reads in HC and CO values. (Peerless Instrument Co.)

Infrared exhaust gas analyzers measure HC and CO by how much infrared energy is absorbed by a sample of the vehicle's exhaust gas. In the infrared block diagram shown in Fig. 5-11, infrared energy generated by an electrically heated element is projected through a sample tube (cell) that has the vehicle's exhaust gas flowing through it. Infrared radiation not absorbed by the exhaust gases hits an infrared detector and is converted to an electronic signal that causes the digital display of the test result to change. With this infrared exhaust gas analyzer, digital readouts have a 0-1999 ppm (parts per million) HC range, and a 0-9.99 percent CO range.

Analyzer operation is simple:
1. Allow analyzer to warm up for 15 minutes in standby mode with probe in clean air.
2. Warm engine to operating temperature. NOTE: Cold engines produce excessive pollutants and water vapor which will quickly clog the filter. See that choke valve is open and fast idle cam is released.
3. Push analyzer ZERO button and adjust zero controls until displays read zero.
4. Insert probe in vehicle's tailpipe.
5. Push analyzer RUN button.
6. Allow displays to stabilize, then read HC and CO values at idle and at 1500-2000 rpm and compare with emissions standards or limits.

FOUR-GAS ANALYZERS are an advanced type of exhaust gas analyzer. These units test for HC, CO, CO_2 (carbon dioxide), and O_2 (oxygen). Some 4-gas analyzers use emissions analysis to determine whether the cause of an engine performance problem is in the fuel system or in the ignition system.

One equipment manufacturer couples the 4-gas analyzer module with an engine analyzer said to provide "all systems" engine diagnosis, Fig. 5-12. This computer test center reportedly is capable of identifying problems such as: rich, lean, or unbalanced air-fuel mixtures; closed loop system malfunctions; air pump or catalytic converter malfunction; carburetor faults, intake manifold leaks; EGR valve leaks; blown head gaskets; air leaks; excessive misfire; excessive spark advance; leaks or restrictions in exhaust systems.

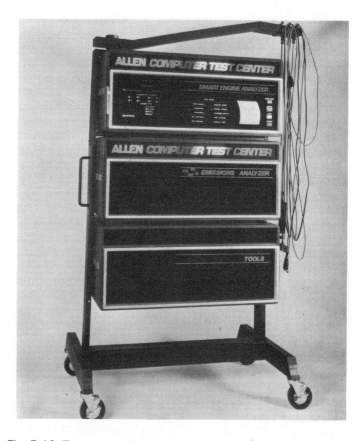

Fig. 5-12. To meet challenge of diagnosing computer controlled engine systems, one test equipment manufacturer couples a 4-gas analyzer with an engine analyzer. Note video monitor and printout. (Allen Testproducts Div., Allen Group)

Another equipment manufacturer produces a digital performance gas analyzer that combines digital display with computer electronics. The unit is microcomputer controlled with automatically timed warmup period and automatically timed gas calibration. The digital display reads 0-2000 ppm HC in 10 ppm increments, and 0-10 percent CO in .05 percent increments.

OSCILLOSCOPES

The OSCILLOSCOPE, Fig. 5-13, is an electronic device used to visually observe and measure the instantaneous voltage in an electrical circuit. Basically, the oscilloscope consists of a cathode ray tube (CRT) and operational circuitry. It operates in much the same manner as a television set.

The "scope" produces a graph-like picture showing voltage values with respect to time. The picture generally is referred to as the pattern or waveform. This pattern on the scope face or screen provides a visual means for comparing the performance of a vehicle's ignition system or charging system to a normal pattern for the system being tested, Fig. 5-14.

Technically, the pattern is produced by the cathode ray, or electron beam, striking a phosphor coating on the inside of the CRT screen. When the electrons strike this material, it gives off a brilliant glow, making it possible to see or trace the path of the beam as it moves across the screen.

The electron beam is moved or deflected by voltage applied to metal plates within the tube. Horizontal deflection or sweep moves the beam from left to right. Vertical deflection or sweep moves the beam up and down on the screen of the CRT. The screen, then, shows "time" on the horizontal axis and "voltage" on the vertical axis. The horizontal axis is called the "X-axis." The vertical axis is called the "Y-axis."

In addition to being able to measure voltage in an electrical circuit, the scope can be used to determine the polarity of the voltage. Polarity is indicated by the vertical movement of the electron beam. When the scope leads are properly connected to the secondary circuit of the ignition system, the voltage (normally negative) will appear above the zero reference line. See Fig. 5-15.

The scope pattern is controlled by the voltage in the electrical system to which it is connected. Scopes can also be connected to non-electrical components by means of special pickups known as transducers. These devices, which convert other forms of energy to electrical impulses, are used to observe engine compression and valve action, and to locate noises and vibrations.

SCOPE CONTROLS AND OPERATION

Today's basic oscilloscope can be used to test conventional and electronic ignition systems, ignition system components, alternator diode condition, and cylinder balance. Scopes can be used to test ignition coil performance, distributor component condition, spark plug circuit firing voltages, resistance, or leakage.

In operating the scope shown in Fig. 5-13, many test patterns can be displayed. Function buttons provide the following pattern selections: 25 kV and 50 kV secondary patterns; secondary superimposed; secondary raster; primary parade; alternator test. Adjustment controls are shown in Fig. 5-13.

ENGINE ANALYZERS

ENGINE ANALYZER is a generic term for a host of testers ranging from a hand-held, ten-function tune-up

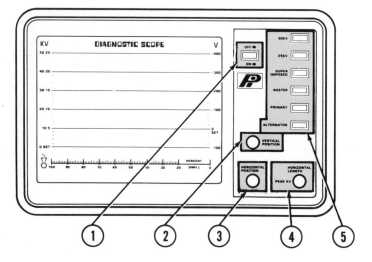

Fig. 5-13. Diagnostic scope can be used as a module of a console or alone. Controls include: 1—On-off. 2—Vertical position. 3—Horizontal position. 4—Horizontal length. 5—Function buttons. (Peerless Instrument Co.)

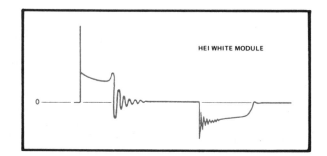

Fig. 5-14. On this particular scope, pattern or waveform is normal for GM High Energy Ignition (HEI) for a single cylinder. (Peerless Instrument Co.)

NORMAL INDICATIONS

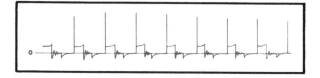

PROBLEMS / CAUSES

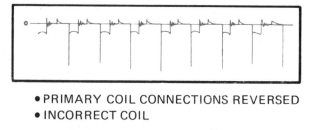

- PRIMARY COIL CONNECTIONS REVERSED
- INCORRECT COIL

Fig. 5-15. In testing spark polarity on scope, normal pattern is above zero reference line (top). Reversed polarity (bottom) means incorrect coil or reversed coil connections. (Peerless Instrument Co.)

analyzer to a massive console of equipment modules that includes a large screen oscilloscope, an automatic computer analyzer, and banks of large scale test meters. In between, a most popular group of compact digital engine analyzers are available for tieing in with GM Computer Command Control (C-3) and other on-board computer systems. These special testers interpret the CCC signals that indicate malfunctions in various engine systems. Data is entered into the tester and specific tests are requested. Trouble codes are digitally displayed for checkout against GM shop manual fault code listings and their meaning.

Oscilloscopes are a well accepted form of engine analyzer. However, to broaden test capabilities, some console manufacturers add a timing light/timing advance unit and a cylinder shorting expanded scale tachometer. Lead sets for these accessories plug into the back of the oscilloscope.

As mentioned earlier, the oscilloscope is often coupled with an infrared exhaust analyzer or 4-gas analyzer. Another popular mobile console with scope includes three banks of large scale meters — dwell/amp, volt/ohm, vacuum gauge, tachometer, HC and CO meters.

Still another oscilloscope console includes a coil, condenser, and cylinder leakage tester module. Coupled with the proper waveform analysis, this module tests coils for reversed polarity, shorts, open circuit, and insulation breakdown. Condenser tests include series resistance, capacity, and leakage. The cylinder leakage tester pinpoints a blown head gasket, cracked block, and bad cylinders and valves.

Console type engine analyzers, then, come in many packages. Some can be built up by adding modules to a basic test stand to suit individual needs. Others are unitized and put on wheels to provide mobility. Still others are suspended from an overhead track and travel from service bay to service bay. Some consoles are used in conjunction with a dynamometer to simulate road testing.

Probably the most sophisticated of modern engine analyzers is the automatic computer analyzer. Factory approved specifications are programmed into the computer. Data is then collected, based on the vehicle's actual operating characteristics. The computer analyzes this information and deduces which components are faulty in any of the major engine systems — starting, charging, fuel distribution, compression, timing, and ignition.

Test results are displayed automatically on the computer terminal. In addition, a hard-copy printout is provided by a multi-copy printer. The printout contains both "specified" and "actual" readings for each test for the technician's and customer's verification.

CHAPTER 5 — REVIEW QUESTIONS

Write your answers on a separate sheet of paper. Do not write in this book.

1. An ohmmeter is used to test:
   a. Current.
   b. Voltage.
   c. Resistance.
   d. Engine speed.
2. Basically, two "types" of meters are used in automotive service work. What are they?
3. When hooking up voltmeter leads to an electrical circuit, they are always connected in _____ (parallel or series).
4. When hooking up ammeter leads to an electrical circuit, they are always connected in _____ (parallel or series).
5. Usually, the D'Arsonval movement is _____ to cut down on friction and insure the accuracy of its readings.
   a. Jeweled.
   b. Calibrated.
   c. Sensitized.
   d. Micro-finished.
6. Why must you use the ammeter leads provided by the meter manufacturer?
7. What is meant by "pegging the meter?"
   a. Having line of sight directly in front of meter pointer to insure an accurate reading.
   b. Allowing pointer to swing hard against high end of meter scale.
   c. Calibrating pointer exactly on zero.
   d. Making incorrect meter lead hookups and reversing polarity.
8. When testing with an ohmmeter, why must the power be OFF in the circuit under test?
9. Four-gas analyzers test exhaust gas for HC, CO, CO_2, and _____ (NOx or O_2).
10. The oscilloscope screen shows time on the horizontal axis and _____ on the vertical axis.
11. The scope pattern is controlled by the voltage in the electrical system to which it is connected. True or False?

Match the question number for each of the following instruments with the letter designated for each correct associated term.

12. ____ Voltmeter.
13. ____ Ammeter.
14. ____ Ohmmeter.
15. ____ Tachometer.
16. ____ Dwell meter.
17. ____ Battery fast charger/tester.
18. ____ Exhaust gas analyzer.
19. ____ Oscilloscope.
20. ____ C-3 digital engine analyzer.

a. Engine rpm
b. Cold cranking amps.
c. Waveform.
d. Vacuum in in. Hg.
e. Series hookup in circuit.
f. Breaker point gap.
g. On-board computer.
h. Parallel hookup in circuit.
i. Resistance in circuit.
j. Cylinder leakage.
k. Infrared.

Chapter 6
ENGINE FUNDAMENTALS

After studying this chapter, you will be able to:
- Identify a water-cooled and air-cooled engine.
- List the sequence of events in a two cycle and four cycle engine.
- Distinguish the difference between an F, L, or I head engine.
- State how crankshafts are designed and why counterweights are needed.

FUNDAMENTALS

Automobiles have been operated successfully by electric motors, steam engines, and internal combustion engines. The internal combustion engine burns fuel within the cylinders, and converts the expanding force of the combustion or "explosion" into rotary force used to propel the vehicle.

There are several types of internal combustion engines: two and four cycle reciprocating piston engines, gas turbines, free piston, and rotary combustion engines. However, the four cycle reciprocating engine has been refined to such a degree that they have almost complete dominance of the automotive field. Engines of other types are described in Chapter 18, DIESEL and OTHER ENGINES.

ENGINE FUELS

Internal combustion engines can be made to operate on almost anything that can be converted into a gas that will burn: wood, coal, alcohol, vegetable oils, mineral oils, etc. However, because of convenience, a wide variety of petroleum products are used as fuel: gasoline, kerosene, fuel oil, liquefied petroleum gas (LP-Gas), etc. When kerosene, fuel oil, or LP-Gas is used, it is necessary to alter the design or equipment of the engine to other than standard gasoline engine practice.

ENGINE DESIGN

Gasoline engines used in automotive vehicles are of two basic types, four cycle and two cycle. Either may be water-cooled, Fig. 6-1, or air-cooled, Fig. 6-2. Four, six, and eight cylinder engines are available.

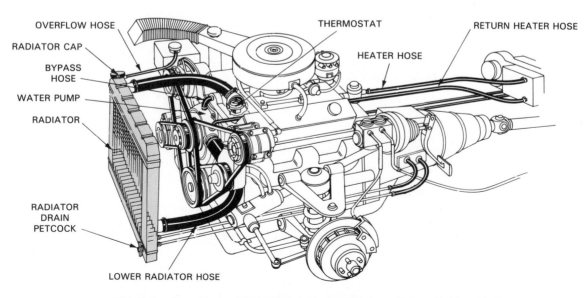

OVERFLOW HOSE

RADIATOR CAP

BYPASS HOSE

WATER PUMP

RADIATOR

RADIATOR DRAIN PETCOCK

LOWER RADIATOR HOSE

THERMOSTAT

HEATER HOSE

RETURN HEATER HOSE

Fig. 6-1. A water-cooled engine has a radiator.   (Gates Rubber Co.)

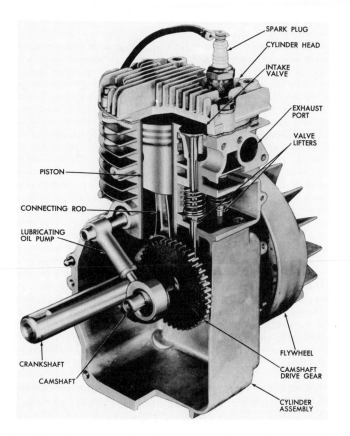

Fig. 6-2. An air-cooled engine has no radiator. However, the engine has cooling fins. The cooling fins are exposed to the air, and heat from the engine is dissipated through the fins.

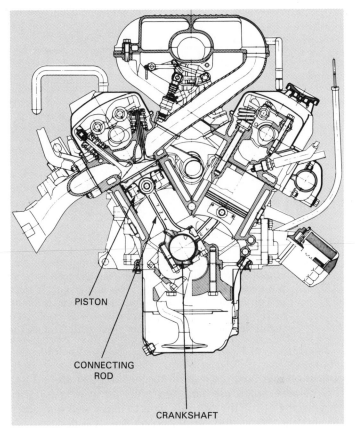

Fig. 6-3. Note the position and arrangement of the various engine parts.   (Chrysler)

The basic automobile engine is the reciprocating piston, four cycle, water-cooled, poppet valve, gasoline engine.

RECIPROCATING ENGINES

Each "cylinder" of the typical automobile engine has a "piston" which reciprocates (moves back and forth) within the cylinder. Each piston is connected to the "crankshaft" by means of a link known as a "connecting rod." See Fig. 6-3.

Other types of reciprocating engines substitute an eccentric, an inclined plate or a cam mechanism for the crankshaft. The "free piston" engine has no crankshaft or connecting rods.

ENGINE OPERATING SEQUENCE

In internal combustion engines, there is a definite series of events that must occur in sequence:
1. Fill cylinder or chamber with an explosive mixture.
2. Compress mixture into a smaller space.
3. Utilize explosive or expansive force for power production.
4. Remove burned mixture from cylinder or chamber.
This series of events must be repeated over and over in the same sequence, automatically in each cylinder, if the engine is to run.

The first need is to fill the cylinder with an explosive

mixture. If gasoline is the fuel, it must be mixed with the proper proportion of 10 to 15 parts of air to each part of gasoline to operate in a gasoline engine. This mixture is compounded automatically and continuously by a carburetor. (See Chapter 23 on Principles of Carburetion.)

If the fuel is fuel oil (diesel engine), it is injected into the cylinders under high pressure. (See DIESEL and OTHER ENGINES.) In diesel engines, the heat generated by compressing the air in the cylinder is used to ignite the fuel. In gasoline engines, an electrical spark is used. (See Chapter 29, Engine Ignition Systems.)

FOUR-STROKE CYCLE

Most automobile engines operate on the four-stroke cycle. This type of engine is known as "four cycle" or "Otto cycle," after the name of its inventor, Nikolaus Otto. The power production cycle consists of four strokes of the piston in a reciprocating engine. See Fig. 6-4. The first stroke draws the combustible mixture into the cylinder. The next stroke compresses the mixture. The third stroke is the power stroke. The final stroke forces burned gases out of the cylinder.

TWO-STROKE CYCLE

In the two-stroke cycle engine, the piston takes over some of the valve function in order to obtain a power stroke each revolution of the crankshaft. Two cycle

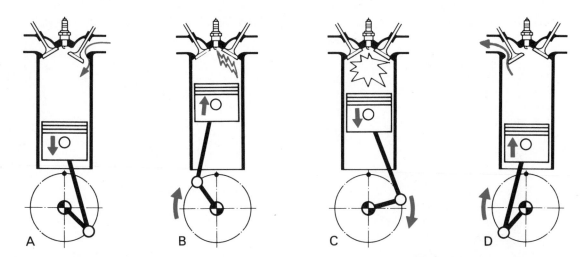

Fig. 6-4. Sequence of a four cycle engine: A—As the piston moves downward, a vacuum is created. The intake valve opens and the air/fuel mixture enters the cylinder. B—The air/fuel mixture is compressed as the piston moves upwards. The spark plug is fired to ignite the air/fuel mixture prior to the piston being at Top Dead Center. Note that both valves are closed. C—The air/fuel mixture explodes, which forces the piston downward. Note that both valves are closed. D—As the piston starts to move upward, the exhaust valve is opened. The piston moving up forces the exhaust gases out of the cylinder. (Robert Bosch)

operation involves the use of ports in the cylinders, Fig. 6-5. These ports are covered and uncovered by the movement of the piston, which acts like a valve in controlling the filling and emptying of the cylinder.

Alternate phases of vacuum and compression in the crankcase can be avoided by using a blower or "supercharger" to push air into the cylinder, Fig. 6-6. In this particular design (used in GM diesel), a row of ports around the bottom of the cylinder serves as the inlet, Fig. 6-5. The piston acts as an inlet valve, and cam-operated

exhaust valves are placed in the cylinder head. In this design, the blower pumps air into the cylinder and diesel fuel is injected under pressure. (See Chapter 18 on Diesel and Other Engines.)

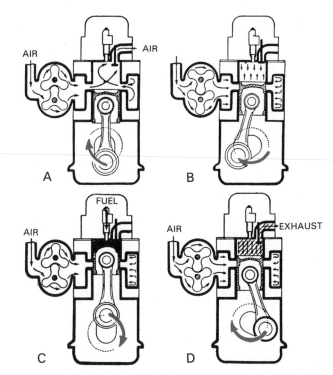

Fig. 6-6. GM's two cycle diesel: A—Piston at BDC. The intake ports are uncovered and the blower forces air into the cylinder. B—As piston moves upward, the ports are closed. The air is compressed, thereby causing the temperature of the air to increase. C—Fuel is injected into cylinder. Temperature of compressed air ignites the fuel mixture; there is no spark plug. D—Explosion forces piston down. Exhaust valve starts to open and exhaust gases are forced out.

Fig. 6-5. The ports of the cylinder allow the air to enter the cylinder when the piston is at Bottom Dead Center. The ports are closed off as piston moves upward. (Detroit Diesel Corp.)

MULTI-CYLINDER ENGINES

Almost all automobile engines, whether water-cooled or air-cooled — four cycle or two cycle, have more than one cylinder. These multiple cylinders are arranged in-line, opposed or in V-form as shown in Fig. 6-7. Engines for other purposes, such as aviation, are arranged as radial, inverted in-line, inverted V, X-shaped, and other assorted forms.

CYLINDER TYPES

The location of the valves in four cycle engines, either water-cooled or air-cooled, is one of the basic elements of design. There are four basic designs, three of which are in current use: L-head, I-head, and F-head, as shown in Figs. 6-8 to 6-10, respectively. The T-head, along with sleeve valves, rotary valves and other variations is not in current use.

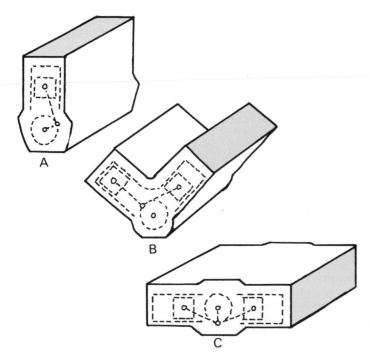

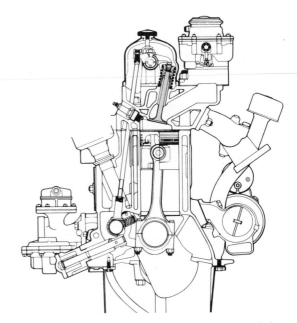

Fig. 6-9. An I-head engine. Both valves are located above the piston.

Fig. 6-7. Arrangement of cylinders: A—In-line. B—V-type. C—Opposed.

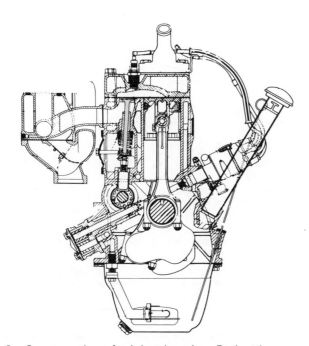

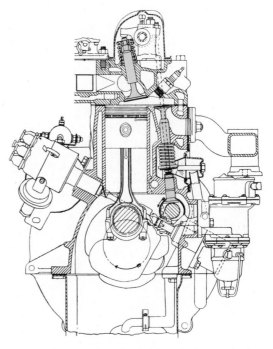

Fig. 6-8. Cross section of a L-head engine. Both valves are located to the side of the piston.

Fig. 6-10. F-head engine. One valve is located above the piston and the other valve is located to side of the piston.

Note that in L-head design, the valve ports and gas passages are built in the cylinder block. In the I-head engine, these passages are built in the detachable cylinder head. The F-head engine has one valve in the head and one in the block, with necessary passages built into both head and block.

CYLINDER BLOCKS

The engine crankcase and cylinder block are cast in one piece. Ordinarily, this is the largest and most intricate single piece of metal in the automobile. Even when the cylinders, cylinder heads, or cylinder sleeves are separate pieces, the crankcase is still the largest single part in the engine. Practically all of the engine parts are attached to the crankcase, directly or indirectly. See Figs. 6-11 and 6-12.

The crankcase houses the crankshaft and, in most cases, the camshaft also. With the oil pan, which goes on the lower surface of the crankcase, it forms on oil-tight housing in which the rotating and reciprocating parts operate. The cylinder block contains the pistons which are attached to the crankshaft by means of the connecting rods, Fig. 6-3.

The crankcase and cylinder block are usually made of high grade cast iron with alloys to improve wear characteristics of the cylinders. This major unit must be extremely strong and rigid to avoid any bending or distortion.

The crankcase and cylinder block is an intricate casting that varies in thickness and does not always cool uniformly. Internal stresses are created that sometimes cause warpage. However, much has been done in the way of design to minimize the effects of warpage of the cylinder bores.

Distortion may occur from incorrect placing of the metal masses around the cylinders, from expansion and contraction due to the heat of operation, or from excessive mechanical stresses placed upon it (unequal or extreme tightening of bolts, etc.). Distortion can occur in several directions. The cylinder head surface can warp or twist. The cylinder bore may warp longitudinally or become out-of-round. The crankshaft or camshaft bearing bores may be warped out of line, etc.

To stiffen and strengthen engine block and crankcase castings, webs or ribs are often added to the casting at the points of greatest stress. In some cases, the crankcase is extended below the center line of the crankshaft, rather than in the same plane as the crankshaft. See Fig. 6-12.

While the metal used for these castings is ordinarily termed "cast iron" or "aluminum," the terminology is rather loose because these metals usually are alloys. In the case of cast iron, small amounts of chromium, molybdenum, or other metals may be added. In the case of aluminum castings, it is customary to add other materials to create an alloy which, along with heat and chemical treatment, increases the strength and wear resisting ability of the metal. In good aluminum engines, a steel sleeve is placed in the cylinder for the rings to move against.

ENGINE CRANKSHAFTS

The crankshaft is regarded as the "backbone" of the engine. It serves to change the reciprocating motion of the piston into rotary motion, and it handles the entire power output. Reciprocating means up and down. Rotary means in a circular motion.

Fig. 6-11. A modern four cylinder engine block and crankshaft.   (Ford)

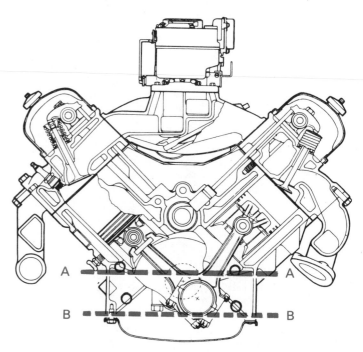

Fig. 6-12. Line A is the center of the crankshaft. Crankshaft extends down to line B. Circles indicate points of reinforcement on the engine block.

The crankshaft revolves in bearings located in the engine crankcase. It must be free to revolve with as little friction as possible, yet have no appreciable looseness in the bearings. Because of the loads imposed, the crankshaft is large in diameter, very accurately machined, and the bearings which support it are of generous size and length.

The number of bearings used will depend upon the number of cylinders in the engine, and the design of the engine. By locating a main bearing journal between throws of the crankshaft, Fig. 6-13, it is possible to use a lighter crankshaft than if two throws are placed between main bearing journals. See Fig. 6-13.

Engine crankshafts vary according to design of the engine. A single cylinder engine will have one throw on the crankshaft, Fig. 6-13. A two cylinder engine will have two throws spaced 180 deg. apart. A three cylinder engine will have three throws spaced 120 deg. apart. A four cylinder engine will normally have cylinders 1 and 4 on the same side and cylinders 2 and 3 on the other side, 180 deg. apart, Fig. 6-14.

CRANKSHAFT BALANCE WEIGHTS

Without special balance weights on the crankshaft, severe vibration would result from:
1. Weight of reciprocating parts.
2. Weight of rotating parts.
3. Inertial force of reciprocating parts.
4. Combustion pressures.
5. Variation in torque.

To reduce or eliminate such vibration, the crankshaft must be balanced. That is, it must be provided with counterweights that extend radially from the crankshaft centerline in the opposite direction of the crank throws or crank arms, Fig. 6-13. In that way, the forces acting on the crankshaft are balanced and vibration is reduced. In addition, bearing life is increased.

SIX CYLINDER IN-LINE CRANKSHAFTS

An in-line six cylinder engine may have a left-hand crankshaft or a right-hand crankshaft, depending on the firing order of the cylinders (to be covered later). The crank throws are spaced 120 deg. apart in both cases, Fig. 6-15. Cylinders 1 and 6 are on the same side in each case. Likewise, cylinders 2 and 5 are in the same plane, and cylinders 3 and 4 are in the same plane.

V-SIX CRANKSHAFTS

If a 90 deg. V-6 engine has a crankshaft with three throws spaced 120 deg. apart (common crankpin for two connecting rods), it will have uneven firing intervals between cylinders. As a result, there will be varying torque impuses with vibration.

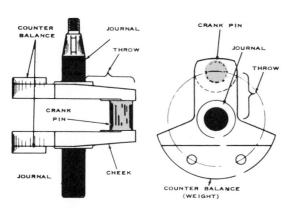

Fig. 6-13. Main bearing journals are in black. Rod journal is in color.

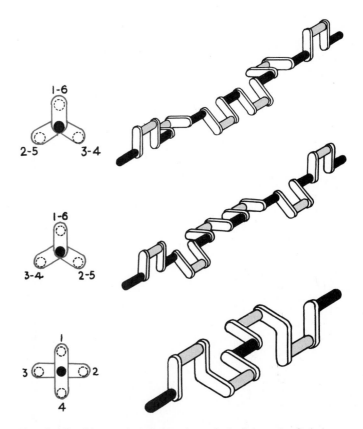

Fig. 6-15. Above. A right hand crankshaft has the 3-4 throw to the right of the 1-6 throw. Center. A left hand crankshaft has the 2-3 throw to the left of the 1-6 arrow. Bottom. Crankshaft for a V-8 engine is similar to a four cylinder engine.

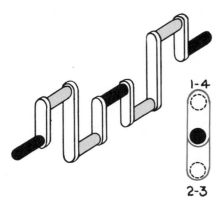

Fig. 6-14. An in-line four cylinder engine normally has two throws 180° apart, with cylinders 1 and 4 on the same plane.

To overcome these problems with its V-6 engine, Buick "split" each crankpin by an included angle of 30 deg. In doing so, Buick advanced the throws of the crankpins for cylinders 2, 4, and 6 by 15 deg. on the right bank, and delayed the throws of the crankpins for cylinders 1, 3, and 5 a similar amount on the left bank. The firing order of the Buick 3.8 liter V-6 is 1-6-5-4-3-2, The firing interval is 120 deg. for all cylinders.

Chevrolet engineers, meanwhile, also decided to "split" the crankpins on the 3.8 liter V-6, but with an included angle of 18 deg. This crankshaft design results in a firing interval of 132-108-132-108-132-108 deg. The firing order is 1-6-5-4-3-2.

V-8 CRANKSHAFTS

A V-8 engine normally has a four throw crankshaft with two cylinders attached to each throw. However, the location of the crankpins will vary. In one case, all four throws may be in the same plane, two on each side of the crankshaft, Fig. 6-14. Or, the throws may be in two planes, each 90 deg. apart as shown in Fig. 6-15.

Chapter 6—REVIEW QUESTIONS

Write your answers on a separate sheet of paper. Do not write in this book.

1. All automobile engines have either six or eight cylinders. True or False?
2. The majority of automobile engines are the _____ cooled type.
3. Is a flat engine the same as an in-line engine? Yes or No?
4. Name the largest single part of the engine.
5. Which engine part changes the reciprocating motion of the pistons to rotary motion?
6. List in proper sequence the events that occur in a four cycle internal combustion engine.
7. A "valve" and a "port" are the same thing. True or False?
8. How does the mixture get into the cylinder?
9. The I-head, valve-in-head, and overhead valve engines are identical. True or False?
10. How is the explosive mixture in the cylinder ignited in a gasoline engine?
11. How is the explosive mixture ignited in most diesels?
12. What is the basic difference between a four cycle engine and a two cycle engine?
13. How many "throws" are on the crankshaft of a V-8 engine? Two, four, or eight?
14. What causes distortion of engine blocks?
15. All four cylinder crankshafts are alike. True or False?
16. List three causes of crankshaft vibration.

Chapter 7

ENGINE CONSTRUCTION

After studying this chapter, you will be able to:
- Describe how and why a cylinder wears.
- Identify the parts of a piston.
- Explain why a piston is cam ground and tapered.
- State why the piston pin is offset.

DESIGN CONSIDERATION

Many things are demanded of an engine used to propel an automobile. Some of the requirements are:
1. Ease of starting regardless of temperature.
2. Reliability.
3. Power.
4. Responsiveness.
5. Economy in fuel, oil, and repairs.
6. Ease of handling.

7. Quiet operation.

Some of these factors conflict. For example, a great amount of power can be had from an engine of sufficient size, but a supersize engine is not economical to operate, so all automobile engines are a compromise in order to obtain the desirable combination of performance and economy.

ENGINE SIZE

The size of an engine is determined by its bore and stroke. Bore is the diameter of the cylinders. Stroke is the length of piston travel, Fig. 7-1. The bore area multiplied by the stroke. Then multiply this number by number of cylinders and then divide by 1,000,000 and this is engine displacement or size. Example:

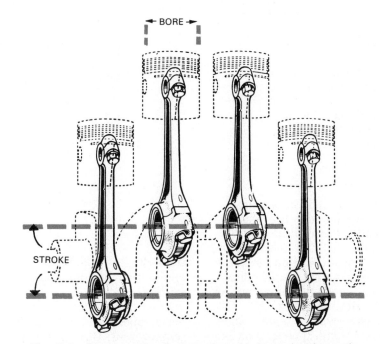

Fig. 7-1. Diameter of cylinder and stroke determine the engine displacement. Stroke is the distance that the piston will move in the cylinder, and is controlled by the length of the throw on the crankshaft.

A four cylinder engine has a bore of 87.5 and a stroke of 92 mm. To determine the displacement of the engine, use the following formula:

Radius of bore = 43.75 mm
Radius² = 1,914.06 mm
1,914.06 × 3.14 (π) = 6,010.15 sq. mm
6,010.15 sq. mm × 92 mm (stroke) =
   552,934.37 cu. mm
552,934.37 cu. mm × 4 (No. of cylinders) =
   2,211,737 cu. mm
2,211,737 ÷ 1,000,000 = 2.2 Liters
2.2 Liters = Engine displacement

Size alone, however, is not an exclusive measurement of power developed by the engine. Many other things need to be taken into consideration:
1. Engine speed.
2. Compression ratio.
3. Valve size, lift, and timing.
4. Internal engine friction.
5. Mechanical condition of parts.

Each item is subject to alteration by service procedures. Each can be altered and must be understood by the technician.

Possibly the most important item is the mechanical condition of the parts and units. Certainly it is the item most directly under the control of the technician. If an engine is badly worn or damaged, with little or no compression in the cylinders, the technician can do little until compression has been restored.

Because the cylinders must be round and true, they are machined and finished within a thousandth of an inch accuracy. This is required so that the piston and rings, which are finished with equal accuracy, will have a true mating surface. Otherwise the compression may leak between the pistons and cylinders on the compression and power strokes, and little power would be developed. Also, the oil might leak through between piston and cylinder wall on the intake stroke, and the oil burned.

CYLINDER WALL WEAR

Cylinder walls do wear, regardless of kind of material from which they are made and how carefully they are designed and finished. This wear may be caused by:
1. Pressure of piston rings against cylinder walls.
2. Amount of water condensed in cylinder.
3. Temperature of operation.
4. Degree of lubrication.
5. Kind of lubricant.
6. Type of fuel being used.
7. Type of service in which the engine is operated.
8. Amount of abrasive in lubricant and in the combustible fuel drawn into cylinder from carburetor.

Cylinders wear to a taper, Fig. 7-2, and also out-of-round. Taper is caused by insufficient lubrication in the upper area of cylinder. Out-of-round wear results primarily from greater side pressure exerted by the piston on its power stroke than on the other strokes, Fig. 7-3. Design features will also affect cylinder wear. Short stroke engines will tend to wear faster than long stroke engines. High engine speeds will also tend to increase cylinder wear because of increased cylinder wall pressure. The design of the water jackets surrounding

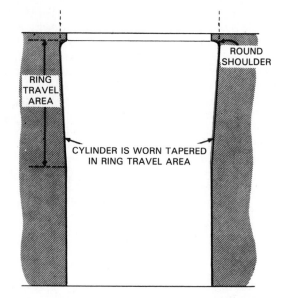

Fig. 7-2. Cylinder wear is greatest at the top of the cylinder. The difference between the top and bottom dimensions of cylinder are referred to as taper.

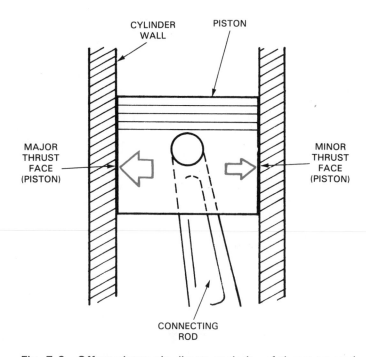

Fig. 7-3. Offset piston pin directs majority of thrust toward one side of piston and cylinder wall.

the cylinder walls is an important factor, as is the accumulation of rust and other sediment in the water jackets.

Most cylinder wear occurs during the first few miles of operation, before the engine has reached full operating temperature. During that period, there is a maximum amount of condensation in the cylinders (a major factor in causing wear). In addition, there is little oil on the cylinder walls when the engine is first started.

In some engines, the cylinders are fitted with sleeves to serve as a bearing surface for the piston rings. These sleeves are of two types, "dry" and "wet." The dry type is simply a sleeve or barrel which is pressed into an oversize bore in the cylinder block. The wet type is a cylinder sleeve which replaces the cylinder wall. With a wet sleeve, the coolant circulates in contact with the outside surface of the sleeve. In this case, seals are required at both ends of the sleeve. See Fig. 7-4.

In some situations, there is a certain service advantage to the wet or dry type of cylinder sleeve. If one cylinder wall becomes damaged, it may be more economical to replace the sleeve than to rebore the cylinder and fit oversize pistons and rings.

CYLINDER HEAD GASKETS

Cylinder head gaskets are by far the most important gaskets on the engine. If the gasket is not sealing properly, engine performance will suffer. In addition, coolant may leak into the combustion chamber. There are several different types of cylinder head gaskets available on the aftermarket.

Perforated steel core cylinder head gasket, Fig. 7-5, has a *very thin* perforated metal core sandwiched between soft material. This soft material does an excellent job of compensating for the irregularities between the mating surfaces. However, this same feature makes it necessary to retorque the head bolts after approximately 500 miles of driving. This is due to the soft material relaxing.

The embossed steel shim cylinder head gasket, Fig. 7-6, is usually used by the manufacturer and can also be purchased in the aftermarket. This design of cylinder head gasket does not require retorquing of the head bolts after any period of driving time. This is due to the steel's resilience. Steel does not relax after a period of time. However, the steel shim cylinder head gasket does not compensate for irregularities between the mating surface, as well as the perforated cylinder head gasket. This is not of any concern on new engines, as the mating surfaces are completely flat.

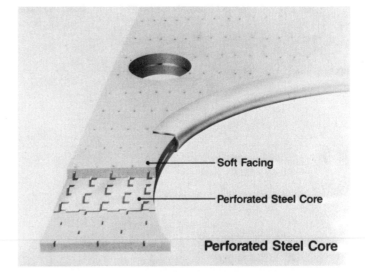

Fig. 7-5. This cylinder head gasket design makes it necessary to retorque, but compensates for irregularities between the mating surfaces. (Fel-Pro, Inc.)

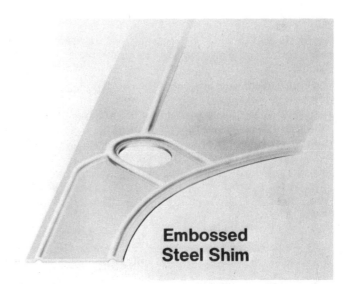

Fig. 7-6. This cylinder head gasket design does not have to be retorqued, but does not do the best job of compensating for irregularities between the mating surfaces. Note that critical sealing areas are raised. (Fel-Pro, Inc.)

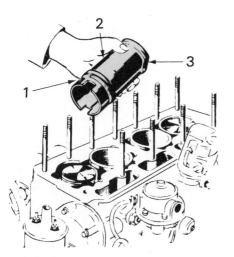

Fig. 7-4. A wet type cylinder sleeve. 1—Sleeve. 2—Sealing ring. 3—Sealing surface.

The multilayered cylinder head gasket, Fig. 7-7, because of its solid steel core, does not have to be retorqued after any period of driving time. This is due to the solid steel core not relaxing. The Teflon serves a dual purpose. First, when the cylinder head is torqued to specifications, the Teflon works its way into the irregularities between the mating surfaces for an effective seal. Aluminum cylinder heads expand at a faster rate than the cast iron block, on which the aluminum head seats. The Teflon provides a slippery surface for the aluminum cylinder head to slide on as it expands and contracts. Currently, this type of gasket is supplied only by the aftermarket.

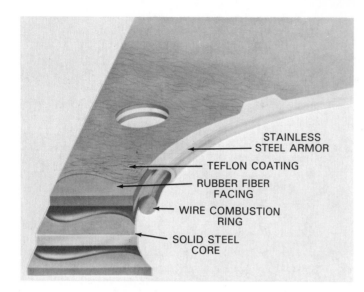

Fig. 7-7. This cylinder head gasket design does not need to be retorqued, and the Teflon provides a very effective seal between the irregularities of the mating surfaces. The Teflon also allows aluminum cylinder heads to slide as they expand and contract. (Fel-Pro, Inc.)

COMBUSTION CHAMBER

The combustion chamber is the space within the cylinder above the piston where the burning of the air-fuel mixture occurs. Improvements have been made, but research continues on design characteristics of the combustion chamber. Combustion chamber design is toward the creation and control of turbulence (movement of air and fuel within cylinder to create a more uniform mixture), Fig. 7-8.

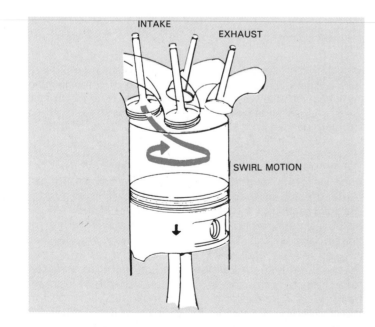

Fig. 7-8. Swirling motion or turbulence improves the combustion characteristics of the air/fuel mixture.

As fuel improved and higher compression ratios were sought, the L-hed engine was largely superseded by the overhead valve (OHV) engine. OHV design permits larger engine valves and increased compression ratio, permitting more power by an engine of a given size.

The shape of the combustion chamber of the overhead valve engine has gone through many changes. It has ranged from the plain cylindrical form to the wedge type and hemispherical design shown in Fig. 7-9.

The wedge shaped combustion chamber is an efficient design used in most engines. It is noted for the turbulence produced in the air-fuel charge as the piston moves up on the compression stroke. Stepped-up efficiency is a further result.

The hemispherical design, or "hemi," provides room for larger valves for a given bore. In addition, the "hemi" design permits a centrally located spark plug, which contributes to more efficient combustion, better heat dissipation and higher thermal efficiency.

With increased emphasis being placed on cleaner exhaust, it is important to note that the unburned hydrocarbons are proportional to the surface of the combustion chamber. As that area is reduced, the unburned hydrocarbons are also reduced. That area, is at a minimum with a hemispherical combustion chamber. Both "wedge" and "hemi" designs feature a reduced tendency toward detonation.

Some engines use a double overhead camshaft to provide a hemispherical combustion chamber. This design permits the use of larger valves, and a resulting increase in power, than in the same size engine with a single overhead camshaft.

Further in this connection, when the cylinder heads and combustion chambers are made of aluminum, the valves operate at approximately 100 °C lower than in comparable cylinder heads of cast iron. In addition, the compresion ratio can be increased approximately 1.0 over the cast iron head (11.0:1 over 10.0:1, for example).

The material from which the combustion chamber is made, and the efficiency of the cooling system, also have a distinct bearing on the compression ratio of a given engine. For example, aluminum cylinder heads and aluminum pistons can operate at higher compression ratios than cast iron or steel. This is made possible by the superior heat transfer ability of aluminum. The heat of combustion is dissipated more rapidly to the cooling water or air.

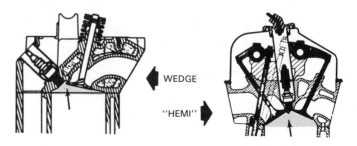

Fig. 7-9. Modern engine combustion chamber shapes: Left. Wedge shape combustion chamber. Right. Hemi or hemispherical shape combustion chamber.

PISTON CONSTRUCTION

The piston head or "crown," Fig. 7-10, is the top surface against which the explosive force is exerted. It may be flat, concave, convex or any one of a great variety of shapes to promote turbulence or help control combustion. In some applications, a narrow groove is cut into the piston above the top ring to serve as a "heat dam" to reduce the amount of heat reaching the top ring.

Piston rings carried in the ring grooves are of two basic types: "compression" rings and "oil control" rings. Both types are made in a wide variety of designs.

The upper ring or rings are to prevent compression leakage; the lower ring or rings control the amount of oil being deposited on the cylinder wall. The lower groove or grooves often have holes or slots to permit oil drainage from behind the rings.

The piston ring lands are the parts of the piston between the ring grooves. The lands provide a seating surface for the sides of the piston rings.

The main section of the piston is known as the skirt. It forms a bearing area in contact with the cylinder wall which takes the thrust caused by the crankshaft.

Some thrust is created on both sides of the piston. "Major" thrust is to the side opposite the crank throw as it is driven down on the power stroke. "Minor" thrust is the side opposite the crank throw as the piston moves up on the compression stroke. Pistons are internally braced to make them as strong as possible. See Fig. 7-11.

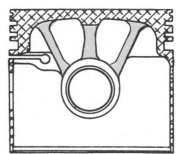

Fig. 7-11. Ribs reinforce piston head.

The piston pin (wrist pin) hole in the piston also serves as a bearing for the piston pin, and is not located exactly in the middle of the piston. It is placed as much as 1/16 in. from the center of the piston, Fig. 7-12.

In some designs, the piston skirt is extended downward on the thrust sides to form what is known as a "slipper" piston, Fig. 7-10. This design feature increases the area of piston contact with the cylinder walls at the thrust faces.

PISTON DESIGN

Cast iron pistons may have the skirts split in a variety of ways, Fig. 7-13. These slots are placed on the thrust sides to provide flexibility in the piston skirt. By this means, the piston can be fitted more closely when cold, so it can expand when hot, without damage.

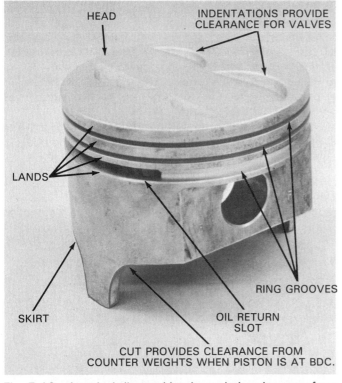

Fig. 7-10. A typical slipper skirt piston derives its name from a portion of skirt that is cut away to provide clearance for counterweights. Lands are areas between the grooves that rings ride against. Note that piston pin hole is recessed, which prevents pin from coming in contact with cylinder wall. (Ford)

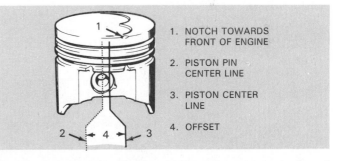

Fig. 7-12. Piston pin is offset 1/16 in. from the centerline of piston. This prevents piston from slapping the cylinder wall as thrust changes from major to minor thrust face of piston. (Oldsmobile)

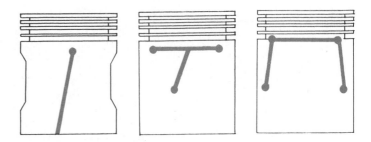

Fig. 7-13. Some pistons may have a slot cut through skirt on minor thrust side of piston.

Some pistons are of the "strut" type shown in Fig. 7-14. In this case, an alloy steel insert is cast into the aluminum piston to control the expansion of the aluminum and maintain more constant clearance. Pistons are usually "skeleton" type and do not contact the cylinder walls around the piston pin holes.

Most aluminum pistons are "cam-ground," or purposely machined with the skirts oval, Fig. 7-15. While the skirts will be out-of-round when cold, the skirt will become more nearly round when the piston expands at operating temperature.

Pistons are also slightly tapered in design, Fig. 7-16. The top of the piston runs much hotter than the skirt, so the top is smaller in diameter, Fig. 7-16. This is particularly true in the area above the top ring.

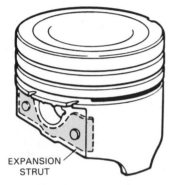

EXPANSION STRUT

Fig. 7-14. Strut helps control the rate and direction of expansion. (Chevrolet)

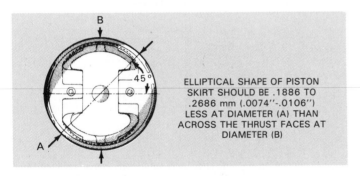

ELLIPTICAL SHAPE OF PISTON SKIRT SHOULD BE .1886 TO .2686 mm (.0074"-.0106") LESS AT DIAMETER (A) THAN ACROSS THE THRUST FACES AT DIAMETER (B)

Fig. 7-15. A cam-ground piston is slightly egg shaped when cold and becomes rounded as the engine reaches operating temperature. (Chrysler)

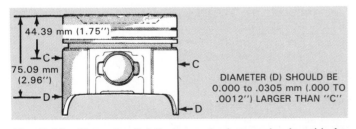

44.39 mm (1.75")

75.09 mm (2.96")

DIAMETER (D) SHOULD BE 0.000 to .0305 mm (.000 TO .0012") LARGER THAN "C"

Fig. 7-16. Piston is slightly tapered when engine is cold. As operating temperature of the engine increases, the amount of taper is reduced. (Chrysler)

PISTON MATERIALS

Cast iron has been used extensively as a piston material. It is strong enough to withstand stresses imposed; has a melting point above the cylinder operating temperature; expands at the same rate as cast iron cylinders; and does not generate excessive friction when properly lubricated. The principal objection is excessive weight, a design factor that becomes more important as engine speeds increase.

Aluminum alloy is now preferred as a material for pistons. It is lighter than cast iron. It is readily cast and machined. It does not generate excessive friction in the cylinder, Fig. 7-17.

Aluminum expands more rapidly than cast iron when subjected to the heat of operation, and also has a much lower melting point. In material and design, the aluminum piston has been developed to a point where its advantages outweigh its disadvantages. Because of this, it is used in almost all automobile engines.

Lighter weight means less inertia for the reciprocating parts and higher speed for the engine along with responsive acceleration. Less inertia also decreases bearing loads at high speeds and reduces side thrust on the cylinder walls. The piston head runs cooler because of the greater heat transfer of aluminum and, in general, it is possible to use higher compression ratios.

Early aluminum pistons were noisy because they had to be fitted in the cylinder with considerably more clearance than cast iron pistons. This resulted in piston slap and rattle when the engine was cold. The difficulty has been largely overcome by designing the piston skirt so it is flexible, by the use of special alloys and by means of steel struts, Fig. 7-14.

Aluminum pistons possess the desirable characteristic of transferring the heat away from the combustion chamber more rapidly than cast iron. However, if the rings are stuck in the groove, the top edge of the piston or the lands between the rings may soften and melt or be blown away by the hot gas, Fig. 7-18.

Severe and continued detonation (too rapid burning or explosion of air-fuel mixture in combustion chamber) is

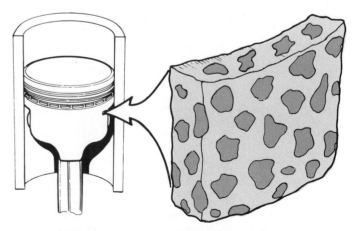

Fig. 7-17. Some piston skirts are impregnated with silicon, which reduces friction and makes the piston more durable. (Chevrolet)

Fig. 7-18. Piston damage when piston becomes overheated.

also responsible for broken piston heads. The aluminum becomes soft when overheated, allowing the ring grooves to deform. Aluminum pistons can be strengthened by alloying the aluminum with other metals and also by special heat treatment. Materials alloyed with the aluminum include copper, magnesium, nickel, and silicon.

Chapter 7—REVIEW QUESTIONS

Write your answers on a separate sheet of paper. Do not write in this book.

1. The power of an automobile engine is determined by the number of cylinders. True or False?
2. The stroke of the engine is determined by:
   a. Length of the cylinder.
   b. Length of the crankshaft throw.
   c. Displacement of the cylinder.
3. How can the displacement of an engine be found?
4. Explain why cylinders wear out-of-round.
5. A wet cylinder sleeve is lubricated, a dry sleeve is not. True or False?
6. Which metal expands the fastest?
   a. Cast iron.
   b. Aluminum.
   c. Either a or b.
   d. Neither a nor b.
7. The combustion chamber is:
   a. Above the piston
   b. Below the piston.
   c. In the crankcase.
8. Piston pins are:
   a. Offset up to 1/16 in.
   b. Centered to the piston.
   c. Both a and b.
   d. Neither a nor b.
9. Which material is used most for pistons?
10. What is a heat dam in a piston?
11. Which side of the piston is the major thrust side?
12. What is meant by piston relief?
13. Pistons are slotted so that they can be more readily inserted in the cylinders. True or False?
14. The tops of pistons are often contoured to provide turbulence. True or False?
15. Describe a cam-ground piston.
16. Multilayered, steel cored cylinder head gaskets:
    a. Never needs to be retorqued.
    b. Provide a surface for the head to slide as it expands and contracts.
    c. Provide an effective seal between mating surfaces.
    d. All of the above.
17. The "hemi" combustion chamber has greater surface area than other designs. True or False?
18. The wedge shape combustion chamber provides good turbulence. Yes or No?
19. How do cylinders wear and why?

Chapter 8

MEASURING ENGINE PERFORMANCE

After studying this chapter, you will be able to:
- Define what is meant by work, inertia, energy, torque, and friction.
- Explain the different types of measurable horsepower.
- Determine the compression ratio of an engine.

ENGINE PERFORMANCE

The study of engine performance deals with ways in which engines are measured dimensionally and the power developed. Many factors enter into this study: the basics of inertia, work, power, torque, and friction; the affect of barometric pressure, temperature, and humidity of the ambient atmosphere; and the engineering decisions that determine engine bore-stroke-displacement, compression ratio, volumetric efficiency, thermal efficiency, and mechanical efficiency.

INERTIA

INERTIA is the force that causes an object to remain stationary, unless acted on by an external force. A car remains in place unless an external force acts on the car. This external force is the engine being started and the transmission placed in gear, Fig. 8-1. Inertia is also the force that causes an object to remain in motion once that object is in motion, unless the object is acted on by an external force. The external force in this case is the brakes being applied, Fig. 8-2, or shifting the transmission into a lower gear. When the transmission is downshifted, the engine speed is reduced, thereby reducing the speed of the vehicle. This is known as engine braking. With a manual transmission, the driver downshifts to second gear. With an automatic transmission, the downshifting is automatic.

Fig. 8-1. For a car to move, the car must overcome inertia.
(Toyota)

Fig. 8-2. For a car to stop, it must overcome inertia.   (Toyota)

WORK

When an object is moved from one position to another, WORK is said to be performed. Work is measured in units of foot pounds (ft. lbs.). For example: if a 3 pound weight is lifted 2 ft., Fig. 8-3, the work performed would be 3 lbs. $\times$ 2 ft. = 6 ft. lbs. In other words, work equals the force (in pounds) required to move the object times the distance in feet. Work is performed when weights are lifted, springs compressed, shafts rotated.

The ability or capacity to do work is known as energy. A lump of coal or a quart of gasoline has energy stored in it, which when released will perform work. A valve spring does the work of closing a valve when it is released after having been compressed.

POWER

POWER is defined as the rate or speed at which work is performed. One horsepower is defined as the amount doing 33,000 ft. lb. of work in one minute. The unit of measurement was originated by an engineer by the name of Watt, who found that a strong horse could hoist 366 lbs. of coal up a mine shaft at the rate of one foot per second. In one minute, the horse would have raised the 366 lbs. 60 feet. This would be equivalent to raising 21,960 lbs., one foot in one minute. Arbitrarily, Mr. Watt raised this figure to 33,000 lbs., one foot in one minute. Expressed as a formula:

$$HP = \frac{ft.\ lb.\ per\ min.}{33,000} = \frac{DW}{33,000\ t}$$

Where D = the distance the weight is to be moved.
   W = Force in pounds required to move the weight through that distance.
   t = time in minutes required to move the weight through the distance D.

For example:
Using this formula, how many horsepower would be required to raise a weight of 5000 lb. a distance of 60 ft. in three minutes?

$$HP = \frac{DW}{33,000\ t} = \frac{60 \times 5000}{33,000 \times 3} = 3.03\ hp$$

ENERGY

ENERGY is the capacity to do work. There are two different kinds of energy. The first type is potential energy. The second type is kinetic energy.

POTENTIAL ENERGY

POTENTIAL ENERGY is energy at rest. An example of potential energy is a piston at TDC, Fig. 8-4. The formula for potential energy is as follows:
   PE = mass of an object $\times$ acceleration of gravity (32.2 ft./sec.²) $\times$ height

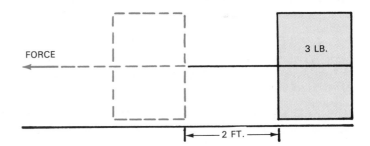

Fig. 8-3. Work is done when an object is moved. The object in the illustration weighs 3 lb. This same object is moved 2 ft. The weight is multiplied by the distance moved. The answer is given in foot-pounds, which, in this case, is 6 ft./lb.

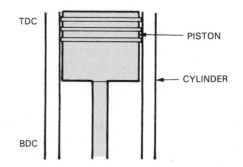

Fig. 8-4. Piston at TDC is an example of potential energy.

KINETIC ENERGY

KINETIC ENERGY is the energy in a moving object at its present velocity until that velocity is terminated. An example of kinetic energy is the downward motion of a piston from TDC until it reaches BDC, Fig. 8-5. The formula for kinetic energy is:

KE = 1/2 the mass of an object × velocity squared

TORQUE

TORQUE is the turning or twisting force on an object. While torque is measured in ft. lb., it differs from work or power as torque does not necessarily produce motion. For example; if a 50 pound force was applied at the end of a 3 ft. lever, there would be 150 ft. lb.

In the case of the automotive engine, torque is low at low engine speeds and increases rapidly with the speed. Automotive engineers make every effort to increase the torque at low speeds and to remain as nearly constant as possible. Note the variation in torque and horsepower, as shown in Fig. 8-6.

FRICTION

FRICTION is the resistance between two bodies in contact with each other, or separated only by a lubricant.

Friction varies not only with different materials, but also with the surface condition of the materials. Friction was originally attributed to the interlocking of projections and depressions on the surfaces, but present day theory is that molecular attraction is the explanation.

The amount of friction is proportional to the pressure between the two surfaces in contact and is independent of the area of the surfaces in contact, Fig. 8-7. It also depends on the relative velocity of the moving surfaces.

In the case of viscous friction, such as that which occurs when solids move through liquids or gases (an automobile moving through air for example), the force of friction varies directly with the relative velocity and rises very rapidly when the velocity becomes very great.

The friction of lubricated surfaces is much less than that of dry surfaces. It is also greatly reduced when rolling friction (ball and roller bearings) is substitued for sliding friction.

Experiments show that dividing the force required to slide one object over the other at a constant speed, by the pressure holding them together, is a constant which is known as the coefficient of friction. The coefficient of friction is always the same for those materials and surfaces, Fig. 8-7.

For example: If a pull of 60 lb. is required to keep a weight of 120 lb. sliding over a surface at a constant speed, the coefficient of sliding friction would be:

$$\frac{60}{120} = 0.5$$

It must be emphasized that more force is required for initial movement than to keep the object moving. Sliding friction is therefore measured after motion has started.

A lubricant is a substance placed or injected between two surfaces to reduce friction. The thin layer of lubricant, adhering to the two surfaces is then sheared by

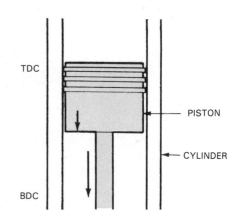

Fig. 8-5. The downward motion of a piston from TDC to BDC is an example of kinetic energy.

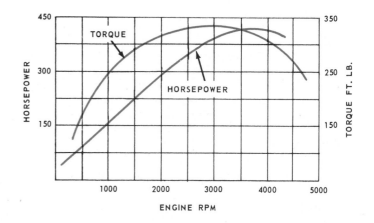

Fig. 8-6. Note the variation in torque and horsepower as engine speed changes.

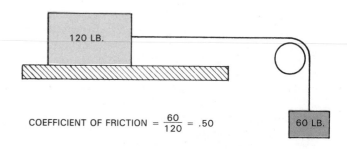

COEFFICIENT OF FRICTION = $\frac{60}{120}$ = .50

Fig. 8-7. A method of determining the coefficient of friction.

the movement. Since the friction within the lubricant is less than that between the two surfaces, less force is required to produce movement.

A simple experiment to determine the coefficient of friction can be easily performed by means of a flat board and a weight. The weight is placed on one end of the board and that end is then raised until the weight starts to slide. At that point, the height of the end of the board is measured and also the base of the triangle formed by the tilted board. Dividing the height by the base equals the coefficient of friction, Fig. 8-8.

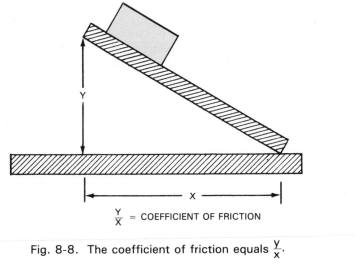

$$\frac{Y}{X} = \text{COEFFICIENT OF FRICTION}$$

Fig. 8-8. The coefficient of friction equals $\frac{Y}{X}$.

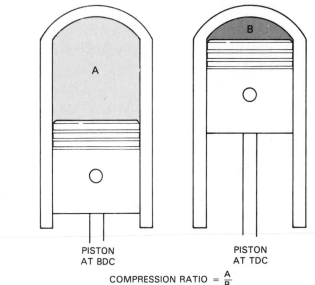

PISTON AT BDC   PISTON AT TDC

$$\text{COMPRESSION RATIO} = \frac{A}{B}$$

Fig. 8-9. Compression ratio is equal to volume of A divided by B.

BORE-STROKE-DISPLACEMENT

The diameter of an engine cylinder is referred to as the bore. The distance the piston moves from bottom dead center to top dead center is called the stroke.

Displacement of an engine is a measurement of its size. It is equal to the number of cubic inches the piston displaces as it moves from bottom dead center to top dead center. In other words, it is equal to the area of the piston times the stroke. In the case of a multi-cylinder engine, it is also necessary to multiply by the number of cylinders.

$$\text{Displacement} = A \times S \times N$$

A is the area of the piston in square inches, S is the length of stroke in inches, and N the number of cylinders. Assuming you have a six cylinder engine with a 4 in. bore and a 4 1/4 in. stroke, the procedure is to first calculate the piston area:

$$\text{Area} = 4 \times 4 \times .7854 = 12.56 \text{ sq. in.}$$

Then the displacement equals

$$12.56 \times 4.25 \times 6 = 320.28 \text{ cu. in.}$$

COMPRESSION RATIO

COMPRESSION RATIO of an engine is the extent to which the combustible gases are compressed within the cylinder, Fig. 8-9. It is calculated by dividing the volume existing within the cylinder with the piston at BDC, by the volume in the cylinder with the piston at TDC. For example: If the volume with the piston at BDC is 45 cu. in. and at TDC is 5 cu. in., the compression ratio is

$$\frac{45}{5} = 9 \text{ to } 1$$

Therefore, the gases are compressed to one-ninth the original volume.

Up to a certain point, the more the fuel charge is compressed, the more power will be obtained. Experiments made by General Motors engineers, indicate that 17 to 1 compression ratio is the peak efficiency for gasoline engines.

In the service field, the compression ratio of an engine can be increased by shaving the cylinder head, installing higher compression pistons, installing thinner gaskets, by increasing the stroke by regrinding the crankshaft, or by increasing the bore of the engine. However, consideration must be given to the possibility of the valves striking the piston.

In case it is desired to increase the compression ratio of an engine, the following formula may be used:

$$\frac{B}{C-1} = A$$

A equals the volume of the combustion chamber, B is the displacement of the cylinder, and C is the desired compression ratio. For example; if the displacement is 36 cu. in., and the desired compression ratio is 10 to 1, then:

$$\frac{36}{10-1} = 3.6 \text{ cu. in.}$$

In that particular engine, the combustion chamber would have to have a volume of 3.6 cu. in. to obtain a compression ratio of 10 to 1.

ENGINE EFFICIENCY

Engine efficiency is the ratio of power obtained to power supplied. There are many energy losses in gasoline engines. Therefore, in relation to the inherent power in the fuel, only about 15 percent appears as useful power, Fig. 8-10. The rest is lost in the cooling system, exhaust system, and friction.

In a turbojet engine, the losses are only about 1 to 2 percent.

The mechanical efficiency of an engine is equal to the relationship of brake horsepower and indicated horsepower.

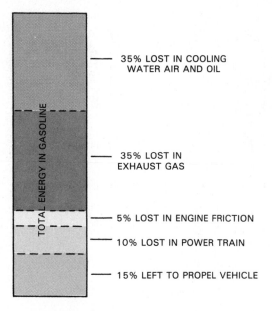

Fig. 8-10. The graph shows where the power goes on a normally aspirated engine. If the engine is turbocharged, less power will be lost in the exhaust, which creates more power for the engine to drive the car.

$$\text{Mechanical efficiency} = \frac{BHP}{IHP}$$

This in most cases is approximately 85 percent.

VOLUMETRIC EFFICIENCY

No engine is 100 percent efficient. One of the factors affecting the efficiency of a gasoline engine is the difficulty of getting a full charge of combustible mixture into the cylinder. Because of restrictions of the intake manifold, atmospheric temperature, valve timing and similar factors, a theoretically full charge does not reach the cylinder. The ratio of the amount of charge actually taken in per cycle to a complete charge is known as the volumetric efficiency.

After a certain engine speed is reached, the volumetric efficiency drops rapidly. In general, maximum volumetric efficiency is reached at approximately the same point where maximum torque is reached. For example, one engine had maximum efficiency 82 percent at 1500 rpm, but at 2500 rpm it had dropped to 65 percent.

One method of increasing volumetric efficiency is to use a supercharger. See Chapter 20.

As atmospheric pressure drops, with an increase in altitude, volumetric efficiency will also decrease as it is the difference in pressure between the pressure outside the cylinder and the pressure inside the cylinder that determines the amount of mixture which will enter the cylinder.

THERMAL EFFICIENCY

The performance of various engines is often compared on the basis of their thermal efficiencies. The ratio of the heat equivalent of work done in an engine to the total heat supplied is referred to as its thermal efficiency.

BRAKE HORSEPOWER

Brake horsepower may be defined as the power that is available for propelling the vehicle. It is the power developed within the cylinder (indicated horsepower) less the power that remains after the effects of friction and the power that is required to drive the fan, water pump, oil pump, and generator.

The term brake horsepower is derived from the equipment first used to determine the power developed by an engine, which is known as the Prony brake, Fig. 8-11.

It will be noted that the Prony brake consists of a large drum and a band type brake which operates on the outer surface of the drum. Attached to the brake is a lever, with its free end bearing on a weighing scale.

The drum is directly connected to the engine crankshaft to be tested. As the drum is rotated, the brake is tightened, imposing a load on the engine, which in turn causes the lever to be pressed against the scale.

When making a Prony brake test, the throttle is first set to operate the engine at some specific speed. The brake is then tightened until the speed drops off, and the weight on the scale is noted. This procedure is repeated, each time at 100 rpm higher speed. Then, using 1 hp = 33,000 lt. lb. per min., calculate the brake horsepower developed at each speed, based on the following formula:

$$BHP = \frac{2\pi LRW}{33,000} = \frac{LRW}{5252}$$

Where L = Length of lever arm in feet.
R = Engine speed in rpm.
W = Load in pounds on scale.

The data thus produced can then be plotted to scale, as shown in Fig. 8-12, which is typical of the horsepower developed by a gasoline engine.

Brake horsepower can also be measured on a dynamometer. Such equipment consists of a resistance creating device, such as an electric generator or a paddle wheel revolving in a fluid, which is so arranged as to absorb and dissipate the power produced by the engine. Suitable gauges are provided to indicate the amount of power absorbed.

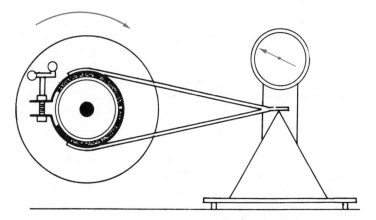

Fig. 8-11. A Prony brake is used in measuring brake horsepower.

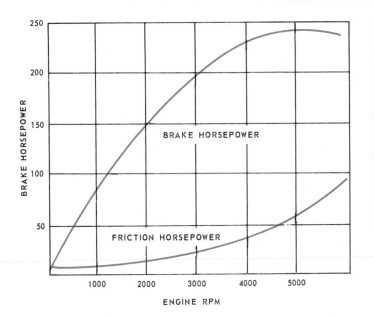

Fig. 8-12. Brake horsepower determined by a Prony brake. Friction horsepower determined by a dynamometer.

Fig. 8-14. Computerized diagnostic machine is used in conjunction with a dynamometer.

In automotive manufacturers' testing laboratories the engines are usually directly connected to the shaft of the dynamometer. When used in service stations, the dynamometer is provided with rollers which are then driven by the wheels of the vehicle, Fig. 8-13.

The drive-on type of dynamometer is now used extensively in diagnostic centers to supply factual information of the performance of the vehicle, Fig. 8-14.

ENGINE TORQUE

As previously described, torque is turning effort. In the case of an automotive engine, the pressure on the piston provides torque. As shown in Fig. 8-15, the torque at idling speed is relatively low, but increases rapidly as the engine speed rises. The torque maintains a high level, but decreases as higher speeds are reached.

In designing the engine, engineers try to have the engine maintain as high a torque as possible throughout the speed range of the engine. Assisting in this are large carburetors, large section manifolds, large valves, and exhaust systems with minimum back pressure. However, as engine speed increases, there is less time for the fuel mixture to fill the cylinders due to inertia of the mixture, resistance to its movement offered by the induction system and the valve timing. As a result, volumetric efficiency is reduced and the torque is similarly reduced. Compare the general form of the curve, shown in Fig. 8-15 which the curve shown in Fig. 8-16, which is that of a Ford turbine developed especially for long distance truck work. Note the turbine starts with maximum torque, whereas the gasoline engine does not attain maximum torque until it reaches higher rpm.

RATED HORSEPOWER

The rated horsepower of an engine is based on a formula developed in the early days of the industry and is based on the assumption of a brake mean effective pressure of 67.2 psi and a piston speed of 1000 rpm.

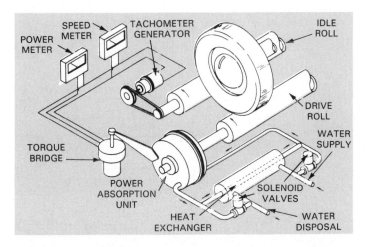

Fig. 8-13. The parts of a chassis dynamometer. Vehicle's drive wheels rest on idle and drive rollers.

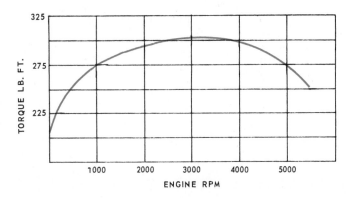

Fig. 8-15. Torque curve of an automotive engine. Note that torque drops off at higher engine speed.

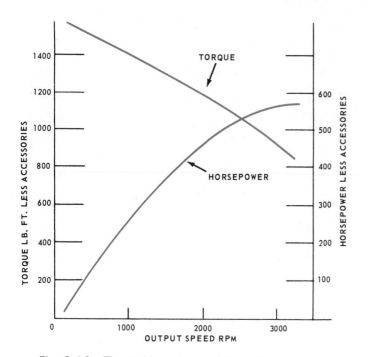

Fig. 8-16. The turbine starts with maximum torque.

N is the number of cylinders and B is the diameter of the engine bore in inches. For example; consider a six-cylinder engine with a bore of 4 in. Then:

$$\text{Rated Horsepower} = \frac{6 \times 4 \times 4}{2.5} = 38.4$$

INDICATED HORSEPOWER

Another method of rating an engine is by the indicated horsepower. This is based on the actual power developed in the engine from an indicator diagram, Fig. 8-17. As the indicated horsepower is the power produced within the engine, it includes the power required to overcome the friction within the engine. Subtracting the friction horsepower from the indicated horsepower gives the brake horsepower:

$$BHP = IHP - FHP$$

The indicator diagram is obtained by means of an oscilloscope or a special instrument which makes an actual drawing of the events that are occurring in the cylinder. It records in diagram form, the pressure existing at each instant of a complete cycle of the engine from the time that the combustible mixture is first drawn into the cylinder until the end of the exhaust stroke. The area of the diagram is then proportional to the power developed, i.e., it is the indicated horsepower.

When calculating the indicated horsepower, it is first necessary to determine the mean effective pressure. This is the average pressure during the power stroke, minus the average pressure during the other three strokes of the cycle. The indicated horsepower is then found by the formula:

Today's engines operate at much higher speeds and pressures. Consequently, the formula no longer gives any indication of the power output of an engine.

It is often incorrectly referred to as the SAE horsepower, but the correct name is rated horsepower. The formula is still used for purposes of licensing automotive vehicles. The formula is as follows:

$$\text{Rated Horsepower} = \frac{NB^2}{2.5}$$

$$IHP = \frac{PLANK}{33,000}$$

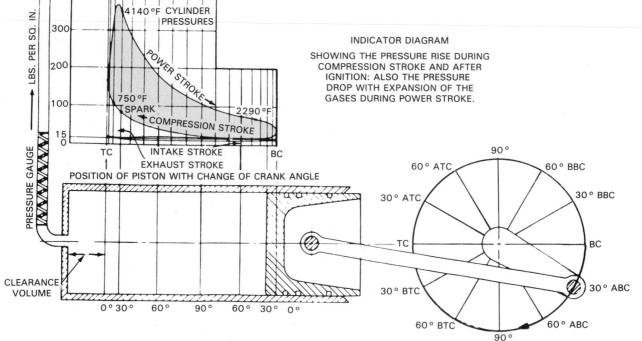

INDICATOR DIAGRAM

SHOWING THE PRESSURE RISE DURING COMPRESSION STROKE AND AFTER IGNITION: ALSO THE PRESSURE DROP WITH EXPANSION OF THE GASES DURING POWER STROKE.

Fig. 8-17. Curve of indicated horsepower of an automotive engine.

Where P = Mean effective pressure in psi.
L = Stroke in feet.
A = Area of cylinder in sq. in.
N = Number of power strokes per minute.
K = Number of cylinders.

FRICTION HORSEPOWER

Friction horsepower is the power required to overcome the friction within the engine. The friction results from the pressure of the piston and rings against the cylinder walls, the friction of the crankshaft and camshaft rotating in their bearings and the friction of other moving parts such as the oil pump, fuel pump, the engine valves, timing gear, or chain.

Friction horsepower increases with the speed of the engine and also the size of the engine. A typical friction horsepower curve was shown in Fig. 8-12.

CURRENT HORSEPOWER RATINGS

Comparison of the brake horsepower ratings listed for 1972 and more recent engines shows a marked drop with the listings for similar engines prior to that date.

For example, in 1972 the 400 cu. in. Chevrolet V-8 with a two-barrel carburetor was rated at 170 hp @3400 rpm. However, in 1971, this same engine was rated at 255 hp at 4400 rpm. In 1970, the ''400'' produced 265 hp at 4400 rpm.

Some of this decrease in 1972 results directly from the extra ''plumbing'' that has been installed to reduce the exhaust emissions of hydrocarbons, carbon monoxide, and oxides of nitrogen. But a major reason for the decrease results from quoting NET horsepower instead of GROSS horsepower, which was used in the past.

Engines are now rated in accordance with SAE Test Standard J245, and this rating is obtained with carburetion and ignition set as required by varying operating conditions.

INCREASING HORSEPOWER

Horsepower of an engine can be increased by: raising the compression ratio; reducing back pressure from the exhaust system; increasing the size or number of the valves and manifolding; installing a cam with a higher lift or longer duration along with a carburetor that flows more fuel and air; using superchargers or turbochargers.

Currently, there is strong interest in turbochargers. These devices utilize the force of exhaust gases to drive more air-fuel mixture into the cylinders. (See Chapter 20.)

Installation of a turbocharger is one of the most effective methods of increasing the output of an engine. A conventional engine with a single barrel carburetor develops 105 hp; with the turbocharger, power output is improved to 165 hp.

Chapter 8—REVIEW QUESTIONS

Write your answers on a separate sheet of paper. Do not write in this book.
1. Define inertia.
2. Brake horsepower is a reliable measure of the power developed by an engine. True or False?
3. How is the displacement of an engine determined?
4. Torque is the same as power. True or False?
5. Friction is dependent on the area in contact. True or False?
6. Indicated horsepower does not take into consideration the friction losses within the engine. True or False?
7. Mean effective pressure is another name for: Explosion pressure _____. Compression pressure _____. Average pressure _____.
8. Define the difference between power and torque.
9. Why does torque decrease above a certain speed?
10. A gas is best measured by: Volume _____. Weight _____.
11. Given the bore of the cylinder and the volume of the combustion chamber, it is possible to determine the compression ratio. True or False?
12. Rated horsepower is the same as brake horsepower. Yes or No?
13. The volume within the cylinder of a certain engine is 50 cu. in., and the volume of the combustion chamber is 5 cu. in.; what is the compression ratio?
    a. 10 to 1.
    b. 6 to 1.
    c. One tenth.
14. Current hp ratings are NET figures. Yes or No?
15. The use of a supercharger will increase volumetric efficiency. True or False?
16. Which is correct? Mechanical efficiency of an engine equals: $\dfrac{BHP}{IHP}$ or $\dfrac{Rated\ HP}{IHP}$

Chapter 9

ENGINE PISTON RINGS AND PINS

After studying this chapter, you will be able to:
- Identify the different types of rings.
- Explain the different design characteristics of piston rings and why they are designed this way.
- List the materials of which rings are made.
- Describe how modern pistons are attached to the connecting rod and why they are connected this way.

PISTON RINGS

Piston rings have been designed in an unbelievable multitude of variations. Originally, they were a simple split ring made of cast iron. Since engine power output has constantly increased and oiling requirements have become more complicated, more efficiency and durability has been demanded of piston rings.

Modern piston rings are made of steel, as well as cast iron. Oil control rings often have multiple sections and are quite complicated in design. Different types of rings are heat treated in various ways and plated with other metals. Today's piston rings, however, still fall into two distinct classifications: compression rings and oil control rings. A typical ring installation is shown in Fig. 9-1.

Latest developments in the design of piston rings tend to reduce emissions, together with reducing oil consumption and improving engine durability. Improvements in hydrocarbon emissions may be obtained by mounting the top compression ring near the top of the piston. Also, reducing ring friction reduces nitrogen oxide emissions because of lower throttle settings for a given load output.

PISTON RING BLOW-BY

Piston rings would be less of a problem if cylinders and pistons did not expand, distort out-of-round, and warp at operating temperatures. The rings must be capable of adapting to these changing conditions.

Furthermore, the rings are exposed to high temperatures of combustion and to alternating pressure and vacuum. Rings are expected to prevent the blow-by of pressure in one direction and to control the flow of oil in the other direction.

Compression pressure and explosion pressure can get by the rings in several ways. "Blow-by" can go through the ring gaps which change in width according to the expansion and contraction of the cylinder and rings. If the rings were fitted so precisely that ring ends touched to seal the gap, the cylinder walls would score when the rings expand.

Blow-by also can occur if it gets behind the compression rings, as shown in Fig. 9-2. If the rings were fitted too tight in the grooves to avoid possible leakage, there would be danger of sticking when the piston and rings expand.

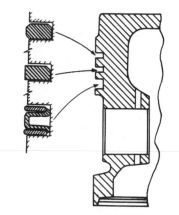

Fig. 9-1. The upper two rings are compression rings, while the bottom ring is an oil control ring.

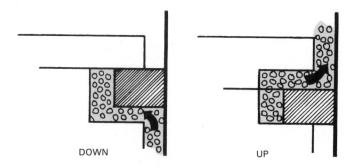

DOWN   UP

Fig. 9-2. Oil can work its way past the ring. Combustion gases also work their way past the ring into the crankcase.

Blow-by is a serious problem when the cylinder walls distort out-of-round at operating temperature. This condition can be caused by improper cooling or unequal tightening of cylinder head bolts adjacent to the cylinders. Distortion may occur in more than one spot on the cylinder wall, and the different spots are often different size and shape. See Fig. 9-3.

Just as compression can leak down past the rings, oil can also pass upward into the cylinder. The result is known as "oil pumping." This condition causes fouling of the spark plugs, excessive deposits of carbon in the combustion chamber, and smoking exhaust as well as loss of oil.

OIL PUMPING

It is easier for oil to pass upward, in some cases, than it is for compression to leak down past the rings. Therefore, it is possible to have an engine with good compression and power, which is also an oil pumper. The oil may seal excessive side clearance in the ring grooves and prevent leakage of compression. Yet, alternating vacuum and pressure in the cylinder may cause the rings to act as a pump. See Fig. 9-4.

This condition is aggravated if the walls of the ring grooves, and the sides of the rings, are not flat and true. The volume of oil leakage past the back of the ring can be much greater than through the tiny ring gaps.

From these explanations of blow-by and oil pumping, you can see that great care is required in reconditioning cylinders to make sure they are round and true when new rings are fitted. Equal care is required in selecting the new rings and fitting them to the pistons and cylinders.

COMPRESSION RINGS

The top compression ring is rectangular in cross section. It may have a bevel cut on the inner top corner, Fig. 9-5. Often the ring is chrome plated, Fig. 9-6, or is molybdenum-filled (moly) cast iron to provide better wearing qualities. The second compression ring is often a coated cast iron ring. Some compression rings have a taper on the face, and they may or may not have an inside bevel.

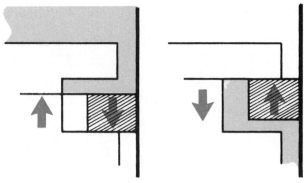

EXHAUST   INTAKE

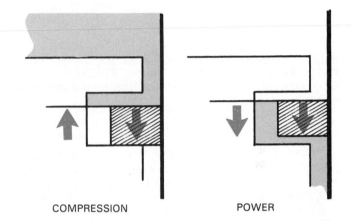

COMPRESSION   POWER

Fig. 9-4. There must be some clearance between the ring and groove to allow for ring movement. However, the ring can then act as a pump drawing oil up into the combustion chamber, and allowing combustion gases down into the crankcase. On the exhaust stroke, the piston moves upward while the ring moves downward due to the exhaust gases. On the intake stroke, engine vacuum holds the ring against the top of the groove while the piston moves downward. On the compression stroke, the pressure forces the ring against the bottom of the groove while the piston moves upward. On the power stroke, the expanding gases push both the piston and the ring downward. This causes the ring to float in the groove.

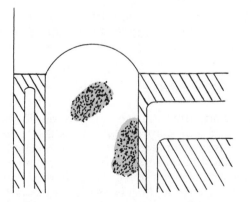

Fig. 9-3. Distortion of cylinder walls can cause the cylinder to be out-of-round in spots.

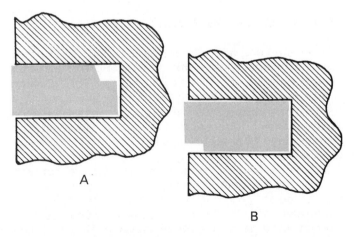

Fig. 9-5. Two methods for cutting a groove or bevel on a piston ring. A—A groove may be cut on the top inside of the ring. B—Or, the groove may be cut on the bottom outside of the ring.   (Perfect Circle)

81

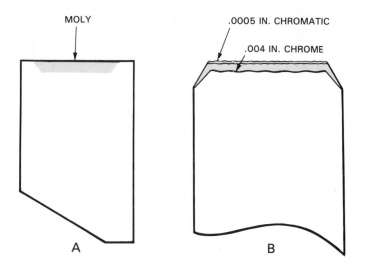

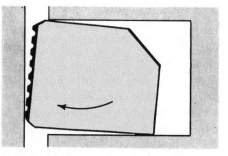

Fig. 9-7. With a bevel on the ring, the ring twists in the groove.

Fig. 9-6. Molybdenum and chrome rings. A—The face of the ring is cut out and molybdenum is added. B—The face of the ring is coated with chrome. Some rings have an additional layer called chromatic. (Perfect Circle)

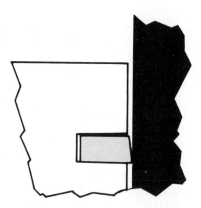

The bevel on the inside upper corner of the ring is to effect a better seal. The bevel causes the ring to twist in the groove so that the outside lower edge presses on the cylinder wall more tightly than the rest of the ring face, Fig. 9-7.

The compression ring with a tapered outer face does the same thing, Fig. 9-8. In both cases, the limited area in contact with the cylinder wall offers a higher pressure at that point for better sealing. Beveled and/or tapered rings must be installed right side up and are usually stamped "TOP" on that side of the ring.

Usually, the second ring is a compression ring, but it may be slightly different in design since it helps in oil control. This difference might be a bevel cut on the inner or outer corner, Fig. 9-5, which might be combined with a taper on either the inside or outside. These second rings are also known as scraper rings, because one or more edges are designed to aid in scraping the oil from the cylinder walls.

Fig. 9-8. A tapered face ring assures lower face contact with the cylinder wall for a positive seal. (Perfect Circle)

SELECTING PISTON RINGS

The piston ring with a CHROME face, Fig. 9-6, comes installed on most engines from the factory. This is a good general purpose ring for passenger cars. While chrome is a hard metal, the advantage of chrome rings is that they resist abrasive wear best. This makes chrome rings the best choice for areas that are dusty. However, the disadvantage of chrome rings is that they can take up to 1000 miles to seat.

MOLYBDENUM is a metal softer than chrome, but with a higher melting point. This higher melting point reduces the chance of "ring scuffing," (ring is momentarily welded to the cylinder wall). This is caused by an excessive amount of heat in the combustion chamber. Since molybdenum is a softer metal, rings made of this metal can seat within 5-10 minutes after the engine is first started. This ring should NOT be used in areas that are extremely dusty.

BREAKING IN NEW RINGS

To aid in seating new rings, especially chrome faced rings, the car should be driven as follows: Accelerate the car rapidly to the maximum speed limit on the highway. As soon as the speed limit is reached, let off of the accelerator and coast to a speed of about 35 mph. Then accelerate rapidly to the maximum speed limit again. Repeat this cycle about 24-36 times. During the rapid acceleration, the rings are forced out against the cylinder wall. During deceleration, a high vacuum is formed in the combustion chamber drawing oil up around the face of the piston rings. These combined actions aid in seating the rings against the cylinder wall. If the rings do not seat, oil will get past the face of the rings. Oil consumption will be excessive, as it will be burned in the combustion chamber.

OIL CONTROL RINGS

The third ring from the top, and the fourth, if four are used, are of the oil-control type, Fig. 9-9. Oil rings vary all the way from simple to extremely complicated types.

Remember that oil scraped from the cylinder wall by the oil ring must have a free passage to the inside of the piston. For this reason, holes or slots are cut in the lower ring grooves. When an inner ring or expander is used, these openings must be kept open if the oil ring is to function as intended. See Figs. 9-10 and 9-11.

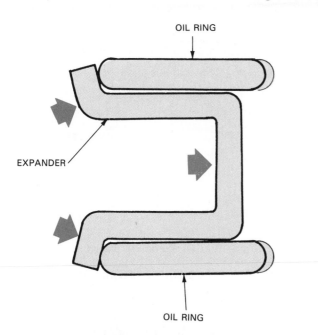

Fig. 9-9. Expander is placed behind the oil control rings. This forces the oil control rings against the cylinder wall. (Perfect Circle)

If the cylinder is worn tapered, the rings will expand and contract as they move up and down in a bore that is larger at one end than the other. If the cylinder is out-of-round in spots, the rings will pump in and out of the grooves as they try to follow the cylinder wall.

Another type of oil control ring is shown in Fig. 9-12. This ring is a cast iron ring with a self expanding stainless steel spring expander. It is designed specifically to prevent oil clogging in heavy duty service. Note that the expander is located above the drainage slots, so oil flow will not be restricted. In addition, drainage slots at the bottom of the ring are curved to eliminate sharp corners. The ring is faced with chrome to reduce wear.

PISTON PINS

Piston pins ("wrist pins") connect the upper end of the connecting rod and the piston, Fig. 9-13.

The proper size for a piston pin presents a design problem. If the pin is large enough in diameter to provide a long wearing bearing surface, the reciprocating weight will be greater and the bearing loads correspondingly increased. If it is as small as permissible to hold down bearing loads, it will be smaller in diameter and have less bearing surface to carry the load.

Fig. 9-10. Oil passes through the slots in oil control ring to oil return holes in the piston groove.

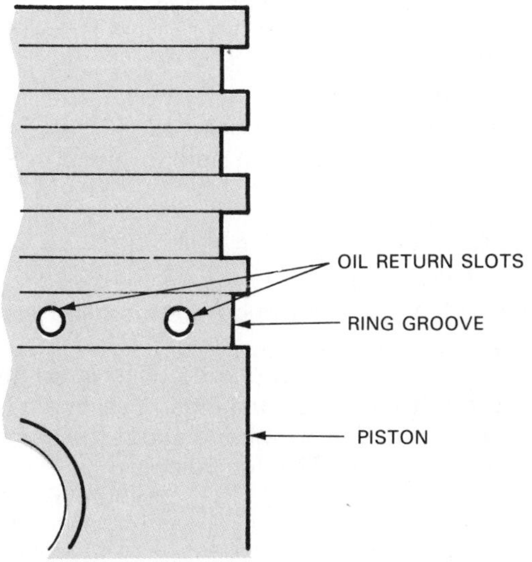

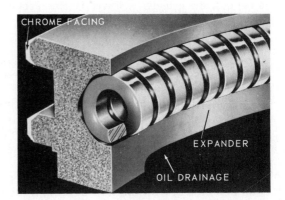

Fig. 9-12. Chrome faced oil control ring with stainless steel coiled spring expander.

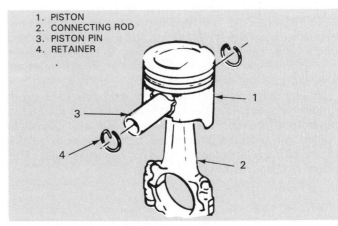

Fig. 9-13. The piston pin joins the piston to the connecting rod. (Cadillac)

Fig. 9-11. After the oil passes through the slots of the oil control ring, it passes through the slots in the groove of the piston. After passing thorugh the piston, the oil flows back to the crankcase.

83

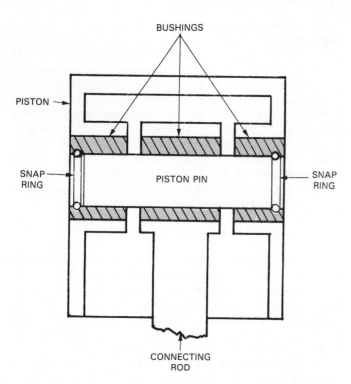

Fig. 9-14. The bushings used in a piston and connecting rod assembly are an older method of retaining pistons pins. If snap rings fall out, the cylinder wall will become scored.

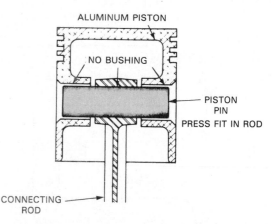

Fig. 9-15. Notice that an aluminum piston has no bushings when the piston pin is pressed into the piston. This provides better heat transfer from the piston. (Sunnen Co.)

Piston pins are case hardened, as they are subject to 2000 pounds per square inch of pressure. Also, they are chrome plated to resist abrasive wear.

One of the methods of connecting the piston to the connecting rod, Fig. 9-14, involves bronze bushings inside of the piston and connecting rod. The piston pin is held in place by a snap ring at each end. The problem with this is that three different metals were involved (aluminum pistons, bronze bushings, and steel piston pins). Each expands at a different rate. Also, if the snap ring fell out, the piston pin would score the cylinder wall.

INTERFERENCE FIT

The modern method of connecting the piston to the connecting rod involves what is known as an IN-TERFERENCE FIT. This means that the bore in the connecting rod (where the piston pin fits in) is slightly smaller in diameter than the piston pin, Fig. 9-15. Since there is a difference of diameter, the piston pin must be pressed into the connecting rod.

In any case, the piston pin is exposed to a great amount of heat. This heat increases wear on the piston pin bore. If the wear becomes excessive, the clearance between the piston pin and the piston pin bore will increase to such an extent that the pin becomes noisy. This noise is a double knock.

Chapter 9—REVIEW QUESTIONS

Write your answers on a separate sheet of paper. Do not write in this book.
1. Name two results of oil pumping.
2. Blow-by may be a serious problem after the engine warms up to operating temperature. True or False?
3. Do piston rings move up and down in the grooves? Yes or No?
4. Why must piston rings be flexible?
5. A piston ring may act as a pump. True or False?
6. Give two reasons for cylinder wall distortion.
7. Do piston rings move in and out in the grooves? Yes or No?
8. More oil leakage occurs:
    a. At the ring gap.
    b. Around behind the ring.
9. If an engine has good compression it will not pump oil. True or False?
10. Chrome rings are best used when:
    a. Excessive oil is consumed.
    b. Engine runs hot.
    c. Both a and b.
    d. Neither a nor b.
11. Describe an "interference fit."
12. Modern piston pins are held in place by:
    a. Snap rings.
    b. Press fit.
    c. Both a and b.
    d. Neither a nor b.
13. Molybdenum-faced rings are installed at the factory. True or False?
14. A hardened steel pin can be used in an aluminum piston without any bushings. Yes or No?
15. Aluminum and bronze have about the same rate of heat expansion. True or False?
16. Piston pins are not _____ for wear.

Chapter 10

ENGINE CRANKSHAFTS AND BEARINGS

After studying this chapter, you will be able to:
- Describe the construction of a bearing.
- Explain the purpose of a vibration damper/balance shaft.
- Define the purpose of engine bearings.

ENGINE BEARINGS

The purpose of any engine bearing is to provide a surface of dissimilar metal for the moving parts to rotate on and reduce friction. Dissimilar metal means that the bearing is made of a metal that is different than that of the metal of the crankshaft or camshaft. When dissimilar metals are used, there is less wear and friction than if two metals of the same type were to rotate against each other. There is even less wear and friction when oil is added between the dissimilar metals. Alloys of copper, tin, and lead do the best job of supporting a cast iron/steel crankshaft or camshaft. Modern engine bearings can be readily replaced.

A one or two cylinder engine usually has two main bearings, one at the front and one at the rear adjacent to the flywheel. A four cylinder engine normally has three main bearings, Fig. 10-1: one at the front; one between cylinders No. 2 and No.3; and one at the rear. However, some four cylinder engines have five main bearings: front, rear, and between crankshaft throws. An in-line six cylinder engine has either three or five mains. A V-6 engine has four mains. A V-8 engine may have three main bearings but usually has five.

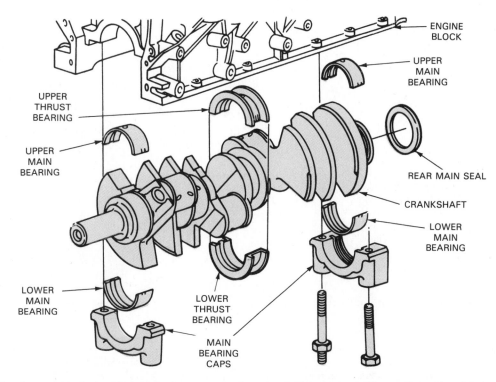

Fig. 10-1. A crankshaft, bearings, bearing caps, and rear seal. The upper and lower thrust bearing is a main bearing with a flange on each side to control the fore and aft movement of the crankshaft. (Oldsmobile)

85

In a previous chapter, reference was made to cylinder block distortion. This can be serious if the crankcase distorts to throw the engine main bearings out of alignment with each other. An example of this is shown in Fig. 10-2.

On engines having less than eight cylinders, it is customary to provide a throw on the crankshaft for each cylinder. On V-type engines, however, the rods are usually placed side by side, two on each throw.

There are two types of bearings used on automobile engine crankshafts. One is known as the poured, cast-in or integral type. It is now virtually obsolete. The other type is known as the precision insert or slip-in type of bearing. The bearing surface is, in all cases, a soft metal with good heat conducting qualities and which will possess a low coefficient of friction in contact with the steel crankshaft journal. The metal must be soft to allow any abrasive material to become imbedded in the bearing, rather than remain between bearing and journal surfaces, which would damage the journal.

PRECISION BEARINGS

The precision or slip-in type of bearing is shown in Fig. 10-3. It has become increasingly popular since engine

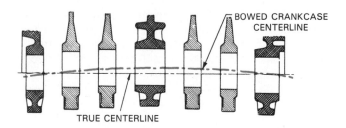
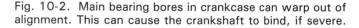

Fig. 10-2. Main bearing bores in crankcase can warp out of alignment. This can cause the crankshaft to bind, if severe.

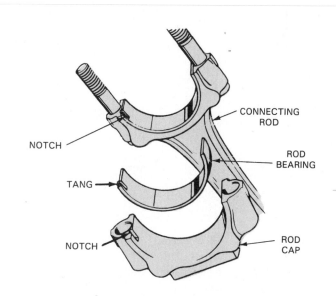

Fig. 10-3. Tang in bearing corresponds to notch in rod bearing cap and rod. This notch prevents mis-alignment of bearing halves. (Oldsmobile)

speeds and loads have been increased so much that a material stronger than babbitt became necessary. It is now used in the majority of automobile engines for both main and connecting rod bearings. The bearing material is an alloy of several metals and may include lead, tin, copper, silver, cadmium, etc. The proportion of the various metals varies considerably, and the development is the result of much experience and experimentation.

The bearing insert or shell, consists of a hard shell of steel or bronze, with additional metal linings or laminations, and a thin lining of anti-friction metal or bearing alloy to form the inner surface, Fig. 10-4. These inserts are manufactured to extremely close dimensions and must be handled carefully to avoid damage. When properly installed they are very durable. When they do wear from continued use, they are discarded and replaced with new inserts.

Precision type bearing inserts, being made to such close dimensions, must be used under closely controlled conditions. Fitting and installing them properly involves measurement in fractions of thousandths of an inch. Careless workmanship in installation cannot be tolerated, as they are not adjustable.

MAIN BEARING CAPS AND SEALS

An exploded view of a typical V-8 crankshaft together with its bearings, caps, and seals is shown in Fig. 10-5. Note that there are two bolts for each cap. In larger engines four bolts are often used. The center main bearing in illustration Fig. 10-1 is designed to take the end thrust as indicated by the flanges on the side. To prevent oil leakage, the rear main bearing is provided with a seal. Seals are either of the wick type or are made of neoprene. See Fig. 10-6.

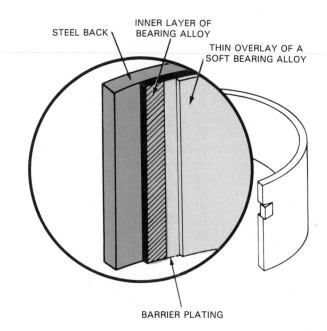

Fig. 10-4. Construction of an engine bearing. On quality undersize bearings, the steel back thickness is increased. On inferior undersize bearings, the bearing alloy material is increased in thickness. (Federal Mogul)

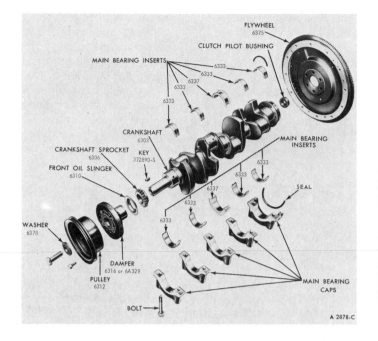

Fig. 10-5. Detailed view shows a V-8 engine crankshaft.

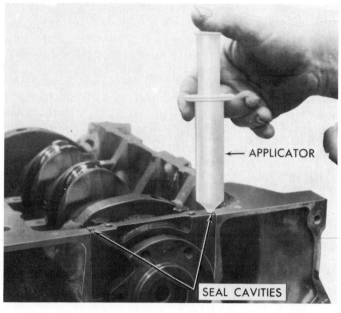

Fig. 10-7. A special sealant is used instead of a conventional rear main seal on a Vega engine.

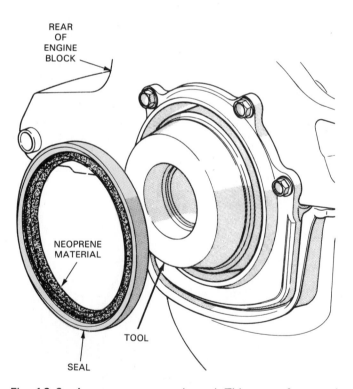

Fig. 10-6. A neoprene rear main seal. This type of rear main seal is the most commonly used in modern engines. (Chrysler)

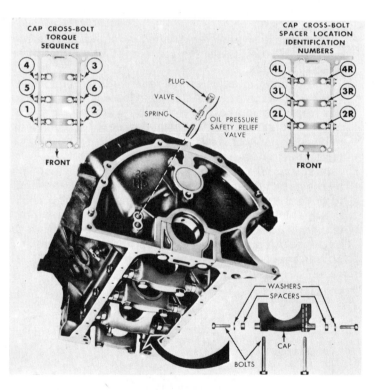

Fig. 10-8. Cross bolts and strength to bearing caps on a Ford high performance engine.

Another method of sealing the rear main bearing cap is employed on the Vega. In this design the sealant is forced into the cavities provided by means of a special applicator, Fig. 10-7.

The upper seal can be removed in most cases, without removing the crankshaft, by first loosening the main bearing cap bolts to lower the crankshaft slightly.

Then remove the rear bearing cap, after which the upper seal can be pushed around the shaft until one end protrudes. The end can then be grasped with pliers and pulled out the rest of the way.

In the case of high performance engines, the main bearing caps are provided with cross bolts, in addition to the usual vertical bolts, Fig. 10-8.

Fig. 10-9. Holes in camshaft bushings provide lubrication to the camshaft and other parts of the engine.

CAMSHAFT BEARINGS

Camshaft bearings are usually made of bronze, and are bushings rather than the split bearings. See Fig. 10-9. Camshaft bushings are not adjustable for wear and are replaced when worn. The degree of wear dictating replacement is more a matter of oil clearance than any tendency toward noise.

ENGINE CRANKSHAFTS

Automobile engine crankshafts are forged out of steel, Fig. 10-10, or they are made out of cast steel by a special process.

The bearing journals are all finished in precise alignment with each other. Also, great care is exercised to see that the journals are absolutely round, and not tapered longitudinally. A high degree of accuracy is necessary in any work that is done with an engine crankshaft or any of the bearings.

In automobile engines, a gear or sprocket is installed on the end of the crankshaft (opposite the flywheel end) to drive the camshaft either by means of a timing chain or a gear arrangement. Also, a torsional vibration damper usually is attached to the same end of the crankshaft to help smooth out vibrations set up in the crankshaft by power impulses that end to twist the shaft.

ENGINE FLYWHEELS

A flywheel ordinarily is mounted near the rear main bearing. This is usually the longest and heaviest of the main bearings, since it must support the weight of the flywheel.

The purpose of the flywheel is to assist the engine to idle smoothly by carrying the pistons through parts of the operating cycle when power is not being produced.

The heavier the engine flywheel, the smoother the engine will idle. However, because of its inertia, an excessively heavy flywheel will cause the engine to accelerate and decelerate slowly. For this reason, heavy-duty or truck engines have large and heavy flywheels, while racing engines or high performance engines have light flywheels.

The rear surface of the flywheel is usually machined flat. This surface is used to mate with one surface of the clutch. With automatic transmissions, where no clutch is used, part of the fluid flywheel or torque converter is attached to and becomes a part of the flywheel.

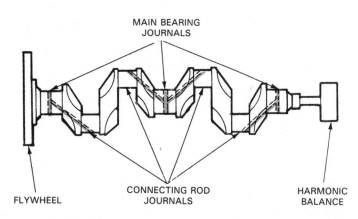

Fig. 10-10. Oil passages, in color, provide lubrication to the engine bearings and other parts of the engine. Note that the main bearing journals are on the same plane.

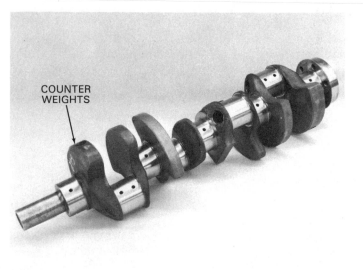
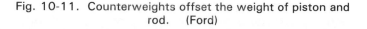

Fig. 10-11. Counterweights offset the weight of piston and rod. (Ford)

Fig. 10-12. A crankshaft with vibration damper and flywheel.

CRANKSHAFT BALANCE

Because of the forces acting on the flywheel and crankshaft, and the speed at which it revolves, the crankshaft must be balanced with great care. The assembly is first balanced statically, then dynamically. Static balance of the crankshaft is obtained when the weight is distributed equally in all directions from the center of the crankshaft while it is at rest.

Dynamic balance means balance while the crankshaft is turning. It is attained when the centrifugal forces of rotation are equal in all directions at any point. The dynamic balancing operation requires special machinery and involves removal of metal at the heavy points or addition of metal at the light points.

To obtain rotating balance, crankshafts are equipped with counterweights, which are usually forged or cast integrally with the crankshaft, Figs. 10-11 and 10-12. Counterweights are located on the opposite side of the crankshaft from the connecting rod to counter balance the weight of the rod and piston.

In addition to balancing the crankshaft itself, the entire rotating assembly must be balanced dynamically, Fig. 10-13. This assembly includes the fan pulley, vibration damper, timing gears, crankshaft, flywheel, and the clutch or converter parts attached to it. In addition, the connecting rod assemblies, including piston pins, pistons, bearings, etc., are all carefully balanced one with another so that the rotating mass will have as little vibration as possible.

For a further discussion on crankshaft balancing and methods used to correct unbalance, see Chapter 14.

TORSIONAL VIBRATION

The explosive forces acting on the pistons, and the inertia forces of the reciprocating parts, vary in intensity as the pistons move up and down in the cylinders. This variation in force, or torque, causes the crankshaft to twist or transmit torsional vibration. It is more noticeable at certain speeds than others. The vibration is of greater intensity on long shafts than on short ones.

When the No. 1 cylinder fires, it tends to turn the front end of the crankshaft instantly. This force is transmitted through the length of the crankshaft to the flywheel, which has considerable inertia. At this point, the crankshaft momentarily "winds up" or twists lengthwise (to a small degree, but enough to create vibration). Any piece of steel, no matter how heavy, can be twisted slightly when enough torque is applied to it.

Twisting of the crankshaft depends upon the forces operating in the engine, so it is more severe at some speeds than others. Vibration dampers are used to help control crankshaft twist, Figs. 10-12 and 10-14.

VIBRATION DAMPERS

Regardless of the type of vibration damper used, they all accomplish the same purpose. They add mass or inertia to the end of the crankshaft opposite the flywheel to minimize crankshaft twist. The simplest vibration dampening device would be a flywheel at each end of the crankshaft. In this case, the weight of both flywheels would be about the same as the weight of a single normal flywheel.

A better way is to use a smaller flywheel on the front end and mount it so that it floats. In one type, Fig. 10-14, rubber is used between the small flywheel and its hub. This permits limited circumferential movement between the crankshaft and small flywheel.

Fig. 10-13. Special equipment is used to check the dynamic balance of an engine while crankshaft, piston, and connecting rods are in place.

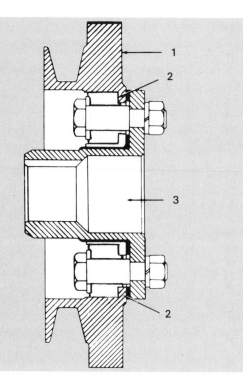

Fig. 10-14. Construction of a vibration damper: 1—Pulley. 2—Rubber insert. 3—Pulley hub.

BALANCE SHAFTS

The balance shaft does the same thing as a vibration damper. Balance shafts are used on large four cylinder engines and some small V-6 engines. On the smaller four cylinder engines neither a vibration damper nor balance shaft is used, as the vibrations are so slight that neither is needed. Some manufacturers locate the balance shaft above the crankshaft, Fig. 10-15A. Other manufacturers locate the balance shaft below the crankshaft, Fig. 10-15B. Also, while some manufacturers use only one balance shaft, others use two, Fig. 10-15C.

CRITICAL SPEEDS

No matter how carefully the crankshaft and parts attached to it are balanced, there will be certain speeds at which some vibration will occur. These are known as critical speeds, where other related parts also vibrate. By careful design and balancing, these critical periods occur at speeds outside the ordinary working speeds of the engine.

In this connection, it is not too difficult to balance rotating parts. However, when reciprocating parts are attached, the problem becomes much more complicated. Consider that each heavy connecting rod and piston assembly must be started, speeded up, slowed down, and stopped twice during each revolution.

OTHER CAUSES OF VIBRATION

Other factors enter into this matter of unbalance. The piston does not accelerate and decelerate uniformly dur-

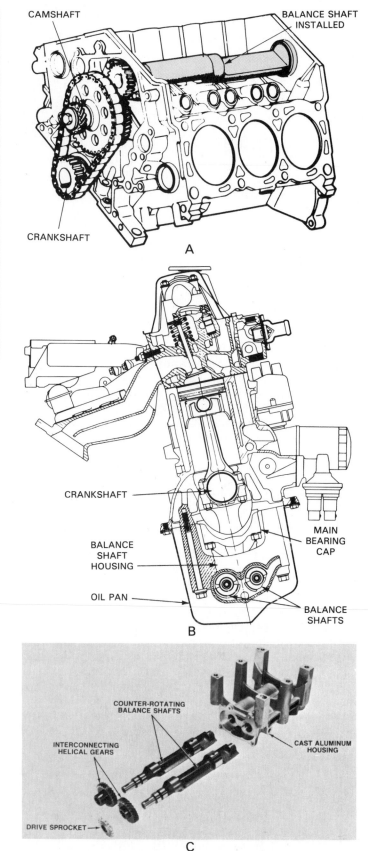

Fig. 10-15. A—The balance shaft on this V-6 engine is located above the crankshaft and camshaft. Only one balance shaft is used. B—The balance shafts on this engine are located below the crankshaft. C—The balance shaft is driven by a chain, which is driven by the crankshaft. (Chrysler and Ford)

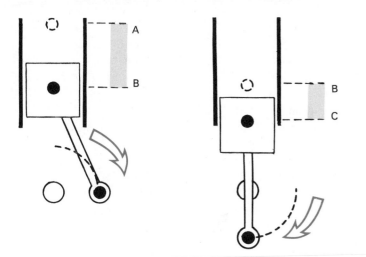

Fig. 10-16. During the first quarter revolution of crankshaft, the piston moves the distance from A to B. During second quarter of revolution, the piston moves from B to C. Crankshaft moves the same amount, but piston movement is less from B to C.

ing each quarter of a revolution. During the first quarter revolution from top dead center (TDC), the connecting rod moves down a distance (length of crank throw) and away from the center of the cylinder. Both the downward and outward motions of the rod cause the piston to travel downward.

During the second quarter of a revolution, there is continued downward motion equal to the crank throw. But, the end of the connecting rod is now moving back toward the center line of the cylinder. During the last portion of this movement, the piston is no longer moving downward. As a result, actual movement of the piston during the second quarter revolution is less than during the first quarter, Fig. 10-16.

When you consider all of these forces acting on the crankshaft, it is easy to see why you cannot add or subtract a fraction of an ounce of weight to any of these parts during a repair operation. Furthermore, the crankshaft, bearings, bearing journals, etc., must be in excellent mechanical condition at all times.

Chapter 10—REVIEW QUESTIONS

Write your answers on a separate sheet of paper. Do not write in this book.

1. Bearings are made of the same type of metal as the crankshaft. True or False?
2. Is an integral bearing the same thing as a precision bearing? Yes or No?
3. Why is bearing metal comparatively soft?
4. Bushings are always used on all camshaft journals. True or False?
5. Slip-in bearings are not adjustable for wear. True or False?
6. Name four metals used in bearing metal alloys.
7. What is the purpose of a flywheel?
8. What is the difference between static and dynamic balance?
9. Give a description of a vibration damper.
10. Small four cylinder engines:
    a. Use a vibration damper.
    b. Use a balance shaft.
    c. Either a or b.
    d. None of the above.
11. When the crankshaft rotational speed is constant, is the distance traveled by the piston during each quarter revolution the same? Yes or No?

Chapter 11

ENGINE CAMSHAFTS AND VALVES

After studying this chapter, you will be able to:
- Explain the purpose of the camshaft.
- State how a camshaft operates.
- Name the parts of a valve and the valve train.
- Explain how the valves are cooled.
- Define the relationship of the camshaft to the crankshaft.
- Determine the difference between an overhead camshaft design and an overhead valve design.
- List the parts of a hydraulic lifter.
- Explain how a hydraulic lifter operates.

CAMS

A cam is a piece of metal that is somewhat egg or wedge shaped, Fig. 11-1. As a cam rotates in an eccentric motion, it can open and close items that it comes in contact with. On a car's engine, the cam opens and closes the valves of the engine as it rotates, Fig. 11-2.

These cams appear to have a simple shape, but actually the exact shape of the cam is a meticulous job of design. The design is worked out after a painstaking and detailed program of mathematical calculation, and checked by lengthy experimentation. If the shape of the cams is altered by wear, the efficiency of the engine deteriorates fast. There is much more to the matter than just opening and closing a valve.

CAM FUNCTIONS

The cam is designed to open the valve at precisely the correct instant in relation to piston travel and hold it open long enough to obtain the most efficient filling and emptying of the cylinder. It exerts considerable control over the volumetric efficiency of the engine.

In a passenger car engine, ramps on the cams are designed to open the valves smoothly and gradually. This avoids shock to the valves, valve springs, etc., and makes for quietness of operation. The final design is usually a compromise between efficiency and quietness of operation.

On racing engines where noise is not important and utmost efficiency is desired, the cams are often shaped with more abrupt ramps, higher lift, flatter flank, and wider nose. The cam is intended to "bat" the valve open

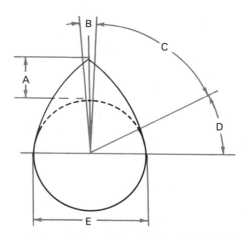

Fig. 11-1. Nomenclature of a cam: A—Height of lift. B-Nose. C—Flank. D—Ramp. E—Diameter of cam.

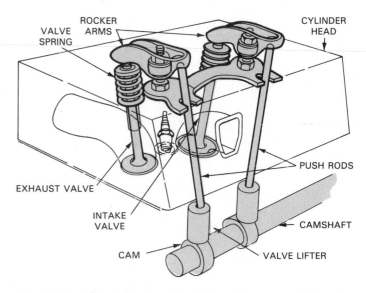

Fig. 11-2. A typical valve train. When the nose or high point of the cam push against the lifter, the lifter pushes up on the push rod to the rocker arm. The rocker arm acts as a lever and transmits this motion downward on the valve, as it overcomes spring pressure, and opens the valve. Note that there is a separate cam for each valve. (Oldsmobile)

quickly, open it wider, hold it open longer, and close it rapidly. Such engines are noisy, idle roughly, and wear more quickly.

If the camshaft is chain or belt driven, Fig. 11-3, it rotates in the same direction as the crankshaft which is clockwise from the front of the engine. If the camshaft is driven by a gear meshed with a mating gear on the crankshaft, the camshaft rotation is counterclockwise, or opposite from the crankshaft.

As the valves must be precisely opened and closed with relation to the piston travel, any wear in the camshaft driving chain or belt will result in the valve not being opened and closed at the exact instant desired and a loss in engine efficiency will be incurred.

TIMING CHAIN WEAR

In a few cases, adjustment is provided by timing chains such as an eccentric mounting for an accessory shaft, automatic slack adjusters, etc. In most cases it is necessary to install a new chain when the old one becomes worn and stretched. In general, a deflection of 1/2 in. is permitted for timing chains when the chain is depressed.

In a gear-driven camshaft, the crankshaft gear is usually made of steel. However, the camshaft gear is often made of nonmetallic composition. This nonmetallic substance is quite durable and also makes for quieter operation. These gears are not adjustable and must be replaced when worn.

The car manufacturers set up specifications as to the amount of wear permissible in the chain or between the gear teeth. They also mark the gears or chains to facilitate correct timing, Fig. 11-3.

TIMING BELT WEAR

The timing belt should be checked periodically for wear. See Fig. 11-4A. The timing belt should be replaced during a valve job or major engine overhaul. Some premature wear can be attributed to wear of the teeth on the timing belt sprocket, See Fig. 11-4B. If the timing belt should break, the engine must be torn down to make sure that none of the valves or connecting rods are bent. If a new timing belt is installed without tearing the engine down first, the car may come back into the shop. The same is true for timing chains.

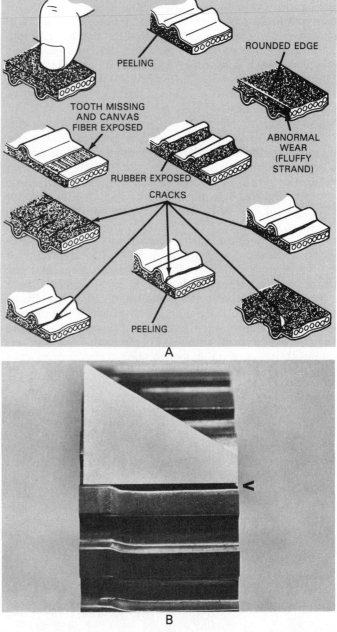

Fig. 11-4. Timing belt wear. A—Inspecting the timing belt for various types of wear. B—Using a straight edge to determine if there is a gap on teeth of timing belt sprocket, as indicated by arrow. This sprocket must be replaced, or timing belt will wear prematurely.   (Gates Rubber Co. and Chrysler)

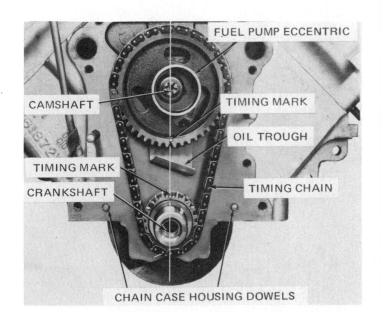

Fig. 11-3. Camshaft is located in the engine block. Note that the size of the camshaft sprocket is twice the diameter of the the diameter of the crankshaft sprocket, which provides a reduction in speed of the camshaft. Also, timing marks on camshaft and crankshaft sprockets must align when first installed.

CAMSHAFT

A camshaft is just that; a shaft that has cams. Since the valves of the engine need to be opened at different times, the nose or high point of the cams are offset from one another. Most camshafts have twice as many cams as there are cylinders. The reason for this is one cam opens and closes the exhaust valve, and another cam opens and closes the intake valve, Fig. 11-2. So, there are two cams per cylinder, which means a V-8 engine would have a total of 16 cams.

The camshaft is made of steel, and only the surface of each cam is hardened to avoid rapid wear. If the entire camshaft were hardened it would snap apart, as it would not be able to absorb the twisting motion.

In a four cycle engine, each valve is opened once for two revolutions of the crankshaft. Therefore, the camshaft turns at one-half the speed of the crankshaft, Fig. 11-3. Since the camshaft runs at a slower speed than the crankshaft, it is not subject to as much wear as the crankshaft.

CAMSHAFT LOCATION

On most I-head engine designs (valves above the piston), the camshaft is usually located above the engine crankshaft in the block, Fig. 11-3. However, to avoid the use of extensive linkage (which wastes power), there is a growing trend to place the camshaft in the cylinder head, Fig. 11-5. With this setup, the camshaft can be driven by a cog belt, Fig. 11-6, or it may be chain driven or gear driven. Some overhead camshaft engines are provided with two camshafts, Fig. 11-7, for each bank of cylinders; one camshaft for the intake valves and the other for the exhaust valves.

Race engines have their overhead camshaft driven either by a shaft or by a series of gears. The cog belt is made of neoprene reinforced with fiber glass. Among the advantages claimed for this construction are heat and oil resistance and the ability to absorb shock and constant flexing. In addition, it is inherently quiet and needs no lubrication.

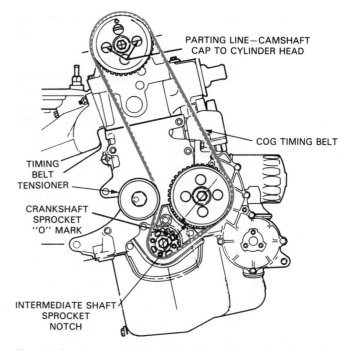

Fig. 11-6. A cogged timing belt drives this overhead camshaft. Belt tensioner provides constant tension on the timing belt. (Chrysler)

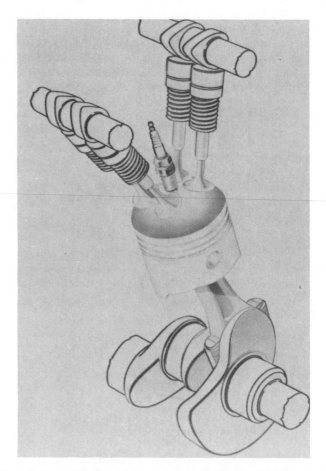

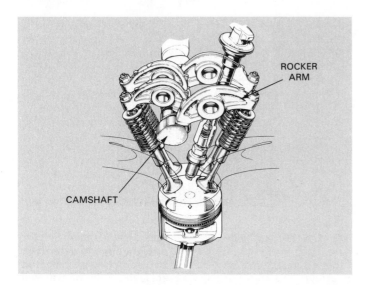

Fig. 11-5. OHC or overhead camshaft. (Honda)

Fig. 11-7. A DOHC or dual overhead camshaft. One camshaft opens only the intake valves, and the other camshaft opens only the exhaust valves. Note that there are two exhaust valves and two intake valves per cylinder. (Saab)

The overhead camshaft is efficient. It eliminates push rods and permits excellent valve action at high speeds since there is little inertia of moving parts.

It is necessary that the camshaft journals be round and true, and the camshaft be straight and true. There should be no measurable wear on the cam surfaces. There must be no appreciable looseness in the bearings, since any radial movement or vibration of the cams would affect the operation of the valves. The location of the cams around the camshaft, along with the design of the crankshaft, determines the firing order of the engine.

FIRING ORDER

A one cylinder, two cycle engine fires once each revolution. A one cylinder, four cycle engine fires once every other revolution. A two cylinder, two cycle engine fires twice each revolution. A two cylinder, four cycle engine fires once every revolution.

In a four cylinder, four cycle engine, the No. 1 piston moves downward on the power stroke, while No. 4 is also moving down on the intake stroke. While No. 1 and 4 are going down, 2 and 3 are, of course going up. One is on the exhaust stroke; the other on the compression stroke. There are therefore two possible firing orders, 1, 2, 4, 3 or 1, 3, 4, 2. In either case, one power impulse is obtained every one-half revolution of the crankshaft, giving two power impulses per revolution. See Fig. 11-8.

The six cylinder, four cycle engine (and a three cylinder, two cycle engine) has the crank throws spaced 120 deg. apart, rather than 180 deg., and gets a power impulse every one-third revolution of the crankshaft. The firing order of a right-hand crankshaft can be 1, 5, 3, 6, 2, 4, or it can be 1, 2, 4, 6, 5, 3. With the left-hand crankshaft, the firing order can be 1, 4, 2, 6, 3, 5, or it can be 1, 3, 5, 6, 4, 2.

With a V-8 engine, the crank throws are spaced 90 deg. apart, and there will be a power impulse every one-quarter revolution of the crankshaft. See diagram at right in Fig. 11-8.

While different firing orders are used, the general idea of an in-line engine firing order is to fire cylinders as nearly as possible at alternate ends of the crankshaft. On a V-8 engine, the objective is to alternate between the ends of the crankshaft and between the left and right banks of cylinders. This tends to distribute the forces throughout the engine and avoid concentrating consecutive power impulses near one point of the crankshaft. This reduces vibration and results in a smoother running engine. A popular cylinder arrangement and typical firing order are shown in Fig. 11-9.

VALVES

Internal combustion engine valves, Fig. 11-10, have a tremendous task to perform and under the very best conditions they are not all that could be desired. The conditions under which the valves operate would seem to impose an impossible task upon them, but they have been developed to a point where they are fairly efficient. A great amount of ingenuity has been expended upon sleeve valves, rotary valves, slide valves, and poppet valves. The poppet valve, despite all its shortcomings, is used almost universally.

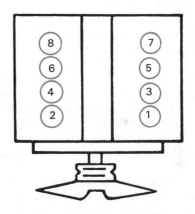

Fig. 11-9. A popular V-8 firing order is 1-8-4-3-6-5-7-2.

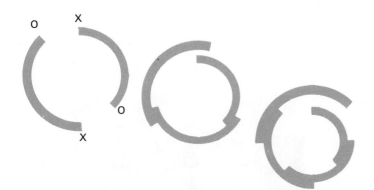

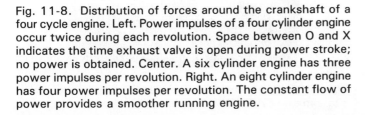

Fig. 11-8. Distribution of forces around the crankshaft of a four cycle engine. Left. Power impulses of a four cylinder engine occur twice during each revolution. Space between O and X indicates the time exhaust valve is open during power stroke; no power is obtained. Center. A six cylinder engine has three power impulses per revolution. Right. An eight cylinder engine has four power impulses per revolution. The constant flow of power provides a smoother running engine.

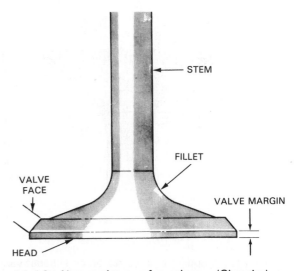

Fig. 11-10. Nomenclature of a valve.   (Chrysler)

Poppet valves are noisy and it is difficult to cool them, but they are simple and do provide an effective seal under operating conditions. These operating conditions are brutal. The valves in the combustion chamber are exposed to the burning gas but not surrounded with cooling water as is the combustion chamber. Neither are they cooled by the oil as is the piston. The explosion temperature within an engine combustion chamber may momentarily approach 5000°F (2700°C), then the exhaust valve must open and permit these hot gases to go past the valve head at high velocity.

It may be readily seen that the exhaust valve head may attain a temperature of 1000°F (540°C), Fig. 11-11, or more under these conditions. The valve cannot readily be cooled directly by the cooling water in the engine. The only cooling comes from contact with the valve guides and with the cylinder head during the short space of time it is in contact with the valve seat.

If an engine is operating at 3000 rpm that means any one cylinder will fire 1500 times per minute. Every time the cylinder fires, the exhaust valve must open to let the burned gas out. In spite of the fact that the valve is lifted off its seat 1500 times each minute, a large portion of the heat passes from the valve head and into the valve seat and then into the water jacket.

VALVE TEMPERATURES

It is not difficult to understand why exhaust valves are prone to cause trouble. In normal operation, the valve head around the seating surface will operate at a temperature of 1000 to 1200°F (540 to 645°C). The central portion of the valve head will run somewhat hotter, 1200 to 1400°F (645 to 760°C) and the stem adjacent to the head is 800 to 1000°F (425 to 540°C). Running at a red heat under normal conditions, it may be seen that the steel valve may melt under abnormal conditions.

The intake valve has a somewhat easier task as it is not exposed to the burning while it is off its seat. The intake valve is also cooled by the incoming gas mixture, which is below atmospheric temperature.

VALVE AND SEAT MATERIALS

Exhaust valves are usually made of heat resistant alloy steel. Quite often they are partially filled with sodium to help transfer the heat. See Fig. 11-12. The valve seat is often also made of heat resistant alloy in the form of an insert which is set into the cylinder head. See the alloy inserts in Fig. 11-13. These inserts are used in cast iron heads as well as aluminum heads.

The particular construction shown in Fig. 11-14 shows how heat is transferred to the water jacket.

INDUCTION HARDENED SEATS

One of the results of lead free fuel is higher valve temperatures along with valve and seat burning.

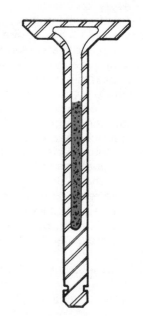

Fig. 11-12. A portion of the hollow valve stem is filled with sodium. When the sodium melts, the liquid bounces between the valve head and the tip of the valve transferring the heat of the valve. This aids in the heat transfer process. This type of valve is usually only found on diesel and high performance engines.

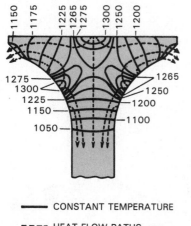

CONSTANT TEMPERATURE

HEAT FLOW PATHS

Fig. 11-11. Various temperatures on an exhaust valve. Hottest location is the valve head.

Fig. 11-13. The valve seat insert can be shrunk by exposing it to extreme cold, and is then placed in the cylinder head.

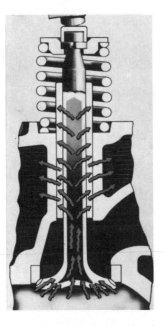

Fig. 11-14. Heat transfer path from valve head and face to the seat. Heat also is tranferred through the valve guide.

In the past the lead in the fuel acted as a lubricant, at least between the valve face and its seat. When there is no lead in the fuel, the cast iron seats become oxidized by the hot exhaust gases. These oxides abrade the valve face and seat, so there is metal transfer from the seat to the valve. Valve seat wear increases rapidly as valve lash becomes greater. When lash increases from 0.001 to 0.040 in. the impact loads increase up to 30 times which increase valve and seat wear.

To overcome this situation, several methods are available. One method is to use alloys for the valve seats or hard noncorrosive inserts. Instead of ethyl lead in the fuel, boron oxide or iron phosphate can be used, but these materials have an adverse effect on catalytic converters. Another method is to aluminize the valve face or chrome plate the valve head. Valve stems are also being chrome plated in order to reduce wear in that area.

Internally cooled valves such as shown in Fig. 11-12 are also being used and extensive research on water filled valve stems is promising, showing temperature reduction up to 600 °F. To further aid in the dissipation of heat, valve stem diameter is sometimes increased.

Induction hardening of valve seats extends the life of the seat, Fig. 11-15. This process heats the valve seats to 1700 °F and hardens them to a depth of 0.05 to 0.08 in. This gives the seats approximately the same durability as is obtained with leaded fuel.

VALVE COOLING

The heat of combustion flows from the valve head to the cooling water. Tests made show that the popular conception that solid exhaust valves are cooled primarily by conduction down the stem is not true.

Most of the heat leaves the valve at the face. In fact, over half of the total heat absorbed by the valve leaves through the face.

It will also be noted that the heat flows from the valve stem to the valve guide and from the guide to the head, Fig. 11-14. As heat will flow more readily through one piece of metal than from one piece to another, the removable valve guide on most passenger car engines has been dispensed with and instead the cylinder head is reamed to form the guide. When it becomes necessary to recondition the valve guide, replacement valves are provided with oversize stems and the guides are then reamed to the desired size. Or, the valve guide can be knurled, if wear is less than .006 in. Also, the guide can be reamed oversize and a bushing pressed into the guide. With the last two methods, the same valve is used.

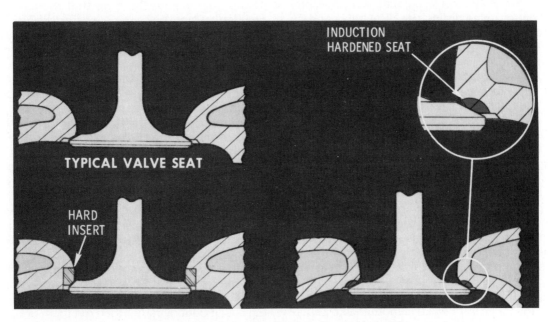

Fig. 11-15. Induction hardened seat is at right.

VALVE SEAT CONTACT AREA

From the foregoing, it should be realized that anything that reduces the area of contact between the valve and the cylinder head will hamper the transfer of heat from the valve. Thus, if the valve seat is too narrow or valve guide worn excessively, the area of contact will be reduced and the valve will overheat.

The area of contact could be increased by widening the valve seat, but it has been found that a wider seat also encourages flakes of carbon to adhere, and hold the valve off its seat causing burning of the valve face. Another method of increasing the contact area would be to increase the diameter of the valve head, the valve stem, or both by installing oversize valves, oversize stems, or longer guides, etc.

There are of course mechanical limitations to the amount of increase in these dimensions. Of more importance however, would be the increase of weight in the valve. The valve is required to move endwise with such speed that it must be kept as light as possible. Any excess weight would add to the inertia and slow down the valve action. So, here again a compromise must be made and a reasonable limitation in size imposed. However, the major factor limiting the size of the valve is the diameter of the cylinder bore and shape of the combustion chamber.

VALVE HEAT DISSIPATION

This matter of valve heat dissipation must be thoroughly understood if automobile engines are to be serviced properly. There are several things to be considered in this connection. Some of them are similar to problems previously discussed in connection with pistons and rings.

For example, the heat of operation causes distortion of cylinder heads, blocks, etc. The same conditions cause distortion of the valve and its seat. Any hot spots in the cylinder head or block near the valves or any unequal tightening of the cylinder head bolts will aggravate distortion and cause valve difficulties. The valve and its seat may be round and true when the engine is cold, but may not be round and true when the engine gets to operating temperature.

The valve head is liable to warp due to the difference in temperture at different points. This warpage will be aggravated if the margin of the valve is thin or uneven. See Fig. 11-16. Furthermore, the temperature may vary around the margin of the valve in some cases due to the difference in volume and velocity of the gas going between the valve and seat as determined by combustion chamber design and valve port shape.

In addition to changes in valve and valve seat shape, the diameter of both may change. The valve head runs hotter than the valve seat because the seat is nearer the circulating coolant. Therefore, the valve head may expand more than the seat and as a result the valve may rise on the seat as shown in Fig. 11-17. This action results in a change in the valve seat area location.

It will be apparent that the dimension between the valve seat and the valve lifter will be lengthened by such expansion. The length of the valve itself between the

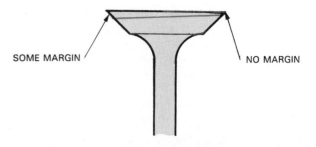

Fig. 11-16. If there is no margin on the valve, the thin edges will become excessively hot and could cause preignition.

Fig. 11-17. Left. Exhaust valve may seat properly when cold. Right. When exhaust valve is hot, the valve will move off of its seat.

seat surface and the end of the stem, will be altered by lengthwise expansion of the valve and valve stem.

One of the most important factors affecting valve temperatures is that of valve lash or tappet clearance. Insufficient clearance will result in the valves contacting the seats for a shorter time and consequently operate at higher temperatures. Excessive clearance will result in noisy operation and loss of power. Great accuracy should be used when adjusting the valve lash.

VALVE TIMING

Anything that occurs to change the time that the valve opens, the duration of the time it is held open, the size of the opening, or the time that it closes, will have a decided affect on engine performance. This fact is seldom fully realized. Many engines run constantly below par because of incorrect valve tappet clearance adjustment.

A full realization of the need for accurate adjustment can come only from a study of valve action and requirements. This study starts with the relation between the crankshaft and camshaft. Due to the difference in the diameter of the circles described by the crank throw and the cam nose, and the difference in the comparative speed of rotation, the crank throw may travel many times as fast as the cam nose. While the cam nose is moving 1/4 in., the crank throw moves 1 1/2 in. If the cam is a few thousandths late in opening the valve, the crank throw and the piston attached to it will move a considerable distance farther than it should before the valve begins to open.

In this manner, the motion of the piston is partially lost, and the power output suffers. A worn timing chain or gears should be replaced as soon as the wear exceeds the specifications rather than run them until they become noisy or break, which is all too often the case.

The extreme accuracy with which it is desired to open and close the valves may be understood when thought is given to the speed at which the valve parts operate. This timing becomes more important as engine speeds are increased. This is the reason for what is known as valve "overlap." Valve overlap means that the intake and exhaust valves are open at the same time in any one cylinder. This, however, is to compensate for the time required by the air or gas to flow through the manifolds.

Many things have to be considered when designing the timing of an engine. In order that the engine may operate satisfactorily at high speeds, it is necessary that the exhaust valve open before the end of the power stroke and close after the completion of the exhaust stroke; also that the intake valve open before the end of the exhaust stroke and close after the completion of the intake stroke. This involves an overlapping of the exhaust and intake periods which is made necessary by the inertia of the gases. Also, the slow opening and closing motions of the valves is made necessary by the demands for quiet operation. See Fig. 11-18.

VALVE SPRINGS

Valve springs, Fig. 11-19, are required to close the valve after it has been opened by the action of the cam. Valve springs are of the coil type and are made of special high grade steel designed to withstand the high rate of stress applications, temperature, and also to keep the valve from bouncing on its seat.

On some engines a single valve spring is used for each valve. On many high performance engines, two valve springs, one within the other, are required in order to obtain the desired pressure characteristics. Usually the end turns of the springs are closer together than the other turns in order to reduce vibrations. Valve springs are also provided with dampers which help to reduce vibrations.

Valve spring pressure varies with the type of engine. Stronger springs are required on high speed engines and also on engines with heavier push rods, valves, rocker arms, etc.

VALVE LIFTERS

The valve lifter is a device in the valve system that transmits the action of the cam to the valve or push rod as the case may be. There are two types of valve lifters, mechanical and hydraulic.

The solid or mechanical lifter is usually of the mushroom type and is provided with an adjusting screw so that the clearance or lash between the valve stem and the lifter is adjustable. This is necessary as engine heat will expand and lengthen the valve stem to such a degree that the valve would not close, with the further result that the combustible charge in the cylinder would not be compressed.

Instead of the mushroom type lifter, some engines are equipped with roller type lifters, Fig. 11-20. In this design the engine cam strikes a roller mounted on the lower face of the lifter. This has the advantage of reducing friction as compared to the mushroom type lifter.

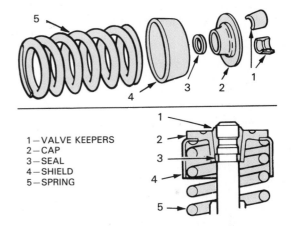

1—VALVE KEEPERS
2—CAP
3—SEAL
4—SHIELD
5—SPRING

Fig. 11-19. A valve spring and related parts. (Oldsmobile)

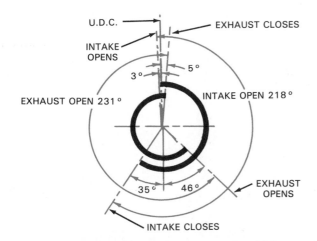

Fig. 11-18. Diagram illustrates valve overlap. Valve overlap is the period that the exhaust valve and intake valve are both open. This is necessary at high speeds to compensate for inertia of the gases moving in and out of the cylinder.

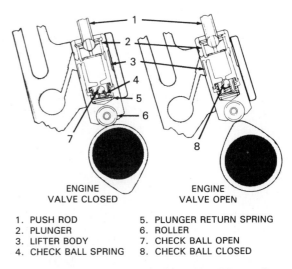

1. PUSH ROD
2. PLUNGER
3. LIFTER BODY
4. CHECK BALL SPRING
5. PLUNGER RETURN SPRING
6. ROLLER
7. CHECK BALL OPEN
8. CHECK BALL CLOSED

Fig. 11-20. Operation of a hydraulic valve lifter; roller type. Roller reduces friction between lifter and camshaft. This type of lifter does not spin in its bore. Note that when engine valve is open, the checkball is seated making the lifter solid. (Oldsmobile)

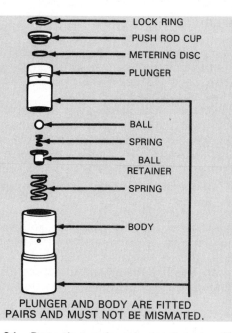

LOCK RING
PUSH ROD CUP
METERING DISC
PLUNGER

BALL
SPRING
BALL RETAINER
SPRING

BODY

PLUNGER AND BODY ARE FITTED PAIRS AND MUST NOT BE MISMATED.

Fig. 11-21. Parts that make a hydraulic valve lifter. (Oldsmobile)

Hydraulic lifters are designed to automatically take up the clearance that exists between the valve and the lifter, Fig. 11-21. The advantage of this type of valve lifter is that it is quiet in operation as it has zero valve lash.

Oil enters each lifter through grooves and oil holes in the lifter body and plunger, flows down into the chamber below the plunger through the feed hole and around the check ball, Fig. 11-22. At the start of the cycle the plunger spring holds all lash clearances out of the valve linkage. As the engine cam starts raising the valve lifter body, oil in the lower chamber and the check ball spring firmly seat the check ball to prevent loss of oil from the lower chamber. The lifting force is then transmitted through the entrapped oil to the check ball and plunger. The plunger and push rod seat move upward with the lifter body to operate the valve linkage which opens the engine valve.

Then as the valve seats, the linkage and lifter plunger stop. The plunger spring forces the body of the lifter to follow the cam downward until it again rests on the cam base circle. Oil pressure against the check ball from the lower chamber ceases when the plunger movement stops. This allows passage of oil past the check ball into the lower chamber to replace the slight amount of oil lost through "leak down," which is the oil that escapes through the clearance between the plunger and the body.

When valve linkage expands due to increased engine temperature, the plunger must move to a slightly lower position in the lifter body to assure full closing of the engine valve. Similarly, when engine temperature drops, the plunger must move to a slightly higher position. In either case, the capacity of the lower chamber changes, and the volume of oil present is automatically controlled by passage of oil through the plunger feed hole.

HYDRAULIC LIFTER PROBLEMS

While hydraulic valve lifters do provide ideal valve operation, they are subject to certain difficulties and require some attention. Clearances between the moving parts must be controlled closely. This has caused some difficulty because of dirt or varnish, causing the lifters to stick.

The plunger and cylinder are held to dimensional tolerances of one-tenth of a thousandth of an inch or less in manufacture. Different plungers are tried in different cylinders until a pair is found that fits closely enough without being too tight. For this reason, lifters should not be mixed up when they are removed for service. Each plunger should be kept with the cylinder in which it operates.

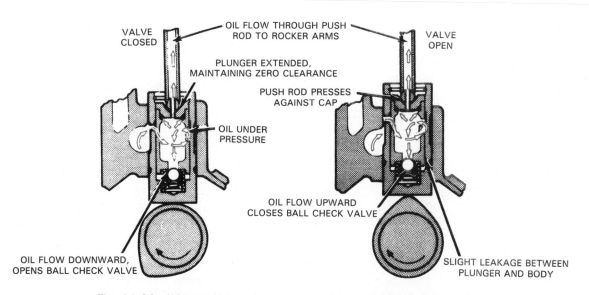

VALVE CLOSED

OIL FLOW THROUGH PUSH ROD TO ROCKER ARMS

VALVE OPEN

PLUNGER EXTENDED, MAINTAINING ZERO CLEARANCE

PUSH ROD PRESSES AGAINST CAP

OIL UNDER PRESSURE

OIL FLOW UPWARD CLOSES BALL CHECK VALVE

OIL FLOW DOWNWARD, OPENS BALL CHECK VALVE

SLIGHT LEAKAGE BETWEEN PLUNGER AND BODY

Fig. 11-22. When the engine valve is closed, the check ball is unseated allowing oil to flow through entire lifter. As the engine valve begins to open, the check ball is seated making hydraulic lifter solid. (Oldsmobile)

With clearances so small, the tiniest fleck of carbon, a fine thread of lint from a wiping cloth, a speck of dust, or any foreign matter could wedge between the plunger and cylinder, and cause them to stick. Anything as large as an eyelash or hair will put it completely out of order.

For this reason, it is necessary to keep the engine oil CLEAN when hydraulic lifters are used. The very best grade of oil must be used in the engine and the oil MUST be changed frequently. Also, oil filters must be replaced regularly.

Another reason for using the best possible engine oil, and changing it frequently, comes about from an increase in driving speeds for long continued periods. Highways and cars are so constructed that car owners do not hesitate to drive at high speeds for hours at a time. This type of operation generates heat, and the inside of the engine and the engine oil reach temperatures that are destructive to the oil.

The engine oil often becomes hot enough to "crack" some of the petroleum fractions (just as in an oil refinery). In decomposing, these elements form a "varnish," which collects on the plunger and in the cylinder, and causes sticking. In many cases this varnish is so thin and clear as to be invisible to the naked eye.

These deposits can be removed mechanically by brushing or friction, but there is a danger of harming the surface of the plunger or cylinder. The safest method of removal appears to be the use of chemical solvents. After cleaning, the units should be dried by air and kept covered to avoid dust until they are installed in the engine. They should not be wiped with a cloth for fear that a thread of lint will adhere to them.

Of course, these parts must be handled with extreme care when out of the engine. If dropped on the floor, or dropped one on another, a nick or scratch could result that would cause them to stick. When clean and dry, the plunger should fall into or drop out of the lifter body of its own weight.

When reinstalled, the clearance should be checked to make sure it is adequate. The tappet clearance dimension is much greater than with mechanical linkage, and it varies considerably among the different makes. The manufacturers' recommendations should be obtained and followed.

As in the case of any other valve tappet adjustment, the lifter must be on the base circle of the cam when measured. The usual procedure is to turn the engine until the ignition distributor rotor is in the firing position for the cylinder to be checked. This assures that the piston is at TDC, and both valves completely closed.

Chapter 11—REVIEW QUESTIONS

Write your answers on a separate sheet of paper. Do not write in this book.

1. How many possible firing orders are there for a four cylinder, four cycle engine? One _____, Two _____, Four _____.
2. A six cylinder, four cycle, in-line engine camshaft has how many lobes on it? Six _____, Twelve _____, Eighteen _____.
3. Mechanic A states that there are two valves per cylinder.

Mechanic B states that there are two cams per cylinder.
Who is right?
a. Mechanic A.
b. Mechanic B.
c. Both mechanic A and B.
d. Neither mechanic A nor B.
4. The timing gears must be aligned when installed. True or False?
5. What is the difference between an I-head engine and an overhead camshaft engine?
6. Name one advantage and one disadvantage of overhead camshaft engines.
7. How many power impulses per revolution occur in an eight cylinder, four cycle engine? Four _____, Eight _____, Sixteen _____.
8. How many power impulses per revolution occur in a three cylinder, two cycle engine? Three _____, Six _____, Twelve _____.
9. Why is the firing order of V-type engines arranged differently than on in-line engines?
10. What is the advantage of the overhead camshaft engine as compared to having the camshaft in the crankcase?
a. Fewer moving parts.
b. Quieter operation.
c. Increase height of engine.
d. Permits larger valves.
11. Valve seats can be too wide. True or False?
12. Valves are sometimes hollow to make them lighter in weight. True or False?
13. Excessive heat gets out of valve by flowing to: The valve seat _____. The valve guide _____. Both _____.
14. Why are valves not made larger?
15. An exhaust valve may reach a temperature of: 500 °F _____. 1000 °F _____. 3000 °F _____.
16. Valve length is not constant. True or False?
17. At what speed does the camshaft operate? Half crankshaft speed _____. Same speed _____. Twice crankshaft speed _____.
18. What is the objection to a long chain in a camshaft drive?
19. The cam nose on the camshaft travels faster than the crankthrow on the crankshaft. True or False?
20. Are timing chains adjustable for wear? Yes _____. No _____. Sometimes _____.
21. What is valve overlap?
22. Are stronger or weaker valve springs used on high performance engines?
23. How many types of valve lifters are there? One _____. Two _____. Three _____. Four _____.
24. What is the great advantage of a hydraulic valve lifter?
a. Better valve action.
b. Closes the valves faster.
c. Quieter valve action.
d. More accurate valve timing.
25. The lead free fuels increase valve seat temperatures. True or False?
26. Lead in the fuel acts as a lubricant. True or False?

Chapter 12

ENGINE RECONDITIONING

After studying this chapter, you will be able to:
- Describe the steps in cleaning, measuring, and examining engine parts.
- List which items of the engine need to be checked for wear.
- Explain how to recondition a cylinder.
- Give examples of a static and dynamically balanced engine, and why it is important.

PROCEDURE

The first step in any job of reconditioning is to clean the assembly. There are many different methods of cleaning, and the one selected depends on the part and the type of dirt that is to be removed.

When overhauling an engine, many shops will remove the engine from the chassis, then steam clean the entire unit with a steam detergent solution. Steam cleaning can be done with a gun type cleaner or in a tank type cleaner.

Cleaning the engine before disassembly will make for an easier disassembly. In addition, cleaning will reveal defects and conditions that will help in diagnosing the cause of the trouble and aid in preventing its early reoccurrence.

Following the removal of the outer dirt and oil, the pan, valve covers, and cylinder head are removed. These parts can be cleaned by a gun or one of the other cleaning methods: tank, jet, and ultrasonic, to remove accumulations of sludge, carbon, dirt, and grease.

CLEANING

A process used extensively for cleaning automotive parts is called "the hot tank method." Briefly, this method utilizes a tank filled with a detergent solution, which is agitated to hasten the cleaning process. The temperature of the solution varies with the type of detergent and particular metal to be cleaned. Parts made of aluminum are cleaned with special detergents at a lower temperature than is used for steel and iron.

Another efficient parts cleaning technique is called the jet method. The cleaning unit has two compartments: the lower chamber holds the solution; the upper chamber provides a revolving platform for the work. A series of jets spray detergent on the slowly revolving part in the upper compartment. Each jet delivers detergent at an extremely high velocity, reaching the work from all sides, top and bottom. Each jet delivers approximately three gallons of hot detergent solution per minute.

Blasting with glass beads is another method used extensively for cleaning automotive parts, Fig. 12-1. Compressed air is the propellant which blasts the beads against the part. Both wet and dry blast machines are available.

Glass beads clean the part down to bare metal, leaving no film of detergent. The beads are round in shape and not abrasive. They do not imbed themselves in the surface to be cleaned. Being round, the beads leave a

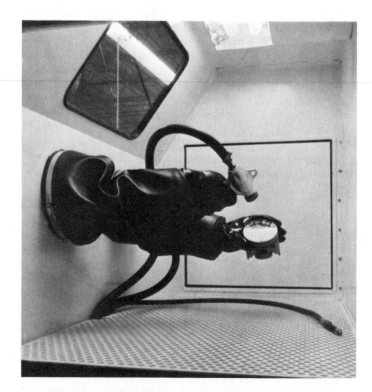

Fig. 12-1. Cleaning a piston with a bead blaster.
(Winona Van Norman)

102

uniform indented surface imparting strength by compressing the metal being cleaned. This method is used in cleaning pistons, valves, and connecting rods.

Ultrasonic energy is a more recent advance. Ultrasonic sound differs from normal sound only in that its pitch is above the human hearing range. When high frequency vibrations are introduced into a liquid, cavitation (extreme agitation) occurs.

Every liquid contains thousands of nuclei in the form of bubbles which range in size from those which are visible to those which are submicroscopic. Under ultrasonic irradiation, these bubbles grow and then collapse. They are said to explode inwardly, at which time pressures up to 15,000 psi and temperatures up to 700 °F area created.

The ultrasonic cleaner consists basically of three parts:
1. A generator which is used to convert the line current into high frequency electrical energy.
2. A transducer which converts this electrical energy into mechanical energy of the same frequency.
3. A tank containing a liquid through which the ultrasonic energy is passed, and which produces the cavitation that blasts away any dirt on parts placed in the solution.

Ultrasonic cleaners are used in production engine rebuilding, shops servicing diesel engine injectors and pumps, and in large jobber machine shops.

Many small auto repair shops use a simple tank with a power sprayer, Fig. 12-2, to clean parts removed from the vehicle to be repaired or replaced. Cleaning parts with a brush and a pan of gasoline is a big fire hazard. In addition, leaded gasoline always carries the threat of lead poisoning if used for cleaning on a regular basis. Instead, use a solvent designed for the cleaning job at hand.

Fig. 12-2. Cleaning parts in a modern parts cleaner. (Safety-Kleen)

Before cleaning a cylinder block or cylinder head, remove the core hole plugs. This will permit the cleaning solution to flush out any accumulation of rust and lime deposits.

EXAMINATION AND MEASUREMENT

After cleaning, it is possible to make a careful examination of the individual parts, along with accurate measurement to spot defects, determine the extent and type of wear, and pinpoint what caused the worn condition.

The starting point for actual engine reconditioning is the cylinder block, because practically all other parts are fitted to it. If the block is damaged in any way, it must be repaired or replaced. There are many things to be inspected and checked.

The engine block or head may be cracked, warped, worn or otherwise damaged. The damage may affect the operation of the crankshaft, pistons, rings, bearings, camshaft, cooling, lubrication, etc. The extent of the damage will determine whether or not the block is repairable. There are many methods of changing the condition or dimensions of metal parts. Several different methods may be used to restore an engine to good condition.

METAL PARTS RESTORATION

If you want to increase the size of a part, you can add metal by soldering, brazing, welding, plating, or spraying. In some cases, you can expand it by heat and pressure. In adding metal, you have a wide choice of materials, each of which possesses certain characteristics which may be desired for the particular purpose. If you want a soft surface, use tin or bronze. If you want a hard surface add steel of any desired degree of hardness by welding. Another method of adding a hard surface is by the electroplating process, such as the chrome surface on a piston ring.

In engine repair work, there is a way to add material to or increase the size of one part without disturbing the mating part. An example of this is to spray molten metal on a worn crankshaft journal to avoid installation of undersize bearings. Or, you may expand a piston with heat or pressure, or both, and reinstall it in the mating cylinder.

If you want to reduce the size of a part, you can cut, grind, or etch the metal away. Or, in some cases, you can shrink it with freezing. In some cases, removing metal from one part and installing an oversize mating part, in order to obtain the proper clearance. Example of this is a rebored cylinder and an oversize piston.

In still other cases, metal is removed for the sole purpose of obtaining better surface fit of two mating parts. An example of this is the correction of a warped cylinder head by surface grinding to restore a flat and true surface.

For all of these operations, special tools and equipment are available. These tools will do the job if they are properly handled. It will be essential to measure, adjust, and operate in accordance with the manufacturer's instructions. If the instructions are not followed, the technician may cause injury to him/herself and their co-workers.

Fig. 12-3. Leaking freeze plugs must be punched out and new freeze plugs installed. Always install new freeze plugs after cleaning a cylinder head or engine block in either a hot or cold tank solution.

Fig. 12-4. Repairs made to cracked water jacket.

EXTERNAL CRACKS

When the cylinder block and head are clean, make a visual inspection for cracks or serious damage. Include a close look at the condition of the freeze plugs, Fig. 12-3. If signs of leakage or corrosion are found, replace the plugs.

If the block was cracked by water freezing in the water jacket, the crack can usually be closed satisfactorily by copper welding, brazing, iron welding, Fig. 12-4, or by one of the patented processes such as the Seal Lock process. Many mechanics prefer electric welding to gas welding, as lower temperatures in the area of repair are not likely to produce warpage of the cylinder block.

In the case of the Seal Lock process the sides of the crack are tied together by driving special keys or locking pins into previously drilled holes. Then the surface is carefully peened and further sealed.

In cases where a panel or section of the water jacket is broken out, it is sometimes possible to shape a metal plate into a patch corresponding to and slightly larger than the opening. The patch is then attached to the block by means of multiple screws around the edge of the patch. Holes are drilled and tapped in the block for the screws.

In the case of small cracks, iron cement can be used for a quick repair, Fig. 12-5. Never repair an area with cement in or by the cylinder or cylinder head.

The choice of the repair method will depend upon the size of the damaged area, the location of the crack, the cost of a new block as well as the value of the automobile.

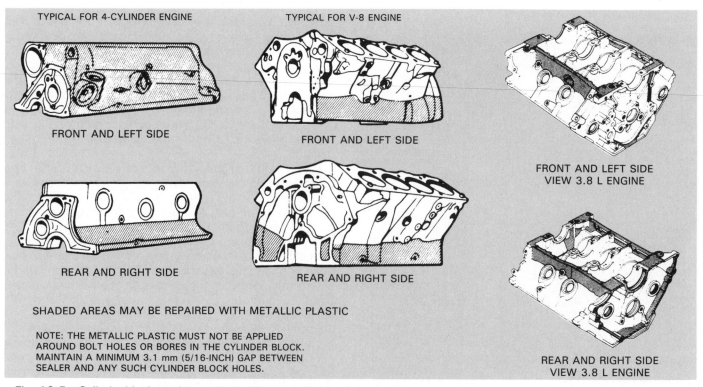

TYPICAL FOR 4-CYLINDER ENGINE

TYPICAL FOR V-8 ENGINE

FRONT AND LEFT SIDE

FRONT AND LEFT SIDE

FRONT AND LEFT SIDE
VIEW 3.8 L ENGINE

REAR AND RIGHT SIDE

REAR AND RIGHT SIDE

REAR AND RIGHT SIDE
VIEW 3.8 L ENGINE

SHADED AREAS MAY BE REPAIRED WITH METALLIC PLASTIC

NOTE: THE METALLIC PLASTIC MUST NOT BE APPLIED AROUND BOLT HOLES OR BORES IN THE CYLINDER BLOCK. MAINTAIN A MINIMUM 3.1 mm (5/16-INCH) GAP BETWEEN SEALER AND ANY SUCH CYLINDER BLOCK HOLES.

Fig. 12-5. Cylinder block can be repaired with a metallic plastic in shaded areas only. Note that the area around the cylinders cannot be repaired; a new short block must be used.   (Ford)

INTERNAL CRACKS

At times, the cylinder wall will crack as shown in Fig. 12-6. Or, the crack may be in the cylinder head. Usually, a cracked cylinder head is replaced, rather than repaired. If the crack is small, it may be possible to peen it shut with a power peening hammer, Fig. 12-7.

Cracks in cylinder heads and blocks are often so fine that they are difficult to see with the naked eye. The procedure is to use special dyes or chemicals which, when painted on the surface of the metal, will quickly make the cracks visible. This procedure is used on aluminum parts. Magnetic and electrical methods are specifically designed to reveal the location of cracks on ferrous metal components. See Fig. 12-8.

CORROSION

In the case of aluminum engine blocks or heads, the visual inspection should be particularly thorough to detect any possible corrosion of the metal. Sometimes, corrosion of the metal around the water circulation openings will occur from chemicals in the cooling water, particularly in localities where the water supply contains more than the usual amount of chloride.

Corrosion from electrolytic action also may occur, because of the dissimilar metals found in the engine cooling system. If corrosion is serious enough, it may interfere with the seal of the gasket between head and block. This would permit coolant to enter the combus-

tion chamber, or allow compression pressure to escape to the water jacket.

CYLINDER HEAD WARPAGE

Cylinder heads often become warped. Sometimes the cylinder block mating surface also warps. These surfaces should be true within .003 in. in any 6 in., or within .006 in. overall. Measurement is made by means of a steel straightedge and feeler gauge strips as shown in Figs. 12-9 and 12-10. If the surfaces are warped or otherwise damaged, they can be reconditioned on special equipment, as shown in Fig. 12-11. If .030 in. is removed from a head on a V-type engine, the other head and intake manifold are also shaved true. If not, the bolt holes connecting the intake manifold to the heads will not align.

Fig. 12-8. A magnetic field is created in this cast-iron cylinder head. Metal filings are dusted on, and outline the crack. If the cylinder head is aluminum, a dye must be used to detect cracks in the head as aluminum is a nonferrous metal.

Fig. 12-6. A crack in the cylinder makes this engine block useless.

Fig. 12-9. Checking a cylinder head for warping. If a .006 in. feeler gauge can be placed between the straightedge and cylinder head, the head is warped and must be shaved true. (Fel-Pro Inc.)

Fig. 12-7. Some cracks may be closed with a peening hammer.

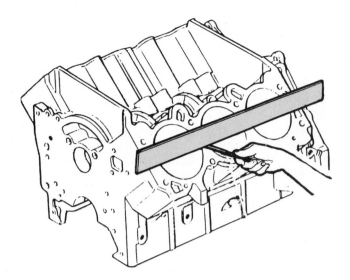

Fig. 12-10. Checking engine block for warpage is the same as checking the head for warpage. (Oldsmobile)

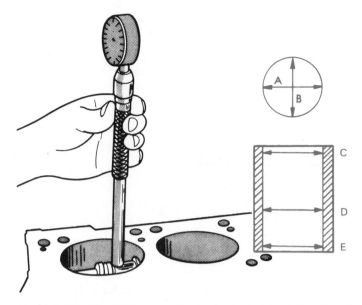

Fig. 12-12. The difference in measurement between line A and line B is the amount cylinder is out-of-round. This measurement must be taken at the top of cylinder. The difference in measurement between line C and line D is the amount of taper in the cylinder. Line E will be the original diameter of the cylinder, as the piston rings do not travel that far down. (Chrysler)

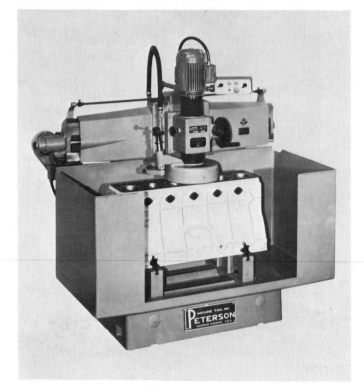

Fig. 12-11. Equipment used to deck engine blocks.

CYLINDER WEAR

The greatest amount of wear in a cylinder occurs at the top of the cylinder. This is due to the lack of lubrication at the top of the cylinder and the side thrust of the piston. The wear at the top of the cylinder is referred to as out-of-round, Fig. 12-12. The difference between the amount of wear at the top of the cylinder and the bottom of the cylinder is referred to as taper, Fig. 12-12.

CYLINDER RECONDITIONING

Cylinder wall wear and the reasons for it were described previously in this text. They wear in tapered form, and also out-of-round. When wear exceeds specifications, the cylinders require machining to restore the wall surface. Maximum wear limitations are .005 in. out-of-round and .010 in. taper.

Either boring bars, Fig. 12-13, or hones, Fig. 12-14, may be used to recondition the cylinder walls. In many shops, the preferred method is to first use a boring bar, and then finish with a hone. Another method is to first use a hone with coarse stones and then finish with stones of about No. 180-220 grit, making sure the stones are clean and sharp.

Before any cylinder is refinished, all main bearing caps must be in place and tightened to the specified torque. Otherwise the crankshaft bearing bores may become distorted from the refinishing operation.

Precautions must be taken to insure that the cylinders be refinished parallel to each other and at right angles to the crankshaft. Special care must be taken when setting up the reconditioning equipment, particularly when the top of the cylinder block is not at right angles to the cylinder bore, Fig. 12-15. When the cylinder block is formed with an angular surface, special adapters must be used with the cylinder boring bar so that the cylinder will be reconditioned parallel to its original centerline.

When dry honing, a vacuum cleaning device is provided. However, regardless of the method used in reconditioning the cylinders, the block must be thoroughly cleaned to remove all cutting and abrasives. Machinists advise scrubbing with soap and water. Oil the cylinders after thoroughly drying them.

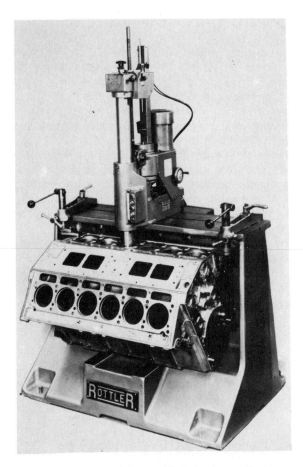

Fig. 12-13. Machine used in reboring cylinders.

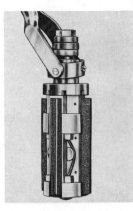

Fig. 12-14. Cylinder hone.

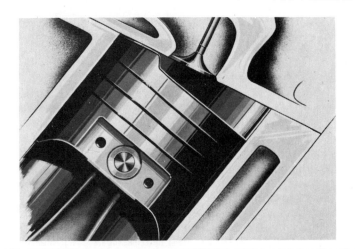

Fig. 12-15. Note the angle of cylinder block at the cylinder head.

Fig. 12-16. A cast-iron engine block being cleaned in a hot tank solution. Aluminum engine parts must be cleaned in a cold tank, or in carburetor type cleaner.

The job of cleaning a cylinder block after reconditioning is not easy. Many jobs which were mechanically correct have been ruined because some abrasives and dirt remained in the cylinders. All oil holes in the block must be cleaned. Core plugs should be removed so the water jacket can be cleaned. The final cleaning is usually done on specialized cleaning equipment, Fig. 12-16.

When reconditioning cylinders, it is best to find out what sizes are available in oversize pistons before starting the operation. Otherwise, the cylinders may be bored to a size for which stock pistons are not available. Then the pistons would have to be reground to the desired size or new ones ordered.

DRY TYPE CYLINDER SLEEVES

If damage is so deep that reboring to fit the largest oversize piston is not sufficient to remove the score marks, it is still possible to recondition the cylinder by installation of a cylinder sleeve.

The dry type cylinder sleeve does not come in contact with the coolant. The cylinder is bored out to an oversize dimension. The sleeve is then installed into the cylinder. An oversize piston is not needed and the standard size piston can be used provided that it is in good shape. However, the transfer of heat is not as efficient as a wet type sleeve or a cylinder that is bored directly into the block.

The procedure is to rebore the cylinder until the score marks are removed. Then a sleeve is prepared with an outside diameter .0001 in. larger than the diameter of the rebored cylinder, and with an inside diameter slightly smaller than required for the available piston. The sleeve is shrunk in dry ice to reduce its diameter, then it is pressed into the cylinder with an hydraulic press.

Finally, the cylinder is finish honed, remove any wrinkles that may have formed when the sleeve was pressed in position.

CYLINDER WALL SURFACE

When new rings are installed in cylinders which have not been reconditioned, the hone should be run through the cylinder a few times to break the glaze formed on the cylinder wall through normal operation.

The desired cylinder wall finish is not a mirror surface, as this type of surface does not produce the best lubricating conditions for the piston rings. The proper finish should have a pattern of diagonal crosshatch scratches, but no longitudinal scratches, Fig. 12-17. This pattern can be obtained with a hone, Fig. 12-18, pulling it up and down in the bore while the hone is rotating. After honing the cylinder, wash it with a warm soap and water solution. Then, rinse thoroughly with clear water. Dry each cylinder and then oil the cylinders so as to prevent rust.

Fine scratches in the cylinder wall surfaces permit rapid seating of rings. The fine scratches retain a film of oil to provide lubrication for the ring face and prevents scoring of the cylinder.

WET TYPE CYLINDER SLEEVES

Passenger car engines built in the U.S.A. usually have the cylinders bored directly in the engine block. Some truck, tractor, and industrial engines use the wet type of cylinder sleeve. A wet sleeve is in the form of a barrel or sleeve which is inserted in the block in contact with the cooling water. Several European passenger car engines have liners or sleeves, Fig. 12-19.

In a wet-sleeve construction, each cylinder barrel is a separate sleeve inserted in the block. Each sleeve is sealed at the bottom of the water compartment by means of a copper or rubber gasket, Fig. 12-20. The cylinder head gasket, of course, provides a seal at the top end of the sleeve.

In the wet sleeve construction, engine coolant circulates directly around and in contact with the sleeve. Since the thickness of the sleeve or cylinder wall is uniform, cylinder wall distortion is minimized.

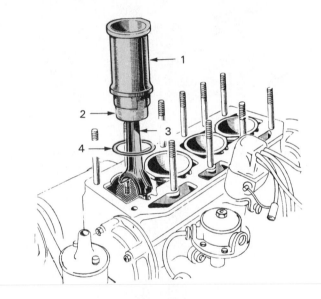

Fig. 12-19. Wet type sleeve used by Renault: 1—Sleeve. 2—Piston. 3—Connecting Rod. 4—Copper sealing ring.

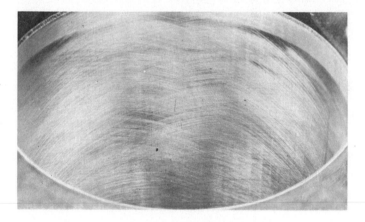

Fig. 12-17. Cylinder walls must look like this after honing. This pattern is called "crosshatch."

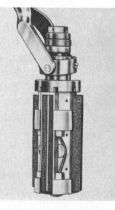

Fig. 12-18. A rigid type cylinder hone is used on cylinders that are perfectly round.

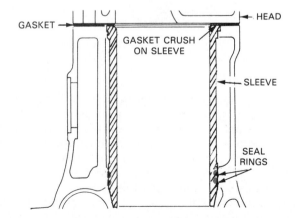

Fig. 12-20. Rubber seals are used at the bottom of sleeves in this Oliver engine.

108

Another advantage of cylinder sleeves is the ease and comparatively low cost of replacing a damaged cylinder sleeve instead of reboring the cylinders and installing oversize pistons. These sleeves quickly pull out, Fig. 12-21, and a new sleeve is slipped in place.

PISTON CLEARANCE

There is no set amount of clearance to be provided between the piston and cylinder. Much depends upon the design of the engine cylinders and the cooling system, the piston design and material, and the conditions under which the engine operates.

For example, if a passenger car engine will be driven mostly at slow speeds in city traffic, the pistons can be fitted with a minimum of clearance. If the engine is in a race car, it may be required to run at full power for hours at a time. Such service would generate a great amount of heat in the cylinders and cause the pistons to expand considerably. Therefore, the internal engine parts would be fitted with maximum clearances.

In general, it is customary to fit solid skirt cast-iron pistons to about .00075 to .001 in. per inch of piston diameter. A 4 in. piston would be .003 to .004 in. smaller than the cylinder. Some aluminum pistons can be fitted more closely, but much depends upon the design of the piston. Instructions given by the manufacturer should be obtained and followed.

Surface treatment will also have a bearing on the piston clearance. Some pistons are tin plated, others have an oxide coating or some other surface treatment. Sometimes the surface is serrated or interrupted to provide minute scratches for the retention of oil. These treatments are intended to lessen the tendency of the piston to stick or score, particularly during the time it is seating to the wall.

CLEARANCE MEASUREMENT

The clearance between cylinder and piston is measured in most cases by means of a feeler gauge inserted between piston and cylinder. See Fig. 12-22. The strip of feeler gauge should be about 1/2 in. wide and long enough to extend the full length of the cylinder. This strip with a thickness equal to the desired clearance should be placed on the thrust side of the skirt. Four to five pounds pull as measured on a spring scale should be required to remove the feeler.

The clearance can also be measured by subtracting the maximum diameter of the piston from the minimum diameter of the cylinder, as measured with inside and outside micrometers. In this case, measurement must be made at several points in the cylinder and on the piston. All piston clearance recommendations are made for use with the temperature at approximately 70 °F.

As pistons wear, or if they become overheated, the skirt is liable to collapse, or become smaller in diameter. When this happens the piston will "slap" in the cylinder. Also, it will allow an excessive amount of oil to pass up to the rings. This, of course, places an undue load on the oil control rings and may result in oil pumping.

PISTON RESIZING

There are several ways to expand or resize the pistons. One method consists of heating the piston, and expanding it with special equipment made for the purpose. Another method requires special equipment for "peening" the inside of the piston with steel shot. This procedure compacts the metal on the inside, and causes it to expand on the outside. Electric and pneumatic peening hammers are made for the purpose.

Various types of equipment, or tools, are available for "knurling" the piston skirt. This method raises the surface of the metal in ridges or patterns along the path of the knurling, increasing the diameter of the piston. An additional claim made for this method is that it creates "pockets" on the piston surface, which gather and retain a film of oil to assist in sealing and lubricating.

HEAD BOLT TORQUE

All threads must be clean and undamaged. The nuts must spin on easily. A thread compound should be used,

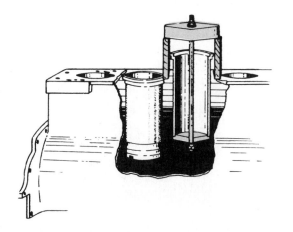

Fig. 12-21. Method of removing wet type sleeves.

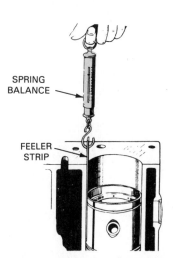

Fig. 12-22. Checking piston clearance with feeler gauge attached to spring scale. The amount of pull required should be between four and five lb.

partically on aluminum heads and cylinder blocks. This will prevent leakage in those cases where the bolt holes enter the water jacket.

Be sure to install the specified bolt in the correct hole as bolt holes frequently vary in depth. A torque wrench should be used to tighten bolts and nuts to specified torque. They should be tightened in the correct sequence to prevent distortion of parts, Fig. 12-23.

The usual procedure is to tighten the bolts in three successive steps. For example, tighten first to 25 ft. lb., then 50 ft. lb. and, finally, 95 ft. lb.

BALANCING ENGINES

With the increase in engine speeds, it becomes increasingly important that all rotating and reciprocating parts of the engine are precision balanced. Unless this is done, wear is accelerated and engine life reduced. In addition, operating costs increase.

Unbalance causes increased bearing loads and greater vibration, both of which absorb power and cause wear and fatigue of parts. In addition, the vibration will cause alternator brackets and other accessory brackets to crack. Driver fatigue also increases.

With precision balancing of engine parts, bearing life has been increased in excess of 200 percent, and horsepower and acceleration have been improved nearly 15 percent. While increased top speed is what interests the speed enthusiast, it is the longer engine life and reduce maintenance cost which interest the truck and fleet operator.

Manufacturers producing parts for their engines specify certain tolerances for the various parts. For example, the weight specification for a piston may be given as 25 oz. plus or minus 1/4 oz. (1/4 oz. is equal to 7.09 grams). Connecting rods may have a similar weight specification and, in addition, the center-to-center length of the rod is held to a close tolerance.

It is therefore possible to have a V-8 engine with eight pistons of different weights, but all within the specified tolerance of 1/4 oz. As an extreme case, one of the pistons may weigh 25 1/4 oz. and other piston 24 3/4 oz.

A set of pistons of varied weights will result in considerable vibration, plus higher loads on the bearings. If similar variations are found in the connecting rods, a very rough running engine will result. As pointed out, not only will top speed be affected, but extreme wear of parts also will result.

Precision balancing will help to eliminate the possibility of wear due to vibration. It also will step up performance and boost economy of operation. With modern balancing equipment, Fig. 12-24, the weight of rotating and reciprocating parts can be brought within 1/2 gram of each other, Fig. 12-25.

In order to achieve the highest output of the engine, greatest fuel economy, longest life of parts, and smoothest operation, the following parts must be precision balanced.

1. Pistons.
2. Piston rings.
3. Piston pins.
4. Connecting rods.
5. Connecting rod bearings.
6. Crankshaft.
7. Front pulley or vibration damper.
8. Clutch and disc.

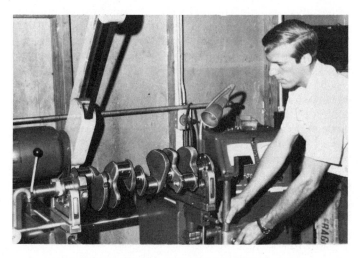

Fig. 12-24. Preparing to balance the crankshaft. This machine can also be used to polish the journals of the crankshaft.

Fig. 12-25. Weighing pistons for proper balance. All pistons in an engine must weigh the same, or a vibration will result.

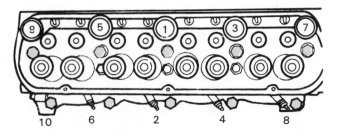

Fig. 12-23. Tightening sequence of a cylinder head. Start from the center and work toward each end of the cylinder head. This will prevent the cylinder bores from distorting and the head gasket from leaking coolant and oil. (Ford)

UNBALANCE

Unbalance is simply the uneven distribution of weight. When a part is rotated, the unbalance becomes a vibration which wastes power output. Even a small amount of unbalance is harmful. Just one ounce placed one inch away from the center of rotation will be multiplied 40 times at a speed of 1200 rpm. At 5000 rpm, the force will reach 45 lb. 10 oz., Fig. 12-26.

STATIC BALANCE

When a rotor has an absolutely even distribution of weight mass around its axis, it will be in static balance. That is there will be no tendency toward rotation about its axis.

View A in Fig. 12-27 shows a rotor and a shaft on two knife edges. A heavy area, indicated by a dot, will turn the rotor until it reaches its lowest point. In view B, this weight is 8 oz. located 2 in. from the center.

To make the rotor in Fig. 12-27 stop in any position, it will be necessary to add a counterweight directly opposite the heavy area, as shown in view C. This would put the rotor in static balance, if the two weights provided the same torque (weight times distance from axis of rotation). Therefore, if the first weight is 8 oz. at a distance of 2 in. from the center, the other weight could be 4 oz. at a distance of 4 in. from the center. Both weights provide the same turning effort of 16 oz. in.

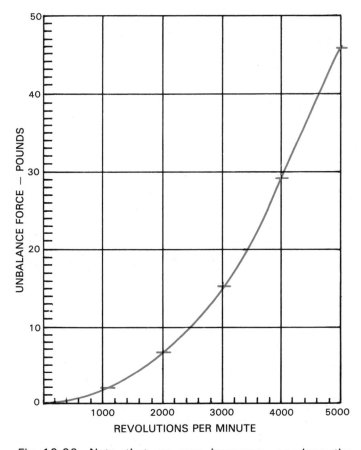

Fig. 12-26. Note that as rpm increases, so does the unbalance.

DYNAMIC BALANCING

A shaft or rotor may be in perfect static balance but, when rotated, will vibrate considerably because it was not in dynamic balance. When the center line of the weight mass of a revolving rotor is in the same plane as the center line of the rotor, it is in dynamic balance.

If there is excess weight on one side of the shaft at one end, which is balanced statically by an equivalent weight on the other side, but at the opposite end, the shaft would not be balanced dynamically, Fig. 12-28. When the shaft with this condition is rotated, a centrifugal couple is formed, resulting in an unbalanced condition with vibration.

In Fig. 12-29, a heavy section W, weighing 9 oz., is located 2 in. from the axis of the cylinder. A counterweight of 6 oz. is located 3 in. from the axis, but at the other end of the cylinder. Both are equal to 18 oz. in., so the cylinder is in static balance. However, because the weights are at opposite ends of the cylinder, a centrifugal couple or twisting action is formed and a dynamic unbalanced condition exists. By adding compensating weights of 3 oz. and 6 oz., as indicated in Fig. 12-29, the cylinder is in static and dynamic balance.

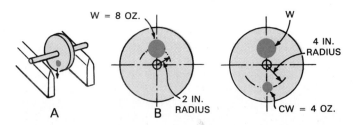

Fig. 12-27. To test balance: A—Place rotor on pointed blocks. B—Unbalance totals 8 oz., 2 in. from center. C—Counterbalancing with a 4 oz. weight that is 4 in. from center corrects the unbalance.

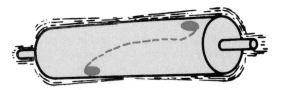

Fig. 12-28. Weights at opposite ends of rotor cause a twisting motion. Rotor is balanced statically, but not dynamically.

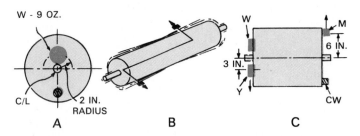

Fig. 12-29. A—Cylinder is balanced statically. B—Cylinder vibrates. C—Additional weights correct unbalance.

BALANCING IN-LINE AND V-TYPE ENGINES

In V-8 and V-12 engines, the crankshaft basically is in an unbalanced condition. To balance a V-type engine, it is necessary to attach weights to each of the crank throws as substitute for the weights of the connecting rods and piston assemblies. Such weights are known as "bob" weights, Fig. 12-30.

When balancing in-line engines, such as the four and six, "bob" weights are not needed because the crankshaft throws are symmetrically arranged.

In the case of two cycle engines, the GMC series 71 diesel requires special consideration. These engines are counterbalanced by a combination of balance weights on the camshafts (on in-line engine, one camshaft and a balance shaft are used), Fig. 12-31. Connected to the crankshaft through a small gear are a pair of shafts driven by gears the same size as that on the crankshaft. On in-line engines the first shaft is the camshaft, the second is the balance shaft.

On V-type engines, both shafts are camshafts, with counterweighted gears. Also, on the far end of each shaft, a counterweight is located diametrically opposed to the counterweight on the gear. The amount of counterweight on one end should counterbalance the counterweight on the other end.

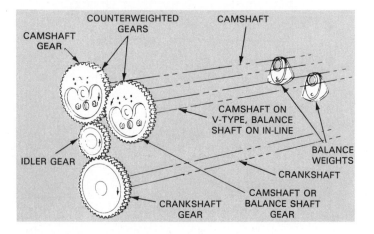

Fig. 12-30. Bob weights attached to crankshaft for balancing purposes.

Fig. 12-31. Balancing two cycle GMC 71 series diesel engine involves counterweighted gears. Balance weights at opposite ends of the shaft counter the weight of the gears.

Theoretically, all four ends, gears, and balance weights should have identical oz.-in. amounts of unbalance. Because these parts (gears and balance weights) are diametrically opposed, the shaft when assembled should have no force (kinetic) unbalance, but a desired high couple (dynamic) unbalance.

Therefore, in order to properly balance a GMC 71 series engine, bob weights must be used on the crankshaft, and the counterweighted gears and the counterbalance weights must be balanced on a special fixture.

BALANCING SINGLE CYLINDER ENGINES

Single cylinder engines, and other inherently unbalanced engines such as outboard, motorcycle, go-cart etc., require special balancing procedures because of their relatively high speeds. These small engines will not be as vibrationless as multi-cylinder engines, but they are precision balanced for smoothest operation.

When determining the bob weight for a single cylinder engine, use 100 percent of the rotating weight (same as for a V-8 engine), but use a higher percentage of the reciprocating weight. V-8 engines usually use 50 percent of the reciprocating weight.

For the single cylinder engine, the weight should range from 55 percent up to 65 percent according to the engine speed.

CRANKSHAFT BALANCING PROCEDURE

The degree of unbalance of the crankshaft is determined by placing the shaft (V-8 with its bob weights or in-line shaft without bob weights) in the balancing machine. As the shaft is rotated, the degree of unbalance and its location will be indicated.

In general, the unbalanced condition can be corrected by removing metal from the counterweight. In those cases where the throws are light, it is necessary to tack weld thin steel sheets to the sides of the counterweights.

Normal weight removal is accomplished by using a 1/2 in. drill. Special fixtures allow the drilling to be performed with the shaft in balancer. If too much metal is removed, the 1/2 in. drilled hole can be plugged with 1/2 in. rod, then redrilled the desired amount.

BOB WEIGHTS

As previously pointed out, bob weights are temporarily attached to the crankshaft while it is being balanced to compensate for the weights of the pistons and connecting rod assemblies.

Part of the piston and connecting rod is a rotating weight and part is a reciprocating weight. The weight of the piston with its pin and rings, along with a portion of the upper end of the connecting rod, is considered as reciprocating weight. The weight of the big end of the connecting rods is considered as rotating weight.

To obtain the actual weight of these parts, weigh all of the pistons with their rings and pins. Then, using the weight of the lightest piston assembly, reduce the weight of the other pistons to conform to the weight of the lightest one.

To reduce the weight of a piston, chuck it in a lathe and remove metal from the inside of the piston skirt. In some piston designs, pads have been provided on the inner surface of the skirt from which the necessary metal can be removed. Take care not to weaken the strength of the piston. To insure that the exterior of the piston is not scored by the jaws of the lathe chuck, first cover the piston with thin sheet steel or copper.

Special weighing scales are used to measure the weights of the pistons. These scales must have an accuracy of less than 1/2 gram, Fig. 12-25. Special weighing scales are also used to weigh the connecting rods. While one end of the rod rests on the scales, the other end is supported. When the weight of the crank ends has been found, the heavier crank ends should be balanced by removing metal so they are equal in weight with the rod with the lightest crank end. Similarly, the weights of the pin ends of the rods must be made to conform to the weight of the rod with the lightest pin end. A grinder or belt sander is usually used to remove metal from the connecting rods. NOTE: The weight of the individual rods and pistons should be carefully recorded.

On V-type engines which carry two rod and piston assemblies on each crank throw, the bob weight for each throw will include:

1. The weight of the crank end of one rod with bearing inserts, lock nuts, and oil in crank throw.
2. The weight of one piston, pin, pin lock, one set of rings, weight of one piston end of rod.
3. The total of weights in 1 and 2 will be the weight of the bob weight to be attached to each crank throw when balancing the crankshaft.

On V-type engines which carry one rod and piston assembly on each throw, the bob weight for each throw will include:

1. The weight of the crank end of one rod with its bearing inserts, lock nuts, and weight of oil in crank throw. This is the rotating weight.
2. The reciprocating weight to be included in the bob weight includes 50 percent of the pin end of the rod, piston, piston pin, pin locks set of rings.
3. The sum of the rotating and the reciprocating weight in 1 and 2 is the bob weight which must be attached to each crankpin when balancing the crankshaft.

As pointed out, in-line four and six cylinder engines do not require bob weights when balancing the engine crankshaft. However, the weights of the piston and rod assemblies must be made equal within a tolerance of 1/2 oz.

BY THE NUMBERS

Prior to disassembly of the engine, the technician should number the main bearing caps, Fig. 12-32, along with the pistons, Fig. 12-33. Once each piston is removed, the rod and cap of each piston should be marked Fig. 12-34. This step, will make reassembly easier. If the piston is installed in the wrong cylinder, or the wrong rod cap installed on a connecting rod, the engine could seize. The same thing can happen if a main bearing cap is installed in the wrong position. Always turn the engine one complete revolution by hand after torquing the main bearing caps. Again, rotate the crankshaft by hand after installing and torquing each rod

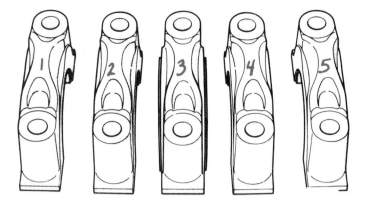

Fig. 12-32. Number the main bearing caps prior to removing. If caps are mixed-up, the engine will seize. (Chrysler)

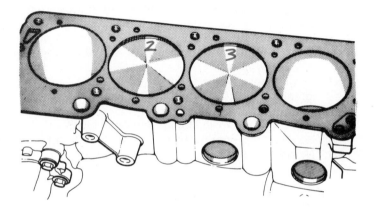

Fig. 12-33. Number the pistons prior to removing. (Chrysler)

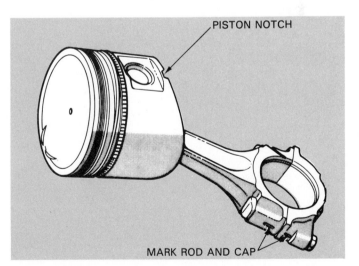

Fig. 12-34. Mark the connecting rod and rod cap where indicated prior to removing. If caps are mixed up, the engine will seize. (Chrysler)

cap. This will determine if rod and main caps are in the right position. If they are not, the crankshaft will not be able to make a complete revolution.

113

Chapter 12—REVIEW QUESTIONS

Write your answers on a separate piece of paper. Do not write in this book.

1. Name five ways of increasing the size of a metal part.
2. An oversize bearing is required on a reground crankshaft journal. True or False?
3. Name five ways of repairing a water jacket cracked by freezing.
4. How much warpage, overall, usually can be tolerated in a cylinder head?
   a. .001 in.   b. .003 in.   c. .006 in.
5. When installing a new dry sleeve in a cylinder, should the sleeve be smaller or larger in diameter than the cylinder?
6. Why do pistons sometimes seize in cylinders?
7. Name two ways of repairing badly scored cylinders.
8. Why must dry cylinder sleeves fit tightly in the block?
9. If a newly installed dry sleeve is round, straight, smooth and free from wrinkles, is it ready for service? Yes or No?
10. A cylinder sleeve should be _____ after installation.
11. The limitation for cylinder wear is .010 in. out-of-round and .005 in. taper. True or False?
12. How can a proper cylinder wall finish be described?
13. Name three ways of expanding pistons.
14. In general, how much clearance, per inch of diameter, should cast iron pistons have in cylinders?
    a. .0075 to .01 in.
    b. .00075 to .001 in.
    c. .00005 to .00015 in.
15. Aluminum cylinder heads can be cleaned:
    a. Bead blaster.
    b. Cold tank solution.
    c. Hot tank solution.
    d. Either a or b.
16. The greatest amount of wear in the cylinder takes place at the _____ of the travel of the piston rings.
17. What is the maximum amount of taper specified for cylinder wear in passenger car engines?
    a. 0.010 in.   b. 0.005 in.   c. 0.075 in.
18. Only static balance of engine parts is required. True or False?
19. Unbalance of engine parts _____ bearing loads.
20. The affect of engine unbalance increases with engine speed. Yes or No?
21. To balance a GMC series 71 diesel, follow the same procedure used for a _____ engine.
22. Aluminum heads can be checked for cracks by:
    a. Using an electromagnet.
    b. Using a dye.
    c. Either a or b.
    d. Neither a nor b.

Chapter 13

PISTON RING
AND PIN FITTING

After studying this chapter, you will be able to:
- Determine if the piston ring groove needs to be reconditioned.
- Explain why and how a piston ring groove wears.
- Tell how to measure the piston ring gap and explain why it is important.
- State how to properly install piston rings.

PISTON RINGS

Piston ring design and purpose was covered in a previous chapter. It included a reference to the fact that a ridge is formed at the top of the cylinder wall as the cylinder wears. To avoid damage to pistons and rings, this ridge must be cut away before an attempt is made to remove the pistons from the cylinders. Special tools are made for this purpose, Fig. 13-1.

Cylinder wall reconditioning and piston fitting have been discussed. Now, some consideration should be given to proper fitting of the rings to the piston and cylinder; also, to fitting piston pins in the pistons.

PISTON RING GAP

It is obvious that the top piston ring runs hotter than the lower rings. Therefore, the top ring will expand the most. This means that the top ring will need more gap clearance at the ends, and more sidewise clearance in the piston grooves than the other rings. The piston ring manufacturer specifies the clearance needed. Manufacturers instructions should be followed.

Piston ring gap clearance is measured as shown in Fig. 13-2. The ring is pushed into the cylinder. An inverted piston without rings is used to push the ring in place since this method locates the ring squarely in the bore. Piston rings of the correct size for the application should be purchased. If necessary, minor increases in gap clearance can be made by filing the ends of the ring. However, if the ring side clearance is not to specifications, do NOT file the width of the ring. New rings are needed.

In case clearance dimensions are not available, it is customary to allow .004 in. gap clearance per inch of piston diameter for the top ring, and .003 in. per inch diameter for the other rings. For example, a 3 in. diameter cylinder would require .012 in. gap in the top ring and .009 in. in the other rings. The exception is the "U" type oil ring, which is extremely flexible. These rings require no gap clearance.

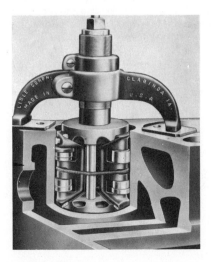

Fig. 13-1. Cutaway view of engine block shows a ridge reamer which removes the ridge at the top of the cylinder.

Fig. 13-2. Measuring piston ring gap. Gap is measured at the bottom of ring travel in cylinder.

RING GROOVE CLEARANCE

The sidewise clearance of the ring in the groove is measured as shown in Fig. 13-3, using a feeler (thickness) gauge. In the absence of instructions, it is customary to allow at least .003 in. side clearance on the top ring and at least .002 in. on the other rings. More than .005 in. side clearance on any ring calls for the grooves in the piston to be reconditioned, or the piston replaced.

New rings should never be installed in worn ring grooves. This practice results in poor oil economy and increased blowby, Fig. 13-4. In addition, ring life will be shortened. No matter how accurately a piston ring is made, it cannot form an effective oil and blowby seal against worn or uneven sides of the piston ring groove. The importance of checking ring grooves for wear cannot be overemphasized. New rings can be purchased in any standard size, oversize, or overwidth as desired. Overwidth rings may be used if the sides of the ring grooves are flat, smooth, and square.

If the grooves are worn excessively, Fig. 13-5, or in tapered fashion, Fig. 13-6, they can be repaired in two ways. One way is to machine the grooves wider and install overwidth rings. The other way is to install spacers with standard width rings, as shown in Fig. 13-7. In either case the ring grooves in the piston will need to be trued up. Special equipment is available for this purpose, Fig. 13-8, or the piston replaced.

Fig. 13-3. Measuring ring side clearance with a new ring installed. If clearance is excessive, ring will twist more than usual, and cause it to break.

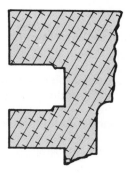

Fig. 13-5. Shoulder in groove may not leave enough clearance for new rings.

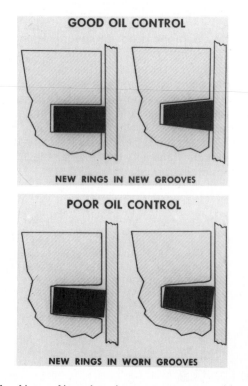

Fig. 13-4. Above. New rings in new grooves provide good oil control. Bottom. New rings in worn grooves increase oil consumption and blowby.

Fig. 13-6. Piston ring grooves: A—New groove is perfectly square. B—Ring grooves wear in a bellmouth shape. This is due to the ring twisting in the groove as the piston moves up and down.

Fig. 13-7. Standard rings may be used with a spacer installed above the ring in remachined grooves.

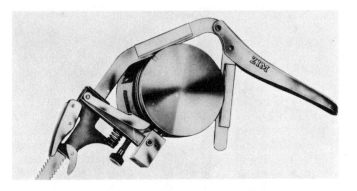

Fig. 13-8. Widening grooves on a piston. Similar equipment is used as a ring groove cleaner.

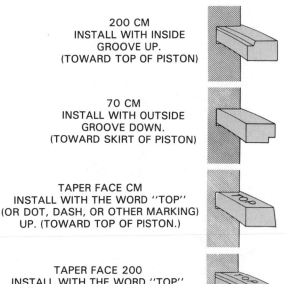

200 CM
INSTALL WITH INSIDE
GROOVE UP.
(TOWARD TOP OF PISTON)

70 CM
INSTALL WITH OUTSIDE
GROOVE DOWN.
(TOWARD SKIRT OF PISTON.)

TAPER FACE CM
INSTALL WITH THE WORD "TOP"
(OR DOT, DASH, OR OTHER MARKING)
UP. (TOWARD TOP OF PISTON.)

TAPER FACE 200
INSTALL WITH THE WORD "TOP"
(OR DOT, DASH, OR OTHER MARKING)
UP. (TOWARD TOP OF PISTON)

Fig. 13-10. If rings are installed in the opposite of specified manner, rings will scrape oil into the combustion chamber. (Perfect Circle)

The depth of the ring groove must also be checked when replacing rings. Sometimes shallow grooves are used with thin rings, and a replacement with normal thickness rings will cause them to "bottom." The groove must be deep enough to allow the ring to enter the groove below the surface of the ring land. If the grooves are too shallow, they can be machined out deeper.

When installing rings, space the gaps around the pistons to avoid any possibility that gaps will align one above the other, and increase blowby, Fig. 13-9. The manufacturers' instructions should always be followed when installing new rings. They know how their own products should be fitted, and they have studied the peculiarities of the different engines, Fig. 13-10.

Piston ring grooves must be thoroughly cleaned before installing new rings. Special tools are available for scraping the carbon from the grooves. A broken segment of a piston ring may also be used for this purpose.

Piston rings are fragile and must be handled carefully. They should be placed in the piston ring grooves with the aid of a ring expander, Fig. 13-11, and not by stretching them by hand over the piston. Even if they do not break, they may become distorted by careless handling. It is also important to use a ring compressor when inserting the piston with rings into the cylinder. Otherwise the sharp edge of the ring may be deformed, and the ring rendered useless. See Fig. 13-12.

If the bearings are worn in a pressure-lubricated engine, excess oil will be thrown upon the cylinders. The engine will pump oil, regardless of how good the rings are, or how well they are fitted. The oil is supplied in such quantities that it is beyond the ability of any ring to control it.

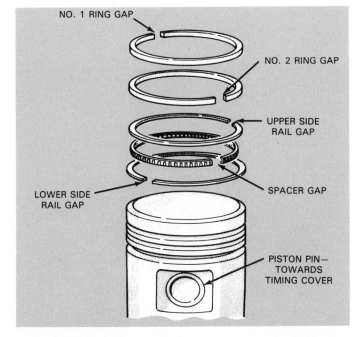

NO. 1 RING GAP

NO. 2 RING GAP

UPPER SIDE
RAIL GAP

LOWER SIDE
RAIL GAP

SPACER GAP

PISTON PIN—
TOWARDS
TIMING COVER

Fig. 13-9. Ring gaps must be staggered when installed on the piston, or blowby will be excessive. (Chrysler)

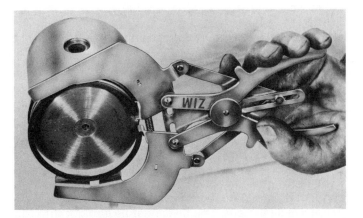

Fig. 13-11. Ring expander must be used to place rings on the piston so that they do not break.

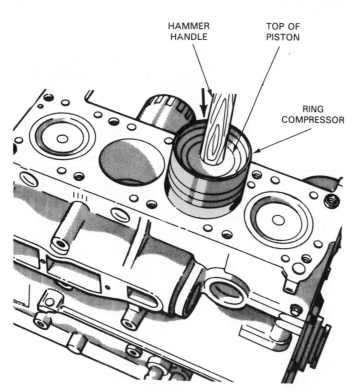

Fig. 13-12. A ring compressor must be used to compress rings so that piston can be inserted into cylinder. After ring compressor is tightened around rings and piston, use the wooden end of a hammer to tap piston downward into the cylinder. (Chrysler)

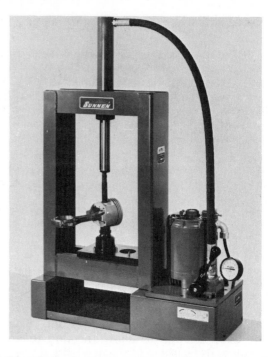

Fig. 13-13. Hydraulic press must be used to remove and insert piston pins. (Sunnen)

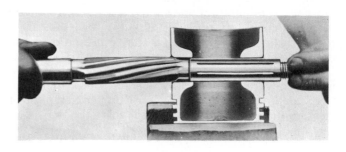

Fig. 13-14. Reamer is used to make sure that holes for piston pin align.

Fig. 13-15. Honing machine is used to recondition piston pin end of connecting rod. (Sunnen)

PISTON PINS

Today, piston pins are an interference fit in the upper end of the rod. That is, the diameter of the piston pin is slightly larger than the diameter in the upper end of the connecting rod. Special equipment, Fig. 13-13, is needed for removing and installing the pins in the piston and rod assembly. In addition to a hydraulic press, equipment needed includes special anvils on which the piston assembly is mounted, pilots, and in some cases, to a spring for the anvil. These differ for each piston design.

The pressing procedure is to mount the piston assembly on the anvil. Then, by means of a pilot and hydraulic press or an electro-hydraulic pin press, Fig. 13-13, the pin is pressed from the assembly. A similar procedure is followed when assembling the piston pin to the rod and piston.

OVERSIZE PISTON PINS

In the full floating type, the installation of new oversize pins will require reaming or honing of the piston bushings or bosses, along with the rod.

In every case where reaming or honing is done on either piston or connecting rod, it is of utmost importance to have the finished hole at precisely a right angle to the connecting rod. Also, both piston boss bearings must be in precise alignment. The hole must be straight through both bosses. Equipment used for reconditioning piston pin holes is shown in Figs. 13-14 and 13-15.

PISTON PIN FITTING

Fitting piston pins is one of the most delicate operations to be found in automobile repair work. Suitable equipment for fitting piston pins properly is available. Furthermore, we are dealing with steel, bronze, and aluminum, each of which has a different rate of heat expansion. We fit the piston pins at room temperature (assumed to be 70 °F) then put them in an engine which quickly attains a temperature of at least 140 °F. This temperature expands the piston.

There must be room for a film of oil around the piston pin. Otherwise, metal-to-metal contact will occur, and the friction generated will score the pin, bushing, or both. This measurement is usually tenths of a thousandths of an inch.

Standards of manufacture have improved, and most piston pins are round and straight within one tenth of a thousandth of an inch. A pin so finished looks perfect and appears to be glass smooth. When the surface is magnified 100 times it does not look so smooth. When magnified 1000 times, it looks rough. See Fig. 13-16.

Reaming, grinding, and honing equipment is now available which will produce a hole which appears to be dead smooth. It is like the pins, accurate to one tenth of a thousandth. When magnified, however, it looks much like the bearing surface on the pins.

With the use of good equipment, it is possible to produce a hole that enables a good working fit to be made. When working with such close dimensions, the clearance will be determined by the surface finish.

Unless the hole finish is practically perfect, the "peaks" will be sheared off when the pin is forced into the hole, Fig. 13-16. The result of such a condition is rapid wear of the peak base, and the pin and bushing are worn OUT before they wear IN to a working fit.

Piston pins must not be fitted too tight, Fig. 13-17.

If the hole is finished to the correct size, there will be room for a film of oil to prevent metal-to-metal contact. When such a fit is obtained, the pin will enter the hole readily without force being applied. It will have sufficient bearing surface to wear satisfactorily. This precision fit can be obtained by a skillful operator using modern equipment in accordance with the manufacturers' instructions. Fig. 13-18 pictures a connecting rod heater for use in press-fit rod work.

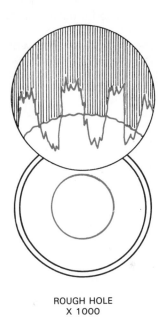

ROUGH HOLE
X 1000

Fig. 13-17. Forcing a smooth piston pin through a rough hole will cause the high points to be sheared off, which will result in metal-to-metal contact.

TO THE EYE

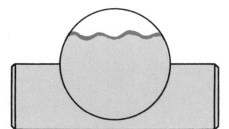

X 100

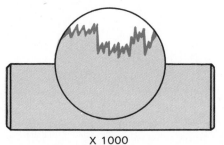

X 1000

Fig. 13-16. A piston pin may be smooth to the naked eye, but when magnified the surface of the piston pin is rough.

Fig. 13-18. Electric heater expands connecting rod eye so that piston pin can be pushed in by hand.   (Sunnen)

Chapter 13—REVIEW QUESTIONS

Write your answers on a separate sheet of paper. Do not write in this book.

1. How much end gap should the top ring have in a four inch diameter cylinder?
   a. .009 in.
   b. .012 in.
   c. .016 in.
2. How much gap should the oil ring have in a cylinder three and one half inches in diameter?
   a. .009 in.
   b. .012 in.
   c. .015 in.
3. The top ring should have at least .005 in. side clearance in the ring groove. True or False?
4. How deep should the ring groove be?
5. Piston pins are case-hardened, so they do not wear. True or False?
6. Can oversize pins be installed when the pin floats in both piston and connecting rod?
7. What is meant by "room temperature?"
8. New piston pins can be expected to be round within:
   a. .002 in.
   b. .0001 in.
   c. .00005 in.
9. Mechanic A states that the ring groove wears in a bellmouth shape.
   Mechanic B states that if a .006 in. feeler gauge can be inserted between a new piston ring and the ring groove, the grooves must be reconditioned or the piston replaced.
   Who is right?
   a. Mechanic A.
   b. Mechanic B.
   c. Neither Mechanic A nor B.
   d. Both Mechanic A and B.
10. Explain how a ring groove wears and why?
11. Ring gaps on a piston should:
    a. Align with one another.
    b. It really doesn't matter.
    c. Depends on many variables.
    d. Be about 90 deg. from any other ring gap.

Chapter 14

CRANKSHAFT AND CONNECTING ROD SERVICE

After studying this chapter, you will be able to:
- Determine when a crankshaft needs reconditioning.
- Discriminate between a good and bad connecting rod.
- List the characteristics and types of engine bearings.
- State when an engine bearing needs replacement.
- Explain why an engine block needs to be align bored.

CRANKSHAFT

In studying the forces applied to a journal of the crankshaft, it will be found that the load is much heavier at some points of rotation than at others. For example, the force of the explosion is several times as strong as the force of the compression stroke. Also, the explosion stroke always applies the force at the same spot on the journal.

Finally, an additional load is imposed by the action of centrifugal force resulting from the rotation of the crankshaft with its connecting rods and pistons. The result is out-of-round crankshaft journals and crankpins.

If a connecting rod is bent, or is out of alignment, it will tend to wear the crankpin journal in a tapered fashion. That is, it will wear more at one end of the bearing surface than the other end. Also any twisting of the engine crankcase or any excessive vibration of the crankshaft will cause the main crankshaft journals to wear in tapered form.

Furthermore, if abrasive material gets into the engine oil, wear may be unequal. It will wear more at one bearing or more on one spot of the bearing, depending on where the abrasive enters in greatest quantity.

Bearings seldom wear equally. One bearing may operate with a smaller volume of oil than another. Likewise, one bearing, because of location in the engine, may operate at a higher temperature than the others. All of these things cause or contribute to unequal wear on the crankshaft journals.

If a connecting rod journal has taper or a flat spot, it simply cannot be used. Either condition would ordinarily cause such an increase in oil consumption that it would be essential to recondition the crank throw.

Because of close clearances in the bearings, a sprung crankshaft cannot be tolerated. The main bearings must fit the crankshaft journals all around the circumference with only enough clearance for a film of lubricating oil. If the bearing journal is scored or other than absolutely round, it must be reconditioned or replaced.

DAMAGED CRANKSHAFTS

Engine crankshafts usually are large and expensive parts, so it is desirable to repair damage rather than replace the shaft. Before any extensive work is started, however, it is well to have the shaft checked by a specialist with proper special magnetic or chemical equipment to make sure there are no cracks in it. See Fig. 14-1.

Fig. 14-1. A magnetic particle inspector is used to detect cracks that cannot be seen by the naked eye. (Kwik-Way)

If damage has occurred to one or more crankpin journals, it is possible to recondition the crankpin with the aid of special equipment made for this specific purpose. See Fig. 14-2.

An engine crankshaft is subjected to terrific vibration and stress. It may develop tiny cracks, particularly at or near the ends of the connecting rod throws or at the ends of the main bearing journals. Occasionally, a crack may develop near the oil feed holes in the shaft.

If the crankshaft is sound, journals worn slightly tapered or out-of-round can be reground and UNDERSIZE BEARINGS fitted. See Fig. 14-3. Here again, it is desirable to check out available sizes of bearing inserts, then have the shaft journals ground to an undersize for which inserts are carried in stock.

A crankshaft journal can be checked for scoring by running a fingernail over the journal. If your fingernail detects the slightest ridge or scoring anywhere, the journal must be reconditioned. Your fingernail should be able to glide over the entire journal surface.

If the shaft is badly damaged, it may be possible to restore the journal by spraying metal on it. The shaft is built up oversize, then reground to the desired size. This type of work usually is done by specialists. See Fig. 14-4.

BEARING CLEARANCES

A previous study of engine lubrication revealed that oil is pumped under pressure to the various bearings in the engine. However, to get this oil into the bearing and lubricate it, clearance for an oil film must exist.

The one most important thing to keep in mind in this connection is that the steel crankshaft journal MUST be separated from the bearing metal when the engine is running or the bearing will melt. The heat generated by friction when steel moves rapidly on soft, dry metal WILL melt the soft metal. Therefore, an automobile engine uses a film of oil between the journal and the bearing.

The oil film serves to hold the two metals apart and also circulates to carry away the heat generated by friction. The space is not great (measured in thousandths), but those thousandths are all important. See Fig. 14-5.

This film thickness will vary with the design of the engine and the type of lubrication system used. In general, a splash lubrication system is less critical of oil clearances than a pressure lubrication system. In the splash system, the oil is churned up by internal parts of the engine into a combination of liquid and mist, which is sprayed over the entire interior of the engine.

In the pressure lubricated engine, the oil is pumped under pressure to the bearings, Fig. 14-6. In this case, the flow of oil must be controlled by maintaining limited clearance all around a ROUND bearing and a ROUND shaft. If there are unequal clearances in the circulation system, too much oil will collect in one place, and not enough in other places. This is because oil under pressure will go through the largest clearance space in the greatest quantity.

CLEARANCE MEASUREMENT

The diameter of the shaft is measured at several points around the circumference to determine the size and to check for roundness. See Fig. 14-7. Measuring each end of the journal will determine the amount of taper, if any.

The inside of the bearing bore, minus the bearing, is measured with the cap bolted in place. Use a telescoping

Fig. 14-2. Special machinery is needed to recondition crankshaft journals.

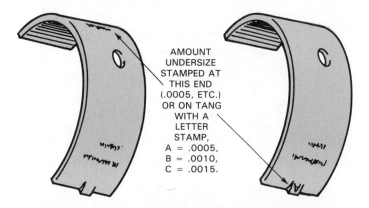

AMOUNT UNDERSIZE STAMPED AT THIS END (.0005, ETC.) OR ON TANG WITH A LETTER STAMP, A = .0005, B = .0010, C = .0015.

Fig. 14-3. When a crankshaft journal is undersized, the bearings are oversized. However, the bearings, like the journal, are also referred to as undersized. (Oldsmobile)

Fig. 14-4. A crankshaft can be reconditioned by spraying metal with special equipment.

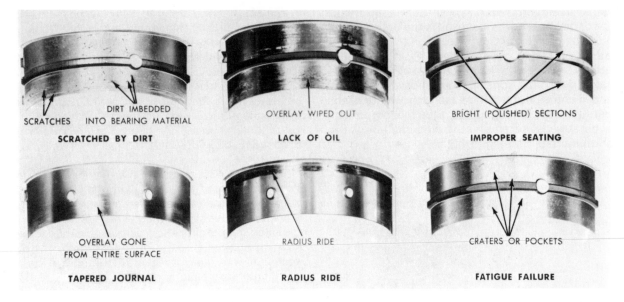

Fig. 14-5. Different types of bearing failure. The most common cause of bearing failure is dirt.

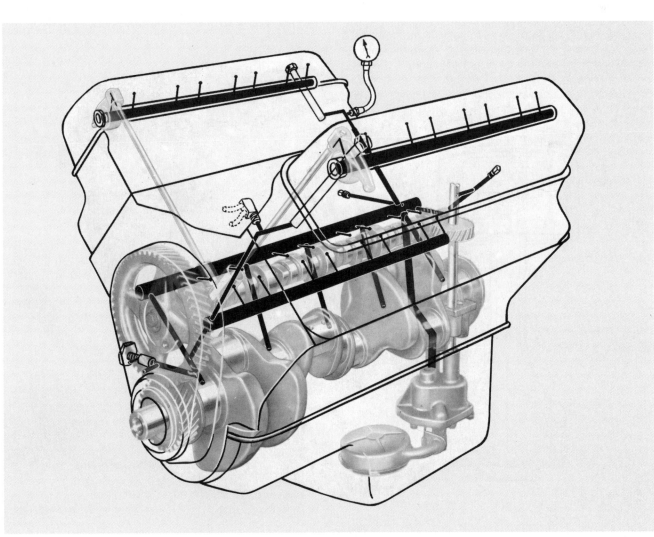

Fig. 14-6. A pressurized lubrication system distributes oil to all parts of the engine.

gauge or an inside micrometer, Fig. 14-8. The difference in these two measurements represents the amount that the bore is out of round.

The use of a plastic material called "PLASTIGAGE," which flattens between the journal and bearing when the cap is drawn down to proper tightness determines the oil clearance. The amount of increase in the width of the plastic material, as it flattens out, is then measured with a furnished gauge to determine the clearance between journal and bearing. See Fig. 14-9.

The amount of diametral clearance on crankshaft bearings is specified by the car manufacturer. In the absence of specifications, use a minimum of .0005 to .001 in. (0.0127 to 0.0154 mm) for small shafts and up to .0015 to .002 in. (0.381 to 0.0508 mm) for large shafts. Clearance in excess of .005 in. (0.1270 mm) on either main bearings or rod bearings usually calls for the installation of new undersize bearings.

ENDWISE CLEARANCE

The crankshaft must not move endwise to any great extent; so one of the main bearings usually is provided with flanges that bear against a machined flange on the crankshaft. See Fig. 14-10. There is always some end thrust on the crankshaft. This may originate in the clutch pushing against the end of the shaft, or the thrust on acceleration or deceleration of the engine.

Just as in the case of diametral clearance, there must be some clearance on the thrust faces. Otherwise, expansion of the shaft and bearings from the normal heat of operation would cause metal-to-metal contact and burning of the thrust bearing. Here again the car manufacturers' instructions should be followed. It is customary to provide a minimum of .004 in. and a maximum of .008 in. clearance. End thrust can be measured with a feeler gauge, as shown in Fig. 14-11.

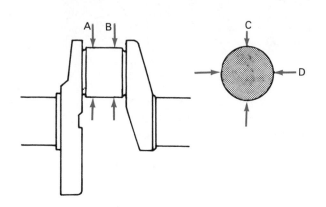

Fig. 14-7. In addition to checking each journal for scoring, taper and out-of-round must also be checked. The difference between A and B is the amount of taper. The difference between C and D is the amount of out-of-round. (Nissan)

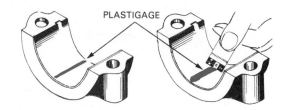

Fig. 14-9. Using Plastigage to check oil clearance.

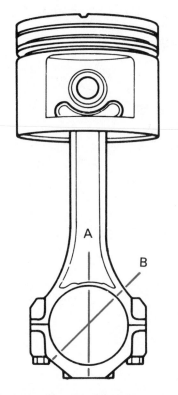

Fig. 14-8. Distance at line A will be the greatest due to wear. The difference between line A and line B is the amount of out-of-round. If a rod is out-of-round more than .001 in., a new one must be used. Use an indicator dial, or telescoping gauge and micrometer. (Oldsmobile)

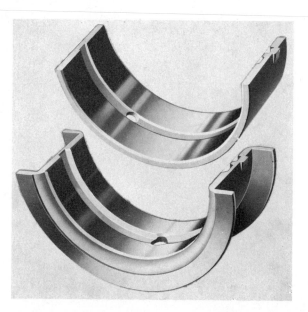

Fig. 14-10. Top. Precision insert bearing. Bottom. Precision insert thrust bearing. Note that thrust bearing has flanges.

Fig. 14-11. A feeler gauge is used to check end clearance of crankshaft. End clearance is controlled by the thrust bearing. A screwdriver is used as a lever to move the crankshaft back and forth to obtain readings. (Oldsmobile)

Fig. 14-13. Number the main and rod caps prior to removing. (Chrysler)

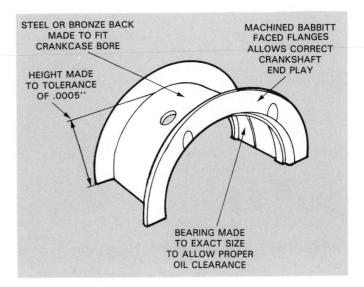

STEEL OR BRONZE BACK MADE TO FIT CRANKCASE BORE

HEIGHT MADE TO TOLERANCE OF .0005"

MACHINED BABBITT FACED FLANGES ALLOWS CORRECT CRANKSHAFT END PLAY

BEARING MADE TO EXACT SIZE TO ALLOW PROPER OIL CLEARANCE

Fig. 14-14. A typical thrust bearing.

BEARING REMOVAL

The first step is ridge reaming to remove the unworn portion of the cylinder wall above piston ring travel, Fig. 14-12. Then the rod caps are removed, and the entire piston and rod assembly is pushed up and out of the cylinder. Rods and their respective caps must be kept together and marked for cylinder location, Fig. 14-13.

REPLACEMENT OF INSERTS

With the insert, or shell type of bearing, it is possible to replace all main and all connecting rod bearings without removing the crankshaft. See Fig. 14-14. These

bearing inserts require no fitting by hand, since they are made to extremely close limits of accuracy. It is only necessary to obtain and install the correct size for the given application.

Even in the case of bushing or sleeve type bearings used in old Volkswagen engines, Fig. 14-15, replacement bearings are available in an assortment of sizes to meet almost any requirement.

If the crankshaft journal has been reduced in diameter so much that a standard insert will not fit and the crankshaft has not been damaged, the journal is reconditioned to an undersize dimension, and an undersize insert is used.

If the crankshaft journal has been reduced in diameter to much that a standard undersize insert will not fit, inserts are available with excess bearing metal that can be bored out to the size desired, Fig. 14-16.

If the bearing bore and journal are round, these new inserts require no fitting or adjustment. If the journal is out-of-round more than .0015 in., it should be trued up or machined until it is round. The same applies to the bearing bore in which the insert seats. Any errors in the bore will distort the bearing shell when the bolts are drawn down to the proper specification. In general, when a connecting rod bearing has worn sufficiently to require replacement, the bore of the connecting rod will have worn to such an extent that replacement is also required.

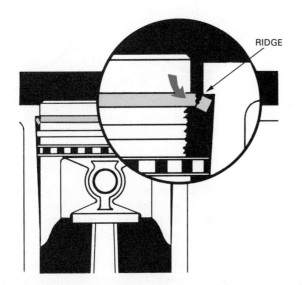

RIDGE

Fig. 14-12. If ridge is not removed before pushing piston upwards, the rings and the piston lands will be broken. (Sealed Power)

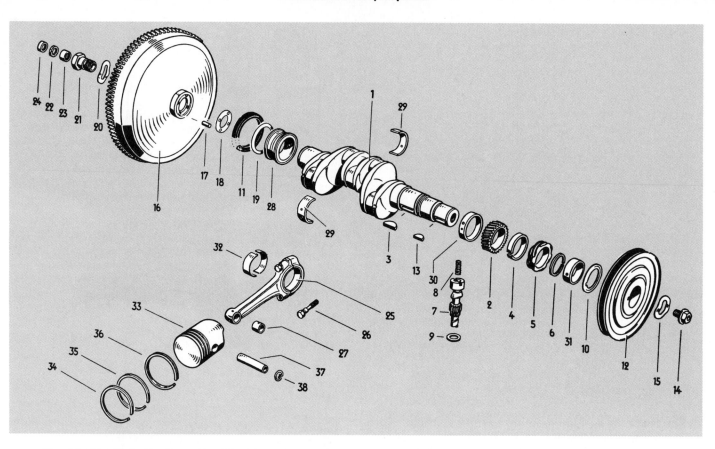

Fig. 14-15. Main bearings, No. 28, 30, and 31, are sleeve type. Center bearing, No. 29, is a split type.   (VW)

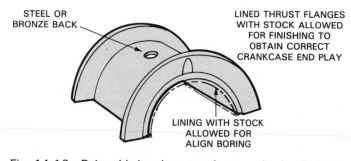

Fig. 14-16. Reborable bearings permit any undersize desired. (Federal Mogul)

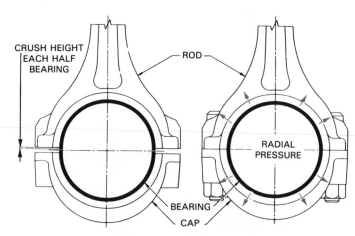

Fig. 14-17. Bearing crush means that bearing sits slightly higher than each half of the bore.

BEARING INSERT SEATING

The bearing seat and bearing insert MUST be round and true, as there MUST be contact between the bearing seat bore and the back of the bearing insert. If contact does not exist, the heat will not flow from the insert to the crankcase or connecting rod, and the bearing may melt. Note that no shims of any sort are used between the insert and seat in an effort to correct for wear or distortion.

This matter of heat dissipation is one reason for BEARING CRUSH. Crush means that the two halves of the bearing shell extend a few thousandths beyond the bearing seat bore, as shown in exaggerated form in Fig. 14-17. When the bearing cap nuts are drawn down to specified tightness, the insert is forced to seat in its bore.

Another reason for crush is to make sure the bearing remains round. If it were not tightly held on the edge it might distort as shown in exaggerated form in Fig. 14-18, enough to allow the edges to touch the journal.

Still another reason for crush is to avoid any possible movement at the insert in the seat. If the shell should become slightly loose, it might oscillate in the seat and wear the bearing back. This would interfere with both oil control and heat transfer. Any dirt between the shell and the bore will have the same effect. See Fig. 14-19.

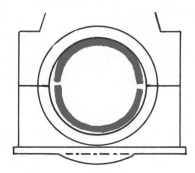

Fig. 14-18. Lack of bearing crush would permit inserts to curl inward.

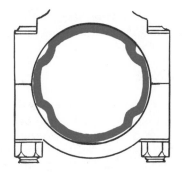

Fig. 14-20. Excessive bearing crush will cause the bearing to distort when the cap is tightened.

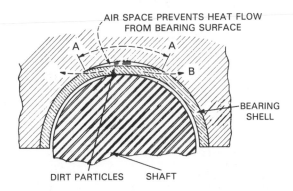

Fig. 14-19. Dirt between insert and bore creates a high spot on bearing surface. In addition, this prevents an effective transfer of heat from the connecting rod, which could cause the bearing to melt.

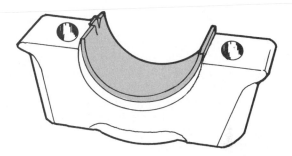

Fig. 14-21. Bearing spread permits the bearing to be snapped into place.

Bearing crush must always be there, so the edges of the insert should not be dressed down flush with the bearing seats. Of course, the amount of crush must not be excessive. If it were, the insert would be distorted when the cap is drawn down and the bearing would be deformed, Fig. 14-20.

The amount of crush is only .001 or .002 in., and is finished to dimension the same as the bore and outside diameter. These inserts are extremely accurate and must be handled with care. They should be purchased to the precise size required, and inserted with no alteration.

BEARING SPREAD

The diameter of the bearing is slightly wider than the bore. This is known as BEARING SPREAD, Fig. 14-21. The bearing spread allows the bearing to remain in its seat during assembly, while the bearing or engine is inverted.

LUBRICATION GROOVES

Lubrication grooves, Fig. 14-22, are sometimes added to the bearing design to help distribute oil over a wider area of the journals. Annular grooves route oil to other oil passages in the engine block. The thumbnail grooves allow the oil to be distributed evenly over the flange of the thrust bearing.

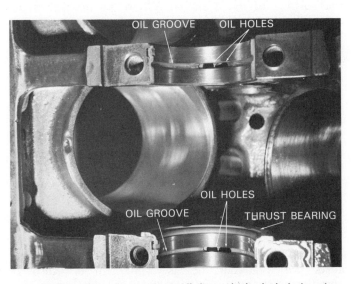

Fig. 14-22. Oil groove routes oil through the hole in bearing, which then flows to other areas within the engine. (Ford)

INSTALLATION

When all bearings are installed properly, and the caps drawn up tight, there should be little resistance toward rotation of the shaft. If there is resistance: one or more bearings are fitted too tightly; there is insufficient end clearance on the thrust bearing; the crankshaft is sprung; the bearings are not in correct alignment; or the bearing caps have been mixed-up.

If the engine is stiff after installing new bearings, it should not be started until the cause of the interference is located and eliminated.

SIDE CLEARANCE

The connecting rod must have some side clearance at the crankpin. If it has too much, the bearing may move sidewise and cause a knock. The clearance is measured by inserting a feeler gauge between the side of the cap and cheek of the crankshaft throw, as shown in Fig. 14-23. Manufacturers' specifications vary somewhat, but the usual side clearance is .005 to .010 in. Since there is no adjustment of the side clearance, excessive clearance requires replacement of the bearing inserts.

MAIN BEARINGS

The replacement of main bearings of the insert type presents a problem only when the cylinder block has become warped, Fig. 14-24, and/or when the crankshaft is scored or badly worn. If the cylinder block is not warped and the shaft is in good condition, all that is necessary is to remove the old bearing inserts and slip in new ones of the correct size.

Main bearing inserts are replaced one at a time. The procedure is to remove the bearing cap and slip out the bearing insert. To remove the upper half of the bearing insert, a ''roll-out'' pin is inserted into the oil hole of the crankshaft. The end of this pin protrudes slightly above the surface of the crankpin. When the crankshaft is rotated, the pin will force out the upper insert. A tool for this purpose can be fashioned from a cotter pin. See Fig. 14-25.

The new bearing insert is slipped into position by hand. In some cases it may be necessary to use the ''roll-out'' pin to complete the installation. After installing the bearing cap and insert, the same procedure is followed with the other bearings.

Bearing cap bolts are not tightened completely until all the bearing inserts are in position. Then the bolts are tightened to the specified torque.

If the crankshaft is scored and the crankcase warped, the engine must be removed to do a complete reconditioning job. This includes regrinding the crankshaft, Fig. 14-2, and align boring the bearing bores, Fig. 14-26.

If the crankcase is not warped, the crankshaft is reground to a standard undersize for which bearing inserts are available. If the crankcase is warped, semifinished bearings are installed in the crankcase. The bearings are align bored and then the crankshaft is reground to size to fit the bearings.

Before align boring the semifinished bearings, make sure caps are properly assembled and bolts tightened to the specified torque. Also, all oil passages should be plugged with substantial pieces of clean cloth to prevent chips and bearings from getting into the lubrication system.

When locating the boring bar, great care must be exercised to insure that the centerline of the finished bearings will be the correct distance from the top of the cylinder block, parallel with it and at right angles to the cylinder bores.

Fig. 14-23. A feeler gauge is used to check side clearance.

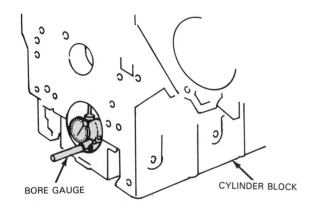

BORE GAUGE   CYLINDER BLOCK

Fig. 14-24. Using a dial indicator to measure out-of-round of main bearing bores. If any one bore exceeds .001 in., the block must be align bored. (Oldsmobile)

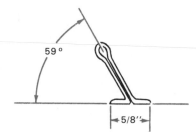

59°

5/8''

Fig. 14-25. Bending cotter pin so that it can be used to remove upper main bearing inserts.

In an engine built with a gear to drive the camshaft, the distance between the centerline of the camshaft and the bore of the main bearings must be very accurately maintained. Otherwise, the crankshasft and the camshaft gears will not mesh properly. More tolerance is permitted if the camshaft is driven by a chain or a cog belt.

After all boring operations are completed, all plugs must be removed from the oil passages and all chips cleaned from the interior of the crankcase. All inside edges of each bored surface should be hand chamfered with a scraper about 1/64th in.

Fig. 14-26. Align boring machine. (Sunnen)

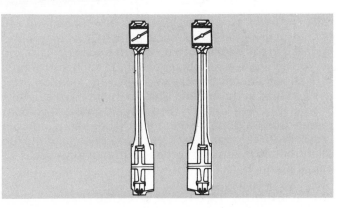

Fig. 14-28. Connecting rods are offset. The short side is closest to the main bearing.

In all bearing work, extreme accuracy and cleanliness are required. Particular attention must be paid to the areas contacting the backs of the bearing inserts, the bearing surfaces, and also the interior of all oil lines and oil passages.

In case of a leaking rear main bearing, it is often possible to replace the bearing seal and bearing without removing the crankshaft. To do this, loosen all the main bearing caps slightly to lower the crankshaft. Then, remove the rear main bearing cap. With a small pin punch, start to drive out the seal. Grasp it with a pair of pliers and pull it out. To replace the upper part of the seal, first lubricate it with engine oil. Start it into the groove by hand and have the crankshaft turned until the seal slides in place.

The upper insert can be removed by first inserting a special tool or a bent cotter pin, Fig. 14-25, into the oil hole of the crankshaft. Then, as the crankshaft is turned, the pin will push out the bearing half. Start removing the seal with a punch, Fig. 14-27, then pull it out with a pair of pliers.

CONNECTING ROD

In addition to the proper fit of the large end of the connecting rod on the crankshaft, and the proper condition of the piston pin at the other end of the rod, the alignment of the rod itself, and the condition of the bearing bore in the big end of the rod must also be checked.

Most V-type and opposed cylinder type engines have the cylinder blocks slightly offset from each other, endwise, to facilitate placement of the rod bearings on the crankshaft. It is also customary to offset the connecting rods, Fig. 14-28, to place the power load as near to the main bearings as possible. This tends to reduce vibration of the crankshaft. On most engines, the connecting rods are marked on the same side. It is something that should be watched during engine assembly. If unmarked, align prick-punch marks on the same side of each rod end and cap, using one mark for cylinder No. 1, two marks for cylinder No. 2, etc.

The piston pin and crankshaft journal must be precisely parallel. If the piston pin is not parallel with the crankshaft, every force on the piston will cause it to try to slide endwise on the piston pin. This will cause PISTON SLAP in the cylinder; a knock created by the piston. The large end of the connecting rod will also have a tendency to knock.

Special equipment is available for checking the connecting rods, Fig. 14-29. This type of equipment checks the

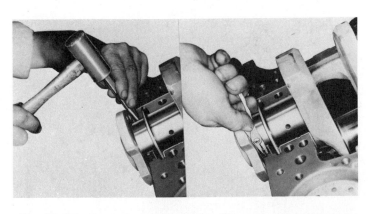

Fig. 14-27. Removing rear main bearing seal while crankshaft is in engine.

Fig. 14-29. Checking the alignment of connecting rod. If connecting rod has any twists, the rod must be replaced. Never attempt to straighten the rod.

rods for twist as well as bends. Every connecting rod should be checked for proper alignment, just before it is installed in the engine. Many hard-to-locate noises in an engine originate in misalignment of the connecting rods.

Each rod should be checked again for location after it is installed in the engine. The rod might have a double bend in it, which would not be noticed on the alignment tester. Such a double bend might leave the piston pin parallel with the crankshaft, yet the upper end of the rod might be close enough to one of the piston bosses to cause a knock.

Chapter 14—REVIEW QUESTIONS

Write your answers on a separate sheet of paper. Do not write in this book.
1. Give three reasons for crankshaft wear.
2. Cracks in steel parts may be found by means of:
   a. Chemical equipment.
   b. Magnetic equipment.
   c. Either.
3. An undersize crankshaft journal can be altered to become oversize. True or False?
4. Clearance between crankshaft and bearing in a splash lubricated engine may be _____ than in a pressure lubricated engine.
   a. More.   b. The same.   c. Less.
5. What happens if oil clearances are unequal in a pressure oiling system?
6. Name two ways of measuring bearing clearance.
7. In general, the diametral clearance in a small engine main bearing should be:
   a. .0005 to .001 in.
   b. .001 to .0015 in.
   c. .0015 to .002 in.
8. In general, endwise clearance for crankshafts should not exceed:
   a. .004 in.   b. .006 in.   c. .008 in.
9. A bearing bore should be trued up if it is out-of-round more than:
   a. .0015 in.   b. .0025 in.   c. .005 in.
10. Name two reasons for bearing crush.
11. The short side of the offset on the No. 1 connecting rod should be toward the _____ of the engine.
12. A piston pin can be properly fitted and parallel with the crankshaft and still cause a knock. True or False?
13. Bearing spread means:
   a. The diameter of the bearing is wider than the bore.
   b. The height of the bearing is higher than the cap.
   c. Both a and b.
   d. Neither a nor b.

Chapter 15

VALVE SERVICE

After studying this chapter, you will be able to:
* List the steps involved in a valve job.
* State the purpose and list types of valve seals.
* Explain why valve guides wear in a bellmouth shape and what can be done to correct this.
* Describe how, why, and when a valve rotator is used.
* Tell what check should be made on valve springs.

VALVES

The condition of the valves has much to do with engine efficiency. Poppet valves lead a hard life, so it is not surprising that valve service is a frequently performed operation in automotive service shops.

Valve service was once a hand lapping procedure using an abrasive paste between the valve face and valve seat. This procedure was assumed to provide a gas-tight valve, and little attention or thought was given to valve seat width, heat dissipation, concentricity of valve with seat, strength of valve springs, wear in valve guides, and all the other things that require attention on the modern high speed engine.

Modern ''valve grinding'' is a true grinding process. Every part of the operation is governed by careful measurement with accurate test equipment. The first step after the valves are removed and cleaned, is to determine whether the valve can be reconditioned or whether it must be replaced. If the stem is scored, pitted, bent, or worn more than .002 in., it should be discarded.

A dial gauge and V-blocks can be used to check the stem for straightness, Fig. 15-1. For other visual checkpoints, see Figs. 15-2 and 15-3. The stem diameter can be checked for wear with a micrometer, Fig. 15-4.

Visual inspection, for example, may disclose a seriously warped valve head, cracked valve face, or lack of margin. If the face is burned, badly warped, or worn to a thin margin, the valve is discarded. See Fig. 15-3. If the valve appears to be in good condition, it is placed in a special grinding machine known as a valve refacer, and a new surface is ground on the face at the proper angle. See Fig. 15-5.

Most valve faces are cut at an angle of 45 deg. with the stem. An angle of 30 deg. is also used. In either case, a slight interference angle, about 1/2 to 1 deg., may be

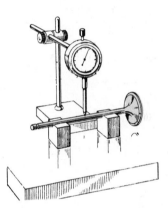

Fig. 15-1. Using a dial indicator to check valve stem straightness. If dial deviates .002 in. while rolling the stem, the valve must be replaced.

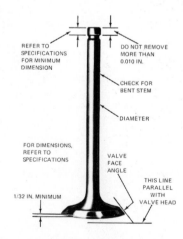

Fig. 15-2. Points to check on a valve for wear. If the valve stem has even the slightest ridge or groove, the valve must be replaced.

cut on either the valve face or valve seat, to improve the seating ability, Fig. 15-6. However, it is invariably cut on the valve face as valve refacers can be adjusted to any desired angle.

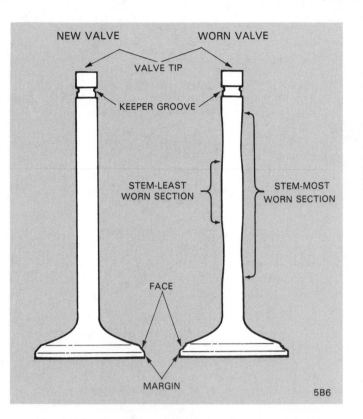

Fig. 15-3. Examples of a good and a worn valve. (Oldsmobile)

Fig. 15-5. If the valve is in good shape, the face of the valve can be resurfaced. (Sioux)

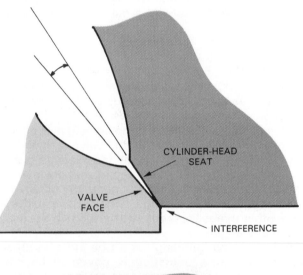

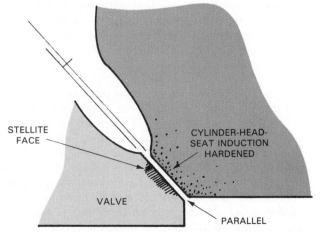

Fig. 15-6. Top. Interference angle is used when engines burn leaded fuels. This chips the deposits off of the valve face. Bottom. With engines that burn unleaded fuels, an interference angle is not needed nor wanted. This is because the unleaded fuels burn hotter and cleaner. (Oldsmobile)

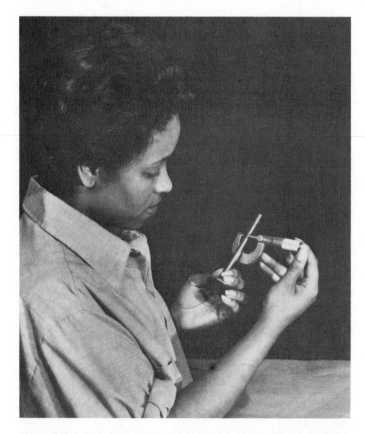

Fig. 15-4. The valve stem must be measured in several different locations to determine wear. If wear at any one point is .002 in., or greater, the valve must be discarded.

VALVE SEAT RECONDITIONING

The seat in the block or head is also resurfaced with the aid of special grinders. First of all, it is necessary to position the tool so it will be located to cut the seat concentric with the valve stem guide, Fig. 15-7. This is difficult to do if the guide is worn. Guides should be replaced or reconditioned if worn bellmouthed.

After reconditioning the valve guides, the seat surface is cut or ground to the proper angle, Fig. 15-8. This cutting or grinding must produce a smooth, true surface if the valve is to be gas-tight. It cannot be true if the seat is not concentric with the valve stem. A method of testing with a dial gauge is shown in Fig. 15-9. The seat should be concentric within .001 in. of the guide.

Valve seats that are too narrow will not dissipate the heat properly. If too wide, they will encourage carbon to adhere to them. In the absence of factory specifications, a seat 1/16 in. wide is usually satisfactory. If the seat is wider than this, the first operation will be to narrow it by cutting an acute angle under the seat, and an obtuse angle above the seat, Fig. 15-10. This is done with special grinders made for the purpose.

To check the valve seat contact area, coat the face of the valve with Prussian blue. Insert the valve into the seat and rotate it with light pressure. Remove the valve and examine the face. A ring of bare metal should be left showing on the valve face. This ring should be approximately 1/16 in. from the margin, as this is the point the valve face meets the seat. If measurement is other than 1/16 in., the seat will have to be recut.

VALVE SEAT INSERTS

Hardened valve seat inserts are ordinarily used in air-cooled automobile engines having aluminum cylinder heads. Induction hardened valve seats are also used in many late model engines having cast iron heads, Fig. 15-6. If the insert is badly worn or burned, it may be easier to replace the insert than to try to recondition it. These seats are made of hard, heat-resisting metal, refaced by grinding with special grinders.

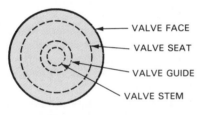

Fig. 15-7. The valve guide must be perfectly round so that valve face can close squarely on the seat. (Sioux)

Fig. 15-9. Checking valve seat concentricity. Dial gauge is used to check that the seat is centered to the valve guide after grinding the seats.

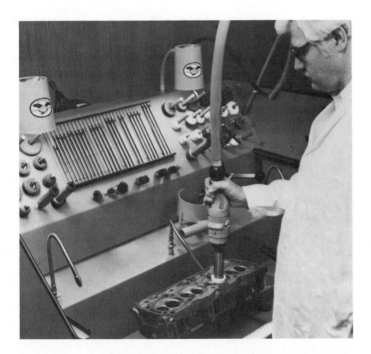

Fig. 15-8. Grinding the valve seats is the last step in a valve grinding operation. (Sioux)

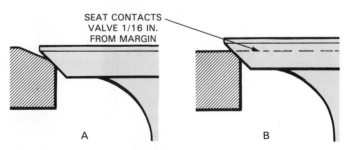

Fig. 15-10. Valve seat contact. A—Valve is sitting too far into the head. The seat must be narrowed using either a 15° or 20° stone, or carbon will collect on the seat. B—The valve face should contact seat 1/16 in. from the valve margin. (Sioux)

If the seat is the old screw-in type, it is a simple matter to unscrew the old seat and screw in the new one. The seating surface is ground after the insert is in place. The pressed-in, or shrunk-in, insert is usually held tightly in place by rolling or peening the metal around the edge of the insert after it is in place.

Since it is sometimes difficult to clean up the peening enough to allow inserts to be pulled, they are usually broken for removal. Whether the old insert is pulled or broken out, it is essential that the hole for the insert be round and true. If the insert does not fully bottom in the hole, or if it does not fit tightly all around the hole, there will be poor heat transfer from the insert to the head or block. Then, of course, the insert will run hotter than it should.

For this reason, the inserts are usually sized to provide an ''interference fit.'' That is, the insert is one or two thousandths larger in diameter than the hole into which it is installed. In this case, to avoid the stresses imposed in pressing them in place, the inserts are often shrunk for insertion.

For service installation, the inserts may be placed in a deep freeze for a few hours, or packed in dry ice for a few minutes. Either of these procedures will shrink them sufficiently for easy insertion. When frozen, the inserts must be handled carefully and quickly, since they are quite brittle and will crack or split easily. After insertion, the metal around the insert may be lightly rolled or peened over the top outside edge of the insert, to help hold it firmly in place. The final step is to grind the valve seat true with the valve guide.

VALVE STEM GUIDES

Older engines have pressed-in valve guides. Now, they are built with the valve stem in direct contact with a hole bored in the cylinder head. Heat dissipation is better where pressed-in guides are not used. Wear in the guides means honing the holes out larger, the using valves with oversize stems. Separate guides are made of cast iron. Bronze is also used because of the superior wearing characteristics and more rapid heat dissipating ability.

Press-in guides are often identical for the exhaust and intake valves, but are sometimes installed differently. In other cases, the exhaust and intake guides are not interchangeable. See Fig. 15-11. In still another case, the guides are identical, but the intake guides are installed upside down from the exhaust guides. Some exhaust guides are cut off shorter in the port opening, and others are counterbored in the port end, to reduce the tendency for carbon to accumulate in the guide.

Carbon does accumulate in the guide bore and on the stem of exhaust valves. This causes them to stick partly open or to slow down in action. The tendency for carbon to accumulate increases as the exhaust valve stem and guide wear, because more hot gas blows by between the stem and guide. Wear on the intake stem and guide is equally undesirable, because it permits air to be drawn in through the clearance to dilute the air and gasoline mixture. Under such conditions, it is impossible to obtain a satisfactory carburetor adjustment.

Also, oil from the valve chamber may be sucked in between valve and guide to increase oil consumption and carbon up the engine. This oil leakage is sometimes pronounced on overhead valve engines, as oil is pumped up on the rocker arms. To discourage this tendency, a special cutter is available to cut a bevel on the end of untapered valve guides.

It is customary to place seals either on the valve stem or in the guide on overhead valve engines to exclude excess oil. Several types are shown in Figs. 15-12 through 15-14.

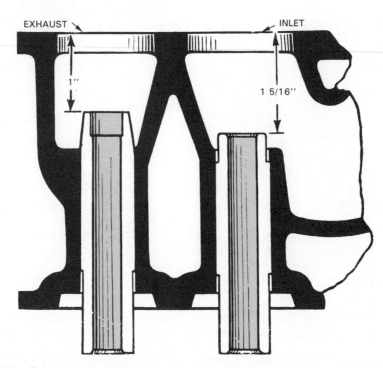

EXHAUST   INLET

1''   1 5/16''

Fig. 15-11. Exhaust valve guide extends farther into the port than the intake valve guide.

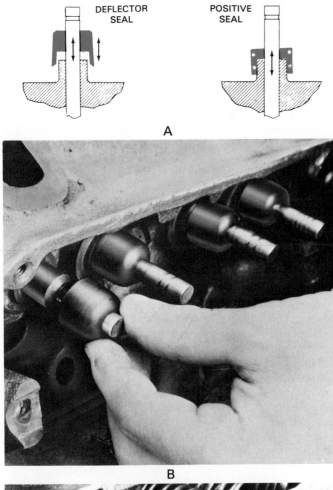

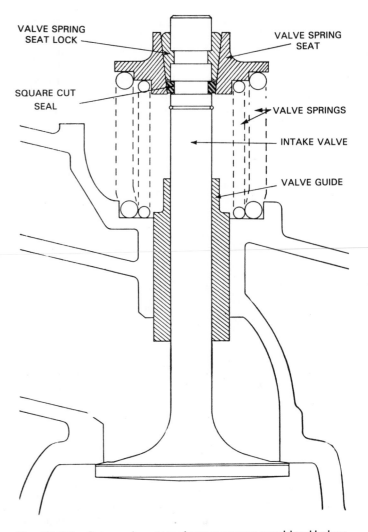

Fig. 15-13. Some valve stems have a groove machined below the keeper grooves. A square cut seal is then placed in this groove and acts as a valve guide seal.

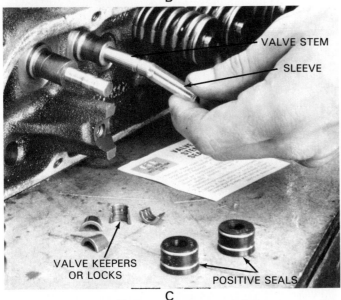

Fig. 15-12. Valve seals. A—Deflector or umbrella valve seal grasps the valve stem and moves up and down with the valve stem. Positive valve seal remains fixed to the valve guide boss. As valve stem moves up and down, the seal wipes excess oil from the stem. B—Umbrella valve seals derive their name because of the shape. C—Positive valve seals have two wire rings around the circumference of the seal. Note that a sleeve is temporarily installed on the valve stem. This sleeve aids in the installation of the seal and prevents the seal from being torn during installation. Once the seal is installed, the sleeve is removed from the valve stem. (Fel-Pro Inc.)

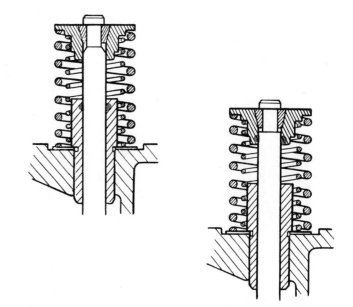

Fig. 15-14. Some older engines use an O-ring as a valve guide seal.

Another undesirable result of excessive valve guide wear is to permit the valve to wobble enough to cause it to ride to one side of the valve seat as shown in Fig. 15-15. Quite naturally, this interferes with proper seating and sealing of the valve and also promotes wear. It is customary to replace the valve guides, valves, or both, whenever more than .005 in. clearance for small valve or .006 in. for large valvee exists between valve stem and guide. One method of measuring clearance is shown in Fig. 15-16.

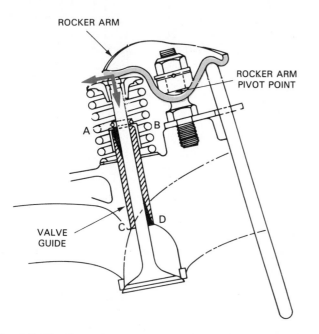

ROCKER ARM

ROCKER ARM PIVOT POINT

VALVE GUIDE

Fig. 15-15. As rocker arm moves downward it forces valve sideways as valve opens. This causes valve stem to be pushed against guide at point A and D. This prevents oil from lubricating these areas, which causes guide to wear to point A and D. Rocker arm action causes bellmouth wear of guides. Note that at point B and C valve stem is forced away from the guide. The valve guides must be reconditioned before grinding the valve seats.   (Oldsmobile)

Fig. 15-16. Checking valve guide wear. If the guide is worn excessively, the valve guide will allow too much oil into the combustion chamber.   (Chrysler)

Before any measurement is made, the valve stem must be cleaned and polished, and the valve stem guide thoroughly cleaned of carbon deposits. Special tools are made for cleaning carbon out of valve guides, Fig. 15-17. The measurement for clearance should be made with the valve slightly off the seat as shown in Fig. 15-16. The valve spring must also be removed while making the measurement.

One repair method for valve guide troubles, that does not involve replacement of the guides, is to displace the metal inside the valve guide bore by rolling a spiral groove through it. See Fig. 15-18. The idea here is to decrease the inside diameter slightly and, at the same time, form a continuous groove for oil to gather and act as a seal. A special tool is made for this purpose. The guide is then reamed to the desired diameter.

When valve guides of the press-in type are replaced, it is important to have them positioned properly in the block or head. See Fig. 15-19. The car manufacturer specifies the proper position with regard to some accessible surface, from which measurement can be made. An example of this is shown in Fig. 15-20.

In cases where an unusual amount of trouble is experienced with exhaust valves sticking because of rapid accumulation of carbon, it has been found helpful to cut off the end of the exhaust guide. This is often done with a drill ground to a flat angle on the end. The guide is cut down even with the opening in the port in which the guide is located.

After the guides are pressed in place, it is usually necessary to ream them to proper size, and provide

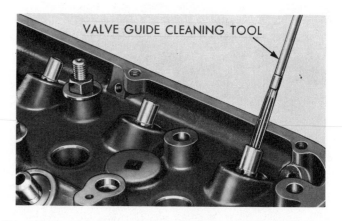

VALVE GUIDE CLEANING TOOL

Fig. 15-17. Prior to checking the valve guides for wear, clean them so that an accurate reading can be obtained.

Fig. 15-18. Knurling can recondition the guide if wear is less than .006 in.

clearance for heat expansion of the valve stem. Special reamers are made for this purpose, Fig. 15-21. This operation must be performed carefully so that the hole will be straight and true with a good surface. Exhaust valve stems require more clearance in the guides than intake valves. Fit intake valves with .001-.003 in. clearance, and exhaust valves with .002 -.004 in. clearance, depending on the size of the valve stem. To reduce reconditioning time, special equipment has been designed to recondition valve guides and seats.

VALVE SPRINGS

Valve springs seldom receive the attention they deserve. They are an exceedingly important part of the engine, and have much to do with the engine performance. They are seldom replaced unless broken, yet they should be replaced when not up to specifications. They work hard, being subjected to millions of cycles of high speed operation, and all of it under shock conditions.

The valves are opened with lightning-like speed by the action of the cam, and the spring closes the valve just as fast as it is opened. If the spring is weak and does not hold the lifter in contact with the cam, noise will be created and the valve, spring, lifter, and cam will be subjected to hammer-like blows that cause metal fatigue. Many broken valves result from shock caused by sticking stems, weak valve springs, or excessive tappet clearance.

The car manufacturer provides specifications on the free length of the spring, and the pressure in pounds that the spring should exert when it is compressed to a measured length, Fig. 15-22. Special tools are available for measuring the length and strength of the spring.

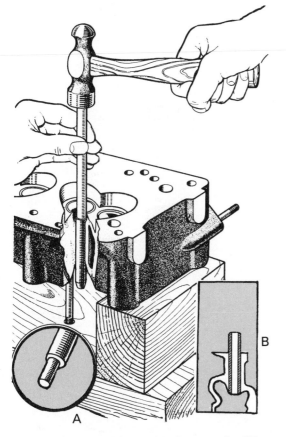

Fig. 15-19. Removing valve guide inserts. A—Pilot end of driver. B—Dimension that guide must be installed above the head.

Fig. 15-21. Reaming to the next larger oversize is another method of reconditioning valve guides. New valves with oversize valve stems must then be used.

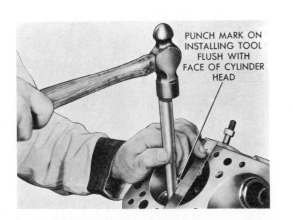

Fig. 15-20. Valve guide inserts must be positioned accurately.

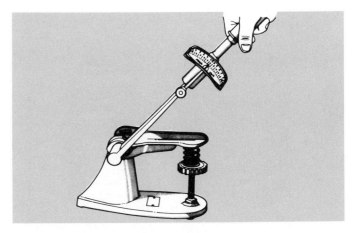

Fig. 15-22. Testing the tension of the valve spring. If valve springs are too weak, the valves will float at high rpm's. (Chrysler)

Valve springs are simple coil wire springs. They should not be expected to last forever.

Valve springs should be square on each end. Otherwise, they will have a tendency to pull the valve stem to one side and cause undue wear on the valve stem and guide. They can be checked for squareness and free length as shown in Fig. 15-23. When the coils of the spring are wound closer together at one end than at the other, the close coils are to be placed next to the engine block or head. See Fig. 15-24. This uneven coiling is done to lessen the tendency of the spring to vibrate at high speeds.

Another method of reducing vibration is to install dampers. Still another method is to taper the spring or to use two lighter springs, one within the other, instead of one heavy spring. See Fig. 15-24. The two springs are usually wound in opposite directions. The final alternative method to control vibrations of the valve spring is to have a stiffer spring. Whatever the construction used, it is important to check the springs whenever they are out, and replace them whenever they are not up to specifications.

Periodic replacement is also good to avoid unexpected failure. Valve springs often become "etched" when the valve chamber is subject to corrosive vapors. Some valve chambers are not well ventilated and steam or moisture containing acids formed from combustion will collect and cause flecks of rust to form on the valve springs. This etching is likely to cause the spring to break, Fig. 15-25.

This corrosive action is similar to the corrosion that causes pits and rust to eat into valve stems. On the valve stems it means wear. A broken valve spring on an overhead valve engine may permit the valve to drop into the cylinder, damaging or ruining a piston or cylinder head.

VALVE SPRING RETAINERS

Valve spring locks, or keepers, are usually of the split cone, horseshoe, or flat rectangular key type. They fit into an appropriate slot in the end of the valve stem. Fig. 15-26 shows the split cone type in position. A washer

Fig. 15-25. Broken valve spring was caused by acid vapors not venting from the crankcase.

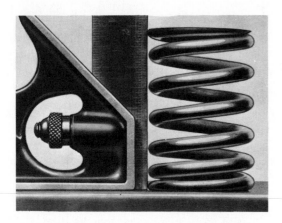

Fig. 15-23. Valve springs must be square, or the pressure will be directed to one area of the valve face.

Fig. 15-24. Left. Valve spring has internal coil spring to damper harmonic vibrations. Right. Tapered valve spring also dampens harmonic vibrations.

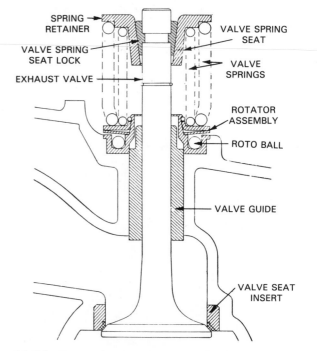

Fig. 15-26. Tapered valve keeper or lock fits into machined groove of valve stem.

called the spring retainer fits over these keepers and the tension of the spring bearing on the retainers holds the locks in place. Other methods are also used: slots cut near the end of the stem; a key or pin pushed through the slot; threads cut on the end of the stem for a nut and locknut; etc.

Removal is accomplished by holding the valve stationary while the spring is compressed enough to allow the retainer to be raised from the locks. See Figs. 15-27 to 15-29. The locks are removed and the valve spring released. This allows the spring and retainer to be removed first. Valves should never be mixed up when removed, unless it is known that new valves or guides are to be installed. The valves should always be replaced in the same guide from which they were removed.

VALVE SPRING INSTALLED HEIGHT

As the result of valve and seat reconditioning, the valve will be recessed further into the cylinder head, with the result the valve spring will not be compressed as much as it normally would be. In other words, the installed height of the spring would be increased. The effect is just the same as weak valve springs. The installed height is measured from the surface of the spring pad to the undersize of the spring retainer, Fig. 15-30. If the height is greater than specifications, then shims will have to be installed under the valve spring.

VALVE ROTATORS

Some retainers are more complicated and are intended to permit or encourage the valve to rotate slightly with regard to the seat. The purpose is to provide a longer lasting seal between valve and valve seat. Rotation of the valve will discourage the formation of carbon deposits, and help prevent valve warpage.

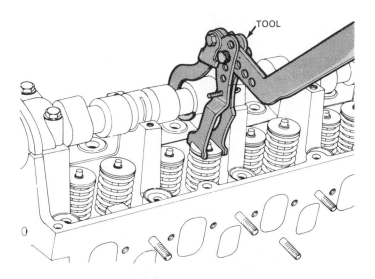

Fig. 15-27. A valve spring compressor must be used to overcome valve spring pressure. Once the valve spring is compressed, the valve keepers can either be removed or installed. (Fel-Pro Inc.)

Fig. 15-29. After removing the valve springs, the valve tip must be dressed with a file to remove the mushroomed burr. After this is done, the valve can then be removed from the head. If the tip is not dressed and the valve is forced through the guide, the guide will break. The mushroomed tip is caused by rocker arm action. (Fel-Pro Inc.)

Fig. 15-28. Compressing valve springs on an overhead camshaft. (Chrysler)

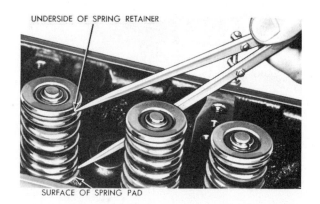

Fig. 15-30. Measuring valve spring installed height should be the last measurement made in a valve job. If the height is greater than the specification, shims must be installed under the valve spring to reduce the height.

Some of these devices release the valve from the valve spring tension at one point in the cycle of operation, so that it is free to rotate slightly. With this type it is important to maintain the clearances between stem and cup and between cup and retainer within specified limits. See Fig. 15-31. If the clearance between stem end and cap is too little, the end of the valve stem is ground off as needed. If the clearance is too great, the skirt of the cap is ground off as required. A special tool is available for measuring the clearance accurately. See Fig. 15-32.

Valve rotators impart a positive rotational effort to the valve once during each cycle of operation. One such device is illustrated in Fig. 15-33.

Valve rotators keep the seat and valve face clean and, in that regard, help maintain emission control. Valve rotators also minimize sticking and wear between guide and stem. Other than cost and complication, the only apparent objection to them is the slightly increased weight of the reciprocating assembly.

The valve rotators can easily be checked to see if they are functioning properly. To check the rotator operation, examine the valve tip, Fig. 15-34 (where the rocker arm contacts the valve). If the rotator is working properly there will be no indentations on the valve tip. When an engine uses unleaded fuel or LP gas, the valves will not have a rotator. If rotators were used on an engine that burned unleaded fuel or LP gas, valve face wear would be accelerated.

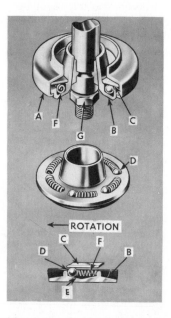

Fig. 15-33. Positive type of valve rotator causes rotation of the valve when ball moves to the valley of the ramp. A—Housing. B—Retainer. C—Cupped washer. D—Ball. E—Ramp. F—Spring. G—Valve lifter.

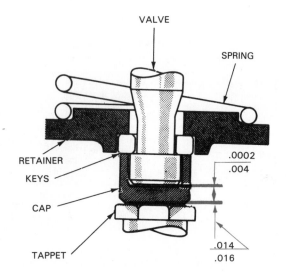

Fig. 15-31. With this type of valve rotator, clearance must be maintained between valve and cap.

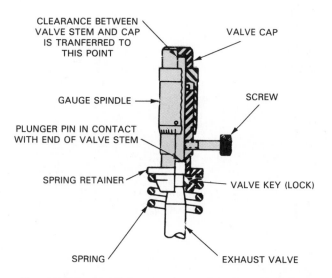

Fig. 15-32. Special gauge is used to measure clearance.

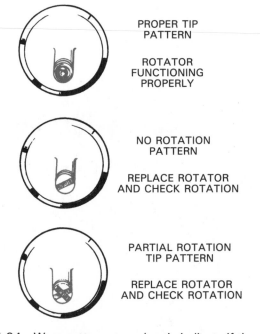

PROPER TIP PATTERN

ROTATOR FUNCTIONING PROPERLY

NO ROTATION PATTERN

REPLACE ROTATOR AND CHECK ROTATION

PARTIAL ROTATION TIP PATTERN

REPLACE ROTATOR AND CHECK ROTATION

Fig. 15-34. Wear patterns on valve tip indicate if the rotator is working. (Cadillac)

Fig. 15-35. Timing gear installation.

VALVE MECHANISMS

It is customary in U.S. built engines to mesh the camshaft drive gear directly with the crankshaft gear or, in the case of chain drive, to locate the sprockets near each other. See Figs. 15-35 and 15-36.

The cog belt used on an overhead camshaft, Figs. 15-37, 15-38, and 15-39, is made of reinforced fiberglass. While this is a relatively long drive, no difficulties have resulted from stretching. The material of which the belt is made is described as being heat resistant as well as oil resistant. It is inherently silent in operation, requires no lubrication, and absorbs the shock of opening and closing the valves.

Where long chains are used to operate camshafts, the

Fig. 15-36. Timing chain on an in-line engine. (Chrysler)

141

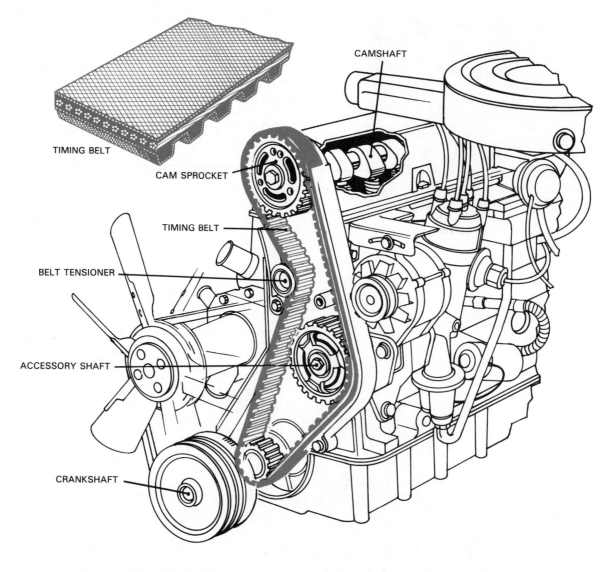

TIMING BELT

CAM SPROCKET

TIMING BELT

BELT TENSIONER

ACCESSORY SHAFT

CRANKSHAFT

CAMSHAFT

Fig. 15-37. Timing belt on an overhead camshaft engine. (Gates Rubber Co.)

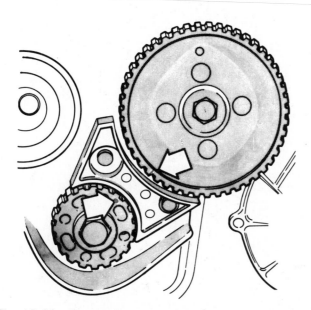

Fig. 15-38. Intermediate and crankshaft sprockets must first be aligned.

Fig. 15-39. After aligning the intermediate and crankshaft sprockets, the camshaft sprocket must be positioned properly prior to installing the timing belt.

problem of slack, Fig. 15-40, or lost motion presents itself. Valve timing must be precise. Sloppy motion cannot be tolerated. Several devices have been tried to control this. One of the most interesting is an automatic hydraulic chain tightener, as used on the English Rover. This design is shown in Fig. 15-41. Engine oil pressure is used in the hydraulic cylinder.

WORN MECHANISMS

The camshaft and camshaft drive are only part of the mechanism used to operate the valves. To continue the study of valve action and timing, consider the operation of parts such as lifters, push rods, rocker arms, etc. Each has something to do with valve timing. Consider, too, that a little wear at each point equals major wear. A little wear at many points in the valve train may be equal, in effect, to considerable wear at one point.

For example, suppose there is .005 in. excess wear between the gear teeth. This will allow the valves to open late and close early. Add to this another .005 in. excess wear in the camshaft bearings. This will reduce valve lift, as well as increase late opening and early closing of the valves. Add another .005 in. worn from the cam contour, which also changes the valve lift, timing, or both.

On an overhead valve engine, additional wearing parts include both ends of the rocker arm operating rod, the rocker arm, rocker arm bushing, and shaft. See Fig. 15-42. Now, on top of all this, add another .005 in. excess wear between the lifter and guide. This results in the lifter moving sidewise in the guide before it starts to lift the valve.

All of this cumulative wear will interfere with efficient operation of the engine. On engines having solid valve lifters, such conditions are often further aggravated by careless adjustment of the valve tappets. Many mechanics who do not understand valve action, adjust the tappets with too much clearance to make sure there is no possibility of the valve holding open. They do not realize that they are restricting the ability of the engine to draw in a full charge of mixture, and to dispose of the exhaust gas properly.

If excess wear exists at all of those points, it becomes a serious matter indeed. For these reasons, the valve tappet clearance on overhead valve engines must be more carefully adjusted.

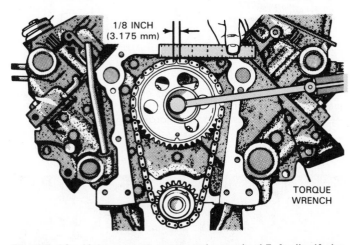

Fig. 15-40. Using a torque wrench, apply 15 ft. lb. if the heads are removed, or 30 ft. lb. if the heads are bolted to the engine. If timing chain moves more than indicated, replace the chain.

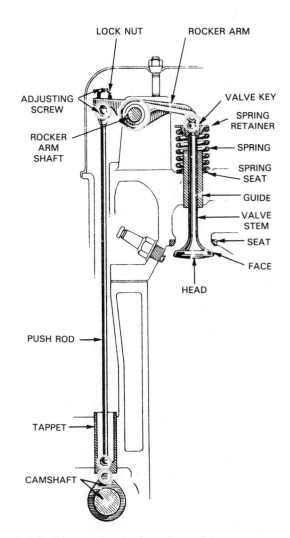

Fig. 15-42. Many points in the valve train are prone to wear. A little wear at each point becomes a significant overall amount in the entire valve train.

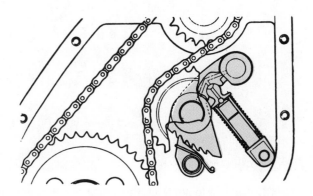

Fig. 15-41. Automatic timing chain tensioner prevents periodic adjustments.

143

It should be evident that accurate adjustment is impossible if the various contacting surfaces are worn to untrue dimensions. See Fig. 15-42. If such parts are not too seriously worn, they can be restored by grinding with equipment made for the purpose. If they are worn enough to be through the case-hardened shell, they should be discarded and replaced with new parts.

When checking valve lifters, it is essential that the surface contacted by the cam, Fig. 15-43, be examined for wear. Fig. 15-44 shows a lifter with normal wear, and others with varying degrees of wear. One method of checking the cam for wear is stated at Fig. 15-43.

PUSH RODS

The push rods on an overhead valve engine are a critical link between the lifters and the rocker arms. If the push rod should become warped or bent, the valve will not open sufficiently. This will cause a loss of power or performance.

To check for warping, place the push rod in a holding fixture. While watching the dial indicator, rotate the push rod, Fig. 15-45. If the dial indicator moves more than .001 in., the push rod will have to be replaced. Make sure to check all push rods, one at a time. Another method for checking push rods is to roll them on a piece of glass. The technician will be able to detect visibly if there is any distortion as the push rods are rolling.

VALVE TAPPET ADJUSTMENT

Adjustment of the tappet clearance is made by means of a feeler gauge as shown in Fig. 15-46, or with the aid of a special dial gauge as shown in Fig. 15-47. In these cases, the adjustment is readily accessible on an overhead valve engine. The adjustments should be made after the engine has reached operating temperatures. The valves must be adjusted properly, as the adjustment compensates for slightly worn valve train parts.

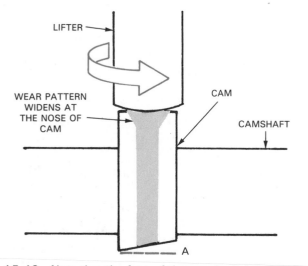

Fig. 15-43. Note that the face of the cam is slightly tapered from true horizontal which is indicated by line A. This taper combined with a crowned lifter bottom causes the lifter to spin in its bore. This prevents the lifter from premature wear. This same spinning action of the lifter is transmitted to the push rod. So, if the push rod is not spinning extremely fast, a new camshaft and new lifters are required.

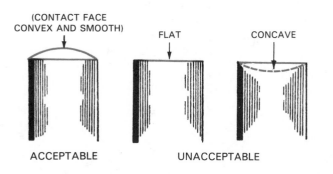

Fig. 15-44. If the bottom of the lifter is other than convex on any lifter, a new set of lifters and a camshaft are required. (Ford)

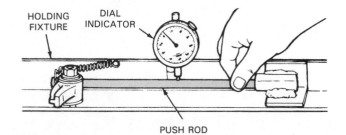

Fig. 15-45. If push rods are bent or warped, the individual push rods must be replaced. Never attempt to straighten a push rod. (Ford)

Fig. 15-46. Using a feeler gauge to adjust mechanical valve lifters. Hydraulic valve lifters do not need adjusting. If hydraulic valve lifters become noisy, they may need to be replaced.

144

Fig. 15-47. By loosening locknut, the adjusting screw can be tightened to quiet noisy valves. Adjustment compensates for wear in the valve train. Make sure engine is hot when adjusting valves, or there will be no clearance between rocker arm and valve tip when the engine reaches operating temperature. Make sure to tighten the locknut after the adjustment is made.

CAMSHAFTS

Some wear does occur on camshafts, as on any other engine part. Since the camshaft operates at slower speed than the crankshaft, wear usually is less pronounced. The cams and journals are hardened, so wear ordinarily occurs in the bushings rather than on the shaft journals. However, because of the weight of push rods, rocker arms, stronger valve springs, and today's higher engine speeds, the load on the cams is greater. Consequently, there is an increased tendency toward wear.

The lift of the cam is the difference in measurements, AA and BB, Fig. 15-48. The amount of wear is then obtained by comparison with specified lift. Cam lift also can be measured by mounting a dial gauge on the cylinder head with its button contacting the upper end of the valve push rod. Then, as the engine is slowly cranked, the distance from the lowest point to the highest will be the lift of the cam, Fig. 15-49.

It is important to measure the lift of all cams in the engine to determine if any are worn, since the cams do not all wear at the same rate.

Worn cams occasionally are the cause of lost power or misfiring, which is often overlooked when troubleshooting. If a check on valve lift shows that it is less than it should be, the cams can be reground on special machinery. In most cases, however, the camshaft is replaced, Fig. 15-50.

CAMSHAFT BEARINGS

Some camshafts bear directly in the metal of the crankcase, but most run in bearings in the form of bronze bushings pressed into the crankcase. These bushings are not adjustable for wear and must be replaced when

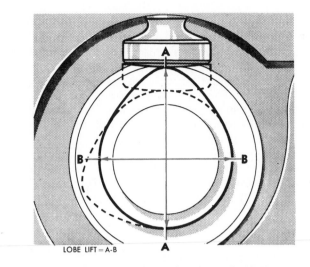

LOBE LIFT = A-B

Fig. 15-48. Difference between line A and line B is the amount of lift.

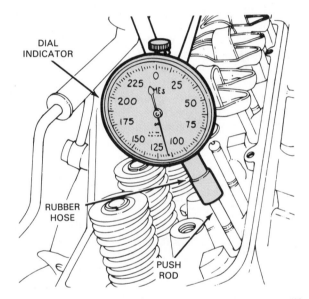

Fig. 15-49. Using a dial gauge to measure cam lift.

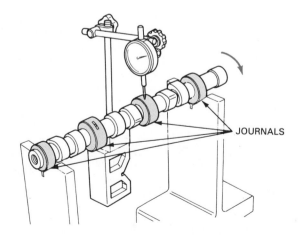

Fig. 15-50. Each journal of the camshaft should also be checked for runout. If runout exceeds .0015 in. on any journal, replace the camshaft. (Nissan)

worn. The degree of wear dictating replacement is more a matter of oil clearance than any tendency toward noise. However, if seriously worn, they may create noise and vibration in the timing gears and valve train.

The camshaft must be removed to replace the camshaft bearings. This involves removal of the valve operating mechanism. It is seldom necessary to replace a camshaft bearing or bearings until the engine is dismantled for other work.

After the camshaft is removed, the bearings are pressed out of their bores with a special tool made for the purpose. However, this special tool will also be needed for inserting the new bushings, Fig. 15-51.

New bushings are available in the proper outside diameter and standard, as well as undersize, inside diameter. If the camshaft has been undersized by regrinding worn journals, the bearings can be align reamed to any size desired by use of the proper equipment, Fig. 15-52.

It is essential to start the bushing squarely in the bore and apply pressure steadily and evenly. If the bushing cocks in the bore, it will be distorted and the inside diameter decreased. The bushings should be pushed fully into the bore. If one end extends, the valve lifter may strike it. It is good policy to check the installation after the valve operating parts are installed to make sure there is sufficient clearance for the lifters. Also, end-play of the camshaft should be checked and corrected if it exceeds the manufacturers' specifications (usually about the same as for crankshafts).

Usually the camshaft is provided with a thrust plate.

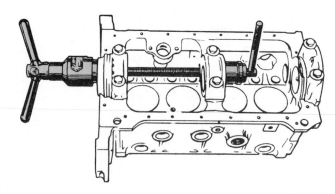

Fig. 15-51. A special tool is needed to remove and install camshaft bushings.

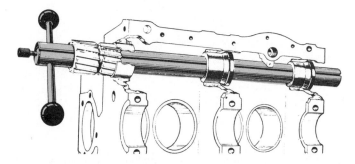

Fig. 15-52. A special tool is used to align bore the camshaft bushings.

This holds the camshaft against a flange to eliminate excessive end-wise movement. The thrust plate must be replaced if end-play is excessive.

Chapter 15—REVIEW QUESTIONS

Write your answers on a separate piece of paper. Do not write in this book.

1. A valve should be discarded if the stem is bent more than:
   a. .002 in.
   b. .004 in.
   c. .006 in.
2. A valve interference angle should be cut on the:
   a. Combustion chamber side.
   b. Port side.
   c. Both sides.
3. A narrow valve seat will dissipate the heat better than a wide one. True or False?
4. The valve seat should be concentric with the guide within:
   a. .001 in.
   b. .002 in.
   c. .003 in.
5. Valve seat inserts are not used in cast iron cylinder blocks or heads. True or False?
6. Describe an interference fit for a valve seat insert.
7. Name two ways of shrinking inserts.
8. Heat dissipation is better when valve guides are not used. True or False?
9. Leaking intake valve guides:
   a. Cause excessive oil consumption.
   b. Upset carburetor adjustment.
   c. Both.
10. Valve stem seals are placed:
    a. In the valve stem.
    b. In the valve guide.
    c. Either.
11. Valve stem to guide clearance should not exceed:
    a. .003-.004 in.
    b. .004-.005 in.
    c. .005-.006 in.
    d. .006-.007 in.
12. Why must valve springs be square on each end?
13. What causes valve stem and valve spring etching?
14. Mechanic A states that the purpose of an interference valve angle is to chip carbon off of the valve face.
    Mechanic B states that the purpose of a valve rotator is to lengthen valve life.
    Who is right?
    a. Mechanic A.
    b. Mechanic B.
    c. Neither Mechanic A nor B.
    d. Both Mechanics A and B.
15. Worn camshaft bearings will cause a valve to open early. True or False?
16. Mechanic A states that valve rotators are used on all valves.
    Mechanic B states that valve rotators are used only on engines that burn unleaded fuel.
    Who is right?
    a. Mechanic A.

b. Mechanic B.
c. Both Mechanics A and B.
d. Neither Mechanic A nor B.

17. Mechanic A states that the rocker arm action causes valve guides to wear in a bellmouth shape. Mechanic B states that the positive valve seal re- mains stationary as the valve moves up and down. Who is right?
a. Mechanic A.
b. Mechanic B.
c. Both Mechanics A and B.
d. Neither Mechanic A nor B.

Chapter 16

ENGINE LUBRICATION

After studying this chapter, you will be able to:
- Explain how a lubricating system operates.
- State the purpose of lubrication.
- List the properties of engine oil.
- Select the proper engine oil.

OIL

Without the aid of friction, an automobile could not move itself. Excessive friction in the engine, however, would mean rapid destruction. We cannot eliminate internal friction, but we can reduce it to a controllable degree by the use of friction reducing lubricants, Fig. 16-1.

These lubricants are usually made from the same crude oil from which we obtain gasoline. The petroleum oils are compounded with animal fats, vegetable oils, and other ingredients to produce satisfactory oils and greases for automotive use. Lubricating oils and greases are also manufactured from silicones and other materials and have no petroleum products in them.

Lubricating oil in an automobile engine has several tasks to perform:
1. Lubricates the moving parts.
2. Seals between piston ring and cylinder wall.
3. Cools as it carries the heat away from engine parts.
4. Carries contamination away from moving parts.

Furthermore, the engine oil must function whether the temperature is below 0°F or above 200°F. This is contrary to the nature of petroleum products since they tend to thicken at low temperatures and thin out at high temperatures. The oil must go through many processes during manufacture to reduce this tendency to change viscosity with changes in temperature.

PROPERTIES OF ENGINE OIL

Engine oil is available in different viscosities. VISCOSITY is considered to be the internal friction of a fluid. An oil of low viscosity will flow more easily than an oil of high viscosity. Sometimes a low viscosity oil is referred to as a light oil and a high viscosity oil as a heavy oil.

Oils of different viscosities have been assigned numbers by the Society of Automotive Engineers. The lower the viscosity, the lower the assigned number. SAE 10 engine oil, for example, is recommended for cold weather operation and SAE 30 for warm weather. The SAE number of an oil has nothing to do with its quality.

SELECTING VISCOSITIES

There are single viscosity and variable or multi viscosity oils. The single viscosity oils are commonly referred to as a straight weight. Straight weights are used in areas where the temperature is consistent. Variable or multi viscosity oils are used in areas where there are seasonal changes, or extreme temperature difference between the morning and the afternoon. See Fig. 16-2. Examples of a single viscosity oil: SAE 10, SAE 20, SAE 30. Ex-

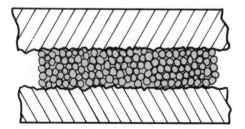

Fig. 16-1. Oil molecules roll over one another to reduce friction. This action is similar to ball bearings.

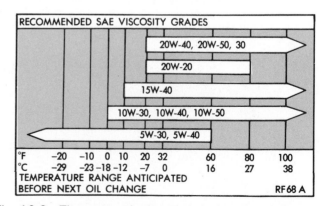

Fig. 16-2. The atmospheric temperature determines the viscosity of oil selected. (Chrysler)

amples of a variable or multi viscosity oil: 5W-20, 10W-30, 10W-40, 20W-50. A low numerical viscosity is needed in cold weather, or the engine will have difficulty in turning over due to the resistance of the thick oil. A high numerical viscosity oil is needed in hot weather, or the oil will thin out and not provide enough protection for the engine components.

The "W" in a 10W-40 oil, for example, means that a viscosity of 10 was obtained when tested at 0 °F. The "W" stands for winter grade. The absence of the "W" after the 40 designates that a viscosity of 40 was obtained when tested at 210 °F.

SELECTING QUALITY

Oil containers carry a logo on their tops, Fig. 16-3. This provides the consumer or technician with the proper data of the type of oil in the container. With this information the right type of oil can be obtained for the type of weather and the specific engine application.

Several groups are responsible for testing the quality of oil. One is the American Society for Testing Materials (ASTM). The American Petroleum Institute (API) and the Society of Autmotive Engineers (SAE) also test oils. However, the API is the only group listed for testing the quality, and the SAE is the only group listed for testing the viscosity. Together, these groups have established the ratings for the quality of oil. They are as follows.
GASOLINE ENGINES:
SA — For engines operating under mild conditions. No special protection capabilities (mineral oil).
SB — For light-duty engine operation. Has anti-scuff capabilities, resists oil oxidation, retards bearing corrosion.
SC — Minimum requirements for all 1964 to 1967 passenter cars and light trucks. Controls high and low temperature deposits. Retards rust and corrosion in gasoline engines.
SD — For 1968 and later engines warranty service. Better high and low temperature deposit control than SC. Also rust/corrosion resistant.
SE — For 1972 and later gasoline engine warranty maintenance service. It provides maximum protection against rust, corrosion, wear, oil oxidation, and high temperature deposits that can cause oil thickening.
SF — For gasoline engines in passenger cars and some trucks beginning with 1980 model operating under engine manufacturers' recommended maintenance procedures.

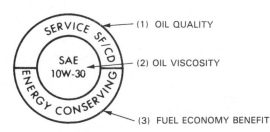

(1) OIL QUALITY
(2) OIL VISCOSITY
(3) FUEL ECONOMY BENEFIT

SERVICE SF/CD
SAE 10W-30
ENERGY CONSERVING

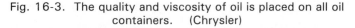

Fig. 16-3. The quality and viscosity of oil is placed on all oil containers. (Chrysler)

SG — This designation is for 1987 and newer car models.
DIESEL ENGINES:
CA — For light-duty normally aspirated diesel engines. Provides protection against high temperature deposits and bearing corrosion.
CB — For moderate-duty, normally aspirated diesel engines operating on high sulphur fuel. Protects against bearing corrosion and high temperature deposits.
CC — For moderate-duty, lightly supercharged diesel engines and certain heavy-duty gasoline engines. Protects against rust, corrosion, and high/low temperature deposits.
CD — For severe-duty supercharged diesel engines using fuels of a wide quality range. Provides highly effective control of corrosion and deposits.
CE — For supercharged, heavy duty diesel engines made since 1983.

If the proper quality of oil is not selected, the owner will experience premature engine failure.

ADDITIVES

The requirements of today's automobile engines are far beyond the range of straight mineral oils. All automobile manufacturers now recommend oils which have been improved by additives. The need for improved oil results from higher engine compression, increased speeds, greater sensitivity to deposit formation, corrosion, and rusting.

There are many different additives in use today. Probably the first one to be used was a POUR POINT DEPRESSANT. At low temperatures, the wax in the oil would crystallize, then form a sort of "honey comb" which in turn would block the flow of oil to the oil pump. Pour point depressants prevent this.

DETERGENT-DISPERSANT additives are used to prevent sludge and varnish deposits, which otherwise would restrict the free flow of oil and cause valves and lifters to stick.

FOAM INHIBITORS are designed to prevent the formation of foam, which would result from the egg beater action of the rotating engine parts. Unless the foaming is stopped, bearings and other parts would receive only foam instead of oil and would soon fail.

OXIDATION INHIBITORS are used to reduce the possibility of oil being oxidized. This oxidation usually occurs at higher operating temperatures attained during sustained high speed, full throttle operation. Series oxidation of the oil results in deposit formation and will occur unless oxidation is prevented.

VISCOSITY INDEX IMPROVERS, as the words imply, improve the viscosity index. The viscosity index is a measure of the rate of change or variation in the viscosity of a liquid with changing temperature.

A high viscosity index indicates a relatively low rate of viscosity change at two different temperatures. A low index indicates a high rate of viscosity change. Oils designed for automotive engine use have a relatively high viscosity index and are suitable for use in both high and low atmospheric temperatures.

CORROSION AND RUST INHIBITORS are designed to

help the detergent-dispersant additives in the prevention of rust and corrosion.

ANTIWEAR ADDITIVES, one of the most important used, have the ability to coat metal surfaces with a strong and slippery film that prevents direct metal-to-metal contact. All modern, top-quality oils contain this additive.

All of these additives combine to produce an oil which not only will withstand heavier loads, reduce corrosion, stop foaming, maintain viscosity, stop sludge, and varnish formation, but will also keep the interior of the engine cleaner and increase its useful life.

Furthermore, many of the additives in the engine oil become depleted due to the heat from the engine and are no longer effective. Unless the oil is changed, wear is accelerated.

OIL CHANGES

When to change oil is a difficult question to answer. Much depends on the conditions under which the vehicle is being operated. Most manufacturers have two recommendations. One is for normal driving and the other for severe conditions.

Severe conditions are described as: short trip driving during which the engine does not reach operating temperature for an appreciable time; towing another vehicle; excessive idling conditions; or driving in dusty areas. Since most cars are operated in cities or towns with a population of 25,000 or greater, it is evident that the cars are used mostly in short trips with much time spent idling. Therefore, most cars are operated under ''severe'' conditions.

Normal driving may be described as cars that are driven on individual trips of 10 miles or more. Also, they do not pull a trailer, and operate in an atmosphere that is relatively free of dust.

Car manufacturers' oil change recommendations show a big difference for vehicles used for normal driving and for those being operated under severe conditions. One manufacturer, for example, recommends that the oil and oil filter should be changed: each 3000 miles or three months under severe conditions; each 7500 miles or once a year under normal driving conditions; turbocharged engines each 3000 miles under all conditions. However, oil change intervals are subject to frequent change, so always consult manufacturers' specifications.

Oil in the crankcase, while performing its many functions of protecting the engine from wear and corrosion, becomes loaded with acids, dirt, and abrasives. Not all of these can be trapped by filters. So, there is only one way of removing this wear-producing contaminant and that is by changing oil. Nondetergent oils and low quality oils are not recommended. Use SF or SG oils and make the prescribed oil filter changes.

OIL FILTERS

Oil filters are placed in the engine oil system to remove dirt and abrasives from the oil. Dilutents, such as gasoline and acids, are not removed. However, by removing the solid materials, the possibility of acids forming is reduced, and the rate of wear of engine parts is greatly reduced.

Oil filters installed on modern passenger car engines are full-flow type; all oil passes through the filter before it reaches the bearings. However, in the event the filter becomes clogged or obstructed, a bypass valve is provided so that oil will continue to reach the bearings. The filters in use today are of the ''throw-away'' type. See Figs. 16-4 through 16-7.

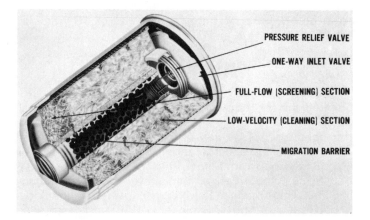

Fig. 16-4. Cartridge type, full flow oil filter. The filter is thrown away and a new one installed at prescribed intervals.

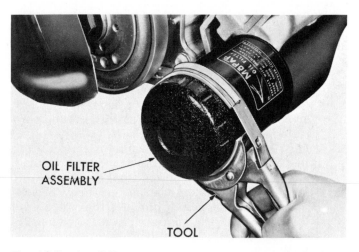

Fig. 16-5. An oil filter wrench is needed to remove the oil filter.

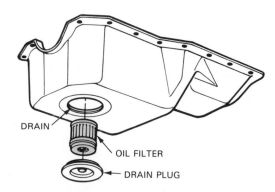

Fig. 16-6. The oil filter on some newer G.M. engines is located inside the oil pan.

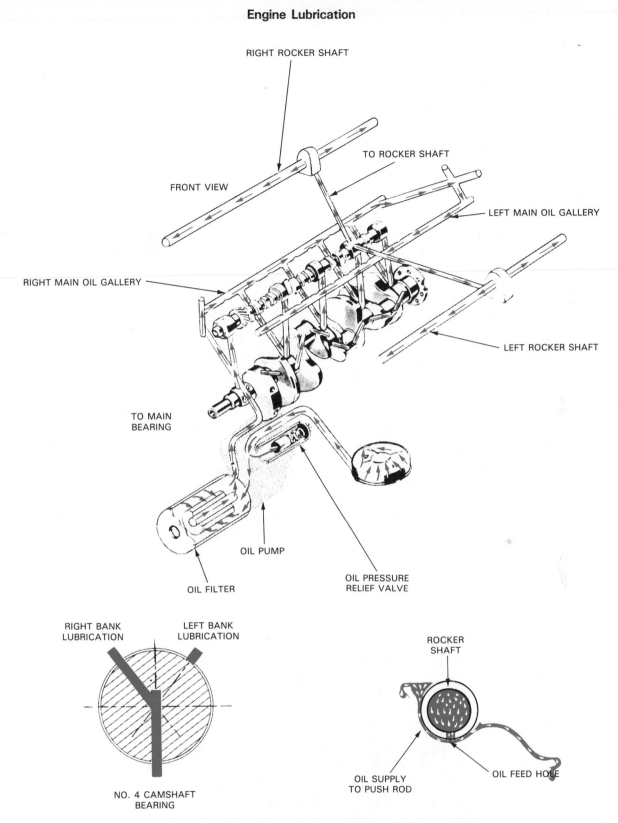

RIGHT ROCKER SHAFT

TO ROCKER SHAFT

FRONT VIEW

LEFT MAIN OIL GALLERY

RIGHT MAIN OIL GALLERY

LEFT ROCKER SHAFT

TO MAIN BEARING

OIL PUMP

OIL FILTER

OIL PRESSURE RELIEF VALVE

RIGHT BANK LUBRICATION

LEFT BANK LUBRICATION

ROCKER SHAFT

NO. 4 CAMSHAFT BEARING

OIL SUPPLY TO PUSH ROD

OIL FEED HOLE

Fig. 16-7. Oil is filtered before delivery through the various passages.

LUBRICATING METHODS

Oil is supplied to moving parts of the engine by pump pressure, splashing, or a combination of both. Splashed oil usually becomes a mist for lubricating parts such as cylinder walls and pistons.

Oil is fed to the majority of engine parts under pressure, especially to main bearings and connecting rod bearings. Leakage or "throw-off" from the rod bearings splashes on other moving parts inside the engine. A typical pressure lubrication system is shown in Figs. 16-8 and 16-9.

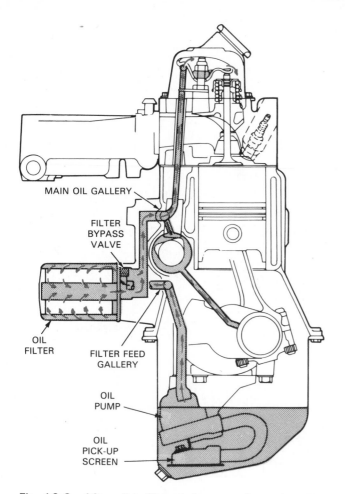

MAIN OIL GALLERY

FILTER BYPASS VALVE

OIL FILTER

FILTER FEED GALLERY

OIL PUMP

OIL PICK-UP SCREEN

Fig. 16-8. After oil is filtered, it enters the main gallery. (Oldsmobile)

PRESSURE SYSTEMS

Figs. 16-8 and 16-9 show the oil pump located in the sump of the oil pan. The oil enters the pump through a screen. Quite often the intake screen is mounted so that it stays on top of or in the middle of the oil in the sump, Fig. 16-8. The idea is to keep the pump intake away from any dirt that might settle in the bottom of the sump.

Figs. 16-8 and 16-9 show the path of the oil from the pump to the oil gallery or distributing tube in the crankcase. The oil is conducted to the main bearings through drilled passages in the crankcase. Passages are also drilled in the crankshaft to carry the oil from the main bearings to the connecting rod journals. The path of the oil to the overhead valve rocker shaft is shown in Figs. 16-8 and 16-9. Some connecting rods have oil passages drilled lengthwise to carry oil to the piston pins, Fig. 16-10. The connecting rods in some engines also have a spurt hole drilled in them on one side. A squirt of oil shoots out on the cylinder wall when the hole aligns with the oil passage in the crankshaft. See Fig. 16-11.

Mercedes, in its turbocharged five cylinder diesel engine, cools the pistons by shooting a stream of oil upward into a collecting hole that carries the lubricating oil into a cooling gallery. See Fig. 16-12. Valves in jets are provided in the Mercedes diesel to shut off the jets of oil when the engine is idling in order to maintain oil pressure when piston cooling is not needed.

OIL PUMPS

The pumps used to circulate the oil are of the positive displacement type in several designs. Vanes, plungers, rotors, and gears are all used to build up the necessary

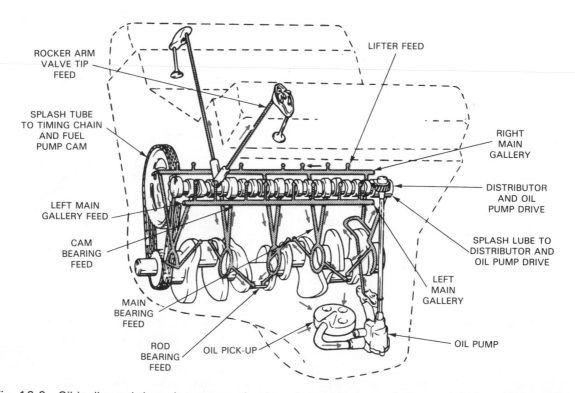

ROCKER ARM VALVE TIP FEED

LIFTER FEED

SPLASH TUBE TO TIMING CHAIN AND FUEL PUMP CAM

RIGHT MAIN GALLERY

LEFT MAIN GALLERY FEED

DISTRIBUTOR AND OIL PUMP DRIVE

CAM BEARING FEED

SPLASH LUBE TO DISTRIBUTOR AND OIL PUMP DRIVE

MAIN BEARING FEED

LEFT MAIN GALLERY

ROD BEARING FEED

OIL PICK-UP

OIL PUMP

Fig. 16-9. Oil is directed through passages that have been drilled out of the crankshaft. (Oldsmobile)

pressure. A rotor and a gear pump are illustrated in Fig. 16-13. These pumps are always positively driven, usually from the camshaft by means of gears.

Since these pumps handle oil, they are well lubricated at all times and do not suffer from excessive wear. They do, in time, develop an excess of clearance and require replacement of parts. The gear teeth or vane contours, as well as the gear ends and housings, may wear. When excessive wear does occur, the oil pressure will drop.

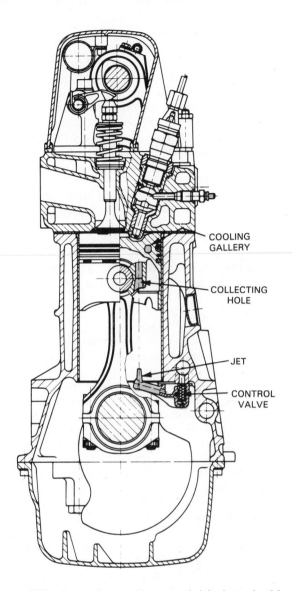

Fig. 16-12. Oil is directed upwards to cool the piston in this Mercedes diesel engine.

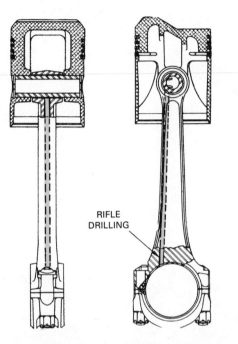

Fig. 16-10. Left. Oil passage is drilled lengthwise through connecting rod. Right. Oil passage provides lubrication to the piston pin.

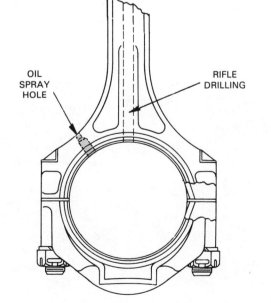

Fig. 16-11. Oil spray hole directs a squirt of oil to the cylinder walls.

Fig. 16-13. Oil pumps are of the rotor or gear type.

OIL PRESSURE

Most cases of lost oil pressure are due to excessive clearance in the bearings of the engine rather than worn oil pumps. If the oil pump is in good condition, the pressure relief valve will regulate the pressure of the oil within limits. However, it will not increase the capacity of the oil pump. The regulator is a simple spring-loaded valve which RELIEVES EXCESS PRESSURE in the circulating system by bypassing the excess oil back to the sump. See Fig. 16-14.

Another reason for lack of oil pressure is stoppage in the oil pump supply line or screen. This prevents oil reaching the pump in sufficient volume to maintain pressure. A typical case of "sludge" accumulation in a screen is shown in Fig. 16-15. This sludge stops up the oil passages, with the result that a bearing may "starve" for oil, then friction will melt the metal.

OIL SLUDGE

SLUDGE is a mayonnaise-like mixture of water, oil, and other products of combustion. It is most likely to form in an engine that seldom reaches a satisfactory operating temperature. For example: a light truck used for postal delivery service in cold weather. Such a vehicle ordinarily runs a short distance at slow speed, stops, and then runs another short distance at slow speed.

Slow speed, stop-and-go operation means that the engine seldom gets hot enough to evaporate the water in the crankcase. The water condenses on the cold walls of the crankcase, or in some cases gets into the crankcase through leaking cylinder head gaskets. This water emulsifies with the oil, carbon, dirt, etc., to form sludge. See Fig. 16-16.

Sludge formation can be held to a minimum by using the correct cooling system thermostat to maintain a high engine operating temperature. Using engine oils of high detergency and making frequent changes of oil and filter are necessary. Adequate crankcase ventilation is also important.

Researchers have found that when the cooling system thermostat was removed from the engine water jacket outlet, temperatures barely exceeded 100 °F when the ambient temperature was 60° to 70 °F. The engine operated at approximately 30 °F above the ambient temperature, resulting in sludge build up.

Water jacket outlet temperature usually corresponds to the setting of the cooling system thermostat. It must be emphasized that oil dilution and sludge formation decrease with 195 °F thermostat as compared to thermostats having a lower opening temperature. Not only is sludge reduced, but production of hydrocarbons and carbon monoxide in the exhaust are also reduced.

Equally important to keeping sludge formation to a minimum is proper crankcase ventilation. Adequate crankcase oil temperature must be maintained to assist in evaporation and purging of volatile blowby contaminants. Oil temperatures are usually only a problem under conditions involving excessive idling or operation in severely cold weather.

Fuel is a major factor in the formation of sludge. Modern oils with their additives help to control the con-

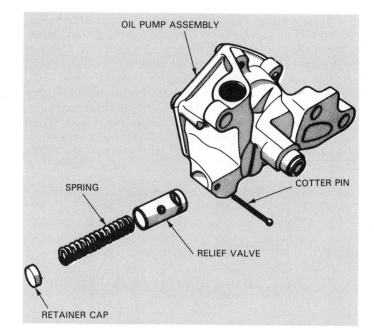

Fig. 16-14. Oil pressure relief valve. If the relief valve sticks in the closed position, the oil filter will burst. If the pressure relief valve sticks in the open position, oil pressure will never develop. (Chrysler)

Fig. 16-15. Left. An accumulation of sludge on this oil pick-up screen will stop the flow of oil. This will cause the engine to seize. Right. An oil pick-up screen in good condition.

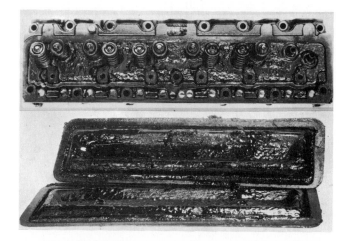

Fig. 16-16. An accumulation of sludge on cylinder head and valve covers.

dition by keeping sludge and other foreign materials in suspension.

POSITIVE CRANKCASE VENTILATION (PCV)

Since venting "blowby" gases into the atmosphere has been illegal since 1968, another method of crankcase venting has been implemented. This method is called POSITIVE CRANKCASE VENTILATION, which is commonly referred to as the PCV system, Fig. 16-17. Blowby is the exhaust gas that works its way past the piston rings and into the crankcase. Blowby mixed with the oil in the crankcase contributes in forming sludge. In the PCV system, blowby gases are forced out of the crankcase, Fig. 16-17, and into the combustion chamber where they are reburned. This prevents sludge from forming in the engine and reduces emissions into the atmosphere simultaneously.

ENGINE VARNISH

Another type of engine deposit is known as VARNISH. Varnish is formed when an engine is worked hard enough to run hot for extended periods of time. The heat causes the oil to break down. Some of the elements separate out and deposit a varnish-like substance on the metal parts inside the engine.

To avoid such deposits, it is necessary to use the best oil obtainable and change the oil regularly. It is also essential to make sure that the cooling system is functioning efficiently.

The importance of regular and frequent oil changes has been emphasized. It is more economical to throw away a quart of oil costing a few cents than to take a chance of damaging an engine worth several hundred dollars.

Chapter 16—REVIEW QUESTIONS

Write your answers on a separate sheet of paper. Do not write in this book.

1. Name four tasks that the lubricating oil in an engine is expected to perform.
2. An SAE 10 oil can be used anywhere that SAE 10-W can be used. True or False?
3. Is a light oil always better than a heavier oil? Yes or No?

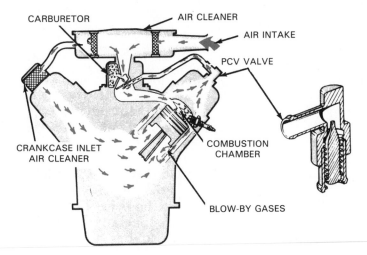

Fig. 16-17. PCV system forces fresh air into the crankcase. Blowby is then forced into intake manifold. PCV valve regulates the amount of blowby that enters intake manifold in relation to engine load.   (Chrysler)

4. What is meant by "oil throw-off?"
5. Oil passages are drilled in the:
   a. Engine block.
   b. Crankshaft.
   c. Connecting rods.
   d. All of the above.
   e. None of the above.
6. Oil pumps are sometimes belt driven. True or False?
7. What is the most frequent cause of low oil pressure?
8. Name three things found in oil sludge.
9. Sludge and varnish are not the same thing. True or False?
10. All engine oils recommended by the automobile manufacturers have been improved by additives. Name three.
11. Slow speed driving is always desirable in order to maintain the best engine lubrication. Yes or No?
12. How does engine oil become diluted?
13. Oil classification SA is for engines operating under mild conditions. True or False?
14. Oil classification _____ is for severe-duty supercharged diesel engines.

Chapter 17

ENGINE COOLING SYSTEMS

After studying this chapter, you will be able to:
- List components of the cooling system.
- Explain how the cooling system operates.
- Describe how the components of the cooling system operate.

COOLING

A cooling system of some kind is necessary in any internal combustion engine. If no cooling system were provided, parts would melt from the heat of the burning fuel, and pistons would expand so much they would seize (could not move in the cylinders).

The pressurized cooling system of a water-cooled engine, Figs. 17-1 and 17-2, consists of the engine water jacket, thermostat, water pump, radiator, radiator cap, fan, fan drive belt, and necessary hoses. It must be designed to operate at temperatures ranging up to the boiling point of the coolant under pressure, which in the case of ethylene glycol antifreeze may exceed 250°F.

As fuel is burned in the engine, about one-third of the heat energy in the fuel is converted into power. Another third goes out the exhaust pipe unused, and the remaining third must be handled by the cooling system. This third is often under-estimated and even less understood.

Perhaps it will be helpful to describe it in readily understood terms rather than by reference to so many Btus (British thermal units). The heat removed by the cooling system of an automobile at normal speed is sufficient to keep a six-room house warm in 0°F weather.

This means that several thousand gallons of water must be circulated in the cooling system every hour to absorb the heat and carry it to the radiator for disposal. It also means that many thousands of cubic feet of air must flow through the radiator every hour in order to dissipate the heat to the air.

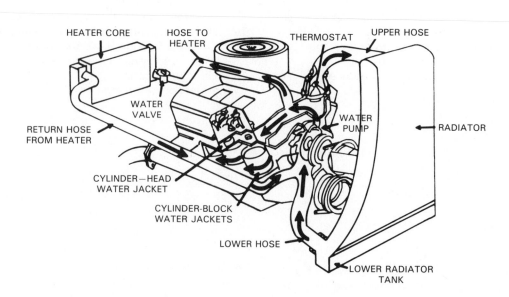

Fig. 17-1. The coolant leaves the radiator through the lower radiator hose. The hot coolant enters the radiator, after circulating through the engine, through the upper radiator hose. The heat that was picked-up is dissipated to the air flowing through radiator fins. This cycle continually repeats. (Everco)

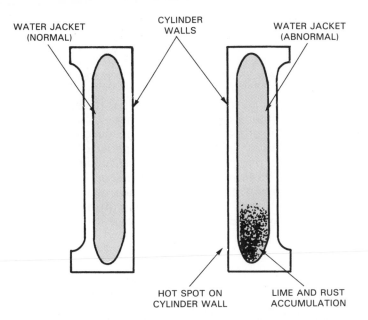

WATER JACKET (NORMAL)   CYLINDER WALLS   WATER JACKET (ABNORMAL)

HOT SPOT ON CYLINDER WALL   LIME AND RUST ACCUMULATION

Fig. 17-2. The cooling system transfers heat from the combustion chamber to the coolant that circulates through the water jackets in the engine block. If an accumulation of rust and/or lime develop in the water jackets, heat from cylinder cannot be transferred to coolant. This creates a "hot spot" within the cylinder. (Perfect Circle)

Considering these cooling factors, it is important at this time to distinguish between HEAT TRANSFER and HEAT DISSIPATION. The heat generated by the mixture burned in the engine must be transferred from the iron or aluminum cylinder to the water in the water jacket. The outside of the water jacket dissipates some of the heat to the air surrounding it, but most of the heat is carried by the cooling water to the radiator for dissipation to the surrounding air. See Fig. 17-1.

HEAT TRANSFER

In an automotive engine, heat flows or transfers from the iron or aluminum cylinder to the cooling water, and from the coolant to the copper or aluminum radiator. Iron, aluminum, copper, and water are all good conductors of heat. If they are in contact with one another, the heat will flow readily from one to another.

If, however, there is a coating of lime or rust between the water and the bare metal, the flow will be retarded since lime and rust are poor heat conductors. There is a great amount of surface within the water circulation system on which this lime and rust can accumulate. Lime is a white deposit formed by the heating of the water. As the water heats up, the lime separates from the water. When the water cools down, the white, powdery lime deposit is left on the metal surfaces which in this case are the water jackets, Fig. 17-2.

An engine is liable to have rust in the cooling system at any time. Rust is a combination of iron, water, and oxygen. We have iron in the engine, water in the engine, and some oxygen in the water. Additional oxygen enters by way of the air that finds its way into the cooling system.

This accumulation of rust and lime combines with a small amount of grease or oil, which often acts as a binder, and soon a coat of insulation forms on the inside surface of the water jacket. Grease or oil gets into the cooling system from water pump lubricant, leaking cylinder head gaskets, etc.

Scale deposits also collect in corners or pockets of the water jacket where the water circulation is sluggish. This often causes HOT SPOTS which, in turn, distort cylinders and valve seats. This type of overheating can and does occur without any indication of overheating on the temperature gauge. The gauge is located at one spot in the water jacket, and the overheating condition is localized in another spot.

The scale that collects in corners and narrow passages is also a deposit point for bits of rubber from the inside of hoses, and other foreign matter that finds it way into the cooling system. The result is a mass of insulating sludge and scale which does considerable harm to the engine. These accumulations can be avoided by proper maintenance of the cooling system, the year-round use of ethylene glycol solutions, and periodic flushing of the cooling system.

WATER PUMPS

Automobile engine water pumps are of many designs, but most are the centrifugal type. They consist of a rotating impeller. Sometimes the fan is installed on the water pump shaft, Fig. 17-3.

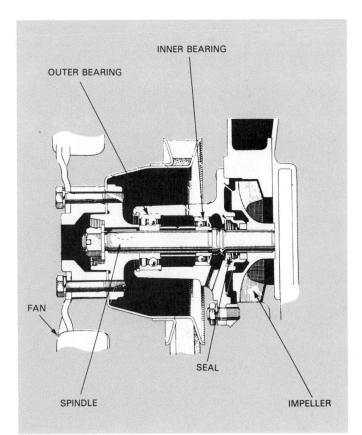

INNER BEARING

OUTER BEARING

FAN

SPINDLE   SEAL   IMPELLER

Fig. 17-3. Nomenclature of a water pump.

An exploded view of a typical water pump assembly with all parts in proper relation to each other is shown in Fig. 17-4. These vanes should not touch the housing. But, at the same time, they should not have excessive clearance. For this reason, excessive endwise motion (end play) of the shaft to which the vane is attached is not permissible.

Impeller type water pumps must turn rapidly to be ef-

Fig. 17-4. The impellers of the water pump force the coolant through the engine block. (Everco)

ficient. Worn or loose belts will permit slippage, Fig. 17-5, which is not readily detected. It is particularly difficult to detect a worn V-belt fan pulley. If the pulley is suspected, the groove can be compared with a new pulley for wear. Also, alignment of the pulley should be checked.

Many water pumps have a spring-loaded seal to avoid leakage of water around the pump shaft. Modern pumps are fitted with prepacked ball bearings, which are sealed at each end to eliminate the need for periodic lubrication.

While most pumps run on sealed ball bearings and the shaft is sealed from the housing, they do occasionally require attention. Sand and grit in the water will wear the impeller blades and pump housing. Also, the sealing surfaces may be scored enough to leak air if not water.

BELTS

The V-belt drives the various accessories by a wedging action in the pulley groove. There are two different types of V-belt design, Fig. 17-6. The banded design is older and shows wear as it ages. The newer bandless d does not show wear as it ages, so it is extremely i tant to change this type of belt periodically, eve belt appears not worn.

SERPENTINE BELTS

The serpentine drive belt is a combination of a V-ribbed belt and a flat back belt, Fig. 17-7. The serpentine belt must be installed properly on the pulley grooves, Fig. 17-8. The purpose of the serpentine belt is to eliminate the number of belts needed to drive the accessories.

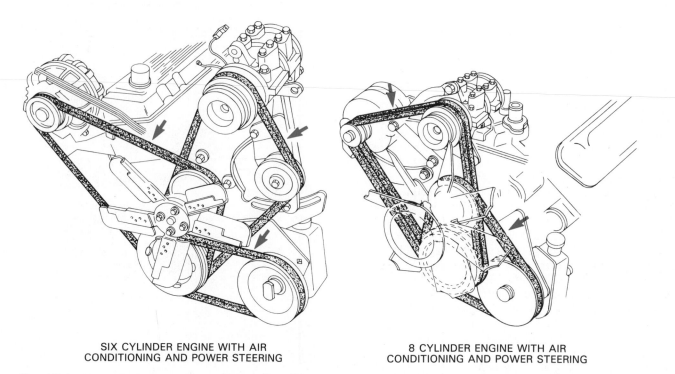

SIX CYLINDER ENGINE WITH AIR
CONDITIONING AND POWER STEERING

8 CYLINDER ENGINE WITH AIR
CONDITIONING AND POWER STEERING

Fig. 17-5. Press the belts at arrows. If the belt deflects more than 1/2'', the belt needs to be tightened. However, the belt must have some free play, or the bearings of the alternator, power steering pump, and water pump will burn out and need replacement. (Chrysler)

With the serpentine belt only one belt is needed. However, if this one belt breaks, all accessories will not operate. This is why it is important to check for wear periodically, Fig. 17-9. Most manufacturers have an automatic tensioning device, Fig. 17-10, when they use a serpentine belt. This eliminates periodic adjustment of the serpentine belt. When the serpentine belt is used, a diagram indicating the routing of the belt is placed in the engine compartment, Fig. 17-11.

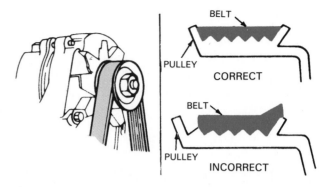

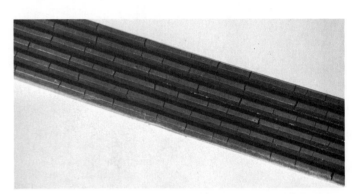

Fig. 17-8. The correct installation of a V-ribbed belt is shown at the top. (Ford)

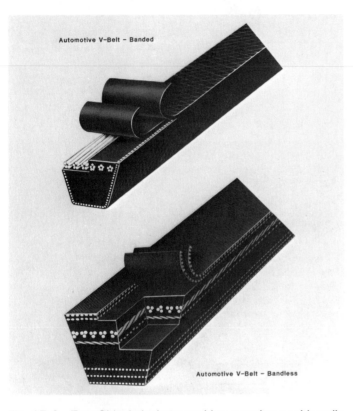

Fig. 17-6. Top. Older belts have a rubber covering on sidewalls to serve as wear indicator. Bottom. Modern belts are bandless, so there is no wear indicator. (Gates Rubber)

Fig. 17-7. The serpentine drive belt is a V-ribbed belt. This combines the traditional V-belt, which drives by a wedging action, and a flat back belt that uses friction to drive the various components. Both sides transmit power on a serpentine drive. (Gates Rubber)

Fig. 17-9. Cracks indicating wear on a V-ribbed belt. (Gates Rubber)

Fig. 17-10. Automatic spring idler provides the proper tension and eliminates periodic adjustment of the belt. (Gates Rubber)

159

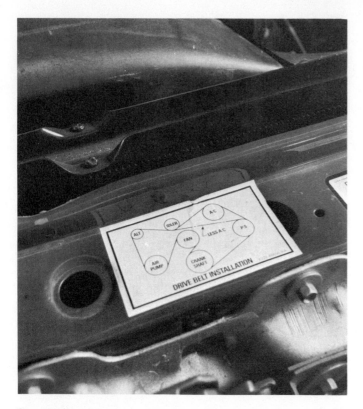

Fig. 17-11. Decal in engine compartment provides routing instructions for replacement of V-ribbed belt on a serpentine drive.   (Gates Rubber)

Fig. 17-12. Various types of hose clamps. From left: twin wire; screw tower; spring or corbin clamp; worm drive clamp.   (Gates Rubber Co.)

Fig. 17-13. Check all hoses their entire length. If there are any soft or hard and brittle spots, the hose will have to be replaced. (Gates Rubber)

HOSES AND CLAMPS

Radiator hoses connect the radiator and engine. These hoses are fastened with hose clamps, Fig. 17-12. The hoses should be inspected at every oil change to prevent problems from arising while traveling. Check the entire length of ALL coolant carrying hoses for either soft or hard and brittle spots, Fig. 17-13. If either condition is found, the hose must be replaced.

Sometimes the simple removal of a radiator hose becomes difficult. Do not attempt to remove the hose by twisting it off with a pair of water pump pliers, as this will destroy the outlet. Instead, use a sharp knife and make an incision on the hose, Fig. 17-14.

LOWER RADIATOR HOSE

The lower radiator hose connects the water pump to the radiator. As the pump turns, it creates a suction. The atmospheric pressure on the coolant forces it to the low pressure area at the water pump. To prevent the lower hose from collapsing, due to the suction, a spring is placed inside the hose.

RADIATORS

The radiator is a device designed to DISSIPATE the heat which the coolant has absorbed from the engine. It is constructed to hold a large amount of water in tubes or passages which provide a large area in contact with the atmosphere.

Fig. 17-14. A sharp knife should be used to cut the radiator hose off if the hose is stuck on the outlet.   (Gates Rubber)

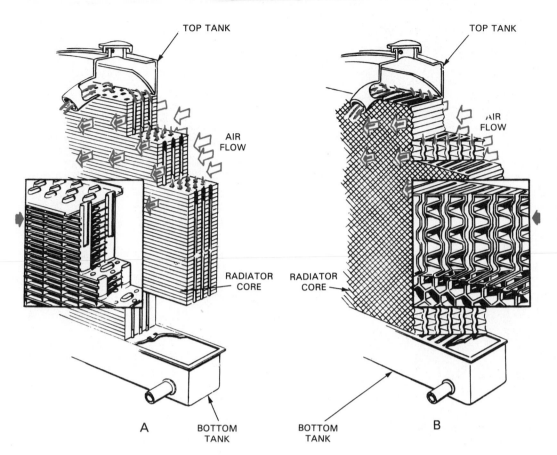

Fig. 17-15. Radiator construction. A—Typical tube type radiator. B—Cellular type radiator.

Construction usually consists of the radiator core, with its water-carrying tubes and large cooling area, which are connected to a receiving tank at the top and to a dispensing tank at the bottom, Fig. 17-15.

Radiator cores are of two basic types, the fin and tube type, Fig. 17-15A, and the ribbon cellular or honeycomb type, Fig. 17-15B.

The popular fin and tube type of radiator core has the advantage of fewer soldered joints and is therefore a stronger construction. It consists of a series of parallel tubes extending from the upper to the lower tank.

Fins are placed around the tubes to increase the area for radiating the heat.

The honeycomb type core consists of a large number of narrow water passages made by soldering pairs of thin metal ribbons together along their edges. These tubes are crimped and the soldered edges form the front and rear of the vertical tubes. These tubes are separated by fins of metal ribbon which help dissipate the heat.

In operation, water is pumped from the engine to the top (receiving) tank where it spreads over the tops of the tubes. As the water passes down through the tubes, it loses its heat to the airstream which passes around the outside of the tubes.

To help spread the heated water over the top of all the tubes, a baffle plate is often placed in the upper tank, directly under the inlet hose from the engine.

While the usual construction of a radiator is to have the water circulate from the top to the bottom, crossflow radiators are designed to have the coolant flow from one side to the other, Fig. 17-16. It is claimed there is more efficient fan coverage of the radiator core with this design.

The core capacity of modern radiators is much smaller than in the past for the same size engine. This is possible because systems now operate at pressures ranging up to 17 psi. Pressurization makes the engine more efficient in terms of heat rejection to the coolant per horsepower developed.

Smaller radiators also are the result of improved heat transfer efficiency of the radiator core. For example: the 1954 Chevrolet 235 cu. in. six cylinder engine developed 115 hp, and had a radiator core capacity of 816 cu. in. Now, the Chevrolet 230 cu. in. six delivers 150 hp, and has a radiator core capacity of 406 cu. in.

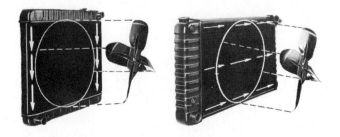

Fig. 17-16. Flow of coolant can be from top to bottom, or from side to side. Side flow radiator allows a lower hood line for better aerodynamic styling.

161

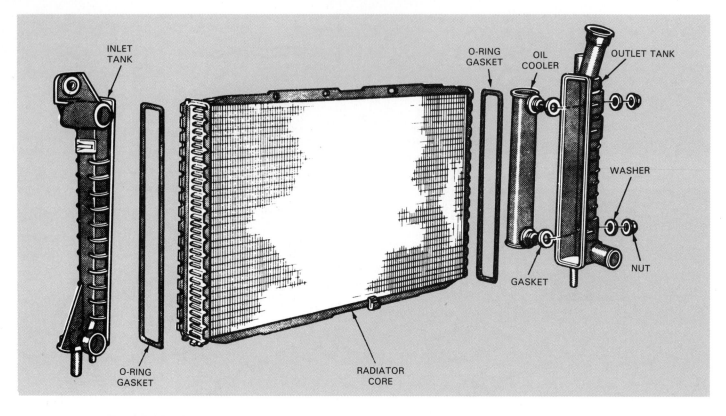

Fig. 17-17. Automatic transmission oil cooler is located in the radiator outlet tank.   (Ford)

AUTOMATIC TRANSMISSION COOLER

On cars that have automatic transmissions, an oil cooler is incorporated into the design of the radiator, Fig. 17-17. This keeps the automatic transmission fluid at a low temperature, which prevents oxidation of the transmission fluid. This not only increases the life of the transmission fluid, but the transmission components as well. If the seams of the oil cooler should leak transmission fluid into the radiator, both the coolant and the automatic transmission fluid will turn into a thick, pink mixture. If this situation occurs, the radiator will have to be removed and the oil cooler repaired. In addition, the cooling system will have to be flushed out, along with the automatic transmission, torque converter, and oil cooler lines.

CLOSED SYSTEM

Most cooling systems today are a CLOSED SYSTEM. This system connects a plastic tank to the radiator through a rubber tube, Fig. 17-18. As the coolant becomes hot and expands, the coolant flows out of the radiator and into this plastic tank or reservoir. This saves coolant from spilling out on the ground. Then as the radiator tank cools, a vacuum is created forcing the coolant from the plastic reservoir back into the radiator, if needed. This brings the radiator to a specified level. Coolant should be added to this plastic tank when necessary.

RADIATOR CAPS

Originally, the radiator cap served only to prevent the coolant from splashing out the filler opening. Today's radiator cap, Fig. 17-19, is designed to seal the system so that it operates under 14 to 17 psi. This improves cooling efficiency and prevents evaporation of the coolant. Losses due to surging are also eliminated.

Since evaporation is reduced or eliminated, it is not necessary to add coolant as often. Consequently, the introduction of rust-forming materials is greatly reduced. Also by operating at higher temperatures, the engine operates more efficiently, as does the car heater.

The higher temperatures result from the higher pressure. Each psi placed on the coolant increases the boiling point about 3.25 °F. Since current radiator caps maintain a pressure of about 15 psi, the boiling point would be raised to 272 °F.

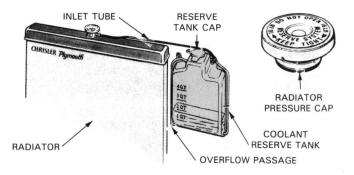

Fig. 17-18. If radiator level is low, coolant is siphoned from the reserve tank as the radiator cools.

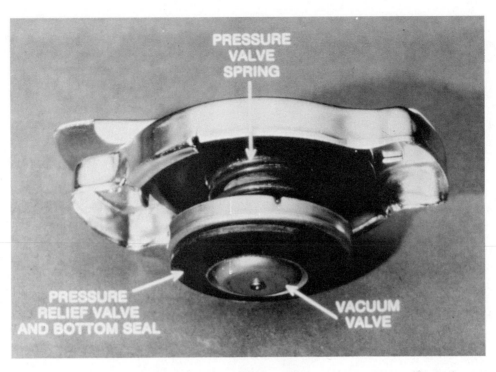

Fig. 17-19. Nomenclature of a modern radiator pressure cap. (Everco)

The pressure cap fits over the radiator filler opening and seals it tightly. Two spring-loaded valves are provided. The larger valve is designed to relieve pressure at a predetermined value. The smaller valve opens to relieve the vacuum that forms when the steam in the system condenses after the engine is stopped, Fig. 17-20. Otherwise, atmospheric pressure (14.7 psi) on the large, flat surface of the upper tank would cause it to buckle and open the seams.

If you must remove a pressure cap soon after the engine is stopped, PROCEED SLOWLY. Use a large, heavy cloth or a special hand guard to turn the cap counterclockwise to the first stop to let the steam escape. Wait awhile, then cautiously remove the cap. Temperature rises rapidly the first few minutes after the engine is stopped, causing coolant to boil.

COOLING FANS

The fan is designed to draw cooling air through the radiator core, Fig. 17-1. This is necessary at slow speeds or when the engine is idling, since there is not enough air motion under those conditions to provide adequate cooling.

So that none of the force of the fan is dissipated, shrouding is often provided. In that way, the full force of the fan is used to draw air through the radiator core.

The fan is usually mounted on an extension of the water pump shaft, Fig. 17-3, and is driven by a V-belt from a pulley mounted on the front end of the crankshaft. Others are driven by an electric motor, Fig. 17-21. Front wheel drive cars use an electric fan motor. It is mounted to a frame, which is connected to the radiator.

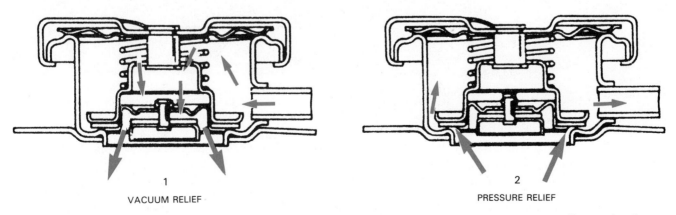

VACUUM RELIEF   **PRESSURE RELIEF**

Fig. 17-20. 1—Vacuum relief valve is lowered allowing atmospheric pressure into radiator to prevent collapse of radiator. 2—Excess pressure in cooling system is vented to atmosphere or reserve tank as pressure relief valve is raised off its seat. (Oldsmobile)

Fig. 17-21. Transversely mounted engine. A—It is impossible for engine to drive a fan on a front wheel drive car. B—Fan switch on radiator allows current to computer or fan relay after coolant has reached operating temperature. Relay or computer then energizes fan motor. C—If fan fails to operate after engine has reached operating temperature, remove electrical connection from fan switch. Then, jump connections from electrical connector and turn the ignition to the ON position. If fan now operates, the fan switch on radiator is defective. D—If fan still fails to operate, disconnect fan motor electrical connection and insert test light as shown. If test light fails to glow, the wiring, relay, or computer is defective. However, if test light should glow, the fan motor is defective.   (Chrysler)

In order to reduce the noise made by the rotating fan, the fan blades are often placed asymmetrically, and with the tips bent and rounded, Fig. 17-22.

At 3000 rpm, an 18 in. fan will consume over 2 hp, and power requirements increase very rapidly with the speed. Since the fan is required primarily at idling and low vehicle speeds, couplings have been devised to disconnect or reduce the speed of the fan above certain engine speeds.

The fan drive clutch is a fluid coupling containing silicone oil. The more silicone oil in the coupling, the greater the speed. In one construction, Figs. 17-23 and 17-24, a bimetallic coil on the front of the fluid coupling regulates the amount of silicone oil entering the coupling. This allows a valve to regulate the flow of oil to and from the reservoir.

THERMOSTATS

Automotive internal combustion engines operate more efficiently when a high temperature is maintained within narrow limits. To attain this objective, a thermostat is inserted in the cooling system. In operation, the thermostat is designed to close off the flow of water from the engine to radiator until the engine has reached the desired operating temperature.

The thermostat is operated by a wax pellet, Fig. 17-25, which expands and contracts with changes in engine temperature to open and close the valve.

Fig. 17-22. A flexible fan blade flattens out as rpms increase. This reduces the amount of drag on the engine, as the fan is not needed at high rpms to draw air through the radiator. (Everco)

Fig. 17-24. A fluid coupling mounted to fan.　(Everco)

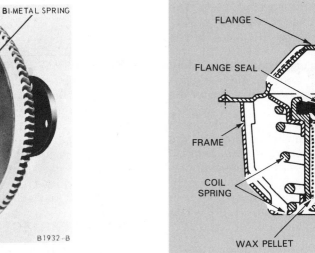

Fig. 17-23. The bimetal spring is sensitive to heat and controls the flow of silicone oil to fluid coupling, which governs fan speed.

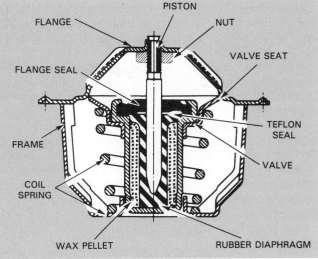

Fig. 17-25. Nomenclature of a modern engine thermostat. (Cadillac)

When the water is cold, the thermostat closes the valve and stops the flow of water to the radiator. Then, as the water becomes hotter, the wax pellet expands to open the valve and allows the water to reach the radiator, Fig. 17-26.

The opening and closing of the thermostatically controlled valve continues as more or less heat is developed by the engine so that its operating temperature is maintained within narrow limits.

Thermostats are calibrated at the time of manufacture, when they are stamped with the temperature at which they are designed to open. A thermostat designed for use with an alcohol type antifreeze usually is calibrated to open at 155° to 160°F (68.3° to 71.1°C), and be fully open at 180°F (82.2°C). Most modern cooling systems are designed to use permanent type antifreeze, and the thermostats are calibrated to open between 188° and 195°F (86.7° and 90.6°C), and be fully open between 210° and 212°F (98.9° and 100°C).

HEATER

The basic hot water heater core used in automobiles is constructed in the same manner as the radiator. In operation, hot water from the cooling system is circulated through it. The heater fan drives air past the hot heater core tubes and through ducts to the passenger compartment, Fig. 17-27. Therefore, it is important to keep the heater water passages free from rust accumulations. When flushing the system, make sure any valves in the line going to the heater are open.

The air which passes through the heater is usually supplied from outside the vehicle through openings provided in the top or sides of the cowl. The motion of the car, aided by the action of the fan, forces fresh air through the heater. Vent air valves operated by Bowden wire controls serve to control the amount of air passing through the heater and into the passenger compartment. Warm air from the heater is also directed to clear the inside of the windshield.

ANTIFREEZE SOLUTIONS

When water freezes, it expands approximately nine percent in volume. Because of this great rate of expansion, it will break or seriously distort the shape of the vessel in which it is contained. Because of this characteristic, it is necessary to use a nonfreezing solution in the cooling system of water-cooled engines operated in climates where the temperature is below the freezing point of water.

The first type of antifreeze that was ever used was alcohol. However, when summer rolled around, the alcohol was flushed from the system. It was replaced entirely with water. This is because of the fast evaporation rate of alcohol when exposed to heat, which is incurred during summer. Pure water also has a higher boiling point than alcohol. When fall came again, the water was flushed from the cooling system and replaced with alcohol.

Today, antifreeze is of the permanent type. This means that the solution of antifreeze and water that makes up engine coolant does not have to be changed at the end

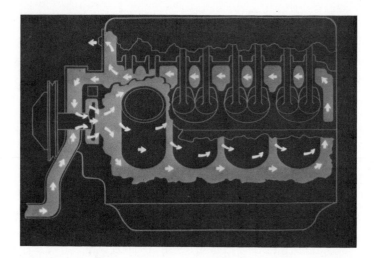

Fig. 17-26. When engine is cold, coolant circulates through engine block only. When engine temperature rises, thermostat opens and coolant flows through upper radiator hose to radiator. (Everco)

Fig. 17-27. A heater core is basically a mini-radiator located within the passenger compartment. (Everco)

of each season. However, engine coolant must be changed at least every two years. This is because the heat from the engine destroys the additives found in the antifreeze. These additives must be replenished, or rust will develop in the cooling system.

Since copper, iron, aluminum, brass, solder, etc. are used in parts of the engine in contact with the coolant, it is important that the antifreeze does not corrode any of these metals. Also, the material should not be harmful to the various types of rubber used in the connecting hoses. The most suitable is ethylene glycol.

FREEZING PROTECTION

The mixing of an antifreeze with water forms a solution that has a lower freezing point than water. The temperature at which an antifreeze will freeze depends on the strength of the solution, Fig. 17-28. This varies with each antifreeze, Fig. 17-29. Pure ethyl alcohol freezes at −174.6 °F; methyl alcohol at −144.2 °F; while, a 68 percent solution of ethylene glycol freezes at −92 °F. Increased concentrations would not further reduce the freezing point of the solution.

EXPANSION OF ANTIFREEZE

Antifreeze solutions will expand slightly more than water when heated, Fig. 17-30. When water is heated from 40 °F to 180 °F, it will expand approximately 1/4 pint per gallon. For the same range of temperature, ethylene glycol will expand 1/3 pint per gallon, methyl alcohol 2/5 pint per gallon and ethyl alcohol 1/2 pint per gallon.

To avoid loss of antifreeze due to expansion, the cooling system must not be completely filled. In the case of a 20 quart capacity cooling system completely filled at −20 °F, there would be a loss of 2 1/3 pints of ethylene glycol; 2 7/8 pints of methyl alcohol; or 3 2/3 pints of ethyl alcohol when the temperature goes up to 180 °F.

BOILING POINT

When ethylene glycol is added to water, the boiling point of the solution is raised. When either methyl alcohol or ethyl alcohol is added to water, the boiling point of the solution is lowered. For example, methyl and ethyl alcohol solutions affording protection to −20 °F will have boiling points of about 180 °F. A solution of ethylene glycol has a boiling point of 223° that is protected to −20 °F. As the pressure that is placed on the coolant is increased, the temperature at which the solution boils is increased, Fig. 17-31.

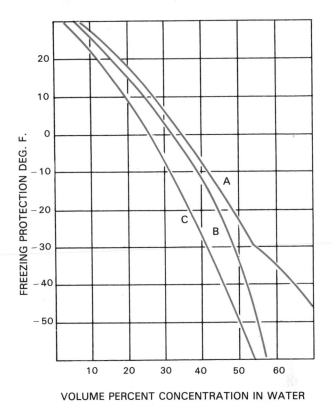

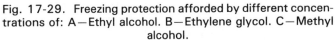

Fig. 17-29. Freezing protection afforded by different concentrations of: A—Ethyl alcohol. B—Ethylene glycol. C—Methyl alcohol.

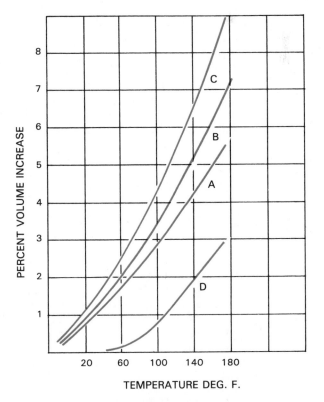

Fig. 17-30. Expansion of antifreeze solutions from −20 °F to 180 °F: A—Ethylene glycol. B—Methyl alcohol. C—Ethyl alcohol. D—Water.

Fig. 17-28. Checking the engine coolant with hydrometer. Coolant should test to at least −20° F. (Everco)

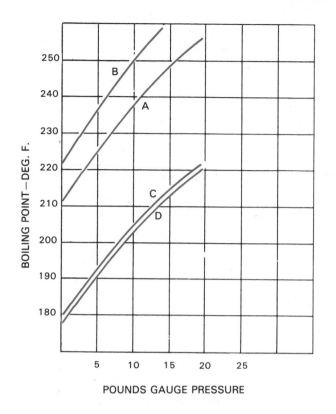

Fig. 17-31. Chart shows effects of pressure on boiling points of various antifreeze solutions. A—Water. B—Ethylene glycol. C—Ethyl alcohol. D—Methyl alcohol.

The normal boiling point of a coolant solution is important, and so is the change in boiling point brought about by placing the solution under pressure. With pressurized cooling systems used today, a coolant with a higher boiling point than water is necessary. Ethylene glycol fills these requirements, and is installed as original equipment in all vehicles built in the United States.

The higher boiling point of ethylene glycol makes it a highly satisfactory coolant for use in warm weather as well as cold. In addition to its higher boiling point, glycol is provided with a rust inhibitor.

Car manufacturers advise against the use of water as a coolant. If it is used, boiling can result, particularly in hot weather, when towing another vehicle, or when the air conditioner is in use.

EVAPORATION

There is virtually no loss of ethylene glycol solution due to evaporation. Any loss of coolant solution that does occur is practically all water. This evaporation loss is greatest under prolonged high speed driving conditions or extended idling periods in heavy traffic. Alcohol based antifreeze solutions have a greater rate of evaporation, so they are sledom used.

RUST INHIBITORS

In order to reduce the formation of rust, commercial antifreeze contains an inhibitor designed to prevent corrosion. Some products also contain antifoaming agents.

The prevention of rust is essential if the cooling system is to be maintained at maximum efficiency. After the cooling system is drained, a rust inhibitor should be added if clear water is used as a coolant. Year-round use of antifreeze is a more practaical answer.

AIR-COOLED ENGINES

Air-cooled engines were used successfully in the early days of the automobile. Today's best example of an air-cooled engine is Volkswagen's "flat four."

Air cooling of a reciprocating piston engine requires constant circulation of a lot of air. Forced air circulation is provided by a fan of generous capacity which is usually driven from the engine crankshaft by a belt, or by fan blades formed in the flywheel, Fig. 17-32.

Radiation fins are provided on the cylinders and cylinder heads, Fig. 17-33. In some aplications, the crankcase also is "finned," Fig. 17-34.

Air-cooled engines usually are surrounded by a metal housing and baffle plates to direct cooling air where desired.

When the engine is running, forced air is directed over and through the fins to dissipate the heat. In order to regulate the engine temperature by controlling the volume of cooling air, a thermostat is installed inside the metal housing which enclosed the engine. The thermostat unit is connected to control flaps, or an air control ring. As the engine becomes hotter the control ring opens wider to admit more air, and closes when the engine is cold. See Figs. 17-35 and 17-36.

With the ring closed, air circulation is restricted, and a cold engine warms up more rapidly. Rapid warm-up is characteristic of air-cooled engines, since they do not have to heat water in cylinder jackets and radiator. This rapid warm-up is helpful in avoiding sludge and crankcase dilution.

Fig. 17-32. Tecumseh air cooled engine. The fan blades are built into flywheel.

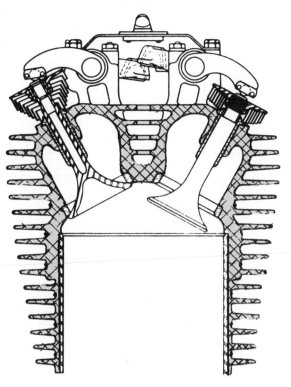

Fig. 17-33. Cooling fins on cylinder head are larger in diameter and heavier than those around cylinder.

Fig. 17-35. Air control ring moves in and out to control volume of air supplied to fan. (Volkswagen)

Fig. 17-34. This Teledyne Wisconsin engine is completely finned.

Fig. 17-36. Air control ring is regulated by cross shaft.

Air-cooled engines normally operate at somewhat higher temperatures than water-cooled engines, but do not overheat if the cooling system is maintained in reasonably good order.

However, air-cooled engines should never be "lugged," If the engine is pulling hard at slow speed,

more heat than usual is generated at the same time than less cooling air is supplied. In this case, there is no reservoir of water to absorb excess heat (as on a water-cooled engine). Therefore, engine speed should be maintained by shifting to a lower gear.

Higher engine operating temperatures mean higher engine efficiency, but this characteristic is also accused of causing noise. One reason given for air-cooled engines being noisier than water-cooled engines is that there is no silencing provided by water jackets. Another reason given is the somewhat greater clearances sometimes provided between operating parts. This relates to the fact that higher temperatures require more room for expansion of the metals.

Regardless of the advantages and disadvantages of air cooling, it has provided to be entirely successful for automobiles, trucks, tractors, airplanes, boats, and all kinds of small engines.

OIL COOLING

While it is unusual for passenger car engines to provide special cooling for the engine lubricating oil, many race car engines have cooling fins on the oil pan to reduce the temperature of the engine oil.

Fig. 17-37 shows a sectional view of an Offenhauser race engine provided with cooling fins on the lower cutside of the oil pan and on the sides of the crankcase. While this is a water-cooled engine, cooling fins are also provided on the exterior of the water jacket.

COOLING SYSTEM TROUBLESHOOTING

The most frequent cooling system complaints are leakage of coolant and overheating. Generally, the best troubleshooting approach is test and inspect, followed by the service or parts replacement required.

Since the system is pressurized, it is logical to test the radiator pressure cap for pressure-holding ability and to pressure-test the entire cooling system for coolant leakage. First, make sure the correct cap for the vehicle is installed on the radiator. The cap must seat properly on the filler neck of the radiator and seal the system so that it operates under 14 to 17 psi.

Next, remove the radiator pressure cap and clean it thoroughly. Check the valves and seating surfaces for damage. Wet the rubber seals with water and install the cap on a pressure tester designed for this purpose.

Operate the tester pump and observe the highest pressure gauge reading, Fig. 17-38. The release pressure should be within the manufacturer's specified limits (12 to 15 psi, for example). Allow the maximum pressure reading to remain on the gauge, and watch for a pressure drop. If the cap holds this pressure for 30 seconds or more, the cap is good. If the pressure drops quickly, a new radiator pressure cap is needed.

Pressure-test the cooling system with the engine at normal operating temperature:

1. Carefully remove radiator pressure cap and check coolant level (should be 1 to 1 1/2 in. below base of filler neck).
2. Test freeze protection level of coolant, using an anti-freeze hydrometer.
3. Wipe inside of filler neck and inspect inside sealing seat for damage.
4. Inspect overflow tube for dents, kinks, or obstruction.
5. Inspect cams on outside of filler neck. Reform cams, if bent.
6. Attach pressure tester to filler neck and operate tester pump to apply specified pressure to system.
7. Observe pressure gauge reading, Fig. 17-39. If system holds this pressure for two minutes, no coolant leakage is indicated. If the pressure drops

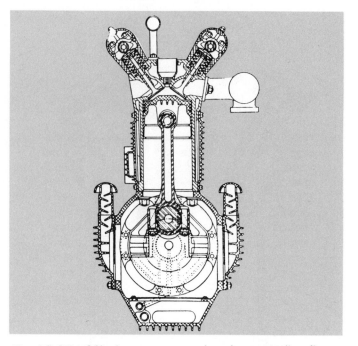

Fig. 17-37. Offenhauser race engine shows cooling fins on oil pan, water jackets around cylinder, and around crankcase.

Fig. 17-38. Testing a radiator pressure cap.　(AC-Delco)

quickly, examine entire cooling system for external coolant leakage. If pressure drops slowly, tighten all hose clamp connections and then retest the cooling system. If no leakage is apparent, check for internal coolant leakage.

TESTING FOR LEAKS

If frequent additions of coolant are required to maintain the proper level in the system, check all units and connections for leakage. Make the inspection when the

Fig. 17-39. Pressure testing the cooling system. Make sure engine is fully warmed up before testing. Pressure should hold for at least two minutes. (AC-Delco)

system is hot and operating. Tell-tale stains of grayish white, rust color, or dye stains from the antifreeze are sure signs of coolant leakage.

Exhaust gas or air trapped in the cooling system may cause the level of the coolant in the system to rise. Air may be drawn into the system through leakage at the seal in the water pump. Exhaust gas may be forced into the system as the result of a defective cylinder head gasket and a cracked or warped head. Extreme overheating can occur.

A piece of rubber tubing and a bottle of clear water can be used to check for air or gas leakage into the cooling system:

1. With cooling system cold, add coolant to bring coolant to proper level.
2. Install a conventional radiator cap (no pressure). Attach a length of rubber tubing to overflow pipe.
3. Operate engine at a safe high speed until it reaches operating temperature.
4. Maintain this speed and insert free end of rubber tubing into bottle of water. A continuous flow of bubbles indicates that air is being drawn into system from water pump seal or being forced into system from blown cylinder head gasket.
5. To determine whether defect is in the pump or head gasket, run a small amount of engine oil through carburetor throat or fuel injector throttle body. This will cause smokey bubbles to appear in the bottle if the gasket is defective.

REMOVING GYLCOL FROM CRANKCASE

If ethylene glycol leaks into the engine oil (milky substance on the oil dipstick), it will clog the oil lines, cause the pistons to seize, and result in severe damage to the engine. When it has been determined that ethylene glycol is in the lubricating system, the first step is to locate the cause of the coolant leak (a blown gasket, cracked head, or cracked block), then make the necessary repairs.

Next, remove the engine oil filter and drain the engine oil. Then, fill the crankcase to the full mark on the dipstick with a mixture of 3 qt. SAE 10W engine oil and 2 qt. of Butyl Cellusolve (can be obtained from a chemical supply house).

Run the engine at idling speed for about 30 minutes, paying particular attention to the oil pressure. Then, drain and flush with 3 qt. of SAE 10W oil and 2 qt. kerosene. Idle the engine with this flushing oil for about 10 minutes. Drain, install filter, and refill crankcase with correct weight and grade of engine oil.

LEAKAGE OF COOLANT

1. Faulty radiator pressure cap.
2. Defective radiator.
3. Bad thermostat housing gasket.
4. Cracked or deteriorated radiator hose.
5. Cracked or deteriorated heater hose.
6. Defective heater core.
7. Faulty heater water control valve.
8. Defective water pump seal or gasket.
9. Rusted out core hole plugs.
10. Damaged coolant reserve tank.
11. Bad cylinder head gasket.
12. Cracked cylinder head, manifold or block.

OVERHEATING

1. Faulty radiator pressure cap.
2. Defective thermostat.
3. Loose, slipping, or broken fan belt.
4. Worn pulleys.
5. Damaged fan.
6. Faulty fan drive clutch.
7. Collapsed lower radiator hose.
8. Obstructed front grille.
9. Clogged radiator fins.
10. Clogged A/C condenser fins.
11. Clogged radiator tubes. (See Fig. 17-40.)
12. Incorrect cooling system components installed.
13. Defective water pump.
14. Low coolant level.
15. Low coolant protection (low boiling point).
16. Water used as coolant (low boiling point).
17. Cooling system capacity inadequate for load being carried or towed.
18. Air trapped in cooling system.
19. Clogged coolant passage in engine block.
20. Excessive use of A/C while vehicle is parked or in stop and go traffic.
21. Retarded ignition timing.
22. Sticking manifold heat control valve.
23. Clogged exhaust system.
24. Low engine oil level.
25. Excessive engine friction.
26. Dragging brakes.

Fig. 17-40. To check if radiator is plugged and the cause of overheating, remove radiator cap after engine has reached operating temperature. Squeeze upper radiator hose after engine is placed on fast idle. If coolant spills out of radiator, it is plugged and must be rodded out. (Everco)

Fig. 17-41. To see if water pump bearings are worn, grip the fan blades 180 degrees apart. Exert an up and down motion on the fan blades. If there is any up and down movement of the fan blades, the water pump bearings are defective; replace the water pump.

LOW OPERATING TEMPERATURE

1. Wrong cooling fan.
2. Wrong radiator.
3. Wrong thermostat.
4. Defective thermostat.
5. Fan pulley too small.

NO COOLANT FLOW THROUGH HEATER CORE

1. Clogged water pump return pipe.
2. Collapsed or clogged heater hose.
3. Clogged heater core.
4. Plugged outlet in thermostat housing.
5. Obstructed heater bypass hole in cylinder head.

INOPERATIVE COOLANT RECOVERY SYSTEM

1. Faulty radiator pressure cap.
2. Coolant level below add mark.
3. Clogged or leaking overflow tube.
4. Plugged vent in recovery reservoir.
5. Pinched or kinked reservoir hose.

NOISE

1. Fan contacting shroud.
2. Loose water pump impeller.
3. Dry fan belt.
4. Loose fan belt.
5. Rough drive pulley.
6. Worn water pump bearing. (See Fig. 17-41.)

COOLING SYSTEM FLUSH

There are several methods for removing the old coolant from the cooling system. The method requiring no special tools is to remove the cylinder block drain plug(s), Fig. 17-42, and let water circulate through the engine while it is left running. Make sure that a garden hose is placed in the radiator while the coolant is circulating and draining.

Another method that is used by most repair facilities is called fast flushing. This method involves the use of a flushing "T" placed in line of the heater hose, Fig. 17-43. A special coupling is then used to connect a hose to the "T" and clear water is forced through the entire cooling system while the engine is left running, Fig. 17-43. Once clear water is flowing out of the radiator neck (radiator cap removed), the flush is complete.

If accumulations of lime and rust must be removed from the system, the engine and radiator must be reversed flushed, Fig. 17-44. This involves using a flushing gun that forces water through at high pressures. Compressed air is used to pressurize the water. In some rare instances when the reverse flushing fails to clean the deposits from the radiator, the radiator must be removed and rodded out by a radiator repair shop.

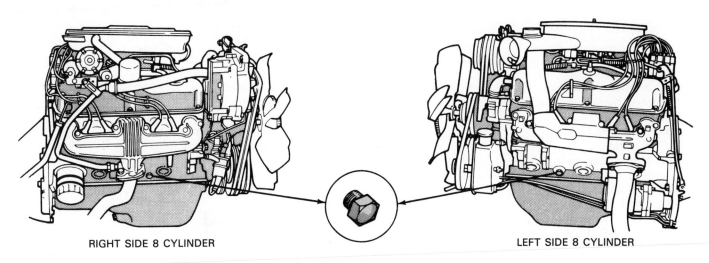

RIGHT SIDE 8 CYLINDER   LEFT SIDE 8 CYLINDER

Fig. 17-42. The cylinder block drain plug is located at the lowest point on the block.   (Chrysler)

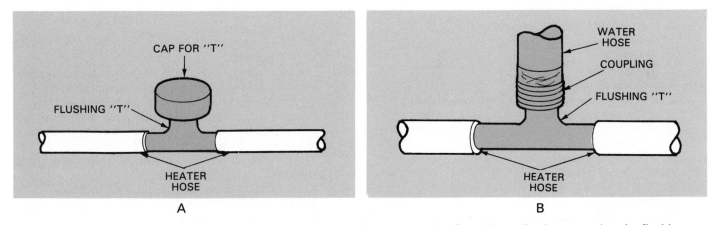

Fig. 17-43. Fast flush. A—The flushing "T" is inserted in the heater hose. B—Special coupling is screwed to the flushing "T", after removing the cap. Water hose is then screwed into the coupling and water is forced through cooling system.

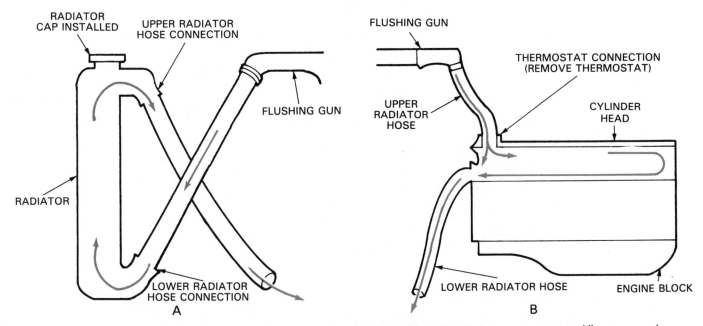

Fig. 17-44. Reverse flushing. A—Flushing gun uses water under high pressure to remove rust and lime accumulation from radiator. B—Flushing gun forces rust and lime accumulation from the engine block.

Chapter 17—REVIEW QUESTIONS

Write your answers on a separate sheet of paper. Do not write in this book.

1. How much of the heat energy in the fuel must be handled by the cooling system?
   a. One fourth.
   b. One third.
   c. One half.
2. What happens to the balance of the heat energy?
3. Several thousand gallons of water are circulated through the cooling system every hour of operation. True or False?
4. The water jackets dissipate most of the heat from the cylinders to the air. Yes or No?
5. What is rust?
6. Name two causes of engine hot spots.
7. Automobile engine water pumps are usually of the positive displacement type. Yes or No?
8. Antifreeze must be mixed with water. True or False?
9. A water pump seal may leak:
   a. Air?
   b. Water?
   c. Both?
10. Thermostats are installed:
    a. Between the pump inlet and the radiator.
    b. Between the pump outlet and the water jacket.
    c. Between the water jacket outlet and the radiator.
11. Where does the water from the engine usually enter the radiator?
    a. Top.
    b. Bottom.
12. When water freezes, it expands approximately:
    a. 4 percent.
    b. 6 percent.
    c. 9 percent.
13. Under pressure, does water boil at a higher or lower temperature?
    a. Higher.
    b. Lower.
14. Why is a vacuum valve needed in a radiator pressure cap?
15. In addition to providing greater capacity, what is the purpose of an auxiliary tank?
    a. Provides additional capacity.
    b. Acts as an expansion chamber.
    c. Connects engine to radiator.
16. Which protects against freezing to the lowest temperature?
    a. Ethylene glycol.
    b. Methyl alcohol.
    c. Ethyl alcohol.
17. An ethylene glycol solution will boil at a lower temperature than water. True or False?
18. In an air-cooled engine, how much of the total volume of cooling air is usually directed to the cylinder heads?
    a. 40 percent.
    b. 60 percent.
    c. 80 percent.
19. How can air-cooled engine with the cooling system in good working order become overheated?
20. What can be done to avoid such overheating?
21. Name two possible reasons why an air-cooled engine might make more noise than a comparable water-cooled engine.
22. What is one distinct advantage of an air-cooled engine?
23. A milky substance on the dipstick indicates:
    a. A normal condition.
    b. Engine overheating.
    c. Coolant has entered the crankcase.
    d. A loose water pump bearing.
    e. None of the above.

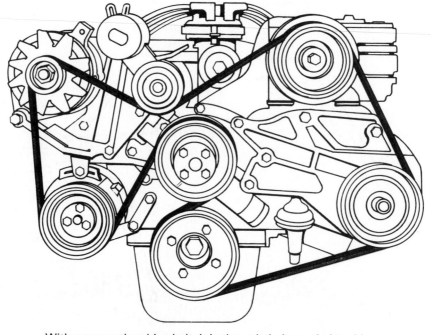

With a serpentine drive belt, it is the only belt needed to drive all accessories. (Gates Rubber Co.)

Chapter 18

DIESEL AND OTHER ENGINES

After studying this chapter, you will be able to:
- List the different types of engines.
- Explain how a diesel engine works.
- Describe how the Wankel engine operates.

DIESEL ENGINES

Diesel engines are similar to gasoline engines, Fig. 18-1. They are built in both two cycle and four cycle designs. They may be water cooled or air cooled. They are heavier in structure than gasoline engines to withstand the higher pressures resulting from the high compression ratios used. In a full diesel engine, the compression ratio may be as high as 22 to 1. What is known as a ''semi-diesel'' engine usually employs a somewhat lower compression ratio and may use spark plugs for ignition.

Previously, it was established that compressing a gas, such as air, generates heat. In the diesel engine, air is compressed so much that it becomes hot enough (1000°-1200°F) to ignite the fuel. The fuel, in this case, is a petroleum product which is lighter than crude oil, but heavier than gasoline. A gasoline-air fuel mixture cannot be used in a diesel because it would start to burn from the heat generated by the high compression long before the piston reached the top of the stroke.

The diesel has no carburetor. The air is compressed in the cylinder and, at the proper time, fuel that is under pressure is sprayed into the heated air. The air-fuel mixture then ignites and burns the same as in a gasoline engine to produce power. The entry of the fuel must be ''timed'' the same as a spark to the spark plug in a gasoline engine.

Fig. 18-1. This 6.2 liter diesel engine is found on some GM passenger cars and light trucks.   (Detroit Diesel Corp.)

TWO CYCLE DIESELS

As two cycle engines are not efficient as air pumps, it is necessary to force air into the cylinder and to force out the burned gas. One means of doing this is to use a supercharger or "blower." The GM two cycle diesel, Fig. 18-2, uses a positive displacement type supercharger, Fig. 18-3. There are two exhaust valves in each cylinder, and no intake valves. The fuel injection nozzle is located between the two exhaust valves. It is operated by a camshaft, push rod, and rocker arm.

Air enters the cylinder through holes in the cylinder liner as shown in Fig. 18-3. The blower forces fresh air into the cylinder through these holes during the time the holes are uncovered by the piston at the bottom of the stroke. At the same time, it forces the exhaust out through the exhaust valves.

Fig. 18-2. A two cycle diesel engine.

FUEL VAPORIZATION

As diesel fuel is more on the order of oil than gasoline, it does not vaporize as readily. This means that it must be broken up into fine particles and sprayed into the cylinder in the form of mist. This is accomplished by forcing the fuel through a nozzle or a series of very fine holes. As it enters the cylinder, the fuel combines more thoroughly with the air in the cylinder to form a combustible mixture.

DIESEL COMBUSTION CHAMBERS

A major difference in the design of the various diesel engines is the form or type of combustion chamber. There are four general types:
1. Open combustion chamber.
2. Precombustion chamber.
3. Turbulence chamber.
4. Energy cell.
Each design has certain advantages.

OPEN COMBUSTION CHAMBER: Probably the most common type of diesel combustion chamber is the open combustion design shown in Fig. 18-4. It is also known as the direct injection type. In addition to the form illustrated (known as the Mexican Hat type), there are many variations in the shape of the piston crown and cylinder head. Such variations range from the flat topped piston head through cylindrical forms made by a ridge around the edge of the piston.

However, the basic characteristic of the open combustion chamber is that the fuel is sprayed directly into the combustion chamber. The form of the combustion chamber, together with the manner in which the air enters and the direction of the fuel spray, are designed to give maximum turbulence and improved combustion. The turbulence is of maximum importance if complete combustion of fuel is to be obtained.

An important variation of the open combustion chamber is the M system, which has a special combustion chamber formed in the piston head, Fig. 18-5. The fuel is directed to the upper portion of the sphericall

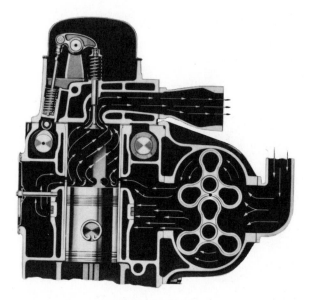

Fig. 18-3. A supercharger or blower forces air into the cylinders.

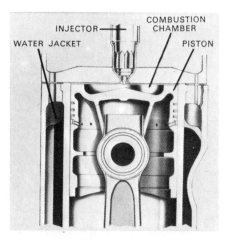

Fig. 18-4. Direct fuel injection is used in this open combustion chamber.

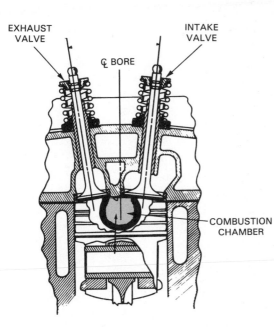

Fig. 18-5. M type combustion chamber.

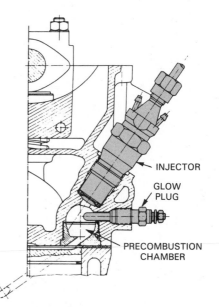

Fig. 18-6. A Volkswagen diesel engine shows the location of the injector and glow plug.

chamber. High turbulence is created by means of the directional intake port, the shape of the chamber, and the direction of the injected fuel.

Advantages claimed for the open combustion chamber include a high degree of efficiency, low manufacturing costs, and high turbulence. A special advantage of the M system is the ability to operate on a wide variety of fuels from gasoline to diesel fuel.

PRECOMBUSTION CHAMBER: A portion of the combustion chamber is contained in the space above the piston and is connected with a small passage. This design is known as a precombustion type, Fig. 18-6.

Thermal efficiency of the precombustion chamber engine is slightly lower than the open chamber type due to the greater heat loss from the larger combustion chamber area. The precombustion chamber contains approximately 30 percent of the total volume. However, cylinder pressure is lower and combustion smoother (particularly important when the engine is used in an automotive vehicle). Another important advantage is that the precombustion chamber engine is not as sensitive to the type of fuel used, and it is not necessary to provide such fine atomization.

TURBULENCE CHAMBER: In the turbulence chamber type of construction, up to 80 percent of the clearance volume is contained in the chamber, Fig. 18-7. The passage to the space over the piston is relatively large, and a high degree of turbulence is developed to provide a good mixture of air and fuel. Like the precombustion chamber engine, it is sensitive to the type of fuel provided. Cold weather starting without a glow plug is difficult.

ENERGY CELL: The energy cell (also known as the air cell) type of combustion chamber has the main combustion chamber located in the cylinder head and an antichamber placed on the opposite side of the combustion chamber from the injection nozzle, Fig. 18-8. This design is used primarily in high speed diesel engines with a cylinder bore less than 5 in.

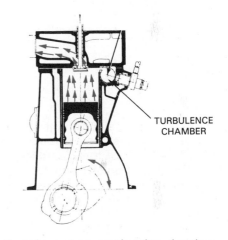

Fig. 18-7. Turbulence type combustion chamber. (Hercules Motor)

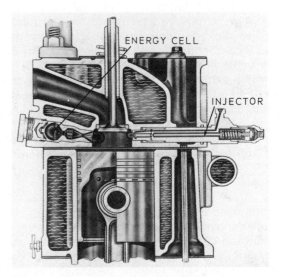

Fig. 18-8. Energy cell type combustion chamber.

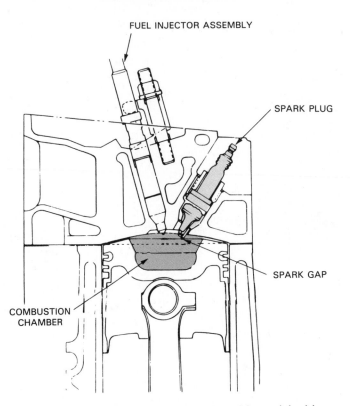

FUEL INJECTOR ASSEMBLY

SPARK PLUG

SPARK GAP

COMBUSTION CHAMBER

Fig. 18-9. Ford experimental diesel engine with spark ignition and open combustion chamber.

Performance compares to that of the open chamber diesel. High peak pressure and rough operation are controlled as the result of the controlled combustion.

FORD ENGINE: In an effort to develop an engine with a marked reduction in exhaust emission gases, Ford has been doing research on a diesel with spark ignition, Fig. 18-9. This engine combines diesel fuel injection and a compression ratio of 11 to 1.

The reduction in exhaust emissions has been achieved basically by using air throttling and exhaust gas recirculating. Nitric oxide formation is controlled within the engine as well as in the exhaust system. The nitric oxide formation is reduced by controlling peak cycle temperatures, exposure time at high temperatures, and availability of oxygen. Recirculation of exhaust gas also plays an important part in reducing nitric oxide by diluting the incoming air-fuel mixture.

Hydrogen oxide emission control is effected, primarily by injecting fuel late in the compression stroke with an overall air fuel ratio of 15.5 to 1. The significance of the air-fuel ratio is the fact that it provides sufficient oxygen for secondary oxidation without additional oxygen for the formation of nitric oxide formation.

TRUCK ENGINES

Engines used in light-duty trucks are very similar to automobile engines. There are some differences in design and operating conditions, but they are rather minor in nature. Actually, many light trucks use passenger car engines without any change whatever. Heavy-duty trucks usually have special engines.

Any changes that are made in a passenger car engine to adapt it to truck use are intended to compensate for the difference in operating conditions. For example, the engine in a truck will be required to move a heavier load, so the axle gearing will be such that the engine can run at higher speed for the same vehicle speed. The result may be that the truck at 60 mph will have a wide-open throttle. Therefore, the truck engine will be operating more of the time at full power.

Under these conditions, the exhaust valves will run hotter; need to be made of heat-resisting steel; and also require special valve seat inserts. The pistons and rings need slightly greater clearance for heat expansion, etc. The cooling system may require a larger water pump, larger radiator, or some increase in capacity. A different bearing material is used on the crankshaft to withstand the higher bearing loads, and an oil pan of larger capcity is usually installed.

Heavy-duty trucks usually have engines that are designed and built for truck use. They may be of either the two cycle or four cycle type, and may operate on gasoline or diesel oil. Such engines are customarily much heavier in construction than passenger car engines. See Fig. 18-10. Crankshafts are larger in diameter and the bearings are wider. Crankcases are heavier and braced with webs at points of strain. The piston displacement is increased and engine speed decreased for a given amount of power.

The GMC series 71 two cycle engine is shown in Fig. 18-11. The "71" is used extensively in automotive trucks. To reduce vibration, it is provided with a balance shaft driven by the camshaft.

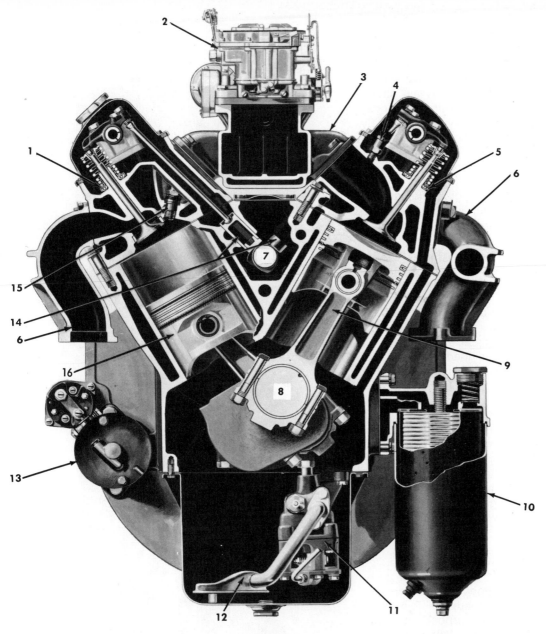

Fig. 18-10. Sectional view of a GMC V-six cylinder gasoline engine.

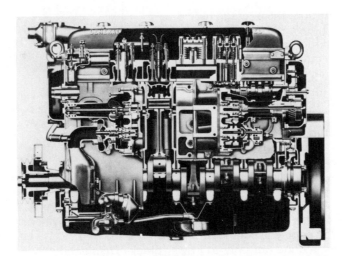

Fig. 18-11. Two cycle GMC series 71 diesel engine has a balance shaft that is driven by the camshaft.

SMALL ENGINES

Air-cooled engines are used almost exclusively for small machinery such as lawn mowers, chain saws, gardening equipment, etc. Single or multiple-cylinder engines of both two cycle and four cycle types are entirely safisfactory, and operate for long periods of time with little attention and few repairs, Figs. 18-12 and 18-13.

These small industrial engines are usually self-contained power units having built-in fuel and ignition arrangements similar to an outboard engine. The ignition is often supplied by a magneto which is a part of, or attached to, the engine flywheel. Rotation of the engine generates electricity for ignition.

Snowmobiling is becoming an increasingly popular sport and profitable service market. Most snowmobile engines are two cycle, air-cooled, single or two cylinder design. The McCulloch "twin," for example, has a displacement of 24.3 cu. in. (398 cm³). This is 1.27 hp per cu. in. displacement, which is approximately twice that of many American passenger car engines.

These "balanced engines" are designed with a balancing cylinder opposite each power cylinder. See Fig. 18-13. The balancing cylinder is about half the size of the power cylinder. Its location increases crankcase capacity and compression ratio of the crankcase, as well as providing dynamic balance. There is no supercharging. The power cylinder has the normal two cycle transfer and exhaust ports, with the exhaust port closing last.

The balance cylinder is primarily used for mechanical balance, but it does control the intake ports much like a rotary intake valve. The basic ignition system utilizes a high tension magneto which, on some installations, includes a 70 watt generator.

RACING ENGINES

The most successful racing engines are designed for the purpose and are made of special materials. Passenger car engines can be adapted for racing purposes, but considerable alteration usually is required. When used for racing, the engine is designed or altered to get the utmost in power and rotational speed regardless of anything else. See Fig. 18-14.

Since noise is a minor consideration, the average race car engine roars and clatters. The clearances are very carefully measured on each working part. Some of this clatter comes from the valve mechanism, which is designed to open the valves quickly, and close them quickly. Large valves with a high lift will expedite the flow of the gases in and out of the cylinders.

The opening and closing time of the valves, as well as the duration of the valve opening, is designed solely for efficiency at high speed. As a result, racing engines seldom idle smoothly. Other reasons, for rough idling are lightweight flywheels for rapid acceleration, and the extremely high compression ratios, which approach that of diesels.

In addition to the greater clearances between all moving parts, each rotating part in the engine is balanced to extremely close tolerances. This is done not only to increase the speed of the engine, but to reduce destructive vibration. Every part of the engine is made of the

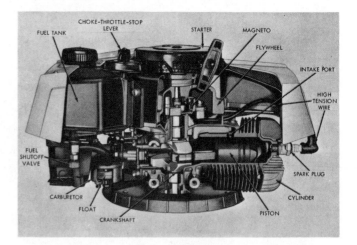

Fig. 18-12. A small, single cylinder, two stroke, gas engine is used in lawn mower applicators. (Jacobsen Mfg.)

Fig. 18-13. Cutaway view of a two cylinder, two-stroke, air cooled engine that is used in snowmobiles. (McCulloch Corp.)

finest material available for the purpose to insure reliability and freedom from mechanical failure.

The race car engine shown in Fig. 18-15 is the Ford-Weslake engine, which developes 455 hp @ 10,000 rpm. It is a 60 deg. V-12 engine with an aluminum cylinder block. Displacement is 182.6 cu. in. (3 liter). Double overhead camshaft operating four valves per cylinder are features.

Fig. 18-14. Ford Indy race engine. Note that there are two camshafts per each bank of cylinders.

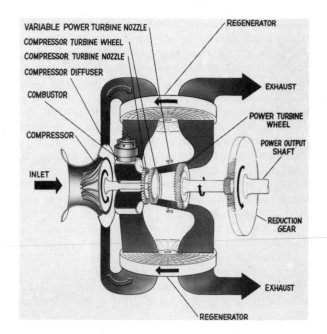

Fig. 18-16. Drawing shows airflow path of a turbine. (Ford)

TURBINES

Gas turbines can be used to propel automobiles, trucks, boats, and airplanes. They also can be designed to serve as stationary power plants. The fundamental principle of a turbine consists of an inclined plane mounted on a rotating shaft, and located in the path of fluid force, Fig. 18-16.

A gas turbine is a heat engine which transforms energy created by the expansion of the burning fuel and air in the combustion chamber to either thrust or shaft power. This power can be utilized directly to push a vehicle, or it can be turned into shaft power to drive an automobile.

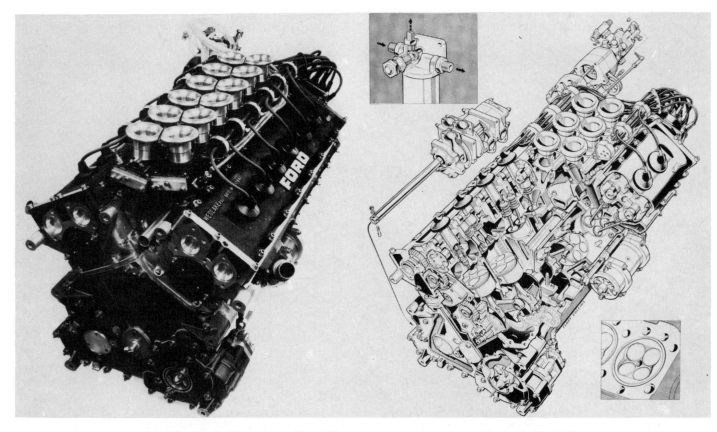

Fig. 18-15. A 12 cylinder Ford Weslake engine develops 455 hp @ 10,000 rpm.

The thrust force developed by a turbine can be shown by using a toy balloon for a demonstration. The balloon is inflated with air, then released. As the air rushes out through the neck of the balloon, the balloon will shoot away in the direction opposite the air flow. The force for propulsion is applied against the inside of the balloon, rather than being supplied by a jet of compressed air pushing against free air. This is the same principle of operation employed in a rocket or jet engine.

The same thrust force can be exerted against a turbine wheel to produce rotary motion, Fig. 18-17. The first stage, or gasifier section, produces the thrust. If shaft power is wanted, the section to the right (power section) is added as a second stage. In this particular turbine, Fig. 18-17, the first turbine wheel drives only the compressor. Fuel is sprayed into the two burners receiving compressed air from the compressor. Only a portion of the air is burned in the burners, and the compressor requires only a portion of the energy in the hot gas. The remainder of air and hot gas is used as a thrust force.

If shaft power is wanted instead of thrust, air and hot gas are directed to the second turbine. Basically, a gas turbine provides rotary power from the expansion of burning gas without the use of reciprocating pistons and connecting rods operating a crankshaft.

The main housing is the principal structural member of the turbine, to which five subassemblies are attached: gasifier, variable power turbine nozzle, power turbine, reduction gear box, combustor, and regenerator. Each is a self-contained unit, and except for the variable power turbine nozzle, can be removed for service without disturbing the remainder of the engine.

Airflow through a turbine engine is shown in Fig. 18-16.

1. Air enters compressor after passing through inlet filter and silencer, then it is discharged into diffuser.

2. After leaving diffuser, where airflow is split, it passes into forward half of regenerator covers, then inward through regenerator coraes.

3. Air heated by passing through regenerators is then directed in and about combustor in a flow pattern developed to give good combustion and an even temperature distribution.

4. Combustor then discharges into plenum chamber which conducts hot gases into gasifier turbine nozzle and wheel.

5. High velocity gases leaving gasifier turbine pass through a transition duct into variable nozzle vanes, which direct flow to power turbine wheel.

6. Gases leaving power turbine wheel are diffused and directed outward through rear half of two regenerator cores where heat is recovered for transfer to compressor discharge air.

7. Cooled gases then collect in regenerator covers and are discharged to exhaust.

WANKEL ROTARY ENGINE

The Wankel rotary engine does not have reciprocating parts. Rotary engines of the Wankel type are being used in virtually all fields, including automotive (Mazda), aircraft, farm equipment, marine, outboard engines, motorcycles, and small electric generators. Air cushion vehicles have also been produced.

The Wankel type rotary engine, Fig. 18-18, is a compact power plant requiring less space than a piston engine of the same horsepower. It is an exceptionally quiet engine with very little vibration.

There are approximately 630 parts in a Wankel engine compared to about 1050 parts for a piston engine. Ports are used instead of valves, eliminating the need for the

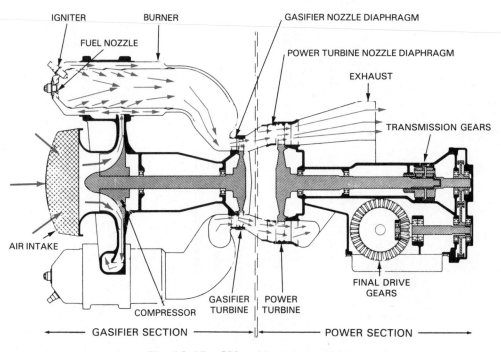

Fig. 18-17. GM turbine arrangement.

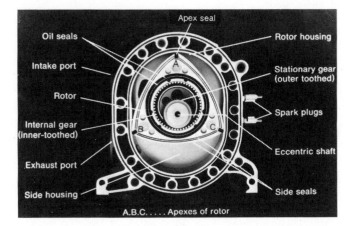

Fig. 18-18. A rotary engine has almost half as many parts as a reciprocating engine. (Mazda)

imately 5.1 cu. ft. of engine compartment space, while the V-8 requires 23.2 cu. ft. Fuel distribution to the rotor chambers is better than the distribution to the piston engine, consequently volumetric efficiency is higher.

Most of the Wankel type rotary engines in production have two rotors. Fig. 18-19, for example, shows the engine which powers the Japanese Mazda. Some rotary engines have three rotors (Mercedes-Benz CIII), and four-rotor engines have been built. Wankel type engines can be built as small as 18.5 cu. in. per working chamber up to 1920 cu. in. per working chamber.

Fig. 18-20 shows heat balance chart of a typical Wankel rotary engine. The percentages compare favorably with the average piston engine.

WANKEL FUNDAMENTALS

The Wankel rotor is triangular in shape with slightly curved sides. It orbits eccentrically on a fixed gear in a housing shaped slightly like a figure eight, Fig. 18-18. That is, the rotor rotates around its own axis while orbiting around the mainshaft. However, the output shaft makes three turns per rotor revolution. As a result, one operating cycle takes place per output shaft revolution.

complicated valve train of the piston engine.

A Wankel engine weighing 237 lbs. will produce approximately the same power as a conventional V-8 weighing over 600 lbs. The Wankel occupies approx-

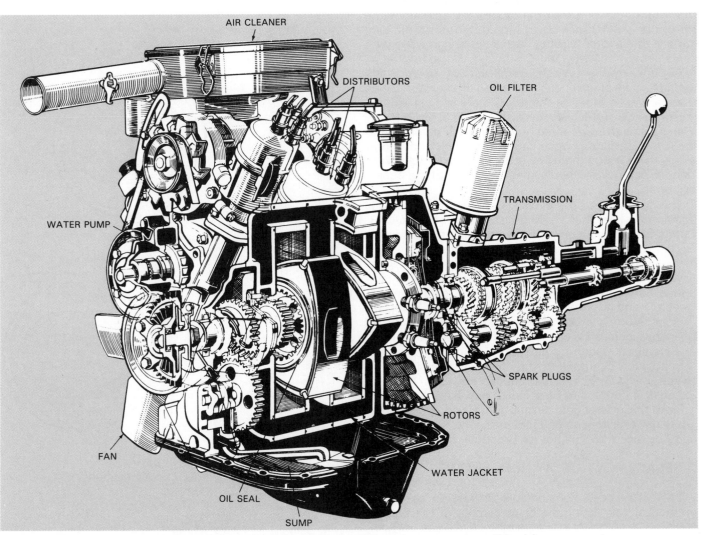

Fig. 18-19. This Wankel engine uses only two rotors. (Mazda)

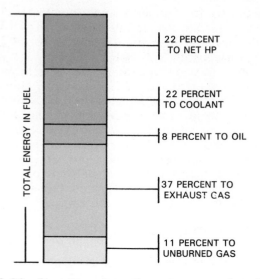

Fig. 18-20. Showing where the power goes in a Wankel engine.

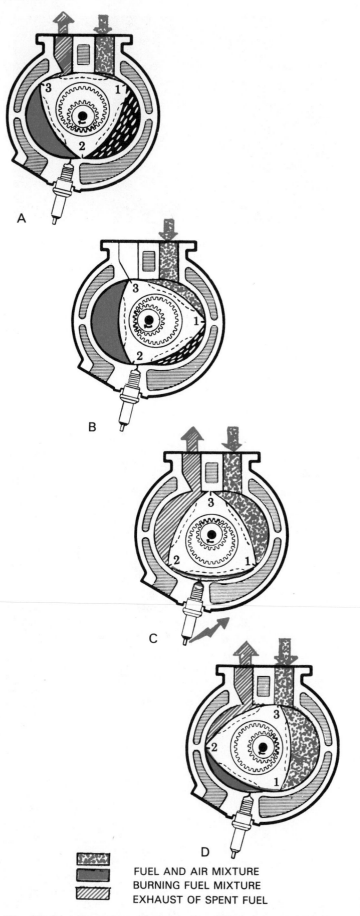

FUEL AND AIR MIXTURE
BURNING FUEL MIXTURE
EXHAUST OF SPENT FUEL

Fig. 18-21. Sequence of events in a Wankel engine. Unlike a reciprocating engine, fuel is always entering a rotary engine.

As the rotor swings around the fixed gear, the internal gear (rotor gear) transmits the rotary motion to the output shaft. The output shaft is an eccentric shaft and the rotation is such that the tips of the apexes of the rotor, Fig. 18-18, are always in contact with the side surface of the rotor housing. These tips are provided with seals shown at A, B, and C.

All four cycles (intake, compression, power, and exhaust) take place in one revolution of the rotor. Since there are three lobes to the rotor, there is a continuous performance of these cycles on every lobe, Fig. 18-21. The crankshaft turns three times for every revolution of the rotor. With one power impulse for each of the rotor sides, there will be three power impulses per rotor revolution, or one power impules per revolution of the eccentric shaft.

The sequence of the cycles is shown in Fig. 18-21, position A, intake is starting between lobes 1 and 3. Compression is occurring between 1 and 2. Power is being produced between 2 and 3. Exhaust is finishing between 3 and 1.

When the rotor has moved to position B, intake continues between 1 and 3. Compression continues between 1 and 2. Power is finishing between 2 and 3.

In position C, intake is finishing between 1 and 3. Spark has ignited the compressed charge between 1 and 2. Exhaust is occurring between 2 and 3.

In position D, intake of the charge is completed between 1 and 3. Power is produced between 1 and 2. Exhaust is continuing between 2 and 3.

From this operational description, it can be seen that when gas pressure on one face turns the rotor, it brings another face into position to produce power.

DISPLACEMENT OF WANKEL ENGINE

There has been considerable discussion as to the method of calculating the displacement of the Wankel engine. The currently accepted method is twice the combustion volume multiplied by the number of rotors.

POWER DEVELOPED

As is the case with the conventional piston engine, horsepower developed by different makes of the Wankel rotary engine varied considerably.

The Audi-NSU model R080 is a 60.7 cu. in. rotary engine that develops 130 hp @ 5500 rpm. Compression ratio is 9 to 1. The Mazda R100 engine has a displacement of 60 cu. in. and develops 100 hp @ 7000 rpm. Compression ratio is 9.4 to 1.

In a rotary engine, the compression ratio is limited by the rotor radius and the eccentricity. When those two dimensions have been selected, the maximum compression ratio is determined. The compression ratio is equal to the radius to eccentricity ratio, or R/e, Fig. 18-22.

PERFORMANCE

The location of intake and exhaust ports are factors in performance and fuel economy. NSU and Mercedes-Benz are advocates of peripheral ports. Toyo Kogyo, manufacturer of the Mazda, prefers side location of ports, claiming better idling, low speed performance, and light load scavenging. In general, the peripheral ports, Fig. 18-23, provide high speed and power while the side ports, Fig. 18-19, provide performance over a wide range.

The fuel used in the Wankel rotary engine is the same kind used in conventional piston engines. Normal fuel ranges from 87 to 91 octane. Leaded fuel is not required. Tests made on the Mazda showed satisfactory operation with 67 octane fuel. Satisfactory operation has also been obtained on some rotary engines with diesel fuels.

Fuel flow from the carburetor, when used, to the Wankel engine is described as being constant. There is no problem of uneven distribution such as encountered in piston engines where some cylinders receive a greater quantity of air/fuel mixture than others.

IGNITION

Two spark plugs per chamber are used. Note the location of the spark plugs in the Mazda rotary engine shown in Fig. 18-19.

Spark plugs differ greatly from those used in the piston engine. Note the side electrodes shown in Fig. 18-24.

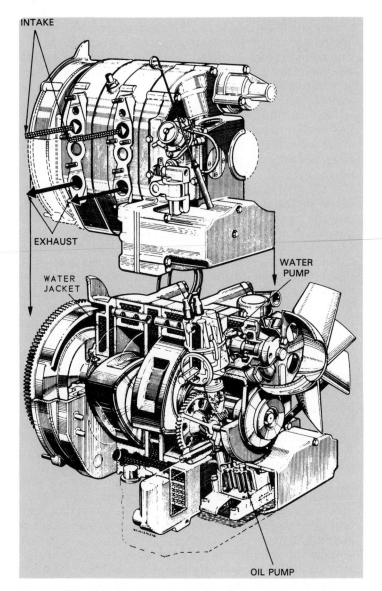

Fig. 18-23. Peripheral intake and exhaust ports provide a higher speed and more power over side ports.

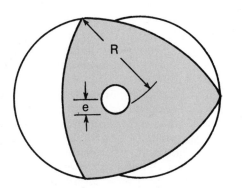

Fig. 18-22. Compression ratio of a Wankel engine is determined by R/e.

Fig. 18-24. A special type spark plug must be used on a rotary engine. Note the two side electrodes.

Location of the spark plugs is as important in rotary engines as it is in piston engines. Research has shown that by using two spark plugs in each chamber, exhaust emissions are reduced, power is increased, combustion is more complete, and duration of combustion is minimizied.

Two distributors, Fig. 18-19, are usually provided. Researchers have found that a spark advance of approximately five degrees usually is required. This corresponds to an advance of approximately 28 degrees on a piston engine.

In piston engines, the spark plugs receive the benefit of the cooling effects of the incoming fuel charge. This is not the case in a rotary combustion engine. Consequently, spark plug temperatures are higher. Spark plugs used in these engines are an extremely cold type plug.

Timing of the ignition on the rotary engines is in relation to the angle of the shaft. Top center is the same as the top center on a piston engine, but the angle of the shaft is greater than the corresponding angle of the piston engine crankshaft.

EMISSIONS

Currently, Mazda and NSU rotary engines have met Federal requirements for low levels of exhaust emissions. Intense combustion chamber turbulence claimed for the Wankel type engine contributes largely to improved exhaust emissions. In addition, the Wankel engine can give satisfactory operation on relatively lean mixtures, which also contributes to improved exhaust emissions.

However, the hydrocarbon emission level of the Wankel rotary engine is higher than a piston type engine of the same general size. The carbon monoxide and nitrous oxide levels are lower than that of a reciprocating piston engine.

As is the case of the piston engine, the exact emission quantity and composition of the Wankel exhaust depends on throttle opening and engine speed. With a rich or lean mixture, there is the possibility of incomplete combustion. The problem is worse under light load conditions. However, the Wankel rotary engine operates well under a lean mixture, and has an advantage over the piston engine in that respect.

Thermal reactors have been shown to produce a reduction in hydrocarbon emission from the Wankel engine. Tests have shown reductions up to 90 percent when a thermal reactor has been used, Fig. 18-25.

COOLING

While air-cooled Wankel type rotary engines have been produced, the water-cooled type is used most extensively. The coolant is primarily for cooling the housing, as oil is used to cool the rotor. Typical water-cooled rotary engines are shown in Figs. 18-19 and 18-23.

Cooling the Wankel engine is required primarily in the area where combustion and expansion take place (area around the spark plugs). The concentration of heat in such a small area tends to cause distortion which makes sealing of oil and fuel mixture difficult. Unless adequate cooling is provided, thermal fatigue or shock cracks may form in the spark plug hole area.

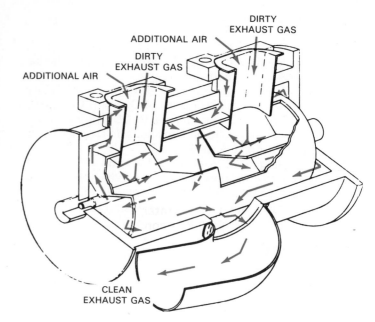

Fig. 18-25. An exhaust gas reactor reduces the level of hydrocarbon emissions in a rotary engine. (Curtiss-Wright)

The cooling of the rotor presents a special problem. It is completely enclosed within the housing and does not have the benefit of the cooling provided by the crankcase in a reciprocating engine. In addition, the rotor turns at one third of the mainshaft speed.

While aluminum is lighter than cast iron and also has excellent heat conductivity, most manufacturers prefer cast iron for rotors. For actual cooling, lubricating oil is circulated from the sump, Fig. 18-19, and then through the rotor. After cooling the rotor, it passes through a filter and heat exchanger, through the hub of the rotor and returns to the sump. The inside is carefully designed, since it effects not only the cooling of the rotor but also engine balance. Excessive rotor temperatures will result in carbon formation on the interior of the rotor. This could cause an unbalanced condition, as well as further increase engine temperature.

The oil seals on the rotor bearings permit a measured amount of oil leakage to provide lubrication for the sides of the rotor.

SEALS

Adequate sealing for the various areas of a rotary engine proved to be one of the most difficult problems in the early stages of development. Apex seal and side seals, Fig. 18-18, must be provided to prevent leakage from the working chambers.

The problem of designing effective seals for the apex of the rotor is complicated by the different forces which act on the seal. Forces include positive and negative centrifugal force, gas pressure, and friction against the working surfaces. In addition, the position of the apex seal varies. When at the major and minor axis, it is perpendicular to the working surface. At other positions of the rotor, the seal is at an angle other than 90 deg. to the surface.

Apex seals are straight and inserted in radius slots at each rotor apex. Side seals are curved to conform to the curvature of the rotor and are placed in grooves in the rotor sides. These seals are provided with interlocking ends to reduce leakage.

Various materials have been used for seals. Mazda, for example, originally used carbon for their apex seals, because of its lubricating qualities. Later, a sintered material impregnated with aluminum was adapted. Ceramic seals have also been used.

LUBRICATION

Since the lubricating oil in a rotary engine is not subject to blowby and consequent contamination, periodic oil changes have been eliminated in most rotary engine service recommendations. However, additional oil occasionally is needed to replace that metered for lubricating the rotor seals and housing. With high speed driving, use of a quart of oil every 1000 miles has been experienced.

Bearings of the output shaft are lubricated with oil from the sump in the normal manner, the oil is supplied under pressure from a gear type pump, Fig. 18-23. The oil supplied to the rotor seals keeps them from sticking. Originally, engine oil was mixed with the fuel, much in the same manner as oil and fuel are mixed for use in two cycle outboard engines. Subsequently, automatic metering of the lubricating oil from the rotor side was adapted. A third method of lubricating the rotor seals consisted of introducing oil into the intake ports in accordance with engine operating conditions.

SERVICING ROTARY ENGINES

While the Wankel type rotary engine is relatively new to the service field, servicing should not present any major problem. First of all, there are no valves to stick or burn. There are no piston rings, but there are seals on the rotor. These, however, should present no problem when replacement is necessary. It can be expected that the life of the seals should equal that of piston rings.

The carburetor, or fuel injection, and ignition systems are readily accessible, which greatly simplifies tune-up work. Ignition units also follow conventional design.

CERAMIC ENGINES

Currently, ceramic engine blocks are being implemented in some diesel applications as an alternative to cast iron or aluminum. The ceramic engine is referred to as an adiabatic engine. An adiabatic engine does not gain or lose heat.

There are several advantages of a ceramic engine. First, it is much lighter than even an aluminum engine block. But like the aluminum engine block, a steel sleeve must be inserted into the cylinder. Second, it is not necessary to have an engine cooling system, radiator, or the associated hoses. Finally, main bearings are not needed. Neither is there a need for an oiling system to the main journals. This is because the ceramic surface becomes quite slippery when hot.

While most engines today remain either cast iron, aluminum, or a combination of the two, ceramics can be used for select components of these engines. Some of the components being tested are parts of the valve, a portion of the piston, and the compressor and turbine blades of a turbocharger. The disadvantage of ceramics is that it can fail suddenly and unexpectedly, which would be catastrophic.

Chapter 18—REVIEW QUESTIONS

Write your answers on a separate sheet of paper. Do not write in this book.

1. Carburetors are used on diesel engines. True or False?
2. Diesel fuel pumps are usually driven by double or triple V belts. Yes or No?
3. Name two purposes of a supercharger on a two cycle diesel engine.
4. How many general types of combustion chambers are used in diesel engines?
   a. Four.
   b. Five.
   c. Two.
   d. Six.
5. In the M system, the combustion chamber is formed in what part of the engine?
   a. Cylinder head.
   b. Piston.
   c. Cylinder bore.
6. Name five alterations that are often made to passenger car engines to adapt them for use in light trucks.
7. Small industrial engines are usually air cooled. True or False?
8. Give three reasons for poor idling of racing engines.
9. The thrust developed by a turbine is similar to a toy balloon. True or False?
10. A turbine:
    a. Converts reciprocating power into rotary.
    b. Uses only reciprocating power.
    c. Uses only rotary power.
    d. All of the above.
11. Mechanic A states that a rotary engine usually has two spark plugs per chamber.
    Mechanic B states that the spark plugs used in rotary engines usually have two side electrodes. Who is right?
    a. Mechanic A.
    b. Mechanic B.
    c. Both Mechanics A and B.
    d. Neither Mechanic A nor B.
12. The Wankel engine must use special spark plugs. True or False?
13. The Wankel engine is a:
    a. Reciprocating engine.
    b. Rotary engine.
    c. Free piston engine.
    d. None of the above.
14. Is special fuel required for the rotary combustion engine used in the Mazda car?
15. The Wankel engine requires more space than a piston engine of the same power. True or False?
16. The Wankel engine is limited to two rotors. Yes or No?

17. What is the shape of the rotor used in the Wankel engine?
    a. Round.
    b. Triangular.
    c. Square.
    d. Elliptical.
18. There are _____ power impulses in a rotary combustion engine for each revolution of the rotor.
19. Fuel injection cannot be used in a Wankel rotary engine. True or False?
20. In general, the hydrocarbon emission level of the Wankel engine is higher than a piston type engine of the same general size. Yes or No?
21. A ceramic engine block must have:
    a. Aluminum sleeves in the cylinders.
    b. Steel sleeves in the cylinders.
    c. Both A and B.
    d. Neither A nor B.
22. Define an adiabatic engine.
23. What are the advantages of a ceramic engine?
    a. Lighter than aluminum.
    b. Needs no cooling system.
    c. Engine main bearings are not needed.
    d. All of the above.

Chapter 19

AUTOMOTIVE FUELS

After studying this chapter, you will be able to:
- Describe detonation and preignition.
- List and explain the characteristics of various fuels.
- Compare the various fuels including alcohol, diesel, LPG, and lead free.

VOLATILITY

The fuel used in most automobiles and internal combustion engines is gasoline. Other fuels include methanol, benzol, alcohol, alcohol-gasoline blends, and liquid petroleum gas (LP-Gas).

Gasoline is a colorless liquid obtained from crude petroleum as a result of a complicated distillation and cracking process. Two important characteristics of gasoline used for fuel in automotive engines are volatility and antiknock characteristics.

The volatility of any liquid is its vaporizing ability. In the case of a simple substance, it is usually determined by its boiling point. For example, the boiling point of water is 212 °F. Gasoline is a mixture of hydrocarbon compounds, each having its own boiling point. Gasoline used for fuel in automobiles has a range of boiling points from approximately 100 °F up to 400 °F, Fig. 19-1.

The fuel must remain a liquid until it enters the air stream in the carburetor or fuel injection throttle body. At this time, it must quickly vaporize and mix uniformly in the correct proportions with the intake air.

The volatility of gasoline affects ease of starting, length of warm-up period, and engine performance during normal operation. For easy starting with a cold engine, the fuel must be highly volatile. In other words, it must vaporize easily. Therefore, when cold weather approaches, fuel refiners increase the percentage of highly volatile fuel contained in gasoline, to insure easier starting under the cold weather operating conditions.

A portion of the fuel must be sufficiently volatile to insure proper vaporization during periods of acceleration. If fuel sprayed from the accelerating pump jet does not vaporize readily, it could result in a lean mixture that would exist only for a moment, and is known as a "flat-spot" or hesitation on acceleration.

If the volatility of fuel is too low, the engine will never start. This is best illustrated by a vehicle that is placed in storage for a long time. Time comes for the vehicle to be removed from storage. The engine turns over but does not start. The troubleshooting process shows that both spark and fuel are present. However, the fuel in the tank has lost its volatility and cannot be ignited in the combustion chamber. Fuel should always be removed from a vehicle prior to any long term storage.

If the volatility of the fuel is too high, it will contribute to a vapor lock condition. In vapor lock, the liquid fuel vaporizes at any point before the metering process of the carburetor or fuel injector. This prevents fuel from reaching the carburetor or fuel injector as a liquid.

VAPOR LOCK

Just as water turns to steam when it is heated, gasoline turns to vapor when sufficient heat is applied.

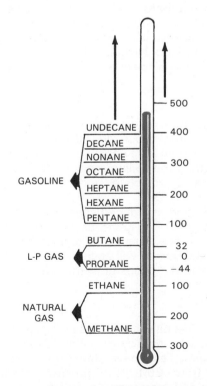

Fig. 19-1. Range of boiling points of various hydrocarbons.

189

Early vaporization of the fuel can cause complete or partial interruption of fuel flow. Since the vapor of motor fuel occupies a greater volume than in liquid form, the amount of fuel flow will be reduced. Loss in power and missing will occur, and under extreme conditions, the engine will stop, or will not start. This condition may occur anywhere in the fuel line.

Whether or not vapor is likely to form depends on vapor pressure, or ease with which the fuel will vaporize. The standardized method of measuring or determining vapor pressure in the laboratory is known as the Reid Method. U.S. Government specifications for motor gasoline require that the Reid vapor pressure at 100 °F should not exceed 12 psi.

Carburetors are vented to a charcoal canister as part of the evaporative emission control system. This also aids in relieving the problem of vapor blocking the flow of liquid fuel.

In another design technique, a molded phenolic resin fuel bowl keeps the fuel about 20 °F cooler than in an all metal fuel bowl. Also in the area of insulation, some manufacturers place an asbestos gasket approximately 1/2 in. thick between the carburetor and manifold. This reduces the transmission of heat to the carburetor.

In addition, fuel pumps are placed where they will be cooled by air blasts and shielded from the heat of the exhaust manifold. Also to reduce the possibility of vapor lock, fuel lines are routed away from the exhaust pipe, catalytic converter, and muffler.

Low pressure on the fuel will also promote vaporization. An electric fuel pump, located in the fuel tank, would avoid the problem that conventional, mechanical type fuel pumps have.

Vaporization is also controlled by gasoline refineries by changing the vapor pressure. During winter months, a fuel that is easily vaporized is supplied to facilitate starting. During summer months, when temperatures are high, a fuel that is not so easily vaporized is provided. However, during unseasonably warm weather in the spring, and before refiners have supplied their summer grade fuel, it is not unusual to encounter early vapor lock.

BOILING RANGE

The boiling temperature of fuel is also the temperature at which it is completely vaporized. Furthermore, fuel can be completely burned in an engine only in vaporized form. Because of this, the boiling range of fuel should be low enough to permit complete vaporization with the existing engine temperature.

For engines operating at reduced speed and load, or in cold weather, lower boiling point fuels will give more satisfactory performance. Fuels that cannot be completely vaporized and burned will accumulate and form sludge and other harmful deposits in the engine.

SULFUR CONTENT

Sulfur content in fuel oil should be as low as possible in order to keep the amount of corrosion and deposit formation at a minimum. Tests have shown that increasing sulfur content from .25 to 1.25 precent increases deposits and wear 135 percent.

HEAT VALUE

The power obtained from any fuel is determined by its heat value, which is measured by burning a unit amount of fuel in an excess of air or oxygen. It is measured in British thermal units per pound of fuel. One British thermal unit (Btu) is the amount of heat required to raise one pound of water 1 °F. One Btu is equal to 778.6 foot-pounds.

Some of the higher heat values of hydrocarbon found in gasoline are as follows:

1. Hexane   20700
2. Heptane   20600
3. Octane   20500
4. Monane   20450
5. Decane   20420
6. Undecane   20375
7. Dodecane. 20350

COMBUSTION OF GASOLINE

Rapidly combining fuel with oxygen produces heat. This is known as combustion. In the case of gasoline, combustion is the rapid oxidation of the carbon and the hydrogen constituting the fuel. The heat produced is the result of the chemical change.

The chemical equation of combustion for octane is:

$$C_8H_{18} + 12.5\ O_2 = 8\ CO_2 + 9\ H_2O$$

In this equation, C_8H_{18} represents the chemical formula for gasoline. The 12.5 O_2 is the oxygen required to burn one part of gasoline. This produces eight parts of carbon dioxide (CO_2) and nine parts of water (H_2O).

However, air is used in actual operation of an engine, instead of pure oxygen. Air consists of a mixture of 1/5 oxygen and 4/5 nitrogen, by volume. From the standpoint of weight, it consists of one part oxygen, and 3 1/2 parts of nitrogen or, more exactly, 23 parts of oxygen and 77 parts of nitrogen.

The atomic weights for the different elements entering into the combustion of octane and air are as follows:
1. Carbon   = 12
2. Nitrogen   = 14
3. Oxygen   = 16
4. Hydrogen   = 1

On a weight basis, the chemical formula of combustion is:

$$114\ C_8H_{18} + 400\ O_2 = 352\ CO_2 + 162\ H_2O$$

Since air is a mixture of oxygen and nitrogen in a ratio of 23 to 77, the nitrogen must also be considered in writing the combustion equation for octane and air. The amount of nitrogen present with 400 weight units of oxygen is:

$$400 \times \frac{77}{23} = 1339$$

This nitrogen is present in the combustible mixture and also in the products of combustion. So, it must be added to both sides of the equation:

$$114\ C_8H_{18} + 400\ O_2 + 1339\ N_2 = 352\ CO_2 + 162\ H_2O + 1339\ N_2$$

For one pound of octane, the formula becomes:

3.09 lb. CO_2 + 1.42 lb. H_2O + 11.76 lb. N_2

1 lb. of fuel + 15.27 lb. air = 16.27 lb. of exhaust gas.

The amount of power developed in an internal combustion engine is dependent on the heat that can be obtained from burning the fuel. This, in the case of gasoline or any of the hydrocarbons, is equal to the total of the heat due to the combustion of the carbon and hydrogen. From that must be subtracted the heat required to break up the hydrocarbon molecules.

When carbon becomes carbon dioxide, due to combustion, 14,542 Btu are liberated for each pound of carbon burned. In the combustion of hydrogen to steam, 62,032 Btu are liberated for each pound of hydrogen. To break up the octane into carbon and hydrogen. To break up the octane into carbon and hydrogen, 1523 Btu are required for each pound of octane.

In octane (C_8H_{18}), the carbon is 84.2 percent, while the hydrogen is 15.8 percent. The heat produced by combustion is:

84.2 percent of 14,542 Btu = 12,244
15.8 percent of 62,032 Btu = 9,801

This makes a total of 22,045 Btu. From this, subtract 1523 Btu required to break up the fuel into carbon and hydrogen. The difference, 20,522 Btu, is the total heat from burning one pound of octane.

COMBUSTION CHAMBER TEMPERATURE

During combustion, temperatures vary through a relatively wide range. Temperatures are affected by compression ratio, combustion chamber contour, cooling system effectiveness, richness of air-fuel mixture, and amount of burned gases remaining in the cylinder from the previous cycle.

At the end of the compression stroke (but before ignition), temperatures of approximately 985 °F may be considered average for an engine with a compression ratio of 9 to 1. Immediately after ignition, the temperature increases very rapidly and will reach a value of approximately 5500 °F.

NORMAL COMBUSTION

The normal combustion process in the combustion chamber, Fig. 19-2, goes through three stages termed formation (nucleus of flame), hatching out, and propagation.

As soon as the ignition spark jumps the gap of the spark plug, a small ball of blue flame develops in the gap. This ball is the first stage or nucleus of the flame. It enlarges with relative slowness, and during its growth, there is no measureable pressure created by the heat.

As the nucleus enlarges, it develops into the hatching-out stage. The nucleus is torn apart, so that it sends fingers of flame into the mixture in the combustion chamber. This causes enough heat to give a slight rise in temperature and pressure in the entire air-fuel mixture. Consequently, a lag still exists in the attempt to raise pressure in the entire cylinder.

It is during the third stage, or propagation, that the effective burning of the fuel takes place. The flame burns in a front which sweeps across the combustion chamber, burning rapidly, and causing great heat with its accompanying rise in pressure. It is this pressure which causes the piston to move downward.

During normal combustion, the burning is progressive. It increases gradually during the first two stages. But, during the third stage, the flame is extremely strong as it sweeps through the combustion chamber. However, there is no violent or explosive action such as when detonation (ordinarily responsible for pinging or knocking) occurs.

DETONATION

If detonation takes place, it occurs during the third stage of combustion, Fig. 19-3. In the propagation stage, flame sweeps from the area around the spark plug toward the walls of the combustion chamber. Parts of the chamber the flame has passed may contain inert, nonburnable gases. The section not yet touched by flame contains highly compressed, heated, combustible gases.

As the flame races through the combustion chamber, the unburned gases ahead of it are still further

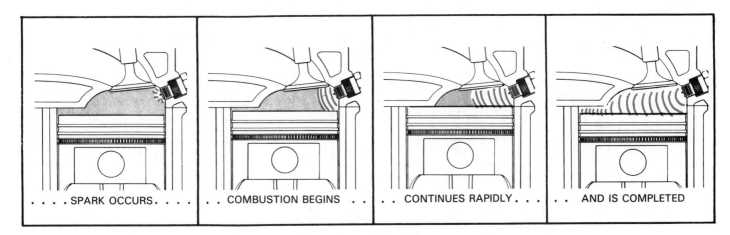

. . . . SPARK OCCURS . . . .   . . COMBUSTION BEGINS . .   . . CONTINUES RAPIDLY . . . .   . . AND IS COMPLETED

Fig. 19-2. During normal combustion, the air-fuel mixture does not burn all at once. Flame front moves rapidly, in a controlled manner. (Perfect Circle)

191

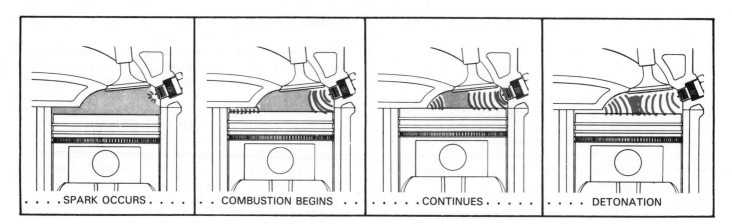

Fig. 19-3. Detonation is the rapid and uncontrolled burning of fuel within the combustion chamber that creates a secondary flame front. The two flame fronts collide and cause a knock or pinging.

compressed and are heated to higher temperatures. Under certain conditions, the extreme heating of the un-burned part of the mixture may cause it to ignite spontaneously and explode.

It is this rapid, uncontrolled buring in the final stage of combustion that is called detonation. It is caused by the rapidly burning flame front compressing the unburned part of the mixture to the point of self-ignition. This secondary wave front collides with the normal flame and makes an audible knock or pining sound.

Detonation harms an engine and hinders its performance in several ways. In extreme cases, pistons may shatter, cylinders burst, or cylinder heads crack. At times, these temperatures resulting from detonation may reach the point where the piston actually melts. Other effects of detonation may be: overheating of the engine, broken spark plugs, overloaded bearings, high fuel consumption, loss of power.

The causes of detonation include:
1. Lean air-fuel mixtures (vacuum leaks).
2. Fuel of too low an octane rating.
3. Ignition timing overadvanced.
4. Lugging the engine (gear is too high for the speed of the engine).
5. Excessive carbon accumulations in the combustion chamber.

PREIGNITION

Preignition is the igniting of the fuel charge before the regular ignition spark. If the premature combustion is completed before the occurrence of the regular spark, there may be no identifying noise. However, if the regular ignition spark follows shortly after the preignition occurs, there will be a pinging noise when the two flame fronts collide, Fig. 19-4. Also, preignition can lead to detonation. These two types of abnormal combustion are closely linked and often it is difficult to distinguish between them.

The main causes of preignition include:
1. Carbon deposits that remain incandescent.
2. Valves operating at higher than normal temperature.
3. Hot spots caused by defects in cooling system.
4. Spark plugs that run too hot.
5. Sharp edges in the combustion chamber.
6. Detonation.

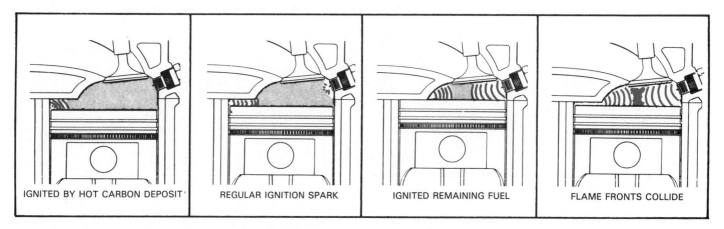

Fig. 19-4. Preignition occurs when a flame front, caused by a localized hot spot, ignites the air-fuel mixture prior to the spark plug. When the two flame fronts meet, a knock or pinging sound can be heard.   (Perfect Circle)

ANTIKNOCK QUALITIES

One of the most important qualities of modern fuel is the ability to burn without causing knocking. The tendency toward knocking is overcome by the addition to the fuel of such compounds as tetraethyl lead or butane. In addition, refining processes also aid in producing knock-free gasoline.

To understand what is meant by antiknock quality, consider the process of combustion. When substance burns, it is actually uniting in rapid chemical reaction with oxygen (one constituent of air). During the burning process, the molecules of the substance and oxygen are set into very rapid motion and heat is produced.

In the combustion chamber of an engine cylinder, the gasoline vapor and oxygen in the air are united and burned. They combine, and the molecules begin to move about very rapidly as the high temperatures of combustion are reached. The molecules bombard the combustion chamber walls and the head of the piston with a rain of fast moving molecules. It is this bombardment that causes the heavy push on the piston, forcing it downward on the power stroke.

OCTANE RATING

The ability of a fuel to resist knocking is measured by its octane rating. The octane rating of a fuel is determined by matching it against mixtures of normal heptane and iso-octane in a test engine under specified test conditions. The test continues until a mixture of these pure hydrocarbons is found which gives the same degree of knocking in the engine as the gasoline being tested.

The octane number of the fuel, then, is the percent of the iso-octane in the matching iso-octane normal-heptane mixture. For example, a gasoline rating of 90 octane is equivalent in its knocking characteristics to a mixture of 90 percent iso-octane and 10 percent normal heptane.

The tendency of a fuel to knock varies in different engines. It even varies in the same engine under different operating conditions. The shape of the combustion chamber is important, but most important of all is the compression ratio.

It should be emphasized that octane number of a fuel has nothing to do with its starting qualities, power, volatility, or other major characteristics. If an engine operates satisfactorily with a fuel of a certain octane rating, its performance will not be improved by using fuel of a still higher octane rating.

CETANE RATING

The delay between the time the fuel is injected into the cylinder and ignition is expressed as a cetane number. Usually, this is between 30 and 60. Fuels that ignite rapidly have high cetane ratings, while slow-to-ignite fuels have low cetane ratings.

A fuel with better ignition quality would assist combustion more than a lower cetane fuel during starting and idling conditions when compression temperatures are cooler. Ether with a very high cetane rating of 85-96 is often used for starting diesel engines in cold weather. The lower the temperature of the surrounding air, the greater the need for fuel that will ignite rapidly.

When the cetane number of the fuel is too low, it may result in difficult starting, engine knock, and puffs of white exhaust smoke, particularly during engine warm-up and light load operation. If these conditions continue, harmful engine deposits will accumulate in the combustion chamber.

FUEL ADDITIVES

Tetraethyl lead is used in some gasoline to reduce or prevent knocking. However, in 1975 it became illegal to use a leaded gasoline except for cars built prior to this date. Also, with the addition of a catalytic converter, it is undesirable to burn leaded fuel. Leaded fuel will clog the converter, which increases the backpressure of the exhaust. This, in turn, reduces the amount of power that the engine can produce. This means that the catalytic converter, which is expensive, will have to be replaced. Methyl Tertiary Butyl Ether (MTBE) is used in unleaded fuel to increase the octane.

DETERGENTS

Gasoline exposed to heat and air oxidizes and leaves a gummy film. Detergents are currently added to gasoline to prevent this. The detergents keep the carburetor passages and fuel injectors free from these deposits, Fig. 19-5. These deposits could cause hard starting and driveability problems.

LEAD-FREE GASOLINE

Lead-free gasoline is motor fuel without tetraethyl lead. Formerly, lead was added to gasoline to improve its octane rating. Now, lead-free gasoline is required because leaded fuel would quickly destroy the catalytic converter. Methyl Tertiary Butyl Ether (MTBE) is usually added to lead-free gasoline to increase the octane instead of lead. These converters are designed to reduce the amount of carbon monoxide and hydrocarbons in the exhaust.

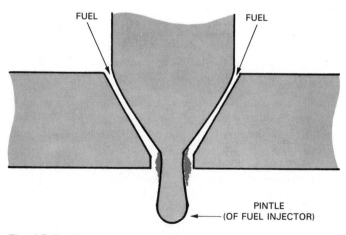

Fig. 19-5. Detergents prevent fuel deposits, in color, from accumulating on the pintle of fuel injector. These deposits can restrict the flow of fuel and cause a rough idle, hesitation on acceleration, surging, stalling, and a lack of power.

Both leaded and lead-free gasolines have certain advantages. In addition to the higher octane rating, leaded gasoline has a good effect on valves and valve seats. With lead in the fuel, valve and valve seat life are lengthened, particularly at high speeds. The lead in the fuel is deposited on the valve seats where it acts as a lubricant.

Valve seat wear has been shown to result from the adhesion of hard abrasive oxide particles from the valve seat onto the valve face. This is followed by the failure of the valve and seat. Tests made by TRW Inc. engineers show a 10 to 20 times greater valve recession rate when lead-free gasoline is used. However, in recent years car manufacturers have improved the valve seats in their engines to better withstand the effect of lead-free gasoline.

ALCOHOL AS A FUEL

The increasing cost and scarcity of gasoline has turned the attention of car and truck designers, and the motoring public, to various substitutes. Chief among the alternate fuels is alcohol.

Considerable research has been done and is being carried on for alcohol in spark ignition engines. In Germany, during World War II, alcohol fuels were used extensively. Currently, alcohol blends are used in many vehicles.

Methanol and ethanol are two forms of alcohol receiving the most attention. Both are made from non-petroleum products. Methanol can be produced from coal. Ethanol can be made from farm products such as sugar cane, corn, and potatoes. Characteristics are compared below.

PROPERTY	METHANOL	ETHANOL	GASOLINE
Heat of vapor-ization	265	216	70-100
Calorific heat value	4200	6400	10,500
Air required	6.4	9.0	14.9
Air-fuel ratio	2.15 to 15.5	3.5 to 17.0	6.0 to 22.0
Self-ignition temperature	478°F	420°F	300-450°F
Research octane number	110	100	92-98
Motor octane	92	89	84-88

Both alcohols have a higher octane number than gasoline. The high heat of vaporization indicates that the use of alcohol could give hard starting problems. The calorific heat values of the alcohols are higher than gasoline, which translates into the need for a larger fuel tank and larger jet sizes in the carburetor. However, the alcohols require less air for combustion, which compensates for the high calorific values. Proportionately, this could result in practically the same air-fuel ratio for all three fuels. In fact, experimental tests have shown that alcohol-fueled spark ignition engines can produce as much or slightly higher power than gasoline.

Alcohol fuels have a higher self-ignition temperature than gasoline, which rates them better from a safety standpoint. However, this same quality bars them from use in a diesel engine that depends on the heat of compression to ignite the fuel.

Currently, only ethanol can be blended in small concentrations (10 percent) with gasoline. Because of the high octane rating, alcohols can be used with relatively high compression ratios ranging from 8.4:1 to 11:1. Experiments also indicate that emissions from alcohol-fueled engines would not require the use of exhaust gas recirculation controls.

ALCOHOL

Alcohol is frequently used as an additive to commercial gasoline. In that way, it will absorb any condensed moisture which may collect in the fuel system.

Water will not pass through the filters in the fuel line. Consequently, when any water collects, it will prevent the free passage of fuel. In addition, water will tend to attack or corrode the zinc die castings of which many carburetors and fuel pumps are made. This corrosion will not only destroy parts, but also clog the system and prevent the flow of fuel. By using alcohol in gasoline, any water present will be absorbed and pass through the fuel filter and carburetor jets into the combustion chamber.

DIESEL FUELS

The type of fuel available for use in diesel engines varies from highly volatile jet fuels and kerosene, to the heavier furnace oil. Automotive diesel engines are capable of burning a wide range of fuel between these two extremes. How well a diesel engine can operate with different types of fuel is dependent upon engine operating conditions, as well as fuel characteristics.

A large variety of fuel oils are marketed by the petroleum industry for diesel engine use. Their properties depend on the refining practices employed, and the nature of the crude oil from which they are produced. Fuel oils, for example, may be produced within the boiling range of 300° to 750°F and have many possible combinations of other properties.

The classification of commercially available fuel oils that has been set up by the American Society for Testing Materials is shown in Fig. 19-6. Grade 1D fuels range from kerosene to what is called intermediate distillates. Grades 2D and 4D each have progressively higher boiling points and contain more impurities.

The fuels commonly known as high-grade fuels, kerosene, and 1D fuels, contribute a minimum amount to the formation of harmful engine deposits and corrosion. There are less impurities present in those fuels. Therefore the tendency to form deposits is kept to a minimum.

While refining removes the impurities, it also lowers the heat value of the fuel. As a result, the higher grade fuels develop slightly less power than the same quantity of low-grade fuel. Often, however, this is more than offset by the maintenance advantages.

LIQUEFIED PETROLEUM GAS (LPG)

A mixture of gaseous petroleum compounds, principally butane and propane, together with smaller quantities

ASTEM DIESEL FUEL CLASSIFICATION DO75-49T

GRADE OF DIESEL FUEL OIL	CETANE NUMBER (MIN.)	SULFUR % BY WT. (MAX.)	DISTILLATION TEMPERATURES, °F		VISCOSITY AT 100°F KINEMATIC CENTISTOKES (OR SUS)	
			90%BOILING POINT (MAX.)	100% BOILING POINT (MAX.)	(MIN.)	(MAX.)
No. 1-D	40	0.50		625	1.4 1.8	5.8
No. 2-D	40	1.0	675		(32.0)	(45)
No. 4-D	30	2.0			5.8 (45)	26.4 (125)

Fig. 19-6. Grade No 1. diesel fuel must be used in the winter. If Grades No. 2 and 4 are used during winter, the fuel will gel and cut off the flow of fuel to the injectors. Grade No. 4 diesel fuel must be used in hot weather, to provide adequate protection.

of similar gases, is known as liquefied petroleum gas (LP-Gas). LP-Gas is used as fuel for internal combustion engines, principally in the truck and farm tractor fields.

Chemically, LP-Gas is similar to gasoline since it consists of a mixture of compounds of hydrogen and carbon. However, it is a great deal more volatile. At usual atmospheric temperatures, it is a vapor. For that reason, when LP-Gas is used as a fuel for internal combustion engines, a special type of carburetor is required.

For storing and transporting LP-Gas, it is compressed and cooled so that it is a liquid. Depending upon conditions, it takes approximately 250 gallons of LP-Gas to be compressed into one gallon of liquid. Because of the pressure it is under, it must be stored in strong tanks. The boiling point of propane is approximately 44°F below zero.

At temperatures below their boiling points, butane and propane exert no pressure. But as the temperature increases, the pressure increases rapidly. At 40°F, liquid propane will have a pressure of 65 lbs.; while butane will have a pressure of about 3 lbs. At 65°F, the pressure of propane will have increased to 100 lbs. and butane to 15 lbs.

LP-Gas is made of surplus material in the oil fields. It is becoming more widely distributed as an increasing number of trucks and tractors are being fitted with the equipment required to make use of it. In addition to its low cost, LP-Gas has the advantage of having a high octane value. Pure butane has a rating of 93 octane, while propane is approximately 100. The octane rating of LP-Gas will range between these two values, depending upon the proportion of each gas used.

Since it is a dry gas, LP-Gas does not create carbon in an engine, and does not cause dilution of the engine oil. As a result, maintenance and internal parts replacement on engines is reduced. In addition, oil changes for the engine can be made at less frequent intervals because LP-Gas is a cleaner burning fuel. Other advantages claimed for LP-Gas are easy cold weather starting, lack of objectionable exhaust odor, and elimination of evaporation.

Chapter 19—REVIEW QUESTIONS

Write your answers on a separate sheet of paper. Do not write in this book.
1. Name three different fuels used in internal combustion engines.
2. The volatility of gasoline is equivalent to its:
   a. Octane rating.
   b. Boiling point.
   c. Cetane rating.
   d. Distillation.
3. What characteristic of fuel affects easy starting?
4. Name the three stages of normal fuel combustion in an internal combustion engine.
5. Describe detonation.
6. Describe preignition.
7. Iso-octane and what other material are used to determine the octane rating of a fuel?
   a. Cetane.
   b. Propane.
   c. Heptane.
   d. Benzol.
8. Alcohol is added to gasoline primarily to:
   a. Provide easier starting.
   b. Absorb any moisture that may be present.
   c. Increase the volatility of the fuel.
9. Automobile diesel engines are capable of burning a wide range of fuels. True or False?
10. Cetane number of a diesel fuel is a measure of:
   a. Volatility.
   b. Viscosity.
   c. Time between fuel injection and ignition.
11. Sulfur content of a fuel should be:
   a. High as possible.
   b. Low as possible.
   c. Does not matter.
12. LP-Gas is a mixture of:
   a. Benzol and heptane.
   b. Butane and propane.
   c. Butane and heptane.
   d. Heptane and cetane.

13. The power of any fuel is determined by its:
    a. Molecular weight.
    b. Heat value.
14. Immediately after ignition, combustion chamber temperatures may reach a value of:
    a. 1500 °F.
    b. 2500 °F.

c. 5500 °F.
d. 7500 °F.

15. Carbon deposits in the combustion chamber are responsible for increased levels of hydrocarbon emissions. Yes or No?
16. Lead-free gasoline promotes longer valve and valve seat life. True or False?

Chapter 20

FUEL SUPPLY SYSTEMS

After studying this chapter, you will be able to:
- List the different types of fuel pumps and gauges.
- Explain how a mechanical and electrical fuel pump operates.
- Describe turbocharger and wastegate operation.

FUEL PUMPS

On small gas engines and many industrial engines, fuel is gravity fed. On automobiles, either mechanical or electric fuel pumps are used.

Mechanical pumps are operated by means of a cam or an eccentric on the camshaft of the engine. Service is limited to replacement.

Electric fuel pumps are energized by a built-in electric motor. Some are designed to be submerged in the fuel in the tank; others are installed in the fuel line between the tank and carburetor or fuel injector. Service is also limited to replacement.

MECHANICAL FUEL PUMP

A typical, single-action, "sealed" mechanical fuel pump is shown in Fig. 20-1. Working parts include an actuating lever, diaphragm, spring, inlet valve, and outlet valve, Fig. 20-2.

In operation, the eccentric presses down on the pump rocker arm, Fig. 20-3, lifting the pull rod and diaphragm

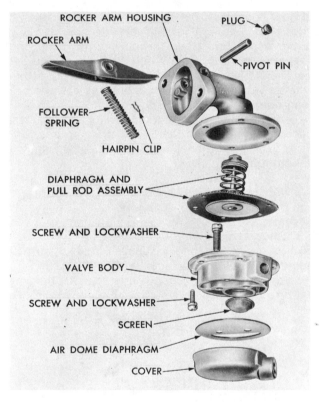

Fig. 20-2. Components of a mechanical fuel pump.

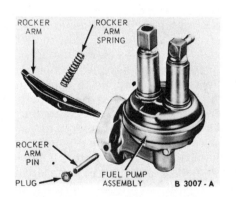

Fig. 20-1. If any part of a mechanical fuel pump is found defective, the entire pump must be replaced. (Carter)

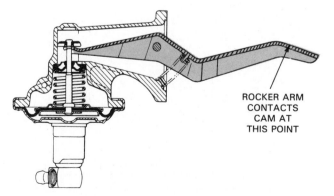

Fig. 20-3. Rocker arm on fuel pump acts as a lever. (Chrysler)

against the tension of the main spring of the pump. This creates a vacuum in the valve housing, opens the intake valve and fuel is drawn into the valve housing chamber, Fig. 20-4.

On the return stroke, the main spring forces the diaphragm down, closing the inlet valve and fuel is pumped from the chamber through the outlet valve to the fuel filter. Each revolution of the camshaft repeats this cycle.

When the carburetor float needle valve closes, fuel pump output is limited to the small amount that bleeds back. The lever keeps working, maintaining fuel pressure in the fuel pump chamber to keep the diaphragm extended and inoperative. Fuel flow to the carburetor is halted until the carburetor needle valve opens. This cycle of operation continues as long as the engine is in operation.

Most mechanical fuel pumps are designed to prevent an oversupply of fuel when the carburetor float rises and fuel flow is shut off by the needle and seat assembly. At this point, the fuel pump diaphragm spring is held in a compressed position and the rocker arm "idles" on the camshaft eccentric. Diaphragm action is reduced to a slight movement, just enough to provide a reduced flow of fuel to replace fuel which enters the carburetor between pump strokes.

In effect, this idling action produces a constant pressure on the fuel in the line to the carburetor. This pressure is proportional to the force exerted by the diaphragm spring.

MECHANICAL FUEL PUMP TROUBLES

Modern fuel pumps give many thousands of miles of trouble-free service without the need for maintenance. When a pump no longer supplies fuel in sufficient volume, it should be replaced with a new unit.

To determine if the fuel pump is at fault, first make sure the supply tank has a sufficient quantity of fuel and that the tank is properly vented. If satisfactory, disconnect the fuel supply line at the carburetor and direct the fuel line into a small container. Then, with the distributor primary wire to the ignition coil grounded, crank the engine by means of the starter. If the fuel pump is in good condition, fuel will spurt from the supply line.

If no fuel is pumped, or only a small quantity, the pump is probably defective and should be replaced. Of course, it must be verified that the fuel line between the pump and supply tank is not clogged, or have an air leak. Also, check the condition of the fuel filter and the flexible fuel line connecting the pump with the end of the rigid fuel line leading to the supply tank. These flexible lines may develop air-leaks or the interior may swell and obstruct the flow of fuel.

An infrequent trouble is when the fuel pump supplies too much fuel. Excessive pressures result in flooding of the carburetor. Fuel pump pressure may be tested with a suitable pressure gauge.

To make the test: Connect the gauge to the outlet side of the pump. When the engine is cranked by the starter, the gauge should register 4 to 6 lbs. pressure. The length of the hose connecting the gauge to the fuel pump should not exceed 6 in., otherwise inaccurate readings may result.

Another fuel pump test can be made by directing fuel flow from the pump into a pint or quart measure. With the engine operating at idling speed, a pint of fuel should be pumped in approximately 45 seconds. The fuel in the float bowl will keep the engine operating long enough to make the test.

It has been established that there are four points where wear or damage will affect the performance of a fuel pump. These points are: worn linkage, worn valves or seats, worn pull rod, and punctured diaphragm.

While a carbureted engine usually uses a mechanical fuel pump, a fuel injected engine uses an electric fuel pump. An electric fuel pump reduces the chances of vapor lock.

ELECTRIC FUEL PUMPS

Electrically operated fuel pumps are of two basic types:
1. Suction type draws fuel from tank in a manner similar to mechanically operated pumps.
2. Pusher type placed in bottom of fuel supply tank "pushes" fuel to carburetor.

An in-tank, pusher type fuel pump is illustrated in Fig. 20-5 and a Bendix electric fuel pump is shown in Fig. 20-6. An advantage of the externally mounted electric pump is that several pumps can be installed, and larger quantities of fuel can be supplied; if one pump should fail, the others would continue to supply fuel.

An important advantage of an electric fuel pump is that there it a considerable reduction in vapor lock problems. The reason is that the vacuum created to "pull" the fuel from the tank reduces the boiling point.

The mechanical pump, on the other hand, is driven by the engine camshaft and must be installed in a location where it will operate at a higher temperature. Another advantage of the electric pump is that as soon as the ignition is turned on it will supply fuel.

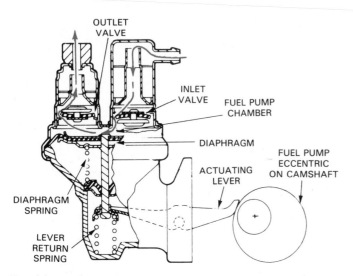

Fig. 20-4. The rocker arm of the fuel pump is depressed by an eccentric on the camshaft. This action causes the diaphragm to be pulled downward against spring pressure. As the diaphragm moves downward, a suction is created. (American Motors)

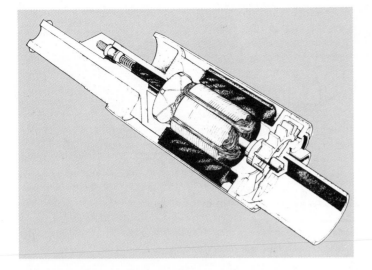

Fig. 20-5. Some electric fuel pumps are mounted inside the gas tank. (AC Spark Plug)

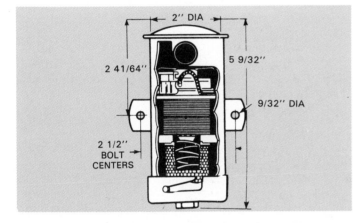

Fig. 20-6. A Bendix electric fuel pump.

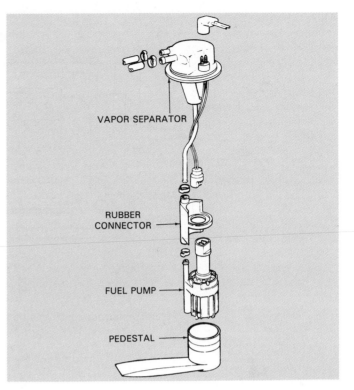

Fig. 20-7. Components of an electric fuel pump (Carter)

There are no valves between the electric pump and the throttle body. Therefore, the fuel drains back into the tank when the engine is stopped. This eliminates pressure buildup and consequent hard starting of a hot engine. The delivery of the fuel is steady and nonpulsating.

IN-TANK ELECTRIC FUEL PUMPS

The electric fuel pump, Fig. 20-7, is located in the fuel tank as part of the electric fuel pump and fuel gauge tank unit assembly. The assembly is installed through the fuel tank access hole in the trunk floor. Electrical connections are by means of two wires to the fuel pump terminals, an outside ground wire, and a two-way connector.

The pump is a turbine type hydraulic unit directly coupled to a permanent magnet motor, Fig. 20-7. Fuel is drawn into the pump through a woven plastic filter, then ''pushed'' through the fuel line. A control switch located near the oil filter is hydraulically connected to the engine oil system, so that oil pressure actuates the diaphragm of the switch.

During cranking of the engine, current for the electric fuel pump control switch is taken from the starter solenoid, as long as engine oil pressure is below 3 psi. Once the engine starts and oil pressure is normal, the pump is energized through the ignition switch, gauge fuse, control switch, and in-line pump fuse. Turning off the ignition switch de-energizes the pump.

If oil pressure drops below 3 psi during engine operation, the pump will be de-energized, and the engine will stop running. When the engine is cranked, current is delivered through a special bypass circuit. Current passes through the oil pressure switch to the pump, delivering the full 12 V. When the engine starts, the current will pass through a resistor, cutting voltage to 8 1/2 to 10 V. Electric fuel pumps are serviced as an assembly.

ROBERT BOSCH

The Bosch electric fuel pump, Fig. 20-8, is of a roller type. As the roller assembly spins, Fig. 20-9, a low pressure area is created on the left side of the pump. Atmospheric pressure pushes fuel from the tank to the low pressure area created within the pump. As the roller continues to spin, the fuel is pushed into an increasingly smaller area within the pump. As this happens, the fuel is pressurized and forced out the pump discharge outlet and into the fuel lines. A fuel pump relay is mounted on the fuse box. The relay acts as a safety device. In the event the car is in an accident, the relay breaks the electrical circuit to the fuel pump, and prevents fuel from being pumped. This reduces the chance of a fire. Electric fuel pump diagnosis is covered in Chapter 26, Fuel Injection.

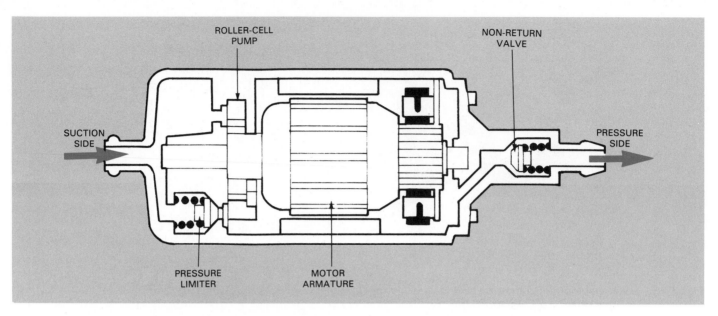

Fig. 20-8. Construction of an electric roller type fuel pump.   (Robert Bosch)

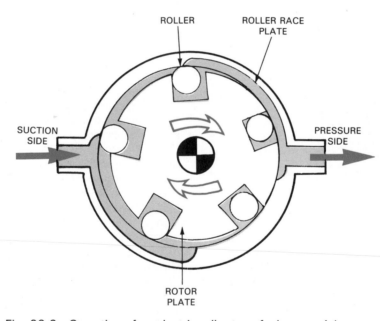

Fig. 20-9. Operation of an electric roller type fuel pump. A low pressure area is created within the pump and fuel is forced to it. The fuel is then forced to an increasingly smaller area and is pressurized.   (Robert Bosch)

FUEL FILTERS

Clean fuel is essential, because of the many small jets and passages in the carburetor and orifices in a fuel injector. To ensure this cleanliness, fuel filters are installed in the fuel line between the fuel pump and carburetor or fuel injector.

Fuel filters of various types and construction are used, all designed to filter out all foreign matter. Some remove water that may be present.

In many cases, the filter is built into the carburetor. A ceramic type filter is shown in Fig. 20-10 and a paper element type filter in Fig. 20-11.

Since accumulations of dirt and water in the filter tend to restrict the flow of fuel, it is essential that the unit is replaced periodically. Usually, this is done once a year. A disposable cartridge type fuel filter is also used, Figs. 20-12 and 20-13. This type of fuel filter is placed in-line. Both types perform the same function.

FUEL GAUGES

There are two basic types of fuel gauges in use, the thermostatic type and the balancing coil type.

Fig. 20-10. A ceramic type fuel filter can be cleaned and reinstalled.

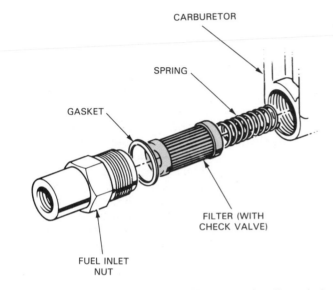

Fig. 20-11. A paper type fuel filter must be discarded and replaced with a new fuel filter. (Oldsmobile)

Fig. 20-12. An in-line fuel filter must also be discarded and replaced with a new filter of the same type.

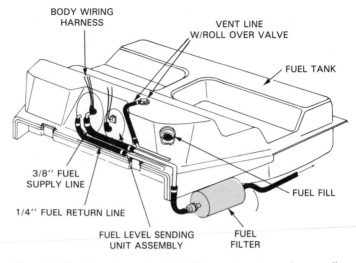

Fig. 20-13. The filter for fuel injected engines is usually located near the fuel tank. (Chrysler)

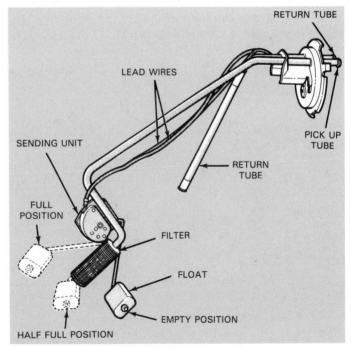

Fig. 20-14. The sending unit is located in the fuel tank. Note that there is an in-tank filter located on the suction side. (Chrysler)

THERMOSTATIC GAUGE

The thermostataic type of fuel gauge consists of a sending unit located in the fuel tank, Fig. 20-14, and the gauge (registering unit) located on the instrument panel. In addition, there is a voltage regulator unit, which is designed to maintain an average value of 5.0 volts at the gauge terminals. It is compensated for temperature variations and is provided with an adjustment which controls the rate at which the contacts make and break. It controls the voltage supplied to the gauge system.

The gauge pointer is controlled by a bimetallic arm and heating coil, Fig. 20-15. The sending unit in the fuel tank has a rheostat that varies its resistance depending on the amount of fuel in the tank.

When the fuel tank is empty, the grounding sliding contact, Fig. 20-15, is at the end of the resistance wire of the rheostat. With all of the resistance in the circuit, only a small amount of current will flow through the heating oil of the gauge unit, and the gauge will register zero.

When the tank is full, the float rises with the fuel, moving the grounded contact toward the beginning of the resistance coil. More current will flow through the heating coil, and the bimetallic arm of the gauge will deflect the pointer to the "Full" position.

BALANCED COIL FUEL GAUGE

The fuel gauge used in some cars and trucks is of the electricallly operated balanced coil type. It consists of a dash unit and a tank unit, Fig. 20-16.

The dash unit is made of two coils placed at 90 deg. to each other. An armature and pointer assembly is mounted at the intersection of the centerline of the two coils. To prevent vibration of the pointer, the armature is provided with a dampening device.

The tank unit consists of a rheostat with a movable contact arm. Position of the contact arm is controlled by a float that rests on the surface of the fuel. To prevent splashing of the fuel from affecting the movement of the float, a torque washer and spring are used.

The tank unit is grounded out of the gauge circuit when the fuel tank is empty, and the float is in its lowest position. Then, current passes through the coil on the empty side of the dash unit ("full coil" is of higher resistance), and the pointer is pulled to indicate zero.

As fuel is added to the supply tank, there is corresponding rise of the float. Movement of the rheostat arm placed resistance in the circuit, and current will flow through the "full" coil. As a result, the pointer will be attracted to indicate the quantity of fuel in the tank.

Since an increase or decrease of battery voltage will affect both coils equally, the accuracy of the gauge will not be affected. Compensation for temperature variation is also provided.

SUPERCHARGERS

The power developed by an internal combustion engine is largely dependent on the amount of combustible mixture reaching the cylinders. The design of manifolds, carburetors, fuel injectors, the size of valves, and valve ports are all important factors in determining the amount of this mixture. Therefore, to overcome friction losses in the intake system and to aid in scavenging the cylinders of burnt gases, superchargers can be used to blow the combustible mixture into the cylinders of spark ignition engines, Fig. 20-17.

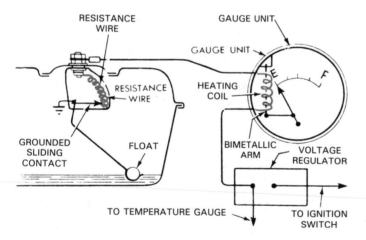

Fig. 20-15. Thermostatic fuel gauge.

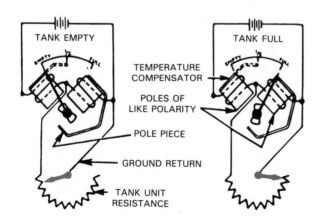

Fig. 20-16. Balanced coil fuel gauge. Left. Conditions for an empty tank. Right. Conditions for a full tank. (AC Spark Plug)

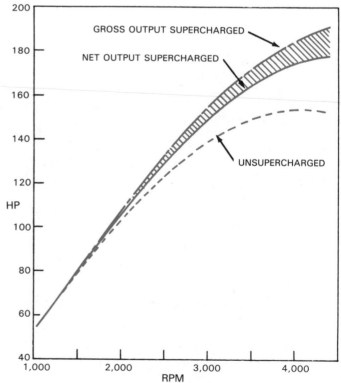

Fig. 20-17. Comparing power output of a nonsupercharged and supercharged engine.

Superchargers were first developed for racing cars and other high performance engines. Later, they found wide application on aircraft. In this application, the power of an engine falls rapidly as the airplane attains higher altitudes. As air density decreases, smaller amounts of air will be drawn into the cylinders. Finally, at an altitude of 18,000 feet, only one half the normal charge will reach the cylinder, and only one half the power will be developed. Superchargers then are used on aircraft to help maintain power at high altitudes.

A supercharger is a compressor. Therefore, a supercharged engine will have higher overall compression than a nonsupercharged engine having the same combustion chamber volume and piston displacement.

However, this higher overall compression will increase the tendency toward detonation of spark ignition engines. So, when a supercharger is used, fuel of higher-than-standard octane rating is required to avoid detonation. However, when a supercharger is installed on a diesel engine, only air is blown into the cylinders, and the tendency toward detonation is reduced.

Superchargers are designed to develop from 4 to 20 lb. pressure. The greater the pressure developed, the more air-fuel mixture or air that will be carried to the cylinders. The power required to drive the supercharger increases rapidly. It may be as much as 50 hp per lb. of air per second.

A supercharged engine will burn more fuel than when it is nonsupercharged. However, the increase in power is not proportional to the increase in fuel consumed.

TYPES OF SUPERCHARGERS

There are two general types of superchargers, the Rootes type and the centrifugal type. The Rootes "blower" has two rotors, Fig. 20-18. The centrifugal supercharger utilizes an impeller rotating at high speed inside a housing.

In most designs of the Rootes supercharger, each of the two rotors has two lobes. In shape, they resemble a figure 8. However, some Rootes units are fitted with rotors of three or more lobes. Fig. 20-18. The shafts of the two Rootes rotors are interconnected through gearing and operate at the same speed with action similar to the gear type oil pump. The rotors do not quite touch each other. There is also a slight clearance between the rotors and the surrounding housing.

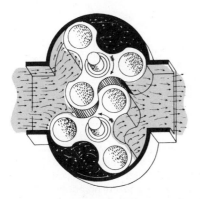

Fig. 20-18. A Rootes type supercharger.

In operation, air enters the housing by the action of the rotors. It passes between the lobes of the rotors and the housing, then is forced through the outlet of the unit.

With the Rootes blower, the rate of delivery varies slightly faster than the speed of rotation, because the leakage decreases as the speed increases. Above a certain minimum speed, the amount of supercharging is almost constant. Rootes blowers are driven at speeds from one to two times engine speed.

The centrifugal type supercharger, used in many racing applications, consists of an impeller rotating at a high speed inside a housing. Clearance between the blades and the housing must be kept at a minimum. Since the speed of rotation is approximately five times engine speed, it can easily attain a speed of 25,000 rpm.

Therefore, it is essential that the rotor is accurately balanced, both statically and dynamically. Furthermore, the rotor blades must be made strong enough so that the centrifugal force at high speeds will not cause them to stretch and strike the housing.

On racing car installations, the air from the impeller first passes to a diffuser, where the force of the moving air is converted to static energy. The diffuser consists of a ring-shaped housing containing blades or vanes.

Coolers are used in conjunction with centrifugal superchargers to reduce the temperature of the air. This is important because the act of compressing the air will increase its temperature. The warm air entering would reduce the efficiency of the engine. The coolers consist of several lengths of finned tubing.

The rate of delivery of the centrifugal supercharger increases as the square of the speed of rotation. As a result, very little supercharging is obtained at lower speeds, and the variation between different speeds is large. Carburetion is more difficult with a centrifugal supercharger than with a Rootes type unit.

LOCATION OF SUPERCHARGER

Superchargers can be placed between the throttle body of the carburetor or fuel injection system and the manifold; or, at the air inlet before the throttle body. Racing cars usually have the supercharger between the throttle body and the manifold.

The throttle body/manifold design has the advantage that the fuel can be supplied through the throttle body without modification to any part of the system. If the supercharger is placed in front of the throttle body, fuel must be supplied under sufficient pressure to overcome the added air pressure created by the supercharger. The advantage of a supercharger over a turbocharger is that there is no lag time of boost; the moment the accelerator pedal is depressed, the boost is increased.

TURBOCHARGER

While turbochargers and superchargers perform the same function, the turbocharger is driven by exhaust gases; the supercharger is driven by belts or gears. However, a turbocharger requires less power to be driven than a supercharger. A turbocharger consists of a turbine and a compressor, Fig. 20-19. The pressure of the hot exhaust gases cause the turbine to spin. Since the turbine is mounted on the same shaft as the compressor, the compressor is forced to spin at the same time, Fig. 20-20. When the compressor spins, 50 percent more air is drawn into the cylinders than without a turbocharger. This creates more power when the air-fuel mixture explodes.

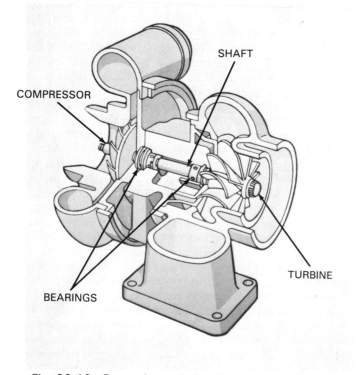

Fig. 20-19. Parts of a typical turbocharger. (Chrysler)

A turbocharged engine's compression ratio must be lowered. This is usually accomplished by using a lower compression piston. If the compression is not lowered, an excessive amount of pressure will be placed on the piston, connecting rods, and crankshaft. Further excessive pressure will cause detonation which can destroy an engine. The connecting rods, crankshaft, and the gears in the transmission must all be strengthened on a turbocharged engine. If this is not done, the engine and transmission will be torn apart by the increased horsepower.

WASTEGATE

The wastegate, Fig. 20-21, controls the amount of BOOST that the turbocharger can put out. Boost is a pressure greater than atmospheric pressure. When the boost pressure reaches a predetermined value, the wastegate opens and bypasses some of the exhaust gases directly into the exhaust manifold. This causes the turbine to reduce its speed, thereby reducing the speed of the compressor. This limits the amount of boost. As pressure is reduced, the wastegate begins to close again. If the boost is not controlled, the turbocharger will explode. In addition, engine components will be damaged from the excessive pressure.

On some computerized engines the wastegate is controlled by a solenoid, which is activated by the computer. This eliminates the pressure-operated wastegate actuator, the rod that connects the actuator to the wastegate, and the rubber hose that connects from the compressor side of the turbo to the actuator. On these engines the boost is monitored through the MAP sensor.

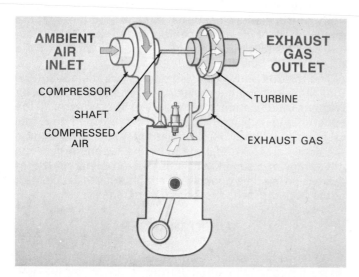

Fig. 20-20. As the exhaust gases leave the cylinder they must pass through the turbine. This causes the turbine to spin. Since the shaft connects the compressor, the compressor spins also. As the compressor spins, air is forced into the cylinder. (Chrysler)

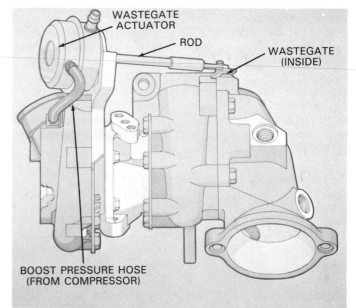

Fig. 20-21. Wastegate is located in the turbo housing. On some computerized engines, the wastegate actuator is a solenoid that sits directly on top of the wastegate. The wastegate limits the amount of boost to approximately 5 to 10 psi on street cars and 50 psi on race cars. (Chrysler)

WASTEGATE OPERATION

The wastegate is held closed by spring pressure, Fig. 20-22. The compressed air from the compressor is routed to the cylinders and the wastegate actuator. As pressure increases, the wastegate begins to open. This is anywhere from 5 to 10 psi on street engines and 50 psi on race engines.

To verify that the wastegate is operating properly, install a vacuum/pressure gauge to a manifold vacuum source. Consult the individual manual for the specified amount of boost. While driving under all different conditions, note the readings. If the specified boost is never obtained, the wastegate is stuck in the open position. If the specified pressure is exceeded, the wastegate actuator is defective or the wastegate is stuck in the closed position.

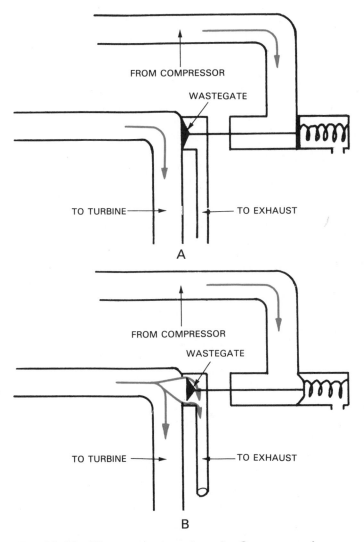

Fig. 20-22. Wastegate operation. A—Compressor is connected to the wastegate actuator by a rubber hose. When boost is low, the wastegate remains closed and allows boost to increase. B—When boost reaches the specified limit, the boost pressure overrides spring pressure in the wastegate actuator, forcing the wastegate to open. Some of the exhaust gases are then diverted past the turbine, reducing the turbine's speed. This then limits the amount of boost.

As stated earlier, some computerized engines replace the wastegate actuator with a solenoid. So, if the correct pressures are not obtained, the solenoid, MAP sensor, or computer are defective. However, the wastegate may also be stuck in either the closed or open position.

INTERCOOLER

While the compressor of the turbocharger is forcing air into the cylinders, the air is pressurized. Pressure is directly related to heat; the greater the pressure, the greater the heat. The air, after being compressed, is extremely hot. Hot air expands and is less dense than cooler air. Therefore, it is desirable to cool down the compressed air before it enters the intake manifold. This is done by an intercooler, Fig. 20-23. The cool compressed air is packed tighter together in the cylinder than if it had not been cooled. Since the air-fuel mixture is packed tighter, more power is created when this air-fuel mixture explodes. Not all turbocharged engines have an intercooler, as this is an added expense.

TURBOCHARGER SERVICE

To provide the proper maintenance for a turbocharged engine, the engine oil must be changed more frequently than a non-turbocharged engine. This is due to the excessive amount of heat generated by the turbocharger. The heat reduces the effectiveness of the oil. Also, the slightest contamination can destroy the bearings in the turbocharger, as the turbo rotates at speeds in excess of 100,000 rpm. The engine oil that should be used must be recommended especially for turbocharged engines. Follow manufacturer's recommendations and specifications carefully.

TURBOCHARGER PROBLEMS

The most common problems associated with a turbocharger is the wastegate or its actuator. If the

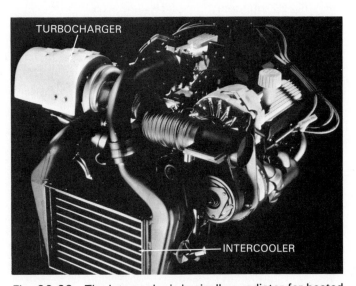

Fig. 20-23. The intercooler is basically a radiator for heated air from the turbo. (Buick)

wastegate remains in the closed position, fuel consumption will be increased and detonation will result. If the wastegate sticks in the open position, there will be a lack of power on acceleration. This is due to a lack of boost. Other problems are:

1. Vibration due to excessive axial play caused by bearing wear in turbo. Nicks or dents on the compressor or turbine wheel can also cause a vibration.
2. Turbo housing becomes cherry red due to an excessively lean air-fuel mixture (vacuum leak), and/or advanced timing.
3. Oil consumption due to a carbon seal defect in the turbo housing. If so, the entire turbocharger will have to be replaced. However, do not consider a small amount of oil inside of the turbo hosuing a problem; this is normal. Since the turbo is increasing the amount of air into the cylinders, there will be an increase of blowby. Blowby carries oil vapors from the crankcase into the turbo housing where they condense. Suspect the carbon seal only if there is an excessive amount of oil in the turbo housing, and no other defects are found for excessive oil consumption.

Chapter 20—REVIEW QUESTIONS

Write your answers on a separate sheet of paper. Do not write in this book.

1. On lawn mower engines, how is fuel usually supplied to the carburetor?
2. On modern passenger cars, what two methods are used to drive the fuel pumps?
3. How much pressure should the conventional mechanical type fuel pump develop?
   a. 5 lb.
   b. 10 lb.
   c. 15 lb.
4. In 45 seconds, how much fuel should be pumped by the average mechanical type fuel pump?
   a. 1 pint.
   b. 2 pints.
   c. 3 pints.
   d. 32 ounces.
5. Mechanic A states that a fuel filter for a fuel injected engine is usually located in the engine compartment.
   Mechanic B states that a fuel filter for a fuel injected engine is located near the fuel tank.
   Who is right?
   a. Mechanic A.
   b. Mechanic B.
   c. Both Mechanics A and B.
   d. Neither Mechanic A nor B.
6. What is a major advantage of using an externally mounted, electrically operated fuel pump?
7. Name two main types of mechanically driven superchargers.
8. Which type of internal combustion engine will tend to detonate more?
   a. Supercharged.
   b. Nonsupercharged.
9. What is a major advantage of the turbocharger over the mechanically driven type?
   a. Little or no power required to drive it.
   b. Develops more pressure.
10. Name the two general types of fuel gauges.
11. Name two types of materials used in fuel filters.
12. Mechanic A states that the wastegate limits the amount of boost.
    Mechanic B states that a wastegate cools the compressed air.
    Who is right?
    a. Mechanic A.
    b. Mechanic B.
    c. Neither Mechanic A nor B.
    d. Both Mechanic A and B.
13. The purpose of the intercooler is to:
    a. Limit the amount of boost.
    b. Limit fuel pressure.
    c. Cool the compressed air.
    d. None of the above.
14. What else must be done to the engine when it is turbocharged?
    a. Lower the compression ratio.
    b. Strengthen the drive train parts.
    c. Both A and B.
    d. None of the above.
15. Fuel moves from a low pressure area to a high pressure area. True or False?
16. What drives the turbocharger?
    a. The camshaft.
    b. The crankshaft.
    c. Incoming air.
    d. Exhaust gas.

Chapter 21

INTAKE MANIFOLDS

After studying this chapter, you will be able to:
- Explain the problems associated with an intake manifold.
- State the purpose for applying heat to the manifold.
- Describe how an intake manifold is heated.
- Tell how fuel is distributed through the intake manifold.

INTAKE MANFOLDS

The intake manifold connects the carburetor to the intake ports of the engine, Fig. 21-1. Intake manifolds were of simple design. Today, however, intake manifold design is much more precise. Also, in order to ensure good distribution of fuel, heat is supplied to the intake manifold.

The problem in designing intake manifolds lies in providing each cylinder with the same quality and quantity of fuel. As was pointed out in the section on fuels, gasoline is a mixture of various hydrocarbons. Some vaporize more easily than others. If the gasoline consisted solely of vaporized fuel, equal distribution of the fuel to each cylinder would be easy.

Heat is applied to aid in vaporization. However, heat tends to reduce the volumetric efficiency of the engine. Smaller amounts of the combustible air-fuel mixture will reach the cylinder and, in that way, power will be reduced. So, heat must be controlled for a given engine.

FUEL DISTRIBUTION PROBLEMS

Even with heat aiding vaporization, the mixture in the intake manifold is not fully vaporized. As a result, the quantity and quality of the fuel charge reaching each cylinder varies. Because of this unequal distribution, some cylinders develop more power than others. Some cylinders are more likely to detonate than others.

Air-fuel distribution varies with the speed of the engine. So, it is necessary to design and adjust the carburetor to provide an adequate mixture for what would otherwise be the weak cylinder. However, the other cylinders will receive a mixture that is too rich.

There are several reasons why the fuel reaching each of the cylinders varies in quality and quantity. When the

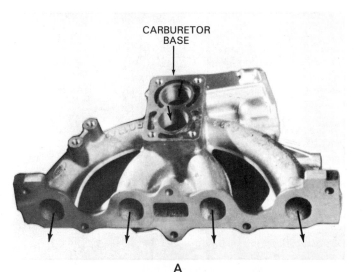

CARBURETOR BASE

A

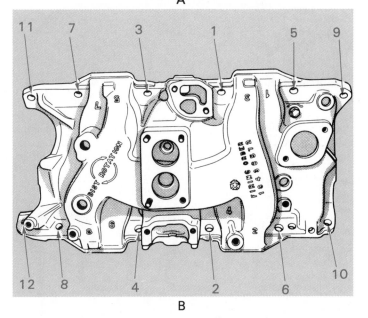

B

Fig. 21-1. Intake manifolds for two barrel carburetors. A—Four cylinder intake manifold. Arrows indicate direction of air-fuel flow. B—V-8 intake manifold. Manifolds, like cylinder heads, must be tightened in a specific sequence to prevent vacuum leaks. (Ford and Chrysler)

throttle valve is partly open, the flow of air and fuel is directed against one side, Fig. 21-2.

Of even greater effect on distribution is that the heavy particles of the air-fuel mixture have greater inertia than the lighter particles. As a result, the heavier particles will tend to continue moving past an intake runner in the manifold, Fig. 21-3. Therefore, the cylinder supplied by that intake runner will receive fewer heavy particles and an excess of lighter particles.

Some cylinders will receive greater quantities of tetraethyl lead, when used, than others. Cylinders receiving the leanest mixture and/or least amount of tetraethyl lead will be more likely to knock.

Fig. 21-4 shows the varied air-fuel ratio of the fuel reaching each of the cylinders. Similar in effect is the varied octane rating of the fuel supplied each cylinder. The shape of the intake manifold, composition of the fuel, heat supplied, and engine speed all effect air-fuel distribution.

Other studies show that, as a result of varied fuel distribution, pressures developed in a six cylinder engine vary from a low of 125 psi to a maximum of 310 psi. It was found that cylinders No. 3 and 4 developed the minimum pressure, cylinder 6 the maximum, and cylinders 1, 2, and 5 approximately 280 psi each.

Increasing the fuel supply rate improved the condition up to a point. Increases resulted in cylinders No. 3 and 4 producing a pressure of 310 psi and the other cylinders developing only 235 psi.

In order to improve the air-fuel mixture distribution to the cylinders, many engines are equipped with carburetors of two or four barrels (Bbl.), or throats. In addition, some engines have more than one carburetor. Two four barrel carburetors or three two barrel carburetors may be used on V-8 engines, Figs. 21-5 and 21-6.

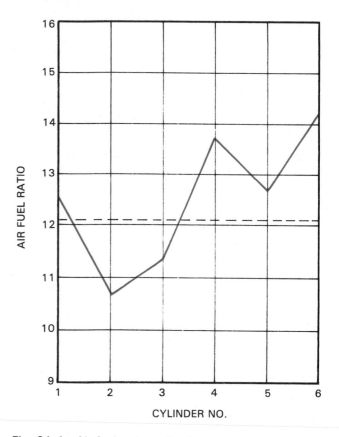

Fig. 21-4. Air-fuel ratio varies from cylinder to cylinder.

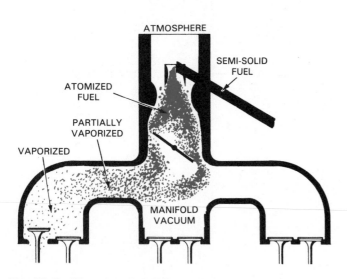

Fig. 21-2. Throttle valve deflects air-fuel mixture to one side.

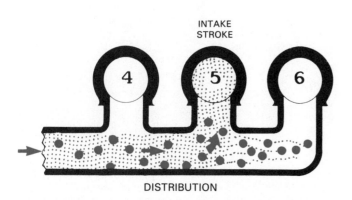

Fig. 21-3. Heavy particles of air-fuel mixture move to end of manifold, rather than enter an intake runner.

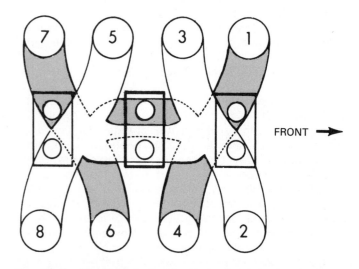

Fig. 21-5. Manifold design for three two barrel carburetors.

There are large variations in air-fuel mixture delivered to the cylinders of an engine equipped with a carburetor. Also, poor fuel mileage and higher exhaust emissions are a problem. Because of this, manufacturers are adopting fuel injection systems, Fig. 21-7.

MANIFOLD DESIGN

Manifolds for engines in passenger cars are usually made of cast iron or aluminum. Manifolds for racing engines are made either of cast aluminum or built up of aluminum tubing with walls approximately 1/8 in. thick.

The number of outlets to the manifolds is dependent on the number of cylinders and valves. For example, each cylinder has its own intake and exhaust ports.

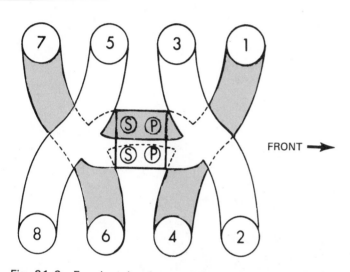

Fig. 21-6. Four barrel carburetor has a primary side, indicated by the ''P,'' and a secondary side indicated by the ''S.'' A two barrel carburetor is the same except for the added fuel from the secondaries.

Fig. 21-7. Intake runner design on a fuel injected engine. Note the long runner design for inertia effect. (Pontiac)

V-8 engines fitted with a two barrel carburetor have the manifolds designed so that each carburetor barrel supplies alternate cylinders in the firing order. One barrel of the carburetor will supply the end cylinders on the left bank and the two central cylinders on the right bank, Fig. 21-6. The other barrel supplies the central cylinders on the left bank and the end cylinders on the right bank.

For example, the firing order of a V-8 is 1R, 1L, 4R, 4L, 2L, 3R, 3L, 2R, or 1-5-4-8-6-3-7-2. One throat of the carburetor will supply 1L, 7L, 6R, and 4R. The other will supply 8R, 3L, 5L, and 2R, Fig. 21-8.

With emission controls, the intake manifold takes on added importance. First, the positive crankcase ventilation system is connected to it. Various emission control devices rely on intake manifold vacuum. These include vacuum-controlled spark timing devices, vacuum-operated motors for heated air cleaners, and intake manifold-based exhaust gas recirculation systems. See Chapter 37, EMISSION CONTROLS for details. SION CONTROLS for details.

MANIFOLD HEAT CONTROL

The purpose of a carburetor is to deliver a metered amount of atomized fuel mixed with air, to the manifold. Regardless of how well mixed and vaporized the fuel mixture is as it leaves the carburetor, it is changed as it passes through the manifold. Cold surfaces in the manifold will cause some of the vaporized fuel to condense. Changes in direction of flow will, through inertia, cause some portions of the mixture to settle out. These conditions have been observed by using glass manifolds.

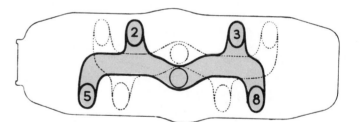

FIRING ORDER
LEFT HAND BARREL OF CARBURETOR
5-8-3-2

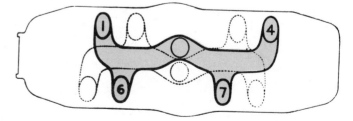

FIRING ORDER
RIGHT HAND BARREL OF CARBURETOR
1-4-6-7

Fig. 21-8. A V-8 engine with a firing order of 1-5-4-8-6-3-7-2. Note the fuel distribution for this firing order.

The problem is further complicated by the fuel itself. Formerly, when the fuel was highly volatile, the problem was not so difficult. Today's fuels are nonvolatile in contrast. It is necessary to supply heat to obtain better vaporization and more equal distribution of the fuel to each cylinder, Fig. 21-9.

Heat to the intake manifold is most needed when the engine is cold and idling. When idling, suction on the carburetor is low, and the fuel is not sprayed very finely.

In order to supply and regulate the amount of heat reaching the intake manifold, a thermostatic manifold heat control valve is installed. Details are shown in Figs. 21-10 and 21-11.

If an engine did not have some way of heating the fuel mixture, the engine would stumble and hesitate until it reached operating temperature. If heat were applied to the air-fuel mixture after the engine had reached operating temperature, exhaust valves would burn and detonation would result.

A typical thermostatic coil spring used on a manifold heat control valve is shown in Fig. 21-12. The thermostat is mounted on the outside of the exhaust pipe or manifold, and it is provided with a counterbalance weight, Fig. 21-10. Often, the valve shaft is mounted on stainless steel bushings. This is important because the high temperatures and acids of the exhaust cause these valves to become rusted in position.

To ensure free operation of the manifold heat control valve, special oils, usually containing graphite, should be applied to the ends of the valve shaft and bushings at regular intervals. To free a stuck valve, penetrating oil should be applied when the manifold is cold. After allowing the oil to penetrate, tap the valve shaft back and forth with a light hammer.

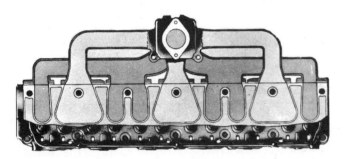

Fig. 21-9. On an in-line engine the exhaust manifold surrounds the intake manifold. This heats the air-fuel mixture.

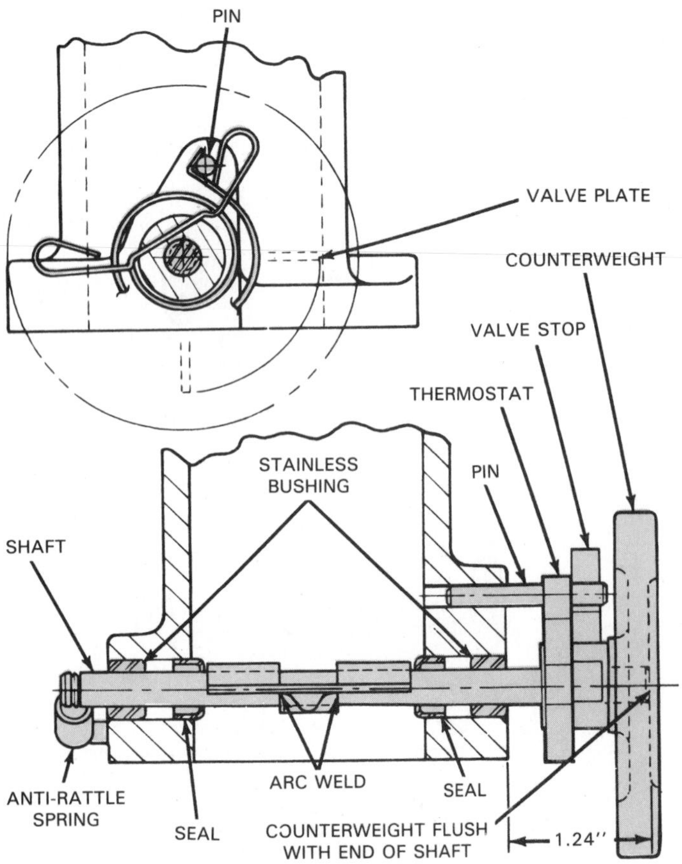

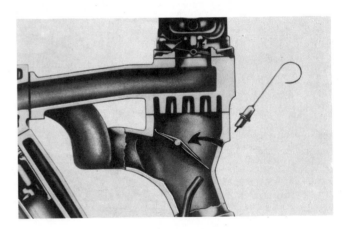

Fig. 21-11. Manifold heat control valve redirects the exhaust gases.

Fig. 21-10. A manifold heat control valve installed in the exhaust manifold.

PIN

VALVE PLATE

COUNTERWEIGHT

VALVE STOP

THERMOSTAT

STAINLESS BUSHING

PIN

SHAFT

ANTI-RATTLE SPRING

SEAL

ARC WELD

SEAL

COUNTERWEIGHT FLUSH WITH END OF SHAFT

1.24"

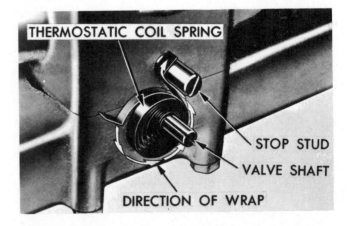

Fig. 21-12. Thermostatic coil spring determines when heat control valve is closed. When the spring is cold, the heat control valve remains closed. This allows the exhaust gases to be redirected to crossover passage in intake manifold.

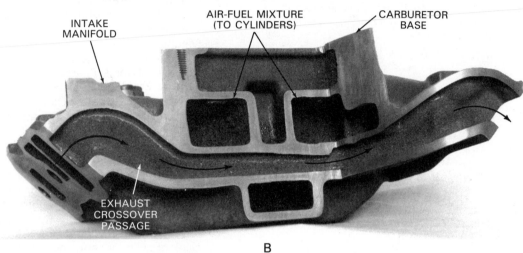

Fig. 21-13. Exhaust gas passages. A—No. 1 indicates the intake ports of cylinder head that align with intake manifold. No. 2 indicates where exhaust gases exit cylinder head when heat control valve is closed. Exhaust gases then enter crossover passage of intake manifold. No. 3 indicates coolant passages. B—Exhaust gases flow through separate passage under carburetor to heat the incoming air-fuel mixture. Exhaust gases then exit through a port in remaining cylinder head on a V-type engine.   (Ford)

The manifold heat control valve is closed by spring pressure of the thermostataic coil when the engine is cold. This forces the exhaust gases through the crossover passage of the intake manifold, Fig. 21-13. The exhaust gas heats the intake manifold. This assists in vaporizing the incoming fuel mixture on a V-type engine. As the engine reaches operating temperature, the thermostatic coil spring unwinds relieving the pressure on the heat control valve. This forces the heat control valve to open, as the heat is no longer wanted or needed.

EARLY FUEL EVAPORATION SYSTEM (EFE)

One of the EFE systems is similar to the thermostatic heat control valve. However, vacuum is used to open the heat control valve instead of a coil spring, Fig. 21-14. Another type of EFE system has an electric grid placed under the throttle body of the carburetor.

The EFE system that uses vacuum to open the heat control valve is regulated by engine coolant temperature, Fig. 21-15. When the coolant is cold, vacuum is allowed to the actuator and the control valve is closed. When

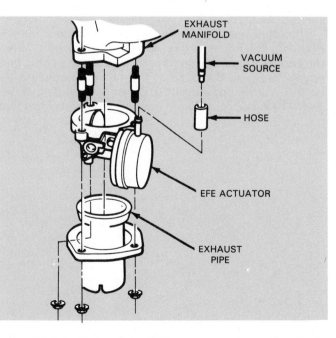

Fig. 21-14. Parts of the EFE vacuum servo.   (Cadillac)

211

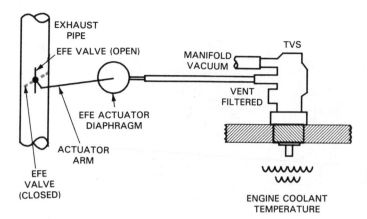

Fig. 21-15. When the coolant is cold, vacuum is allowed to pass through the TVS valve and the heat control valve is closed. (Cadillac)

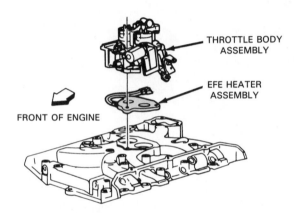

Fig. 21-16. Electric grid EFE system. (Cadillac)

engine coolant reaches operating temperatures, no vacuum is allowed to the actuator and the heat control valve is opened.

The other type of EFE system uses a ceramic electric grid, Fig. 21-16, which is also the base gasket. When the engine is cold, current is permitted to the electric grid, which heats up the base of the throttle body. As the engine warms up, current is no longer supplied to the grid. The manifold is warm enough to vaporize the fuel.

Chapter 21—REVIEW QUESTIONS

Write your answers on a separate sheet of paper. Do not write in this book.

1. What is the purpose of the intake manifold?
2. Why is heat applied to the intake manifold?
3. Where is the intake manifold on a V-type engine located?
   a. Between the two banks of cylinders.
   b. On each side of the engine, on the outside.
   c. On the front of the cylinder block.
4. Mechanic A states that the EFE system uses a vacuum contolled servo to redirect exhaust gases through the crossover passage.
   Mechanic B states that the EFE system uses an electric grid placed under the throttle body.
   Who is right?
   a. Mechanic A.
   b. Mechanic B.
   c. Both Mechanics A and B.
   d. Neither Mechanic A nor B.
5. What causes unequal distribution of fuel?
6. All cylinders receive fuel of the same octane rating. Yes or No?
7. Which cylinders of a V-8 engine do the barrels of a two barrel carburetor supply?
   a. Both barrels supply all cylinders.
   b. Left barrel supplies cylinders on left side of engine, and right barrel supplies cylinders on right.
   c. Right barrel will supply center cylinders on right bank of cylinders and end cylinders on left bank. Left barrel will supply center cylinders of left bank of cylinders and end cylinders on right bank.
8. The manifold heat control valve is designed for what purpose?
9. Why are carburetors of more than one barrel used on some multi-cylinder engines?
10. The intake manifold serves as part of the positive crankcase ventilation system. True or False?
11. The intake manifold is incorporated in which of the following emission control systems?
    a. Exhaust gas recirculation.
    b. Air injection.
    c. Thermal reactor.
    d. All of the above.
    e. None of the above.

Chapter 22

AIR CLEANERS

After studying this chapter, you will be able to:
- State the purpose of an air cleaner.
- List the components of a heated air intake system.
- Explain how the heated air intake system works.
- Tell why a crankcase breather is needed.

AIR FILTERS

Air that is drawn into the cylinders must be clean. If dust or other foreign matter enters the engine, it acts to grind away machined parts to a rough finish. Under extreme conditions, it results in the need for complete engine reconditioning.

To reduce the amount of dust entering the engine, an air cleaner is installed at the air intake. The air cleaner houses an element that filters all incoming air.

There are several types of air cleaners. These include:
1. Oil wetted mesh.
2. Oil bath.
3. Polyurethane.
4. Paper element.

Today, car engines are fitted with air cleaners of the paper element type, Fig. 22-1. The pleated paper element was found to be more efficient than any other type, and it is compatible with emission control devices.

PAPER ELEMENT

The paper element, or dry type, air cleaner is the most efficient. To service this type of filter, replacement is all that is needed. However, the filter can be cleaned by tapping it against a hard, flat surface to shake loose the dirt. Then, direct compressed air to the inner circle of the filter. Make sure that the nozzle of the compressed air remains at least 2 in. from the filter, Fig. 22-2. Never dip the filter in a solvent to clean it.

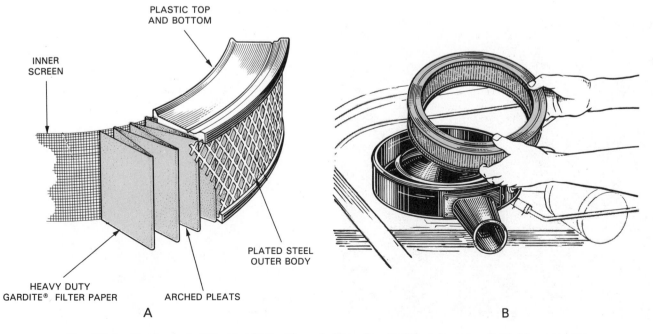

Fig. 22-1. Dry type air filter. A—Parts of an air filter. B—Air filters for rear wheel drive cars are circular. (Wix Division of Dana Corp.)

FRONT WHEEL DRIVE CARS

Air filters on cars with front wheel drive have a shape other than the typical circle found on rear wheel drive cars. These cars have a rectangular shaped filter, Figs. 22-3 and 22-4. This shape is suited for the smaller engine compartment found on front wheel drive cars.

CRANKCASE BREATHERS

The positive crankcase ventilation system directs atmospheric pressure to the crankcase. The atmospheric pressure then pushes the blowby gases to a low pressure area, which is at the PCV valve. The air that is directed into the crankcase must first be filtered, Figs. 22-5 and 22-6. If it is not, the airborne particles will destroy the engine parts. Also, when blowby is excessive, it is routed back through the crankcase breather element, Fig. 22-7. It then enters the carburetor or throttle body with the incoming fresh air to be burned in the cylinders. In addition, the breather helps keep the regular air filter cleaner for a longer period of time, as blowby contains oil vapor from the crankcase.

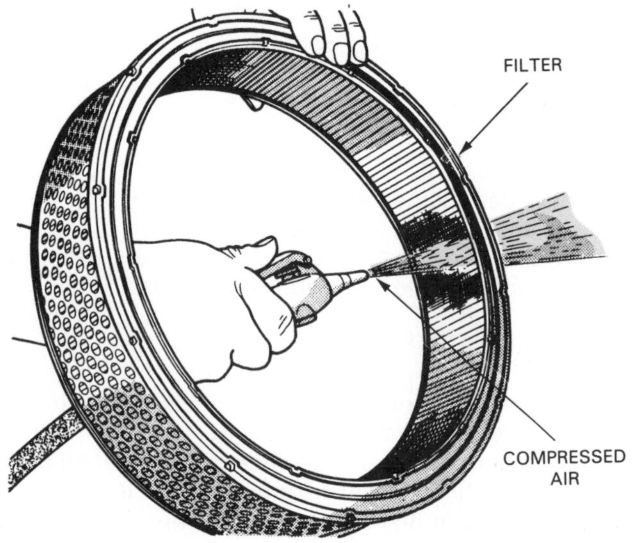

FILTER

COMPRESSED AIR

Fig. 22-2. Using compressed air to clean an air filter. Note that compressed air is directed to the inner circle of the filter. (Chrysler)

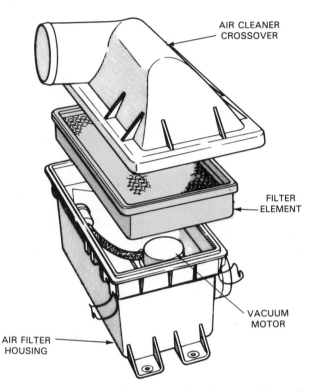

AIR CLEANER CROSSOVER

FILTER ELEMENT

VACUUM MOTOR

AIR FILTER HOUSING

Fig. 22-4. Air filter is of a rectangular shape on front wheel drive cars. (Chrysler)

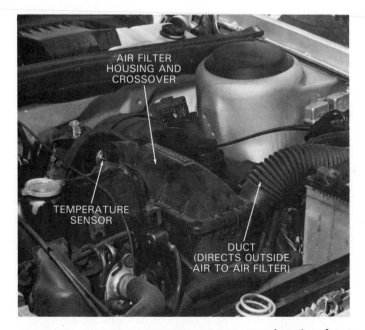

AIR FILTER HOUSING AND CROSSOVER

TEMPERATURE SENSOR

DUCT (DIRECTS OUTSIDE AIR TO AIR FILTER)

Fig. 22-3. Air cleaner housing and crossover found on front wheel drive car.

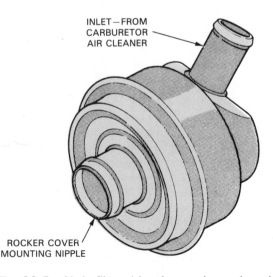

INLET—FROM CARBURETOR AIR CLEANER

ROCKER COVER MOUNTING NIPPLE

Fig. 22-5. Air is filtered by the crankcase breather prior to entering crankcase. (Chrysler)

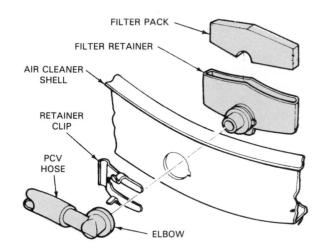

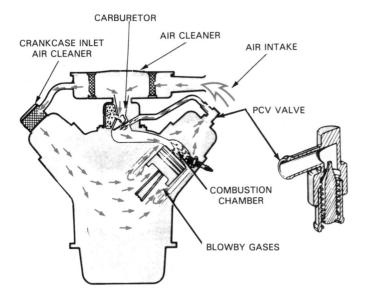

Fig. 22-6. Crankcase breather element also prevents frequent replacement of the regular air filter. (Ford)

Fig. 22-7. During high vacuum conditions, fresh air is directed through crankcase breather to the crankcase. During periods of low vacuum, blowby gases are forced from crankcase through the crankcase breather element instead of through PCV valve. The blowby gases then enter the carburetor along with the incoming fresh air. (Chrysler)

HEATED AIR INTAKE

The heated air intake system forms part of the air cleaner, Figs. 22-8 and 22-9. It is an essential part of the exhaust emission control system.

A temperature sensor is attached to the air cleaner. It controls the temperature of air that enters the air cleaner. The assembly takes the heated air from a shroud around the exhaust manifold. The heated air is then passed through the air cleaner.

The temperature sensor, Figs. 22-8 and 22-9, in the air duct is exposed to the heated air. This action of the sensor controls the position of the valve so that the hot and cold air are blended to maintain 100°F.

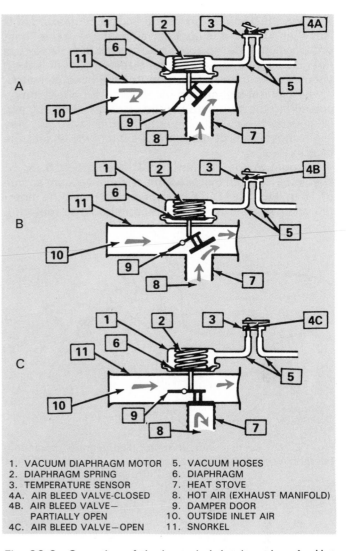

1. VACUUM DIAPHRAGM MOTOR
2. DIAPHRAGM SPRING
3. TEMPERATURE SENSOR
4A. AIR BLEED VALVE-CLOSED
4B. AIR BLEED VALVE— PARTIALLY OPEN
4C. AIR BLEED VALVE—OPEN
5. VACUUM HOSES
6. DIAPHRAGM
7. HEAT STOVE
8. HOT AIR (EXHAUST MANIFOLD)
9. DAMPER DOOR
10. OUTSIDE INLET AIR
11. SNORKEL

Fig. 22-8. Operation of the heated air intake valve. A—Hot air delivery. B—Modulating hot and cold air. C—Valve is closed blocking off hot air that would cause detonation. (Oldsmobile)

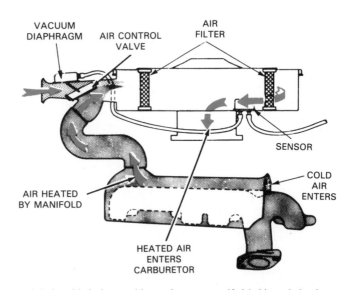

Fig. 22-9. Air is heated by exhaust manifold. Hot air is then directed to snorkel of air cleaner. (Chrysler)

When the temperature in the engine compartment is less than 100 °F, the duct valve should be in the "heat on" position. If the engine is cold and the duct valve does not close during idle, check for disconnected or leaking vacuum lines to the vacuum motor and bimetal switch.

The bimetal switch can be checked for operation by subjecting the switch to heated air or, by removing and immersing the switch in water heated to 80 °F. Only slight movement of the bimetal switch will unseat the bleed valve.

Vacuum at the vacuum motor should be 15 in. To check the vacuum motor, connect it to a vacuum source of 15 in, Fig. 22-10. The motor should move the motor rod one-half inch. If not, the motor should be replaced.

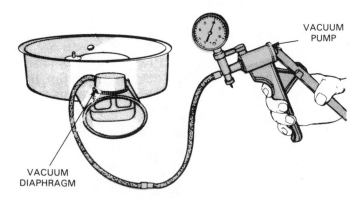

VACUUM PUMP

VACUUM DIAPHRAGM

Fig. 22-10. Testing vacuum motor diaphragm with vacuum pump. If motor fails to hold a vacuum, it is defective and must be replaced. (Chrysler)

Chapter 22 — REVIEW QUESTIONS

Write your answers on a separate sheet of paper. Do not write in this book.

1. Name four types of air cleaners.
2. Where is the air cleaner installed?
   a. Between the carburetor and the manifold.
   b. At the air intake of the carburetor or throttle body.
   c. On the carburetor air bleed.
3. Which type of air cleaner is most efficient?
4. How should a paper element air filter be cleaned?
   a. Washed in cleaning solvent.
   b. Throwing it away.
   c. Tapping against some hard flat surface and compressed air.
5. The duct valve in the vacuum-operated air cleaner system should be open when the engine is not operating. True or False?
6. The damper on the thermostically controlled air cleaner used on some cars should open when incoming air temperature reaches 85 to 115 °F. True or False?
7. Mechanic A states that the crankcase breather filters the air prior to entering the crankcase.
   Mechanic B states that the crankcase breather filters the blowby prior to entering the carburetor or throttle body.
   Who is right?
   a. Mechanic A.
   b. Mechanic B.
   c. Both Mechanic A and B.
   d. Neither Mechanic B nor B.

Chapter 23

PRINCIPLES OF CARBURETION

After studying this chapter, you will be able to:
- State the purpose of the carburetor.
- List the circuits of the carburetor.
- Explain Bernoulli's Principle.
- Describe how each circuit of the carburetor works.
- Define what is meant by closed and open loop.

FUEL SYSTEM

The purpose of the fuel system, Fig. 23-1, is to provide a mixture of fuel and air to the engine. The air-fuel mixture must be in proportion to the speed and load placed on the engine. Major parts of the system include: fuel tank and cap, emission controls, fuel lines, fuel pump, fuel filter, carburetor, and intake manifold. Also, the fuel gauge, which indicates the amount of fuel in the tank.

CARBURETOR

The purpose of the carburetor is to supply and meter the mixture of fuel vapor and air in relation to the load and speed of the engine. Because of engine temperature, speed, and load, perfect carburetion is difficult to obtain. When a cold engine is first started, a richer than normal air-fuel mixture is needed. When the engine reaches operating temperature, the fuel is easily vaporized and the rich fuel mixture is not needed or wanted. The engine will not run as well with a rich fuel mixture after the engine has warmed up.

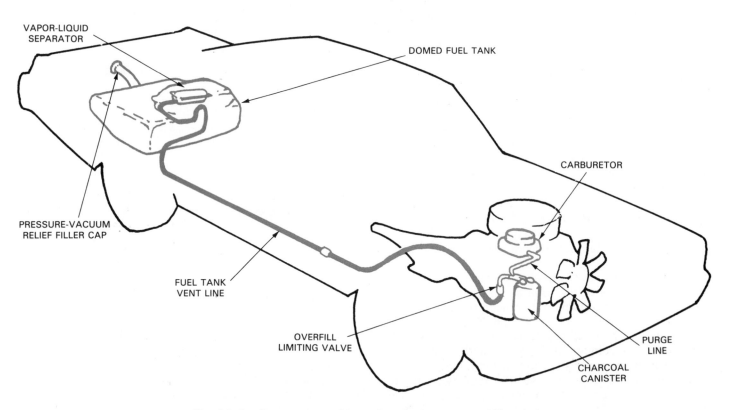

VAPOR-LIQUID SEPARATOR

DOMED FUEL TANK

CARBURETOR

PRESSURE-VACUUM RELIEF FILLER CAP

FUEL TANK VENT LINE

OVERFILL LIMITING VALVE

PURGE LINE

CHARCOAL CANISTER

Fig. 23-1. Components of a modern fuel system.   (Chrysler)

Another problem must be overcome by the carburetor. When the engine is at an idle or low speeds, a richer mixture is needed than when at medium speeds. When maximum power is needed, the air-fuel mixture must be as rich as possible. The problem in designing carburetors is the fact that the airflow rate through the carburetor changes more than 100 to 1. This is a result of change in engine speed. At low speeds, the airflow through the carburetor is at a minimum. At maximum engine speed, it will be 100 times greater.

Fuels also present problems in carburetor design. Gasoline is a blend of fractions of crude oil. As a result, some fractions contained in gasoline will boil at 100 °F. Others have boiling points ranging up to 400 °F. Depending on the temperature of the intake manifold, some cylinders will receive a mixture fully vaporized; others may be in a liquid form. Also, some cylinders receive fuel having greater antiknock qualities than others. When the intake manifold is cold, the problem is greater.

AIR-FUEL RATIO

The best economy is obtained by a mixture of 1 part gasoline to between 16 to 17 parts of air. For quick acceleration and maximum power, a richer mixture of about 1 part gasoline to 12 to 13 parts of air is needed. For idling, a richer mixture is also needed. When starting a cold engine, an extremely rich mixture is needed. See Chapter 24, CHOKE SYSTEMS.

CARBURETION PRINCIPLES

To cause a liquid to flow there must be a high pressure area, which in this case is atmospheric pressure, and a low pressure area. See Fig. 23-2. A low pressure is less than atmospheric pressure. The average person refers to a low pressure area as a vacuum. Since atmospheric pressure is already present, a low pressure area can be created by air or a liquid flowing through a venturi, Fig. 23-3. The downward motion of the piston also creates a low pressure area.

Likewise, air and gasoline are drawn through a carburetor and into the engine by suction created as the piston moves downward. As the piston moves down, a partial vacuum is created in the cylinder. The difference between this low pressure within the cylinder and atmospheric pressure outside of the carburetor causes air and fuel to flow into the cylinder from the carburetor.

BERNOULLI'S PRINCIPLE

The effect of Bernoulli's Principle is summarized as follows.

A venturi is a specially designed section of pipe, line, or tube. The area of the tube at the center is reduced in diameter. This reduction increases the speed of the air that is passing through the tube. The same volume of air or fluid flows through all sections of the tube. Therefore, the velocity of the air or fluid must increase as it passes through the reduced diameter.

The venturi not only increases the velocity of the flow of air which passes through it, but it also produces a low pressure at its point of reduced diameter, Fig. 23-3. The

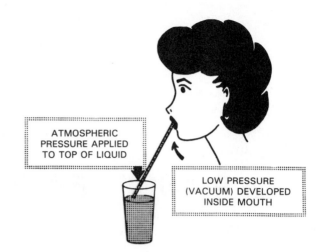

Fig. 23-2. Liquid moves from a high pressure area to a low pressure area. (Rochester)

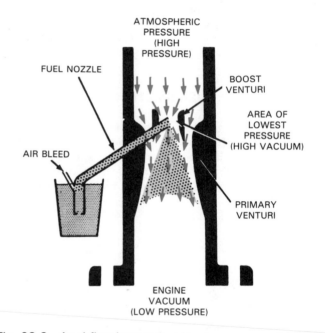

Fig. 23-3. As airflow increases, a low pressure area is created within the venturi. (Rochester)

Fig. 23-4. Carburetor operates on the same principle as a spray gun.

outlet of a fuel jet is placed at that point. Fuel is drawn from the jet and mixes with the passing air. This mixing of the fuel with air is known as vaporization, and it closely resembles the action of a spray gun, Fig. 23-4.

Some carburetors have as many as three venturis. This design permits a more precise metering of the flow of air and fuel for different conditions. It improves combustion, which has become increasingly important in reducing exhaust emissions.

The difference between the pressure at the venturi and atmospheric pressure on the fuel in the float bowl, Fig. 23-3, causes the fuel to flow.

CHANGE OF STATE

All substances, whether solid, liquid, or gas, are made of molecules. In solids such as steel and copper, the particles are so close together they seem to have no motion. In liquids, the molecules are not held together so tightly, as a result, liquids flow. In gases, such as air, it is less likely for the molecules to hold together, so they move quite freely.

When molecules of a liquid move from the liquid into the air, the liquid is said to evaporate. As this continues, the liquid disappears from its container and forms vapor in the air. Evaporation varies with a number of factors. These factors, include temperature, the pressure above the liquid, the amount of liquid that has already evaporated into the air, and the volatility of the liquid. The term volatility refers to the ease with which a liquid vaporizes. For example, alcohol and benzene are more volatile than water because they evaporate more easily. A highly volatile liquid evaporates rapidly. A liquid of low volatility evaporates slowly.

At higher temperatures, molecules move faster. As a result, the rate of vaporization is increased. When there is little pressure above the liquid, the molecules can escape from the liquid easily. If evaporation takes place in a closed chamber, the evaporation of the liquid will soon stop because the limited space above the liquid becomes filled with vaporized molecules of the liquid. When this occurs, the space above the liquid is said to be saturated.

If a liquid is broken up into tiny particles, it will vaporize more easily. Breaking a liquid into tiny particles is known as vaporization. Spray guns of the type used for spraying insecticides or paint will vaporize a liquid. If gasoline is placed in an ordinary spray gun, Fig. 23-4, the fuel will be broken into a fine mist that will change into vapor almost instantly.

It is impossible for liquid gasoline to burn, until it is changed into a vapor. So, it is only the vapors of gasoline that burn. In order for gasoline to be of any use in a modern engine, the liquid gasoline is changed into a vapor. Whenever atmospheric pressure is reduced on the gasoline, it undergoes a change of state from a liquid to a mist or vapor.

CARBURETOR CIRCUITS

In order to supply an air-fuel mixture suitable for all conditions of low to high speeds, and light loads to full loads, a carburetor must be equipped with many circuits and controls. These circuits include: choke, float, idle, transfer, main metering, acceleration, and power. Under controls, there are: the choke unloader, anti-icing, hot idle compensator, and anti-stall dashpot.

CHOKE CIRCUIT

The purpose of the choke circuit is to provide a richer than normal fuel mixture for a cold engine. A richer mixture is needed as some of the fuel is condensed on the walls of the cold carburetor. So, a rich fuel mixture compensates for the lack of vaporized fuel.

The choke coil forces the choke valve closed and adjusts the linkage to increase the idle speed, Fig. 23-5.

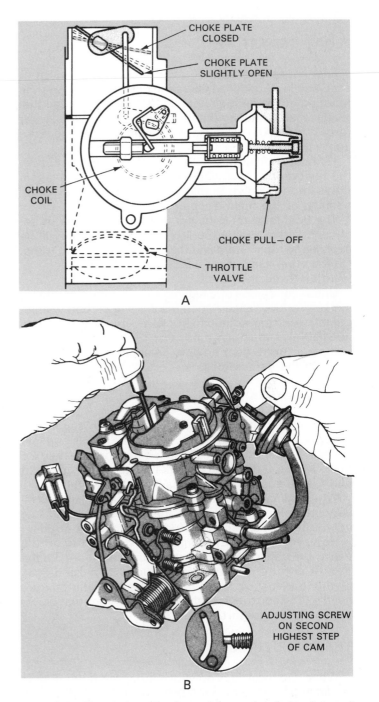

Fig. 23-5. The choke coil, when cold, sets the choke plate and fast idle speed. A—Choke plate reduces the amount of cold air that enters carburetor, until the engine reaches operating temperature. B—Fast idle speed is obtained by a wedge shaped cam. Fast idle allows more fuel to flow. (Chrysler)

The choke plate blocks or reduces the amount of cold air that enters the carburetor. This action assists in the evaporation of the fuel in cold weather. The increased idle speed provides the extra fuel needed to compensate for the fuel that is condensed on the walls of the carburetor.

If both actions were not take, the engine would stall and be hard to start until it had reached operating temperature. Once the engine reaches operating temperature, the choke plate is fully opened and the idle speed is reduced. This is caused by the choke coil relaxing due to the engine heat.

FLOAT CIRCUIT

Fuel in the carburetor must be maintained at a specified level under all operation conditions. This is the function of the float circuit, Fig. 23-6. The needed fuel level is maintained by the float. When its attached lever forces the needle valve closed, the flow of fuel from the pump is stopped.

Then, as soon as fuel is discharged from the float bowl, the float drops. The needle valve opens and fuel again flows into the bowl. In that way the fuel is level to the opening of the main discharge nozzle.

The float level must be set with a high degree of accuracy. If the level is too low, not enough fuel will be supplied to the system and the engine will stall on turns. On the other hand, if the level is too high, too much fuel will flow from the nozzle.

Under conditions of a high fuel level in the float bowl, excessive fuel consumption results and carbon will accumulate in the combustion chambers. The float and needle valve maintain a position that permits the fuel coming into the float bowl to balance the fuel passing through the carburetor jets.

IDLE CIRCUIT

The idle circuit, Fig. 23-7, is designed to supply the proper amount of mixture for the engine at idle and low speeds. It operates from idle speed to approximately 25 mph. Above that speed, the idle system is phased out and fuel is supplied by the main metering system.

When the throttle valve is almost closed, there will be very little air passing through the venturi. There will be very little vacuum to draw fuel from the fuel nozzle.

However, on the intake manifold side of the throttle valve, the vacuum will be at a maximum as long as the throttle is in the closed position. Fuel is then discharged at this port below the throttle valve. An idle mixture needle is used to adjust the amount of fuel that flows to the discharge port.

TRANSFER CIRCUIT

When the throttle is opened a little, the flow of air is too limited for the venturi to discharge fuel from the main nozzle, Fig. 23-7. However, with the increased movement of air through the carburetor more fuel must be supplied in order to maintain the correct air-fuel mixture.

To supply the needed fuel during this stage, another port is positioned slightly above the closed position of

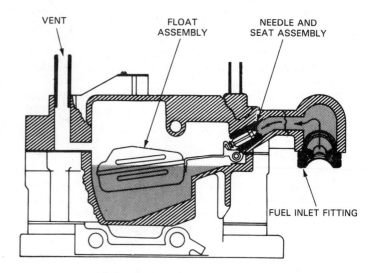

Fig. 23-6. Typical float circuit. (Chrysler)

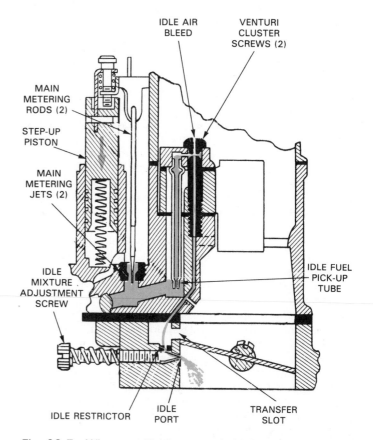

Fig. 23-7. When manifold vacuum is high, step-up piston is pulled downward. Since metering rod is attached to step-up piston, metering rod is pulled into jet. This limits the flow of fuel to idle port. Low pressure area is created by the downward motion of piston, as velocity of air is not great enough to cause a low pressure area with venturi. As throttle blade opens slightly, fuel begins to flow out of transfer slot. (Chrysler)

the throttle valve, Fig. 23-7. As soon as the valve is opened a small amount, the port will be exposed to manifold vacuum. This will cause fuel to flow from this port also and the needed fuel will be obtained.

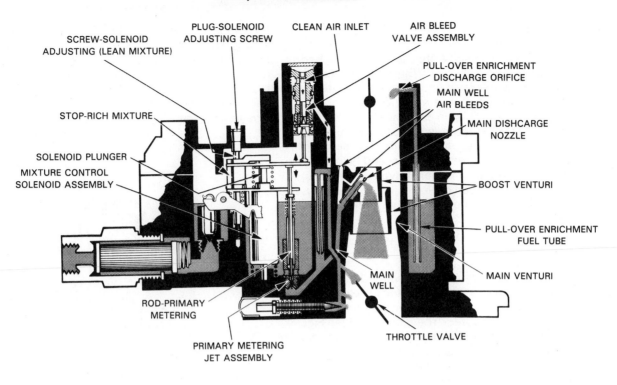

Fig. 23-8. Main metering system provides just enough fuel to maintain a constant cruising speed.   (Rochester)

MAIN METERING CIRCUIT

As the throttle is opened, vacuum at the venturi increases. So, fuel starts to flow from the main circuit. The main circuit consists of the main nozzle, which is centered in the venturi, Fig. 23-8. Fuel is discharged from the nozzle during part throttle through full throttle positions.

As the airflow through the carburetor increses, the flow of fuel also increses at a faster rate. This is because the density of the fuel does not change, while that of the air does. So, the mixture in a simple carburetor will be too rich under wide open throttle (WOT).

Since the correct air-fuel mixture on a simple carburetor would be supplied at only one position of the throttle valve, steps must be taken to provide the correct mixture of all positions of the throttle valve.

METERING ROD

A metering rod varies the size of the carburetor jet opening. In this design, Fig. 23-9, fuel from the float bowl is metered through the jet and the metering rod within it. The fuel is forced from the jet to the nozzle extending into the venturi.

As the throttle valve is opened, its linkage raises the metering rod from the jet. The rod has several steps, or tapers, on the lower end. As it is raised in the jet, it makes the opening of the jet greater in size. This allows more fuel to flow through the jet to the discharge nozzle. The metering rod must keep pace with the slightest change in the throttle valve position so that the correct air-fuel mixture is obtained through all engine speeds.

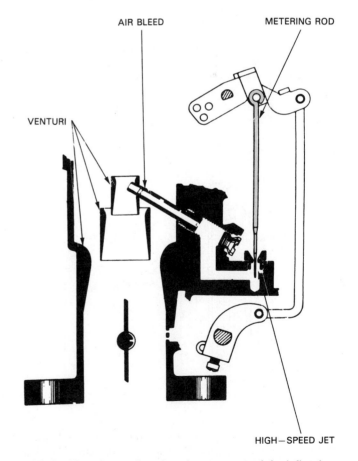

Fig. 23-9. Metering rod varies the amount of fuel flowing through the jet. As speed increases, the metering rod is lifted out of the jet, allowing more fuel to flow.

POWER CIRCUIT

The power circuit consists of a step-up piston fastened to metering rods, Fig. 23-10. When high vacuum develops in the intake manifold (part throttle operation), atmospheric pressure holds the step-up piston down against spring pressure. This, in turn, holds the metering rod down in the main metering jet, closing the jet.

When no vacuum is in the intake manifold (wide-open throttle), the difference in pressure above and below the piston is the same. The piston is then moved up by spring pressure and the rod is raised out of its jet. In this way, additional fuel is allowed to flow through the jet for maximum power.

POWER VALVE

Other power circuits use a power valve instead of metering rods attached to a step-up piston. The concept is the same, which allows the increased flow of fuel to provide the necessary power. The power valve, Fig. 23-11, is held closed during normal operation. As vacuum drops, due to the increased load placed on the engine, the piston located above the power valve is pushed downward. This piston pushes on the power valve, which opens it allowing more fuel to flow. When vacuum increases again, the piston is forced up off the power valve. This shuts off the flow of fuel from the power valve.

ACCELERATOR PUMP

When a throttle valve is opened quickly to produce rapid acceleration, the carburetor fuel mixture tends to become too lean and a hesitation occurs. This results from the fact that the fuel is of greater weight than air. When the accelerator is opened suddenly the flow of fuel will lag behind the flow of the air.

To supply the extra fuel needed to overcome this, an accelerator pump is part of the carburetor design, Fig, 23-12. This pump is operated by the throttle linkage. In some designs, the stroke of the pump can be adjusted to any one of three positions. The longest stroke provides the most amount of fuel. So, this is the setting usually used during cold weather.

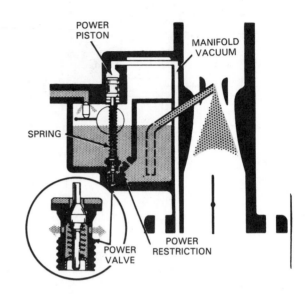

Fig. 23-11. When manifold vacuum is reduced, the piston is forced down against the power valve. The power valve is opened and the flow of fuel is increased. When manifold vacuum increases, the piston is pulled up and off of power valve. This reduces the flow of fuel. (Rochester)

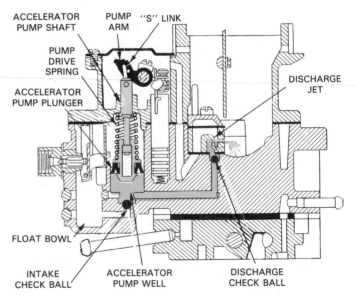

Fig. 23-12. Accelerator pump circuit. When the accelerator pump moves upward, intake check ball is unseated allowing fuel from float bowl to fill accelerator pump well. When accelerator pump moves downward, intake check ball is seated and discharge check ball is unseated allowing a squirt of fuel into the airstream. Discharge check ball prevents fuel siphoning from accelerator pump well, which would deplete the needed fuel for smooth acceleration. (Chrysler)

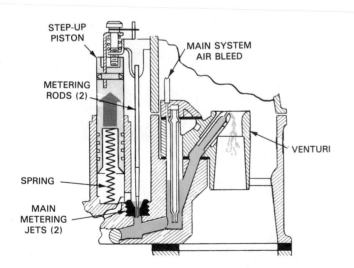

Fig. 23-10. Power circuit. As speed is increased, vacuum drops and spring pushes step-up piston upward. This brings metering rod out of the jet, which allows the needed fuel to provide the necessary power. Velocity of air is now great enough to create a pressure drop within venturi. (Chrysler)

The accelerating pump circuit generally consists of:
1. A pump well.
2. A plunger, mechanically actuated by a lever connected to the throttle shaft.
3. An intake check ball located in bottom of pump well to control passage of fuel from bowl to pump cylinder.
4. A discharge check ball located in the discharge passage. This prevents fuel in the accelerator pump well from being siphoned into the air stream.
5. Discharge nozzle (pump jets) located in the throat of the carburetor.

As the throttle is opened, the pump plunger moves downward. The downward movement is obtained by linkage with the throttle. The downward travel of the plunger forces fuel past the discharge check ball. Fuel is then supplied to the pump cylinder through the intake check ball at the bottom. This checkball permits a supply of fuel to reach the cylinder, but closes on the down stroke of the plunger to prevent fuel in the well from being pushed back into the float bowl.

AIR BLEED PRINCIPLE

The use of air bleeds is a method to compensate for the increased richness of the mixture caused by increased air velocity through the carburetor. Fig. 23-13 shows the air bleed system used on a carburetor.

Air at that point reduces the surface tension of the fuel and helps fuel flow at low pressures. This bleed also prevents fuel flow through the main jets under high vacuum conditions. These two factors control the air-fuel mixture. The increased richness of a mixture occurs when a plain nozzle is exposed to increased air velocity.

BALANCED PRESSURE

A tube connects the top of the float bowl chamber to the upper section of the air horn, Fig. 23-14. This tube vents the vapors from the fuel bowl into the airstream through the air horn. These vapors are also burned with the fuel that is discharged at the various ports within the carburetor. Venting the carburetor in this manner relieves any pressure in the float bowl. Also, the atmospheric pressure directed to the float bowl through the balance or vent tube will equalize the pressure in the float bowl if the air filter is too dirty.

A dirty air filter will cause a greater pressure difference at the venturi. This is because the airflow through a dirty

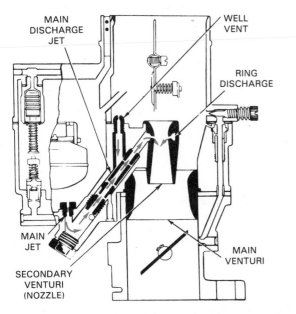

Fig. 23-13.Well vent acts as an air bleed on this Zenith carburetor.

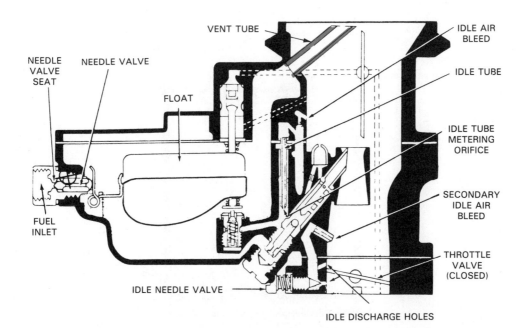

Fig. 23-14. Vent tube directs atmospheric pressure to float bowl after air has been filtered. This equalizes the effects of a partially clogged air filter and prevents an overly rich fuel mixture.

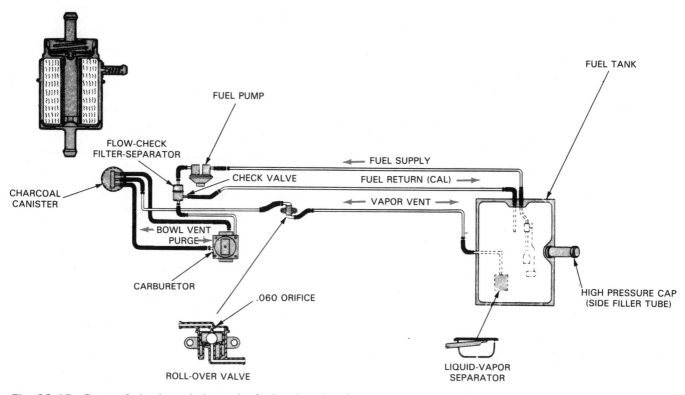

Fig. 23-15. Due to federal regulations, the fuel tank and carburetor can no longer be vented to the atmosphere. All fuel vapors are routed to a charcoal canister and then later purged through the carburetor. (Chrysler)

air filter will be reduced. This causes a drop in pressure on the inner side of the filter. However, atmospheric pressure in the fuel bowl will remain the same. The greater pressure difference will cause more fuel to flow than needed if not compensated. So, a balance tube routes the pressure from the inner side of the air filter to the fuel bowl. This prevents a richer fuel mixture. The

balance tube compensates for a partially restricted air filter.

Today, fuel vapors from the float bowl are externally vented to a charcoal canister, Figs. 23-15 and 23-16. At the proper time the vapors are purged through the carburetor. However, the internal vent or balance tube remains.

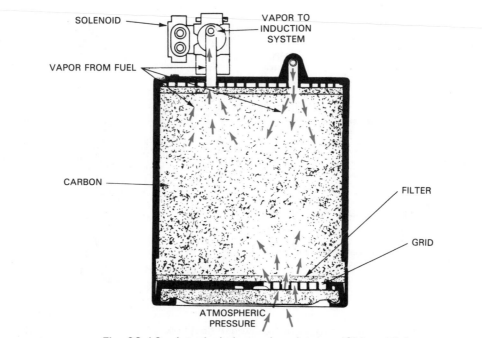

Fig. 23-16. A typical charcoal canister. (Oldsmobile)

CHOKE UNLOADER

When an engine does not start immediately, prolonged cranking will result in a flooded condition. The air-fuel mixture in the engine is so rich that it is no longer a vapor. The spark plugs cannot ignite liquid gasoline. To overcome this, linkage is provided on the carburetor which will hold the choke valve open when the accelerator is pushed to the floor, Fig. 23-17. Then, as the engine is cranked again, air will enter the cylinders to clear excessive gasoline from the system while the engine is cranked. This is accomplished by linkage between the throttle and choke levers, Fig. 23-17.

ANTI-ICING

As fuel evaporates, the temperature is decreased and it absorbs heat from the air and metal parts. When the humidity of the air is high and temperatures are at the freezing point, the evaporation of fuel in the carburetor often causes "icing." The ice forms around the closed position of the throttle plate. The idle port becomes closed with ice. This, in turn, will cause the engine to stall at low speeds.

To overcome this icing condition, some carburetors are provided with passages that carry hot exhaust gases around the carburetor, heating the area around the throttle plate, Fig. 23-18.

HOT IDLE COMPENSATOR

During long periods of idling with an extremely hot engine, the fuel in the carburetor bowl becomes hot enough to form vapors. These vapors enter the carburetor bores by way of the inside bowl vents or balance tube. Mixing with the idle air causes an extremely rich mixture. This will result in loss of engine rpm and stalling. To overcome this condition, a hot idle compensator valve is placed in some of the carburetors. This permits extra air to enter the manifold below the throttle valve, Fig. 23-19, where it mixes with the fuel vapors to provide a leaner fuel mixture.

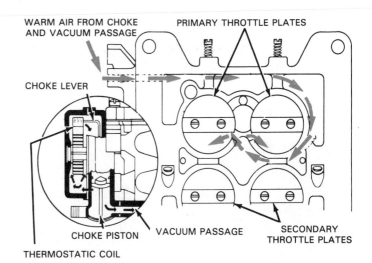

Fig. 23-18. Path of hot air is directed around throttle valves to prevent ice formation.

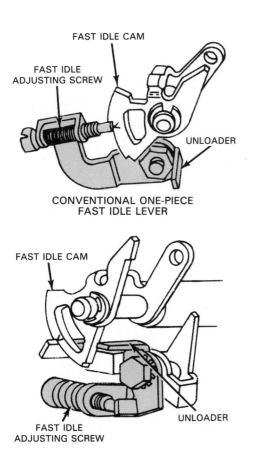

Fig. 23-17. Choke unloader action causes choke plate to open. This allows a flooded engine to be cleared.

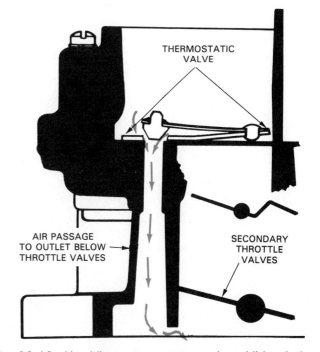

Fig. 23-19. Hot idle compensator permits additional air to enter carburetor under extreme hot conditions.

ANTI-STALL DASHPOT

Most older cars with automatic transmissions have an anti-stall dashpot connected to the carburetor linkage, Fig. 23-20. The purpose of this dashpot is to prevent the throttle valve from closing too fast. Too rapid closing often causes the engine to stall. The dashpot prevents the throttle from being closed too quickly, thereby avoiding stalls.

This condition would not occur with a manual transmission since the momentum of the vehicle would continue to drive the engine through the stall period.

SINGLE-BARREL CARBURETOR

A carburetor is classified by the number of throats, or barrels. A single-barrel carburetor, Fig. 23-21, has one outlet to the intake manifold. It is designed to take care of all the needs of the engine for all conditions. This is used on engines having six cylinders or less.

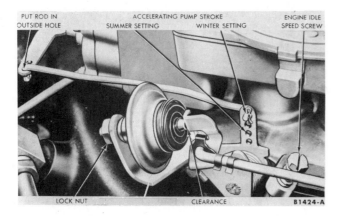

Fig. 23-20. A typical anti-stall dashpot. (Ford)

TWO-BARREL CARBURETOR

Carburetors with two outlets to the intake manifold are known as two-barrel carburetors, Fig. 23-22. These units are two single-barrel carburetors in one, with two complete idling circuits, two high-speed circuits, two power circuits, two accelerator discharge passages, two throttle valves, but only one float system.

With a two-barrel carburetor, each barrel supplies alternate cylinders in the firing order. In a six cylinder engine, one barrel supplies cylinders 1, 3, and 2. The other barrel supplies cylinders 5, 6, and 4.

FOUR-BARREL CARBURETOR

In the four-barrel carburetor there are four openings to the intake manifold. Some systems, such as the float system, may be common to all four barrels. In four-barrel designs, half of the carburetor operates as a two-barrel unit during light load and cruising speeds. The other half of the carburetor is supplemental for top speed and full-throttle. The two barrels that supply fuel for light load are known as the primary side. The supplementary two barrels are known as the secondary side, Fig. 23-23.

In this design, the secondary throttle plates remain closed at lower engine speeds. As engine speed increases, the throttle plates of the secondary barrels are opened.

In some designs, the secondary throttle plates are operated mechanically through linkage. On other models, the secondary throttle plates are controlled by a vacuum-operated diaphragm. The secondary throttle plates will start to open when the primary plates are open 50 deg.

Manifolding for both two-barrel and four-barrel carburetors is designed as follows: One half of the carburetor supplies fuel to the end cylinders on one side of the engine and two center cylinders on the other side. The other half of the carburetor supplies fuel to the remaining cylinders.

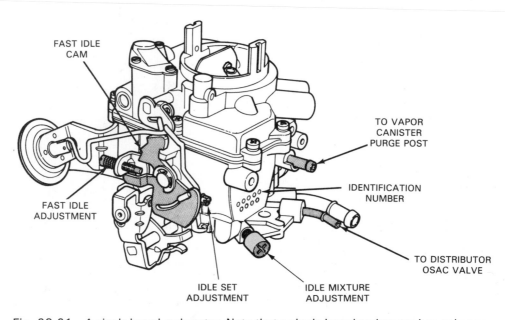

Fig. 23-21. A single barrel carburetor. Note that a single barrel carburetor has only one idle mixture adjustment screw. (Chrysler)

226

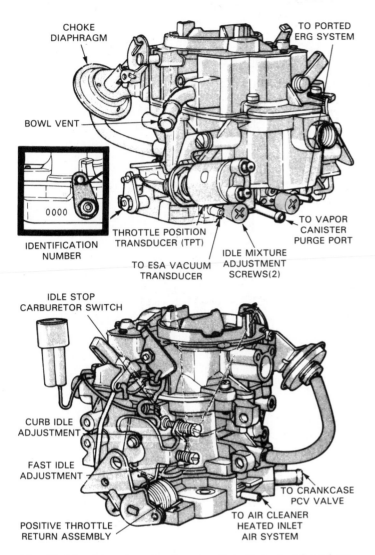

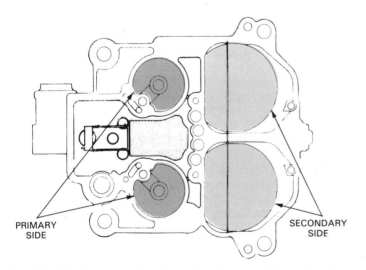

Fig. 23-22. A two-barrel carburetor. Note that a two-barrel carburetor has two idle mixture adjustment screws. However, a four-barrel carburetor also has only two idle mixture adjustment screws, which are located on the primary side. (Chrysler)

Fig. 23-23. A typical four-barrel carburetor. Note that the primary side bores are smaller than the secondary bores. (Rochester)

In a four-barrel carburetor on a V-8 engine, the primary and secondary barrels supply cylinders 1-7-4-6. The other primary and secondary barrels supply fuel to cylinders 3-5-2-8. However, this applies only to an engine having a firing order of 1-8-4-3-6-5-7-2.

VARIABLE VENTURI CARBURETOR

Ford's Motorcraft model 2700 variable venturi carburetor, Figs. 23-24 and 23-25, varies the area of the venturi as a function of speed and load. Most carburetors have venturis that are fixed. In this design, changing the size of the venturi maintains enough air velocity and pressure drop to the main metering system. This is accomplished by means of tapered metering rods attached to the venturi valve, which changes the area of the venturi.

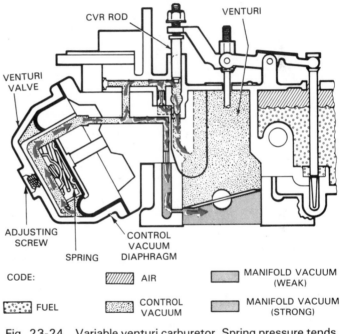

Fig. 23-24. Variable venturi carburetor. Spring pressure tends to close venturi valve and control vacuum acts to open it. (Ford)

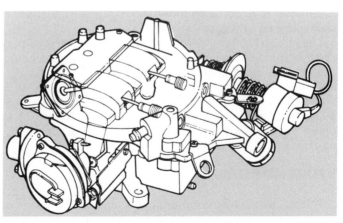

Fig. 23-25. Ford's variable venturi carburetor.

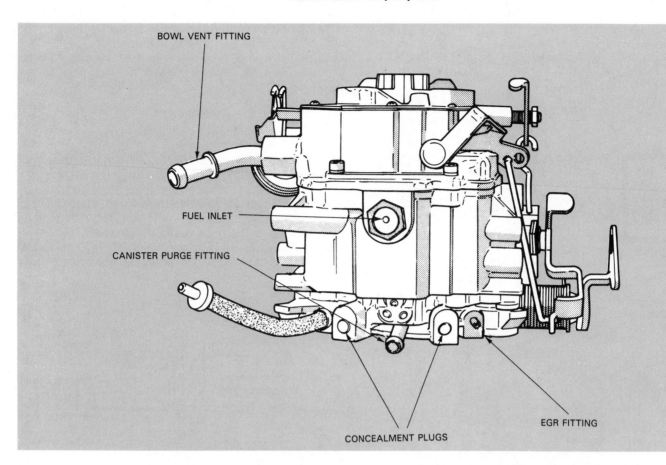

Fig. 23-26. Air-fuel mixture screws are located behind lead concealment plugs. Plugs must be drilled out in order to gain access to fuel mixture screws. This usually involves removing the carburetor from the engine. (Chrysler)

There is one rod and one jet for each bore of the carburetor. The rod moves back and forth in the jet when the air valve moves. When the venturi valve is closed, the largest diameter of the rod is in the jet. When the valve is wide open, the smallest diameter of the rod is in the jet. In that way, metering of the fuel is controlled by the position of the rod, Fig. 23-25.

AIR-FUEL MIXTURE

Carburetors have been modified to provide leaner air-fuel mixtures to conform to federal regulations that concern exhaust emissions.

These leaner mixtures result from better control of the idle mixture. In some cases the idle mixture screws have a finer pitch, making for more accurate control of the air-fuel ratio.

On 1980 and newer car models, the air-fuel mixture adjustment screws have been sealed, Fig. 23-26. This prevents tampering with the air-fuel mixture adjustment, as this will affect emissions.

STOICHIOMETRIC

A lean air-fuel mixture produces a high level of nitrous oxides (NO_x) in the exhaust. A rich air-fuel mixture produces a high level of hydrocarbons (HC) and carbon monoxide (CO) in the exhaust. However, the byproducts of perfect combustion produce water (H_2O) and carbon dioxide (CO_2) in the exhaust. This is provided that the engine is 100 percent efficient. The best designed and built engine is not 100 percent efficient.

A STOICHIOMETRIC air-fuel mixture is as close as you can get in obtaining the byproducts of perfect combustion. A stoichiometric air-fuel mixture is neither too rich nor too lean. It is 14.7 parts air to 1 part fuel. However, even with this desired air-fuel mixture, hydrocarbons, carbon monoxide, and nitrous oxides remain, but only in small percentages. To achieve this, the combustion process, along with other engine variables, must be measured.

COMPUTERIZED SYSTEM

The only practical method for monitoring all of the engine variables at once is with the use of an on-board computer. The on-board computer receives information from the various sensors located near or on the engine, Fig. 23-27. Once the computer receives all of the sensor signals, it then processes the signals. Once the computer processes the input signals, it then adjusts the fuel mixture, timing, and other actuators. This process is continuous, as long as the engine is running.

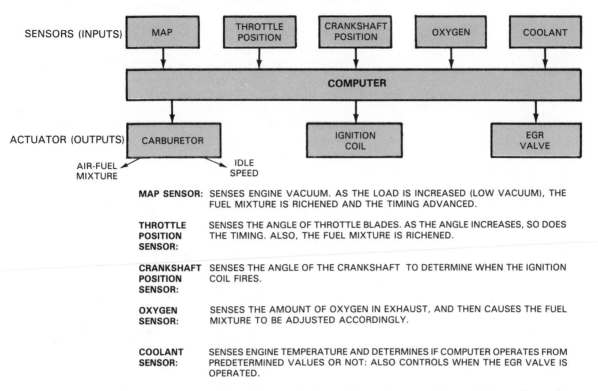

MAP SENSOR: SENSES ENGINE VACUUM. AS THE LOAD IS INCREASED (LOW VACUUM), THE FUEL MIXTURE IS RICHENED AND THE TIMING ADVANCED.

THROTTLE POSITION SENSOR: SENSES THE ANGLE OF THROTTLE BLADES. AS THE ANGLE INCREASES, SO DOES THE TIMING. ALSO, THE FUEL MIXTURE IS RICHENED.

CRANKSHAFT POSITION SENSOR: SENSES THE ANGLE OF THE CRANKSHAFT TO DETERMINE WHEN THE IGNITION COIL FIRES.

OXYGEN SENSOR: SENSES THE AMOUNT OF OXYGEN IN EXHAUST, AND THEN CAUSES THE FUEL MIXTURE TO BE ADJUSTED ACCORDINGLY.

COOLANT SENSOR: SENSES ENGINE TEMPERATURE AND DETERMINES IF COMPUTER OPERATES FROM PREDETERMINED VALUES OR NOT: ALSO CONTROLS WHEN THE EGR VALVE IS OPERATED.

Fig. 23-27. Computer receives information from the various sensors and then adjusts the actuators.

ELECTRO-MECHANICAL CARBURETORS

The modern electro-mechanical carburetor is controlled by the computer. The fuel mixture is controlled by an oxygen feedback (mixture control) solenoid located within the carburetor, Figs. 23-28 and 23-29. The idle speed is maintained by an electric motor that automatically adjusts the idle speed, Fig. 23-30. When the engine is cold, the computer operates from predetermined values and the fuel mixture is fixed at full rich. When operating temperatures have been reached, the fuel mixture varies, Fig. 23-31.

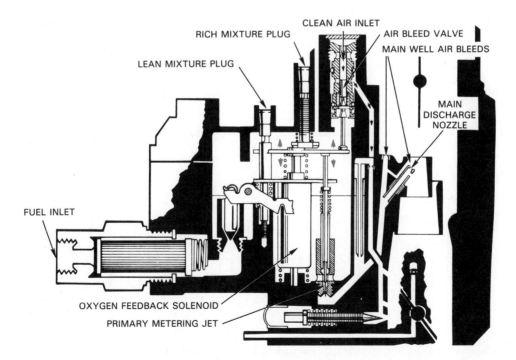

Fig. 23-28. When oxygen feedback solenoid is energized, the metering rod is pushed into the jet reducing the flow of fuel. (Rochester)

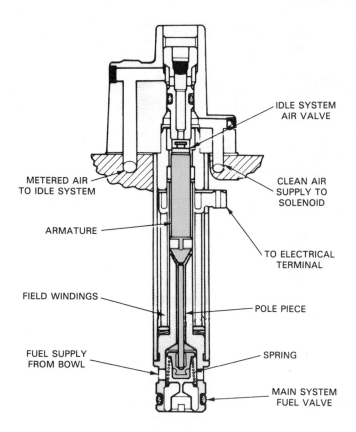

IDLE SYSTEM
AIR VALVE

METERED AIR
TO IDLE SYSTEM

CLEAN AIR
SUPPLY TO
SOLENOID

ARMATURE

TO ELECTRICAL
TERMINAL

FIELD WINDINGS

POLE PIECE

FUEL SUPPLY
FROM BOWL

SPRING

MAIN SYSTEM
FUEL VALVE

Fig. 23-29. When de-energized, the pole piece is pushed up-wards by spring pressure allowing more fuel to flow through the jet. (Chrysler)

OPEN LOOP

When the temperature of the exhaust gases are below 600°F, the computer operates from predetermined values. Or, if the driver depresses the accelerator to the floor (Wide Open Throttle) after the exhaust gases have reached the specified temperature, the signal from the oxygen sensor is ignored by the computer. When the oxygen sensor signal is ignored by the computer it is referred to as OPEN LOOP.

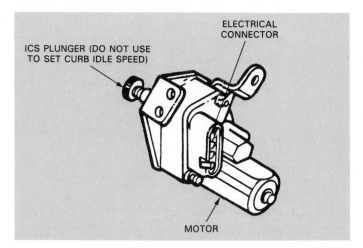

ELECTRICAL
CONNECTOR

ICS PLUNGER (DO NOT USE
TO SET CURB IDLE SPEED)

MOTOR

Fig. 23-30. Idle speed motor is controlled by the computer and automatically adjusts the idle. (Oldsmobile)

RELATIONSHIP OF DWELLMETER READINGS TO MIXTURE CONTROL SOLENOID CYCLING

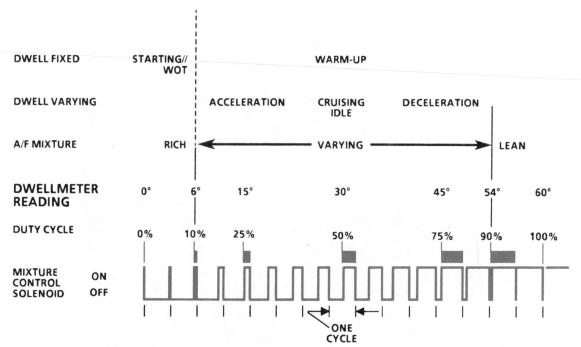

Fig. 23-31. When engine is cold, the air-fuel mixture is set to full rich. The mixture control or oxygen feedback solenoid is energized only 10 percent of the time. When the engine reaches operating temperature, the fuel mixture will vary. (Cadillac)

CLOSED LOOP

After the exhaust gases have reached a temperature of 600 °F, the computer energizes and de-energizes the oxygen feedback solenoid within the carburetor at the rate of 10 times per second. The computer decides which to do after receiving the signal from the oxygen sensor, Fig. 23-32. When the computer uses this signal to decide if the fuel mixture should be leaned out or richened, it is referred to as CLOSED LOOP, Fig. 23-33.

OXYGEN SENSOR OPERATION

If the fuel mixture is too rich (a lack of oxygen in the exhaust), the sensor produces a 1 volt signal. The computer then energizes the oxygen feedback solenoid. This causes the fuel flowing through the metering jets to be reduced or leaned out.

If the fuel mixture is too lean (an excess of oxygen in the exhaust), the sensor does not produce any voltage. The computer de-energizes the oxygen feedback solenoid. This causes more fuel to flow through the metering jets to richen the mixture.

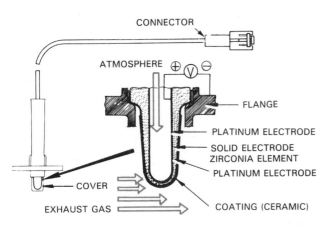

Fig. 23-32. Oxygen sensor compares oxygen in atmosphere to the amount of oxygen in exhaust. Sensor provides a 1 volt signal to computer when there is a lack of oxygen in exhaust. No voltage signal is sent to the computer when there is an excess of oxygen in the exhaust. (Toyota)

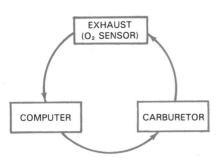

Fig. 23-33. Closed loop cycle. Oxygen sensor monitors combustion process and relays this information to the computer. The computer then adjusts the fuel mixture in the carburetor. This cycle is continuous after the engine reaches operating temperature, except during wide open throttle.

Chapter 23—REVIEW QUESTIONS

Write your answers on a separate sheet of paper. Do not write in this book.

1. What is the purpose of the fuel system in an internal combustion engine?
2. List the main parts of a fuel system.
3. The rate of flow through a carburetor is the same under all operating conditions. True or False?
4. When starting an internal combustion engine, the fuel mixture should be:
   a. Rich.
   b. Lean.
   c. Average.
5. Which speed requires a richer mixture?
   a. Idling.
   b. 30 mph.
6. Will all cylinders of a multi-cylinder engine receive an air-fuel mixture having the same octane rating?
7. For normal operating conditions, what air-fuel ratio will give the best economy?
   a. 16 to 1.
   b. 20 to 1.
   c. 25 to 1.
8. For quick acceleration, what is the best air-fuel ratio?
   a. 5 to 1.
   b. 10 to 1.
   c. 12 to 1.
   d. 20 to 1.
9. Are the molecules forming a gas held more tightly together than those of a metal?
10. Name two factors affecting evaporation.
11. What causes the air-fuel mixture to be drawn into the combustion chamber of an internal combustion engine?
12. The purpose of a venturi in a carburetor is to:
    a. Increase speed of air passing through carburetor.
    b. Maintain correct air-fuel ratio.
    c. Provide extra fuel for acceleration.
13. There are five main circuits in a modern carburetor. Name four of them.
14. In a carburetor venturi, which point has the highest vacuum?
    a. Entrance to the venturi.
    b. Narrowest point of the venturi.
    c. Point one inch beyond the venturi.
15. The idle system of a carburetor supplies fuel at which speeds?
    a. Idle speed only.
    b. Speeds up to 40 mph.
    c. Speeds up to 25 mph.
16. How many fuel discharge ports does the conventional idle system have?
    a. One.
    b. Two.
    c. Three.
    d. Four.
17. When the idle system is no longer supplying fuel to the engine, which system then supplies fuel?
    a. Air bleed system.
    b. Main system.
    c. Vaporizing system.

18. The purpose of a power valve is to supply more or less fuel?

19. The metering rod is designed to vary the size of:
    a. The float.
    b. The venturi.
    c. The accelerator pump.
    d. The carburetor jets.

20. Under what conditions is ice most likely to form in a carburetor?
    a. 20 °F below zero and high humidity.
    b. 32 °F above zero and high humidity.
    c. 0 °F and low humidity.

21. On what type of car are you most likely to find an anti-stall dashpot?
    a. Cars with automatic transmission.
    b. Cars with conventional transmission.
    c. Cars fitted with 1 Bbl. carburetors.
    d. Cars fitted with 4 Bbl. carburetors.

22. What is the purpose of an oxygen sensor?

23. Explain what is meant by closed loop.

24. In your own words, define what is meant by a stoichiometric air-fuel ratio?

Chapter 24

CHOKE SYSTEMS

After studying this chapter, you will be able to:
● List the types and components of the choke circuit.
● State the purpose of each part of the choke system.
● Explain how the choke operates.

CHOKE

To start a cold engine, a rich fuel mixture is needed. This is because not all of the fuel will vaporize when the engine is cold. The rich fuel mixture compensates for the fuel that condenses in the throat of the carburetor.

When the choke coil is cold, and after the accelerator is depressed, it forces the choke plate closed and at the same time positions the fast idle cam. When the choke plate is closed it blocks out the cold air. With the cold air blocked, it is easier for the fuel to vaporize. However, once the engine is started, the choke plate opens slightly. The choke plate is placed slightly off-center in relation to the shaft, Fig. 24-1. This helps open the choke plate. The amount that the choke plate opens is controlled by the choke pull-off, Fig. 24-2. After the fast idle cam has been positioned, fuel flows out of all ports, Fig. 24-1. This provides the needed rich fuel mixture. As the engine warms up, the choke plate opens and the fast idle speed is reduced.

CHOKE CONTROLS

The opening and closing of the choke valve can be controlled manually or automatically. When it is manually controlled, a push-pull cable is used. It extends from the choke on the carburetor to the instrument panel. The driver closes the choke when starting the engine. Then it opens gradually as the engine reaches operating temperature.

The problem with a manual choke is that the driver is likely to forget to open the choke fully. A rich mixture will result, and cause carbon to form in the combustion chambers and on the spark plugs.

To correct this problem, the automatic choke was developed. Some automatic chokes depend on exhaust manifold heat for their operation; others combine manifold heat with intake manifold vacuum, and the velocity of air acting on the offset choke valve for their operation.

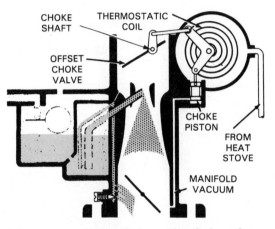

Fig. 24-1. Thermostatic coil closes the choke valve or plate. Note that shaft is not centered to the valve. Also, fuel is discharged at all ports to provide the needed rich fuel mixture. (Rochester)

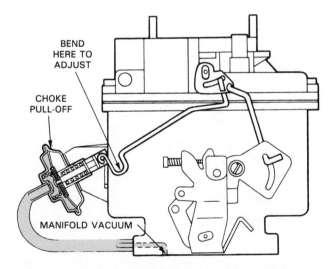

Fig. 24-2. Choke pull-off assists in opening the choke plate a fraction of an inch. The "U" shape bend in the link determines how far the choke valve is opened. To increase the choke valve opening, decrease the width of the "U." To decrease the choke valve opening, increase the width of the "U." Make sure a vacuum source is applied to choke pull-off prior to making adjustments. (Chrysler)

AUTOMATIC CHOKE OPERATION

The automatic choke depends on the unwinding of a thermostatic coil spring as heat is supplied. As the spring unwinds, it causes the choke valve in the carburetor air horn to open. This permits more air to pass through the carburetor.

Heat for the thermostatic coil, in most cases, is obtained from the exhaust gases. The thermostatic coil is mounted in a well in the exhaust crossover passage of the intake manifold, Fig. 24-3. Movement of the bimetal spring is relayed to the choke valve shaft by means of linkage and levers.

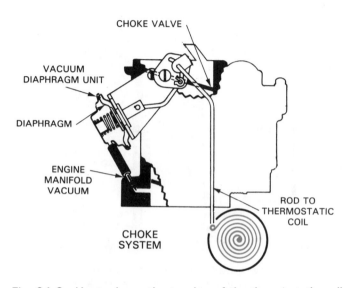

Fig. 24-3. Heat relaxes the tension of the thermostatic coil spring. This allows choke valve to fully open.

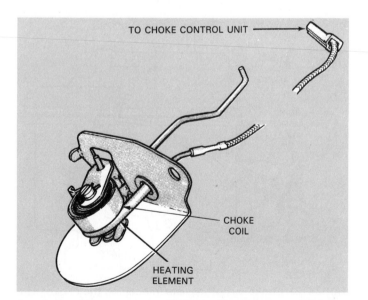

Fig. 24-4. One type of electrically heated choke coil. The problem with some electric choke coils is that with the ignition ON and the engine not running, the coil will heat up. Then, if the engine is cold and is started, the choke plate will be open when it should be closed. This will cause hard starting and stalling until the engine has warmed up.   (Chrysler)

The choke valve is helped open by a vacuum break unit or choke pull-off, Fig. 24-2. Some carburetors have two choke pull-offs. This vacuum controlled unit adjusts the choke valve in relation to the load placed on the engine. The load on the engine is reflected by the drop in manifold vacuum. The rush of air past the off-center choke valve provides the extra needed force to open the choke valve.

As the engine warms up, manifold heat is transmitted to the choke housing. The heat causes the bimetal spring to relax. An electric heating coil in the automatic choke shortens the length of time that the choke valve is closed, Figs. 24-4 and 24-5. This reduces the emissions in the exhaust and is part of the emission controls.

CHOKE UNLOADER

Should the engine become flooded during the starting period, the choke valve can be opened by pushing the accelerator pedal to the floor. This is accomplished by means of the choke unloader, Fig. 24-6, which rotates the fast idle cam and opens the choke valve.

SECONDARY LOCKOUT

On four barrel carburetors, it is necessary to prevent the secondaries from opening while the engine is cold. If the secondary side were permitted to open on a cold engine, there would be a severe hesitation and stumble on acceleration until the engine warmed up. The secondary side is prevented from opening by a secondary lockout lever, Fig. 24-7.

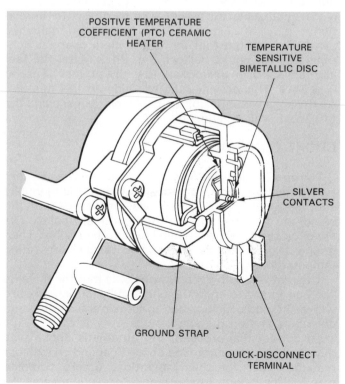

Fig. 24-5. This type of choke coil receives current from the alternator.   (Ford)

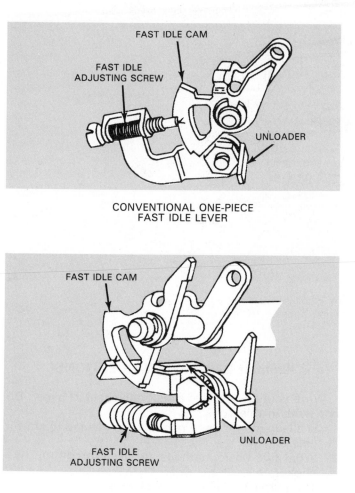

CONVENTIONAL ONE-PIECE
FAST IDLE LEVER

Fig. 24-6. Choke unloader causes the choke valve to open when the accelerator is pressed to the floor.

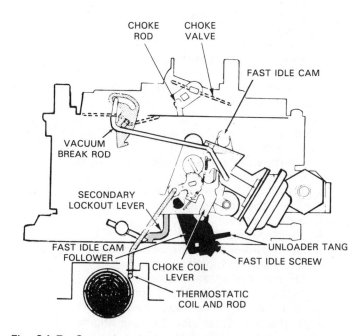

Fig. 24-7. Secondary lockout lever prevents the secondary side of a four barrel carburetor from engaging while the engine is cold. (Rochester)

EXHAUST-HEATED CHOKES

The crossover type of automatic choke is thermostatically controlled. The thermostatic coil, Fig. 24-8, is mounted in a well in the exhaust crossover passage in the intake manifold on V-type engines. The choke valve is controlled by the thermostatic spring.

As the thermostatic coil gains heat, it unwinds and allows the choke valve to open. At the same time, the choke pull-off, connected by a rod to the valve, keeps a constant pull on the valve against the tension of the spring. This continues as long as the engine is running, so the choke valve opens slowly. Also, the offset choke valve assists in opening the valve.

When the thermostatic coil is mounted on the side of the carburetor, Fig. 24-9, heat is conducted from the exhaust manifold to the choke housing and coil. This is done by passing a tube through the exhaust manifold.

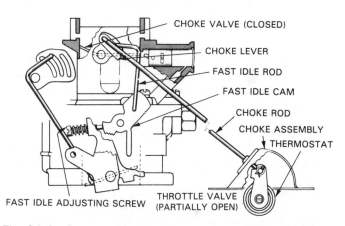

Fig. 24-8. Crossover type choke has thermostatic coil placed in a well on the intake manifold. This well sits directly above the exhaust crossover passage.

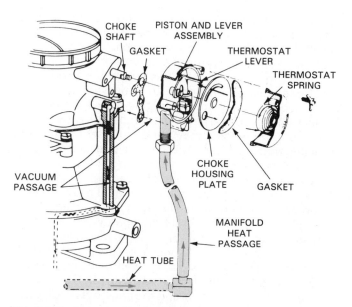

Fig. 24-9. Heat for thermostatic coil mounted on the side of the carburetor is directed through a tube from the exhaust manifold.

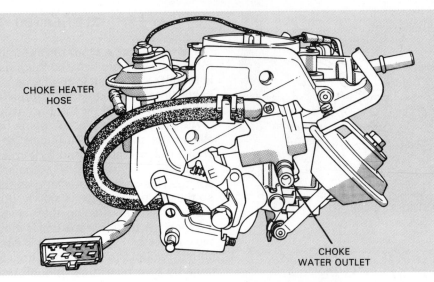

CHOKE HEATER
HOSE

CHOKE
WATER OUTLET

Fig. 24-10. Heat for this thermostatic coil is supplied by the
hot coolant carried through the heater hoses. (Chrysler)

Air drawn through the choke tube is heated by exhaust gases passing around the tube. In this way, the tube serves to supply heated air to the choke housing and thermostatic coil.

WATER-HEATED CHOKE

Instead of using exhaust heat to control the automatic choke, some engines use coolant from the engine water jacket. By this design, the choke will remain open as long as the water in the water jacket remains hot, Fig. 24-10. Coolant, in some ways, is better than heated air. This is because water retains heat longer than air. This prevents overchoking.

CHOKE TROUBLESHOOTING

The basic check for choke operation is to make sure the choke valve is closed when the engine is cold. When the engine is hot, the choke valve should be open.

Choke troubles may be the cause for:

1. Hard or no starting cold. This could be caused by the choke valve remaining in the open position. If the temperature is mild, the engine may start but stall as soon as it is started. If the temperature is extremely cold, the engine may not even start if the choke valve remains open. This may be due to a defective choke coil spring.

2. No starting cold. This could be caused by the choke valve remaining closed, which would allow no air to enter the carburetor. This may be caused by the choke coil spring being set too tight. When the choke coil is set too tight, the spring coil exerts more pressure on the choke valve keeping it closed. To determine if this is the cause, wedge the choke valve open with the shank of a screwdriver. The car will start if this is the cause and the engine is not flooded.

Chapter 24—REVIEW QUESTIONS

Write your answers on a separate sheet of paper. Do not write in this book.

1. Is a lean mixture or a rich mixture needed to start a cold engine?
2. What two basic methods are used to control the choke?
3. The purpose of the choke plate is:
   a. To block out cold air.
   b. To block out hot air.
   c. Both a and b.
   d. Neither a nor b.
4. Where is the heat obtained to open an automatic choke valve?
5. When thermostatic coil is mounted on side of carburetor, how is heat supplied?
   a. Electrically.
   b. Through tubing which passes through the exhaust manifold.
   c. From hot water obtained from the radiator.
6. Explain how air velocity is used to open the choke valve.
7. What carburetor linkage prevents stalling during the warmup of an engine?
8. The purpose of the secondary lockout is to:
   a. Increase horsepower.
   b. Prevent air from entering the secondary side when the engine is cold.
   c. Both a and b.
   d. Neither a nor b.
9. In the crossover type automatic choke, where is the thermostatic coil located?
   a. On the side of the carburetor.
   b. In a well in the intake manifold.
   c. In a well in the exhaust manifold.
   d. In the hot water jacket of the engine.

Chapter 25

CARBURETOR ADJUSTMENT, SERVICE

After studying this chapter, you will be able to:
- Diagnose carbureted related problems.
- Describe the procedure for adjusting carburetor idle speed and air/fuel mixture.
- List which parts of a carburetor should be cleaned and which should be replaced.

CARBURETORS

Modern carburetors are designed to work with a specific engine. In the past, carburetors needed a great amount of time and skill to adjust. After these adjustments were made, prolonged road testing under all speeds and conditions were needed. Today, the adjustments are few and can be done in a short amount of time by a technician.

ADJUSTMENTS

Before making carburetor adjustments, see that the ignition system is in good shape, and that compression is within 10 percent of specifications for all cylinders. There must be no leaks in the intake manifold. The carburetor float level must be to specifications. The engine must be at operating temperature so that the idle speed can be set. Then, connect the red lead of the tachometer to the negative side of the coil and the black lead to a good ground. With manual shift cars in "neutral" and automatic transmission cars in "drive," the idle speed can be checked and adjusted, Figs. 25-1 to 25-3.

Fig. 25-1. A decal placed in the engine compartment provides the necessary information for timing, idle speed, and fuel mixture.

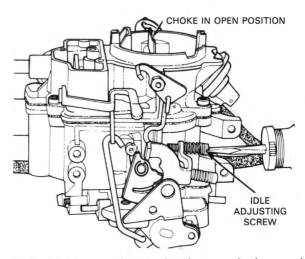

Fig. 25-2. Make sure that engine has reached operating temperature and the choke plate is wide open prior to adjusting the idle. Turn the screw clockwise to increase idle speed and counterclockwise to decrease the speed. (Chrysler)

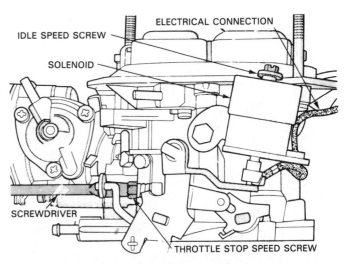

Fig. 25-3. Some idle speed adjustments are a two step process. First, the idle speed screw on the solenoid is adjusted. Then, the solenoid is de-energized by removing the electrical connection. The final adjustment is made by turning the throttle stop speed screw to the specified speed. The electrical connection at the solenoid is then reconnected. (Chrysler)

The choke spring coil forces the choke valve closed when it is cold, after depressing the accelerator pedal. At the same time, the fast idle cam is positioned by linkage connected to the choke valve shaft, Fig. 25-4. So, the fast idle screw is adjusted after touching the fast idle cam with the engine running. When the choke valve is wide open, the fast idle screw will not touch the fast idle cam. The engine will then be at a "curb" idle speed.

NOTE: On some computerized engines, the computer controls the idle and fast idle speed. No attempt should be made to adjust the idle or fast idle speed on these engines. Consult the individual service manual.

IDLE MIXTURE CHECK

An infra-red exhaust gas analyzer is used to check the idle mixture. Always consult the individual service manual for specifications. The following procedure is an example:

1. Set parking brake and place transmission or transaxle in neutral. Turn off all lights and accessories. Connect a tachometer to start and run engine until operating temperature is reached.
2. On feedback-equipped cars, turn engine off and then disconnect negative battery cable for 10 seconds before reconnecting cable. Disconnect oxygen sensor electrical connection. Restart the engine and run at 2500 rpm for 10 seconds before returning to curb idle.
3. Disconnect electrical connection at radiator fan, if so equipped. Allow engine to idle for two minutes.

4. Insert probe from exhaust gas analyzer into tailpipe, Fig. 25-5.
5. Adjust idle speed, if possible, to specified idle rpm.
6. Check reading of carbon monoxide at the exhaust gas analyzer. Reading should be between 0.1 to 0.3 percent. If is it not, the idle mixture may need adjustment. It is possible that a high float level, dirty air filter, etc. may also cause a high percentage of carbon monoxide in the exhaust.
7. If reading is within specified range, turn engine off and reconnect fan motor and oxygen sensor wire. Disconect tachometer.

NOTE: If an infra-red machine is not available, an alternate (but not as accurate) method, adds propane to the carburetor to temporarily enrich the fuel mixture.

IDLE MIXTURE ADJUSTMENT

If the carbon monoxide reading is not within specifications, the fuel mixture may have to be adjusted. Prior to adjustment, the concealment plugs must be removed to gain access to the mixture screws, Figs. 25-6 and 25-7. This requires removing the carburetor from the intake manifold. After the plugs have been removed, the carburetor must be reinstalled on the engine. With the engine running and test equipment hooked up, the fuel mixture screws can be adjusted.

To lean the fuel mixture, turn the mixture screws clockwise. To richen the fuel mixture, turn the mixture screws counterclockwise. The mixture screws should be turned only 1/16 of a turn at a time. This allows for a precise adjustment.

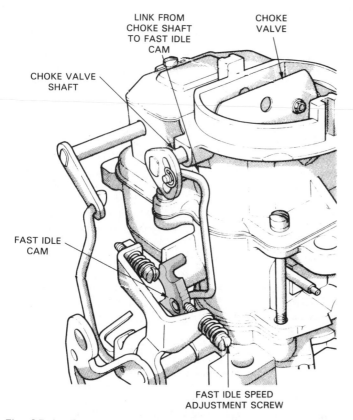

Fig. 25-4. To set the fast idle speed, the fast idle cam must be placed under the fast idle screw. (Chrysler)

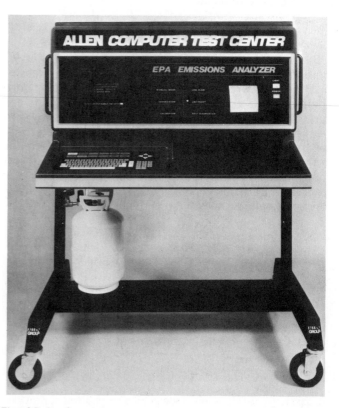

Fig. 25-5. Special equipment is needed to analyze exhaust gases.

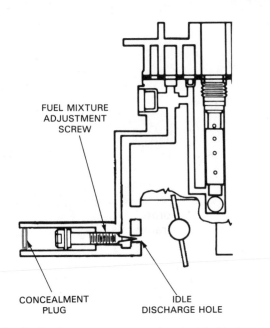

Fig. 25-8. Check throttle body for warpage using a straightedge.

Fig. 25-6. Fuel mixture screws are located behind concealment plugs. (Chrysler)

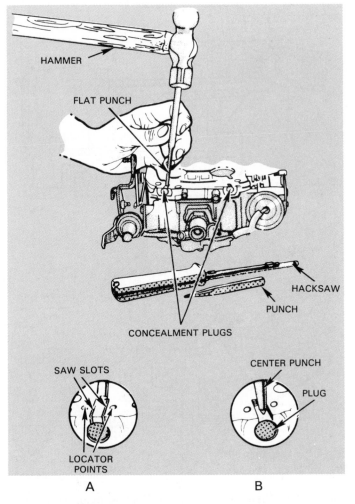

Fig. 25-7. Gaining access to the fuel mixture screws. A—Turn the carburetor upside down and saw where indicated. B—Using a punch, drive the plug out. The carburetor is now ready to reinstall and adjust. (Rochester)

On two and four barrel carburetors, both fuel mixture screws must be turned the same amount and in the same direction. Alternate between fuel mixture screws after each adjustment. For example, if you turn one fuel mixture screw clockwise 1/16 of a turn, then, the other must be turned 1/16 of a turn in the same direction. When you do this the engine will run smoothly at idle.

WARNING! Idle mixture screws are sealed for a purpose. Federal laws prohibit the tampering with these screws, unless an infra-red machine is used while adjusting the fuel mixture. If caught, a mechanic can expect stiff fines and a possible jail sentence.

CARBURETOR CLEANING

Cleaning the carburetor is the first step in rebuilding it. Carburetor cleaning solutions dissolve the gum that accumulates on the inside and outside of carburetors. This gum is formed by heat acting on the fuel.

Carburetors are disassembled and then individual parts are washed in special carburetor cleaner. This also provides the opportunity for inspection and replacement of worn parts, Fig. 25-8.

Some import carburetors can be damaged by immersion in a "dunk type" carburetor cleaner. This is because of a thermo-wax element at the end of drilled passage. The dunk type carburetor cleaning solution will dissolve the thermo-wax element. This will cause the carburetor to malfunction. If you are not sure that a carburetor has a thermo-wax element, use a spray type carburetor cleaner.

Wash all parts except the accelerator pump diaphragm or plunger, power valve diaphragm, and anti-stall dashpot assembly. Do not wash parts made of fabric or rubber. They could be injured by the cleaning solution.

After cleaning, wash all traces of the cleaning solution with HOT water. Then, blow the parts dry with compressed air. Force compressed air through all passages of the carburetor to be sure they are clean and dry. Do not use a wire brush. Do not run a fine wire through any jets. This may damage the ports. Once this is complete, the carburetor is ready to be rebuilt.

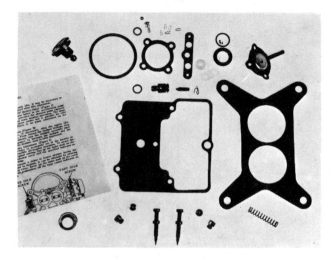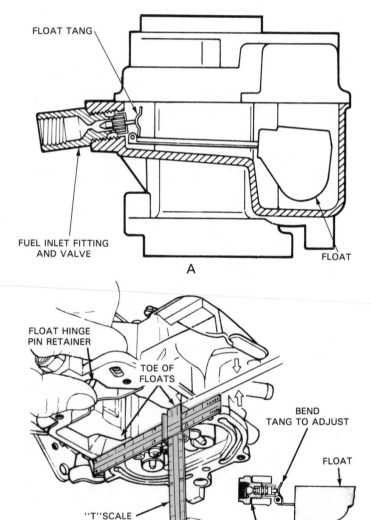

CARBURETOR OVERHAUL

After cleaning and inspecting the parts of a carburetor, it is time to reassemble it. Also, all adjustments are made during this time. A carburetor rebuild kit, Fig. 25-9, is used in the process. This kit contains new gaskets, accelerator pump, needle and seat, check balls, and instructions which include specifications for all of the adjustments.

Carburetor floats are either mounted in the fuel bowl, Fig. 25-10, or attached to the air horn assembly, Fig. 25-11. The float assembly should also be replaced during a rebuild. This is inexpensive insurance, since the floats can absorb gasoline as they age. This makes the float heavier. It rides lower in the fuel bowl and allows more fuel into the bowl than specified. This causes an overly rich fuel mixture. A new fuel and air filter completes the carburetor rebuild.

QUESTIONS BEFORE TESTING

Prior to testing and making a diagnosis of the problems, a GOOD technician is a detective. Asking the driver questions will eliminate guessing where to start the testing procedure. This reduces diagnostic time and replacing needless parts. Some of the questions the technician should ask:

1. Is the engine hot or cold when the problem occurs? How long and how far do you drive before experiencing problems?
2. When does the problem occur?
   a. At idle?
   b. Acceleration—full or part throttle?
   c. At a constant low speed?
   d. At a constant high speed?
   e. During deceleration (foot off gas pedal)?
   f. Making a left or right turn?
   g. Hauling cargo?
3. Are atmospheric conditions a factor?
   a. Is it raining, snowing, or is high humidity present when the problem occurs?
   b. What is the temperature when the problem occurs? (Hot or Cold)
   c. Is there a strong head wind?
4. Where does the problem occur?
   a. Going up a gradual or steep grade?
   b. On a level grade?
   c. At high altitudes?
   d. Near high power lines?
5. What is the fuel tank level when the problem occurs?
6. What type of gas did you last purchase? Where was it purchased?
7. Other factors:
   a. Were any recent repairs made? (Were they done correctly with quality parts?)
   b. Has there been any modifications to the fuel or ignition system?
   c. Is the problem intermittent?
8. Verify that the problem exists:
   Some drivers mistake a surging condition for:
   a. The air conditioning clutch cycling on and off.
   b. The torque converter clutch (TCC) locking and unlocking. If this is severe, a problem may exist with the TCC system.

Fig. 25-9. A carburetor rebuild kit is primarily made up of gaskets.

Fig. 25-10. Float mountings. A—Float is mounted in fuel bowl. B—When floats are mounted in fuel bowl, the bowl, along with the floats, must be inverted to take float measurement. Place carburetor upright and then bend tang to adjust float level. (Chrysler)

240

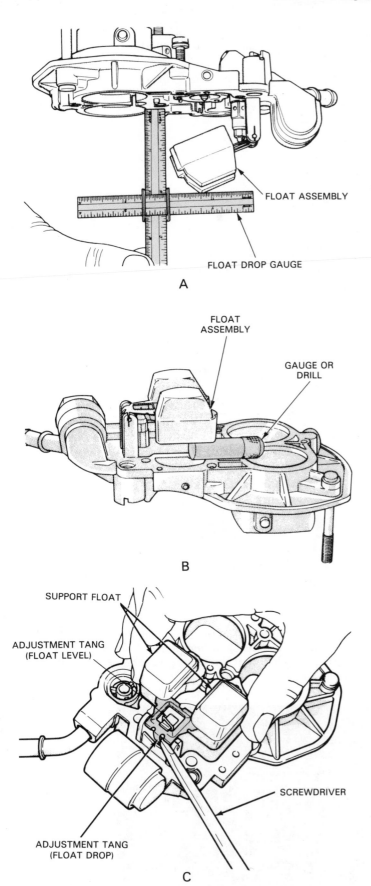

Fig. 25-11. Float mountings. A—Floats mounted to the airhorn must have the float drop also measured. B—Measuring float level. C—Adjustment points for float drop and float level. (Chrysler)

TROUBLESHOOTING CARBURETOR/FUEL SYSTEM

A defective or poorly adjusted carburetor will affect the economy and performance of the car. Failure of the engine to perform is seldom in the carburetor. Therefore, when the engine fails to start or perform, check the ignition, compression, choke, and supply of fuel to the carburetor before disassembling it.

If the above mentioned inspections fail to detect a problem, the following procedure should be used. Operate the throttle lever by hand while looking in the carburetor. Fuel should squirt from the accelerator pump jets. If no fuel is seen squirting from the accelerator pump jets, there is no fuel in the carburetor float bowl. This could mean that fuel pump is bad, the fuel filter is clogged, a leaky or clogged fuel line, or there is no atmospheric pressure in the tank pushing on the fuel. Disconnect the fuel line at the carburetor and direct the line into a small bottle. Fuel should flow in heavy spurts. Also, check the fuel line by blowing air back to the fuel tank. A gurgling sound should be heard back at the tank or the fuel line is clogged.

DWELL READINGS

On GM carbureted engines that are computerized, a dwell meter can be used in the troubleshooting process, Fig. 25-12. If the engine is cold and/or has just been started, the dwell should be fixed at 6 deg. for about two minutes. After this time dwell will be around 30 deg. at idle and will vary as the engine is accelerated or decelerated.

The technician should be able to hear the mixture control solenoid "click" after starting the engine. If not, the mixture control solenoid may be defective. After the engine has reached operating temperature, remove a vacuum hose. The dwell should decrease. Then, reconnect the vacuum hose and choke the engine. The dwell should increase. If not, consult the individual service manual for test procedures.

TROUBLE CODES

A light may appear on the dash that informs the driver to "CHECK ENGINE" or "SERVICE ENGINE SOON," Fig. 25-13. This same light is used by the technician to pull Trouble Codes from the computer by flashing out numbers. Look in the service manual to find what the Trouble Code means. Not all computerized systems have Trouble Codes. For more information on Trouble Codes, see Chapter 29, Engine Ignition Systems.

CARBURETOR TROUBLESHOOTING

While the basic causes of carburetor trouble will vary with different makes and designs, the usual problems and their causes are outlined below.

POOR ENGINE PERFORMANCE

1. Air leak at carburetor or manifold.
2. Air leak in fuel line.

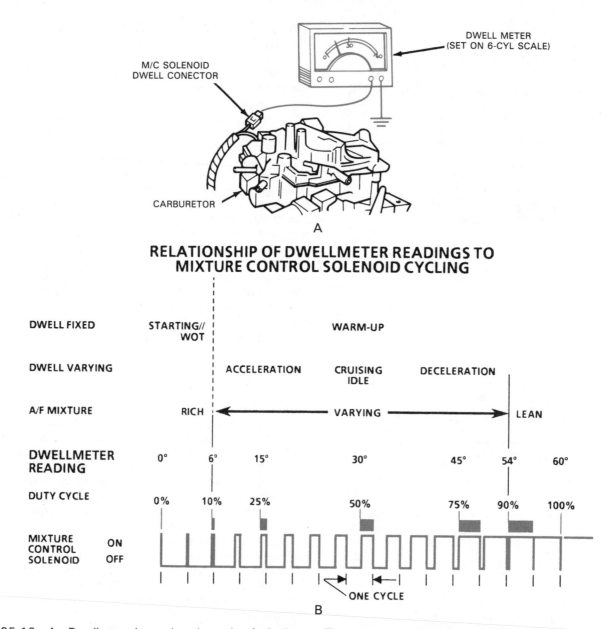

RELATIONSHIP OF DWELLMETER READINGS TO MIXTURE CONTROL SOLENOID CYCLING

Fig. 25-12. A—Dwellmeter is used to determine fuel mixture. The meter must be set on the six cylinder scale regardless of the number of cylinders. B—Dwell reading of 6 deg. indicates a rich fuel mixture; solenoid is energized 10 percent of the time. Dwell reading of 54 deg. indicates a lean mixture; solenoid is energized 90 percent of the time.   (Cadillac and Oldsmobile)

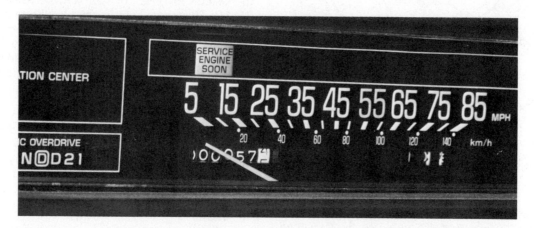

Fig. 25-13. CHECK ENGINE or SERVICE ENGINE SOON light indicates a problem. The technician uses this same light to pull trouble codes from the computer.

3. Clogged or dirty carburetor air filter.
4. Clogged fuel lines or fuel filter.
5. Defective fuel pump.
6. Incorrect fuel level in fuel bowl.
7. Automatic choke incorrectly set.
8. Dirt in carburetor jets and passages.
9. Worn or inoperative accelerating pump.
10. Wrong or incorrectly set metering rod (Carter carburetor).
11. Inoperative power valve, economizer or jet.
12. Damaged or wrong size main metering jet.
13. Worn idle needle valve and seat.
14. Loose jets in carburetor.
15. Defective gaskets in carburetor.
16. Worn throttle valve shaft.
17. Clogged exhaust system.
18. Defective manifold heat control valve.
19. Leaking vacuum lines to accessory equipment.
20. Defective sensors.
21. Defective computer.

POOR IDLING

1. Incorrect adjustment of idle needle valve.
2. Incorrect float level.
3. Sticking float needle valve.
4. Defective gasket between carburetor and manifold.
5. Defective gaskets in carburetor.
6. Loose carburetor-to-manifold nuts.
7. Loose intake manifold attaching bolts.
8. Idle discharge holes partly clogged.
9. Defective automatic choke.
10. Loose jets in carburetor.
11. Leaking vacuum lines to accessory equipment.
12. Vacuum leaks which are partly compensated for by a rich idle adjustment.
13. Worn main metering jet.
14. Restricted or clogged air cleaner.
15. High float level.
16. Defective sensors.
17. Defective computer.
18. Defective O_2 feedback solenoid.

HARD STARTING

1. Incorrect choke adjustment.
2. Defective choke.
3. Incorrect float level.
4. Incorrect fuel pump pressure.
5. Sticking fuel inlet needle.
6. Improper starting procedure.

POOR ACCELERATION

1. Accelerator pump incorrectly adjusted.
2. Accelerator pump inoperative.
3. Corroded or bad seat on accelerator bypass jet.
4. Accelerator pump leather hard or worn.
5. Clogged accelerator jets or passages.
6. Defective ball checks in accelerator system.
7. Incorrect fuel level.
8. Misadjusted throttle position sensor.

CARBURETOR FLOODS

1. Float level too high.
2. Stuck float needle valve.
3. Defective gaskets in carburetor.
4. Cracked carburetor body.
5. Excessive fuel pump pressure.

EXCESSIVE FUEL CONSUMPTION

There are many causes of excessive fuel consumption other than defective carburetion. Consider: Poor engine compression. Excessive engine friction. Dragging brakes. Misaligned wheels. Clogged muffler. Defective ignition. Quick starts. High speed driving.

1. Adjustment of idle mixture.
2. Fuel leaks in carburetor or lines.
3. Dirty air cleaner.
4. High float level.
5. Defective fuel economizer.
6. Defective manifold heat control valve.
7. Dirty carburetor.
8. Turbo wastegate stuck closed.
9. Excessive fuel pressure.
10. Sticking fuel inlet needle.

Chapter 25—REVIEW QUESTIONS

Write your answers on a separate sheet of paper. Do not write in this book.

1. Which should be adjusted first?
   a. Ignition.
   b. Carburetor.
2. Describe briefly the procedure for adjusting a single throat carburetor.
3. Describe the procedure for adjusting a two barrel carburetor.
4. What is the advantage of analyzing the exhaust gas?
5. On engines with emission controls, adjustment of _____ and _____ is important.
6. Which of the following parts should not be washed in carburetor cleaning solution?
   a. Carburetor float.
   b. Anti-stall dashpot.
   c. Idle needle valve.
   d. Accelerator pump diaphragm.
   e. Accelerator pump plunger.
   f. Main jets.
   g. Throttle valve.
7. List three causes for carburetor flooding.
8. List three causes for hard starting that start in the fuel system.
9. List five causes of excessive fuel consumption that start in the fuel system.
10. A dwell meter is used to determine if a problem exists in the computer, carburetor, or oxygen sensor. True or False?
11. Mechanic A states that the "CHECK ENGINE" light informs the driver of a problem.
    Mechanic B states that the "CHECK ENGINE" light is used by the technician to pull Trouble Codes from the computer.

Who is right?
a. Mechanic A.
b. Mechanic B.
c. Both Mechanics A and B.
d. Neither Mechanic A nor B.

Chapter 26

FUEL INJECTION

After studying this chapter, you will be able to:
- List the various types of fuel injection systems.
- Describe the three sub-groups of an EFI system.
- Explain how the pressure regulator and fuel injector operate.
- Troubleshoot the fuel injection system.
- Tell why fuel pressure must be released, and explain how and when it is released.

GASOLINE INJECTION

Fuel injection has been around for a period of time. The cost factor did not make it practical until now. With modern carburetors using a fuel mixture control solenoid, the carburetor has become as expensive as fuel injection. Fuel injection is much more precise in metering fuel. Also, there are less parts in a fuel injected system, compared to a carbureted system, making it easier to troubleshoot.

Other advantages of fuel injection include:
1. Increased power.
2. Higher torque.
3. Improved fuel economy.
4. Quicker cold weather starting.
5. Faster warmup.
6. No need for manifold heat.
7. Lower intake temperatures.

CLASSIFYING GASOLINE INJECTION SYSTEMS

The types of fuel injection systems are:
1. SINGLE POINT/CONTINUOUS.
2. MULTI-POINT/INTERMITTENT.
3. DIRECT.

SINGLE POINT/CONTINUOUS

Single point injection is also referred to as Throttle Body Injection (TBI). Single point refers to a centrally located fuel injector. One or two fuel injectors are in the throttle body, Figs. 26-1 and 26-2. Fuel is sprayed into an intake manifold, and then delivered to the cylinders.

Continuous fuel injection means that the fuel is sprayed constantly from the fuel injector into the intake manifold. The injector is pulsed on and off so fast that

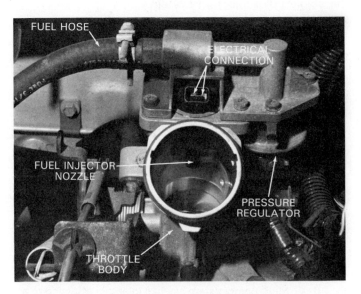

Fig. 26-1. Single point or Throttle Body Injection.

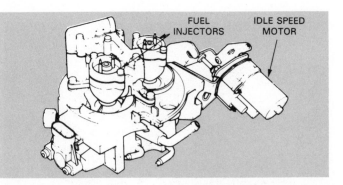

Fig. 26-2. Some single point systems have two injectors. Both injectors are pulsed on and off at the same time. With TBI, an intake manifold is still needed.   (Cadillac)

it sprays a steady stream of fuel. Single point injection, whether one or two injectors are used, is pulsed on for each intake stroke. This means there are two pulses per crankshaft revolution on a four cylinder engine; 26 pulses per second at idle.

MULTI-POINT/INTERMITTENT

Multi-point injection refers to many fuel injectors used on the engine. This means that there are as many injectors as there are cylinders. On this system, the fuel injectors are attached to a fuel rail, Fig. 26-3.

Most multi-point systems are intermittent. This means that the injectors are not energized at the same time. There are different types of intermittent injection. The injectors can be turned on and off:
1. In pairs.
2. In a specific sequence (Sequential Injection).
Most, but not all, multi-point systems are ported. Ported injection means that the fuel is sprayed directly into an intake runner, Figs. 26-4 and 26-5. This eliminates the problems associated with intake manifolds. This contrasts to fuel being sprayed in the intake manifold as in the single point injection system.

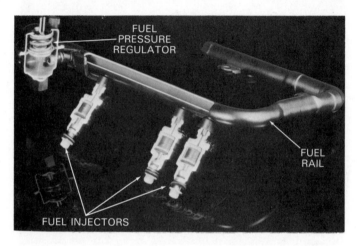

Fig. 26-3. Multi-point system has fuel injectors attached to a fuel rail. Fuel flows through the rail to all fuel injectors.   (Buick)

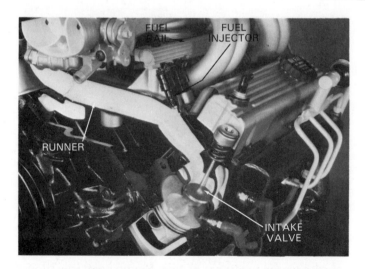

Fig. 26-4. With a ported fuel system, fuel is sprayed directly into the individual intake runners. There are as many intake runners as cylinders, as there is no intake manifold. Ported injection is used only on multi-point systems.
(Pontiac)

DIRECT

Direct fuel injection means that the fuel is sprayed directly into the combustion chamber. The fuel injector nozzle is located in the combustion chamber. This system is used by diesel engines.

CLASSIFYING THE CONTROL SYSTEMS

There are three methods for controlling the delivery of fuel to the injectors. Mechanical fuel injection is the oldest of the fuel injection systems. This system uses throttle linkage and a governor. It is now used mainly on diesel engines. Hydraulic fuel injection is used by some of the imports. Hydraulic pressure is applied to a fuel distributor. It is used as a switching device to route fuel to a specific injector. Currently, the most common method on gas engines is Electronic Fuel Injection (EFI). This system is divided into three sub-groups. They are:
1. AIR INDUCTION.
2. FUEL INJECTION.
3. ELECTRONIC CONTROLS.

AIR INDUCTION

The incoming air is regulated by the throttle valve. It is located in the throttle body, Fig. 26-6. The throttle valve is connected by linkage to the accelerator pedal. As the accelerator pedal is depressed, the valve is opened allowing air to enter the intake. Fuel is added to the incoming air.

FUEL INJECTION

The fuel from the tank is carried under pressure to the fuel injector(s). This is done by an electric fuel pump, which is located in or near the fuel tank. The excess fuel is returned to the fuel tank, Fig. 26-7. A relay for the electric fuel pump, Fig. 26-8, is used to complete the circuit to the fuel pump. This cuts off the current to the fuel pump in the event of an accident.

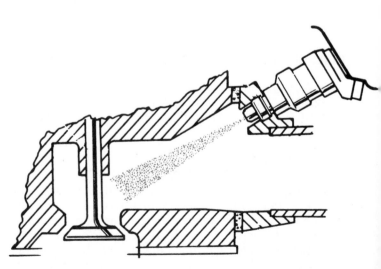

Fig. 26-5. Ported injection sprays fuel into the intake port.
(Oldsmobile)

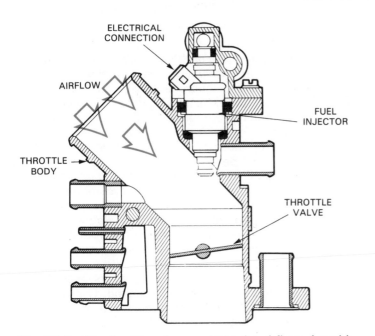

Fig. 26-6. The throttle valve regulates the airflow. A multi-point system uses a throttle body, minus the fuel injector. (Chrysler)

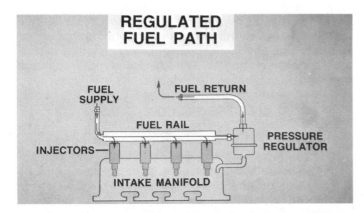

Fig. 26-7. Path showing flow of fuel. Unused fuel is returned to the tank through the fuel pressure regulator. Note that this system is a multi-point, but still uses an intake manifold. (Chrysler)

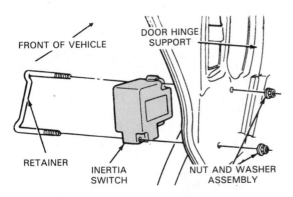

Fig. 26-8. Some fuel systems use a switch in addition to a fuel pump relay. The inertia switch stops the electrical current to the fuel pump in the event of an accident. The inertia switch can be reset. (Ford)

REGULATOR

The fuel pressure regulator, Fig. 26-9, keeps the fuel pressure at the injectors constant under all different driving conditions. A diaphragm inside of the regulator is held in place by spring pressure. Vacuum from the engine is applied to the spring side of the diaphragm. When vacuum is high, (idle and low load conditions), it overrides the spring pressure and lifts the diaphragm from the return port. The unused fuel is returned to the tank. During low engine vacuum, for example WOT, the engine needs all of the fuel it can get. Spring pressure is greater than the vacuum, and the spring forces the diaphragm against the return port. This prevents fuel returning to the tank, as all of the fuel is needed by the engine. The diaphragm is constantly opening and closing to maintain the desired fuel pressure.

INJECTOR

The fuel injector, Fig. 26-10, is an electromechanical device that sprays and atomizes the fuel. The fuel injector is nothing more than a solenoid through which gasoline is metered. When electric current is applied to the injector coil, a magnetic field is created. This causes the armature to move upward. This action pulls a spring-loaded ball or pintle valve off its seat. Then, fuel (under pressure) can flow out of the injector nozzle. The contour of the ball or pintle valve causes the fuel to be sprayed in a cone shaped pattern. When the injector is de-energized, the spring pushes the ball or pintle valve onto its seat, stopping the flow of fuel.

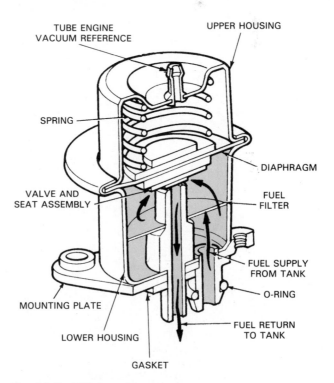

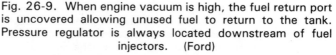

Fig. 26-9. When engine vacuum is high, the fuel return port is uncovered allowing unused fuel to return to the tank. Pressure regulator is always located downstream of fuel injectors. (Ford)

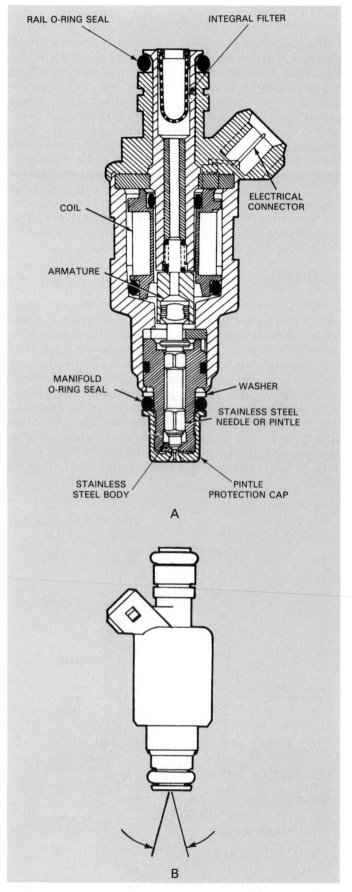

RAIL O-RING SEAL

INTEGRAL FILTER

ELECTRICAL CONNECTOR

COIL

ARMATURE

MANIFOLD O-RING SEAL

WASHER

STAINLESS STEEL NEEDLE OR PINTLE

STAINLESS STEEL BODY

PINTLE PROTECTION CAP

A

B

Fig. 26-10. Fuel injectors. A—When energized, fuel flows through the injector. B—Fuel spray pattern should always be cone shaped. (Ford and Delco-Rochester)

CONTROLLING THE FUEL INJECTORS

A lean air-fuel mixture produces a high level of nitrous oxides (NO_x) in the exhaust. A rich air-fuel mixture produces a high level of hydrocarbons (HC) and carbon monoxide (CO) in the exhaust. However, the byproducts of perfect combustion produce water (H_2O) and carbon dioxide (CO_2) in the exhaust, provided that the engine is 100 percent efficient. The best designed and built engine is not 100 percent efficient.

A STOICHIOMETRIC air-fuel mixture comes closest in providing the byproducts of perfect combustion. A stoichiometric air-fuel mixture is neither too rich nor too lean. It is 14.7 parts air to 1 part fuel. However, even with this desired air-fuel mixture, hydrocarbons, carbon monoxide, and nitrous oxides remain, but only in small percentages.

To achieve this, the combustion process, along with other engine variables, must be measured. The variables determine the length of time that the injectors are turned ON to provide the desired mixture.

SENSORS/ACTUATORS

Most, not all, sensors are supplied a reference voltage. A sensor is a device that measures. The measurement is then converted into an electrical signal. This signal is then compared, by the computer, to the reference voltage. This determines the amount of time that an actuator is energized. An actuator is a device that is controlled by the computer. The idle speed motor, ignition coil, and fuel injector are examples of actuators.

ELECTRONIC CONTROLS

The computer, or microprocessor, receives information from the various sensors, Fig. 26-11, and then adjusts the actuators accordingly. The fuel injector is one of the actuators that the computer controls. The longer the fuel injector is energized, the richer the fuel mixture becomes. The injector pulse width, Fig. 26-12, is the length of ON time. The pulse width is determined by the:
1. Crankshaft position sensor. This determines when the injector is energized. Most crankshaft position sensors double as an engine speed sensor. The higher the rpm, the more times the injector(s) is energized.
2. Manifold Absolute Pressure (MAP) sensor. This senses the engine load. The greater the load, (low vacuum), the longer the injector is energized.
3. Throttle position sensor. This determines the angle of the throttle blades. The greater the angle, the longer the fuel injector is energized.
4. Coolant temperature sensor. This senses the temperature of the engine. A cold engine needs the injector(s) to be energized longer. Other systems provide a cold start valve to richen the fuel mixture on a cold engine, Fig. 26-13.
5. Manifold air temperature sensor. This senses the temperature of the incoming air. Colder air is denser. To compensate for the denser air, the injector ON time must be increased.
6. Oxygen sensor. This senses the amount of oxygen in the exhaust. When there is an excess of oxygen

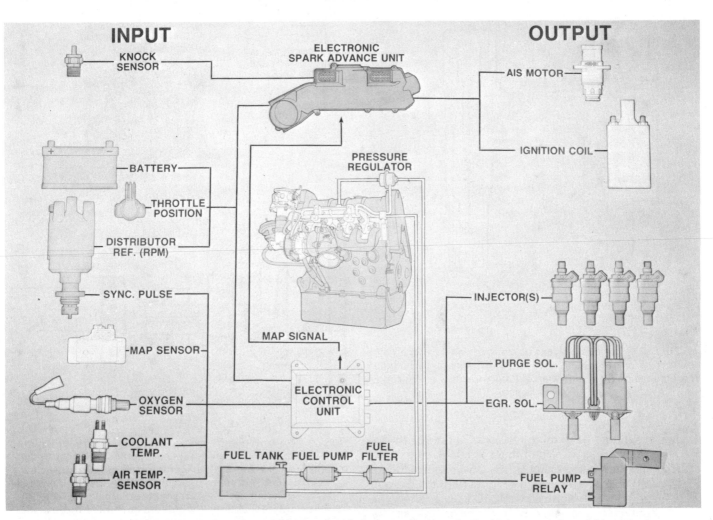

Fig. 26-11. The computer processes many input signals before adjusting the fuel injectors pulse width and other output devices. (Chrysler)

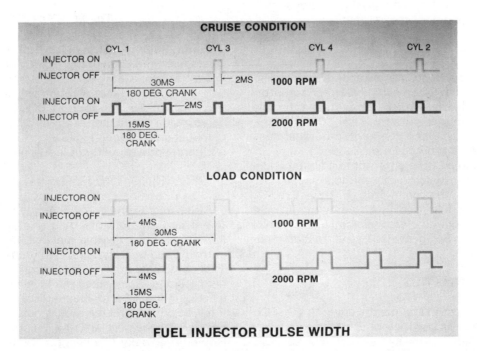

Fig. 26-12. The ON time or pulse width of the injector is measured in milliseconds. The higher the rpm, the more times a fuel injector is energized. Also, the greater the load, the longer the fuel injector is energized. (Chrysler)

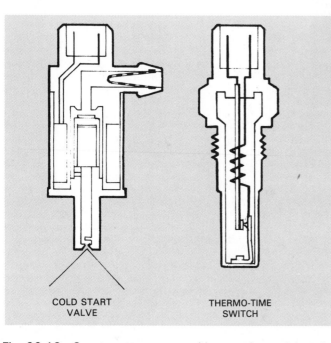

Fig. 26-13. Some systems use a cold start valve to richen the fuel mixture on a cold engine. The thermo-time switch limits the amount of time that the cold start valve is energized. (Robert Bosch)

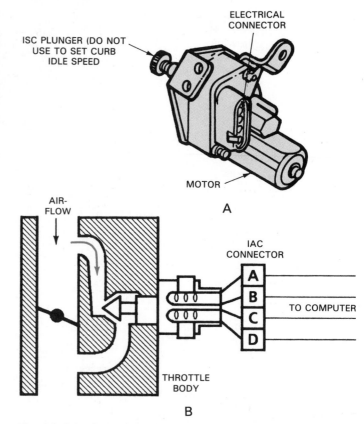

Fig. 26-14. Automatic idle speed adjustment. A—Some systems use a motor that retracts or extends a plunger to control idle speed. When the plunger is extended, idle speed is increased. B—Other systems use a motor that retracts or extends a valve regulating airflow past the throttle blades. When the valve is retracted, airflow is increased past the throttle blades increasing the idle speed. No attempt should be made to adjust the idle speed on either system. (Cadillac)

in the exhaust (lean mixture), and ON time of the injector is increased. When there is a lack of oxygen (rich mixture) in the exhaust, the ON time is reduced. When the computer uses the signal from the oxygen sensor, it is referred to as CLOSED LOOP. When the exhaust gases are below 600°F, the oxygen sensor does not provide the computer with a signal. The computer operates from predetermined values. This is referred to as OPEN LOOP. Also, when the throttle is wide open (WOT), the signal from the sensor is ignored, regardless of the temperature.

AUTOMATIC IDLE ADJUSTMENT

On computerized systems, the idle speed is controlled by a motor, Fig. 26-14. The motor is another actuator. The computer decides to increase or decrease the idle rpm after receiving input signals from all of the sensors. This keeps the idle speed at a constant rpm, regardless of the load placed on the engine while idling.

The technician should never attempt to adjust the idle speed. If there is a problem with the idle speed, the motor, sensors, or the computer is defective. A mechanical defect could also interfere with the idle speed. This could be due to a large vacuum leak. A small vacuum leak would be compensated by automatically adjusting the idle speed.

ON BOARD DIAGNOSTICS

When a light on the dash informs the driver to "CHECK ENGINE," a problem has been detected by the computer. Any of the components of the system could be at fault. For detailed information on diagnosing the cause, see Chapter 29, ENGINE IGNITION SYSTEMS.

DUAL STAGED

Some fuel injected engines that are equipped with a Dual Overhead Camshaft (DOHC) engine have what is known as a dual staged intake runner. When the rpm is below 5000, air flows through only a portion of the runner, Fig. 26-15. As soon as 5000 rpm is obtained, a valve inside of the runner opens allowing more air to the combustion chamber, Fig. 26-15. This increases low-to-mid-range power, without losing power at higher rpm's.

SERVICING THE FUEL INJECTION SYSTEM

A fuel injector has only one moving part, but if defective it can create more than one symptom. The most common problem with a fuel injector is that the orifices in the nozzle become dirty and restrict the flow of fuel. This can cause stalling, hesitation on acceleration, and hard starting. Sometimes the fuel injector can be cleaned by adding fuel injector cleaner to a full gas tank. The car must be driven until the tank is nearly empty. If this does not correct the problem, the injector must be replaced. However, a leaky fuel injector will flood the engine and may cause the engine to run on after the key has been turned to the OFF position.

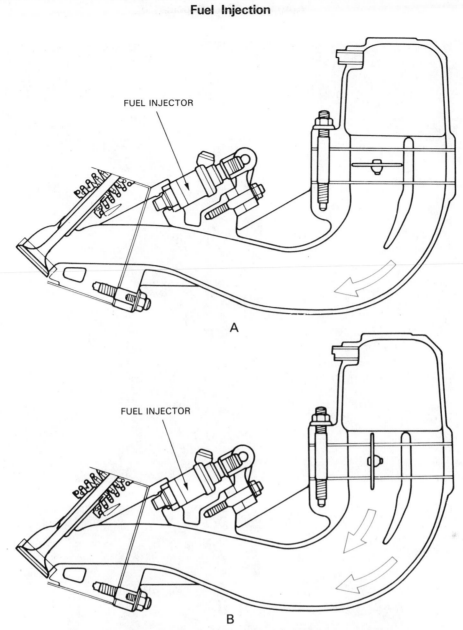

FUEL INJECTOR

FUEL INJECTOR

A

B

Fig. 26-15. Dual staged intake runner. A—When rpm is below 5000, valve remains closed and air flows through only a portion of runner. B—When rpm is 5000 or above, valve opens allowing more air through intake runner. (Honda)

LOW FUEL PRESSURE

Low fuel pressure creates a lean air-fuel mixture. This can cause a surging while driving at a steady speed. Causes for low fuel pressure:
1. A plugged fuel filter.
2. Defective fuel pump.
3. Fuel pump hose coupling (inside gas tank) leaking.
4. Defective fuel pressure regulator (stuck open).
5. Defective fuel pump check valve or accumulator.
6. Fuel line leaking.

TESTING FUEL PRESSURE

Connect a fuel pressure gauge to the test port, Fig. 26-16. Fuel pressure should register as soon as the ignition is turned ON (engine not running). Note the pressure and compare to specifications. If pressure is good, then start the engine and note the operating pressure. Fuel pressure should drop about 5 to 10 psi after engine has started and is idling. If fuel pressure does not drop, remove the vacuum hose from the pressure regulator. Make sure that a suction can be felt at the end of vacuum hose. If not, locate and repair the leak. If a suction is felt, reconnect the vacuum hose to the pressure regulator. Fuel pressure should drop about 3 to 6 psi after reconnecting the vacuum hose. If pressure does not drop, the pressure regulator is bad.

If the fuel pressure starts to fall shortly after connecting the gauge, with the ignition ON and the engine not running, the:
1. Fuel pump check valve or accumulator is bad; or
2. Fuel pump coupling hose is leaking; or
3. Fuel injector is leaking.

Fig. 26-16. Testing fuel pressure. A—Remove dust cap to access Schrader valve. B—Screw threaded adapter to Schrader valve. Lever is then lowered to allow pressurized fuel to gauge. C—If fuel pressure is at specified level, no further testing is needed. Note the drain valve and drain tube. To relieve fuel pressure, open drain valve with the ignition to the OFF position. (Rochester)

To determine which is at fault, energize the fuel pump, Fig. 26-17. Then, pinch shut the fuel return line or flex hose located in the fuel return line, Fig. 26-18. Fuel pressure should be around 75 to 100 psi with the pump energized and the fuel return line pinched. If not, the fuel pump or filter is bad. However, if fuel pressure is good and now fails to fall, the fuel pump check valve or accumulator is bad, or the pump coupling hose is leaking. On the other hand, if fuel pressure continues to fall, one or more injectors are leaking.

Sometimes a leaky fuel injector can be detected by removing all of the spark plugs from the engine. Note the condition of the porcelain insulator. If any are wet, the injector for that cylinder is leaking. However, an injector balance test may be needed to detect a leaky injector.

HIGH FUEL PRESSURE

If fuel pressure is above specifications, the fuel return line is restricted or the pressure regulator is defective. If there are no restrictions in the return line, replace the regulator.

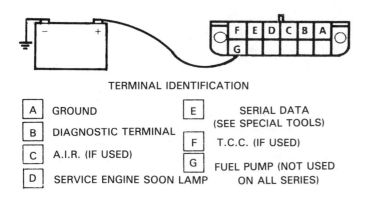

TERMINAL IDENTIFICATION

A	GROUND	E	SERIAL DATA (SEE SPECIAL TOOLS)
B	DIAGNOSTIC TERMINAL		
C	A.I.R. (IF USED)	F	T.C.C. (IF USED)
D	SERVICE ENGINE SOON LAMP	G	FUEL PUMP (NOT USED ON ALL SERIES)

Fig. 26-17. To energize the pump on some computerized GM engines, connect a jumper wire from a hot source to terminal G of diagnostic connector.
(Cadillac)

NOTE: Always consult the individual service manual for test procedures and specifications. If fuel is found in the vacuum hose connection of the pressure regulator, the regulator is bad.

CHECKING MULTI-POINT

Checking the fuel injectors on a multi-point system needs more time and special tools for testing. A defective fuel injector on a multi-point system may create an engine miss, dieseling, and a flooded engine. An oscilloscope can detect an injector that is only partially defective, Fig. 26-19. An injector balance test is another method for detecting bad fuel injectors, Fig. 26-20.

HARD STARTING

Sometimes a hard start will be experienced on fuel injected engines. This can be caused by many things. If a fuel injector is leaking it will flood the engine. A fuel pump check valve that is bad will allow fuel to drain back into the tank. Other systems may have a fuel pressure accumulator that prevents fuel from draining back into the tank. If the accumulator or check valve is bad, it will take time for the fuel to pressurize in the lines.

To determine if a fuel injector or check valve is causing a hard start, connect a fuel pressure gauge and start the engine. As soon as maximum pressure is reached, turn the engine off. Watch the gauge pressure. If pressure maintains for at least 15 min., all is fine. However, if pressure drops during that time, the injector, check valve, or accumulator is defective. A leaky fuel injector will show up in an injector balance test as shown in Fig. 26-20. A pressure regulator may also cause a hard start. The test for this was covered earlier in the chapter.

A defective fuel pump relay may also cause a hard start. The fuel pump is also wired in parallel with the oil pressure switch. This acts as a back-up for the relay. It will take a lot of cranking for the engine to build up enough oil pressure to close the switch. The closed switch then allows current to the fuel pump motor.

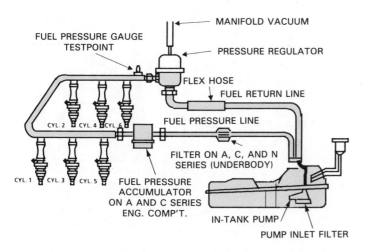

Fig. 26-18. Pinch the flex hose or return line closed. With pump energized, fuel pressure should be at lest 75 psi. Note fuel pressure accumulator.   (Oldsmobile)

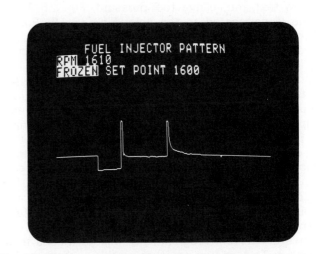

Fig. 26-19. An oscilloscope can be used to detect even a sticking fuel injector.   (Snap-On)

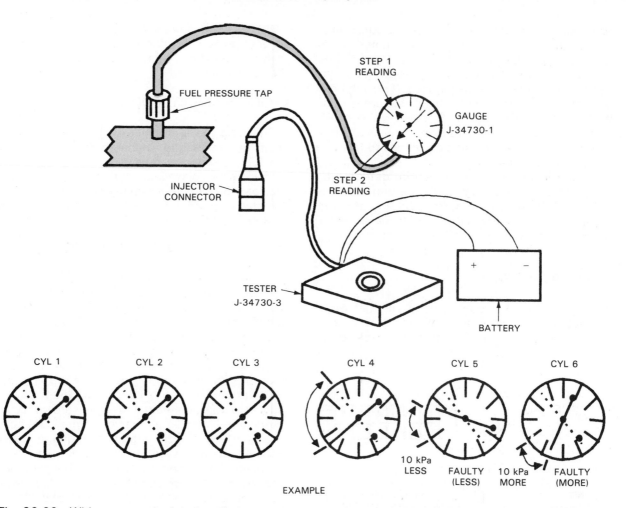

FUEL PRESSURE TAP

STEP 1
READING

GAUGE
J-34730-1

INJECTOR
CONNECTOR

STEP 2
READING

TESTER
J-34730-3

BATTERY

| CYL 1 | CYL 2 | CYL 3 | CYL 4 | CYL 5 | CYL 6 |

10 kPa
LESS

FAULTY
(LESS)

10 kPa
MORE

FAULTY
(MORE)

EXAMPLE

Fig. 26-20. With gauge and tester installed, note the drop in pressure after energizing the injector with the use of tester. Before moving tester to electrical connection at next injector, turn ignition to the OFF position. Once tester has been connected, the ignition is again turned to the ON position. After testing all injectors, compare readings. If any reading is more or less than 10 kPa, the corresponding injector is defective. (Oldsmobile)

RELEASING FUEL PRESSURE

The high fuel pressure in the lines of a fuel injection system can cause serious harm if opened without first releasing pressure. Most fuel injection systems have a port to test and relieve fuel pressure, Fig. 26-21. A gauge is connected to the port, Fig. 26-16. Fuel is discharged through drain tube, after opening the drain valve. Make sure that the pump is not energized and that the ignition is at the OFF position.

On systems that do not have a port to relieve fuel pressure (Chrysler), the electrical connection at the injector must be removed, Fig. 26-22. Attach two jumper wires at the electrical connections of the injector, Fig. 26-23. Attach the other end of one jumper wire to a good ground. Touch the other end of the remaining jumper wire to the battery positive post for no longer than 10 seconds to avoid shorting out the injector, Fig. 26-24. The energized injector will discharge the fuel through the injector. The system will then be safe to open and service, whether a fuel pump, filter, accumulator, pressure regulator, or injector needs to be replaced. To test fuel pressure on this system, a ''T'' must be inserted in the fuel return line.

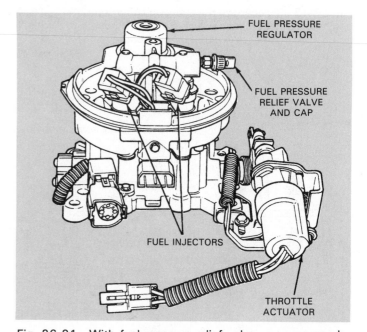

FUEL PRESSURE
REGULATOR

FUEL PRESSURE
RELIEF VALVE
AND CAP

FUEL INJECTORS

THROTTLE
ACTUATOR

Fig. 26-21. With fuel pressure relief valve, a gauge can be easily connected to this point. Fuel is then discharged through gauge. (Ford)

Fig. 26-22. On systems that do not provide a port to test or relieve pressure, disconnect electrical connection at injector.

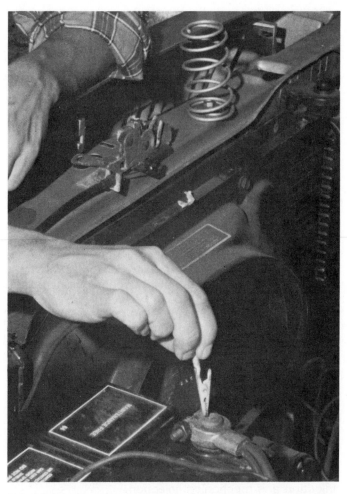

Fig. 26-24. Connect other end of one jumper wire to a good ground. With the remaining jumper wire end, touch it to the battery positive post for no longer than 10 seconds. Fuel will be discharged through injector into the intake manifold.

FUEL INJECTION HOSES/CLAMPS

The fuel hose on fuel injection systems is of a special type. Use only a fuel hose that is marked ''EFM/EFI.'' Regular fuel hose cannot be used on a fuel injection system. Also, use only fuel hose clamps that have a ''rolled edge.'' If regular worm type clamps are used, the sharp edges can cut into the fuel hose. The fuel is under greater pressure than a carbureted system. A small nick or cut in the fuel line will have a serious, if not fatal, effect in a fuel injected system.

STARTING EFI

On carbureted engines, the driver has to depress the accelerator once or twice before turning the ignition switch to start the engine. This action sets the choke and squirts a shot of fuel into the manifold.

On EFI systems the accelerator pedal is NEVER depressed before or during the start of the engine; there is no choke to set. The driver can depress the accelerator pedal all day and fuel will NOT come out of the injector. The fuel injector is energized by the computer when it sees a signal from the crankshaft position sensor.

Fig. 26-23. Connect one end of each jumper wire to fuel injector electrical connection.

If the accelerator is held to the floor while cranking the engine, the computer interprets this as a flooded engine. The computer then shuts off the supply of fuel. Therefore, no fuel is supplied during cranking. This would cause an engine NOT to start even if it was not flooded. If the engine does not start by turning the key, there is something wrong with the system. So, it is also possible for a misadjusted throttle position sensor to cause a NO START condition.

DIESEL INJECTION

A diesel engine compresses air and, at the point of maximum compression, fuel is injected into the combustion chamber. Ignition takes place as a result of the high temperature.

The fuel is forced into the combustion chamber of a diesel engine by means of a pump and injector. Since high pressures exist in the combustion chamber at the time of injection, the injection system must develop pressures in excess of combustion chamber pressure.

In delivering the fuel to the combustion chamber, a diesel fuel injection system must fulfill five main needs:
1. Meter or measure correct quanitity of fuel injected.
2. Time of fuel injection.
3. Control rate of fuel injection.
4. Atomize fuel into fine particles.
5. Properly distribute fuel in combustion chamber.

METHODS OF INJECTION

There are two different methods of fuel injection: air injection and mechanical injection.

In the air injection system, a blast of air from an external source forces a measured amount of fuel into the cylinder.

In the mechanical injection system, fuel is forced into the cylinder by hydraulic pressure on the fuel. This is the most common.

There are four types of mechanical fuel injection:
1. Common rail system.
2. Pump controlled (or jerk pump) system.
3. Unit injection system.
4. Distributor system.

COMMON RAIL SYSTEM: The common rail system consists of a high-pressure pump which distributes fuel to a common rail or header to which each injector is connected by tubing, Fig. 26-25.

PUMP CONTROLLED SYSTEM: This is also known as the jerk pump system. It gives a single pump for each injector. The pump is mounted separately. It is driven by an accessory shaft. Connection to the injectors is made by suitable tubing.

UNIT INJECTOR SYSTEM: This system combines the pump and the injector into a single unit. High-pressure fuel lines are not needed. Operation of the unit injector is by means of push rods and rocker arms.

DISTRIBUTOR SYSTEM: There are several types of distributor systems. One type provides a high-pressure metering pump with a distributor. Another design provides a low-pressure metering and distribution. High pressure needed for injection is met by the injection nozzles, which are cam operated.

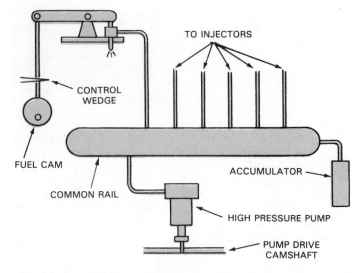

Fig. 26-25. Simple drawing of a common rail system of mechanical fuel injection.

MECHANICAL INJECTION PUMPS

The mechanical fuel injection pump performs many functions. It times, meters, and forces the fuel at high pressure through the spray nozzle.

Most designs are of the plunger type and are cam operated, but there is variation in the method used to control the quantity of fuel delivered. Among the methods of controlling the amount of fuel are:
1. Variable stroke.
2. Throttle inlet.
3. Throttle bypass.
4. Timed bypass.
5. Control of port opening.

Current design favors the port opening type of control.

VARIABLE STROKE DESIGN: The stroke is changed by sliding a cam plate in or out of its slot in the hollow camshaft. Axial movement of the camshaft is governor controlled, which in turn creates radial displacement of the cam plate.

THROTTLE INLET DESIGN: The flow of fuel into the pumping cylinder is throttled. This is done by rotation of a metering valve, which varies the port opening into the plunger bore.

THROTTLE BYPASS DESIGN: Metered fuel in the plunger chamber is discharged to the nozzle. At the same time it is bypassed through a throttle valve back to the inlet. The size of the bypass port opening is varied by governor action controlling a needle valve.

TIMED BYPASS DESIGN: Fuel is controlled by spilling the excess to a mechanically operated bypass valve. The amount of fuel discharged is controlled by rotation of an eccentric shaft on which a rocking lever pivots. Fuel delivery starts on the upstroke of the plunger, and stops when the bypass valve is lifted by contact with the rocking lever.

PORT CONTROL DESIGN: A portion of the plunger functions as a valve to cover and uncover ports in the plunger barrel. A groove on the plunger is designed to rotate so that the plunger stroke can be varied, thus controlling the amount of fuel delivered on each stroke.

AMERICAN BOSCH DIESEL SYSTEMS

The American Bosch Arma Corporation produces fuel injection pumps for single and multi-cylinder engines. The pumps for single cylinder engines are of the constant stroke, lapped plunger, port controlled type. For multi-cylinder engines, American Bosch produces the constant stroke type and the single plunger distributor type pump.

Typical of the port controlled type are the APE and the APF series. A pump of the APE series is shown in Fig. 26-26. Each pump element is so accurately fitted in the barrel that it provides a seal without any packing, even at high pressures and low speeds. The plunger jacket is milled out along a helical line to provide for the control helix on the plunger. The plunger has two opposing radial holes through which the fuel oil reaches the delivery chamber of the barrel. See Fig. 26-27.

The pump plunger is actuated by a cam on the compression stroke; by the plunger spring on the suction stroke. The valve is closed by a spring-loaded delivery valve, connected with the delivery pipe to the respective nozzles in the engine cylinder.

To vary pump output, the pump valve has a control sleeve with a toothed quadrant clamped on the upper end. A control rod meshes with the toothed quadrant so that the pump plunger can be rotated during operation.

Various positions of the plunger are shown in Fig. 26-28. In its upward movement, the plunger closes the intake port, shown at 2 in Fig. 26-28. This forces the fuel through the delivery valve to the delivery pipe. Fuel delivery stops as soon as helix and inlet port align. The delivery chamber of the barrel is (from that moment) connected to the suction chamber through the longitudinal

and annular grooves. The fuel is forced back into the suction chamber. If the plunger is turned far enough for the longitudinal groove and inlet port to meet, as at 6 in Fig. 26-28, the fuel in the delivery chamber is not subjected to pressure, and no fuel will be delivered.

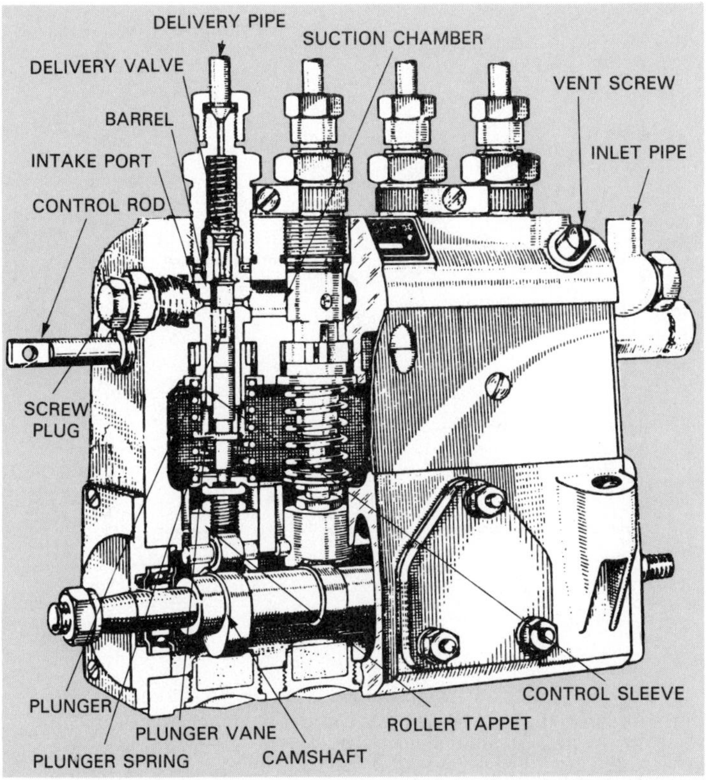

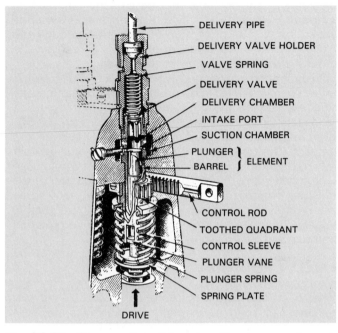

Fig. 26-27. Cross section of American Bosch pump element.

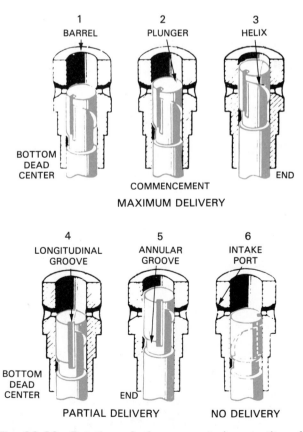

Fig. 26-28. Rotation of plunger controls quantity of fuel delivered.

Fig. 26-26. Bosch type APE diesel injection pump.

The injection nozzle used in the diesel system made by American Bosch is designed to control the mixture in the combustion chamber. American Bosch nozzles are of the pintle type or hole type, Figs. 26-29 and 26-30.

In the case of the pintle type, the nozzle valve carries an extension on the lower end in the form on a pin called a ''pintle,'' which protrudes through the closely fitting hole in the nozzle bottom. This requires the injected fuel to pass through a round orifice to produce a hollow-cone shaped spray. The projection of the pintle through the nozzle creates a self cleaning effect. This reduces the amount of carbon build-up at that point.

The hole type nozzle has no pintle, but is similar to the pintle type. The hole type nozzle has one or more spray orifices which are straight round roles through the tip of the nozzle body beneath the valve seat, Fig. 26-30. Spray from each individual orifice is relatively dense and compact. The spray pattern is determined by the number and arrangement of the holes. As many as 18 holes can be provided in the the larger nozzles. The diameter of the individual orifices may be as small as .006 in. The spray pattern may or may not be symmetrical (regular in shape), depending on the contours of the combustion chamber and fuel distribution needs.

NOZZLE OPERATION

The operation of the nozzle is controlled by the fuel pressure. As soon as pressure is exerted during the delivery stoke, the injection pump exceeds the tension of the pressure spring in the nozzle holder. Pressure acting on the taper of the nozzle needle causes the needle to be lifted off its seat. Fuel in then injected into the combustion chamber.

Nozzle opening pressure (which is adjustable) is determined by the tension of the pressure spring in the nozzle holder, Fig. 26-29. The needle stroke is limited by the plane surface on the nozzle holder.

When injected, fuel flows through the delivery pipe, connector, and pressure passage of the nozzle holder, Fig. 26-29. Then, through the groove and passage of nozzle, the out of the injection hole or holes of the nozzle into combustion chamber.

Delivering only clean fuel to the nozzles cannot be stressed enough. Because of the closely fitted parts, even microscopic size foreign matter can cause problems and wear of the parts. Because of this, two or more filters are installed, Fig. 26-31. The first, or primary, filter is designed to remove the larger and heavier particles. Often, it is the cleanable metal edge type. The final filter should be capable of removing particles down to 3 to 5 microns (0.00012 to 0.00020 in.).

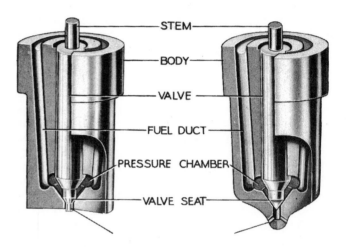

Fig. 26-30. Pintle and hole type fuel injectors.

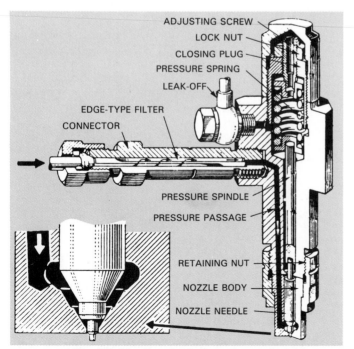

Fig. 26-29. Bosch pintle type nozzle.

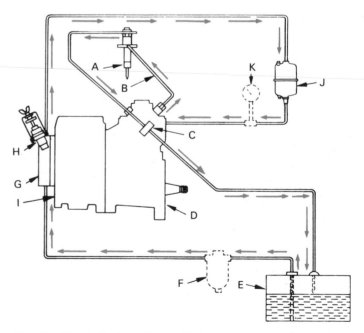

Fig. 26-31. American Bosch PSJ system. A—Injector. B—High pressure fuel. C—Overflow valve. D—Injection pump. E—Tank. F—Primary filter. G—Supply pump. H—Priming pump. I—Governor housing. J—Final filter. K—Fuel pressure gauge, if used.

AMERICAN BOSCH DISTRIBUTOR TYPE PUMPS

There are two American Bosch distributor type pumps, the PS series and the series 100. These pumps utilize a single hardened steel plunger that moves back and forth for pumping action. It also rotates for constant distribution of the fuel to the discharge outlets and from there to the engine.

The model 100 is a flange mounted, high speed (up to 3200 rpm) variable timing, governor controlled, high-pressure, single plunger, distributor type injection pump. It is designed for off-highway vehicles, and for marine and industrial use.

The replaceable hydraulic head, Fig. 26-32, contains a delivery valve and a plunger which, in addition to being actuated by a multi-lobe cam, is continuously rotated to serve as a fuel distributor.

Fuel distribution does not need to be adjusted. Therefore, the only adjustments are for average fuel deliveries. Changes in fuel delivery are controlled by the vertical movement of the plunger metering sleeve. This sleeve is actuated by the control unit which, in turn, is operated by the control rod.

A centrifugal, mechanical type governor actuates the control rod. The governor controls idle speed, maximum no-load speed, and fuel delivery throughout the speed range for any given throttle position.

The fuel supply pump draws fuel from the supply tank, through a primary filter, then supplies the fuel through a final filter to the hydraulic head sump area. Fuel pressure in the sump area is controlled by the overflow valve assembly. The fuel supply pump contains an integral pressure relief valve which prevents fuel system damage in the event of downstream restriction.

An internal timing device, known as the Intravance® automatically advances or retards the beginning of fuel injection as engine speed changes. Also, there is an internal, excess fuel starting device which provides increased fuel at cranking speeds.

GM DIESEL INJECTION SYSTEM FOR COMMERCIAL VEHICLES

This General Motors diesel engine operates on the two cycle principle and has a unit injector fuel system. In this system, a single unit measures the amount of fuel to be injected under varying conditions of speed and load. Next, it builds up the high pressure needed to inject the fuel into the combustion chamber, which is filled with air at a pressure of 1000 lbs. per sq. in. Then, it atomizes the fuel. There is no central metering or pressure pump and, therefore, high-pressure fuel distributing lines are not needed.

In the GM unit injection system, high pressures exist only at the tip of the injector. Each injector is complete. After repair work, or having run dry, it is not necessary to prime the GM injector.

The complete fuel system, Fig. 26-32, consists of the fuel supply tank, fuel line, fuel filters, fuel pump, fuel line manifold, and the fuel injector. A separate injector is needed for each cylinder. From the supply tank, fuel is drawn through the first fuel strainer or filter by the fuel pump. Then, the fuel is forced through the second filter to the fuel intake manifold that supplies fuel to each of the injectors. The unused fuel is returned through the outlet manifold to the supply tank.

The cross-sectional view of the engine, Fig. 26-33, shows the injector mounted in the cylinder head, and Fig. 26-34 shows details of the injector.

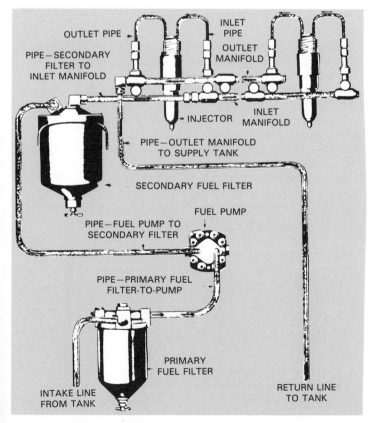

Fig. 26-32. Fuel system for two-cycle GM diesel engine.

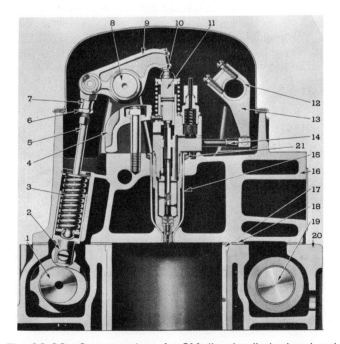

Fig. 26-33. Cross section of a GM diesel cylinder head and injector.

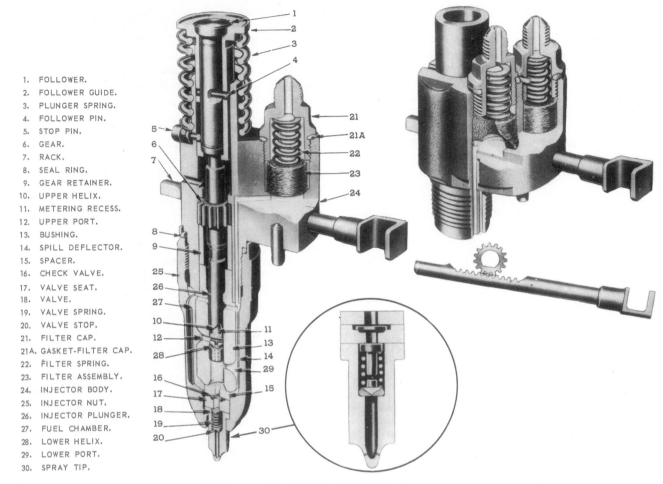

1. FOLLOWER.
2. FOLLOWER GUIDE.
3. PLUNGER SPRING.
4. FOLLOWER PIN.
5. STOP PIN.
6. GEAR.
7. RACK.
8. SEAL RING.
9. GEAR RETAINER.
10. UPPER HELIX.
11. METERING RECESS.
12. UPPER PORT.
13. BUSHING.
14. SPILL DEFLECTOR.
15. SPACER.
16. CHECK VALVE.
17. VALVE SEAT.
18. VALVE.
19. VALVE SPRING.
20. VALVE STOP.
21. FILTER CAP.
21A. GASKET-FILTER CAP.
22. FILTER SPRING.
23. FILTER ASSEMBLY.
24. INJECTOR BODY.
25. INJECTOR NUT.
26. INJECTOR PLUNGER.
27. FUEL CHAMBER.
28. LOWER HELIX.
29. LOWER PORT.
30. SPRAY TIP.

Fig. 26-34. A GM injector.

In the GM unit injector, Fig. 26-34, fuel is supplied to the injector at about 20 psi and enters the body through the filter cap. The fuel passes through the filter and fills the chamber between the bushing and the spill deflector. The plunger moves up and down by means of the engine camshaft, push rods, and rocker arms. It operates in a bushing connected by means of ports to the fuel supply in the annular chamber.

The motion of the injector rocker arm is relayed to the plunger by means of the follower that bears against the return spring. By means of the gear and rack, the plunger can be rotated. An upper and lower helix are machined into the lower end of the plunger for the purpose of metering fuel. As the plunger is rotated, the relation of the two helices with the plunger ports is changed.

As the plunger moves downward, fuel in the injector high-pressure cylinder is displaced through two ports, back into the supply chamber until the lower edge of the plunger closes the port. The remainder of the oil is then forced upward through the central passage in the plunger into the recess between the two helices. From there, it can still flow back into the supply chamber of the injector until the upper helix closes the upper port.

At this point, both upper and lower ports are closed. The fuel remaining under the plunger is then forced through the spray tip and into the combustion chamber of the engine. Changing the position of the helices by

rotating the plunger retards or advances the closing of the ports. It also signals the beginning and ending of the injection while, at the same time, controlling the desired amount of fuel that remains under the plunger for injection into the combustion chamber.

The positions of the plunger from no injection to full injection are shown in Fig. 26-35. Full injection is obtained with the control rack pushed in. In this position, the upper port is closed shortly after the lower port has been covered. In this way, a full effective stroke and maximum injection is produced. When the control rack is pulled out completely, the upper port is not closed by

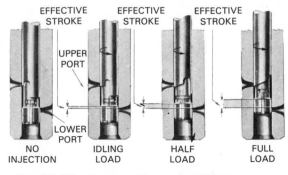

Fig. 26-35. Four positions of a GM injector.

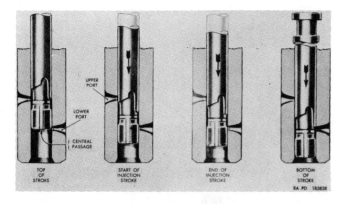

Fig. 26-36. Four positions of downward travel of a GM injector.

the helix until after the lower port is uncovered. As a result, all of the fuel charge is forced back into the supply chamber and no injection of fuel occurs.

The four positions for the downward travel of the plunger are shown in Fig. 26-36. On downward travel, the plunger forces the metered amount of fuel through the valve assembly, through the check valve, Fig. 26-34, and against the spray tip valve.

When enough pressure has been built up on the fuel, the spray tip valve is lifted from its seat and fuel is forced

through the small orifices in the spray tip into the combustion chamber. The check valve prevents air leakage from the engine combustion chamber into the injector. If the valve is held open by carbon or dirt, the check valve permits the injector to operate until the foreign matter works through the valve.

On the upward return movement of the plunger, the high-pressure cylinder is again filled with fuel through the ports. The constant circulation of fresh fuel oil in the fuel supply chamber helps maintain even operating temperatures. Also, all traces of air are done away with.

Each injector control rack is operated by a lever on a common control shaft. This shaft, in turn, is linked to the governor and the throttle. These levers can be rotated independently on the control shaft by the adjustment of two screws, and permits an even setting of the injector racks.

CUMMINS PRESSURE TIME SYSTEM

The Cummins PT system for diesel engines operates on the pressure time principle. This principle is based on the fact that by changing the pressure of a liquid flowing through a pipe, the amount of liquid coming out the open end is changed. Raising the pressure increases the amount of liquid delivered. This system consists of the fuel pump (with governor), the supply and drain lines, and the injectors, Fig. 26-37.

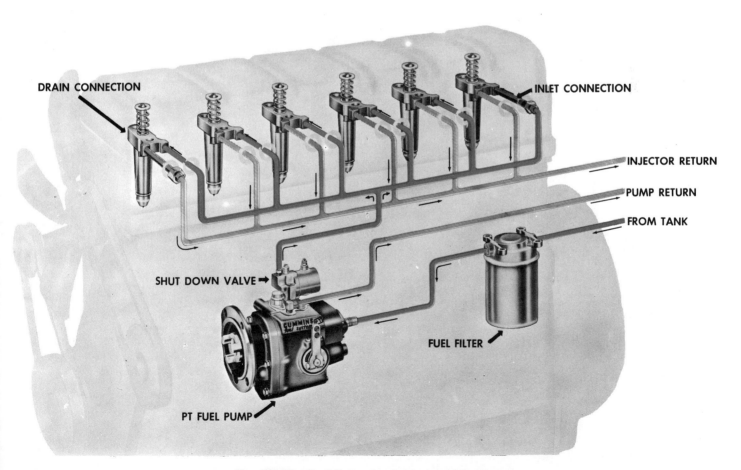

Fig. 26-37. Fuel flow of a Cummins PT system.

The fuel pump, Fig. 26-38, is made of three units:

1. Gear pump that draws fuel from the supply tank and delivers it under pressure through pump and supply lines to each injector.
2. Pressure regulator limits pressure of fuel to injectors.
3. Governor and throttle that act independently of pressure regulator to control fuel pressure to regulators. Fuel pump is driven at crankshaft speed.

The gear pump is located at the rear of the fuel pump, Fig. 26-38. It consists of one set of gears which pick-up and deliver fuel throughout the system, Fig. 26-37.

The pressure regulator is a bypass valve to regulate the fuel under pressure to the injectors. Fuel for the engine flows past the pressure regulator to throttle shaft, Fig. 26-39. The fuel passes around the shaft to the idle jet in the governor. For operation above idle, fuel passes through the throttling hole in the shaft and enters the governor through the primary jets.

Mechanical governor action is met by a system of springs and weights, Fig. 26-39. The governor maintains enough fuel for idling and cuts it off above rated rpm. Governors vary according to engine needs.

CUMMINS INJECTORS

The injector used with Cummins PT system is shown in Fig. 26-40. Fuel constantly circulates through the injector, except during a short period following injection into the combustion chamber. From the inlet connection, fuel flows down the inlet passage of the injector, around the injector plunger, between the body end and cup, up the drain passage to the drain connections and manifold and back to the supply tank.

As the plunger comes up, the injector feed passage is opened and fuel flows through the metering orifice into the cup. At the same time, fuel flows past the cup and out the drain orifice. The amount of fuel entering the cup is controlled by the fuel pressure against the metering orifice. Fuel pressure is controlled by the fuel pump.

During injection, Fig. 26-41, the plunger comes down until the orifice is closed. The fuel in the cup is injected into the cylinder. While the plunger is seated in the cup, all fuel flow in the injector is stopped. The flow diagram of this system is shown in Fig. 26-42.

CUMMINS METERING PUMP INJECTION SYSTEM

Another Cummins system employs a metering pump to measure each charge of fuel delivered at low pressure to the injectors. The injectors build up pressure of the fuel and injects it into the combustion chamber.

The Cummins diesel fuel pump performs four functions:

1. Draws fuel from supply tank.
2. Meters fuel in equal charges for each cylinder.
3. Distributes and delivers metered fuel at correct instant to each injector.
4. Provides a governor for control of idling and maximum engine speeds.

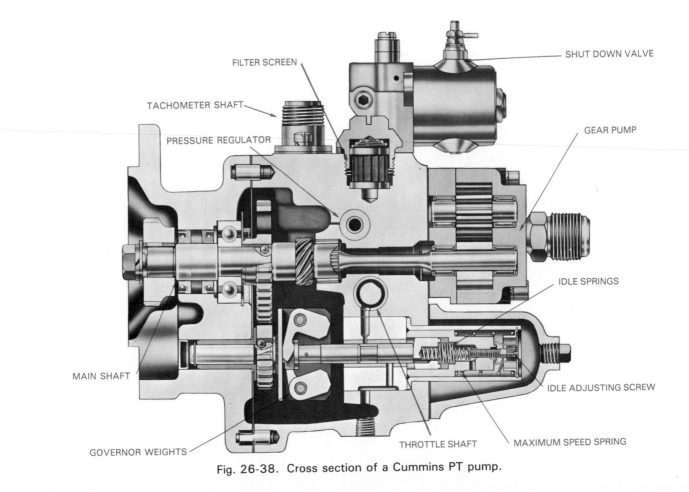

Fig. 26-38. Cross section of a Cummins PT pump.

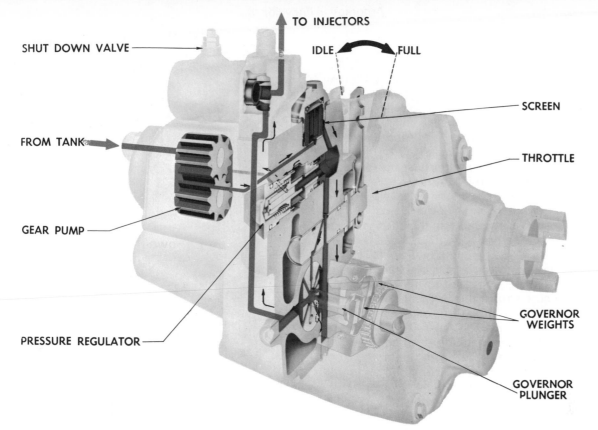

SHUT DOWN VALVE

TO INJECTORS

IDLE   FULL

SCREEN

FROM TANK

THROTTLE

GEAR PUMP

GOVERNOR
WEIGHTS

PRESSURE REGULATOR

GOVERNOR
PLUNGER

Fig. 26-39. Fuel flow through pump.

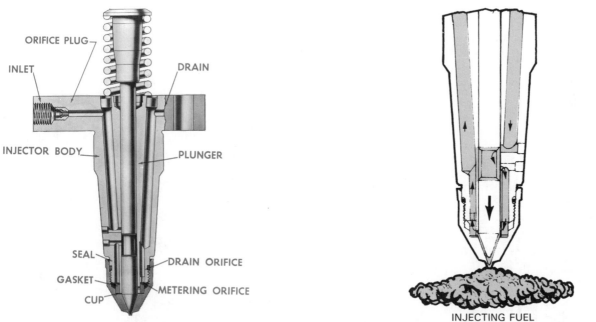

ORIFICE PLUG

INLET   DRAIN

INJECTOR BODY   PLUNGER

SEAL   DRAIN ORIFICE
GASKET   METERING ORIFICE
CUP

Fig. 26-40. Cross section of a Cummins injector.

INJECTING FUEL

Fig. 26-41. Fuel flow through injector.

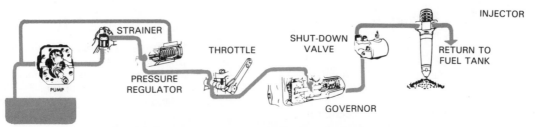

INJECTOR

STRAINER

SHUT-DOWN
VALVE

THROTTLE

RETURN TO
FUEL TANK

PUMP

PRESSURE
REGULATOR

GOVERNOR

Fig. 26-42. Fuel flow of a Cummins PT system.

ROBERT BOSCH INJECTION SYSTEM

The diesel fuel injection pump installed on many engines is a PE series type, Figs. 26-43, 26-44, and 26-45. The PE pump contains one pump element, consisting of a cylinder and plunger for each engine cylinder. The plunger is lapped in the cylinder and has a clearance of two to three thousandths of a millimeter. This small clearance serves to stress the importance of extreme cleanliness when working on injectors.

Plungers and cylinders are interchangeable only in complete sets. An injection timing device is built into the drive assembly of the pump, so fuel injection is timed to engine speed. The control rod, 11 in Fig. 26-45, is geared to the pinion, 12. The pump plunger, 9, can be turned with the control rod, and the discharge rate of the pump can be varied from zero to maximum.

During the pressure stroke, the plunger is lifted by the cam. During the suction stroke, the plunger is forced down again by the plunger spring, 15 in Fig. 26-45. The stroke of the pump plunger cannot be varied. The suction space, 8, is constantly filled with fuel and is kept under pressure by the feed pump. If the pump plunger is at bottom dead center, the control port, 7, is opened and the pressure space, 5, is filled with fuel.

During the upward motion, the plunger closes the control port and pushes fuel through the pressure valve, 4 in Fig. 26-45, into the pressure line, 1. The delivery ends as soon as the upper control edge has reached the control port, since the pressure space is connected with the suction space by the compensating hole in the plunger. The discharge rate is varied by turning the plunger, Fig. 26-45. The plunger opens the control port sooner or later, depending on the amount the plunger is rotated.

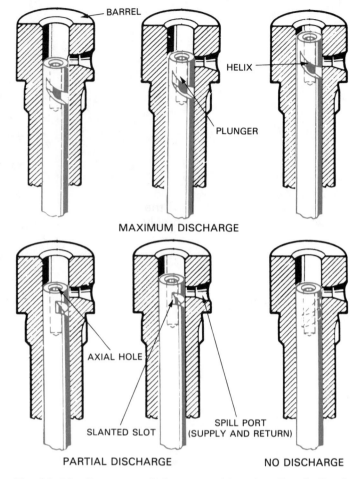

Fig. 26-44. Sequence of plunger positions in a Bosch diesel injection pump.

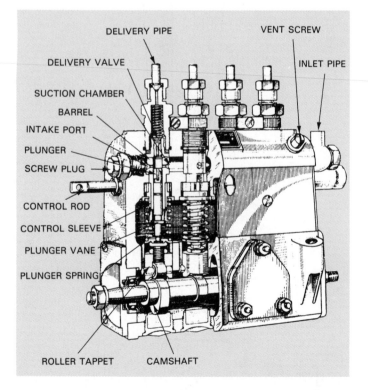

Fig. 26-43. Bosch model PE diesel injection pump.

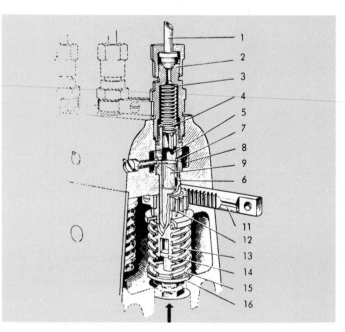

Fig. 26-45. Drive mechanisms of a Bosch PE type fuel injection pump. 1—Pressure line. 2—Connection. 3—Valve spring. 4—Pressure valve. 5—Pressure space. 6—Pump cylinder. 7—Control port. 8—Suction space. 9—Plunger. 11—Control Rod. 12—Pinion. 13—Control rod. 14—Plunger. 15—Plunger spring. 16—Spring retainer.

STANADYNE FUEL INJECTION PUMP

The Stanadyne fuel injection pump is a single cylinder, opposed plunger, inlet metering, distributor type unit. Fig. 26-46. It is used largely in high speed diesel engines. The main components are: drive shaft, distributor rotor, transfer pump, pumping plunger, internal cam ring, hydraulic ring, end plate, and governor.

The Stanadyne fuel injection pump is a self-lubricated unit, with the filtered fuel it pumps. There are no spring-loaded lapped surfaces, no ball bearings, and no gears. The rotating members revolve on a common axis. These are the drive shaft, distributor rotor (containing plungers and mounting governor), and the transfer pump.

Fuel is drawn from the supply pump into the inlet strainer, Fig. 26-46, by the vane type fuel transfer pump. Excess fuel is bypassed through the regulating valve back to the inlet side. The amount of flow bypassed increases in proportion to the speed, and the regulating valve is designed so that transfer puressure also increases with speed.

Fuel, under transfer pump pressure, is forced through an axial passage to the head and into an annular groove milled around the rotor shank. The fuel flows around the groove and through the metering valve in an amount determined by engine demands.

As the rotor revolves, one of its charging ports aligns with a passage, permitting the fuel to enter the axial passage. Inflowing fuel forces the plungers outward for a distance that is equal to the amount of fuel to be injected on the following stroke.

If only a small amount of fuel is admitted into the pumping cylinder, as at idling, the plungers move out very little. As extra fuel is admitted, the plunger stroke increases to the maximum amount allowed by a leaf spring arrangement. See Fig. 26-46.

At this point of the cycle, the rollers are in the "valley" of the cam. The fuel is trapped in the cylinder for a short period of time after charging is complete. During this time, the charging port is no longer aligned with the passage and the rotor discharge port has not yet aligned with an outlet port in the hydraulic head. Once it is aligned, fuel is injected into the line.

Chapter 26—REVIEW QUESTIONS

Write your answers on a separate sheet of paper. Do not write in this book.
1. When the fuel injector is located in the throttle body, the system is referred to as:
   a. Multi-point.
   b. Single point.
   c. Ported.
   d. Direct.
2. Intermittent fuel injection is associated with:
   a. Multi-point.
   b. Single point.
   c. Both a and b.
   d. Neither a nor b.
3. Continuous fuel injection is associated with:
   a. Multi-point.
   b. Single point.

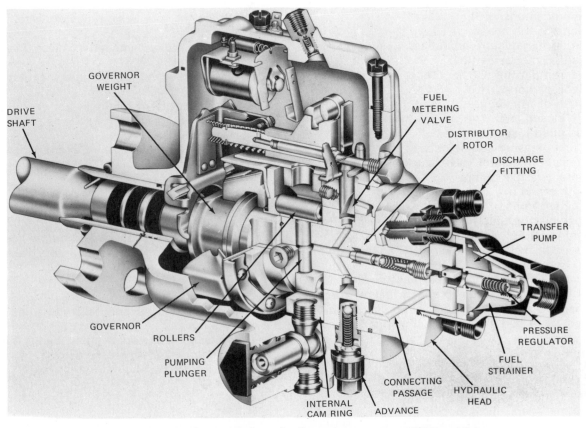

Fig. 26-46. Cross section of a Stanadyne pump. (Oldsmobile)

c. Neither a nor b.

d. Both a and b.

4. When the injector sprays fuel directly into a runner instead of an intake manifold, the system is:
   a. Multi-point.
   b. Single point.
   c. Ported.
   d. Direct.

5. Electronic fuel injection includes:
   a. Air induction.
   b. Fuel injection.
   c. Electronic controls.
   d. All of the above.
   e. None of the above.

6. Mechanic A states that the MAP sensor measures the load placed on the engine.
   Mechanic B states the airflow meter measures the load placed on the engine.
   Who is right?
   a. Mechanic A.
   b. Mechanic B.
   c. Both Mechanic A and B.
   d. Neither Mechanic A nor B.

7. Hot air is denser than cold air. True or False?

8. Cold air needs a richer fuel mixture. True or False?

9. A stoichiometric air-fuel ratio in an engine that is 100 percent efficient produces:
   a. Water.
   b. Carbon dioxide.
   c. Both a and b.
   d. Neither a nor b.

10. A lean air-fuel mixture produces:
    a. Carbon monoxide (CO).
    b. Carbon dioxide (CO_2).
    c. Hydrocarbons (HC).
    d. None of the above.

11. A rich air-fuel mixture produces:
    a. Carbon monoxide (CO).
    b. Carbon dioxide (CO_2).
    c. Hydrocarbons. (HC).
    d. None of the above.

12. Define closed loop.

13. Define open loop.

14. Low fuel pressure can be caused by:
    a. Pressure regulator valve stuck open.
    b. Defective fuel pump.
    c. Both a and b.
    d. Neither a nor b.

15. Before replacing a fuel filter, the pressure in the fuel system must be released. True or False?

16. Any type of fuel hose and clamps can be used on a fuel injection system. True or False?

17. Mechanic A states that low fuel pressure can cause a surging condition, due to a lean fuel mixture.
    Mechanic B states that low fuel pressure can be caused by a bad fuel pump or a bad pressure regulator.
    Who is right?
    a. Mechanic A.
    b. Mechanic B.
    c. Mechanic A and B.
    d. Neither Mechanic A nor B.

18. Mechanic A states that removing the vacuum hose from the pressure regulator should cause a drop in fuel pressure.
    Mechanic B states that removing the vacuum hose from the pressure regulator should cause fuel pressure to increase.
    Who is right?
    a. Mechanic A.
    b. Mechanic B.
    c. Mechanic A and B.
    d. Neither Mechanic A nor B.

19. Mechanic A states that a leaking injector may cause hard starting or diesling.
    Mechanic B states that the fuel pump relay, if defective, can cause hard starting.
    Who is right?
    a. Mechanic A.
    b. Mechanic B.
    c. Mechanic A and B.
    d. Neither Mechanic A nor B.

20. Mechanic A states that the accelerator pedal must be pumped several times prior to and during the starting of an EFI engine.
    Mechanic B states that only the key has to be turned to start an EFI engine.
    Who is right?
    a. Mechanic A.
    b. Mechanic B.
    c. Mechanic A and B.
    d. Neither Mechanic A nor B.

21. On the compression stroke, what does a diesel engine compress?
    a. Air.
    b. Air-fuel mixture.
    c. Diesel fuel.

22. What are the four basic types of diesel fuel injection used?

23. What five requirements must a diesel fuel injection system fulfill?

24. In the Bosch system, what does the rotation of the pump plunger control?
    a. The quantity of fuel delivered.
    b. Timing of injection.
    c. Compression.

25. What type engines are the General Motors diesel?
    a. Four cycle.
    b. Two cycle.
    c. Sleeve valve.

26. What type of injector system is used ont he General Motors diesel engine?

27. How many high pressure distributing lines are used on a four cylinder General Motors diesel engine?
    a. Four.
    b. Eight.
    c. None.

28. After repair work, is it necessary to prime a General Motors injector?

29. In the General Motors system, fuel is supplied to the injector at what pressure?
    a. 5 lb.
    b. 10 lb.
    c. 15 lb.
    d. 20 lb.

30. Describe the Cummins PT diesel system.

Chapter 27

EXHAUST SYSTEMS

After studying this chapter, you will be able to:
- List the components of the exhaust system.
- Explain the purpose of each component of the exhaust system.
- Describe what back pressure is and how it affects the operation of the engine.

EXHAUST GASES

The exhaust system of an engine, Figs. 27-1 and 27-2, is designed to conduct the burned gases (exhaust) to the rear of the car and into the air. This system also serves to silence the sounds of combustion.

Major parts of the exhaust system include the exhaust manifold, exhaust pipe, catalytic converters, muffler, and tailpipe. Also, V-type engines have a crossover pipe, and an intermediate pipe (connecting the crossover pipe to the muffler). Sometimes a resonator, a secondary silencing device, is installed. If the exhaust valve was closed during the entire combustion process, there would not be a need for the muffler and resonator.

Catalytic converters have been used in the exhaust systems of most cars since 1975. They are emission control devices that contain chemically treated substances that convert harmful emissions into harmless carbon dioxide and water vapor.

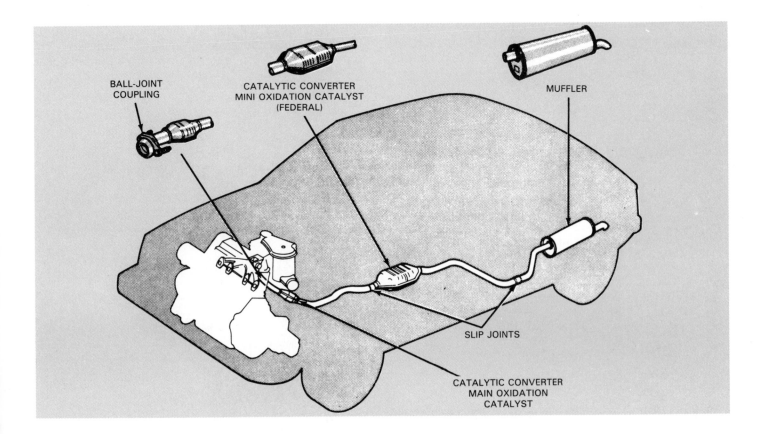

Fig. 27-1. Illustration shows location of muffler and catalytic converter. (Chrysler)

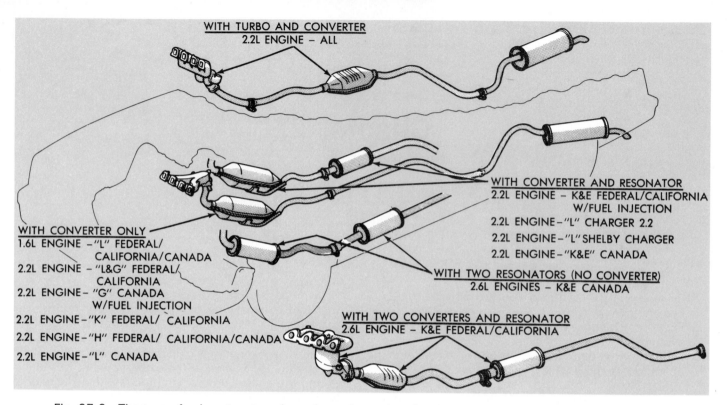

Fig. 27-2. The type of exhaust system depends on the engine size, if it is normally aspirated or turbocharged, and where the car will be sold. (Chrysler)

EXHAUST MANIFOLD

Exhaust manifolds are of many types. On an in-line engine, the manifold is bolted to the side of engine. On V-8 engines, separate manifolds are used for each side of the "V," Figs. 27-3 and 27-4. In V-8 applications, a separate exhaust system may be provided for each side of the engine. Or, the two sides may be joined together by means of a "crossover pipe."

Regardless of the design, the passages forming the manifold are made as large in size as practical. This reduces the resistance to the flow of the burned gases.

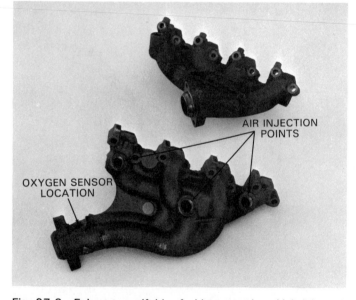

Fig. 27-3. Exhaust manifolds of a V-type engine. Air is injected into the exhaust manifold on some engines. This dilutes the exhaust gases and provides the needed air for catalytic converter operation. (Ford)

Fig. 27-4. Cutaway view of an exhaust port and manifold. (Ford)

Included in the design of the exhaust manifold on some engines is the manifold heat valve. This, together with special passages, conducts heat to the intake manifold to improve the vaporization of the fuel.

MUFFLERS

In order to reduce the noise of the combustion of an engine, exhaust gases from the engine are passed through a muffler, Fig. 27-5. The muffler is designed so that the gases expand slowly.

Muffler design must be such that there is the least amount of back pressure developed. Back pressure prevents free flow of the exhaust gases from the engine. As a result, not all of the burned gases will be forced from the cylinders. Remaining exhaust gases dilute the incoming air-fuel mixture and engine power is reduced. The exhaust of a car passes into the exhaust manifold, Figs. 27-3 and 27-4. Then, the gas passes through the exhaust pipe into the muffler. From the muffler, it passes into the tailpipe and from there into the air. Also, some cars use resonators in the system, Fig. 27-2.

A certain amount of room for expansion and cooling of the exhaust gas is designed into the exhaust manifold and exhaust pipe. They provide from two to four times the exhaust volume of a single cylinder of the engine. Additional expansion is provided for in the muffler.

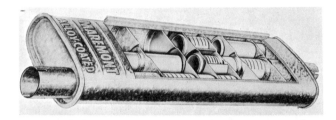

Fig. 27-5. Cutaway view of a muffler. Note that pipes are not connected with one another.

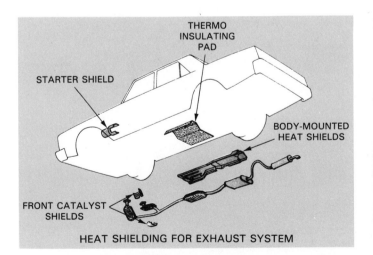

Fig. 27-6. Heat shields prevent higher than normal temperatures, created by catalytic converter, from being transferred into passenger compartment. Undercoating material should never be applied to heat shields.   (Chrysler)

CATALYTIC CONVERTERS

The catalytic converter is installed to reduce hydrocarbons (HC), carbon monoxide (CO), and nitrous oxides (NO_X). The catalytic converter does this by operating at temperatures in excess of 1500°F. The high temperature burns the unwanted byproducts of combustion. This is the reason heat shields are installed at varied points around the car, Fig. 27-6. Some catalysts are honeycomb shaped, Fig. 27-7. Other catalysts use beads, Fig. 27-8. If leaded fuel is used, it will clog the catalyst. This will create an excessive amount of back pressure in the exhaust system. A restrictor is placed in the fuel filler tube, Fig. 27-9, that prevents a larger diameter fuel nozzle, (leaded gasoline) from being inserted.

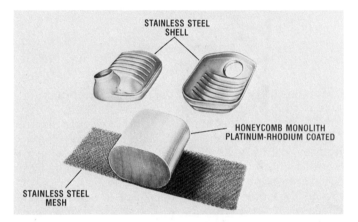

Fig. 27-7. A honeycomb type catalytic converter. If leaded fuel is used, passages will become plugged.   (Chrysler)

Fig. 27-8. Some catalysts use beads or pellets instead of a honeycomb.   (Universal Oil Products)

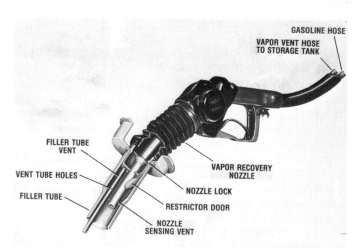

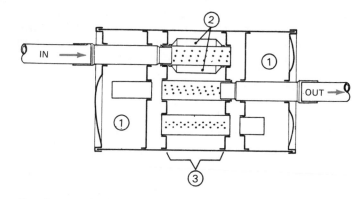

Fig. 27-11. Reverse flow muffler. 1—Helmholtz tuning chambers. 2—High frequency turning chamber. 3—Reversing crossover passages. (Maremont)

Fig. 27-9. Catalytic equipped cars have a restrictor in the fuel filler tube. This prevents the accidental use of leaded fuels, which have a larger diameter fuel nozzle.

MUFFLER DESIGN

The design of the muffler varies with manufacturers. One is the straight through type. See B in Fig. 27-10. In this design, a straight path for the gases extends from the front to the rear of the unit. With the straight through muffler, centrally located pipe with holes is provided. Surrounding this pipe is a sheet metal shell three times the diameter of the pipe. In some cases, the space between the outer shell and inner pipe is open. In other cases, it is filled with steel wool or some other heat-resistant sound deadener material.

Another type of muffler reverses the flow of the exhaust gases, Fig. 27-10, and has the advantage of saving space. The double shell and two shell designs are other forms of modern mufflers.

In order to reduce the noise of the exhaust below that attained by a single muffler, many systems are equipped with two mufflers in each line, Fig. 27-2. This design is needed on cars with a long wheelbase and a high output engine. The extra unit is called a resonator.

The design of a muffler is precise. The size and shape of the different chambers will affect the noise level and back pressure. In Fig. 27-11, chambers marked 1 are known as Helmholtz tuning chambers. These areas within the muffler are precisely tuned. Chamber volume, tuning tube size, and temperature of the gases in the chamber are taken into account.

If the exhaust pipe is the right length and diameter, the frequency of the explosions can cause a resonance in that pipe. This is the same as blowing across the neck of a bottle. These Hemholtz tuning chambers can be designed to absorb resonance and reduce the noise level of the exhaust system.

The high frequency tuning chanber, marked 2 in Fig. 27-11, reduces the sound level of the high frequencies

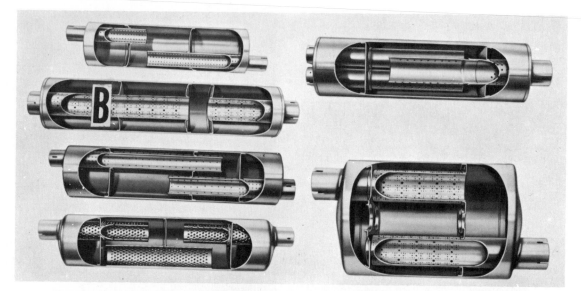

Fig. 27-10. Muffler B is a straight through design, which reduces the amount of back pressure. However, this is the noisest of the muffler designs. All other mufflers shown as of the reverse flow type, which are quieter in operation.

present in the exhaust system. (Helmholtz chambers primarily affect low frequency sounds.) The high frequencies can be generated by exhaust flow past a sharp edge in the exhaust system, venturi noise in the carburetor, and friction between the forceful exhaust flow and the pipes. High frequencies show up as a whistling noise. So, each hole in the inner tube of the high frequency tuning chamber acts as a small tuning tube.

The reversing unit crosswover shown at 3 in Fig. 27-11 is most effective in removing or reducing the midrange frequencies missed by the high and low frequency chambers. The amount of crossover is determined by the size and amount of holes in the adjacent tubes.

BACK PRESSURE

In Fig. 27-12, the loss in engine power due to back pressure from the exhaust system is charted. Note that as the speed of the car increases, back pressure increases. For a given car speed, the loss in power increases very fast with the increase in back pressure. For example, with 2 lb. back pressure at 70 mph, the power loss is 4 hp. When the back pressure is 4 lb., power loss has increased 8 hp.

Also, fuel consumption is increased as back pressure increases. This is shown in Fig. 27-13.

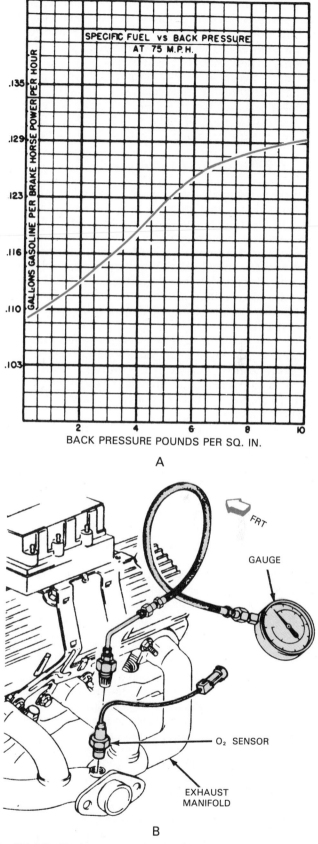

A

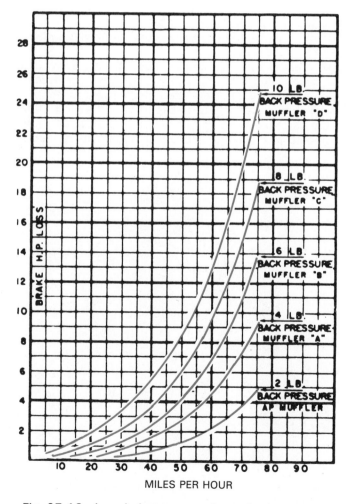

Fig. 27-12. Loss in horsepower due to back pressure.

Fig. 27-13. Back pressure. A—Fuel consumption increases as back pressure increases. B—Remove oxygen sensor and install pressure gauge in its place. Operate engine at 2500 rpm. If pressure exceeds specifications, then back pressure is a problem. A vacuum gauge can also be used to detect back pressure. (Oldsmobile)

Care must be used so that there are no kinks or flattened areas in the exhaust system that would obstruct the free flow of the exhaust gases. Any obstruction caused by internal blockage, will reduce power and fuel economy. This could be caused by:

1. A defective EGR valve/system.
2. Clogged catalytic converter.
3. Collapsed muffler.
4. Frozen heat control valve.
5. Kink in exhaust pipes.

EXHAUST SYSTEM CORROSION

Mufflers, tailpipes, and exhaust pipes wear out due to corrosion. External rusting is due to rain, snow, and humidity. In some northern states, this external rusting is speeded up by the use of salt on icy roads.

The greatest amount of corrosion occurs inside the exhaust system, mostly in the muffler. This is because a gallon of water is formed for every gallon of fuel burned. Acids are also formed in the combustion process. The acids and water combined quickly rust the inside of the exhaust system.

Until the exhaust system has reached operating temperature, much of the moisture will condense on the cool surfaces and collect in the muffler. Then, as the muffler becomes hot, the moisture will evaporate. On short drives, the muffler will not get hot enough and corrosion will occur.

To reduce corrosion, most manufacturers are using rust-resisting coatings and/or special alloys in the design of the mufflers and pipes. Stainless steel is used or a ceramic coating is applied to the inside of the muffler and pipes.

DEADLY EXHAUST GAS

It is important that no leaks occur in the exhaust system. Exhaust gases contain carbon monoxide (CO). When CO finds its way inside the car, it causes headaches, drowsiness, and nausea. As the amount of CO is increased, unconsciousness and, then, death results.

Surveys show that about 5 percent of the cars on the road contain enough carbon monoxide to cause drowsiness and impair driver judgment and reflexes if the windows are rolled up. Any leaks that occur in the exhaust system, from the exhaust manifold to the tailpipe, should be repaired as soon as possible.

Not only is exhaust gas deadly to the people inside the car, but to the technicians working in the shop as well. Engines should never run in the shop unless there is enough ventilation. In large shops, special ducts are used. These ducts are connected to the tailpipe of the car. The exhaust is then transferred outside.

SERVICING EXHAUST SYSTEMS

Because of the rusting that occurs in the exhaust system, parts in the exhaust system often need to be replaced. The parts most often replaced are the muffler and tailpipe. Their life depends on the type of service in which the car is used. If it is used for short trips, it is

not uncommon for the muffler and tailpipe to be replaced by 20,000 miles. This is true in dual exhaust systems of V-8 engines, as one pipe does not attain as high a temperature as the other.

The joint between the manifold and exhaust pipe is of the flange-and-gasket type. Brass nuts are used to hold the flanges together. Brass nuts are used as they will not rust to the stud, which makes removal easy.

PARTS REPLACEMENT

Exhaust system parts can be obtained from a supplier, or by keeping a supply of parts in the shop. However, stocking enough exhaust pipes, mufflers, and tailpipes takes much space and involves a large amount of money.

To help overcome these problems, tube bending equipment is available. With this equipment, only straight tubing in various diameters is stocked. The straight pieces are then bent to the desired shape, as needed.

The tube bender in Fig. 27-14, is fully automatic with foot pedal controls. This equipment is designed to produce bends through 3 in. outside diameter tubing. A heavy duty expander is used on the ends of the cut to form slip connections.

The exhaust pipe is designed with the lower end slightly larger in diameter than the opening in the muffler. The muffler opening can then be slipped into the end of the exhaust pipe. A clamp is placed around the end of the exhaust pipe. When tightened, the two parts are held together. Metal or metal-and-fabric straps are used to hold the muffler and pipes in proper alignment and with leak-proof connections.

To replace a muffler and tailpipe, remove the clamps and straps holding the tailpipe in place. Next, remove the tailpipe from the muffler. The tailpipe rusts to the muffler, which makes it hard to separate at the joint. If any of the parts are to be used again, penetrating oil should be applied to the joints before pulling them apart. In most

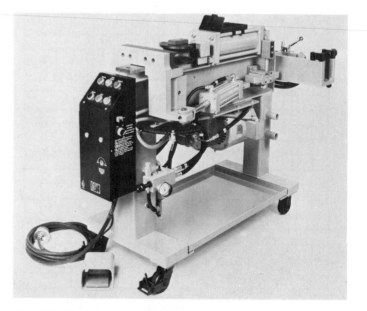

Fig. 27-14. Equipment designed for bending exhaust system tubing. (Huth Mfg. Co.)

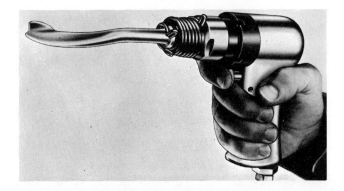

Fig. 27-15. An air chisel can be used to reduce the amount of time in remvoing exhaust pipes and mufflers.

Fig. 27-16. An expander is used to slightly increase the diameter of exhaust pipe for muffler installation.

cases, exhaust systems are not used again, and, therefore, can be cut apart.

Hacksaws can be used for muffler removal, but power-driven tools, Fig. 27-15, will do the job much more quickly. It is necessary to expand the end of a muffler pipe, tailpipe, or exhaust pipe. This is so the pipes can be assembled. A special tool for this purpose is shown in Fig. 27-16.

Chapter 27—REVIEW QUESTIONS

Write your answers on a separate sheet of paper. Do not write in this book.

1. What four parts form the exhaust system on a car?
2. On an in-line engine, where is the exhaust manifold attached?
3. What affect does back pressure have on the operation of an engine?
   a. Reduces power.
   b. Increases power.
   c. Increases the amount of carbon monoxide.
4. What affect does back pressure have on fuel economy?
   a. None.
   b. Reduces it.
   c. Increases it.
5. What is a major factor in the rusting of a muffler?
   a. Short distance driving.
   b. Long distance driving.
   c. High speed.
   d. Idling for extended periods.
6. What material is used in making the nuts used to bolt the manifold to the cylinder head?
   a. Cast iron.
   b. Steel.
   c. Castellated.
   d. Brass.
7. Mechanic A states that the catalytic converter is a secondary silencing device.
   Mechanic B states that the catalytic converter burns the unwanted byproducts of combustion, and thereby reduces them.
   Who is right?
   a. Mechanic A.
   b. Mechanic B.
   c. Both Mechanic A and B.
   d. Neither Mechanic A nor B.

The exhaust manifold on this engine is made of stainless steel tubing. This reduces the weight compared to a conventional cast iron exhaust manifold. The entire exhaust system, from the manifold to the tailpipe, is also stainless steel to increase its life.
(Buick)

Chapter 28
FUNDAMENTALS OF ELECTRICITY, MAGNETISM, AND ELECTRONICS

After studying this chapter, you will be able to:
- Explain the makeup of matter in terms of the molecular theory.
- State the basics of the electron theory of electricity.
- Employ Ohm's Law in troubleshooting electrical circuits.
- Describe the characteristics of series, parallel, and series-parellel circuits.
- Give the theory of permanent magnets and electromagnets.
- Explain construction and operation of diodes, transistors, and silicon controlled rectifiers.
- Recognize the tremendous effect of electronics on automotive advances.

ELECTRICITY

Electricity and electronics play a vital role in the safe and reliable operation of modern automotive vehicles. Demands range from a simple door switch and courtesy lamp to an engine electrical system so complex that a 40-way bulkhead disconnect may be required between the instrument panel and the engine compartment.

It logically follows that anyone who expects to successfully maintain, troubleshoot, and repair today's vehicles must have a thorough knowledge of the fundamentals of electricity and electronics.

STATIC ELECTRICITY

The ancient Greeks had a word for it. ELECTRIC is derived from a Greek word meaning amber. They found that by rubbing a piece of amber with a piece of silk, bits of paper, straw, and dry leaves were attracted to it. Later experiments showed that the same effect can be produced by rubbing a rod of glass or hard rubber with a handkerchief. In fact, many other nonmetallic materials are found to have this property called STATIC ELECTRICITY.

For example, if you rub a rod of hard rubber with a piece of fur, then hold it close to a pith ball suspended on a thread, the pith ball will be attracted to the rod. But if you allow the rod to touch the ball, the ball will bounce away. You can get the same effect by rubbing a glass rod with a piece of silk.

ATTRACTION AND REPULSION

Further experiments show that all electrified materials behave either as glass or rubber. Glass is said to have a POSITIVE CHARGE; hard rubber has a NEGATIVE CHARGE. If you electrify two strips of hard rubber by rubbing them with fur, they will repel each other. Two glass rods will behave in a similar manner. However, if you electrify a rod of rubber and suspend it near an electrified rod of glass, they will attract each other.

This simple experiment demonstrates one of the most important laws of electricity: BODIES WITH SIMILAR CHARGES REPEL EACH OTHER; BODIES WITH OPPOSITE CHARGES ATTRACT EACH OTHER. This law also applies to magnets (to be covered later).

ELECTRON THEORY OF ELECTRICITY

People have experimented with and controlled the use of electricity for scores of years, yet no one can explain just what electricity is. Many different theories have been advanced regarding the nature of electricity. Today, the ELECTRON THEORY is generally accepted.

In essence, the electron theory proposes that all matter (the earth, rocks, minerals, chemicals, elements, etc.) consists of tiny particles called MOLECULES. These molecules, in turn, are made of two or more smaller particles called ATOMS. These atoms are further divided into even smaller particles called protons, neutrons, and electrons.

These particles — protons, neutrons, and electrons — are the same in all matter, whether a gas, a liquid, or a solid. The different properties or characteristics of the matter take form according to the arrangement and number of protons, neutrons, and electrons that make up the atoms.

The PROTON has a natural positive charge of electricity. The ELECTRON has a negative charge. The NEUTRON has no charge at all, but adds weight to the matter.

CENTRAL CORE OF ATOM

Protons and neutrons form the nucleus (central core) of the atoms about which the electrons rotate, Fig. 28-1.

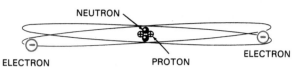

Fig. 28-1. Electrons rotate about central core of atoms, much like earth and other planets rotate about the sun.

Electrons carry small negative charges of electricity, which neutralize the positive charges of the protons.

The simplest atom of all is the hydrogen atom. It consists of one positively charged proton and one negatively charged electron, Fig. 28-2. Other atoms, such as those forming copper, iron, or silicon, are much more complicated. Copper, for example, has 29 electrons circling about its nucleus in four different orbits, Fig. 28-3.

SIZE OF ATOM

It is difficult to conceive the size of the atom. Research by physicists has established that the mass of one electron is about .000,000,000,000,000,000,000,000,-000,911 of a gram. If you assume that the size of a proton in a hydrogen atom is the size of a baseball, located in Kansas City, then its orbit would reach from the Atlantic coast to the Pacific.

So, along with the extremely small size of electrons and protons, they are separated by relatively vast distances. An appreciation of the distance between the proton and electron is necessary to understand the electron flow.

INSULATORS

In most elements, the nucleus is composed of protons and neutrons, which are surrounded by closely held electrons that never leave the atom. These are called BOUND ELECTRONS. When bound electrons are in the majority in an element or compounded material, the material is called an INSULATOR or a NONCONDUCTOR of electricity.

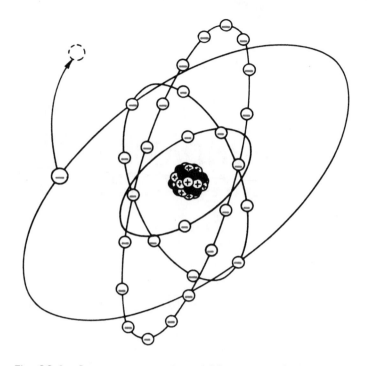

Fig. 28-3. Copper atom consists of 29 electrons circling about its nucleus of neutrons and protons in four different orbits.

CONDUCTORS

In other types of material, the nucleus is surrounded by another group of electrons which can be freed to move from one atom to the other when electricity is applied, Fig. 28-3. Electrons of this kind are known as FREE ELECTRONS, and the materials made up of these atoms are called CONDUCTORS of electricity.

SPEED OF ELECTRICITY

The speed of electricity is 186,000 miles per second. However, the electrons do not travel at this tremendous speed. Free electrons, which are available because electron orbits overlap in conducting materials, are pulled from one atom to another. As they move, the free electrons temporarily rotate about each new center. Since an electron carries a negative charge of electricity, electron flow (current flow) is assumed to be from negative to positive.

ELECTRON DRIFT

The rate at which the free electrons drift from atom to atom determines the amount of CURRENT. In order to create a drift of electrons through a circuit, it is necessary to have an electrical pressure, or VOLTAGE.

ELECTRIC CURRENT, then, is the flow of electrons. The more electrons in motion, the stronger the current. In terms of automotive applications, the greater the concentration of electrons at a battery or generator terminal, the higher the pressure between the electrons. The greater this pressure (voltage) is, the greater the flow of electrons.

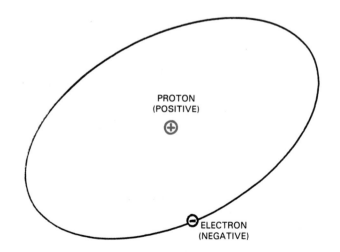

Fig. 28-2. Simple hydrogen atom consists of one positively charged proton and one negatively charged electron.

VOLTS, AMPERES, OHMS

The pressure between the electrons is measured in VOLTS. The flow of electrons (current) is measured in AMPERES. Opposing the flow of electrons is the RESISTANCE of the conductors, which is measured in OHMS.

Some materials offer greater resistance to electron flow than others: iron more than copper; copper more than silver. The length of the connecting wiring also contributes to the amount of resistance in a circuit. And, finally, the size of the wiring is also a resistance factor. A conductor of small diameter will offer greater resistance to the flow of electrons than will a conductor of large diameter.

OHM'S LAW

Ohm's Law is the mathematical relationship between voltage, resistance, and the amount of current in an electrical circuit. Each affects the other, and the relationship is stated as follows:

$$E = IR$$

E is the voltage. I is the current in amperes. R is the resistance in ohms. Also, by transposing the factors:

$$R = E \div I \text{ or } I = E \div R$$

As a memory aid in learning to make good use of Ohm's Law, try writing the basic equation as follows:

$$\frac{E}{IR}$$

Then cover the unknown factor with a fingertip, and you will have the formula you need to get your answer. For example:

If you cover the E, the formula is I × R.
If you cover the I, the formula is E ÷ R.
If you cover the R, the formula is E ÷ I.

Ohm's Law is used extensively in checking and troubleshooting electrical circuits and parts in automobiles. For example: the current flowing through the coils of a 12V alternator is 3.0 amperes. What is the resistance of the coils? Answer: 4 ohms (12 ÷ 3.0).

Studying Ohm's Law reveals exactly how a change in one factor affects the others. If the resistance of a circuit increases and the voltage remains constant, current will decrease.

To cite a practical example: If the connections of a starting battery are loose or corroded, a high resistance will be caused. The result will be insufficient current reaching the starting motor, lights, or other units to provide for proper operation.

TYPES OF CIRCUITS

There are three general types of electrical circuits:
1. Series, Fig. 28-4.
2. Parallel, Fig. 28-5.
3. Series-parallel, Fig. 28-6.

All circuits, regardless of type, consist of a source of electricity (battery or alternator), pieces of electrical equipment or devices, and electrical conductors that con-

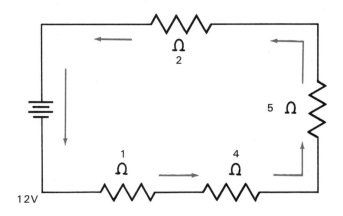

Fig. 28-4. In a series circuit, total resistance is sum of individual resistances shown by Greek letter Omega.

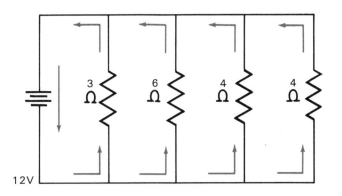

Fig. 28-5. Note how current divides through different branches of this parallel circuit.

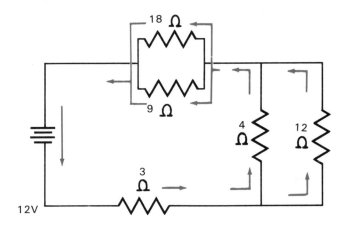

Fig. 28-6. A series-parallel circuit has some electrical devices connected in series, others in parallel.

nect the equipment or devices to the source.

In a SERIES CIRCUIT, Fig. 28-4, the current passes from the power source (battery, in these examples) to each device in turn, then back to the other terminal of the battery. The current has only one path to flow. The amount of current (amperage) will be the same in all parts of the circuit.

In PARALLEL CIRCUITS, Fig. 28-5, there will be more than one path for the current to flow. In this type of circuit, one terminal of each device is connected to a common conductor, which leads to one terminal of the battery. The remaining terminals of each device are connected to another common conductor which, in turn, is connected to the other terminal of the battery.

SERIES-PARALLEL CIRCUITS, Fig. 28-6, are those which have some electrical devices connected in series and others in parallel.

MEASURING RESISTANCE

To find the total resistence of a series circuit, add the resistance of each device. In Fig. 28-4, this would be:

$$R_T = R_1 = R_2 + R_3 + R_4$$
$$R_T = 2 + 5 + 4 + 1$$
$$R_T = 12 \text{ ohms}$$

The current flowing in this series circuit can be found by applying Ohm's Law as follows:

$$I = \frac{E}{R}$$
$$I = 12 \div 12$$
$$I = 1 \text{ ampere}$$

In a parallel electrical circuit, there is more than one "path" for the current to take. Therefore, the total resistance of all the devices will be less than the resistance of any single device.

There are several ways to compute total resistance in a parallel circuit. Probably the simplest way is to utilize the "conductance" formula. CONDUCTANCE is the reciprocal (opposite) of resistance. It is the current-carrying ability of any wire or electrical component. Resistance, as mentioned, is the ability of any wire or electrical component to oppose the flow of current.

To find total resistance, then, use this conductance formula and invert the answer:

$$\frac{1}{R_T} = \frac{1}{R_1} + \frac{1}{R_2} + \frac{1}{R_3} + \frac{1}{R_4}$$

To solve total resistance of the parallel circuit shown in Fig. 28-5, substitute the resistance values for R factors in the equation given:

$$\frac{1}{R_T} = \frac{1}{3} + \frac{1}{6} + \frac{1}{4} + \frac{1}{4}$$
$$\frac{1}{R_T} = \frac{4}{12} + \frac{2}{12} + \frac{3}{12} + \frac{3}{12} = \frac{12}{12}$$

Invert both sides of the equation (equal factors):

$$R_T = \frac{12}{12} = 1 \text{ ohm}$$

The total current flowing through the circuit will be:

$$I_T = E \div R_T$$
$$I_T = 12 \div 1$$
$$I_T = 12 \text{ amperes}$$

The circuit flowing through any single branch of a parallel circuit is found by dividing the voltage by the resistance of that particular path or branch. In Fig. 28-5, the current flowing in each branch would be as follows:

First — 12 ÷ 3 = 4 amperes
Second — 12 ÷ 6 = 2 amperes
Third — 12 ÷ 4 = 3 amperes
Fourth — 12 ÷ 4 = 3 amperes

Adding these values gives 12 amperes, which checks with the value found for the total circuit.

To make the calculations for a series-parallel circuit, treat each portion separately. Then, having calculated the resistance of each parallel branch, add those resistances as you would in a simple series circuit.

In Fig. 28-6, the resistance of the upper parallel circuit is 3 ohms. The parallel circuit on the left of the diagram is 6 ohms. Adding these values to 3 ohms of the series circuit at the right makes a total of 12 ohms.

VOLTAGE DROP

The decrease in voltage as current passes through a resistance is known as VOLTAGE DROP. The sum of the individual "drops" is equal to the total voltage impressed on the circuit.

Ohm's Law can be used to calculate voltage drop in different parts of the circuit. In Fig. 28-4, assume that 1 ampere of current is flowing:

Voltage drop E = IR
First part = 1 × 2 = 2
Second part = 1 × 5 = 5
Third part = 1 × 4 = 4
Fourth part = 1 × 1 = 1

Adding these drops in voltage, you have 2 + 5 + 4 + 1 = 12 volts, which checks with the voltage impressed on the circuit.

ELECTRICAL WORK AND POWER

The electrical unit for measuring work is called the "joule." One JOULE is equal to one ampere flowing for one second under the pressure of one volt.

First bear in mind that work is done when energy is expended. WORK is the product of force multiplied by the distance through which it acts in overcoming resistance.

An electrical force may exist without work being done. This is the condition that exists between the terminals of a battery when no equipment is connected to them. When a piece of equipment is connected to the terminals of the battery, current will flow and work will be done.

POWER is the rate of doing work:

$$\text{Power} = \frac{\text{work}}{\text{time}}$$

$$\text{Electrical power} = \frac{\text{electrical work}}{\text{time}}$$

The WATT is the electrical unit of power and is equal to one joule of electrical work per second.

$$\text{Watt} = \frac{\text{Joules}}{\text{Seconds}} = \frac{\text{Volts x Amperes x Seconds}}{\text{Seconds}}$$

$$\text{Watts} = \text{Volts x Amperes}$$

For example: In an automotive lighting circuit, the current is 8 amperes and the voltage is 12. The number of watts is 8 x 12 = 96 watts.

The unit for measuring mechanical power is HORSEPOWER (hp). Experimentally, it has been found that one horsepower is equal to 746 watts.

MAGNETISM

MAGNETISM, like electricity, is still a mystery. We know many laws governing its behavior and have applied it in the automotive field to starting motors, alternators, ignition coils, voltage regulators, etc. However, no one knows just what magnetism is.

The effects of magnetism were first discovered when it was found that pieces of iron ore from certain parts of the world would attract each other and also other pieces of iron. In addition, it was found that fragments of this ore, when suspended in air, would always point toward the North Star. The end of the ore that pointed toward the north was called the "north pole," the other end became the "south pole."

MAGNETIC FIELDS

All magnets have a magnetic field, which is evidenced by LINES OF FORCE, or MAGNETIC FLUX, around the magnet, Fig. 28-7. The strength of the magnetic field varies. It is strongest close to the magnet and gets progressively weaker away from it.

The area or extent of the magnetic field can be determined by means of a compass, which also shows the direction of the lines of force. In Fig. 28-7, note how the lines of force leave the north pole of the magnets (and coil), and reenter at the south pole. Also note that the lines of force exerted by the horseshoe magnet are more concentrated between the two poles of magnet.

THEORY OF PERMANENT MAGNETS

The effects, direction, and extent of magnetic fields can be studied. However, there is no actual knowledge as to why certain materials have magnetic properties and others do not. The ELECTRON THEORY generally is accepted as the best explanation of magnetism. It is also known as the DOMAIN THEORY.

According to this theory, an electron moving in a fixed circular orbit around the proton creates a magnetic field with the north pole on one side of the orbit and a south pole on the other side, Fig. 28-8. It is assumed that the

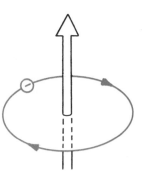

Fig. 28-8. An electron, moving in a fixed circular orbit, creates a magnetic field.

orbiting electron carries a negative charge of electricity, which is the same as electrical current flowing through a conductor. Current flow, then, is from negative to positive.

When a number of magnetized orbiting electrons exist in a material, they interact with each other and form "domains" or groups of atoms having the same magnetic polarity. However, these domains are scattered in random patterns throughout and the material is, in effect, unmagnetized. See Fig. 28-9.

Under the influence of a strong external magnetic field, these domains become aligned and the total material is magnetized, Fig. 28-9. The strength of its magnetic field depends on the number of domains that are aligned.

In magnetic substances (iron, cobalt, and nickel), the domains align themselves in parallel planes and in the same direction when placed in a magnetic field, Fig. 28-9. This arrangement of the electron-created magnets produces a strong magnetic effect.

It is also interesting to note that soft iron will lose virtually all of its magnetic effect as soon as it is removed from the magnetic field. Hard steel will retain its

MAGNETIC FIELDS

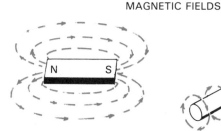

BAR MAGNET   CURRENT CARRYING CONDUCTOR

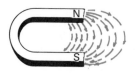

HORSESHOE MAGNET   CURRENT CARRYING COIL

Fig. 28-7. Note that lines of force leave magnet or loop of wire at north pole, reenter at south pole.

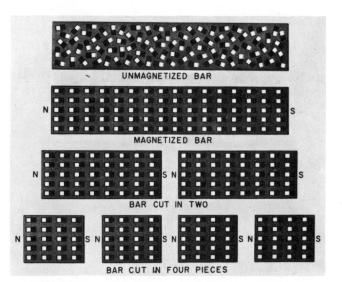

Fig. 28-9. In magnetic substances, "domains" align themselves in parallel planes and in same direction when placed in a magnetic field.

magnetic characteristics for an indefinite period. Special alloys of tungsten, chromium, and cobalt produce magnetic fields of considerably greater strength than other materials. They also retain their magnetism for a longer period. These alloys are used to form the magnets used in specialized electrical equipment where a strong magnetic field is required.

Magnetic lines of force seem to penetrate all substances. They are deflected only by magnetic materials or by another magnetic field. There is no insulator for magnetism or lines of force.

Another interesting property of magnets is illustrated by the following experiment. Cut a magnet in two and check the individual pieces for north and south poles. You will find that each piece has north and south poles, situated as in the original magnet. See Fig. 28-9.

ATTRACTION AND REPULSION

When two permanent magnets are placed so that the north pole of one is close to the south pole of the other, the magnets attract each other. Also, if the magnets are placed with similar poles close together, they repel each other, Fig. 28-10. This attraction and repulsion of magnets forms a fundamental law of magnetism: LIKE POLES OF MAGNETS REPEL EACH OTHER; UNLIKE POLES ATTRACT EACH OTHER.

PRODUCING MAGNETS, MAGNETIC FIELDS

If you stroke a piece of hardened steel with a natural magnet, the piece of steel will become a magnet. (Steel railroad tracks laid in a north-to-south direction become magnetized because they lie parallel to the magnetic lines of the earth.) Much stronger magnets and magnetic fields can be produced by electrical means. Placing a piece of steel in any strong magnetic field will cause it to become magnetized.

A magnetic field surrounds any conductor carrying an electrical current. The discovery of that fact resulted in the development of much of our electrical equipment. The FIELD OF FORCE is always at right angles to the conductor. This can be shown by placing a magnetic compass close to a conductor of electricity, Fig. 28-11.

Since a magnetic force is the only force known to attract a compass needle, it is obvious that a flow of electric current produces a magnetic field similar to that pro-

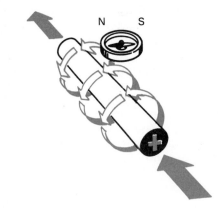

Fig. 28-11. A magnetic field surrounds any conductor carrying an electric current. Field is at right angles to conductor.

duced by a permanent magnet. When making this experiment, pass direct current through the conductor. Alternating current will cause the magnetic field to change with each alternation of the current.

Not only is the field of force at right angles to the conductor, but the field of force also forms concentric circles about the conductor, Fig. 28-12. Also, when the current in the conductor increases, the field of force is increased. Doubling the current will double the strength of the field of force.

LEFT HAND RULE

In many cases, it is helpful to know the direction of the lines of force that surround a conductor. Their direction is dependent on the direction the current is traveling in the conductor. Use the LEFT HAND RULE to make this determination.

To determine the direction of the lines of force, grasp the conductor with the left hand with the thumb extended in the direction the current is flowing. The fingers will

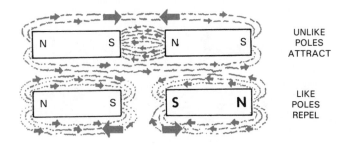

Fig. 28-10. Lines of force leaving north pole of one magnet will enter south pole of an adjacent magnet since all lines of force are in same direction. Lines leaving similar poles are repelled since they have opposite direction.

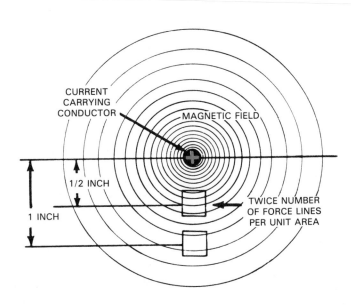

Fig. 28-12. A magnetic field forms concentric circles around a conductor carrying an electric current.

then indicate the direction in which the lines of force surround the conductor, Fig. 28-13. This left hand rule can be used to determine the direction the current is flowing after having first determined the direction of the magnetic field by means of a compass.

STRENGTHENING THE FIELD

As mentioned, the magnetic field surrounds the conductor, which is carrying an electric current. If this conductor is formed into a loop, Fig. 28-14, the lines of force on the outside of the loops spread out into space; lines on the inside of the loop are confined and crowded together. This increases the DENSITY OF LINES OF FORCE in that area. A much greater magnetic effect is produced with the same amount of current flowing.

In this setup, one side of the loop will be a north pole and the other side will be a south pole. By increasing the number of loops, the magnetic field will be greatly increased. By winding the loops or coils on a core of soft iron, the field is further intensified.

COMBINING MAGNETIC FIELDS

Another interesting experiment with magnetism is COMBINING MAGNETIC FIELDS. Figs. 28-7 and 28-10 show the fields of horseshoe magnets and the fields resulting from similar and unlike poles. Fig. 28-15 shows magnetic fields surrounding adjacent conductors. In accompanying drawings, the + mark on the end of the conductor simulates the butt end of an arrow. It indicates that the current is moving away from you. The dot on the other end is the point of the arrow. The current is coming toward you.

Current flowing in the same direction, and in opposite directions, in two adjacent and parallel conductors are shown in Fig. 28-15. A field of force surrounds each conductor, and the direction of the field can be determined by applying the left hand rule. The field will be clockwise around one conductor and counterclockwise around the other. However, in the area between conductors, the

MAGNETIC FIELD AROUND A LOOP

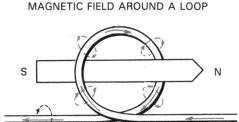

MAGNETIC FIELD AROUND A COIL

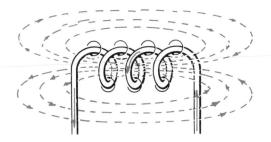

Fig. 28-14. Illustrating magnetic field surrounding a single loop carrying current, and field surrounding a coil of wire.

lines of force move in the same direction.

Since the amount of current is the same in both conductors, the number of lines of force between the conductors is the same as the number of lines outside the conductors. And, since the distance between the conductors is limited, the lines of force will be more dense in that area than beyond the conductors. This condition is known as UNBALANCED DENSITY, which will cause forces to act on the conductors.

When current is moving in the same direction in two parallel conductors, the unbalanced density will tend to draw the conductors together, as in A in Fig. 28-15. If

MAGNETIC EFFECT
OF PARALLEL CONDUCTORS

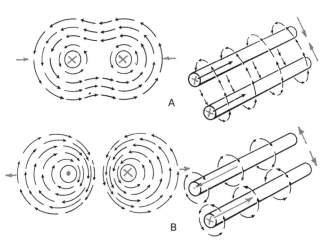

Fig. 28-15. A—With current flowing in same direction in adjacent conductors, resultant magnetic field tends to draw conductors together. B—If current is flowing in opposite direction, magnetic field will force conductors apart.

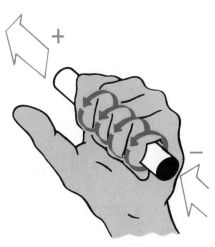

Fig. 28-13. Fingers of left hand around conductor show direction of lines of force, and extended thumb shows direction of current in conductor.

the current is moving in opposite directions in two parallel conductors, the unbalanced density will tend to force the conductors apart, as shown in B.

As illustrated in A in Fig. 28-15, two parallel conductors carrying current in the same direction will tend to move closer together. The two conductors act basically like a single conductor carrying a current equal to the sum of the two currents. As a result, twice as many lines of force are created than would be produced by either conductor with its original current. When several more current-carrying conductors are placed side by side, Fig. 28-16, the lines of force join and surround all of the conductors. This kind of magnetic pattern is obtained in coils of an alternator, starter solenoid, or ignition coil.

The STRENGTH OF THE MAGNETIC FIELD surrounding the coil of wire is directly proportional to the number of turns of wire in the coil and the strength of the current. To calculate the magnetizing force created, multiply the amperes flowing by the number of turns of wire. This force is known as AMPERE-TURNS.

DETERMINING POLARITY

To determine the MAGNETIC POLARITY of any coil or electromagnet when the direction of current flow is known, use the left hand rule for coils. Grasp the coil with your left hand so that your fingers extend in the direction the coil is wound and in the direction of current flow, Fig. 28-17. The thumb will then point toward the north pole created by the current flow through the coil. Remember that both the direction of current flow and the direction of coil winding determine the polarity of a coil.

MAGNETIC CONDUCTIVITY

The conductivity of air for lines of force has been adopted as a standard, so air is rated as having a permeability of one. ''Permeability of a substance,'' as defined by Kelvin, ''is the ease with which lines of force may be established in any medium as compared with a vacuum.'' Basically, PERMEABILITY is the magnetic conductivity of a substance.

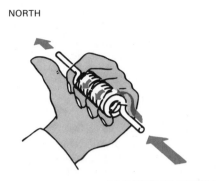

NORTH

DIRECTION OF CURRENT FLOWING

Fig. 28-17. Left-hand rule for coils may be used to determine polarity of a current-carrying coil.

When a soft iron core is inserted in a coil to form a true electromagnet, Fig. 28-18, the lines of force, or magnetic flux, will be increased several hundred times. By means of the better conductor (iron core), more lines of force are created. Field coils in starters, regulator windings on iron cores, and ignition coils all use this same principle.

SOLENOIDS

A SOLENOID is a tubular coil of wire with an air core. It is designed to produce a magnetic field. In most cases, the solenoid also includes an iron core that is free to move in and out of the tubular coil, Fig. 28-19. The movement of the iron core is used to operate some mechanism or switch. Its major application in the automotive field is to shift a starting motor drive into engagement with the flywheel ring gear. When a solenoid is used to close the contacts of an electrical switch, it is called a MAGNETIC SWITCH.

In Fig. 28-19, note that the south pole of the iron core is adjacent to the north pole of the coil. The polarity of the movable iron core is induced by the lines of force from the coil. Because the adjacent poles of the coil and the core are of opposite polarity, there is an attraction which draws the movable core into the center of the coil whenever current flows through the coil.

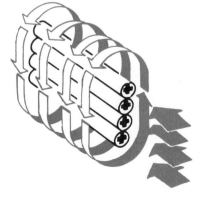

Fig. 28-16. When several current-carrying conductors are placed side by side, magnetic lines of force join and surround all conductors.

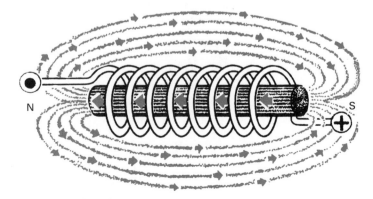

Fig. 28-18. Magnetic field of a coil can be strengthened by winding coil on a core of soft iron to form an electromagnet.

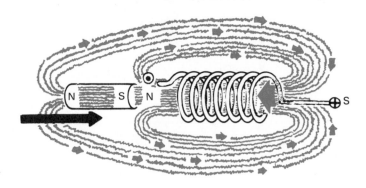

Fig. 28-19. A solenoid usually consists of a tubular coil of wire and an iron core.

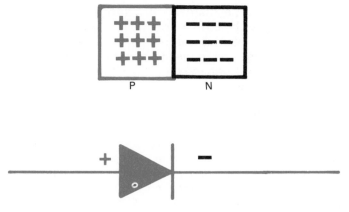

Fig. 28-21. Top. With P and N materials joined at PN junction, diode is ready to pass current in one direction only. Bottom. Diode symbol is shown.

ELECTRONICS

Electronics refers to any electrical component, assembly, circuit, or system that uses solid state devices. SOLID STATE means that these devices have no moving parts, other than electrons. Examples of solid state devices include semiconductor diodes, transistors, and SCRs (silicon controlled rectifiers). These and many more have broad application in automotive electronics.

SEMICONDUCTORS

In the electrical portion of this chapter, you learned that conductors are materials that will pass an electric current. You also learned that nonconductors, or insulators, are materials through which it is difficult to pass an electric current.

Now, in electronics, you will study semiconductors. SEMICONDUCTORS are made from material somewhere between the range of conductors and nonconductors. Semiconductors, basically, are designed to do one of three things:

1. Stop flow of electrons.
2. Start flow of electrons.
3. Control amount of electron flow.

SEMICONDUCTOR DIODES

A SEMICONDUCTOR DIODE is a two-element solid state electronic device. It contains what is termed a P type material connected to a piece of N material. See Fig. 28-20. The union of the P and N materials forms

a PN junction with two connections. The ANODE is connected to the P material; the CATHODE is connected to the N material, Fig. 28-21.

A diode is, in effect, a one-way valve. It will conduct current in one direction and remain nonconductive in the reverse direction. When current flows through the diode, it is said to be FORWARD BIASED. See Fig. 28-22. When current flow is blocked by the diode, it is REVERSE BIASED, AS SHOWN IN Fig. 28-23.

NOTE: When a diode is reverse biased, there is an extremely minute current flow. In practice, however, reverse bias current flow is said to be ''negligible.''

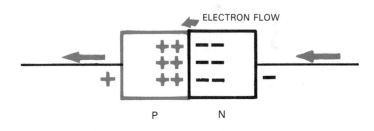

Fig. 28-22. With current flow from − to +, electrons in N material are repelled toward PN junction to meet ''hole flow.'' Current will flow through diode.

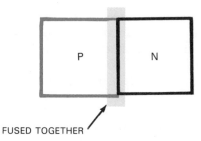

FUSED TOGETHER

Fig. 28-20. Positive and negative semiconductor materials must be fused together to form a diode.

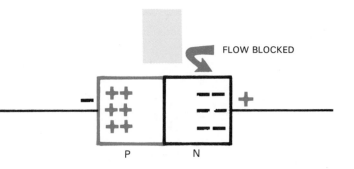

Fig. 28-23. With current flow from + to −, electron flow and hole flow will be away from PN junction. Current will not flow through diode.

With the P and N materials fused together to form a diode, it can be placed in a circuit. The P material is connected to the positive side of the battery and the N material is connected to the negative side of the battery. See Fig. 28-24. Connected in this manner, current will flow. If connections are reversed, current will not flow.

DIODE POLARITY

Because of the "one way" characteristic of a semiconductor diode, it is obvious that it must be placed in the circuit with correct polarity. Otherwise, it will block current flow or even by damaged by a surge of voltage above peak inverse voltage. PEAK INVERSE VOLTAGE (PIV) is the amount of voltage a diode can take in the reverse direction (reverse bias) without being damaged.

Generally, diodes are labeled plus (+) and minus (−). Those that are not labeled can be tested with an ohmmeter and properly labeled before being placed in the circuit. Simply hook the positive lead from the ohmmeter to one end of the diode and the negative lead to the other end. See Fig. 28-25. If you get a low resistance reading, you are forward biasing the diode. Mark a minus sign on the end of the diode hooked to the negative lead from the ohmmeter. Mark a plus sign on other end of diode.

If the ohmmeter reads high resistance, Fig. 28-26, you are reverse biasing the diode. Polarity is incorrect. Just reverse the leads and retest, then mark the ends of the diode for correct polarity.

TRANSISTORS

A TRANSISTOR is a solid state device used to switch and/or amplify the flow of electrons in a circuit. A typical automotive switching application would be a transistorized ignition system in which the transistor switches the primary system off and on. An amplifying application could be in a stereo system where a radio signal needed strengthening.

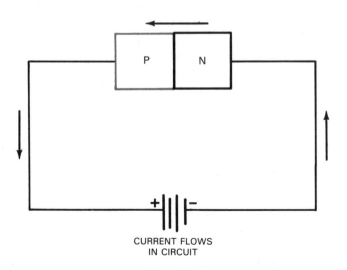

Fig. 28-24. When a battery is connected to a diode with positive side to P material and negative side to N material, current will flow.

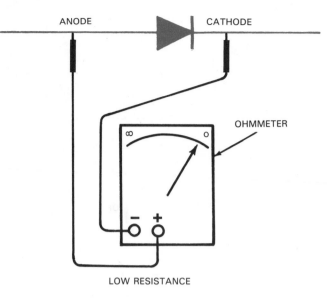

Fig. 28-25. To test polarity, connect ohmmeter leads as shown. Low resistance indicates that diode is forward biased.

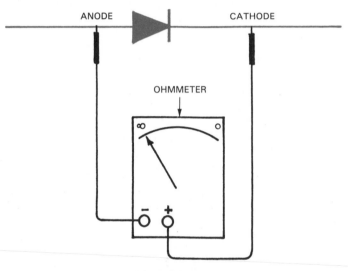

Fig. 28-26. If ohmmeter test for diode polarity results in high resistance, diode is reverse biased.

A transistor is a three-element device made of two types of semiconductor materials. The three elements are called "emitter," "base," and "collector." See Fig. 28-27. The outer two elements (collector and emitter) are made of the same material; the other element (base) is different. Each has a conductor attached.

The materials used are labeled for their properties. P is for positive, meaning a lack of electrons. It has "holes" ready to receive electrons. N is for negative, which means the material has a surplus of electrons.

The HOLE THEORY is based on the assumption that the movement of a free electron from atom to atom leaves a hole in the atom it left. This hole is quickly filled by another free electron. As this electron movement is

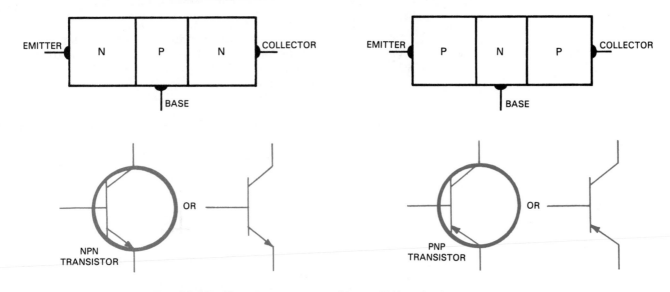

Fig. 28-27. Transistors are manufactured in two basic types. Left. PNP transistor. Right. NPN transistor. Symbols are shown below.

transmitted throughout the conductor, an electric current is created from negative to positive.

At the same time, the "hole" has been moved backward in the conductor as one free electron after another takes its place in sort of a chain reaction. "Hole flow" is from positive to negative. Current flow in a transistor, then, may be either electron movement or hole flow, depending on the type of material.

TRANSISTOR TYPES

Transistor types are either PNP or NPN, and their operation is basically the same. The differences are in the current carriers (electrons or holes) and direction of current flow. In either case, the polarity of the source voltage must be reversed to make a transistor operate. Symbols for PNP and NPN transistors are illustrated in Fig. 28-27.

TRANSISTOR LEADS

Transistor leads (wires) are known as EMITTER, BASE, and COLLECTOR. The PNP transistor will have its leads labeled as shown in Fig. 28-28. Note that the emitter lead in the symbol always has an arrow. In order to identify the PNP symbol, think of the PNP as "pointing in" with reference to the arrow.

The NPN transistor leads will be labeled as shown in Fig. 28-29. To identify the NPN transistor symbol, think of NPN as "not pointing in." Using these catchwords will be a help when you work with transistors and transistorized circuit drawings.

When transistors are placed in a circuit, the emitter-base (E-B) junction is forward biased. Forward biasing of the E-B junction will cause current to flow in the normally reverse-biased base-collector (B-C) junction.

In order to turn on a PNP transistor in a lamp circuit,

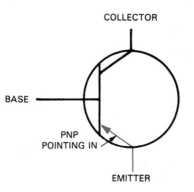

Fig. 28-28. On PNP transistor symbol, arrow is "pointing in." Leads are emitter, base, and collector.

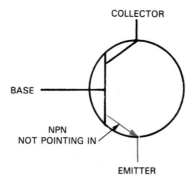

Fig. 28-29. On NPN transistor symbol, arrow is "not pointing in." Leads are emitter, base, and collector.

Fig. 28-30, a negative signal must be placed on the base. When this happens the flow of electrons is from the collector to the emitter. Note that the flow of electrons is against the direction indicated by the arrow on the emitter, Fig. 28-31.

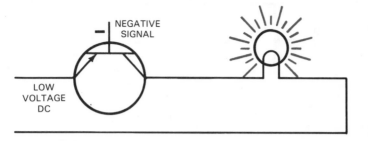

Fig. 28-30. In a low voltage dc circuit with PNP transistor and lamp, putting a negative signal on base of transistor will turn on transistor and light lamp.

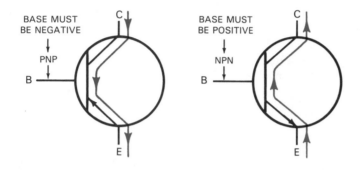

Fig. 28-31. When transistor is forward biased, flow of electrons is against direction indicated by arrow on emitter.

With an NPN transistor, a positive signal must be placed on the base to make it conduct. This will let the electrons flow from emitter to collector, Fig. 28-31. Again, the flow of electrons is against the direction indicated by the arrow on the emitter.

SILICON CONTROLLED RECTIFIERS

A SILICON CONTROLLED RECTIFIER combines two diodes so that their junctions appear as shown in Fig. 28-32. With this arrangement, junction 1 is forward biased, junction 2 is reverse biased, and junction 3 is forward biased.

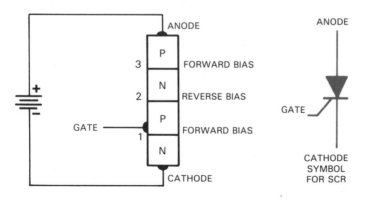

Fig. 28-32. Left. Schematic of silicon controlled rectifier construction and placement in a simple dc circuit. Right. Symbol for SCR.

The anode is positive in Fig. 28-32 and the cathode is negative, but the SCR will not conduct because one of the junctions will be reverse biased. A third connection made to the SCR is called the GATE. If dc is applied to the gate, it will "trigger" the SCR into conduction.

After initiating the induction, the gate will lose control until the anode-cathode path to the source is broken momentarily. Then the gate is again in control for the next triggering action. The triggering capability of the SCR makes it suitable for use in electronic ignition systems and in battery chargers.

SENSORS

Many electronic circuits use sensors to trigger a control signal. A SENSOR is a solid state semiconductor that controls electron flow as its temperature or pressure changes.

A typical automatic temperature control (ATC) automotive air conditioner uses three sensors:
1. For outside (ambient) temperature.
2. For in-car temperature.
3. For air discharge duct temperature.

ELECTRONIC ADVANCES

In the automotive field, electronics have touched on almost all operating systems:

1. Electronic ignition with sensors that "read" engine speed, load, and temperature and feed these signals to a micromputer. The microcomputer adjusts spark timing once per crankshaft revolution to a programmed setting to match engine operation requirements.
2. Electronic fuel injection (EFI) for intermittent, continuous or throttle body systems, each under the precise control of key sensing units and an electronic control unit (ECU).
3. An electronic data processing center for the engine that combines digital control of individual systems such as fuel injection and ignition in a single unit. Sensors deliver data on engine rotational speed, crankshaft position, and ambient air temperature to determine ideal spark advance and fuel quantity.
4. Electronically controlled diesel fuel injection that uses a digital electronic control unit to process inputs from various sensors into electrical outputs. These outputs, in turn, are translated into mechanical actions that regulate the fuel injection pump by means of a transducer.
5. Electronic control for automatic transmission. Input sensors sense engine and transmission rotational speeds and engine loads. The selector lever position, kickdown switch, and "program switch" are taken into account. Based on this information, the transmission's electronic program selects the best gear for operating conditions. It also smooths shifts, cuts fuel consumption, and protects engine and transmission from driver mistakes.

6. An electronically controlled anti-skid braking system that utilizes rotational speed sensors, an electronic control unit, and a hydraulic modulator to control braking. Magnetic valves in the modulator can lower line pressure, hold it steady, or increase it again because of electronic signal processing. With this pulsating application of the brakes, no wheel actually skids. The vehicle retains its directional stability.

7. Electronic trigger unit for passive restraint systems with an oscillator inside that measures vehicle deceleration. Its sensor signal is compared electronically with pre-programmed values. If these values are exceeded (in an accident), the trigger's electronic control signals the air bag to inflate. Or, in the case of an automatic shoulder/lap belt tensioner, the ECU triggers the tensioning.

8. Electronic thermostatic control for auto heating systems. The desired interior temperature is set and the ETC system maintains it, independently of vehicle speed, engine temperature, or ambient conditions. Heat delivery and blower speed are controlled as required.

9. Trip computers that deliver information on: fuel consumption; average speed since beginning this particular journey; estimated distance to the next fuel stop; exact trip time; time of day; and outside temperature.

10. Other electronic functions in some passenger cars include: Voice Alert systems; Information Centers; Keyless Entry; Alternator Voltage Regulators; Automatic Level Control; Headlight Dimmer; Off-On Headlight Control; Security Systems; Clocks; Radios; Tape Players; Automatic Temperature Control; On-Board Self-Diagnosis; Cruise Control; Variable Speed Cooling Fans; Electronic Control of Exhaust Gas Recirculation; Air Injection; Canister Purge; and Early Fuel Evaporation.

With engine operation, fuel economy, emission control, and safe braking under electronic control, it appears that the next breakthrough will be in the area of total information systems for the automobile. The "total" system would integrate all driver-information functions into a single display unit, eventually leading to replacement of today's instruments.

For situations that could endanger the driver or vehicle, a multi-purpose display would signal the threat. If more than one threat is imminent, the system would decide which threat has priority. And, it probably would provide the information audibly.

Whatever direction future automotive advances take, you can be sure that electronics will be deeply involved.

Chapter 28—REVIEW QUESTIONS

Write your answers on a separate sheet of paper. Do not write in this book.

1. How will an electrified piece of rubber react when placed close to an electrified piece of glass:
   a. Attract.
   b. Repel.
2. Similarly charged electrified bodies attract each other. True or False?
3. What tiny particles form an atom?
4. Electrons have a _____ (positive or negative) charge.
5. The nucleus of atoms consists of:
   a. Protons and electrons.
   b. Protons and neutrons.
   c. Neutrons and electrons.
   d. Electrons.
6. Electrons in a conductor are _____ (bound or free).
7. Electron flow is from _____ to _____.
8. Electric current is the _____.
9. The pressure between the electrons is measured in _____.
   a. Amperes.
   b. Ohms.
   c. Volts.
   d. Watts.
10. State Ohm's Law.
11. Write the Ohm's Law formula for finding voltage (E).
12. Write the Ohm's Law formula for finding current in amperes (I).
13. Write the Ohm's Law formula for finding resistance in ohms (R).
14. What is the total resistance in a series circuit having four individual resistances of 4 ohms, 8 ohms, 6 ohms, and 2 ohms?
15. When you place the fingers of your left hand around a current-carrying conductor, with extended thumb showing direction of current, the fingers will then indicate the direction in which _____ surround the conductor.
16. In an automotive circuit, how many watts are there if the current is 4 ampers and the voltage is 12 volts?
   a. 3 watts.
   b. 16 watts.
   c. 48 watts.
   d. 72 watts.
17. How many watts are there in an electrical horsepower?
   a. 764.
   b. 464.
   c. 746.
   d. 674.
18. The area surrounding a magnet is called the _____.
19. Which of the following metals are magnetic substances?
   a. Iron.
   b. Brass.
   c. Nickel.
   d. Lead.

20. The magnetic field of force surrounding any conductor carrying electrical current is always _____ (parallel or at right angles) to the conductor.

21. Basically, _____ is the magnetic conductivity of a substance.

22. If you insert an iron core in a coil or wire carrying electrical current, the magnetic field is _____.

23. When using the left-hand rule as applied to a current-carrying coil, what does the direction of the thumb indicate?
    a. Direction of current flow.
    b. Direction of electron flow.
    c. North pole.
    d. South pole.

24. A solenoid is a tubular coil of wire with an _____ or _____ core.

25. Electronics refers to any electrical component, assembly, circuit, or system that uses _____ devices.

26. Semiconductors are made from material somewhere between the range of _____ and _____.

27. Semiconductors are designed to:
    a. Stop flow of electrons.
    b. Start flow of electrons.
    c. Control amount of electron flow.
    d. All of the above.

28. A semiconductor diode is a _____ element solid state electronic device.
    a. One -
    b. Two -
    c. Three -
    d. Four -

29. A semiconductor diode contains P material and N material. The _____ is connected to the P material; the _____ is connected to the N material.

30. When current flows in a diode, it is said to be _____ (forward biased or reverse biased).

31. What is peak inverse voltage?

32. What instrument is used to test the polarity of a diode?
    a. Ohmmeter.
    b. Ammeter.
    c. Voltmeter.

33. A transistor is a solid state device used to _____ and/or _____ the flow of electrons in a circuit.

34. A transistor is a _____ element device made of _____ types of semiconductor materials.

35. Transistor types are either _____ or _____.

36. Many electronic circuits use _____ to trigger a control signal.

37. The polarity of the source voltage must be reversed to make a transistor operate. True or False?

38. Transistor _____ are known as emitter, base, and collector.

39. A silicon controlled rectifier combines _____ diodes.

40. On an SCR, anode is positive, cathode is negative. A third connection made to the SCR is called the _____.
    a. Emitter.
    b. Base.
    c. Collector.
    d. Gate.

Chapter 29

ENGINE IGNITION SYSTEMS

After studying this chapter, you will be able to:
- Distinguish between the primary and secondary side of the ignition.
- Describe how battery voltage is transformed into 20,000 or more volts.
- Explain how the different types of ignition systems operate.
- List the different types of sensors and explain their operation.
- Troubleshoot the computerized ignition system.

IGNITION

The first section of this chapter is on the components in the secondary side of the ignition system. The secondary side of the ignition is the same on most ignition systems, whether it is a breaker point or computerized ignition system. The primary side of the ignition is discussed to an extent, but will be covered in depth in the second section.

The primary side of the ignition system is that which carries battery voltage. The primary side controls the secondary side of the ignition. The design of the primary side can vary from manufacturer to manufacturer. The secondary side of the ignition system is where battery voltage has been transformed into 20,000 or more volts.

IGNITION COILS

The ignition coil, Fig. 29-1, is a transformer designed to increase primary voltage (received from battery) of 12 V to at least 20,000 V. It is composed of a primary winding, secondary winding, and core of soft iron.

The primary winding is made up of 200 turns of heavy wire (No. 18 gauge). The secondary winding may have as many as 22,000 turns of fine wire, (No. 38 gauge). The construction is to have the secondary winding wound around the soft iron core, and the primary winding surrounds the secondary. The purpose of the core is to concentrate the magnetic field.

This coil assembly is placed in a steel case with a cap of molded insulating materials that carries the terminals. Some ignition coils have their windings immersed in oil or paraffin-like material. This is done to improve insulation and reduce the effects of moisture. Oil-filled coils can better withstand corona (faint glow) and heat. Oil has the advantage of healing itself if any breakdown in insulation occurs.

To prevent coils from absorbing moisture, they are hermetically sealed. Heavy-duty coils are built with larger cores and provided with greater insulation. The higher inductance of these coils limits top speed performance, but their life is lengthened.

The current flowing through the primary winding of the ignition coil produces a magnetic field in the coil. When the primary circuit is interrupted to the coil, the magnetic field collapses, and the movement of the magnetic field induces current in the secondary winding of the coil. Since there are many more turns of wire in the secondary winding than there are in the primary winding, the battery voltage is increased to 20,000 or more volts.

NEGATIVE POLARITY

Most manufacturers consider negative polarity of the high tension outlet of the ignition coil as a means of saving electrical energy. This is because the center electrode is the hottest part of the spark plug.

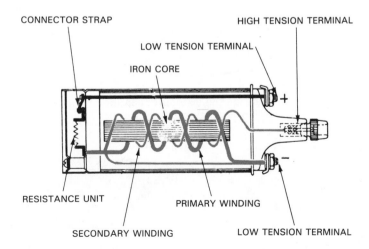

Fig. 29-1. The ignition coil is constructed of primary and secondary windings wound around a soft iron core.

When the center electrode is connected to the negative high tension voltage, the spark gap becomes ionized more readily and forms a lower resistance path for the spark. Therefore, a lower voltage is needed to fire the same plug gap.

A simple means of testing coil polarity on a car can be made with a voltmeter. The positive lead is connected to a good ground and the negative lead is connected to the spark plug terminal of No. 1 cylinder. With this connection, the voltmeter is connected across the coil high tension windings. Run the engine at idle. If the voltmeter indicates ''up'' scale, the coil has a negative polarity.

Also, a lead pencil can be used to check polarity. Insert the pencil point in the gap between the end of disconnected spark plug cable and the spark plug terminal. If the flare appears on the plug side, the polarity is correct.

DISTRIBUTOR CAP

The distributor cap should be checked to see that sparks have not been arcing from point to point within the cap. The inside of the cap must be clean. The firing points should not be eroded, Fig. 29-2, and the inside of the towers must be clean and free from corrosion.

If needed, the inside of the distributor cap towers can be cleaned by means of a round wire bristle brush. When cleaning distributor caps, never use any cleaning solu-

tion that would injure the cap, which is made of Phenol-resin.

There are two methods of holding the distributor cap in place on the distributor housing. One is by means of clips or cap springs and the other is by means of a latch. The clips can be pulled back, permitting the cap to be lifted from the distributor housing. To release the latch, a screwdriver is inserted in upper slotted end of cap retainer, pressed down and turned until the latch is disengaged.

ROTOR

A distributor rotor is designed to rotate and distribute the high tension current to the towers of the distributor cap. The firing end of the rotor, Fig. 29-3, from which the high tension spark jumps to each of the cap terminals in turn should not be worn. Any wear will result in excessive resistance to the high tension spark.

Rotors are mounted on the upper end of the distributor shaft, Fig. 29-4. In this connection, the rotor must have a snug fit on the end of the shaft. On another design, two screws are used to attach the rotor to a plate on the top of the distributor shaft. Built-in locators on the rotor, and holes in the plate, insure correct reassembly. One locator is round; the other is square. A method to hold the rotor in place is shown in Fig. 29-5.

SPARK PLUG WIRES

The spark plug wire carries 20,000 or more volts from the distributor cap to the spark plug. Spark plug wires, Fig. 29-6, are made of various layers of materials. The fiber core, inside the spark plug wire carries the high voltage. The older design of spark plug wires used a metallic wire to carry the high voltage. This caused an electrical interference with radio and TV reception.

Some spark plug wires have a locking connection at the distributor cap, Fig. 29-7. The distributor cap must first be removed and the terminals squeezed together, and then the spark plug wire can be removed from the distributor cap.

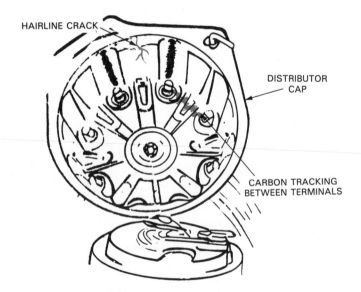

Fig. 29-2. Check inside the distributor cap for carbon tracking and hairline cracks.

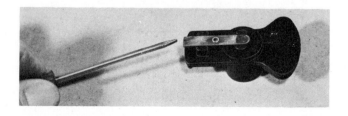

Fig. 29-3. The firing end of the rotor must not be worn, or it will have to be replaced.

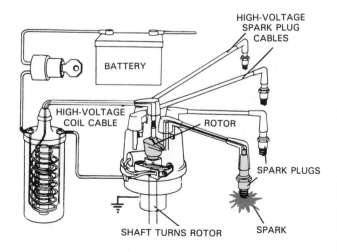

Fig. 29-4. As the rotor rotates inside the distributor cap, it delivers the high voltage from the ignition coil to each of the spark plugs.

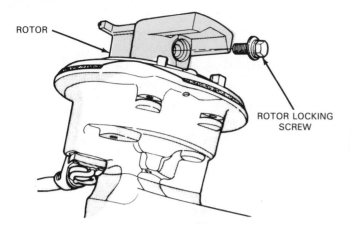

Fig. 29-5. This rotor is held in place by a screw on its side. (Chrysler)

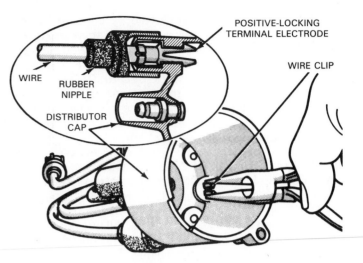

Fig. 29-7. This type of distributor cap is found on four cylinder Chrysler products. After removing the cap from the distributor, squeeze the locking terminal together before removing the spark plug wire from the cap. If not, the spark plug wire may be ruined along with the distributor cap.   (Chrysler)

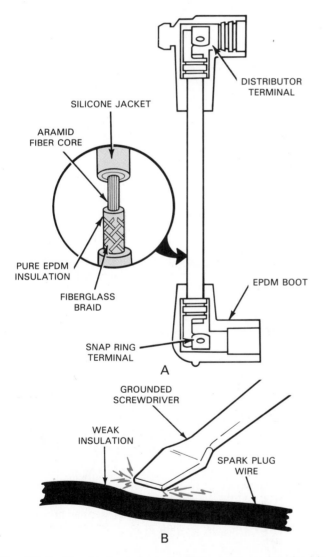

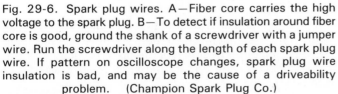

Fig. 29-6. Spark plug wires. A—Fiber core carries the high voltage to the spark plug. B—To detect if insulation around fiber core is good, ground the shank of a screwdriver with a jumper wire. Run the screwdriver along the length of each spark plug wire. If pattern on oscilloscope changes, spark plug wire insulation is bad, and may be the cause of a driveability problem.   (Champion Spark Plug Co.)

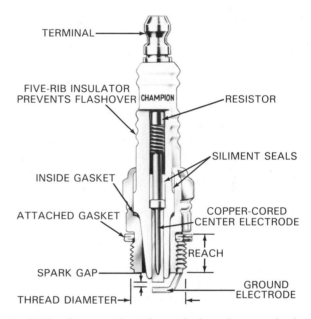

Fig. 29-8. Construction of a typical modern spark plug. (Champion)

SPARK PLUGS

The spark plug in a spark ignition (SI) engine provides the gap across which the high tension voltage jumps, to create the spark that ignites the compressed air-fuel mixture.

The spark plug, Fig. 29-8, consists of a center electrode, which is connected to the ignition coil secondary through the distributor. The center electrode is insulated from the spark plug shell by means of a porcelain insulator. The side electrode protrudes from the bottom edge of the spark plug shell. It is positioned so that there is a gap between it and the center electrode.

The spark plug gap is adjusted by bending the side electrode. Fig. 29-9 shows a combined spark plug gauge and tool for adjusting the gap by bending the side electrode.

Spark plug gaps range from .020 to .080 in. (0.501 to 2.032 mm). The gap must be set to the manufacturer's specification. The size of the gap depends on the compression ratio of the engine, design of the combustion chamber and ignition system.

Today, manufacturers specify gaps of .030, .035, .060, and .080 in. (0.762, 0.890, 1.52, and 2.03 mm). A wider gap includes more air-fuel mixture than a narrow gap, so there is more to ignite.

The shell of the spark plug is threaded, so it can be removed and reinstalled with ease. All but tapered seat plugs require a gasket. The following thread sizes are used: 10 mm, 14 mm, and 18 mm. The spark plug must extend into the combustion chamber the correct amount (reach). The correct point for the spark plug electrodes in the combustion chamber is determined by the engineer.

Using plugs with a longer reach may result in the valves or piston striking the spark plug. If a plug with a short reach is installed, the electrodes become partly sheltered by the spark plug hole in the cylinder head. In this case, engine roughness and missing may result.

HEAT RANGE

Spark plugs must be designed so the temperature of the firing end of the plug is high enough to burn off any carbon or other deposits. Yet, the plug must not get too hot or it will cause preignition, deterioration of the insulator or electrodes. This is difficult since the temperature of the spark plug tip varies with different engines and conditions. The center electrode temperatures range from a low of 200 °C at 10 mph to a high of 800 °C at 80 mph.

The temperature of the spark plug insulator depends on the design of the spark plug and on the burning fuel in the combustion chamber. The latter temperature will, of course, vary with the design of the engine, compression ratio, cooling system, and air-fuel ratio.

As the tip of the spark plug absorbs heat from the burning air-fuel mixture, the heat travels up the insulator to the spark plug shell, then to the cylinder head and to the water jacket. The path the heat travels is shown in Fig. 29-10. The heat absorbed by the insulator increases as the temperature in the combustion chamber rises. More heat will be absorbed as the area of the insulator exposed to the hot gases is increased.

If the path the heat must follow to reach the cooling system is short, the tip will have a low temperature. Therefore, plugs with short paths for the heat to travel are known as cold plugs. Plugs with long paths for the heat to travel are known as hot plugs.

The length of the path traversed by the heat in reaching the cooling system, insulator material, and insulator shape will affect its temperature. As a result, some spark plug insulators have a narrow neck just above the tip. Another design will have recessed tip sections that more readily follow temperature changes in the combustion chamber.

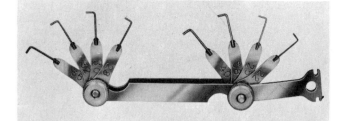

Fig. 29-9. Wire type spark plug gauge is more accurate. The gap adjuster is at the right end of the gauge. The gap is adjusted by bending the side electrode.

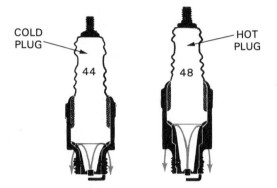
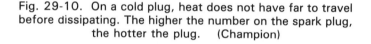

Fig. 29-10. On a cold plug, heat does not have far to travel before dissipating. The higher the number on the spark plug, the hotter the plug.　(Champion)

Fig. 29-11. Special spark plug with booster gap provides protection against fouling at low temperatures.

Other designs provide increased volume between the shell and the insulator to permit more cooling, Fig. 29-11. Still other design has the tip of the insulator protruding beyond the end of the shell for improved heat characteristics.

The heat range of any spark plug is its ability to transfer heat from the firing end up through the insulator, gasket, and shell to the cylinder head and water jacket. Heat range is also known as the "Thermal Characteristic."

Fig. 29-12 shows typical heat flow in an auto spark plug. A spark plug designed for the Mazda rotary engine is shown in Fig. 29-13. Note the dual firing points.

Engine designers select spark plugs that will give good performance for average driving conditions. However, if the engine is run for a long time under full load conditions, the standard plug will run at too high a temperature, and preignition will result. Therefore, a colder plug is needed to carry off the heat faster.

On the other hand, if the engine is run for a long time at part throttle opening, the standard plug will tend to foul. The insulator tip will become covered with carbon and other products of combustion. As a result, high tension voltage will leak across the carbon (because of their lower resistance) rather than jump the gap at the electrodes. In this case, a hotter plug (one with a longer heat path) should be used.

SPARK PLUG FOULING

As mentioned, products of combustion accumulate on the portion of the insulator of the spark plug within the combustion chamber. As a result, there are three types of spark plug fouling:
1. Carbon fouling.
2. High speed or lead fouling.
3. Oil and carbon fouling.

Carbon fouling, Fig. 29-14, results from extended low speed operation and when the fuel mixture is rich. Carbon fouling causes missing or roughness, creates soft black soot that is easy to remove from the spark plug.

Lead fouling, Fig. 29-15, results from the tetraethyl lead used in the fuel to improve its antidetonating characteristics. Lead fouling is caused by extended high speed operation. Spark plugs with lead fouling will work at low and medium loads. When full load is applied, however, missing will occur. This results from the higher temperatures melting the lead salts. This increases their electrical conductivity, and the plug will short out.

Led compounds added to gasoline have a bad effect on some spark plug insulators. they react with the silica in the insulator to form lead silicate glass, which has a low melting point. At high temperatures, it is a good conductor of electricity. For this reason, a spark plug may give good results under light loads, but fail when full loads and high combustion chamber temperatures are reached.

In some cases of lead fouling, it is possible to run the engine at a speed just below the point where missing will occur. Then, by increasing the speed (always keeping below "missing" speed), it will be possible to burn off the lead fouling. Lead fouling will appear as a heavy, crusty formation, or as tiny globules. The form it takes will depend on fuel, operating conditions, and time.

The third type of fouling, Fig. 29-14, is found on engines that are so badly worn that excess oil reaches the combustion chamber past the piston ring, or the valve guides.

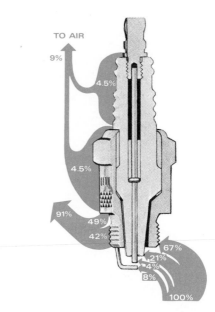

Fig. 29-12. Heat flow from a spark plug.

Fig. 29-13. Spark plug for a rotary engine has two ground electrodes.

Another condition that affects spark plug operation is the condition of the gap across which the spark jumps. Fig. 29-14 shows a spark plug with extreme electrode erosion, resulting from high temperatures and prolonged use of the plug. High capacity of the system also affects electrode life.

REQUIRED VOLTAGE

There are many factors which will affect the voltage needed to jump a certain gap. These factors include the shape of the electrodes forming the gap, the conductivity of the gases in the gap, temperature, pressure, and the air-fuel ratio existing within the gap.

GAP BRIDGED

IDENTIFIED BY DEPOSIT BUILD—UP CLOSING GAP BETWEEN ELECTRODES.

CAUSED BY OIL OR CARBON FOULING, REPLACE PLUG, OR IF DEPOSITS ARE NOT EXCESSIVE. THE PLUG CAN BE CLEANED.

OIL FOULED

IDENTIFIED BY WET BLACK DEPOSITS ON THE INSULATOR SHELL BORE ELECTRODES.

CAUSED BY EXCESSIVE OIL ENTERING COMBUSTION CHAMBER THROUGH WORN RINGS AND PISTONS, EXCESSIVE CLEARANCE BETWEEN VALVE GUIDES AND STEMS, OR WORN OR LOOSE BEARINGS. REPLACE THE PLUG.

CARBON FOULED

IDENTIFIED BY BLACK, DRY FLUFFY CARBON DEPOSITS ON INSULATOR TIPS, EXPOSED SHELL SURFACES AND ELECTRODES.

CAUSED BY TOO COLD A PLUG, WEAK IGNITION, DIRTY AIR CLEANER, DEFECTIVE FUEL PUMP, TOO RICH A FUEL MIXTURE, IMPROPERLY OPERATING HEAT RISER ON EXCESSIVE IDLING. CAN BE CLEANED.

NORMAL

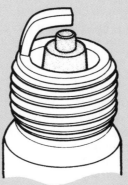

IDENTIFIED BY LIGHT TAN OR GRAY DEPOSITS ON THE FIRING TIP.

PRE-IGNITION

IDENTIFIED BY MELTED ELECTRODES AND POSSIBLY BLISTERED INSULATOR METALLIC DEPOSITS ON INSULATOR INDICATE ENGINE DAMAGE.

CAUSED BY WRONG TYPE OF FUEL, INCORRECT IGNITION TIMING OR ADVANCE, TOO HOT A PLUG, BURNT VALVES OR ENGINE OVERHEATING. REPLACE THE PLUG.

OVERHEATING

IDENTIFIED BY A WHITE OR LIGHT GRAY INSULATOR WITH SMALL BLACK OR GRAY BROWN SPOTS AND WITH BLUISH-BURNT APPEARANCE OF ELECTRODES.

CAUSED BY ENGINE OVER-HEATING, WRONG TYPE OF FUEL, LOOSE SPARK PLUGS, TOO HOT A PLUG, LOW FUEL PUMP PRESSURE OR INCORRECT IGNITION TIMING. REPLACE THE PLUG.

FUSED SPOT DEPOSIT

IDENTIFIED BY MELTED OR SPOTTY DEPOSITS RESEMBLING BUBBLES OR BLISTERS.

CAUSED BY SUDDEN ACCELERATION. CAN BE CLEANED IF NOT EXCESSIVE, OTHERWISE REPLACE PLUG.

Fig. 29-14. Examples of spark plug fouling. (Ford)

Fig. 29-15. Lead fouling due to additives in gasoline combined with prolonged high speed driving.

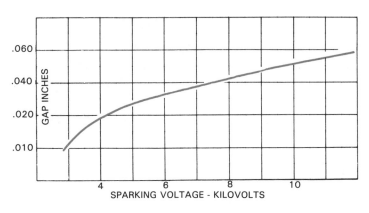

Fig. 29-16. Voltage needed to jump different spark plug gaps.

When fuel mixtures are lean, voltage needed may be as much as 40 percent higher than normal. The highest voltage needs exist at low engine speed under very light acceleration. Missing under such conditions indicates that there is not enough voltage to fire the plug.

In Fig. 29-16, note that voltage required to jump a gap increases rapidly until 12,000 V is needed to jump a gap of .060 in. The measurements were made in an auto engine at road load.

The current delivered to the plugs depends on the current flowing in the primary, and the amount of current decreases as the engine speed increases. The voltage at the plug also depends on the cleanliness of the spark plug electrode. For example, an ignition system that can deliver 20,000 V to a clean plug may only deliver one half that amount to a plug that is partly fouled.

The reason plug fouling cuts down on peak voltage is because it takes time for the voltage to build up to a value where it can jump the plug gap. This high voltage is not reached instantaneously. It is built up to a maximum and then drops to zero, which needs a long time (electrically speaking), or about 1/20,000 sec.

The secondary voltage increases until it reaches a value that is capable of jumping the gap at the spark plug. However, if the plug is partly fouled, some current will flow across the coating on the insulator, which acts as a shunt across the gap. This loss of current reduces peak voltage to the point that it will not jump the gap of a badly fouled plug, Fig. 29-17.

The faster the high tension voltage is built up, the less effect fouling will have. One method of attaining fast electrical buildup is by means of high frequency ignition systems. Another method is by means of a series gap.

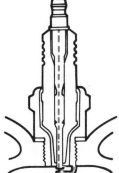

Bridged Electrodes
Fouling deposits between the electrodes "ground out" the high voltage needed to fire the spark plug. The arc between the electrodes does not occur and the fuel air mixture is not ignited. This causes a power loss and exhausting of raw fuel.

Flashover
A damaged spark plug boot, along with dirt and moisture, could permit the high voltage charge to short over the insulator to the spark plug shell or the engine. AC's buttress insulator design helps prevent high voltage flashover.

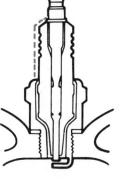

Tracking Arc
High voltage arcs between a fouling deposit on the insulator tip and spark plug shell. This ignites the fuel/air mixture at some point along the insulator tip, retarding the ignition timing which causes a power and fuel loss.

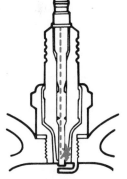

Cracked Insulator
A crack in the spark plug insulator could cause the high voltage charge to "ground out." Here, the spark does not jump the electrode gap and the fuel air mixture is not ignited. This causes a power loss and raw fuel is exhausted.

Fouled Spark Plug
Deposits that have formed on the insulator tip may become conductive and provide a "shunt" path to the shell. This prevents the high voltage from arcing between the electrodes. A power and fuel loss is the result.

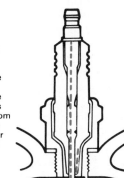

Wide Gap
Spark plug electrodes are worn so that the high voltage charge cannot arc across the electrodes. Improper gapping of electrodes on new or "cleaned" spark plugs could cause a similar condition. Fuel remains unburned and a power loss results.

Fig. 29-17. Abnormal voltage paths at the spark plug cause problems. (Cadillac)

SPARK PLUG GAPS

Spark plug gaps do not remain constant, but increase in size. The amount of increase is dependent on mileage, chemical characteristics of the fuel, combustion chamber temperatures, and the action of the electrical spark which tears off portions of the electrode.

The electrical characteristics of the ignition system also effect the rate of wear of the spark plug electrodes. The electrical capacity of the ignition coil and the wiring is an important factor. Systems with high capacity will cause more rapid gap wear than systems with low capacity. Inserting a resistor in or near the spark plugs will tend to counteract this condition. Resistors reduce the peak current which passes through the electrodes when the capacity of the system is being discharged.

Some engines operate better with wider spark plug gaps than others. Many engineers agree that the explanation is in the characteristics of the air-fuel mixture in the vicinity of the plug gap. The mixture varies in different parts of the combustion chamber. This is due to the design form of the combustion chamber, the turbulence imported to the mixture, and the amount of burned gases that remain in the combustion chamber from the last cycle.

SPARK PLUG LIFE

Under good conditions, the life of a spark plug ranges from 15,000 to 30,000 miles. Beyond that, they lose efficiency and should be replaced. Plug condition is important in the maintenance of low emission levels. Higher engine temperatures, added emission controls, and greater loads have made the conditions under which the spark plug operates severe.

Higher voltages are needed to fire a spark plug with worn electrodes. As shown in Fig. 29-18, higher voltage is needed to fire a used spark plug than a new plug. This is true at low speeds where the difference may be as much as 4000 V.

SECONDARY CIRCUIT CHECK

In the event of a "no start" condition, the ignition system will have to be checked in the following manner (provided the ignition coil is externally mounted). Remove the coil wire from the distributor cap. Hold the coil wire about 1/4 in. from a good ground and crank the engine, Fig. 29-19. If there is no spark, a check of the primary side of the ignition system is needed. Start by checking voltage at the positive terminal of the ignition coil with the ignition switch to the ON position, Fig. 29-20. Repeat the process at the negative terminal. Battery voltage should be observed, within one volt, at each terminal. If battery voltage is not obtained at the positive terminal, this wire will have to be traced to the point that the circuit is open. If battery voltage is obtained at the positive terminal, but not at the negative terminal, replace the ignition coil.

If a spark was observed jumping this gap, reconnect the coil wire to the distributor cap. Then, remove a spark plug wire from a spark plug and hold it about 1/4 in. from a good ground. Crank the engine. If no spark is observed

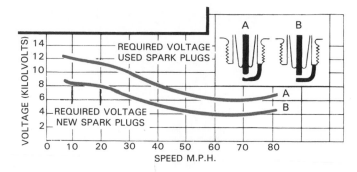

Fig. 29-18. Voltage needed to fire new and old spark plugs.

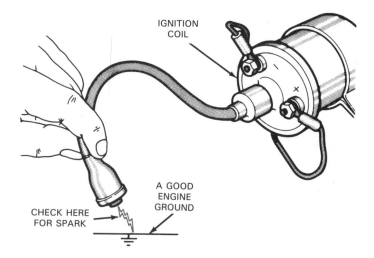

Fig. 29-19. Hold the coil wire about 1/4 in. from a good ground while cranking the engine.   (Chrysler)

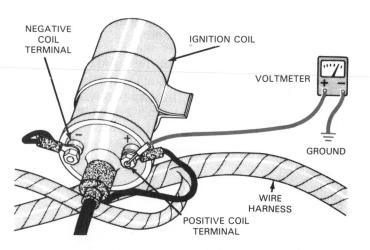

Fig. 29-20. If spark was not observed while cranking the engine, check the voltage at the positive terminal, then at the negative terminal.   (Chrysler)

now, the distributor cap and rotor, or spark plug wire is at fault. Use an ohmmeter to test spark plug wire for continuity. If a spark was observed, remove and examine the spark plug. If the plug appears normal, a check of the fuel system is needed.

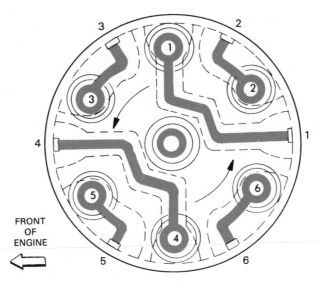

Fig. 29-21. Note that the electrodes inside of this distributor cap are offset from the outside terminals. (Chrysler)

FIRING ORDER

In order to reduce engine vibration and secure an even flow of power, the cylinders of an engine must fire in the correct sequence. On in-line engines, the No. 1 cylinder is behind the timing gears. On GM and Chrysler V-8 engines, the front cylinder on the left bank is No. 1. The front cylinder on the right bank would be No. 2.

The firing order of in-line six cylinder engines in the United States is 1-5-3-6-2-4, Fig. 29-21. The most popular firing order of a V-8 is 1-8-4-3-6-5-7-2, Other firing orders used on V8 engines are: 1-5-6-3-4-2-7-8, 1-5-4-2-6-3-7-8, and 1-3-7-2-6-5-4-8. The firing order of four cylinder in-line engines can be either 1-3-4-2 or 1-2-4-3.

IGNITION TIMING

The ignition system must be timed so that the spark occurs in the combustion chamber at the correct instant. Incorrect timing results in loss of efficiency and power. If the spark "fires" too early, preignition and "pinging" occurs. If continued, the engine will be damaged. If the spark "fires" too late, both fuel economy and power will be reduced.

Timing of the spark varies in engines. For this reason, specifications must be observed. The spark is timed in relation to the position of the No. 1 piston in most engines. Timing is specified as so many degrees before top center (BTC). The top center referred to is at the end of the compression stroke. Timing marks are placed on the flywheel or the vibration damper at the front of the crankshaft. A timing mark setup is shown in Fig. 29-22.

To time the ignition of an engine, use a timing light, Fig. 29-23. The timing light is connected to the battery and to No. 1 spark plug wire. The beam of the timing light is then directed to the timing marks on the engine. With the engine running, the light will flash each time the spark occurs. The timing marks will appear to stand still, so that the time the spark occurs is easily noted.

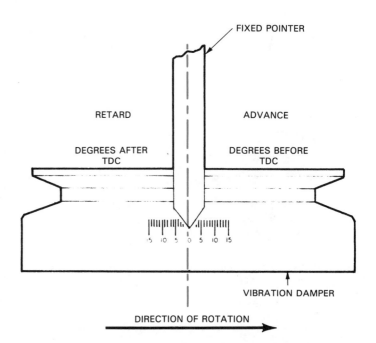

Fig. 29-22. Timing marks on a vibration damper.

Fig. 29-23. Timing light with advance control and meter. Meter indicates amount of advance.

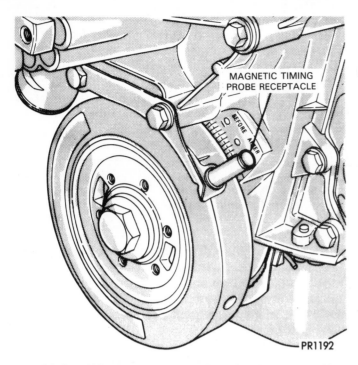

ig. 29-24. When using a magnetic timing device, an offset angle must be entered into the diagnostic machine. (Chrysler)

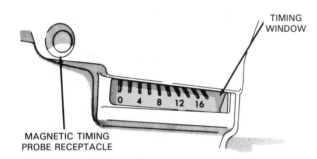

Fig. 29-25. These timing marks are located at the flywheel end of a transversely mounted engine. (Chrysler)

The timing mark should align with the index mark. If not, the clamp screw of the distributor is loosened and the distributor is rotated to the correct position. Moving the distributor housing against shaft rotation advances the timing. Moving it with shaft rotation retards timing.

Special timing setups exist. For example, the notch, Figs. 29-24 and 29-25, is designed to receive a magnetic probe when timing the engine. With the aid of this device, precision timing is assured for the lowest emission levels.

SPARK ADVANCE

When the engine is idling, the spark is timed to occur just before the piston reaches the top of the compression stroke. Idling, or when driving at a sustained speed under part throttle conditions, cylinders take in only part of the full charge. As a result, compression pressures are low and combustion is slow. With lower pressures, the mixture does not burn as rapidly. To obtain maximum efficiency under such conditions, the spark has to be advanced. Also, at higher engine speeds, there is a shorter interval of time for the mixture to ignite. Therefore, in order to obtain maximum power at higher speeds, the spark must occur slightly earlier in the cycle.

FACTORS GOVERNING SPARK ADVANCE

Many variables affect spark advance, Fig. 29-26, in an engine and ignition system. Consider these factors:
MANIFOLD PRESSURE
    High Vacuum (low manifold pressure): Combustion is slower and more spark advance needed.
    Low Vacuum (high manifold pressure): Combustion is faster and less spark advance needed.
ENGINE SPEED
    Low Speed and Load: Combustion slower and more spark advance needed.
    Low Speed and Full Load: Combustion faster and less spark advance needed.
    High Speed and Full Load: Combustion slower and more spark advance needed.

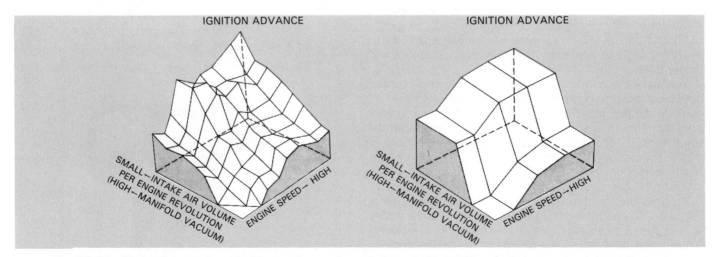

Fig. 29-26. Right. Conventional ignition, points and condenser or electronic, calculates spark advance for load and speed only. Left. Computerized ignition systems calculate many variables before advancing the spark. This creates more horsepower and reduces emissions for an efficient engine. (Toyota)

ENGINE TEMPERATURE

Cold Engine: Combustion slower and more spark advance needed.

Hot Engine: Combustion faster and less spark advance needed.

CYLINDER BORE

Larger Bore: Combustion slower and more spark advance needed.

Smaller Bore: Combustion faster and less spark advance needed.

COMPRESSION RATIO

Low Compression Ratio: Combustion slower and more spark advance needed.

High Compression Ratio: Combustion faster and less spark advance needed.

CHARACTER OF FUEL

Low Volatile Fuel: Combustion slower and more spark advance needed.

High Volatile Fuel: Combustion faster and less spark advance needed.

THROTTLE ANGLE

Small Angle: Combustion faster and less spark advance needed.

Large Angle: Combustion slower and more spark advance needed.

OCTANE RATING

High Octane Fuel: Combustion slower and more spark advance needed.

Low Octane Fuel: Combustion faster and less spark advance needed.

In addition to the above factors that affect spark timing, others include:

1. The shape of the combustion chamber.
2. Location of the spark plug, Fig. 29-27.
3. Amount of carbon in the combustion chamber.
4. Fuel distribution to each of the cylinders.

SPARK ADVANCE CONTROLS

On breaker point and electronic ignitions, the spark advance is controlled by the centrifugal advance and vacuum advance. The amount of centrifugal advance is determined by engine rpm. Vacuum advance is supplied in addition to centrifugal advance. However, the amount of vacuum advance is determined by engine load or manifold pressure.

On computerized ignition systems, the amount of advance is determined by the throttle angle, manifold pressure, engine rpm, coolant temperature, and atmospheric temperature and pressure. The computer processes this information from the sensors. The computer then advances the timing accordingly.

SPECIFIC SYSTEMS

This section of the chapter will discuss breaker point, electronic, and computerized ignition systems. The most common type systems are included.

BREAKER POINT IGNITION

The ignition distributor, Fig. 29-28, makes and breaks the primary ignition circuit. It also distributes high tension current to the proper spark plug at the correct time. The distributor is driven at one half crankshaft speed on four cycle engines. It is driven by the camshaft.

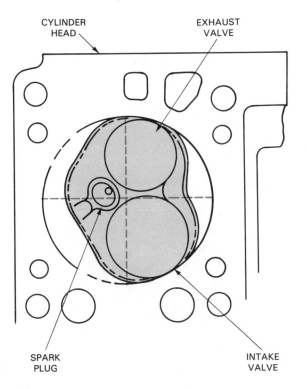

CYLINDER HEAD   EXHAUST VALVE

SPARK PLUG   INTAKE VALVE

Fig. 29-27. The spark plug is located almost in the center of a wedge shaped combustion chamber. (Oldsmobile)

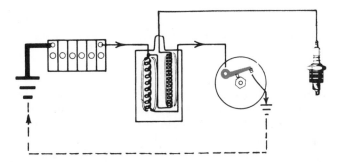
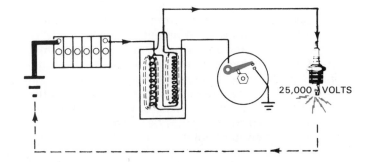

25,000 VOLTS

Fig. 29-28. Left. Breaker points are closed allowing current to flow through primary windings creating a magnetic field. Right. As points begin to open, the magnetic field collapses and induces a high voltage in secondary circuit.

Detailed construction of the ignition distributor varies with the manufacturers, Fig. 29-29. It consists of a housing into which the distributor shaft and centrifugal weight assembly are fitted with bearings. In most cases, these bearings are of the bronze bushing type.

In this distributor, Fig. 29-30, the contact set is attached to the movable breaker plate. A vacuum advance unit attached to the distributor housing is mounted under the breaker plate. The rotor covers the centrifugal advance mechanism, which consists of a cam actuated by two centrifugal weights, Fig. 29-29.

As the breaker cam rotates, each lobe passes under the rubbing block, causing the breaker points to open. Since the points are in series with the primary winding of the ignition coil, current will pass through that circuit when the points close. The period that the points are closed is referred to as *dwell.* When the points open, the magnetic field in the coil collapses and a high tension voltage is induced in the secondary windings of the coil by the movement of the magnetic field through the secondary windings, Fig. 29-28.

The design is to provide one lobe on the breaker cam for each cylinder of the engine. A six cylinder engine will have a six lobe cam in the distributor, and a V-8 will have an eight lobe cam. As a result, every revolution of the breaker cam will produce one spark for each cylinder of the engine.

On a four cycle engine, each cylinder fires every other revolution. Therefore, the distributor shaft must revolve at one half crankshaft speed.

After the high tension surge is produced in the ignition coil by the opening of the breaker points, the current passes from the coil to the center terminal of the distributor cap. From that point, it passes down to the rotor mounted on the distributor shaft and revolves with it. The current passes along the rotor, then jumps the minute gap to the cap electrode under which the rotor is positioned at that instant. This cap electrode is connected by high tension wiring to the spark plug. As the rotor continues to rotate, it distributes current to each of the cap terminals in turn.

CONDENSER

Primary current produces a magnetic field around the coil windings. However, this does not occur instantly. It takes time for the current and the magnetic field to reach maximum value.

This time element is determined by the resistance of the coil winding or the length of time the distributor contacts are closed. The current does not reach the maximum because the contacts remain closed for such a short time, and more so at higher engine speeds.

When the breaker points begin to open, the primary current will continue to flow. This condition in a winding is increased by means of the iron core. Without an ignition condenser, the induced voltage causing this flow of current would create an arc across the contact points and the magnetic enengy would be consumed in this arc. As a result the contact points would be burned and ignition would not occur.

The condenser prevents this arc by making a place for the current to flow. As a result of condenser action, the

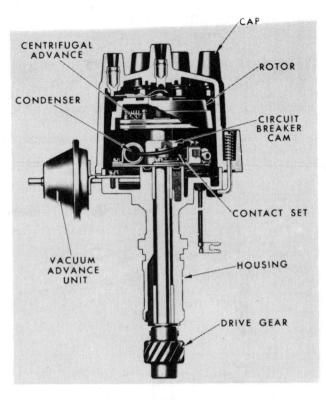

Fig. 29-29. A Delco-Remy distributor.

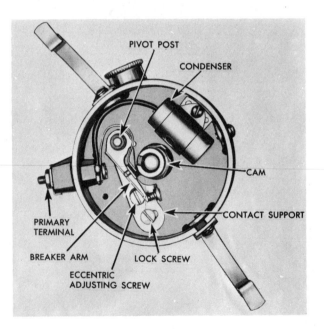

Fig. 29-30. Eccentric adjustment is used to control point gap.

magnetic field produced and continued by the current flow will quickly collapse. It is this rapid cutting out of the magnetic field that induces high voltage in the secondary windings. So, if the condenser should go bad, the high voltage needed to jump the gap at the spark plugs will not be possible. This could cause a no-start condition or a driveablity problem.

RESISTORS

In most 12 V systems, a resistor is connected in series with the primary circuit of the ignition coil. However, during the cranking period, the resistor is cut out of the circuit so that full voltage is applied to the coil. This insures a strong spark during cranking, and, in that way, quicker starting is provided.

Contacts on the cranking motor solenoid are used to cut the resistor out of the primary circuit during the cranking period. The ignition coil and its windings are designed to operate at a voltage lower than full battery voltage. So, when full battery voltage is applied, a hotter than normal spark is provided. During cranking, the excessive load applied on the battery will reduce the voltage reaching the ignition coil. On some systems, the resistor is of the block type. Other systems, Fig. 29-31, use a wire that is sensitive to heat. As the temperature of the wire increases, so does its resistance. As a result, when the engine reaches operating temperature, its resistance is six volts applied to the coil.

However, the starting circuit is designed so that as long as the starting motor is in use, full battery voltage is applied to the coil. When the starter is not cranking the engine, the resistance wire is cut into the circuit to reduce the voltage applied to the coil.

If the engine starts when the ignition switch is turned on, but stops when the switch is released to the run position, it can indicate that the resistor is bad and should be replaced. At no time should the resistor be bypassed out of the circuit, as that would supply constant battery voltage and burn out the coil.

Resistors and resistor wires should be checked whenever the breaker points are burned, or when the ignition coil is bad. With the ignition switch turned on, the voltage reading from the resistor side of the coil to the ground should be about 5 to 7 V, unless other specifications are available. Resistance of a resistor used on 12 V systems is about 1.5 ohms.

ELECTRONIC IGNITION

The short-lived electronic ignition system was a transition from the points and condenser system to the computerized ignition system. It came into widespread use in the mid-1970s and was overshadowed by the computerized ignition system by the late 1970s. However, there are still a few engines that use the electronic ignition system.

CHRYSLER ELECTRONIC IGNITION

The basic circuits of the Chrysler electronic ignition system are shown in Fig. 29-32. The primary circuit consists of the battery, ignition switch, compensating side of the dual ballast resistor, primary winding of the ignition coil, the power switching transistor of the control unit, and the car frame acting as a ground. The secondary circuit consists of the ignition coil secondary winding, distributor cap, rotor, and spark plugs.

The resistance serves the same purpose as in the contact ignition system. It maintains constant primary current with variation in engine speed. While starting, this

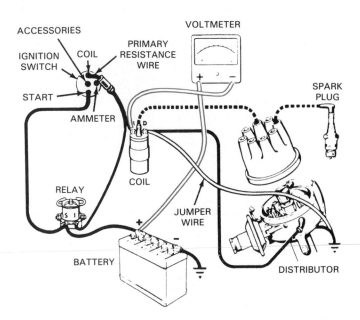

Fig. 29-31. Diagram shows checking the voltage drop at ignition coil. If voltage drop is excessive, a loose connection, ignition switch, or resistance wire is at fault. (Ford)

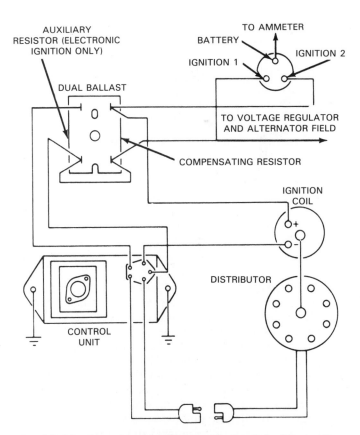

Fig. 29-32. Diagram of the Chrysler electronic ignition system.

resistance is bypassed, applying full battery voltage to the ignition coil. The compensating resistance is in series with both the control unit feed and the auxiliary ballast circuits, Figs. 29-33 and 29-34.

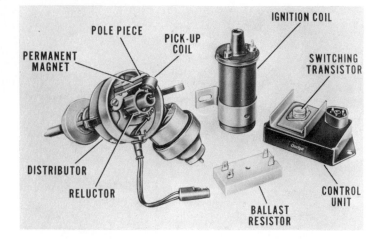

Fig. 29-33. The Chrysler electronic ignition system.

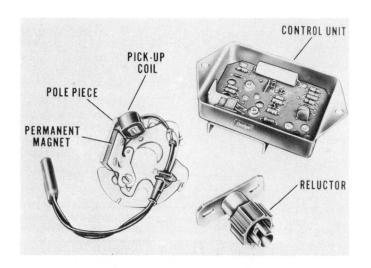

Fig. 29-34. Pick-up coil and reluctor create a voltage signal, which is sent to the control unit. The control unit interrupts the primary current at the ignition coil. (Chrysler)

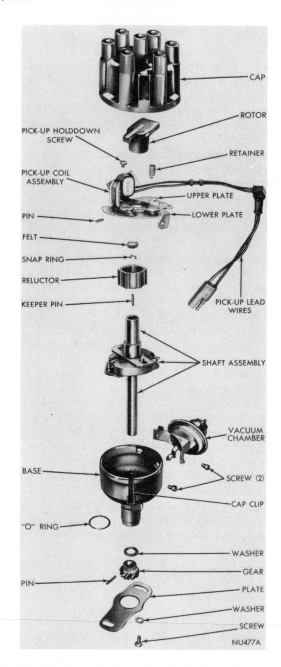

Fig. 29-35. Chrysler's electronic ignition distributor.

In addition to the two basic circuits, there are the pick-up circuit, control unit feed circuit, and auxiliary ballast circuits. Two circuits are used to operate the circuit of the control unit. These are the auxiliary ballast circuit (which uses 5 ohm section of dual ballast resistor) and the control unit feed circuit.

The pick-up circuit is used to sense the proper timing for the control unit switching transistor, Figs. 29-34 and 29-35. The reluctor, rotating with the distributor shaft, produces a voltage pulse in the magnetic pick-up each time a spark plug is to be fired. This pulse is transmitted through the pick-up coil in the power switching transistor in the control unit, causing the transistor to interrupt current flow through the primary circuit. This break in the primary circuit induces high voltage in the secondary coil and fires a spark plug.

The length of time that the switching transistor blocks the flow of current to the primary circuit is determined by the electronic circuitry in the control unit. Even though dwell may be read with a dwell meter, there is no means

provided to change it.

The magnetic pick-up and the control unit have replaced the function of the breaker points and, unlike the breaker points, show no signs of wear, as there is an airgap between the two. Therefore, checks of timing and dwell are not needed. Ignition maintenance is reduced to inspection of wiring, and cleaning and changing of spark plugs as needed.

DELCO HIGH ENERGY IGNITION (HEI)

Some General Motors engines are equipped with the Delco-Remy high energy ignition (HEI) system, Fig. 29-36. It is an electronic system that does not use ignition breaker points and condenser.

All HEI components are mounted in or on the dis-

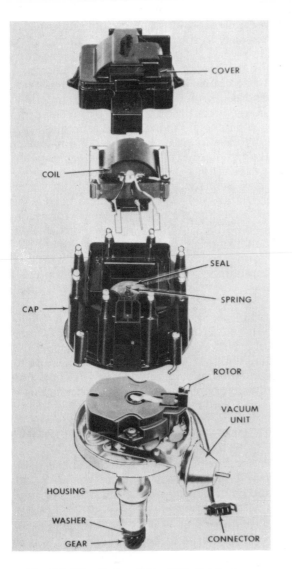

Fig. 29-36. Parts of the HEI distributor.

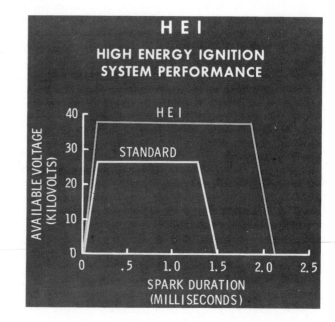

Fig. 29-37. Voltage comparison between HEI and points/condensor ignition system.

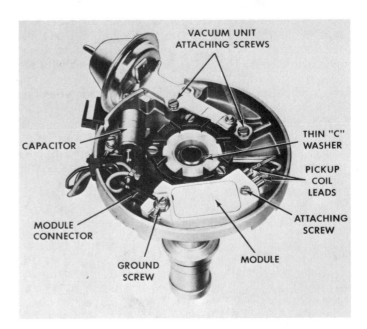

Fig. 29-38. Parts of the HEI distributor under the rotor. Silicone grease must be placed under the module, or intermittent stalling will occur with high temperatures.

tributor. The coil is built into the distributor cap. This results in increased energy at the spark plugs. Also, contributing to the high efficiency of this ignition system is the use of improved silicone leads and boots.

With a breaker point ignition system, less than 30 kilovolts with a duration of 1.5 milliseconds is available at the plug points. With HEI, the kilovoltage is increased to nearly 40, with a duration in excess of 2.0 milliseconds, Fig. 29-37.

This system includes a magnetic pulse distributor with integrated electronics and a high energy ignition coil. These parts form a single unit, Fig. 29-36, except on the in-line six cylinder engine application in which the coil is mounted separately.

The basic HEI distributor contains a pick-up coil, permanent magnet, and a pole piece with internal teeth. In the case of V-8 models, there are eight equally spaced teeth. The in-line six has six equally spaced teeth. The V-6 has three banks of teeth with two teeth per bank. These teeth are located and retained on the distributor shaft upper bushing. See Fig. 29-38. The distributor also contains an electronic module, a condenser for noise sup-

pression, and a vacuum advance unit. Attached to the lower part of the centrifugal advance weight base is a timer core. External teeth on the timer core are spaced in the same manner as those on the pole piece.

When the distributor shaft rotates, the teeth of the timer core align with the teeth of the pole piece to induce voltage in the pickup coil. This signals the all-electronic module to open the ignition coil primary circuit. Maximum inductance occurs at the instant the timer core teeth are aligned with the teeth on the pole piece.

At the instant the timer core teeth start to pass the teeth on the pole piece, the primary current decreases. This results in a collapse of the magnetic field, which induces a current in the primary coil winding. This, in turn, induces a high voltage in the secondary winding of the coil. The rotor then carries the current to spark plugs in corect firing order.

NOTE: There are no breaker points, and the condenser is used only for radio noise suppression.

The HEI system operates for many miles without needing any replacements since there are no breaker points. Spark plugs also last much longer because the higher secondary voltage will fire larger than normal spark plug gaps.

The vacuum diaphragm is connected by linkage to the pole piece. When the diaphragm moves against spring pressure, it rotates the pole piece, allowing the poles to advance relative to the timer core. The timer core is rotated about the shaft by advance weights, which provide centrifugal advance.

FORD SOLID STATE IGNITION

Ford's solid state system has a coil, high tension wiring, spark plugs, a permanent magnet, low-voltage generator, plus the solid state unit, Fig. 29-39.

The generator consists of an armature with six or eight gear-like teeth (one for each cylinder) mounted on top of the distributor shaft, and a permanent magnet located inside a small coil. The coil is riveted in place to provide a preset air gap with the armature. The distributor base, cap, rotor, vacuum, and centrifugal spark advance mechanisms are the same as in the breaker point ignition system.

The distributor is connected to the solid state module, which is located in the engine compartment. The module is 4 in. square and 2 in. deep. Its aluminum housing has cooling fins. Inside are the resistors, capacitors, transistors, and diodes.

The module performs two functions that are done mechanically in the breaker point ignition system. The module senses a signal from the magnetic generator to perform the "switching function" of the breaker points, and it also controls "dwell." Some of the module parts are used as protective devices, so the module will not be damaged from high voltage or reversed polarity.

The permanent magnet generator sends alternating current to the module, with the current changing from positive to negative each time one of the gear teeth on the armature passes the permanent magnet in the coil.

When a gear tooth is exactly opposite the coil, there is zero voltage. The electronic module senses this and cuts off current to the coil. This causes the magnetic field surrounding the coil to collapse, and high tension current generated is directed to the cylinders by a rotor.

Performance characteristics of Ford's solid state ignition compared to a breaker point ignition system:

	SPARK PLUG VOLTAGE	
	Start	Run
	10 V @	14 V @
	200 rpm	800 rpm
Solid State	32,000	26,000
Conventional	26,000	25,000

In addition to providing improved starting, Ford's solid state ignition system has no breaker points that wear and need replacement.

COMPUTER THEORY/COMPONENTS

This section of the chapter discusses how a computerized ignition system operates. Also, the various sensors and actuators are discussed at length. The sensors, along with the computer, make up the primary side of the ignition system. All of the actuators are controlled with battery voltage.

THE MOVE TO COMPUTERS

Since the car was first invented, a breaker point ignition has been used to transform battery voltage into 20,000 volts to fire the spark plugs. This system lasted until the mid-1970s. The problem with a breaker point ignition system is that a rubbing block, Fig. 29-40, attached to the arm of the points would wear down. This rubbing block followed the cam as it revolved, inside of the distributor, opening and closing the points. As the

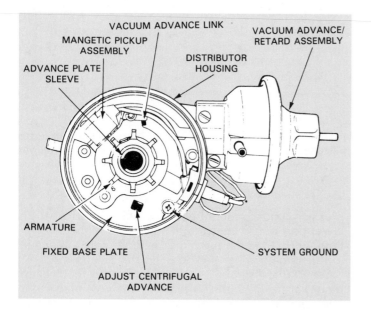

Fig. 29-39. Parts of the Ford electronic ignition distributor. Misalignment by one-half tooth causes a 7 3/4 degree timing error.

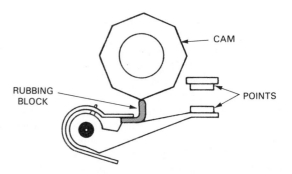

Fig. 29-40. As the rubbing block wears down, the dwell and timing change.

rubbing block would wear, the length of time that the points were opened was shortened. This would cause spark plugs to misfire and the timing to change. When this occurred, performance suffered along with an increased emission level. With government intervening and regulating the amount of emissions, along with a minimum mpg, a system more advanced than breaker points was needed. This system had to meet emission levels, gas mileage, and provide a smooth and continuous operation. Auto manufacturers found the answer in an on-board computer.

THE COMPUTER

The computer found on modern cars has two components. One is the hardware. The second is the software.

HARDWARE

The hardware consists of the Central Processing Unit (CPU). The CPU, when made in an integrated circuit (IC), is referred to as a microprocessor.

An Integrated Circuit (IC) combines transistors, diodes, and capacitors that are placed on a tiny chip of semiconductor material that is smaller and thinner than an eraser

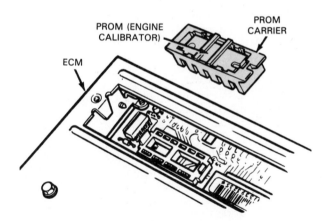

Fig. 29-41. The PROM can be serviced separately from the ECM. If the PROM is installed backwards, it will be destroyed. (Oldsmobile)

at the end of a pencil. This semiconductor material, most of the time, is silicon. Silicon, like any semiconductor material, does not conduct electricity until either voltage, a magnetic field, heat, or light is directed to the semiconductor. The microprocessor receives instructions from a program.

SOFTWARE

The software consists of a program. A program tells the computer what to do, and when to do it in a specific sequence. The program is stored in a permanent memory, which is referred to as Read Only Memory (ROM). The computer knows only what is placed in its memory. General Motors has a variation of the ROM. This is called a Programmable Read Only Memory (PROM). The PROM , Fig. 29-41, can be readily removed and replaced while the ROM cannot. This makes it less expensive if the memory should become defective, then only the PROM has to be replaced and not the entire microprocessor. If the microprocessor should become defective, the PROM is transferred to a new microprocessor. An auto microprocessor contains a ROM or PROM and a RAM.

RAM stands for Random Access Memory. This type of memory can be accessed without going through a specific sequence. The technician interfaces with the RAM whenever trouble codes are accessed. However, not all computerized ignition systems have trouble codes.

Some computers have the ability to learn. This is referred to as an adaptive memory. When a value falls outside of a specified limit, due to engine wear, the adaptive memory makes a slight adjustment in the program to compensate. The car must be driven from 20 to 30 miles, as it take the computer this long to learn. Any time that power is disconnected to the computer, it will have to relearn everything.

COMPUTER OPERATION

The computer receives many (input) voltage signals at once from the various sensors, Fig. 29-42. Once the computer receives this information from the sensors, the signal is processed with information from the program. Once it is processed, the computer energizes the various actuators (outputs).

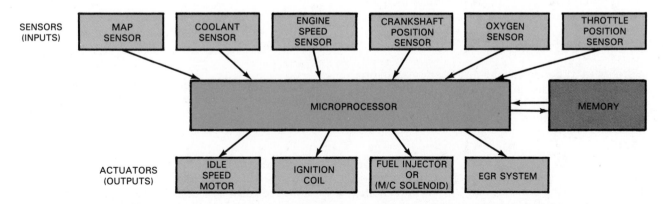

Fig. 29-42. Without the information that sensors provide, the computer is of limited use.

COMPUTER TYPES

There are two different types of computer. The first type is an analog. The second type is digital.

ANALOG

The analog computer is designed to imitate the signal it receives. The analog computer receives different strength voltage signals from the sensors and adjusts the actuators proportionately. The biggest problem with analog computers is that they are not consistent as the temperature and the supply voltage change.

DIGITAL

The digital computer can be referred to as an ON-OFF computer. The digital computer turns an actuator on, or it remains in the off position. There is no inbetween like an analog computer. The problem of temperature and voltage change found to be a problem in analog computers is remedied by using a digital computer.

CONVERSIONS

Most sensors send an analog signal to the computer. A digital computer cannot use an analog signal. So, the analog signal must first be converted into a digital signal. This is done with an analog-to-digital converter within the integrated circuit (IC).

Some actuators are an analog device, and therefore are adjusted proportionately. So, the signal that a digital computer provides must be converted into an analog signal for the specific output device. This is done by a digital-to-analog converter.

WARNING! It is very important to keep the charging system in top shape, as the voltage affects the operation of the computer. If the voltage falls below 12 V, the computer will malfunction until the needed repairs are made to the charging system. Also, if voltage exceeds 15 V, the computer may be destroyed.

SENSOR OPERATION

The sensor measures and then converts that measurement to an electrical signal. This signal is then sent to the computer where it is compared to the voltage supplied to the sensor. The voltage supplied to the sensor is called reference voltage. This section describes sensor design and operation.

CRANKSHAFT POSITION SENSOR

There are many types of crankshaft position sensors. However, they all tell the computer the position of the crankshaft so that the spark plug (and fuel injectors) can be fired at the proper time, Fig. 29-43.

MAGNETIC

The magnetic crankshaft position sensor, Fig. 29-44, produces an alternating current, Fig. 29-45. This is the most common type. Each of the metal tabs corresponds

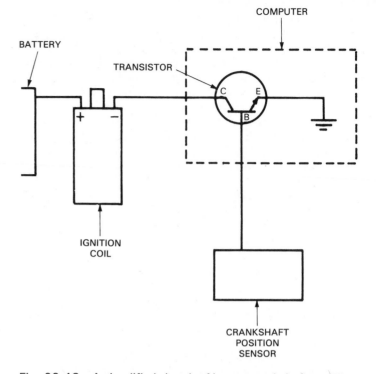

Fig. 29-43. A simplified sketch of how a crankshaft position sensor is connected to the base of a transistor in the computer. The transistor increases battery voltage to the coil primary windings. It also breaks the flow of current to the coil much faster than a set of points. These two facts combined produce a higher secondary voltage than a points and condenser ignition system.

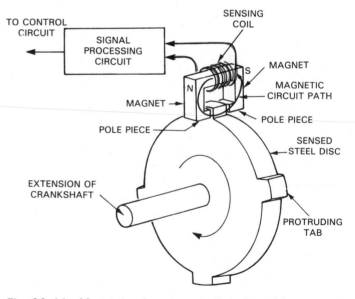

Fig. 29-44. Magnetic reluctance crankshaft position sensor. Voltage signal is sent to the computer through windings around magnet.

to a cylinder at TDC of the compression stroke. This type would be used on an eight cylinder engine. This can also be adapted to fit in a distributor. Then, there will be as many metal tabs as there are cylinders.

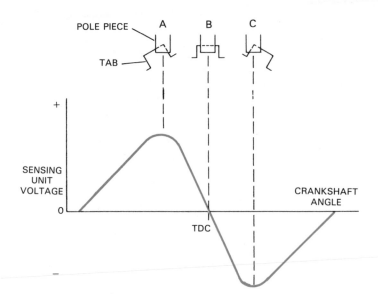

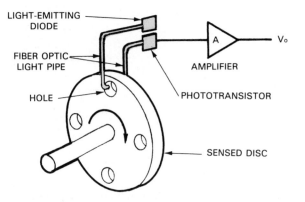

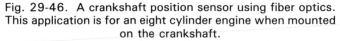

Fig. 29-45. An alternating current is produced by this crankshaft position sensor. A—Voltage is peaked just prior to metal tab aligning with magnet. If transistor is the NPN type, voltage is applied to the base of the transistor. This turns transistor ON and allows current to flow through it to the primary windings of the coil. B—Metal tab aligns with magnet and voltage drops to zero. The lack of voltage at the transistor base turns the transistor OFF and interrupts current to the coil primary windings. The coil then fires 20,000 or more volts to the spark plug. C—As the metal tab begins to leave the magnetic field, the polarity is reversed. This portion of the signal is irrelevant unless the transistor is the PNP type.

Fig. 29-46. A crankshaft position sensor using fiber optics. This application is for an eight cylinder engine when mounted on the crankshaft.

OPTICAL

An optical crankshaft position sensor, Fig. 29-46, can be mounted in the distributor or at the back end of the crankshaft. The light from the LED is carried through fiber optics. The beam of light is interrupted by a steel disk, except when a hole in the disk aligns between the two fiber optic light pipes. When this occurs, the beam of light is directed to the base of a phototransistor. Current is then allowed to flow through the phototransistor to the primary windings of the ignition coil. When the steel disk interrupts the beam of light, the current flowing to the primary windings is interrupted and a spark plug is fired. Each hole in the disk represents TDC of a compression stroke. The problem with fiber optics is that they must be protected from dirt and/or oil so that they can perform their job. If dirt collects at one end of a light pipe, the beam of light will never reach the phototransistor and the coil will not be able to fire the spark plugs.

HALL EFFECT

The Hall Effect sensor, most of the time, does not measure the position of the crankshaft directly. However, it does measure the position of the camshaft which rotates at half the speed of the crankshaft. This sensor is mounted in the distributor, Fig. 29-47. It is a thin slab of semiconductor material that has voltage supplied to it constantly. When the metal tab passes between the magnet and the sensor, the magnetic field is

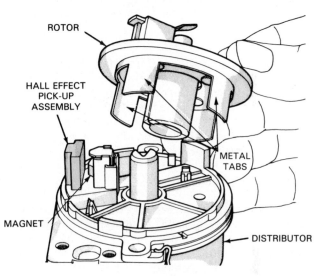

Fig. 29-47. A typical Hall Effect sensor. The disadvantage of locating the sensor in the distributor, is that it cannot compensate for wear in the timing chain or belt. (Chrysler)

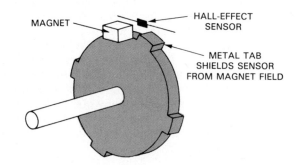

Fig. 29-48. The metal tabs interrupt the magnetic field to the sensor.

interrupted and the voltage at the sensor, that is sent to a transistor in the computer, is lowered. See Figs. 29-48 and 29-49. Each metal tab corresponds to TDC of a compression stroke. So, a spark plug is fired when a metal tab is between the magnet and the sensor.

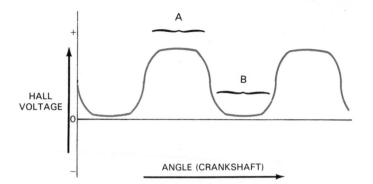

Fig. 29-49. Hall voltage. A—Metal tab has passed between sensor and magnet. This voltage turns transistor ON and allows current to flow through transistor to primary windings in coil. B—Metal tab aligns with magnet and sensor; voltage is decreased at sensor. The lower voltage is not great enough to turn transistor ON and current flowing through transistor is interrupted. The ignition coil then fires 20,000 or more volts. Note that voltage never reaches zero.

NOTE: The reverse is true on some Hall Effect sensors. The magnetic field in the ignition coil is built up when the metal tab is between the magnet and the sensor. So, a spark plug is fired when the metal tab has passed between the magnet and sensor. This is due to the type of Hall Effect sensor design used, as it passes the magnetic field to the sensor instead of interrupting it.

ENGINE SPEED SENSOR

Most crankshaft position sensors double as an engine speed sensor. This establishes engine rpm for the computer. The computer counts the number of times it receives a voltage signal from the sensor. However, the computer must be programmed for how many voltage signals or ''pulses'' equal one crankshaft revolution.

VEHICLE SPEED SENSOR

This sensor tells the computer how fast the car is traveling. The vehicle speed sensor is driven by the speedometer cable, Fig. 29-50. The speedometer cable drives a pulse generator in the speedometer pinion housing. Some cars have the speedometer pinion drive the pulse generator. As the pulse generator makes one revolution, a certain number of pulses or voltage signals are sent to the computer. The computer must be programmed to ''know'' how many pulses equal one revolution of the speedometer cable. This information is also used for a digital dash and trip computer, if the vehicle is so equipped.

AIRFLOW METER

The rate at which the air enters the engine has to be measured to determine the precise amount of fuel, in relation to the amount of air entering the intake system. The airflow meter, Fig. 29-51, has a spring loaded flap, which is deflected as air flows through the intake system. As the airflow is increased, the flap is deflected to an increasingly smaller angle.

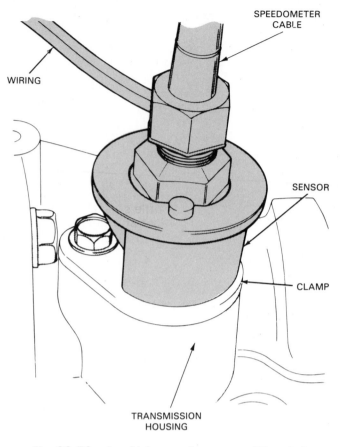

Fig. 29-50. A vehicle speed sensor. (Chrysler)

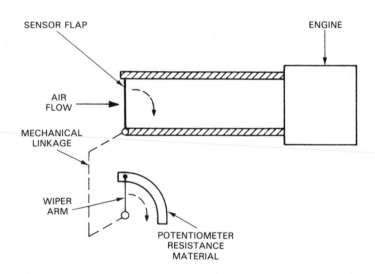

Fig. 29-51. A cross section of a simplified airflow meter.

The flap is mechanically linked to a wiper arm, which rides on a variable resistor. As the flap moves, so does the wiper arm. As the wiper arm moves, the resistance varies and adjusts the voltage signal accordingly. As the volume of air increases, the output voltage from the sensor drops. However, some systems increase the voltage signal to the computer as the volume of air increases. Some systems use a MAP sensor instead of an airflow meter.

THROTTLE POSITION SENSOR

The purpose of the throttle position sensor is to send a voltage signal to the computer indicating the angle of the throttle; the greater the angle, the richer the fuel mixture. Also, the greater the angle, the more the timing has to be advanced. The sensor tells the computer when the throttle is wide open, at an idle position, or somewhere inbetween. The sensor is located at one end of the throttle shaft, Fig. 29-52. If mis-adjusted it will send the computer the wrong information, possibly a cause of a no-start condition. The sensor, Fig. 29-53, works on the same principle as the airflow meter. The wiper arm is connected directly to the throttle shaft. As the throttle shaft moves, so does the wiper arm. The other end of the wiper arm rides on a variable resistor. As the throttle angle changes, so does the resistance. The voltage signal sent to the computer is adjusted by the amount of resistance encountered at the sensor.

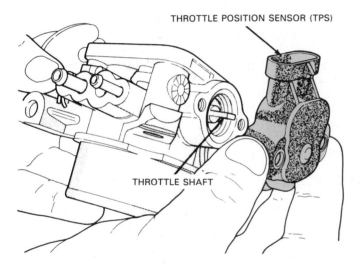

Fig. 29-52. The throttle position sensor fits over one end of the throttle shaft. (Chrysler)

MANIFOLD ABSOLUTE PRESSURE (MAP)SENSOR

Absolute pressure is different than regular gauge pressure. Gauge pressure does not include atmospheric pressure as part of the reading. Absolute pressure adds atmospheric pressure (14.7 psi at sea level) to the reading. So, an absolute pressure reading of 14.7 psi equals 0 psi on a regular gauge. By using an absolute scale, the reduced pressure (less than atmospheric pressure) is read as a lower pressure instead of as a vacuum.

The MAP sensor tells the computer how much pressure is in the manifold. The port for a MAP sensor is located below the throttle plate, Fig. 29-54. The higher the manifold pressure (low or no vacuum), the higher the voltage signal sent to the computer. This would indicate that a load has been applied to the engine. The greater the load on the engine, the richer the fuel mixture must be, and the more the timing must be advanced. A low manifold pressure (high vacuum) equals a low voltage signal sent to the computer. This would indicate a low or no load applied to the engine. The fuel mixture would be as lean as possible, and the timing would be advanced very little or not at all.

There are different types of MAP sensor designs. They include: strain gauge, capacitor capsule, and aneroid types.

STRAIN GAUGE

The Strain Gauge, Fig. 29-55, is the most common MAP sensor. The lower silicon dioxide chip is cemented to a Pyrex plate, thereby forming a vacuum chamber between the plate and the chip. Four sensing resistors are placed on top of the n-silicon. These are connected to external metal bonds on top of the silicon dioxide chip. The electrical connections are made at these metal bonds. When manifold pressure is applied and causes the diaphragm to deflect, the sensing resistors vary their resistance. This variance in resistance adjusts the voltage sent to the computer.

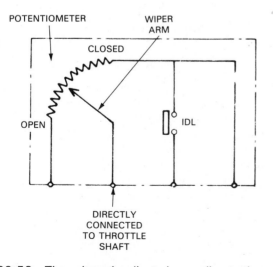

Fig. 29-53. The voltage is adjusted according to the angle of the throttle opening. (Toyota)

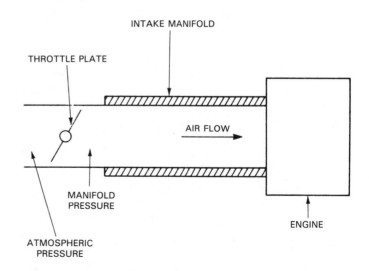

Fig. 29-54. The MAP sensor port is located below the throttle plate.

309

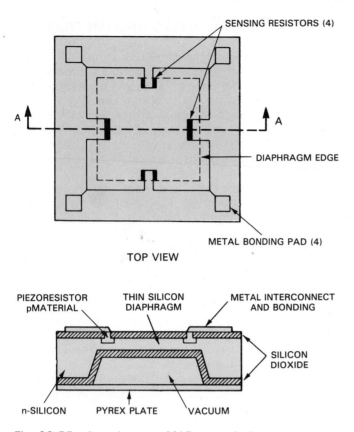

SENSING RESISTORS (4)

A ← ← → A

DIAPHRAGM EDGE

METAL BONDING PAD (4)

TOP VIEW

PIEZORESISTOR pMATERIAL

THIN SILICON DIAPHRAGM

METAL INTERCONNECT AND BONDING

SILICON DIOXIDE

n-SILICON   PYREX PLATE   VACUUM

Fig. 29-55. A strain gauge MAP sensor is the most common.

CAPACITOR-CAPSULE

The capacitor-capsule MAP sensor is shown in Fig. 29-56. This design has alumina plates on the top and bottom. These are cemented to an insulating washer. A film electrode is placed on the inside of each alumina plate, and each electrode has an external lead.

The capacitor-capsule is placed in a sealed unit exposed only to manifold pressure. As the alumina plates flex due to manifold pressure, the distance between the two electrodes varies. As the distance between the electrodes vary, so is the voltage signal sent to the computer.

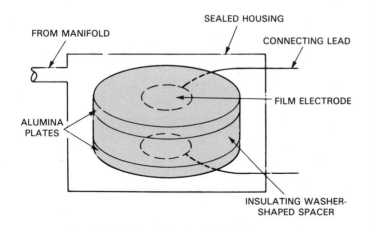

SEALED HOUSING

CONNECTING LEAD

FROM MANIFOLD

FILM ELECTRODE

ALUMINA PLATES

INSULATING WASHER-SHAPED SPACER

Fig. 29-56. Capacitor-capsule MAP sensor.

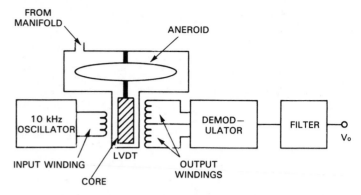

FROM MANIFOLD

ANEROID

10 kHz OSCILLATOR

DEMOD-ULATOR

FILTER

Vo

INPUT WINDING   LVDT   OUTPUT WINDINGS

CORE

Fig. 29-57. An aneroid MAP sensor. The oscillator produces a 10 kHz signal at the input winding. The signal is adjusted by the position of the core, and the output windings, then, receive the signal.

ANEROID

The aneroid MAP sensor, which is being phased out, is shown in Fig. 29-57. It uses a linear variable differential transformer (LVDT). The core of the LVDT is attached to an aneroid bellows, which is exposed to manifold vacuum. When the engine is off, the core is in the mid-position. As the core of the LVDT is raised and lowered, due to manifold pressure, between the input and output windings, the voltage at the output windings is adjusted accordingly. The voltage signal is then sent to the computer.

BAROMETRIC PRESSURE SENSOR

The BARO sensor measures atmospheric pressure, Fig. 29-58. When barometric pressure drops, due to weather or altitude, the timing needs to be advanced and the fuel mixture leaned. This sensor can be similar in design to any MAP sensor.

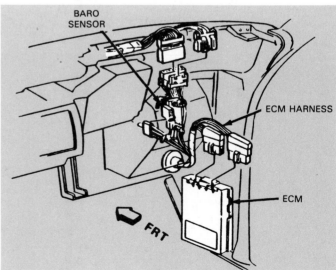

BARO SENSOR

ECM HARNESS

ECM

FRT

Fig. 29-58. Location of the BARO sensor on one car. (Cadillac)

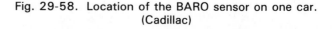

COOLANT TEMPERATURE SENSOR

The coolant sensor measures the temperature of the coolant. This information is used to determine the amount of spark advance, as more spark advance is needed when the engine is cold. Also, the fuel mixture is made richer, idle speed increased, and no vacuum is allowed to the EGR valve when the engine is cold.

Once the engine temperature warms up, the fuel mixture is leaned out, spark advance and idle speed are reduced, and vacuum is allowed to the EGR valve. The coolant sensor is located in the engine block where its tip can be exposed to the coolant, Fig. 29-59.

A coolant sensor is a thermistor, which is made of a semiconductor material, Fig. 29-60. The resistance of the thermistor varies inversely to the temperature of the coolant. When the coolant is cold, the thermistor has a greater amount of resistance than when the coolant is hot. This is referred to as Negative Temperature Coefficient. The voltage signal sent to the computer is increased when the resistance is high. So, the voltage signal sent to the computer is decreased as the engine reaches operating temperature.

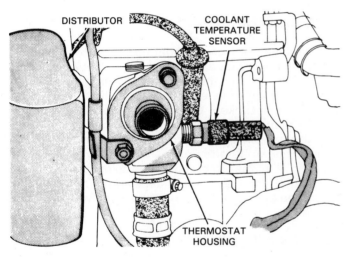

Fig. 29-59. Coolant temperature sensor location. (Chrysler)

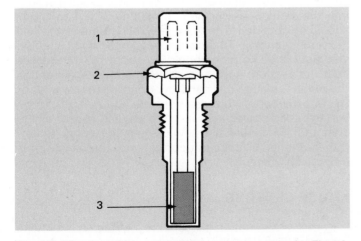

Fig. 29-60. A typical coolant temperature sensor. 1—Electrical connect. 2—Case. 3—Thermistor. (Robert Bosch)

MANIFOLD AIR TEMPERATURE SENSOR

The manifold air temperature sensor, Fig. 29-61, senses the temperature of the incoming air. Cold air is much denser than hot air. With colder air, a richer mixture is needed. The design of this sensor can be identical to the coolant sensor.

STOICHIOMETRIC

A lean air-fuel mixture produces a high level of nitrous oxides (NO_x) in the exhaust. A rich air-fuel mixture produces exhaust with high levels of hydrocarbons (HC) and carbon monoxide (CO). However, the byproducts of perfect combustion produce water (H_2O) and carbon dioxide (CO_2) in the exhaust, provided that the engine is 100 percent efficient. The best designed and built engine is not 100 percent efficient.

A STOICHIOMETRIC air-fuel mixture provides the closest in obtaining the byproducts of perfect combustion. A stoichiometric air-fuel mixture is neither too rich nor too lean. It is 14.7 parts air to 1 part fuel. However, even with this desired air-fuel mixture, hydrocarbons, carbon monoxide, and nitrous oxides remain, but only in small percentages. To achieve this, the combustion process, along with other engine variables, must be measured.

OXYGEN SENSOR

The oxygen sensor, Figs. 29-62 to 29-64, is made of two platinum electrodes with zirconia oxide (ZrO_2) between the two electrodes. The ZrO_2 attracts the oxygen in the air. The platinum electrode on the air side has a much higher concentration of oxygen exposed to it than the electrode on the exhaust side. This makes the electrode on the air side have a negative charge. A lack of oxygen in the exhaust, due to a rich fuel mixture, causes the electrode on the exhaust side to become positively charged. This causes the oxygen sensor to become a battery by producing voltage. The computer then causes the fuel mixture to be leaned out by reducing the amount of time that the individual fuel injector is energized.

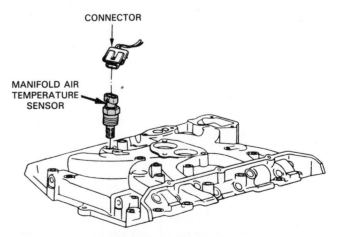

Fig. 29-61. The manifold air temperature sensor is located on the intake manifold. (Cadillac)

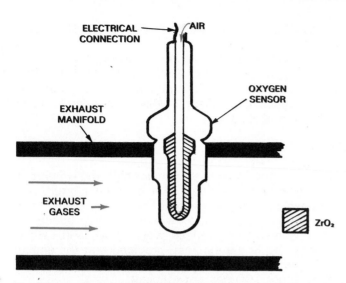

Fig. 29-62. The zirconia oxide in the oxygen sensor is exposed to exhaust gases and outside air. The oxygen content makes it produce a negative charge. So, if the oxygen content level is high in the exhaust, no voltage is produced.

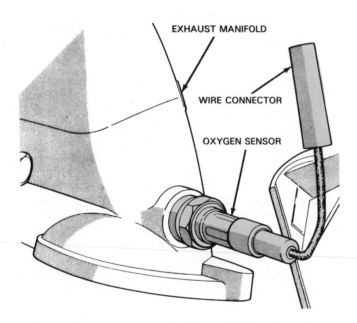

Fig. 29-63. The oxygen sensor is located in the exhaust manifold. When servicing an oxygen sensor, coat the threads with an anti-seize compound. (Chrysler)

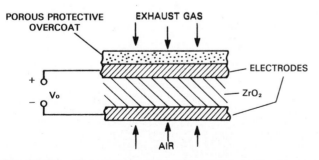

Fig. 29-64. The air side of the oxygen sensor tip always has a negative charge. The lack of oxygen causes a positive charge on the exhaust side.

However, if the exhaust gases have a high concentration of oxygen, due to a lean fuel mixture, the electrode on the exhaust side also becomes negatively charged. Since both electrodes are negatively charged, no voltage is produced and no voltage signal is sent to the computer. The computer, not receiving a voltage signal, causes the fuel mixture to be richened by increasing the amount of time that the individual fuel injector is energized.

OPEN/CLOSED LOOP

The oxygen sensor does not provide a voltage signal to the computer to control the fuel mixture while the engine is cold. The computer then operates from predetermined values during this time, and is known as "open loop." Once the exhaust gases reach 600 °F, the oxygen sensor provides a voltage signal to the computer. When the computer uses this signal to adjust the fuel mixture, it is known as "closed loop." The only time that the signal from the oxygen sensor is overridden, once in the "closed loop" mode, is during wide open throttle (WOT). During this time the fuel mixture is fixed at full rich. Once the driver lets off the accelerator, the system reverts to "closed loop."

OXYGEN SENSOR WIRE

The oxygen sensor wire that runs from the sensor to the computer carries anywhere from 0 to 1 V. Since this voltage is so low, the oxygen sensor wire must be isolated from all other electrical wires. If this preventive measure is not taken, the magnetic flux lines that surround the other electrical wiring may induce a voltage into the oxygen sensor wire. The computer uses this voltage signal, from the oxygen sensor, to control fuel delivery. The false signal sent to the computer may cause an intermittent deep sag on acceleration. This can be prevented by isolating the oxygen sensor wire in a foam sleeve.

OXYGEN SENSOR TESTING

After the engine is in closed loop, which should take about two minutes once the engine is started, the sensor can be checked. With a digital voltmeter probe inserted into the oxygen sensor wire, a reading of 0.1 to 1.0 V should be obtained. The voltage will fluctuate as the fuel mixture changes. To confirm readings, disconnect a vacuum hose. Voltage should be about 0.1 V. Reconnect the vacuum hose and choke the engine. To choke the engine, place your hand over part of the air inlet at the throttle body. Voltage should be about 1.0 V. If the voltage does not correspond, the oxygen sensor or the computer is bad. Install a new oxygen sensor and retest. If the voltage still does not correspond, the computer is most likely at fault.

KNOCK SENSORS

Knock or detonation sensors are located on the intake manifold, Fig. 29-65. The purpose of this sensor is to eliminate the knock that is associated with detonation

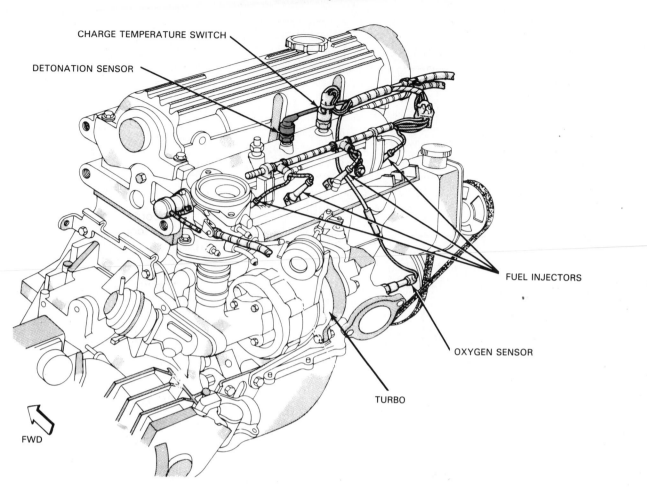

CHARGE TEMPERATURE SWITCH

DETONATION SENSOR

FUEL INJECTORS

OXYGEN SENSOR

TURBO

FWD

Fig. 29-65. The detonation sensor is located on the intake manifold. The charge temperature sensor senses incoming air temperature. (Chrysler)

or pre-ignition. This reduces power and destroys pistons and valves.

The magnetostrictive rods, Fig. 29-66, which are placed in a magnetic field, change the density of the magnetic field when a knock is detected. This change in the density of the magnetic field creates a variation in voltage in the coil. This voltage is sent to the computer. The computer then retards the timing. This eliminates the engine knock. However, there are problems with this sensor in picking up other engine noises, unless an electronic filter is used.

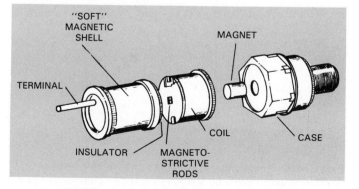

"SOFT" MAGNETIC SHELL

MAGNET

TERMINAL

COIL

CASE

INSULATOR

MAGNETO-STRICTIVE RODS

Fig. 29-66. Construction of a detonation sensor.

SENSOR MULTIPLEXING

With recent technical advances it has become possible to connect all of the engine-monitoring sensors to the computer with one wire, Fig. 29-67. This is referred to as multiplexing (MUX). It reduces the amount of wiring that is needed. This single wire is called a data bus, and all sensors transmit a signal to it. This data bus can even be composed of fiber optics. The use of fiber optics is even more desirable than copper wiring, as there will be no interference of the signal by other electrical devices.

Each sensor receives a signal at a separate and predetermined time. Only one sensor is sending and receiving signals at a time, Fig. 29-67. The concept of multiplexing can be used not only for sensors, but throughout the entire car.

ACTUATOR OPERATION

An actuator is an (output) device that is controlled by the computer. An actuator can control the idle speed, adjust ignition timing, regulate fuel mixture, and the EGR system. The time and duration that each actuator is energized is controlled by the computer. The computer determines this with the information from the various sensors.

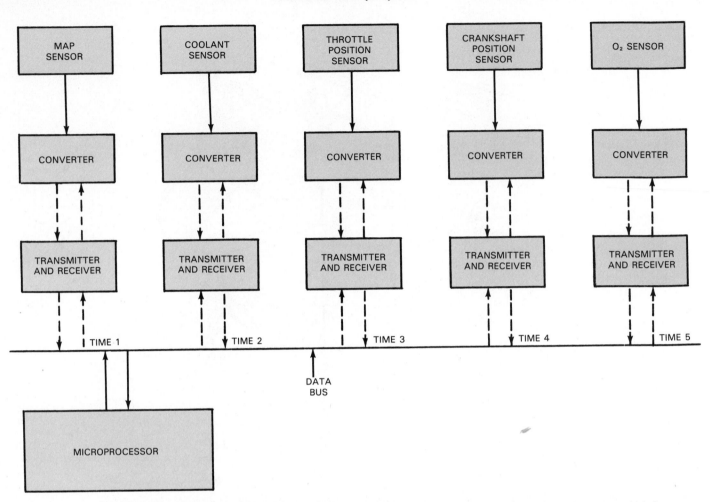

Fig. 29-67. The converter changes the analog signal of the sensor to a digital signal. When the computer needs information from a specific sensor, a signal is sent on the data bus to the individual transmitter/receiver. Only one sensor signal interacts with the computer at a time. Each sensor has a designated time to interact with the computer.

A computerized engine system includes a number of actuators. Among them are:

1. Automatic idle adjustment.
2. Ignition coil.
3. Fuel injectors.
4. Mixture control solenoid.
5. EGR system valve.
6. Fuel pump relay.

AUTOMATIC IDLE ADJUSTMENT

The idle speed on a computerized ignition system is controlled by an electric motor (an actuator), Fig. 29-68. The plunger on the idle speed motor is automatically extended when the idle speed needs to be increased. This prevents the engine from stalling during idle. An increased load placed on the engine while idling would normally cause the idle speed to drop. Also, the plunger will automatically retract once the load has been removed from the engine. This idle speed motor will also automatically increase the idle speed if there is a small vacuum leak. Increasing the idle speed, which increases the fuel supply, compensates for the added air intake (vacuum leak). The driver may never even know that there is a small problem.

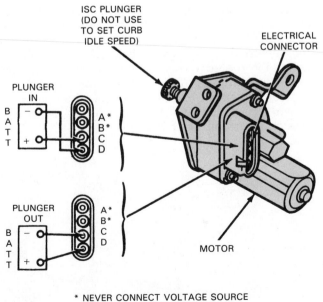

* NEVER CONNECT VOLTAGE SOURCE
ACROSS TERMINALS "A" AND "B"

Fig. 29-68. The plunger is retracted or extended automatically. This is determined by the load on the engine while idling. (Oldsmobile)

IGNITION COIL

Current flows from the battery through a transistor to the primary windings of the ignition coil, Fig. 29-69. The flow of the current to the ignition coil is then interrupted, by the transistor, whereby the magnetic field is collapsed across the secondary windings in the coil. Voltage is then induced in the secondary windings in the coil. When voltage is induced in the secondary windings, voltage is increased to over 20,000 volts. This voltage is then delivered to the spark plug to fire the fuel mixture in the combustion chamber.

FUEL INJECTORS

The fuel injector, Fig. 29-70, delivers the fuel supply, under pressure, to the combustion chamber. Once the fuel injector is energized, the fuel is sprayed in a fine mist into the intake runner or manifold where it is delivered to the combustion chamber. The length of time that the fuel injector remains energized is determined by the load placed on the engine, along with other variables. The greater the load placed on the engine, the longer it stays energized. The longer it is energized, the more fuel that is delivered to the combustion chamber.

MIXTURE CONTROL SOLENOID

The mixture control solenoid, Fig. 29-71, which is also referred to as an oxygen feedback solenoid, is an actuator if the engine is carbureted. This solenoid controls the fuel mixture. The mixture control solenoid operates just the opposite of a fuel injector. This means that when the mixture control solenoid is energized, the fuel mixture is lean. This contrasts to the fuel injector that provides fuel when energized.

EGR SYSTEM

The vacuum to the EGR valve, Fig. 29-72, is controlled by a solenoid. This allows a more precise metering of the exhaust gases that are recirculated. When the solenoid is energized, vacuum is routed to the EGR valve. The EGR valve then opens, which allows the exhaust gases to be mixed with the incoming air-fuel mixture.

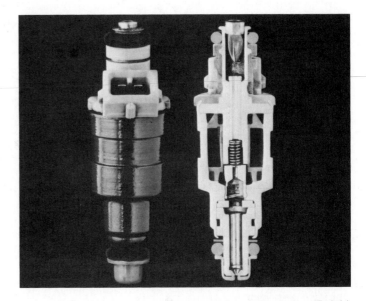

Fig. 29-70. The fuel injector is another actuator. (Buick)

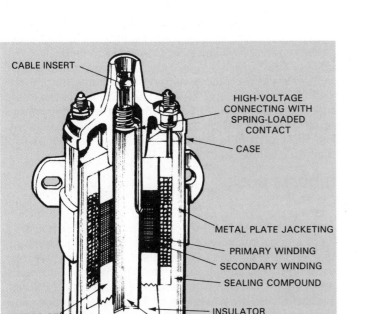

Fig. 29-69. A cross section of an ignition coil.

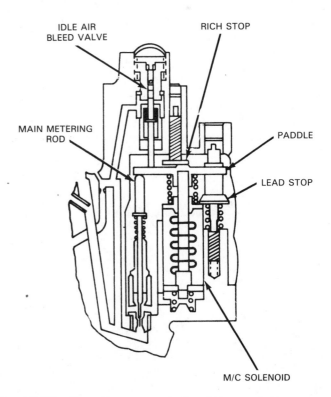

Fig. 29-71. The mixture control solenoid is an actuator on carbureted engines. The mixture control solenoid is opened and closed at the rate of 10 times per second. (Cadillac)

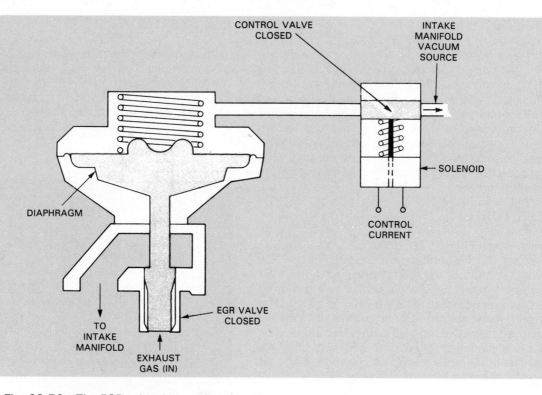

Fig. 29-72. The EGR solenoid is an actuator. The computer decides when to energize or de-energize the solenoid. The EGR solenoid allows vacuum to the EGR valve.

FUEL PUMP RELAY

Some manufacturer's incorporate the fuel pump relay, Fig. 29-73, as an actuator. The fuel pump relay automatically opens electrical contacts upon loss of signal from the computer. This interrupts current to the electric fuel pump, and turns off the supply of fuel, reducing the chance of fire in the event of an accident.

COMPUTERIZED IGNITION SYSTEMS

This final portion of the chapter covers the steps in checking the timing, accessing trouble codes, and diagnosing the specific computerized ignition systems.

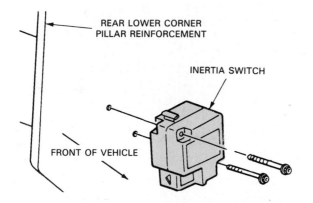

Fig. 29-73. The inertia switch is opened in the event of an accident. This interrupts current to the electric fuel pump. (Ford)

Due to the wide variety of systems, only Ford, GM, and Chrysler can be covered. However, only the most common of these systems will be discussed, as each has many types of computerized ignition systems.

COMPUTER COMMAND CONTROL

The Computer Command Control (CCC) system is one of GM's computerized ignition systems. The computer is referred to as an Electronic Control Module (ECM), Fig. 29-74. The ECM is a digital microprocessor and can be located in various places within the passenger compartment, Figs. 29-75 and 29-76. The ECM is located in the passenger compartment since there is less temperature variation and vibration than in the engine compartment. The CCC system is used on carbureted as well as fuel injected engines.

TROUBLE CODES

When the CHECK ENGINE or SERVICE ENGINE SOON light appears, Fig. 29-77, the driver is informed that there is a problem with the system. This light will appear while the engine is being started to let the driver know that the bulb is good. This light will not come on again unless there is trouble with the system. If it does, the technician must use the on-board diagnostics. This means that the computer has the ability to diagnose the components to determine the trouble in the system. The ECM continually receives signals from the sensors. If the sensors do not give the proper signal, the CHECK ENGINE or SERVICE ENGINE SOON light appears and remains on until the proper repairs are made.

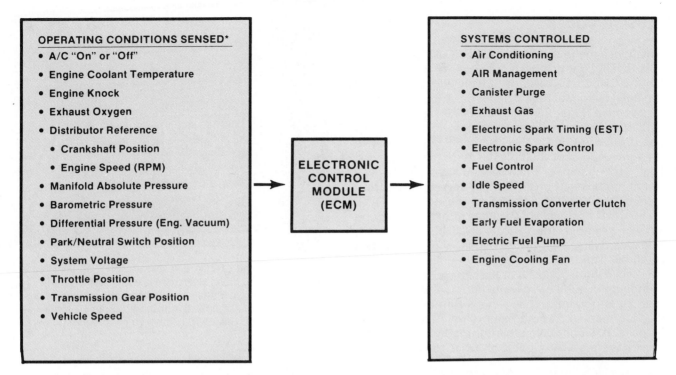

OPERATING CONDITIONS SENSED*	SYSTEMS CONTROLLED

OPERATING CONDITIONS SENSED*
- A/C "On" or "Off"
- Engine Coolant Temperature
- Engine Knock
- Exhaust Oxygen
- Distributor Reference
  - Crankshaft Position
  - Engine Speed (RPM)
- Manifold Absolute Pressure
- Barometric Pressure
- Differential Pressure (Eng. Vacuum)
- Park/Neutral Switch Position
- System Voltage
- Throttle Position
- Transmission Gear Position
- Vehicle Speed

ELECTRONIC CONTROL MODULE (ECM)

SYSTEMS CONTROLLED
- Air Conditioning
- AIR Management
- Canister Purge
- Exhaust Gas
- Electronic Spark Timing (EST)
- Electronic Spark Control
- Fuel Control
- Idle Speed
- Transmission Converter Clutch
- Early Fuel Evaporation
- Electric Fuel Pump
- Engine Cooling Fan

Fig. 29-74. All of the items that the ECM senses before adjusting any of the actuators. (Delco-Remy)

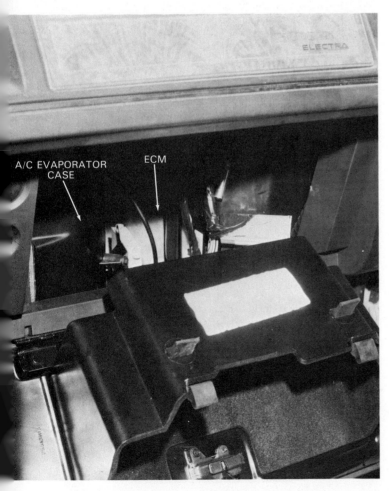

Fig. 29-75. The ECM is buried behind the glovebox in this application.

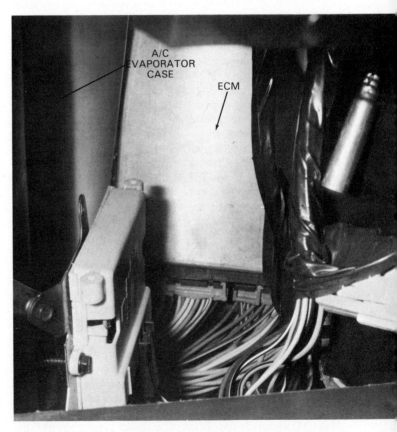

Fig. 29-76. A close-up view of the ECM. Note the electrical connections. The connections must be clean and tight, or it will appear is if the computer is malfunctioning. Never disconnect the electrical connections when the ignition switch is at the ON position. If you do, the computer may be destroyed. Also, never reroute wiring to or from computer, as this will create driveability problems.

ACCESSING CODES

To diagnose the fault, the CHECK ENGINE or SERVICE ENGINE SOON light will flash out codes, Fig. 29-77. To enable the CHECK ENGINE or SERVICE ENGINE SOON light to flash out codes, the diagnostic terminal will have to be grounded, Figs. 29-78 and 29-79. Turn the ignition to ON, but do not start the engine. The first set of flashes, from the CHECK ENGINE or SERVICE ENGINE SOON light, represent multiples of ten. Then there will be a half second pause, and a second set of flashes will represent multiples of ones. If there are any other trouble codes, the CHECK ENGINE or SERVICE ENGINE SOON light will flash out these codes after a four second pause. For example, the CHECK ENGINE, Fig. 29-77, light flashes twice, then a brief pause, and then flashes twice again. The first set of flashes equal the number twenty, while the second set of flashes equal the number two. Adding the numbers twenty and two together, the number 22 is obtained. Using this information, look in the service manual to determine what "Trouble Code 22" means. After obtaining this information, the technician will have a starting point of what to check.

CAUTION ON THE TROUBLE CODES

After determining the trouble codes and which fault is represented, some additional problem solving must be used. If the trouble code indicates that the coolant sensor is faulty, the problem may be elsewhere in the cooling system. For example, the coolant level may be low causing the trouble code for a faulty coolant sensor. Or, the thermostat may be stuck closed causing the engine to overheat. This will also cause a trouble code for a faulty coolant sensor. A short circuit or an open circuit can cause any of the sensors to produce a trouble code while the sensor is good.

Sometimes there are NO trouble codes indicated and a problem exists. When this occurs the computer may be at fault, or a mechanical defect may be the cause. Or, if there are more than several trouble codes indicated, the computer is probably at fault.

NOTE: The computer should be replaced only after all other components of the system test good. If it is replaced, test all the relays and solenoids that the computer operates. A shorted relay will cause the computer to go bad.

CLEARING TROUBLE CODES

Once the trouble code has been determined and the needed repairs made, the trouble codes must be cleared from the system. If the codes are not cleared, they will remain and the SERVICE ENGINE SOON or CHECK ENGINE light will remain lit. To clear the trouble codes, simply remove the quick disconnect near the battery. After 10 seconds reconnect the bullet type connection.

FIELD SERVICE MODE (Fuel Injected Engines Only)

If the engine is started and then the diagnostic terminal is grounded, Figs. 29-78 and 29-79, it will be in the field service mode. The field service mode will enable the SER-

Fig. 29-77. The CHECK ENGINE or SERVICE ENGINE SOON light informs the driver that there is a problem with the system. The technician uses this same light to pull trouble codes from the computer to diagnose the problem. Code 12 should always flash. However, this code is ignored for diagnostic purposes.

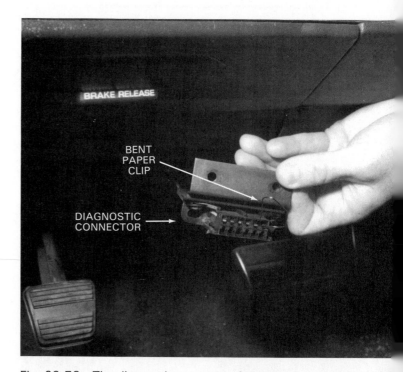

Fig. 29-78. The diagnostic connector for accessing trouble codes is located under the dash. Jump the diagnostic terminal to the ground terminal using a paper clip. Always refer to the individual service manual.

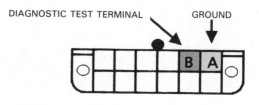

Fig. 29-79. Identifying the diagnostic and ground terminals of the connector. (Cadillac)

VICE ENGINE SOON light to tell the technician if the engine is in closed or open loop. If the SERVICE ENGINE SOON light, Fig. 29-77, flashes twice each second, the engine is in open loop. When the SERVICE ENGINE SOON light flashes once every second, the engine is in closed loop. If the engine should stay in open loop for more than two minutes after the engine is started, the oxygen sensor and/or its circuit, the coolant temperature sensor, or the computer is defective.

If the SERVICE ENGINE SOON light, Fig. 29-77, remains OFF all or most of the time while in the field service mode, a lean mixture is indicated. This could be caused by a vacuum leak, a shorted oxygen sensor wire, or a bad coolant temperature sensor. However, if the SERVICE ENGINE SOON light remains ON all or most of the time while in the field service mode, a rich mixture is indicated. This could be caused by the coolant temperature sensor, fuel in the charcoal canister, oxygen sensor contaminated, or a defective computer.

COMPONENT FAILURE

In the event of a part failure within the computerized ignition system, the car can be driven. However, the performance of the car will be limited and the CHECK ENGINE light will appear. This will allow the driver to bring the car in for service wihtout being towed or stranded.

Some systems have a backup called the CALPAK, Fig. 29-80. The CALPAK takes over in the event of failure in the circuit within the ECM that controls the fuel related items. The CALPAK is serviced in the same manner as the PROM.

CHECKING TIMING

Before checking the timing on this system, the diagnostic terminal must be grounded after the engine is started, Fig. 29-81. This is the same procedure for accessing the field service mode. After checking the timing, and making any needed adjustments, remove the paper clip grounding the diagnostic terminal. If the diagnostic terminal remains grounded, it may be the cause of hard starting and other driveability problems.

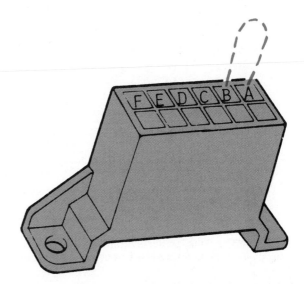

Fig. 29-81. Prior to checking and adjusting the timing, the diagnostic terminal must be jumped to the ground terminal. This is the same procedure as for accessing the field service mode. (Cadillac)

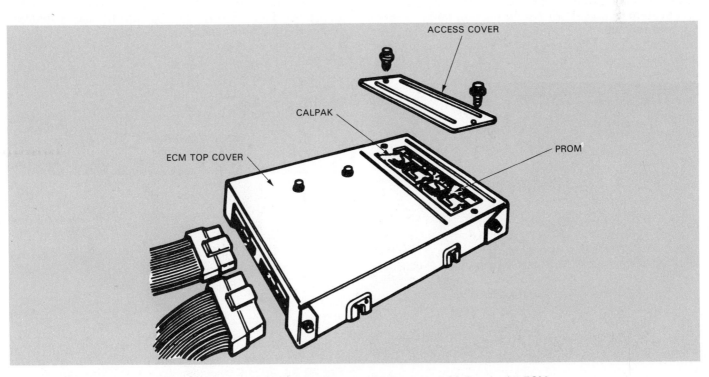

Fig. 29-80. The CALPAK takes over in the event of failure in the ECM circuit that controls fuel delivery. (Cadillac)

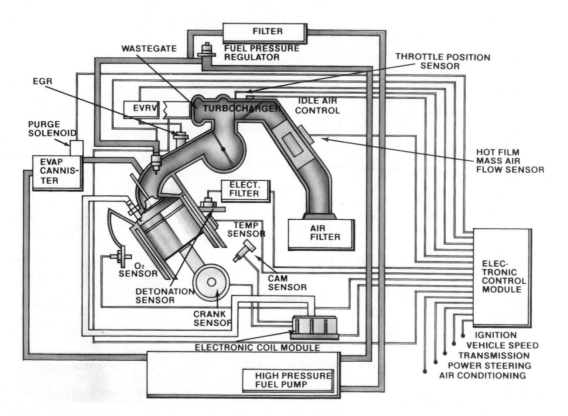

Fig. 29-82. This ignition system uses a hot film mass airflow sensor. The crankshaft position sensor on some six cylinder engines is a Hall Effect device. The camshaft sensor is not used on all engine applications. (Buick)

DIRECT IGNITION

The direct ignition system is characterized by the absence of a distributor, Fig. 29-82. The advantage of this system is that there are no moving parts to wear out and replace.

The direct ignition system carries the high voltage from the ignition coils to the spark plugs through spark plug wires, Fig. 29-83. The four cylinder engine uses two ignition coils, while a six cylinder engine uses three ignition coils, Fig. 29-84. The ignition module is located under the ignition coils, Fig. 29-85.

Fig. 29-83. This C3I ignition system has three ignition coils; each ignition coil services two cylinders. (Buick)

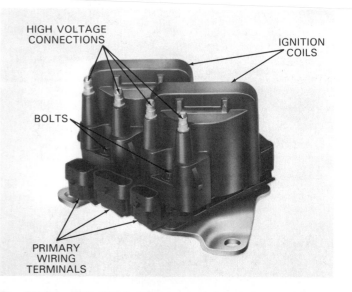

Fig. 29-84. This C3I ignition system has only two ignition coils, which means the engine has four cylinders. (Delco-Remy)

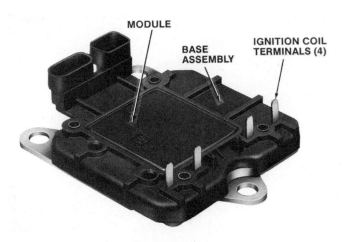

Fig. 29-85. The module is located under the ignition coils. The module interacts with the ECM. (Delco-Remy)

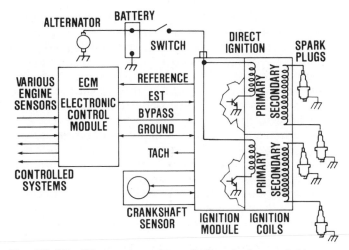

Fig. 29-86. When voltage is applied to the base of this transistor, current can flow from battery through transistor to primary windings of ignition coil.

The ignition module, Fig. 29-85, receives a voltage signal from the crankshaft position sensor. Sometimes a camshaft position sensor is also used. The ignition module then sends a voltage signal to the ECM and then transmits the voltage signal back to the ignition module, Fig. 29-86.

OPERATION

On engines that have a firing order of 1-3-4-2, one of the ignition coils *fires the spark plugs at cylinders 1 and 4 at the same time.* This means that the spark plug at cylinder 1 is fired near the end of the compression stroke, while the spark plug at cylinder 4 is fired at the end of the exhaust stroke. On the next cycle, the same ignition coil will fire the spark plug at cylinder 4 near the end of the compression stroke, while firing the spark plug at cylinder 1 at the end of the exhaust stroke. The other ignition coil fires cylinders 2 and 3 in the same manner. Since very little voltage is needed to fire a spark plug during the exhaust stroke, most of the available voltage is directed to the spark plug firing on the compression stroke. The ECM controls the timing during normal operating conditions, Fig. 29-87.

CAUTION! This system can produce 100 watts, which is far greater than a conventional ignition system. This amount is enough to kill you!

HOT FILM MASS AIRFLOW SENSOR

The hot film mass airflow sensor, Fig. 29-88, is used with this system. It combines the function of an air temperature sensor and airflow meter.

The air temperature sensor, which works the same way as a coolant temperature sensor, uses a thermistor in the middle of the wire. This is placed in the middle of the airflow in front of the hot film element. It is placed in front of the element because the element is heated. If it was placed behind the heated element, the heat from the element would be carried across the thermistor with the airflow and cause a false temperature reading. However, the air temperature sensor is electrically connected to the hot film element.

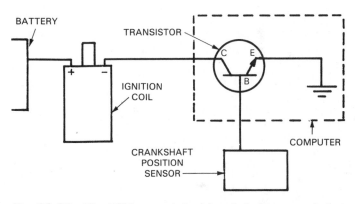

Fig. 29-87. The ECM controls ignition timing, except during cranking and ECM failure. The crankshaft position sensor controls ignition timing in those cases. (Delco-Remy)

Fig. 29-88. The hot film mass airflow sensor measures the temperature and the mass of incoming air. This determines the amount of spark advance, as well as the fuel mixture. (Buick)

The hot film element is electrically heated to a constant temperature. As the airflow increases, due to the speed of the car, the element is cooled and its resistance is adjusted. The amplifier then increases the voltage to the element to keep it at the prescribed temperature. The computer monitors the voltage that is sent from the amplifier. Its voltage, a digital signal, is equal to the mass of air flowing through the sensor.

A bad mass airflow sensor might be detected by the on-board diagnostics. However, the symptoms of a bad mass airflow sensor causes stalling as soon as the car is started or a no-start condition. Disconnecting the electrical connection at the sensor will determine if the sensor is at fault. If the stalling is eliminated or the car now starts, the mass airflow sensor is bad.

INTEGRATED DIRECT IGNITION

The Integrated Direct Ignition system operates in the same manner as the direct ignition, except that there are no spark plug wires, Fig. 29-89. The spark plugs, ignition module, ignition coils, and secondary conductors are all located under the cover, Fig. 29-90. The high voltage from the coils is carried to the spark plugs through the secondary conductors, Fig. 29-91.

CHECKING TIMING

The timing cannot be adjusted, as there is nothing to adjust. However, when the camshaft position sensor is used in this system, it is adjustable, Fig. 29-92. If the sensor is mis-adjusted, engine performance will be affected.

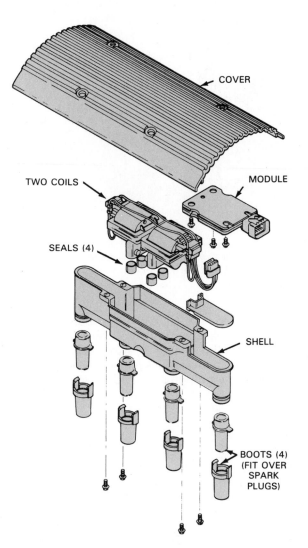

Fig. 29-90. The Integrated Direct ignition system. (Delco-Remy)

Fig. 29-89. All of the ignition components are located under the cover. Note that the spark plugs are not visible. (Pontiac)

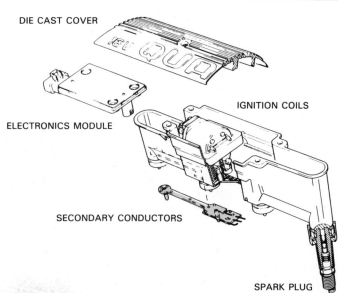

Fig. 29-91. The secondary conductor carries the high voltage from the ignition coils to the spark plugs. (Pontiac)

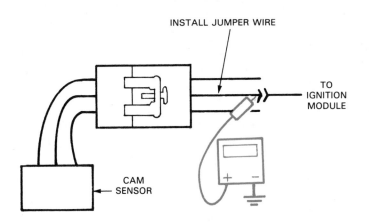

Fig. 29-92. Rotate the crankshaft so that No. 1 cylinder is at TDC of the compression stroke. Mark the harmonic balance, and then rotate the crankshaft to 25 degrees ATDC. Using a digital voltmeter, rotate the camshaft sensor counterclockwise until a reading of 2 to 0 V is obtained. This should only be checked if there is a driveability problem. (GM)

CHRYSLER'S COMPUTERIZED IGNITION SYSTEM

On Chrysler products with fuel injection, a logic module is used. The logic module is the heart of the computerized ignition system and is a digital microprocessor, Fig. 29-93. The logic module is located behind the right kick panel, Fig. 29-94. The MAP sensor is located in the logic module and can be removed for servicing, Fig. 29-95. The various sensors and actuators are shown in Fig. 29-96.

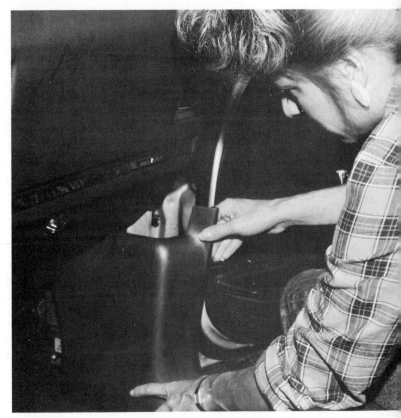

Fig. 29-94. To gain access to the logic module, the right kick panel must be removed.

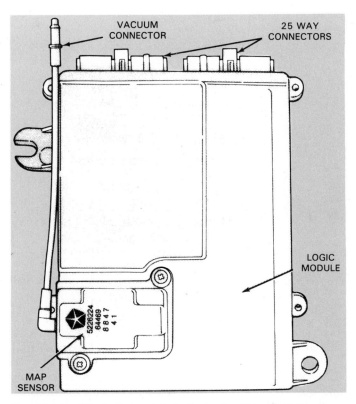

Fig. 29-93. The logic module is the brain of the Chrysler computerized system.

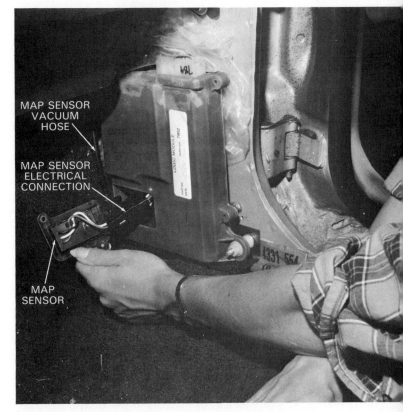

Fig. 29-95. The MAP sensor is located in the logic module on some applications, and can be serviced separately.

323

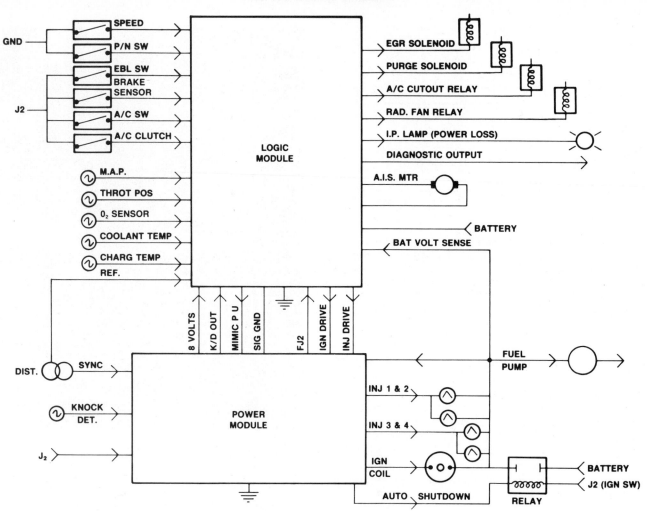

Fig. 29-96. The various sensors and actuators of Chrysler's computerized system.

LOGIC MODULE

The logic module controls ignition timing by measuring anti-dwell. Anti-dwell is the time during which the ignition coil fires the spark plug. The reason anti-dwell is measured, instead of dwell, is that anti-dwell can be measured faster. This causes the ignition spark advance to be more responsive to engine needs for increased power. Remember, "dwell" is the amount of time that the primary current is building the magnetic field in the ignition coil.

POWER MODULE

The power module, Figs. 29-96 and 29-97, receives a voltage signal from the distributor. As long as the power module receives this signal, it energizes:
1. Automatic Shutdown Relay (electric fuel pump relay).
2. Ignition Coil.
3. Fuel Injector(s).

The power module also reduces battery voltage to 8.0 volts. This reduced voltage, from the power module, energizes the Hall Effect sensor, in the distributor, and the logic module. The power module is located near the battery, Fig. 29-98.

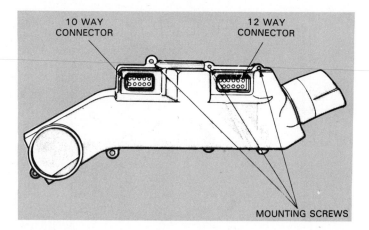

Fig. 29-97. The power module controls the fuel injectors, fuel pump, ignition coil, and logic module.

SINGLE MODULE ENGINE CONTROLLER (SMEC)

In 1988, Chrysler combined the function of the logic and power modules, Fig. 29-99. The SMEC module is in the same location that the power module used to occupy.

Fig. 29-98. The power module is located between the left front fender and the battery.

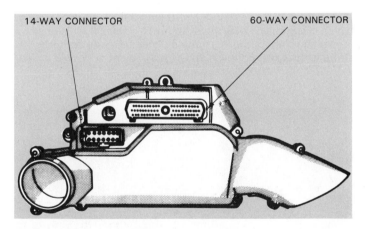

Fig. 29-99. The SMEC occupies the same space the power module once used, near the battery.

OPTICAL DISTRIBUTOR

On the 3.0 liter engine, a V-6 type, an optical distributor is used, Fig. 29-100. There are two light emitting diodes (LED) that transmit light to two photo diodes. When the photo diode senses the beam of light, a voltage signal is sent to the SMEC. This beam of light is interrupted by a disc driven at camshaft speed. This disc contains two slots, Fig. 29-101. One LED sends a beam of light through the HIGH DATA RATE SLOTS, Fig. 29-102. The HIGH DATA RATE SLOTS control the timing for speeds up to 1200 rpm. The other LED sends a beam of light through the LOW DATA RATE SLOTS.

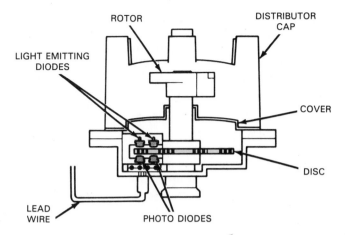

Fig. 29-100. The LED sends a beam of light to the photo diodes. (Chrysler)

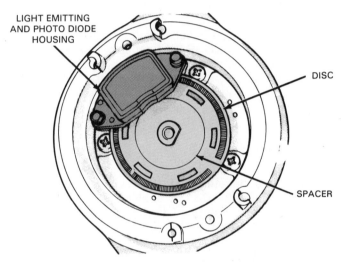

Fig. 29-101. The beam of light is sent through the slots in the disc. (Chrysler)

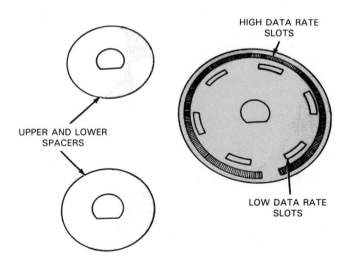

Fig. 29-102. The HIGH DATA RATE SLOTS control timing for speeds up to 1200 rpm. The LOW DATA RATE SLOTS control timing for speeds over 1200 rpm. The LOW DATA RATE SLOTS correspond to TDC of the compression stroke, and are also used to control the fuel injectors. (Chrysler)

The LOW DATA RATE SLOTS control the timing at speeds above 1200 rpm. Each of the LOW DATE RATE SLOTS SLOTS also represents TDC of the compression stroke for each cylinder. The LOW DATA RATE SLOTS are also used to determine when each of the fuel injectors are energized, and for the length of time that they are energized.

COMPONENT FAILURE

In the event of a part failure within the computerized system, the car will be driveable. However, the performance of the car will suffer greatly, and the POWER LOSS light will appear.

TROUBLE CODES

When the POWER LOSS light comes on, Fig. 29-103, it is time to use the on-board diagnostics. This means that the computer has the ability to diagnose trouble in the system. The computer continually receives signals from the sensors. If the sensors do not give the proper signal, the POWER LOSS light appears and remains on until the proper repairs are made. This light will appear while the engine is being started to let the driver know that the bulb is good. This light will not come on again unless there is trouble with the system.

ACCESSING CODES

To diagnose the fault, the POWER LOSS light will flash out codes, Fig. 29-103. To enable the POWER LOSS light to flash out codes, cycle the ignition switch ON, OFF, ON, OFF, ON, Fig. 29-104. This sequence must be completed within five seconds. Do not start the engine while cycling the key. The first set of flashes from the POWER LOSS light represent multiples of ten. Then, there will be a very brief pause, and a second set of flashes will represent multiples of ones. If there are any other trouble codes, the POWER LOSS light will also flash the specific code after a longer pause. For example, the POWER LOSS light, Fig. 29-103, flashes twice, then a brief pause, and then flashes twice again. The first set of flashes equal the number twenty, while the second set of flashes equal the number two. Adding the numbers twenty and two together, the number 22 is obtained. Using this information, look in the service manual to determine what ''Trouble Code 22'' means. After obtaining this information, the technician will have a starting point for diagnosis.

CAUTION ON THE TROUBLE CODES

After determining the trouble code and which fault is represented, some additional problem solving must be used. If the trouble code indicates that the coolant sensor is faulty, the problem may be elsewhere in the cooling system. For example, the coolant level may be low causing the trouble code for a faulty coolant sensor. Or, the thermostat may be stuck closed causing the engine to overheat. This will also cause the trouble code for a faulty coolant sensor. A short circuit or an open circuit can cause any of the sensors to produce a trouble code while the sensor is good.

Sometimes there are NO trouble codes indicated but a problem exists. When this occurs, the computer may be at fault, or a mechanical defect may be the cause. If there are more than several trouble codes indicated, the computer is probably at fault.

Fig. 29-103. The POWER LOSS light informs the driver that there is a problem with the system. This same light is used by the technician for pulling trouble codes from the computer. A trouble code of 55 means end of test, no more trouble codes.

Fig. 29-104. To enable the POWER LOSS light to flash out trouble codes, the ignition switch must be cycled OFF and ON three times within five seconds. The POWER LOSS light will glow for a short time before flashing out trouble codes.

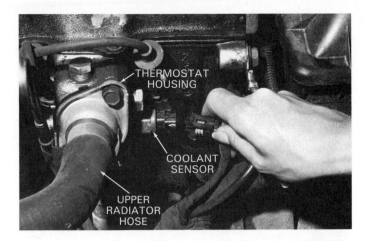

Fig. 29-105. Before checking and adjusting the timing, the coolant sensor must be disconnected. After checking the timing, make sure to reconnect the coolant sensor.

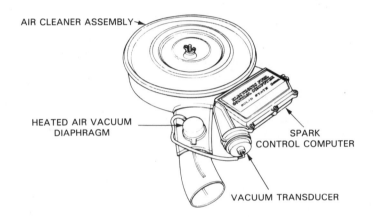

Fig. 29-106. The computer, on carbureted engines, is located on the air filter housing for rear wheel drive cars. The vacuum transducer measures the load. (Chrysler)

CLEARING TROUBLE CODES

Once the trouble code has been determined and the needed repairs made, the trouble codes must be cleared from the system. If the codes are not cleared, the POWER LOSS light will remain lit. To clear the trouble codes, simply remove the quick disconnect at the battery. After 10 seconds, reconnect the bullet type connector.

CHECKING TIMING

On this system, the coolant sensor electrical connection must be disconnected from the sensor before checking and adjusting the timing, Fig. 29-105. Once this has been done, the timing can be checked and adjusted in the normal fashion. Make sure to reconnect the sensor after checking the timing, or engine performance will suffer.

SPARK CONTROL COMPUTER

The spark control computer is used on Chrysler carbureted engines. The computer is of the digital type and is located on the air filter housing on the rear wheel drive cars, Fig. 29-105, and near the battery on the front wheel drive cars. The sensors are located on the engine. See Fig. 29-107:
1. Oxygen sensor.
2. Coolant sensor.
3. Vacuum transducer.
4. Camshaft position/engine speed sensor, Fig. 29-108.
5. Throttle position sensor.
6. Detonation sensor.

This specific system cannot flash out trouble codes. The preliminary step for checking engine timing is to disconnect and plug the vacuum hose from the vacuum transducer.

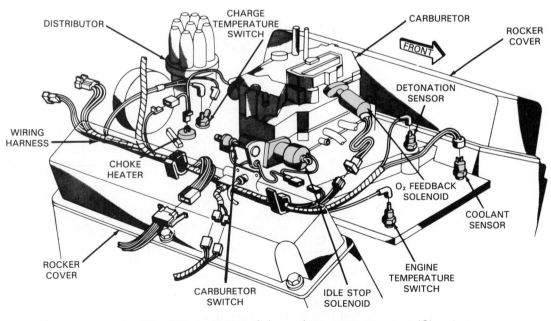

Fig. 29-107. Location of the various components. (Chrysler)

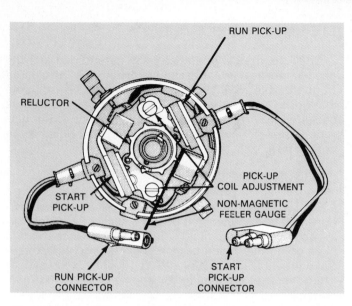

Fig. 29-108. The camshaft position sensor is located in the distributor, and uses two magnetic pick-up coils.   (Chrysler)

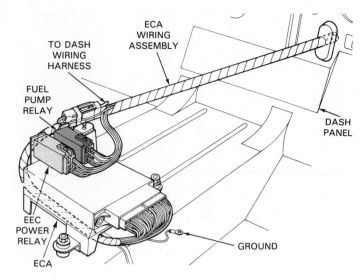

Fig. 29-109. The ECA is located under the front section of the center console. Note the location of the fuel pump relay and the power relay.   (Ford)

EEC IV

Ford has many computerized ignition systems. The Electronic Engine Control (EEC) IV is the most advanced computerized ignition system that Ford has to offer. The microprocessor, Fig. 29-109, is referred to as an Electronic Control Assembly (ECA).

The ECA is energized by the EEC Power Relay, Fig. 29-110. The EEC Power Relay, which is protected by a fuse, also allows current to the fuel pump relay. The fuel pump relay allows current to the inertia switch, which then allows current to the electric fuel pump, Fig. 29-110. The inertia switch interrupts current to the electric fuel pump in the event of an accident.

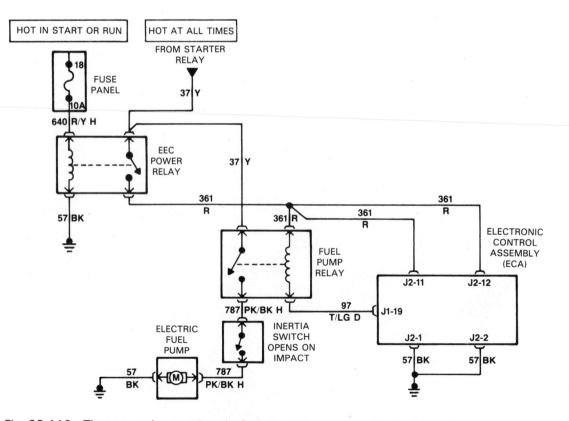

Fig. 29-110. The power relay energizes the fuel pump relay and the ECA. The fuel pump realy energizes the inertia switch, which then completes the circuit to the electric fuel pump.   (Ford)

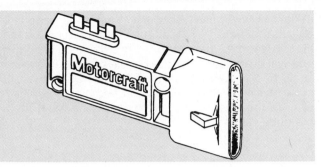

Fig. 29-111. Thick Film Ignition module type IV. The TFI module determines the duration of the spark. (Ford)

The Thick Film Ignition (TFI) Module, Figs. 29-111 and 29-112, Type IV is used on this ignition system. The TFI module sends and receives information from the ECA. The TFI module determines the duration of the spark.

The sensors used in the ECC IV system are:
1. Engine Coolant Temperature (ECT).
2. Profile Ignition Pick-up, Fig. 29-113.
3. Air Vane Meter Assembly, Fig. 29-114.
4. Throttle Position Sensor (TPS).
5. Oxygen Sensor.
6. A/C Clutch Signal.
7. Neutral/Drive Signal.

COMPONENT FAILURE

In the event of component failure, the car will still operate, but the ignition timing will be fixed at 10 degrees BTDC. This will cause a noticeable loss of power. However, no CHECK ENGINE light will appear.

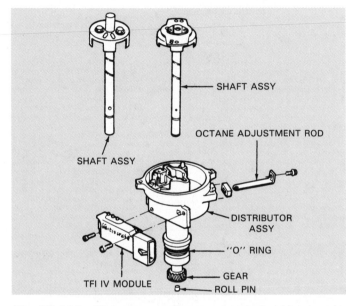

Fig. 29-112. The octane adjustment rod should never be replaced with a different length rod, as this would upset emissions requirement. (Ford)

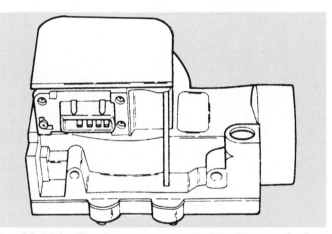

Fig. 29-114. The air vane meter assembly measures the flow of incoming air, as well as its temperature. (Ford)

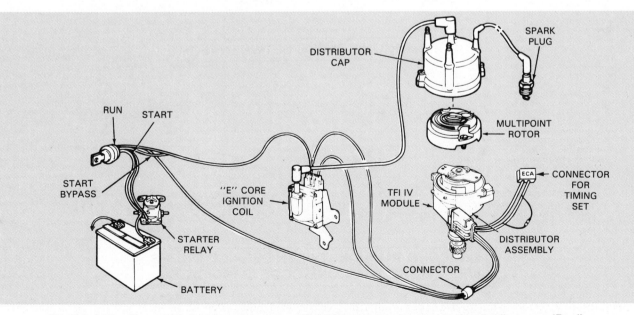

Fig. 29-113. The profile ignition pick-up is a Hall Effect sensor located in the distributor. (Ford)

ACCESSING CODES

To access the trouble codes, an analog voltmeter is needed. Ford dealerships have the use of a special tester that reads the trouble codes directly, Fig. 29-115.

The voltmeter red lead is clipped to the positive post of the battery. The negative lead from the voltmeter is inserted into PIN 4 of the Self-Test Connector, Fig. 29-116. The self-test connector is located at various points on different models. Consult the service manual for specific location. Then, jump PIN 2 to PIN 5 at the self-test connector, Fig. 29-116.

READING TROUBLE CODES

With the key to the ON position and the engine OFF, watch the voltmeter. The needle on the voltmeter will deflect very slightly. This is a "fast code" and is used only at the factory. This should be ignored by the technician. After the "fast code," the trouble codes will start and will be indicated by the needle moving to about mid-scale of the voltmeter, Fig. 29-117. Once the trouble code has been determined, the technician will have to refer to the service manual to determine what the trouble code means.

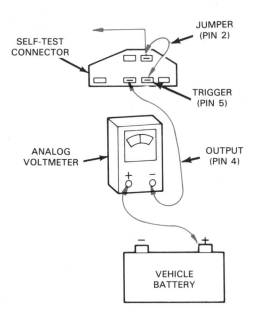

Fig. 29-116. Connections at the self-test connector used to access trouble codes. (Ford)

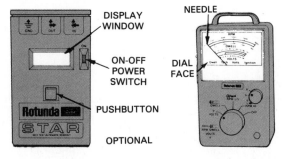

Fig. 29- 115. The STAR tester reads the trouble codes directly. If the STAR tester is not available, an analog voltmeter must be used. (Ford)

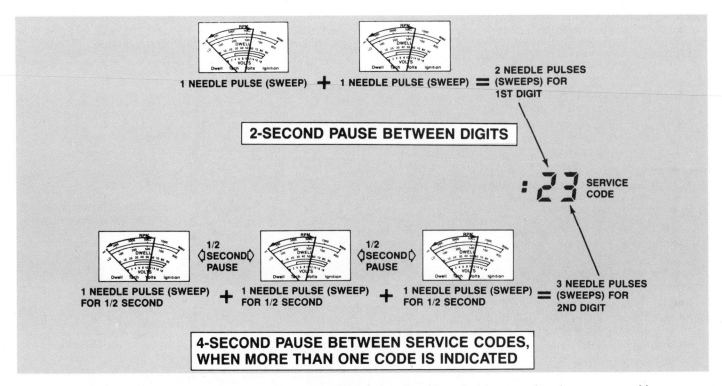

Fig. 29-117. Reading the trouble codes on an analog voltmeter. Trouble code 11 means that there are no problems with the system. (Ford)

ENGINE RUNNING

If there are no trouble codes indicated, and a problem still exists, check for trouble codes with the engine running. Once the engine is started, the engine must idle at least two minutes at 2000 rpm. After the engine is warmed-up, turn the engine OFF and install the jumper wire between PIN 2 and PIN 5 at the self-test connector, Fig. 29-116. Restart the engine. The trouble codes will start one minute after the needle is deflected twice to mid-scale on the voltmeter, which is known as an identification process and is used only by the factory. The trouble codes are read in the same manner as mentioned earlier.

CAUTION ON THE TROUBLE CODES

After determining the trouble code and which fault is represented, some additional problem solving must be used. If the trouble code indicates that the coolant sensor is faulty, the problem may be elsewhere in the cooling system. For example, the coolant level may be low causing the trouble code for a faulty coolant sensor. Or, the thermostat may be stuck closed causing the engine to overheat. This will also cause the trouble code for a faulty coolant sensor. A short circuit or an open circuit can cause any of the sensors to produce a trouble code while the sensor is good.

Sometimes there are NO trouble codes indicated and a problem exists. When this occurs, the computer may be at fault, or a mechanical defect may be the cause. Or, if there are more than several trouble codes indicated, the computer is probably at fault.

INTERMITTENT PROBLEMS

If the problem is intermittent, disconnect the jumper wire between PIN 2 and PIN 5 at the self-test connector while the ignition switch is at the OFF position. Then, turn the ignition switch to the ON position. With the ignition switch in the ON position, the engine can be OFF or running, wiggle and tap all sensor connections and the harness connection at the computer while observing the voltmeter. If the needle on the voltmeter deflects while tapping and wiggling the connections, the trouble code will be stored and can be accessed in the same manner as mentioned earlier. However, DO NOT turn the ignition key OFF or the trouble codes will be erased.

PERFORMANCE TESTING

Start the engine and connect a jumper wire between PIN 2 and PIN 5 of the self-test connector. The timing should be between 27 and 33 degrees BTDC. If the timing is not between 27 and 33 degrees BTDC, the technician must refer to PINPOINT testing in the Engine/Emissions Diagnosis Manual for the year of the car that is being serviced. The only time the technician is to start with the PINPOINT testing is if the engine does not start.

Pinpoint testing involves a logical step-by-step testing of all parts of the computerized ignition system. The technician should not deviate from the sequence.

CHECKING THE TIMING

To check the base timing, disconnect the yellow wire with green dots that is located at the distributor. The timing can then be checked in the normal fashion. The initial timing should be 10 degrees BTDC. Also, make sure to re-connect this wire after checking the timing. A timing light with an inductive pick-up must be used with this system.

DIGITAL VOLT/OHMMETERS

A digital volt/ohmmeter, Fig. 29-118, with at least 10,000 ohms (10 Megohms) input impedance must be used to check the sensors, or the computer will be damaged. Also, some voltage specifications are given in tenths of a volt for computerized ignition systems. This is impossible to read with an analog voltmeter. A narrow range may also be given that would be extremely hard to read on an analog volt/ohmmeter.

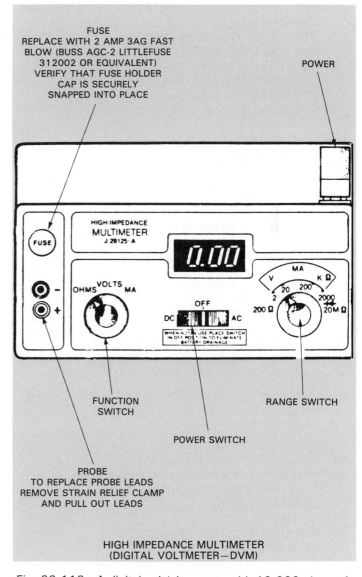

Fig. 29-118. A digital volt/ohmmeter with 10,000 ohms of impedance must be used when testing a computerized system. (Cadillac)

Chapter 29—REVIEW QUESTIONS

Write your answers on a separate sheet of paper. Do not write in this book.

1. Which are components of the secondary side of the ignition?
   a. Distributor cap, rotor, ignition coil, and the spark plugs.
   b. Points and condenser.
   c. Computer.
   d. Battery.
   e. All of the above.

2. The rotor:
   a. Is located under the distributor cap.
   b. Moves at camshaft speed.
   c. Distributes high voltage at the proper time.
   d. All of the above.
   e. None of the above.

3. Briefly explain how battery voltage is transformed into 20,000 volts.

4. If the spark plugs are fouled, the technician should first diagnose the cause before replacing the plugs. True or False?

5. The timing marks are located only on the harmonic balance. True or False?

6. On a computerized system, the spark is advanced proportionately in relation with many factors. True or False?

7. The computerized ignition system consists of:
   a. Software.
   b. Hardware.
   c. Both a and b.
   d. Neither a nor b.

8. The digital computer is the only type of computer. True or False?

9. The crankshaft position sensor tells the computer:
   a. That the piston is at TDC of a compression stroke.
   b. That the piston is at BDC of a compression stroke.
   c. Both a and b.
   d. Neither a nor b.

10. Most of the time the Hall Effect device is located in the distributor and measures the position of the crankshaft indirectly. True or False?

11. There are how many different types of crankshaft position sensors described in this chapter?
    a. 1.
    b. 2.
    c. 3.
    d. 4.
    e. 5.

12. The airflow meter is used to:
    a. Sense the load placed on the engine.
    b. Sense the position of the throttle.
    c. Both a and b.
    d. Neither a nor b.

13. The throttle position sensor:
    a. Is adjustable.
    b. Tells the computer how much spark advance is needed.
    c. Tells the computer how much fuel is needed.
    d. All of the above.
    e. None of the above.

14. The MAP sensor:
    a. Is located above the throttle plate.
    b. Measures the load placed on the engine.
    c. Both a and b.
    d. Neither a nor b.

15. The input from the MAP sensor is used to:
    a. Advance the timing.
    b. Richen the fuel mixture.
    c. Both a and b.
    d. Neither a nor b.

16. There are how many different MAP sensor designs?
    a. 1.
    b. 2.
    c. 3.
    d. 4.
    e. 5.

17. The voltage signal sent to the computer from the coolant temperature sensor is increased as the engine warms-up. True or False?

18. Information from the coolant sensor is used to:
    a. Determine the amount of spark advance.
    b. Determine the fuel mixture.
    c. Control some of the actuators.
    d. All of the above.

19. The oxygen sensor signals the computer to control the fuel mixture when in the closed loop mode. True or False?

20. When there is a lack of oxygen in the exhaust, the oxygen sensor becomes a battery and produces voltage. True or False?

21. Which are actuators?
    a. Ignition coil.
    b. Fuel injectors.
    c. EGR solenoid.
    d. Idle speed motor.
    e. All of the above.

22. Mechanic A states that to access trouble codes in the GM CCC system, the diagnostic terminal must be grounded.
    Mechanic B states that to access the trouble codes in Chrysler's computerized ignition system, the ignition switch must be cycled ON and OFF three times within five seconds.
    Who is right?
    a. Mechanic A.
    b. Mechanic B.
    c. Both Mechanics A and B.
    d. Neither Mechanic A nor B.

23. Mechanic A states that prior to checking the timing on the GM computerized ignition system, the coolant sensor must first be disconnected.
    Mechanic B states that prior to checking the timing on GM's computerized ignition system, the electrical connection at the distributor must first be disconnected.
    Who is right?
    a. Mechanic A.
    b. Mechanic B.
    c. Both Mechanics A and B.
    d. Neither Mechanic A nor B.

Chapter 30

AUTOMOTIVE BATTERIES

After studying this chapter, you will be able to:
- State three functions of an automotive battery.
- List basic parts of a typical automotive battery.
- Describe chemical reactions within battery cells during discharge and charge.
- Give two methods of rating battery performance.
- Explain three methods of testing an automotive battery.
- List safe battery servicing practices.
- Identify four methods of charging a battery.
- State sequence of steps of procedure for jump starting an engine.

The LEAD-ACID STORAGE BATTERY used in automobiles and other vehicles is an electrochemical device that converts chemical energy into electrical energy. When the battery is connected to an external load, such as a starting motor, the energy conversion takes place and electricity flows through the circuit.

BATTERY FUNCTIONS

The lead-acid automotive battery, Figs. 30-1 and 30-2, has three main functions:
1. It serves as a source of power for the starting motor and ignition system for cranking and starting an internal combustion engine.
2. It acts as a stabilizer of voltage for the entire automotive electrical system.
3. It furnishes current for a limited time whenever electrical demands exceed alternator output.

SIZES AND TYPES

Storage batteries used in automobiles vary in size, capacity, and cranking power. In addition, there are CONVENTIONAL (wet, moist, or dry charged) BATTERIES and MAINTENANCE-FREE (Freedom, low water loss) BATTERIES. Yet, their basic construction is very similar.

BATTERY CONSTRUCTION

A typical 12 volt, lead-acid automotive battery is made up of six CELLS connected in series, Fig. 30-3, and filled

Fig. 30-1. Typical conventional battery for use in cranking, starting, and lighting passenger cars.

with ELECTROLYTE (sulfuric acid diluted with water). Each cell will produce approximately two volts.

CELLS

Each battery cell contains PLATES composed of special active materials contained in cast grids. The PLATE GRIDS usually are rectangular, flat, lattice-like castings with a relatively heavy framework around a hexagonal, diagonal, or vertical and horizontal mesh. See Fig. 30-4. The POSITIVE PLATES generally contain lead dioxide (PbO_2), which is chocolate brown. The NEGATIVE PLATES contain sponge lead (Pb), which is gray.

PLATES AND PLATE GROUPS

Each cell of a storage battery is made up of alternate positive and negative plates. A PLATE GROUP is made by welding a number of plates of the same polarity to a post strap. During assembly, plate groups of opposite polarity are interlaced, Fig. 30-4.

Usually, negative plate groups contain one more plate than the positive plate group within the same cell to help equalize the chemical activity.

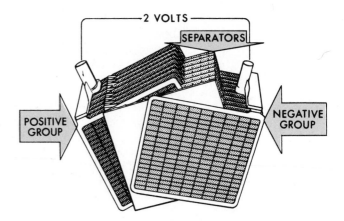

Fig. 30-4. One element of a battery consists of a group of positive plates, and a group of negative plates, plus separators.

Fig. 30-2. General Motors "Freedom" battery has a sealed-in lifetime supply of electrolyte. Test indicator shows state of charge.

SEPARATORS

To insure that adjacent plates do not touch each other, SEPARATORS are placed between them. See Fig. 30-4. This assembly of positive and negative plates and separators is called an ELEMENT. There is one element per cell.

Separators are made of sheets of porous, nonconducting material such as resin impregnated cellulose fibers, various plastic materials, rubber, or fiberglass. Battery separators must be chemically resistant to sulfuric acid. They must be strong, yet porous enough to permit free passage of the electrolyte. The separators prevent the active chemicals in the plates from touching each other through expansion.

Some maintenance-free batteries use ENVELOPE SEPARATORS rather than sheets. See Fig. 30-5. Each plate is contained in an envelope that is closed on three sides. The envelopes extend to the bottom of the battery case, avoiding the need for sediment chambers.

ELEMENTS AND CASE

The elements of positive and negative plates and separators are placed in each cell of the outside case or shell of the battery, between partitions built into the

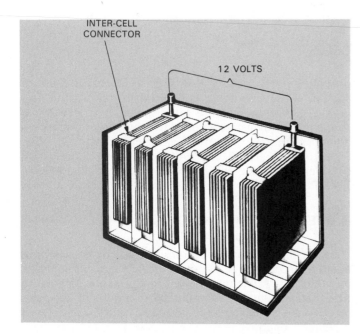

Fig. 30-3. Typical arrangement of cells and straight-through cell connectors in a 12 volt battery.

Fig. 30-5. Envelope separators are used in many maintenance-free batteries instead of "sheet" separators.
(ESB Incorporated)

case. Generally, the case is molded polypropylene (impact and acid-resistant) or hard rubber.

The lower edge of each element of conventional batteries is supported on ''bridges'' or element rests at the bottom of the case, running the full length of each cell. See Fig. 30-3. The plates are positioned at right angles to the element rests. The spaces between the rests are sediment chambers designed to collect active material shed from the plates.

Most battery cases are formed with hold-down ramps on two sides at the bottom. See Figs. 30-1 and 30-2. Many cases are designed for top or bottom hold-down mounting.

INTERCELL CONNECTORS

With the elements in place in the battery case, INTERCELL CONNECTORS (element terminal posts) are inserted either through holes in the case partitions or over the partitions. This design provides a short, low resistance path through the battery. See Fig. 30-6.

In conventional batteries, the intercell connectors are placed on the top side of the plates on the side opposite the posts and post straps. In some maintenance-free batteries, the through-the-partition intercell connectors are centered for increased vibration protection.

ELECTROLYTE

The battery is ACTIVATED by the addition of electrolyte, a mixture of sulfuric acid and water. This solution causes the chemical actions to take place between the lead dioxide of the positive plate and the sponge lead of the negative plate. The electrolyte is also the carrier that moves electric current between the positive and negative plates through the separators.

Lead-acid storage batteries use a fairly concentrated solution of sulfuric acid and water having a ''fully charged'' specific gravity of 1.265 corrected to 80°F (27°C). SPECIFIC GRAVITY is the weight of a given volume of a liquid divided by the weight of an equal volume of water. Water has arbitrarily been assigned a value of 1.000. Therefore, electrolyte with a specific gravity of 1.265 means it is 1.265 times heavier than an equal volume of pure water when both liquids are at the same temperature.

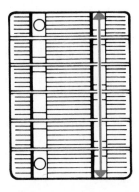

Fig. 30-6. Intercell connectors provide a direct, low resistance path through or over battery case partitions.
(ESB Incorporated)

FORMING CHARGE

Batteries may be produced as ''charged and wet,'' or ''charged and moist,'' or ''dry charged.'' When a battery is CHARGED AND WET, it has been given a FORMING CHARGE at the factory, and it is shipped filled with electrolyte of 1.265 specific gravity.

When a battery is CHARGED AND MOIST, it has been given the forming charge, but practically all of the electrolyte was removed. After draining, the cells were sealed and the battery was shipped. Upon being placed in service, it must be ''activated'' with electrolyte of 1.265 specific gravity.

When a battery is DRY CHARGED, it received the forming charge, then the plates or elements were washed and dried before the battery was sealed. Dry charged batteries must be filled with electrolyte and BOOST CHARGED (light finishing charge of 5 to 15 amps.) before being placed in service.

Some maintenance-free batteries are dry charged. These batteries feature an access vent on the cover that can be opened for activation, testing, or to replace water if overcharging has occurred.

COVERS AND TERMINALS

Cell covers usually are made of plastic material or hard rubber, Figs. 30-1 and 30-2. The one-piece cover is bonded (usually heat-sealed) to the case, and the battery posts (terminals) are sealed at the cover.

There are three major types of posts or terminals:
1. Tapered posts. The positive post is slightly larger in diameter at the top than the negative post to help guard against installing the battery in reverse.
2. Side terminals. Internally threaded terminals are molded into the side wall of the battery near the top edge. Each battery cable is attached to the proper terminal by means of a bolt that threads into the terminal.
3. ''L'' terminals. L-shaped metal terminals are mounted on top of the battery. The upright portion of the ''L'' has a hole. The battery cable is attached to the terminal by means of a bolt and a wing nut.

VENT PLUGS AND VENTS

Vent plugs of various designs are used. Usually, the vent plugs are baffled so gas can escape, but electrolyte splashed into the vent will drain into the cell. The plugs may be screw type or push-in type. The push-in type may be a single plug or a gang vent plug (three-plug-manifold).

Most maintenance-free batteries do not use vent plugs, Fig. 30-7. Instead, the gas is vented through baffled passages and small vent holes in the cover. Most conventional batteries have flame arrester vent plugs, Fig. 30-8. In maintenance-free batteries, the flame arresters are located at the exits of the baffled passages.

MAINTENANCE-FREE BATTERIES

While the internal construction of maintenance-free batteries appears to be similar to conventional batteries, differences may include the use of envelope separators,

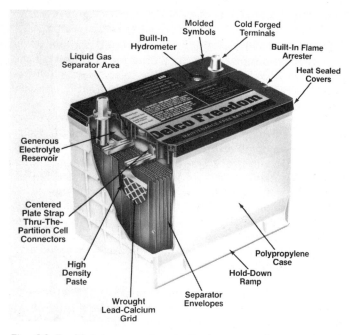

Fig. 30-7. Maintenance-free batteries generally are vented through baffled passages and vent holes in cover.

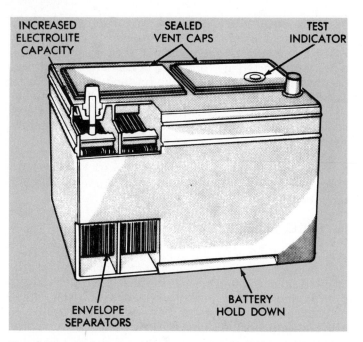

Fig. 30-9. Maintenance-free batteries provide many advantages over conventional automotive batteries. (Chrysler Corp.)

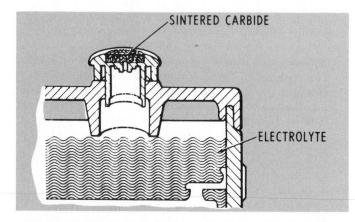

Fig. 30-8. This Chevrolet vent cap has a flame arrestor of sintered carbide that disperses fumes and protects battery from flame entry.

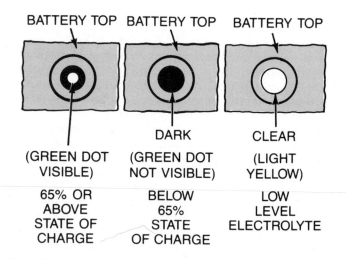

Fig. 30-10. Maintenance-free batteries usually have a temperature-compensated hydrometer built into top of battery. (Cadillac Motor Div., General Motors Corp.)

Figs. 30-5 and 30-9, and expanded plate grids containing calcium, cadmium, or strontium to reduce gassing and self-discharge. Also, activation is eliminated, as is boost charging, prior to installation.

Maintenance-free batteries also have a greater electrolyte reserve above the plates, better overcharge resistance, and less tendency toward terminal corrosion than conventional batteries.

With maintenance-free batteries, no electrolyte level checks or additions are necessary. Most have a built-in hydrometer or a visual test indicator in the cover. See Fig. 30-10.

CHEMICAL ACTIONS

The CHEMICAL ACTIONS that take place during charging and discharging of a lead-acid automotive bat-

tery are shown in Fig. 30-11. In a charged condition, the positive plate material is essentially pure lead dioxide, PbO_2. The active material of the negative plates is spongy lead, Pb. The electrolyte is a solution of sulfuric acid, H_2SO_4, and water. The voltage of the cell depends upon the chemical difference between the active materials. The concentration of the electrolyte also has an affect on voltage.

DISCHARGE CYCLE

The DISCHARGE CYCLE occurs when an electric load is connected to the battery and current flows. The cur-

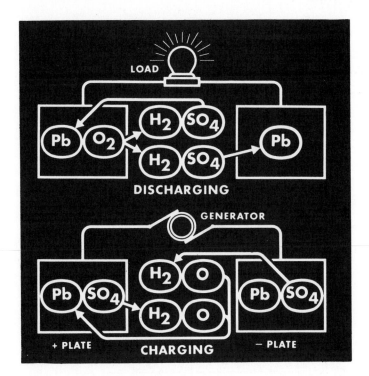

Fig. 30-11. Chemical reactions within lead-acid automotive battery are graphically shown.

rent is produced by the chemical reactions between the active materials of the two kinds of battery plates and the sulfuric acid. As shown in Fig. 30-11, the oxygen in the PbO_2 combines with the hydrogen, H_2, from the sulfuric acid to form water, H_2O. At the same time, the lead, Pb, in the lead dioxide combines with the SO_4 portion of the sulfuric acid to form lead sulfate, $PbSO_4$.

A similar action takes place at the negative plate, where the lead, Pb, of the negative active material combines with the SO_4 of the sulfuric acid to form $PbSO_4$, lead sulfate. As the discharge continues, the plates are becoming more alike and the electrolyte is getter weaker. Therefore, the voltage is becoming lower since it depends on the difference between the two plate materials and the concentration of the electrolyte.

While there is an electric load on the battery, lead sulfate is formed on both positive and negative plates and the electrolyte becmes diluted with water. As the discharge continues, the accumulation of lead sulfate on the plates and the dilution of the electrolyte lowers the specific gravity. When the chemical action can no longer take place, the battery is said to be discharged.

CHARGE CYCLE

The lead-acid storage battery is chemically reversible. A discharged battery can be charged by passing current through the plates in a direction opposite to the direction of discharge. See Fig. 30-11. Its active chemicals will be restored to a charged condition.

During the CHARGE CYCLE, the chemical reactions are basically the reverse of those which occur during discharge. The $PbSO_4$, lead sulfate, on both plates is split into Pb and SO_4, while the H_2O, water, is split into

hydrogen, H_2, and oxygen, O. The passage of the charging current, which is in the reverse direction of the discharging current, forces the SO_4 from the plates and combines with the H_2 to form H_2SO_4, sulfuric acid. At the same time, the oxygen combines with the lead at the positive plate to form PbO_2.

The specific gravity of the electrolyte decreases during discharge for two reasons. Not only is the sulfuric acid used up, but new water is formed. Since the water is formed at the positive plates and diffuses slowly through the electrolyte, the positive plates are more likely to be damaged during freezing weather. When the battery is fully charged, the specific gravity of the solution increases, sulfuric acid is formed, and the water is used up. As a result, there is little danger of a fully charged battery freezing.

BATTERY VOLTAGE AND CAPACITY

The OPEN CIRCUIT VOLTAGE (no load voltage) of a fully charged automotive battery is 12.6 volts or more for electrolyte of approximately 1.265 specific gravity. This is true regardless of the number of plates per cell, or their area. The voltage is determined only by the character of the chemicals in the plates and the specific gravity of the electrolyte.

The CAPACITY of a battery is the amount of current it will deliver. Capacity depends on the number and area of plates in the cells and also on the amount of electrolyte present. Cells having a large number of plates will deliver more current than cells having a smaller number. Automotive lead-acid batteries are built with large, porous, low density plates so the electrolyte will have quick access to as much active plate surface area as possible.

Battery capacity drops rapidly as the temperature drops. This "drop" occurs because the battery is an electrochemical device and, like virtually all chemical actions, it is aided by heat. For example, if the capacity of cranking power of a battery at 80°F (26.7 °C) is given as 100 percent, at 32 °F (0 °C) the capacity will be only 65 percent. At 0 °F (− 17.8 °C), it will be only 40 percent. See Fig. 30-12.

BATTERY RATINGS

Two methods of rating the performance of lead-acid batteries have been established by the Battery Council

COMPARISON OF CRANKING POWER AVAILABLE FROM FULLY CHARGED BATTERY AT VARIOUS TEMPERATURES

Temperature	Cranking Power
80°F (26.7°C)	100 %
32°F (0°C)	65 %
0°F (−17.8°C)	40 %

Fig. 30-12. Capacity of cranking power falls off sharply with a drop in temperature. (Battery Council International)

International (BCI). These standards are designed to indicate a battery's power-delivering capability:
1. Cold cranking rating.
2. Reserve capacity rating.

The COLD CRANKING RATING determines the amount of current (amps.) a battery can deliver for 30 seconds at 0°F (−17.8°C) and still maintain a terminal voltage of 7.2 volts, or 1.2 volts per cell. The rating is given as amps. @ 0°F (−17.8°C). The cold cranking rating provides a means of determining whether a battery will crank a given engine (based on amperage draw of starter) over a wide range of ambient (surrounding air) temperatures.

The RESERVE CAPACITY RATING is the time required to reduce a fully charged battery's terminal voltage below 10.2 volts, or 1.7 volts per cell, at a continuous discharge rate of 25 amps. at approximately 80°F (26.7°C). The test is a straight draw on the battery, without any charging system input.

The reserve capacity rating appears on the battery as a time interval. For example, a rating of 100 minutes means that once the indicating lamp comes on, the driver has one hour and 40 minutes of driving time under minimum electrical load to get to a service facility.

BATTERY INSPECTION

The first test of the condition of any used battery is a visual inspection, backed by a manual check for loose cable connections and/or loose battery posts. Look carefully for defective cables, eroded cable clamps, accumulated corrosion deposits, cracks in the battery cover or case, and for a loose or broken hold-down device. Clean, repair, or replace parts as required.

The next consideration — when servicing conventional batteries — is an electrolyte level check. If necessary, add distilled water or a good grade of drinking water (not mineral water). Refill to the electrolyte level indicator or to 1/2 in. (13 mm) above the top of the separators. Do not overfill.

BATTERY TESTING

There are several methods used to test the state of charge and condition of an automotive battery. In general, these methods include:
1. Hydrometer test.
2. Heavy load test.
3. Open circuit voltage test.

HYDROMETER TEST

The HYDROMETER, Fig. 30-13, is an instrument used to test state of charge of a battery.

The STATE OF CHARGE of a conventional lead-acid battery can be determined by testing the specific gravity of the electrolyte. Do not, however, make the hydrometer test immediately after water has been added to the electrolyte. Measurement should be made before the water is added in order to obtain a representative sample. If the level is too low to obtain a sample, water should be added as needed. Then, after the battery has been in use long enough to thoroughly mix the

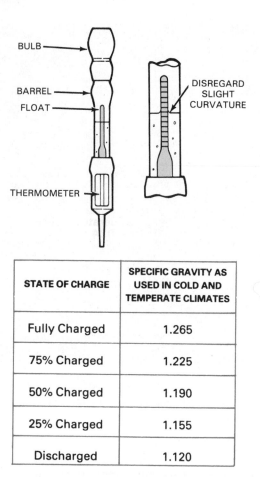

STATE OF CHARGE	SPECIFIC GRAVITY AS USED IN COLD AND TEMPERATE CLIMATES
Fully Charged	1.265
75% Charged	1.225
50% Charged	1.190
25% Charged	1.155
Discharged	1.120

Fig. 30-13. To read hydrometer, squeeze bulb to draw enough electrolyte from cell to raise float. Float should not touch barrel of hydrometer. Release pressure on bulb and observe specific gravity reading on float. Check thermometer and compute temperature-corrected specific gravity of electrolyte.

water with the electrolyte, the sample may be taken with the hydrometer.

See Fig. 30-13 for instructions on how to read the hydrometer. To make the hydrometer test, check the specific gravity of each cell. The generally accepted full charge reading is 1.265. Compare the lowest and highest readings. If there is more than .050 difference in the readings, replace the battery. If the readings are about the same, they can be checked against the chart in Fig. 30-13 to determine percent of full charge or, in effect, state of charge.

Note that hydrometer readings should not be taken while the battery is gassing. This condition would affect the accuracy of the reading.

Remember, too, when checking the specific gravity of a battery cell, you must check the temperature of the electrolyte and make the necessary correction. Fill, empty, and refill the hydrometer tube with samples of electrolyte to get a sample of the proper temperature. See Fig. 30-14.

As mentioned earlier, most maintenance-free batteries have a built-in hydrometer or a visual test indicator in the cover. When making a visual test, for example, a green, black, clear or yellow color code is used on General Motors Freedom batteries. Green signals a 65

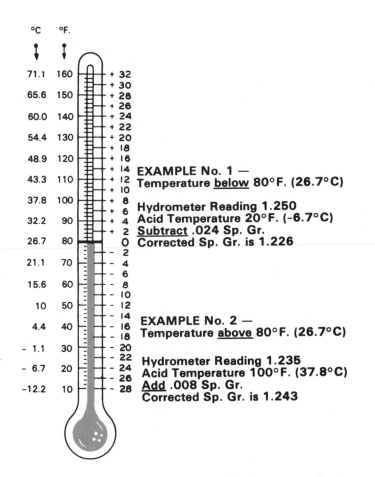

EXAMPLE No. 1 —
Temperature below 80°F. (26.7°C)

Hydrometer Reading 1.250
Acid Temperature 20°F. (-6.7°C)
Subtract .024 Sp. Gr.
Corrected Sp. Gr. is 1.226

EXAMPLE No. 2 —
Temperature above 80°F. (26.7°C)

Hydrometer Reading 1.235
Acid Temperature 100°F. (37.8°C)
Add .008 Sp. Gr.
Corrected Sp. Gr. is 1.243

Fig. 30-14. Temperature correction of hydrometer reading involves changing reading .004 points of specific gravity for each 10°F (5.5°C) electrolyte temperature is above or below 80°F (26.7°C).

equipped, and install a thermometer in electrolyte.
2. Connect a battery load tester, Fig. 30-15 and 30-16, or a battery starter tester, directly to battery posts: positive to positive; negative to negative.
3. Turn carbon pile knob to apply a load equal to 50 percent of cold cranking rating of battery being tested.
4. Read voltmeter while load is being applied for 15 seconds. Turn carbon pile knob to OFF position. Record voltage.
5. Read thermometer, record temperature, and check temperature and voltage against chart in Fig. 30-15.
6. Replace battery if minimum voltage is below specification.
7. If reading is the same or greater than voltage shown on chart, clean and fully charge. The battery should remain in service.

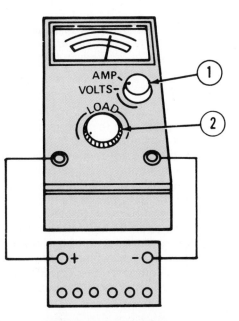

LOAD TEST CHART		
Minimum Voltage	**Temperature**	
	F°	C°
9.6	70 and above	21 and above
9.5	60	16
9.4	50	10
9.3	40	4
9.1	30	−1
8.9	20	−7
8.7	10	−12
8.5	0	−18

Fig. 30-15. Battery load tester has carbon pile to impose heavy load of three times ampere hour rating of battery. Voltage reading after 15 sec. under load determines battery condition. See minimum voltage values at temperatures shown in chart. (American Motors Corp.)

percent-or-above state of charge. Black indicates below 65 percent state of charge. Clear means a low electrolyte level. See Fig. 30-10.

On late model Chrysler products, the visual test indicator uses a green, black, red, and yellow color code. Green indicates a 75 percent-or-above state of charge. Black means a state of charge between 50 and 75 percent. Red signals a state of charge below 50 percent. Yellow indicates a low electrolyte level.

These readings merely reveal "state of charge," not battery condition. Various tests must be made to establish whether recharging or battery replacement is required.

HEAVY LOAD TEST

The HEAVY LOAD TEST (also called "high rate discharge" or "capacity" test) is a good test of the battery's ability to perform under load. In this test, a good battery will produce current equal to 50 percent of its cold cranking rating (or equal to three times its ampere hour rating) for 15 seconds and still provide minimum voltage to start the engine.

To make the heavy load test:
1. Charge battery, if necessary, until all cells are at least 1.225 Specific gravity. Remove vent caps, if so

OPEN CIRCUIT VOLTAGE TEST

If the battery fails the heavy load test, check its state of charge by making a stabilized OPEN CIRCUIT

Fig. 30-16. Heavy load tester has adjustable load control up to 500 amps, battery temperature compensation, and state of charge reading. (Christie Electric Corp.)

VOLTAGE test. Allow at least 10 minutes after the load test for the battery voltage to stabilize, then measure and record open circuit voltage.

There are many types of test equipment available for making the open circuit voltage test. In general, a voltmeter is used by connecting its positive lead to the positive post of the battery and its negative lead to the negative post of the battery. See Fig. 30-17.

To analyze the open circuit voltage test result, consider that a battery at a temperature of 60 to 100 °F (16 to 38 °C) in good condition should show approximately 12.4 volts on the voltmeter. See Fig. 30-17. If the state of charge is 75 percent or more, the battery is considered

"charged."

However, if the state of charge is under 75 percent, the battery should be recharged, then load tested again. If it fails the load test again, the battery should be replaced. If it passes, the battery should remain in service.

SAFETY PRECAUTIONS

Working with batteries poses several safety problems. Spilled electrolyte can "eat" holes in clothing and burn the skin. Electrolyte splashed into the eyes is sight-threatening. Also, explosive gases are generated within the battery cells. For safety sake, it pays to wear safety goggles or a face shield and observe all safe servicing practices when working on or near batteries.

HANDLING ELECTROLYTE

Avoid contact with the battery electrolyte, if possible. If electrolyte does get on your clothing, body, or finish of the car being serviced, neutralize it immediately with a solution of baking soda and water, then rinse with clean water.

If electrolyte is splashed into the eyes, flood the eyes with cool, clean water for about five minutes and get medical help as quickly as possible. If electrolyte is accidentally swallowed, drink large quantities of water or milk, followed by milk of magnesia or vegetable oil. Call a doctor immediately.

If you are mixing sulfuric acid and water to make up an electrolyte solution of a certain specific gravity:
1. Use a lead, lead-lined, or nonmetallic container.
2. Always pour acid slowly into water. Do not pour water into acid.
3. Add small amounts of acid at a time while stirring solution.
4. Repeatedly test specific gravity with a hydrometer until solution reaches desired gravity reading.

DANGER OF EXPLOSION

Chemical reactions within the battery create explosive mixtures of hydrogen and oxygen. These gases are generated within the cells during normal battery operation. Even a battery standing idle self-discharges and produces a small amount of hydrogen. There is always the danger of an external spark or flame setting off an explosion of the gases within the cells and possibly shattering the battery.

Another danger is that the generated gases may escape through the battery vents and form an explosive atmosphere around the battery. In these situations, a match being struck, a lighted cigarette, or any spark or flame could ignite the gases and cause an explosion.

Most vent plugs on conventional batteries have flame arresters designed to prevent the ignition of gases within the battery by external sparks or flames. See Fig. 30-8. Maintenance-free batteries have flame arresters at exits of the baffled passages in the cover. See Fig. 30-7. In spite of these preventive measures, an external spark may ignite the gases within the battery and result in an explosion.

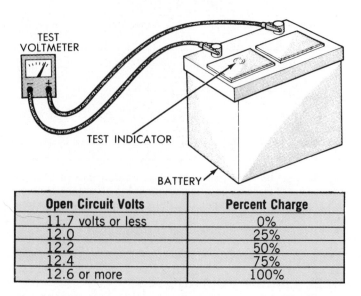

Open Circuit Volts	Percent Charge
11.7 volts or less	0%
12.0	25%
12.2	50%
12.4	75%
12.6 or more	100%

Fig. 30-17. An open circuit voltage test is made by connecting voltmeter leads across battery terminals. Voltage reading indicates percent charge as shown in chart. (Chrysler Corp.)

SAFE SERVICING PRACTICES

With these dangers of a battery explosion in mind, always observe the following safe battery servicing practices:

1. Never lean over a battery when charging, testing, or jump-starting an engine. Wear goggles or a face shield.
2. Do not "break" live circuits. For example, do not disconnect positive cable first when working on a battery. Always disconnect negative cable first and reconnect it last, Fig. 30-18.

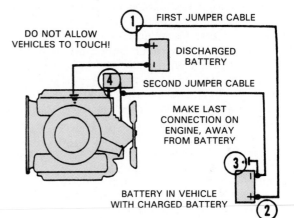

MAKE CONNECTIONS IN NUMERICAL ORDER

Fig. 30-19. Proper jumper cable hookup stresses need to connect second jumper cable from negative terminal of booster battery to engine, away from discharged battery.

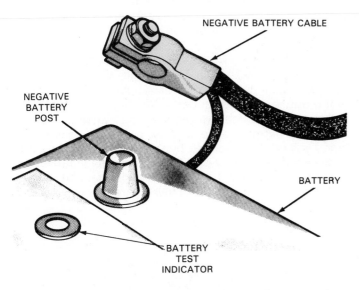

Fig. 30-18. When it becomes necessary to disconnect battery cables: always disconnect negative cable first; reconnect it last. (Chrysler Corp.)

3. Avoid accidental "grounds" and resulting sparks caused by dropped tools or metal parts bridging a live circuit and any grounded part.
4. Charge batteries only in a well ventilated area.
5. Never attempt to charge a frozen battery. Allow battery to warm to 60 °F (15.5 °C) before charging.
6. When preparing to charge a battey, see that charger ac (alternating current) lead is unplugged or switch is turned off before attaching, readjusting, or removing charger clamps.
7. Never connect jumper cables to a frozen battery in an attempt to jump-start an engine. Allow battery to warm to 40 °F (4.4 °C) and add water if necessary before proceeding with jumper cable hookup.
8. See that battery charger cable clamps or jumper cable clamps are clean and make good connections. Poor connections can cause an electrical arc.
9. If violent gassing occurs when charging a battery, or battery case feels hot (125 °F or 52 °C), reduce charging rate or temporarily stop charging.
10. Strictly observe directions for jumper cable hookup sequence. See Fig. 30-19. An improper hookup could result in an explosion of one of the batteries.

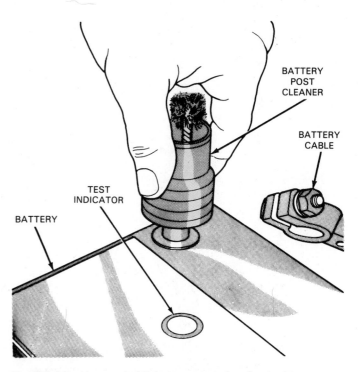

Fig. 30-20. Use a suitable battery post cleaning tool to remove dirt and corrosion from posts and mating surfaces of cable clamps. (Chrysler Corp.)

BATTERY SERVICE TIPS

Observe all safety suggestions given earlier and use proper tools when performing battery service. Proper tools include correct size open end wrenches, a cable clamp puller, cable clamp spreader, tapered post and cable clamp cleaning brush, scraper, and wire brush. Also convenient and necessary are a "filling" device (either self-leveling type or syringe type water dispenser), a battery carrier, and jumper cables.

When servicing batteries:

1. Use a fender cover.
2. Inspect and/or test cables, hold-down, and battery.
3. Repair or replace parts as required.
4. Remove cables from battery (ground cable first), using an open end wrench and cable clamp puller.
5. Spread clamps with cable clamp spreader.
6. Clean tapered posts and mating surfaces of cable clamps with special cleaning brush, Fig. 30-20. Use a baking soda and water solution to clean side terminals or "L" terminals.
7. Clean battery cover with a scraper and wire brush.
8. If necessary, remove battery and clean corrosion and rust from hold-down and battery tray.
9. Reinstall battery, tighten hold-down (do not over-tighten), and finish cleaning with baking soda and water solution. See Fig. 30-21.
10. Connect cables to battery posts or terminals (ground cable last), tighten securely, and coat with high temperature grease.
11. Use open end wrench to tighten nuts at starter relay and/or solenoid switch and at ground cable connection at engine block.
12. Check level of electrolyte in cells of conventional batteries. Refill to level indicator or to 1/2 in. (13 mm) above tops of separators with distilled water or good grade of drinking water.

BATTERY CHARGING METHODS

Battery charging methods vary, based on several considerations:
1. Electrical capacity of battery being serviced.
2. Temperature of electrolyte.
3. Battery state of charge at start of charging period.
4. Battery age and condition.

BATTERY CHARGING METHODS include high rate fast charging, constant potential charging, constant current slow charging, and trickle charging.

HIGH RATE FAST CHARGING provides a high charging rate for a short time. See Fig. 30-22. Usually, the intent of a fast charge is to give the battery the "boost" it needs (70 to 90 percent of full charge) until the vehicle charging system can bring it to a full state of charge. In keeping with this, a battery with electrolyte specific gravity of 1.225 or above should not be "fast charged."

The fast charging rate should be limited to 60 amperes for 12 volt batteries. Generally, the rate is set at 40 to 60 amperes for 30 minutes. To completely recharge a battery, the high rate fast charger should be adjusted to "slow charge," preferably at a rate of one ampere per positive plate per cell. If, for example, the battery has nine plates per cell (four positive, five negative), the charging rate would be four amperes.

CONSTANT POTENTIAL CHARGING, as the name implies, maintains the same voltage on the battery throughout the period of the charge. As a result, the current is automatically reduced as the battery approaches full charge. This feature reduces the amount of overcharge the battery can receive, so batteries in good condition will not be damaged by this method of charging. However, if the battery is badly sulfated, the temperature may rise soon after it is placed on charge. These batteries should be placed on slow charge.

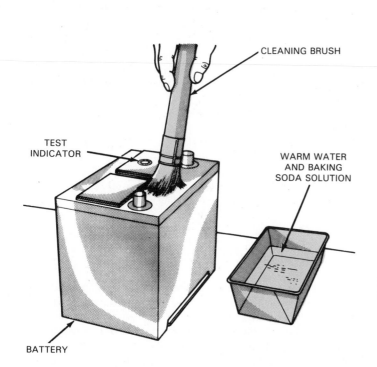

TEST INDICATOR

CLEANING BRUSH

WARM WATER AND BAKING SODA SOLUTION

BATTERY

Fig. 30-21. Finish battery maintenance service by cleaning cover with a stiff bristle brush and a solution of baking soda and warm water. (Chrysler Corp.)

Fig. 30-22. High rate fast chargers provide convenience of an in-car "boost charge" of battery to get vehicle back on road. (Christie Electric Corp.)

CONSTANT CURRENT SLOW CHARGING uses a low charging rate for a relatively long time, Fig. 30-23. Charging rates of three to five amperes or one percent of cold cranking rating are typical. Another acceptable

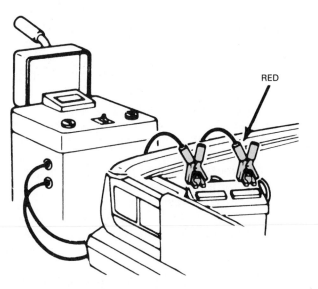

Fig. 30-23. Battery charging hookup is: charger red cable to positive post of battery; charger black cable to negative post of battery. (American Motors Corp.)

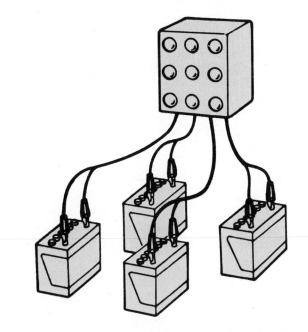

Fig. 30-24. While trickle chargers have a low charging rate, continuous overcharging can cause grids of positive plates to disintegrate. Follow battery charger manufacturer's instructions. (Battery Council International)

charging rate for slow charging is one ampere per positive plate per cell.

Constant current slow charging periods as long as 24 hours may be needed to bring the battery to full charge. To check the progress of the charge, hydrometer readings should be taken every hour. The battery is fully charged when the cells are gassing freely, and there is no increase in the hydrometer reading for three successive hourly tests.

TRICKLE CHARGING, Fig. 30-24, is designed to charge batteries at a rate of approximately one ampere. Trickle charges are used primarily for maintaining displays and stocks of batteries in fully charged condition.

While the trickle charging rate is extremely low, batteries can be damaged if left on trickle charge for long periods. Common practice is to leave the batteries on a trickle charge during the day and take them off charge during the night. In that way, the danger of severe overcharging is lessened.

When preparing to charge a battery, be aware of all of the safety precautions you should observe during the charging operation. Familiarize yourself with the manufacturer's battery charger guide and follow the step-by-step instructions in the sequence given.

Ideally, use an automatic battery charger that senses battery voltage and automatically shuts off — or almost shuts off — when the battery reaches or approaches the fully charged state. These chargers include temperature sensing and, usually, also sense polarity to help avoid sparks if the charger clamps are connected in reverse.

ACTIVATING DRY CHARGED BATTERIES

A DRY CHARGED AUTOMOTIVE BATTERY contains no electrolyte until it is placed in service. The cell elements are given an initial charge on special equipment at the factory. Then they are thoroughly washed, dried,

and assembled into battery cases. The batteries are shipped in the dry state.

A dry charged battery will retain its full charge indefinitely if moisture does not enter the cells. When ready for service, the battery is filled with electrolyte and, generally, is given a boost charge.

When filling a dry charged battery with electrolyte, the manufacturers advise that protective glasses be worn. Then follow this procedure:

1. Remove vent plugs and discard restrictors, if used.
2. Open container of electrolyte, cut a small opening in plastic bag.
3. Using a glass or acid-proof funnel, fill each cell with electrolyte, Fig. 30-25, to top of separators.

Fig. 30-25. To activate a dry charged battery: fill cells with electrolyte to top of separators; boost charge battery; fill cells with electrolyte to 1/2 in. (13 mm) above top of separators.

4. Boost charge battery at 15 amperes until specific gravity of electrolyte is 1.250 or higher and temperature is at least 60°F (15.5°C).
5. After boost charge, check level of electrolyte in all cells. Add electrolyte to bring level to level indicator of 1/2 in. (13 mm) above top of separators.
6. After battery has been put in service, add only distilled water or a good grade of drinking water. Do not add electrolyte.

JUMP STARTING AN ENGINE

JUMP STARTING an engine is a common procedure whereby jumper cables are used to transfer power from a good (booster) battery, Fig. 30-26, to a discharged battery.

Fig. 30-26. Mobile car starting equipment is available. This setup includes two-wheel cart, high capacity booster battery, jumper cables, and battery charger. (Ford Motor Co.)

The key to safe and effective jump starting is the correct hookup of the jumper cables. See Fig. 30-19. The following steps must be performed in sequence:
1. Position vehicle with booster battery next to vehicle with discharged battery so that jumper cables can reach batteries in both vehicles.
2. Vehicles must not touch each other.
3. Turn off electrical loads; set parking brake; place automatic transmission in PARK, manual transmission in neutral.
4. See that vent plugs are tight and place a damp cloth over plugs of each battery.

5. Connect positive jumper cable to positive post or terminal of discharged battery, Fig. 30-19.
6. Connect other end of positive jumper cable to positive post of booster battery.
7. Connect negative jumper cable to negative post or terminal of booster battery.
8. Connect other end of negative jumper cable — away from discharged battery — to engine block, car frame, or other good metallic ground.
9. See that cables are clear of fan blades and other moving parts of both engines, then start engine of vehicle with booster battery.
10. Allow a few minutes of engine operation, then try to start engine of vehicle with discharged battery.
11. After starting, allow engine to return to idle speed and remove negative jumper cable at engine block or other ground connection.
12. Remove other end of negative jumper cable from booster battery.
13. Remove positive jumper cable from discharged battery.
14. Remove other end of positive jumper cable from booster battery.
15. Discard damp cloths that were placed over vent plugs of both batteries.

NOTE: If engine in vehicle with discharged battery fails to start after cranking for 30 seconds, stop jump starting procedure. A second problem, in addition to the discharged battery, must be solved.

Chapter 30—REVIEW QUESTIONS

Write your answers on a separate sheet of paper. Do not write in this book.
1. Define "lead acid" storage battery.
2. The sole function of an automotive battery is to serve as a source of power for the starting motor and ignition system for cranking and starting an internal combustion engine. True or False?
3. A typical 12 volt automotive battery is made up of _____ cells connected in series and filled with _____.
4. An _____ is an assembly of positive and negative plates and separators.
5. The _____ of a battery is the amount of current it will deliver.
6. Name two methods of rating the performance of lead-acid batteries.
7. A hydrometer is an instrument used to test which of the following:
   a. Open circuit voltage.
   b. Closed circuit voltage.
   c. Specific gravity of electrolyte.
   d. Level of electrolyte in cells.
8. When checking a color-coded, built-in hydrometer in the cover of a maintenance-free battery, which color indicates 3/4 to full charge?
   a. Yellow or clear.
   b. Green.
   c. Red.
   d. Black.

9. When mixing sulfuric acid with water to make up an electrolyte solution of a certain specific gravity, should you pour the acid into the water or pour the water into the acid?

10. When testing the specific gravity of a battery electrolyte, what is the generally accepted "full charge" reading?
   a. 1.265.
   b. 1.275.
   c. 1.285.
   d. 1.295.

11. The specific gravity readings merely reveal _____, not battery condition.

12. When comparing the lowest and highest specific gravity readings, if there is more than _____ difference in the readings, replace the battery.
   a. .025.
   b. .050.
   c. .075.
   d. .100.

13. When making a heavy load test, what is the maximum length of time the test load should be applied?
   a. 5 seconds.
   b. 10 seconds.
   c. 15 seconds.
   d. 20 seconds.

14. When making a stabilized open circuit voltage test, a battery is considered to be in good condition if the voltmeter reading is:
   a. 12 volts.
   b. 12.2 volts.
   c. 12.4 volts.
   d. 12.6 volts.

15. When disconnecting battery cables, do not "break" live circuits. Always disconnect _____ (positive/negtive) cable first and reconnect it last.

16. What is the correct level of electrolyte in the battery cells in relation to tops of separators?

17. Battery charging methods include: _____ constant potential charging, constant current slow charging, and trickle charging.

18. The battery is fully slow charged when the cells are _____, and there is no increase in the hydrometer reading for _____ successive hourly tests.

19. When filling a dry charged battery with electrolyte, the manufacturers recommend that protective _____ be worn.

20. The key to safe and effective jump starting is the _____ of the jumper cables

Match the question number for each of the following descriptive phrases with the letter designated for each correct term.

21. ____ Sulfuric acid diluted with water.
22. ____ Assembly of positive plates, negative plates, and separators in a battery cell.
23. ____ "Bridges" at bottom of case.
24. ____ Lead dioxide.
25. ____ Active materials contained in cast grids.
26. ____ Spongy lead.
27. ____ Element terminal posts.
28. ____ When specific gravity of the electrolyte increases.
29. ____ Nonconducting material between plates.
30. ____ When specific gravity of the electrolyte decreases.

a. Specific gravity.
b. Intercell connectors.
c. Electrolyte.
d. Separators.
e. Element.
f. Element rests.
g. Plate group.
h. Positive plate.
i. Plates.
j. Discharge.
k. Charge.
l. Negative plate.

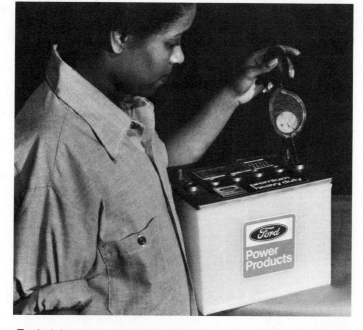

Technician uses a special hydrometer to test specific gravity of electrolyte in cells of a conventional automotive battery.

Despite underhood clutter of parts and assemblies, typical right side location of battery, cables, and starting motor permits ease of accessibility for testing, charging, servicing, or replacement. Special colorable thermoplastic rubber allows extensive color coding of underhood components.   (Monsanto Chemical Co.)

Chapter 31

STARTING MOTOR FUNDAMENTALS

After studying this chapter, you will be able to:

- Explain the principles of electric motor operation.
- Describe how the cranking system works.
- Cite the function of an overrunning clutch.
- List the various steps of starter maintenance.
- Give examples of possible causes of cranking system problems.
- Describe ways of testing a starting motor to determine its operating condition.

The AUTOMOTIVE STARTING MOTOR, Fig. 31-1, is an electromagnetic device that converts electrical energy into mechanical energy. It is designed specifically for cranking internal combustion engines at speeds which will permit starting.

A typical starting motor, Fig. 31-2, is made up, basically, of a frame and field assembly, an armature, drive mechanism, drive end housing, brush and holder assembly, and a relay and/or solenoid switch. The starting motor mounts on the flywheel housing or on a flange at the rear of the engine. See Fig. 31-3. The solenoid operates a starter drive mechanism having a small pinion

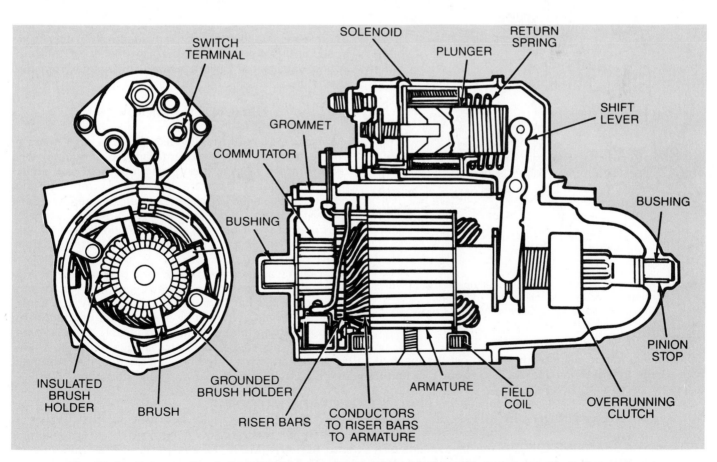

Fig. 31-1. Cross-sectional views reveal internal parts of a typical, positive engagement starting motor. (Chevrolet Motor Div., General Motors Corp.)

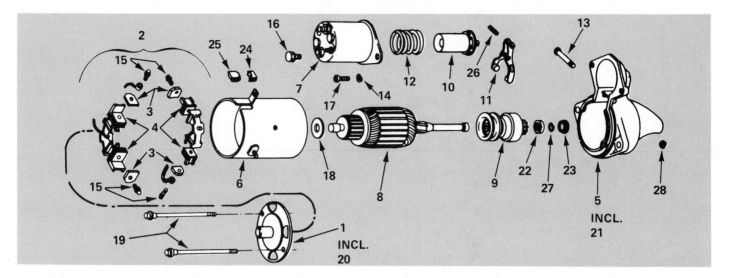

Fig. 31-2. Parts of disassembled starting motor include: 1—Commutator end frame. 2—Brush and holder package. 3—Brush. 4—Brush holder. 5—Drive end housing. 6—Frame and field assembly. 7—Solenoid switch. 8—Armature. 9—Drive assembly. 10—Plunger. 11—Shift lever. 12—Plunger return spring. 13—Shift lever shaft. 14—Lock washer. 15—Brush attaching screw. 16—Field lead to switch screw. 17—Switch attaching screw. 18—Leather washer. 19—Through bolt. 20—Commutator end bushing. 21—Drive end bushing. 22—Pinion stop collar. 23—Thrust collar. 24—Grommet. 25—Grommet. 26—Plunger pin. 27—Pinion stop retaining ring. 28—Lever shaft retaining ring. (Cadillac Motor Car Div., General Motors Corp.)

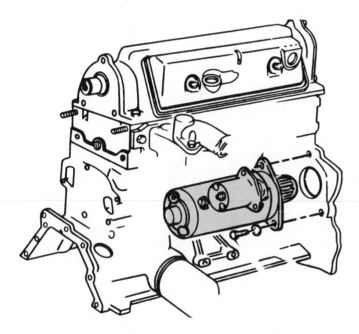

Fig. 31-3. Starter assembly is installed in opening in flywheel housing or in a flange at rear of engine. (Chevrolet Motor Div., General Motors Corp.)

gear (having about eight teeth) which can be meshed with a large flywheel ring gear (having about 100 teeth) to crank the engine. See Fig. 31-4.

CRANKING CIRCUIT

The engine CRANKING CIRCUIT mainly consists of a battery, starting motor, ignition switch, and related electrical wiring. See Fig. 31-4. When the ignition switch is placed in "start" position, the solenoid windings are energized and the resulting shift lever movement causes the drive pinion gear to engage the flywheel ring gear, Fig. 31-4, and cranking takes place.

When the engine starts, an overrunning clutch (part of drive assembly) protects the armature from excessive speed until the switch is opened. At this point, a return spring causes the pinion gear to disengage from the flywheel.

OPERATING PRINCIPLES

Electric motors of the type used in "starters" operate on the principle that a current-carrying conductor will tend to move from a strong magnetic field to a weak magnetic field. To illustrate, if a single current-carrying conductor is placed in a magnetic field created by a permanent magnet, as in Fig. 31-5, the flow of current in the conductor will cause a magnetic field to encircle the conductor in a clockwise direction (left-hand rule applies).

This circular magnetic field will tend to cancel out and weaken those lines of force between the poles of the permanent magnet *below* the conductor. At the same time, both fields will combine *above* the conductor to create a strong magnetic field. In effect, there is more magnetism above the conductor and less below it. Then, as the distorted lines of force tend to straighten out, they exert a downward thrust on the conductor.

ROTARY MOTION

To further illustrate how downward thrust is converted into ROTARY MOTION, assume that the conductor in Fig. 31-5 is bent into a loop, as shown in Fig. 31-6. This rotating part is known as the ARMATURE. The ends of

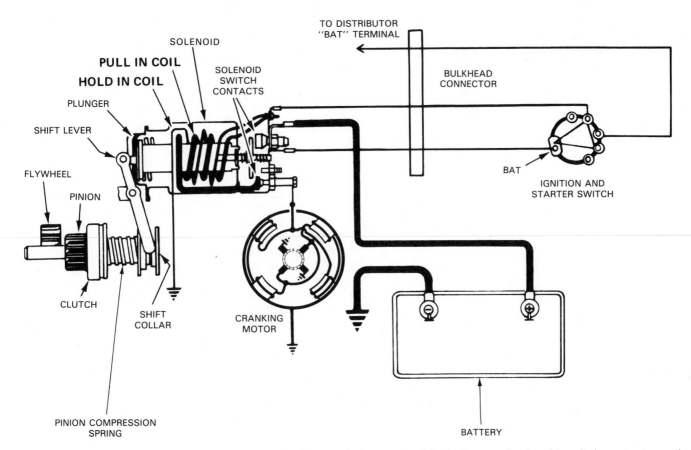

Fig. 31-4. Trace cranking circuit from battery to ignition switch to solenoid windings and solenoid switch contacts, and to starting motor. Also note shift lever and starter drive mechanism at left. (Oldsmobile Div., General Motors Corp.)

Fig. 31-5. When a current-carrying conductor is placed in a magnetic field, the conductor will tend to move in direction indicated.

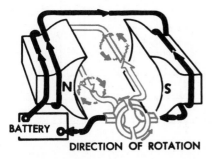

Fig. 31-6. Drawing depicts simple electric motor using a single loop of wire for an armature. Note direction of current flow (outlined arrows) and field around conductor (solid arrows).

the armature are connected to two semicircular brass bars called the COMMUTATOR. The magnetic field of the two magnetic poles (marked N and S) is created by two electromagnets. Current for the electromagnets — called FIELD COILS in this setup — is provided by a battery.

The current flowing through the field coils, Fig. 31-6, produces a strong magnetic field which flows from the north pole (N) to the south pole (S). At the same time, current flowing through the armature coil produces a circular magnetic field which surrounds the armature, as shown by the arrows in Fig. 31-6. This circular magnetic field is in a clockwise direction on the left-hand conductor of the armature, and counterclockwise around the right conductor. Note that the current in the left-hand side of the armature coil is flowing toward the commutator, which is the same direction shown in Fig. 31-5. This results in a downward thrust on the armature. Since the current is flowing in the opposite direction in the right-hand side of the armature coil, the thrust will be in the opposite direction, or upward, Fig. 31-7.

The combination of the two thrusts causes the armature to rotate. This rotation will continue because each time the armature coil passes the vertical position, the commutator (which rotates with the armature) will automatically connect the armature coil so the current will continue to flow away from the commutator in the right-hand coil, and toward the commutator in the left-hand coil.

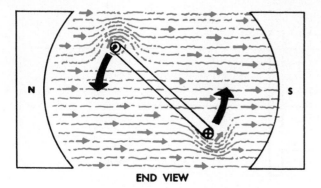

Fig. 31-7. Lines of force react to distortion of magnetic field to create a downward thrust at left and an upward thrust at right, causing armature coil to rotate.

The tendency for a current-carrying coil to move when placed in a magnetic field can be easily demonstrated by means of a permanent magnet, a battery, and some wire. See Fig. 31-8. First, connect the battery to points A and B. Then, reverse the connections and the wire bent in the form of a yoke will swing in the opposite direction. Turning the horseshoe magnet over from its original position will also change direction of thrust on yoke.

EFFECT OF COUNTER EMF

As pointed out in Chapter 29, Fundamentals of Electricity, when any conductor is moved through a magnetic field, a voltage will be induced in the conductor. This condition also occurs in a motor when the conductor is being supplied with current. However, the voltage *induced* in the conductor (by cutting magnetic lines of force) will be in the opposite direction to voltage being supplied to the motor. Such voltage is known as a BACK VOLTAGE, or COUNTER ELECTROMOTIVE FORCE (CEMF).

The effect of CEMF is to limit the current in the armature. When the speed of the armature increases, the

CEMF also increses. Since CEMF is opposed to the voltage applied to the motor, it has the effect of decreasing the effective voltage. As a result, the voltage that is forcing current through the armature is the difference between the applied voltage and the CEMF.

SPEED AND TORQUE CHARACTERISTICS

A reason for using a series-wound motor for cranking internal combustion engines is that it has extremely high torque. Torque varies with the strength of the magnetic field and the current in the armature. With the armature and field coils in series, any increase in current will produce an increase in the strength of the field. As the load on the motor increases, the current through the fields and armature will also increase. As a result, the torque will keep increasing as the load increases. See Fig. 31-9.

The speed of a series-wound motor will vary with the load. For any particular load which a given series motor is driving, there will be a certain definite speed. With heavy loads, series-wound motors will operate at a relatively slow speed. With a light load, these motors will operate at very high speeds. This is because any armature always tends to operate at a speed where the voltage used in overcoming its resistance, plus the CEMF, will be equal to the voltage being applied to the motor. At heavy loads, the current — and the voltage consumed in overcoming the internal resistance — will be large. Consequently, the armature will not have to rotate at very high speed to produce the required CEMF to equal the applied voltage.

However, under light loads, the motor speeds up, inducing a higher CEMF and decreasing the current through the field and armature coils. This weakens the strength of the field, causing a further increase in armature speed, which again decreases the CEMF.

With no load, the speed of a series-wound motor will continue to increase to such an extent that centrifugal force will destroy the armature. Series-wound motors

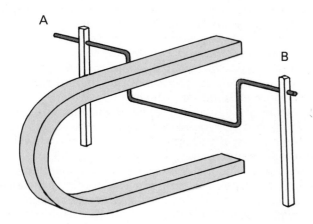

Fig. 31-8. Simple equipment shown will demonstrate basic principles of electric motor operation. Connecting a battery to ends of loop of wire, at A and B, will cause loop to swing.

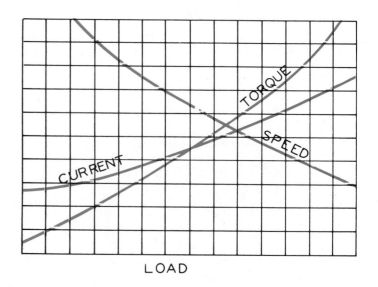

Fig. 31-9. Chart curves illustrate fact that increased load on a series motor will cause its speed to drop, while current and torque will rise.

used for cranking internal combustion engines should never be operated without a load except under controlled conditions.

STARTING MOTOR TYPES

Starting motors basically operate on the same principle: first using a light current to energize the relay and/or solenoid, then using a heavy current to power the starting motor. The solenoid serves to actuate the drive

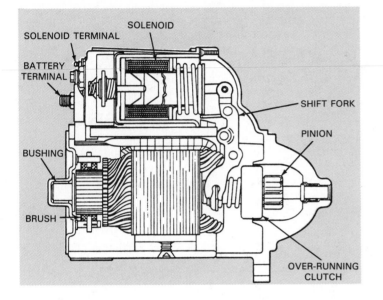

Fig. 31-10. Sectional view of a typical Ford positive engagement starting motor gives details of solenoid and solenoid-actuated shift fork, starter drive, and overrunning clutch.

mechanism, causing a pinion gear to engage with the flywheel ring gear and crank the engine.

To accomplish this, various types of starting motors are currently in use. Conventional field motor designs feature current-carrying, wire-wound field coils. Newer designs utilize permanent magnets and gear reduction.

Figs. 31-1 and 31-10 illustrate POSITIVE ENGAGEMENT STARTING MOTORS. These motors incorporate a shift fork or lever connected by linkage to the solenoid plunger. When the ignition switch is turned to the "start" position, the solenoid windings are energized. Electromagnetic action moves the solenoid plunger and shift fork, causing the pinion gear on the drive mechanism to engage the flywheel. At the same time, the main contacts close in the solenoid switch and heavy current cranks the engine.

Fig. 31-11 presents an exploded view of a MOVABLE POLE SHOE type of starting motor. With this arrangement, the pole shoe is attached to the starter drive yoke. When heavy current passes through a grounded field coil, the pole shoe moves and the yoke pushes the starter drive pinion gear into mesh with the flywheel ring gear.

Fig. 31-12 shows a Chrysler starting motor equipped with a 3.5 to 1 reduction gearset. The GEAR REDUCTION MECHANISM adds to starter size and weight because one gear goes above the other. However, the gear reduction principle boosts cranking speed, a plus for below zero starts. Again, a solenoid assembly and shift fork are used to actuate the drive mechanism.

Fig. 31-13 pictures a PERMANENT MAGNET STARTING MOTOR. The permanent magnets, which replace the conventional wound fields, reportedly increase starter performance by 16 percent. In addition, a PLANETARY GEARSET is used to transmit power between the motor and the output shaft. The use of six per-

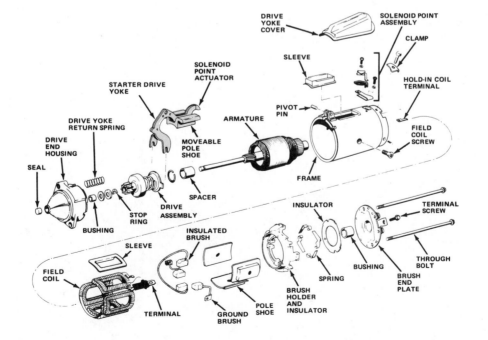

Fig. 31-11. American Motors starter has a movable pole shoe attached to starter drive yoke. When heavy current passes through a grounded field coil, pole shoe moves and yoke pushes starter drive into mesh with flywheel.

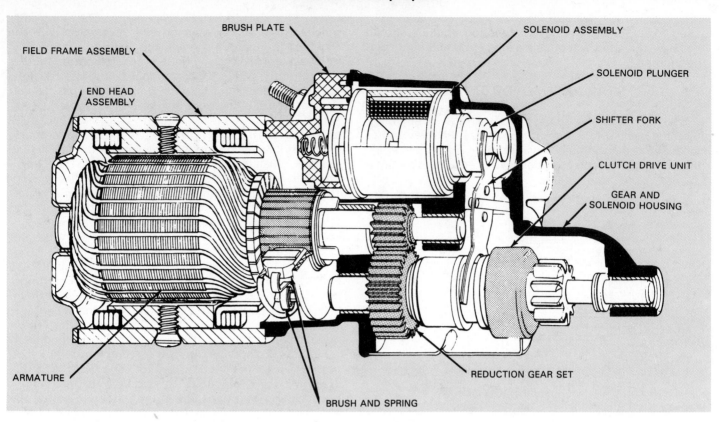

Fig. 31-12. Some Chrysler starters are reduction gear type, using either a 2.0 to 1 or a 3.5 to 1 reduction gearset.

manent magnets reduces starter current draw. The planetary reduction gearing permits compact, lightweight design and increases cranking speed.

STARTING MOTOR INTERNAL CIRCUITS

While the basic characteristics of the conventional, series-wound motor is used in many starting motors, there are some modifications of the method of connecting the field coils to each other and to the armature. Some variations in the internal circuits of starting motors are shown in Figs. 31-14, 31-15, and 31-16.

Fig. 31-14 (left) shows a four-pole, two-field coil design used on many motors. The two windings are connected in parallel to each other and in series with the armature, permitting the high current to divide in equal

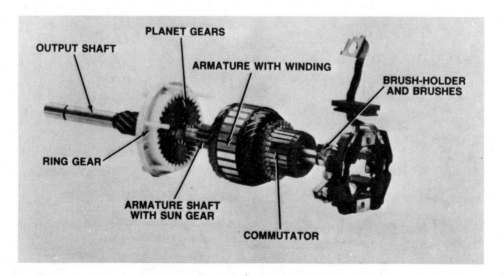

Fig. 31-13. Permanent magnets are used in place of wound field coils in certain late model applications. Also featured is reduction type planetary gearing. (Chrysler Corp.)

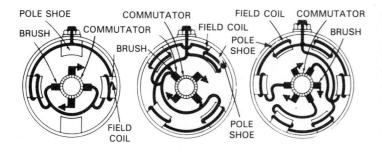

Fig. 31-14. Three typical starting motor circuits include: Left. Four-pole, two-field coil design. Center. Four-pole, four-field coil design. Right. Six-pole, six-field coil design.

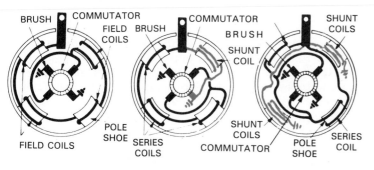

Fig. 31-15. Four-pole starting motor circuits also in use are: Left. Four field coils all in series. Center. Three series-wound field coils and one shunt field coil. Right. Two series-wound field coils and two shunt field coils.

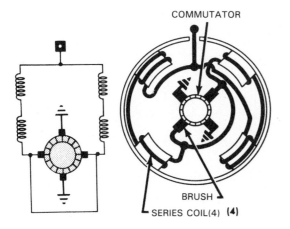

Fig. 31-16. Oldsmobile uses a starting motor with four field coils on certain engines. Wiring arrangement is termed a "series compound winding." Note separate lead between insulated brushes.

rent flows through one pair of windings to one of the insulated brushes. The other half flows through another pair of windings to the other insulated brush. The current then combines at the commutator and goes through the armature. Four field coil windings of low resistance create stronger magnetic fields and produce starting motors with greater torque and cranking ability.

A variation of this principle of dividing the current is found in starting motors having six poles and six field windings paired off three ways, Fig. 31-14 (right). In this motor, one-third of the current flows through each of three pairs of field windings to one of three insulated brushes. Increasing the number of circuits through the starting motor keeps resistance low, so that high horsepower can be developed for use in heavy-duty service.

As mentioned earlier, a starting motor with all field coils connected in series, Fig. 31-15 (left), would crank up to an extremely high top free speed if not controlled. With this in mind, shunt connections are used on many 12 volt starting systems, Fig. 31-15 (center and right). Two or three heavy field coils are connected in series and carry current to the armature. The remaining field coil, or coils, are shunt coils connected between the starting motor terminal and ground. The shunt coil has two purposes: first to assist the series coils to build up and maintain a high magnetic field; second to prevent excessive motor speed and noise when the armature is not subjected to cranking load.

When the motor is cranking the engine, heavy current flows through the series windings to form the magnetic field. The ampere turns in the shunt field provide additional strength under this condition. When the engine starts, the load on the starter immediately drops. Less current flows through the armature and series field, which makes this field weaker. This would result in high rotational speed if the shunt field was not used. The shunt field continues to produce its maximum field strength so that the motor is held to a safe speed.

Oldsmobile has a variation of the internal circuit with four field coils in series between the terminal and armature. Note in Fig. 31-16 that, in addition to windings connecting the four poles of the motor, a separate lead connects the insulated brush leads. Therefore, this winding is not a straight series circuit, and it is not a straight shunt hookup. Oldsmobile calls it a "series compound winding."

CONTROL MECHANISMS AND CIRCUITS

The starting motor armature must revolve at a fairly high speed to produce sufficient torque (turning effort) to rotate the engine. As soon as the engine starts, its speed is much greater than cranking speed. If the starter drive pinion gear remained engaged with the flywheel, the starter rpm would be excessive and ruin the armature.

To prevent this problem, various mechanisms have been developed which permit the gears to mesh during the cranking period and to demesh as soon as the engine is started. Most modern starters use a positive engagement or pre-engagement drive mechanism, Fig. 31-10, a moving pole shoe, Fig. 31-11, or a reduction

amounts and pass through each field winding. All of the current then passes through the armature, with the result that high cranking torque is produced. The two poles which have no windings serve to complete the magnetic circuits.

The starting motor in Fig. 31-14 (center) has four field coils on four poles. With this setup, one half of the cur-

mechanism, Figs. 31-12 and 31-13.

Electrically, most starting motor control circuits use a relay and/or solenoid switch connected in series with the ignition switch. When the ignition switch is turned to the "start" position, the solenoid operates and the circuit between the battery and starter is completed.

The solenoid switch also shifts the starter pinion gear into engagement with the flywheel ring gear. This is accomplished by means of linkage between the solenoid plunger and the shift lever on the starter. When the circuit is completed to the solenoid, current from the battery passes through two separate windings, known as the "pull-in" and "hold-in" windings. The combined magnetic field of these windings pulls in the plunger, the drive pinion gear is shifted into mesh, and the main contacts of the solenoid switch are closed. See Fig. 31-17.

The heavy pull-in winding is used to complete the plunger movement, but when the air gap is decreased, the hold-in winding is sufficient to retain the plunger. The closing of the main contacts closes the circuit between the battery and the starter and, at the same time, shorts out the pull-in winding.

When the control circuit is opened, after the engine is started, current no longer reaches the hold-in winding. However, current flows from the battery through the main contacts, through the pull-in winding (in reverse direction), and then through the hold-in winding to the ground. See Fig. 31-17. With an equal number of turns of winding in both coils and the same current, the magnetic forces are equal but opposed and counteract each other. Tension of the return spring then causes the plunger to return to the "at rest" position and break the circuit.

Reduction gear starters, Fig. 31-12, differ in construction from positive engagement starters, but electrical circuitry is basically the same. Two separate circuits are used: a supply circuit to power the starting motor; a light duty circuit to energize the solenoid control circuit.

OVERRUNNING CLUTCH

Positive engagement starters use an OVERRUNNING CLUTCH, Fig. 31-18, to provide positive meshing and demeshing of the starter drive pinion gear and flywheel ring gear. The overrunning clutch transmits cranking torque from the starter to the flywheel gear, but permits the pinion gear to run faster or overrun the armature once the engine has started. This protects the armature from excessive speed during the brief period that the starter drive pinion gear remains enmeshed and the engine has started.

The overrunning clutch consists of a shell and sleeve assembly which is splined internally to match the splines on the armature shaft. Both shell and sleeve assembly and armature shaft turn together. A pinion gear and collar assembly fits loosely into the shell, and the collar is in contact with four hardened steel rollers assembled into notches cut in the inner face of the shell. The notches taper inward slightly and are spring loaded, Fig. 31-18.

When the shift lever is operated, the clutch assembly is moved along the armature shaft until the pinion gear meshes with the flywheel ring gear. If the teeth should butt against each other instead of meshing, the clutch spring compresses so that the pinion gear is spring loaded against the ring gear teeth. Then, as the armature starts to rotate, the gears are forced into engagement.

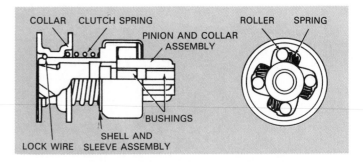

Fig. 31-18. Sectional view of overrunning clutch reveals details of construction and location of rollers and springs in clutch shell and sleeve assembly.
(Pontiac Motor Div., General Motors Corp.)

As movement of the shift lever is completed, the starter switch is closed and the starter armature begins to rotate. This rotates the shell and sleeve assembly, causing the rollers to jam tightly in the smaller sections of the shell rotator. The rollers are jammed between the pinion collar and the shell, and the pinion gear is forced to rotate with the armature and crank the engine.

When the engine starts, it tries to drive the starter armature through the pinion gear. This causes the pinion gear to overrun the shell and armature. The rollers are turned back toward the larger section of the shell notches and the pinion gear is free to overrun. The shift

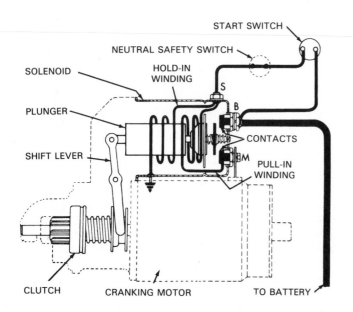

Fig. 31-17. Schematic of Chevrolet positive engagement starting motor shows windings of solenoid circuit and details of shift lever and overrunning clutch type starter drive mechanism.

lever spring then pulls the overrunning clutch out of mesh with the flywheel ring gear. Movement of the shift lever also opens the starting motor main switch.

NEUTRAL SAFETY SWITCH

All cars equipped with an automatic transmission are provided with a NEUTRAL SAFETY SWITCH, Fig. 31-19. This switch eliminates the possibility of starting the engine when the transmission selector lever is in gear to drive the car. Note in Fig. 31-19 that the neutral safety switch is connected between the ignition switch and the solenoid.

On some applications, the transmission selector lever may be placed either in PARK or NEUTRAL position before the circuit to the starter is completed. In other installations, the lever must be placed in PARK position.

STARTER MAINTENANCE

Periodically checking the condition of the starting motor and cranking system helps reduce the possibility of failures on the road. The frequency of inspection is dependent on type of operation. However, a visual inspection of the cranking system, an operational test of starting motor performance, and a test of neutral safety switch operation should be done annually and as part of an engine tune-up.

Modern starters do not permit thorough inspection unless disassembled. A visual inspection for clean, tight electrical connections, Fig. 31-19, and secure mounting at the flywheel housing is about the extent of a maintenance check. Then, operate the starter and note speed of rotation and steadiness of operation. To prevent the starting motor from overheating, do not operate the starter for more than 15 seconds at a time.

If necessary, remove the starter for cleaning and careful inspection. Steps for removal generally include:
1. Disconnect cable from battery negative terminal.
2. Remove wires from solenoid.
3. Remove starter upper mounting bolt.

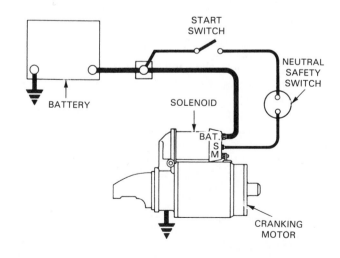

4. Raise and support vehicle.
5. Remove brackets or shields that may interfere with starter removal.
6. Remove starter.

NOTE: On some transaxle applications, disconnect speedometer cable at transaxle and remove transaxle rear strut.

Disassemble the starter, Fig. 31-20, and examine the commutator and brushes. If the commutator is dirty, clean it with a strip of No. 00 sandpaper. If the commutator is rough, pitted, or out of round, or if the mica (insulation between commutator bars) is high, chuck the armature in a lathe and recondition the commutator. Also, undercut the mica 1/32 in.

Brushes should be at least half of full length. If not, replace them. The brushes should have free movement in the brush holders. They should have the specified spring tension and make full contact with the commutator.

Do not use a grease-dissolving or high temperature cleaning solution on the commutator and field windings. It could damage the insulation. The same caution goes for the overrunning clutch drive units.

Test the operation of the drive pinion gear on the overrunning clutch drive unit. It should turn freely in the overrunning direction, and it should not slip in the driving direction.

When reassembling the starter, use a special lubricant to coat the armature shaft, drive end bushing, and commutator end bushing. Make sure the brushes are fully seated. Align the housing and end frame, Fig. 31-20, and securely install the through bolts. Reinstall the starter in the opening in the flywheel housing and tighten the mounting bolts to specified torque tightness. Connect the cables and wire leads firmly to clean terminals. See Fig. 31-19.

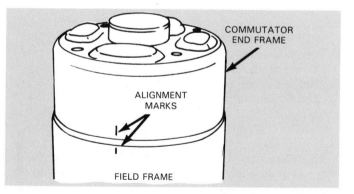

Fig. 31-20. Before disassembly of starting motor, scratch alignment marks on field frame and end frame to ease reassembly. (Oldsmobile Div., General Motors Corp.)

TROUBLESHOOTING CRANKING SYSTEM

INOPERATIVE STARTER

1. Loose or corroded battery terminals.
2. Discharged battery.

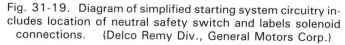

Fig. 31-19. Diagram of simplified starting system circuitry includes location of neutral safety switch and labels solenoid connections. (Delco Remy Div., General Motors Corp.)

3. Dead battery.
4. Open cranking circuit.
5. Inoperative solenoid or relay.
6. Faulty ignition switch.
7. Defective starter.
8. Inoperative neutral safety switch.

INOPERATIVE STARTER AND HEADLIGHTS DIM

1. Weak battery or dead cell.
2. Loose or corroded battery connections.
3. Internal ground in starting motor windings.
4. Grounded starting motor field.
5. Armature rubbing on pole shoes.

STARTER TURNS BUT DRIVE DOES NOT ENGAGE

1. Broken teeth in flywheel ring gear.
2. Rusted starter drive shaft.
3. Defective starter drive.
4. Slipping overrunning clutch.

SLOW CRANKING SPEED

1. Discharged battery or defective cell.
2. Excessive resistance in starter.
3. Excessive resistance in cranking circuit.
4. Engine oil too heavy for prevailing conditions.
5. Excessive engine friction.
6. Burned solenoid contacts.
7. Bent armature.
8. Loose pole shoe screws.
9. Worn bearings.

STARTER DOES NOT DISENGAGE

1. Faulty ignition switch.
2. Short circuit in solenoid.
3. Stuck solenoid contact switch plunger.
4. Broken solenoid plunger spring.
5. Faulty starter relay.
6. Loose starter mounting bolts.
7. Worn drive end bushing.
8. Broken drive yoke return spring.
9. Defective overrunning clutch.

STARTING MOTOR TESTS

There are many ways of testing a starting motor to determine its operating condition. Begin by making on-car tests, follow up with a no-load test, then pinpoint the cause of the problem with bench tests.

ON-CAR STARTING MOTOR TESTS

The following tests will reveal EXCESSIVE RESISTANCE in the cranking circuit. Use an expanded-scale voltmeter to test voltage drop across the various points shown in Fig. 31-21. Remove the primary lead from the ignition coil and crank the engine.

Maximum allowable voltage drop, typically, is as follows:

1. With voltmeter leads connected to positive post of

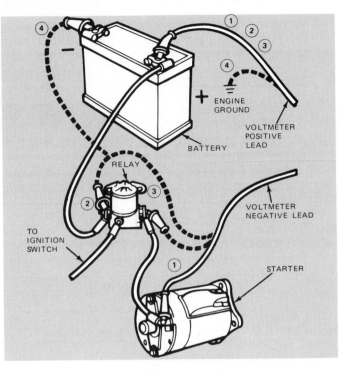

Fig. 31-21. To test for high resistance in cranking system, use an expanded scale voltmeter (0.1 volt calibrations) to test voltage drop between four sets of points indicated by numbers.   (Ford Motor Co.)

battery and to starter terminal — 0.5 volt.
2. With voltmeter connected to positive post of battery and to battery terminal of starter relay — 0.1 volt.
3. With voltmeter connected to positive post of battery and to starter terminal of starter relay — 0.3 volt.
4. With voltmeter connected to negative terminal of battery and to ground — 0.3 volt.

The following test of the starting motor on the car under load gives a result in AMPERAGE DRAW. The engine must be at normal operating temperature.

1. Disconnect and ground ignition coil secondary wire.
2. Connect a remote control switch between battery positive terminal and S terminal on starter solenoid.
3. Connect load tester as shown in Fig. 31-22 and place tester load control knob in full counterclockwise position (decrease).
4. Close remote control switch and observe voltage indicated on voltmeter after starter has reached maximum rpm.
5. Do not crank engine more than 15 seconds, then open remote control switch.
6. Turn tester load control knob clockwise (increase) until voltmeter indicates same voltage as obtained when starter cranked engine.
7. Read amperage draw on ammeter scale and compare with manufacturer's specification — typically 150-250 amps.

NO-LOAD TEST

The NO-LOAD TEST will determine how fast the armature will revolve and the amount of current draw at

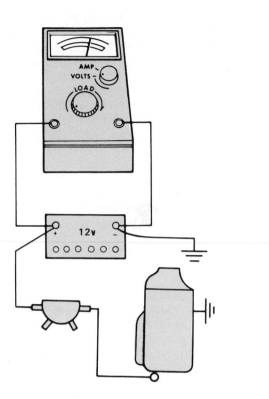

Fig. 31-22. Hookup of test equipment is shown for making an amperage draw test of an American Motors starting motor operation.

a specified voltage. To make the test, connect test equipment leads as shown in Fig. 31-23, using a tachometer attached to the end of the armature shaft.
1. Adjust variable resistance control to obtain given voltage value.

2. Starter will run at no-load speed.
3. Read amperage and rpm values and compare these readings with specifications — typically at 10 volts: 50-75 amps; 6000-11,500 rpm (reduction gear starters: 3700 minimum rpm).

ANALYZING NO-LOAD TEST RESULTS

If, under no-load conditions, the starter rotates at normal rpm at specified voltage and amperage draw, the starting motor is in good condition. However, if trouble is indicated, consider the following:
1. If starter fails to rotate under no-load tests and shows high amperage draw, there may be a direct ground in armature or field windings or ''frozen'' armature shaft bearings.
2. Low no-load speed and a high amperage draw indicate a dragging armature, worn bearings, or tight and dirty bearings.
3. Low no-load speed and a low current draw point to high resistance in starting motor. One of the field windings may be ''open.'' Other causes could be broken brush springs, badly worn brushes, high insulation between commutator bars, or an extremely dirty or oily commutator.
4. High no-load speed and high current draw are signs of ''shorted'' field windings.

BENCH TESTS

When your analysis of no-load test results indicate that trouble exists in the starting motor, perform the following bench tests to pinpoint the cause.

ARMATURE AND FIELD OPEN CIRCUIT TESTS

An open circuit armature may be detected by examining the commutator for evidence of burning. The spot burned on the commutator is caused by an arc formed

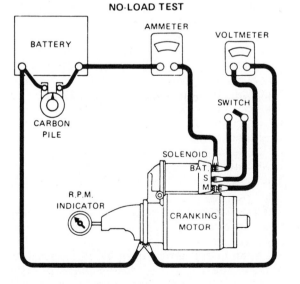

Fig. 31-23. Schematic shows ammeter and voltmeter lead connections and attachment of tachometer for making a no-load test of Chevrolet starting motor operation.

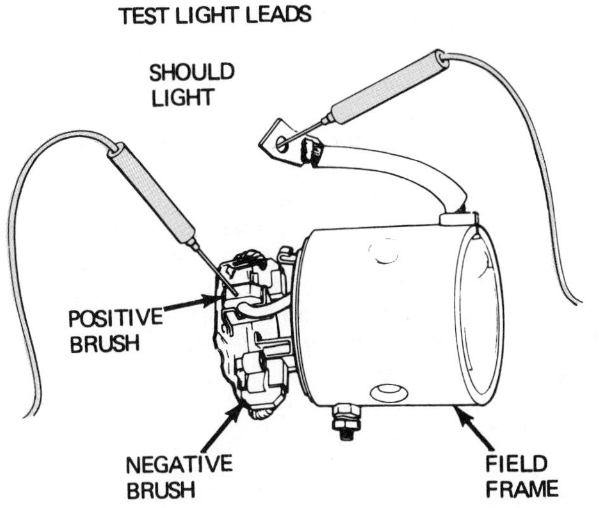

Fig. 31-24. Bench tests of starting motor circuitry include testing field windings for an open circuit by means of a 120 volt test lamp. If lamp fails to light, field winding is open. (Oldsmobile Div., General Motors Corp.)

every time the commutator segment connected to the open circuit winding passes under a brush.

An open circuit test of the field can be made by means of a 120 volt test lamp, Fig. 31-24, or by connecting a jumper lead from the positive post of a battery to the starter terminal, the voltmeter negative lead to the negative post of the battery, and the voltmeter positive lead to each field brush in turn. If the lamp fails to light or no reading is obtained on the voltmeter, the field winding is open.

ARMATURE AND FIELD GROUNDED CIRCUIT TESTS

If the armature or field coil insulation has failed, it would permit a conductor to touch the starter frame or armature core. This test can be made with a 120 volt test lamp or by using a voltmeter.

To test the armature with a test lamp, touch one test prod to the armature shaft and touch the other prod to each commutator bar in turn. If the lamp lights, the armature winding is grounded.

To make the test with a voltmeter, connect a jumper lead from the positive post of a battery to the armature shaft. Connect the voltmeter leads to the negative post of the battery and to each commutator bar in turn. If any voltage is indicated, the winding is grounded.

To test for grounded field circuit windings, connect a jumper lead from one terminal of the starter to one post of the battery. Contact the other post of the battery with a test prod while keeping the brushes away from the frame of the starter. Then touch the other test prod to the field frame of the starter. If the lamp lights, or if any voltage is indicated on the meter, the field windings are grounded.

Chapter 31—REVIEW QUESTIONS

Write your answers on a separate sheet of paper. Do not write in this book.

1. In which direction does a current-carrying conductor tend to move when placed in a magnetic field?
   a. From a strong magnetic field to a weak one.
   b. From a weak magnetic field to a strong one.
2. The rotating part of an electric motor is known as an _____.
3. To what are the ends of an armature coil connected?
4. In an electric motor, the rotating coils are cutting magnetic lines of force, thereby generating voltage. Relative to applied voltage, in which direction does the induced voltage cause the current to flow?
   a. In the same direction as applied voltage.
   b. In the direction opposed to the applied voltage.
5. Why is a series-wound starting motor used for cranking an internal engine?
   a. High speed.
   b. High torque.
   c. Low speed.
   d. Low torque.
6. The speed of a series-wound motor will vary with the load. True or False?
7. What is the purpose of the overrunning clutch in a positive engagement starter drive mechanism?
8. What is the purpose of the neutral safety switch on cars equipped with an automatic transmission?
9. Give three starting motor and cranking system maintenance procedures that should be done annually or as part of an engine tune-up.
10. When attempting to start an engine or when testing starting motor performance, do not operate the starter for more than _____ seconds at a time.
    a. 15.
    b. 20.
    c. 25.
    d. 30.
11. When examining the components of a disassembled starting motor, if the commutator is dirty, clean it with a strip of No. _____ sandpaper.
12. When checking internal parts of a starting motor, brushes should be at least half of full length. True or False?
13. Test the operation of the drive pinion gear on the overrunning clutch unit. It should turn freely in the _____ direction, and it should not slip in the _____ direction.
14. A car brought in for service was tested and mechanics found that the starter turned but the starter drive did not engage. Mechanic A said it could be caused by broken teeth in the flywheel ring gear. Mechanic B said it could be caused by a slipping overrunning clutch. Who is right?
    a. Mechanic A.
    b. Mechanic B.
    c. Both mechanic A and mechanic B.
    d. Neither mechanic A nor mechanic B.
15. A customer complained that the starter did not disengage when the engine started. Mechanic A said it could be caused by a faulty ignition switch. Mechanic B said it could be caused by loose starting motor mounting bolts. Who is right?
    a. Mechanic A.
    b. Mechanic B.
    c. Both mechanic A and mechanic B.
    d. Neither mechanic A nor mechanic B.
16. In testing a stalled vehicle, it was found that the starter would not crank the engine and the headlights dimmed when the ignition switch was turned to "start" position. Mechanic A said it could be caused by a defective starter drive mechanism. Mechanic B said it could be caused by a grounded starting motor field. Who is right?
    a. Mechanic A.
    b. Mechanic B.
    c. Both mechanic A and mechanic B.
    d. Neither mechanic A nor mechanic B.
17. The no-load starting motor test will determine how fast the _____ will revolve.
18. The no-load starting motor test also will determine the amount of _____ at a specified _____.
19. An open circuit armature may be detected by examining the _____ for evidence of burning.
20. Using a 120 Volt test lamp, how would you test for a grounded armature? Describe the process.

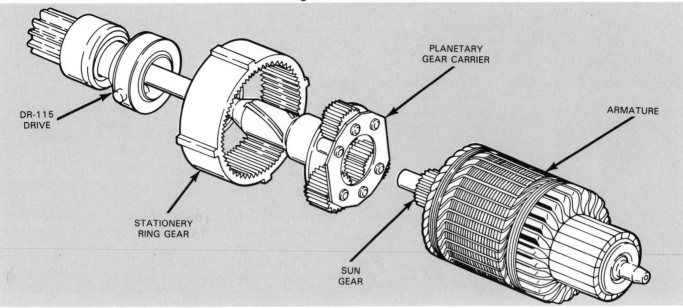

DR-115
DRIVE

STATIONERY
RING GEAR

PLANETARY
GEAR CARRIER

ARMATURE

SUN
GEAR

Exploded view shows major elements of a permanent magnet, planetary gear starting motor. Newly developed permanent magnets allow size and weight reductions. Planetary gearset provides high speed and low torque.   (Delco Remy Div., General Motors Corp.)

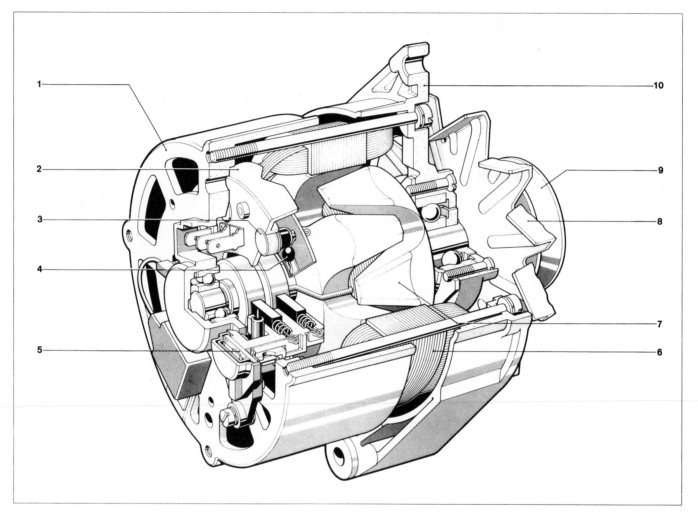

Line drawing points out basic construction features of a claw-pole alternator: 1—Collector-ring end shield. 2—Rectifier. 3—Power diode. 4—Exciter diode. 5—Regulator, brush holder, and carbon brushes. 6—Stator. 7—Rotor. 8—Fan. 9—Pulley. 10—Drive end shield.   (Robert Bosch Corporation)

Chapter 32

GENERATORS AND ALTERNATORS

After studying this chapter, you will be able to:
- Explain the principle of electromagnetic induction.
- Describe how alternators differ from dc generators.
- Name the major components of an alternator.
- Tell how an alternator produces alternating current within, then converts it to direct current at the output terminal.
- Give some examples of alternator design and construction differences.

An AUTOMOTIVE GENERATOR, Fig. 32-1, is an electromagnetic device that converts the mechanical energy supplied by the engine into electrical energy. In operation, the generator maintains the storage battery in fully charged condition and supplies electrical power for the ignition system and accessory equipment.

The various generator manufacturers have different names for their products, including ALTERNATOR, AC GENERATOR, DELCOTRON, and even CHARGING SYSTEM when the generator has a built-in voltage regulator. "Alternator" is the most common terminology.

ELECTROMAGNETIC INDUCTION

The operation of the automotive ALTERNATOR is based on the principle of electromagnetic induction. That is, when a coil of wire is moved through a magnetic field, a voltage will be induced, or generated, in the coil.

Actually, voltage can be induced in either of two ways:
1. By moving a coil of wire through a magnetic field.
2. By keeping the coil stationary and moving the

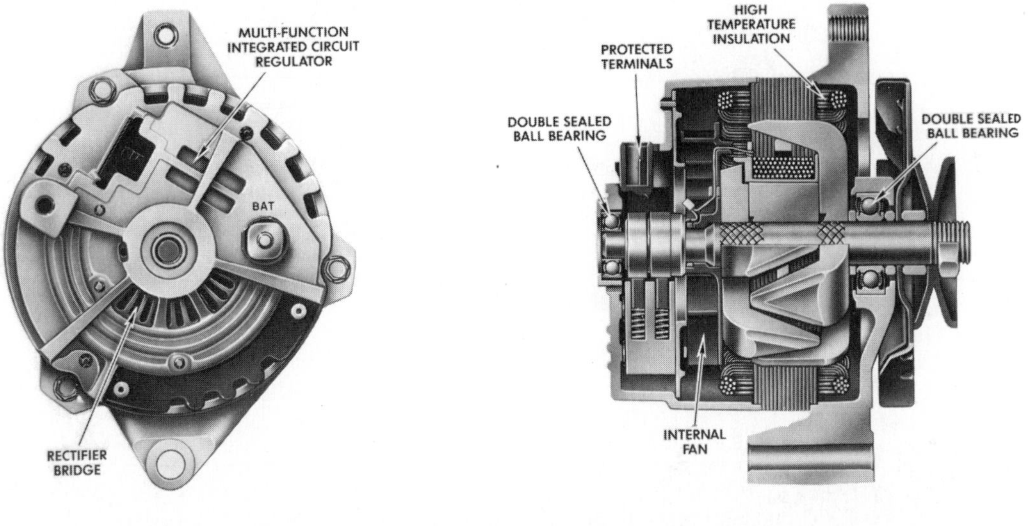

Fig. 32-1. Late model alternator features digital integrated circuit voltage regulator and capacitor, "chip" type bridge rectifier (diode assembly), dynamically balanced rotor, and internal and external fans.   (Delco Remy Div., General Motors Corp.)

magnetic field.

The old dc (direct current) generator operated on principle No. 1. The DC GENERATOR induced voltage in coils of wire as the assembly (armature) rotated in a stationary magnetic field. See Fig. 32-2.

The ac (alternating current) generator operates on principle No. 2. The magnetic field, or ROTOR, is rotated and voltage is generated in the stationary coils, or STATOR. See Fig. 32-1.

In general, then, voltage is induced in a coil whenever there is a change in the lines of force passing through the coil. Fig. 32-3 illustrates what happens when lines of force are cut by a rotating coil.

When the coil is in the vertical position, as shown at A in Fig. 32-3, the lines of force surrounding the conductor are balanced. For that instant, no lines of force are being cut. Therefore, no voltage will be induced in the coil.

As the coil approaches position B, an increasing number of lines of force will be cut. The generated voltage will continue to increase until it reaches a maximum of position B.

After passing position B, the voltage will start to decrease as fewer lines of force are being cut. It will become zero when position C is reached. As rotation continues, another maximum will be reached at position D. However, the lines of force are now being cut in the opposite direction to that of position B. Therefore, the current generated will flow in the opposite direction.

Since the current keeps changing its direction as the loop of wire is rotated, it is called an ALTERNATING CURRENT. The variations in the value and direction of the generated voltage are shown in the lower portion of Fig. 32-3.

To make use of the electrical energy that is being generated, each end of the coil is connected to a ring which rotates with the coil of wire. Contact with these rotating slip rings is made by brushes which bear against the rings.

ALTERNATING CURRENT GENERATOR

All automotive generators produce alternating current which, in turn, must be rectified (converted) to direct current to satisfy the needs of the storage battery and the various electrical systems and accessories.

In an ac generator, or alternator, Fig. 32-4, the magnetic field is rotated and voltage is generated in the stationary coils. Rectifiers, or diodes, are built into the alternator to limit current flow to one direction only to provide direct current at the output terminal.

DIRECT CURRENT GENERATOR

A DC GENERATOR, Fig. 32-2, operates basically the same as an alternator in that it produces alternating current. However, the dc generator works on the principle that voltage is generated in a coil, or coils, of wire (armature) as it is rotated in a stationary magnetic field. Instead of using a rectifier to convert the ac to dc, a

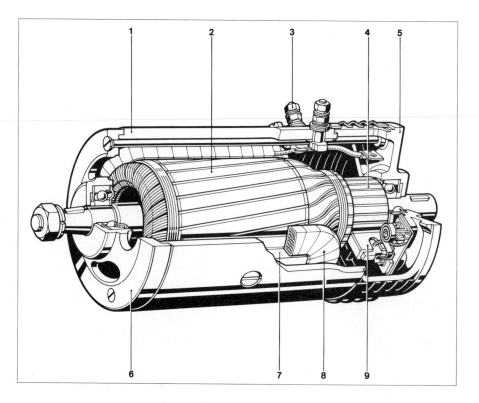

Fig. 32-2. Construction of a dc generator: 1—Stator frame. 2—Armature. 3—Terminal. 4—Commutator. 5—Commutator end shield. 6—Drive end shield. 7—Pole shoe. 8—Excitation winding. 9—Brush holder and carbon brush. (Robert Bosch Corporation)

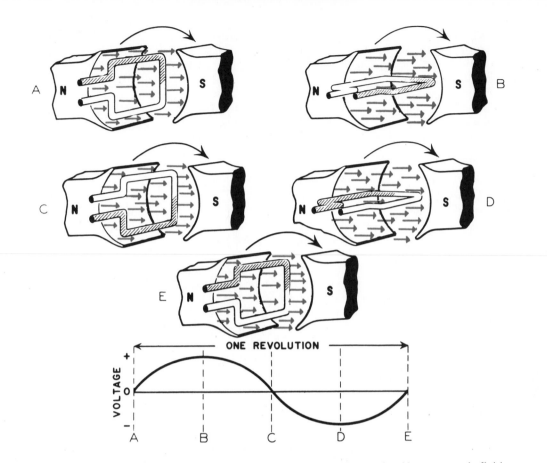

Fig. 32-3. Illustrating how voltage is induced in a coil that is revolved in a magnetic field.
Curve at bottom shows variation in voltage for each position of revolving coil.

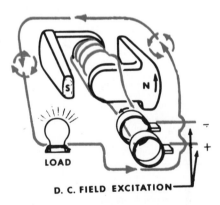

Fig. 32-4. Current for field excitation of an alternator is supplied by battery through brushes and slip rings.

mechanical switch (brushes and commutator) is provided.

In operation, the armature rotates between pole shoes wound with field coils. The spinning armature builds voltage in the field coils, and the field coils, in turn, produce more voltage and current in the armature.

The commutator is attached to the armature shaft and rotates with it. Coils of the armature are connected to bars or segments of the commutator. Each segment is insulated from the other, and spring-loaded brushes ride

on the commutator and transmit the voltage and current to the generator terminals, then to the battery and other electrical accessories.

A shortcoming of dc generators is that low speed output is limited. As a result, the battery does not receive a charge at idling and low speed operation. In addition, there is insufficient current for the operation of other electrical equipment. These are the main reasons why the dc generator was replaced by the alternator.

VOLTAGE REGULATORS

Some means of controlling generator output must be provided to prevent voltage from exceeding predetermined values. Voltage regulators are covered in detail in Chapter 33.

ALTERNATOR CONSTRUCTION

An alternator, Fig. 32-5, consists of three major units:
1. A ROTOR which provides the magnetic field.
2. A STATOR in which voltage and current is produced.
3. A DIODE (rectifier) ASSEMBLY which changes ac to dc.

The rotor assembly incorporates an iron core on a shaft with a wire coil wound around it. The coil is enclosed between two iron pole pieces with interspaced fingers or claws. The ends of the coil are connected to two slip rings mounted on one end of the rotor shaft.

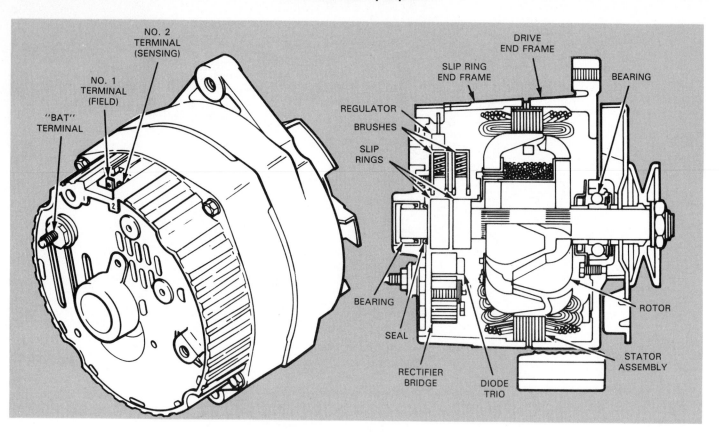

Fig. 32-5. Rear view and sectional side view of a typical alternator reveal all major components. (Chevrolet Motor Div., General Motors Corp.)

Small brushes ride on the slip rings. One brush is grounded, the other is insulated and connects to the alternator field terminal. This terminal, in turn, is connected through the alternator regulator and ignition switch to the battery.

The stator has three sets of windings assembled around the inside circumference of a laminated core, Fig. 32-5. This core forms part of the exterior frame in most alternators, and it provides a path for the flow of magnetic flux between two adjacent poles of the rotor.

Each winding of the stator generates a separate voltage, Fig. 32-6. One end of each winding is connected to a positive and negative diode. The other ends of the stator windings are connected to form a "Y" arrange-

ment. See Fig. 32-7. On heavy-duty applications, the windings are connected to form a triangle (delta-connected stator). See Fig. 32-8.

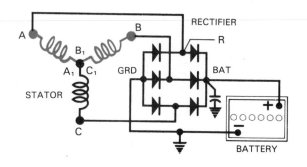

Fig. 32-7. When stator leads A, B, and C are connected together at A_1, B_1, and C_1, a three-phase "Y" circuit stator is formed.

The diode assembly basically consists of six diodes mounted at the slip ring end of the alternator housing, Fig. 32-9. The three negative diodes are mounted in the end frame or in a heat sink bolted to the end frame. The three positive diodes are mounted in a heat sink insulated from the end frame. Some alternators use DIODE TRIO assemblies.

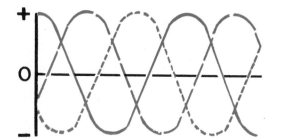

Fig. 32-6. Each winding of stator generates a separate voltage, making alternator a three-phase unit.

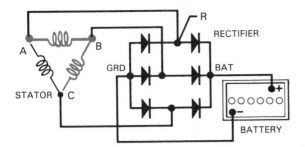

Fig. 32-8. When stator lead A is connected to B, B to C, and C to A, a triangular, three-phase "delta-connected" stator is formed.

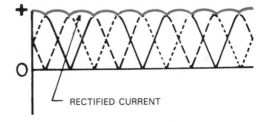

Fig. 32-10. Rectifier (diode assembly) permits current to pass through in one direction only. Rectified three-phase current is shown.

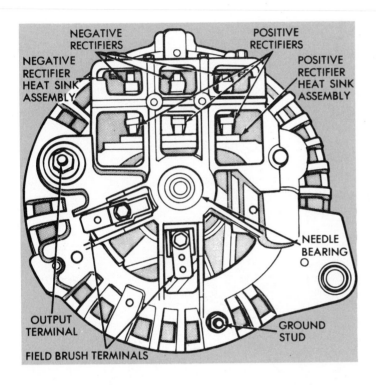

Fig. 32-9. Rear view of alternator rectifier (diode assembly) end shield shows location of positive and negative rectifiers and heat sink assemblies. (Chrysler Corp.)

The DIODES are connected to the stator leads and serve as one-way valves that permit current to flow through in one direction only. Each phase of the three-phase output of the alternator ranges from positive to negative and back to positive again. The diodes convert this alternating current to direct current at the alternator output terminal.

Note in Fig. 32-10 that while the voltage of each phase ranges from zero to maximum, the effective voltage of all phases maintains a reasonably even current output.

The front and rear housings, or frames, of the alternator generally are held together by "through bolts." A fan mounted on the front of the rotor shaft draws air through the housing for cooling. The housings support the bearings, usually a sealed thrust ball bearing at the front and an axial roller bearing at the rear.

ALTERNATOR OPERATION

Basically, an alternator produces alternating current within, then converts it to direct current at the output terminal. But before an alternator will begin to charge, direct current must flow through the rotor field coil to magnetize the pole pieces, Fig. 32-4. That is, the rotor (alternator field) must be externally excited before it will deliver voltage and current.

To help provide field excitation, some alternators utilize an ISOLATION DIODE and a CHARGE INDICATOR LAMP hooked up in parallel. This extra diode acts as an automatic switch between the battery and alternator to block current flow back to the alternator and regulator when the alternator is not operating.

When the ignition switch is turned ON, voltage is supplied to one side of the indicator lamp on the dash. This causes a small amount of current to pass through the regulator to the insulated brush. It flows through the slip ring, field coil, other slip ring, and other brush to ground. This direct current passing through the coil creates a magnetic field in each section of the rotor and lights the charge indicator lamp.

Then, as the rotor turns, its magnetic field induces voltage in the stator windings. Because the rotor sections have alternate north and south poles, and because current direction is reversed each half revolution of the rotor, alternating current is produced. See Fig. 32-6.

The stator sends this three-phase alternating current to the diode assembly, which permits current to pass through in one direction only to provide direct current at the alternator output terminal. See Fig. 32-10.

Fig. 32-11 shows the circuitry of a late model Ford alternator application with charge indicator light and electronic voltage regulator. When the ignition switch is turned ON, the warning lamp control circuit passes current to the warning lamp. When the voltage at terminal S rises to a preset value, current is cut off to the warning lamp. With input voltage present at terminal S, a switching circuit energizes the voltage control circuit which, in turn, controls the output circuit.

In this charging system application, current is supplied from the alternator-regulator system to the rotating field of the alternator through two brushes and two slip rings. The alternating current is rectified to direct current by six diodes. Typically, this alternator is self-current limiting. Note in Fig. 32-11 that the charging system contains a FUSE LINK at the starter relay battery ter-

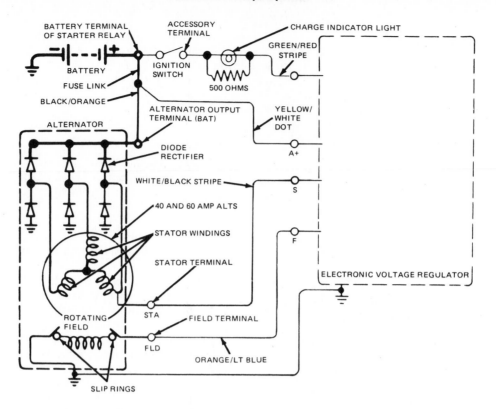

Fig. 32-11. Wiring diagram of a typical alternator charging system includes a charging indicator light circuit and an electronic voltage regulator. (Ford Motor Co.)

minal. Ford utilizes this fuse link to prevent damage to the wiring harness and alternator if the wiring harness becomes grounded or if booster battery cables are connected to the charging system with the wrong polarity.

ALTERNATOR DESIGN DIFFERENCES

Alternator design and construction varies according to vehicular application and electrical demands of the vehicle. Passenger car alternators range in rated output from 40 to 85 amps. Some special applications, such as fleet operations or police cars, have alternators that put out from 90 to 120 amps. Heavy-duty truck alternators are generally 105 to 160 amps.

In addition to higher output, design differences affect internal make-up, size, shape, and mounting configuration of the alternator. For example, open frame (vented) alternators are generally used in passenger cars, Fig. 32-12. Closed units are used in marine and off-the-road applications. Some models feature enclosed brushes and slip rings for use where explosive mixtures may be present. Oil cooled, totally enclosed units with stationary conductors are available for use on motor coaches.

Some alternators have 12 claw-pole rotors; others have 14 or 16 claw poles. The rotors may be riveted or welded. Voltage regulators may be built-in or mounted away from the alternator. Drive-end and rectifier-end bearings may be ball type or roller type or one of each. Diodes may be pressed-in, screwed-in, or come as a "trio" assembly. Heavy-duty alternators may have dual internal fans or an internal fan and an external fan. Some alternators have rear terminals; others have side ter-

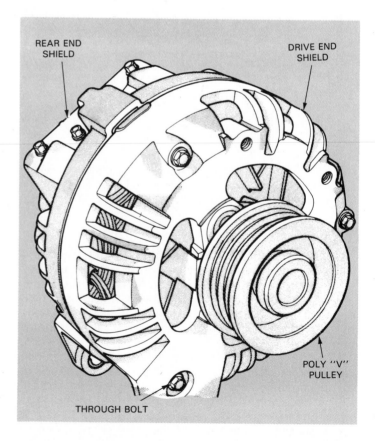

Fig. 32-12. External view of alternator assembly calls attention to finned, "open frame" design of passenger car alternators. (Chrysler Corp.)

minals. See Fig. 32-13.

Some alternators have dual brush sets; others are brushless. BRUSHLESS ALTERNATORS have no moving electrical connections. Both stator and field are stationary, eliminating shorts or grounds from rotor windings. The rectifier bridge, integrated voltage regulator, and other parts are located under a removable service access cover. The location of special features is indicated in Fig. 32-14.

These design differences only serve to emphasize that whatever the alternator design, diodes change alternating current from the stator windings to a flow of direct current at the output terminal of the alternator. The rotor (magnetic field), stator (conductors), and diodes (rectifiers) act as a team to produce direct current electricity to keep the battery fully charged and to supply electrical energy to the vehicle's current-consuming devices.

Chapter 32—REVIEW QUESTIONS

Write your answers on a separate sheet of paper. Do not write in this book.
1. What is an automotive generator?
2. What is the purpose of an automotive generator?

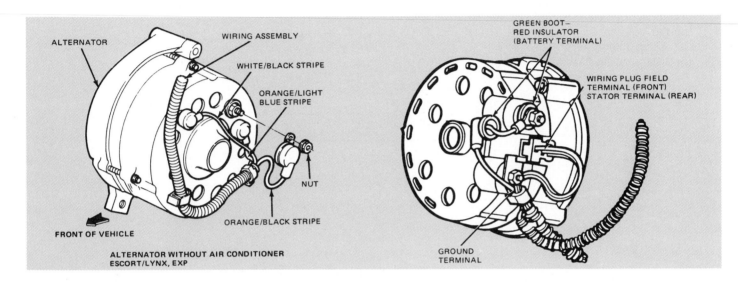

Fig. 32-13. Alternators have either rear terminals. A, or side terminals, B, as influenced by internal design or for compatibility with location at front of engine. (Ford Motor Co.)

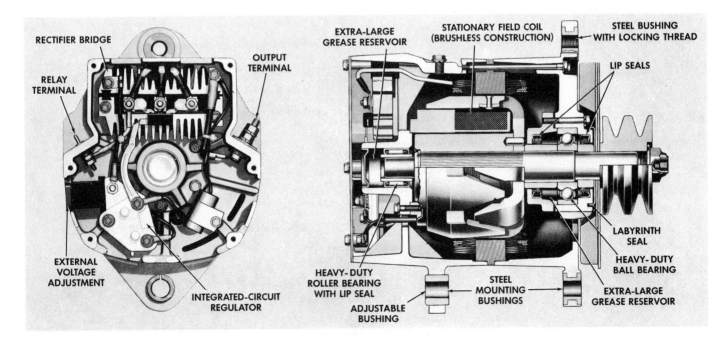

Fig. 32-14. Both stator and field coil in this brushless alternator are stationary, eliminating shorts and grounds more likely to occur when field winding must rotate. (Delco Remy Div., General Motors Corp.)

3. When rotating a coil of wire through a horizontal magnetic field, maximum voltage will be produced in the _____ (horizontal/vertical) position of the coil.

4. Voltage can also be produced by keeping the coil stationary and moving the magnetic field. True or False?

5. Name the three major units of an alternator.

6. The _____ has three sets of windings around the inner circumference of a laminated core.
   a. Armature.
   b. Rotor.
   c. Field coil.
   d. Stator.

7. What means of controlling generator output is provided to prevent voltage from exceeding predetermined values?
   a. Cutout relay.
   b. Voltage regulator.
   c. Integral transistor.
   d. Diode rectifier.

8. In most alternators, which part is the rotating magnetic field?
   a. Armature.
   b. Rotor.
   c. Field coil.
   d. Stator.

9. In an alternator, which part changes the current from alternating to direct?
   a. Commutator.
   b. Converter.
   c. Regulator.
   d. Diode.

10. Ford's charging system utilizes a _____ at the starter relay battery terminal to prevent damage to the wiring harness if it becomes grounded.
    a. Isolation diode.
    b. Slip ring.
    c. Fuse link.
    d. Cutout relay

11. Name the two types of generators.

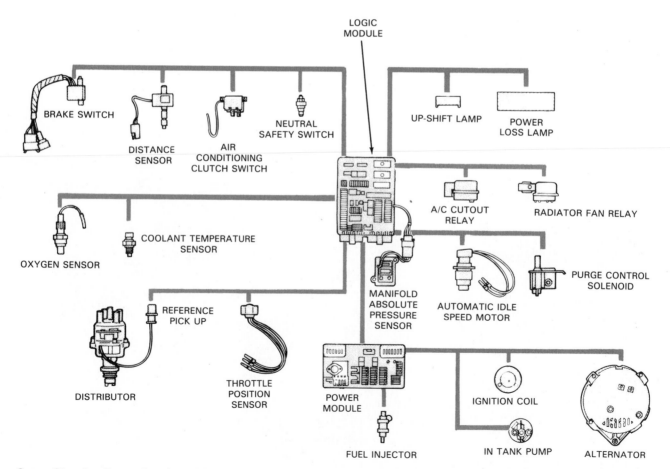

Some Chrysler Corp. charging systems are regulated by functions of engine computer logic module and power module. No internal or externally mounted voltage regulator unit is used.

Chapter 33

CHARGING SYSTEM REGULATORS AND RELAYS

After studying this chapter, you will be able to:
- Tell why and how voltage regulation is necessary in a charging system.
- Discuss the three basic phases of voltage regulator development.
- Describe the makeup and operating principles of a typical electromagnetic alternator voltage regulator.
- Describe the makeup and operating principles of a typical electronic voltage regulator.
- Explain how modules in the engine spark control computer determine and control alternator voltage output.

The automotive alternator produces the electricity needed to charge the battery and to operate electrical equipment. By design, however, its output continues to rise as its speed increases. Therefore, the charging system is provided with a voltage regulator.

Basically, the ALTERNATOR VOLTAGE REGULATOR is an automatic switch that controls charging system output so that voltage and current will not exceed predetermined values. Regulation is needed or excessively high current will damage the battery, alternator, or other elements of the charging system.

The task of the voltage regulator, then, is to sense the amount of voltage present . . . determine when the battery needs to be charged . . . then control alternator output accordingly.

VOLTAGE REGULATOR TYPES

Voltage regulators are in their third phase of development. First, there were ELECTROMAGNETIC VOLTAGE REGULATORS, used in both dc generator and alternator charging systems. See Figs. 33-1 and 33-2.

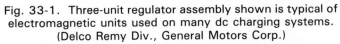

Fig. 33-1. Three-unit regulator assembly shown is typical of electromagnetic units used on many dc charging systems. (Delco Remy Div., General Motors Corp.)

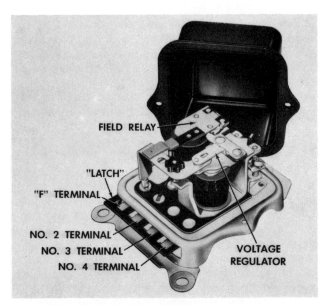

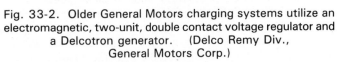

Fig. 33-2. Older General Motors charging systems utilize an electromagnetic, two-unit, double contact voltage regulator and a Delcotron generator. (Delco Remy Div., General Motors Corp.)

Then, ELECTRONIC VOLTAGE REGULATORS were introduced, and they continue to be used in most late model applications. These solid state devices, Fig. 33-3, did away with wire-wound coils, contact points, and bimetallic hinges. The manufacturers state that the electronic units are more reliable, durable, and less affected by temperature changes.

Now, in certain applications, the voltage regulator

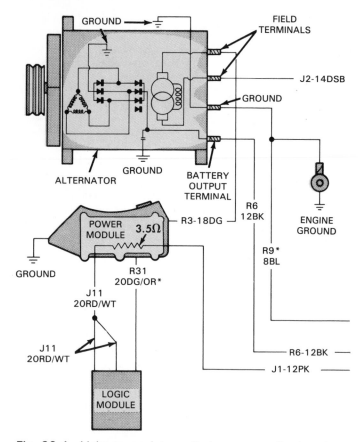

Fig. 33-4. Voltage regulator units in some applications have been replaced by functions within engine computer modules. (Chrysler Corp.)

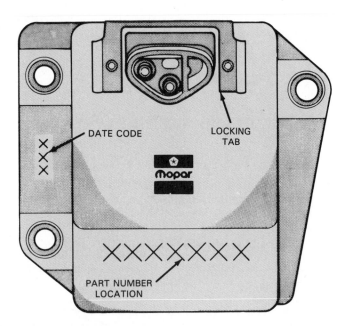

Fig. 33-3. Electronic voltage regulators generally contain sealed-in transistors, diodes, resistors, and capacitors. (Chrysler Corp.)

function has become part of the ENGINE COMPUTER CONTROL SYSTEM. Chrysler, for example, controls the alternator output voltage by means of two computer modules. See Fig. 33-4.

Regardless of type, however, the voltage regulator controls voltage and current output of the alternator by automatically cutting resistance in or out of the field circuit. Varying the resistance alters the amount of current passing through the field. This changes the strength of the magnetic field and alternator output is regulated.

DC GENERATOR REGULATOR OPERATION

Electromagnetic regulators used on many dc generator charging systems consist of three elements: cutout relay, current regulator, and voltage regulator, Fig. 33-1. Others utilize a cutout relay and a step-voltage control unit. Still others use a cutout relay with a vibrating voltage regulator or a cutout relay with a combined current-voltage unit.

The purpose of the CUTOUT RELAY is to prevent the battery from discharging through the generator when the engine is stopped or turning over at slow speed.

The CURRENT REGULATOR is a magnetic switch in the charging circuit designed to protect the dc generator from overload by limiting current output to a safe value.

The VOLTAGE REGULATOR controls charging circuit

voltage from exceeding a safe value. When the battery needs charging, the voltage regulator cuts resistance out of the field circuit, which increases the flow of current and boosts generator output. When the battery becomes fully charged, the resistance is cut into the field circuit and the charging rate is decreased.

Because of increased electrical loads, many dc charging system regulators are provided with voltage regulator units of the double contact type. These units are equipped with two sets of contact points to accomodate the high field currents in the generator.

REGULATORS FOR ALTERNATORS

Regulators most commonly used with alternators are the electromagnetic, transistorized, and electronic types (including integral type). Carbon pile regulators are also used, but mainly in heavy-duty, high-output applications.

In electromagnetic regulators, Fig. 33-2, the voltage regulator unit limits voltage output by controlling the amount of current applied to the rotating field (alternator rotor). The field relay, on regulators so equipped, connects the alternator field windings and voltage regulator windings directly to the battery. In some cases, it also serves as an indicator lamp relay.

The conventional cutout relay unit is eliminated by the diodes in the alternator. The current limiter (regulator) is eliminated by the current-limiting characteristic of alternator design.

Transistorized and electronic regulators, Fig. 33-3, have no moving parts. Consequently, they have a long life. These regulators usually consist of transistors, diodes, resistors, and capacitors, all working together to regulate alternator field current and thereby limit alternator output voltage to a safe value.

Integral regulators, as the name implies, are built into the alternator. In most applications, the integral regulator is small, flat, transistorized, and attached to the inside of the slip ring end frame.

ELECTROMAGNETIC ALTERNATOR REGULATORS

ELECTROMAGNETIC REGULATORS used on earlier alternator charging systems also utilized a voltage regulator unit to limit voltage output to a predetermined value. This unit is incorporated in single, two, or three-unit regulators in many standard equipment applications. The single-unit regulator is used only in circuits with an ammeter. The two-unit, double contact regulator is suitable for use in circuits containing either an ammeter or indicator lamp. The three-unit, double contact regulator contains a voltage regulator, field relay, and indicator lamp relay.

Regulator terminals usually are slip-connection type. Slots in the regulator base are keyed to mating surfaces of a connector on the wiring harness to insure correct connections.

The two-unit regulator consists of a double contact voltage regulator unit and a field relay. If an indicator lamp is used in the charging circuit, Fig. 33-5, it lights when the ignition switch is turned ON and goes out when the alternator begins to produce charging voltage.

A voltage regulator actually has many stages of operation. A typical GENERAL MOTORS TWO-UNIT, DOUBLE CONTACT REGULATOR, Fig. 33-5, operates as follows:

1. Field relay points close when engine starts and alternator stator windings put out voltage. As soon as points close, field current is supplied directly from battery instead of through ignition switch and resistance wire.

2. When engine speed is low and battery or accessories need a lot of current, lower contacts of voltage regulator unit remain closed to allow full field current (about 2 amps) to flow.

3. As engine speed increases, or load lessens, lower contacts vibrate between open and closed position to reduce field current to between 2 amps and 3/4 amp.

4. When speed and load requirement reach a point where exactly 3/4 amp field current provides needed output, voltage regulator armature will "float" between upper and lower contacts. In this situation, entire field current passes through a resistor that limits current to 3/4 amp.

5. When engine speed is high and load is low, increased voltage in charging circuit will cause voltage regulator armature to be drawn down, closing upper set of contacts to ground circuit and no field current will flow.

6. As engine speed is reduced and load again calls for a small charge, upper contacts will vibrate and field current will flow at from 0 to 3/4 amp, depending on rate of vibration.

FORD MOTOR COMPANY ELECTROMAGNETIC TWO-UNIT ALTERNATOR REGULATORS consist of a field relay and a double contact voltage limiter (regulator), Fig. 33-6. As is generally the case with alternator-equipped charging systems, a cutout relay and a current regulator are not needed.

The field relay connects the battery and alternator output to the field circuit when the engine is running. The double contact voltage limiter controls the amount of current supplied to the rotating field.

At low engine speed and with a load applied, the upper contacts of the voltage limiter are closed, full system

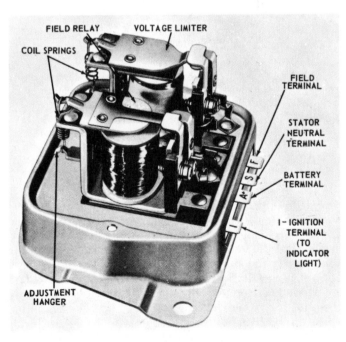

Fig. 33-6. Some Ford electromagnetic alternator regulators have two control units and four slip-on terminals coded as shown.

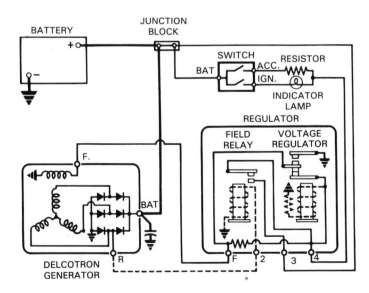

Fig. 33-5. Schematic details charging system circuitry of Delcotron generator and double contact regulator shown in Fig. 33-2. (Delco Remy Div., General Motors Corp.)

371

voltage is applied to the field, and maximum field current will flow. At high engine speed and with little or no load, the lower contacts are closed and no current flows to the field. A resistor is connected from the field terminal to ground to absorb electrical surges when the voltage limiter armature vibrates on the contacts or floats between them.

On Ford cars with charge indicator light on the dash, battery current flows through the indicator light and a parallel resistor, and through the voltage limiter contacts to the field coil. When the ignition switch is turned on, this small current permits the alternator to start charging. On cars with ammeters, closing of the field relay contact connects battery and alternator output to the field through the voltage limiter contacts.

CHRYSLER ELECTROMAGNETIC REGULATORS generally are single-unit, double contact voltage regulators. See Fig. 33-7 for construction features. Underneath, these regulators have three resistance units, two of which are connected in series with the field circuit.

AMERICAN MOTORS ELECTROMAGNETIC REGULATORS are used on cars equipped with a V-8 engine. These regulators are mounted on the wheelhouse panel near the battery. They are nonadjustable.

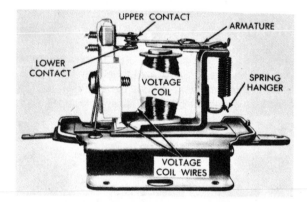

Fig. 33-7. Some Chrysler Corp. cars are equipped with electromagnetic, single-unit, double contact voltage regulators with resistance units mounted underneath.

TRANSISTORIZED/ELECTRONIC REGULATORS

Each of the various models of GENERAL MOTORS TRANSISTORIZED REGULATORS is matched to the alternator field circuit it must control and to the vehicle application. See Fig. 33-8. Internal construction is similar, but the various models are not interchangeable.

Basically, the transistor is "switched" on and off to control alternator field current. The frequency of switching depends on alternator speed and accessory load, with the possibility that the "on-off cycle" may be repeated as often as 7000 times per second.

FORD TRANSISTORIZED AND ELECTRONIC VOLTAGE REGULATORS are used in late model applications. Both operate on the principle of controlling alternator voltage output by regulating the alternator field cur-

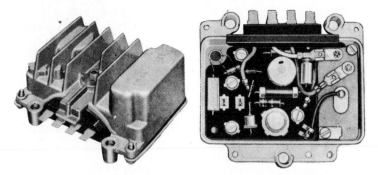

Fig. 33-8. Delco Remy transistorized regulators are similar in appearance but internal construction may differ.

rent. The transistorized units have a voltage limiter adjustment. The electronic units are factory calibrated, sealed, and nonadjustable.

Ford's transistorized voltage regulators, Fig. 33-9, control alternator voltage output electronically by the use of transistors and diodes. The voltage sensing element is a zener diode which changes its resistance to suit voltage requirements.

Ford electronic regulators consist of transistors, diodes, and resistors. These parts are arranged in four different circuits or stages: output, voltage control, solid state relay, and field current overprotection.

Closing the ignition switch turns on the warning lamp and output stage. See Fig. 33-10. The alternator receives maximum field current, and output terminal

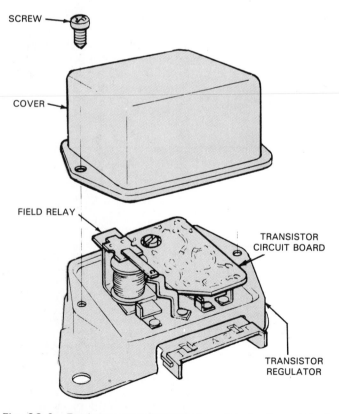

Fig. 33-9. Ford uses an adjustable transistorized regulator in charging system of certain engine applications.

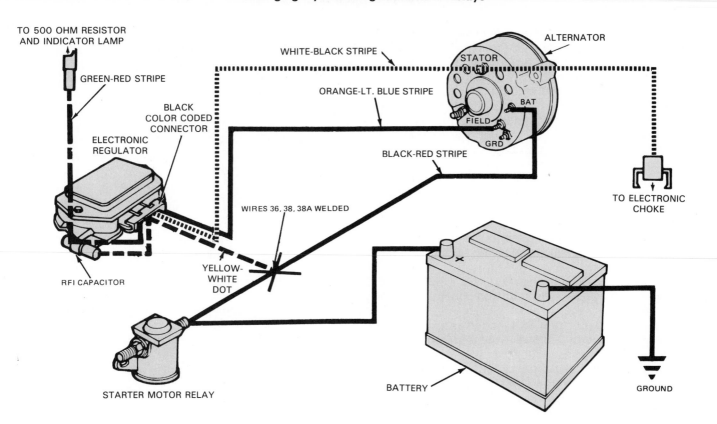

Fig. 33-10. Wiring diagram shows color-coded wiring of a Ford alternator charging system equipped with an electronic voltage regulator and indicator lamp.

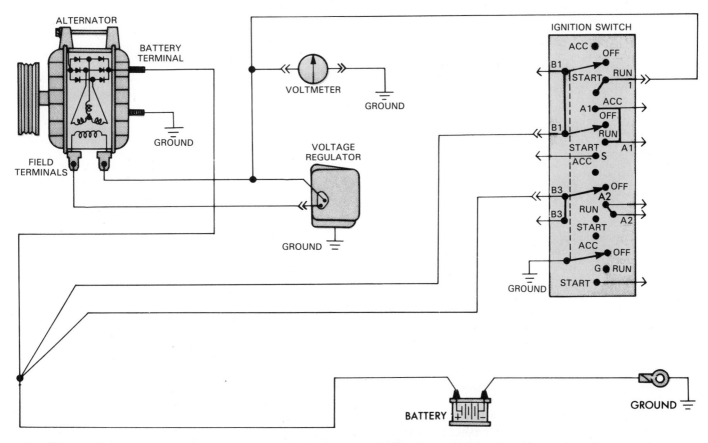

Fig. 33-11. Typical Chrysler Corp. charging system features a six-diode alternator and an electronic voltage regulator as shown in Fig. 33-3.

voltage increases from zero to a level determined by the voltage control stage. The stator terminal voltage is one-half of output voltage and turns off the indicator lamp by way of the solid state relay circuit.

When the ignition switch is switched off, the solid state relay circuit turns off the output stage, thus turning off all current flow through the regulator. With that, there is no current drain on the battery.

The field current overprotection stage protects the regulator against damage that could be caused by a ''short'' in the field circuit.

Chrysler Corporation engines have a variety of alternators and electronic voltage regulators in their charging systems. See Fig. 33-11. As with earlier systems, the electronic units limit alternator output voltage by controlling the amount of current passing through the alternator field winding.

CHRYSLER ELECTRONIC VOLTAGE REGULATORS are made up of several solid state components, including a large transistor placed in series with the alternator field winding. These regulator units function as a voltage sensitive switch. A control circuit in the regulator turns the transistor on and off as required by speed and load conditions. In addition, the control circuit is designed to vary regulated voltage up or down with temperature changes.

A Bosch alternator used in some Chrysler high output charging systems has 16 built-in rectifiers. A compact electronic voltage regulator, Fig. 33-12, is built into the rear housing of the alternator.

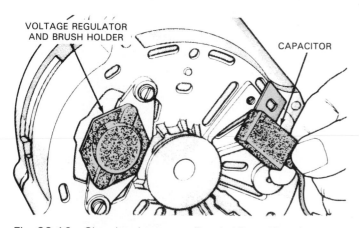

Fig. 33-12. Chrysler also uses a Bosch 16-rectifier alternator having an electronic voltage regulator and capacitor attached to its rear end shield.

A Mitsubishi alternator installed on certain other Chrysler applications has 15 built-in rectifiers. An internal electronic voltage regulator unit, Fig. 33-13, is used.

GENERAL MOTORS ELECTRONIC VOLTAGE REGULATORS utilize solid-state circuitry to regulate current applied to the generator field. These nonadjustable electronic units and the brush holder assembly are attached inside the rear housing of the generator. See Fig. 33-14. Some American Motors cars with four cylinder or six cylinder engines use a similar generator/regulator setup, Fig. 33-15.

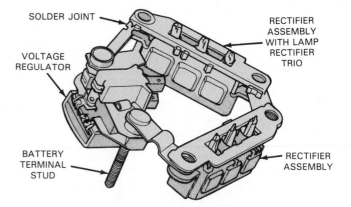

Fig. 33-13. Chrysler also uses a Mitsubishi 15-rectifier, high output alternator with internal electronic voltage regulator.

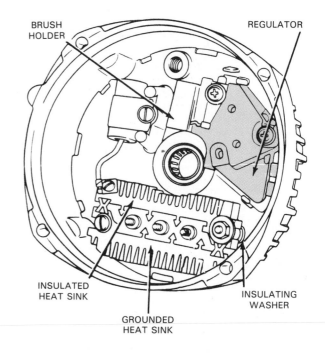

Fig. 33-14. General Motors cars use a variety of Delco Remy generators. An integrated circuit electronic voltage regulator is mounted inside generator rear housing. (Chevrolet Motor Div., General Motors Corp.)

COMPUTER CONTROLLED VOLTAGE REGULATION

Voltage regulator units have been replaced by functions within two engine computer modules on certain late model Chrysler Corporation applications. The regulator functions are shared by circuits in the power and logic modules in the engine spark control computer. See Fig. 33-4. This, Chrysler claims, eliminates the possibility of ''blowing'' computer circuits if a charging system terminal is accidentally grounded.

In operation, the field is turned on by a ''driver'' in the power module. The driver is controlled by a ''predriver'' in the logic module. The logic module also checks battery temperature as a means of determining and con-

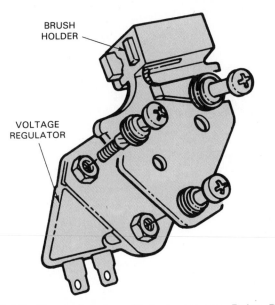

BRUSH HOLDER

VOLTAGE REGULATOR

Fig. 33-15. Some American Motors cars use Delco Remy generators with integral voltage regulator, similar to installation shown in Fig. 33-14. (American Motors Corp.)

trolling alternator output voltage. Again, this method of alternator voltage control limits output by controlling the amount of current allowed to pass through the alternator field windings.

Chapter 33—REVIEW QUESTIONS

Write your answers on a separate sheet of paper. Do not write in this book.

1. What is the purpose of the voltage regulator?
2. What is the function of the voltage regulator unit when the battery is low in charge?
   a. To maintain a constant charging rate.
   b. To prevent battery from discharging through generator (alternator).
   c. To cut resistance out of field circuit.
   d. To cut resistance into field circuit.
3. Why are two sets of contact points used on some electromagnetic voltage regulators?
4. Name the two major basic types of voltage regulators.
   a. Single and double contact.
   b. Two-unit and three-unit.
   c. Integral and externally mounted.
   d. Electromagnetic and electronic.
5. Now, in certain applications, the voltage regulator function has become part of the _____.
   a. Electronic ignition system.
   b. Engine computer control system.
   c. Emission control system.
   d. Electronic fuel injection system.
6. Transistorized and electronic voltage regulators have no moving parts. True or False?
7. The voltage sensing element in Ford's transistorized voltage regulator is a _____ which changes its resistance to suit voltage requirements.
   a. Resistor.
   b. Capacitor.
   c. Field relay.
   d. Zener diode.
8. Ford electronic voltage regulator parts are arranged in four different circuits or stages; output, voltage control, solid state relay, and _____.
9. Chrysler electronic voltage regulators are made up of several solid state components and function as a _____.
10. General Motors electronic voltage regulators utilize a _____ circuit to regulate current applied to the alternator field.

Chapter 34

CHARGING SYSTEM TESTING AND SERVICING

After studying this chapter, you will be able to:
- State precautions concerning charging system testing and servicing.
- Give quick checks for solving charging system problems.
- Explain need for follow-up current output and circuit resistance tests.
- Recognize importance of service manual information.
- Describe bench testing of charging system components.
- Interpret step-by-step testing and servicing procedures.

Alternator charging systems require regular inspection and maintenance. The frequency of inspection depends on operating conditions. High-speed operation, high temperatures, dust, and dirt all tend to increase wear on alternator components.

CHARGING SYSTEM INSPECTION

Inspect alternator systems visually and manually at approximately 5000 mile intervals to make sure that brushes, slip rings, and bearings are in good operating condition. Also test the battery's state of charge and the condition of starting and charging system cables, wires, and connections. It pays to check the condition of the battery and starting system before performing charging system electrical tests.

Check for tightness of starter, alternator, and regulator mounting bolts to insure good ground circuits. Look over the alternator drive belt for signs of wear or slippage. See that the tension adjustment is correct. The belt should deflect 1/4 in. in the center of a long span. Belt tension testers generally show color-coded GOOD and BAD ranges, Fig. 34-1. If not, check the tester tension reading against manufacturer's specifications.

CHARGING SYSTEM PRECAUTIONS AND TESTS

Alternator testing and servicing call for special precautions since the alternator output terminal is connected to the battery at all times.

1. Use care to avoid reverse polarity when performing battery service of any kind. A surge of current in opposite direction could burn out alternator diodes (rectifiers) and damage vehicle wiring.
2. Do not purposely or accidentally "short" or "ground" system when disconnecting wires or connecting test leads to terminals of alternator or regulator. For example, grounding of field terminal at either alternator or regulator will damage regulator. Grounding of alternator output terminal will damage alternator and/or charging circuit.
3. Never operate an alternator on an open circuit. With no battery or electric load in circuit, alternators are capable of building high voltage (50 to over 110 volts) which may damage diodes and could be dangerous to anyone who might touch the alternator output terminal.
4. Do not try to polarize an alternator. Polarity of alternator systems cannot be lost or damaged, so attempts to polarize system serve no purpose and may cause damage to diodes, wiring harness, or other system components.

Fig. 34-1. Alternator drive belt condition and tension are two primary considerations in alternator maintenance.

Maintenance is minimized by the use of prelubricated rotor bearings and long brushes in most modern alternators. If a problem exists, such as low output or overcharging, check for a complete field circuit (rotor) by placing a large screwdriver on the alternator rear bearing surface. If the field circuit is complete, there will be a strong magnetic pull on the blade of the screwdriver. This indicates that the field windings are energized. If there is no field circuit, an alternator will not charge because the field windings must be "excited" by battery voltage.

QUICK CHECKS

Generally, certain other quick checks for possible sources of charging system problems can be made before getting into extensive electrical tests.

If the charging system has a fuse (fusible) link, Fig. 34-2, check it for appearance and continuity. The link is designed to "blow" if heavy current flows in the circuit. If the link is blackened or "open" (no continuity), replace it with a "matching" link. Do not bypass it or replace it with "any piece of wire."

Also check the charge indicator lamp on the dash. The only time the lamp should light is when the ignition switch is in the "run" position and the engine is off. Once the engine starts and the alternator begins to produce voltage, the indicator lamp should turn off. If it stays on, there is a malfunction in the charging system. If the lamp fails to light in any ignition key position, the indicator lamp bulb is probably at fault.

On General Motors and American Motors alternators with integral voltage regulator, make the following checks on charging systems having an indicator lamp outage: Unplug No. 1-2 connector and ground the No. 1 wire. If the lamp fails to light, check for an "open" in the No. 1 wire. If the lamp lights, reconnect the No. 1-2 connector and "ground" the tab in the alternator end frame access hole. See Fig. 34-3. If the light stays on, replace the regulator. If the light turns off when the tab is "grounded," check the rotor, brushes, and slip rings for an "open."

If the problem is "undercharging," a good way to begin electrical tests of the charging system is to bypass the voltage regulator (called "full fielding" because the alternator field winding is receiving full current input). FULL FIELDING can be accomplished by use of a little plastic "full fielder," a piece of "jumper" wire, or a screwdriver. See Fig. 34-3.

If full fielding allows the alternator to produce at least a normal charging voltage (13.8-14.9 volts), the voltage regulator is at fault. If the alternator is still "undercharging," there is a problem in the alternator or wiring.

Before condemning any particular component or assembly in the charging system, make further tests of current output and circuit resistance. A specific procedure for each test follows.

CURRENT OUTPUT TEST — CHRYSLER

Specifically, make test connections shown in Fig. 34-4 to measure a Chrysler alternator's ability to produce its rated current output at specified speed and voltage at normal operating temperature.

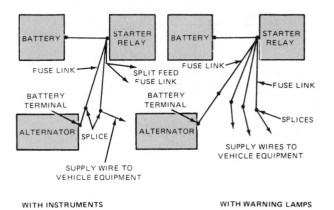

WITH INSTRUMENTS   WITH WARNING LAMPS

Fig. 34-2. Note fuse link between starter relay terminal and alternator battery terminal. Open circuit usually means fuse link has "blown." (Ford Motor Co.)

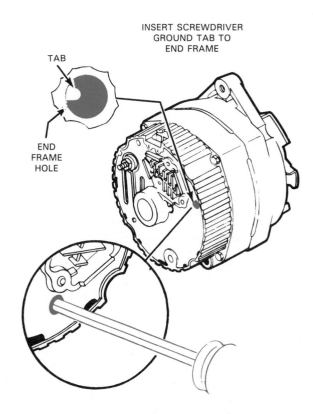

Fig. 34-3. Delcotron generators have a test hole that provides a point of access for using a screwdriver to ground field winding. (Chevrolet Motor Div., General Motors Corp.)

1. Make sure battery is fully charged.
2. Disconnect battery ground cable.
3. Disconnect BAT lead wire at alternator output terminal.
4. Connect a 0-150 amp (minimum) ammeter in series between disconnected wire and output terminal.
5. Connect positive lead of 0-18 volts (minimum) voltmeter to BAT terminal of alternator.
6. Connect negative lead of voltmeter to ground.
7. Connect a tachometer to engine, then reconnect battery ground cable.

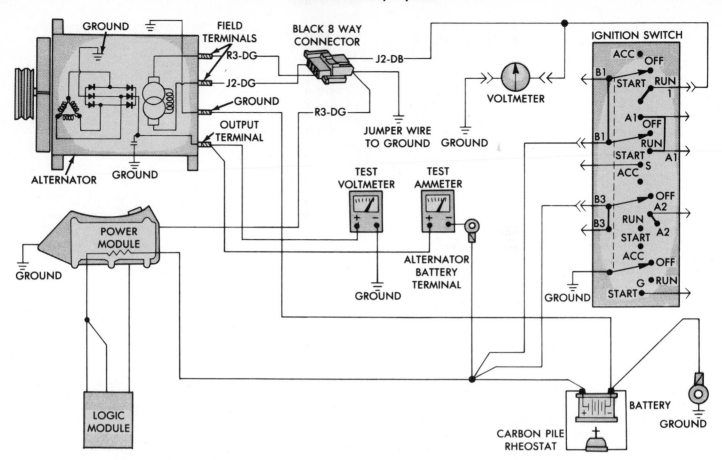

Fig. 34-4. Diagram shows testers and carbon pile rheostat hookups for making a current output test on a Chrysler Corp. alternator with voltage regulated by computer modules.

8. Install a variable pile rheostat (with carbon pile OFF) between battery terminals.

9. Remove air hose between power module and air cleaner.

10. Ground one end of "jumper" wire and use other end to probe green R3 lead wire of black 8-way connector. See Fig. 34-5.

11. Start engine and operate at idle speed.

12. Gradually adjust carbon pile and engine speed until a speed of 1250 rpm (typical setting — check specifications) and voltmeter reading of 15 volts are obtained. NOTE: Do not exceed 16 volts.

13. Ammeter reading (current output) must be within limits given for alternator being tested:

    a. Chrysler Corp. 60 amp alternator with external or internal electronic voltage regulator: 47 amps minimum.

    b. Corporate 78 amp alternator with external or internal electronic voltage regulator: 58 amps minimum.

    c. Corporate 90 amp alternator regulated by power and logic modules: 96 amps minimum. See Fig. 34-6.

    d. Corporate 114 amp alternator with external electronic voltage regulator: 92 amps minimum (13.5 volts at 900 rpm).

    e. Bosch 65 amp alternator with Chrysler Corp. external electronic voltage regulator: 50 amps minimum.

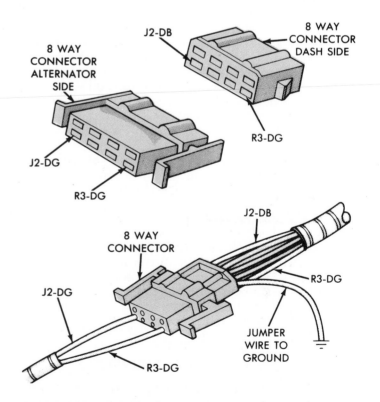

Fig. 34-5. Key step in making alternator current output and charging circuit resistance tests is grounding of green R3 lead at 8-way connector. (Chrysler Corp.)

CHRYSLER 40/90 AMP ALTERNATOR WITH VOLTAGE REGULATOR IN ELECTRONICS

Output	40/90
Rotation	Clockwise (as viewed from pulley end)
Voltage	12 Volt System
Current Output	Design Controlled
Voltage Output	Limited by Voltage Regulator in Electronics
Brushes (Field)	2
Condenser Capacity	0.5 Microfarad plus or minus 20%
Field Current Draw (Bench Test)	
Rotating by Hand	2.5 to 5.0 Amperes @ 12V
Current Rating	**Current Output**
40/90 Amp	96 Amp Minimum
Current output is measured at 1250 engine rpm and 15 volts at the alternator. Voltage is controlled by variable load (carbon pile) across the battery.	

Fig. 34-6. Sample specification chart from Chrysler Corp. service manual gives alternator identification details, test requirements, and performance specifications.

f. Bosch 90 amp alternator with internal electronic voltage regulator: 78 amps minimum (13.5 volts at 1000 rpm).

g. Bosch 90 amp alternator regulated by power and logic modules: 87 amps minimum.

h. Mitsubishi 75 amp alternator with internal electronic voltage regulator: 63 amps minimum (13.5 volts at 1000 rpm).

CHARGING CIRCUIT RESISTANCE TEST — CHRYSLER

If the current output test indicates that a problem exists in the charging circuit, make the circuit resistance test with the hookup shown in Fig. 34-7. This test will reveal whether the problem lies in the insulated circuit, ground circuit, or alternator:

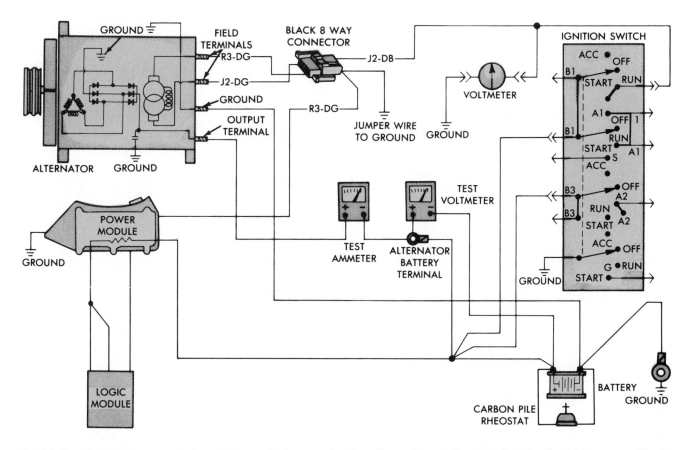

Fig. 34-7. Diagram shows tester and carbon pile rheostat hookups for making a charging circuit resistance test on a Chrysler Corp. alternator with voltage regulated by computer modules.

1. Make sure battery is fully charged.
2. Disconnect battery ground cable.
3. Disconnect BAT lead wire at alternator output terminal.
4. Connect a 0-150 amp (minimum) ammeter in series between disconnected wire and terminal.
5. Connect positive lead of low range voltmeter to alternator BAT terminal.
6. Connect negative lead of voltmeter to disconnected alternator BAT terminal wire.
7. Remove air hose between power module and air cleaner.
8. Ground one end of a ''jumper'' wire and use other end to probe green R3 lead wire of black 8-way connector. See Fig. 34-5.
9. Connect a tachometer to engine, then reconnect battery ground cable.
10. Install a variable pile rheostat (with carbon pile OFF) between battery terminals.
11. Start engine and operate at idle speed.
12. Adjust carbon pile and engine speed to obtain a 20 amp current flow in charging circuit.
13. Check voltmeter reading. It should not exceed 0.5 volt (voltage drop).

If higher voltage drop is indicated, clean and tighten all connections in the charging circuit. If necessary, make voltage drop tests at each connection in the circuit. A higher than normal voltage may indicate a poor ground connection.

IMPORTANCE OF SERVICE MANUALS

When making tests or performing service operations, consult the car manufacturer's SERVICE MANUALS for step-by-step instructions, test equipment and tools needed, test procedures, and acceptable values or ranges for a comparison with test results. See Fig. 34-6.

The alternator rated amp output and current output minimum values given in the preceding test results are condensed from information contained in one particular Chrysler Corp. service manual. The fact that the various alternators listed are available in different vehicle applications during the same model year certainly emphasizes the need for consulting service manuals for complete and authoritative service information and specifications.

ALTERNATOR REMOVAL

If the charging system fails to meet current output specifications, and ''full fielding'' (bypassing voltage regulator or computer modules) shows the alternator at fault, remove the alternator for disassembly and bench tests. See Fig. 34-8.
1. Place ignition switch in OFF position.
2. Remove ground cable from negative post of battery.
3. Disconnect leads from alternator output terminal (BAT) and from two field terminals. (FLD).
4. Disconnect ground lead from alternator.
5. Remove wiring retainer nut and disengage retainer from alternator.
6. Unscrew mounting bolts and adjusting arm bolts.
7. Slip off drive belt, or belts, and remove alternator from engine.

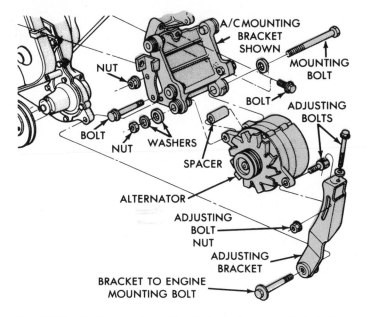

Fig. 34-8. Exploded view of a typical alternator installation shows arrangement of brackets, mounting bracket, adjusting bracket, bolts, and nuts.   (Chrysler Corp.)

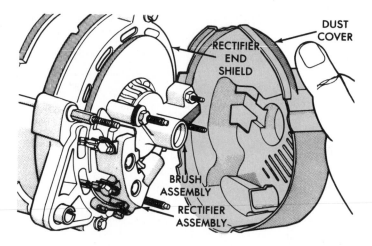

Fig. 34-9. Disassembly of Chrysler Corp. alternator with voltage regulated by electronics begins with removal of dust cover.

ALTERNATOR DISASSEMBLY

To disassemble alternator:
1. Scribe marks on front and rear housings or end shields and stator frame to aid reassembly.
2. Remove dust cover, Fig. 34-9.
3. Remove brush holder mounting screws and brush holder assembly, Fig. 34-10.
4. Remove three stator-to-rectifier attaching screws.
5. Remove two rectifier assembly mounting screws.
6. Remove rectifier insulator.
7. Remove condenser (capacitor) mounting screw and remove rectifier assembly.
8. Remove through bolts, then separate end shields by using two screwdrivers to pry gently between

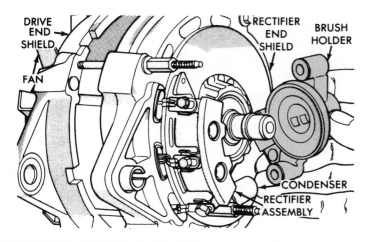

Fig. 34-10. Removal of brush holder assembly permits access to rectifier assembly and condenser. (Chrysler Corp.)

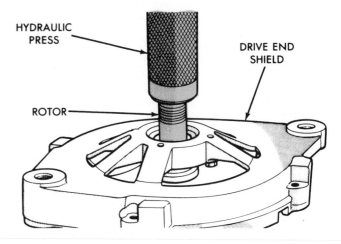

Fig. 34-12. If rotor removal is necessary, support drive end shield on bed of hydraulic press, and press out rotor. (Chrysler Corp.)

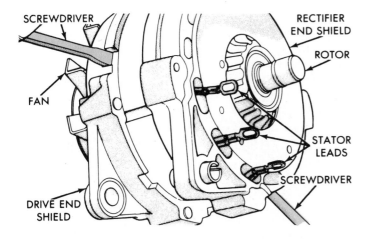

Fig. 34-11. To separate end shields, use two screwdrivers to pry between stator and drive end shield. (Chrysler Corp.)

Fig. 34-13. Remove stator from rectifier end shield for making bench tests. (Chrylser Corp.)

drive end shield and stator. See Fig. 34-11. Stator should remain with rear end shield.

9. Remove pulley nut, pulley washer, pulley, and fan.
10. Remove bearing spacer and press rotor out of drive end shield, Fig. 34-12.
11. Remove stator from rear end shield, Fig. 34-13.

BENCH TESTS

With all major parts disassembled, they may be tested for condition by making various "bench tests."

ROTOR TESTS

To test the rotor for an "open" circuit: Connect test lamp leads to each slip ring. If the lamp fails to light, the circuit is incomplete or "open."

To test for a "short" circuit: Connect one test lamp lead to the rotor shaft. Connect other lead to one slip ring, Fig. 34-14. If the lamp lights, there is a "short to ground" between the windings or slip rings and the rotor shaft.

If the rotor fails either test, replace it.

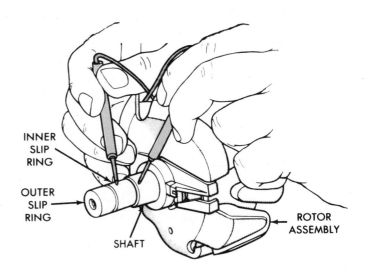

Fig. 34-14. To test for a "short to ground," touch test lamp probes to rotor shaft and slip ring. If lamp lights, rotor is grounded. (Chrysler Corp.)

STATOR TESTS

To test the stator for a "grounded" circuit: Connect one test lamp lead to the stator core (remove varnish first). With other test lead, prod each of three stator leads. If the test lamp lights, the stator lead is "grounded."

To test stator windings for an "open" circuit: Use a test lamp to contact each of three stator leads in turn, two at a time. See Fig. 34-15. If the lamp fails to light, there is an "open" in the stator coil.

If the stator fails either test, replace it.

DIODE TESTS

Several testers on the market permit diode testing without removing the stator leads; others require that the leads be disconnected.

To make a positive diode test: Clip one test lead to output (BAT) terminal of alternator. Clip other test lead to metal strap or pin of each positive diode in turn. See Fig. 34-16. Meter readings should fall in GOOD band and in relatively close range of each other.

To test negative diodes: Move test lead from output terminal of alternator to rectifier end shield. Touch other test lead to each negative diode in turn. Again, meter readings should be in the GOOD zone and relatively close.

To test individual diodes: Connect one test lamp clip to diode base and other lead to diode lead. Note whether or not lamp lights. Then reverse connections. Lamp should light only once, and in same direction for each diode. If lamp lights both times, diode is "shorted." If lamp does not light at all, diode is "open."

REPAIRS/REPLACEMENT

Slip rings that need cleaning may be polished with 00 sandpaper or a 400 grain polishing cloth. Scored or worn slip rings usually necessitate replacement of the rotor assembly.

Diode replacement generally requires removal of four screws holding positive and/or negative diode and heat sink assemblies to alternator end shield. Reverse procedure to install new diode assemblies.

DIODE REPLACEMENT

On some older alternators, diode replacement can be handled by disconnecting, cutting, or unsoldering the diode lead, then pressing out the defective unit. Special diode removing tools are available and the end housing must be supported during the pressing operation to avoid distortion.

ALTERNATOR REASSEMBLY

After all bench tests have been completed, defective parts replaced, and diodes connected to stator leads, the parts can be reassembled in reverse order of disassembly. See Fig. 34-17.

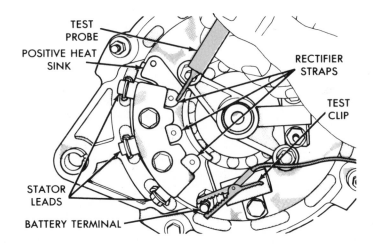

Fig. 34-16. To test positive rectifier (diode) condition, clip one test meter lead to alternator battery terminal. Touch other lead to each rectifier strap in turn. Meter readings should be in GOOD range and relatively close. (Chrysler Corp.)

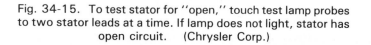

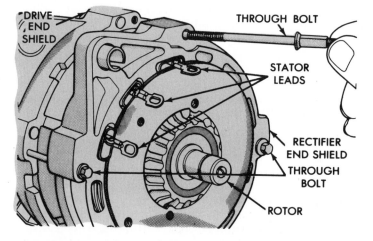

Fig. 34-15. To test stator for "open," touch test lamp probes to two stator leads at a time. If lamp does not light, stator has open circuit. (Chrysler Corp.)

Fig. 34-17. Reassemble alternator in reverse order of disassembly. Manually compress stator and end shields, and install through bolts. Make sure rotor turns freely and fan does not hit stator winding leads. (Chrysler Corp.)

ALTERNATOR REINSTALLATION

To install alternator, position assembly on engine and install pivot bolt and nut and outer mounting bracket bolts, Fig. 34-8. Install alternator drive belt and adjusting bracket bolt. Adjust alternator drive belt to specified tension, Fig. 34-1, but do not pry against stator section of alternator.

Then tighten all alternator mounting bolts and nuts. Connect lead wires to alternator field (FLD) terminals, output (BAT) terminal, and ground terminal, Fig. 34-18. Reconnect ground cable to negative post of battery. Alternator will be polarized when the ignition switch is turned ON.

Start and operate engine. Check alternator operation. Test current output and compare test result with manufacturer's specification.

GENERATOR OVERHAUL — GM and AMC

If a General Motors or American Motors generator with integral voltage regulator is found to be at fault, it should be replaced or overhauled. See Fig. 34-19. Replacement is a simple R & R (remove and replace) operation. However, the pulley and fan must be removed from the defective generator and installed on the replacement generator.

To overhaul a GM or an AMC generator, Fig. 34-20, proceed as follows:
1. Scribe across generator front housing, stator frame, and rear housing to aid reassembly.
2. Remove four through bolts.
3. Pry between housings with a screwdriver to separate front housing and rotor assembly from rear housing and stator assembly.
4. Use pressure-sensitive tape to cover rear housing bearing and rotor shaft at slip ring end to keep out contaminants.
5. Place rotor in a vise and remove pulley nut, lock washer, pulley, fan, and outer collar.
6. Separate front housing from rotor.
7. Remove three stator winding terminal nuts and washers, Fig. 34-20, and remove stator winding terminals from bridge rectifier terminal studs.
8. Separate stator from rear housing.
9. Remove diode trio from brush holder, Fig. 34-20.
10. Disconnect and remove capacitor from bridge rectifier.
11. Remove bridge rectifier and battery wire terminal (output) stud. Inspect insulator used between heat sink and rear housing.
12. Unscrew last two brush holder screws, remove brush holder, and note location of all insulator washer/sleeves to aid reassembly.
13. Remove voltage regulator.
14. Remove front bearing retainer plate screws, retainer plate, and inner collar, Fig. 34-20.
15. Press out front bearing (if worn or rough) and slinger from front housing.
16. Press rear bearing from inside-out (if dry, worn, or rough).
17. Clean rotor poles and stator with oleum spirits or equivalent. Do not use a degreasing solvent.

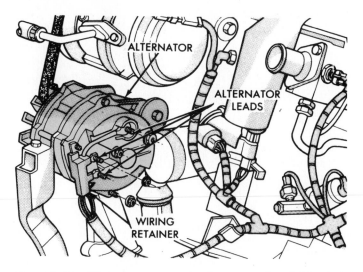

Fig. 34-18. With alternator securely mounted and drive belt adjusted, connect leads to alternator battery terminal, field terminals, and ground terminal. (Chrysler Corp.)

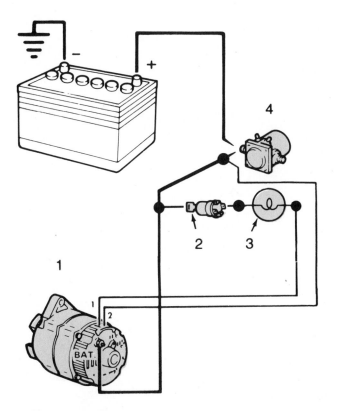
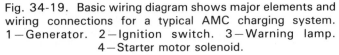

Fig. 34-19. Basic wiring diagram shows major elements and wiring connections for a typical AMC charging system. 1—Generator. 2—Ignition switch. 3—Warning lamp. 4—Starter motor solenoid.

18. Test rotor (field) winding for internal short circuit (see Chrysler procedure) and for an "open" circuit. See Fig. 34-21. Replace rotor if short circuited or "open."
19. If rotor passes tests, spin it in a rotatable support and clean and finish slip ring surfaces with commutator paper or a 400 grain polishing cloth.

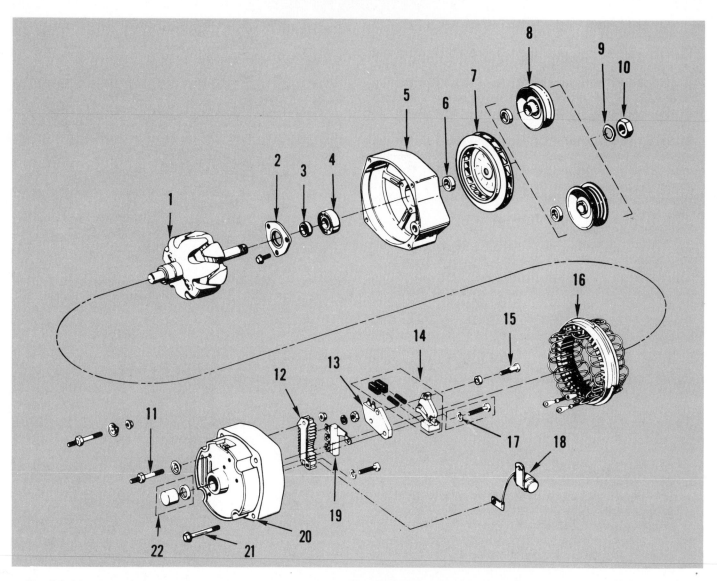

Fig. 34-20. Exploded view of typical GM or AMC generator features: 1—Rotor. 2—Front bearing retainer plate. 3—Collar (inner). 4—Bearing. 5—Front housing. 6—Collar (outer). 7—Fan. 8—Pulley. 9—Lock washer. 10—Pulley nut. 11—Terminal assembly. 12—Bridge rectifier. 13—Voltage regulator. 14—Brush assembly. 15—Screw. 16—Stator. 17—Insulating washer. 18—Capacitor. 19—Diode trio. 20—Rear housing. 21—Through bolt. 22—Bearing and seal assembly. (American Motors Corp.)

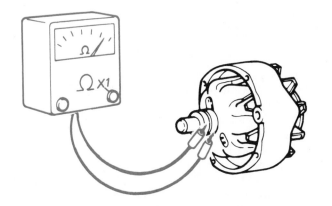

Fig. 34-21. Use ohmmeter to test rotor winding for "open." Touch probes to slip rings. Ohmmeter should read 2.2-3.0 ohms. If infinite resistance, winding has "open" circuit. (American Motors Corp.)

20. Test stator windings for short circuit to ground, Fig. 34-22, and for an "open" circuit (see Chrysler procedure). Replace stator if short circuited or "open."
21. Replace brush springs if damaged or corroded.
22. Replace brushes if worn or contaminated.
23. Clean bridge rectifier, diode trio, and voltage regulator with a brush and high pressure air.
24. Test diode trio (see Chrysler procedure).
25. Replace defective bearings and seals.
26. Reassemble generator in reverse order of disassembly.
   NOTE: Tighten pulley nut with 50 ft. lb. (68 N·m) torque, Fig. 34-23. Insert wooden or plastic toothpick into hole at bottom of brush holder to retain brushes during reassembly. Replace voltage regulator if proved defective by off-car test, Fig. 34-24, or by earlier, on-car "full fielding" test.

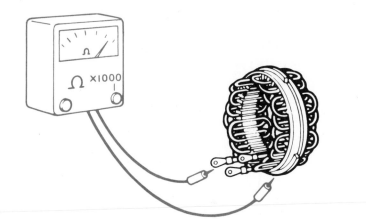

Fig. 34-22. Use ohmmeter to test stator windings for short circuit to ground. Touch one probe to stator core (bare metal). Touch other probe to end of one stator winding. Ohmmeter should indicate infinite resistance. If not, stator windings are "shorted" to core. (American Motors Corp.)

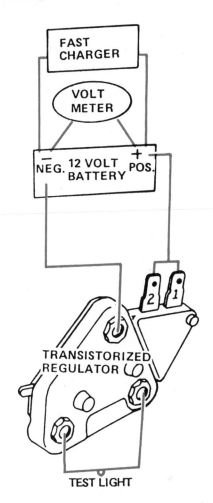

Fig. 34-24. To test voltage regulator: Connect voltmeter, fast charger, 12 volt battery, and test lamp as shown. Test lamp should light. Turn on charger and increase charge rate. Lamp will go out at regulator setting, which should be 13.5-16.0 volts. (Chevrolet Motor Div., General Motors Corp.)

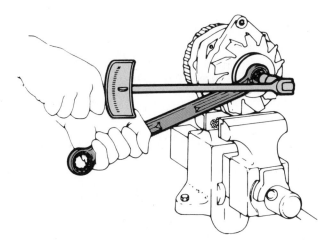

Fig. 34-23. With rotor and front housing assembly held in vise, tighten pulley nut to manufacturer's torque specification. (American Motors Corp.)

Remove tape from rotor shaft. Join front and rear housings with scribe marks aligned. Remove toothpick from brush holder assembly. Rotate rotor to check freedom of operation.

ALTERNATOR/REGULATOR TESTS — FORD

Basically, Ford Motor Company uses two alternators in its charging systems. One is a rear terminal unit; the other is a side terminal unit. See Fig. 34-25.

Ford uses three different voltage regulators:
1. Black color-coded regulators are used in systems which have a warning lamp indicator.
2. Gray color-coded regulators are used in systems which have an ammeter.
3. Neutral color-coded regulators are used with either system. Most of the information contained in earlier general service paragraphs is applicable for Ford charging systems. This includes material under

CHARGING SYSTEM INSPECTION, ON-CAR CHARGING SYSTEM TESTS, QUICK CHECKS, and BENCH TESTS.

However, certain troubleshooting tests that require jumper wire connections are unique to Ford charging systems. See Figs. 34-25 and 34-26.

To test Ford charging system performance:
1. Connect voltmeter leads across battery terminals and record "base voltage" (battery voltage).
2. Connect tachometer to engine.
3. Start engine and increase speed to 1500 rpm. Voltmeter should show higher voltage, but no more than 2.0 volts above base voltage.
4. Turn blower motor on high speed and operate headlamps on high beam.
5. Increase speed to 2000 rpm. Voltmeter should read a minimum of 0.5 volt above base voltage.
6. If test indicates an over voltage problem, connect jumper wire between regulator base and alternator frame. Repeat test outlined in 4 and 5. If over voltage condition persists, clean and tighten all ground connections on alternator, regulator, and from engine-to-dash panel, and to battery.

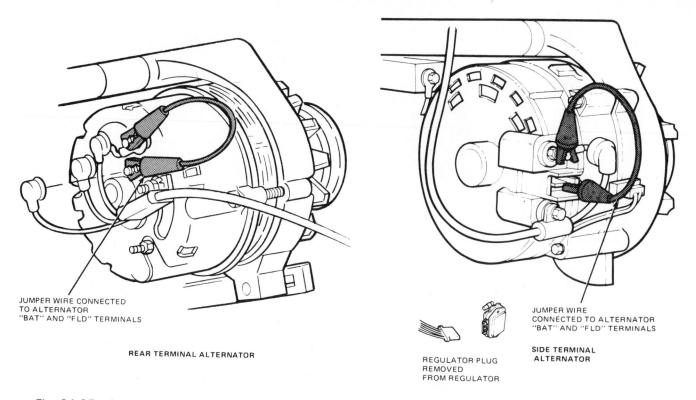

JUMPER WIRE CONNECTED
TO ALTERNATOR
"BAT" AND "FLD" TERMINALS

REAR TERMINAL ALTERNATOR

JUMPER WIRE
CONNECTED TO ALTERNATOR
"BAT" AND "FLD" TERMINALS

REGULATOR PLUG
REMOVED
FROM REGULATOR

SIDE TERMINAL
ALTERNATOR

Fig. 34-25. Jumper wire connections are shown for making performance tests on Ford charging systems.
(Ford Motor Co.)

7. If test indicates an under voltage condition, disconnect wiring connector from regulator and connect ohmmeter leads from terminal F of connector to ground. Ohmmeter should indicate more than 2.4 ohms.

8. If less than 2.4 ohms, test for grounded field circuit in wiring harness or alternator.

9. If more than 2.4 ohms, connect jumper wire from A to F terminals of wiring connector, Fig. 34-26, and repeat test outlined in 4 and 5.

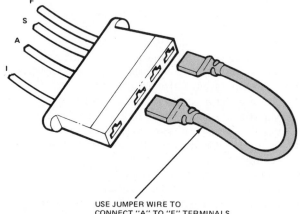

USE JUMPER WIRE TO
CONNECT "A" TO "F" TERMINALS
AT REGULATOR PLUG

Fig. 34-26. Jumper wire is connected to A and F terminals of regulator plug for making Ford charging system tests under load. (Ford Motor Co.)

10. If more than 0.5 volt above base voltage, regulator or wiring is worn or damaged.

11. If under voltage persists, remove jumper wire, Fig. 34-26, from regulator connector and leave connector disconnected from regulator.

12. Disconnect alternator FLD terminal, pull cover from BAT terminal, and connect jumper wire to FLD and BAT terminals. See Fig. 34-25.

13. Repeat test outlined in 4 and 5. If voltmeter now shows 0.5 volt or more above base voltage, test wiring harness from alternator to regulator.

14. If voltmeter still reads under voltage, stop engine and move positive voltmeter lead to BAT terminal of alternator.

15. If voltmeter now reads base voltage, alternator is not generating.

16. Remove and replace alternator or remove alternator, disassemble, and make bench tests of components.

TROUBLESHOOTING CHARGING SYSTEMS

Charge Indicator Light Flickers
1. Loose or worn alternator belt.
2. Loose or corroded wiring connections.
3. Faulty alternator.
4. Defective voltage regulator.
5. Corroded or loose battery cable clamps or terminals.
6. Loose alternator ground wire or strap.
7. Poor ground at voltage regulator.

Charge Indicator Light Stays On
1. Loose, worn, or broken alternator belt.
2. Open or grounded wiring from battery to alternator.

3. Faulty alternator (rotor, stator, diodes, or brushes).
4. Defective voltage regulator.
5. Corroded or loose battery cable clamps or terminals.
6. Grounded field circuit.
7. Malfunction in other electrical systems.

Unsteady or Low Charging
1. Too high charging circuit resistance.
2. Corroded or shorted cables.
3. High resistance across fusible link.
4. Defective alternator diodes.
5. Open stator winding.
6. Excessive carbon on slip rings.

Excessive Charging
1. Defective voltage regulator.
2. Grounded alternator field wire, field terminal, or connections.
3. Internally grounded alternator field.

Lights and/or Fuses Burn Out
1. Too high alternator output.
2. Defective charging circuit wiring.
3. Faulty voltage regulator.
4. Grounded alternator field wire, field terminal, or connections.
5. Internally grounded alternator field.

Noisy Alternator
1. Loose or worn alternator belt.
2. Bent pulley flanges.
3. Loose alternator mounting.
4. Interference between rotor fan and stator leads.
5. Worn or defective alternator bearings.
6. Open or shorted diodes.
7. Open or shorted wiring in stator.

TESTING AND SERVICING

Charging system testing, then, could entail: checking battery state of charge; performing visual and manual inspections of charging system components; taking special precautions to avoid reverse polarity or accidental "shorting" or "grounding" of the system; doing quick checks and current output and circuit resistance tests to aid in problem diagnosis; making bench tests of electrical parts.

Charging system servicing could include: cleaning and tightening battery, starter, alternator, and voltage regulator terminals and connections; removing alternator, disassembling, replacing faulty parts; reassembling and reinstalling alternator.

Chapter 34—REVIEW QUESTIONS

Write your answers on a separate sheet of paper. Do not write in this book.

1. Alternator charging systems require regular _____ and _____.
2. Dust and dirt tend to increase wear on alternator components. Give two operating conditions that also contribute to component wear.
3. When checking alternator drive belt tension, how much should the belt deflect in the middle of a long span?
   a. Zero deflection.
   b. 1/4 inch.
   c. 1/2 inch.
   d. 1 inch.
4. If there is no field circuit, an alternator will not charge because the field windings must be _____ by battery voltage.
   a. Charged.
   b. Regulated.
   c. Controlled.
   d. Excited.
5. If the charging system has a fusible link, check it for appearance and _____.
   a. Amperage draw.
   b. Voltage.
   c. Continuity.
   d. Resistance.
6. If a fusible link has "blown," replace it with a _____ link.
7. What on/off warning device is used in the charging system?
8. What term is used to describe a charging system circuit that is "incomplete?"
   a. Open.
   b. Closed.
   c. Shorted.
   d. Grounded.
9. What is normal charging voltage?
   a. 12.2-12.6 volts.
   b. 12.5-13.0 volts.
   c. 13.0-13.8 volts.
   d. 13.8-14.9 volts.
10. The charge indicator lamp should light when the ignition switch is in the "run" position and the engine is off. True or False?
11. If a current output test indicates that a problem exists in the charging circuit, what follow-up test will reveal whether the problem lies in the insulated circuit, ground circuit, or alternator?
12. What is the term used for bypassing the voltage regulator or computer modules in order to test unregulated alternator voltage output?
13. What electrical value is the result of a charging circuit resistance test?
   a. Voltage output.
   b. Voltage drop.
   c. Current draw.
   d. Infinite ohms.
14. Which one of the following component "condition" tests usually is NOT a bench test?
   a. Voltage regulator test.
   b. Rotor test.
   c. Diode or rectifier test.
   d. Stator test.
15. As the final step of alternator reinstallation, reconnect the _____ cable to the _____ post of battery.
16. What is the purpose for inserting a wooden or plastic toothpick into a hole at the bottom of the brush holder during GM alternator reassembly?

17. What distinguishes the design of each of the two Ford alternators?
18. What is "base voltage," according to the Ford Motor Company?
19. A car in for service has a charge indicator light that flickers.
    Mechanic A says is could be caused by a loose or worn alternator drive belt.
    Mechanic B says it could be caused by open or grounded wiring from battery to alternator.
    Who is right?
    a. Mechanic A.
    b. Mechanic B.

c. Both mechanic A and B.
d. Neither mechanic A nor mechanic B.

20. Tests show that a vehicle's charging system has an excessive charging rate.
    Mechanic A says it could be caused by a defective voltage regulator.
    Mechanic B says it could be caused by a grounded alternator field.
    Who is right?
    a. Mechanic A.
    b. Mechanic B.
    c. Both mechanic A and mechanic B.
    d. Neither mechanic A nor mechanic B.

High-mounted ac generator driven by serpentine belt simplifies charging system service operations on this 3.8 liter V-6 engine. (Buick Motor Div., General Motors Corp.)

Chapter 35

ENGINE TROUBLESHOOTING

After studying this chapter, you will be able to:
- Explain the process of engine troubleshooting.
- Tell why modern engine analyzers should be used to supplement visual inspection and manual checks.
- Describe the function of "plug-in" diagnosis.
- Give an example of "self diagnosis."
- List various engine troubles and identify possible causes.
- Elaborate on more common causes of engine overheating, excessive oil consumption, and engine noises.

ENGINE TROUBLESHOOTING is a process of studying the symptoms of the existing trouble and reasoning possible causes and corrections. This process is supported throughout by analysis, deduction, and elimination.

Since a defect in one part or a maladjustment may have a definite relationship to trouble in another area, you need to have the ability to keep functions of the entire automobile in mind at all times. This aspect of troubleshooting requires mental alertness as well as specific knowledge.

TEST EQUIPMENT

Troubleshooting in its most basic form consists of "shorting out" spark plugs to locate a misfiring cylinder. In its most advanced form, it involves the use of an elaborate diagnostic computer engine analyzer. See Fig. 35-1. In addition, many late model vehicles feature a plug-in diagnostic connection so that a special tester can be plugged into the circuit to quickly locate existing trouble.

Fig. 35-1. Latest computerized engine and emissions analyzers provide diagnostic help needed to pinpoint causes for engine performance complaints and for excess emissions. Operator can "freeze" data on screen, display readouts of test results, and obtain emissions printouts.   (Allen Testproducts Div., Allen Group)

In some situations, trouble areas can be located by visual inspection and manual checks. However, this method of attempted problem solving should be supplemented by tests made with modern engine testing equipment. Then, the "hidden" sources of trouble can be pinpointed more quickly and with greater accuracy.

Typical modern engine analyzers are shown in Figs. 35-1, 35-2, and 35-3. With this equipment, it is possible to test everything from condition of the spark plugs to 4-gas emissions (carbon monoxide, carbon dioxide, oxygen, and hydrocarbons).

In some cases, the tester is actually a diagnostic computer that provides visual and/or "voice" instructions, Fig. 35-2. The computer is preprogrammed with test specifications. In operation, it displays the vehicle's actual performance readings on a screen. A printout of these readings is also furnished for the technician and for the car owner to substantiate the need for repairs. This specialized equipment is covered in detail in Chapter 5, Meters, Testers, and Analyzers.

AFFECT OF EMISSION CONTROLS

Troubleshooting has become more difficult since numerous emission control systems were added or incorporated into the various engine systems. Limits for the emission of carbon monoxide, nitrogen oxides, and hydrocarbons have been set by the Government. So modern engines must be tuned and adjusted to conform to these stringent limits. Therefore, latest test equipment includes necessary instruments for checking chemical content of the exhaust gases. See Chapter 36, Engine Tune-Up, and Chapter 37, Emission Controls.

PLUG-IN DIAGNOSIS

Special test equipment is also available that plugs into a diagnostic connection on the vehicle. In that way, a series of programmed tests can be made to check the condition of various units and systems on the car.

One of the pioneers of this method of engine diagnosis is Volkswagen. The original setup consisted of a computer, a card reader, a hand control unit, an umbilical cord for connecting the test equipment to the vehicle's diagnostic connection, a tachometer, and a timing light.

A more sophisticated diagnostic arrangement is used on many U.S. cars. Chrysler, for example, utilizes an electronic spark advance computer that has been programmed to monitor several different systems. If a problem is detected in a monitored circuit, its fault code is stored for display on a diagnostic readout tool, Fig. 35-4.

To make a series of tests, the readout tool is attached to a test connector located under the hood at the left shock tower. The readout tool can be used to check out three different modes:

1. Diagnostic test mode which retrieves fault codes stored in the computer.
2. Circuit actuation test mode used to check out specific system components.
3. Switch test mode used to check certain switch circuits.

As code numbers appear on the readout tool, they are recorded for later reference to a listing of problem areas related to those particular code numbers. When the problems area corrected, the electronic spark advance computer cancels the fault codes. Also see Fig. 35-5.

Fig. 35-2. Diagnostic computer will analyze six major engine systems. Test instructions are visual and "voice." Remote control keypad permits operator to work in-car or under-hood. Computer identifies problems, possible causes, and logical solutions. (Sun Electric Corp.)

Fig. 35-3. Four-gas infrared analyzer uses emissions analysis to determine whether cause of engine performance problem is in fuel system or in ignition system. (Peerless Instrument Co.)

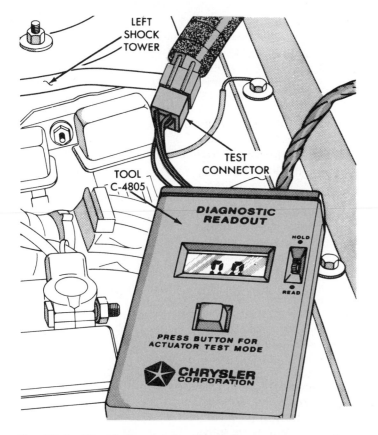

Fig. 35-4. Chrysler's plug-in diagnosis requires use of a diagnostic readout tool attached to vehicle's test connector. Fault code numbers that appear on screen of tool indicate where problems exist. (Chrysler Corp.)

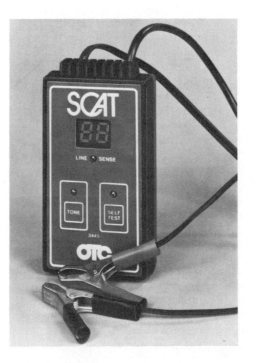

Fig. 35-5. Various diagnostic testers are available that provide access to on-board computers. This Service Code Automatic Tester will retrieve stored service codes from Ford MCU and EEC-IV computerized control systems and display them in high intensity digits. (OTC Tools and Equipment)

SELF DIAGNOSIS

The next step up from plug-in diagnosis is SELF DIAGNOSIS. On vehicles so equipped, there are several electronic components that can be controlled by the service technician to provide valuable self diagnosis.

Cadillac, for example, uses a computer module called an ECM (electronic control module) to provide self diagnosis in the area of engine electronics. The ECM monitors operating conditions for possible malfunctions. It compares system conditions against standard limits. A two digit numerical Trouble Code is stored in the computer memory.

When a malfunction is detected by the self diagnostic system, the trouble codes can be displayed by the service technician. The technician then consults trouble code Diagnostic Charts to determine what service is required to correct the problem found by the system.

TROUBLESHOOTING CHARTS

TROUBLESHOOTING CHARTS have been a traditional means of relating specific symptoms of trouble to possible causes. A series of engine problems are covered in this manner in the following troubleshooting charts.

ENGINE DIAGNOSIS

Engine Will Not Start
1. Weak battery.
2. Corroded or loose battery connections.
3. Loose engine and/or battery ground connection.
4. Defective ignition switch.
5. Faulty starter or solenoid.
6. Faulty ignition coil.
7. Moisture on high tension wiring and distributor cap.
8. Faulty ignition distributor.
9. Faulty high tension wiring.
10. Incorrect spark plug gap.
11. Incorrect ignition timing.
12. Dirt, water, or ice in fuel line or carburetor.
13. Faulty fuel pump.
14. Obstructed air filter.
15. Flooded carburetor.
16. Sticking choke.
17. Maladjusted choke.
18. Incorrect carburetor float setting.
19. Empty fuel tank.
20. Defective neutral starting switch.
21. Faulty emission control unit.
22. Faulty engine computer control system.

Engine Starts But Will Not Run
1. Back pressure in exhaust system.
2. Obstructed air filter.
3. Restricted or inadequate fuel supply to fuel pump.
4. Weak fuel pump pressure or volume.
5. Clogged fuel filter.
6. Misaligned distributor rotor.

Hard Starting
1. Maladjusted choke.
2. Faulty fuel pump.

391

3. Clogged fuel filter.
4. Maladjusted or faulty carburetor.
5. Clogged electronic fuel injection system injectors.
6. Air leak into intake manifold or vacuum hoses.
7. Obstructed air filter.
8. Defective exhaust gas recirculation (EGR) valve.
9. Sticking positive crankcase ventilation (PCV) valve.
10. Faulty ignition coil.
11. Faulty spark plugs or incorrect gap.
12. Incorrect ignition timing.
13. Moisture on high tension wiring and distributor cap.
14. Incorrect valve timing.

Rough Idle
1. Maladjusted carburetor.
2. Obstructed air filter.
3. Faulty evaporative emission control (EEC) system.
4. Improper feedback system operation.
5. Air leak into intake manifold or vacuum hoses.
6. Back pressure in exhaust system.
7. Faulty EGR valve.
8. Faulty PCV system operation.
9. Faulty ignition coil.
10. Defective distributor rotor or cap.
11. Leaking engine valves.
12. Incorrect valve timing.

Engine Stalls
1. Too low idle speed.
2. Incorrect choke adjustment.
3. Too lean or too rich idle mixture setting.
4. Incorrect carburetor float level.
5. Inoperative carburetor float needle valve.
6. Air leak into intake manifold or vacuum hoses.
7. Loose engine and/or battery ground connection.
8. Faulty ignition coil.
9. Worn distributor rotor.
10. Moisture on high tension wiring and spark plugs.
11. Incorrect valve lash (solid lifters).

Engine Stalls on Quick Stops
1. Too low idle speed.
2. Incorrect choke adjustment.
3. Incorrect carburetor float level.
4. Faulty carburetor accelerator pump.
5. Corroded or loose EEC connections.
6. Clogged electronic fuel injection system injectors.
7. Defective EGR valve.
8. Incorrect ignition timing.

Loss of Power
1. Dirt or water in fuel line.
2. Faulty fuel pump.
3. Obstructed air filter.
4. Low carburetor float level.
5. Too lean air-fuel mixture.
6. Improper feedback system operation.
7. Defective or maladjusted emission control system.
8. Faulty ignition coil.
9. Worn distributor shaft.
10. Loose trigger wheel (reluctor) in distributor.
11. Worn or burned distributor rotor.
12. Fouled or incorrectly gapped spark plugs.

13. Leaking engine valves.
14. Incorrect valve lash (solid lifters).
15. Weak valve springs.
16. Incorrect valve timing.
17. Blown cylinder head gasket.
18. Back pressure in exhaust system.

Engine Hesitates on Acceleration
1. Restricted fuel line.
2. Improper thermostatic air cleaner operation.
3. Clogged fuel filter.
4. Maladjusted choke.
5. Faulty carburetor accelerator pump operation.
6. Improper feedback system operation.
7. Faulty ignition coil.
8. Faulty spark plugs.
9. Incorrect ignition timing.
10. Leaking engine valves.

Engine Misses on Acceleration
1. Too lean air-fuel mixture.
2. Dirt in carburetor.
3. Defective carburetor accelerator pump.
4. Faulty ignition coil.
5. Fouled or incorrectly gapped spark plugs.
6. Incorrect ignition timing.
7. Weak valve springs.
8. Sticking engine valves.
9. Leaking engine valves.

Engine Misses Under Load
1. Too low fuel pump pressure or volume.
2. Improper feedback system operation.
3. Air leak into intake manifold or vacuum hoses.
4. Faulty ignition coil.
5. Worn or burned distributor rotor.
6. Faulty distributor cap or moisture on cap.
7. Defective high tension wiring.
8. Fouled or incorrectly gapped spark plugs.
9. Worn camshaft lobes.
10. Sticking hydraulic lifters.
11. Bent push rod.
12. Weak valve springs.
13. Blown cylinder head gasket.

Engine Misses at High Speed
1. Dirt in fuel line.
2. Clogged carburetor jets.
3. Faulty ignition coil.
4. Worn or burned distributor rotor.
5. Worn distributor shaft.
6. Fouled or incorrectly gapped spark plugs.
7. Incorrect ignition timing.
8. Worn camshaft lobes.
9. Worn valve lifters.
10. Sticking engine valves.
11. Leaking engine valves.
12. Incorrect valve lash (solid lifters).

Engine Backfires
1. Air leaks into intake manifold or vacuum hoses.
2. Incorrect ignition timing.
3. Incorrect valve timing.

4. Low compression pressure.

Engine Speed Surges
1. Low fuel pump pressure or volume.
2. Clogged fuel filter.
3. Obstructed air filter.
4. Improper thermostatic air cleaner operation.
5. Sticking carburetor linkage.
6. Incorrect carburetor float level.
7. Malfunctioning carburetor.
8. Air leak into intake manifold or vacuum hoses.
9. Faulty ignition timing advance and retard.
10. Faulty PCV system.
11. Defective EGR valve.

Excessive Fuel Consumption
1. Obstructed air filter.
2. Improper thermostatic air cleaner operation.
3. Maladjusted or sticking choke.
4. High carburetor float level.
5. Faulty carburetor accelerator pump.
6. Maladjusted carburetor.
7. Fouled or faulty spark plugs.
8. Incorrect ignition timing.
9. Back pressure in exhaust system.
10. Incorrect vacuum hose connection.
11. Owner's driving habits.

Engine Vibration
1. Loose or collapsed engine mounts.
2. Defective vibration damper.
3. Loose mounting of belt-driven accessories.
4. Out-of-balance cooling fan.

Engine Runs Cold
1. Defective cooling system thermostat.
2. Defective temperature gauge or warning light circuit.

Engine Overheats
1. Low coolant level.
2. Faulty temperature gauge or sending unit.
3. Air in cooling system.
4. Too much antifreeze in coolant.
5. Collapsed radiator hose.
6. Blocked radiator airflow.
7. Faulty radiator cap.
8. Defective cooling fan or fan clutch.
9. Inoperative electric fan.
10. Slipping fan belt.
11. Faulty water pump.
12. Loose water pump belt.
13. Defective cooling system thermostat.
14. Incorrect ignition timing.
15. Excessive engine friction.

Excessive Oil Consumption
1. Too high oil level.
2. Plugged drainback in cylinder head.
3. Excessive bearing clearance.
4. Worn crankshaft journals.
5. Excessive oil throw-off from engine bearings.
6. Worn piston rings.

7. Clogged drain holes in rings.
8. Incorrect ring gap.
9. Ring gaps incorrectly spaced.
10. Compression rings installed upside down.
11. Too little piston ring side clearance.
12. Wrong size rings installed.
13. Worn pistons and cylinder walls.
14. Damaged or missing valve seals.
15. Worn valve stems and guides.
16. Sticking PCV valve.
17. Overheated engine.

External Oil Leakage
1. Defective fuel pump gasket.
2. Defective cylinder head cover gasket.
3. Defective oil filter gasket.
4. Defective oil pan gasket or end seal.
5. Defective timing chain (or gear) cover gasket.
6. Worn timing chain (or gear) cover oil seal.
7. Worn rear main bearing oil seal.
8. Loose oil gallery plug.
9. Improperly seated engine oil pan drain plug.
10. Improperly seated camshaft rear plug.

Low Oil Pressure
1. Low oil level.
2. Diluted oil or excessive oil temperature.
3. Faulty oil pressure sending unit.
4. Clogged oil filter.
5. Worn oil pump.
6. Excessive bearing clearance.
7. Sticking oil pump relief valve.
8. Loose, bent, or cracked oil pump suction tube.

Ping or Spark Knock
1. Too low octane fuel or poor fuel quality.
2. Low compression pressure.
3. High compression pressure.
4. Excessive combustion chamber deposits.
5. Sharp edges in combustion chamber.
6. Air leak into intake manifold.
7. Incorrect ignition timing.
8. Malfunctioning ignition distributor advance.
9. Wrong spark plugs for application.
10. Faulty EGR valve.

Engine Knocks
1. Noisy connecting rods or bearings.
2. Noisy pistons, piston pins, or piston rings.
3. Noisy main bearings.
4. Detonation.
5. Preignition.

Noisy Connecting Rods or Bearings
1. Insufficient oil in crankcase.
2. Defective oil pump.
3. Low oil pressure.
4. Thin or diluted oil.
5. Excessive connecting rod bearing clearance.
6. Bent connecting rods.
7. Out-of-round connecting rod bearing journals.

Noisy Pistons, Pins, or Rings

1. Excessive piston-to-cylinder wall clearance.
2. Collapsed piston skirt.
3. Loose piston strut.
4. Incorrectly fitted piston pin.
5. Misaligned connecting rods.
6. Excessive carbon deposits on pistons.
7. Piston rings striking ridge at top of cylinder wall.
8. Broken ring.
9. Incorrect ring gap.
10. Excessive ring-to-groove side clearance.

Noisy Main Bearings

1. Insufficient oil supply.
2. Low oil pressure.
3. Worn main bearings.
4. Out-of-round crankshaft journals.
5. Excessive end play of crankshaft.
6. Loose flywheel.
7. Loose or damaged vibration damper.

Noisy Valves

1. High or low oil level in crankcase.
2. Thin or diluted oil.
3. Low oil pressure.
4. Dirt in hydraulic lifters.
5. Excessive hydraulic lifter leakdown.
6. Worn valve lifters.
7. Excessive valve lash (solid lifters).
8. Bent push rods.
9. Excessive runout of valves or seats.
10. Worn rocker arms and/or pivots or shafts.
11. Broken or cocked valve spring.
12. Bent valve.

Burned Valves and Seats

1. Too lean air-fuel mixture.
2. Insufficient valve lash (solid lifters).
3. Too thin valve head margin.
4. Too narrow valve seat.
5. Loose valve seat insert.
6. Warped valve head.
7. Worn valve stems and guides.

Dieseling

1. Too high engine idle speed.
2. Poor quality fuel.
3. Excessive carbon in combustion chamber.
4. Wrong type spark plugs for application.
5. Defective exhaust emission control system.

DIESEL ENGINE DIAGNOSIS

Hard Starting

1. Air in fuel system.
2. Clogged fuel filter.
3. Blocked fuel supply line.
4. Blocked injection lines.
5. Defective injection pump.
6. Blocked injection pump.
7. Incorrect injection timing.
8. Defective preheating device.
9. Low engine compression.

Engine Surges While Idling

1. Incorrectly adjusted governor.
2. Defective fuel injection pump.

Loss of Power

1. Clogged fuel filter.
2. Blocked or leaking injection lines.
3. Defective injection pump.
4. Incorrect injection timing.
5. Defective timing device.
6. Obstructed air filter.
7. Maladjusted low idle.

Engine Misses Under Load

1. Air in fuel system.
2. Clogged fuel filter.
3. Blocked fuel supply line.
4. Blocked injection lines.
5. Defective fuel injector.
6. Incorrect injection timing.
7. Defective overflow valve.

Excessive Fuel Consumption

1. Leaking fuel lines.
2. Defective injection pump.
3. Incorrect injection timing.
4. Defective timing device.
5. Defective injection nozzle.
6. Obstructed air filter.
7. Uneven engine compression.

Engine Cannot Be Shut Off

1. Defective shutoff device.
2. Defective injection pump.
3. Incorrect governor setting.

Black Smoke and Poor Performance

1. Air in fuel system.
2. Defective injection pump.
3. Defective governor.

White or Blue Smoke

1. Blocked fuel tank vent.
2. Air in fuel supply line.
3. Clogged fuel filter.
4. Blocked injection lines.
5. Defective injector or injection nozzle.
6. Obstructed air filter.
7. Defective governor.
8. Uneven engine compression.

EXHAUST SYSTEM BACK PRESSURE

Certain troubles and possible causes listed in the Engine Diagnosis charts deserve further explanation. Exhaust system back pressure, for example, appears as a possible cause for many different engine problems.

If the exhaust pipe, muffler, catalytic converter, or tailpipe is partially restricted, the hot exhaust gases will be unable to escape readily and a back pressure will be created in the exhaust system. As a result, the combustible charge will be severely diluted and full engine power will not be developed. In extreme cases, the exhaust valves will burn.

ENGINE OVERHEATS

There may be many "conditions" that result in engine overheating. The degree of overheating is indicated by the temperature gauge on the instrument panel. Or, a signal lamp on the panel lights as a warning when a prescribed high temperature is reached. Certain of these conditions will cause only a slight change in recorded temperature. Other causes will result in a rapid rise in temperature and violent boiling of the coolant.

When troubleshooting the cause for engine overheating, the first step is to make a careful visual inspection to see if there is any evidence of external leakage of coolant. Check all surfaces of the radiator and its hose connections. Leaks generally cause corrosion, which is easily seen. Also check the heater, heater hoses, and hose connections.

The engine also needs careful inspection. Pay particular attention to the core hole plugs and edges of the cylinder head gasket. Check the cooling fan, water pump, and drive belts. The belts must be in good condition and adjusted to proper tension. Test the radiator cap, Fig. 35-6. Test the operation of the thermostat, Fig. 35-7. A thermostat "frozen" in the closed position will also cause extreme overheating.

To test for restrictions in the radiator, first bring the system up to operating temperature. Then shut off the engine and feel the front surface of the radiator. On cross flow radiators, the radiator should feel hot along the left side and warm along the right side with an even temperature rise from right to left and bottom to top. On vertical flow radiators, the radiator should feel warmer at the top than at the bottom. Any cold spots would indicate clogged sections.

Water pump operation can be checked by running the engine while squeezing the radiator upper hose. A pressure surge should be felt. Also check for a plugged vent hole in the pump housing.

Not all coolant leakage is external. Severe cases of overheating and coolant loss can result from leaks into the combustion chamber. When the cylinder head is cracked, or there is a blown cylinder head gasket, the hot gases of combustion can enter the cooling system. Coolant temperature rises rapidly and boiling takes place.

To test for an internal coolant leak, use a combustion leakage tester, Fig. 35-8. This is a chemical test. The tester is applied to the filler neck of the radiator. Then, with the engine running, any gas from the combustion chamber that enters the coolant will be drawn into the tester and cause the chemical to change its color.

Making a compression test of the engine cylinders will also be helpful in checking for internal coolant leaks, particularly in the case of a blown head gasket. (Low readings on adjacent cylinders indicate blown gasket.)

EXCESSIVE OIL CONSUMPTION

Excessive oil consumption can result from external leakage of oil or as the result of oil passing through the engine. It will be necessary to determine the exact source of the oil loss or whether the oil is passing through the combustion chambers of the engine.

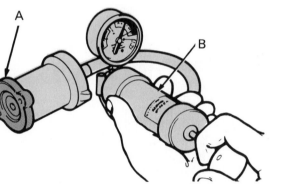

Fig. 35-6. To test condition of radiator cap (A), attach it to a low range, pump type pressure gauge (B). Test cap for pressure "hold" (at least 30 sec.) and for pressure release point, usually marked on cap. (American Motors Corp.)

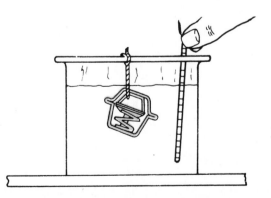

Fig. 35-7. To test operation of thermostat, suspend it in a boiling 50/50 solution of antifreeze and water. Record opening and closing temperatures and compare these readings with manufacturer's specifications. (Ford Motor Co.)

Fig. 35-8. To test for combustion leakage, use a special tester that attaches to radiator filler opening. Combustion gases in sample of coolant will cause color of chemical in tester to change.

EXTERNAL LOSS OF OIL

If there is an external loss of oil, the exterior of the engine will be coated with oil, particularly in the area of the source of the leakage. The usual procedure for locating the source of the oil leak is to first carefully clean the exterior of the engine. Then, take the vehicle for a short drive. Stop the vehicle over a clean area and examine the engine for evidence of oil leakage. See Fig. 35-9. Also see if oil has dripped on the pavement. This will aid in locating the source of the leakage, front or rear, left or right.

It is not unusual to confuse an oil leak at the rear main bearing seal with oil leakage from some other point. To determine the exact source of the leakage, plug the oil filler pipe. With the engine idling, blow compressed air into the dipstick tube or hole in the block. Watch for oil leakage and trace it to its source.

INTERNAL CONSUMPTION OF OIL

When oil is being consumed by passing through the engine, it usually will cause heavy blue smoke to come from the tailpipe, particularly after the engine has idled for several minutes. After the idling period, the engine should be raced briefly and blue smoke should appear.

While worn piston rings and tapered cylinder walls can cause excessive oil consumption, there are a great number of other problem areas that could be at fault, either singly or in combination. In most cases of internal consumption of oil, the oil is leaking out of one or more of the pressure lubricated engine bearings (connecting rod, main, or camshaft bearings). The oil is being splashed or thrown up into the cylinders under the pistons in such large quantities that no piston ring can control the excess.

RELATED TROUBLES

It is obvious that many engine defects are common to both engine overheating and excessive oil consumption. There is a definite relationship between the two engine problems. Searching for the cause of either trouble will often disclose the need for correction in either or both the engine oil circulation system and coolant circulation system.

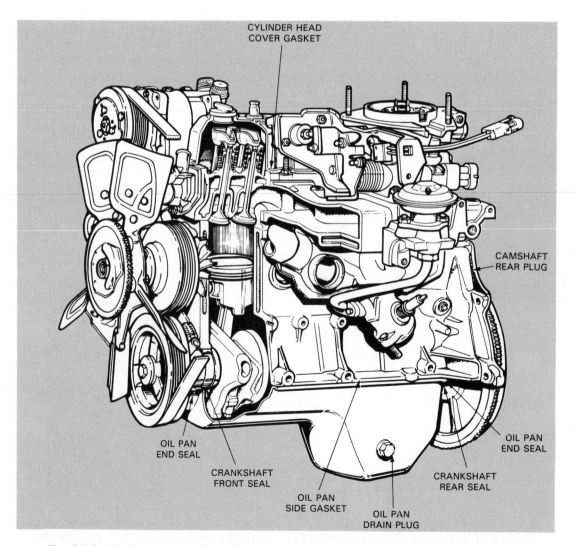

Fig. 35-9. Various points of possible external leakage of engine oil are shown on pictorial drawing of a typical fuel injected four cylinder engine.   (American Motors Corp.)

COMPRESSION PRESSURE LIMIT CHART

Maximum PSI	Minimum PSI	Maximum PSI	Minimum PSI	Maximum PSI	Minimum PSI	Maximum PSI	Minimum PSI
134	101	164	123	194	145	224	168
136	102	166	124	196	147	226	169
138	104	168	126	198	148	228	171
140	105	170	127	200	150	230	172
142	107	172	129	202	151	232	174
144	108	174	131	204	153	234	175
146	110	176	132	206	154	236	177
148	111	178	133	208	156	238	178
150	113	180	135	210	157	240	180
152	114	182	136	212	158	242	181
154	115	184	138	214	160	244	183
156	117	186	140	216	162	246	184
158	118	188	141	218	163	248	186
160	120	190	142	220	165	250	187
162	121	192	144	222	166		

Fig. 35-10. Typical compression pressure limit chart provided by engine manufacturer is calculated so that lowest reading on compression tester is 75 percent of highest reading. (Ford Motor Co.)

COMPRESSION TEST

Testing the compression pressure of each cylinder while the engine is warm and cranking is a well accepted method of checking the condition of internal components of the engine. The compression pressure of each cylinder is taken and recorded, then the readings are compared with compression values supplied by the engine manufacturer. See Fig. 35-10. Compression loss in excess of stipulated values usually means that the engine valves need service or the engine requires an overhaul.

A typical compression testing gauge kit for gasoline fueled engines is shown in Fig. 35-11. Since the compression ratio of a diesel engine may be as high as 23 to 1, a gauge which will check pressures up to and exceeding 650 psi (4 500 kPa) is needed.

VACUUM GAUGE TEST

The use of a vacuum gauge is another basic method of determining the operating condition of an engine. The test is made with the engine running at normal operating temperature and with the vacuum gauge attached to the intake manifold. If the gauge needle is steady at 15 to 20 in. Hg, and if it drops sharply when the throttle is opened quickly, the engine is in good condition.

If the vacuum gauge reading does not drop on sudden acceleration, then recover, the piston rings may be worn. If the reading occasionally drops 1 to 5 in. Hg, an engine valve is sticking or a spark plug is not firing. If the gauge reading shows a steady drop of several inches, a burned valve is indicated.

A steady but low vacuum gauge reading in the 12 to 15 in. Hg range is a signal that the spark may be retarded. If the reading is steady but below 12 in. Hg, the engine valve timing may be incorrect or there is an in-take manifold leak. If, while holding engine speed at 2500 rpm, the gauge reading drops slowly but steadily downward, there could be back pressure in the exhaust system. A large variation in readings at different engine speeds is a sign that the valve springs may be weak. Wide sweeping readings while holding the engine speed constant could mean that the cylinder head gasket is leaking.

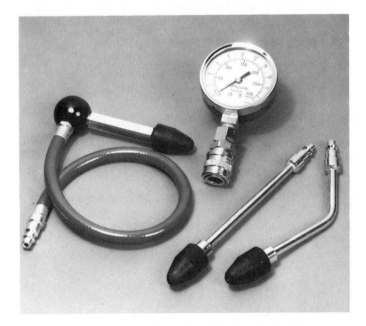

Fig. 35-11. This compression tester is designed for testing compression pressure of gasoline fueled engines. Quick connect-disconnect attachments will adapt tester to most engine applications. (Accurate Instruments)

ENGINE NOISE

One of the most difficult of all troubleshooting jobs is to locate the source of noise or "knocks" in an engine. Actually, every rotating or reciprocating part in the engine is a potential source of noise. In many cases, however, certain noises possess characteristics which help identify their origin.

These characteristics vary somewhat between different engines. In most cases, it will be helpful to utilize an instrument of the stethoscope type to localize the noise at some definite section of the engine. See Fig. 35-12. These instruments magnify the intensity of the noise, and the sound become louder as the tip of the instrument nears the origin of the noise.

CONNECTING ROD BEARING KNOCK

The conditions of operation under which the connecting rod bearing noise is heard and the "timing" of the noise are also useful in determining the source. Some noises are louder as the engine speed is increased, or while the engine is under load. For example, a connecting rod bearing that is slightly "loose" will usually knock loudest around an engine speed of 40 mph and, of greatest intensity, just as the engine goes from a pull to a coast (as driver releases accelerator).

A pronounced rod knock will be heard at all speeds and under both idle and load conditions. One rod will make a distinct noise. If all rods are loose, the noise becomes a rattle or clatter. In many cases, rod bearing knocks are confused with piston slap or loose piston pins. This is particularly true when all rods are loose, and experience will be helpful in deciding which part is at fault. It is not of too much importance to decide definitely, because the remedy for either fault involves removal of the piston and rod assemblies in practically all cases. Measurement and inspection of the parts will then disclose where the trouble lies.

PISTON PIN NOISE

Using a stethoscope is sometimes helpful, since piston or pin may sound loudest when the instrument prod is placed on the cylinder head or block. The rod knock is often loudest with the prod on the crankcase. Shorting out the spark plug on one cylinder may change the intensity of the knock, but it will not always eliminate it. Shorting will help locate which cylinder or rod is at fault in cases where a single knock exists.

Loose piston pins usually, but not always, produce a double rap each revolution of the crankshaft. They rap once at the top of the stroke and again at the bottom. On most engines, the knock is loudest at idling speed, and it will become even louder if the spark is advanced. Often, the knock will be louder if the spark plug is shorted out in cases where not all pins are loose.

PISTON SLAP

There is much confusion between the noise caused by a piston with excessive clearance in the cylinder and a loose piston pin. Either defect produces a click which

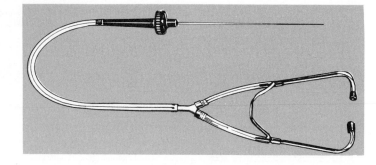

Fig. 35-12. A stethoscope type tool can be used to good advantage in checking for approximate location of engine noises. Stethoscope generally has a built-in diaphragm to amplify sounds.

is quite distinct. If noisy in all cylinders, it becomes a rattle. One indication of piston slap is a decrease in the noise as the engine warms up. A piston slap is always louder when the engine is cold.

PISTON RING NOISE

New piston rings will cause a knock if the ridge at the top of the cylinder bore is not removed before the new rings are installed. Somewhat similar is the condition where the cylinders have been rebored oversize, and the standard cylinder head gasket extends into the combustion chamber. The piston strikes the gasket and makes a distinct knock.

Piston rings that are loose in the grooves will not ordinarily make any noise, since the oil tends to cushion them. If they are excessively loose, particularly the top rings, they may cause a clicking noise similar to a worn valve lifter. There is a difference in the timing of the click. The piston rings will click twice each revolution of the crankshaft, while the valve click will be heard once every other revolution.

MAIN BEARING KNOCK

A main bearing knock is more of a bump than a knock. It can be located by shorting out the plugs near it. The noise is loudest when the engine is "lugging" (pulling hard at slow speed). The sound is heavier and more dull than a connecting rod knock.

CRANKSHAFT END PLAY

Excessive end play in the crankshaft will produce an intermittent rap or knock that is sharper than a main bearing knock. The noise usually will be affected by applying or releasing the clutch. If the car is equipped with an automatic transmission, the noise is more difficult to diagnose. It will rap once, loudly, on sudden acceleration.

LOOSE FLYWHEEL

If the flywheel is loose on the crankshaft flange, the noise will be similar to a main bearing knock. Ordinarily, it will not change when the plugs are shorted out. Furthermore, the noise may come and go rather than being constant. One sure test is to turn off the ignition, then turn it on again just as the engine is about to stop. The sudden twist applied to the crankshaft will produce a definite knock.

NOISY ENGINE MOUNTINGS

If the rubber engine mountings are drawn down too tight, or, if the rubber had deteriorated enough to allow the metal parts of the mounting to contact each other, a knock may occur. This particular knock appears under high torque conditions during rapid acceleration.

VALVE NOISES

Valves are a common source of noise for two reasons. There are several points in each unit of the valve train that can create noise. Usually, it is easy to determine which valve (or valves) are causing the noise by inserting a feeler gauge of suitable thickness between the end of the valve and the rocker arm pad with the engine running.

Clicking caused by wear between the valve lifter and lifter guide, or by damage on the end of the lifter next to the camshaft, is not readily located. Here, the timing of the click is helpful, as well as the use of a stethoscope.

Hydraulic valve lifters often will be noisy when the engine is first started, because oil has leaked from the unit. The noise should disappear after a few minutes operation, during which the lifter will be filled with oil. If the noise does not disappear, the defective lifter can be located by means of a stethoscope.

DIESEL ENGINE DIAGNOSIS

Since the diesel engine does not have an ignition distributor or a carburetor, the troubleshooting procedure is simplified. Basically, it includes checking compression pressure and fuel injector performance.

Checking compression requires the removal of the injectors and testing compression pressure at each cylinder with a compression gauge. Special equipment is necessary to check the injectors and the pattern of spray.

TROUBLESHOOTING ELECTRONIC SYSTEMS

For details concerning electronic ignition and fuel injection, see Chapter 26, Fuel Injection, and Chapter 29, Engine Ignition.

Test equipment manufacturers continually upgrade their products to keep pace with automotive advances. Latest models provide complete on-board computer testing, make diagnostic circuit checks, and display and define car manufacturers' trouble codes. In effect, each tester is designed to simplify engine troubleshooting.

Chapter 35—REVIEW QUESTIONS

Write your answers on a separate sheet of paper. Do not write in this book.

1. What is engine troubleshooting?
2. What advantage does a diagnostic computer engine analyzer have over visual inspection and manual checks?
   a. Pinpoints "hidden" sources of trouble more quickly and with greater accuracy.
   b. Displays performance readings on a screen.
   c. Furnishes a printout of performance readings.
   d. All of the above.
3. Name the four gases that a 4-gas emissions tester will analyze.
4. Chrysler's "plug-in" diagnostic setup utilizes a computer programmed to monitor several different engine systems. To make the tests, a _____ is attached to a test connector located under the hood.
   a. Diagnostic readout tool.
   b. Diagnostic pick-up meter.
   c. Diagnostic printout unit.
   d. Diagnostic computer module.
5. Cadillac's self diagnosis uses a computer module called an _____, which monitors operating conditions for possible malfunctions.
6. An engine starts but will not run. Mechanic A says it could be caused by back pressure in the exhaust system. Mechanic B says it could be caused by an obstructed air filter. Who is right?
   a. Mechanic A.
   b. Mechanic B.
   c. Both mechanic A and mechanic B.
   d. Neither mechanic A nor mechanic B.
7. An engine hesitates on acceleration. Mechanic A says it could be caused by a faulty PCV system. Mechanic B says it could be caused by a faulty carburetor accelerator pump. Who is right?
   a. Mechanic A.
   b. Mechanic B.
   c. Both mechanic A and mechanic B.
   d. Neither mechanic A nor mechanic B.
8. The first step in troubleshooting the cause of engine overheating is to make a careful _____ to see if there is any evidence of external coolant leakage.
9. Not all coolant leakage is external. Severe cases of overheating and coolant loss can result from leaks into the _____.
10. Testing the _____ of each cylinder while the engine is warm and cranking is a well accepted method of checking the condition of internal components of the engine.
    a. Vacuum.
    b. Compression pressure.
    c. Combustion leakage.
    d. Coolant leakage.

Chapter 36

ENGINE TUNE-UP

After studying this chapter, you will be able to:
- Define engine tune-up.
- Explain the close relationship of engine tune-up and emission control.
- Describe test equipment needed to tune-up late model engines.
- State necessary preliminary tests and inspections required to determine whether or not an engine is "tuneable."
- List steps of a logically sequenced engine tune-up test procedure.
- Assess the value of compression pressure tests and the use of a vacuum gauge to diagnose engine problems.

An ENGINE TUNE-UP is a service operation designed to restore the engine's best level of performance while maintaining good fuel economy and minimum exhaust emissions. A tune-up consists of a series of tests, checks, and corrections made according to a prescribed tune-up test procedure.

In the past, peak engine performance was the only goal sought by the tune-up technician. Today, the technician must try to meet two new objectives:
1. Fulfill the obligation to tune the engine to meet Federal and state emissions standards.
2. Satisfy the car owner's demand for economy of operation.

As a result, car maintenance services, including engine tune-up, are more complex and costly. See Fig. 36-1. In some applications, even spark plug replacement has become a tune-up specialist's chore. On the positive side, the more difficult-to-service emission control engines have taken tune-up from the hands of the do-it-yourselfer and given it back to the trained automotive service technician.

Today's auto technician must be able to test and correct problems that exist in compression, ignition, and carburetion or fuel injection; see that the various emission control systems are operable (working as designed); and maintain all related systems (induction, exhaust, temperature control, electronic engine controls, etc.) in good working order. An auto technician must constantly read to keep up with these changes.

Fig. 36-1. In spite of maintenance-free systems and extended service intervals, today's engine tune-ups are more complex. More elaborate equipment is needed to perform required tests and components are less accessible.
(Pontiac Motor Div., General Motors Corp.)

ENGINE TUNE-UP AND AIR POLLUTION

Automobile exhaust emissions are said to be one of the main sources of air pollution in the U.S. Combustion of the air-fuel mixture gives off hydrocarbons (HC), carbon monoxide (CO), oxides of nitrogen (NOx), and other unburned gases that pollute the atmosphere. See Chapter 37, Emission Controls.

Even a well-tuned, clean-burning engine emits some pollutants. If the engine operates inefficiently because of maladjustments (incorrect settings) or malfunctions (improper operation), it will discharge excessive exhaust emissions. According to the results of research conducted by a spark plug manufacturer, a tuned engine, on the average, produces 57 percent less carbon monoxide at idle and 48 percent less hydrocarbons than an untuned engine.

In the past, engine tune-up data and specifications charts provided enough information to help the tune-up technician get maximum performance from a vehicle. However, with today's governmental regulations covering emissions limits, more detailed tests and finer adjustments are necessary — along with regional recommendations for vehicles in different climates and altitudes.

Today's engine tune-up specifications vary from car to car — even for the same make and model — based on the type of fuel system, ignition system, and accessory equipment installed on the vehicle. As a result, the engine tune-up specifications and emissions control information for each particular vehicle are provided on a label (decal) placed conveniently under the hood. See Fig. 36-2.

The tune-up and emissions label contains up-to-date emissions specifications and setting procedures along with a vacuum hose schematic with emission components identified. In order to tune-up a late model engine, the SPECIFICATIONS LABEL must be duly noted and diligently followed.

TUNE-UP EQUIPMENT

An engine tune-up requires the use of certain types of gauges, testers, and test equipment. Fig. 36-3. With this instrumentation, you can perform tests that will reveal weak or defective components that should be replaced. On the other hand, test results will also verify the satisfactory condition of good used units that need not be replaced.

In still another valuable application, you can connect these testers to a given system or circuit to see if a particular setting is as specified. If it is not, the reading on the tester will serve as a means of guiding you in making adjustments to obtain the correct setting.

Tune-up test equipment in the list that follows will permit you to perform all of the checks and tests described later in the TUNE-UP TEST PROCEDURE. They will assist you in making precise settings to manufacturer's specifications.

Compression tester
Vacuum gauge or hand-operated vacuum pump
Fuel pressure gauge
Voltmeter (or volt-amp tester)
Ammeter
Ohmmeter
Digital volt-ohmmeter
Tachometer (or tach-dwell meter)
Dwell meter (see above)
Battery-starter tester
Alternator-regulator tester
Emissions tester (infrared exhaust gas analyzer or 4-gas analyzer)

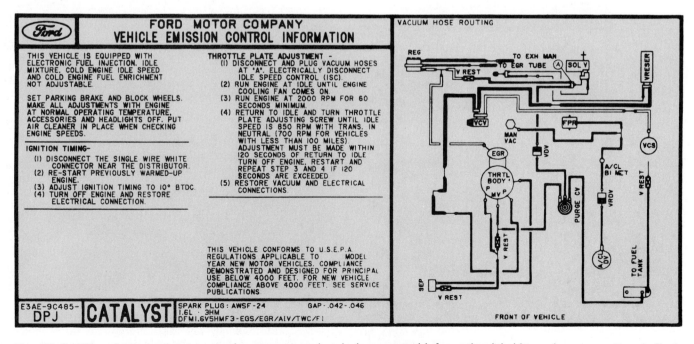

Fig. 36-2. All modern cars have an engine tune-up and emissions control information label in engine compartment. Each label contains specifications for that particular engine application. (Ford Motor Co.)

Engine analyzer or diagnostic computer
Electronic engine controls tester
Distributor tester
Stroboscopic timing light
Hydrometer
PCV (positive crankcase ventilation) system tester
Cooling system pressure tester
Fuel injection pressure gauge
Cylinder leakage tester
Solid state circuit testers
Belt tension gauge
Unpowered test lamp
Jumper wires

In addition, more sophisticated instrumentation is available, Fig. 36-4, that will speed the process and, in some cases, provide more precise readings of a unit's capacity, output, range or level of performance.

TUNE-UP TEST PROCEDURE

Most of the work involved in an engine tune-up job is concerned with tests of the engine electrical systems, fuel system, electronic engine controls, and emission controls. Each is a complete subject in itself, and each is covered in detail in separate chapters of this text.

To illustrate the broad scope of an engine tune-up, the procedure that follows gives brief descriptions of the key steps, arranged in the most logical sequence for doing an efficient and effective job. Tests requiring a more in-depth explanation are spelled out in detail after the basic steps have been covered.

A. **Preliminary Tests and Inspections**
  1. Check engine oil, coolant, and automatic transmission fluid levels.
  2. Note where vacuum hoses to carburetor and air cleaner attach. Use color-coded tags, if necessary. Disconnect vacuum hoses and air intake ducting, and remove air cleaner assembly.
  3. Make a general visual inspection of engine and accessories, including battery condition and possible need for carburetor cleaning or fuel injection system service. If any fluid levels are low, look for evidence of oil, fuel, or coolant leaks.
  4. Use an oscilloscope, ignition system analyzer, or diagnostic computer engine analyzer to make area checks of ignition system operation. See Chapter 29, Engine Ignition, and Chapter 35, Engine Troubleshooting.
  5. Observe ''Check Engine'' lights on vehicles so equipped. If lamp lights when engine is running, self-diagnostic system has detected a problem. Follow through with attachment of diagnostic tester and use manufacturer's diagnostic charts to find problem.

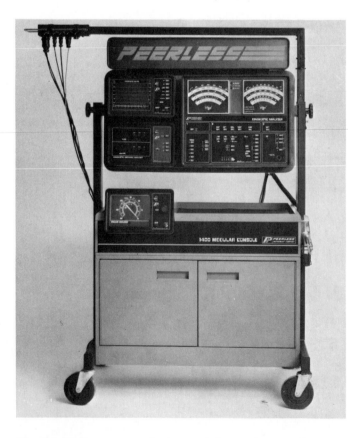

Fig. 36-3. To meet today's need for engine tune-up test instrumentation, this modular console contains a diagnostic, two-meter ignition systems analyzer, infrared gas analyzer, vacuum systems analyzer, carburetor tester, and gimbal (overhead track) mount. (Peerless Instrument Co.)

Fig. 36-4. Computerized Automotive Maintenance System (CAMS) automatically analyzes information from vehicle's engine computer control and tells service technician where problems exist. (Buick Motors Div., General Motors Corp.)

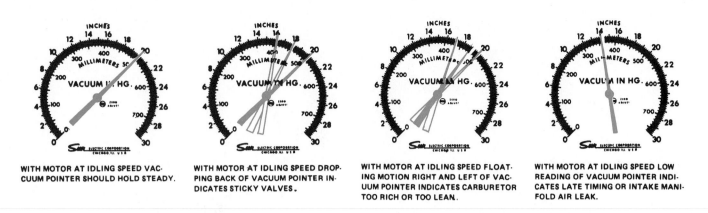

WITH MOTOR AT IDLING SPEED VAC-
CUUM POINTER SHOULD HOLD STEADY.

WITH MOTOR AT IDLING SPEED DROP-
PING BACK OF VACUUM POINTER IN-
DICATES STICKY VALVES.

WITH MOTOR AT IDLING SPEED FLOAT-
ING MOTION RIGHT AND LEFT OF VAC-
UUM POINTER INDICATES CARBURETOR
TOO RICH OR TOO LEAN.

WITH MOTOR AT IDLING SPEED LOW
READING OF VACUUM POINTER INDI-
CATES LATE TIMING OR INTAKE MANI-
FOLD AIR LEAK.

Fig. 36-5. Diagrams show typical action of vacuum gauge needle when various conditions exist in engine under test.
(Sun Electric Corp.)

B. **Internal Engine Condition**

1. Use a voltmeter to test battery voltage while cranking engine. (Should be 9 volts or more.) Also listen to sound of cranking engine. (Should be strong and steady.) Remove spark plugs. Use a compression gauge and remote starter switch to test compression pressure of individual cylinders (with choke and throttle valves wide open). If remote cranking will damage ignition switch in LOCK or OFF position, turn key ON. Also, GM cautions: On HEI systems, disconnect "BAT" terminal from distributor (or coil on some engines) when cranking engine for compression testing.

2. Use a cylinder leakage tester to test for leakage of air under pressure into intake or exhaust manifold, crankcase, or cooling system.

3. Use a vacuum gauge to check for vacuum leaks, Fig. 36-5. Start with manifold vacuum test, with throttle valve closed and vacuum gauge connected directly to intake manifold. (Should hold steady reading.) Then check vacuum to emission control units. See Chapter 37, Emission Controls.

C. **Test and Service Battery**

1. Clean posts, cable clamps, and top of battery.

2. Check level of electrolyte in cells, if possible, and use a hydrometer to check specific gravity of each cell. (Should be at least 1.250, corrected to 80 °F (27 °C) with no more than 25 points of gravity difference between high and low cells.)

3. Load test battery at a load equal to 50 percent of cold cranking rating, noting voltmeter after 15 seconds discharge. (Should be 9.5 volts or more.) Make an open circuit voltage test to verify battery state of charge.

4. Recharge weak battery. Replace defective battery.

D. **Check Starting System**

1. Inspect condition of cables and wires, mounting of components.

2. Test for voltage drop in battery cables, connections, switch, solenoid, and starting motor. See Fig. 36-6.

3. Test for amperage draw of starting motor. Remove high tension coil wire from distributor cap tower. Ground coil wire to metal part of engine. Connect leads of battery-starter tester to battery terminals. Crank engine for 15 seconds and note voltmeter reading. Stop cranking and adjust resistance unit on tester to obtain voltage previously noted, then read amperage draw on ammeter. (Check reading against manufacturer's specifications.)

E. **Test Ignition Coil**

1. With ignition switch OFF, use ohmmeter to test coil primary resistance between + and − terminals. Test secondary resistance between center tower and + terminal. Check readings against manufacturer's specifications. If an oscilloscope or a special coil tester is available, check maximum and required high tension voltages. Also, high tension polarity should be negative. See Chapter 29 for details and tips on General Motors Computer Controlled coil Ignition, a system that incorporates three ignition coils and no distributor.

Fig. 36-6. Digital readout electrical systems analyzer checks batteries, starting motors, starter switches, and cables. It has a carbon pile and automatic 15-second load switch. Analyzer simulates a discharged battery when testing charging system.
(Peerless Instrument Co.)

403

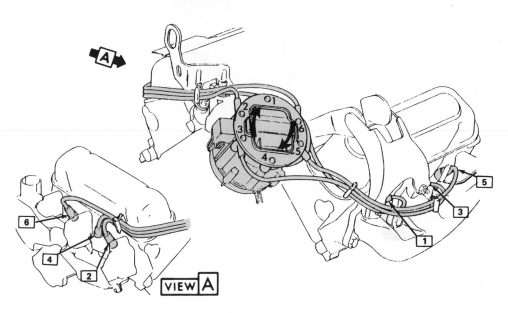

Fig. 36-7. Simplified diagram gives routing of high tension wiring from HEI distributor to spark plugs on a 3.0 liter or 3.8 liter V-6 engine. (Oldsmobile Div., General Motors Corp.)

2. Test resistance of high tension cables with an ohmmeter. (Typically, readings should be at least 3000 ohms/ft. and no more than 5000 to 7200 ohms/ft., depending on application. Check manufacturer's specifications.)

F. Service GM HEI Systems

1. To test operation of earlier HEI systems, disconnect a spark plug wire and use an insulated pliers to hold the wire 1/4 in. (6.0 mm) from a grounded surface. Crank engine. A heavy blue spark should jump the gap.

2. Check for loose or corroded connections and/or poor ground.

3. Check routing of high tension wires through brackets, Fig. 36-7. Note that coil is built into distributor on V-6 and V-8 engines, Fig. 36-8.

4. Disconnect ignition switch feed wire at distributor (V-6 and V-8) or coil (4 and L6). Connect voltmeter leads to wire and ground. With ignition switch ON, test voltage in the START and RUN positions. Both readings should be battery voltage.

5. Remove distributor cap.

6. Wiggle distributor shaft to check for bushing wear. Reluctor and pickup coil must not touch. HEI distributor shaft bushings do not need periodic lubrication.

7. Apply vacuum to vacuum advance unit to test diaphragm operation. Leave vacuum hose disconnected and plugged for ignition timing check.

8. Connect leads of low reading ammeter: one to disconnected switch wire; other to distributor (V-6 and V-8) or coil (4 and L6) terminal. Turn on ignition switch: ammeter should read 0.1 to 0.2 amp. (Crank engine: ammeter should read 0.5 to 1.5 amps. If not, test pickup, module, and coil primary current.)

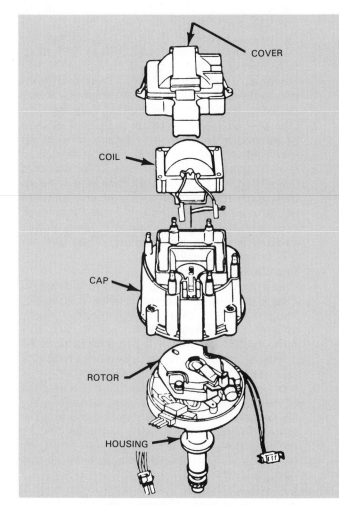

Fig. 36-8. Typically, ignition coil is built into HEI distributor on V-6 and V-8 GM engines. Coil is mounted separately on four and six cylinder inline engines. (Cadillac Motor Car Div., General Motors Corp.)

Fig. 36-9. Hand-held tester is designed to connect to GM vehicle's on-board Computer Command Control (CCC) and cigarette lighter. Tester will troubleshoot system and help pinpoint problems via 49 test modes. (OTC Tools and Equipment)

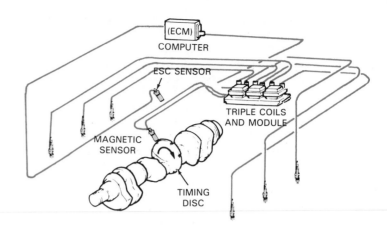

Fig. 36-10. Computer Controlled Coil Ignition (C³I) features triple coils and ignition module. System shown is for use in 2.8 liter multiport fuel injection V-6 engine.
(Chevrolet Motor Div., General Motors Corp.)

9. Use silicone dielectric compound on primary wire connections. Also use this compound on underside of module and on distributor base where module seats.

10. Use prescribed instruments to test electronic ignition components, Fig. 36-9. Note, too, that later GM systems have plug-in or self-diagnostic connectors.

11. On engine speed tests, use a tachometer that is compatible with system. Do not connect tachometer lead to ground, nor allow tach terminal on distributor to touch ground. Damage to module or ignition coil could result.

12. NOTE: When making tests that call for a spark plug to be shorted out, do not run engine longer than necessary. Otherwise, catalyst in catalytic converter will be damaged.

13. See Chapter 29, ENGINE IGNITION, for more information on testing and servicing GM ignition systems with computer engine controls.

14. (C-4—Computer Controlled Catalytic Converter system; CCC—Computer Command Control system.) These later models have EST (Electronic Spark Timing), which is controlled by the ECM (Electronic Control Module) to electronically signal spark timing changes. No vacuum advance or mechanical advance units are used. ESC (Electronic Spark Control) is used on some engines to modify spark advance when detonation occurs.

15. Certain engines have a Computer Controlled Coil Ignition (C³I) system that eliminates need for an ignition distributor. See Fig. 36-10. C³I works in conjunction with CCC and EST systems. C³I consists of an ECM, coil pack, ignition module, and crankshaft and camshaft positioners. Input from sensors provide ignition module with information to select and sequentially trigger each of three interconnected coils to fire spark plugs at proper crankshaft position. For details, see Chapter 29.

G. Service Ford Duraspark Systems

1. To test system operation, remove coil high tension cable and insert a spark tester, Fig. 36-11, into cable. Ground plug shell and crank engine to check for spark.

2. Use an oscilloscope to test ignition system performance. No adjustments are to be made to Duraspark systems except initial ignition timing and spark plug gap.

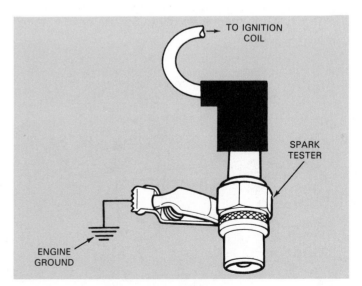

Fig. 36-11. On Duraspark systems, connect spark tester between high tension ignition coil wire and ground. Crank engine, using ignition key, and check for intensity of spark.
(Ford Motor Co.)

3. Check for loose or corroded connections and/or poor ground. Clean and tighten connections.

4. Remove and inspect distributor cap for cracks, burned contacts, broken carbon button, carbon tracking, or corroded tower contacts. NOTE: On Duraspark II systems, when ignition switch is ON, so are the control module and coil. Therefore, before removing distributor cap, be sure that ignition switch is OFF.

5. Inspect rotor for breaks, carbon tracking, or burns on tip.

6. When installing a new distributor cap and rotor, coat (about 1/32 in. or .80 mm thick) brass electrode surfaces on all sides (away from plastic and including outer edge) with silicone grease. See Fig. 36-12. Also, do not remove silicone from new distributor cap electrodes.

7. Inspect distributor components. See that all snap rings are in place. Test pickup assembly for free movement on fixed base plate. Use compressed air to blow out dirt, filings, or metal chips. (Be sure to wear goggles.)

8. Apply vacuum to vacuum advance unit to test diaphragm operation. Leave vacuum hose disconnected for ignition timing operation. NOTE: On some air conditioned cars, a fast idle compensator applies intake manifold vacuum to primary side of diaphragm during hot engine conditions. This causes an increase in engine idle speed, which aids cooling.

9. Also check centrifugal advance unit located below distributor base plate. Inspect condition of springs. Weights should freely pivot outward and inward.

10. On Duraspark II systems, a vacuum switch is used (at module) to sense intake manifold vacuum and provide an automatic spark retard signal to distributor under heavy engine load.

11. Duraspark I systems automatically shut down in one second after control module senses no distributor rotation. To reestablish the module cycle, turn ignition key to START or OFF, then ON again.

12. When servicing Duraspark systems, maintain at least 3/4 in. (19.0 mm) clearance at distributor cap mounting edge, plug terminals, and coil tower to prevent high voltage arc to ground. NOTE: Wires are positioned in brackets on valve rocker arm covers in special order from front to rear to prevent cylinder crossfire. Be sure to reinstall wires in that special order.

13. Ignition coil connector on Duraspark II systems allows hookup of tachometer test lead to DEC (Distributor Electronic Control) terminal without removing connector. See Fig. 36-13.

14. Ford Duraspark II UIC systems include a breakerless distributor, Electronic Control Module (ECM), Universal Integrated Circuit (UIC), and various wiring harnesses. UIC system can be identified by a three-wire harness that connects ECM to a special sensor that adjusts base ignition timing to compensate for altitude and engine load. Duraspark II UIC distributors have centrifugal advance and either single diaphragm or dual diaphragm vacuum advance units.

15. Ford TFI-I systems use a horizontally mounted Thick Film Ignition (TFI) distributor, Fig. 36-14, with mechanical and vacuum advance. It has a concentric pickup coil assembly and a reinforced base to house TFI module. Thick film technology reduces size of module and eliminates long wire leads.

16. Ford TFI-IV distributor uses a Hall Effect vane switch mechanism to induce primary voltage and effect discharge of high secondary voltage. At this point, sensors signal crankshaft position, engine load, and octane calibration to Electronic Engine Control (EEC-IV) for computing proper amount of spark advance. Distributor calibration is controlled by an octane adjusting rod. TFI-IV systems have no mechanical or vacuum advance mechanisms. See Chapter 29 for more details on testing and servicing these Ford ignition systems.

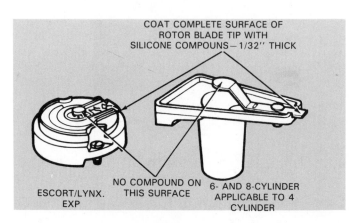

Fig. 36-12. On Duraspark systems, coat distributor cap electrodes and rotor blade tip with silicone dielectric compound. Do not use silicone compound on multipoint rotors. (Ford Motor Co.)

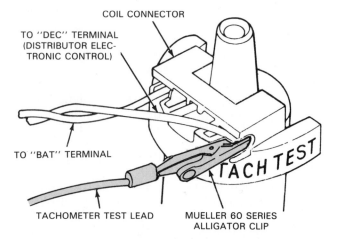

Fig. 36-13. To connect a tachometer to a Duraspark II system, clip one lead to tach test terminal of coil connector and ground other lead. (Ford Motor Co.)

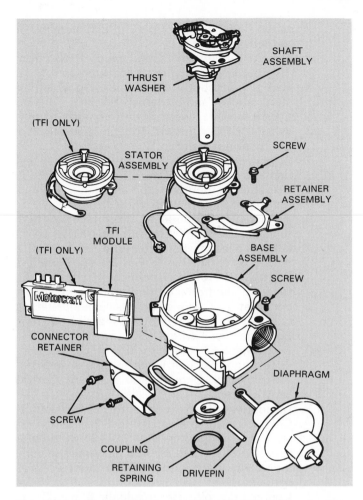

Fig. 36-14. Exploded view of Ford's Thick Film Ignition distributor reveals location of TFI module mounted at base of distributor housing. (Ford Motor Co.)

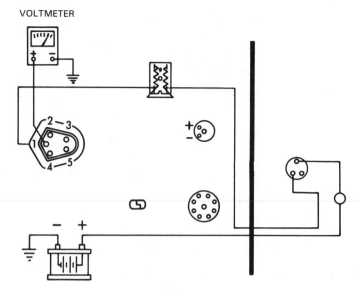

Fig. 36-15. On earlier Chrysler electronic ignition systems, test available voltage at wiring harness connector cavity No. 1. (Chrysler Corp.)

H. Service Chrysler Electronic Ignition Systems

1. On earlier Chrysler systems, inspect condition of wiring harness and connections, secondary cables, and ballast resistor. With ignition switch OFF, remove multiwiring connector from control unit. NOTE: Later ignition systems are equipped with diagnostic plug-in connectors. See Chapter 35, Engine Troubleshooting.

2. With ignition switch ON, hook up a voltmeter with a 20,000 ohm/volt rating: negative lead to ground; positive lead to wiring harness connector cavity No. 1. See Fig. 36-15. Available voltage should be at least 11 volts with all accessories OFF. NOTE: Later models have 10-way dual connector from spark control computer.

3. Repeat primary system test at connector cavities. No. 2 and No. 3.

4. Use an ohmmeter with 1 1/2 volt battery to test pickup coil. Connect leads of ohmmeter to wiring harness connector cavity No. 4, then No. 5. Resistance should be between 150 and 900 ohms.

5. If resistance is out of limits, disconnect dual lead connector from distributor. Using ohm-meter, test resistance at dual lead connector. If resistance is still out of limits, replace pickup coil assembly.

6. Connect one ohmmeter lead to ground, other lead to either connector of distributor. Ohmmeter should show open circuit (infinity). If not, replace pickup coil.

7. Check electronic control unit: Connect one ohmmeter lead to ground; other lead to control unit connector pin No. 5. Ohmmeter must show continuity. If not, tighten control unit mounting bolts and retest. If no continuity, replace control unit.

8. With ignition switch OFF, reconnect wiring harness at control unit and distributor.

9. Remove distributor cap. Inspect cap for cracks, burns, flashover, worn or grooved terminals. Clean or replace cap.

10. Inspect rotor for cracks, burns, and tension of spring terminal. Clean or replace rotor.

11. Check centrifugal advance unit for free operation.

12. Apply vacuum to vacuum advance unit to test diaphragm operation. Leave vacuum hose disconnected and plugged for ignition timing operation.

13. Check air gap between reluctor tooth and pickup coil. Adjust gap to .006 in. (.15 mm), if necessary.

14. Reinstall distributor rotor and cap.

15. Check ignition secondary circuit. Remove high voltage cable from center tower of distributor cap. Hold cable approximately 3/16 in. (4.75 mm) from grounded surface of engine. Crank engine. If arcing does not occur, replace control unit.

16. Crank engine again. If arcing does not occur, replace ignition coil.

17. Later Chrysler Electronic Spark Control (ESC) systems are governed by a Spark Control Computer (SCC), Fig. 36-16, a special calibrated carburetor, a dual pickup distributor ("Start" and "Run"), and up to seven engine sensors. Computer receives signals from all sensors, then immediately computes proper spark advance or retard. "Start" pickup coil signals computer to cause spark plugs to fire at a fixed advance during cranking only. When engine runs, "Run" pickup coil supplies advance information to computer, which modifies spark advance based on information from other sensors.

18. Hall Effect Electronic Spark Control on late model engines features a Hall Effect distributor, Fig. 36-17, an SCC, and up to five sensors. Hall Effect pickup sends direct current signals to computer. Computer uses these signals and signals from other sensors to adjust ignition timing to suit engine operating conditions. Computer has a different advance schedule for a hot and a cold engine. No adjustments can be made to Hall Effect pickup unit. Dwell and spark timing cannot be adjusted. Fixed timing can be adjusted by changing distributor position.

19. See Chapter 29 for more information on testing and servicing Chrysler ESC and Hall Effect ESC systems.

I. **Service AMC (Motorcraft) SSI Systems**

1. AMC Solid State Ignition (SSI) systems feature a solid state ignition distributor and Electronic Control Unit (ECU) that work in conjunction with a Micro Computer Unit (MCU) to control ignition timing to suit engine operating conditions.

2. Inspect primary ignition system for loose or corroded terminals, poor ground connections, or defective wiring.

3. Check routing of spark plug wires from distributor cap towers to spark plugs.

4. Remove distributor cap. Check cap for corrosion, cracks, and/or carbon tracks.

5. Check rotor for wear or deterioration of tip.

6. Wiggle distributor shaft. Trigger wheel and sensor must not touch.

7. Apply vacuum to vacuum advance unit to test condition of diaphragm.

8. Reinstall distributor rotor and cap. Recheck routing of high tension wires.

9. To test system operation, disconnect coil high tension wire from distributor cap. Use an insulated pliers to hold coil wire 1/2 in. (12.7 mm) from engine block, Fig. 36-18. Turn ignition switch ON and disconnect 4-wire connector from electronic control unit. Spark should occur at coil wire. Apply silicone dielectric compound to connector blades and cavities. Reconnect coil wire.

10. Disconnect J2 connector from MCU and connect ohmmeter test leads to pins 3 and 5 of J2 connector. Ohmmeter should indicate 400 to 800 ohms.

11. Disconnect 3-wire connector at distributor. Connect ohmmeter leads to B2 and B3 terminals of connector, Fig. 36-19. Ohmmeter should read 400 to 800 ohms. Apply silicone dielectric compound. Reconnect 3-wire connector.

12. Connect dc voltmeter test leads to pins 3 and 5 of J2 connector. Crank engine. Voltmeter needle should fluctuate if trigger wheel and sensor in distributor are operating properly. Apply silicone dielectric compound. Reconnect J2 connector.

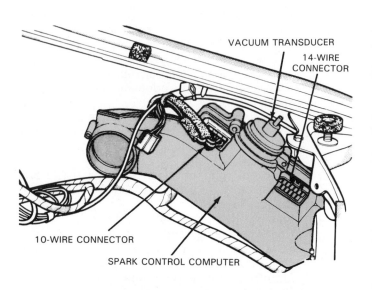

Fig. 36-16. On later Chrysler electronic ignition systems, a Spark Control Computer (SCC) takes sensor signals and computes correct spark timing for operating conditions. (Chrysler Corp.)

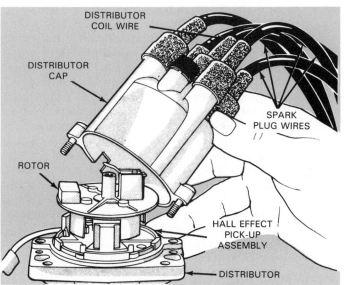

Fig. 36-17. Hall Effect pickup assembly in ignition distributor of Chrysler late model four cylinder engines supplies basic timing signal to Spark Control Computer. (Chrysler Corp.)

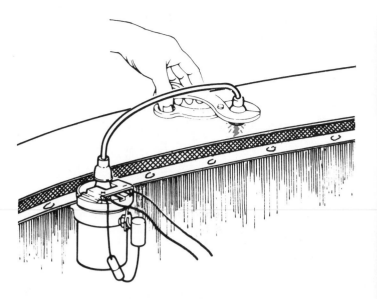

Fig. 36-18. On AMC Solid State Ignition (SSI) systems, hold disconnected high tension ignition coil wire 1/2 in. from grounded surface. Spark should occur with ignition switch ON when 4-wire connector from electronic control unit is disconnected. (American Motors Corp.)

CONNECT OHMMETER TO B2 and B3 TERMINALS OF DISTRIBUTOR CONNECTOR

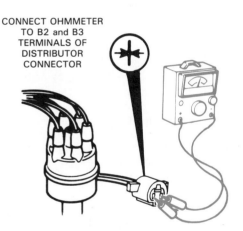

Fig. 36-19. To test AMC Solid State Ignition (SSI) system operation, disconnect 3-wire connector at distributor and apply ohmmeter probes to connector as shown. Ohmmeter should read 400 to 800 ohms. (American Motors Corp.)

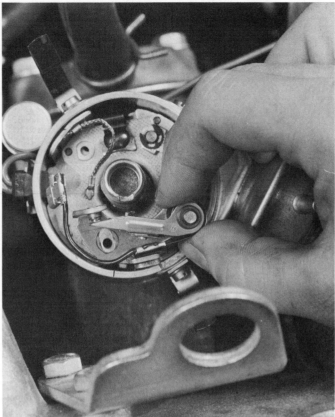

Fig. 36-20. Generally, replace breaker points and condenser when performing an engine tune-up on any old vehicle having this type of ignition system.

13. Connect an oscilloscope to ignition system. Start engine and check secondary voltage. Remove one spark plug wire from distributor cap, again using insulated pliers. (Do not remove wires from plugs for cylinders one or five of a six cylinder engine or for cylinder three of a four cylinder engine). Check open circuit output voltage to disconnected plug wire on oscilloscope. Spark output should be 24,000 volts at 1000 rpm.

J. **Service Ignition Distributor (breaker point type)**
    1. Check condition of distributor cap (inside and out) and rotor.
    2. Note position of rotor and remove distributor from engine.

3. Clean distributor and check condition of lead wires, plate, cam, bushings, and advance mechanism.
4. Replace breaker points and condenser, Fig. 36-20. Align points, if necessary, and adjust gap to manufacturer's recommended setting.
5. Test breaker arm spring tension.
6. Lubricate wick in center of cam assembly with two drops of engine oil. Lubricate cam lobes with light coating of high melting point grease; or, replace cam lubricator.
7. Check operation of mechanical and vacuum advance units. Free or replace inoperative units. Check emission controls that affect timing advance. See Chapter 37.
8. Use a dwell meter to test distributor point dwell (cam angle) and readjust point gap, if necessary. Test dwell variation. (Generally, variation should not exceed 3 deg. from 250 rpm to 2000 rpm.)
9. Install distributor in engine with rotor in original position.
10. Leave spark advance vacuum line(s) disconnected, but plug open end(s).

K. **Inspect Spark Plugs**
    1. Examine all spark plug electrodes for wear. Check insulators for breakage.
    2. Analyze deposits to pinpoint source of problem.

3. Clean electrodes, then file and regap good used plugs. See Fig. 36-21. Or, replace defective plugs with a new set of specified type and proper heat range. (Use new gaskets unless plugs have a tapered seat.)

4. Install spark plugs to correct torque tightness. Typical torque values for various types and sizes are:
   a. Gasketed:
      18 mm — 25-30 ft. lb. (33-38 N·m)
      14 mm — 22-26 ft. lb. (30-35 N·m)
      10 mm — 10-12 ft. lb. (14-18 N·m)
   b. Tapered seat:
      18 mm — 15-20 ft. lb. (20-27 N·m)
      14 mm — 7-15 ft. lb. (10-20 N·m)
      10 mm — 5-11 ft. lb. (8-16 N·m)

5. Apply silicone dielectric compound to inside of spark plug boots, if recommended. Connect spark plug cable terminals securely to plugs in correct firing order. Make sure boots fit firmly over plug porcelains.

L. Check Cooling System

1. Inspect condition of radiator, hoses, and clamps, including transmission oil cooler lines and fittings.
2. Test radiator cap for pressure release point and pressure-hold.
3. Check level of coolant in radiator or in coolant reserve tank and degree of antifreeze protection.
4. Use pressure tester to test cooling system for leaks. Pressurize system to pressure release point of cap and observe reading for at least two minutes. (Drop in pressure indicates leak in system.)
5. Check condition and tension of V-belts. See Chapter 17, Engine Cooling Systems.

M. Inspect Fuel System

1. Torque-tighten intake manifold attaching bolts.
2. Check freedom of operation of manifold heat control valve, if so equipped, Fig. 36-22.
3. Check components of thermostatically controlled air cleaner. See Chapter 22, Air Cleaners.
4. Service all air filters and fuel filters. Clean or replace elements as required.
5. Tighten carburetor or fuel injection system attaching nuts or bolts and cover screws. See Chapter 25, Carburetor Adjustment and Service.
6. Clean automatic choke mechanism and check choke valve and linkage for freedom.
7. Check adjustment of choke, unloader, and kickdown. See Fig. 36-23. See Chapter 24, Automatic and Electric Chokes. Tighten heat tube fittings, if so equipped. Test continuity (current flow) of circuit on electric choke applications.
8. Check components of throttle body injection (TBI) system or individual port injection system, including various sensors and sensor circuitry to engine electronic control system. See Chapter 26, Fuel Injection.

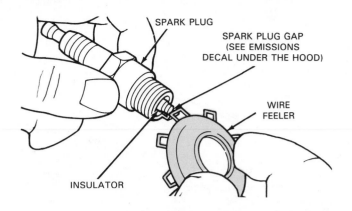

Fig. 36-21. Always check spark plug gap with a round wire feeler gauge. Adjust gap measurement by bending side electrode. (Ford Motor Co.)

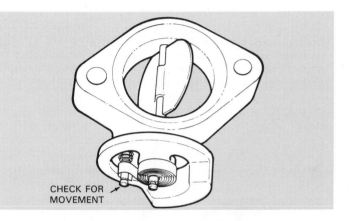

Fig. 36-22. Exhaust manifold heat control valve provides quick warmup of induction system. If valve counterweight does not move freely, use penetrating oil and tap lightly with a hammer. (American Motors Corp.)

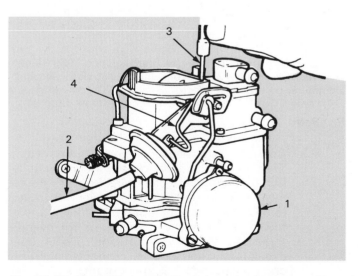

Fig. 36-23. Typically, to check choke valve clearance: Place fast idle speed screw on high step of cam and turn choke housing (1) to 1/4 turn rich. Apply vacuum to force diaphragm against stop (2). Insert specified plug gauge (3) as shown. Adjust clearance between choke valve and air horn wall by bending vacuum diaphragm connector link (4). Readjust cover index to specified lean/rich position. (American Motors Corp.)

9. Inspect fuel lines, hoses, and connections for fuel leaks, kinks, restrictions, or deterioration.
10. Check operation of accelerator linkage. Clean, lubricate, and adjust as required.
11. Check fuel tank for fuel leaks. Check condition of fuel tank filler cap.
12. Check evaporative emissions control system hoses, canister, and filter. See Chapter 37, Emission Controls.
13. Test fuel pump pressure, capacity (volume), and vacuum.
14. Service positive crankcase ventilation (PCV) system. Replace PCV valve if defective or if required by manufacturer's service interval.
15. Check condition of all emission control systems, Fig. 36-24. See Chapter 37.

N. Start Engine and Make Preliminary Adjustments
1. Run engine. Check choking action and fast idle operation.
2. Connect timing light, Fig. 36-25, or other pickup equipment to ignition system and check initial (base) timing. Reconnect vacuum line, if disconnected, and recheck advance with timing light. NOTE: Many late model engines have computer controlled spark timing.
3. Examine entire exhaust system for leaks.
4. Run engine to normal operating temperature and check cooling system thermostat operation.
5. Install tachometer and vacuum gauge. Adjust air-fuel mixture and engine idle speed. Adjust throttle stop solenoid and/or vacuum break on carburetors so equipped.
6. Connect an emissions tester (infrared exhaust gas analyzer, 4-gas analyzer, etc.) to engine and tailpipe of car. Test HC and CO emission levels at various speeds recommended by equipment manufacturer. Check results against specifications.
7. Adjust valve lash, if engine has solid lifters.

O. Test Charging System
1. Use an alternator tester to test voltage and current output of alternator. See Fig. 36-6.
2. Check operation of voltage regulator. See Chapter 34, Charging System Testing and Servicing.

P. Road Test Car
1. Check starting and idle. Warm engine to normal operating temperature and test engine performance at all speeds.
2. Check automatic transmission shift points and kickdown operation.
3. Make final adjustments to obtain best possible engine performance, fewest emissions, and most fuel mileage.

CHECKING COMPRESSION PRESSURE

Never attempt to tune-up an engine having worn piston rings, faulty valves, incorrect valve timing, worn camshaft lobes, or an internal coolant leak. If internal parts are not sound (not in good working order), poor engine performance usually results. This performance

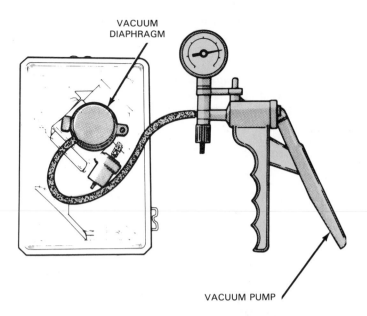

Fig. 36-24. In one of many tests of emission controls during an engine tune-up, use a hand-operated vacuum pump to test operation of vacuum diaphragm on thermostatically controlled air cleaner. (Chrysler Corp.)

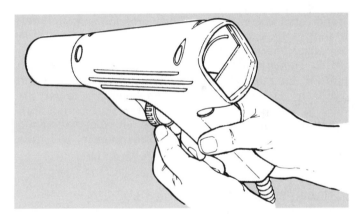

Fig. 36-25. Generally, to check ignition timing, connect stroboscopic timing light leads to ground and to an adapter placed between No. 1 spark plug and No. 1 spark plug wire. (Chrysler Corp.)

problem, however, is beyond the corrective powers of an engine tune-up.

Most internal engine problems can be detected by making a compression pressure test, which is one of the first and most important steps of an engine tune-up. Manufacturers provide minimum/maximum compression pressure charts. See Chapter 35, Engine Troubleshooting. Most specify that the lowest compression reading must be 70 or 75 percent of the highest.

To use the chart, first record compression pressures for each engine cylinder. Use a special compression gauge to make the test. The engine should be at normal operating temperature. The engine oil should be of the proper grade and not seriously diluted.

Make the test with all spark plugs removed and with choke and throttle valves of the carburetor wide open.

Use a remote starter switch to crank over the engine while holding the tip of the compression gauge in each spark plug port in turn. Crank the engine for at least four revolutions, recording the highest reading on the gauge for each cylinder. Compare the high and low figures on your list with the satisfactory ranges shown on the manufacturer's specification chart, Fig. 35-10. If one or more cylinders is "out-of-specification," there is no use tuning up the engine until the cause has been determined and corrected. See Chapter 35.

USING A VACUUM GAUGE

In the hands of an experienced operator, a vacuum gauge can provide considerable useful information about the condition of the internal parts of an engine. However, it is easy to misinterpret the readings of the instrument and reach false conclusions. In using the gauge on an engine, it is much more important to note the action of the needle (floating or vibrating, for example) rather than the numbers on the dial.

When properly used and understood, a vacuum gauge will indicate: incorrect carburetor adjustment; ignition timing errors; ignition defects; improper valve action; restricted exhaust system; cylinder leakage; intake system leakage.

If an engine is in good internal condition and operating properly, the vacuum gauge needle will hold steady at a reading between 15 and 20 at idling speed. See Fig. 36-5. There will be some variation with changes in altitude and atmospheric conditions. For example, each 1000 ft. (304.8 m) above sea level will lower the reading about one point (or one inch of mercury). Vacuum gauges are manufactured with dials marked in inches of mercury (in. Hg.) to correspond to "U" tube laboratory instruments that serve as a standard.

INTERPRETING THE READINGS

With the engine warmed up to operating temperature and running slightly higher than at low idling speed, attach a vacuum gauge to the intake manifold. Attach it directly to the manifold, in order to avoid any air leaks that might exist in vacuum-operated systems or connections. Then make the following analysis of the various readings.

NORMAL: Needle will be steady between 15 and 20 in. Hg. while idling. When the throttle is suddenly opened and closed, the needle will drop to below 5, then bounce up to around 25.

LEAKING RINGS: Needle may be fairly steady, but will read 3 to 4 points lower than normal. When throttle is suddenly opened and closed, needle may not drop.

LATE TIMING: If compression is good and needle reads low, ignition timing may be late, Fig. 36-5. If reading is considerably lower than it should be, valve timing may be late. If adjusting carburetor will not increase vacuum to normal, make a check to see if either or both, ignition or valve timing, should be advanced.

LEAKING INTAKE: If needle is steady but from 3 to 9 points low, throttle valve is not closing or an air leak exists in carburetor or intake manifold.

LEAKING CYLINDER HEAD GASKET: If needle floats regularly between a low and a high reading, the cylinder head gasket probably is "blown" between two adjacent cylinders.

CARBURETOR OUT OF ADJUSTMENT: Needle floats slowly over a range of 4 to 5 points.

SPARK PLUG GAPS: If needle floats slowly over a narrower range, perhaps 2 points, the spark plug gaps may be spaced too close.

RESTRICTED EXHAUST: If needle reads in normal range when engine is first started, sinks to zero, then rises slowly to below normal, the muffler may be clogged or the tailpipe kinked or plugged.

DEFECTIVE VALVE ACTION: Experience will help you to distinguish between valve troubles such as leaking, burned, sticking valves, weak valve springs, or worn valve guides. Action of the needle and range of motion are indications of which is at fault, Fig. 36-5. Since the valve must be removed in most cases to remedy the defect, correctness of diagnosis can be determined.

ENGINE MECHANICAL CONDITION: If vacuum gauge indicates loss of compression or improper valve action, do not proceed with tune-up until all faults are corrected. If, however, tests indicate timing errors, intake leaks, carburetor out of adjustment, or a restricted exhaust system, correct these defects as the next step.

HIGH SPEED TUNING

An engine tune-up can be carried to extremes if you want to get maximum speed and power from a given engine. A high performance tune-up procedure often involves extensive mechanical alteration of the engine. Typical modifications include: enlarging the valves and seats; porting and relieving the cylinder heads; altering the bore and stroke of the engine; increasing the compression ratio; installing a custom camshaft.

Additional changes are: revising valve timing and ignition timing; enlarging and streamlining intake and exhaust manifolds; installing multiple carburetors or fuel injection. High performance tuning is a separate and complicated subject, not within the scope of this text.

TUNING EMISSION CONTROLS

Great care, methodical checks, and precise adjustments are required when tuning emission controlled engines. Failure to follow factory instructions and specifications may result in rough idle, surging, loss of power, increased emissions, and dieseling (run-on after ignition key is turned off).

These devices must be in good working order and properly adjusted to function as designed — as emission controls. Also worth noting, government regulations forbid removing, disconnecting, disengaging, or otherwise rendering emission controls inoperative. Set them up as specified by the manufacturer to maintain the controls at maximum operating efficiency to help fight air pollution. These are federal regulations and must be followed.

REVIEW QUESTIONS

Write your answers on a separate sheet of paper. Do not write in this book.

1. What is an engine tune-up?
2. Combustion of the air-fuel mixture gives off _____, _____, _____ and other unburned gases that pollute the atmosphere.
3. Engine tune-up specifications and emission control information are provided on a tune-up and emissions _____ placed in a convenient location under the hood.
4. Most of the work involved in an engine tune-up job is concerned with tests of the engine electrical system, fuel system, electronic engine controls, and _____.
5. If ''Check Engine'' display lights when engine is running on a vehicle so equipped, what is indicated?
6. What is maximum engine cranking time when making an amperage draw test?
   a. 5 seconds.
   b. 10 seconds.
   c. 15 seconds.
   d. 30 seconds.
7. Use an ohmmeter to test ignition coil primary resistance by connecting leads between:
   a. Center tower and + terminal.
   b. Center tower and − terminal.
   c. Center tower and ground.
   d. + and − terminals.
8. When making tests that call for a spark plug to be shorted out, do not run engine longer than necessary. Why?
   a. Engine may backfire and damage throttle body fuel injection mechanism.
   b. Catalyst in catalytic converter may be damaged.
   c. Ignition coil may be damaged.
   d. Engine computer control unit may be damaged.
9. A power timing light can be used to check ignition timing. Also, certain engines have a hole in the timing case cover for using a _____.
10. What check is required on a manifold heat control valve?
    a. Valve lash measurement.
    b. Torque tightness.
    c. Freedom of operation.
    d. Opening temperature.
11. If an engine is in good condition and operating properly, the vacuum gauge needle will hold a steady reading of _____ in. Hg.
    a. 5 to 10
    b. 10 to 15
    c. 15 to 20
    d. 20 to 25

Match the question number for each of the following engine tune-up tests with the letter designated for each piece of test equipment required to perform the test.

12. ____ Specific gravity of each battery cell.
13. ____ Amperage draw of starting motor.
14. ____ Air leak at intake manifold.
15. ____ Ignition system performance.
16. ____ Charging system output.
17. ____ Emission levels.
18. ____ Resistance of high tension cables.
19. ____ Breaker point cam angle.
20. ____ Engine speed.

a. Ohmmeter.
b. Tachometer.
c. Alternator-regulator tester.
d. Dwell meter.
e. Hydrometer.
f. Vacuum gauge.
g. Oscilloscope.
h. Exhaust gas analyzer.
i. Battery-starter tester.

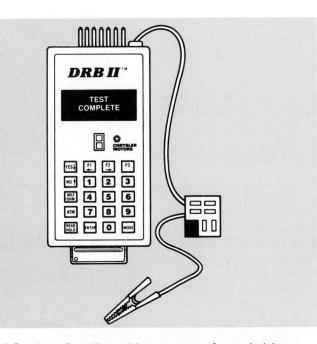

Digital Readout Box II provides a means for technician to analyze fault codes on vehicles having on-board diagnostic capability. (Chrysler Corp.)

Chapter 37

EMISSION CONTROLS

After studying this chapter, you will be able to:
- Name noxious automotive emissions that created need for car manufacturers to install emission controls.
- Explain function of positive crankcase ventilation system.
- Cite various engine design modifications made to combat emissions.
- Classify precombustion and post-combustion emission control systems.
- Give examples of emission control failures and services required.

Many factors, natural and otherwise, contribute to pollution of the air we breathe. Our atmosphere is being polluted daily by the growing and decaying processes of nature, by emissions from motor vehicles, and by smoke from factories, power plants, and the heating of homes, commercial buildings, industrial plants, and institutions.

Industry contributes the largest share of air contaminants, mostly in the form of sulfur compounds and particulates (solid matter). Motor vehicle emissions, on the other hand, are carbon monoxide (CO), hydrocarbons (HC), and oxides of nitrogen (NO_x). These are noxious. This means they are harmful to the body. They can cause damage to the lungs as well as skin irritation and other problems.

AUTOMOTIVE EMISSION STANDARDS

In 1970, the U.S. Government moved to combat the steadily increasing level of air pollutants. The Federal Clean Air Act was passed. This Act was the first of a series of legislative steps aimed at ridding the atmosphere of harmful automotive emissions. In addition, the U.S. Environmental Protection Agency (EPA) was assigned to implement the Clean Air Act.

Automotive emission standards (limits) were set, and through the ensuing years, regularly revised downward. The car manufacturers responded with great strides in engine engineering and in the development of emission control systems and devices. Today's stringent (tight) emission standards are being met and motor vehicle emissions are on the decline.

POSITIVE CRANKCASE VENTILATION

First of the emission controls adopted by the automotive industry, and still in use, is the crankcase ventilation system that routes blow-by gases, condensation vapors, and crankcase fumes to the combustion chambers of the engine. See Fig. 37-1.

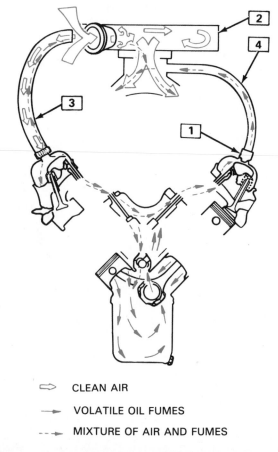

⇨ CLEAN AIR

→ VOLATILE OIL FUMES

--→ MIXTURE OF AIR AND FUMES

Fig. 37-1. Positive Crankcase Ventilation system controls flow of gases and vapors from crankcase into engine combustion chambers, 1—PCV valve. 2—Air cleaner. 3—Crankcase vent hose. 4—PCV valve hose.
(Chevrolet Motor Div., General Motors Corp.)

Called the POSITIVE CRANKCASE VENTILATION (PCV) SYSTEM, the early version is classified as the "open" type because it uses an oil filler cap that is open to the atmosphere. Fresh air enters the oil filler cap and filler pipe. It passes through the crankcase, picks up blow-by gases, enters the cylinder head cover chamber, flows through the PCV valve and hose, and into the intake manifold. The incoming mixture of fresh air and crankcase gases blends with the air-fuel charge, and the mixture is distributed to the cylinder combustion chambers and burned.

The open type of PCV system was satisfactory — to a point. As long as the PCV valve was working and the hoses and intake manifold port were open, blow-by gases were recycled to the combustion chambers. However, a sticking valve or clogged hoses would cause pressure to build in the crankcase. With no other place to go, the blow-by gases would be forced through the "open" oil filler cap, polluting the atmosphere.

Recognizing the problem, the emission control engineers came up with the "closed" type of PCV system, Fig. 37-1. In the closed system, incoming air first passes through the carburetor air cleaner before entering the cylinder head cover. A separate air filter is incorporated in the air cleaner for this system. See Fig. 37-2. The fresh incoming air circulates in the crankcase, picking up blow-by gases and vapor. This mixture is drawn through the PCV valve and hose to the intake manifold.

The PCV valve, Fig. 37-3, meters the flow in the system at a rate that depends on manifold vacuum. The function of the PCV valve is to restrict the flow of crankcase emissions when vacuum is high to preserve satisfactory engine idle. If excessive blow-by occurs, it back flows through the vent hose to the air cleaner to be consumed by normal combustion.

Several different PCV systems are shown and decribed in Figs. 37-4, 37-5, and 37-6. The setups differ but all function to recycle blow-by gases to the combustion chambers.

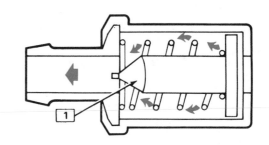

Fig. 37-3. PCV valve (1) meters flow of mixture of crankcase gases and fresh air into intake manifold, based on strength of vacuum. (Chevrolet Motor Div., General Motors Corp.)

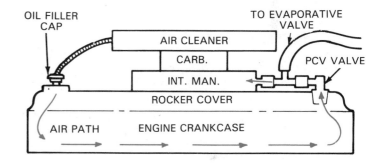
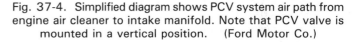

Fig. 37-4. Simplified diagram shows PCV system air path from engine air cleaner to intake manifold. Note that PCV valve is mounted in a vertical position. (Ford Motor Co.)

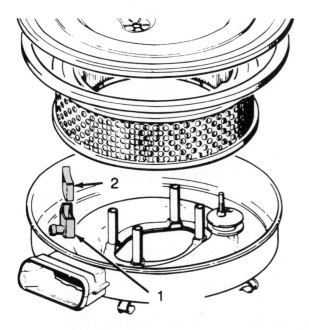

Fig. 37-2. Fresh air is supplied from air cleaner to crankcase through a special PCV air filter: 1—Retainer. 2—Filter. (American Motors Corp.)

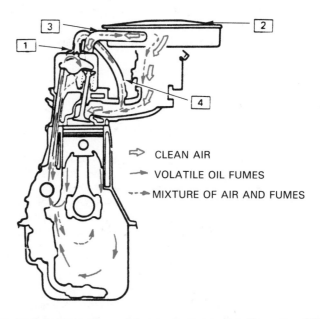

Fig. 37-5. End view of four cylinder engine illustrates PCV system flow as clean air picks up oil fumes from crankcase. 1—PCV valve. 2—Air cleaner. 3—Crankcase vent hose. 4—PCV valve hose. (Cadillac Motor Car Div., General Motors Corp.)

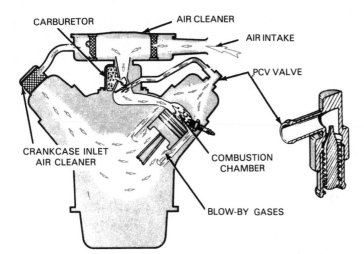

Fig. 37-6. End view of V-8 engine shows cross flow of fresh air and blow-by gases. Note filter at engine oil crankcase inlet. (Chrysler Corp.)

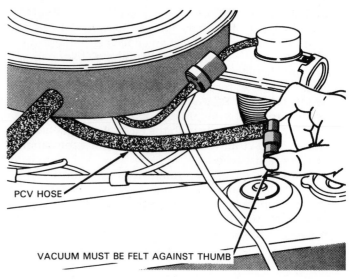

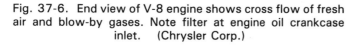

Fig. 37-7. Test PCV system vacuum by idling engine, removing PCV and hose assembly from cylinder head cover, and placing thumb over valve inlet. A strong vacuum should be felt. (Chrysler Corp.)

PCV SYSTEM SERVICE

If the PCV valve is sticking, or hoses are plugged, the engine will have a rough idle, idle too slow, or stall. Also check for oil in the air cleaner and sludge (black, mushy deposits of oil, dirt, and water whipped together by moving parts) in the engine. If the PCV valve or hose leaks, the engine will have a rough idle, idle too fast, or stall.

To diagnose PCV system operation:
1. Lift PCV valve from cylinder head cover with hose intact.
2. Run engine at idle.
3. Place thumb over end of PCV valve to check for vacuum. See Fig. 37-7. If no vacuum, check for plugged hose or intake manifold port. Replace defective hoses and/or clean port.
4. Remove PCV valve from hose and shake valve vigorously back and forth.
5. Listen for rattle of check needle inside valve. If valve does not rattle, replace it.
6. Check and clean or replace PCV filter in air cleaner.

EXHAUST EMISSION CONTROLS

With crankcase emissions eliminated by positive crankcase ventilation, engine engineers concentrated their efforts on the control of exhaust emissions from the vehicle tailpipe and on gasoline vapors being emitted from the fuel tank and carburetor. This vapor loss problem has been solved by Evaporative Emission Controls (EEC — to be covered later), but the struggle to reach near-zero exhaust emissions goes on.

Since 1970, a substantial improvement in exhaust emission levels has been accomplished through changes and modifications in internal engine design. Interim standards for emission levels were met by the use of a wide array of emission control systems and devices. Then, the emission standards became so low-level, meeting them required the installation of catalytic converters in the exhaust system. CATALYTIC CONVERTERS chemically transform noxious emissions into harmless carbon dioxide and water.

SYSTEMS AND DEVICES

There are several different methods of precombustion control of exhaust emissions. Attempts have been made to eliminate the emissions problem at its source by modification of engine design, carburetion, and ignition.

To comply with Federal regulations for the control of exhaust emissions, the car manufacturers and their suppliers developed and installed many different systems and devices. Eventually, they were led to switch to some form of electronic fuel injection, electronic ignition, and engine computer control systems. See Fig. 37-8.

In their original design, these "controls" can be grouped into two broad classes:
1. PRECOMBUSTION CONTROLS designed to reduce or eliminate the *formation* of harmful pollutants in the engine.
2. POST-COMBUSTION CONTROLS designed to destroy or otherwise alter the pollutants *after* they have been formed.

PRECOMBUSTION CONTROLS

The difficulties to overcome in solving the emissions problem can be appreciated by considering the many different conditions that help produce the pollutants:
1. Combustion chamber design.
2. Displacement of cylinders.
3. Coolant temperature.
4. Engine temperature.
5. Inlet air temperature.
6. Air-fuel charge temperature.
7. Air-fuel ratio.
8. Engine speeds.
9. Manifold vacuum.

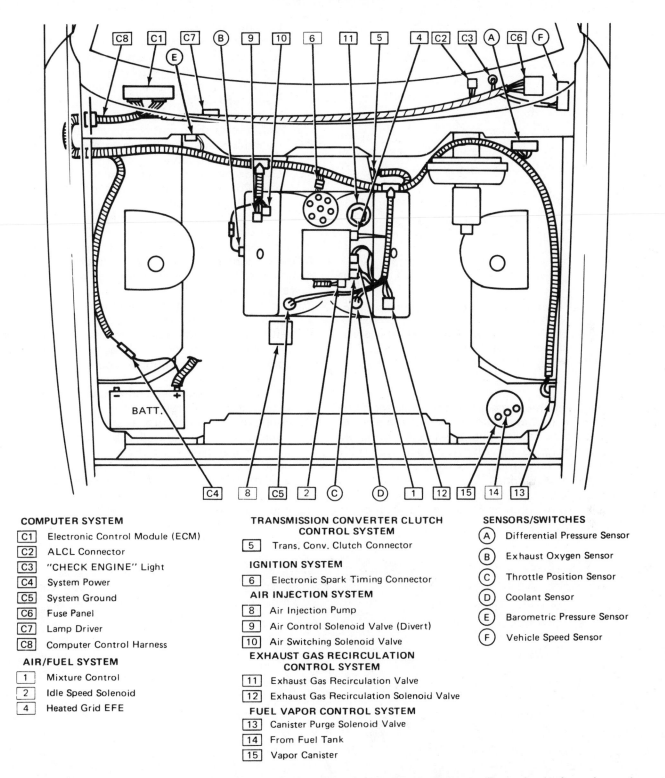

COMPUTER SYSTEM

C1	Electronic Control Module (ECM)
C2	ALCL Connector
C3	"CHECK ENGINE" Light
C4	System Power
C5	System Ground
C6	Fuse Panel
C7	Lamp Driver
C8	Computer Control Harness

AIR/FUEL SYSTEM

1	Mixture Control
2	Idle Speed Solenoid
4	Heated Grid EFE

TRANSMISSION CONVERTER CLUTCH CONTROL SYSTEM

5	Trans. Conv. Clutch Connector

IGNITION SYSTEM

6	Electronic Spark Timing Connector

AIR INJECTION SYSTEM

8	Air Injection Pump
9	Air Control Solenoid Valve (Divert)
10	Air Switching Solenoid Valve

EXHAUST GAS RECIRCULATION CONTROL SYSTEM

11	Exhaust Gas Recirculation Valve
12	Exhaust Gas Recirculation Solenoid Valve

FUEL VAPOR CONTROL SYSTEM

13	Canister Purge Solenoid Valve
14	From Fuel Tank
15	Vapor Canister

SENSORS/SWITCHES

A	Differential Pressure Sensor
B	Exhaust Oxygen Sensor
C	Throttle Position Sensor
D	Coolant Sensor
E	Barometric Pressure Sensor
F	Vehicle Speed Sensor

Fig. 37-8. Underhood component locations are broken down by systems and sensors. Trace circuits from electronic control module to various emissions control systems. (Pontiac Motor Div., General Motors Corp.)

10. Spark retard and advance.
11. Valve timing.
12. Exhaust back pressure.
13. Type of transmission.
14. Lack of maintenance.

ENGINE MODIFICATIONS, a primary means of precombustion control, have brought about many new

advances in internal engine design. Areas affected:

1. Compression ratios lowered for compatibility with no-lead gasoline.
2. Combustion chamber configuration redesigned for better surface-to-volume ratio (area of combustion chamber surface compared to its volume with piston at top dead center).

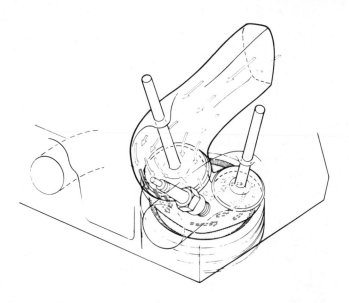

Fig. 37-9. Cylinder head design with cyclonic port induction increases air-fuel mixture velocity. Fast-burn mixture and centrally located spark plug speed combustion process and lower exhaust emission levels.
(Chevrolet Motor Div., General Motors Corp.)

3. Combustion chamber modifications made for more efficient flow rate and burning time of the air-fuel charge, such as ''swirl'' chambers. See Fig. 37-9.
4. Pistons redesigned in crown contour and with smaller upper ring lands, moving top piston ring closer to top of piston.
5. Intake manifolds redesigned for better air-fuel flow and balanced distribution of charge to each com-

bustion chamber.
6. Exhaust gas recirculation incorporated in manifolds to provide a metered amount of exhaust gas for recirculation with air-fuel mixture to slow combustion and reduce combustion chamber temperatures.
7. Camshafts redesigned to modify valve timing and to increase valve overlap periods.
8. Valve ports given soft curves and smooth surfaces.
9. Cylinder heads modified to permit air injection near each exhaust valve.
10. Cylinder head gaskets engineered for correct construction and design for each engine and improved ''fit'' and no-retorque.
11. Spark plug port location changed to suit combustion chamber design. See Fig. 37-9.

Also incorporated in most late model engines are the following conditions, modes of operation, or ''controls'' designed to provide more complete combustion and/or fewer emissions:
1. Higher engine operating temperatures.
2. Ignition distributor recalibrations, modified ignition advance, and better correlation with speed and load.
3. Leaner carburetor recalibrations with higher curb idle speeds, idle stop solenoids, and limiter caps on idle mixture screws.
4. Electric assist automatic chokes with more sensitive action and faster release.
5. Fuel evaporation control systems.
6. Thermostatically controlled air cleaners.
7. Electronic engine control systems which precisely control fuel metering and ignition spark timing based on signals from key sensing elements.
8. Electronic fuel injection systems for more efficient combustion control, Fig. 37-10.

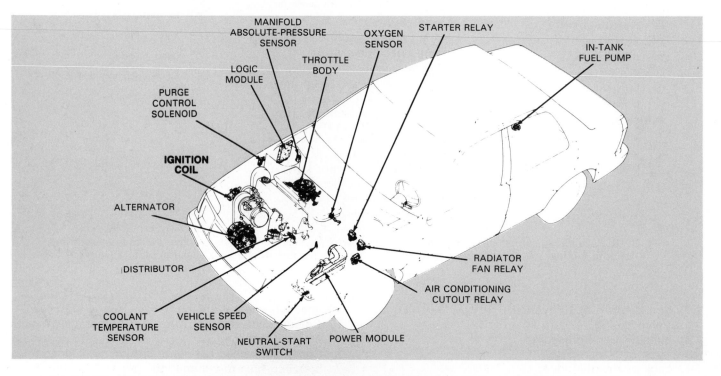

Fig. 37-10. Adoption of low-pressure, single point, electronic fuel injection system on 2.2 liter four cylinder engine improves combustion efficiency and reduces emissions. (Chrysler Corp.)

THERMOSTATICALLY CONTROLLED AIR CLEANERS

All domestic emission control engines are equipped with thermostatically controlled air cleaners. By controlling the temperature of the air entering the carburetor or fuel injection system, air-fuel mixtures can be made leaner and hydrocarbon emissions will be reduced.

The various thermostatically controlled air cleaners in use differ in makeup but provide the same effect — a uniform inlet air temperature. The names differ, too. General Motors calls theirs THERMAC. Ford uses INLET AIR TEMPERATURE SYSTEM. Chrysler has HEATED INLET AIR SYSTEMS. American Motors thermostatic air cleaner is TAC.

A common GM Thermac system includes:
1. A heat stove or shroud built around exhaust manifold.
2. Ducting from heat stove to air cleaner snorkel.
3. Ducting from outside air vent to air cleaner snorkel.
4. Damper door in snorkel and vacuum diaphragm motor to control movement of damper door, Fig. 37-11.
5. Temperature sensor in air cleaner.
6. Vacuum hoses from intake manifold to sensor and from sensor to vacuum motor.
7. Air bleed valve.

THERMAC OPERATION

When temperature is below 86 °F (30 °C), sensor allows vacuum to vacuum motor. Motor raises damper door, A in Fig. 37-12, cutting off outside airflow and passing only heated air from heat stove into air cleaner.

When temperature is between 86 °F (30 °C) and 131 °F (55 °C), damper door is partially open to both outside air and heated air, B in Fig. 37-12.

When temperature is above 131 °F (55 °C), damper door drops down, cutting off heated airflow and passing only outside air into air cleaner. See C in Fig. 37-12.

THERMAC SERVICE

To check operation of GM's Thermac system:
1. Inspect for kinked, plugged, or deteriorated hoses.
2. Check connections of all hoses and ducting.
3. Check condition of air cleaner to TBI (throttle body injection) seal.
4. Check air cleaner cover seal.
5. Check for loose cover or loose air cleaner.
6. With air cleaner in place, damper door should be open to outside air.
7. Start engine. Damper door should move and close off outside air.
8. As air cleaner warms up, damper door should gradually open to outside air.
9. If system fails to operate in this manner, test vacuum motor operation.
   a. Shut off engine. Disconnect hose at vacuum diaphragm motor.
   b. Use vacuum pump to apply at least 7 in. Hg. (23.8 kPa) of vacuum to motor.
   c. Damper door should close to outside air.
   d. If not, check linkage hookup and inside of snorkel for corrosion.

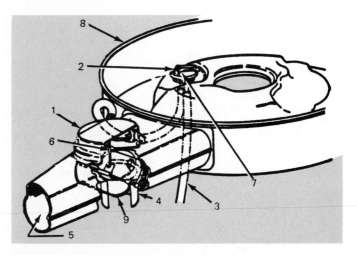

Fig. 37-11. Key elements of Thermac thermostatically controlled air cleaner are: 1—Vacuum diaphragm motor. 2—Temperature sensor. 3—Vacuum hose to intake manifold vacuum. 4—Heat stove duct. 5—Snorkel. 6—Linkage. 7—Air bleed valve. 8—Air cleaner assembly. 9—Damper door. (Cadillac Motor Car Div., General Motors Corp.)

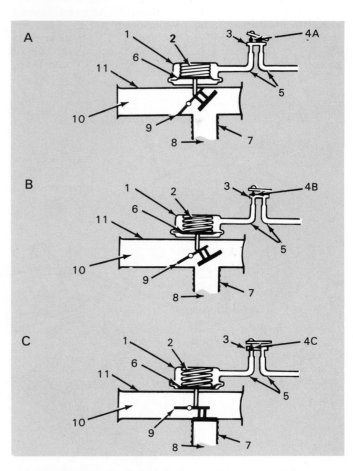

Fig. 37-12. Thermac components related to A, B, C operational description in text: 1—Vacuum diaphragm motor. 2—Diaphragm spring. 3—Temperature sensor. 4A—Air bleed valve-closed. 4B—Air bleed valve-partially open. 4C—Air bleed valve-open. 5—Vacuum hoses. 6—Diaphragm. 7—Heat stove. 8—Hot air from exhaust manifold. 9—Damper door. 10—Outside inlet air. 11—Snorkel. (Chevrolet Motor Div., General Motors Corp.)

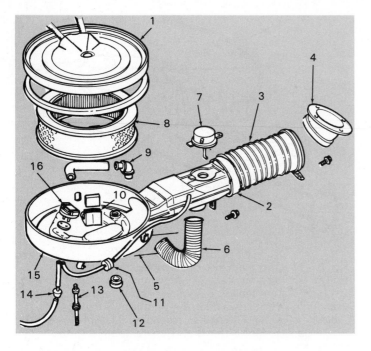

Fig. 37-13. Typical AMC Thermostatic Air Cleaner: 1—Cover. 2—Air duct adapter. 3—Flexible duct. 4—Adapter. 5—Heat stove. 6—Heated air tube. 7—Vacuum motor. 8—Filter element. 9—Elbow. 10—PCV filter retainer. 11—Reverse delay valve. 12—Grommet. 13—Stud. 14—Check valve. 15—Air cleaner body. 16—Thermal switch. (American Motors Corp.)

e. With vacuum applied, bend hose to trap vacuum in motor. Damper door should remain closed.

f. If not, replace vacuum diaphragm motor assembly.

10. If driveability problem is during warmup, make temperature sensor check:

    a. Allow air cleaner temperature to fall below 86 °F (30 °C). Place thermometer close to sensor.

    b. Reinstall air cleaner cover.

    c. Start engine. Damper door should close to outside air, then gradually open as engine warms up.

    d. Remove air cleaner cover and check thermometer reading. It should be about 131 °F (55 °C).

    e. If not, replace temperature sensor.

Two other thermostatically controlled air cleaner systems are shown and described in Figs. 37-13 and 37-14. The setup of system valves, sensors, and vacuum controls differ, but all function to maintain uniform inlet air temperature.

EARLY FUEL EVAPORATION SYSTEM

Some carbureted engines are equipped with an early fuel evaporation (EFE) system as an aid to engine warmup and cold driveaway. The system consists of an EFE heater underneath the primary base of the carburetor, Fig. 37-15, and a temperature switch located at the rear of the intake manifold. When engine temperature is

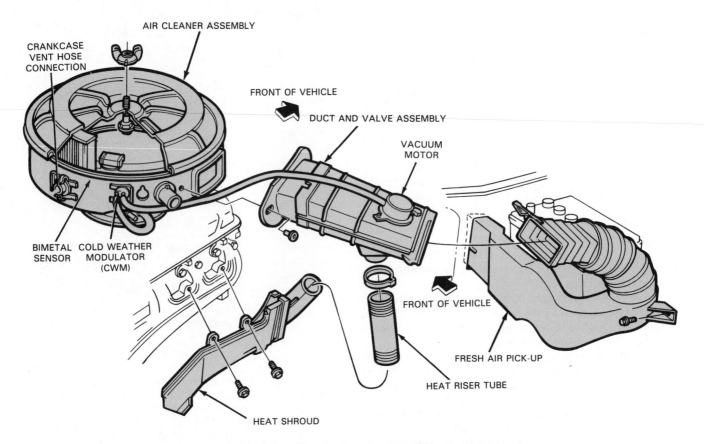

Fig. 37-14. Exploded view of typical Ford Inlet Air Temperature System shows major assemblies in detail: air cleaner; duct, valve, and motor; heat shroud and riser tube; fresh air pickup. (Ford Motor Co.)

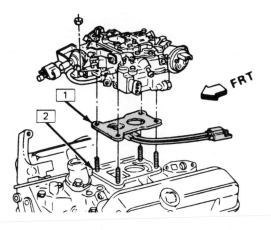

Fig. 37-15. Early Fuel Evaporation system involves use of an electrically heated grid between intake manifold and carburetor to help vaporize fuel when engine is cold. 1—EFE heater. 2—Intake manifold.
(Pontiac Motor Div., General Motors Corp.)

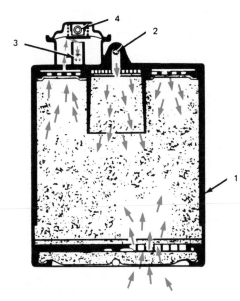

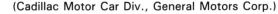

Fig. 37-16. On GM engines with electronic control module, ECM actuates solenoid valve to purge or prevent purging of fuel vapor from Evaporative Emission Control canister. 1—Charcoal canister. 2—To fuel tank. 3—Purge valve to ported vacuum. 4—Control valve to manifold vacuum.
(Cadillac Motor Car Div., General Motors Corp.)

below a calibrated number of degrees, electrical current is supplied to the heater and quick fuel evaporation is provided.

Since the EFE system reduces the length of time carburetor choking is required, it helps to reduce exhaust emissions.

MANIFOLD HEAT CONTROL VALVE

Some carbureted six cylinder and V-8 engines are equipped with a manifold heat control valve. This unit is sandwiched between the exhaust manifold outlet and exhaust pipe. Its thermostatically controlled damper valve circulates heated exhaust gases in a heat chamber of the intake manifold under the carburetor.

The hot gases help vaporize the air-fuel mixture during engine warmup. After warmup, the damper valve redirects the exhaust gases into the exhaust pipe.

EVAPORATIVE EMISSION CONTROL SYSTEMS

EVAPORATIVE EMISSION CONTROLS (EEC) prevent the escape of gasoline vapors from the fuel tank and carburetor, whether or not the engine is running. All late model engines use an activated charcoal canister to trap the vapors when the engine is shut off. On restarting, a flow of filtered air through the canister purges the vapors from the charcoal. The mixture goes through one or more tubes feeding into the intake manifold, carburetor, and/or carburetor air cleaner, and it is burned in the engine. On electronic control module-equipped GM engines, an ECM-controlled solenoid valve permits manifold vacuum to purge evaporative emissions from the charcoal canister. See Fig. 37-16.

Certain late model Chrysler engines also use a secondary damping canister on the intake manifold side of the primary canister as a purge control device. See Fig. 37-17. The damping canister cushions the effect of the sudden charge of fuel vapors when the control valve

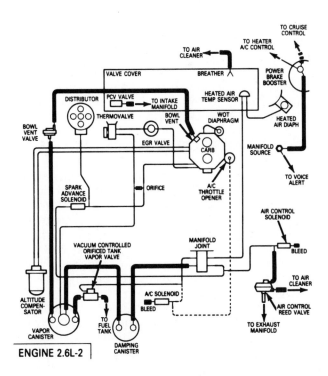

Fig. 37-17. On typical Chrysler vacuum hose routing diagram, heavy lines represent hoses and hose connections. Note vapor canister and connecting damping canister at lower left.
(Chrysler Corp.)

releases them from the primary canister. The vapors are momentarily held, then gradually phased into the intake manifold.

IGNITION TIMING AND FUEL MIXTURE CONTROLS

Over the years, car manufacturers have concentrated their emission control efforts in two areas: ignition timing (and timing advance) and air-fuel mixture control to suit operating conditions. Since ignition timing and air-fuel ratio in all modes of engine operation have a strong influence on combustion efficiency, a wide variety of control devices have been introduced and regularly improved upon.

Most of the timing and fuel mixture control systems and devices proved to be interim answers to the emission control problem. As the emission control standards became more stringent, the car manufacturers' engineers solved the problem by developing electronic ignition systems, electronic fuel injection systems, engine computer control modules, and tie-ins with various sensors, switches, actuators, and vacuum controls. See Figs. 37-8 and 37-10. The computer monitors the input signals, evaluates them, and provides output signals to control ignition timing and air-fuel ratio to match changing operating conditions.

The entire monitoring process takes split seconds, and it is constant. For further details on these various engine computer controls, see Chapter 26, Fuel Injection Systems, and Chapter 29, Engine Ignition Systems.

POST-COMBUSTION CONTROLS

Emission controls designed to reduce carbon monoxide, hydrocarbons, and oxides of nitrogen *after* the combustion process can be termed POST-COMBUSTION CONTROLS. These controls include:
1. Exhaust gas recirculation.
2. Air injection.
3. Catalytic converters.

EXHAUST GAS RECIRCULATION SYSTEMS

The exhaust gas recirculation (EGR) system is specially designed to lower NO$_x$ (oxides of nitrogen) emission levels caused by high combustion temperatures. The system uses an EGR valve operated by intake manifold or ported vacuum to feed exhaust gas back into the combustion chambers. See Fig. 37-18. This recirculation of exhaust gas into the air-fuel mixture tends to slow down the combustion process and absorb heat, thereby reducing NO$_x$.

Only a small amount of exhaust gas is allowed to pass through the EGR valve and only when the engine is warm and operating above idle speed. Otherwise, the entry of the exhaust gas would halt combustion. Various supplemental controls, valves, or switches are used to limit EGR valve actuation to proper operating conditions.

Exhaust gas recirculation valves vary in construction and operation. The PORTED EGR VALVE, Fig. 37-19, uses ported vacuum taken from above the carburetor throttle valve to overcome the pressure of a large, single spring. Movement of the diaphragm opens the valve in the exhaust gas port and allows exhaust gas to be drawn into the intake manifold and engine cylinders.

General Motors engines also use a POSITIVE BACK-PRESSURE EGR VALVE, Fig. 37-20, or a NEGATIVE

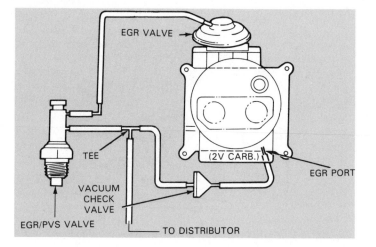

Fig. 37-18. Drawing of typical Exhaust Gas Recirculating valve installation illustrates how EGR system is vacuum actuated. EGR/PVS (ported vacuum switch) unit controls vacuum, based on coolant temperature. (Ford Motor Co.)

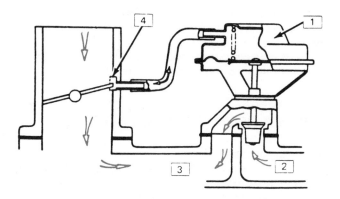

Fig. 37-19. Ported EGR valves operate on ported vacuum taken from above carburetor throttle valve: 1—EGR valve. 2—Exhaust gas. 3—Intake manifold. 4—Calibrated carburetor port or throttle body injection port. (Chevrolet Motor Div., General Motors Corp.)

BACKPRESSURE EGR VALVE to meter the flow of exhaust gas. An air bleed inside the EGR valve acts as a vacuum regulator by bleeding vacuum to the atmosphere when the valve is open. When the EGR valve receives a prescribed amount of exhaust backpressure (through a hollow shaft), it closes the bleed. Then, maximum available vacuum is applied to the diaphragm and the EGR valve opens.

In this way, the air bleed controls the amount of vacuum in the vacuum chamber. If the vacuum chamber has little or no vacuum — such as idle or wide open throttle, or if there is little or no backpressure in the exhaust manifold — the EGR valve will not open.

The negative backpressure EGR valve is similar to the positive backpressure valve in construction. The difference is in the location of the bleed valve spring. It is above the diaphragm on the positive backpressure valve, Fig. 37-20, and below the diaphragm on the negative backpressure valve.

Chrysler uses two types of EGR valves, a ported vacuum unit and a DUAL EGR CONTROL VALVE, Fig. 37-21. The "dual" EGR valve has primary and secondary valves controlled by different carburetor vacuums. The primary valve controls EGR flow over a narrow range of lower speeds. The secondary valve takes effect at higher speeds. EGR flow is suspended at idle and wide open throttle operation. A SUB EGR CONTROL VALVE is directly opened and closed in response to throttle valve opening to further modulate EGR flow controlled by the EGR valve.

Vacuum applied to the dual EGR valve is controlled by a thermo valve, which prevents EGR flow until engine temperature reaches a prescribed level.

American Motors uses a double-diaphragm, ported vacuum EGR valve mounted on the side of the intake manifold. A coolant temperature override (CTO) switch in the EGR system cuts off recirculation of exhaust gases until a prescribed coolant temperature level is reached.

Ford uses four basic types of EGR valves:
1. Ported valve.
2. Integral backpressure valve.
3. Valve and transducer assembly.
4. Electronic valve.

The ELECTRONIC EGR VALVE assembly, Fig. 37-22, is used in EEC (Electronic Engine Control) systems where EGR flow is controlled according to computer demands. The computer controls an EGR Valve Position (EVP) sensor attached to the valve. The EGR valve is operated by a vacuum signal from dual EGR SOLENOID VALVES.

The VALVE AND TRANSDUCER ASSEMBLY consists of a ported EGR valve and a remote transducer, Fig. 37-23. This EGR valve operates the same as Ford's integral backpressure valve, controlling EGR flow by means of ported vacuum and exhaust backpressure.

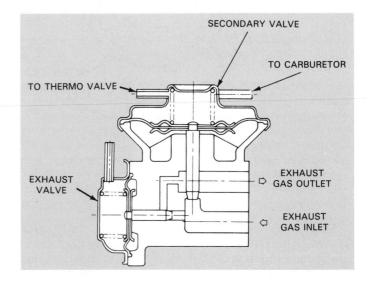

Fig. 37-21. Dual EGR control valve has primary and secondary valves actuated by two different vacuum sources to improve driveability and reduce NO$_x$.   (Chrysler Corp.)

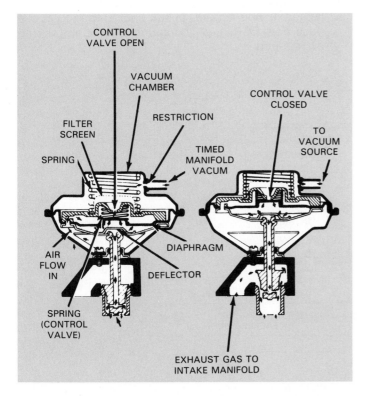

Fig. 37-20. Positive backpressure EGR valve uses exhaust backpressure fed through hollow shaft to actuate spring-loaded control valve. When backpressure increases, valve bleed closes, and vacuum applied to diaphragm opens EGR valve. (Cadillac Motor Car Div., General Motors Corp.)

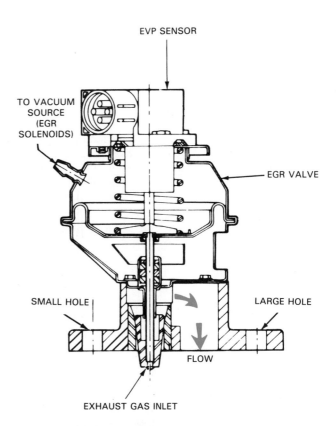

Fig. 37-22. Electronic EGR valve assembly is operated by computer-controlled solenoid valves. Exhaust gas flow is through opening in base of this base entry type EGR valve.   (Ford Motor Co.)

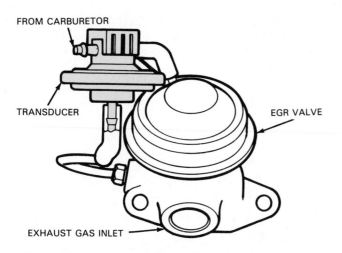

Fig. 37-23. Valve and Transducer EGR assembly requires vertical positioning of transducer. Nipple of transducer must point straight down after installation. (Ford Motor Co.)

Ford also uses a BACKPRESSURE VARIABLE TRANSDUCER (BVT) system, Fig. 37-24. It consists of a vacuum regulator, EGR valve, and a flow control orifice. The regulator, Fig. 37-24, modulates EGR vacuum by using two backpressure inputs.

ELECTRONIC VACUUM REGULATOR VALVE

Buick introduced an ELECTRONIC VACUUM REGULATOR VALVE (EVRV) designed to modulate the strength of the vacuum that reaches the EGR valve. These valve actions, in turn, regulate the amount of exhaust gas to be recirculated to the intake manifold.

In operation, the Electronic Control Module (ECM) computes the required amount of exhaust gas flow, based on signals concerning rpm, load, torque converter clutch engagement, and engine temperature. These signals are evaluated by the ECM and sent to a CONSTANT CURRENT ELECTRONIC CIRCUIT (part of EVRV system). The CCEC interprets the ECM data and converts it to signals that are transmitted to the vacuum regulator.

The regulator body has vacuum inlet and outlet ports and a vented port at one end and an electromagnetic diaphragm at the other end. A steel disc is spring-loaded against a brass seat that surrounds the vented port. Vacuum at the inlet port tends to pull the disc away from the seat. Vacuum is then precisely modulated to the EGR valve as the stator (plunger) attracts the disc toward the vented port at a rate of 128 cycles per second.

EGR SYSTEM SERVICE

To check an EGR SYSTEM for faulty operation:
1. Check routing of all vacuum hoses and lines (see vacuum hose diagram on emissions and tune-up decal in engine compartment).
2. Check vacuum hoses for condition and secure connections.
3. Disconnect hose at vacuum port of EGR valve. There should be *no* vacuum when engine is cold or at warm curb idle.
4. There *should be* vacuum to EGR valve at higher rpm (generally 2000-3000) at normal operating temperature. See manufacturer's specifications.
5. If there is no vacuum, check back through vacuum hose from EGR valve to vacuum source and correct as required.

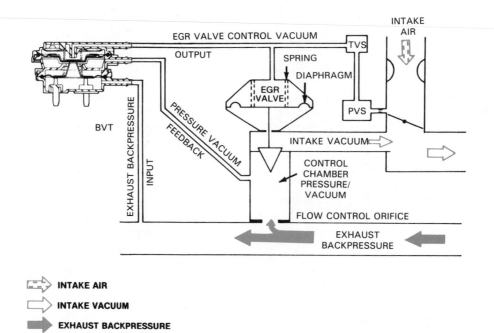

Fig. 37-24. Backpressure Variable Transducer schematic shows relationship of ported EGR valve to vacuum regulator at top left. Vacuum tests are made at top, center, and bottom ports of regulator. (Ford Motor Co.)

To check operation of PORTED VACUUM EGR VALVE, Fig. 37-19:

1. Start engine and warm up to normal operating temperature.
2. Allow engine to idle in neutral for one minute, then abruptly accelerate engine to about 2000-3000 rpm (check manufacturer's specifications). EGR valve stem should move (use a mirror, if necessary).
3. If not, remove EGR valve and clean inlet and outlet ports with a wire brush. Do not wash assembly in solvents. Also clean mounting surfaces of EGR valve and manifold.

To check operation of EXHAUST BACKPRESSURE EGR VALVE, Fig. 37-20:

1. Temporarily plug tailpipe of vehicle with a socket wrench slightly smaller in diameter than inside of tailpipe.
2. Start and warm engine to normal operating temperature.
3. With engine idling, disconnect vacuum hose from EGR valve port and plug hose.
4. Use a hand-operated vacuum pump to apply vacuum to EGR valve port.
5. EGR valve stem *should* move, and engine idle *should* become rough.

To check operation of DUAL EGR VALVE, Fig. 37-21:

1. Cold start engine and run at idle speed.
2. Abruptly accelerate engine to 2500 rpm. Secondary valve (at top of EGR valve) should *not* operate. If it does, replace thermo control valve.
3. Warm engine to normal operating temperature.
4. Abruptly accelerate engine to 2500 rpm. Secondary valve *should* operate.
5. Disconnect hose from secondary valve port to carburetor — at carburetor.
6. Connect a hand-operated vacuum pump to disconnected hose.
7. Pull open sub EGR valve and apply above 6 in. Hg. (20.4 kPa) of vacuum to secondary valve hose. Idle speed *should* become rough.
8. If not, replace EGR valve or thermo control valve.
9. Disconnect vacuum pump and reconnect hose to carburetor.
10. Disconnect hose from primary valve port to carburetor — at carburetor.
11. Repeat steps 6, 7, and 8.

To check operation of SOLENOID VACUUM CONTROL EGR SYSTEMS, Fig. 37-25:

1. With ignition ON and engine stopped, solenoid *should not* be energized and vacuum *should not* pass to EGR valve.
2. Ground diagnostic terminal. Solenoid *should* be energized and allow vacuum to pass.

To check operation of BACKPRESSURE VARIABLE TRANSDUCER EGR SYSTEM, Fig. 37-24:

1. Disconnect one hose at a time from vacuum regulator ports and use a hand-operated vacuum pump to apply at least 5 in. Hg. (17.0 kPa) of vacuum to each of three ports in turn.
2. Top port in Fig. 37-24 *should not* hold vacuum.
3. Center and bottom ports *should* hold vacuum.
4. If test at top, center, or bottom port fails, replace BVT assembly.

AIR INJECTION SYSTEMS

AIR INJECTION SYSTEMS are a form of post-combustion emission control devised to reduce HC and CO emissions by injecting fresh air into the hot gases in the exhaust manifold. Basically, either one of two air injection systems is used:

1. AIR PUMP INJECTION that supplies air to exhaust manifold by means of a belt-driven air pump and air distribution system. See Fig. 37-26.

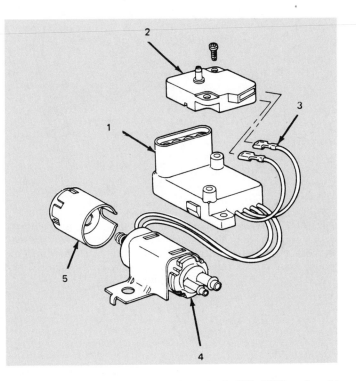

Fig. 37-25. Exploded view of typical GM EGR solenoid vacuum control assembly: 1—Base. 2—EGR vacuum diagnostic switch. 3—Diagnostic switch connectors. 4—EGR solenoid. 5—Filter. (Cadillac Motor Car Div., General Motors Corp.)

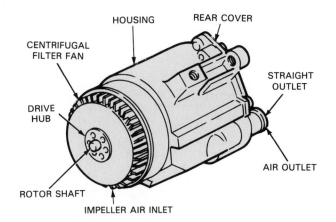

Fig. 37-26. Typical Thermactor air supply pump uses an impeller type air filter fan to separate contaminants from intake air by centrifugal force. (Ford Motor Co.)

2. PULSE AIR that uses natural pulses present in exhaust system to pull air into exhaust manifold through pulse air valves. See Ford system in Fig. 37-27. Chrysler's pulse air setup is termed AIR ASPIRATOR SYSTEM.

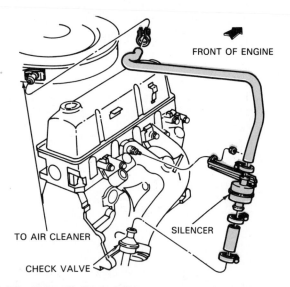

TO AIR CLEANER

FRONT OF ENGINE

SILENCER

CHECK VALVE

Fig. 37-27. Pulse Air System does not use an air supply pump. It is a setup of hoses and pulse air valves that uses "pulses" in exhaust system to draw fresh air from air cleaner into exhaust manifold for injection into hot gases to reduce HC and CO. (Ford Motor Co.)

Earlier single-purpose air injection systems performed the job of reducing the amount of HC and CO in the exhaust gases by injecting air directly into the exhaust port of each cylinder. The air, added to the hot gases, causes further oxidation (burning) of the gases before they enter the exhaust pipe.

The equipment usually incorporated in this air injection system consists of: a belt-driven pump; air hoses, metal tubing air manifold, and injection tubes or internal drilled passages to the rear of each exhaust valve; diverter valve, check valve, pressure relief valve, and silencer.

The DIVERTER VALVE prevents backfire by sensing an increase in manifold vacuum on deceleration. It opens to divert air under pressure to pass through the valve and SILENCER to the atmosphere. The CHECK VALVE prevents hot exhaust gases from backing up into the hose and pump. The PRESSURE RELIEF VALVE controls pressure in the system by releasing excessive pump output to the atmosphere at higher engine speeds.

Most later air injection systems work in conjunction with engine computer control units and THREE-WAY CATALYST catalytic converters.

Ford's MANAGED AIR THERMACTOR SYSTEM is used to divert air under pressure to either the exhaust manifolds or to the dual catalyst in the catalytic converter. See Fig. 37-28. The system also has an AIR BYPASS VALVE to divert air to the atmosphere during certain operating modes.

Ford also uses a COMBINED BYPASS/CONTROL VALVE in electronically controlled air injection systems.

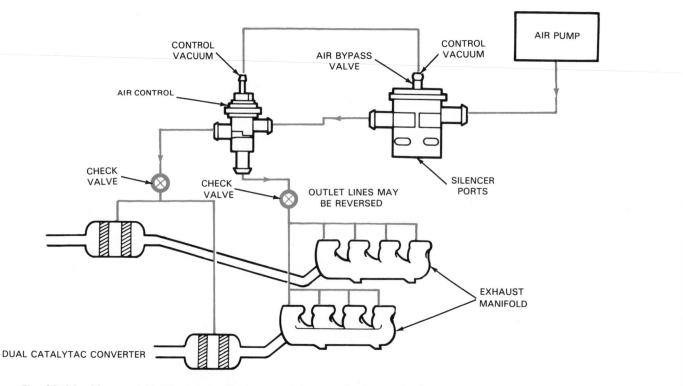

CONTROL VACUUM

AIR BYPASS VALVE

CONTROL VACUUM

AIR PUMP

AIR CONTROL

CHECK VALVE

CHECK VALVE

OUTLET LINES MAY BE REVERSED

SILENCER PORTS

EXHAUST MANIFOLD

DUAL CATALYTAC CONVERTER

Fig. 37-28. Managed Air Thermactor System uses air control valve to direct thermactor air either upstream to exhaust manifold or downstream to dual catalytic converter. During certain operating modes, air bypass valve dumps air to atmosphere. (Ford Motor Co.)

As indicated by its name, this combination air bypass and air control valve is installed in line with the air pump. Air under pressure and vacuum (controlled electronically by two solenoids) operate the combination valve. Air under pressure, then, is diverted either to the intake manifolds or to dual catalytic converters.

The General Motors AIR INJECTION REACTION (A.I.R.) SYSTEM is shown in Fig. 37-29. The A.I.R. system uses a vacuum-operated, ECM-controlled ELECTRIC DIVERT/ELECTRIC AIR SWITCHING VALVE that combines "divert" and "switching" functions in a single housing. See Fig. 37-30. The divert valve diverts air to the air cleaner for converter protection or passes air to the switching valve. The switching valve directs air to exhaust ports during cold engine operation or to a pipe between the two calalyst beds in the converter to heat up the catalysts quickly on engine start-up.

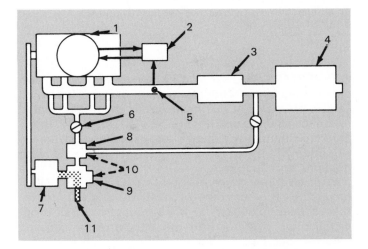

Fig. 37-29. Typical GM Air Injection Reaction System: 1—Closed loop fuel control. 2—ECM. 3—Reducing catalyst. 4—Oxidizing catalyst. 5—O₂ sensor. 6—Check valve. 7—Air pump. 8—Air switching valve. 9—Air divert valve. 10—Electrical signals from ECM. 11—Bypass air to air cleaner. (Pontiac Motor Div., General Motors Corp.)

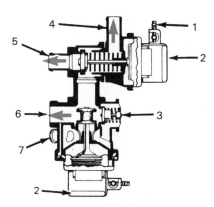

Fig. 37-30. Electric Divert/Electric Air Switching Valve diverts air to air cleaner or switches air to either exhaust ports or dual catalytic converter. 1—Vacuum signal. 2—Solenoid. 3—Relief valve. 4—Converter air. 5—Port air. 6—Air from pump. 7—Divert air. (Pontiac Motor Div., General Motors Corp.)

Some GM engines also use a DECELERATION VALVE to help prevent backfiring during high vacuum conditions. Attached to the air cleaner, this valve opens under high vacuum, allowing air from the air cleaner to flow into the intake manifold and "lean" the air-fuel mixture.

AIR INJECTION SYSTEM SERVICE

The air injection system requires little maintenance. The air pump, Fig. 37-26, is permanently lubricated. It cannot be disassembled and serviced. If the pump fails to provide sufficient air for satisfactory system operation, it should be replaced.

If airflow from the pump does not enter the exhaust stream at the exhaust ports or at the catalytic converter, HC and CO emissions levels will read high on the emissions tester.

If airflow from the pump is constant to the exhaust ports, the ECM unit will command a richer mixture, causing increased temperature of the converter and possible damage.

Noise complaints may be checked out by operating the engine with the air pump drive belt removed. If the noise disappears, inspect for a seized air pump. Also check all hoses and tubes for improper routing. Inspect all connections for leaks. Check the air pump for improper mounting and incorrect bolt torque.

To test the air pump output:
1. Start engine and accelerate to about 1500 rpm.
2. Disconnect pump air outlet hose and observe airflow as engine is accelerated.
3. If airflow increases with rising rpm, pump is operating satisfactorily.
4. If not, listen to pump for air leaking, shut off engine, and check drive belt tension.
5. If pressure relief valve is not leaking, shut off engine, and check drive belt tension.

To check air injection system components:
1. Check all hoses for deterioration or wear at points of interference in routing.
2. See that all hose clamps are tight.
3. Check all pipes for holes, loose fittings, and improper routing.
4. If a leak is suspected on pressure side of system, run engine and use a soap water solution to check for bubbles at connections.
5. To test a check valve: blow through valve toward cylinder head, then suck back through valve. Flow should only be in one direction (toward head). If not, replace check valve.
6. To test other valves in air injection system (switching, divert, deceleration, pressure relief, air bypass valves), see manufacturers' service manuals for procedures.

CATALYTIC CONVERTERS

Major air pollutants contained in exhaust gas are hydrocarbons (HC), carbon monoxide (CO), and oxides of nitrogen (NO$_x$). To help reduce the volume of these pollutants during the post-combustion stage, the car manufacturers use CATALYTIC CONVERTERS.

Basically, a catalytic converter is a container of chemically treated pellets or honeycomb element that

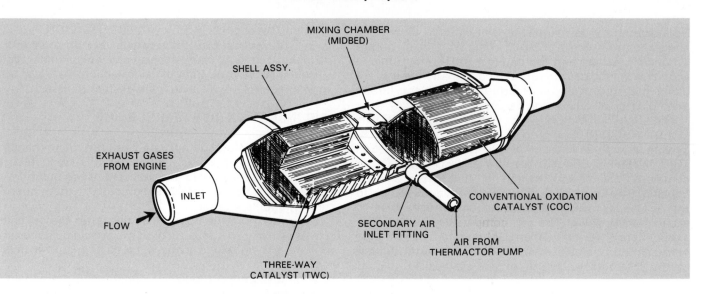

Fig. 37-31. Widely accepted dual catalytic converter uses upstream three-way catalyst to reduce HC, CO, and NO$_x$. Downstream catalyst and air provided by air injection system further reduce HC and CO emissions. (Ford Motor Co.)

is incorporated in the exhaust system. Earlier converters utilized pellets coated with platinum or with platinum and palladium to reduce HC and CO. Operating at about 1500°F (815°C), these catalysts provided a heated chemical reaction to transform noxious emissions into harmless carbon dioxide (CO$_2$) and water vapor (H$_2$O).

The heated chemical reaction of the platinum and palladium worked well in reducing HC and CO, but had the opposite effect on NO$_x$ emissions. High heat serves to increase NO$_x$ emissions.

Then, as NO$_x$ limits were drastically reduced, the manufacturers' engineers turned to DUAL CATALYTIC CONVERTERS, Fig. 37-31. Dual converters contain two catalyst elements. The "upstream" element is termed THREE-WAY CATALYST because it is chemically treated to reduce all three pollutants—HC, CO, and NO$_x$. In addition to platinum or platinum and palladium to decrease HC and CO, the three-way catalyst is treated with rhodium to reduce NO$_x$.

With all three major pollutants (HC, CO, and NO$_x$) reduced by the upstream catalyst, HC and CO are further reduced (oxidized) by the introduction of air (from air injection system) into the downstream oxidizing catalyst. See Fig. 37-32.

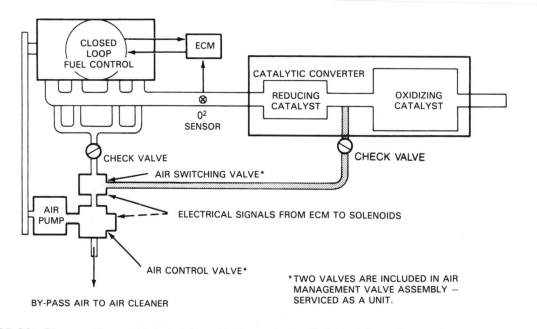

Fig. 37-32. Diagram illustrates how air switching valve switches airflow from exhaust manifold to downstream oxidizing catalyst of catalytic converter. "Switches" are signalled by ECM. (Cadillac Motor Car Div., General Motors Corp.)

CATALYTIC CONVERTER MAINTENANCE

Catalytic converters require little attention as long as unleaded gasoline is used (to avoid "lead poisoning" of catalysts). Also important to converter life is the positioning of the converter in relation to underbody heat shields and surrounding underbody parts. See Fig. 37-33. If clearances are too small, overheating of the converter could result. In addition, excessive floor pan temperature could damage passenger compartment carpets.

Anytime a car is hoisted for service, it pays to check the general condition of the catalytic converter, along with other exhaust system components. If exhaust system work is performed on GM cars, a special sealer should be used at all slip joint connections *except* at the catalytic converter. The sealer cannot withstand converter temperatures.

Occasionally, because of age, high mileage, or contamination of catalysts in the catalytic converter, engine performance may be sluggish due to backpressure in the exhaust system. If the catalyst elements are damaged or become heavily coated with contaminants, the resulting restriction of exhaust gas flow could cause loss of power and, finally, engine stalling and failure to restart.

A primary cause of catalyst damage or contamination is an overly rich air-fuel mixture. As mentioned, failure of the air injection system to supply air under pressure to the catalytic converter could cause the ECM unit to command a richer air-fuel mixture. Also, a "missing" engine will allow unburned gases to travel to the catalytic converter and damage the catalysts. Likewise, do not "fast idle" engine for more than five minutes. CAUTION: If there is a diagnostic need to "short" out a spark plug, do not allow the engine to run more than one minute while "missing."

If the existing catalytic converter is damaged or contaminated, replace it with an original equipment converter—or the equivalent. While external appearance may be similar, there may be internal differences in some replacement converters. Also be sure to observe clearance specifications between converter and heat shields, Fig. 37-33. Connect air line securely to air injection port on a dual catalytic converter.

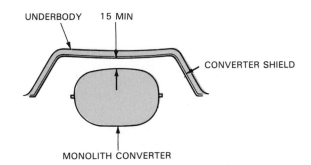

Fig. 37-33. Exhaust system clearances are more critical since catalytic converters were added to system. Typical converter-to-underbody heat shield clearance is 5/8 in. (15 mm). (Cadillac Motor Car Div., General Motors Corp.)

Chapter 37—REVIEW QUESTIONS
EMISSION CONTROLS

Write your answers on a separate sheet of paper. Do not write in this book.

1. Name three noxious automotive emissions.
2. The _____ type of positive crankcase ventilation system has eliminated the emission of crankcase fumes, blow-by gases, and vapors.
   a. Open.
   b. Closed.
   c. Pressure.
   d. Bypass.
3. What is the purpose of the PCV valve?
4. To test a PCV valve: remove hose and valve assembly from cylinder head cover and shake valve vigorously. If it rattles, the valve is defective. True or False?
5. _____ emission controls solve the problem of fuel vapors being emitted from the fuel tank and carburetor.
6. Catalytic converters _____ transform noxious emissions into harmless carbon dioxide and water.
   a. Chemically.
   b. Statically.
   c. Electromagnetically.
   d. Electronically.
7. What are precombustion emission controls?
8. _____ controls are designed to destroy or otherwise alter the pollutants after they have been formed.
9. What is the objective of a thermostatically controlled air cleaner?
10. What is the "effect" of a thermostatically controlled air cleaner?
11. Some carbureted engines are equipped with an _____ system as an aid to engine warmup and cold driveaway.
12. Evaporative emission controls prevent the escape of fuel vapors whether or not the engine is running. True or False?
13. Over the years, car manufacturers have concentrated their emission control efforts in two areas: _____ and air-fuel mixture control.
   a. Internal engine modifications.
   b. Ignition timing.
   c. Exhaust gas recirculation.
   d. Catalytic converters.
14. For what purpose does the exhaust gas recirculating system feed exhaust gas back into the combustion chambers of the engine?
15. The ported EGR valve uses ported vacuum taken from _____ (above, below) the carburetor throttle valve.
16. An engine has a rough idle and is sluggish when cold. The EGR system appears to be at fault. Mechanic A says the EGR valve is stuck in the open position. Mechanic B says the vacuum hose from the EGR valve to the vacuum source may be clogged or deteriorated. Who is right?
   a. Mechanic A.
   b. Mechanic B.
   c. Both mechanic A and mechanic B.

d. Neither mechanic A nor mechanic B.
17. Name two types of air injection systems.
18. Air injection systems are designed to reduce HC and CO emissions by injecting air into the _____ in the _____.
19. Dual catalytic converters contain two catalyst elements, one ''upstream'' and the other ''downstream.'' Why is the ''upstream'' element called a three-way catalyst?
20. The ''downstream'' catalyst element in a dual catalytic converter and air provided by the air injection system further reduce _____.
a. NO_x.
b. HC.
c. CO.
d. HC and CO.

Chapter 38

CLUTCHES

After studying this chapter, you will be able to:
- Explain the purpose of an automotive clutch.
- Describe the operation of major components of a clutch assembly and its actuating parts.
- Give examples of various cable-operated clutch control mechanisms.
- List typical clutch service procedures and precautions.
- Recognize symptoms of pending clutch failure.

A CLUTCH is a friction device used to connect and disconnect a driving force from a driven member. In automotive applications, the clutch is designed to provide smooth and positive engagement and disengagement of the engine and manual transmission or manual transaxle. See Figs. 38-1 and 38-2.

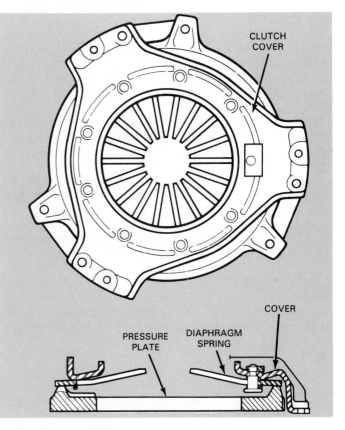

Fig. 38-2. Typical diaphragm type clutch pressure plate used in conjunction with clutch driven plate shown in Fig. 38-1. (American Motors Corp.)

PURPOSE OF THE CLUTCH

The clutch is needed because an internal combustion engine develops little power or torque at low rpm. It must gain speed before it will move the vehicle. At higher speeds, however, a violent engagement would occur if the rapidly rotating engine were suddenly connected to the driveline of a stationary vehicle.

Therefore a gradual application of load and some slowing of engine speed are needed to provide reasonable and comfortable starts. In vehicles equipped with a manual

Fig. 38-1. Typical clutch driven plate (dry disc) used in cars equipped with a manual transmission or transaxle. (American Motors Corp.)

transmission or manual transaxle, this is accomplished by means of a mechanical clutch.

Engagement of the engine and transmission provides the necessary linkup of engine and drivetrain that permits power transfer to the driving axles and wheels. Disengagement provides the necessary halt to power transfer that allows the engine to operate while the transmission does not.

DESIGN AND CONSTRUCTION

Most cars equipped with a manual transmission or manual transaxle use a single plate, dry clutch disc, a diaphragm type pressure plate and cover assembly, a clutch release bearing (throwout bearing), and a clutch release fork. See Figs. 38-3 through 38-5.

PARTS LOCATION AND RELATIONSHIP

In its operating position in the engine/transmission or transaxle linkup, the clutch disc is sandwiched between the engine flywheel and the clutch pressure plate. The pressure plate is bolted to the engine flywheel, and a strong clamping force is developed between the heavy plate and cover.

Engagement and disengagement of the clutch assembly is controlled by a foot pedal and linkage (rods or cable) that must be properly adjusted and relatively easy to apply.

The machined surfaces of the flywheel and pressure plate (against which the clutch facings bear) must be flat, true, and free from cracks or score marks.

The transmission, pressure plate, flywheel housing, clutch disc, flywheel, and crankshaft must be properly aligned to prevent slippage, vibration, and noise.

CLUTCH DISC

The CLUTCH DISC or DRIVEN PLATE consists of a circular metal plate attached to a reinforced splined hub.

Often the hub is mounted on coil springs to provide cushioned engagements. See Fig. 38-1.

The splined hub is free to slide lengthwise along the splines of the transmmission input shaft. See Fig. 38-6. When engaged, the clutch disc drives the input shaft through these splines.

The outer half of the clutch disc has a friction material facing on each side. Generally, the facings are riveted or bonded to the clutch disc. The thickness of the disc assembly must be uniform and its friction facings must be smooth.

WARNING: Be aware that dust created when servicing clutch assemblies may contain asbestos fibers. Breathing this dust may cause serious bodily harm. Asbestos is a known carcinogen—a substance which tends to cause cancer. When working on clutches, wear a mask with a government approved filter and flush clutch parts with water or use a vacuum source.

PRESSURE PLATE

The clutch disc operates in conjunction with a PRESSURE PLATE or CLUTCH COVER, Fig. 38-2. The pressure plate assembly usually consists of a heavy plate, a diaphragm spring with release fingers, and a cover. See Fig. 38-5. The pressure plate diaphragm is shaped like a dished plate. It utilizes over-center action in applying and releasing pressure on the pressure plate and clutch disc.

The cover serves to contain the pressure plate assembly. Most covers are vented to allow heat to escape and cooling air to enter. Some are designed to provide a fan action for forced circulation of air to help cool them. Even proper use of the clutch generates some heat because of normal slippage while it is being engaged.

CLUTCH RELEASE BEARING AND FORK

The CLUTCH RELEASE BEARING or THROWOUT BEARING, in most cases, is a ball bearing assembly with

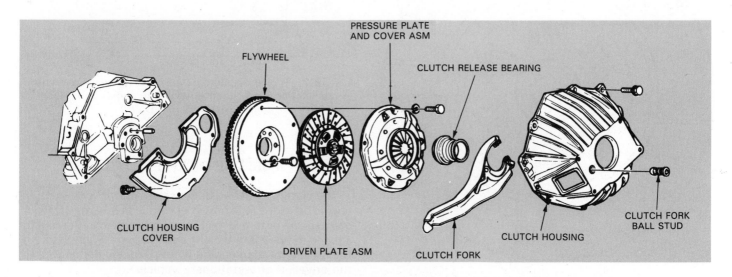

Fig. 38-3. Exploded view of mechanical clutch system used with manual transmission. Operational components include flywheel, driven plate, pressure plate, release bearing, and fork.
(Chevrolet Motor Div., General Motors Corp.)

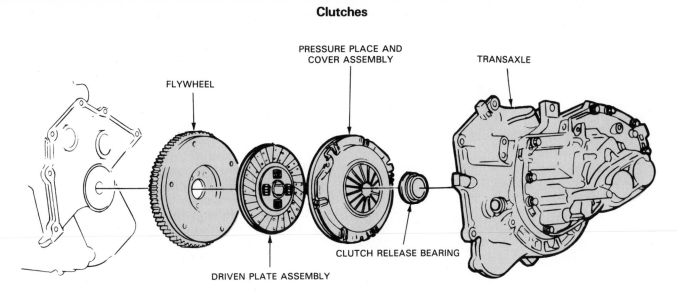

Fig. 38-4. Exploded view of mechanical clutch system used with manual transaxle. (Oldsmobile Div., General Motors Corp.)

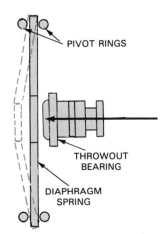

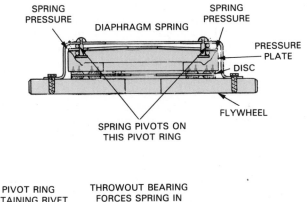

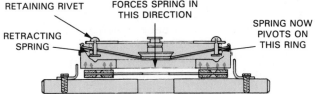

Fig. 38-5. Three diagrammatic views illustrate how pivot rings give diaphragm spring an over-center action when clutch release bearing forces spring toward engine flywheel.

a machined face on one side that is designed to contact the pressure plate diaphragm release fingers during disengagement. See Figs. 38-7 and 38-8. The release bearing is mounted on a sleeve that is designed to slide back and forth on the transmission input shaft bearing retainer whenever the clutch pedal is depressed or released.

The sleeve is grooved or has raised flat surfaces and retaining springs that hold the inner ends of the CLUTCH FORK in place. The fork and connecting linkage provide the means of converting the up-and-down movement of the clutch pedal to the back-and-forth movement of the clutch release bearing assembly. See Fig. 38-5.

Transaxle clutch assemblies generally use a different arrangement of connecting the linkage to the clutch fork and the fork to the clutch release bearing. In transaxle applications, Fig. 38-9, the release bearing is constantly engaged with the release fingers of the pressure plate diaphragm. A clutch fork and a release lever are utilized in conjunction with the clutch cable to depress the pressure plate diaphragm and release the clutch disc. See Fig. 38-9.

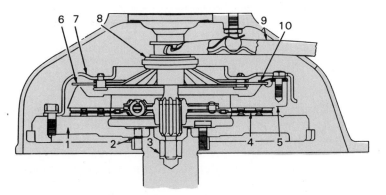

Fig. 38-6. Cross section of clutch assembly: 1—Flywheel. 2—Dowel hole. 3—Pilot bushing. 4—Driven plate. 5—Pressure plate. 6—Diaphragm spring. 7—Clutch cover. 8—Clutch release bearing. 9—Clutch fork. 10—Retracting spring. (Chevrolet Motor Div., General Motors Corps.)

Fig. 38-7. Various clutch release bearings are pictured, along with ball bearing cage and ball bearing assembly.

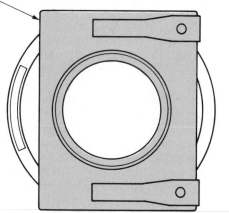

SLEEVE AND SUPPORT

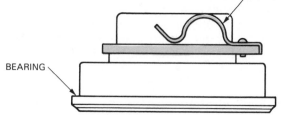

RETAINING SPRINGS

BEARING

Fig. 38-8. Side view of a typical clutch release bearing fitted to a sleeve and support assembly. (American Motors Corp.)

Also note that this setup does not require a pilot bearing. In most cars, a clutch PILOT BEARING or PILOT BUSHING is placed in the back end of the crankshaft or in the center of the flywheel. This bearing or bushing is used to support the outer end of the manual transmission input shaft.

CLUTCH LINKAGE

The CLUTCH LINKAGE connects the brake pedal to the outer end of the clutch fork. Earlier model cars and

some current models use a series of rods, shafts, levers, and springs to make up the linkage arrangement, Figs. 38-10 and 38-11. Many domestic and import models use cable operation. See Figs. 38-12 through 38-15.

ROD-AND-SHAFT CLUTCH CONTROL

A typical pedal rod and cross shaft (torque shaft) clutch control linkage setup is shown in Fig. 38-10. It also incorporates a fork push rod, clutch and brake pedal bracket, and an over-center spring.

Basically, depressing the clutch pedal causes the pedal rod to move a lever attached to the cross shaft. The cross shaft starts to rotate, causing another lever on the shaft to move the fork push rod and, in turn, the clutch fork and release bearing.

When the clutch pedal reaches the end of its travel, the clutch fork will have moved the clutch release bearing enough to completely release the clutch disc. At this point, the driver is able to shift gears in the transmission without difficulty.

When the clutch pedal is released, the "tensioned" over-center spring returns the linkage to original position. With that, the clutch fork moves the release bearing away from the pressure plate and the clutch disc is again clamped into engagement.

Fig. 38-11 presents another rod-and-shaft clutch control system.

CABLE CLUTCH CONTROL— MANUAL TRANSMISSION

Cable control of clutch operation is common in many manual transmission applications. A simple setup is shown in Fig. 38-12. A circlip (1) holds the pedal in place on the shaft. The cable fork end (4) is attached to the top end of the pedal shank by a pin (3) that extends through the fork end and a hole in the pedal shank. A return spring (2) is attached to the pin by passing the spring hook through a hole in the pin. The cable is held firmly in place by a cable stop at the firewall.

The other end of the clutch control cable is connected to the outer end of the clutch release fork, Fig. 38-13. This end is threaded and fitted with an adjusting nut and a locknut to provide a means of adjusting clutch pedal free play.

When the clutch pedal is depressed, the cable is drawn inward, forcing the end of the release fork to actuate the clutch release bearing to disengage the clutch disc.

CABLE CLUTCH CONTROL— MANUAL TRANSAXLE

Various systems have been devised to provide self-adjustment of the clutch cable mechanism on manual transaxle applications. Since the clutch release bearing is a constant running bearing, the self-adjustment feature primarily affects the cable release mechanism.

CHRYSLER'S SELF-ADJUSTING CLUTCH RELEASE

Chrysler's manual transaxle clutch cable release mechanism is self-adjusting; it cannot be adjusted

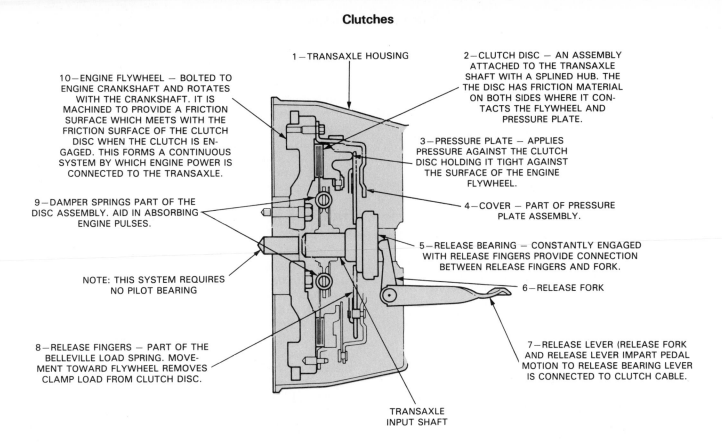

10—ENGINE FLYWHEEL — BOLTED TO ENGINE CRANKSHAFT AND ROTATES WITH THE CRANKSHAFT. IT IS MACHINED TO PROVIDE A FRICTION SURFACE WHICH MEETS WITH THE FRICTION SURFACE OF THE CLUTCH DISC WHEN THE CLUTCH IS ENGAGED. THIS FORMS A CONTINUOUS SYSTEM BY WHICH ENGINE POWER IS CONNECTED TO THE TRANSAXLE.

9—DAMPER SPRINGS PART OF THE DISC ASSEMBLY. AID IN ABSORBING ENGINE PULSES.

NOTE: THIS SYSTEM REQUIRES NO PILOT BEARING

8—RELEASE FINGERS — PART OF THE BELLEVILLE LOAD SPRING. MOVEMENT TOWARD FLYWHEEL REMOVES CLAMP LOAD FROM CLUTCH DISC.

1—TRANSAXLE HOUSING

2—CLUTCH DISC — AN ASSEMBLY ATTACHED TO THE TRANSAXLE SHAFT WITH A SPLINED HUB. THE THE DISC HAS FRICTION MATERIAL ON BOTH SIDES WHERE IT CONTACTS THE FLYWHEEL AND PRESSURE PLATE.

3—PRESSURE PLATE — APPLIES PRESSURE AGAINST THE CLUTCH DISC HOLDING IT TIGHT AGAINST THE SURFACE OF THE ENGINE FLYWHEEL.

4—COVER — PART OF PRESSURE PLATE ASSEMBLY.

5—RELEASE BEARING — CONSTANTLY ENGAGED WITH RELEASE FINGERS PROVIDE CONNECTION BETWEEN RELEASE FINGERS AND FORK.

6—RELEASE FORK

7—RELEASE LEVER (RELEASE FORK AND RELEASE LEVER IMPART PEDAL MOTION TO RELEASE BEARING LEVER IS CONNECTED TO CLUTCH CABLE.

TRANSAXLE INPUT SHAFT

Fig. 38-9. Top view shows clutch components in a manual transaxle application. Ten notes provide complete operational information.   (Ford Motor Co.)

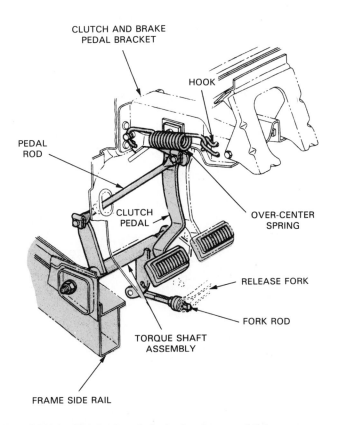

CLUTCH AND BRAKE PEDAL BRACKET

HOOK

PEDAL ROD

CLUTCH PEDAL

OVER-CENTER SPRING

RELEASE FORK

FORK ROD

TORQUE SHAFT ASSEMBLY

FRAME SIDE RAIL

Fig. 38-10. This rod-and-shaft clutch control linkage arrangement features clutch pedal, pedal rod, and over-center spring. Pedal free play adjustment is at end of fork rod. (Dodge Div., Chrysler Corp.)

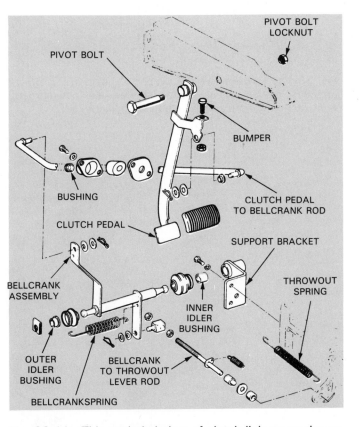

PIVOT BOLT LOCKNUT

PIVOT BOLT

BUMPER

BUSHING

CLUTCH PEDAL TO BELLCRANK ROD

CLUTCH PEDAL

SUPPORT BRACKET

THROWOUT SPRING

BELLCRANK ASSEMBLY

INNER IDLER BUSHING

OUTER IDLER BUSHING

BELLCRANK TO THROWOUT LEVER ROD

BELLCRANKSPRING

Fig. 38-11. This exploded view of clutch linkage works on same principle as linkage shown in Fig. 38-10. Both have a cross shaft with opposed bellcrank levers. (American Motors Corp.)

435

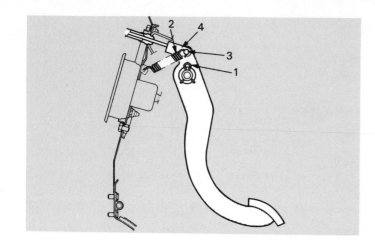

Fig. 38-12. This cable-operated clutch control system simply connects clutch pedal with outer end of clutch fork: 1—Circlip. 2—Return spring. 3—Pin. 4—Cable fork end.

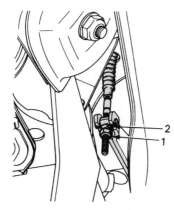

Fig. 38-13. Lower end of clutch cable shown in Fig. 38-12 provides means of clutch pedal free play adjustment: 1—Locknut. 2—Adjusting screw.

manually. A heavy-duty spring between the clutch pedal assembly and the positioner adjuster, Fig. 38-14, holds the clutch cable in the proper position, regardless of clutch disc wear.

Key elements in the self-adjusting mechanism are the clutch pedal spring, the position adjuster, and the adjuster pivot, Fig. 38-14. When the clutch pedal is depressed, the adjuster pivot meshes with and moves the positioner adjuster to hold the clutch release cable in place to effect complete clutch release.

GENERAL MOTORS' CLUTCH SELF-ADJUSTING MECHANISM

General Motors' cars equipped with a manual transaxle utilize a cable-operated system with a self-adjusting mechanism mounted on the clutch pedal and bracket assembly. See Fig. 38-15.

When the clutch pedal is in the released position, a pawl is lifted free of the quadrant. Meanwhile, a spring in the hub of the quadrant causes the quadrant to rotate. This movement automatically adjusts cable length to balance the force being applied at the clutch release bearing. This system, too, employs a constant running clutch release bearing in the normal driving position.

When the clutch pedal is applied, the pawl moves downward to mesh its teeth in the quadrant, Fig. 38-16. The quadrant pulls on the end of the cable, and the clutch fork forces the release bearing against the release fingers of the pressure plate. This disengages the clutch disc, and the transaxle is disengaged from the engine.

When the clutch pedal is released, the pedal and quadrant return to the "rest" mode. The pawl is again lifted free of the quadrant and the spring in the hub of the quandrant applies just enough tension on the cable to keep a constant light pressure against the clutch release bearing. The clutch disc is fully engaged and the engine is transferring power to the transaxle.

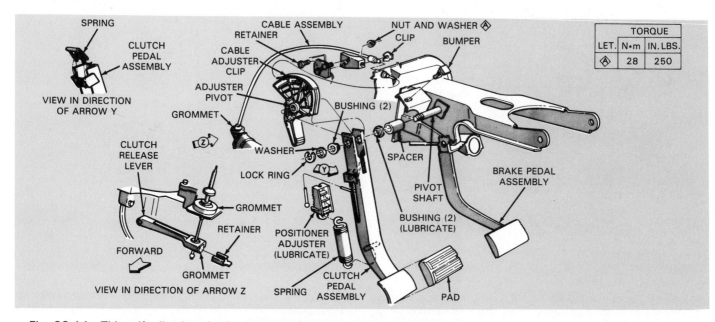

TORQUE		
LET.	N•m	IN. LBS.
⬙	28	250

Fig. 38-14. This self-adjusting clutch release mechanism is used on late model Chrysler-Plymouth cars equipped with either four speed or five speed transaxle.

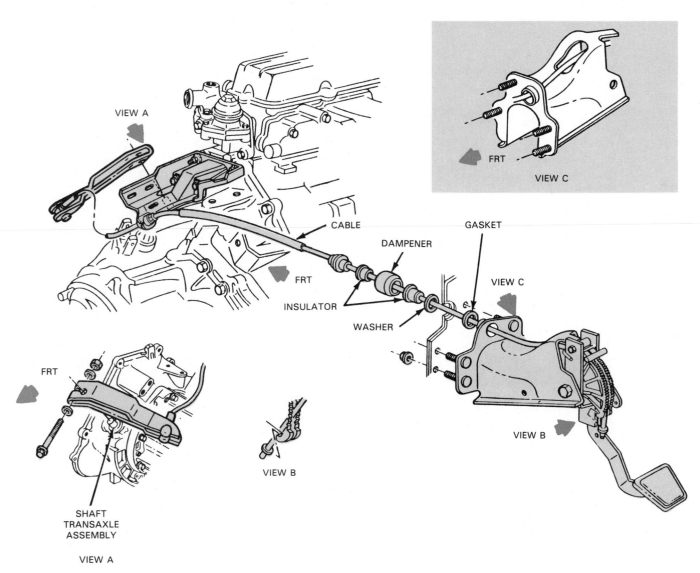

VIEW A

VIEW C

FRT

CABLE

GASKET

DAMPENER

FRT

VIEW C

INSULATOR

WASHER

VIEW B

FRT

VIEW B

SHAFT
TRANSAXLE
ASSEMBLY

VIEW A

Fig. 38-15. General Motors' cars equipped with manual transaxle also use a cable-operated, self-adjusting clutch mechanism. (Oldsmobile Div., General Motors Corp.)

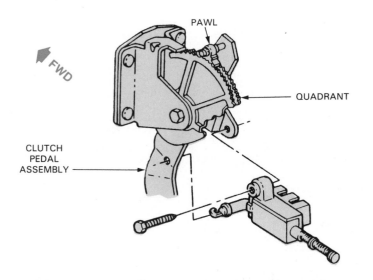

PAWL

FWD

QUADRANT

CLUTCH
PEDAL
ASSEMBLY

Fig. 38-16. Key to operation of GM self-adjusting clutch mechanism is a quadrant, spring, and pawl arrangement. (Oldsmobile Div., General Motors Corp.)

FORD'S SELF-ADJUSTING CLUTCH PEDAL

Ford's self-adjusting clutch control mechanism is very similar to the General Motors' setup. It, too, is cable-actuated and fitted with a pawl-and-quadrant self-adjustment mechanism.

Study Fig. 38-17 to familiarize yourself with the relationship of the parts of the mechanism. After proper installation of the cable, initial adjustment of the cable is made by pulling the clutch pedal all the way up. In this position, the pawl is disengaged from the quadrant. The quadrant position, then, is governed by the position of the clutch pressure plate release fingers.

As the clutch disc facings wear, the pressure plate release fingers gradually move away from the flywheel. This movement is transferred to the quadrant, which automatically adjusts itself to keep the clutch release bearing in constant contact with the pressure plate release fingers. This is the clutch control system employed with the clutch assembly shown in Fig. 38-9.

Ford also incorporates a starter/clutch interlock switch

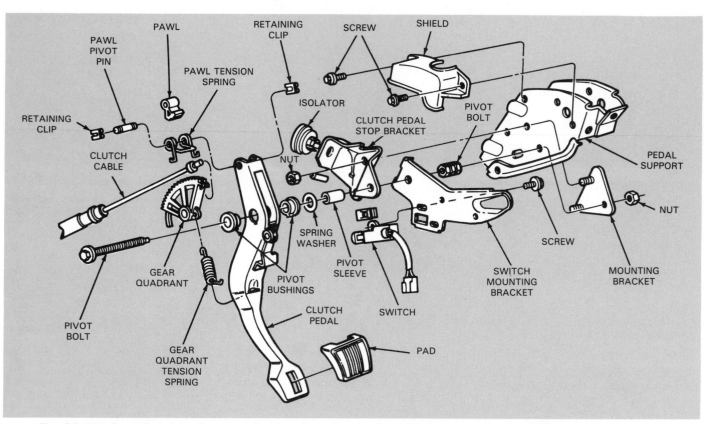

Fig. 38-17. Exploded view shows relative locations of parts that make up a typical self-adjusting, cable-operated clutch control linkage arrangement for Ford manual transaxle applications.

in the clutch control system. This switch is designed to prevent starting the engine with the clutch engaged. The switch, Fig. 38-18, is connected between the ignition switch and starter motor relay coil. It maintains an open circuit with the clutch pedal up (clutch engaged). The first time the clutch pedal is pressed to the floor, it automatically adjusts itself to close the starter circuit.

The starter/clutch interlock switch is located on a bracket alongside the clutch pedal stop bracket and pedal shank. Note the instructions in Fig. 38-18 for installing the switch. If the self-adjusting clip is out of position, the switch will not operate properly. Once the clip is properly installed on the switch bar, the switch can be reset by pressing the clutch pedal to the floor.

AMERICAN MOTORS' HYDRAULIC CLUTCH

Some American Motors cars equipped with a manual transmission use a hydraulic clutch operating mechanism. See Fig. 38-19. The system uses a remote reservoir, a clutch cylinder, and a slave cylinder. The clutch cylinder is mounted on the dash panel, and it is operated directly off the clutch pedal. The slave cylinder is mounted on the clutch housing.

When the clutch pedal is depressed, hydraulic fluid under pressure created in the slave cylinder causes its push rod to extend. Since the outer end of the push rod is connected to the outer end of the clutch release fork, the fork pivots and forces the clutch release bearing to disengage the clutch.

The hydraulic clutch mechanism is self-adjusting.

When the clutch pedal is released, hydraulic pressure falls off and the slave cylinder push rod retracts. A spring keeps the outer end of the clutch release fork in contact with the push rod, so the fork and release bearing are returned to their released positions.

Fig. 38-20 shows the clutch hydraulic system used on various Chevrolet cars. Note that this system also uses a reservoir, master cylinder, and slave cylinder.

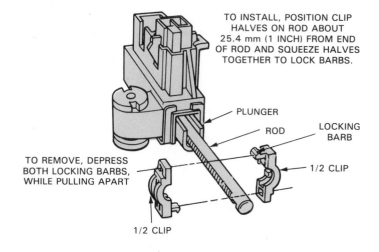

Fig. 38-18. Self-adjusting clutch control mechanism shown in Fig. 38-17 also includes a starter/clutch interlock switch. See directions for switch removal and installation. (Ford Motor Co.)

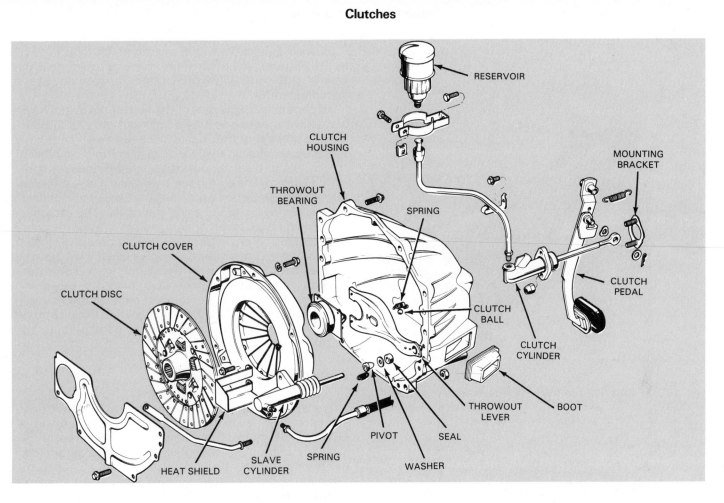

Fig. 38-19. Hydraulic clutch mechanism used on American Motors cars is self-adjusting. Depressing clutch pedal pressurizes system; releasing pedal relieves pressure.

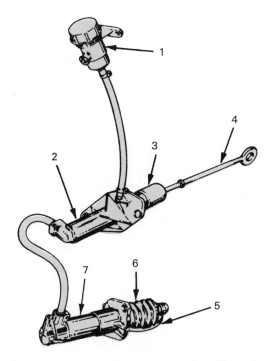

Fig. 38-20. Clutch hydraulic system used on Chevrolet cars: 1—Fluid reservoir. 2—Clutch master cylinder. 3—Boot. 4—Push rod. 5—Shipping strap. 6—Boot. 7—Clutch slave cylinder.

If the reservoir requires fluid, remove boots and check for leakage past the pistons. If excessive leakage is evident, replace the entire system. The Chevrolet clutch hydraulic system must be serviced as a complete unit.

CLUTCH SERVICE

One of the most common causes of clutch trouble is misalignment. The transmission input shaft (which supports the clutch disc) should be in perfect alignment with the engine crankshaft and at right angles to the flywheel face. A worn transmission input shaft bearing or excessive wear in the pilot bearing or bushing will permit the input shaft to run untrue.

Another frequent cause of misalignment is a sprung input shaft or clutch disc. This problem usually is caused by carelessness in removing or replacing the transmission. If the transmission is unsupported while being removed or installed, the weight of the unit is liable to spring the shaft of disc. For this reason, a transmission lift or jack should always be used to aid in moving the transmission in or out of place. See Fig. 38-21.

To check clutch housing alignment, use a dial indicator attached to a special tool installed in the pilot bearing or bushing. See Figs. 38-22 and 38-23. Then check the flywheel for proper alignment by mounting the dial indicator on the clutch housing.

439

Fig. 38-21. This 1/2 ton hydraulic transmission jack safely cradles transmission during removal and reinstallation. (Lincoln Div. of McNeil Corp.)

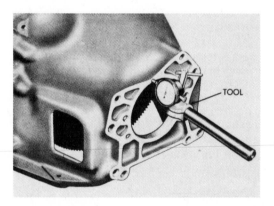

Fig. 38-22. To check clutch housing face alignment, dial indicator is mounted on special tool installed in pilot bushing; then flywheel is turned one revolution.

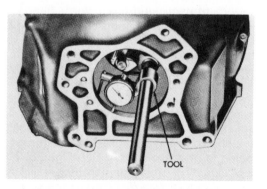

Fig. 38-23. To check housing bore for runout, use dial indicator with tool installed in pilot bushing; then rotate flywheel one revolution.

In most applications, the misalignment limit is .010 in. (0.25 mm), although some manufacturers hold the limit to .005 in. (0.1270 mm). Check the manufacturer's specification.

To correct misalignment of the face of the clutch housing, shims must be installed between the clutch housing and the rear of the engine block. Some engines have offset dowel pins on the rear face, permitting adjustment to compensate for runout of the clutch housing bore.

Distortion of the clutch cover will also cause misalignment. Such distortion or warpage is caused by carelessness in removing or installing the cover. The attaching bolts must be loosened or tightened evenly, or the cover may be sprung or distorted by spring pressure.

Also bear in mind that the engine usually is balanced by the manufacturer with the clutch installed. Before removing the clutch cover, punch mark the cover and flywheel, Fig. 38-24, so you can reinstall the cover in the same relative position. Otherwise, the rotating balance of the engine assembly may be disturbed, and vibration will occur.

CLUTCH ADJUSTMENT

The principal cause of a damaged clutch release bearing in manual transmission applications is neglect of clutch adjustment to compensate for disc wear.

As the friction material gradually wears from the disc in normal use, the pressure plate moves closer to the flywheel and the clutch release fingers of the pressure plate move outward. This forces the clutch release bearing backward and the clutch pedal with it. If the pedal is forced against the pedal stop, the bearing will contact the release fingers and turn at all times. This continuous pressure on the clutch release bearing will tend to partially disengage the clutch disc, causing the friction facings to slip and wear rapidly.

So it pays to check clutch pedal free play regularly, and adjust the clearance when necessary. Clearance, or pedal free play, should be about 1 in. That is, when you depress the clutch pedal, it should travel approximately 1 in. before you feel the contact of the release bearing

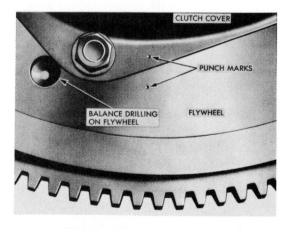

Fig. 38-24. Before removing pressure plate and clutch disc, prick punch flywheel face and clutch cover to maintain balance if original pressure plate is reinstalled.

against the fingers of the clutch diaphragm.

The adjustment of clutch pedal free play usually can be made at the clutch fork push rod, Fig. 38-10 through 38-12, or at the outer end of the clutch pedal rod.

CLUTCH OVERHAUL

Corrective clutch service usually consists of repair, adjustment, or replacement of the faulty part or assembly. To inspect and correct major troubles in clutch operation, proceed as follows:

1. Remove drive shaft(s) and transmission or transaxle. See Fig. 38-25.
2. Remove flywheel cover or clutch bell housing, if so equipped.
3. Locate X marks on flywheel and clutch cover, or put aligned prick-punch marks on these units to insure proper reinstallation if existing clutch assembly is to be reused. See Fig. 38-24.
4. Unhook clutch return spring, back off clutch adjustment, if necessary, and remove clutch release bearing assembly.
5. Loosen clutch cover-to-flywheel attaching bolts in alternate order, one turn at a time, until spring pressure has been released.
6. Remove bolts and clutch assembly.
7. Remove pilot bushing wick, if so equipped. Soak a new wick in engine oil.
8. Clean flywheel face and check it for runout.

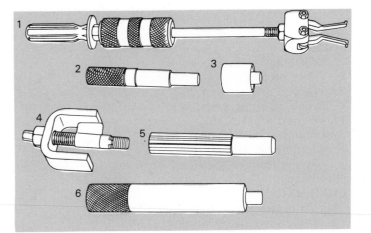

Fig. 38-26. Clutch special tools: 1—Bearing puller. 2—Clutch disc aligner. 3—Pilot bearing installer. 4—Pilot bearing remover. 5—Clutch disc aligner. 6—Pilot bearing installer. (Oldsmobile Div., General Motors Corp.)

9. Inspect pilot bearing or bushing for wear or score marks. Replace bearing or bushing, if necessary, using special tools. See Fig. 38-26.
10. Pack pilot bearing with lubricant, or coat bushing with engine oil. Install new pilot bushing wick.
11. Check clutch housing bore and face alignment. Correct as required.
12. Check fit of new clutch disc on transmission or transaxle input shaft spline.
13. Install clutch disc and clutch cover, using an aligning tool, Fig. 38-26, or an old transmission input shaft. Generally, install the clutch disc with the damper springs offset toward the transmission or transaxle. In some applications, stamped letters on the disc identify the "flywheel" side."
14. Tighten clutch cover-to-flywheel bolts evenly, one turn at a time to correct torque tightness, then remove aligning tool or input shaft.
15. Install new clutch release bearing on bearing sleeve, using care to insure proper seating and to avoid damage to bearing. Or, use a new sleeve and release bearing assembly. Check sliding fit of bearing assembly on transmission input shaft bearing retainer. Wipe a film of lubricant on retainer.
16. Wipe a light coating of lubricant on face of release bearing and pack lubricant in inner recess of the sleeve. Use care to avoid getting lubricant on clutch disc. Also wipe a film of lubricant on arms of clutch release fork, and lubricate clutch fork ball and socket.
17. Install clutch bell housing, if so equipped.
18. Install transmission or transaxle and drive shaft(s), torquing bolts to specified value. See Fig. 38-25.
19. Adjust clutch release fork push rod, or other point of clutch pedal free play adjustment, Figs. 38-10 through 38-12.
20. Install flywheel cover, if so equipped.
21. When servicing hydraulic clutches, check fluid level in the reservoir. Refill to level indicated with SAE-approved brake fluid.
22. Test clutch operation.

Fig. 38-25. Service technician positions transmission on 1/4 ton high-lift transmission jack. Adaptors permit jack to handle all passenger car transmissions and transaxles. (Lincoln Div. of McNeil Corp.)

CLUTCH TROUBLESHOOTING

SLIPPING
1. Worn clutch disc facing.
2. Oil or grease on disc facing.
3. Warped or distorted disc.
4. Weak diaphragm spring in clutch cover.
5. Warped pressure plate surface.
6. Improper linkage adjustment.
7. Clutch disc overheated.
8. Binding, broken, bent, or worn clutch linkage.

DRAGGING
1. Oil or grease on clutch disc facing.
2. Warped or distorted disc.
3. Broken disc facing.
4. Splined disc hub sticking on splined transmission input shaft.
5. Accumulation of dust in clutch assembly.
6. Warped pressure plate surface.
7. Excessive clutch pedal free play.
8. Sticking pilot bearing or bushing.
9. Sticking release bearing retainer.
10. Misalignment of clutch housing or clutch assembly.

CHATTERING
1. Oil or grease on clutch disc facing.
2. Glazed or worn facing.
3. Warped clutch disc.
4. Binding, worn, bent, or broken clutch linkage.
5. Worn or loose splines in disc hub or on transmission input shaft.
6. Splined disc hub sticking on splined shaft.
7. Warped pressure plate surface.
8. Cracked or scored pressure plate or flywheel face.
9. Broken or collapsed diaphragm spring.
10. Bent transmission input shaft.
11. Worn, loose, or spongy engine mounts.
12. Worn or loose universal joint, differential, or torque rod mounting.
13. Loose clutch housing-to-engine and/or clutch housing-to-transmission attaching bolts.
14. Misalignment of clutch housing or clutch assembly.

GRABBING
1. Oil or grease on clutch facing.
2. Glazed or worn clutch disc facing.
3. Splined disc hub sticking or binding on splined transmission input shaft.
4. Sticking or binding clutch pedal linkage.
5. Misalignment of clutch housing or clutch assembly.
6. Loose engine mounts.
7. Warped or distorted pressure plate.
8. Clutch release fork and bearing improperly assembled.

SQUEAKS
1. Dry clutch release bearing.
2. Dry release bearing sleeve bore.
3. Worn or dry pilot bearing.
4. Misalignment of clutch housing or clutch assembly.
5. Release fork shaft improperly installed.

RATTLES
1. Loose hub in clutch disc.
2. Broken or loose coil springs in clutch disc.
3. Worn splines in disc hub or in transmission input shaft.
4. Worn release bearing.
5. Loose release fork.
6. Worn pilot bearing or bushing.
7. Bent transmission input shaft.
8. Worn transmission bearings.
9. Wear in transmission or driveline.
10. Misalignment of clutch housing or clutch assembly.

FAILURE
1. Disc hub torn out.
2. Friction facing torn off or worn off.
3. Splined disc hub stuck on splined transmission input shaft.
4. Broken springs in pressure plate.
5. Insufficient clutch pedal free play.

VIBRATION OR PULSATION
1. Defective clutch disc.
2. Dust in clutch assembly.
3. Broken or collapsed pressure plate diaphragm spring.
4. Improper installation of clutch assembly.
5. Bent transmission input shaft.
6. Misalignment of clutch housing or clutch assembly.
7. Loose engine mountings.

Chapter 38—REVIEW QUESTIONS

Write your answers on a separate sheet of paper. Do not write in this book.
1. A clutch is a friction device used to _____ and _____ a driving force from a driven member.
2. The clutch disc is sandwiched between the engine _____ and clutch _____.
3. The outer half of the clutch disc has a friction material facing on each side. True or False?
4. Most cars with a manual transmission or manual transaxle use a _____ type pressure plate.
5. The pressure plate is bolted to the engine _____.
   a. Crankshaft.
   b. Flywheel.
   c. Rear face.
   d. Flex plate.
6. The clutch _____ is designed to contact the pressure plate diaphragm release fingers during disengagement.
   a. Disc.
   b. Release fork.
   c. Release bearing.
   d. Pilot bearing.
7. The machined surfaces of the flywheel and pressure plate must be flat, true, and free from _____ or _____.
8. The transmission, pressure plate, flywheel housing, clutch disc, flywheel, and crankshaft must be properly _____ to prevent slippage or vibration.

9. How does a transaxle clutch release bearing function differ from a transmission clutch release bearing in the clutch engaged position?
10. Where is the clutch pedal free play adjustment usually located?
   a. At clutch cross shaft.
   b. At clutch pedal stop.
   c. At clutch release bearing.
   d. At clutch fork push rod.
11. Rule-of-thumb figure for clutch pedal free play is:
   a. Zero.
   b. 1/2 in.
   c. 1 in.
   d. 1 1/2 in.
12. What is the function of the clutch pilot bearing?
13. Various systems have been devised to provide self-adjustment of the clutch _____ mechanism on manual transaxle applications.
14. General Motors and Ford use a similar self-adjusting clutch control mechanism. It is fitted with a _____ self-adjustment mechanism.
   a. Pawl and quadrant.
   b. Rod and shaft.
   c. Lever and cross shaft.
   d. Clutch pedal and bracket.
15. One of the most common causes of clutch trouble is misalignment. True or False?
16. A transmission _____ should always be used to aid in moving the transmission in or out of place.
17. Where should a dial indicator be mounted to check runout of the flywheel?
   a. Clutch housing.
   b. Pilot bushing.
   c. Rear face of engine.
   d. Front face of transmission.
18. Where should the dial indicator be mounted to check alignment of clutch housing?
   a. Clutch housing.
   b. Pilot bushing.
   c. Rear face of engine.
   d. Front face of transmission.
19. Generally, what is the maximum allowable runout on the machined face of the flywheel housing?
   a. .003 in.
   b. .007 in.
   c. .010 in.
   d. .015 in.
20. Why should you put aligned prick-punch marks on the flywheel and clutch cover if existing clutch assembly is to be reinstalled?

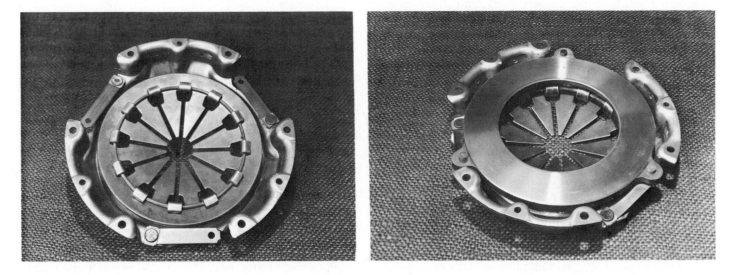

Diaphragm spring turnover (DST) clutch features 12 turnover tabs to locate diaphragm spring in clutch cover, replacing rivets, sleeves, and fulcrum ring support usually used in diaphragm type clutches. Left. Turnover tabs locate spring and are pressed in place. Right. Pressure plate is riveted to drive straps. (Automotive Products Limited)

Chapter 39

MANUAL TRANSMISSION FUNDAMENTALS

After studying this chapter, you will be able to:
- Explain the function of a transmission in an automotive vehicle.
- Give examples of various gear combinations that provide different ratios to produce more power and less speed or more speed and less power at the output shaft of the transmission.
- Trace the power flow through each "gear" of three speed and four speed manual transmissions.
- Tell how the three basic elements of a planetary gearset work together to provide gear reduction or direct drive.
- Trace the power flow through each "gear" of a five speed manual transmission, including fifth gear overdrive.

A TRANSMISSION is a speed and power changing device installed at some point between the engine and driving wheels of the vehicle. It provides a means for changing the ratio between engine rpm (revolutions per minute) and driving wheel rpm to best meet each particular driving situation.

Given a level road, an automobile without a transmission could be made to move by accelerating the engine and engaging the clutch. However, a start under these conditions would be slow, noisy, and uncomfortable. In addition, it would place a tremendous strain on the engine and driving parts of the automobile.

So in order to get smooth starts and have power to pass and climb hills, a power ratio must be provided to multiply the torque (turning effort) of the engine. Also required is a speed ratio to avoid the need for extremely high engine rpm at high road speeds. The transmission is geared to perform these functions.

APPLICATION OF TORQUE

POWER is the rate or speed at which work is performed. (See Chapter 8.) TORQUE is turning or twisting effort.

Torque is derived from power. However, because of operating characteristics, a gasoline engine does not attain maximum torque at the peak of power output. The engine section of this text makes it clear that the amount of torque obtainable from a source of power is proportional to the distance from the center of rotation at which it is applied.

It follows, then, that if we have a shaft (engine

crankshaft) rotating at any given speed, we can put gears of different sizes on the shaft and obtain different results. If we put a large gear on the shaft, we will get more speed and less power at the rim than with a small gear.

If we place another shaft parallel to our driving shaft and install gears or pulleys on it in line with those on the driving shaft, we can obtain almost any desired combination of speed or power within the limits of the engine's ability. That is exactly what an automobile transmission does by means of gears and devices.

GEAR USAGE

Gears are simply a means of applying leverage to rotating parts. An ordinary lever, for example, has more power as the fulcrum gets closer to the object of power application, Fig. 39-1. The closer the fulcrum approaches the object, the longer the distance the lever end has to be moved. The same principle applies to gears and pulleys. The smaller the number of teeth on the driving gear, the slower the driven gear rotates, but with multiplied power.

A modern transmission provides both speed and power. The engineers who designed it selected the gear sizes that would give the best all around performance. It is geared to a power ratio that puts the car in motion, then it shifts, or is shifted, to one or more speed ratios that keep it rolling.

A Frenchman named Levassor is generally credited with developing the first sliding gear transmission. It consisted of two shafts mounted parallel to each other and fitted with sliding spur gears of different sizes. The gears were arranged to mesh with each other to provide a

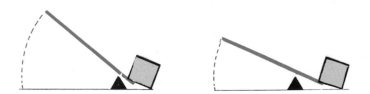

Fig. 39-1. Principle of lever and fulcrum can be compared to gear ratios. Distance between fulcrum and object is comparable to distance between center of a gear and its rim. Therefore, a small gear will drive a large gear slowly, but with great power.

change in the relative speed of the driving and driven shafts, Fig. 39-2. Levassor's transmission had a first, second, and third gear, as well as reverse. It was an ingenious ''first.''

GEAR RATIOS

Gear ratios in transmissions are not standardized, but are engineered to fit changes in the engine, car weight, etc., in order to obtain maximum performance.

A typical automobile manual transmission has ratios as follows:

        Reverse gear . . . . 3.8 to 1
        First gear . . . . 2.8 to 1
        Second gear . . . . 1.7 to 1
        Third gear . . . . 1.0 to 1
        Overdrive . . . . 0.7 to 1

Note that high gear output is direct drive or a 1.0 to 1 ratio. To figure other ratios, compute each meshing of gears in a given speed as a separate ratio. Then, the overall transmission gear ratio for that speed would be a mathematical computation of all of these values.

The gear ratio can be determined by counting the teeth on a pair of gears. If the driving gear has 20 teeth and the driven gear 40 teeth, the ratio would be 2.0 to 1. If the driving gear had 40 teeth and driven gear 20 teeth, the ratio would be 1.0 to 2.

Transmission gear ratios should not be confused with the final drive ratio or car gear ratio which refers to the overall ratio between the engine revolutions and the driving axle revolutions. This, of course, includes the gear reduction in the differential.

In third gear, for example (1.0 to 1 ratio), the output shaft of the transmission turns at the same speed as the engine crankshaft. In overdrive, the output shaft turns faster. In all other gear combinations, the output shaft turns more slowly, but provides greater power.

THREE SPEED MANUAL TRANSMISSION

To illustrate gear arrangement, a simplified, spur gear, three speed transmission is shown in Fig. 39-2. The clutch attaches to the input shaft at the left; the drive shaft attaches to the output shaft at the right. The transmission gears are in the neutral position.

NEUTRAL POSITION

In neutral position: The clutch turns the input shaft, which rotates the countershaft gear, second speed, first, and reverse gears. The output shaft does not revolve. See Fig. 39-3.

REVERSE GEAR

In order to engage reverse gear: First and reverse sliding gear A on the output shaft is moved backward to engage reverse gear B, which is driven by gear C on the countershaft. Interposing idler gear B between gears A and C reverses the rotation of the output shaft. See Fig. 39-4.

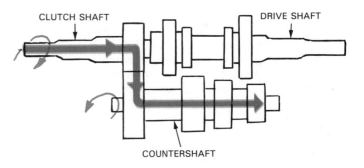

Fig. 39-3. NEUTRAL: With engine running and three speed manual transmission in neutral position, input shaft turns countershaft, but no power is applied to output shaft.

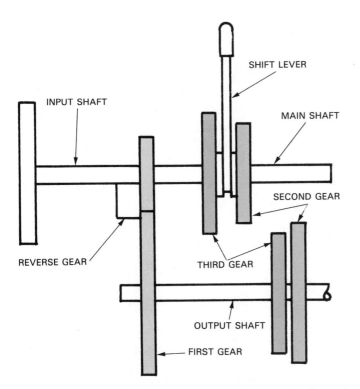

Fig. 39-2. In diagrammatic form: A small gear on main shaft is meshed with a large ''low'' gear for maximum power. Second gears are nearly same size for more speed on drive shaft. High speed gear on main shaft is larger than high gear on drive shaft, so higher speed on driven shaft would result.

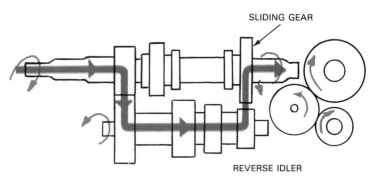

Fig. 39-4. REVERSE: When shift lever is moved to reverse position, an idler gear is interposed between countershaft and output shaft to reverse direction of rotation of output shaft.

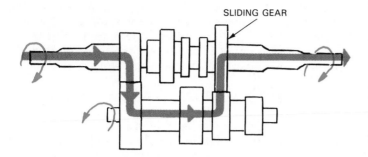

Fig. 39-5. FIRST GEAR: When shift lever is placed in first gear, power is transmitted through countershaft to first and reverse sliding gear to output shaft.

FIRST GEAR

To engage first gear: The first and reverse sliding gear on the output shaft is moved forward into mesh with the first gear. With this move, the input shaft turns the countershaft gear, which turns the first and reverse gear. The first gear on the countershaft, being smaller than the mating gear on the output shaft, provides a gear reduction. Therefore, it turns the output shaft at slower speed with greater power. See Fig. 39-5.

SECOND GEAR

To shift into second gear: The first and reverse sliding gear is returned to neutral, Fig. 39-3, and the output shaft second speed gear is moved backward into mesh with the second speed gear on the countershaft. Since there is less difference in the size of these gears, the output shaft will turn at a higher rate of speed than in first gear. The principle gear reduction is now between the input shaft gear and the countershaft gear, Fig. 39-6.

THIRD GEAR

For third gear: The output shaft second speed gear is disengaged from the second speed gear on the countershaft and moved forward until projections on the rear face of the input shaft gear engage with matching indentations or notches in the forward face of the output shaft second speed gear. This locks the input shaft and output shaft together, and they turn at the same speed.

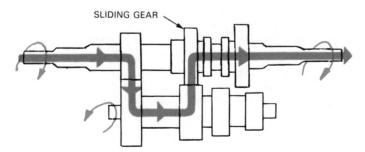

Fig. 39-6. SECOND GEAR: With shift lever in second gear, power flow is through countershaft to second speed sliding gear to output shaft.

The gears on the countershaft continue to rotate, but do not carry power since they are not coupled to any of the gears on the output shaft. See Fig. 39-7.

All shift operations on the output shaft are controlled by collars or forks. The forks are attached to two parallel shafts, and the gear shift lever can be moved to the side, forward, or backward to engage either shifting shaft as desired. An interlocking device is placed between the shafts so that only one shaft can be moved at a time to avoid engaging more than one pair of gears at a time.

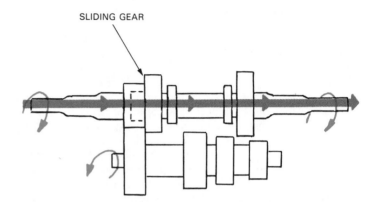

Fig. 39-7. THIRD GEAR: In third gear, power does not go through gears but is transmitted directly from input shaft to output shaft.

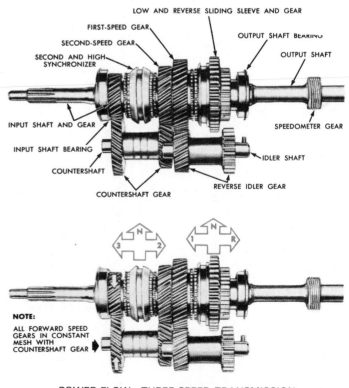

POWER FLOW—THREE-SPEED TRANSMISSION

Fig. 39-8. Above. Gear setup in a typical, helical gear, synchromesh three speed transmission features constant mesh gears with synchronized shifts. Below. Position of shift forks is indicated for neutral, first, second, third, and reverse.

HELICAL GEARS

Today's helical gear synchromesh transmissions, Fig. 39-8, are somewhat similar to the spur gear type. The principal differences are:
1. The shape of the gear teeth.
2. The addition of synchronizing clutches to the second and third speed gears (first gear, too, in many cases).
3. The fact that some of the output shaft gears are free to turn on bearings until engaged.

SYNCHRONIZING CLUTCH

The synchronizing clutch is a drum or sleeve that slides back and forth on the splined output shaft by means of the shifting fork. Generally, it has a bronze cone on each

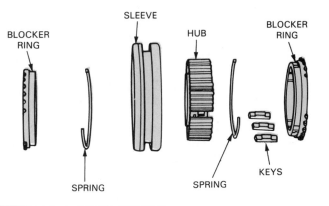

Fig. 39-9. Exploded view of synchronizer assembly shows relative positions of internal and external splined hub, sleeve keys, springs, sleeve, and blocker rings.

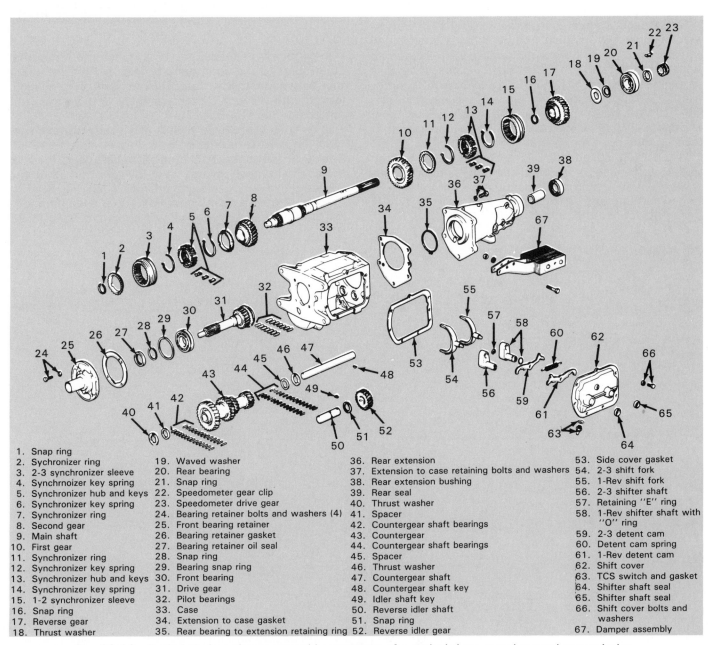

1. Snap ring	19. Waved washer	36. Rear extension	53. Side cover gasket
2. Sychronizer ring	20. Rear bearing	37. Extension to case retaining bolts and washers	54. 2-3 shift fork
3. 2-3 synchronizer sleeve	21. Snap ring	38. Rear extension bushing	55. 1-Rev shift fork
4. Synchronoizer key spring	22. Speedometer gear clip	39. Rear seal	56. 2-3 shifter shaft
5. Synchronizer hub and keys	23. Speedometer drive gear	40. Thrust washer	57. Retaining "E" ring
6. Synchronizer key spring	24. Bearing retainer bolts and washers (4)	41. Spacer	58. 1-Rev shifter shaft with "O" ring
7. Synchronizer ring	25. Front bearing retainer	42. Countergear shaft bearings	59. 2-3 detent cam
8. Second gear	26. Bearing retainer gasket	43. Countergear	60. Detent cam spring
9. Main shaft	27. Bearing retainer oil seal	44. Countergear shaft bearings	61. 1-Rev detent cam
10. First gear	28. Snap ring	45. Spacer	62. Shift cover
11. Synchronizer ring	29. Bearing snap ring	46. Thrust washer	63. TCS switch and gasket
12. Synchronizer key spring	30. Front bearing	47. Countergear shaft	64. Shifter shaft seal
13. Synchronizer hub and keys	31. Drive gear	48. Countergear shaft key	65. Shifter shaft seal
14. Synchronizer key spring	32. Pilot bearings	49. Idler shaft key	66. Shift cover bolts and washers
15. 1-2 synchronizer sleeve	33. Case	50. Reverse idler shaft	67. Damper assembly
16. Snap ring	34. Extension to case gasket	51. Snap ring	
17. Reverse gear	35. Rear bearing to extension retaining ring	52. Reverse idler gear	
18. Thrust washer			

Fig. 39-10. Exploded view shows assembly sequence of a typical three speed manual transmission. (Pontiac Motor Div., General Motors Corp.)

447

side that engages with a tapered mating cone on the second and third speed gears. When this drum is moved along the output shaft, the cones act as a clutch. Upon touching the gear which is to be engaged, the output shaft is speeded up or slowed down as required until the speeds of the output shaft and the gear are synchronized.

This action occurs during partial movement of the shift lever. Completion of lever movement then slides the drum and gear into complete engagement. This action can be readily understood by remembering that the hub of the drum slides on the splines of the output shaft to engage the cones, then the drum slides on the hub to engage the gears. See Fig. 39-9. Fig. 39-8 shows the synchronizers and all other parts in their assembled positions. Fig. 39-10 shows an exploded view of a typical three speed transmission.

FOUR SPEED MANUAL TRANSMISSION

Four speed manual transmissions and high performance engines are popular combinations. Generally, all four forward speeds are synchronized and engineered with closely spaced gear ratios to provide minimum loss of engine speed at shift points. All gears are in constant mesh with the exception of the reverse sliding gear, Fig. 39-11. With four speed transmissions, manual gear shifting is usually accomplished with a floor-type shift lever mounted on a console.

When a four speed manual transmission is in neutral, with clutch engaged, the input shaft drives the countershaft. However, with all synchronizers neutrally positioned and the reverse sliding gear out of mesh, power does not flow to the output shaft. See Fig. 39-11.

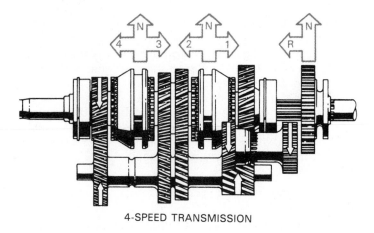

4-SPEED TRANSMISSION

Fig. 39-11. Four speed manual transmission is a favorite of sports car enthusiasts. Fully synchronized, all upshifts and downshifts can be made while car is in motion.

In all forward speeds, power is transmitted from the input shaft to the countershaft gear and to first gear, then to second, third or fourth speed gears, in turn, each locked with a synchronizer assembly to drive the output shaft. See Fig. 39-12.

In reverse, the reverse sliding gear is moved into mesh with the reverse rear idler gear. Power is transmitted from the input shaft to the countershaft gear, then to the constant mesh reverse front idler gear and through splines and reverse gearing to the main shaft. Fig. 39-12.

To illustrate all components of a four speed manual transmission, an exploded view is shown in Fig. 39-13.

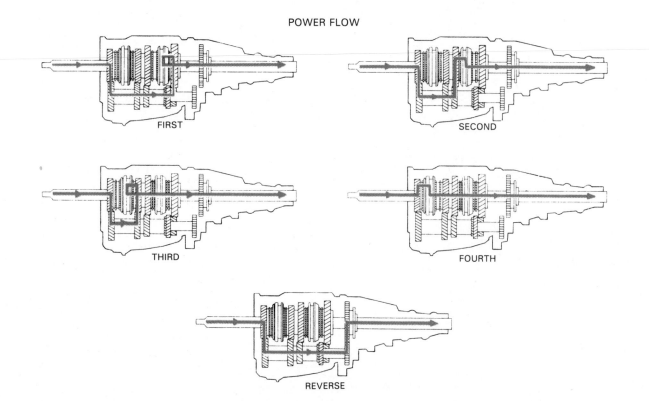

POWER FLOW

FIRST SECOND THIRD FOURTH REVERSE

Fig. 39-12. Power flow in four speed manual transmission is illustrated in each drive position forward, and also in reverse.

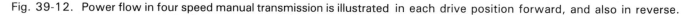

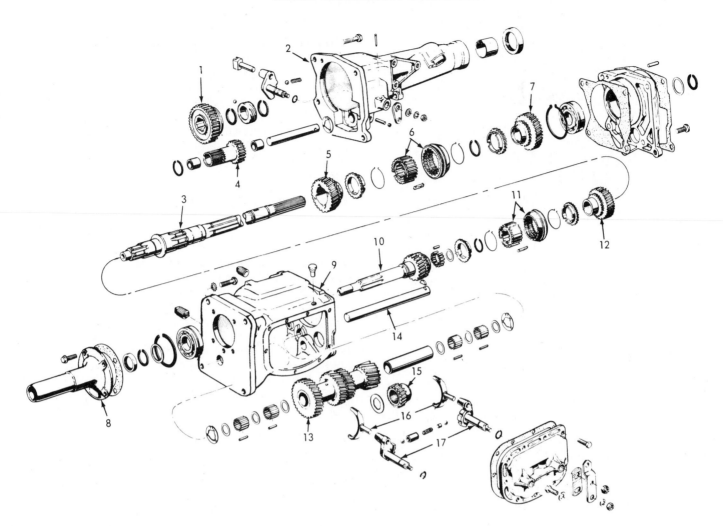

Fig. 39-13. Major elements of a typical four speed manual transmission include: 1—Reverse gear. 2—Reverse gear housing. 3—Main shaft. 4—Reverse idler gear. 5—Second gear. 6—First and second clutch assembly. 7—First gear. 8—Front bearing retainer. 9—Case. 10—Pinion gear. 11—Third and fourth clutch assembly. 12—Third gear. 13—Countershaft gear. 14—Countershaft. 15—Reverse idler gear. 16—Shifter forks. 17—Shifter fork shafts.

With the four speed setup, we have the following typical gear ratios:

Reverse gear	4.0	to 1
First gear	4.0	to 1
Second gear	2.14	to 1
Third gear	1.42	to 1
Fourth gear	1.0	to 1

All components of a four speed manual transmission are shown in Fig. 39-13.

OVERDRIVE REVIVAL

After a lengthy lull, overdrive units are popular again. Either the ''planetary'' type or those with built-in or built-on gears and synchronizers are available from almost all automobile manufacturers.

OVERDRIVE is an arrangement of gearing which produces more revolutions of the driven shaft than the driving shaft. That is: the engine rpm will be reduced about 30 percent while the vehicle maintains the same road speed. As a result, fuel consumption will be reduced and engine life prolonged.

PLANETARY GEAR SYSTEMS

PLANETARY GEARS are sometimes used in one form or another in overdrive transmissions. The name ''planetary'' is derived from this system's similarity to our solar system. The pinions or planet gears each turn on their own axis while rotating around the sun (central) gear. These gears are surrounded by a ring gear, Fig. 39-14, to complete the gearset.

Basically, planetary gearsets are used as a reduction gear. They are used for reverse and are used in multiple sets where more than two forward speeds are desired.

When a planetary gearset is installed in an overdrive application, it is used as an overgear. That is: output rpm exceeds input rpm. Or, as stated earlier, the arrangement of gearing (planetary gearset) produces more revolutions of the driven shaft than the driving shaft.

METHODS OF CONNECTING PARTS

In a planetary gearset, the gears are in mesh at all times and are never shifted in and out of engagement.

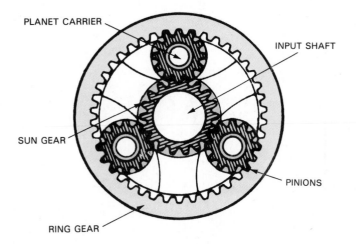

Fig. 39-14. This end view of a planetary gearset shows a three-pinion arrangement. Note that gears are in mesh at all times. As different elements are "held" from turning, different gear ratios are affected.

The gears are attached to different drums which, in turn, are attached to other operating parts of the system. This enables the gears to function in different ways as the various drums are held from rotation by brake bands.

A simple form of planetary gearset, Fig. 39-14, has three pinions mounted between, and meshed with, both the sun gear and ring gear at all times. The pinions revolve on pins or axles which are a part of the planet carrier drum. The pinions are held in spaced relationship with one another, yet can turn freely on their own pins and also can rotate around the sun gear and within the ring gear.

Basically, we have three units:
1. Sun gear.
2. Planet carrier, drum, and pinions.
3. Ring gear and drum.

The gears can be arranged so that they will function as driving elements or driven elements to provide different results by connecting them in different ways.

For example, if the engine is connected to the sun gear and the planet or pinion carrier is connected to the drive shaft, the entire assembly will rotate as a unit (pinions do not turn on their pins). In this case, there will be no gear reduction. The drive shaft will rotate at the same speed as the engine crankshaft.

If, however, a brake band is placed around the ring gear to hold it from turning, the pinions will be forced to travel around inside the ring gear, carrying the pinion carrier along at reduced speed. In this case, the pinion gears turn on their pins in the opposite direction of rotation of the sun gear, while the pinion carrier turns in the same direction as the sun gear but at reduced speed.

With these few gears and a band to hold the drum, we have a basic transmission of the planetary type with gear reduction for low gear and direct drive for high gear.

TRANSMISSION OVERDRIVES

Utilizing the same fundamental gears used in planetary transmissions, we can change the hookup to get an overdrive. If we attach the engine to the planet carrier instead

of the sun gear and attach the drive shaft (or driven shaft) to the ring gear instead of the planet carrier, we would change the entire operation.

By holding the sun gear, we can reverse the action of the gearing and get an increase in gear ratio instead of a reduction. This combination is light in weight, not too expensive to build, and it could be attached to the transmission where it would be carried by the car springs as part of the sprung weight. Furthermore, it could be controlled by the driver and could be made automatic in operation.

ARRANGING OVERDRIVE

There are several ways of hooking up planetary gearing to accomplish different results. One method is to increase gear ratio by attaching the driven shaft to the ring gear, while holding the sun gear from rotating. However, when the sun gear is released, the pinions will simply chase around between the sun gear and ring gear in the opposite direction and no power will be transmitted.

This problem was solved by installing a free-wheel unit on the transmission output shaft. Then, when drive shaft speed exceeds engine speed (coasting), the rollers release. When accelerating the engine, the rollers are wedged on the cam and power is transmitted. See Fig. 39-15.

METHODS OF CONTROL

Older overdrive assemblies were considered an auxiliary unit because they were attached to the rear of a three speed manual transmission. Control of these overdrive transmissions is in the hands of the driver. A control handle is pushed in to engage overdrive; it is pulled out to "lock out" overdrive. The entire operation is controlled by a solenoid, a mechanical centrifugal governor, a kickdown switch, and a locking pawl and balk ring assembly. See Fig. 39-16.

Other planetary type overdrive transmissions were introduced, but the trend in overdrives turned toward "built-in" gears and synchronizers. This trend, plus a

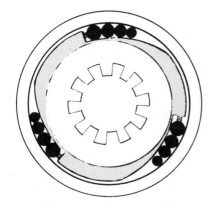

Fig. 39-15. On an overrunning clutch: If outer rim turns clockwise, rollers will roll up on cams and hub will turn at same speed as rim. If rim turns counterclockwise, rollers roll down cams against springs and hub will "free wheel" (cease to rotate).

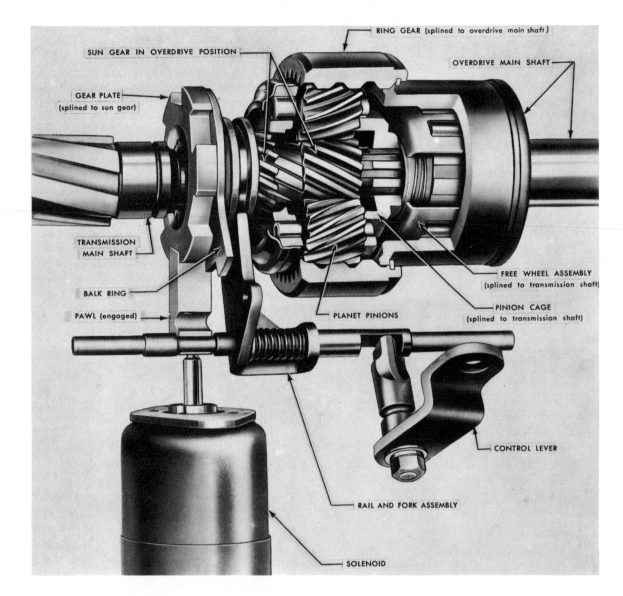

Fig. 39-16. Planetary type overdrive transmission in overdrive: Sun gear is locked in place by pawl in balk ring. Planet gears drive internal ring gear. Ring gear drives overdrive main shaft.

strong move toward transaxle applications, has resulted in the development of four speed and five speed overdrive transmissions.

FIVE SPEED OVERDRIVE TRANSMISSION

A typical five speed transmission is a fully synchronized unit with blocker ring synchronizers and a constant mesh reverse gear. It has the shift lever mounted on top of the extension housing.

In NEUTRAL with clutch engaged, Fig. 39-17, the input shaft turns the countergear, which then turns the fifth, fourth, third, second, first, and reverse idler gears. However, since the clutch sleeves are neutrally positioned, power will not flow through the output shaft. See Fig. 39-17.

In FIRST SPEED, Fig. 39-18, the first and second speed clutch sleeve assembly is moved rearward to mesh with the first speed gear (which is being turned by countergear). Since the first and second speed clutch

5 SPEED TRANSMISSION

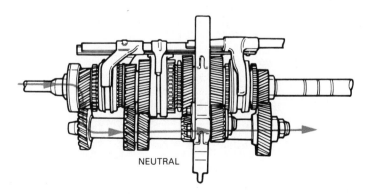

Fig. 39-17. NEUTRAL: Although input shaft at left drives countergear and countershaft, no power flows to output shaft because clutch sleeves are neutrally positioned. (Chevrolet Motor Div., General Motors Corp.)

hub is splined to the output shaft, power flows from the first speed gear through the clutch assembly to the output shaft. See Fig. 39-18.

In SECOND SPEED, Fig. 39-19, the first and second speed clutch sleeve assembly is moved forward to mesh with the second speed gear (which is being turned by countergear). Since the first and second speed clutch hub is splined to the output shaft, power flows from the second speed gear through the clutch assembly to the output shaft. See Fig. 39-19.

In THIRD SPEED, Fig. 39-20, the third and fourth speed clutch assembly is moved rearward to mesh with the third speed gear (which is being turned by countergear). Since the third and fourth speed clutch hub is splined to the output shaft, power flows from the third speed gear through the clutch assembly to the output shaft. See Fig. 39-20.

In FOURTH SPEED, Fig. 39-21, the third and fourth speed clutch sleeve assembly is moved forward to mesh with the input shaft main drive gear. This engagement

results in "direct drive" from input shaft to output shaft. See Fig. 39-21.

In FIFTH SPEED, Fig. 39-22, or overdrive, the reverse and fifth speed clutch sleeve assembly is moved rearward to mesh with the fifth speed gear. This engagement results in power flow from the fifth speed gear through the reverse and fifth speed clutch assembly to the output shaft. See Fig. 39-22.

In REVERSE GEAR, Fig. 39-23, the reverse and fifth speed clutch sleeve assembly is moved forward to mesh with the reverse gear. This engagement results in power flow from the countershaft and reverse idler to the reverse gear and directly to the output shaft, Fig. 39-23.

To illustrate all components of a five speed manual transmission, an exploded view is shown in Fig. 39-24. This transmission is designed for use in a four wheel drive application. Therefore, it features an adapter housing (rather than an extension housing) to adapt the transmission to the transfer case. An exploded view of a four speed overdrive transmission is shown in Fig. 39-25.

5 SPEED TRANSMISSION

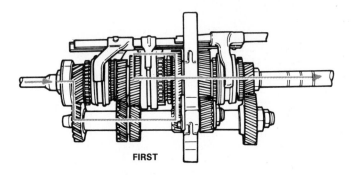

FIRST

Fig. 39-18. FIRST GEAR: Follow power flow lines in color from input shaft to countergear to first speed gear to first and second speed clutch sleeve to output shaft.
(Chevrolet Motor Div., General Motors Corp.)

5 SPEED TRANSMISSION

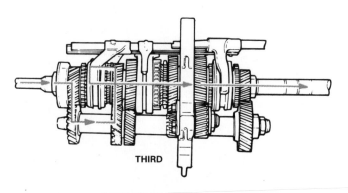

THIRD

Fig. 39-20. THIRD GEAR: Power flow is from input shaft to countergear to third speed gear to third and fourth speed clutch sleeve to output shaft.
(Chevrolet Motor Div., General Motors Corp.)

5 SPEED TRANSMISSION

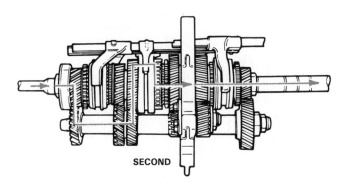

SECOND

Fig. 39-19. SECOND GEAR: Power flow as indicated is from input shaft to countergear to second speed gear to first and second speed clutch sleeve to output shaft.
(Chevrolet Motor Div., General Motors Corp.)

5 SPEED TRANSMISSION

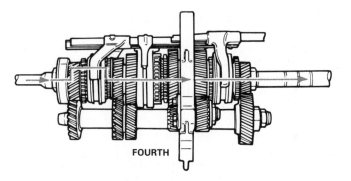

FOURTH

Fig. 39-21. FOURTH GEAR: Power flow is from input shaft to third and fourth speed clutch assembly to output shaft. This is "direct drive" or 1.0 to 1 ratio.
(Chevrolet Motor Div., General Motors Corp.)

5 SPEED TRANSMISSION

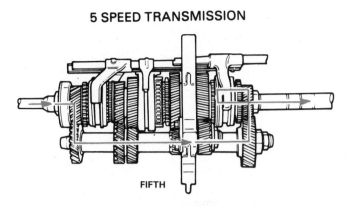

FIFTH

5 SPEED TRANSMISSION

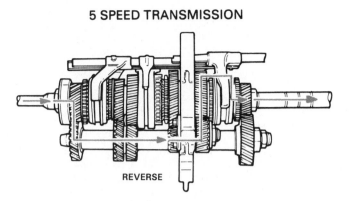

REVERSE

Fig. 39-22. FIFTH GEAR: Power flow is from input shaft to countergear to fifth speed gear to reverse and fifth speed clutch assembly to output shaft. This is "overdrive." (Chevrolet Motor Div., General Motors Corp.)

Fig. 39-23. REVERSE GEAR: Power flow is from input shaft to countergear to reverse gear to reverse idler to reverse and fifth speed clutch assembly to output shaft. (Chevrolet Motor Div., General Motors Corp.)

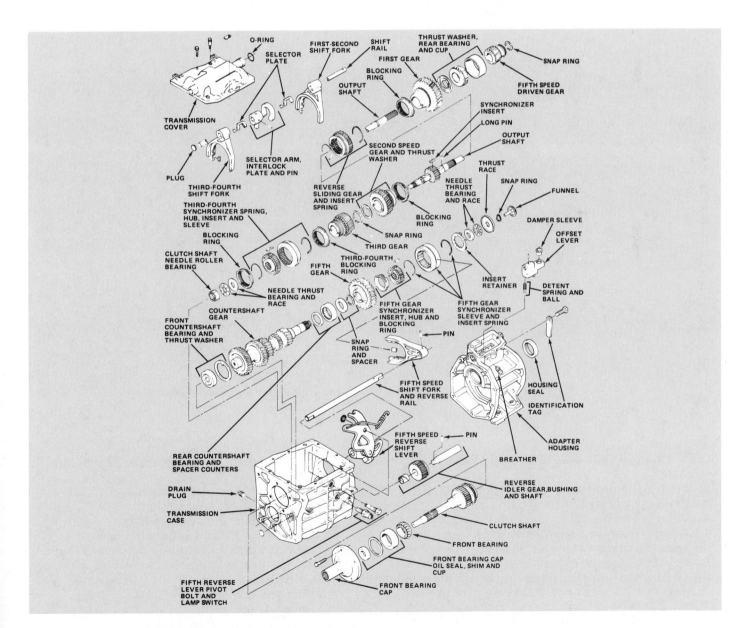

Fig. 39-24. Exploded view shows assembly sequence of a typical five speed manual transmission with overdrive. (American Motors Corp.)

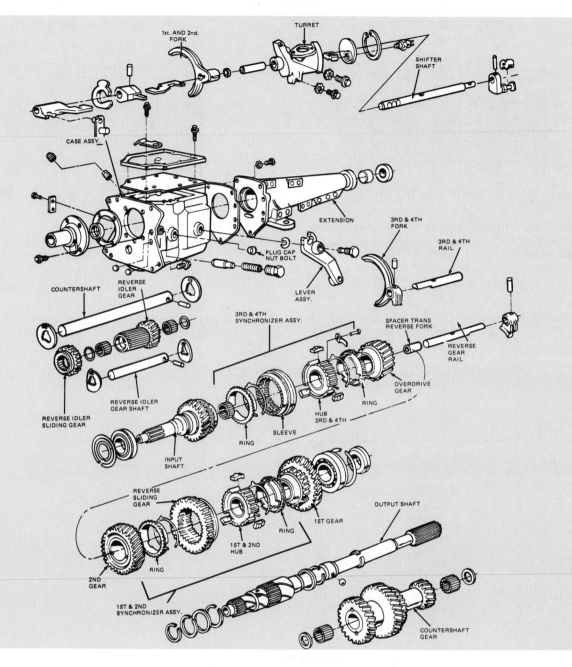

Fig. 39-25. Exploded view of a four speed overdrive transmission.

Chapter 39—REVIEW QUESTIONS

1. What function does a transmission perform?
2. What is "power"?
3. What is "torque"?
4. A larger gear on the driving shaft will increase the speed of rotation of the driven shaft. True or False?
5. How can the ratio of mating gears be determined?
6. What is the gear ratio of a setup where the driving gear has 20 teeth and the driven gear has 40?
   a. 2.0 to 1.
   b. 1 to 2.0.
   c. 4 to 2.0.
   d. 2.0 to 4.

7. Which two manual transmission shafts turn in neutral?
   a. Input shaft and output shaft.
   b. Input shaft and countershaft.
   c. Output shaft and countershaft.
   d. Countershaft and drive shaft.
8. When a manual transmission is shifted into reverse, what extra gear is interposed to reverse the direction of the output shaft?
   a. Low and reverse sliding gear.
   b. Reverse idler gear.
   c. Reverse synchromesh ring.
   d. Overrunning gear.
9. Name the three major units in a planetary gearset.

10. In an overdrive planetary transmission: If the ring gear is held and the pinion carrier is driven by the sun gear and pinions, will this increase or decrease the speed of the driveshaft?

11. What is the function of an overrunning clutch in an overdrive transmission?
    a. Eliminates the clutch.
    b. Disengages the overdrive unit.
    c. Restricts drive to one direction only.
    d. Permits drive in both directions.

12. Which control device on an auxiliary overdrive transmission operates the locking pawl?
    a. Solenoid.
    b. Governor.
    c. Relay.
    d. Kickdown unit.

13. Which control device connects and disconnects the overdrive unit?
    a. Solenoid.
    b. Governor.
    c. Relay.
    d. Balk ring.

14. What is the purpose of the balk ring in an overdrive?

15. When a planetary gearset is installed in an overdrive application, it is used as an _____.

16. With overdrive, output rpm _____ input rpm.

17. In a planetary gearset, the gears are in mesh at all times. True or False?

18. What is the function of a blocker ring synchronizer?

19. Match the numbers of the following "gear positions" at the left with the typical gear ratios at the right in a three speed manual transmission with overdrive.

1. Reverse.	A. 1.0 to 1.	_____
2. First gear.	B. 0.7 to 1.	_____
3. Second gear.	C. 3.8 to 1.	_____
4. Third gear.	D. 2.8 to 1.	_____
5. Overdrive.	E. 1.7 to 1.	_____

20. Match the numbers of the following "gear positions" with the typical gear ratios at the right in a five speed manual transmission.

1. Reverse.	A. 0.68 to 1.	_____
2. First gear.	B. 1.0 to 1.	_____
3. Second gear.	C. 1.29 to 1.	_____
4. Third gear.	D. 1.93 to 1.	_____
5. Fourth gear.	E. 3.15 to 1.	_____
6. Fifth gear.	F. 3.35 to 1.	_____

21. In a four speed manual transmission without overdrive, which "gear" would have a 1.0 to 1 ratio?
    a. First.
    b. Second.
    c. Third.
    d. Fourth.

22. With fifth-speed overdrive, the engine rpm will be reduced about_____ percent while the vehicle maintains the same road speed.
    a. 5.
    b. 10.
    c. 20.
    d. 30.

23. How was the name "planetary" derived?

24. Planetary type overdrive transmissions were popular but the trend in overdrives has turned toward "built-in" _____ and _____.

25. This trend in overdrives has resulted in the development of _____ overdrive transmissions.

In performing a key step of manual transmission maintenance procedure, service technician prepares to remove drain plug and empty used transmission fluid into portable drain barrel. (Lincoln Div. of McNeil Corp.)

Chapter 40

MANUAL TRANSMISSION SERVICE

After studying this chapter, you will be able to:
- Name six manual transmission maintenance operations.
- List various manual transmission troubles and identify possible causes.
- Explain general procedure for manual transmission removal and reinstallation.
- Describe procedures for manual transmission disassembly and internal parts cleaning and inspection.
- Describe procedure for manual transmission reassembly.

MANUAL TRANSMISSIONS are durable, dependable, positive engagement power transfer mechanisms that require little maintenance. Modern "manuals" have helical-cut gears that are in constant mesh in all forward gear ranges. See Fig. 4-1. This feature, plus synchromesh engagement, generally avoids clashing of gears and the resulting gear tooth wear or breakage.

Basically, manual transmission maintenance involves the following routines:
1. Make periodic "fluid" level checks, Fig. 40-2.
2. Make an external inspection of transmission for possible fluid leaks.

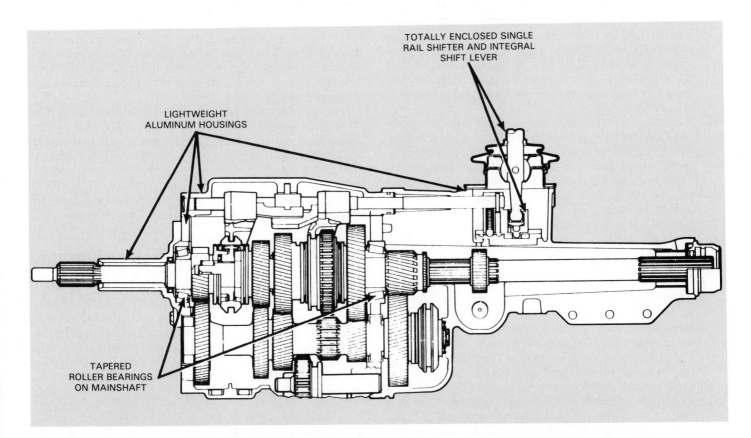

Fig. 40-1. Typical five speed manual transmission has aluminum housing, single rail enclosed shift mechanism, helical gears, and 0.78 to 1 fifth gear overdrive.   (Pontiac Motor Div., General Motors Corp.)

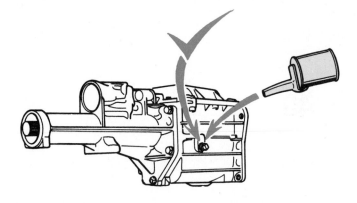

Fig. 40-2. Manual transmission check and refill point generally is located at fill plug hole in side of transmission case. (American Motors Corp.)

3. Test gearshift operation through all gear ranges.
4. Check clutch pedal free play.
5. Examine condition of transmission mount.
6. Test torque tightness of transmission-to-clutch housing attaching bolts.

CHECK FLUID LEVEL

To check fluid level in a manual transmission:
1. Raise vehicle on a hoist.
2. Clean area around fill plug, Fig. 40-2, before removing it.
3. Remove fill plug and insert little finger in fill hole. Fluid level should be even with or just below lower edge of fill hole. NOTE: Some manual transmissions have specified levels 1/2 in. to 1 in. below lower edge of fill hole. Check manufacturer's specification for fluid level and fluid change interval. Drain and refill if fluid is contaminated.
4. If fluid level is low, add recommended type and grade of lubricant to bring level up to lower edge of fill hole. NOTE: Lubricant recommendations vary. Generally, three speed and four speed transmissions call for 75W or 80W-90 gear oil; five speed transmissions require 5W-30SF engine oil or automatic transmission fluid (ATF).
5. Reinstall and tighten fill plug.
6. Lower hoist.

REPLACE REAR SEAL

If fluid is leaking from the transmission at the rear end of the extension housing:
1. Mark drive shaft and rear axle flange for reference on reassembly. Remove drive shaft.
2. Pry out oil seal or use a screw type pulling tool to remove seal from extension housing.
3. Clean counterbore of extension housing.
4. Coat outer diameter of a new seal with cement and — with sealing lip facing inward and using a special installing tool — drive seal into housing until it bottoms in counterbore.
5. Reinstall drive shaft.

TEST GEARSHIFT OPERATION

A methodical run-through of gearshift operation in all gear ranges should be part of any manual transmission maintenance routine. See Fig. 40-3.

Test gearshifting effort and proper engagement in each forward position and in reverse position. If binding is noted or if shift lever fails to indicate a firm detent, place the lever in NEUTRAL and check for a smooth and free crossover. If necessary, make adjustments of floor-mounted gearshift or steering column-mounted shift linkage.

NOTE: Adjusting procedures vary. Check shop manual instructions for specific make and model.

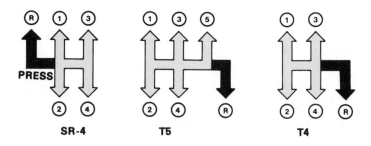

Fig. 40-3. Gearshift patterns vary with make and model of vehicle. Three different four speed and five speed patterns are diagrammed. (American Motors Corp.)

CHECK CLUTCH PEDAL FREE PLAY

To check clutch pedal free play, depress the pedal slowly while noting at what point in its travel it first meets resistance. The resistance occurs when the clutch release bearing makes contact with the clutch pressure plate diaphragm.

The usual clutch pedal free play specification is 1 in. This play is necessary to insure that the clutch release bearing is not in constant contact with the pressure plate diaphragm and partially releasing the clutch disc.

If free play adjustment is necessary, adjust the length of the rod that engages the clutch release fork. NOTE: Occasionally, the adjustment is located elsewhere in the clutch control linkage setup. See Chapter 38, CLUTCHES.

MANUAL TRANSMISSION TROUBLESHOOTING

Transmission Noisy in Neutral

A noise in Neutral may be a growl or hum that can be stopped by depressing clutch pedal. In some cases a bump or thud also will be present, indicating a broken gear or bearing. Defects in output shaft (main shaft), other than pilot bearing, are not included in this group because output shaft does not rotate when transmission is in Neutral.
1. Low lubricant level.
2. Abnormal end play in countershaft gears, reverse idler gear, or input shaft.
3. Input shaft gear badly worn or broken.
4. Input shaft bearing badly worn or broken.

5. Misalignment between engine and transmission.
6. Wear in countershaft drive gear.
7. Wear in reverse and/or reverse idler gear.
8. Countershaft bearings badly worn.
9. Reverse idler shaft bearings badly worn.
10. Countershaft sprung or bent.
11. Pilot shaft bearing worn or broken.
   NOTE: If replacement of a gear is required, mating gear should be replaced too.

Transmission Noisy in Gear

Most causes of noises in Neutral will also appear when transmission is in gear. Same parts are still in operation, plus output shaft (main shaft) which adds the following:
1. Output shaft rear bearing worn or broken.
2. Gears badly worn or broken.
3. Excessive end play of output shaft.
4. Badly worn speedometer gears.

Transmission Noisy in Reverse

1. Worn or damaged reverse idler gear or idler bushing.
2. Worn or damaged reverse gear on main shaft.
3. Damaged or worn reverse countergear.
4. Damaged shift mechanism.

Transmission Slips Out of Gear

Principal cause is misalignment between transmission and engine. Front end of input shaft runs in a bearing in crankshaft, and rear end in transmission case. If this shaft is not in a straight line with engine crankshaft, it will create an angular contact. Less frequent causes are:
1. Input shaft gear teeth worn or tapered.
2. Input shaft gear bearing badly worn.
3. Improper adjustment of shift linkage.
4. Worn shift detent parts.
5. Damaged output shaft pilot bearing.
6. Pilot bearing loose in crankshaft.
7. Transmission loose on clutch housing.
8. Input shaft gear retainer broken or loose.
9. Badly worn or broken gear.
10. Badly worn transmission bearings.
11. Excessive end play of output shaft or countershaft.
12. Output shaft splines worn or distorted.

Transmission Difficult to Shift

1. Engine clutch not releasing.
2. Distorted or burred output shaft splines.
3. Improper adjustment of shift linkage.
4. Misalignment of column control levers.
5. Incorrect clutch adjustment.
6. Internal bind in transmission, caused by shift forks or synchronizer assemblies.
7. Binding shift rail.
8. Incorrect lubricant.

Transmission Leaks Oil

1. Damaged oil seals.
2. Damaged O-rings at speedometer driven gear.
3. Damaged or missing gaskets.
4. Case or cover bolts loose or missing.
5. Case plugs loose or threads stripped.
6. High lubricant level.
7. Vent stopped up.

8. Use of lubricant that foams excessively.
9. Loose or broken input shaft bearing retainer.
10. Worn shift lever seals.

Transmission Gears Clash When Shifting

1. Incorrect clutch adjustment.
2. Binding clutch cable or linkage.
3. Worn or damaged synchronizer assemblies.
4. Low lubricant level.
5. Engine idle speed too high.
6. Misaligned clutch housing.

Transmission Will Not Shift Into One Gear

1. Worn or damaged gearshift selector plates, interlock plate, or selector arm.
2. Worn shift rail detent plunger or broken spring.
3. Worn or damaged gearshift lever assembly.
4. Worn or damaged synchronizer assembly.

Transmission Locked In One Gear

1. Worn or broken shift rail.
2. Bent shifter fork.
3. Broken gear teeth.
4. Worn or broken gearshift lever assembly.
5. Broken shift mechanism in cover.

MANUAL TRANSMISSION SERVICE

The need for major transmission service usually is signaled by noisy operation or gear clash, or transmission jumps out of gear, will not shift gears, or is locked in one gear.

Note that most of the corrections for these complaints call for transmission removal and disassembly. With this in mind, typical procedures are given for removing and reinstalling a manual transmission. In addition, general procedures and precautions are included for disassembling and reassembling a three speed unit, four speed unit, and five speed overdrive unit.

REMOVAL OF TRANSMISSION FROM CAR

1. Shift transmission into Neutral.
2. Remove screws attaching gearshift lever bezel and boot to floor or console.
3. Slide bezel and boot upward on lever and remove lever mounting cover screws.
4. Pull gearshift lever up and out of transmission case, Fig. 40-4.
5. Raise hood.
6. Raise vehicle on hoist.
7. On steering column shift transmissions, disconnect shift rods from shift levers.
8. Place alignment marks on drive shaft and rear axle yoke or flange, Fig. 40-5, for reference on reassembly.
9. Remove drive shaft.
10. Disconnect speedometer cable from extension housing, and remove backup lamp switch wires.
11. Install jack or support stand under clutch housing to support engine.
12. Remove nuts and bolts attaching rear crossmember to frame. See Fig. 40-6.

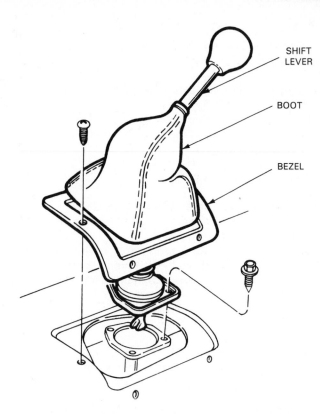

SHIFT LEVER

BOOT

BEZEL

Fig. 40-4. Often, first step in removal of a manual transmission is to unscrew bezel screws and lift gearshift lever from transmission case. (American Motors Corp.)

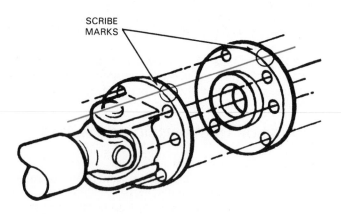

SCRIBE MARKS

Fig. 40-5. Before drive shaft removal, end yoke and rear axle companion flange are marked to insure proper positioning of drive shaft on reassembly. (Ford Motor Co.)

13. Remove catalytic converter support bracket, and disconnect exhaust pipe from manifold.
14. Remove nuts and bolts attaching transmission mount to crossmember.
15. Remove crossmember-to-frame attaching screws and drop crossmember.
16. Remove transmission-to-clutch housing attaching bolts, Fig. 40-7.
17. Pull transmission straight back, holding it level to avoid damaging input shaft, pilot bushing, or clutch disc.

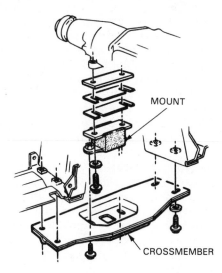

MOUNT

CROSSMEMBER

Fig. 40-6. Rear cross member and transmission mount are removed. (Ford Motor Co.)

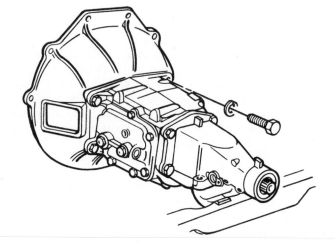

Fig. 40-7. Final step is to unscrew transmission-to-clutch housing attaching bolts and remove transmission. (Chevrolet Motor Div., General Motors Corp.)

18. Remove clutch release bearing and pilot bushing lubricating wick, if so equipped.
19. Soak wick in engine oil.

DISASSEMBLY: THREE SPEED MANUAL TRANSMISSION

Study exploded view illustration, Fig. 40-8.
1. Remove case cover.
2. Remove input (clutch) shaft bearing cap and snap rings.
3. Align notch in input shaft gear (notch down) with countershaft gear and use a puller to remove input shaft and bearing as an assembly.
4. Use a puller to pull bearing from input shaft. See Fig. 40-9.
5. Use a seal remover to pull oil seal from extension

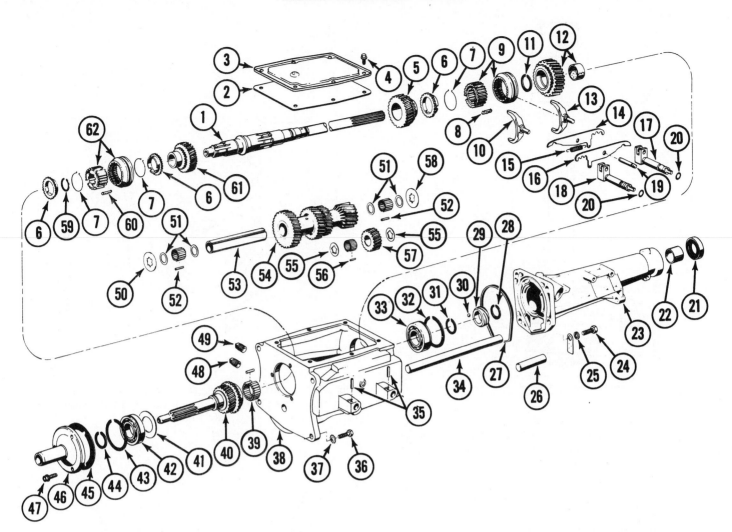

1. **MAIN SHAFT**
2. **GASKET**
3. **CASE COVER**
4. **BOLT**
5. **FIRST GEAR**
6. **CLUTCH FRICTION RING SET**
7. **SHAFT PLATE RETAINING SPRING**
8. **CLUTCH SHAFT FIRST AND REVERSE SHIFT PLATE**
9. **FIRST AND REVERSE CLUTCH ASSEMBLY**
10. **SHIFTER SECOND AND HIGH FORK**
11. **CLUTCH FIRST AND REVERSE GEAR SNAP RING**
12. **REVERSE GEAR**
13. **SHIFTER FIRST AND REVERSE R FORK**
14. **SHIFTER INTERLOCK FIRST AND REVERSE LEVER**
15. **INTERLOCK POPPET SPRING**
16. **SHIFTER INTERLOCK SECOND AND THIRD LEVER**
17. **SHIFTER FORK FIRST AND REVERSE SHAFT**
18. **SHIFTER FORK SECOND AND THIRD SHAFT**
19. **SHIFTER FORK INTERLOCK LEVER PIVOT PIN**

20. **SHIFTER FORK SHAFT SEAL**
21. **OIL SEAL**
22. **BUSHING**
23. **EXTENSION HOUSING**
24. **BOLT**
25. **LOCK WASHER**
26. **IDLER GEAR SHAFT**
27. **GASKET**
28. **SPEEDOMETER DRIVE GEAR RING**
29. **SPEEDOMETER DRIVE GEAR**
30. **SPEEDOMETER DRIVE GEAR BALL**
31. **REAR BEARING LOCKRING**
32. **REAR BEARING LOCKRING**
33. **REAR BEARING**
34. **COUNTERSHAFT**
35. **SHIFTER FORK RETAINING PIN**
36. **BOLT**
37. **LOCK WASHER**
38. **CASE**
39. **SPLINE SHAFT PILOT BEARING ROLLER**
40. **CLUTCH SHAFT**
41. **FRONT BEARING WASHER**
42. **FRONT BEARING**
43. **FRONT BEARING LOCKRING**
44. **FRONT BEARING SNAP RING**
45. **GASKET**

46. **FRONT BEARING CAP**
47. **BOLT**
48. **DRAIN PLUG**
49. **FILLER PIPE PLUG**
50. **FRONT COUNTERSHAFT GEAR THRUST WASHER**
51. **COUNTERSHAFT GEAR BEARING ROLLER WASHER**
52. **COUNTERSHAFT GEAR BEARING ROLLER**
53. **COUNTERSHAFT GEAR ROLLER BEARING SPACER**
54. **COUNTERSHAFT GEAR**
55. **REVERSE IDLER GEAR BEARING ROLLER WASHER**
56. **REVERSE IDLER GEAR BEARING ROLLER**
57. **REVERSE IDLER GEAR**
58. **REAR COUNTERSHAFT THRUST**
59. **CLUTCH SECOND AND THIRD SNAP RING**
60. **CLUTCH SHAFT SECOND AND THIRD SHIFT PLATE**
61. **SECOND AND THIRD CLUTCH ASSEMBLY**
62. **SECOND GEAR**

Fig. 40-8. Exploded view of three speed manual transmission provides good reference information for disassembly and reassembly. (American Motors Corp.)

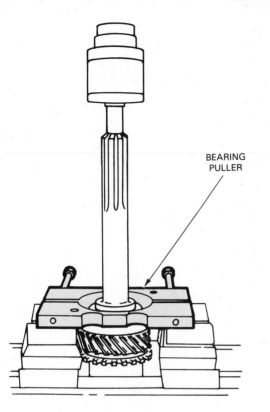

Fig. 40-9. A special bearing puller is used in conjunction with a press to pull front bearing from input (clutch) shaft. (American Motors Corp.)

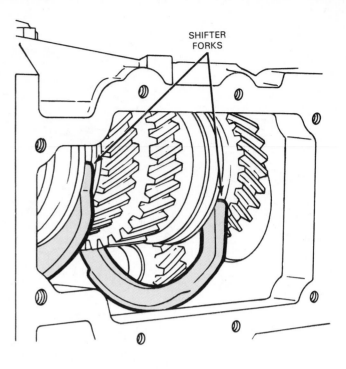

Fig. 40-10. After rear bearing is pulled from output shaft assembly, shaft is moved to one side and both shifter forks are removed.

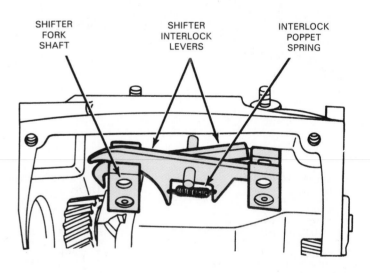

Fig. 40-11. Roll pins are driven from shifter shafts and assembly is lifted from case. (American Motors Corp.)

housing.

6. Remove speedometer drive gear snap ring and remove drive gear.

7. Check condition of pilot bushing; replace, if necessary.

8. Remove rear extension housing and gasket. Inspect condition of bushing. Replace when transmission is reinstalled in vehicle, if necessary.

9. Remove snap rings and use a bearing puller to pull rear bearing.

10. Move output shaft (main shaft) assembly aside and remove both shifter forks, Fig. 40-10.

11. Move front synchronizer to second speed position and lift output shaft assembly from transmission by tilting front of shaft upward.

12. Use a punch to drive pins from shifter fork shafts and push shafts into case, Fig. 40-11, then remove shafts and detent assembly from case.

13. Tap reverse idler gear shaft and countershaft toward rear of case to permit removal of shaft lock plate on rear of case.

14. Use a brass drift to drive reverse idler gear shaft from case, Fig. 40-12.

15. Use a dummy shaft to drive countershaft from case and lift countershaft gear with dummy shaft from case to retain roller bearings in proper position within the countershaft.

16. Remove output shaft front snap ring, second and third speed snychro-clutch assembly, and second gear from shaft. See Fig. 40-8.

17. Slide reverse gear from rear of output shaft, then remove rear snap ring, rear synchro-clutch assembly, and first gear.

CLEAN AND CHECK

Wrap bearings in a clean cloth or paper until washed. Use a fresh solvent to clean transmission case and all parts. Examine case for cracks and all bearing surfaces on case and front face for nicks, wear, or scoring. Check cover for warpage or distortion. Smooth nicks

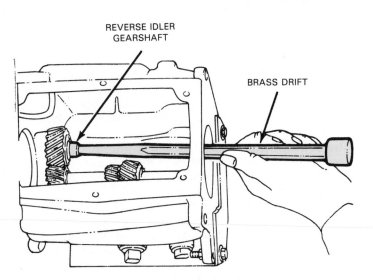

Fig. 40-12. A long brass drift is used to tap reverse idler gear shaft from case. (American Motors Corp.)

with a fine stone (on cast iron) or a fine file (on aluminum), or replace parts.

Check all gears for worn, cracked, or chipped teeth. Replace defective gears; also replace mating gears. Test fit of gears on output shaft. Replace gears that are too loose. Slide synchro-clutch and blocker rings on cones of gears and on input shaft. See Fig. 40-13 for typical minimum clearance between the face of the blocker ring and the clutch teeth on the gear. Replace worn or pitted parts.

Wash bearings in a fresh cleaning solution, rotating each bearing to flush away oil and dirt. Dry bearings with a clean lint-free cloth. Check condition of shift levers, forks, shift rails, and shafts. Check splines of output shaft and input shaft for wear, scoring, or distortion.

REASSEMBLY: THREE SPEED MANUAL TRANSMISSION

1. Install first speed gear and friction ring on main shaft. See Fig. 40-8. Friction ring hub must face

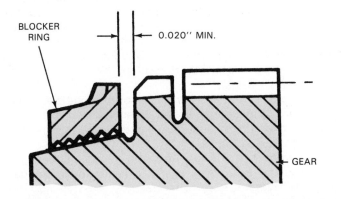

Fig. 40-13. An important step in Clean and Check Procedure is inspecting synchro-clutches and blocker rings for wear. (Ford Motor Co.)

rear of output shaft. (Some installation procedures vary, consult manufacturer's service manual.)

2. Assemble first speed synchro-clutch, place it on output shaft, then install thickest snap ring that will fit into groove.
3. Place second speed gear and friction ring on front of output shaft.
4. Assemble second speed synchro-clutch, Fig. 40-14, place it on output shaft, then install thickest snap ring that will fit into groove.

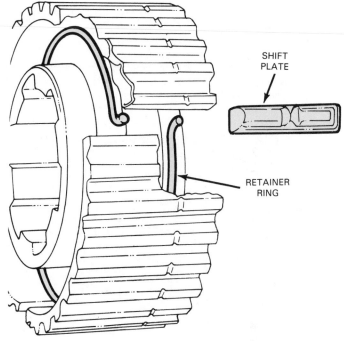

Fig. 40-14. Assembly of synchro-clutch unit requires installation of retainer rings in clockwise direction to insure smooth shifts. (American Motors Corp.)

5. Install dummy shaft in countershaft gear. Coat roller bearings with petroleum jelly and install spacer washers and roller bearings in countershaft gear.
6. Place countershaft gear in transmission case, then position thrust washers at each end of gear so that tabs align with slots in transmission.
7. Use a plastic mallet to install countershaft, driving out dummy shaft.
8. Install roller bearings in reverse idler gear. Use petroleum jelly to hold bearings in place.
9. Place reverse idler gear in case and position thrust washers at each end of gear, then install reverse idler gear shaft. Install lock plate.
10. Partially install shifter fork shafts in case, Fig. 40-11, then position shift levers so that notches are located to rear of case stud.
11. Align shift detent assembly with shifter fork shafts and transmission case stud, then push detent assembly and shifter fork shafts into place and install roll pins.

12. Install front synchronizer in second speed position and place output shaft assembly in case.
13. Move output shaft assembly to one side and install shift forks, Fig. 40-10.
14. Move output shaft assembly to center of case and install pilot end support, Fig. 40-15. Install front bearing cap to hold support in place.
15. Use a driving tool or 1 1/4 in. pipe to drive rear bearing on output shaft. Install thickest rear bearing

MAIN SHAFT PILOT
END SUPPORT

Fig. 40-15. After shift forks are installed, output shaft is centered in case and pilot end support is installed over pilot end of shaft. (American Motors Corp.)

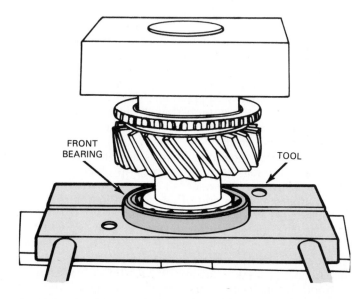

FRONT
BEARING

TOOL

Fig. 40-16. Special tool and press are used to install front bearing on input shaft. (American Motors Corp.)

snap ring that will fit into groove.
16. Install speedometer drive ball, drive gear, and snap ring.
17. Press front bearing on input shaft, Fig. 40-16.
18. Install roller bearings in input shaft cavity. Use petroleum jelly to hold bearings in place.
19. Remove front bearing cap and output shaft pilot end support.
20. Install friction ring on output shaft and slide input shaft into position through front of case.
21. Install thickest front bearing snap ring that will fit into groove.
22. Install new cap gasket and cap, aligning cap with lubrication hole in transmission case.
23. Install rear extension housing and rear oil seal.
24. Install shift levers and check transmission operation in all gears.
25. Install case cover and gasket. Be sure vent is open.

DISASSEMBLY: FOUR SPEED MANUAL TRANSMISSION

1. Study exploded view illustration of transmission being serviced, Fig. 40-17.
2. Drive access plug from extension housing, Fig. 40-18, remove nut from offset lever assembly, then remove assembly.
3. Unscrew remaining extension housing bolts and remove extension housing from case.
4. Remove cover, shifter forks, and shift rod assembly.
5. Remove front bearing retainer.
6. Remove spring clip retaining reverse lever to pivot bolt, unscrew pivot bolt, and remove bolt and reverse lever.
7. Remove snap rings from input shaft and use a puller to pull bearing from input shaft.
8. Remove snap ring holding speedometer gear to output shaft and slide gear and lock ball from shaft.
9. Remove snap rings from output shaft and bearing. Use a puller to pull output shaft bearing from case.
10. Remove input shaft from front of case.
11. Lift output shaft and gear train through top of case.
12. Slide reverse idler gear shaft out rear of case and remove reverse gear.
13. Insert a dummy countershaft through front of case to drive countershaft out rear of case. Lift countershaft gear, thrust washers, and dummy shaft through top of case.
14. Disassemble cover assembly, Fig. 40-19.
15. Scratch alignment marks on synchronizer and blocker rings.
16. Remove front snap ring from output shaft and slide third and fourth speed synchronizer assembly, blocker rings, and third speed gear from output shaft. See Fig. 40-17.
17. Remove next snap ring and second speed gear thrust washer from shaft. Slide second speed gear and blocker ring from shaft.
18. Remove first speed gear thrust washer and roll pin from rear of output shaft. Slide first gear and blocker ring from shaft.
19. Disassemble synchronizer assemblies.

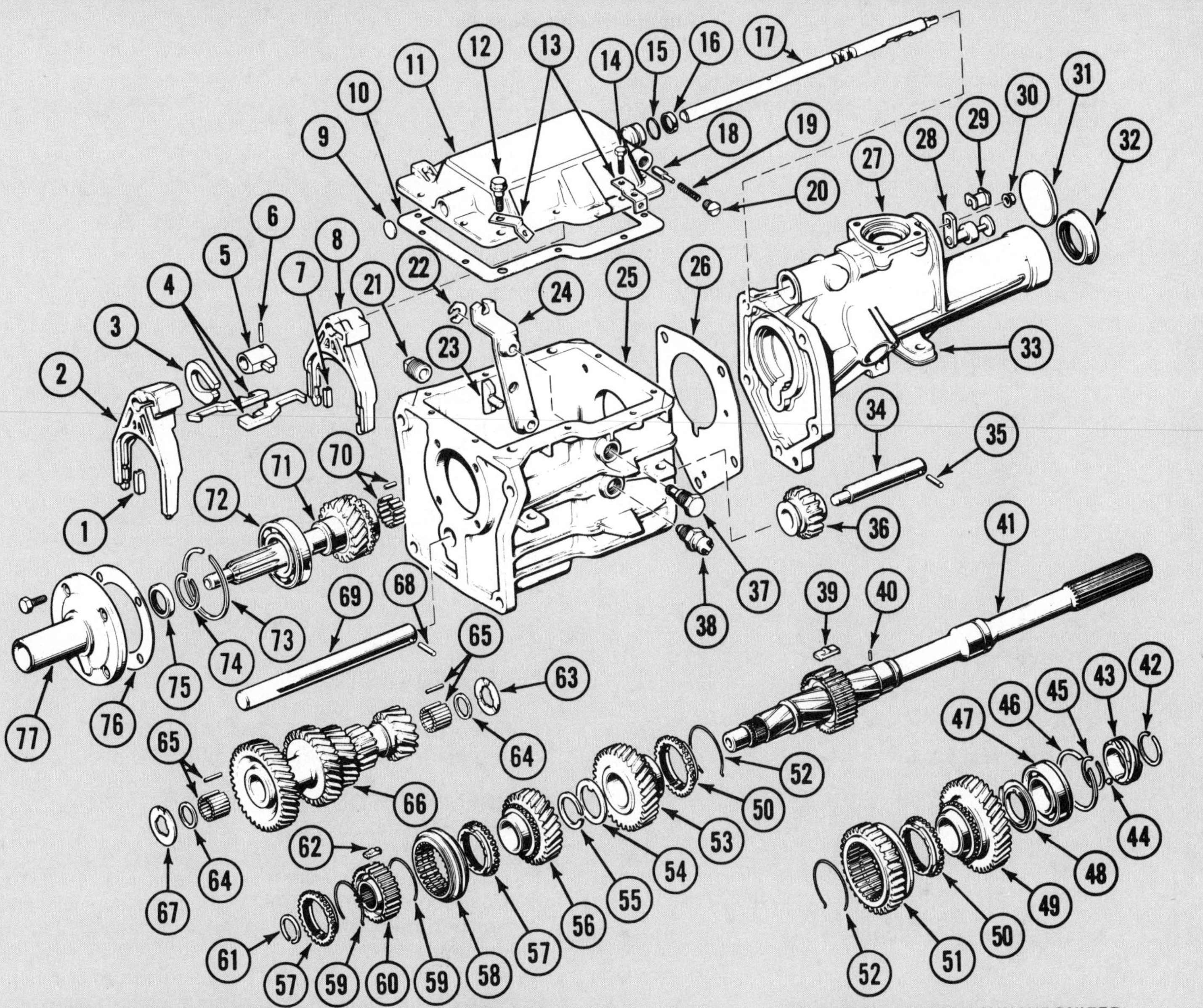

1. THIRD – FOURTH SHIFT FORK INSERT
2. THIRD – FOURTH SHIFT FORK
3. SELECTOR INTERLOCK PLATE
4. SELECTOR ARM PLATE (2)
5. SELECTOR ARM
6. SELECTOR ARM ROLL PIN
7. FIRST – SECOND SHIFT FORK INSERT
8. FIRST – SECOND SHIFT FORK
9. SHIFT RAIL PLUG
10. TRANSMISSION COVER GASKET
11. TRANSMISSION COVER
12. TRANSMISSION COVER DOWEL BOLT (2)
13. CLIP
14. TRANSMISSION COVER BOLT (8)
15. SHIFT RAIL O-RING SEAL
16. SHIFT RAIL OIL SEAL
17. SHIFT RAIL
18. DETENT PLUNGER
19. DETENT SPRING
20. DETENT PLUG
21. FILL PLUG
22. REVERSE LEVER PIVOT BOLT C-CLIP
23. REVERSE LEVER FORK
24. REVERSE LEVER
25. TRANSMISSION CASE
26. EXTENSION HOUSING GASKET
27. EXTENSION HOUSING
28. OFFSET LEVER
29. OFFSET LEVER INSERT
30. OFFSET LEVER RETAINING NUT

31. ACCESS PLUG
32. EXTENSION HOUSING OIL SEAL
33. EXTENSION HOUSING SUPPORT
34. REVERSE IDLER SHAFT
35. REVERSE IDLER SHAFT ROLL PIN
36. REVERSE IDLER GEAR
37. REVERSE LEVER PIVOT BOLT
38. BACKUP LAMP SWITCH
39. FIRST – SECOND SYNCHRONIZER INSERT (3)
40. FIRST GEAR ROLL PIN
41. OUTPUT SHAFT AND HUB ASSEMBLY
42. SPEEDOMETER GEAR SNAP RING
43. SPEEDOMETER GEAR
44. SPEEDOMETER GEAR DRIVE BALL
45. REAR BEARING RETAINING SNAP RING
46. REAR BEARING LOCATING SNAP RING
47. REAR BEARING
48. FIRST GEAR THRUST WASHER
49. FIRST GEAR
50. FIRST – SECOND SYNCHRONIZER BLOCKING RING (2)
51. FIRST – REVERSE SLEEVE AND GEAR
52. FIRST – SECOND SYNCHRONIZER INSERT SPRING (2)
53. SECOND GEAR
54. SECOND GEAR THRUST WASHER (TABBED)
55. SECOND GEAR SNAP RING
56. THIRD GEAR

57. THIRD – FOURTH SYNCHRONIZER BLOCKING RING (2)
58. THIRD – FOURTH SYNCHRONIZER SLEEVE
59. THIRD – FOURTH SYNCHRONIZER INSERT SPRING (2)
60. THIRD – FOURTH SYNCHRONIZER HUB
61. OUTPUT SHAFT SNAP RING
62. THIRD – FOURTH SYNCHRONIZER INSERT (3)
63. COUNTERSHAFT GEAR REAR THRUST WASHER (METAL)
64. COUNTERSHAFT NEEDLE BEARING RETAINER (2)
65. COUNTERSHAFT NEEDLE BEARING (50)
66. COUNTERSHAFT GEAR
67. COUNTERSHAFT GEAR FRONT THRUST WASHER (PLASTIC)
68. COUNTERSHAFT ROLL PIN
69. COUNTERSHAFT
70. CLUTCH SHAFT ROLLER BEARINGS (15)
71. CLUTCH SHAFT
72. FRONT BEARING
73. FRONT BEARING LOCATING SNAP RING
74. FRONT BEARING RETAINING SNAP RING
75. FRONT BEARING CAP OIL SEAL
76. FRONT BEARING CAP GASKET
77. FRONT BEARING CAP

Fig. 40-17. Exploded view of four speed manual transmission shows relative positions of all internal parts. (American Motors Corp.)

20. Remove dummy shaft from countershaft gear, bearing retainer washers, and needle bearings as shown in Fig. 40-20.

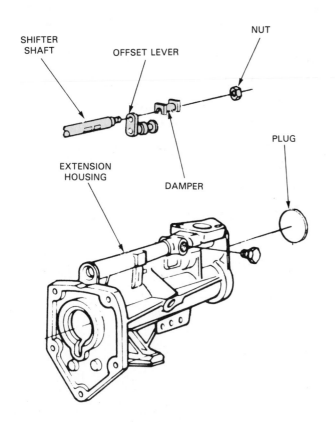

Fig. 40-18. Locations of access plug at rear of extension housing, shifter shaft, and offset lever assembly are shown. (Ford Motor Co.)

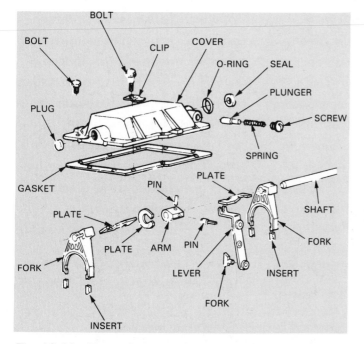

Fig. 40-19. Transmission cover assembly primarily includes cover, shifter shaft, shifter forks, selector arm lever, and plates. (Ford Motor Co.)

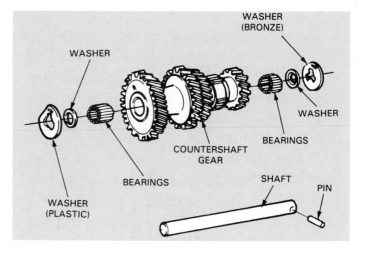

Fig. 40-20. Countershaft assembly requires use of a dummy shaft to hold roller bearings in place during installation. (Ford Motor Co.)

CLEAN AND CHECK

1. See instructions for CLEAN AND CHECK: THREE SPEED MANUAL TRANSMISSION.

REASSEMBLY: FOUR SPEED MANUAL TRANSMISSION

1. Install reverse idler gear and shaft, Fig. 40-17.
2. Coat countershaft washers with petroleum jelly and position them on countershaft gear assembled on dummy shaft.
3. Align countershaft gear bore and thrust washers with bore in case and install countershaft from rear of case.
4. Assemble gears, thrust washers, synchronizers and blocker rings on output shaft. See Fig. 40-17.
5. Position output shaft assembly in case through cover opening, then slide a dummy bearing on shaft to support assembly in case.
6. Assemble input shaft and position shaft and fourth gear blocker ring through front of case.
7. Install snap ring on input shaft bearing and press bearing into position on shaft.
8. Install a new bearing retaining snap ring on input shaft.
9. Install front bearing retainer and new gasket.
10. Remove dummy output shaft bearing. Install a new snap ring on output shaft bearing and press bearing on output shaft.
11. Install a new output shaft rear bearing retaining snap ring.
12. Install reverse idler gear lever assembly.
13. Install offset lever assembly, reverse lever, and retaining spring clip. See Fig. 40-18.
14. Assemble cover assembly, Fig. 40-19, and install new gasket and cover.
15. Install speedometer drive gear lock ball, drive gear, and snap ring.

16. Install extension housing and new gasket; drive oil seal in place, Fig. 40-21.
17. Install offset lever assembly on shift shaft and secure assembly with nut.
18. Insert gearshift lever in position and check all gear positions.
19. Install access plug into rear of extension housing, Fig. 40-18.

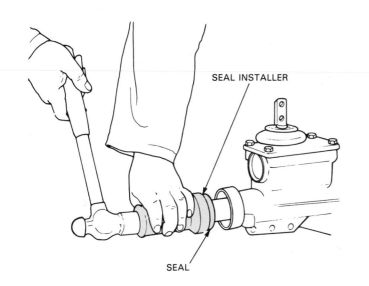

SEAL INSTALLER

SEAL

Fig. 40-21. A special driving tool is used to install seal in transmission extension housing. (Ford Motor Co.)

DISASSEMBLY: FIVE SPEED MANUAL TRANSMISSION

Study exploded view illustration of transmission being serviced, Fig. 40-22.
1. Punch out roll pin attaching offset lever to shift rail.
2. Remove extension housing and offset lever as an assembly, Fig. 40-23.
3. Remove detent ball and spring from offset lever and roll pin from extension housing.
4. Remove plastic funnel, Fig. 40-24, thrust bearing race, and thrust bearing from rear of countershaft.
5. Remove cover assembly, Fig. 40-25.
6. Drive roll pin from fifth gearshift fork.
7. Remove fifth synchronizer gear snap ring, shift fork, fifth gear synchronizer sleeve, blocking ring, and fifth speed gear from rear of countershaft. See Fig. 40-22.
8. Remove snap ring from fifth speed gear.
9. Punch mark front bearing cap and case for assembly reference.
10. Remove bearing cap, bearing race, and end play shims.
11. Rotate input (main drive) shaft until flat surface faces countershaft, then pull input shaft from case, Fig. 40-26.
12. Remove reverse lever C-clip and pivot bolt, then remove output shaft rear bearing race, tilt output

shaft assembly upward, and remove assembly from case. See Fig. 40-27.
13. Unhook overcenter link spring from front of case.
14. Rotate fifth gear-reverse shift rail to disengage rail from reverse lever assembly, then remove rail from rear of case.
15. Remove reverse lever and fork assembly from case.
16. Drive roll pin from forward end of reverse idler shaft, then remove shaft, O-ring, and gear from case. See Fig. 40-28.
17. Remove rear countershaft snap ring and spacer, then insert brass drift through front of case and use an arbor press to remove rear countershaft bearing.
18. Move countershaft assembly toward rear of case, tilt assembly upward, and remove it from case. Also remove countershaft front thrust washer and rear bearing spacer.
19. Use an arbor press to remove front bearing from case.
20. Disassemble output shaft, Fig. 40-22.
21. Remove bearing race, thrust bearing, and roller bearings from input shaft, and use arbor press to remove bearing from input shaft.
22. Disassemble cover. See Fig. 40-22.

CLEAN AND CHECK

1. See instructions for CLEAN AND CHECK: THREE SPEED MANUAL TRANSMISSION.

REASSEMBLY: FIVE SPEED MANUAL TRANSMISSION

1. Assemble transmission cover, Fig. 40-22.
2. Assemble input shaft, Fig. 40-29.
3. Assemble output shaft, Fig. 40-22.
4. Use arbor press to install front countershaft bearing flush with front facing of case.
5. Coat countershaft thrust washer with petroleum jelly and install washer so tab engages depression in case.
6. Install countershaft in front bearing bore.
7. Install countershaft rear bearing spacer. Coat rear bearing with petroleum jelly and use a driving sleeve and tool to install bearing.
8. Position reverse idler in case with shift lever groove facing rear and install shaft from rear of case. Install roll pin in idler shaft, Fig. 40-28.
9. Install assembled output shaft, Fig. 40-27, and install rear output shaft bearing in case.
10. Install assembled input shaft in case, Fig. 40-26, and engage it in third-fourth synchronizer sleeve and blocker ring.
11. Install front bearing race in front bearing cap (no shims).
12. Temporarily install front bearing cap.
13. Install fifth speed-reverse lever, pivot bolt, and retaining clip, making sure that reverse lever fork engages reverse idler gear.
14. Install countershaft rear bearing spacer and retaining snap ring.
15. Install fifth speed gear on countershaft.
16. Install fifth speed-reverse rail in rear of case. Rotate

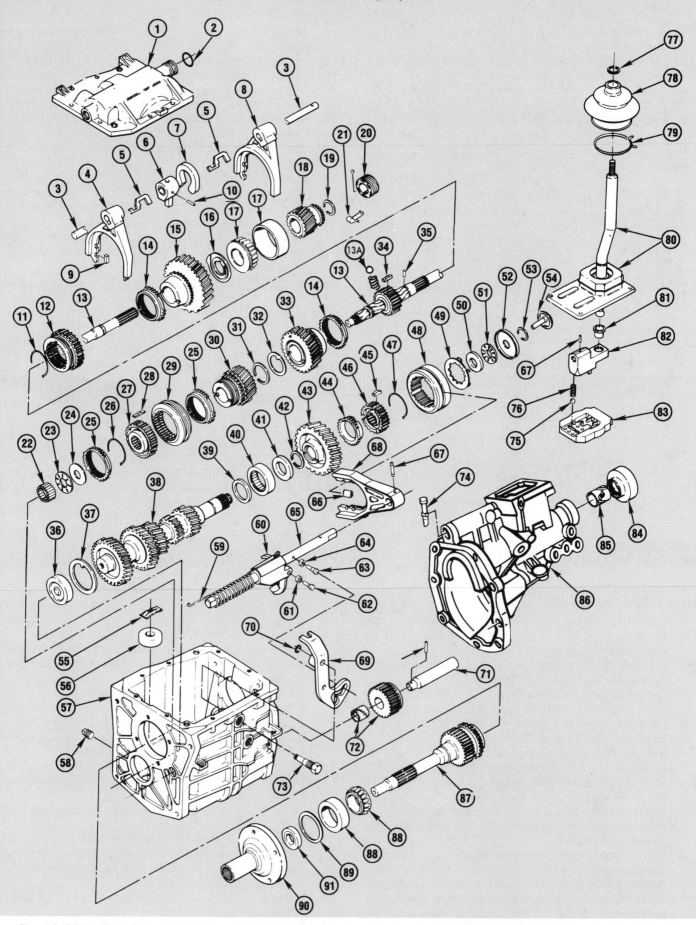

Fig. 40-22A. Exploded view locates and identifies all components and makeup of a typical five speed manual overdrive transmission. (Chevrolet Motor Div., General Motors Corp.)

1. COVER, Trans
2. SEAL, "O" Ring, Cvr to Ext.
3. SHAFT, Shift
4. FORK, 3rd & 4th Shift
5. PLATE, Shift Fork
6. ARM, Control Selector
7. PLATE, Gear Sel Intlk
8. FORK, 1st & 2nd Shift
9. INSERT, Shift Fork
10. PIN, Roll
11. SPRING, Syn
12. GEAR, Rev Sldg
13. SHAFT, Output, W/1 & 2 Syn
13A. SPRING/BALL, Anti-Rattle
14. RING, 1 & 2 Syn Blkg
15. GEAR, 1st Speed
16. WASHER, 1st Spd Gr Thrust
17. BEARING, Rear
18. GEAR, 5th Spd Drvn
19. RING, Snap
20. GEAR, Speedo Dr
21. CLIP, Speedo Dr Gr
22. BEARING, Main Shf Rir
23. BEARING, Main Dr Gr Thr Ndl
24. RACE, Main Dr Gr Ghr Brg
25. RING, 3 & 4 Syn
26. SPRING, 3 & 4 Syn
27. HUB, 3 & 4 Syn
28. KEY, 3 & 4 Syn
29. SLEEVE, 3 & 4 Syn
30. GEAR, 3rd Speed

31. RING, Snap
32. WASHER, 2nd Spd Gr Thr
33. GEAR, 2nd Speed
34. KEY, 1 & 2 Syn
35. PIN, 1st Spd Gr Thr Wa Ret
36. BEARING, Cntr Gr Frt
37. WASHER, Cntr Gr Frt Thr
38. GEAR, Counter
39. SPACER, Counter Gr Brg Frt
40. BEARING, Cntr Gr Rr
41. SPACER, Counter Gr Brg Rr
42. RING, Snap
43. GEAR, 5th Spd Drive
44. RING, 5th Syn
45. KEY, 5th Syn
46. HUB, 5th Syn
47. SPRING, 5th Syn
48. SLEEVE, 5th Syn
49. RETAINER, 5th Syn Key
50. RACE, 5th Syn Thr Brg Frt
51. BEARING, 5th Syn Ndl Thr
52. RACE, 5th Syn Thr Brg Rr
53. RING, Snap
54. FUNNEL, Trans Oiling
55. NUT, Magnet
56. MAGNET
57. CASE, Trans
58. PLUG, Fill & Drain
59. SPRING, Rev Lock
60. FORK, Rev Shift
61. ROLLER, Fork

62. PIN, Rev Fork
63. PIN, Shift Rail
64. ROLLER, Rail pin
65. RAIL, 5th & Rev Shft
66. INSERT, Shift Fork
67. PIN, Roll
68. FORK, 5th Shift
69. LEVER, 5th & Rev Relay
70. RING, Rev. Relay Lever Ret
71. SHAFT, Rev Idler Gr
72. GEAR, Rev Idler (Incl Bshg)
73. PIN, 5th Spd Shft Lvr Piv
74. VENTILATOR, Ext
75. BALL, Steel
76. SPRING, Detent
77. RETAINER, Cont Lvr Boot
78. BOOT, Cont Lvr
79. RETAINER, Cont Lvr Boot Lwr
80. CONTROL, Trans Lvr & Hsg
81. SLEEVE, Shft Lvr Dmpr
82. LEVER, Offset Shift
83. PLATE, Detent & Guide
84. SEAL, Ext Rr Oil
85. BUSHING, Extension Housing
86. HOUSING, Extension
87. GEAR, Main Drive
88. BEARING, Front
89. SHIM, Brg Adj
90. RETAINER, Drive Gr Brg
91. SEAL, Drive Gr Brg Oil

Fig. 40-22B. Check numbered components in Fig. 40-22A with numbers and component names in this list.

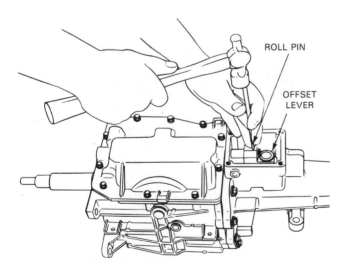

Fig. 40-23. After punching out roll pin holding offset lever to shift rail, extension housing and offset lever can be removed as a unit. (Chevrolet Motor Div., General Motors Corp.)

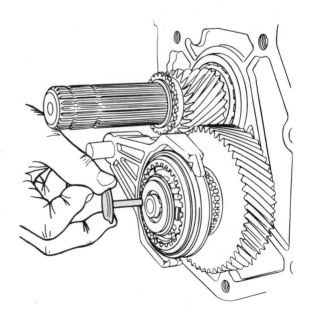

Fig. 40-24. Plastic funnel, thrust bearing, and thrust bearing race slide off back end of countershaft. (Chevrolet Motor Div., General Motors Corp.)

rail while installing it in fifth speed-reverse lever. Connect spring to front of case.

17. Position fifth gear shift fork on fifth gear synchronizer assembly. Install synchronizer on countershaft and place shift fork on shift rail, Fig. 40-30. Align roll pin holes in fork and rail, then install pin.

18. Install thrust race against fifth speed synchronizer hub and install snap ring. Install thrust bearing against race on countershaft. Coat bearing and race

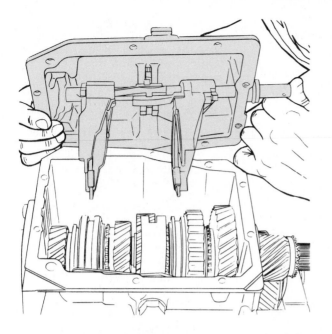

Fig. 40-25. With transmission cover attaching bolts removed, cover and shifter fork assembly may be lifted from case. (Chevrolet Motor Div., General Motors Corp.)

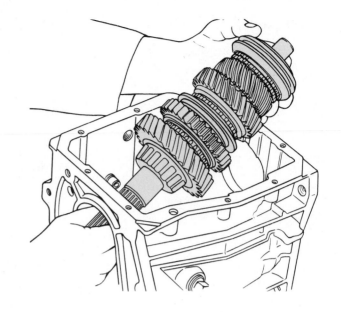

Fig. 40-27. With output shaft rear bearing race removed, output shaft assembly can be tilted up and removed from case. (Chevrolet Motor Div., General Motors Corp.)

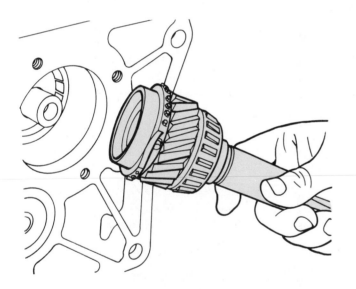

Fig. 40-26. With flat surface of input shaft (main drive) gear facing countershaft, input shaft can be pulled from front of transmission case. (Chevrolet Motor Div., General Motors Corp.)

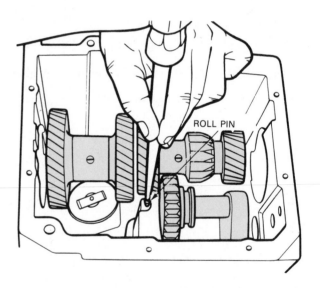

Fig. 40-28. After punching out roll pin from reverse idler shaft, shaft assembly can be lifted from case.

with petroleum jelly.

19. Install lipped thrust race over needle thrust bearing and insert plastic funnel in hole in end of countershaft gear, Fig. 40-24.

20. Temporarily install extension housing. Use dial indicator to measure output shaft end play. Install shim pack to establish correct output shaft bearing preload.

21. Remove front bearing cap and front bearing race. Install shims to obtain desired bearing preload and

reinstall bearing race. Install front bearing cap.

22. Remove extension housing.

23. Move shift forks on assembled transmission cover and synchronizer sleeves in transmission to Neutral position. Install cover, Fig. 40-25.

24. Install extension housing over output shaft and shift rail to where it just enters shift cover opening.

25. Install detent spring into offset lever and steel ball in neutral guide plate detent. Position offset lever on steel ball, Fig. 40-31, apply pressure on lever, and install extension housing.

26. Align and install roll pin in offset lever and shift rail.

27. Check transmission operation in all gears.

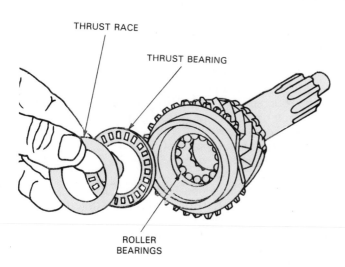

Fig. 40-29. Input shaft reassembly requires use of petroleum jelly to hold roller bearings in shaft cavity. Thrust bearing and race are installed and input shaft is pushed into place in front of case. (Chevrolet Motor Div., General Motors Corp.)

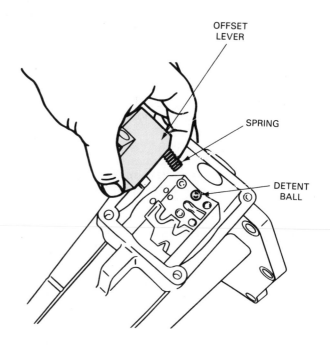

Fig. 40-31. While holding offset lever and spring in position over detent ball, extension housing can be installed. (Chevrolet Motor Div., General Motors Corp.)

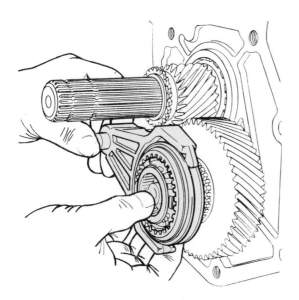

Fig. 40-30. Fifth gear synchronizer assembly is placed on shift fork, then installed on countershaft with fork installed on shift rail. (Chevrolet Motor Div., General Motors Corp.)

REINSTALLATION OF TRANSMISSION IN CAR

1. Remove excess oil from pilot bushing lubricating wick, then install it in bushing.
2. Install clutch release bearing on fork.
3. Place transmission in gear, lift and align it with hub hole in clutch disc.
4. Slide transmission forward while slowly rotating output shaft to align splines in transmission input shaft with splines in clutch disc hub.
5. When splines align, slide transmission into place against clutch housing.
6. Install transmission-to-clutch housing attaching

bolts and lock washers; tighten to manufacturer's torque specification.
7. Install exhaust pipe to manifold and converter bracket to transmission.
8. Connect clutch cable and adjust clutch, if necessary, to provide correct pedal free play.
9. Position rear crossmember to frame and loosely install attaching bolts.
10. Lower jack to seat transmission mount on crossmember; install and tighten attaching bolts or nuts to correct torque specification.
11. Torque-tighten crossmember-to-frame attaching bolts.
12. Install speedometer cable in transmission extension housing connect backup lamp switch.
13. Install drive shaft, aligning marks on drive shaft and rear axle yoke or flange to insure proper reassembly. See Fig. 40-5.
14. On steering column shift transmissions, connect shift rods to shift levers.
15. Refill transmission with recommended lubricant, Fig. 40-2.
16. Lower vehicle to floor.
17. On floor-mounted shift transmissions, install gearshift lever. Make sure fork is properly engaged in grooves, then bolt gearshift lever assembly to extension housing.
18. Install gearshift lever bezel and boot; tighten attaching screws.
19. Test gearshift for smooth and free crossover in Neutral and satisfactory operation through complete range, Fig. 40-3. Recheck clutch pedal free play; make necessary final adjustments.
20. Road test car and check transmission performance in all gears.

Chapter 40—REVIEW QUESTIONS

Write your answers on a separate sheet of paper. Do not write in this book.

Name six manual transmission maintenance routines:

1. Make periodic _____ checks.
2. Make an external inspection of transmission for possible _____.
3. Test gearshift operation in all _____.
4. Check clutch pedal _____.
5. Examine condition of transmission _____.
6. Test _____ of transmission-to-clutch housing attaching bolts.
7. Modern manual transmissions have _____ gears that are in constant mesh in all forward speeds.
   a. Worm.
   b. Spur.
   c. Helical.
   d. Planetary.
8. Fluid level should be even with or just below lower edge of _____ in side of transmission case.
9. Why should you place alignment marks on drive shaft and rear axle flange before removing drive shaft?
10. A car equipped with a manual transmission is noisy in Neutral. Mechanic A says the noise could be caused by worn or broken input shaft gear. Mechanic B says it could be caused by a worn or broken output shaft bearing. Who is right?
    a. Mechanic A.
    b. Mechanic B.
    c. Both mechanic A and B.
    d. Neither mechanic A nor B.
11. What is the principal cause for a manual transmission slipping out of gear?
12. What is probable cause if manual transmission gears clash when shifting?
13. When removing a manual transmission from a car, pull transmission straight back and on the level to avoid damaging input shaft, pilot bushing, or _____.
14. If an aluminum transmission case has nicks on the front face, smooth out the nicks with a _____ (fine stone/fine file).
15. Why is a dummy countershaft used when removing or reinstalling the countershaft assembly?
16. When installing roller bearings in reverse idler gear, use _____ to hold bearings in place.
17. With input shaft and bearing in place in front of three speed transmission case, install thickest snap ring that will fit into groove. True or False?
18. When reinstalling cap (front bearing retainer) on front face of transmission, align cap with _____ in case.
19. In final step of reassembly of three speed manual transmission, install case cover and gasket. Be sure _____ is open.
20. In four speed manual transmission disassembly, removing access plug from extension housing permits access to:
    a. Offset lever assembly.
    b. Rear seal.
    c. Shifter lever.
    d. Reverse idler gear shaft.
21. Which gear assembly is reinstalled first in reassembly of a four speed manual transmission?
    a. Input shaft main drive gear.
    b. Fourth speed gear.
    c. Countergear.
    d. Reverse idler gear.
22. When installing output shaft assembly in transmission case, a dummy bearing is installed on output shaft to _____ assembly in case.
23. Speedometer drive gear assembly includes drive gear lock ball, drive gear, and _____.
    a. Roll pin.
    b. Nylon bushing.
    c. Snap ring.
    d. Lock nut.
24. When removing front bearing cap from a five speed transmission, also remove bearing race and _____ shims.
25. To remove input shaft from transmission case, rotate shaft until _____ faces countershaft, then pull shaft from case.
    a. Notch.
    b. Flat surface.
    c. Cutaway.
    d. Alignment mark.
26. A dial indicator is used to measure output shaft end play. True or False?
27. When installing assembled transmission cover, shift forks should be placed in _____ position.
    a. Neutral.
    b. First gear.
    c. Fifth gear.
    d. Reverse.
28. When reinstalling transmission in vehicle, place transmission in Neutral, lift and align it with hub hole in clutch disc. True or False?
29. After transmission is installed and gearshift lever assembly is bolted in place, test gearshift for _____ crossover in Neutral.
30. Also, check for satisfactory _____ throughout complete range.

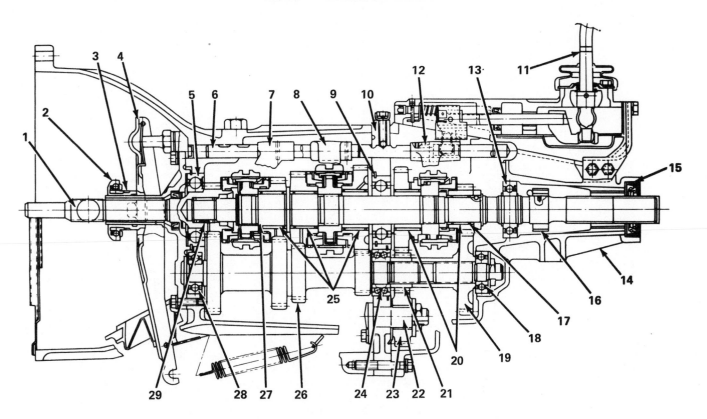

Five speed manual transmission uses blocker ring synchronizers with all forward gears. Reverse gear is sliding mesh type. Components include: 1—Drive gear. 2—Release bearing. 3—Bearing retainer. 4-Shift fork. 5—Drive gear bearing. 6—Shifter shaft. 7—Third and fourth shift fork. 8—First and second shift fork. 9—Mainshaft bearing. 10—Center support. 11—Shift lever. 12—Fifth and reverse shift fork. 13—Mainshaft rear bearing. 14—Extension housing. 15—Rear seal. 16—Speedometer drive gear. 17—Fifth gear assembly. 18—Counter gear rear bearing. 19—Fifth counter gear. 20—Needle bearing. 21—Reverse counter gear. 22—Reverse idler shaft. 23—Reverse idler gear. 24—Counter gear bearing. 25—Needle bearings. 26—Counter gear. 27—Mainshaft. 28—Counter gear front bea ng. 29—Needle bearing.   (Chevrolet Motor Div., General Motors Corp.)

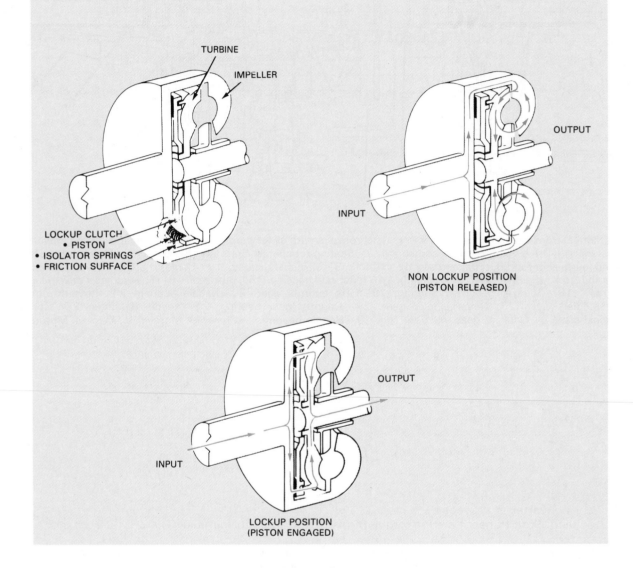

TURBINE

IMPELLER

OUTPUT

INPUT

LOCKUP CLUTCH
• PISTON
• ISOLATOR SPRINGS
• FRICTION SURFACE

NON LOCKUP POSITION
(PISTON RELEASED)

OUTPUT

INPUT

LOCKUP POSITION
(PISTON ENGAGED)

Schematic shows elements of Chrysler's electronically controlled lockup torque converter and power flow when hydraulically operated clutch is in released and engaged positions.   (Chrysler Corp.)

Chapter 41

AUTOMATIC TRANSMISSIONS PRINCIPLES OF OPERATION

After studying this chapter, you will be able to:
- State the primary differences between a fluid coupling and a torque converter.
- Explain how a torque converter multiplies engine torque.
- Tell how a converter clutch locks the turbine to the impeller in direct drive.
- Discuss the function of clutches and bands in automatic transmission operation.
- Detail the principles of planetary gearset operation.
- Trace power flow in the various modes of operation in a three speed automatic transmission.
- Point out the path of power flow in the overdrive mode of a four speed automatic transmission.

Automatic transmissions are installed in over 85 percent of U.S. cars coming off the assembly lines. Car buyers want the comfort and convenience afforded by these labor-saving, automatically controlled, power transfer devices.

FLUID COUPLINGS

Basic, two element fluid couplings were once widely used with semiautomatic and automatic transmissions. Today's torque converter is a direct decendent of the basic fluid coupling. Both transmit engine torque (turning or twisting force) to the gear train of the transmission. The difference is: the TORQUE CONVERTER multiplies that turning power; the FLUID COUPLING does not.

A typical fluid coupling has two facing halves called "torus members." Each member is divided into many sections by designed arrangement of inner and outer shells and vanes. The torus members are splined to separate shafts and operate in a fluid-filled housing, Fig. 41-1. The drive side of the fluid coupling is attached to the engine. The driven side connects to the drive shaft of the vehicle.

In operation, a fluid coupling acts like an automatic clutch. It "slips" at idle speed; "holds" to transmit power as engine speed is increased. Power is transmit-

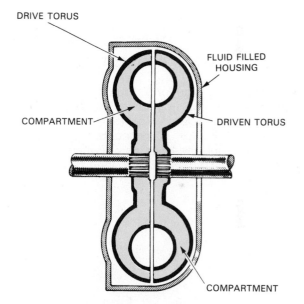

Fig. 41-1. A typical fluid coupling has two torus members. Drive torus is connected to engine crankshaft. Driven torus transmits engine torque to transmission input shaft.

ted through the fluid. There is no mechanical connection between the engine and the drive shaft.

The automatic transmission fluid is circulated by pump pressure to the fluid coupling as well as to other parts of the automatic transmission. Rotation of the drive torus causes the fluid within it to be forced radially outward against vanes of the driven torus. See Fig. 41-2. When the engine runs fast enough, the increased force of the fluid being thrown by the drive torus causes the driven torus to rotate in the same direction.

In addition to the use of fluid couplings in conjunction with automatic transmissions, a fluid coupling was used in the past with a semiautomatic sliding gear transmission. In this application, the fluid coupling served to reduce slippage and wear of the dry clutch disc and eased the shifting of gears.

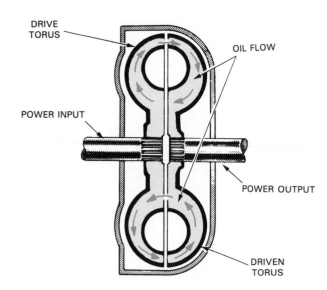

Fig. 41-2. Rotation of drive torus forces fluid against vanes of driven torus, which transmits engine torque to transmission gear train.

TORQUE CONVERTERS

Typically, the conventional torque converter consists of a front cover (housing), impeller (pump), turbine, stator, and stator overrunning (one-way) clutch, Fig. 41-3. The IMPELLER is connected to the engine crankshaft through the front cover (which is welded to the impeller). The TURBINE is splined to the transmission input shaft.

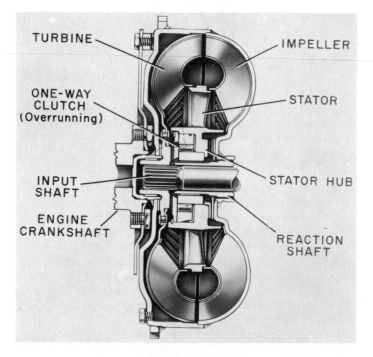

Fig. 41-3. Cross-sectional view of a typical torque converter shows attachment of converter to engine crankshaft and relationship of three major elements: impeller (pump), turbine, and stator.

The STATOR is splined to a reaction shaft or to the stationary hub shaft of the OVERRUNNING CLUTCH. See Figs. 41-3 and 41-4.

OPERATING PRINCIPLES

Basically, all torque converters utilize the rotating elements in a fluid-filled housing to multiply engine torque. All use the engine to drive the impeller which, in turn, impels the fluid against the vanes of the turbine. The turbine is connected through transmission gears to the drive shaft of the automobile. The third (middle) element—the stator—serves to redirect oil flow from the turbine against the impeller vanes to boost impeller action and multiply engine torque. See Fig. 41-4.

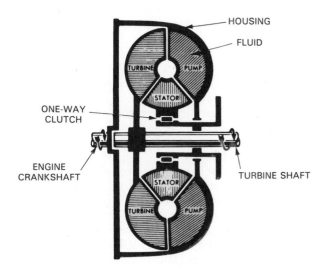
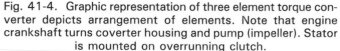

Fig. 41-4. Graphic representation of three element torque converter depicts arrangement of elements. Note that engine crankshaft turns coverter housing and pump (impeller). Stator is mounted on overrunning clutch.

This action of centrifugal force within the torque converter sets up a vortex flow of oil, while the angle of the vanes tends to set up a rotary flow, Fig. 41-5. The combined flow results in a corkscrew action, which sets up a pattern something like a coil spring with the ends connected. See Fig. 41-6.

This whirling ring of oil emerges from the twisting passages of the turbine in a direction opposite to impeller rotation. If directed into the impeller at this time, it would cause a loss of power. Instead, it is directed against the curved face of the stator blades, Fig. 41-7. The impact of the oil flow creates reaction torque since the stator is held stationary by the overrunning clutch. This multiplies engine torque at variable ratios up to at least 2:1 when the turbine is in start-up stall (not rotating).

When enough torque is developed by the impeller, the turbine begins to rotate, along with the transmission input shaft. As turbine speed approaches impeller speed, torque multiplication lessens, since the angle of fluid flow against the face of the stator blades becomes less efficient. Then, just before turbine speed equals impeller

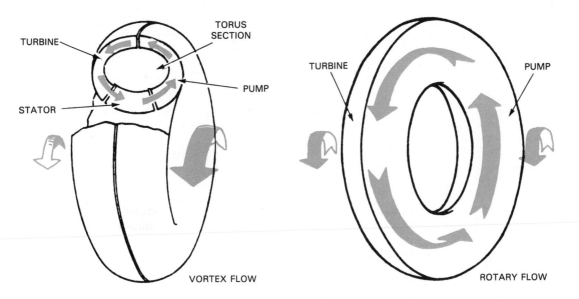

Fig. 41-5. When torque converter is in operation, there are two types of oil circulation within unit: vortex flow and rotary flow.

speed, the fluid strikes the *back face* of the stator blades, which releases the overrunning clutch and permits the three elements to rotate together as a fluid coupling. See Fig. 41-8 for details.

VARIABLE PITCH STATOR

In most torque converters, the stator blades are "fixed" at a predetermined angle. In special designs, a VARIABLE PITCH STATOR assembly is used. For normal operation in drive range, the stator blades are automatically set at a low angle. For increased acceleration, greater torque is obtained by setting the stator blades at a high angle.

The angle of the variable pitch stator blades usually is controlled by a switch mounted on the throttle linkage, a stator solenoid, and a stator valve. At engine idle speed, the switch activates the solenoid, which exhausts line pressure and the stator valve shifts the blade angle from low to high. At light or medium throttle, the solenoid is not activated and line pressure on the stator valve puts

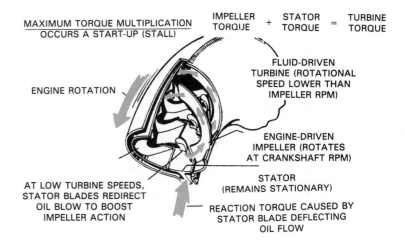

Fig. 41-7. Torque converter cutaway view pictures impeller, turbine, and stator in operation at point of start-up stall. Stator is stationary and torque multiplication is at maximum.

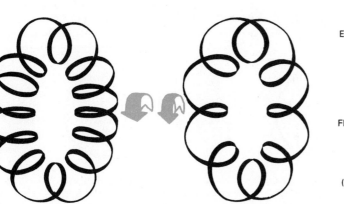

Fig. 41-6. Vortex flow and rotary flow within torque converter combine to produce a spiral action or "coil spring" effect.

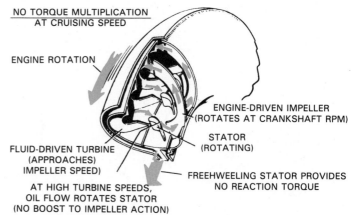

Fig. 41-8. In this operation, car is at cruising speed and overrunning clutch permits stator to free wheel and rotate with impeller and turbine.

477

the blades at a low angle. At about 3/4 throttle opening or under heavy acceleration, the solenoid again exhausts line pressure and the stator valve moves the stator blades to the high angle for maximum performance.

LOCKUP TORQUE CONVERTER

In a conventional torque converter, there is always some slippage between the impeller and turbine in direct drive. Since the impeller is connected to the engine crankshaft, it always rotates at engine speed. As engine speed increases, the turbine gradually builds up rotational speed as oil flow between the elements intensifies. However, the turbine only *approaches* impeller speed, Fig. 41-8. It never quite catches up, so several percentage points of efficiency are lost to slippage.

To overcome this slippage, LOCKUP TORQUE CONVERTERS were introduced. These converters are equipped with an internal locking mechanism called a ''converter clutch'' that locks the turbine to the impeller in direct drive. See Fig. 41-9.

Various types of lockup mechanism are used. One application consists of a sliding clutch piston, torsion springs, and clutch friction material, Fig. 41-10. The friction material is attached to the front cover of the converter. The clutch piston is mounted on the turbine. The torsion springs are located on the forward side of the turbine where they absorb engine power pulses and shock loads that occur during lockup.

HOW LOCKUP OCCURS

When the vehicle reaches approximately 40 mph, transmission fluid is channeled through the transmission input shaft into the area between the clutch piston and the turbine. See Fig. 41-10. This fluid under pressure forces the clutch piston against the front cover friction

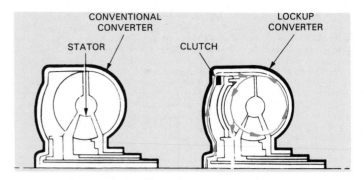

Fig. 41-9. Cross-sectional views compare conventional torque converter to lockup unit. Clutch mechanism locks turbine to impeller in direct drive at predetermined car speed. (American Motors Corp.)

material, locking the turbine to the impeller. When vehicle speed drops below 40 mph or the transmission shifts out of direct drive, fluid pressure is released and the clutch piston retracts. The torque converter returns to conventional operation.

The lockup torque converter has several advantages over the conventional converter:
1. Greater efficiency in direct drive.
2. Reduced fluid operating temperatures.
3. Improved fuel economy for vehicles so equipped.

AUTOMATIC TRANSMISSION OPERATION

Design and construction differs between makes, but all modern automatic transmissions—with rare exceptions—make use of the following key elements:
1. A fluid coupling called a ''torque converter'' that connects the transmission to the engine and serves to

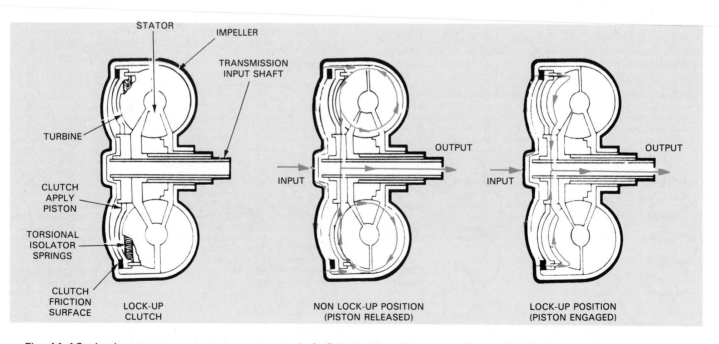

Fig. 41-10. Lockup torque converter components: Left. Relationship of elements. Center. Non-lockup position (piston released). Right. Lockup position (piston engaged). Arrows denote direction of power flow. (American Motors Corp.)

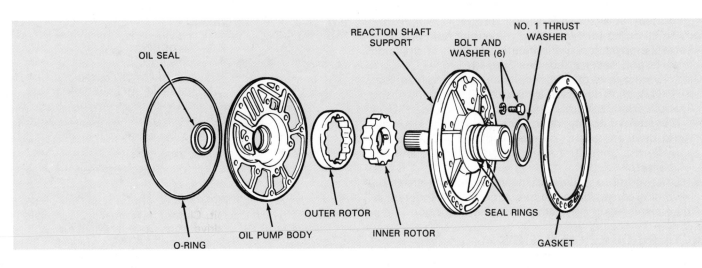

Fig. 41-11. Exploded view of automatic transmission rotor type oil pump shows assembly/disassembly sequence. Gear type and vane type oil pumps are also used. (American Motors Corp.)

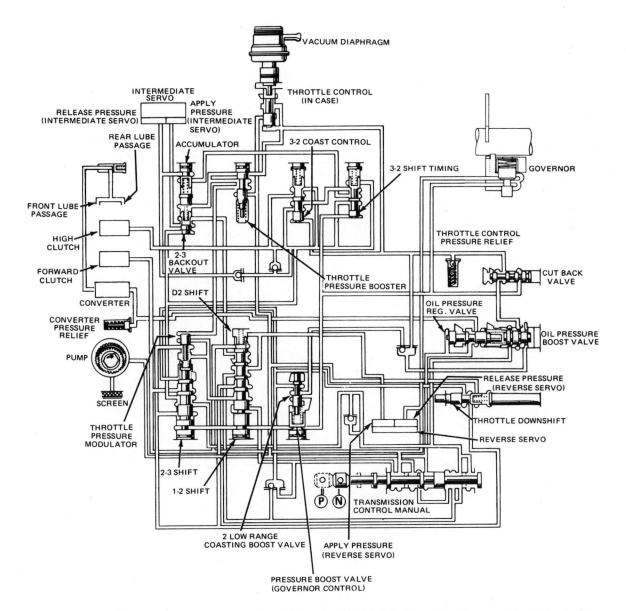

Fig. 41-12. Diagram details hydraulic control system of Ford C-3 three speed automatic transmission. Note oil pump at left; oil pressure regulator at right; manual control valve at lower right. (Ford Motor Co.)

multiply and transmit engine torque.

2. An oil pump (or two) which develops fluid pressure for the operation and lubrication of the transmission parts and assemblies. See Fig. 41-11.

3. A system of hydraulic circuits and spool valves, Fig. 41-12, that directs the flow of ATF to control the application of bands and clutches.

4. A system of holding devices called "bands" and driving devices called "clutches" that are used selectively to control the operation of the planetary gearsets.

5. One—or more—planetary gearsets which receive incoming torque from the torque converter and multiply it still further by means of gear reduction.

ACTIONS OF KEY ELEMENTS

TORQUE CONVERTER construction and principles of operation have been described and explained. See Fig. 41-3. Basically, a torque converter multiplies and transmits engine torque to the input shaft and planetary gearsets of the automatic transmission.

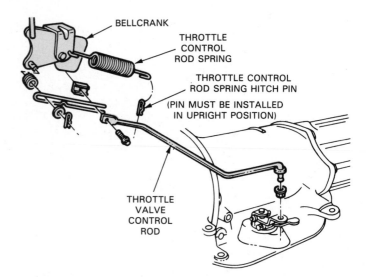

Fig. 41-13. Drawing shows typical throttle rod arrangement and points of adjustment on AMC cars equipped with six cylinder engine and automatic transmission. (American Motors Corp.)

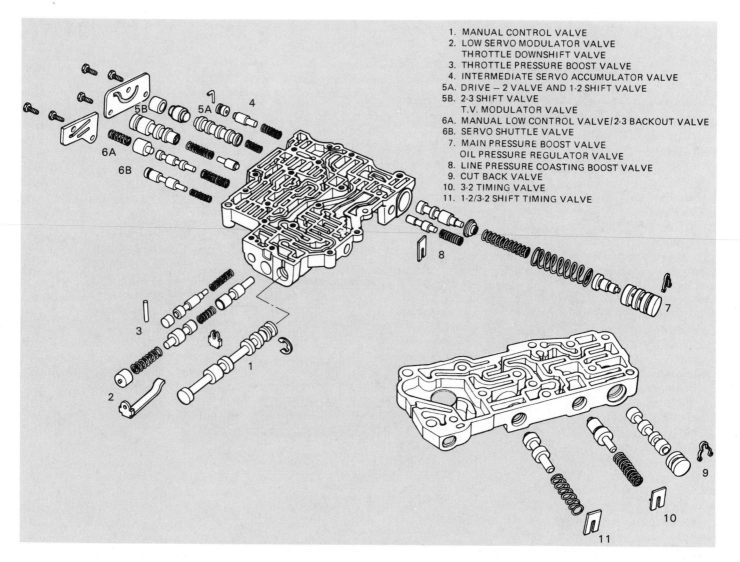

1. MANUAL CONTROL VALVE
2. LOW SERVO MODULATOR VALVE
   THROTTLE DOWNSHIFT VALVE
3. THROTTLE PRESSURE BOOST VALVE
4. INTERMEDIATE SERVO ACCUMULATOR VALVE
5A. DRIVE — 2 VALVE AND 1-2 SHIFT VALVE
5B. 2-3 SHIFT VALVE
   T.V. MODULATOR VALVE
6A. MANUAL LOW CONTROL VALVE/2-3 BACKOUT VALVE
6B. SERVO SHUTTLE VALVE
7. MAIN PRESSURE BOOST VALVE
   OIL PRESSURE REGULATOR VALVE
8. LINE PRESSURE COASTING BOOST VALVE
9. CUT BACK VALVE
10. 3-2 TIMING VALVE
11. 1-2/3-2 SHIFT TIMING VALVE

Fig. 41-14. Valve body on Ford C-3 automatic transmission contains fluid passages and valves that control flow of fluid and regulate pressure. (Ford Motor Co.)

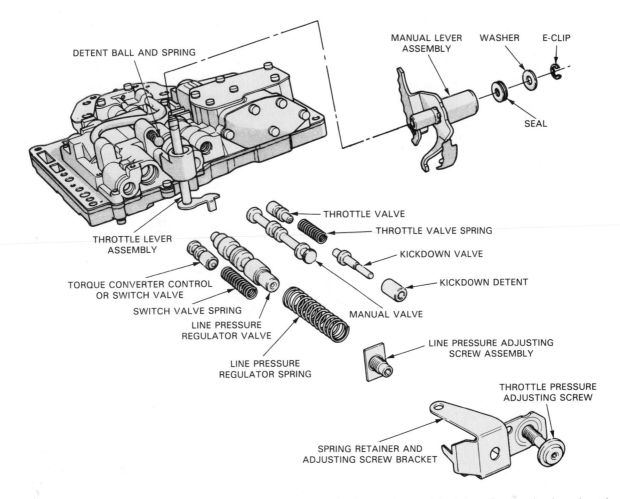

Fig. 41-15. Exploded view of part of control valve body reveals shape, size, and location of manual valve, throttle valve, kickdown valve, and line pressure regulator valve. (American Motors Corp.)

The OIL PUMP, Fig. 41-11, usually is located immediately behind the torque converter. It is driven by the converter and serves as the pressure supply system for the automatic transmission. The pump circulates automatic transmission fluid to the torque converter and provides working oil pressure needed to operate valves, valve controls, and friction elements.

The PRESSURE REGULATOR VALVE, Fig. 41-12, controls the output of the oil pump. It maintains line pressure at a psi (pounds per square inch) value according to the degree of throttle opening. Its output pressure exceeds predetermined psi, the regulator valve opens and bypasses oil back to the oil sump in the transmission. In that way, main line oil pressure is constantly maintained.

VALVES and VALVE CONTROLS range from simple mechanical linkage, Fig. 41-13, to a complicated control valve body assembly, Fig. 41-14. The control valves are needed to direct the flow of ATF, to turn the flow off and on, and to regulate pressure. This built-in hydraulic control system provides a combination of balanced pressures predicated on car speed, engine speed, and the demands of the driver.

A MANUAL CONTROL VALVE, Figs. 41-12 and 41-14, establishes the particular range of transmission operation selected by the driver. For example, when the manual valve is opened, fluid pressure actuates the low band servo and the vehicle will move forward in low gear.

SHIFT VALVES automatically permit 1-2 or 2-1 shifts, 2-3 or 3-2 shifts, etc. depending on vehicle operation. See Fig. 41-15.

The GOVERNOR VALVE ASSEMBLY is connected to the output shaft of the transmission, it controls line pressure and shift speeds. Governor pressure is almost in direct proportion to vehicle speed.

At a predetermined speed, the governor valve will open and fluid under pressure will travel to the shift valve. At a certain level of pressure, the tension of the shift valve spring will be overcome, the shift valve will open, and fluid will flow to a multiple disc clutch.

In any case, the various valves and valve controls in automatic transmissions operate independently or in combination to compensate for changes in car speed, load, and the demands of the driver.

The THROTTLE VALVE usually is indirectly connected to the accelerator pedal through linkage (TV rod), so that pressure on the pedal will automatically operate the valve. Movement of the throttle valve, in turn, regulates pressure to the transmission to control upshift, downshift, and "lockup" speeds.

A VACUUM MODULATOR VALVE, rather than a TV rod, is used on some automatic transmissions to con-

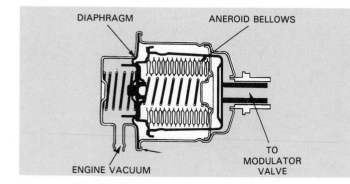

Fig. 41-16. Vacuum modulator is a pressure regulating device operated by engine vacuum and spring action. (Cadillac Motor Car Div., General Motors Corp.)

trol the throttle valve, Fig. 41-12. The vacuum modulator valve, Fig. 41-16, usually is attached to the outside of the transmission case and is connected to the engine intake manifold. As the vacuum modulator diaphragm reacts to changes in engine vacuum, the modulator constantly alters throttle valve pressure to meet engine needs.

For example, the vacuum modulator increases TV pressure at full throttle or under heavy load (low vacuum) to provide more "holding" power for the clutches. Under light load (high vacuum), the vacuum modulator reduces TV pressure to promote smooth shifts.

A DETENT VALVE or KICKDOWN VALVE—sometimes part of the throttle valve—allows a forced downshift from 3 to 2 or 2 to 1 (breakaway), depending on vehicle speed. The detent valve is actuated by pressing the accelerator to near wide open throttle.

The THROTTLE PRESSURE PLUG, Fig. 41-15, on certain automatic transmissions, provides a 3 to 2 downshift at various vehicle speeds. It is used in conjunction with the limit valve, which determines the maximum speed at which a part throttle 3 to 2 kickdown can be made.

The SHUTTLE VALVE provides for fast release of the kickdown band. It allows smooth clutch engagement when the driver lightly lifts his foot from the accelerator pedal to permit a 2 to 3 shift. The shuttle valve also regulates application of the kickdown servo and band for making 3 to 2 kickdowns.

The LOCKUP VALVE, Fig. 41-17, automatically applies the converter clutch if the vehicle speed is above a predetermined mph (30-40) in direct drive.

The FAIL-SAFE VALVE, on TorqueFlite 904 and AMC 998 transmissions, restricts oil flow to the converter clutch if the front clutch pressure drops. The fail-safe valve permits lockup only in third gear and provides for a quick release of the converter clutch during kickdown. See Fig. 41-17.

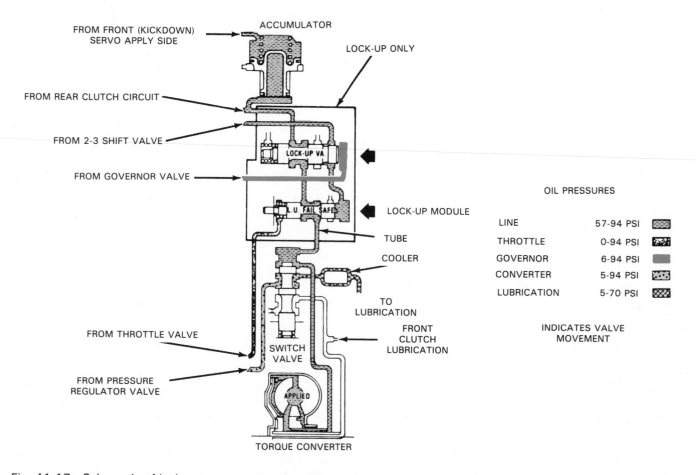

Fig. 41-17. Schematic of lockup torque converter control system shows valves, lines, and oil pressure values in various circuits of system. (American Motors Corp.)

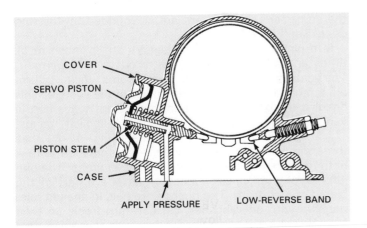

Fig. 41-18. Cross-sectional view gives details of low--reverse band setup in Ford C-4 automatic transmission. Note servo assembly at left and band adjustment screw at right. (Ford Motor Co.)

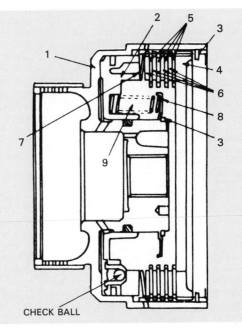

Fig. 41-19. Sectional view of forward clutch assembly on typical three speed automatic transmission: 1—Forward clutch drum. 2—Piston. 3—Snap ring. 4—Retaining plate. 5—Drive plate. 6—Driven plate. 7—Dish plate. 8—Coil spring retainer. 9—Coil spring.

The SWITCH VALVE is a multi-purpose control valve: It directs oil flow to apply the converter clutch in one position and releases it in the other position. It directs oil flow to the cooling and lubricating circuits within the transmission. It regulates the oil pressure to the torque converter and limits maximum oil pressure.

SERVOS, Fig. 41-18, apply and release bands that control the operation of drive shells and planetary gearsets.

MULTIPLE DISC CLUTCHES, Figs. 41-19 and 41-20, are the "drive" members of the team. They are applied by hydraulic pressure. Heavy springs release the clutch discs when hydraulic pressure drops.

The multiple discs are arranged in alternate fashion. The driving discs are splined to the clutch hub. The driven discs are splined to the clutch drum. In operation, a piston in the clutch drum squeezes the clutch discs together when hydraulic pressure is applied. A heavy spring releases the discs when hydraulic pressure drops.

PLANETARY GEARSETS, Fig. 41-21, operate by means of PINION GEARS turning on their own axis — while rotating around a SUN GEAR — and with a RING GEAR (annulus gear) having internal teeth.

When planetary gearsets are used in combination with multiple disc clutches, bands, valve controls, and valves, they automatically provide all of the forward and reverse gear ratios needed for efficient operation under normal driving conditions.

OVERRUNNING CLUTCHES are used both in the torque converter, Fig. 41-4, and in the planetary gearsets

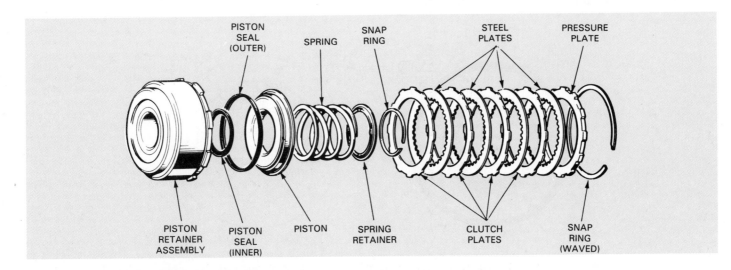

Fig. 41-20. Exploded view shows assembly sequence of front clutch on Model 998 automatic transmission used on American Motors cars. Note alternate arrangement of clutch plates and steel plates. (American Motors Corp.)

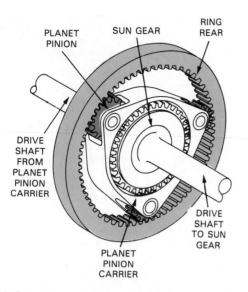

Fig. 41-21. Key parts of a single planetary gearset are sun gear, pinion carrier and planet pinions, and a ring gear. All gears are in constant mesh.

the sun gear. These gears are surrounded by the ring gear. See Fig. 41-21.

In a planetary gearset, the gears are in mesh at all times and are never shifted in or out of engagement. The gears are attached to different drums which, in turn, are attached to other operating parts of the system. This enables the gears to function in different ways as the various drums are held from rotation by "applied" bands.

A simple form of planetary gearset, Fig. 41-21, has three pinions mounted between—and meshed with—both the sun gear and the ring gear at all times. The pinions revolve on pins or axles which are a part of the planet carrier drum. The pinions are held in spaced relationship with one another, yet can turn freely on their own pins and also rotate around the sun gear and within the ring gear.

The gears can be arranged so that they will function as driving elements or driven elements to provide different results by connecting them in different ways. In this manner, planetary gears for forward speeds are used where they act as one-way driving elements. See Fig. 41-22. One type of overrunning clutch, the SPRAG CLUTCH, uses special shape sprag segments, Fig. 41-22, to lock inner and outer races together in one direction only. The ROLLER CLUTCH, another popular type of overrunning clutch, utilizes rollers and ramps to provide lockup one way and freewheeling in the other direction.

PLANETARY GEARSET CONSTRUCTION

Basically, a planetary gearset has three major elements:
1. Sun gear.
2. Planet carrier, drum, and pinions.
3. Ring gear and drum.

The name "planetary gears" is derived from their similarity to our solar system, since the pinions (planet gears) each turn on their own axis while rotating around

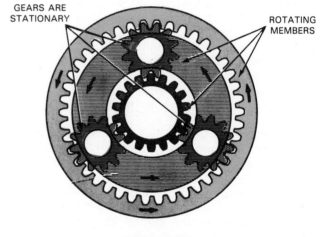

DIRECT GEAR

Fig. 41-23. Chrysler TorqueFlite planetary gearset is shown in direct drive. Entire gearset is locked together and rotates as a unit. (Chrysler Corp.)

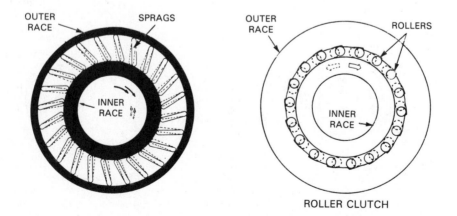

ROLLER CLUTCH

Fig. 41-22. Overrunning clutches: Left. Principle of sprag clutch is illustrated by tipping action of sprag segments to lock inner and outer races in one direction. Right. Principle of roller clutch is shown by rollers moving up ramps to lock races together in one direction.

in one form as a reduction gear and in another form as an overgear. In still another form, the planetary gears are used for reverse. Multiple planetary gearsets are needed where more than two forward speeds are wanted.

PLANETARY GEARSET OPERATION

With a single planetary gearset, there are a number of possible gear combinations: direct drive, reduction, reverse, and neutral. Study Figs. 41-23 and 41-24 and follow these planetary gear actions.

DIRECT DRIVE is accomplished by locking together any two planetary gearset members. In Fig. 41-23, assume that the engine is connected to the sun gear and the pinion carrier is splined to the output shaft of the transmission. Then, if the sun gear and the ring gear are locked together and driven through the gearset, the entire assembly will rotate as a unit. The output shaft will rotate at the same speed as the engine crankshaft (high gear—ratio of 1.0 to 1).

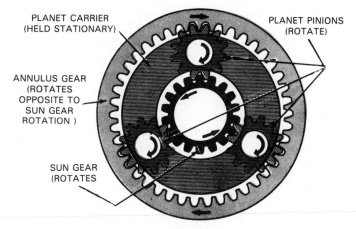

REVERSE GEAR

Fig. 41-24. Chrysler TorqueFlite planetary gearset is pictured in REVERSE. Planet carrier is stationary and pinions rotate, driving annulus gear in opposite direction.   (Chrysler Corp.)

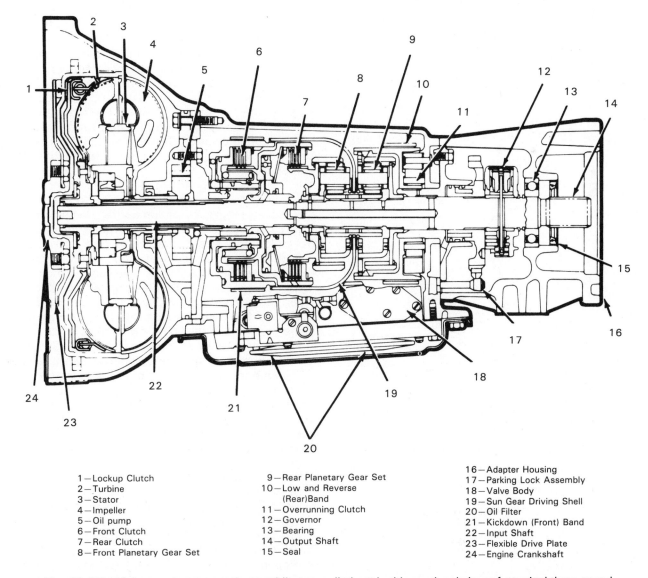

1—Lockup Clutch
2—Turbine
3—Stator
4—Impeller
5—Oil pump
6—Front Clutch
7—Rear Clutch
8—Front Planetary Gear Set

9—Rear Planetary Gear Set
10—Low and Reverse (Rear) Band
11—Overrunning Clutch
12—Governor
13—Bearing
14—Output Shaft
15—Seal

16—Adapter Housing
17—Parking Lock Assembly
18—Valve Body
19—Sun Gear Driving Shell
20—Oil Filter
21—Kickdown (Front) Band
22—Input Shaft
23—Flexible Drive Plate
24—Engine Crankshaft

Fig. 41-25. Major components and assemblies are called out in this sectional view of a typical three speed automatic transmission.   (American Motors Corp.)

REDUCTION means operating at a reduced gear ratio (low gear). Usually, in this forward position, an applied band holds the ring gear from turning. The pinions, in turn, are forced to rotate on their pins and travel around inside the ring gear. In this action, the pinions turn in the opposite direction of rotation of the sun gear, while the pinion carrier turns in the same direction as the sun gear, but at reduced speed. Since the pinion carrier is connected to the output shaft of the transmission, the output shaft will turn more slowly than the engine crankshaft.

REVERSE operation requires that the pinion carrier is held stationary. Then, when torque is applied to the sun gear, the pinions rotate on their pins, causing the ring gear to rotate in the opposite direction. See Fig. 41-24.

In NEUTRAL, no clutches or bands are applied.

Specific examples of how various automatic transmissions operate, and how they are controlled, will be given in the remainder of this chapter. A careful reading of the descriptive copy and follow-up study of the power flow arrows in the accompanying illustrations will provide you with a basic understanding of automatic transmission operation.

THREE SPEED AUTOMATIC TRANSMISSIONS

Consider the operation of clutches, bands, and planetary gears in a typical three speed, fully automatic transmission, Fig. 41-25. This Model 998 transmission used in many American Motors cars has two multiple disc clutches, two bands and servos, an overrunning clutch, and two planetary gearsets. The sun gear is in-

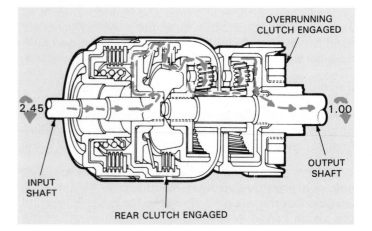

Fig. 41-27. Arrows trace power flow in DRIVE-FIRST gear from input shaft to output shaft. Note gear reduction of 2.45 to 1.0 through rear planetary annulus gear to output shaft. (American Motors Corp.)

terconnected to the multiple disc clutches through a driving shell that is splined to the sun gear and front clutch retainer. See Fig. 41-25.

In NEUTRAL and PARK positions, with the engine running, power flow is from the input shaft to the front clutch hub and rear clutch retainer, Fig. 41-26. Since none of the clutches or bands are applied, power flow stops at the rear clutch retainer. The rear clutch plates (splined to the rear clutch retainer) rotate with the retainer at engine speed. The rear clutch discs (splined to front annulus gear) and the output shaft remain stationary.

In DRIVE-FIRST gear, Fig. 41-27, the rear clutch is applied and the overrunning clutch "holds" the rear planetary gear carrier (pinion carrier). When shifted into DRIVE, the rear clutch retainer, front annulus gear, and front planetary gears rotate at engine speed.

Both front and rear planetary gears are in mesh with the sun gear. See Fig. 41-27. The sun gear has a reverse helix that causes it to revolve opposite engine rotation when turned by the front planetary gears. However, the design of the helix also causes it to revolve the rear planetary gears in the same direction as engine rotation.

Power flow, then, is through the rear clutch and front annulus gear, into the front planetary gears, and to the rear planetary gears by way of the counter-rotating sun gear. At this point, the rear overrunning clutch locks up and prevents the rear planetary carrier and low/reverse drum from turning opposite to engine rotation. With the carrier and drum held stationary, power flow is transferred through the rear annulus gear to the output shaft of the transmission.

Power flow in MANUAL-FIRST GEAR is the same as in DRIVE-FIRST except that, in MANUAL-FIRST, the rear band is applied to provide for engine braking.

In DRIVE-SECOND GEAR, Fig. 41-28, the rear clutch is still applied from DRIVE-FIRST and the overrunning clutch freewheels. The front servo applies the front band in response to increased speed and hydraulic pressure signals from the governor and throttle linkage. This completes the 1-2 upshift.

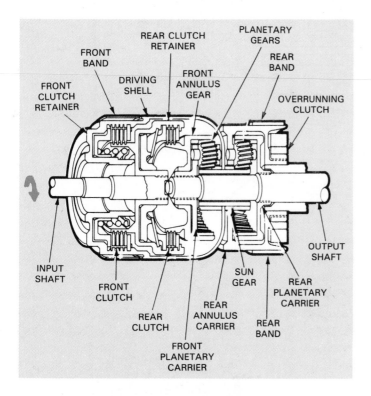

Fig. 41-26. With clutch, band, and gear system in NEUTRAL, input shaft turns and output shaft remains stationary. (American Motors Corp.)

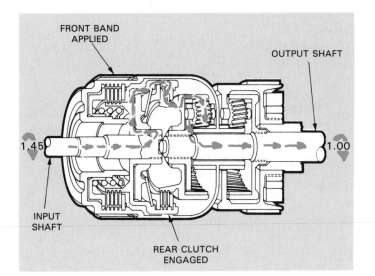

Fig. 41-28. Power flow in DRIVE-SECOND results in 1.45 to 1.0 gear reduction through front planetary pinions and pinion carrier to output shaft. (American Motors Corp.)

The applied front band keeps the front clutch retainer from turning, which prevents the driving shell and sun gear from turning. The applied rear clutch permits power flow through the rear clutch retainer to the front annulus gear, turning it at engine speed and in the same direction of rotation.

Since the sun gear is stationary, front annulus gear rotation causes the front planetary gears and carrier to turn in the direction of engine rotation, but at reduced speed. Power flow is then transferred directly to the output shaft of the transmission. See Fig. 41-28.

In DRIVE-SECOND GEAR, the rear planetary gears are "idling" and the low/reverse drum is freewheeling with the overrunning clutch.

In MANUAL-SECOND GEAR, the transmission components are used in the same sequence and with the same response as in DRIVE-SECOND, except that there is no 2-3 shift. This transmission only performs a 1-2 shift.

In DRIVE-THIRD GEAR, Fig. 41-29, the rear clutch is still applied from DRIVE-SECOND. When car speed reaches the 2-3 upshift range, the front servo releases the front band and the front clutch retainer is applied. Power flow is then transmitted through the front clutch retainer, rear clutch retainer, front annulus gear, rear driving shell, and sun gear, causing it to turn at engine speed and in the same direction of rotation. The front planetary gears are stationary (do not turn on their pins), but are forced by the sun gear to transmit engine torque to the front planetary carrier which, in turn, rotates the output shaft at engine speed.

DRIVE-THIRD GEAR is "direct drive" from input shaft to output shaft. All connecting transmission components rotate as a unit.

In REVERSE GEAR, Fig. 41-30, the front clutch and rear band are applied. Power flow is from the front clutch retainer to the driving shell, which is locked to the retainer and turns the sun gear in the direction of engine rotation. The sun gear, in turn, rotates the planet pinions in a direction opposite to engine rotation.

The rear planetary pinion carrier is "held" by the rear band. This permits power flow from the sun gear through the rear planetary pinions to the rear annulus gear and to the output shaft of the transmission. The front planetary gears are "idling" during REVERSE operation.

TORQUEFLITE THREE SPEED AUTOMATIC TRANSMISSIONS

The operation of clutches, bands, and planetary gearsets in Chrysler TorqueFlite A-727 and A-904 three speed automatic transmissions is very similar to Model

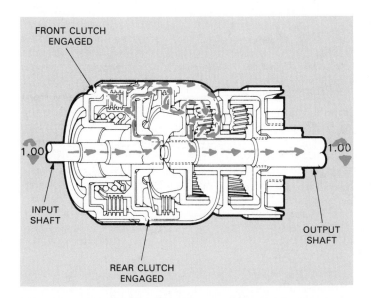

Fig. 41-29. Power flow in DRIVE-THIRD is through locked-together front planetary gearset to rear output shaft to produce direct drive or a 1.0 to 1 gear ratio. (American Motors Corp.)

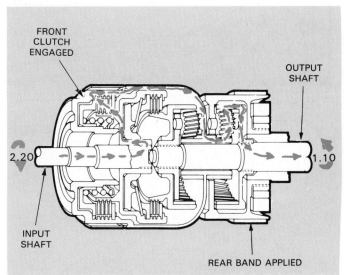

Fig. 41-30. Power flow in REVERSE is through rear planetary pinions and annulus gear to output shaft in a direction opposite to engine rotation. Note gear reduction of 2.20 to 1. (American Motors Corp.)

CLUTCH AND BAND APPLICATION CHART								
DRIVE POSITION	P	R	N	D			2		1
				1	2	3	1	2	
Front Clutch		•				•			
Front Band					•			•	
Rear Clutch				•	•	•	•	•	•
Rear Band		•							•
Overrunning Clutch				•			•		•
Converter Lockup Clutch						•			

Fig. 41-31. Typical clutch and band application chart gives quick and clear indication of "applied" and "released" members in each mode of automatic transmission operation. (Chrysler Corp.)

998 just described. See Fig. 41-31. Basically, the A-904 with conventional torque converter is used in vehicles with four cylinder engine. The A-904 and 998 transmissions equipped with lockup torque converter are used in vehicles with six cylinder engines. The A-727 Torque-Flite automatic transmission is designed for use in larger passenger cars and in conjunction with high performance engines. See Fig. 41-32.

TURBO HYDRA-MATIC TRANSMISSIONS

TURBO HYDRA-MATIC is an old, familiar name for a series of related torque converter automatic transmissions used in broad application in General Motors cars for decades. The older three speed Turbo Hydra-Matic transmissions incorporated a three element torque converter, at least one planetary gearset, three multiple disc

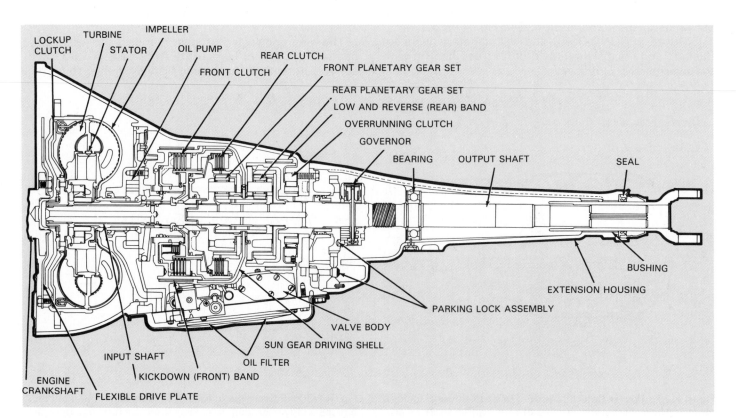

Fig. 41-32. Sectional view details key elements of TorqueFlite A-727 automatic transmission and torque converter. (Chrysler Corp.)

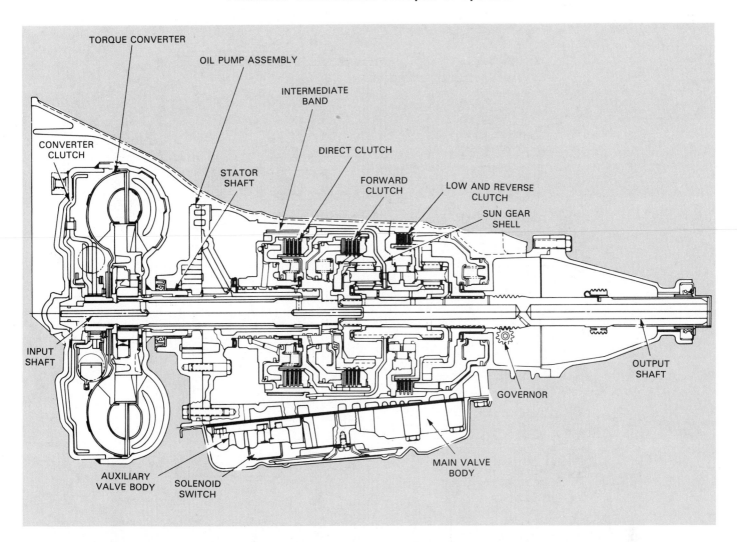

Fig. 41-33. Sectional view of Model 250-C Turbo Hydra-Matic transmission shows location of major components and assemblies from converter clutch to output shaft. (Oldsmobile Div., General Motors Corp.)

clutches, two bands, and two roller clutches. Modifications in this arrangement occurred across various General Motors lines but, generally, these were the basic elements.

In later versions of the Turbo Hydra-Matic, Figs. 41-33 and 41-39, further changes were made in the clutch, band, and gear arrangement, and a converter clutch was added (lockup torque converter) to eliminate slippage.

The MODEL 250-C, for example, shown in Fig. 41-33, is a fully automatic unit consisting principally of a four element torque converter, two planetary gearsets, three multiple disc clutches, one roller clutch, and one adjustable intermediate band.

With the engine running and the Turbo Hydra-Matic 250-C in NEUTRAL position, Fig. 41-34, oil from the pump is directed to the pressure regulator valve. Pump output above line pressure flows from the pressure regulator valve to the converter feed passage to fill the converter.

Oil at full line pressure is routed to the manual valve, 2-3 accumulator, detent pressure regulator, 1-2 accumulator, and vacuum modulator valve. See Fig. 41-34. All clutches and bands are released.

In DRIVE-LOW range, power flow is from the transmission input shaft through the forward clutch to the input ring gear, Fig. 41-35. Clockwise rotation of the input ring gear and output planet pinions causes the sun gear and shaft to rotate counterclockwise. This causes the reaction (rear) carrier planet pinions to rotate clockwise, thereby turning the output ring gear and output shaft in the same direction at a reduction ratio of about 2.52 to 1.

In DRIVE-INTERMEDIATE range, the intermediate band is applied to hold the drive shell and sun gear stationary. Power flow is from the input shaft through the forward clutch to the input ring gear. See Fig. 41-36. Clockwise rotation of the input ring gear causes the output planet pinions to "walk" around the stationary sun gear. This, in turn, causes the output shaft to rotate clockwise at a reduction ratio of about 1.52 to 1.

In DRIVE-HIGH range (direct drive), power flow is from the input shaft through the forward clutch to the input ring rear in a clockwise direction. See Fig. 41-37. The direct clutch is applied, transmitting power through the sun gear drive shell to the sun gear in a clockwise direction. Since the input ring gear and the sun gear are turning in the same direction at the same speed, the

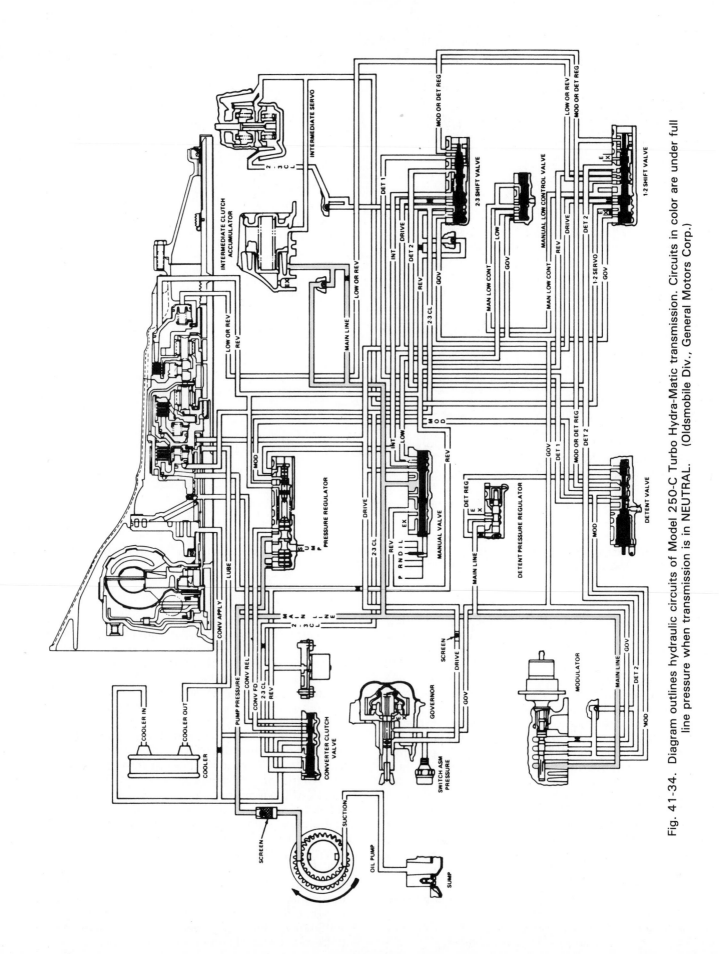

Fig. 41-34. Diagram outlines hydraulic circuits of Model 250-C Turbo Hydra-Matic transmission. Circuits in color are under full line pressure when transmission is in NEUTRAL. (Oldsmobile Div., General Motors Corp.)

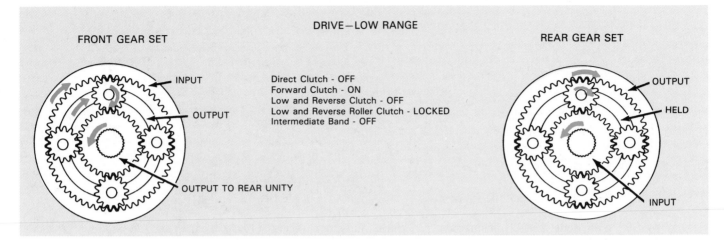

DRIVE—LOW RANGE

FRONT GEAR SET

INPUT

OUTPUT

OUTPUT TO REAR UNITY

Direct Clutch - OFF
Forward Clutch - ON
Low and Reverse Clutch - OFF
Low and Reverse Roller Clutch - LOCKED
Intermediate Band - OFF

REAR GEAR SET

OUTPUT

HELD

INPUT

Fig. 41-35. Arrows point out direction of rotation of various members of front and rear planetary gearsets of Model 250-C transmission in DRIVE-LOW range. (Oldsmobile Div., General Motors Corp.)

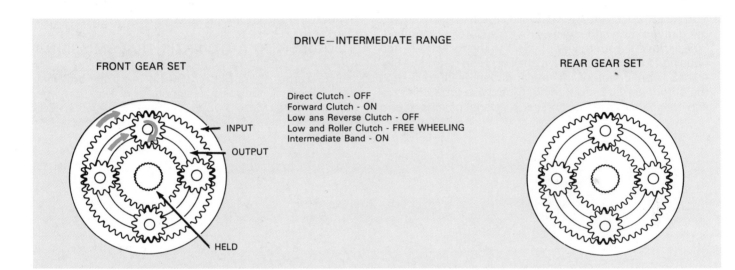

DRIVE—INTERMEDIATE RANGE

FRONT GEAR SET

INPUT

OUTPUT

HELD

Direct Clutch - OFF
Forward Clutch - ON
Low ans Reverse Clutch - OFF
Low and Roller Clutch - FREE WHEELING
Intermediate Band - ON

REAR GEAR SET

Fig. 41-36. Arrows indicate direction of rotation of members of planetary gearsets of Model 250-C transmission in DRIVE-INTERMEDIATE range. (Oldsmobile Div., General Motors Corp.)

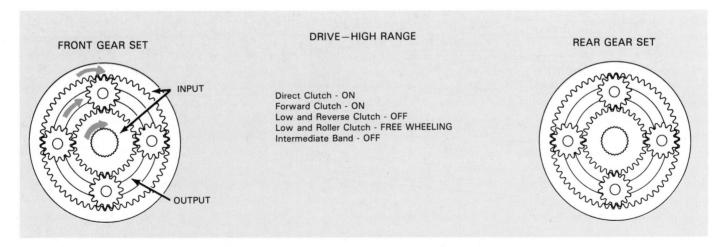

DRIVE—HIGH RANGE

FRONT GEAR SET

INPUT

OUTPUT

Direct Clutch - ON
Forward Clutch - ON
Low and Reverse Clutch - OFF
Low and Roller Clutch - FREE WHEELING
Intermediate Band - OFF

REAR GEAR SET

Fig. 41-37. Arrows show that all members of planetary gearsets of Model 250-C transmission rotate clockwise as a unit in DRIVE-HIGH range. (Oldsmobile Div., General Motors Corp.)

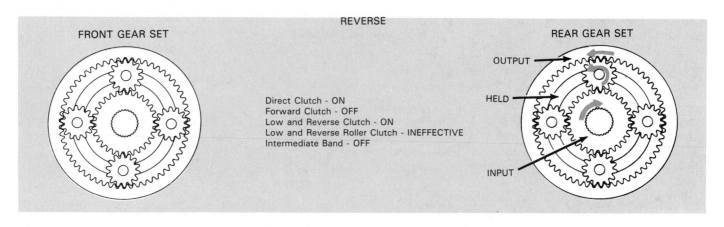

FRONT GEAR SET

REVERSE

REAR GEAR SET

OUTPUT

HELD

INPUT

Direct Clutch - ON
Forward Clutch - OFF
Low and Reverse Clutch - ON
Low and Reverse Roller Clutch - INEFFECTIVE
Intermediate Band - OFF

Fig. 41-38. With Model 250-C transmission in REVERSE, forward clutch is OFF, direct clutch and low and reverse clutch are ON, causing output ring gear and output shaft to rotate counterclockwise. (Oldsmobile Div., General Motors Corp.)

planetary gearset members are locked together and turn at a ratio of 1.0 to 1.

In REVERSE range, the forward clutch is released and the direct clutch and low and reverse clutch are applied. Power flow is from the input shaft to the forward clutch housing to the sun gear drive shell and sun gear. See Fig. 41-38. Application of the low and reverse clutch keeps the output carrier from turning. Clockwise rotation of the sun gear causes the reaction carrier planet pinions to turn

counterclockwise. This, in turn, causes the output ring gear and output shaft to rotate counterclockwise at a reduction ratio of about 1.93 to 1.

FOUR SPEED AUTOMATIC TRANSMISSIONS

The Turbo Hydra-Matic 700-R4 is a fully automatic four speed transmission designed for use on rear wheel drive General Motors vehicles. See Fig. 41-39. Major

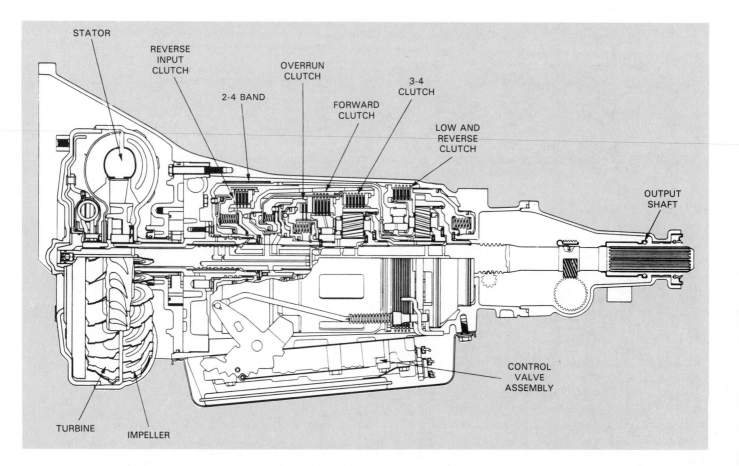

STATOR

REVERSE INPUT CLUTCH

2-4 BAND

OVERRUN CLUTCH

FORWARD CLUTCH

3-4 CLUTCH

LOW AND REVERSE CLUTCH

OUTPUT SHAFT

CONTROL VALVE ASSEMBLY

TURBINE

IMPELLER

Fig. 41-39. General Motors' Model 700-R4 Turbo Hydra-Matic transmission provides four speeds forward with fourth speed geared to a 0.70 to 1 overdrive ratio. (Chevrolet Motor Div., General Motors Corp.)

components of the 700-R4 include: three element torque converter, converter clutch, vane type oil pump, 2-4 band, five multiple disc clutches, two planetary gearsets, one sprag clutch, one roller clutch, and a valve body assembly.

Gear ratios for the 700-R4 are: first—3.06 to 1; second—1.62 to 1; third—1.0 to 1; fourth (overdrive)—0.70 to 1; reverse—2.29 to 1.

Note in the Clutch Applications Chart in Fig. 41-40 that the 2-4 band is applied in overdrive range (fourth, DR4). Also engaged are the forward clutch and the 3-4 clutch. These are the friction elements required to control the operation of the compound planetary gearset to provide the 0.70 to 1 overdrive gear ratio.

FORD'S AUTOMATIC OVERDRIVE TRANSMISSION

Ford's four speed automatic overdrive (AOD) transmission, Fig. 41-41, provides fully automatic operation in D (overdrive) or D (third gear — overdrive lock-out position). In addition, it permits manual upshifting and

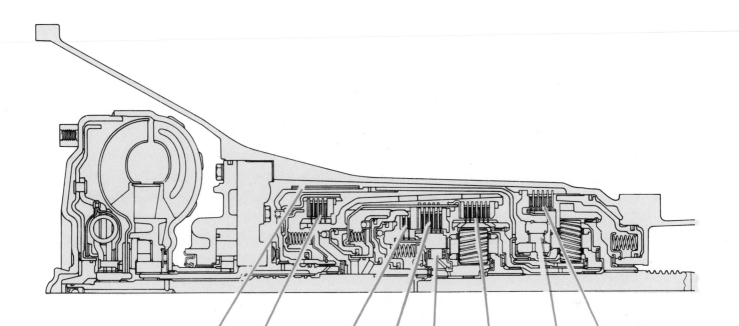

GEAR RANGE	2-4 BAND	REVERSE INPUT CLUTCH	OVERRUN CLUTCH	FORWARD CLUTCH	FORWARD SPRAG CL. ASSEMBLY	3-4 CLUTCH	LO ROLLER CLUTCH	LO-REV. CLUTCH
1ST DR4				ON	ON		ON	
2ND DR4	ON			ON	ON			
3RD DR4				ON	ON	ON		
4TH DR4	ON			ON		ON		
3RD DR3			ON	ON	ON	ON		
2ND DR2	ON		ON	ON	ON			
1ST LO			ON	ON	ON		ON	ON
REV.		ON						ON

Fig. 41-40. Illustration of upper half of Model 700-4R Turbo Hydra-Matic transmission correlates location of friction elements in transmission with Clutch and Band Application Chart. (Chevrolet Motor Div., General Motors Corp.)

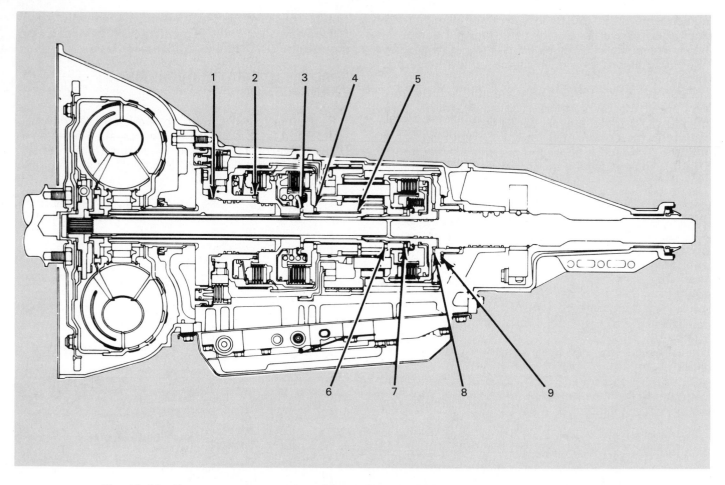

Fig. 41-41. Key parts and assemblies of Ford's Model AOD four speed automatic transmission includes: 1—Intermediate clutch. 2—Reverse clutch and overdrive band. 3—Forward clutch. 4—Reverse sun gear and drive shell assembly. 5—Forward sun gear. 6—Planetary gearset. 7—Direct clutch. 8—Output shaft. 9—Ring gear and park gear. (Ford Motor Co.)

CLUTCH AND BAND APPLICATION CHART

	Interm. Friction Clutch	Interm. One-Way Clutch	Overdrive Band	Reverse Clutch	Forward Clutch	Planetary One-Way Clutch	Low-Reverse Band	Direct Clutch
1st Gear Manual Low					Applied	Holding	Applied	
2nd Gear Manual Low	Applied	Holding	Applied		Applied			
1st Gear — Ⓓ (OVERDRIVE) or D(3)					Applied	Holding		
2nd Gear — Ⓓ (OVERDRIVE) or D(3)	Applied	Holding			Applied			
3rd Gear — Ⓓ (OVERDRIVE) or D(3)	Applied				Applied			Applied
4th Gear — Ⓓ (OVERDRIVE)	Applied		Applied					Applied
Reverse (R)				Applied			Applied	
Neutral (N)								
Park (P)							Applied	

Fig. 41-42. Chart lists each Ford AOD transmission gear selector position and indicates whether clutches and bands are released, applied, or holding. (Ford Motor Co.)

downshifting in all forward drive positions. The gear ratios are: first—2.40 to 1; second—1.47 to 1; third—1.0 to 1; fourth (overdrive)—0.67 to 1. The gear selector quadrant is marked P-R-N- D -D1 (P-R-N- D -3-1).

The AOD transmission basically consists of a three element torque converter, front pump, intermediate clutch, one-way clutch, reverse clutch, overdrive front band, forward clutch, rear (low-reverse) band, direct clutch, planetary one-way clutch, and compound planetary gearset. Study the Clutch and Band Application Chart in Fig. 41-42, then check the location of these assemblies in Fig. 41-41.

In D position with the engine running, the car starts moving in first gear, then the transmission automatically upshifts to second, third, and fourth gear as the engine accelerates. The transmission automatically downshifts as car speed decreases. The AOD transmission will not shift into overdrive, nor remain in the overdrive mode, when the accelerator pedal is "floored." On forced downshifts from 50 mph to 20 mph, in D or D position, the transmission will downshift to second gear. It will not downshift at car speeds above 50 mph.

Note that in D position, Fig. 41-42, the following friction elements are supplied: intermediate friction clutch, direct clutch, and overdrive band.

The AOD transmission planetary gearset operates in fourth gear (0.67 to 1) except when shifted into the D position. Then, the fourth gear is locked out. The D posi-

tion provides better performance and greater engine braking. Also, manual shifts from D to D or from D to D are possible at any car speed.

In the D position, Fig. 41-42, the intermediate friction clutch and direct clutch are applied. In D, however, the overdrive band is released and the forward clutch is applied.

In 1 (first gear) position, maximum engine braking is attained. On shifts to 1 from D or D at car speeds above 20 mph, the transmission will downshift to first gear. On shifts to 1 position on "driveaway," the transmission will remain in first gear until the selector lever is moved to another position.

Power flow in the AOD transmission is as follows:

In operation in overdrive mode, power is transmitted from the engine crankshaft to the flex plate at the front of the torque converter (flex plate is mechanically attached to input shaft). At the same time, the overdrive band is engaged, locking the forward sun gear in the rear planetary gearset. This causes the planetary carrier to rotate around the front sun gear, thereby driving the ring gear and output shaft.

OTHER AUTOMATIC TRANSMISSIONS

Other three speed and four speed automatic transmissions are shown in Figs. 41-43 - 41-45, 41-50, and 41-51. Study the parts and assemblies that make up

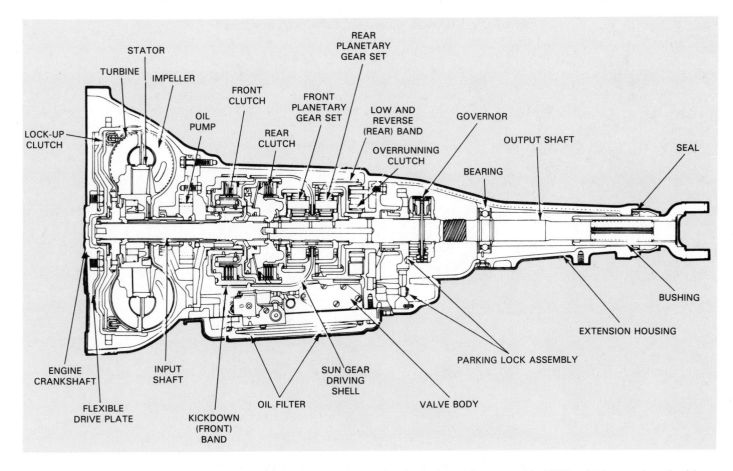

Fig. 41-43. This Model 904 three speed automatic transmission is designed for use with AMC vehicles equipped with four cylinder engine.   (American Motors Corp.)

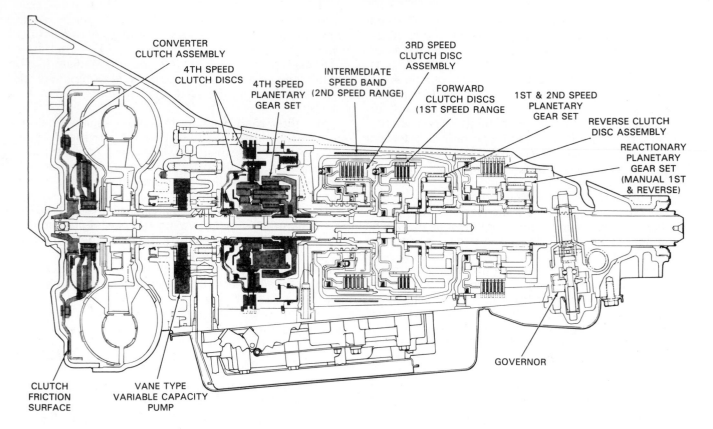

CONVERTER
CLUTCH ASSEMBLY

4TH SPEED
CLUTCH DISCS

4TH SPEED
PLANETARY
GEAR SET

INTERMEDIATE
SPEED BAND
(2ND SPEED RANGE)

3RD SPEED
CLUTCH DISC
ASSEMBLY

FORWARD
CLUTCH DISCS
(1ST SPEED RANGE

1ST & 2ND SPEED
PLANETARY
GEAR SET

REVERSE CLUTCH
DISC ASSEMBLY

REACTIONARY
PLANETARY
GEAR SET
(MANUAL 1ST
& REVERSE)

GOVERNOR

CLUTCH
FRICTION
SURFACE

VANE TYPE
VARIABLE CAPACITY
PUMP

Fig. 41-44. This Model 200-4R Turbo Hydra-Matic is a fully automatic overdrive transmission with three element torque converter and a computer controlled converter clutch. Note 4th speed clutch and planetary gearset in shaded area. (Chevrolet Motor Div., General Motors Corp.)

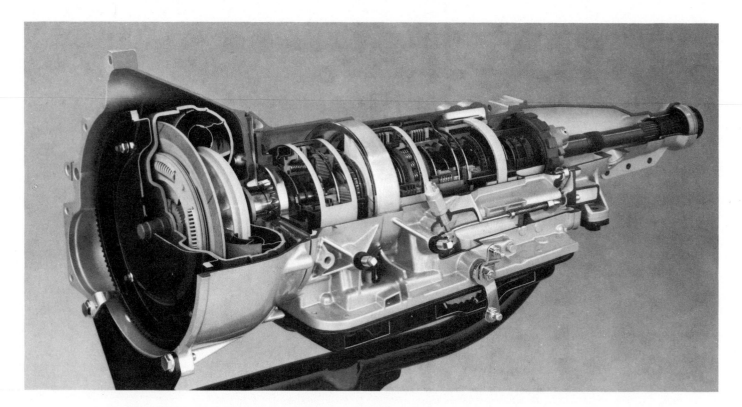

Fig. 41-45. Ford's Model A4LD four speed automatic overdrive transmission features an electronically controlled torque converter clutch. Study the similarities—and differences—between the A4LD and the four speed transmission shown in Fig. 41-47. (Ford Motor Co.)

496

the units and try to visualize power flow to the output shaft. Note, too, that the numbers called out in Figs. 41-50 and 51 are utilized in the Review Questions.

CONTINUOUSLY VARIABLE TRANSMISSIONS

CONTINUOUSLY VARIABLE TRANSMISSIONS (CVT) have been under development for many years. Now these compact, "stepless" transmissions are being installed in motorscooters, Fig. 41-46, commuter cars of up to one-liter engine displacement, Fig. 41-47, and in a subcompact, front wheel drive foreign car with transverse engine.

Industrial use of CVTs is broadening, too. The design problems of mechanical, adjustable-speed industrial drive systems are similar to those of the automotive CVTs. High-power/density rubber belts used in automotive CVT development are being adapted to industrial use. See Fig. 41-48.

The CVT is called "stepless" because it allows almost unlimited ratio changes between engine and final drive. The advantage of a CVT is that it permits the engine to run at near-constant speed, within its most fuel-efficient rpm range, regardless of load or driver's demands.

FOREIGN CAR CVT

In the subcompact, foreign car application mentioned earlier, two multiple disc wet clutches take up engine torque and transmit it to a planetary gearset and transmission input shaft for forward and reverse operation. Key elements are a primary pulley, a steel drive belt,

Fig. 41-47. This CVT setup consists of a high-power/density rubber belt, a hydraulically operated driving sheave (upper right), and a mechanical torque-sensing driven sheave, with microprocessor control of sheave actuation based on driver demand, road load, and engine state. (Dayco Corp.)

and an output pulley. A hydraulic unit controls all operations, including compression of the steel belt "blocks" in response to variations in drive torque and ratio.

The CVT transmission operates by varying the working diameters of two pulleys. See Fig. 41-49. The pulleys

Fig. 41-46. With motorscooter on test stand, its continuously variable transmission (CVT) is under evaluation for shifting characteristics and load-handling capability. (Dayco Corp.)

Fig. 41-48. An industrial CVT belt developed from automotive CVT belt technology is tested on a dynamometer. (Dayco Corp.)

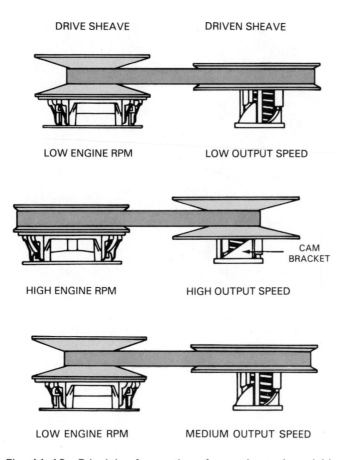

DRIVE SHEAVE   DRIVEN SHEAVE

LOW ENGINE RPM   LOW OUTPUT SPEED

HIGH ENGINE RPM   HIGH OUTPUT SPEED

CAM BRACKET

LOW ENGINE RPM   MEDIUM OUTPUT SPEED

Fig. 41-49. Principle of operation of a continuously variable transmission is shown in these four pulley sheave arrangements. Note that spacing of sheaves and working diameter of pulleys determines output ratio and speed.

have V-shaped grooves in which the steel belt rides. The continuous range of transmission ratio changes is effected by changing the belt position in the groove between the pulley sheaves. The input gearset drives the primary pulley, which is linked to the secondary pulley and output gear by the steel drive belt.

The pulleys each have a fixed cone and a movable cone, with a hydraulic cylinder built in. Actuation of the hydraulic cylinders causes the pulleys to move axially and change the space between the fixed and movable cones. This, in turn, creates a "pinching" action on the steel belt anywhere along the pulley grooves. Basically, the deeper the belt rides in the groove, the smaller the working diameter of the pulleys.

During startup, the primary pulley is automatically set for maximum spacing and minimum working diameter. Conversely, the secondary pulley is set for minimum spacing and maximum diameter, which gives the equivalent of a very low gear ratio. Spacing of the two pulleys changes in reverse proportion as the car speed increases, giving continuous shifts in ratio. Since the pulleys shift V-groove spacing in unison, the steel belt loop is always taut.

The variations in cone spacing—and the resulting variations in working diameters of the pulleys—is controlled automatically by a system of hydraulic valves. These valves are regulated by input signals that register throttle position, engine speed, and torque demand.

In operation, the CVT generally is slower to respond to engine torque than a conventional automatic transmission or transaxle. However, its makers claim that it has better acceleration than the conventional units after 25 mph, thanks to its smooth transition to the most suitable ratio for the given need.

Fig. 41-50. This Ford four speed automatic overdrive transmission is specifically designed to take advantage of 2.4 liter turbo diesel engine characteristics. It has a fourth gear ratio of 0.72 to 1. Can you identify the various clutch assemblies by the number? See Review Questions.   (Ford Motor Co.)

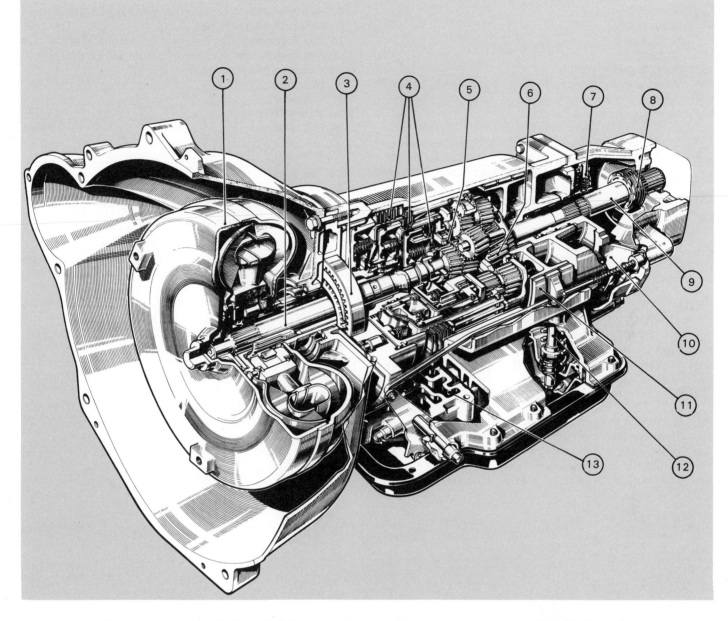

Fig. 41-51. Study the makeup of this typical three speed automatic transmission. Can you identify the various elements by the number? See Review Questions. (Peugeot, Inc.)

Chapter 41—REVIEW QUESTIONS

Write your answers on a separate sheet of paper. Do not write in this book.

1. What purpose does a fluid coupling accomplish in an automatic transmission?
   a. Serves as hydraulic clutch.
   b. Multiplies engine torque.
   c. Builds up hydraulic pressure to operate valves.
   d. Effects gear changes in transmission.

2. Which of these factors is used to control automatic transmission operation?
   a. Ignition timing.
   b. Engine speed.
   c. Engine compression.
   d. Engine temperature.

3. Which of these factors is NOT used to control automatic transmission operation?
   a. Shift lever.
   b. Throttle rod linkage.
   c. Manifold vacuum.
   d. Ignition timing.

4. What is the difference between a fluid coupling and a torque converter?

5. What are the three major rotating elements in most torque converters?

6. Torque multiplication in a torque converter is greater at what speed?
   a. Start-up stall.
   b. Low speed.
   c. Cruising speed.
   d. High speed.

7. Which element creates reaction torque in a torque converter?
   a. Impeller.
   b. Turbine.
   c. Stator.
   d. Converter clutch.
8. What is the purpose of a torque converter clutch?
9. What is the primary function of automatic transmission clutches and bands?
   a. Smooth transmission shifts.
   b. Transmit engine torque through planetary gears.
   c. Provide various gear ratios selected by driver.
   d. Engages and disengages torque converter from engine.
10. Name three principal elements of a planetary gearset.
11. What is the primary function of a planetary gearset in an automatic transmission?
    a. Connects engine to automatic transmission.
    b. Cushions effect of gear changes in transmission.
    c. Provides suitable gear ratios for efficient operation.
    d. Engages and disengages torque converter
12. Servos apply and release bands that control the operation of the elements of a planetary gearset. True or False?
13. An accumulator permits smooth _____ and _____ engagements.
14. Can more than one multiple disc clutch be used in an automatic transmission? Yes or No?
15. What is the purpose of a manual valve in an automatic transmission?
16. The output of the oil pump is controlled by a _____ valve.
17. In a planetary gearset, the gears are in mesh at all times. True or False?

In the following three questions, name the various clutches and bands that are engaged in the given gear range shown here and in Fig. 41-31.

18. Neutral _____.
19. Reverse _____.
20. Drive-Third _____.

In the following seven questions, name the various clutches pointed out in Fig. 41-50.

21. 1. _____.
22. 2. _____.
23. 3. _____.
24. 4. _____.
25. 5. _____.
26. 6. _____.
27. 7. _____.

To answer the following 13 questions, match each numbered assembly in Fig. 41-51 with identifying letter given alongside its correct name.

28. 1. _____ A. Multiple disc clutches.
29. 2. _____ B. Output shaft.
30. 3. _____ C. Speedometer drive gear.
31. 4. _____ D. Planetary gearset.
32. 5. _____ E. Governor.
33. 6. _____ F. Servo.
34. 7. _____ G. Oil pump.
35. 8. _____ H. Overrunning clutch.
36. 9. _____ I. Input shaft.
37. 10. _____ J. Band.
38. 11. _____ K. Torque converter.
39. 12. _____ L. Control valve body.
40. 13. _____ M. Parking pawl.

Chapter 42

AUTOMATIC TRANSMISSION SERVICE

After studying this chapter, you will be able to:
- Name maintenance checks, adjustments, and services that will keep automatic transmissions in satisfactory operating condition.
- Demonstrate how to check level and condition of ATF.
- Determine by inspection where an automatic transmission is leaking ATF.
- Change ATF and replace the filter.
- Explain how to adjust automatic transmission bands.
- Describe throttle linkage and gearshift linkage adjustments.
- Explain road testing, hydraulic pressure and air pressure testing, and stall testing procedures.

Automatic transmissions have been engineered into highly desirable, highly reliable mechanisms for transmitting engine torque to the driveshaft of rear wheel drive vehicles. See Fig. 42-1. They also have been very successfully incorporated into automatic transaxles for front wheel drive vehicles, Fig. 42-2. A TRANSAXLE is a power transmission device that combines the transmission and differential assemblies in a single housing.

That automatic transmissions *are desirable* is proven by the fact that over 86 percent of new car buyers choose ''automatic'' over ''manual.'' That automatic transmissions *are reliable* is evidenced by the typical car owner's lack of concern for transmission maintenance. It takes a very sizable oil slick on the garage floor or pronounced slippage in direct drive to cause the car owner to seek out a service technician for help. By then, it usually is too late for maintenance, and possibly too late for repair.

AUTOMATIC TRANSMISSION MAINTENANCE

While an automatic transmission requires little maintenance, that ''little'' amount is vital to its continued trouble-free operation. Basically, the following checks,

Fig. 42-1. Phantom view of a rear wheel drive Chevrolet Camaro reveals automatic transmission at front end of drive train. (Chevrolet Motor Div., General Motors Corp.)

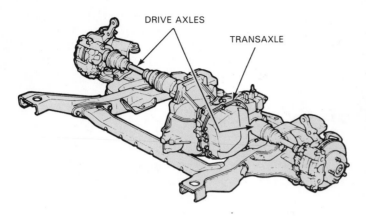

Fig. 42-2. Front wheel drive Buick Skylark transmits engine power to front wheels by way of an automatic transaxle and two drive axles. (Buick Div., General Motors Corp.)

Fig. 42-4. If car manufacturer recommends periodic ATF changes, fluid must be drained when hot. This service technician prepares to empty fluid into a portable 15 gal. oil drain. Only specified ATF or equivalent should be installed. (Lincoln Div. of McNeil Corp.)

adjustments, and services will keep the automatic transmission in satisfactory operating condition, possibly for the life of the vehicle barring driver abuse:

1. Regularly check automatic transmission fluid level. See Fig. 42-3.
2. Check condition of ATF on dipstick.
3. Inspect transmission housings, oil pan, and cooler lines for fluid leakage.
4. Check transmission mount for possible separation of rubber from metal plate.
5. Make periodic ATF changes, Fig. 42-4.
6. Check residue in bottom of transmission oil pan.
7. Replace filter or clean fine mesh wire screen.
8. Adjust bands on transmissions that require it.
9. Refill transmission, using only manufacturer's recommended ATF or the equivalent.
10. Adjust engine curb idle speed to specified rpm.
11. Check gearshift linkage adjustment.
12. Check throttle or TV linkage or cable adjustment.

CHECK ATF LEVEL

The car manufacturers recommend regular checks of the automatic transmission fluid level. A fairly common

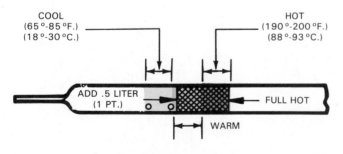

COOL
(65°-85°F.)
(18°-30°C.)

HOT
(190°-200°F.)
(88°-93°C.)

ADD .5 LITER (1 PT.)   FULL HOT

WARM

DO NOT OVERFILL. IT TAKES ONLY ONE PINT TO RAISE LEVEL FROM "ADD" TO "FULL" WITH A HOT TRANSMISSION.

Fig. 42-3. Typical automatic transmission dipstick markings include ADD line and FULL HOT line. Note difference hot temperature makes in level of fluid on dipstick. (Oldsmobile Div., General Motors Corp.)

recommendation is "Check ATF level at each oil change." A good practice is to check the ATF level whenever making any underhood inspection.

To check the automatic transmission fluid level:

1. Drive car or run engine until transmission fluid is at normal operating temperature (about 175-200°F or 80-88°C).
2. Park car on a level surface.
3. Shift transmission into Neutral and apply parking brake.
4. Operate engine at curb idle speed.
5. Move transmission selector lever through all gear ranges, pausing momentarily at each detent to allow complete circulation of fluid through valves and passages. Return shift lever to Neutral.
6. Wipe dirt from transmission fluid filler cap and tube, then remove dipstick (usually located at extreme right rear or engine compartment).
7. Wipe dipstick clean, then reinsert it in filler tube until fully seated.
8. Remove dipstick and check fluid level reading. Fluid level should be between ADD mark and FULL mark. See Fig. 42-3.
9. If fluid appears to be in good condition, but level is low, add manufacturer's specified ATF, or the equivalent, through filler tube to bring level to FULL mark on dipstick.

CAUTION: Do not overfill. Overfilling can result in fluid loss, foaming, or erratic shifting.

502

CHECK ATF CONDITION

When making the fluid level check, always inspect the fluid adhering to the dipstick for evidence of the condition of the fluid. Check the color of the fluid. It should be bright cherry red (transmissions using DEXRON©-II) or dark red (transmissions using Type F fluid). NOTE: Some ATF contains a detergent which may have a darkening effect.

Fluid that is a deep reddish brown could be contaminated. Very dark brown or black fluid carrying a burnt odor indicates that the transmission has overheated because of slipping bands and clutches. Fluid that is milky pink is contaminated by engine coolant, usually caused by a leak between the radiator and transmission oil cooler.

Next, wipe the fluid sample from the dipstick with your thumb and index finger and "feel" the condition of the fluid. It should be smooth and slippery with no evidence of solid contaminants. Then, wipe the fluid from your fingers on a clean white cloth or tissue and inspect the oil stain for metal particles or friction material. If one or both of these conditions exist, the transmission may require an overhaul.

Finally, make a careful, closeup inspection of the lower end of the dipstick for signs of varnish buildup or gum deposits. Varnish or gum on the dipstick is a good indication that a similar condition exists within the control valve body. If, in fact, the internal working parts and passages of this assembly are coated with varnish, it could result in sticking valves and consequent erratic and/or delayed upshifts and downshifts. See Fig. 42-5.

Gum deposits on internal parts of the transmission are caused by antifreeze contamination of the fluid. The varnish buildup results from high temperatures attacking the ATF and causing severe oxidation of the fluid. The high temperatures could result from underfilling or overfilling the transmission with ATF. Either of these conditions could cause foaming of the fluid which, in turn, could create the high temperatures and resulting varnish formation.

INSPECT FOR ATF LEAKS

When preparing to check for the source of an automatic transmission fluid leak, place the vehicle on a lift, and start by cleaning the underside of the transmission and torque converter housing cover. If the leak seems to be in the area of the converter, you need to use care in identifying the type of fluid it is. Although it probably *is* ATF, it could be engine oil leaking past the rear main bearing oil seal or down from the rocker arm cover; or power steering fluid blown back around the converter housing by road draft.

With this in mind, remove the torque converter housing cover. Then, clean the fluid: from the top and bottom of the converter housing; from the front of the transmission case; from the rear face of the engine; and from the engine oil pan. Finally, spray some foot powder on the areas cleaned for inspection.

Then, proceed to carefully look for the source of the automatic transmission fluid leak as follows:

1. Check transmission case breather vent for clogging. If clogged, clean vent and recheck.
2. Check ATF filler tube connection at transmission case (on some applications). If a leak is evident, remove tube, replace O-ring, and reinstall tube.
3. Examine perimeter of oil pan in gasketed area. If leaking ATF, replace gasket and torque-tighten pan attaching screws.
4. Check for ATF leakage at downshift control lever shaft and at manual lever shaft. Replace seals, if necessary.
5. Check connection between transmission case and extension housing. If a leak is evident, replace gasket or seal. See Fig. 42-6.
6. Inspect pressure test port plugs for leakage. Fig. 42-7. If leaking: remove plug, coat threads with sealant, reinstall plug, and retighten.

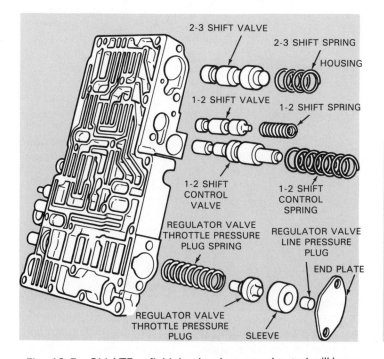

Fig. 42-5. Old ATF or fluid that has been overheated will leave deposits of varnish or gum on dipstick and on valves in control valve body. (American Motors Corp.)

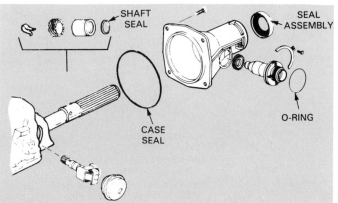

Fig. 42-6. Exploded view of extension housing of a typical automatic transmission helps pinpoint "sealed" areas where ATF leakage may occur.

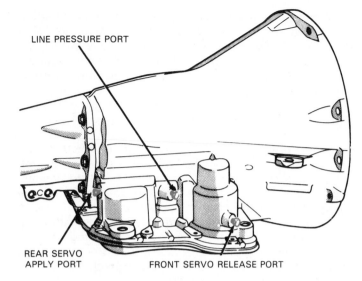

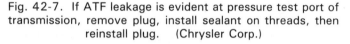

Fig. 42-7. If ATF leakage is evident at pressure test port of transmission, remove plug, install sealant on threads, then reinstall plug. (Chrysler Corp.)

7. Inspect speedometer cable connection to transmission. If ATF is leaking, replace oil seal.
8. Check for ATF leak at transmission output shaft seal in extension housing or adapter housing. Replace oil seal if necessary.
9. Check entire length of ATF lines—and fittings—between transmission and oil cooler in radiator for looseness, wear, or damage. See Fig. 42-8. Replace line and/or fitting as required.
10. Operate engine at 2000 rpm for two minutes, then check for ATF leakage at front of transmission and around torque converter housing. See Fig. 42-9. If source of leakage is at oil pump seal, pump body, oil pump-to-case gasket, or oil pump-to-case bolt, repair requires removal of transmission.
11. Check engine coolant in radiator for contamination by ATF. If contaminated, oil cooler in radiator probably is leaking. Remove radiator for repairs.

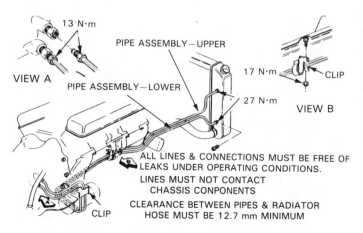

Fig. 42-8. Inspect for ATF leakage along entire length of each oil cooler line and at fittings at transmission and radiator. (Oldsmobile Div., General Motors Corp.)

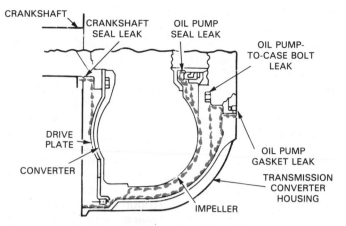

Fig. 42-9. Diagram of torque converter housing pinpoints possible areas where leakage of ATF or engine oil may occur. (American Motors Corp.)

TEST FOR BROKEN TRANSMISSION MOUNT

While the vehicle is on the lift, test the condition of the transmission mount, Fig. 42-10. If it is broken or col-

Fig. 42-10. Service technician uses a high-lift transmission jack to aid in checking condition of transmission mount. Foot pedal operation relieves weight of transmission, permitting closer inspection of mount for breakage or collapse. (Lincoln Div., of McNeil Corp.)

lapsed, replace the mount.

To test the condition of the mount, push up (or pry up) and pull down on the tailshaft of the transmission. At the same time, observe whether or not the rubber part of the mount has separated from the metal plate.

Continue to push up and pull down. If the transmission moves up but not down, the mount has ''bottomed out.'' It has lost its resiliency and collapsed. In either case, replace the mount.

If the mount appears to be whole and resilient during these tests, watch for movement between the metal plate of the mount and its attaching point (usually a crossmember). If there is any movement, tighten the screws or bolts attaching the mount to the transmission and to the crossmember. Torque specifications for this varies by make and model. Check the manufacturer's service manual for exact torque specifications for the vehicle being serviced.

CHANGING AUTOMATIC TRANSMISSION FLUID

Periodic ATF changes are generally recommended by the vehicle manufacturers. Once the pan has been removed and the fluid drained, always remove the filter for cleaning or replacement. Usually, screen type filters can be cleaned and reinstalled. Filters made of paper, fiber, and cloth should be replaced whenever the oil pan is removed. See Fig. 42-11.

A general procedure for draining automatic transmission fluid is as follows:

1. Run engine to bring fluid to normal operating temperature of about 175-200°F (80-88°C).
2. Turn off ignition key and raise vehicle on a lift. See Fig. 42-4.
3. Position drain drum with large funnel under transmission oil pan.
4. Some transmissions can be drained by removing a drain plug or transmission dipstick filler tube, but most require pan removal.

5. Loosen pan screws in a pattern that lets pan tilt at one corner and slowly drain fluid.
6. When most of fluid has drained out, remove screws completely (observing each for varying lengths).
7. Remove pan and carefully inspect inside surface and remaining fluid for metal particles or bits of friction material that signals clutch and band wear.
8. Clean pan thoroughly, especially gasket flanges. Also clean mating surfaces on transmission case.
9. Clean fine mesh wire screen (if so equipped) in nonflammable solvent. Dry with compressed air (wiping with a rag may leave lint on screen). If screen has any holes, replace screen.
10. Replace filter (if so equipped), Fig. 42-11.
11. Reinstall pan, using a new gasket, without cement or sealer. Place longer screws in holes from which they were removed. Torque attaching screws in a crisscross pattern to manufacturer's specification.
12. If fluid was drained by removing a drain plug or dipstick filler tube, reinstall these parts and tighten to manufacturer's torque specifications.
13. Fill transmission with proper type ATF and quantity shown in specifications. If you need to flush transmission oil cooler, add one quart of fluid.
14. Disconnect cooler return line at transmission. Start engine and let it idle until about one quart of fluid has been pumped from cooler return line into a drain pan. Shut off engine and reconnect cooler return line. (NOTE: A more involved back-flushing procedure using mineral spirits is required if considerable foreign matter was discovered in transmission oil pan.)
15. Start engine and let it idle. With foot on brake pedal, move gear selector lever to each position, pausing momentarily to allow full circulation of ATF and purging of air from hydraulic circuits.
16. Return gear selector lever to Neutral or Park position, as specified by manufacturer, and add fluid to bring level to ADD mark on dipstick.
17. Run engine until transmission reaches normal operating temperature, then adjust fluid level to FULL mark on dipstick.
18. Inspect underside of transmission, torque converter housing, oil cooler lines and fittings for leaks, as shown in Fig. 42-8.

ADJUST BANDS

A general procedure for automatic transmission band adjustment involves: tightening the band adjusting screw to a given torque tightness; backing off the adjusting screw a specific number of turns; holding the adjusting screw from turning while torque-tightening the locknut.

Tightening the band adjusting screw, in effect, simulates correct band-apply pressure. The backing off operation represents the band servo travel during application. Study the following examples of specific band adjusting procedures.

Front (kickdown) Band—AMC/Chrysler

1. Raise automobile.
2. Locate front band adjusting screw on left side of

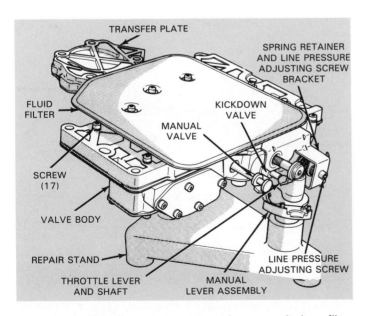

Fig. 42-11. Install a new automatic transmission filter whenever the pan is removed. (Chrysler Corp.)

transmission case above manual valve and throttle lever control levers, Fig. 42-12.

3. Loosen band adjusting screw locknut about four or five turns.
4. Check adjusting screw for freedom of rotation.
5. Tighten band adjusting screw to 72 in. lb. (8 N·m) torque, using a 5/16 in. (8 mm) square socket. See CAUTION in Fig. 42-13.
6. Back off adjusting screw three turns. (Check service manual for adjustment variations from model to model.)
7. Hold adjusting screw from turning and tighten adjusting screw locknut to 35 ft. lb. (47 N·m).

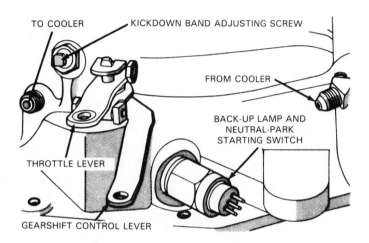

Fig. 42-12. On AMC/Chrysler automatic transmissions, kickdown band adjusting screw is located high on left side of transmission case. (Chrysler Corp.)

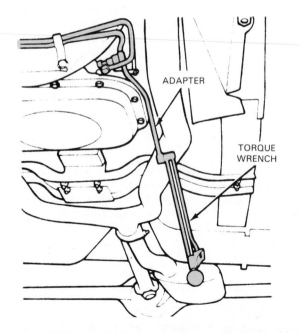

Fig. 42-13. Adjusting kickdown band on AMC/Chrysler transmissions requires use of in. lb. torque wrench and adapter tool. If adapter tool is not used, torque specification must be doubled. (American Motors Corp.)

Rear (low/reverse) Band—AMC/Chrysler

1. Loosen transmission oil pan, drain ATF, remove pan.
2. Remove band adjusting screw locknut.
3. Tighten band adjusting screw to 41 in. lb. (5 N·m), using torque wrench and 1/4 in. hex socket as shown in Fig. 42-14.
4. Back off adjusting screw seven turns (check shop manual).
5. Holding adjusting screw from turning and tighten locknut to 35 ft. lb. (47 N·m).
6. Install oil pan and replacement pan gasket. Torque-tighten attaching bolts to 150 in. lb. (17 N·m).
7. Lower automobile.
8. Fill transmission with recommended ATF. (See CHANGING ATF.)

Intermediate Band—Ford

1. Locate intermediate band adjusting screw on the left side of the transmission case in front of shift levers.
2. Remove locknut from band adjusting screw and discard locknut, which also serves to seal-in fluid.
3. Install a new locknut loosely on adjusting screw.
4. Tighten band adjusting screw to 10 ft. lb. (13.5 N·m).
5. Back off adjusting screw exactly 4 1/4 turns. (Check manufacturer's shop manual.)
6. Hold adjusting screw from turning and tighten locknut to 40 ft. lb. (54 N·m).

Low/Reverse Band—Ford

1. Locate low/reverse band adjusting screw on right side of transmission case above rear pan bolts.
2. Remove locknut from adjusting screw and discard locknut.
3. Install a new locknut loosely on band adjusting screw.
4. Tighten adjusting screw to 10 ft. lb. (13.5 N·m).

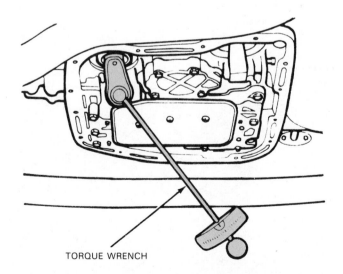

Fig. 42-14. Adjusting rear band on AMC/Chrysler transmissions calls for draining of ATF and pan removal for access to adjusting screw. (American Motors Corp.)

5. Back off band adjusting screw exactly three turns. (Check shop manual.)

6. Hold adjusting screw from turning and tighten locknut to 40 ft. lb. (54 N·m).

Intermediate Band—GM Turbo Hydra-Matic

Band adjustment on late model Turbo Hydra-Matic transmissions calls for the use of safety glasses and specialty tools. Checking band adjustment on certain GM 200/200 C/200 4R transmissions, for example, requires removal of the intermediate servo, disassembly of the servo, testing of the length of the band apply pin by means of a dial indicator and a special pin gage. If adjustment is necessary, a new band apply pin of the correct length is installed.

ADJUST ENGINE CURB IDLE SPEED

There are so many different engine idle speed adjusting procedures, reference to specific manufacturer's service manuals is required. Some of the simpler engine curb idle speed adjustments are given in Chapter 25.

WARNING: When engine is operating during warmup and while making tests and adjustments of curb idle speed, do not stand in direct line with the fan. Do not put your hands near the pulleys, belts, or fan. Do not wear loose clothing.

On later models, idle speed adjustment generally has become increasingly complex. Air conditioning, electric cooling fans, throttle modulators, throttle solenoid positioners, dashpots, and carburetor-related emission controls all contribute to the complexity.

To illustrate a typical late model Ford curb idle speed adjustment on a 4.2 liter engine equipped with a 2150-2 barrel carburetor, study Fig. 42-15 as you follow along with this procedure:

1. Place transmission selector lever in Neutral or Park position.
2. Connect a tachometer to coil negative terminal.
3. Run engine to normal operating temperature.

4. Place A/C-Heat selector in OFF position.
5. Place transmission in specified position (see manufacturer's service manual).
6. Check curb idle speed. If adjustment is required, adjust saddle bracket adjusting screw.
7. Place transmission in Neutral or Park. Accelerate engine momentarily. Place transmission in specified position and recheck curb idle speed. Readjust if required.
8. Check/adjust dashpot clearance (see manufacturer's service manual).
9. Remove tachometer.

Also consider Fig. 42-16 and the more involved steps of this American Motors curb idle speed adjustment on a 4.2 liter engine equipped with a Model BBD-2 barrel carburetor:

1. Connect a tachometer to ignition coil negative (TACH) terminal.
2. Run engine to normal operating temperature (choke and manifold heater must be off).
3. Turn all accessories off and place transmission in Drive position.

WARNING: Set parking brake firmly and do not accelerate engine.

4. Disconnect vacuum hose from Sole-Vac vacuum actuator and plug hose.
5. Disconnect Sole-Vac holding solenoid wire connector.
6. Adjust carburetor curb idle speed adjusting screw, if necessary, to obtain 450-550 engine rpm.
7. Apply a direct source of vacuum to vacuum actuator.
8. When Sole-Vac throttle positioner is fully extended, turn vacuum actuator adjusting screw on throttle lever until 750-850 engine rpm is obtained.
9. Disconnect vacuum source from vacuum actuator.
10. Use a jumper wire to apply battery voltage to energize holding solenoid.
11. Hold throttle open manually to allow throttle positioner to fully extend.

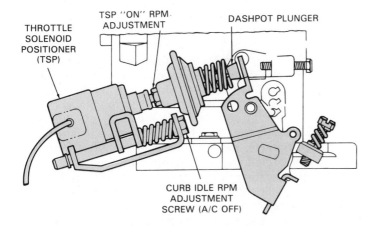

Fig. 42-15. Idle speed setting is important to automatic transmission operation. In one of many Ford idle speed setting arrangements, adjustment is made at saddle bracket adjusting screw. (Ford Motor Co.)

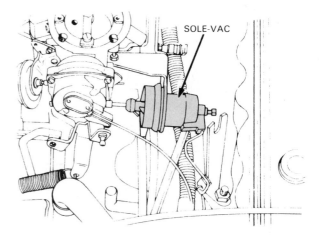

Fig. 42-16. Key element of an AMC idle speed setup is a SOLE-VAC throttle positioner that consists of a closed throttle switch, a holding solenoid, and a vacuum actuator. (American Motor Corp.)

12. If holding solenoid idle speed is not within 600-700 rpm, adjust Sole-Vac throttle positioner (hex-head adjusting screw) to obtain specified rpm.
13. Remove jumper wire from Sole-Vac holding solenoid wire connector.
14. Connect original vacuum hose to vacuum actuator.
15. Remove tachometer.

The correct adjustment of engine curb idle speed is of utmost importance to proper performance of any automatic transmission. One manufacturer states that "Whenever it is required to increase speed by more than 100 rpm, or for any decrease in idle speed, the automatic transmission throttle linkage must be readjusted."

THROTTLE LINKAGE ADJUSTMENT

The throttle linkage adjustment is critical to proper operation of the automatic transmission. Correct adjustment of the linkage will position a valve that controls shift speed, shift quality, and part of throttle downshift control.

If the throttle linkage setting is too short, early shifts and slippage between shifts may occur. If the throttle linkage setting is too long, shifts may be late and the part throttle downshifts may be overly sensitive.

The general rule for adjusting throttle linkage is to remove all slack from the linkage. The particular adjusting procedure shown in Figs. 42-17 and 42-18 requires the use of an extra spring to remove slack from the linkage:

1. Disconnect throttle control rod spring, shown at 1 in Fig. 42-18.
2. Connect this spring so that it holds adjusting link 2 forward against nylon washer 3.
3. Block choke valve open and set carburetor throttle off of fast idle cam.
4. Raise vehicle.
5. Loosen both bolts 4 on throttle control adjusting

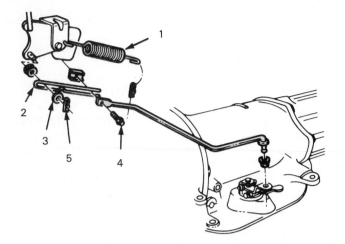

Fig. 42-18. Step 2 in preparing for proper adjustment of throttle linkage is to unhook throttle control rod spring 1 and connect it to adjusting link 2 to hold it forward against nylon washer 3. (American Motors Corp.)

link. NOTE: Do not remove spring clip 5 and nylon washer 3.
6. Connect a spare throttle return spring, shown in Fig. 42-17, so that it holds transmission throttle lever 2 forward against a stop.
7. Push on end of adjusting link 2 in Fig. 42-18 to eliminate lash and pull clamp assembly so bolt 4 bottoms in rear of slot in rod.
8. Tighten forward bolt to clamp link in place.
9. Pull throttle control rod to rear so bolt in rod bottoms in front of slot. Tighten rear retaining bolt.
10. Remove spare return spring from throttle lever.
11. Lower vehicle.
12. Remove throttle control rod spring from adjusting link and install it on control rod.

GEARSHIFT LINKAGE ADJUSTMENT

The correct gearshift linkage adjustment properly positions the transmission manual valve in the valve body. Incorrect adjustment will cause creeping in Neutral, excessive clutch wear, delayed shifts, or failure to start in Neutral or Park. When removing a transmission from a car, place the selector in Neutral.

A check of neutral start switch operation will confirm or condemn the gearshift linkage adjustment. Turn the ignition key to ON position. Move the gearshift lever slowly to Park position. It should click into place in this detent in the shift selector gate.

Next, turn the key to START position and start the engine. If it starts, the Park position setting is correct.

Stop the engine and slowly move the gearshift lever into Neutral position. It should click into place in this detent. If the engine starts, the Neutral position is correct and the gearshift linkage setting is satisfactory.

However, if the starter failed to operate in Park or Neutral, or if the gearshift lever had to be moved back and forth to cause the starter to operate, a gearshift linkage adjustment is required.

Study Fig. 42-19 as you follow along with this

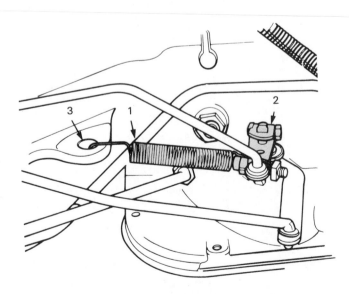

Fig. 42-17. Rule of thumb for making throttle linkage adjustments is to remove all slack in linkage before making adjustment. In this step of procedure, a spare spring 1 holds transmission throttle lever 2 forward against stop. (American Motors Corp.)

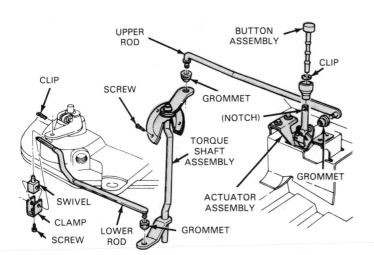

Fig. 42-19. Chrysler uses a swivel block in gearshift linkage. To adjust linkage: loosen lockscrew, move shift lever on transmission to Park position, tighten swivel block. (Chrysler Corp.)

Chrysler console gearshift linkage adjusting procedure:
1. Make sure adjustable swivel block is free to turn on shift rod. Clean or repair parts if necessary.
2. Place console gearshift lever in Park position.
3. With all linkage assembled and swivel block lock screw loose, move shift lever on transmission to rear detent position (Park).
4. Tighten swivel block screw to 90 in. lb. (10 N·m).
5. Test adjustment: Detent positions for Neutral and Drive should be within limits of console gearshift lever gate stops. Key start must occur only when console lever is in Park or Neutral.

A Cadillac gearshift linkage adjusting procedure is illustrated and described in Fig. 42-20. Later models are equipped with a transmission control cable rather than mechanical linkage.

TROUBLESHOOTING TIPS

Automatic transmission problems usually are created by one or more of the following causes:
1. Poor engine performance.
2. Low or high fluid level.
3. Incorrect throttle linkage or gearshift linkage adjustment.
4. Incorrect band adjustment.
5. Incorrect hydraulic control pressure adjustments.
6. Malfunction of hydraulic system.
7. Malfunction of mechanical parts.

Knowing the basics of automatic transmission operation and understanding the importance of correct fluid level and the various key adjustments helps greatly in diagnosing transmission problems. Road testing, then, is the next step after fluid level and adjustments have been checked and corrected.

ROAD TESTING

Road testing is a quick way to begin diagnosis of an automatic transmission problem. Operate the transmission in each gear range and check for slippage, shift points, harsh or spongy shifts, and speeds at which upshifts and downshifts occur. Slippage or engine speed flare-up in any gear usually signals clutch, band, or overrunning clutch problems.

The key to diagnosing the source of a transmission problem during a road test is to know which elements of the transmission are in use in the various gear ranges. This information is available in Clutch and Band Application Charts contained in manufacturers' service manuals. A sample chart is shown in Fig. 42-21.

To put the chart to use, note that both clutches are applied in Drive, third gear only, Fig. 42-21. Therefore, if the transmission slips in third gear, either the front or rear clutch is slipping. To determine which clutch is slipping, select another gear—such as Reverse—which does

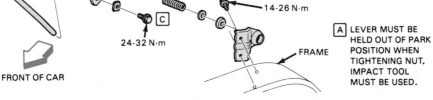

Fig. 42-20. A Cadillac column shift adjustment procedure is given. Note warning at A. (Cadillac Motor Car Div., General Motors Corp.)

ELEMENTS IN USE AT EACH POSITION OF THE SELECTOR LEVER

Lever Position	Standard Ratio	Wide Ratio	Start Safety	Parking Sprag	Clutches Front	Clutches Rear	Clutches Over-running	Lock-up	Bands (Kickdown) Front	Bands (Low-Rev.) Rear
P—PARK			X	X						
R—REVERSE	2.21	2.21			X					X
N—NEUTRAL			X							
D—DRIVE										
First	2.45	2.74				X	X			
Second	1.45	1.54				X			X	
Direct	1.00	1.00			X	X		X		
2—SECOND										
First	2.45	2.74				X	X			
Second	1.45	1.54				X			X	
1—LOW (First)	2.45	2.74				X				X

Fig. 42-21. Study this Clutch and Band Application Chart to learn which elements are in use in various gear ranges. This application chart is especially useful in conjunction with road test results. (Chrysler Corp.)

not use one of these units. Then, if the transmission slips in reverse, the front clutch is slipping. See Fig. 42-21. If the transmission does not slip in reverse, the rear clutch is slipping.

Road testing and use of the Clutch and Band Application Chart provide a means of diagnosis by the process of elimination. By this process, you can pinpoint the malfunctioning unit. However, hydraulic pressure tests must be performed to find the cause.

HYDRAULIC PRESSURE TESTING

All automatic transmissions have pressure testing ports, Fig. 42-7, to which a pressure gauge may be attached, Fig. 42-22. Then, with fluid level and fluid condition checked—and control linkage adjustments found to be correct—pressure test procedures are followed and diagnosis charts consulted to determine the cause of problems within the transmission. The car manufacturers' service manuals carry this information, along with full details on transmission disassembly, parts replacement, and reassembly.

STALL TESTING

Stall testing provides a means of checking the holding ability of the converter-stator overrunning clutch and front and rear clutches of the transmission. It basically determines the maximum engine rpm available at full throttle with the rear wheels locked and the transmission in Drive.

To make the stall test:
1. Connect a tachometer to engine.
2. Check and adjust transmission fluid level.
3. Run engine until ATF reaches normal operating temperature.
4. Block front wheels.
5. Apply parking brakes.
6. Apply service brakes.

WARNING: Do not allow anyone to stand in front of vehicle under test.

7. Accelerate engine to wide open throttle and note maximum engine rpm on tachometer.
WARNING: Do not hold throttle open any longer than five seconds at a time. If more than one stall test is required, cool transmission fluid between tests by operating engine at 1000 rpm with transmission in Neutral for at least 20 seconds.

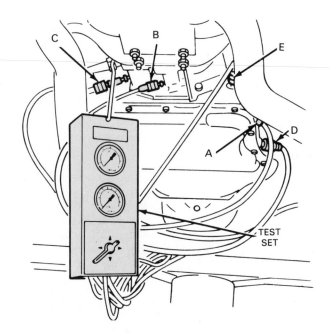

Fig. 42-22. To make hydraulic pressure tests, test set is connected to: A—Accumulator line pressure port. B—Governor pressure port. C—Lubrication pressure port. D—Front servo release pressure port. E—Rear servo apply pressure port. (American Motors Corp.)

8. If engine exceeds rpm indicated on stall speed chart for vehicle under test, release the accelerator immediately; transmission clutch slippage is occurring.
9. Shift transmission into Neutral, operate engine for 20 seconds at 1000 rpm.
10. Stop engine, shift into Park, and release parking and service brakes.
11. Check test results with Stall Speed Charts. (Example: Six cylinder engine—three speed automatic transmission—1850-2150 rpm.)

AIR PRESSURE TESTING

As a followup diagnostic "tool," air pressure testing before automatic transmission removal will confirm suspected improper clutch, band, and servo operation. Also, after repairs have been made, repeat air pressure testing will confirm proper operation of these units.

The air pressure testing procedure involves substituting air pressure for hydraulic pressure at appropriate transmission case passages after the control valve body has been removed. See Fig. 42-23. Generally, pressures of 30 to 100 psi (210 to 690 kPa) are required to perform the air pressure tests.

CAUTION: Use dry, filtered compressed air only when performing air pressure tests.

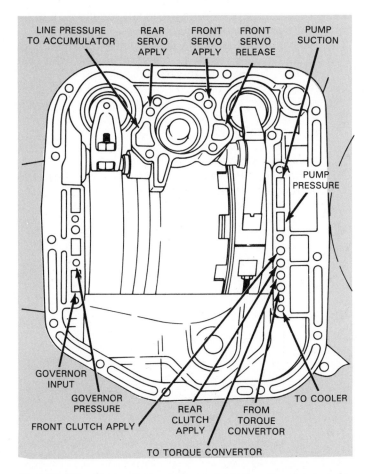

Fig. 42-23. Air pressure tests substitute air pressure for hydraulic pressure in testing for proper or improper operation of transmission control mechanism.   (American Motors Corp.)

Basically, the tests require the introduction of air pressure to specific passages while placing two fingers on the transmission case in the general area where movement of a piston being applied can be felt. An example of typical passage locations and identification is given in Fig. 42-23.

WORKING WITH SERVICE MANUALS

Car manufacturers' service manuals provide quick-reference troubleshooting charts for automatic transmission problem diagnosis. A step-by-step approach to solving automatic transmission problems is used.

In-Automobile Diagnostic Procedures are given first, listing problem conditions that can be corrected with the transmission in the automobile. Out-of-Automobile Diagnostic Procedures list problems that call for transmission removal and disassembly.

Familiarize yourself with both types of troubleshooting charts and the service procedures required to return the automatic transmission to normal operating efficiency.

Chapter 42—REVIEW QUESTIONS

Write your answers on a separate sheet of paper. Do not write in this book.
1. Automatic transmissions transmit _____ to the drive shaft of rear wheel drive vehicles.
2. A transaxle combines the _____ and _____ assemblies in a single housing.
3. When transmission trouble occurs, check _____ first.
4. What color is "normal" for automatic transmission fluid?
   a. Dark brown.
   b. Milky pink.
   c. Cherry red.
   d. Clear.
5. Technician A says that varnish buildup on the transmission dipstick is caused by high temperatures and severe oxidation of the ATF. Technician B says that varnish buildup on the transmission dipstick is caused by antifreeze contamination of the ATF. Who is right?
   a. A only.
   b. B only.
   c. Both A and B.
   d. Neither A nor B.
6. Technician A says that gum deposits on the transmission dipstick are caused by high temperatures and severe oxidation of the ATF. Technician B says that gum deposits on the transmission dipstick are caused by antifreeze contamination of the ATF. Who is right?
   a. A only.
   b. B only.
   c. Both A and B.
   d. Neither A nor B.
7. With the vehicle up on a lift, what is the first step in looking for an ATF leak?
   a. Drain the fluid.
   b. Check tightness of transmission drain plug.
   c. Clean underside of engine oil pan, torque

converter housing, and transmission case and extension housing.

   d. Check oil cooler lines and fittings.

8. Technician A says that a low level of ATF can cause foaming of the fluid. Technician B says that over-filling the transmission with ATF can cause foaming. Who is right?
   a. A only.
   b. B only.
   c. Both A and B.
   d. Neither A nor B.

9. If the source of ATF leakage is at the oil pump seal, pump body, oil pump-to-case bolt, repair requires removal of the transmission. True or False?

10. When the vehicle is on the lift, check the condition of the engine mount. If it is _____ or _____, replace the mount.

11. Once the transmission oil pan has been removed, always remove the _____ for cleaning or replacement.

12. Most late model automatic transmissions have a drain plug in the oil pan. True or False?

13. When service is completed, reinstall the oil pan using a new gasket without _____ or _____.

14. A general procedure for automatic transmission band adjustment is:
   a. Tighten band adjusting screw to a specified torque tightness.
   b. Tighten band adjusting screw to a specified torque tightness, then back it off a given number of turns.
   c. Tighten band adjusting screw to the point where the torque wrench just begins to indicate no clearance and no torque tension.
   d. Back off band adjusting screw two turns.

15. Transmission band adjusting screws are always externally accessible for adjustment. True or False?

16. When adjusting bands on certain Ford automatic transmissions, _____ and _____ locknut from band adjusting screw because it also serves to seal in fluid.

17. Name four reasons why engine idle speed adjustment generally has become increasingly complex.

18. The throttle linkage adjustment is critical to proper operation of the _____.

19. Technician A says that if the throttle linkage setting is too short, early shifts may occur. Technician B says that if the throttle linkage setting is too short, slippage between shifts may occur. Who is right?
   a. A only.
   b. B only.
   c. Both A and B.
   d. Neither A nor B.

20. The general rule for throttle linkage adjustment is to remove all _____ from the linkage.

21. The correct gearshift linkage adjustment properly positions the _____ in the valve body.
   a. Throttle valve.
   b. Manual valve.
   c. Governor valve.
   d. Regulator valve.

22. A check of _____ operation will confirm or condemn gearshift linkage adjustment.

23. Name four common causes of automatic transmission problems.

24. _____ is a quick way to begin diagnosis of an automatic transmission problem.
   a. Hydraulic pressure tests.
   b. Air pressure tests.
   c. Road test.
   d. Stall test.

25. _____ Application Charts show which elements of the transmission are in use in the various gear ranges.

26. _____ pressure tests require ATF drain and transmission oil pan removal.

27. _____ pressure tests do not require ATF drain and transmission oil pan removal.

28. The stall test basically determines the maximum _____ available at full throttle with the rear wheels locked and the transmission in drive.

29. During the stall test, do not hold the throttle open and longer than _____ at a time.
   a. Five seconds.
   b. Ten seconds.
   c. Twenty seconds.
   d. Thirty seconds.

30. Generally, air pressure of _____ psi is used to perform air pressure tests of clutch, band, and servo operation.
   a. 10-50.
   b. 30-100.
   c. 50-150.
   d. 100-200.

With car on four-post electric lift, service technician adjusts position and tilt of lifting head and load support arms to insure safe and efficient automatic transmission removal. (Lincoln Div., of McNeil Corp.)

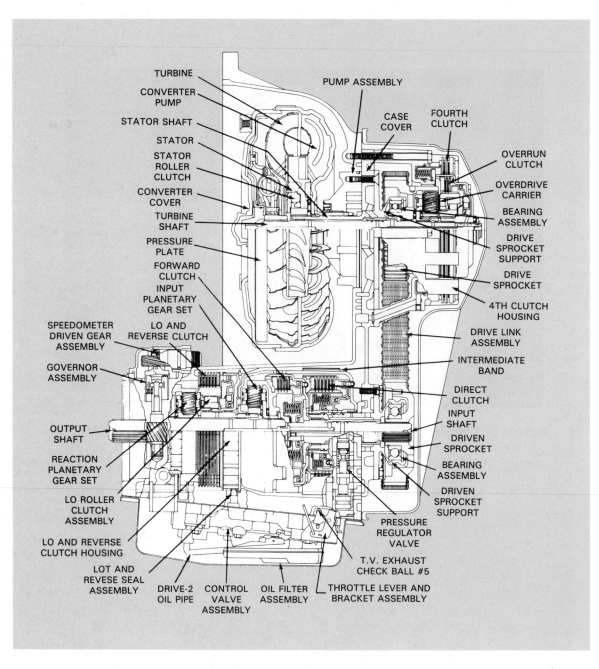

TURBINE

CONVERTER PUMP

STATOR SHAFT

STATOR

STATOR ROLLER CLUTCH

CONVERTER COVER

TURBINE SHAFT

PRESSURE PLATE

FORWARD CLUTCH

INPUT PLANETARY GEAR SET

SPEEDOMETER DRIVEN GEAR ASSEMBLY

LO AND REVERSE CLUTCH

GOVERNOR ASSEMBLY

OUTPUT SHAFT

REACTION PLANETARY GEAR SET

LO ROLLER CLUTCH ASSEMBLY

LO AND REVERSE CLUTCH HOUSING

LOT AND REVESE SEAL ASSEMBLY

DRIVE-2 OIL PIPE

CONTROL VALVE ASSEMBLY

OIL FILTER ASSEMBLY

THROTTLE LEVER AND BRACKET ASSEMBLY

T.V. EXHAUST CHECK BALL #5

PRESSURE REGULATOR VALVE

DRIVEN SPROCKET SUPPORT

BEARING ASSEMBLY

DRIVEN SPROCKET

INPUT SHAFT

DIRECT CLUTCH

INTERMEDIATE BAND

DRIVE LINK ASSEMBLY

4TH CLUTCH HOUSING

DRIVE SPROCKET

DRIVE SPROCKET SUPPORT

BEARING ASSEMBLY

OVERDRIVE CARRIER

OVERRUN CLUTCH

FOURTH CLUTCH

CASE COVER

PUMP ASSEMBLY

A transaxle found on front wheel drive cars.

Chapter 43

TRANSAXLES

After studying this chapter, you will be able to:
- Define transaxle and state its function.
- Explain how transaxle gear ratios are determined.
- Describe the makeup and operation of a typical manual transaxle.
- Describe the makeup and operation of a typical automatic transaxle.
- Tell how to perform common maintenance checks and adjustments.
- Discuss the many ways in which manufacturers' service manuals provide mechanics with helpful automotive service information.

A TRANSAXLE is an engine power transfer mechanism that combines a transmission assembly and a differential (final drive) assembly in a single unit. It receives power from the engine and transmits it to the drive axles at the gear ratio selected by the driver. The transaxle is used mainly in front wheel drive applications, Fig. 43-1.

Some mid-engine cars and some with rear wheel drive are also equipped with a transaxle.

TRANSAXLE CONSTRUCTION

Like conventional transmissions, transaxles may be either manual or automatic. Generally, manual transaxles are either four speed or five speed units. Automatic transaxles are either three speed or four speed units. In front wheel drive applications, the transaxle may be mounted transversely (crosswise) or longitudinally (lengthwise) in the engine compartment.

A typical four speed manual transaxle, Fig. 43-2, consists of an aluminum transaxle case, a gear selector lever, input cluster gear (shaft), main shaft with various gears and synchronizer assemblies, output gear (shaft), differential housing, and a differential assembly.

A typical five speed manual transaxle is similar in design and function to a four speed unit employed by the same manufacturer. The five speed transaxle,

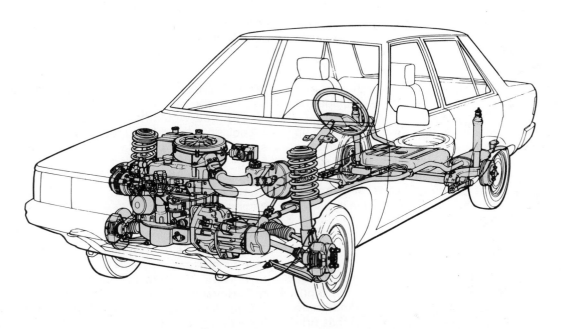

Fig. 43-1. Phantom view of front wheel drive sedan shows typical application of a transverse mounted engine and manual transaxle. (Renault—American Motors Corp.)

515

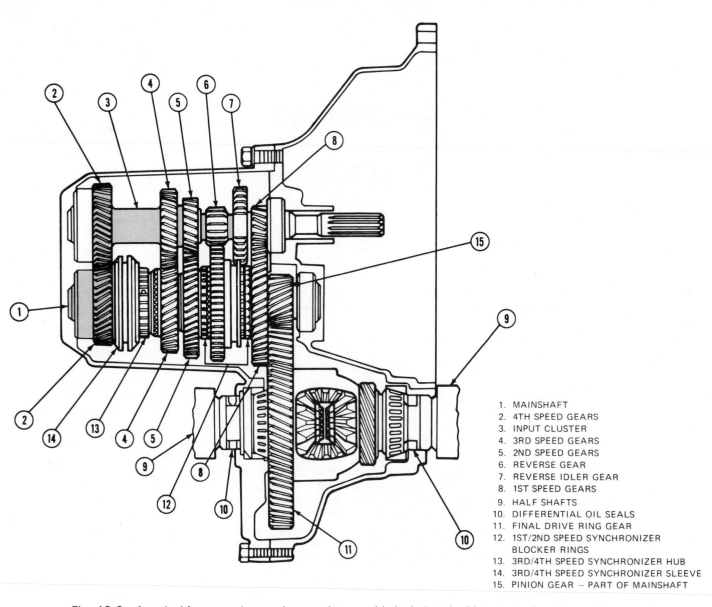

1. MAINSHAFT
2. 4TH SPEED GEARS
3. INPUT CLUSTER
4. 3RD SPEED GEARS
5. 2ND SPEED GEARS
6. REVERSE GEAR
7. REVERSE IDLER GEAR
8. 1ST SPEED GEARS
9. HALF SHAFTS
10. DIFFERENTIAL OIL SEALS
11. FINAL DRIVE RING GEAR
12. 1ST/2ND SPEED SYNCHRONIZER
    BLOCKER RINGS
13. 3RD/4TH SPEED SYNCHRONIZER HUB
14. 3RD/4TH SPEED SYNCHRONIZER SLEEVE
15. PINION GEAR — PART OF MAINSHAFT

Fig. 43-2. A typical four speed manual transaxle assembly includes: 1—Main shaft. 2—4th speed gears. 3—Input cluster.   (Ford Motor Co.)

however, has an additional fifth gear, a fifth gear and synchronizer assembly, and a shifter fork to provide the fifth gear drive range.

A typical three speed automatic transaxle is made up of an aluminum transaxle case, a gear selector lever, a torque converter, valve body, input shaft, output shaft, two multiple disc clutches, an overrunning clutch, front and rear planetary gearsets, drums, bands, and servos, a transfer shaft, governor assembly, extension housing, and differential assembly.

TRANSAXLE GEAR RATIOS

As with manual transmissions, transaxle gear ratios are determined by how many teeth are on the input cluster gear and how many teeth are on the matching gear on the main shaft. For example, assume that first gear on the input cluster has 13 teeth. Next, assume that the first gear on the main shaft has 42 teeth. See Fig.

43-2. Then, by dividing the number of teeth on the main shaft by the number of teeth on the input cluster (42 ÷ 13), you would have a gear ratio of 3.23 to 1.

Looking at actual gear ratios in current use, Ford's four speed manual transaxle has the following gear ratios: First—3.23 to 1. Second—1.92 to 1. Third—1.23 to 1. Fourth—0.81 to 1. Reverse—3.46 to 1. Note that fourth speed is overdrive. The 0.81 to 1 ratio permits engine speed to be reduced by 20 percent over the conventional 1.0 to 1 direct drive of three and four speed manual transmissions.

Oldsmobile's five speed manual transaxle has the following gear ratios: First—3.91 to 1. Second—2.15 to 1. Third—1.45 to 1. Fourth—1.03 to 1. Fifth—0.74 to 1. Reverse—3.50 to 1. Here, fifth speed is overdrive.

Chrysler's three speed automatic transaxle has the following gear ratios: First—2.69 to 1. Second—1.55 to 1. Third—1.00 to 1. Reverse—2.10 to 1. Here, there is no overdrive. Third speed is direct drive.

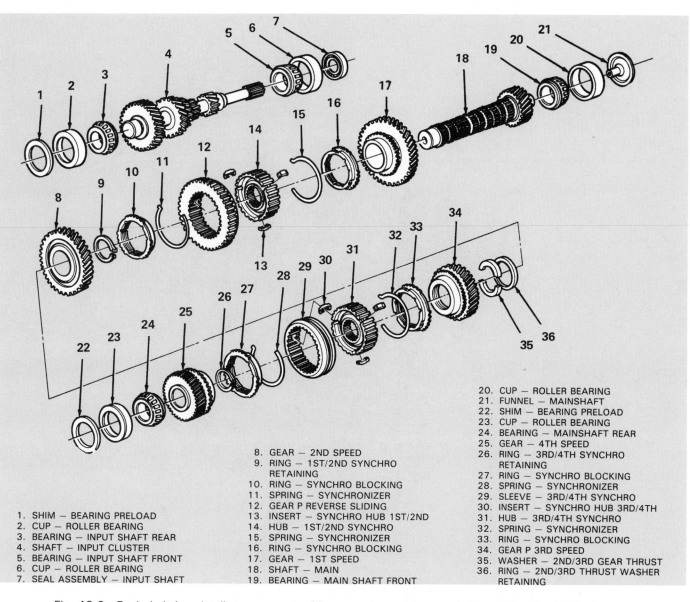

1. SHIM — BEARING PRELOAD
2. CUP — ROLLER BEARING
3. BEARING — INPUT SHAFT REAR
4. SHAFT — INPUT CLUSTER
5. BEARING — INPUT SHAFT FRONT
6. CUP — ROLLER BEARING
7. SEAL ASSEMBLY — INPUT SHAFT

8. GEAR — 2ND SPEED
9. RING — 1ST/2ND SYNCHRO RETAINING
10. RING — SYNCHRO BLOCKING
11. SPRING — SYNCHRONIZER
12. GEAR P REVERSE SLIDING
13. INSERT — SYNCHRO HUB 1ST/2ND
14. HUB — 1ST/2ND SYNCHRO
15. SPRING — SYNCHRONIZER
16. RING — SYNCHRO BLOCKING
17. GEAR — 1ST SPEED
18. SHAFT — MAIN
19. BEARING — MAIN SHAFT FRONT

20. CUP — ROLLER BEARING
21. FUNNEL — MAINSHAFT
22. SHIM — BEARING PRELOAD
23. CUP — ROLLER BEARING
24. BEARING — MAINSHAFT REAR
25. GEAR — 4TH SPEED
26. RING — 3RD/4TH SYNCHRO RETAINING
27. RING — SYNCHRO BLOCKING
28. SPRING — SYNCHRONIZER
29. SLEEVE — 3RD/4TH SYNCHRO
30. INSERT — SYNCHRO HUB 3RD/4TH
31. HUB — 3RD/4TH SYNCHRO
32. SPRING — SYNCHRONIZER
33. RING — SYNCHRO BLOCKING
34. GEAR P 3RD SPEED
35. WASHER — 2ND/3RD GEAR THRUST
36. RING — 2ND/3RD THRUST WASHER RETAINING

Fig. 43-3. Exploded view details components of four speed manual transaxle input and main shaft clusters. (Ford Motor Co.)

TRANSAXLE OPERATION

A typical four speed manual transaxle uses a cable to operate the clutch. It connects the clutch pedal to the clutch lever on the transaxle. See Chapter 38. When the driver depresses the clutch pedal, the cable moves the clutch lever which, in turn, moves the clutch release bearing to disengage the clutch. When the driver lets up on the clutch pedal, the cable relaxes the tension of the release bearing against the pressure plate fingers, and the clutch is re-engaged. However, in transaxle applications — unlike manual transmission applications — the release bearing remains in light contact with the pressure plate under normal driving conditions.

FOUR SPEED MANUAL TRANSAXLE

A typical Ford four speed manual transaxle is shown in Fig. 43-2. Study the list of parts of the assembly, iden-

tify those parts on the accompanying illustration, and follow this description of four speed transaxle operation.

From the clutch, engine power is transmitted to the main shaft by way of the input cluster gear. Each gear on the input shaft is in constant mesh with a matching gear on the main shaft. These matching gearsets provide the four forward gear ratios as each is put into operation by shifting synchronizers into and out of engagement with the selected gear. See Fig. 43-3.

When the engine is running, the input cluster shaft will turn, too. The main shaft gears, however, will freewheel unless locked to the main shaft by one of the synchronizers. In Neutral, the main shaft gears will turn freely, and the engine torque will not be transmitted to the pinion gear on the end of the main shaft. See Fig. 43-3.

If one of the synchronizers is shifted, the gear it controls will be locked to the main shaft. The main shaft will turn at a speed determined by engine speed and the gear ratio of the gear selected.

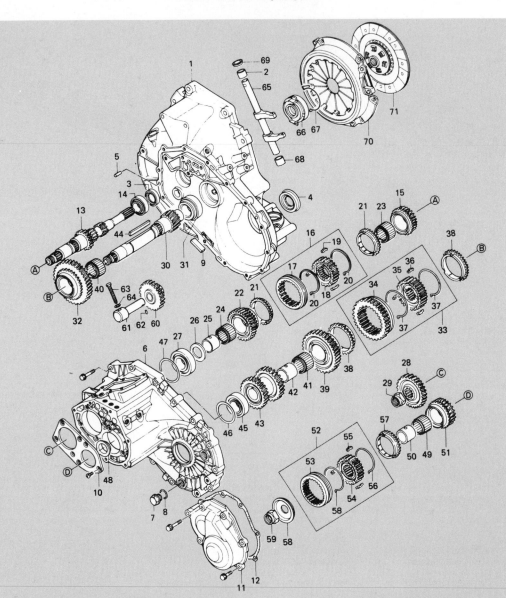

1.	CLUTCH AND DIFF. HOUSING	
2.	CLUTCH SHAFT BUSHING	
3.	INPUT SHAFT OIL SEAL	
4.	DRIVE SHAFT OIL SEAL	
5.	STRAIGHT KNOCK PIN	
6.	TRANSAXLE CASE	
7.	DRAIN PLUG	
8.	GASKET	
9.	MAGNET	
10.	BEARING RETAINER	
11.	REAR COVER	
12.	GASKET	
13.	INPUT SHAFT	
14.	INPUT SHAFT FRONT BEARING	
15.	3RD GEAR ASSEMBLY	
16.	3RD/4TH SYNCHRONIZER ASM.	
17.	SYNCHRONIZER SLEEVE	
18.	CLUTCH HUB	
19.	INSERT	
20.	INSERT SPRING	
21.	3RD/4TH BLOCKER RING	
22.	4TH GEAR ASSEMBLY	
23.	3RD NEEDLE BEARING	
24.	4TH NEEDLE BEARING	
25.	4TH COLLAR	
26.	4TH GEAR THRUST WASHER	
27.	INPUT SHAFT REAR BEARING	
28.	5TH GEAR	
29.	INPUT SHAFT END NUT	
30.	OUTPUT SHAFT	
31.	OUTPUT SHAFT FRONT BEARING	
32.	1ST GEAR ASSEMBLY	
33.	1ST/2ND SYNCHRONIZER ASSEMBLY	
34.	REVERSE GEAR	
35.	CLUTCH HUB	
36.	INSERT	
37.	INSERT SPRING	
38.	1ST/2ND BLOCKER RING	
39.	2ND GEAR ASSEMBLY	
40.	1ST NEEDLE BEARING	
41.	2ND NEEDLE BEARING	
42.	2ND COLLAR	
43.	3RD/4TH OUTPUT GEAR	
44.	KEY	
45.	OUTPUT SHAFT REAR BEARING	
46.	OUTPUT SHAFT BEARING SHIM	
47.	INPUT SHAFT BEARING SHIM	
48.	5TH GEAR THRUST WASHER	
49.	5TH NEEDLE BEARING	
50.	5TH COLLAR	
51.	5TH GEAR ASSEMBLY	
52.	5TH SYNCHRONIZER ASSEMBLY	
53.	SYNCHRONIZER SLEEVE	
54.	CLUTCH HUB	
55.	INSERT	
56.	INSERT SPRING	
57.	5TH BLOCKER RING	
58.	INSERT STOPPER PLATE	
59.	OUTPUT SHAFT END NUT	
60.	REVERSE IDLER GEAR ASM.	
61.	REVERSE IDLER SHAFT	
62.	STRAIGHT PIN	
63.	REVERSE IDLER SHAFT BOLT	
64.	GASKET	
65.	CLUTCH FORK SHAFT ASM.	
66.	CLUTCH RELEASE BEARING	
67.	RELEASE BEARING SPRING	
68.	CLUTCH SHAFT BUSHING	
69.	CLUTCH SHAFT SEAL	
70.	CLUTCH PRESSURE PLATE ASM.	
71.	CLUTCH DISK ASSEMBLY	

Fig. 43-4. Exploded view shows relationship of parts in a typical five speed manual transaxle. (Chevrolet Motor Div., General Motors Corp.)

The pinion gear on the end of the main shaft is part of the shaft. It is also in constant mesh with the ring gear of the differential assembly. Therefore, both the pinion gear and ring gear will rotate when the main shaft is rotating. See Fig. 43-2.

The power flow from the engine, then, is from the input cluster gear to the matching gear on the main shaft; from the main shaft and pinion gear to the differential ring gear; through the differential assembly to the half shafts to the driving wheels. The differential is a conventional final drive arrangement of gears that divides the torque between the drive axles and allows them to rotate at different speeds.

FIVE SPEED MANUAL TRANSAXLE

A typical Oldsmobile five speed manual transaxle is shown in Fig. 43-4. Study the lists of parts of the assembly, identify the parts by the number on the accompanying illustration, and follow this description of five speed transaxle operation.

As with the four speed manual transaxle, engine power is transmitted from the clutch to the five speed transaxle output shaft by shifting a synchronizer assembly into engagement with a selected gear on the input shaft. This causes the output shaft to turn at a speed determined by engine speed and the gear ratio selected.

The difference in five speed transaxle makeup is the addition of a fifth speed gear at the rear end of the input shaft, which is in mesh with a fifth speed gear and synchronizer assembly at the rear end of the output shaft. See Fig. 43-5.

Power flow, then, in fifth gear, would be from the clutch to the input shaft, to the fifth gear on the output shaft; from the integral pinion gear on the front end of the output shaft to the ring gear of the differential, Fig. 43-6; through the differential assembly to the half shafts to the driving wheels.

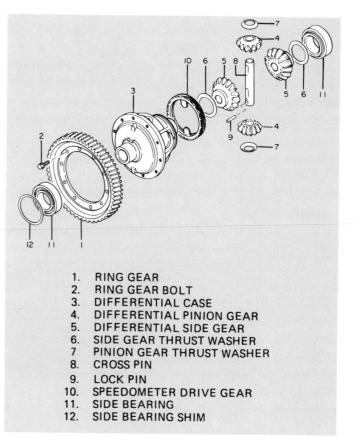

1. RING GEAR
2. RING GEAR BOLT
3. DIFFERENTIAL CASE
4. DIFFERENTIAL PINION GEAR
5. DIFFERENTIAL SIDE GEAR
6. SIDE GEAR THRUST WASHER
7. PINION GEAR THRUST WASHER
8. CROSS PIN
9. LOCK PIN
10. SPEEDOMETER DRIVE GEAR
11. SIDE BEARING
12. SIDE BEARING SHIM

Fig. 43-6. Parts of differential assembly of a five speed manual transaxle are pictured and identified. (Oldsmobile Div., General Motors Corp.)

THREE SPEED AUTOMATIC TRANSAXLE

A typical Chrysler three speed automatic transaxle is shown in Fig. 43-7. Study the parts identified in this illustration, and follow the description of three speed automatic transaxle operation.

Engine power is transmitted to the torque converter. From the converter, power flow is through the input shaft to the multiple disc clutches. Flow continues to the planetary gearsets based on which clutches are engaged and which bands are applied. See chart of "Elements in Use at Each Position of the Selector Lever" shown in Fig. 43-8.

The common sun gear of the two planetary gearsets is connected to the front clutch by a driving shell, which is splined to the sun gear and the front clutch retainer. Consulting the chart in Fig. 43-8, you can see that in first gear, the rear clutch is engaged and the rear band is applied. Also note that in reverse gear, the front clutch is engaged and the rear band is applied. Output direction and gear ratio are determined by which parts of the planetary gearsets are held and which parts are driven.

Output from the planetary gearsets is by way of the output shaft, Fig. 43-7. The output shaft gear then drives the transfer shaft gear. An integral gear on the other end of the transfer shaft drives the ring gear of the differential. From here, the differential distributes power flow to the axle shafts as required by vehicle operation.

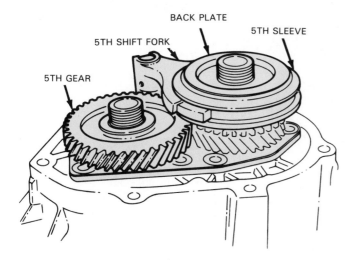

Fig. 43-5. Makeup of this five speed manual transaxle is similar to four speed unit, but includes a fifth speed gear and fifth speed gear and synchronizer assembly at rear of transaxle. (Oldsmobile Div., General Motors Corp.)

BACK PLATE
5TH SHIFT FORK
5TH SLEEVE
5TH GEAR

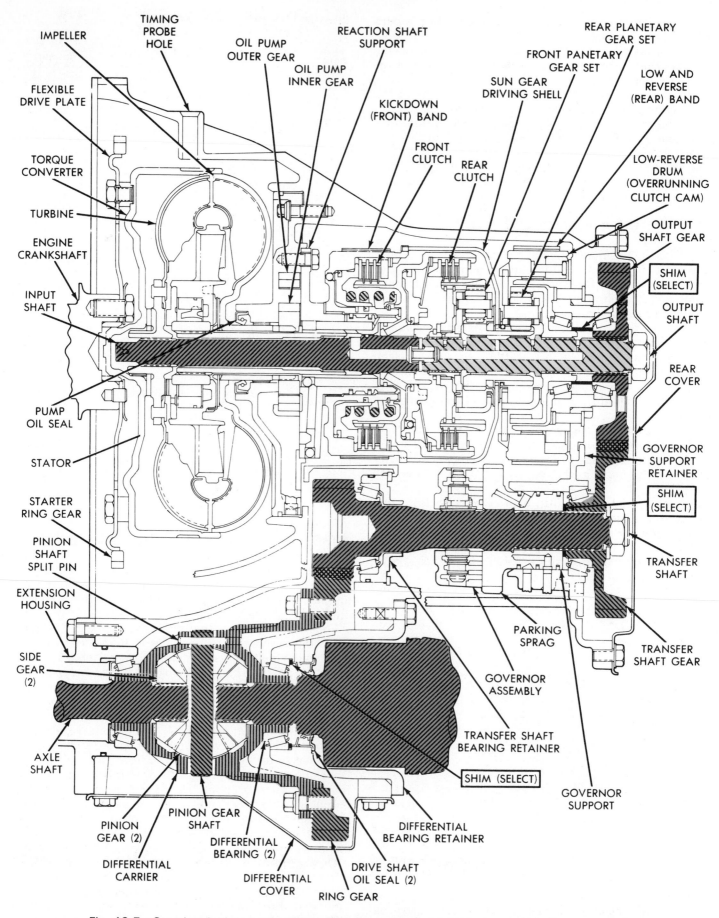

Fig. 43-7. Crosshatched parts of a TorqueFlite three speed automatic transaxle indicate power flow. (Chrysler Corp.)

ELEMENTS IN USE AT EACH POSITION OF THE SELECTOR LEVER

Lever Position	Start Safety	Parking Sprag	Clutches			Bands	
			Front	Rear	Over-running	(Kickdown) Front	(Low-Rev.) Rear
P—Park	X	X					
R—REVERSE			X				X
N—NEUTRAL	X						
D—DRIVE:							
First				X	X		
Second				X		X	
Third			X	X			
2—SECOND:							
First				X	X		
Second				X		X	
1—LOW (First)				X			X

Fig. 43-8. Chart provides means for a quick check to determine which elements of a three speed manual transaxle are in use in each shift lever position. (Chrysler Corp.)

FOUR SPEED AUTOMATIC TRANSAXLE

A General Motors four speed automatic transaxle of unusual design is shown in Fig. 43-9. Study the parts identified in this illustration and note the "different" features of this unit.

The GM four speed, front wheel drive, automatic overdrive transaxle uses only two planetary gearsets to perform all functions. Shifting is accomplished by the application and release of clutches that connect specific gearset components.

From input to output, Fig. 43-9, the four speed unit consists of: torque converter with converter clutch; sprocket and drive link assembly; 1-2 and reverse band assemblies; input, 3rd, 2nd, and 4th multiple disc clutches; input sprag and 3rd roller clutch, compound planetary gearset; differential/final drive assembly.

When engine power is applied to this GM transaxle in first gear, high reduction is achieved through components in both planetary gearsets. Each gear in use helps step down the gear ratio to 2.92 to 1.

In first gear, the input sun gear drives the pinion carrier and internal gear of the input gearset. This assembly, in turn, drives the internal gear and pinion carrier of the reaction gearset. A servo applies the 1-2 band, locking the reaction sun gear, and power output is by way of the reaction gearset pinion carrier, Fig. 43-10.

In second gear, the second clutch becomes the power input to the input gearset. Power flow takes place when the input clutch housing drives the second clutch housing by means of splined clutch plates. From here, power flow is transmitted to the reverse reaction drum. This drum drives the input gearset internal gear, which turns the reaction gear pinion carrier gearset as the final drive output.

In third gear, the third clutch is engaged and drives the input gearset sun gear at the same speed as the torque converter turbine. The input gearset is still driven by the second clutch. In this setup, Fig. 43-9, the input sun gear and carrier pinion gears are rotating at the same speed. This forces the internal gear to turn with them, which results in direct drive. Output is by way of the internal gear of the reaction gearset at a 1.0 to 1 ratio.

In fourth gear, power flow is from the second clutch to the input gearset. The input sun gear is held stationary, causing the input carrier to drive the reaction gearset carrier. The reaction internal gear then becomes the output in overdrive. The large size internal gear drives the final drive sun gear to achieve an overdrive ratio of .70 to 1.

In reverse, the reverse band is applied to hold the input carrier assembly. With the carrier held stationary, the carrier pinion gears react as idler gears to drive the internal gear in the opposite direction.

The differential/final drive is also of unusual construction. It utilizes a planetary gearset (instead of conventional ring and pinion gears) to actuate the differential side gears and differential pinion gears. See Fig. 43-11. The side gears are connected to the axle shafts. The pinion gears act as idlers to transfer power from the carrier to the side gears, while allowing unequal speeds of axle rotation when the vehicle is rounding a curve.

AUTOMATIC TRANSAXLE ADVANCES

"Lockup torque converters" in automatic transmissions were described in detail in Chapter 41. These converters are equipped with an internal locking mechanism called a "converter clutch" that locks the converter turbine to the impeller in direct drive. In effect, the converter clutch provides a direct, mechanical drive to eliminate hydraulic converter slippage for greater efficiency and economy.

Some transaxles, too, are equipped with converter clutches to provide these advantages. Ford Motor Company, for example, has a three speed automatic transaxle with "CLC" (centrifugally linked converter). See Fig. 43-12. This converter has a bypass clutch that is actuated when centrifugal force causes it to lock up.

Ford also developed a four speed automatic overdrive transaxle with an electronically controlled torque converter bypass clutch. This converter clutch is controlled

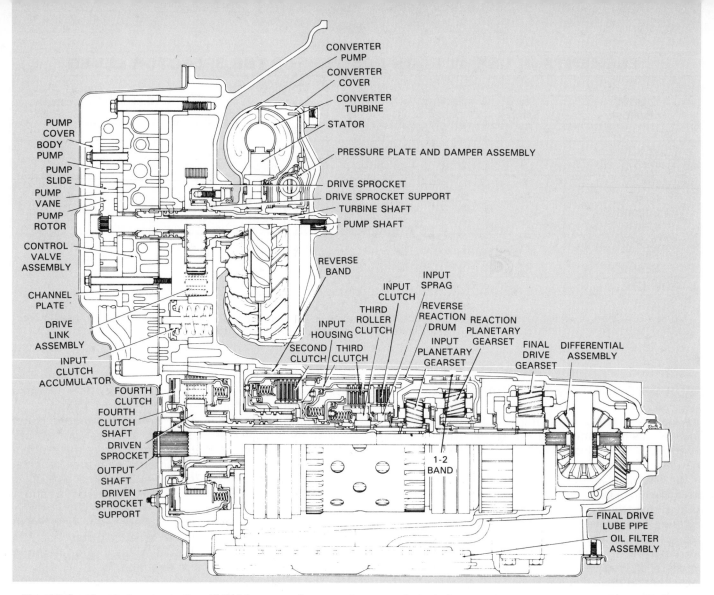

CONVERTER PUMP
CONVERTER COVER
CONVERTER TURBINE
STATOR
PRESSURE PLATE AND DAMPER ASSEMBLY
DRIVE SPROCKET
DRIVE SPROCKET SUPPORT
TURBINE SHAFT
PUMP SHAFT

PUMP COVER
BODY PUMP
PUMP SLIDE
PUMP VANE
PUMP ROTOR
CONTROL VALVE ASSEMBLY
CHANNEL PLATE
DRIVE LINK ASSEMBLY
INPUT CLUTCH ACCUMULATOR
FOURTH CLUTCH
FOURTH CLUTCH SHAFT
DRIVEN SPROCKET
OUTPUT SHAFT
DRIVEN SPROCKET SUPPORT

REVERSE BAND
INPUT CLUTCH
INPUT SPRAG
THIRD ROLLER CLUTCH
REVERSE REACTION DRUM
REACTION PLANETARY GEARSET
INPUT HOUSING
INPUT PLANETARY GEARSET
FINAL DRIVE GEARSET
DIFFERENTIAL ASSEMBLY
SECOND CLUTCH
THIRD CLUTCH
1-2 BAND
FINAL DRIVE LUBE PIPE
OIL FILTER ASSEMBLY

Fig. 43-9. Unusual construction of GM four speed automatic transaxle includes a reverse reaction drum, input planetary gearset, reaction planetary gearset, and final drive planetary gearset. (Buick Motor Div., General Motors Corp.)

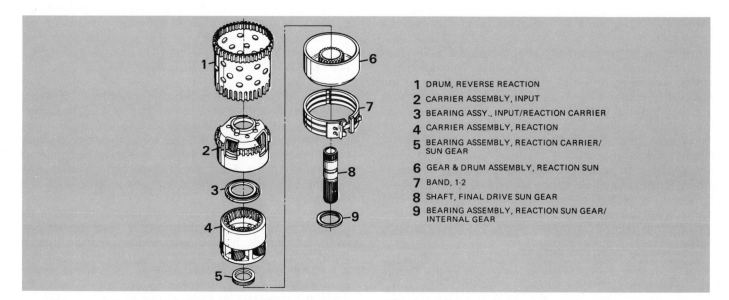

1 DRUM, REVERSE REACTION
2 CARRIER ASSEMBLY, INPUT
3 BEARING ASSY., INPUT/REACTION CARRIER
4 CARRIER ASSEMBLY, REACTION
5 BEARING ASSEMBLY, REACTION CARRIER/ SUN GEAR
6 GEAR & DRUM ASSEMBLY, REACTION SUN
7 BAND, 1-2
8 SHAFT, FINAL DRIVE SUN GEAR
9 BEARING ASSEMBLY, REACTION SUN GEAR/ INTERNAL GEAR

Fig. 43-10. Exploded view shows reverse reaction drum and reaction planetary gearset elements of four speed automatic transaxle. (Buick Motor Div., General Motors Corp.)

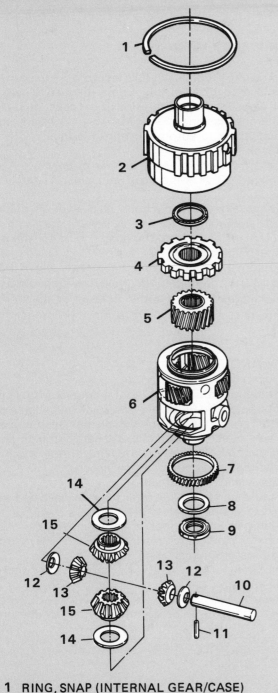

1. RING, SNAP (INTERNAL GEAR/CASE)
2. GEAR, FINAL DRIVE INTERNAL
3. BEARING ASSEMBLY, (INTERNAL GEAR/PARK GEAR)
4. GEAR, PARKING
5. GEAR, FINAL DRIVE SUN
6. CARRIER, FINAL DRIVE
7. GEAR, GOVERNOR DRIVE
8. WASHER, CARRIER/CASE SELECTIVE
9. BEARING ASM., (SELECTIVE WASHER/CASE)
10. SHAFT, DIFFERENTIAL PINION
11. PINION, DIFFERENTIAL PINION SHAFT RET.
12. WASHER, PINION THRUST
13. PINION, DIFFERENTIAL
14. WASHER, DIFFERENTIAL SIDE GEAR THRUST
15. GEAR, DIFFERENTIAL SIDE

Fig. 43-11. Exploded view reveals individual parts arrangement of final drive planetary gearset and final drive assembly of GM four speed automatic transaxle.
(Buick Motor Div., General Motors Corp.)

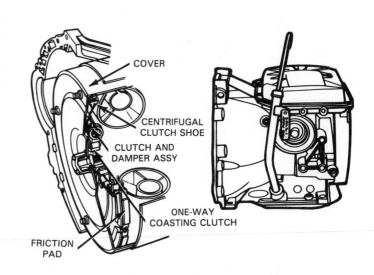

Fig. 43-12. This three speed automatic transaxle torque converter has a bypass clutch that "locks up" to provide a mechanical connection from flywheel to gear train.
(Ford Motor Co.)

by the EEC-IV engine control system to provide direct, mechanical torque flow in third and fourth gear ranges under certain conditions.

AMC/Renault also has a computer controlled automatic transaxle. It utilizes a computer to actuate two electric solenoid ball valves that route the hydraulic pressure to effect gear shifts as car speed increases. A "shift schedule" stored in the computer's memory establishes which gear range is required for any given situation.

This automatic transaxle computer receives inputs from four sensors and switches: a multifunction switch; engine load sensor; road speed sensor; kickdown switch. The computer compares these inputs with those stored in the shift schedule, then turns the solenoid valves on or off as needed to obtain the proper gear range.

MANUAL TRANSAXLE TROUBLESHOOTING

Noise in Neutral
1. Neutral rollover rattle (normal).
2. Damaged input gear bearings.
3. Damaged clutch release bearing.

Noise in Forward Gears
1. Low lubricant level.
2. Binding external shift mechanism.
3. Improperly installed clutch disc.
4. Worn or damaged input/output bearings.
5. Worn or damaged gear teeth.
6. Worn or damaged synchronizer.
7. Gear rattle.

Difficult to Shift
1. Improper clutch disengagement.
2. Binding external shift mechanism.
3. Improperly installed clutch disc.
4. Damaged synchronizers or shift mechanisms.
5. Incorrect lubricant.
6. Sticking blocker ring.

Slips Out of Gear
1. Damaged or binding gearshift linkage.
2. Stiff or blocked floor shift.
3. Broken or loose engine mounts.
4. Worn or damaged internal components.
5. Transaxle loose on engine housing.

Gear Clash in Forward Speeds
1. Improper clutch disengagement.
2. Improperly installed clutch disc.
3. Worn or damaged shift forks or synchronizers.

Locked in One Gear
1. Damaged external shift mechanism.
2. Worn or damaged internal shift components.
3. Burred synchronizers.

Will Not Shift Into One Gear
1. Damaged external shift mechanism.
2. Blocked floor shift.
3. Restricted travel of internal shift components.

Will Not Shift Into Reverse
1. Damaged external shift mechanism.
2. Worn or damaged internal components.

Leaks Lubricant
1. Excessive lubricant in transaxle.
2. Damaged drive axle seals.
3. Damaged shift lever seal.
4. Damaged input gear bearing retainer seals.

MANUAL TRANSAXLE MAINTENANCE

Maintenance checks and services on manual transaxles are quite simple. Basically, they include checking fluid level, inspecting for fluid leakage, draining and refilling the transaxle, torque tightening the transaxle-to-engine attaching bolts, and inspecting the condition of the transaxle mounts.

CHECK FLUID LEVEL

The procedure for making fluid level checks varies with make and model of vehicle. Some manual transaxles have fill plugs located on the side of the case, much like manual transmissions. See Fig. 43-13. Others have dipsticks similar to automatic transmissions.

To check fluid:
1. Locate transaxle dipstick at rear of engine.
2. Remove dipstick, wipe clean, and reinstall it until fully seated.
3. Remove dipstick and check fluid level on marked blade. It should be between the ADD mark and the FULL mark. If not, add specified fluid to maintain proper fluid level.
4. Or, remove fill plug on side of transaxle, Fig. 43-13, and insert little finger in fill hole. Level should be at lower edge of hole or within 3/16 in. of lower edge. If not, add specified fluid to maintain proper fluid level.

DRAIN AND REFILL

Most manufacturers state that manual transaxle fluid need not be changed, unless the fluid has become contaminated by water or if the vehicle has been operated under severe service conditions (sustained high speed driving during hot weather, towing a trailer, etc.).

If drain and refill becomes necessary:
1. Raise vehicle on a hoist.
2. Remove pan from side of differential case and allow fluid to drain completely.
3. Clean pan and magnet, if so equipped.
4. Reinstall pan, using prescribed gasket or RTV (room temperature vulcanizing) sealer.
5. Tighten attaching screws to manufacturer's torque specification.
6. Lower hoist.
7. Refill transaxle to proper level with manufacturer's

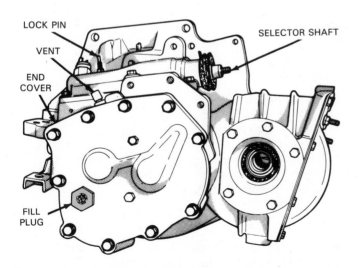

Fig. 43-13. Some manual transaxles have a fill plug located partway up on side of case. When plug is removed, threaded hole serves as an access point for checking fluid level and as a "fill" hole. (Chrysler Corp.)

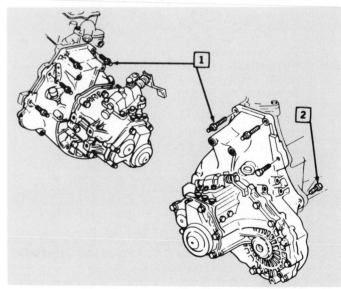

Fig. 43-14. Correct torque tightness of transaxle-to-engine attaching bolts is essential. Torque specification for this five speed manual transaxle is 60 ft. lb. (75 N·m). (Oldsmobile Div., General Motors Corp.)

approved fluid, or refill with a fluid having equivalent properties.

TIGHTEN ATTACHING BOLTS

An important consideration in maintaining manual transaxles is checking the torque tightness of the transaxle-to-engine attaching bolts. Looseness could result in transaxle slipping out of gear. See Fig. 43-14.

The transaxle-to-engine attaching bolts — correctly tightened — help insure the integrity of the power train. They serve to preserve the proper alignment of engine and transaxle. Tighten the attaching bolts to manufacturer's torque specification.

TIGHTEN TRANSAXLE MOUNTS

Any maintenance procedure on manual transaxles requires a check of the condition of the mount (or mounts) and the torque tightness of the mount-to-transaxle case attaching screws or nuts. See Fig. 43-15.

To check the condition of the transaxle mount:
1. Raise car on hoist.
2. Push up or pull down on transaxle case while observing mount.
3. If rubber separates from metal plate of mount, replace mount.
4. If case moves up but not down, mount has collapsed. Replace mount.
5. If mount appears to be intact, tighten screws or nuts attaching mount to crossmember and to transaxle case. Observe manufacturer's torque specifications.

AUTOMATIC TRANSAXLE TROUBLESHOOTING

No Drive Forward
1. Hydraulic pressures too low.
2. Low fluid level.

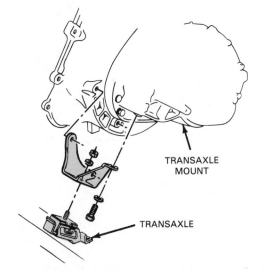

Fig. 43-15. Transaxle mounts vary in design and location, but all support, position, and cradle transaxle assembly in back of engine.
(Buick Motor Div., General Motors Corp.)

3. Valve body malfunction or leakage.
4. Worn or broken input shaft seal rings.
5. Faulty overrunning clutch.
6. Worn or faulty rear clutch.
7. Broken or seized planetary gearset.

No Drive in Reverse
1. Hydraulic pressures too low.
2. Worn low-reverse band.
3. Valve body malfunction or leakage.
4. Low-reverse servo, band, or linkage malfunction.
5. Incorrect gearshift control linkage setup or cable adjustment.
6. Worn or faulty front clutch.

No Drive In Any Position
1. Low hydraulic pressures.
2. Malfunctioning valve body.
3. Low fluid level.
4. Clogged oil filter.
5. Faulty oil pump.
6. Broken or seized planetary gearsets.

Slips In All Positions
1. Low hydraulic pressures.
2. Malfunctioning valve body.
3. Low fluid level.
4. Clogged oil filter.
5. Worn or broken input shaft seal rings.
6. Aerated fluid.

Harsh Engagement
1. Too high engine idle speed.
2. Malfunctioning valve body.
3. Too high hydraulic pressures.
4. Worn or faulty rear clutch.
5. Poor engine performance.

Erratic Shifts
1. Low hydraulic pressures.
2. Malfunctioning valve body.
3. Low fluid level.
4. Incorrect gearshift control linkage setup or cable adjustment.
5. Clogged oil filter.
6. Faulty oil pump.
7. Aerated fluid.
8. Incorrect throttle linkage adjustment.
9. Worn or broken seal rings.
10. Worn or faulty front clutch.

Drives In Neutral
1. Malfunctioning valve body.
2. Incorrect gearshift control linkage setup or cable adjustment.
3. Insufficient clutch plate clearance.
4. Worn or faulty rear clutch.
5. Dragging rear clutch.

Grating, Scraping, Growling Noise
1. Worn low-reverse band.
2. Maladjusted kickdown band.
3. Damaged drive shaft bushings.

4. Broken or seized planetary gearsets.
5. Worn, broken, or seized overrunning clutch.

Buzzing Noise
1. Malfunctioning valve body.
2. Low fluid level.
3. Too low engine idle speed.
4. Damaged overrunning clutch.

Oil Blows Out Filler Hole
1. Clogged oil filter.
2. Aerated fluid.
3. High fluid level.

MAINTENANCE

A quick review of these problems will reveal that certain causes repeatedly appear. Among common causes are: low fluid level, aerated fluid, clogged oil filter, and incorrect gearshift control linkage or cable adjustment.

It follows that regular checks of fluid level, fluid condition, and gearshift control linkage or cable adjustment — with corrective steps taken if necessary — will help avoid problems. See Figs. 43-16 and 43-17.

CHECK FLUID LEVEL

Always check fluid level at normal operating temperature (180-200 °F or 83-93 °C). To check:
1. Park car on level surface.
2. Apply parking brake.
3. Run engine at slow idle.
4. Move gear selector through all gear positions.
5. Shift selector to Park and read fluid level on dipstick (wipe dipstick clean, reinsert until seated, then remove and read level).
6. If fluid is hot, reading should be in "crosshatched" or "marked" area as shown in Fig. 42-16.

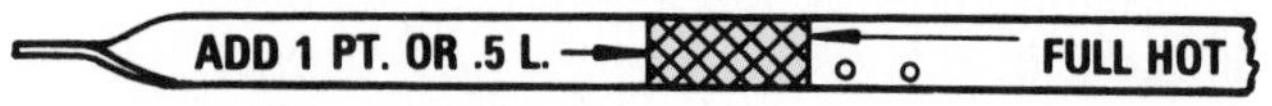

ADD 1 PT. OR .5 L. — ▨▨▨ ∘ ∘ FULL HOT

Fig. 43-16. Transaxle dipsticks are marked to indicate a safe operating area immediately below "full hot" level. Maintain fluid level in this area.
(Cadillac Motor Car Div., General Motors Corp.)

7. Check fluid for burnt smell, indicating overheating of transaxle.
8. Wipe some fluid from dipstick with thumb and index finger and feel for metal particles from worn internal parts.
9. Wipe remainder of fluid on a clean, white cloth and check stain for evidence of contaminants.
10. If hot fluid passes these tests but fluid level is low, add enough recommended fluid through dipstick tube or filler hole to bring level within "marks" on dipstick. See Fig. 43-16.
11. Wait at least 60 seconds, then recheck fluid level. Do not overfill.
12. Install dipstick in tube or filler hole, making sure that

it is fully seated to prevent dirt and/or water from entering dipstick tube or filler hole.

DRAIN AND REFILL

If the fluid level is low, inspect the area all around the bottom of the transaxle for signs of fluid leakage. Leakage at the pan gasket, extension housing oil seal, or at the speedometer pinion adapter can be corrected without removing the transaxle from the vehicle.

Fluid coming from the transaxle vent usually indicates that the transaxle has been overfilled with fluid. When overfilled, the operation of the transaxle aerates the fluid, and foamy fluid is forced from the vent. When this occurs, the transaxle should be drained and refilled with the manufacturer's approved fluid or fluid with equivalent properties.

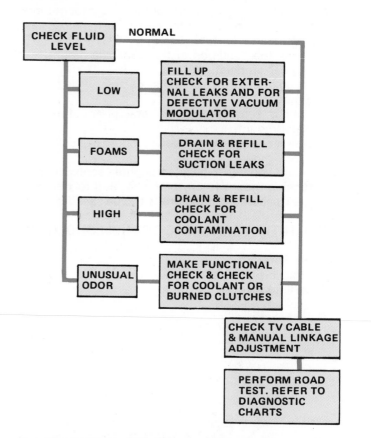

Fig. 43-17. Chart lists recommended steps for checking automatic transaxle fluid level and condition.
(Cadillac Motor Car Div., General Motors Corp.)

If the fluid needs to be changed:
1. Raise vehicle on a hoist.
2. Place oil drain barrel with large opening under transaxle oil pan.
3. Loosen pan bolts and tap pan at one corner to break it loose from gasketed surface and allow fluid to drain into barrel. NOTE: Certain transaxles have a drain plug, Fig. 43-18, simplifying drain procedure.
4. Remove oil pan and dump remainder of fluid into barrel.

5. Remove and replace filter with a new filter.
6. Clean and reinstall pan, using prescribed gasket or RTV (room temperature vulcanizing) sealer. Tighten pan attaching screws to manufacturer's in. lb. torque specification.
7. Lower hoist.
8. Refill transaxle with manufacturer's approved fluid or fluid with equivalent properties.

NOTE: Some transaxles have separate sumps (fluid reservoirs) for transmission fluid and final drive fluid. In others, the final drive sump is integral with the transmission sump. Check manufacturer's service manual for details.

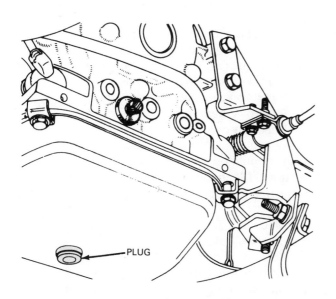

Fig. 43-18. Automatic transaxle fluid drains usually require pan removal. This transaxle has a drain plug. Drain fluid when it is hot to help remove as much old fluid as possible. (Renault-American Motors Corp.)

ADJUST GEARSHIFT CONTROL LINKAGE OR CABLE

Checking and adjusting the gearshift control linkage are key steps of automatic transaxle maintenance. Some setups only require a simple positional adjustment of the cable at the gearshift lever end, Fig. 43-19. Others require a step-by-step procedure from securing body bolts to torque tightening the cable pin attaching nut.

ADJUST TV CONTROL LINKAGE

On certain Ford automatic transaxles, the key linkage adjustment is in the TV (throttle valve) control linkage. Correct positioning of the sliding trunnion block, Fig. 43-20, will insure proper actuation of the internal TV control mechanism that regulates TV control pressure.

To adjust typical TV control linkage for a Ford automatic transaxle:

1. Run engine to normal operating temperature with all accessories turned off.
2. Check to see that hot engine curb idle speed is set to specifications.
3. Use care when working near hot exhaust gas recirculation valve.
4. Loosen bolt on sliding trunnion block.
5. Remove corrosion from TV control rod so that trunnion block slides freely.
6. With engine idling in Park, use one finger to rotate TV control lever upward with light force to bring lever against its internal idle stop.
7. Holding firm, light upward pressure on lever, tighten bolt on trunnion block to 7-11 ft. lb. (9-14 N·m).

CONSULT SERVICE MANUALS

Refer to manufacturers' service manuals for major service operations. Detailed procedures are given for points of inspection, analysis of problems, parts replacements, fits and adjustments with the transaxle in car or out-of-

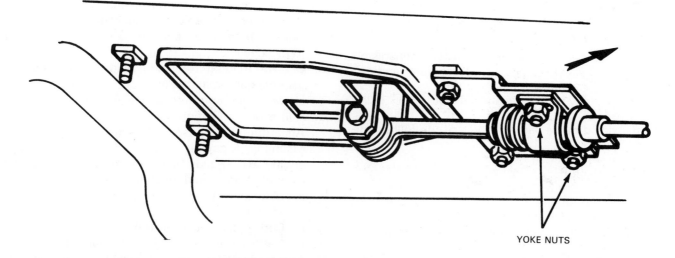

YOKE NUTS

Fig. 43-19. One simple automatic transaxle gear selector cable adjustment only requires that yoke and cable be shifted forward to remove slack in cable. Yoke nuts secure adjustment. (Renault-American Motors Corp.)

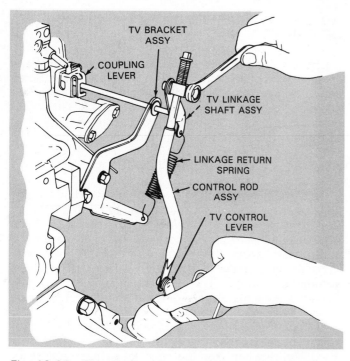

Fig. 43-20. This diagram and specific adjustment procedure given in text reference are typical of service and repair information contained in manufacturers' service manuals. (Ford Motor Co.)

car. Exploded views and step-by-step procedures are spelled out for transaxle removal from the vehicle, for disassembly and reassembly of internal parts, and for transaxle reinstallation.

Service manuals contain directions and specifications for air pressure checks, control pressure tests, shift point checks, and for torque tightening attaching nuts and bolts. Special service tools are listed. Fluid capacities are given. In-depth troubleshooting charts are furnished and road test diagnosis is described in detail.

Service manuals are generally recognized as the ultimate authority for service information for specific makes and models of vehicles.

Chapter 43—REVIEW QUESTIONS

1. A transaxle is an engine power transfer mechanism that combines a _____ assembly and a _____ assembly in a single unit.
2. Transaxles may be either manual or automatic. True or False?
3. Transaxles may be used in which of the following applications:
   a. Front wheel drive cars.
   b. Mid-engine cars.
   c. Rear wheel drive cars.
   d. All of the above.
4. How are transaxle gear ratios determined?
5. Which of the following gear ratios is overdrive?
   a. 0.81 to 1.
   b. 1.23 to 1.
   c. 1.92 to 1.
   d. 3.23 to 1.

6. In transaxle applications, the _____ remains in light contact with the clutch pressure plate under normal driving conditions.
7. Trace power flow in a Ford four speed manual transaxle from engine to driving wheels.
8. The differential (final drive) assembly divides the torque between the _____ and allows them to rotate at different speeds.
9. In transaxles, the differential is also called:
   a. Drive axle.
   b. Final drive.
   c. Torque divider.
   d. Torque converter.
10. Power flow to the planetary gearsets in a Chrysler three speed automatic transaxle is based on which _____ are engaged and which _____ are applied.
11. A General Motors four speed automatic transaxle of unusual design utilizes a _____ instead of conventional ring gear and pinion differential gears.
    a. Sprocket and drive link assembly.
    b. Synchronizer and blocker ring.
    c. Planetary gearset.
    d. Reaction gearset.
12. A manual transaxle slips out of gear. Mechanic A says it could be caused by broken or loose engine mounts. Mechanic B says it could be caused if transaxle is loose on the engine housing. Who is right?
    a. Mechanic A.
    b. Mechanic B.
    c. Both mechanic A and mechanic B.
    d. Neither mechanic A nor mechanic B.
13. A manual transaxle has gear clash in forward speeds. Mechanic A says it could be caused by burred synchronizers. Mechanic B says it could be caused by an improperly installed clutch disc. Who is right?
    a. Mechanic A.
    b. Mechanic B.
    c. Both mechanic A and mechanic B.
    d. Neither mechanic nor mechanic B.
14. Name three maintenance checks on manual transaxles.
15. Change manual transaxle fluid if the fluid has become contaminated by _____ or if the vehicle has been operated under _____.
16. Name two indications of faulty transaxle mounts.
17. An automatic transaxle has harsh engagement. Mechanic A says it could be caused by too high engine idle speed. Mechanic B says it could be caused by low fluid level. Who is right?
    a. Mechanic A.
    b. Mechanic B.
    c. Both mechanic A and mechanic B.
    d. Neither mechanic A nor mechanic B.
18. Automatic transaxle fluid coming from the transaxle vent usually indicates that fluid level is _____.
19. Some transaxles have separate sumps for transmis-

sion fluid and final drive fluid. True or False?
20. Refer to manufacturers' service manuals for:
   a. Major service operations.
   b. Analysis of problems.

c. Specifications for fits and adjustments, fluid capacities, and torque tightness values.
d. All of the above.

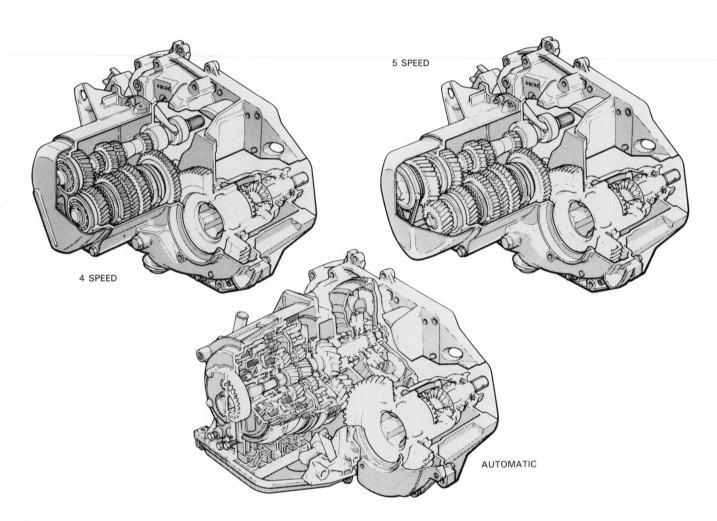

Renault transaxles. Top left. Four speed manual. Top right. Five speed manual. Bottom. Three speed automatic.   (Renault-American Motors Corp.)

Chapter 44

DRIVELINE, UNIVERSAL JOINTS, DIFFERENTIALS, DRIVING AXLES

After studying this chapter, you will be able to:
• Trace the transfer of power in the drive train of a rear wheel drive vehicle.
• Discuss the need for universal joints in the driveline.
• State the principles of operation of the differential.
• Distinguish between Hotchkiss drive, torque tube drive, and control arm drive.
• Explain the types and functions of various constant velocity joints.
• Give examples of several different front wheel drive driving axle systems.

In basic passenger car design, the DRIVELINE connects the transmission with the driving axles. In effect, the driveline transmits engine power to the driving wheels. See Fig. 44-1.

REAR WHEEL DRIVE DRIVELINE

In rear wheel drive applications, the driveline consists of one or more universal joints, the drive shaft, and differential drive pinion gear. The DRIVE TRAIN, on the other hand, includes the engine, transmission, driveline, differential assembly, and driving axles.

In rear wheel drive cars, the engine and transmission are mounted on the frame or unit body crossmembers, and the driving wheels are free to move up and down in relation to the frame. This causes constant changes in the angularity of the line of drive. Therefore, flexibility is needed in the drive train, and it usually is provided by universal joints. See Fig. 44-2.

UNIVERSAL JOINTS

A UNIVERSAL JOINT, Fig. 44-3, is a mechanical device that can transmit torque and/or rotational motion from one shaft to another at fixed or varying angles. Most cars utilize a universal joint at front and rear of the drive shaft. See Fig. 44-4. A third "U-joint" is used on applications having two drive shafts.

The front universal joint is connected to the transmission output shaft. The rear universal joint is connected by a yoke to the differential drive pinion gear shaft. This balanced arrangement of power transfer components serves to compensate for any changes in the line of drive.

DRIVE SHAFT

The DRIVE SHAFT or PROPELLER SHAFT on rear wheel drive vehicles usually is tubular steel with a yoke (slotted end that straddles another part) aligned and welded to each end. See Fig. 44-4 and 44-5. Most drive shafts are of solid tube, one-piece construction. In certain rather rare applications, the drive shaft is made up of two concentric (having a common center) tubes separated by molded rubber rings to absorb vibrations.

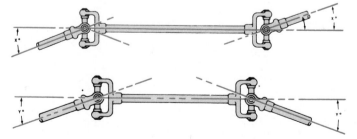

Fig. 44-1. Driveline angle is difference of alignment between transmission output shaft, drive shaft, and drive pinion shaft centerlines. (Ford Motor Co.)

Fig. 44-2. Universal joints at both ends of drive shaft compensate for changes in angularity of driveline. Here X° = X° and Y° = Y°. (Chevrolet Motor Div., General Motors Corp.)

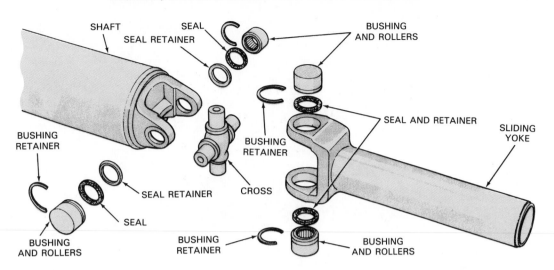

Fig. 44-3. Exploded view shows typical cross and roller universal joint that permits changes in angularity between drive shaft yoke and sliding or slip yoke that connects to transmission output shaft. (Chrysler Corp.)

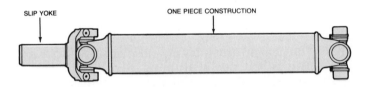

Fig. 44-4. Usually, a one-piece drive shaft with universal joints front and rear is used on rear wheel drive passenger cars. (Chevrolet Motor Div., General Motors Corp.)

DIFFERENTIAL

The DIFFERENTIAL is a gear system that transfers power from the drive shaft to the driving axles. Since the driving axles are splined to the differential side gears at right angles to the line of drive, the differential assembly uses a drive pinion gear and ring gear to redirect the transfer of power to the driving axles. See Fig. 44-6.

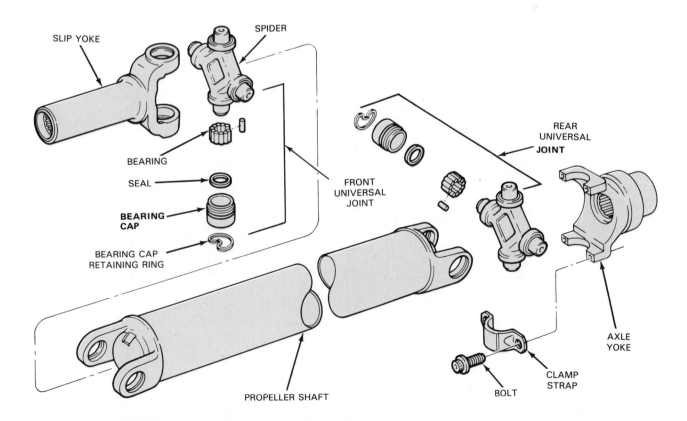

Fig. 44-5. Exploded view of complete drive shaft assembly includes shaft, universal joints, front slip yoke, and rear axle yoke that connects to differential drive pinion shaft. (American Motors Corp.)

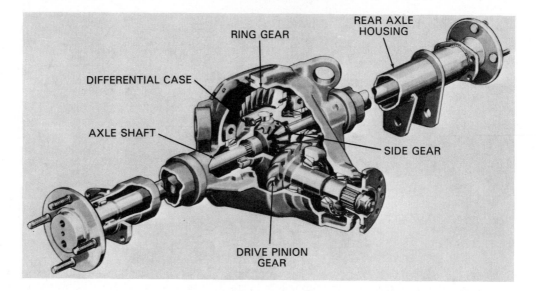

Fig. 44-6. Cutaway view of complete differential and rear axle assembly details right angle drive of drive pinion gear to ring gear. Also note "spline mesh" of side gears and axle shafts. (Ford Motor Co.)

The differential assembly also permits one driving wheel to turn faster than the other to prevent skidding and scuffing of rear tires on turns. See explanation in Figs. 44-7 and 44-8.

DRIVING AXLES

The DRIVING AXLES of a rear wheel drive passenger car are used to hold, align, and drive the rear wheels and support the weight of the vehicle. These SEMI-FLOATING AXLES generally are flanged on the outer end, Fig. 44-9, and fitted with press-fit bolts for use with lug nuts for installing the brake drums and the wheels.

The rear axle shaft wheel bearings usually are the straight roller type, Fig. 44-9, and roll directly on the axle shaft. The bearing assembly is held in position in the axle housing by the axle shaft seal.

The inner ends of the axle shafts are externally splined for meshing with the internally splined differential side gears that drive the axle shafts. See Fig. 44-6.

In another design of semi-floating rear axle, the axle shaft is tapered at the outer end to fit into a tapered hub. The shaft is also keyed in place and secured by a nut on the threaded end of the axle shaft. To remove the hub from this type of axle, it is necessary to use a wheel puller.

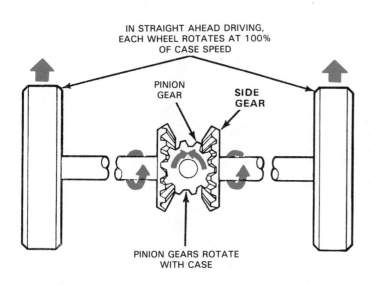

Fig. 44-7. In straight ahead driving, entire differential assembly rotates as a unit with side gears and pinion gears locked together in case. (American Motors Corp.)

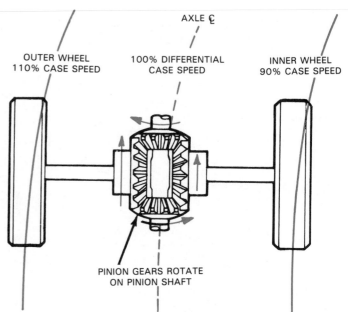

Fig. 44-8. On turns, pinion gears turn on their axes and roll around side gears to permit driving wheels to rotate at unequal speeds. (American Motors Corp.)

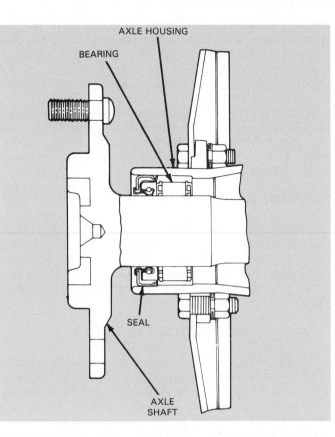

Fig. 44-9. Rear axle shaft bearing and seal installed in axle housing ride on machined surface of axle shaft. (Chevrolet Motor Div., General Motors Corp.)

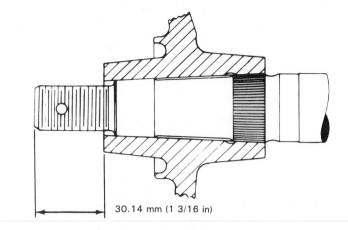

Fig. 44-10. In this rear axle shaft design, axle has external serrations; hub has internal serrations. Note specification given for how far hub must be pressed on axle shaft. (American Motors Corp.)

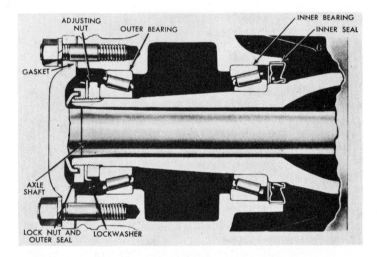

Fig. 44-11. Full-floating rear axle and hub is used in truck applications. Weight of vehicle rests on roller bearings mounted on axle housing.

In still another tapered axle and hub design, a key is also used to align the keyway in the hub with the keyway in the axle shaft. Also note in Fig. 44-10 that the hub and axle shaft are serrated. In order to fully engage the hub serrations with the axle shaft serrations, the hub must be installed to a specified dimension from hub outer face to the end of the axle shaft.

A FULL-FLOATING REAR DRIVE AXLE used primarily on trucks drives the wheel, but it does not hold the wheel nor support the weight of the vehicle. See Fig. 44-11. The axle housing is fitted with two roller bearings that carry the weight of the vehicle.

The axle shaft in full-floating applications is flanged on the outer end and bolted to the hub. A full-floating axle can be removed from the axle housing without disturbing the wheel.

DRIVELINE TO DRIVING WHEELS

In tracing the driveline, differential, driving axles, and driving wheels, power is transferred:
1. From transmission output shaft through front universal joint to drive shaft.
2. From drive shaft through rear universal joint to differential drive pinion gear.
3. From drive pinion gear to ring gear.
4. From ring gear to attached differential case, pinion gears, and side gears.
5. From side gears to driving axles.
6. From driving axles to driving wheels.

TORQUE EFFECT ON DRIVELINE

As mentioned, the balanced arrangement of power transfer components (universal joints and drive shaft) serves to compensate for any changes in the line of drive. However, when engine power is applied to the drive train, torque is developed in the driving wheels. See Fig. 44-12. This twisting action creates further changes in the angularity of the line of drive.

When power is transmitted by the drive shaft, the drive pinion gear tries to turn the ring gear. The ring gear must turn the axle shafts and the wheels, so it resists being moved. The pinion gear then attempts to "roll around" the ring gear. Since is cannot, the pinion gear transfers the torque to the axle housing. The obvious visible effect of this torque is the tendency of the back end of the car to dip when power is suddenly applied to the driving wheels.

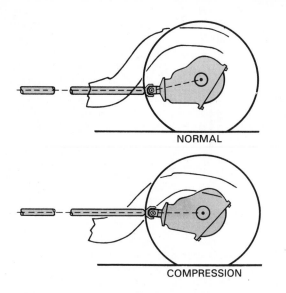

Fig. 44-12. Differential housing will tilt upward when engine torque is relayed from drive shaft to drive pinion to rear axle housing.

TORQUE TRANSFER OR DRIVE

When torque force from the engine is applied to the drive train, power to drive the vehicle is transferred from the drive pinion shaft to the rear axle housing and from the axle housing to either the springs, torque tube, or control arms, depending upon which type of "drive" is built into the vehicle.

HOTCHKISS DRIVE

The HOTCHKISS type of drive features leaf spring rear suspension and an open drive shaft with two universal joints to compensate for variations in road surfaces, load conditions, and power application (torque) that cause changes in alignment between the transmission output shaft and the drive pinion shaft. When the Hotchkiss type of drive is used, the vehicle is moved forward by driving wheel force on the front end of the springs pushing against the frame. See Fig. 44-13.

TORQUE TUBE DRIVE

In cars equipped with TORQUE TUBE DRIVE, the pushing action is at the front end of the torque tube. Only one universal joint is used in the driveline at the front

end of the drive shaft. In this case, the drive shaft is within a long, large tube which is anchored to the axle housing. The torque tube does not permit the axle housing to twist when engine power is applied. Also, the springs do not absorb any torque and are required only to cushion the ride.

With torque tube drive, the engine usually is mounted as low as possible in the frame or at an angle with the rear end lower than the front end. The object is to obtain a line of drive as straight as possible for power transmission.

CONTROL ARM DRIVE

In CONTROL ARM DRIVE, driving and braking forces are transferred to the front end of heavy-duty control arms, Fig. 44-14. The torque transfer effect is similar to Hotchkiss drive, but coil springs are used at the rear rather than leaf type springs. Some cars use three control arms, most use four.

DRIVE SHAFT LENGTH

In addition to line of drive problems caused by angularity of the drive shaft, the distance between the transmission output shaft and the drive pinion shaft is subject to change. This creates the need for some flexibility in the length of the drive shaft.

In referring to the Hotchkiss drive in Fig. 44-15, the front end of the drive shaft is attached to the transmission shaft at B. The rear end is attached to the drive pinion shaft at C. As the wheels move up and down, the drive shaft swings up and down in arc A-A around pivot

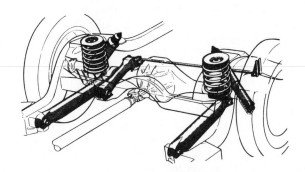

Fig. 44-14. Ford-Mercury rear suspension features control arm drive. Two parallel lower arms extend forward to rubber-bushed anchors for transfer of driving force.
(Ford Motor Co.)

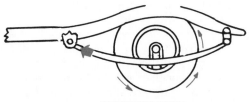

HOTCHKISS DRIVE

Fig. 44-13. In a Hotchkiss drive setup, driving force is transmitted from rear wheels to front of rear springs.

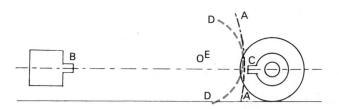

Fig. 44-15. In Hotchkiss drive, length of drive shaft varies because of changes in wheelbase as rear wheels move up and down with road surface irregularities.

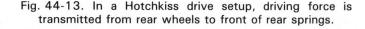

B. At the same time, the pinion shaft C — being attached to the rear axle — swings in an arc D-D around the pivot where the spring is anchored to the frame at E. Therefore, as the arcs A-A and D-D do not coincide, it will be necessary for the drive shaft to alternately lengthen and shorten as the wheels move up and down in relation to the frame.

SLIP JOINTS

One method of lengthening or shortening the drive shaft is by means of a splined shaft coupling or ''slip joint.'' See Fig. 44-16. When this type of slip joint is used, it is possible to assemble it incorrectly because of the many different ways in which the splines can be aligned. This results in an annoying vibration. These slip joints usually are marked for correct assembly. If not, the splines must be aligned so that both yokes are in the same plane, or ''in phase.'' See Fig. 44-16.

EFFECT OF VARYING SHAFT SPEEDS

When the two yokes of the drive shaft are ''in phase,'' the speed of the transmission output shaft and pinion shaft will be constant and the same if the line of drive of both shafts is uniform. The velocity of the drive shaft will not be constant, but this is unimportant as long as the velocity of the driving and driven shafts is uniform.

When the two yokes are ''out of phase,'' the rotational speed of the shafts will be uniform only if the shafts are operated in a straight line. When operating at an angle with the yokes ''out of phase,'' a conventional universal joint will cause the driven shaft to speed up and slow down each revolution. The number of turns per shaft will be the same, but the velocity of the driven shaft will fluctuate.

CONSTANT VELOCITY JOINTS

The fluctuation of speed of the driven shaft is further emphasized in the design of driving axles. In the case of front wheel drive vehicles, the universal joints used in the driving axle assemblies must transfer driving power to the front wheels and, at the same time, compensate for steering action on turns.

To solve this fluctuation problem, special universal joints known as CONSTANT VELOCITY JOINTS were developed, Fig. 44-17. In the example shown, rolling balls in curved grooves are utilized to obtain uniform motion. The balls, which are the driving contact, move laterally as the joint rotates. This permits the point of driving contact between the two halves of the coupling to remain in a plane which bisects the angle between the two shafts. See Fig. 44-17. By this means, the fluctuation in speed of the driven shaft is avoided.

In a parallel development for use in rear wheel drive shafts, Figs. 44-18 and 44-19, two yoke-and-cross universal joints are placed adjacent and connected to form a constant velocity joint. A similar design of constant velocity joint called ''double cardan,'' with lubrication fittings, is shown in Fig. 44-20.

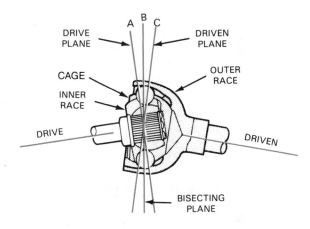
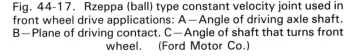

Fig. 44-17. Rzeppa (ball) type constant velocity joint used in front wheel drive applications: A—Angle of driving axle shaft. B—Plane of driving contact. C—Angle of shaft that turns front wheel. (Ford Motor Co.)

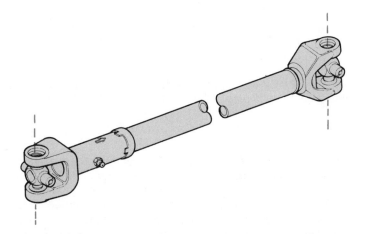

Fig. 44-16. Front and rear drive shaft yokes must be ''in phase.'' Shaft must be assembled into front yoke so marks align and yokes are in same plane. (American Motors Corp.)

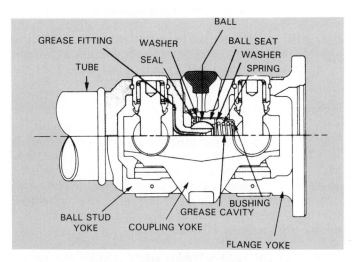

Fig. 44-18. This rear wheel drive constant velocity universal joint consists of two single joints connected by a link yoke and maintained in relative position by a center ball and socket.

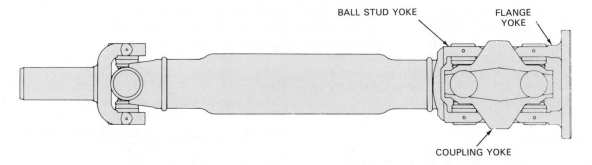

Fig. 44-19. Constant velocity joint (at right) cancels out vibration that could occur from speed fluctuation with single universal joints at both ends of drive shaft.

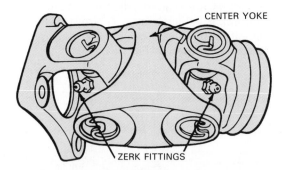

Fig. 44-20. Double cardan constant velocity joint consists of two cross and roller universal joints with ball studs and centering spring in between and coupled by a center yoke. (Ford Motor Co.)

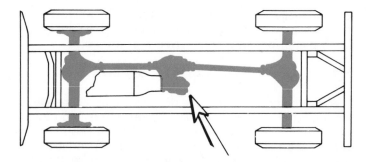

Fig. 44-21. Engine torque goes from transmission to transfer case where it is applied to drive shafts extending to each driving axle. (Americal Motors Corp.)

TRANSFER CASES

When a vehicle is driven by both front and rear wheels (four wheel drive), it is equipped with a "power takeoff" to drive both axles. This auxiliary device is known as a TRANSFER CASE, Fig. 44-21. It is customary to provide a shifting device on these units so that the front drive can be disengaged if desired.

On FOUR WHEEL DRIVE vehicles, the angularity of the drive shafts between front and rear wheels changes constantly. Therefore, the transfer case is positioned in the best possible compromise to serve both axles. Each drive shaft is fitted with a slip joint to accommodate changes in distance between axles and transfer case as the wheels move up and down.

CENTER BEARINGS

In some full size passenger cars, the drive shaft is divided into two sections and a supporting "center bearing" is utilized. The center bearing serves to stabilize the shaft and reduces vibration and "whip." The whip comes from centrifugal force aided by any unbalance that may exist in the shaft. For this reason, all drive shafts are carefully balanced.

DIFFERENTIALS AND AXLES

Early automobiles were driven by means of belts or ropes around pulleys mounted on the driving wheels and

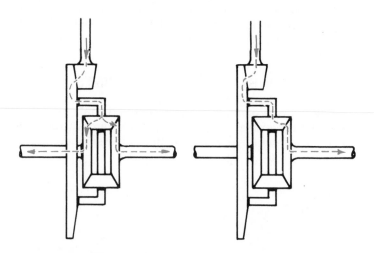

Fig. 44-22. Differential gearing shown in diagrammatical view indicates flow of power: Left. Straight ahead. Right. During left turn.

engine shaft or transmission shaft. Because there always was some slippage of the belts, one wheel could rotate faster than the other when turning a corner.

When belts proved unsatisfactory, the builders borrowed an idea from bicycle design and applied sprockets and chains. This was a positive driving arrangement, so it was necessary to provide differential gearing to permit one driving wheel to turn faster than the other, Figs. 44-8 and 44-22.

DIFFERENTIAL GEARS

In a typical differential gear arrangement, Fig 44-22, the drive pinion gear turns the ring gear and the differential case attached to it. The differential pinion gears mounted in the case mesh with the differential side gears that are splined to the rear axle shafts.

In straight ahead operation, the ring gear and differential case (with enclosed differential pinion gears and side gears) rotate as a unit. The differential pinion gears do not turn about their own axes, but apply equal effort to each of the differential side gears and axle shafts.

On turns, the resistance against the rotation of one axle increases as the wheels turn at different speeds. This causes the differential pinion gears to turn on their own axes and roll around the differential side gear on the reluctant one of the two axles.

This action allows the reluctant axle to slow down or stand still, causing a corresponding increase in the speed of rotation of the other axle. If one axle does not turn at all, the other axle will turn at almost twice the normal speed. So, it is possible for the drive wheels to turn at unequal speeds while the same amount of power is applied to both of them.

BEVEL GEARS

Pinion and ring gears have different tooth designs. The original type was known as a "straight bevel." The teeth were straight, like a spur gear, Fig. 44-23. Another type is known as a "spiral bevel." In this case, the teeth are curved and operate quietly because the curved teeth make a sliding contact. The spiral bevel ring gear and pinion setup is stronger because more than one tooth is in contact at all times.

HYPOID GEARS

Note that the pinion shaft in Fig. 44-23 is in line with the center of the ring gear. Fig. 44-24 shows a hypoid gear with the pinion shaft below the center of the ring

gear. The advantage of this design is that it allows the drive shaft to be placed lower to permit reducing the hump in the floor.

DIFFERENTIAL MOUNTING

Passenger car differentials ordinarily use two differential pinions on a straight shaft. The exploded illustration, Fig. 44-25, shows the differential case and gears.

The differential assembly is mounted either on a differential carrier, Fig. 44-26, or directly in the rear axle housing, Fig. 44-27. In all cases, there is a bearing and shim on each side of the assembly which provides a means of adjustment to move the ring gear toward or away from the drive pinion gear. See Fig. 44-28.

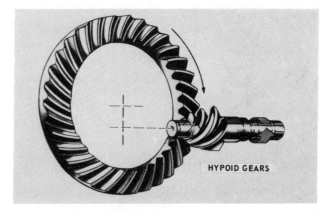

Fig 44-24. Hypoid gears are spiral bevel design, but center of pinion shaft is below center of ring gear.

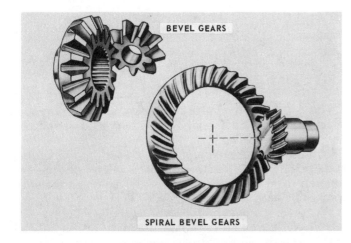

Fig. 44-23. Left. Bevel gear has straight teeth and makes tooth-to-tooth contact. Right. Spiral bevel gear has curved teeth, which places more than one tooth in contact at all times.

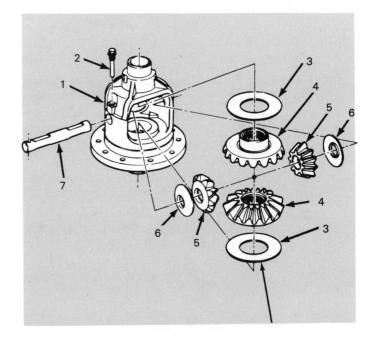

Fig. 44-25. Typical differential case assembly: 1—Case. 2—Screw. 3—Side gear thrust washer. 4—Side gear. 5—Differential pinion gear. 6—Pinion gear thrust washer. 7—Shaft. (Pontiac Motor Div., General Motors Corp.)

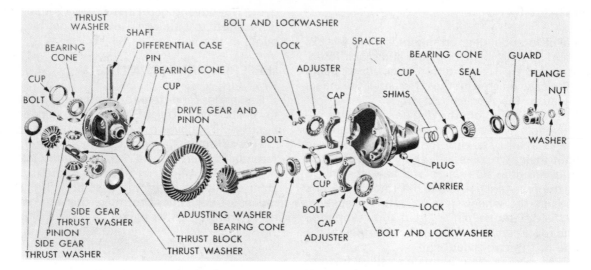

Fig. 44-26. Exploded view of hypoid type differential assembly shows arrangement in which differential is assembled and adjusted, installed in "carrier," then carrier is installed in rear axle housing.

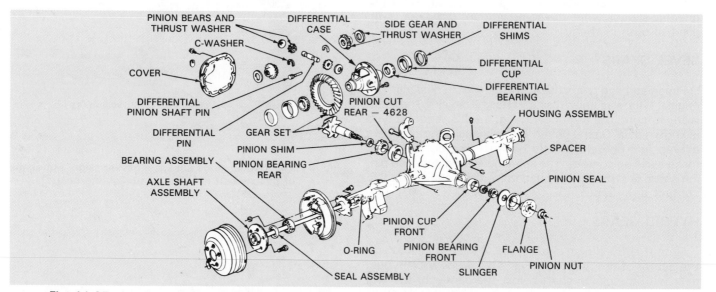

Fig. 44-27. In this "integral carrier" rear axle setup, parts and subassemblies must be installed in axle housing, then adjusted and torqued to specifications. (Ford Motor Co.)

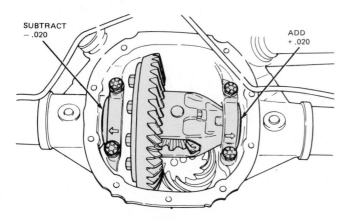

Fig. 44-28. Generally, differential bearing preload and ring gear backlash are adjusted by shims located between differential bearing cup/races and carrier housing. Caps lock bearings in place when adjustment is correct. (Ford Motor Co.)

When the setting is completed, the bearings are locked in place by heavy caps, Figs. 44-26 and 44-28.

DRIVE PINION MOUNTING

The drive pinion gear that meshes with the ring gear is also mounted on bearings in the pinion carrier or axle housing, Fig. 44-29.

If the torque tube type of drive is used, the mounting is quite similar. Or, instead of using a pair of opposed tapered roller bearings, some constructions consist of a roller bearing and a ball bearing.

Whatever the construction, the bearings must prevent any endwise motion of the pinion shaft. In the case of the opposed angular roller bearings, the bearings themselves handle both radial and thrust loads. In the case of the ball bearing-roller bearing setup, the ball bearing is a combination radial and thrust design.

538

Fig. 44-29. Pinion shaft and bearing assembly is arranged in proper sequence of assembly. Note special preload spacer at center.

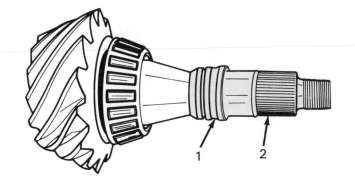

Fig. 44-30. A collapsed bearing spacer (1) is shown on drive pinion shaft (2). Obviously, a new spacer must be installed each time assembly is taken apart and reassembled. (Pontiac Motor Div., General Motors Corp.)

PINION BEARING PRELOAD

Many car manufacturers specify "preloading" of drive pinion bearings. In some cases, this is done by the use of a special bearing spacer or sleeve. See Fig. 44-29. The spacer between the two bearings is made with a weakened section. After installation, the bearings are pulled together by heavy torquing of the pinion shaft nut, causing the spacer to collapse, Fig. 44-30. Equally important, there should be no radial movement of the pinion.

LIMITED SLIP DIFFERENTIALS

Limited slip differentials are a popular option on a number of different makes of automobiles under a number of different names. Some use disc clutches to direct power flow to the axle of the wheel having the best traction. At the same time, less power is applied to the wheel that tends to slip, so better traction is obtained for both driving wheels. See Figs. 44-31 and 44-32.

An earlier limited slip design has beveled ends on the differential pinion shafts and corresponding "ramps" cut in the shaft openings of the differential case. With this construction, the differential pinions and pinion shafts float between the differential side gears and the case. When power is applied, the ramps tend to force the side gears apart and apply pressure to the clutch assembly having the best traction.

Another more popular limited slip differential utilizes cone clutches that are preloaded with five springs. The

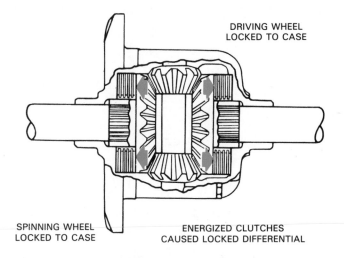

Fig. 44-31. In wheel spinning situations with a disc clutch type limited slip differential, power is transmitted through side gears and energized clutches to driving wheel having best traction.

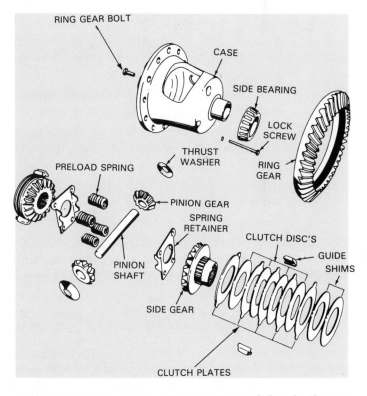

Fig. 44-32. Exploded view shows makeup of disc clutch type limited slip differential. Note preload springs and alternate placement of clutch plates and clutch discs. (Oldsmobile Div., General Motors Corp.)

frictional surface of the cones contain a coarse spiral thread that provides passages for the flow of lubricant, Fig. 44-33. In straight ahead operation, the pressure of the springs and separating force created by the pinion gears pushes each clutch cone/side gear against the case. On turns, the axles are automatically unlocked by differential action, overcoming the spring load on the clutch cones and permitting them to overrun.

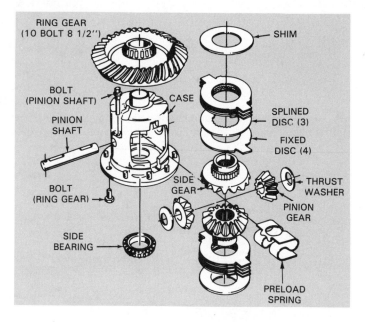

Fig. 44-34. Exploded view gives disassembly/assembly order of parts in a disc clutch type limited slip differential having an S-shaped preload spring.
(Oldsmobile Div., General Motors Corp.)

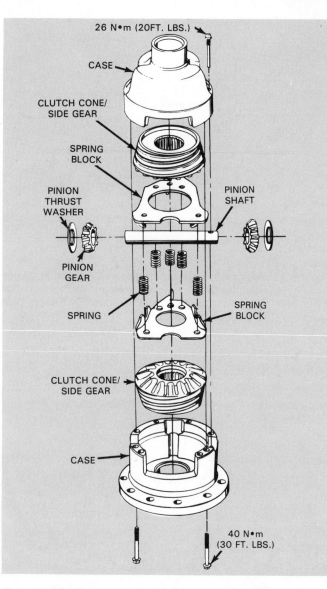

Fig. 44-33. Exploded view details sequence of components of a cone type limited slip differential. Note clutch cone/side gear construction. (Oldsmobile Div., General Motors Corp.)

Another disc clutch type of limited slip differential is shown in Fig. 44-34. In this unit, a one-piece, S-shaped spring is used to apply initial force to the side gears and clutch packs. Additional force is provided by side gear thrust loads. When the vehicle is cornering, the clutches slip and allow normal differential action. When one rear wheel slips, friction between the clutch plates transfers torque to the wheel having the most traction.

PLANETARY DIFFERENTIALS

A PLANETARY DIFFERENTIAL is used on certain front wheel drive cars to provide an axle gear package of minimum width alongside the engine. Early models of the Oldsmobile Toronado, for example, coupled a spiral bevel ring gear with a spiral bevel drive pinion gear that is straddle mounted by two tapered roller bearings. During straight ahead driving, the ring gear, planet pinions, and sun gear rotate as a unit. On turns, the planet gears and

sun gear rotate within the ring gear and allow the drive axles to rotate at different speeds.

FRONT WHEEL DRIVE DRIVELINE

A key element in the driveline — and drive train — of a front wheel drive vehicle is a power transfer mechanism called a TRANSAXLE. The transaxle is attached to the rear of the engine which, in most cases, is mounted crosswise in the engine compartment. The transaxle combines transmission and differential (final drive) in a single unit. See Fig. 44-35.

In front wheel drive vehicles, the DRIVE TRAIN is compacted into an engine/transaxle/driving axles (halfshafts) "package" that provides torque force to the front wheels.

The DRIVELINE probably is best described as extending from the mainshaft pinion gear to the final drive ring gear, and through the rotating differential case assembly (during straight ahead operation) to the driving axles. See Figs. 44-35 and 44-36.

For basic transaxle operation and service information, see Chapter 43, Transaxles. Emphasis in this chapter will be placed on front wheel drive CONSTANT VELOCITY JOINTS and DRIVING AXLES.

CONSTANT VELOCITY JOINTS

The main purpose of the driving axles is to transmit engine torque from the final drive unit to the front (driving) wheels. As part of the driving axle assembly, the CV joints are designed to operate at varying angles, both vertically and to accommodate wheel turning angles. Some CV joints also permit shaft length changes caused by up and down movement of the front wheels and by engine movement due to torque reaction.

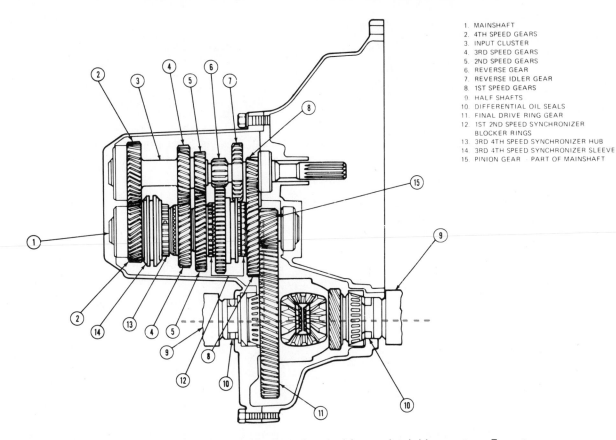

1. MAINSHAFT
2. 4TH SPEED GEARS
3. INPUT CLUSTER
4. 3RD SPEED GEARS
5. 2ND SPEED GEARS
6. REVERSE GEAR
7. REVERSE IDLER GEAR
8. 1ST SPEED GEARS
9. HALF SHAFTS
10. DIFFERENTIAL OIL SEALS
11. FINAL DRIVE RING GEAR
12. 1ST 2ND SPEED SYNCHRONIZER
    BLOCKER RINGS
13. 3RD 4TH SPEED SYNCHRONIZER HUB
14. 3RD 4TH SPEED SYNCHRONIZER SLEEVE
15. PINION GEAR - PART OF MAINSHAFT

Fig. 44-35. Dashed line indicates driveline of typical front wheel drive system: From trans-axle mainshaft pinion gear (15). To final drive ring gear (11). To differential side gears, pinion gears, and case. To halfshaft assemblies (9). See Fig. 44-36. (Ford Motor Co.)

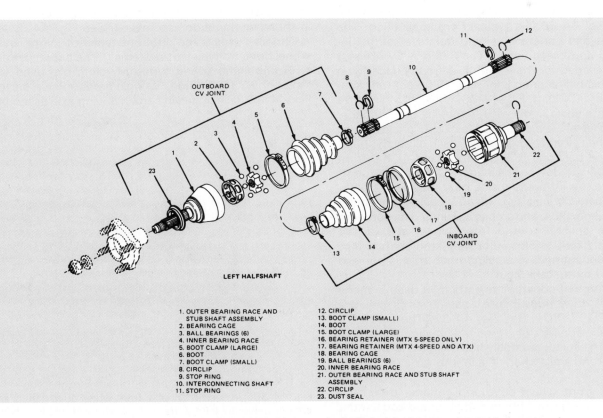

1. OUTER BEARING RACE AND
   STUB SHAFT ASSEMBLY
2. BEARING CAGE
3. BALL BEARINGS (6)
4. INNER BEARING RACE
5. BOOT CLAMP (LARGE)
6. BOOT
7. BOOT CLAMP (SMALL)
8. CIRCLIP
9. STOP RING
10. INTERCONNECTING SHAFT
11. STOP RING

12. CIRCLIP
13. BOOT CLAMP (SMALL)
14. BOOT
15. BOOT CLAMP (LARGE)
16. BEARING RETAINER (MTX 5-SPEED ONLY)
17. BEARING RETAINER (MTX 4-SPEED AND ATX)
18. BEARING CAGE
19. BALL BEARINGS (6)
20. INNER BEARING RACE
21. OUTER BEARING RACE AND STUB SHAFT
    ASSEMBLY
22. CIRCLIP
23. DUST SEAL

Fig. 44-36. Exploded view of typical left driving axle (halfshaft) of front wheel drive system is a continuation of driveline shown in Fig. 44-35. (Ford Motor Co.)

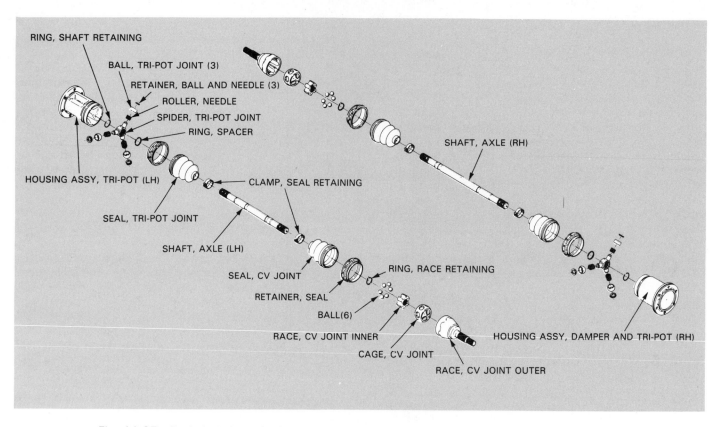

Fig. 44-37. Exploded view of left (top) and right (bottom) driving axles shows details of constant velocity joint construction. Note Rzeppa CV joints are outboard; tripod joints are inboard. (Oldsmobile Div., General Motors Corp.)

The front wheel drive HALFSHAFT (driving axle) shown in Fig. 44-36 is a typical Ford application. The driving axle has constant velocity joints at both "inboard" and "outboard" ends. The RZEPPA CV JOINTS shown are named for the inventor, Alfred Rzeppa, who patented this ball bearing joint over half a century ago.

The inboard CV joint, Fig. 44-36, consists of an outer race and stub shaft, inner race, cage, six ball bearings, and a ball retainer. The outer race is called "plunge" type because it has elongated grooves which allow the bearing cage and bearings to slide in and out as the front wheels go up and down. The inboard CV joint stub shaft is splined to the differential side gear. See Fig. 44-35.

The outboard CV joint, Fig. 44-36, consists of an outer race, cage, inner race, and six ball bearings. The outboard CV joint is splined to the front wheel end of the driving axle. The CV joint outer race stub shaft is also splined to accommodate a splined hub that is pressed on and held by a staked nut.

Another type of constant velocity joint used in many front wheel drive driving axle assemblies is called a FIXED TRIPOD JOINT. See Fig. 44-37. The tripod CV joint basically consists of a grooved housing and spider assembly. The spider assembly has three trunnions, needle rollers, and balls that ride in the grooves of the housing.

On some front wheel drive applications, tripod CV joints are used at both inboard and outboard ends of the driving axles. In other cases, the tripod joint is used at the inboard end only with a "plunge" type race. A Rzeppa CV joint is used at the outboard end of the shafts in these driving axle assemblies. See Fig. 44-37.

Chrysler uses three different types of joints in front wheel drive "drive shaft systems." The constant velocity Rzeppa and tripod types of joints are used in all "systems." In addition, a single cardan universal joint, Fig. 44-38, is included in certain driving axle assemblies.

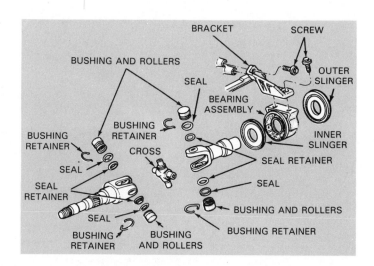

Fig. 44-38. In certain Chrysler front wheel drive cars, a single cardan universal joint is used. Stub shaft at left is splined to transaxle side gear to transmit torque force to driving axle. (Chrysler Corp.)

DRIVING AXLES

"Driving axles" is a generic term for front wheel drive shaft-and-joint assemblies that extend from in-board CV joints to outboard CV joints.

Chrysler Corporation uses two different driving axle systems on front wheel drive vehicles. Because of design differences, one is called an "equal length" system; the other is called an "unequal length" system.

The "equal length" system shown in Fig. 44-39 has short, solid interconnecting shafts of equal length in the left and right driving axle assemblies. The right axle also has a tubular intermediate shaft attached to a cardan universal joint with a stub shaft splined into the transaxle side gear. A tripod CV joint is splined to the other transaxle side gear. Another tripod joint is used between the intermediate shaft and right interconnecting shaft. Rzeppa CV joints are used at the wheel hubs.

The second driving axle system utilized by Chrysler is shown in Fig. 44-40. Note that two "unequal length" interconnecting shafts are used along with tripod inboard CV joints and Rzeppa outboard CV joints.

The Oldsmobile Division of General Motors has an unusual front wheel drive setup on Toronado models. See Fig. 44-41. The Toronado system consists of a final drive unit bolted to the transmission, right and left output shafts, and right and left drive axles. The output shafts are splined to the final drive side gears. The right output shaft is longer than the left output shaft and requires a support bracket and bearing, Fig. 44-41. The output shafts bolt to the drive axles. The inboard CV joints are tripod design; the outboard CV joints are Rzeppa type.

A typical Ford Motor Company driving axle setup on front wheel drive vehicles is shown in Fig. 44-36. An exploded view of right and left driving axle assemblies typical of General Motors front wheel drive applications is shown in Fig. 44-37.

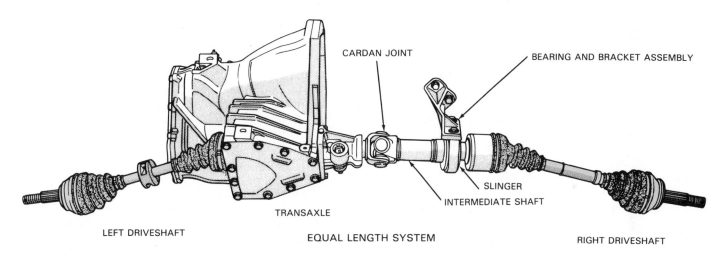

Fig. 44-39. Equal length drive shaft system includes cardan universal joint in right driving axle. Left and right drive shafts are "equal length." (Chrysler Corp.)

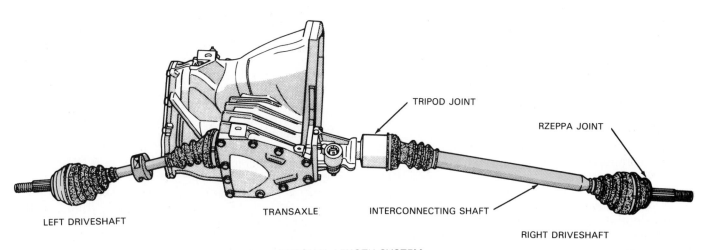

Fig. 44-40. Unequal length front wheel drive shaft system does away with intermediate shaft and cardan universal joint. Left and right drive shafts are "unequal length." (Chrysler Corp.)

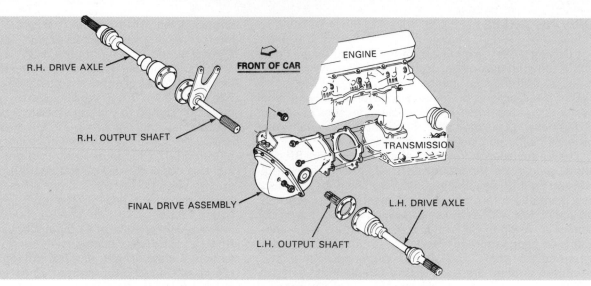

Fig. 44-41. Oldsmobile Toronado driving axle setup features left and right output shafts of different lengths and equal length left and right drive axles. (Oldsmobile Div., General Motors Corp.)

Chapter 44—REVIEW QUESTIONS
DRIVELINE, UNIVERSAL JOINTS, DIFFERENTIALS, DRIVING AXLES

Write your answers on a separate sheet of paper. Do not write in this book.

1. In rear wheel drive applications, the _____ (driveline or drive train) consists of one or more universal joints, the drive shaft, and differential drive pinion gear.
2. Flexibility in the drive train usually is provided by _____ _____.
3. The differential assembly uses a drive pinion gear and _____ _____ to redirect the transfer of power to the driving axles.
   a. Differential gear.
   b. Differential pinion gear.
   c. Ring gear.
   d. Planetary gear.
4. The differential assembly prevents one driving wheel from turning faster than the other to avoid skidding and scuffing of rear tires on turns. True or False?
5. What type of driving axles are generally used in rear wheel drive passenger cars?
6. On acceleration, engine torque will cause differential housing to _____ _____ (tilt downward or tilt upward).
7. Driving force is transmitted to the front of the rear leaf springs on cars equipped with:
   a. Hotchkiss drive.
   b. Torque tube drive.
   c. Open drive shaft drive.
   d. Control arm drive.
8. What is the purpose of the slip joint in the driveline?
9. In straight ahead operation, the ring gear and differential case assembly rotate as a unit. True or False?
10. In differential assembly, what is the purpose of the

spacer or sleeve between the two drive pinion bearings?
11. Name two types of limited slip differentials.
12. A key element of a front wheel drive driveline — or drive train — is a power transfer mechanism called a _____.
   a. Transmission.
   b. Differential.
   c. Transaxle.
   d. Final drive unit.
13. The main purpose of the driving axles on front wheel drive cars is to transmit engine torque from the _____ _____ _____ to the driving wheels.
14. Constant velocity joints are designed to operate at varying angles, both vertically and to accommodate _____ _____ angles.
15. Some CV joints also permit shaft length changes caused by up and down movement of the front wheels. True or False?
16. A _____ (Rzeppa or tripod) CV joint is ''ball bearing'' type.
17. A _____ (Rzeppa or tripod) CV joint is ''spider'' type.
18. What is a ''plunge'' type CV joint?
19. What type of splined shaft is used at outboard CV joints to accommodate the installation of splined wheel hubs?
   a. Interconnecting.
   b. Intermediate.
   c. Output.
   d. Stub.
20. In addition to Rzeppa and tripot CV joints, Chrysler uses a cardan universal joint in which one of its front wheel drive driving axle assemblies?
   a. Equal length system.
   b. Unequal length system.
   c. Interconnecting drive shaft system.
   d. Output shaft/drive axle system.

Chapter 45

DRIVELINE SERVICE

After studying this chapter, you will be able to:
- Identify elements of rear wheel drive and front wheel drive drivelines.
- Describe differential pinion gear/ring gear adjusting procedures for obtaining correct tooth contact.
- Tell how to check angularity of drive shaft on rear wheel drive vehicles.
- Cite driveline lubrication requirements.
- Explain driving axle services, both on rear wheel drive and front wheel drive systems.
- Recommend need for skill and care and attention to detail when performing driveline services.

The DRIVELINE of a rear wheel drive vehicle consists of one or more universal joints, the drive shaft, and differential drive pinion gear. Each of these elements must be maintained properly in order to provide a smooth running, relatively quiet, vibration-free power transfer system.

DRIVE SHAFT

The DRIVE SHAFT is a long, usually tubular steel member of the driveline that connects the transmission output shaft to the differential drive pinion shaft. The UNIVERSAL JOINTS are considered to be part of the drive shaft assembly, Fig. 45-1. This assembly rotates at fluctuating speeds and operates at constantly changing angles. Therefore, it is susceptible (subject) to vibration. Add to this any rotating imbalance and the result is a serious vibration that will shake the entire vehicle.

For example, a one ounce weight placed on a drive shaft 2 in. from the center of rotation will exert a force of 50 lb. at 3750 rpm. At that speed, this force will be exerted in opposite directions 62 1/2 times per second, causing a heavy vibration.

From this example, it is easy to see why all drive shafts must be balanced, properly mounted assemblies with all working parts lubricated by a special, high melting point lubricant.

Also, on cross and roller universal joints, Fig. 45-2, the cross must be centered within the bearing cups. Most bearing assemblies are held in place by snap rings, others by trunnion straps or bearing plates. Some original equipment universal joints have trunnions retained by a plastic material injected into a groove in the yoke. See Fig. 45-1.

In any case, all parts must be ''opposed identical

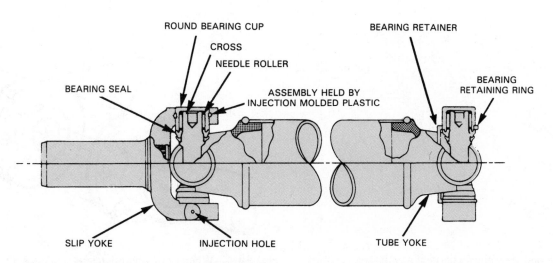

Fig. 45-1. Cross and roller universal joints at both ends of one-piece driveshaft provide flexibility needed in line of drive of rear wheel drive vehicle. (Pontiac Motor Div., General Motors Corp.)

pairs'' to help maintain drive shaft balance. In addition, all bolts, nuts, washers, seals, and retainers used to assemble the joints and flanges must be the same weight as the opposed pair.

DRIVE SHAFT REQUIREMENTS

It follows, then, that drive shafts must be:
1. Carefully and accurately manufactured.
2. Correctly assembled.
3. Straight.
4. Balanced.
5. Properly mounted in the automobile.
6. Frequently checked.

Even when all these things are done, the shaft still can get out of balance when in use. Journal cross bearings can wear. Splines wear. Bolts and keys get loose. The drive shaft can become bent. Balance weights can fall off. Lubricant becomes misplaced or leaks out. Sometimes a drive shaft is thrown out of balance by careless spraying of undercoating.

The drive shaft may have incorrect angularity. It may be dented. A weld may be cracked. The universal joints may bind or ''clunk'' on shifts into reverse. There may be burrs or nicks on support yokes or excessive looseness at slip yoke splines.

However, new developments in universal joint design and the use of constant velocity joints, Fig. 45-3, have eliminated the need for regular maintenance service. The joints are prelubricated and sealed at the time of manufacture. Note: The manufacturers specify frequent inspections for universal joint wear or lubricant leakage.

UNIVERSAL JOINT SERVICE

If a universal joint becomes worn or noisy, a service kit may be installed. Replacement parts in the kit usually include a cross, bearing cup assemblies, seals, washers, and snap rings, Fig. 45-2.

The drive shaft must be removed from the car to service or repair the universal joints. Mark the relationship of the yoke or companion flange to the drive shaft.

Disconnect the rear universal joint by removing bearing straps or unscrewing bolts from the companion flange, Fig. 45-4. Then tape bearing caps, if necessary, and remove the drive shaft.

If a double drive shaft is used, handle it with care to avoid jamming the joints, and keep it in a relatively straight line. Clamp the drive shaft in a vise by the universal joint yoke.

Disassemble the universal joints by means of a special tool set or press, Fig. 45-5. Constant velocity joints, in particular, require special service equipment to do the job right. Inspect the bearing cups for wear, roughness, pitting, or brinelling (rippled effect). If wear or damage is evident, install a complete service kit.

Reassemble the drive shaft carefully to maintain balance. See that the newly installed joints operate freely in all directions. Tap the yoke with a hammer, if necessary, to seat parts. Reinstall the drive shaft, align the scribe marks, Fig. 45-4, and tighten the attaching bolts to the proper torque value.

Then, check the angularity of the drive shaft and universal joints against manufacturer's specifications.

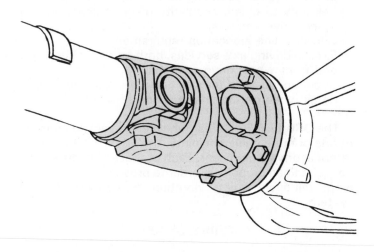

Fig. 45-3. Constant velocity joints used in rear wheel drive applications usually are double universal joints separated by a centering ball. (Chevrolet Motor Div., General Motors Corp.)

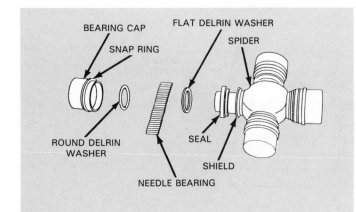

Fig. 45-2. Exploded view shows parts of a typical replacement cross and roller universal joint. (Chevrolet Motor Div., General Motors Corp.)

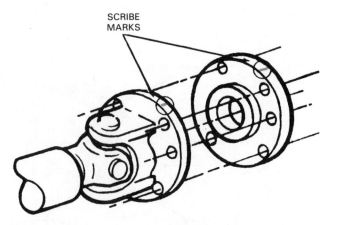

Fig. 45-4. When removing drive shaft, place scribe marks on drive shaft and companion flange to aid in reinstallation and to maintain balance. (Ford Motor Co.)

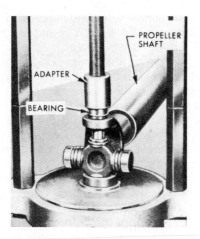

Fig. 45-5. Special tools or a press and adapters are needed to disassemble and assemble cross and roller universal joints.

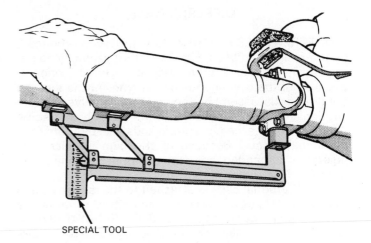

Fig. 45-7. Special tool (inclinometer) is used to measure universal joint angle at rear axle. (Chrysler Corp.)

See Fig. 45-6. Angularity can be checked with a protractor or inclinometer, Fig. 45-7:

1. Rotate drive shaft until universal joint cups on axle yoke and transmission yoke are facing straight down.
2. Clean cup surfaces and install inclinometer magnet against cup surface.
3. Work inclinometer contact shoe firmly against drive shaft until both tabs contact bottom of shaft.
4. Read indicated angle.

If front universal joint angle is incorrect, place shims between the transmission extension housing and the engine rear mount. If the rear universal joint angle is incorrect, place a tapered wedge between rear leaf spring and rear axle housing spring seat. See Fig. 45-8.

CENTER BEARING SERVICE

The CENTER BEARING is usually attached to a cross-member mounted between the left and right side rails of the frame. Center bearings on older models and some double cardan constant velocity joints are equipped with lubrication fittings. Most late models have prepacked bearings that do not require maintenance. If service is required, the center support can be disassembled by use of a special puller.

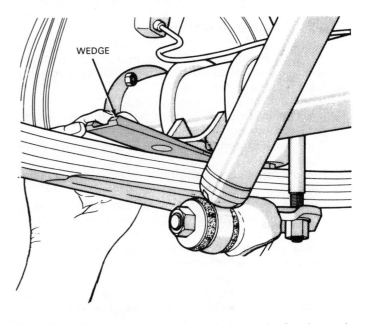

Fig. 45-8. Placing a tapered wedge between leaf spring and rear axle housing spring seat is one method of correcting rear universal joint angle. (Chrysler Corp.)

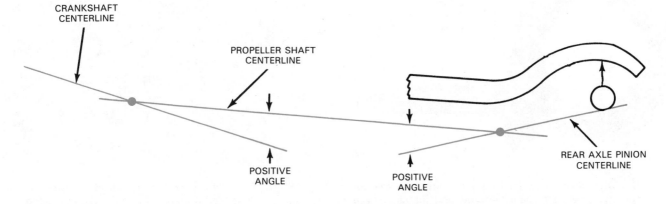

Fig. 45-6. Diagram depicts angles formed by crankshaft, propeller shaft, and drive pinion centerlines. Positive angles of front and rear universal joints are shown. (American Motors Corp.)

DIFFERENTIALS

DIFFERENTIALS are heavy-duty, precision-produced, mated-gear assemblies, Fig. 45-9, that generally do not require maintenance other than occasional lubricant. Because of the tremendous power transmitted through the differential assembly, the pressures involved are exceptionally high. The pressures are so high that some distortion of the heavy and, in most cases, hardened parts may occur. Because of the high standards of quietness demanded, adjustments must be made to extremely close dimensions.

The differential case is attached to the ring gear, and the entire propelling force is transmitted through the drive pinion gear and the DIFFERENTIAL CASE ASSEMBLY. This assembly also includes side gears, pinion gears, pinion shaft, pinion shaft lock bolt. To insure a tight union of parts, a series of eight to 12 special bolts extend through precisely machined holes in the case and screw into threaded holes in the ring gear. Torque tightness is in the area of 70 to 85 ft. lb. (95 to 115 N·m).

TROUBLES AND REMEDIES

Service problems with differentials usually are limited to lubricant leakage at the drive pinion oil seal or noisy operation of the differential.

To replace the drive pinion oil seal:
1. Mark relationship of yoke or flange to drive shaft.
2. Disconnect rear universal joint.
3. Tape bearing caps, if necessary, and remove drive shaft.
4. Remove drive pinion shaft nut, washer, and yoke or flange.
5. Use a special puller to remove drive pinion oil seal.

Reassemble in reverse order, but observe the following precautions:
1. Install oil seal with sealing lip facing lubricant.
2. Coat OD (outside diameter) of seal with nonhardening sealing compound.
3. Use special driving tool to bottom seal against shoulder in rear axle housing. See Fig. 45-10.

4. Make sure machined bearing surface of drive pinion yoke or flange is not worn, scored, or nicked in area where it rotates against seal.
5. Tighten drive pinion shaft nut to original position, plus 1/8 turn to preload pinion bearings (typical).
6. Refill rear axle housing to correct level with recommended lubricant.

Noisy operation of a differential unit is usually caused by worn or damaged gears or bearings. However, a thorough test should be made to pinpoint where the noise is coming from: rear axle assembly; rough road surface; underinflated tires, or tires with unevenly worn tread; front or rear wheel bearings; engine or transmission. Noises telegraph to other parts of the car, so establishing the source of the noise is of first importance.

If the differential assembly is noisy, check for: low level of lubricant in rear axle housing (howl and whine); excessive backlash between teeth of drive pinion gear and ring gear (chuck); looseness of drive pinion bearings (howl and whine); worn differential side and pinion gears (howl and whine on turns). Removal and complete disassembly of the differential probably is required.

DISASSEMBLY AND INSPECTION

When disassembling the differential, Figs. 45-11 and 45-12, be sure to mark mating parts to that they can

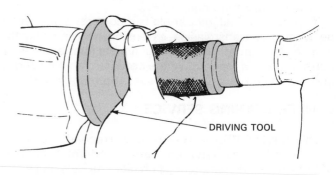

Fig. 45-10. Drive pinion oil seal replacement calls for use of a special puller and a special driving tool as shown. (Ford Motor Co.)

Fig. 45-9. Drive pinion gear and ring gear comprise a mated-gear assembly. They are manufactured and installed as a matched set. Nodular iron hypoid gears are shown. (Central Foundry Div., General Motors Corp.)

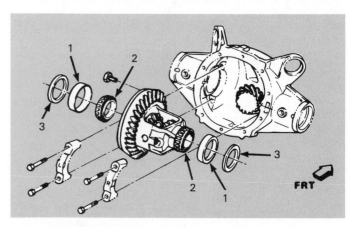

Fig. 45-11. Exploded view of standard differential case assembly is illustrated outside of carrier: Other related parts include: 1—Race. 2—Roller Bearing. 3—Shim. (Oldsmobile Div., General Motors Corp.)

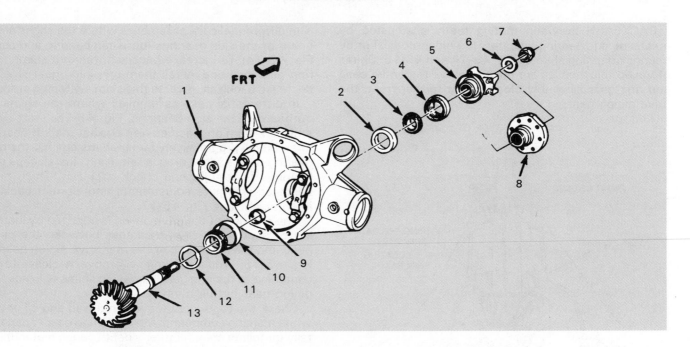

Fig. 45-12. Exploded view of drive pinion gear and related parts include:
1—Carrier. 2—Pinion front race. 3—Pinion front roller bearing. 4—Seal.
5—Flange. 6—Washer. 7—Nut. 8—Flange (some applications). 9—Spacer.
10—Pinion rear race. 11—Pinion rear roller bearing. 12—Shim (as required).
13—Drive pinion gear. (Oldsmobile Div., General Motors Corp.)

be reassembled on the correct side and in the proper position. For example, carrier bearing caps are marked L and R to prevent a mix-up. Since gears and bearings are a press fit in many cases, avoid the use of hammers and drifts. Use a suitable press or puller to prevent chipping and distortion of parts, Fig. 45-13.

After the parts have been disassembled and thoroughly cleaned, carefully inspect them for scuffed surfaces, cracks, warpage, or any other visible defects. If the surfaces of the gear teeth are scratched or scuffed, the gears must be replaced. If there are any cracks visible in the differential case, the case should be replaced. If the differential pinion bushings or shaft are worn or loose, new parts are required.

Pay particular attention to the pinion shaft and differential side bearings. Check the shaft or housings on which, and in which, the bearings seat. The inside cone of the bearings must be a tight fit on the shaft or housing upon which they are mounted. The outer race or cone must be a snug fit in the housing in which it seats. The bearings must not show any indication of wear. The races and rollers or balls and cups must be absolutely smooth and polished on the contact surfaces.

Hardened anti-friction bearings are used. No other type of bearing could stand the speeds and pressures and continue to maintain correct alignment of the gears.

REASSEMBLY AND ADJUSTMENT

When reassembling, use new shims, spacers, washers, gaskets, and oil seals. Thoroughly clean the inside of the housing of all grease and oil to make sure that no metal chips or abrasive material is left inside to be circulated by the lubricant.

The manufacturer's instructions concerning whether or not the bearings are to be preloaded, and how much, are needed for proper assembly. Also required is the method of adjusting gear contact by measurement with special gauges or micrometers. Necessary, too, are specifications on the amount of torque to be applied to all the bolts and nuts.

Two adjustments can be made which will affect tooth contact pattern between the drive pinion gear and the ring gear: backlash and the position of the drive pinion gear in relation to the ring gear.

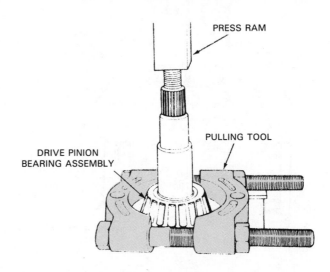

Fig. 45-13. Differential disassembly requires special pullers, drivers, and use of a press to remove and install bearings and certain gears. (Ford Motor Co.)

BACKLASH between mating teeth is adjusted by means of side bearing adjusters (on older models) or by bearing adjusting shims, Figs. 45-14 and 45-15. Shims of varied thicknesses are used to move the entire case and ring gear assembly closer to, or farther from, the drive pinion gear.

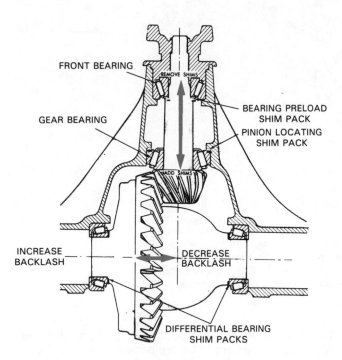

Fig. 45-14. Some differential designs require placement of shims under side bearings to adjust backlash between drive pinion gear and ring gear. (Ford Motor Co.)

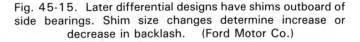

Fig. 45-15. Later differential designs have shims outboard of side bearings. Shim size changes determine increase or decrease in backlash. (Ford Motor Co.)

In differential case assemblies where the shims are inboard of the side bearings (between bearing and case), Fig. 45-14: To increase backlash, remove shims from ring gear side and install them on pinion gear side. To decrease backlash, reverse this shim switching process.

In differential case assemblies where the shims are outboard of the side bearings, Fig. 45-16, start by installing a shim of specified size against the left bearing. Then install progressively larger shims against the right bearing until a slight drag is felt. Next, install caps over bearings fingertight and check backlash. Then, make balanced shim size adjustments until correct backlash is obtained. See Fig. 45-17.

The position of the drive pinion is adjusted by increasing or decreasing shim thickness between the pinion head and the inner face of the rear drive pinion bearing, Fig. 45-15. Adding shims will move it closer to the centerline of the ring gear; removing shims will move the pinion gear farther away.

Check the tooth contact with red lead and oil or with white marking compound. Move the ring gear experimentally (or follow manufacturer's depth gauge method) until proper contact is obtained. See Fig. 45-18. Tighten all bolts gradually and equally to specified torque tightness.

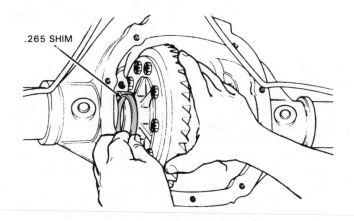

Fig. 45-16. First step of backlash adjustment is placement of a shim of specified size against left side bearing. (Ford Motor Co.)

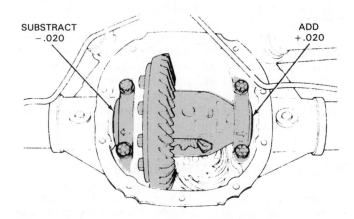

Fig. 45-17. After shimming against right side bearing, shim size adjustments, left and right, are made until backlash amount meets specification. (Ford Motor Co.)

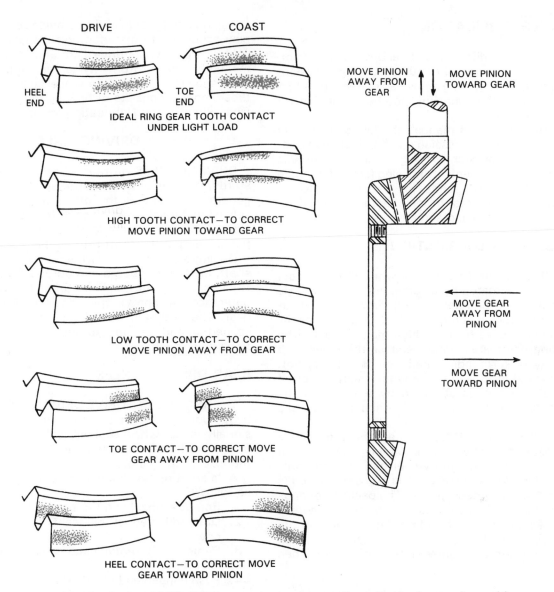

Fig. 45-18. Pattern of drive pinion gear-to-ring gear tooth contact is shown, along with corrective steps required to improve contact.

Correct adjustment of hypoid gears is of paramount importance because they will often wear excessively without making any noise. There is such a pronounced wiping action between the gear teeth, they can overheat and gall very quickly unless correctly adjusted and lubricated by a special hypoid lubricant.

GEAR AND BEARING LUBRICATION

Proper lubrication is of utmost importance. The straight bevel and spur gears were successfully lubricated with a heavy mineral gear oil. When spiral bevel gears were adopted, it was found necessary to add some ingredients to the oil to enable it to withstand the high pressure sliding or wiping action of the gear teeth.

With the adoption of hypoid gears, the sliding action was greatly increased, and previously used straight gear oils and extreme pressure gear oils were found inadequate. Special hypoid lubricants were developed and must be used with these gears. The vehicle manufacturer furnishes specific recommendations for type of lubricant, proper level, and frequency of change.

The ring gear acts as a circulating pump to distribute the lubricant over the gear teeth and to the bearings. Since the oil is in constant circulation when the vehicle is in motion, any abrasive material or metal chips will be promptly carried to the working surfaces. If abrasive, undue wear of gear teeth and bearings will occur. If a metal chip goes through the gears, it probably will break gear teeth, spring parts out of alignment, or both. Care must be exercised to keep the oil clean before and during refilling.

In any case, clean the area around the fill plug before removing it. Remove the plug and check the level of lubricant in the differential housing. The proper level in most applications (check manufacturer's recommendation) is at the lower edge of the fill hole. When adding or changing lubricant, use the recommended type and grade. The type of lubricant is specified in the service manual. Reinstall and tighten the fill plug.

TRANSAXLE LUBRICATION

In transaxles, the differential (final drive) unit is combined with either a manual or automatic transmission. While some types of gearing require an extreme pressure type of lubricant, this lubricant may be unsuitable for other types of gears.

When the transaxle is manual, the lubricant usually flows between the transmission and the final drive unit, with a single level check and fill plug provided. Automatic transaxles may have a separate housing for the final drive gears. Then, the two units may require different lubricants. Always refer to the manufacturer's specifications for the vehicle being serviced.

WHEEL BEARING LUBRICATION

REAR WHEEL BEARINGS on rear wheel drive cars are automatically lubricated by oil creeping along the axle shafts from the differential housing. Front wheel bearings call for repacking at regular intervals with a special wheel bearing grease having a high melting point. The high melting point is essential because the wheel hub and brake rotor surrounding the bearings get very hot. Not all this heat is applied to the wheel bearings, but a considerable amount is absorbed by the hub. If the grease melts, it may get by the oil seal and ruin the brake lining.

FRONT WHEEL BEARINGS on rear wheel drive cars may be "packed" by hand or, preferably, by the use of a bearing packer. After the wheel hub is thoroughly cleaned, a thin film of wheel bearing grease is placed in the hub and on the wheel spindle. The packed bearings are put in place and a new seal is installed. The wheel and tire assembly is reinstalled on the spindle and the bearings are seated by tightening the wheel nut, usually to a prescribed torque tightness. See Fig. 45-19. Then

the spindle nut is adjusted to provide zero preload or end play according to manufacturer's specifications.

Most front wheel drive cars are equipped with permanently sealed front wheel bearings. No periodic lubrication is required. Rear wheel bearing lubrication on these models consists of bearing repacking, much like front wheel bearing lubrication on rear wheel drive cars.

DRIVING AXLES

DRIVING AXLES on rear wheel drive cars are long, sturdy, one-piece steel shafts, splined at one end and generally flanged at the other end, Fig. 45-20. The splined end meshes with the differential side gear. The side gear transfers torque force to the axle shaft. The flanged end of the shaft rotates the rear driving wheel.

Driving axles on front wheel drive cars consist of a shaft, or shafts, inboard and outboard constant velocity joints, and boots. See Fig. 45-21. The inboard CV joint outer race stub shaft is splined to the final drive unit side gear. The outboard CV joint outer race stub shaft is splined to, and transfers torque force to, the hub of the front driving wheel.

REAR DRIVING AXLES

The REAR WHEEL DRIVE DRIVING AXLE is a durable, heavy-duty part that seldom requires service. Occasionally, a rear wheel seal will leak differential lubricant or a rear wheel bearing will fail. In rare circumstances, the axle shaft will break.

Axle shaft removal and installation are accomplished as follows:

1. Remove wheel and tire assembly and brake drum.
2. Drain differential lubricant by removing carrier cover.
3. Remove differential pinion shaft lock bolt and pinion shaft.
4. Push flanged end of axle shaft toward center of car and remove C-lock from inboard end of axle shaft. See Fig. 45-22.
5. Pull axle shaft from rear axle housing.
6. Use a special puller to remove axle bearing and seal.
7. Lubricate new bearing with differential lubricant and use a special driving tool to seat bearing in rear axle housing bore.
8. Install new axle shaft seal, using special driving tool, and apply grease between lips of seal.

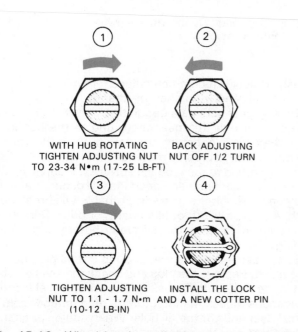

Fig. 45-19. Wheel bearing adjusting procedure is given in views 1, 2, 3, and 4 for tightening hub nut and locking it in place. (Ford Motor Co.)

1 — WITH HUB ROTATING TIGHTEN ADJUSTING NUT TO 23-34 N•m (17-25 LB-FT)

2 — BACK ADJUSTING NUT OFF 1/2 TURN

3 — TIGHTEN ADJUSTING NUT TO 1.1 - 1.7 N•m (10-12 LB-IN)

4 — INSTALL THE LOCK AND A NEW COTTER PIN

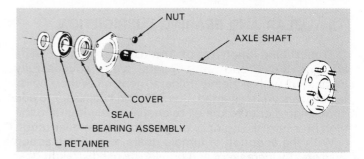

Fig. 45-20. Axle shaft and related outboard parts are typical of rear wheel drive driving axle construction. (Cadillac Motor Car Div., General Motors Corp.)

NUT
AXLE SHAFT
COVER
SEAL
BEARING ASSEMBLY
RETAINER

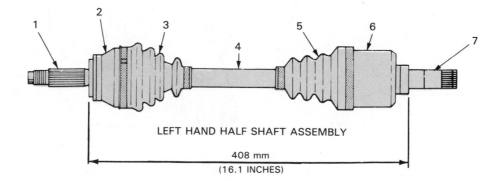

Fig. 45-21. Front wheel drive driving axle consists of: 1—Stub shaft. 2—Outboard CV joint outer race. 3—Boot. 4—Interconnecting shaft. 5—Boot. 6—Inboard CV joint outer race. 7—Stub-shaft. (Ford Motor Co.)

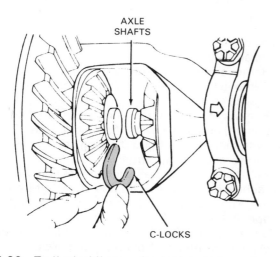

Fig. 45-22. To "unlock" rear wheel drive driving axle, push axle inward and remove C-lock from groove at inboard end of axle. (Ford Motor Co.)

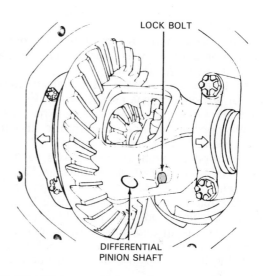

Fig. 45-23. With rear driving axle "locked" in place, install differential pinion shaft and lock bolt. (Ford Motor Co.)

9. If called for, install O-ring on spline end of axle shaft.
10. Slide axle shaft into rear axle housing, taking care not to damage seal or bearing.
11. Start axle shaft spines into side gear splines, then push shaft into differential case.
12. Install C-lock on end of axle shaft spline and push shaft outboard until C-lock seats in counterbore (recess) in differential side gear.
13. Install pinion shaft and shaft lock bolt, Fig. 45-23.
14. Apply sealant to face of clean carrier cover, install cover, and tighten bolts to specified torque value.
15. Fill differential housing to proper level with prescribed hypoid gear lubricant.
16. Install brake drum and wheel and tire assembly.

FRONT DRIVING AXLES

FRONT WHEEL DRIVE DRIVING AXLES are of many different designs and arrangements of components. Service problems mainly stem from ruptured constant velocity joint boots, which permits loss of CV joint lubricant and entry of dirt and contaminants.

Service procedures for driving axle assemblies vary among the many different front wheel driving axle systems. This holds true to the extent that driving axle removal differs for a given manufacturer's manual and automatic transaxle applications. Therefore, the manufacturer's service manual should be consulted for detailed procedures and cautions for the driving axle system being serviced.

DRIVING AXLE HANDLING HINTS

Certain general recommendations are given for handling and servicing front wheel drive driving axles:

1. During removal and installation, always support free end, or ends, of driving axle assemblies at CV joint housings, See Fig. 45-24.
2. Do not allow CV joints to "over angle" beyond their capacity.
3. Do not pry against, press on, or cut into CV joint boots.
4. Use care to see that machined surfaces and splines are not nicked or damaged in any way.
5. Use special tools when removing and installing pressed-on components. Never use a metallic hammer.

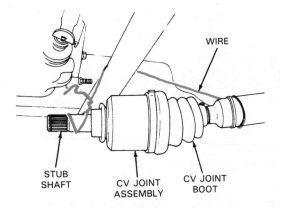

Fig. 45-24. When removing a front wheel drive driving axle from final drive unit or wheel hub, always support free end at CV joint housing. (Ford Motor Co.)

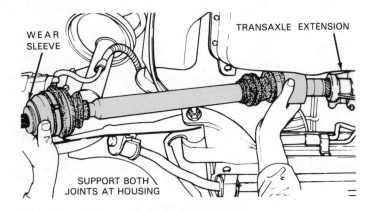

Fig. 45-26. Handle front wheel drive driving axles with care to avoid damage to boots, CV joints, or shafts. (Chrysler Corp.)

6. CV joint components are matched. Do not interchange components with components from another CV joint. See Fig. 45-25.

7. When replacing a boot, CV joint, shaft, or complete right or left driving axle assembly, know vehicle's transaxle type, transaxle ratio, engine size, and specify right or left side, inboard or outboard end when requesting replacement parts.

8. Do not drop assembled driving axle, or bump it against adjacent parts during installation, Fig. 45-26.

9. During installation, do not "over-plunge" outward on assembled inboard "plunge" type CV joint.

10. When replacing a boot, thoroughly clean CV joint and refill housing and boot with special CV joint lubricant, Fig. 45-27. Always use new boot clamps to seal-in lubricant and seal-out contaminants.

FRONT DRIVING AXLE SERVICE

Front wheel drive driving axle removal and installation procedures vary with make, model, and driving axle system. Very general procedures for removal, disassembly and reassembly, and reinstallation follow, with numerous "Notes" calling out exceptions. See Figs. 45-28 and 45-29.

Front driving axle removal:
1. Raise vehicle.
2. Remove wheel and tire assembly.
3. Remove hub nut and washer. Discard nut if torque prevailing type.
4. Remove brake caliper (wire it to underbody component) and brake rotor, if required. Note: On some systems, remove bolt attaching brake hose routing clip to suspension strut.
5. Remove nut from ball joint-to-steering knuckle attaching bolt, Fig. 45-30, and drive bolt from steering knuckle. Note: Discard nut and bolt, if so specified.
6. Separate ball joint from steering knuckle. Note: Use pry bar with care if prying is required.

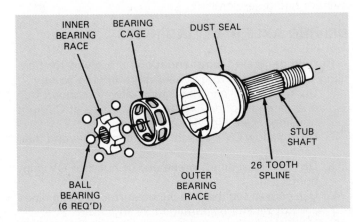

Fig. 45-25. CV joints are "matched" assemblies. Components cannot be interchanged with components from another CV joint. (Ford Motor Co.)

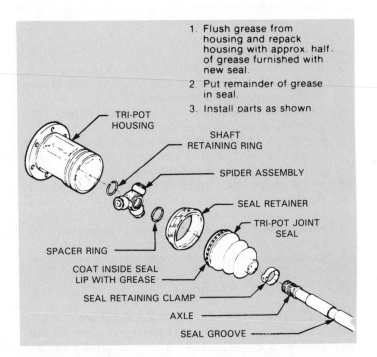

1. Flush grease from housing and repack housing with approx. half of grease furnished with new seal.
2. Put remainder of grease in seal.
3. Install parts as shown.

Fig. 45-27. Exploded view of inboard CV joint reveals "plunge" type tri-pot housing and matched internal parts. Note CV joint lubricant repacking instructions. (Oldsmobile Div., General Motors Corp.)

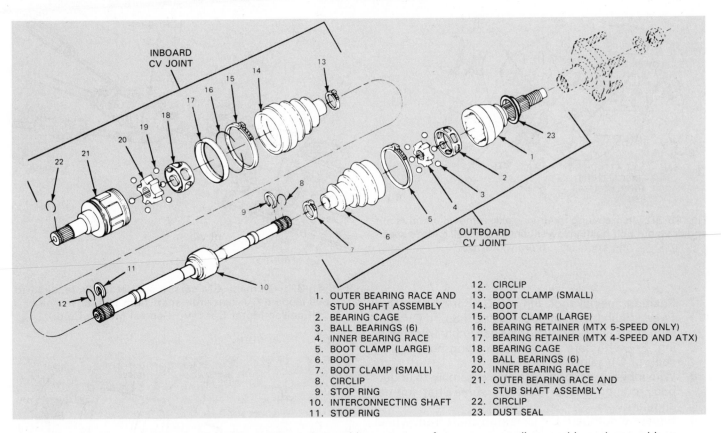

1. OUTER BEARING RACE AND STUD SHAFT ASSEMBLY
2. BEARING CAGE
3. BALL BEARINGS (6)
4. INNER BEARING RACE
5. BOOT CLAMP (LARGE)
6. BOOT
7. BOOT CLAMP (SMALL)
8. CIRCLIP
9. STOP RING
10. INTERCONNECTING SHAFT
11. STOP RING
12. CIRCLIP
13. BOOT CLAMP (SMALL)
14. BOOT
15. BOOT CLAMP (LARGE)
16. BEARING RETAINER (MTX 5-SPEED ONLY)
17. BEARING RETAINER (MTX 4-SPEED AND ATX)
18. BEARING CAGE
19. BALL BEARINGS (6)
20. INNER BEARING RACE
21. OUTER BEARING RACE AND STUD SHAFT ASSEMBLY
22. CIRCLIP
23. DUST SEAL

Fig. 45-28. Exploded view of right driving axle provides sequence for component disassembly and assembly. (Ford Motor Co.)

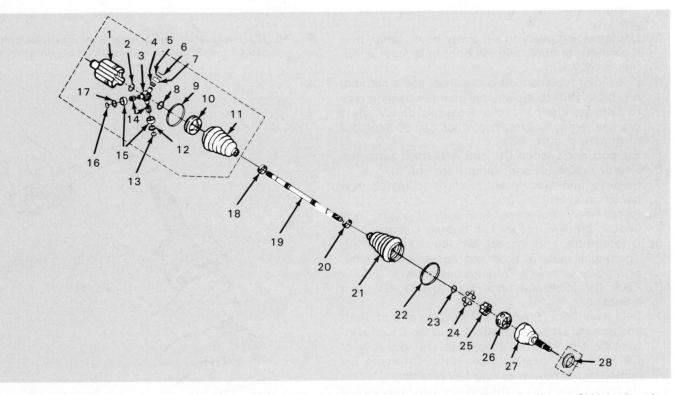

Fig. 45-29. Exploded view of typical GM right driving axle shows following parts arrangement: 1—Tri-pot CV joint housing. 2—Retaining ring. 3—Spider. 4—Needle rollers. 5—Retainer. 6—Ring. 7—Ball. 8—Spacer ring. 9—Clamp. 10—Bushing. 11—Boot. 12—Retainer. 13—Ring. 14—Needle rollers. 15—Ball. 16—Ring. 17—Retainer. 18—Clamp. 19—Axle shaft. 20—Clamp. 21—Boot. 22—Clamp. 23—Ring. 24—Ball. 25—Rzeppa CV joint inner race. 26—Cage. 27—Outer race. 28—Deflector ring. (Cadillac Motor Car Div., General Motors Corp.)

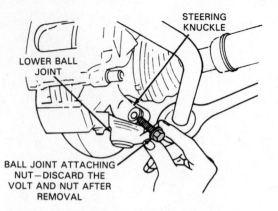

Fig. 45-30. In preparing for driving axle removal, remove nut and drive out bolt holding lower control arm ball joint to steering knuckle. (Ford Motor Co.)

7. Position special tool, Fig. 45-31, or pry bar, between final drive unit housing and inboard CV joint stub shaft and pry driving axle assembly from housing. Pry with care to avoid damaging housing, oil seal, or CV joint.
8. Wire inboard end of driving axle assembly to underbody component to maintain somewhat normal angularity.
9. Separate outboard CV joint stub shaft from wheel hub. Note: On some systems, a special puller is required.
10. Remove driving axle assembly from vehicle.

Front driving axle disassembly and reassembly:
1. Clamp interconnecting shaft of driving axle in a soft jaw vise.
2. Use a cutting pliers to cut away boot clamp, peel it away from boot, and roll boot back over shaft.
3. Inspect CV joint.
4. If CV joint replacement is required, use a hammer and brass drift to tap sharply on inner bearing race to dislodge internal circlip. Note: Some CV joints use a wire ring ball retainer which can be pried out of groove in outer race.
5. Support parts when CV joint and shaft separate.
6. Remove old boot and clamp from shaft.
7. Remove and discard old circlip and install new circlip on shaft.
8. Install new small clamp and boot on shaft. Seat boot in groove in shaft and tighten clamp.
9. Disassemble and inspect CV joint, Fig. 45-32. Thoroughly clean all parts and reassemble CV joint, or replace complete CV joint assembly.
10. Pack CV joint and boot with special CV joint lubricant.
11. Peel back boot. Position CV joint on end of shaft and use a plastic-tipped hammer to tap CV joint into place, Fig. 45-33. Circlip must seat in groove of CV joint inner bearing race. Note: On some CV joints, install new wire ring ball retainer.
12. Remove excess lubricant and position large end of boot over CV joint housing. Install and tighten new large clamp.
13. Move plunge type CV joint in or out to adjust driving axle to length specified. See Fig. 45-21.

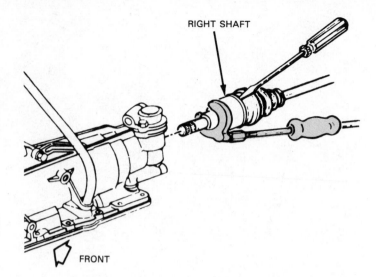

Fig. 45-31. On many GM cars, a special tool is required to pull inboard CV joint stub shaft from final drive unit. (Cadillac Motor Car Div., General Motors Corp.)

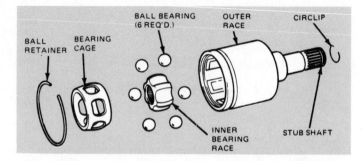

Fig. 45-32. Disassembly of constant velocity joint permits careful inspection of matched components. (Ford Motor Co.)

Fig. 45-33. To install CV joint on shaft, peel back boot, position CV joint assembly on end of shaft, and tap it in place. (Ford Motor Co.)

14. Relieve any trapped air from boot, then install boot clamp.
Front driving axle reinstallation:
1. Place new circlip on inboard CV joint stub shaft.
2. Carefully align splines of inboard CV joint stub shaft with splines in final drive unit side gear, Fig. 45-34.
3. Push CV joint into final drive unit until circlip seats in side gear.
4. Carefully align splines of outboard CV joint stub shaft with splines in wheel hub, Fig. 45-35.
5. Push shaft into hub as far as possible. Note: On some systems, use special puller and adapters to complete installation of shaft in hub.
6. Connect control arm to steering knuckle and install new bolt and nut to specified torque value.

7. Install brake caliper and rotor. Note: On some systems, install bolt attaching brake hose routing clip to suspension strut.
8. Install washer and new torque prevailing nut, finger-tight, on outboard CV joint stub shaft. Note: Some hub nuts have a nut lock and cotter pin.
9. Install wheel and tire assembly.
10. Lower vehicle and final-tighten wheel nuts.
11. Tighten hub nut to specified torque value, and make sure that locking tab on nut aligns with slot in CV joint stub shaft. See Fig. 45-36. Note: On some hub nuts, after proper torque tightening, install nut lock and cotter pin.
12. Fill transaxle to correct level with recommended transaxle lubricant.

CARE IN SERVICING DRIVELINES

When servicing drivelines and driving axles, bear in mind that you are working with parts and assemblies designed, produced, and quality controlled to meet exacting standards of size, shape, and finish. Such high standards of manufacture deserve equally high standards of skill and care and attention to detail when performing services.

When working on these important elements of the drive train, you are dealing with low-to-high speed rotating parts, centrifugal force, and the effects of engine torque and power transfer. With shafts, you need to maintain proper angularity and balance to avoid vibration. With constant velocity joints, you are involved with matched parts, opposed identical pairs, and a special CV joint lubricant.

Likewise, you must provide special and specified lubricants for transaxles, transmissions, differentials, universal joints, and wheel bearings. In all areas, you must insure freedom of operation of moving parts to help eliminate friction and wear, and to furnish maximum power transfer to the driving wheels.

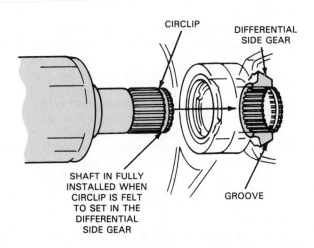

Fig. 45-34. During installation of driving axle assembly, splines on inboard CV joint stub shaft are aligned with, and fully installed in, splines of final drive unit side gear. (Ford Motor Co.)

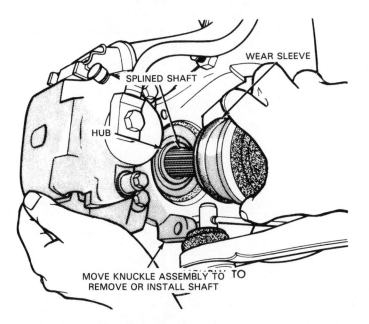

Fig. 45-35. With inboard CV joint locked in place, outboard CV joint stub shaft splines are meshed with wheel hub splines. (Chrysler Corp.)

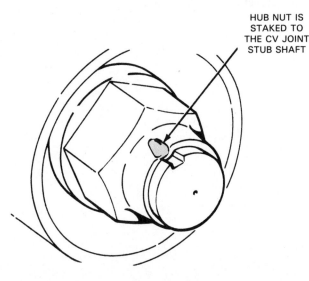

Fig. 45-36. After new torque prevailing nut is tightened to specified torque value, it must be "staked" to outboard CV joint stub shaft. (Ford Motor Co.)

Chapter 45—REVIEW QUESTIONS
DRIVELINE SERVICE

Write your answers on a separate sheet of paper. Do not write in this book.

1. The driveline of a rear wheel drive vehicle consists of one or more universal joints, the drive shaft, and _____.
   a. Transmission output shaft.
   b. Transaxle side gears.
   c. Differential drive pinion gear.
   d. Driving axles and wheels.
2. The universal joints are considered to be part of the drive shaft assembly. True or False?
3. All drive shafts must be balanced, properly mounted assemblies with all working parts lubricated by a special, _____ lubricant.
4. After installing new universal joints, why should you reassemble the drive shaft carefully?
5. What measuring device should you use to check the angularity of the drive shaft and universal joints?
6. The differential drive pinion gear and ring gear comprise a _____ assembly.
7. The differential case is attached to the _____.
   a. Drive pinion gear.
   b. Ring gear.
   c. Drive shaft.
8. Service problems with differentials usually are limited to lubricant leakage. Where?
9. What two adjustments can be made which will affect tooth contact between the drive pinion gear and the ring gear?
10. Front wheel bearings on front wheel drive cars require periodic lubrication much like front wheel bearings on a rear wheel drive car. True or False?
11. Driving axles on rear wheel drive cars are splined at one end and generally _____ (flanged or tapered) at the other end.
12. The splined end of the rear driving axle meshes with:
    a. Differential side gear.
    b. Differential pinion gear.
    c. Ring gear.
    d. Drive pinion gear.
13. A car owner complained of a "clunk" at the rear of a rear wheel drive car. Mechanic A says it could be caused by a faulty rear universal joint. Mechanic B says it could be caused by too much backlash between the differential drive pinion gear and ring gear. Who is right?
    a. Mechanic A.
    b. Mechanic B.
    c. Both mechanic A and mechanic B.
    d. Neither mechanic A nor mechanic B.
14. In most rear wheel drive cars, the driving axles are retained in the differential by:
    a. C-locks.
    b. Circlips.
    c. Snap rings.
    d. Stop rings.
15. In many front wheel drive systems, the driving axles are retained in the final drive unit by _____ (C-locks or circlips).
16. Constant velocity joint components are matched. You _____ (may or may not) interchange components with components from another CV joint.
17. What type of nut or bolt should be discarded once it is removed from a shaft or spindle?
18. After assembly of front wheel drive driving axle, move plunge type CV joint in or out to adjust driving axle to specified length. True or False?
19. A car owner complained of vibration under a rear wheel drive car. Mechanic A says it could be caused by an out-of-balance drive shaft. Mechanic B says it could be caused by over-angularity of the drive shaft and universal joints. Who is right?
    a. Mechanic A.
    b. Mechanic B.
    c. Both mechanic A and mechanic B.
    d. Neither mechanic A nor mechanic B.
20. In performing driveline service, you must insure freedom of operation of moving parts to help eliminate friction and wear, and to furnish maximum _____ to the driving wheels.

Chapter 46

FOUR WHEEL DRIVE

After studying this chapter, you will be able to:
- Define four wheel drive.
- Explain how four wheel drive and all wheel drive differ.
- Tell how a viscous coupling in a four wheel drive system builds internal resistance and provides "limited slip" action.
- State why differential "locks" are used in four wheel drive systems.
- Identify some typical four wheel drive troubles and give possible causes.

FOUR WHEEL DRIVE is a power transfer system that permits a vehicle to be driven by all four wheels. The principal advantages of four wheel drive (4WD) are better traction and greater control of the vehicle in adverse conditions such as muddy roads, wet or oily highways, snow or ice-covered roads, loose surfaces, or hazardous off-road terrain.

FOUR WHEEL DRIVE/ALL WHEEL DRIVE

Four wheel drive has a long history. It was pioneered in 1910 with the introduction of the truck-like 4WD "Duplex" power car. In 1913, the Jeffrey Quad was produced as a 4WD commercial vehicle. Later, it was adapted for military use and became the Nash Quad, the most famous Army truck of World War I.

Then, the "go anywhere" World War II Jeep established the superior flexibility and capability of 4WD vehicles in adverse conditions. The Jeep, however, was created as a dual-purpose vehicle. It not only had a rigidly connected 4WD system, but was equipped with a transfer system that permitted the vehicle to be shifted into a two wheel drive mode for on-highway use.

Today, the dual-mode (2WD/4WD) system is used in a wide-range of large and compact pickup trucks, large and sports utility vehicles, vans, station wagons, and passenger cars. The versatility of 4WD and its added safety aspects of better traction and greater control have made it an ever-expanding part of the new vehicle market.

Also contributing to 4WD popularity is a relatively recent development termed ALL WHEEL DRIVE. See Fig. 46-1. All wheel drive (AWD) systems automatically react to normal or adverse situations without the need for the

driver to decide when or when not to shift into 4WD.

In all wheel drive applications, then, the shifting is automatic. Most four wheel drive vehicles, however, have a shifting device so that the front wheel drive or rear wheel drive can be disengaged if desired and the vehicle becomes two wheel drive. See Fig. 46-2. In some cases, the vehicle must be stopped with the engine idling when the "shift" is made, either from 2WD to 4WD or from 4WD to 2WD. In other applications, the driver can "shift on the fly."

A study of various 4WD systems as they evolved should provide a basic understanding of how these systems operate and why advanced 4WD and AWD designs have improved the "breed."

AMC/JEEP 4WD SYSTEMS

In 1973, the introduction of the Jeep Quadra-Trac system brought full-time four wheel drive into an expanding market. The Quadra-Trac 4WD system uses an inter-drive shaft differential that has an unloading cone type limited slip action. It restricts the difference in rotational speeds between the two drive shafts, thus delivering better traction.

Quadra-Trac II was introduced on American Motors Eagle 4WD vehicles. It, too, uses an inter-drive shaft differential with limited slip action — but by way of a viscous coupling, Fig. 46-3. The viscous coupling is part of a single-speed transfer case. The rear drive shaft is driven directly from the rear of the transfer case. The front drive shaft is offset to the left, driven by a chain.

When the drive shafts operate at different rpm (when a wheel, or pair of wheels, tends to spin), the liquid silicone in the viscous coupling interacts with 43 closely spaced plates alternately attached to the housing and the hub of the coupling. This builds resistance and effectively "locks" the drive shafts together to prevent all of the power from going to the axle with the spinning wheel (or wheels).

SELECT DRIVE

American Motors went to a SELECT DRIVE system, Fig. 46-4, on Eagle models with a dash-mounted switch that controls two vacuum motors to provide either 2WD

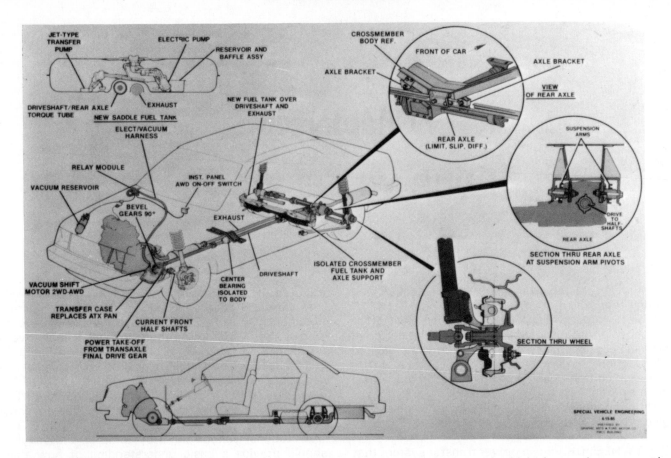

Fig. 46-1. Major elements of Ford all wheel drive system are shown in phantom views of vehicle. Insets give construction details of related assemblies. Note front-to-rear alignment of driveline (bottom left), brought about by mounting transfer case under automatic transaxle and use of a new design, specially contoured fuel tank (top left). (Ford Motor Co.)

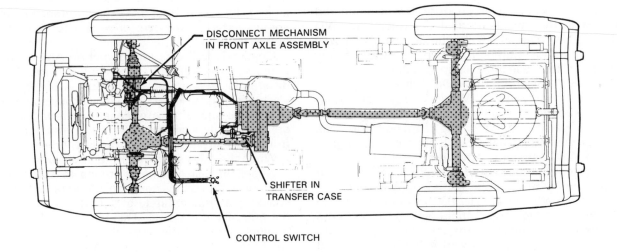

Fig. 46-2. AMC Eagle 4WD drive train is highlighted by dot formation. System has direct drive through transfer case to rear differential. Chain drive in transfer case powers front differential when control switch and front axle disconnect mechanism are in 4WD mode. (American Motors Corp.)

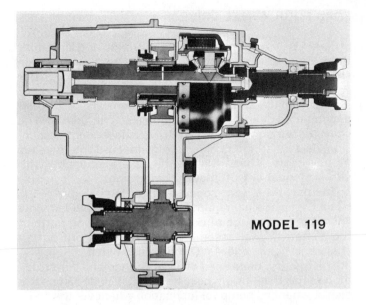

Fig. 46-3. Eagle transfer case has viscous coupling in case to provide "limited slip" action to drive shafts. (American Motors Corp.)

or 4WD capability. For 2WD operation, one motor disengages the front axle drive chain in the transfer case, Fig. 46-5. The other motor actuates a front axle disconnect mechanism. A "shift on the fly" feature on later models permits shifts while the vehicle is in motion.

On later Eagle models, a switch was made in the transfer case to a four pinion, open type differential instead of the viscous coupling. A vacuum control system, actuated by a selector switch on the dash panel, is used to change drive mode. The name, Select Drive, also applies to the later four-pinion gear system.

COMMAND-TRAC

Some Jeep models use a COMMAND-TRAC part-time, dual range, chain-driven, gear type 4WD system. Later models feature "shift-on-the-fly." Shifting into or out of 4WD while the vehicle is moving is made possible by use of a synchronizer assembly in the sliding spline clutch that locks the front axle drive chain sprocket to the transfer case. See Figs. 46-6 and 46-7. Also in later models, a front axle disconnect mechanism is employed for 2WD, which eliminates the need for locking hubs.

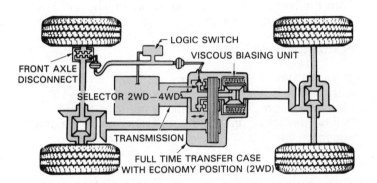

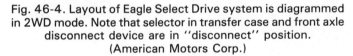

Fig. 46-4. Layout of Eagle Select Drive system is diagrammed in 2WD mode. Note that selector in transfer case and front axle disconnect device are in "disconnect" position. (American Motors Corp.)

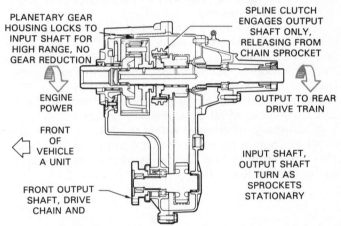

Fig. 46-6. Diagram of internal features of Jeep Command-Trac transfer case shows elements in 2WD mode. (AMC Jeep Corp.)

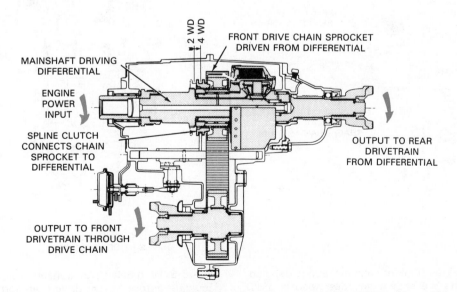

Fig. 46-5. Sectional view gives particulars of Select Drive transfer case operation in 4WD mode. (American Motors Corp.)

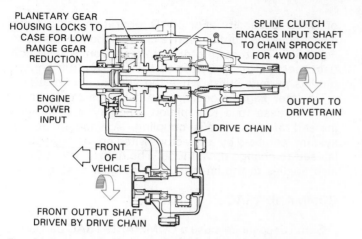

Fig. 46-7. Command-Trac transfer case elements are pictured in 4WD mode. Note in this mode that spline clutch engages input shaft to chain sprocket. (AMC Jeep Corp.)

Some Jeep models adopted the viscous coupling setup in the SELEC-TRAC full-time 4WD/2WD system. This system is similar to Select-Drive, but it also has a low-range, or two-speed, capability in the transfer case when extra torque is needed.

The low range mode is activated by a floor-mounted lever, but only when the vehicle is in 4WD. Figs. 46-8 and 46-9 reveal how the Selec-Trac system operates.

In later models, Jeeps are equipped with a redesigned transfer case within the Selec-Trac 4WD system. This transfer case affords the use of a five-position shift lever: 2WD, Hi Lock, 4WD, Neutral, and Lo Lock.

A planetary differential within the transfer case provides a constant torque split to the front and rear axles. The differential action can be overidden, or locked, in either high or low range.

FORD FOUR WHEEL DRIVE

Ford 4WD systems are used on Bronco and light duty truck models. One system uses the front driving axle shown in Fig. 46-10 in conjunction with the transfer case shown in an exploded view in Fig. 46-11.

The front driving axle assembly consists of two independent yoke and arm assemblies. The driving axle shafts utilize universal joints to give independent suspension. The steering knuckles are connected to the yokes by ball joints. These 4WD vehicles are equipped with either manual or automatic locking hubs.

The part-time, two-speed transfer case, Fig. 46-11, has a two-piece aluminum housing. This exploded view shows the sequence of components, including parts of the planetary gear assembly, shift levers, front output shaft and yoke, and 4WD indicator switch.

The transfer case used on later Bronco and light truck models has magnesium case halves. It includes a positive displacement oil pump for lubrication whenever the mainshaft is turning. A ''Touch Drive'' electrical shift selector system is available. See Fig. 46-12. With this system, shifts between 2WD and high-range 4WD can be made at any speed or with the vehicle stopped. Shifts into or out of low-range 4WD require that the vehicle is stopped with the transmission in neutral. Obviously, the Touch Drive system uses automatic locking front wheel hubs.

FORD ALL WHEEL DRIVE

An All Wheel Drive system is offered on some Ford front wheel drive passenger cars. See Fig. 46-13. It is intended to provide improved on-the-road traction and can be 'switched' into and out of all wheel drive at any speed or when the vehicle is standing still.

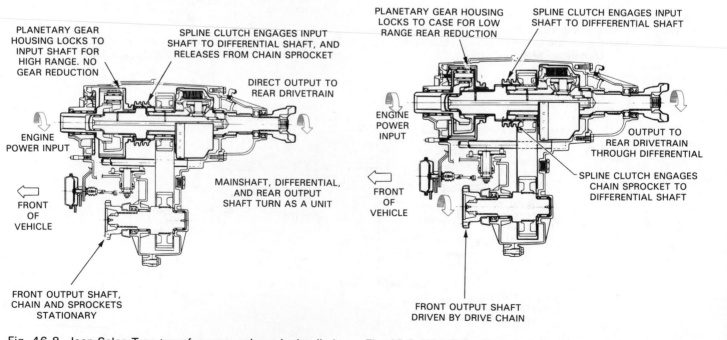

Fig. 46-8. Jeep Selec-Trac transfer case makeup is detailed. Transfer case elements are shown and described in 2WD ''high'' mode. (AMC Jeep Corp.)

Fig. 46-9. With Selec-Trac transfer case in 4WD mode, arrows indicate output to rear drive train and front output shaft. (AMC Jeep Corp.)

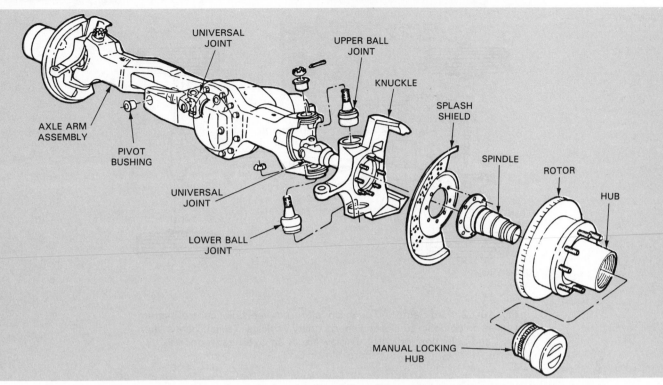

Fig. 46-10. Three-quarter front view shows details of Ford Bronco front driving axle, including steering knuckle, wheel spindle, hub and rotor assembly, and locking hub. (Ford Motor Co.)

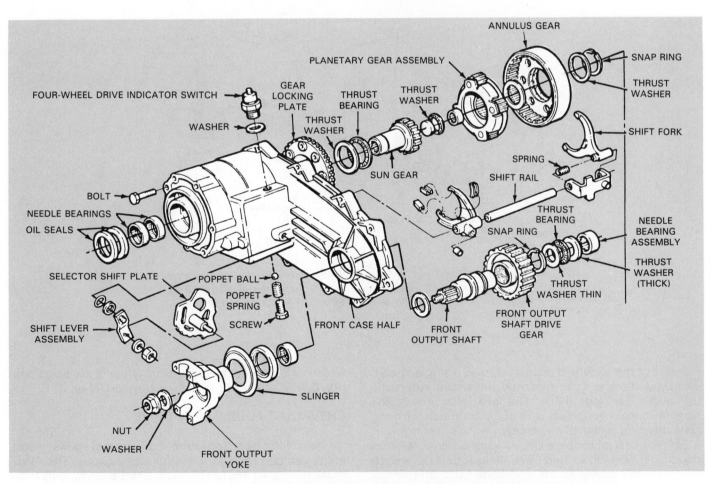

Fig. 46-11. Exploded view gives disassembly/assembly sequence of Ford Bronco transfer case. (Ford Motor Co.)

563

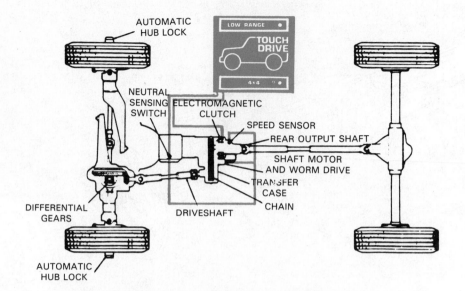

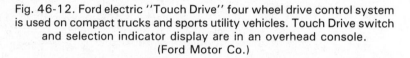

Fig. 46-12. Ford electric "Touch Drive" four wheel drive control system is used on compact trucks and sports utility vehicles. Touch Drive switch and selection indicator display are in an overhead console. (Ford Motor Co.)

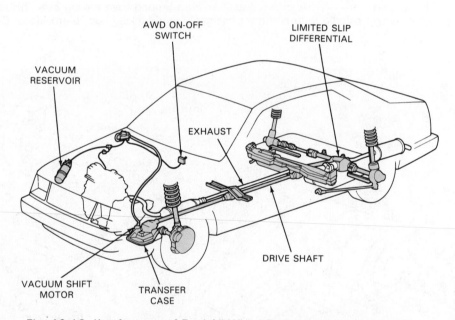

Fig. 46-13. Key features of Ford All Wheel Drive system are pointed out in phantom view of Tempo/Topaz. A two-piece drive shaft transmits power to rear limited slip differential when AWD switch is ON. (Ford Motor Co.)

Heart of the all wheel drive system is a single-speed, part-time transfer case mounted under the automatic transaxle. See Fig. 46-1. The gear that drives the transfer case mechanism is in constant mesh with the final drive ring gear of the transaxle.

For all wheel drive operation, a sliding clutch collar links the driving gear with a two-piece, hollow tube drive shaft that transfers power to the rear limited slip differential. The sliding clutch collar is engaged and disengaged by a shift fork. The fork is activated by a vacuum motor, which is actuated by solenoids when a two-position (2WD/AWD) electric switch is turned ON or OFF.

CHEVROLET FOUR WHEEL DRIVE

Chevrolet offers four wheel drive on wagons, sport utility vehicles, compact and full size pickups. The 4WD system is called INSTA-TRAC. It lets the driver shift from 2WD to 4WD "high" and back again without stopping. This provides convenience for the driver.

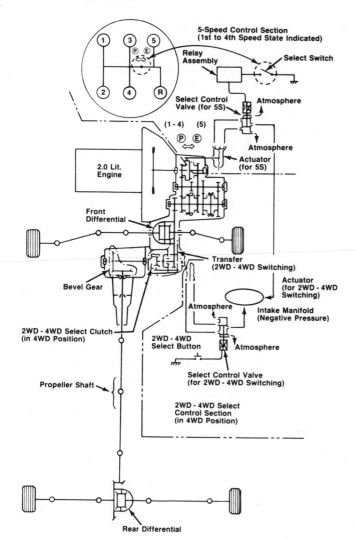

The full size Blazer has an automatic locking hub system that allows the driver to shift into or out of 4WD without leaving the cab.

CHRYSLER/MITSUBISHI 4WD

The Colt Vista four wheel drive wagon is imported by Chrysler for the Plymouth and Dodge lines. Fig. 46-14 calls out all of the 2WD/4WD mechanisms. Trace the system in this schematic from select button to select control valve, actuator, transaxle, front differential, transfer case (for 2WD/4WD switching), bevel gear setup, propeller shaft, and rear differential.

AUDI FOUR WHEEL DRIVE

The Audi Quattro four wheel drive system is permanently engaged, freeing the driver from reacting to rapidly changing road conditions. Power is transmitted through a five-speed manual transaxle to the front wheel drive driveline and front wheels. Power to the rear wheels is by way of a two-piece drive shaft, differential, and driving axles. The axles are supported by fully independent rear suspension members. See Fig. 46-15.

For even greater traction, a differential lock control can be triggered by a rotating knob to lock the center differential. This locks or synchronizes the rotation of the front wheels to the rotation of the rear wheels. Under worst conditions, the rear differential also can be locked for maximum traction.

VOLKSWAGEN ALL WHEEL DRIVE

Volkswagen has introduced an automatically engaging, permanent all wheel drive system for use on certain Vanagon models. The system is based on the use of a viscous coupling, Fig. 46-16, designed to enhance the positive traction already provided by the Vanagon's rear engine, rear wheel drive setup.

Fig. 46-14. Schematic shows 2WD/4WD mechanisms on Colt Vista wagon. Arrows point out features and functions of 4WD system and related components. (Chrysler Corp.)

Fig. 46-15. Audi has engineered permanently engaged all wheel drive for its sports coupes and sedans. AWD system utilizes a unique differential between front and rear wheels that provides added traction when needed. (Audi of America, Inc.)

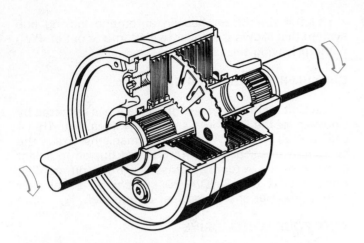

Fig. 46-16. Volkswagen uses a sealed viscous coupling unit in front differential of four wheel drive Vanagon models. When required by driving conditions, silicone fluid thickens and gives direct drive to plates in coupling, thus transmitting power to front wheels. (Volkswagen of America, Inc.)

The viscous coupling is mounted in the front final drive housing, where it operates constantly and automatically to transmit power to the front differential as required by the need for greater traction.

The viscous coupling is filled with a patented silicone fluid. In operation, the coupling allows up to six percent speed difference between the drive shaft and front axle before the thick silicone fluid effects a rigid connection.

An optional rear differential lock is offered. It is designed for use at low speeds only when the vehicle is in danger of being stuck in the mud or snow. A shift valve on the dash panel controls the engagement and disengagement of a lock sleeve in the differential housing.

Certain Volkswagen Quantum models have All Wheel Drive. This 4WD system has three differentials, one for each driving axle and one between the front and rear axles. The center differential is integrated into the transmission, where it provides the 4WD handling characteristics. The three differentials can be locked in different positions to suit difficult or hazardous driving conditions.

SUBARU FOUR WHEEL DRIVE

Some older Subaru models have "On Demand" part-time four wheel drive. One system setup uses an electric 4WD engagement switch in the manual transmission shift lever. Another setup has an auxiliary two-speed transfer case operated by a second shift lever. Moving the 4WD shift lever an extra notch gives the vehicle 46 percent more low speed pulling power.

Later models couple 4WD with a microprocessor controlled air spring suspension system. This system automatically raises the vehicle one inch when 4WD is engaged. It lowers the vehicle at a speed of 50 mph.

Subaru's newer, full-time 4WD system uses a mechanical center differential to transfer power to the front and rear driving axles. Under hazardous driving conditions, the center differential can be locked to provide power to each axle.

HONDA FOUR WHEEL DRIVE

Certain Honda models offer "Real Time" 4WD and improved traction by pressing a push button switch. Also featured is a "special low" gear in a six-speed manual transmission.

The 4WD system uses a viscous coupling in the drive shaft to the rear axle. The coupling has interlaced plates and is filled with a silicone fluid. If the front wheels slip, the fluid heats up and expands, causing the coupling to lock and transfer power to the rear wheels.

FOUR WHEEL DRIVE SERVICE

Servicing four wheel drive systems can be the end result of lengthy processes of elimination. Since all 4WD systems affect or are affected by at least two drivelines and all four driving axles, pinpointing a problem area is a wide-ranging, systematic search for the source of trouble.

Manufacturers warn that, "Before attempting to repair a suspected transfer case malfunction, check all other driveline components. The actual cause of the problem may be related to the axles, hubs, propeller shafts, transmission or transaxle, wheels and tires."

Also consider the many 4WD types in present use. Some are designed around a front-mounted engine and rear wheel drive. These require the use of a transfer case to send power forward to the front differential.

Other 4WD designs are based on an engine in front and front wheel drive. With this basic layout, the primary drive remains at the front axle and power goes back to the rear wheels by way of a "power takeoff," which can be connected or disconnected. Most are "part-time," selector-engaged, or "on demand" 4WD.

Some 4WD systems utilize three differentials with "lock-up" capabilities for improved traction. Others have manual or automatic locking hubs. Still others use a viscous coupling to provide "full-time" or "all wheel drive."

With this in mind, always refer to the manufacturer's service manual for diagnostic information and step-by-step service procedures.

A listing of four wheel drive troubles and possible causes follows. This list is general, touching on a variety of types of 4WD, but it could serve to sharpen your problem solving ability.

Vehicle Tends to Wander
1. Unequal or incorrect tire pressures. (Pressure should be within 1/2 to 1 psi [3.50 to 7.0 kPa] wheel to wheel.)
2. Unequal or mismatched tire sizes and types.
3. Incorrect front wheel caster angle.

Noisy Operation
1. Incorrect or insufficient lubricant in transfer case or differential. Check manufacturer's specifications.
2. Worn gears or bearings in transfer case.
3. Worn gears or bearings in differential.
4. Worn or damaged wheel bearings.
5. Unequal or incorrect tire pressure.
6. Unequal or mismatched tire sizes or types.

Lubricant Leaks

1. Overfill condition in transfer case.
2. Vent closed or restricted.
3. Yoke seals worn or damaged.
4. Yoke seal-bearing surfaces rough or worn.
5. Silicone fluid from viscous coupling. (Replace entire unit.)

System Will Not Shift Into 2WD

1. No vacuum at mode selector harness.
2. No vacuum at storage tank or vacuum hose from storage tank.
3. No vacuum at intake manifold supply fitting.
4. Defective select control valve or actuator.
5. Inoperative transfer case vacuum motor.
6. Malfunctioning transfer case shift linkage.
7. Inoperative front axle shift vacuum motor.
8. Automatic locking front hubs not unlocking.

System Will Not Shift Into 4WD

1. No vacuum at mode selector harness.
2. No vacuum at storage tank or vacuum hose from storage tank.
3. No vacuum at intake manifold supply fitting.
4. Defective select control valve or actuator.
5. Inoperative transfer case vacuum motor.
6. Malfunctioning transfer case shift linkage.
7. Inoperative front axle shift motor.
8. Automatic locking front hubs not locking.

Vibration or Shudder

1. Defective or loose steering linkage.
2. Defective steering damper.
3. Faulty universal joints.
4. Bent wheels.
5. Low level of silicone fluid in viscous coupling. (Replace entire unit.)
6. Runout or unbalance of propeller shaft.

REVIEW QUESTIONS — FOUR WHEEL DRIVE

1. Define the term "four wheel drive."
2. What are the principle advantages of four wheel drive?
3. With "All Wheel Drive" systems, the "shifts" from 2WD to 4WD and from 4WD to 2WD are:
   a. Manual, with vehicle stopped.
   b. Manual, and "on the fly."
   c. Semiautomatic.
   d. Automatic.
4. Key element of the Quadra-Trac 4WD system is:
   a. Viscous coupling.
   b. Two-speed transfer case.
   c. Front axle disconnect.
   d. Automatic locking front wheel hubs.
5. Jeeps equipped with a redesigned transfer case within the Selec-Trac 4WD system have a five-position shift lever. True or False?
6. The Ford All Wheel Drive system for passenger cars has a single-speed, part-time transfer case mounted under the _____.
   a. Manual transaxle.
   b. Automatic transaxle.
   c. Front differential.
   d. Rear differential.
7. The Audi Quattro has a _____ 4WD system.
   a. Real time.
   b. Part-time.
   c. On-demand.
   d. Permanently engaged.
8. A driver complained that a four wheel drive pickup truck with transfer case and automatic locking front hubs would not shift into two wheel drive. Mechanic A says it could be caused by an inoperative transfer case vacuum motor. Mechanic B says it could be caused by the automatic locking hubs not locking. Who is right?
   a. Mechanic A.
   b. Mechanic B.
   c. Both mechanic A and mechanic B.
   d. Neither mechanic A nor mechanic B.
9. Manufacturers warn that, "Before attempting to repair a suspected transfer case, check all other _____ components.
10. Give two possible causes why a 4WD vehicle would tend to wander.

Chapter 47

SUSPENSION AND STEERING SYSTEMS

After studying this chapter, you will be able to:
- Explain the function of the various front and rear suspension components and assemblies.
- Name the three basic types of front and rear suspension systems.
- Tell how a typical ''automatic level control system'' works.
- Describe the makeup of manual rack and pinion and recirculating ball types of steering systems.
- State the operating principles of a power rack and pinion steering gear assembly and the integral power steering gear assembly.
- Identify some typical suspension and steering system troubles and give possible causes.

The modern automobile has come a long way since the days when ''just being self-propelled'' was enough to satisfy the car owner. Improvements in suspension, Figs. 47-1 and 47-2, and steering, increased strength and durability of components, and advances in tire design and construction have made large contributions to riding comfort and driving safety.

SUSPENSION SYSTEMS

Basically, SUSPENSION refers to the use of front and rear springs to suspend a vehicle's frame, body or unitized body, engine, and power train above the wheels. These relatively heavy assemblies constitute what is known as ''sprung'' weight. The ''unsprung'' weight, on the other hand, includes wheels and tires, brake assemblies, the rear axle assembly, and other structural members not supported by the springs.

The SPRINGS used on today's cars and trucks are engineered in a wide variety of types, shapes, sizes, rates, and capacities. Types include leaf springs, coil springs, air springs, and torsion bars. These are used in sets of four per vehicle, or they are paired off in various combinations and are attached to the vehicle by a number of different mounting techniques.

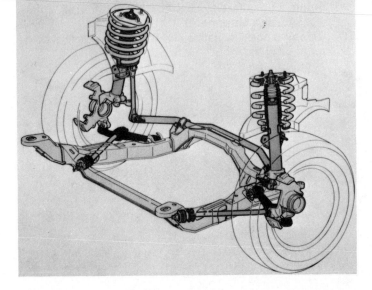

Fig. 47-1. A typical MacPherson strut front suspension system features long shock absorber struts surrounded by coil springs. Lower control arms, wheel spindles, a stabilizer bar, and diagonal struts are part of MacPherson design. (Ford Motor Co.)

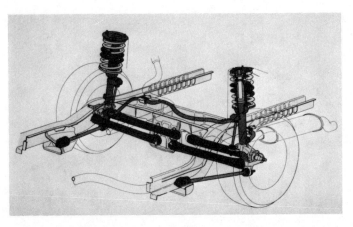

Fig. 47-2. MacPherson strut suspension is also well suited for use at rear of front wheel drive vehicles. Here, four transverse, parallel control arms are used in conjunction with a stabilizer bar and tie rods attached to spindle and knuckle assemblies. (Ford Motor Co.)

COIL SPRINGS

Many front and rear suspension systems incorporate compression type COIL SPRINGS. Some front coil springs are mounted between the lower control arm and spring housing or seat in the frame, Figs. 47-3 and 47-4.

Other front suspension systems have the coil springs mounted above the upper control arms, compressed between a pivoting spring seat bolted to the control arm and a spring tower formed in the front end sheet metal. See Fig. 47-5.

When coil springs are used in both front and rear suspension, three or four control arms are placed between the rear axle housing and the frame to carry driving and braking torque. The lower control arms pivot in the frame members and sometimes support the rear coil springs to provide for up and down movement of the axle and wheel assembly.

In addition, a SWAY BAR (track bar) is usually attached from the upper control arm to the frame side rail to hold the rear axle housing in proper alignment with the frame and to prevent side sway of the body. However, if the rear coil springs are mounted between the frame and a swinging half axle, the independently suspended rear wheels have a sturdy axle housing attached to the differential housing which, in turn, is bolted to the frame.

Coil springs are also used in MacPherson strut suspension systems. The spring is installed between a spring seat insulator on the strut and the top mount of the strut assembly. See Fig. 47-6.

Coil springs are made of steel or steel alloy. Some have evenly spaced coils, others have variable spacing. Each is manufactured to meet the prescribed Rated Suspension Spring Capacity for the particular vehicle application. This rating is designed to provide for adequate coil spring durability and vehicle stability under all intended load conditions.

LEAF SPRINGS

Front LEAF SPRINGS are used in conjunction with solid axle beams in most truck applications. Corvettes use single-leaf, filament-wound, glass/expoxy front and rear springs mounted transversely (crosswise to vehicle centerline).

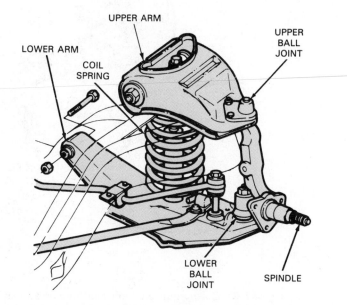

Fig. 47-4. Short and long arm front suspension generally includes ball (spherical) joints as "swivel points" for each front wheel. (Ford Motor Co.)

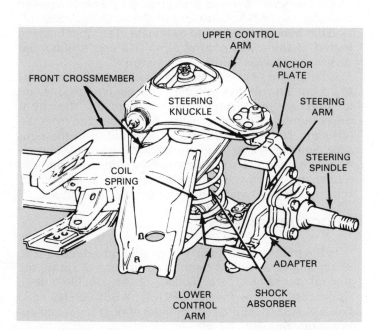

Fig. 47-3. Independent front suspension with coil springs and control arms of "short and long arm" type is used on most rear wheel drive passenger cars. (American Motors Corp.)

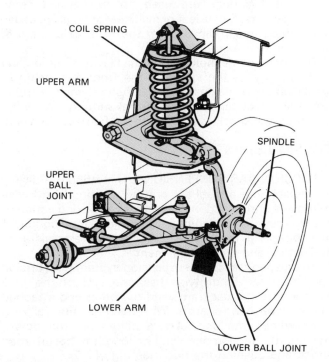

Fig. 47-5. In front suspension systems of some subcompact and compact cars, coil springs are mounted above upper control arms. Note use of strut to support lower control arm. (Ford Motor Co.)

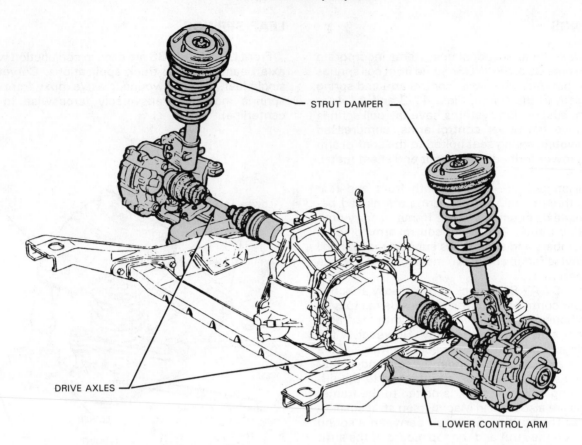

STRUT DAMPER

DRIVE AXLES

LOWER CONTROL ARM

Fig. 47-6. Coil springs are high-mounted on strut in typical MacPherson strut fashion on this front wheel drive application. Note relative positioning of transaxle and drive axles.
(Pontiac Motor Div., General Motors Corp.)

Rear leaf springs are used on trucks and some passenger cars. Single leaf or multi-leaf springs are usually mounted longitudinally over the front axle beam or under the rear axle housing.

The spring center bolt fastens the leaves together, and its head locates the spring in the front axle beam or saddle on the rear axle housing. U-bolts clamp the spring firmly in place and keep it from shifting. Eyebolts, brackets, and shackles attach it to the frame at each end.

TORSION BARS

TORSION BAR SUSPENSION is a method of utilizing the flexiblity of a steel bar or tube twisting lengthwise to provide spring action. Instead of the flexing action of a leaf spring, or the compressing-and-extending action of a coil spring, the torsion bar twists to exert resistance against up-and-down movement.

An independent front suspension system with torsion bars mounted lengthwise has one end of the bars anchored to the car frame and the other end attached to the lower control arms. With each rise and fall of a front wheel, the control arm pivots up and down, twisting the torsion bar along its length to absorb road shock and cushion the ride. See Fig. 47-7.

Some independent front suspension systems on rear wheel drive cars have transverse (crosswise) torsion bars. On Chrysler cars so equipped, two bars of modified L-shape are used. See Fig. 47-8.

The straight end of each torsion bar is anchored in the front crossmember opposite the wheel its spring action affects. Each bar extends parallel to the transverse part of the crossmember and is supported by a pivot cushion bushing, Fig. 47-8. Outboard of the bushing, each torsion bar bends backward to terminate in another bushing bolted to the lower control arm. This end of each bar serves as a lower control arm "strut."

Adjustment of the torsion bars controls the height of the front end of the vehicle. The adjusting bolts are located at the torsion bar anchors in the front crossmember. The right torsion bar is adjusted from the left side. The left torsion bar is adjusted from the right side. See Fig. 47-8. The inner ends of the lower control arms are bolted to the crossmember and pivot through a bushing. When the control arm pivots up and down, the torsion bar twists and absorbs the road shock.

SHOCK ABSORBERS

In the past, a wide variety of direct and indirect shock absorbing devices has been used to control spring action of passenger cars. Today, direct, double-acting, "telescoping" hydraulic SHOCK ABSORBERS and SHOCK ABSORBER STRUTS have almost universal application. See Fig. 47-9.

The operating principle of direct-acting hydraulic shock absorbers consists of forcing fluid through restricting orifices in the valves. The restricted flow serves to slow

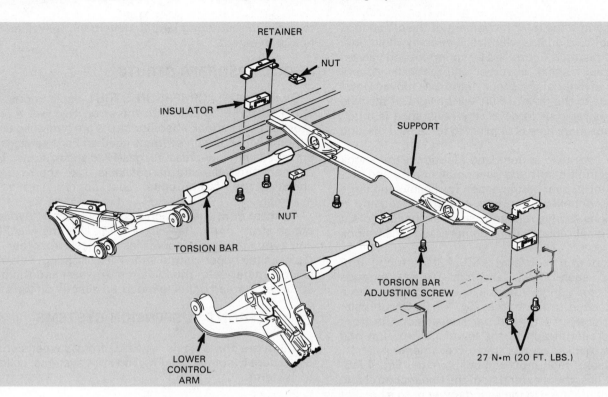

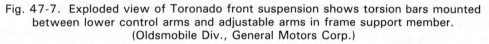

Fig. 47-7. Exploded view of Toronado front suspension shows torsion bars mounted between lower control arms and adjustable arms in frame support member. (Oldsmobile Div., General Motors Corp.)

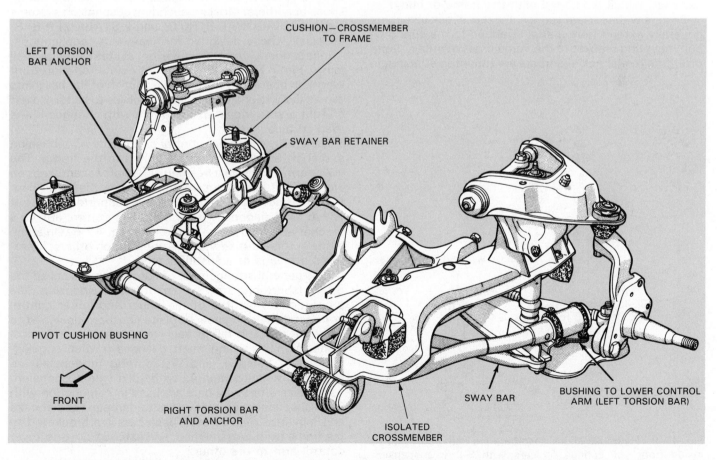

Fig. 47-8. Some Chrysler rear wheel drive cars have transverse torsion bar front suspension. Each torsion bar provides a twisting reaction on outboard end of opposite lower control arm. (Chrysler Corp.)

down and control the rapid movement of the car springs as they react to road irregularities. Generally, fluid flow through the piston is controlled by spring-loaded valves.

The hydraulic shock absorber automatically adapts itself to the severity of the shock. If the axle moves slowly, resistance to the flow of fluid will be light. If the axle movement is rapid or forceful, the resistance is much stronger since more time is required to force fluid through the orifices.

By these hydraulic actions and reactions, the shock absorbers permit a soft ride over small bumps and provide firm control over spring action for cushioning large bumps. The double-acting units operate effectively in both directions. Spring rebound can be almost as violent as the original action that compressed the shock absorber.

At the front of a vehicle with S.L.A. (short-long arm) suspension, each shock absorber usually extends through the coil spring from the lower control arm to a bracket attached to the frame, Fig. 47-9. On Chrysler cars with transverse torsion bar suspension, the front shock absorbers attach to the lower control arm and mount to a bracket on the frame crossmember.

In the case of high-mounted coil springs, Fig. 47-5, front shock absorbers extend from the upper control arm to a platform mounted in the spring tower or to a bracket on the wheel housing in the engine compartment.

At the rear, the lower end of the shock absorber usually is attached to a bracket welded to the axle housing. The upper end is fastened to the frame or coil spring upper seat, which is integral with the frame or body.

On cars with rear leaf springs, the rear shock absorbers generally extend from a stud attached to the spring U-bolt mounting bracket to the frame cross member. Quite often the rear shock absorbers are mounted at an angle

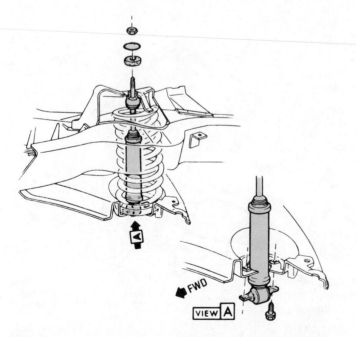

Fig. 47-9. Hydraulic shock absorbers are commonly placed inside front coil springs on cars with S.L.A. suspension systems. Typical upper and lower mountings are shown. (Chevrolet Motor Div., General Motors Corp.)

to assist in restricting lateral movement as well as vertical movement.

SHOCK ABSORBER STRUTS

On typical MACPHERSON STRUT applications, the shock absorber is built into the strut. See Fig. 47-10. Most of these shock absorber struts are hydraulic units.

Some MacPherson systems used on Ford vehicles are equipped with low-pressure, gas-filled shock struts. They are nonadjustable and nonrefillable. Like the hydraulic shock struts, faulty units must be replaced as an assembly.

A similar front suspension system is termed "hydraulic shock strut" type. See Fig. 47-11. Like the MacPherson type, this strut serves as a shock absorber and replaces the upper control arm. The coil spring, however, is located between the lower control arm and the body structure instead of being mounted directly on the strut.

FRONT SUSPENSION SYSTEMS

There are three basic types of front suspension: independent systems; MacPherson strut systems; solid axle systems.

INDEPENDENT FRONT SUSPENSION

INDEPENDENT FRONT SUSPENSION SYSTEMS, Fig. 47-3, usually operate through coil springs or torsion bars, upper and lower control arms, and direct, double-acting shock absorbers. Most independent suspension systems also use DIAGONAL STRUTS and a STABILIZER BAR, especially those designed for heavy-duty applications.

Independent front suspension systems utilize ball joints, Fig. 47-4, to provide pivot points for each front wheel. In operation, the swiveling action of the ball joints allows the wheel-and-spindle assemblies to be turned left or right and to move up and down with changes in the road surface.

Generally, the upper control arm pivots on a bushing and shaft assembly which is bolted to the frame. The lower arm pivots on a bushing and shaft assembly or on a bolt in the frame crossmember. When the lower control arm is not the A-frame type, it is supported by a strut which runs diagonally from the lower control arm to a bracket attached to the frame. See Fig. 47-5. On some models, this strut serves as a support; on others, it provides a means of adjusting caster.

This general arrangement of control arms is called the S.L.A. (short-long arm) system of front suspension. The proportionate lengths of the upper and lower control arms (and their engineered placement) are designed to keep the rise and fall of each front wheel in a vertical plane. With this arrangement, changes in wheel angularity, weight balance, and tire-scuffing tendencies are negligible when compared with solid axle suspension.

Stabilizers or sway bars are used in conjunction with front suspension on many cars to dampen road shocks and minimize road sway. These bars are bracketed to the frame front crossmember and extend from one lower control arm to the other.

Independent suspension is designed to provide anti-dive characteristics during braking.

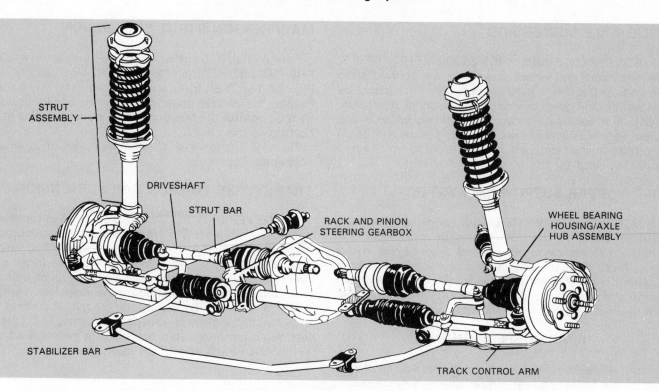

Fig. 47-10. Front wheel drive, rack and pinion steering, and MacPherson struts have been used on imported cars for many years. Also note typical application of stabilizer bar and strut bars.
(Toyota Motor Sales, U.S.A. Inc.)

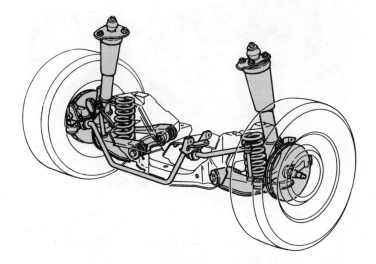

Fig. 47-11. Ford's "shock strut" front suspension is a modified MacPherson strut type. Difference lies in separate location of coil springs and shock strut setup.
(Ford Motor Co.)

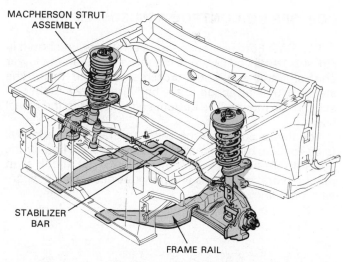

Fig. 47-12. Typical General Motors MacPherson strut arrangement on compact cars is outlined against phantom view of vehicle's engine compartment.
(Chevrolet Motor Div., General Motors Corp.)

MACPHERSON STRUT SUSPENSION

The MACPHERSON STRUT SYSTEM, Fig. 47-12, is used on most subcompact and compact cars with front wheel drive. The MacPherson system features a long, telescopic shock absorber strut surrounded by a coil spring. The upper end of the strut is isolated by a rubber mount that contains an oilless ball bearing for wheel turn- ing. The lower end attaches to the steering knuckle or lower control arm ball joint.

The lower control arm is attached to the underbody side apron or lower side rails and to the steering knuckle. A stabilizer bar usually is connected to both lower control arms and the front crossmember. See Fig. 47-12. Some systems also include adjustable strut bars, Fig. 47-10, connecting the control arms to the subframe.

SOLID AXLE SUSPENSION

In SOLID AXLE SUSPENSION SYSTEMS, Fig. 47-13, the axle beam and wheel assemblies are connected to the vehicle (usually a medium or heavy-duty truck) by leaf springs and direct or indirect-acting shock absorbers.

With the solid axle setup, the steering knuckle and wheel spindle assemblies are connected to the axle beam by bronze-bushed king pins, or spindle bolts, which serve as pivot points for the steering knuckles.

REAR SUSPENSION SYSTEMS

REAR SUSPENSION SYSTEMS are engineered in many different designs. The primary design consideration is whether the vehicle is front wheel drive or rear wheel drive. Next, does the vehicle require a solid rear axle or independently suspended wheels? Should it have coil spring and control arm suspension, MacPherson struts, leaf springs, or transverse torsion bars?

REAR SUSPENSION/FWD

Front wheel drive vehicles generally are equipped with one of the following rear suspension arrangements:
1. Coil springs and control arms or trailing arms with a solid axle and independently suspended wheels.
2. MacPherson struts and independently suspended wheels.
3. Transverse torsion bars and suspension arms.

COIL SPRING/CONTROL ARM SUSPENSION

The FWD Ford rear suspension arrangement shown in Fig. 47-14 has coil springs mounted between the lower control arms and body crossmember/side rails. The shock strut is attached to the body panel by a rubber insulated top mount. The bottom end is bolted to the wheel spindle.

The lower control arms serve to stabilize the lateral (side-to-side) movement of the rear wheels. The tie rods control fore-and-aft wheel movement. The shock strut reacts to braking forces and provides necessary suspension damping.

MACPHERSON STRUT SUSPENSION

Ford mid-size, front wheel drive models have MAC-PHERSON STRUT INDEPENDENT REAR SUSPENSION, Fig. 47-15. The struts are gas-filled (later: hydraulic). Parallel, transverse lower control arms and longitudinal tie rods control the position of the wheel spindles at the bottom of the struts.

Fig. 47-2 shows and describes this unusual rear suspension system.

TRANSVERSE TORSION BAR SUSPENSION

TRANSVERSE TORSION BARS are used at the rear on some American Motors front wheel drive subcompact cars. See Fig. 47-16. This system utilizes trailing suspension arms attached to a crossmember at inner pivot points and to torsion bar ends at outer pivot points.

A stabilizer bar is mounted on the suspension arms in back of the torsion bars. The shock absorbers are attached to the body and suspension arms. The right and left non-interchangeable torsion bars are marked with symbols on each end to aid identification.

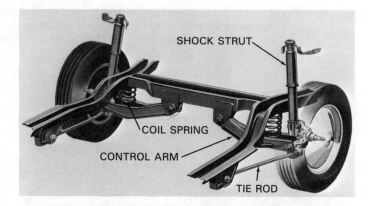

Fig. 47-14. Ford independent rear suspension utilizes coil springs mounted on lower control arms attached to underbody and to forged spindles. Shock struts also bolt to wheel spindles. (Ford Motor Co.)

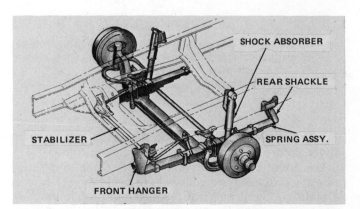

Fig. 47-13. A solid front axle beam and leaf springs are used on most medium and heavy-duty trucks.

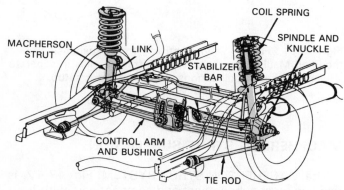

Fig. 47-15. This MacPherson strut rear suspension on certain front wheel drive, mid-size models locates struts by means of four parallel control arms and diagonal tie rods. (Ford Motor Co.)

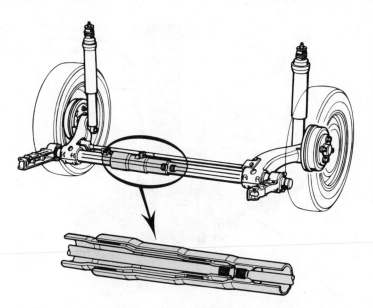

Fig. 47-16. Certain subcompact AMC models use transverse torsion bar rear suspension. Note detail of splined bar inner ends. (AMC-Renault, Inc.)

REAR SUSPENSION/RWD

Rear wheel drive automobiles usually are produced with one of the following rear suspension setups:
1. Coil spring and control arms with fixed rear axle housing.
2. Longitudinal leaf springs with fixed rear axle housing.
3. Transverse leaf spring with independently suspended rear wheels.

COIL SPRING/CONTROL ARM SUSPENSION

Some Ford rear wheel drive cars have a rear suspension system that includes coil springs between upper seat brackets in the frame rails and integral seats in the lower suspension arms. See Fig. 47-17.

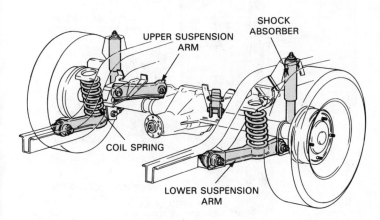

Fig. 47-17. Some rear wheel drive cars with coil spring rear suspension use four suspension arms to provide for stability and coil spring support. Note vertical mounting of shock absorbers. (Ford Motor Co.)

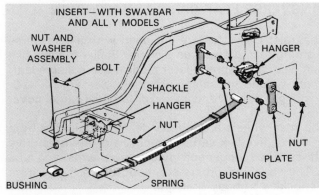

Fig. 47-18. Some rear wheel drive cars are equipped with rear leaf springs that suspend vehicle body above rear axle housing. Typical spring and mounting hardware and bushings are shown. (Chrysler Corp.)

The longitudinal lower suspension arms extend from brackets on the rear axle housing to brackets welded to the outboard side of the frame rails. The lower arms control front-to-rear movement. Diagonally mounted upper suspension arms control side-to-side movement.

The shock absorbers are mounted vertically from shock brackets welded to the axle housing and to shock towers on the floorpan.

LONGITUDINAL LEAF SPRING SUSPENSION

Certain Dodge/Plymouth rear wheel drive models are equipped with semi-elliptical leaf springs (one main leaf plus progressively shorter spring leaves) at the rear. The springs are attached to mounting brackets bolted to the body at the front and to spring shackles at the rear. See Fig. 47-18.

Each spring center bolt seats in a hole in a bracket welded to the rear axle tube. U-bolts and a spring plate hold the spring securely in place against the bracket. The shock absorbers are mounted between the spring plate and a frame crossmember. See Fig. 47-19.

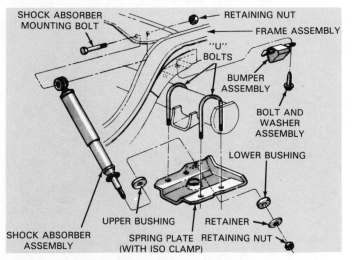

Fig. 47-19. Exploded view reveals position of rear shock absorber and additional leaf spring hardware, including U-bolts and spring plate. (Chrysler Corp.)

TRANSVERSE LEAF SPRING SUSPENSION

Chevrolet Corvettes are equipped with a transverse leaf spring rear suspension system. Earlier models use a multi-leaf steel spring; later models use a single-leaf, filament-wound, glass/epoxy spring. See Fig. 47-20. The spring is mounted to a fixed differential carrier cover beam.

The rear wheels are independently suspended by a four-link or five-link setup composed of a wheel drive shaft, strut rod, upper and lower control arms, and a tie rod. The shock absorbers are mounted vertically from the knuckles to body brackets.

AUTOMATIC LEVEL CONTROL

Various automatic leveling systems are in use. Ford's microprocessor controlled AIR SUSPENSION system, for example, replaces conventional coil spring suspension with automatic front and rear load leveling by means of four rubber and plastic air springs. Most leveling systems, however, are designed to automatically extend or compress the rear shock absorbers or shock struts. This brings the rear of the car back to design level when the car is loaded with additional passengers and/or luggage.

GM's ELECTRONIC LEVEL CONTROL system includes a compressor assembly, air dryer, exhaust solenoid, compressor relay, height sensor, air adjustable shock absorbers or shock struts, Fig. 47-21, wiring, air tubing, and pressure limiter valve.

The air adjustable shock strut is basically a conventional unit constructed with a sleeve attached to the dust tube and reservoir. This sleeve forms a flexible chamber that will extend the shock strut when air pressure in the chamber is increased. When the pressure is reduced, the weight of the car will cause the shock strut to compress to a "minimum pressure" level.

When weight is added to the rear suspension, an arm on the height sensor signals the compressor relay to turn on the compressor and pump air to the air chambers of the shock struts. The shock struts extend, raising the rear of the car. At the proper level, the arm signals the

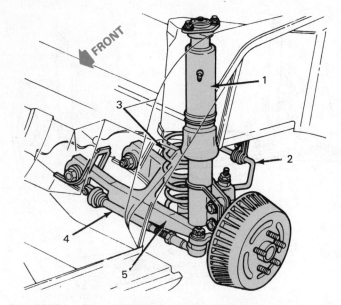
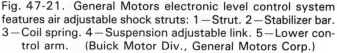

Fig. 47-21. General Motors electronic level control system features air adjustable shock struts: 1—Strut. 2—Stabilizer bar. 3—Coil spring. 4—Suspension adjustable link. 5—Lower control arm. (Buick Motor Div., General Motors Corp.)

relay to turn off the compressor.

Some Chrysler Corporation models are equipped with an ELECTRONIC AUTOMATIC LOAD LEVELING system, Fig. 47-22. An electronic sensor linked to the rear suspension track bar detects changes in rear suspension height and directs the system to either add or exhaust air from rubber bladders on the rear shock absorbers. See inset in Fig. 47-22. The sensor also allows for normal ride motions to prevent unnecessary height adjustments.

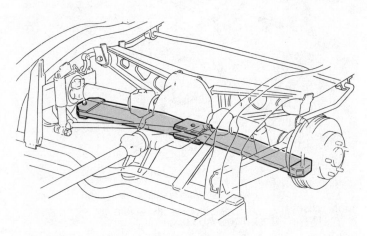

Fig. 47-20. Corvettes use a composite, single leaf rear spring, transversely mounted.
(Chevrolet Motor Div., General Motors Corp.)

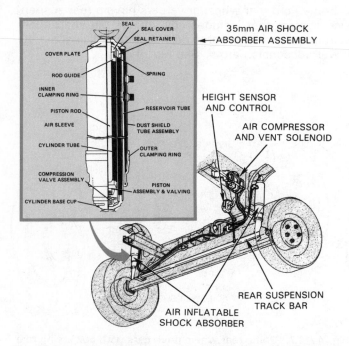

Fig. 47-22. Chrysler's electronic load leveling system uses air inflatable shock absorbers to automatically adjust rear of vehicle to design height. (Chrysler Corp.)

Air for the shock absorbers is provided by a sealed air compressor driven by an electric motor. The combination compressor and motor is mounted behind the right rear wheel well. A flexible air hose connects the compressor with the special shock absorbers.

AUTOMATIC RIDE CONTROL

Certain Ford models are provided with an electronically operated AUTOMATIC RIDE CONTROL system. It consists of a two-position mode selector switch, sensors (for speed, steering, brake application, and acceleration force input), shunt motor actuators (on top of each front shock strut and rear shock absorber), an electronic control module (ECM), and the wiring harness. See Fig. 47-23.

The mode selector switch provides positions for "Auto" or "Firm" ride control. In the automatic mode, the system provides a "soft ride" until sensor input indicates the need for firm ride control. Then, the ECM

simultaneously operates all four actuators to increase the shock struts resistance to vehicle motion. A specific time lag for the return to "soft ride" is programmed into the ECM.

STEERING SYSTEMS

There are two basic types of steering systems on passenger cars: manual and power. In the manual system, the driver's effort to turn the steering wheel is the primary force that causes the front wheels to swivel to the left or right on the steering knuckles. With power steering, the driver's turning efforts are multiplied by a hydraulic or an electrohydraulic assist.

The MANUAL STEERING SYSTEM incorporates: a steering wheel; shaft and column; either a manual gearbox and pitman arm or a rack and pinion assembly, Fig. 47-24; linkage; steering knuckles and ball joints; and wheel spindle assemblies.

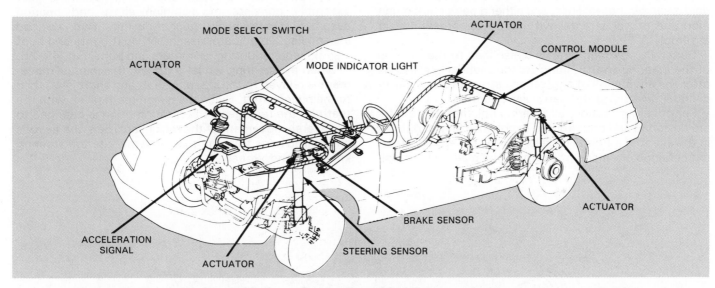

Fig. 47-23. Phantom view highlights major elements of Ford's automatic ride control system. Soft ride is provided until firm ride is needed for good handling. (Ford Motor Co.)

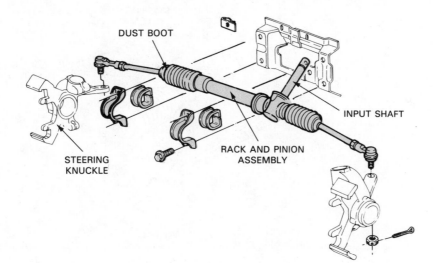

Fig. 47-24. Simplified drawing shows a typical manual rack and pinion steering gear assembly, mounting insulators and brackets, and tie rod assemblies. (Ford Motor Co.)

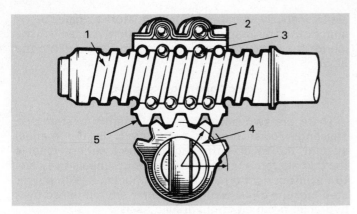

Fig. 47-25. Cross-sectional view of ball nut reveals details of manual recirculating ball steering gear. 1—Worm gear. 2—Return guides. 3—Ball bearing. 4—Sector gear. 5—Ball nut.

The power steering system adds: a hydraulic pump; fluid reservoir; hoses; lines; and either a power assist unit mounted on, or integral with, a power steering gear assembly.

Generally, steering wheels are splined to the top end of the steering shaft. Tilting steering wheel assemblies offer the advantage of angular adjustment to suit the individual driver and the particular situation.

For driver protection, all steering columns and shafts are designed and constructed to collapse and/or deform in the event of a frontal collision. Some collapsible steering columns are made of slotted steel mesh. Other col-

umns, steering shafts, and shift shafts are two-piece, telscoping type, interconnected by plastic inserts or collars and shear pins.

MANUAL STEERING GEARS AND LINKAGE

There are several different manual steering gears in current and recent use. The RACK AND PINION type is the current choice of most manufacturers. See Fig. 47-24. The RECIRCULATING BALL type is a past favorite because the balls act as a rolling thread between the wormshaft and the ball nut, Fig. 47-25. Another manual steering gear once popular in imported cars is the WORM AND SECTOR type. Other manual gears are the WORM AND TAPERED PIN STEERING GEAR and the WORM AND ROLLER STEERING GEAR.

MANUAL RACK AND PINION STEERING

A typical manual rack and pinion steering gear assembly consists of a pinion shaft and bearing assembly, rack gear, gear housing, two tie rod assemblies, an adjuster assembly, dust boots and boot clamps, and mounting grommets and bolts, Fig. 47-26.

When the steering wheel is turned, this manual movement is relayed to the steering shaft and shaft joint, then to the pinion shaft. Since the pinion teeth mesh with the teeth on the rack gear, the rotary motion is changed to transverse movement of the rack gear. Then, the tie rods and tie rod ends transmit this movement to the steering knuckles and wheels.

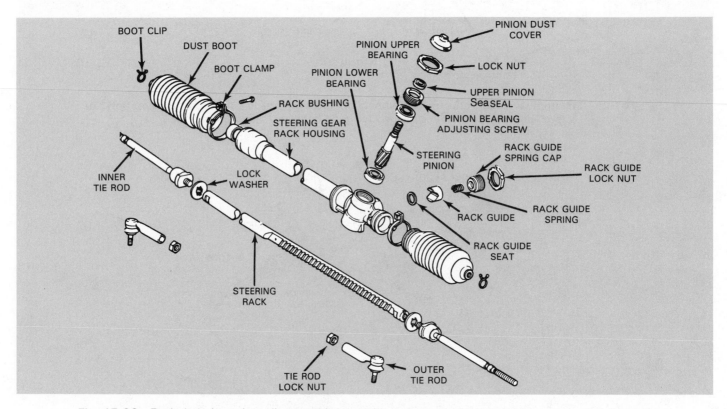

Fig. 47-26. Exploded view gives disassembly/assembly sequence of components of a typical General Motors manual rack and pinion steering gear assembly. Study relationship of parts. (Chevrolet Motor Div., General Motors Corp.)

MANUAL RECIRCULATING BALL STEERING

A typical manual recirculating ball steering gear assembly is shown in Fig. 47-27. With this steering gear, turning forces are transmitted through ball bearings from a worm gear on the steering shaft to a sector gear on the pitman arm shaft. A ball nut assembly is filled with ball bearings which "roll" along grooves between the worn teeth and grooves inside the ball nut.

When the steering wheel is turned, the worm gear on the end of the steering shaft rotates, and movement of the recirculating balls causes the ball nut to move up and down along the worm. Movement of the ball nut is carried to the sector gear by teeth on the side of the ball nut. The sector gear, in turn, moves with the ball nut to rotate the pitman arm shaft and activate the steering linkage. The balls recirculate from one end of the ball nut to the other through ball return guides, Fig. 47-28.

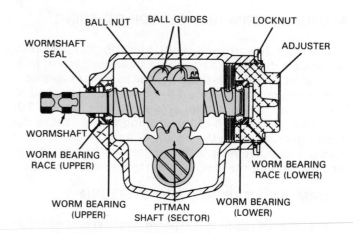

Fig. 47-28. Principle of worm and recirculating ball steering gear is revealed by this sectional view. Note ball return guides that permit ball bearings to recirculate.

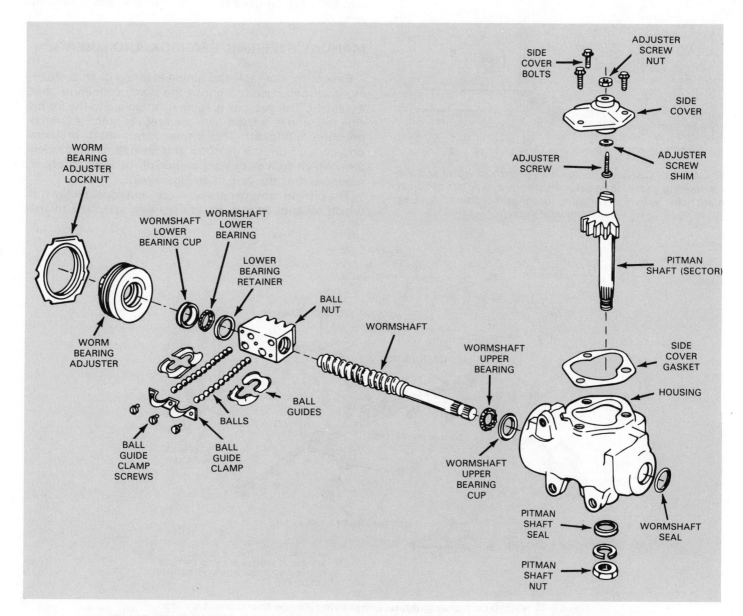

Fig. 47-27. Exploded view shows relative positioning of parts that make up a recirculating ball type of manual steering gear used mainly on rear wheel drive cars. (American Motors Corp.)

MANUAL WORM AND SECTOR STEERING

The manual worm and sector steering gear assembly employs a steering shaft with a three-turn worm gear supported by, and straddled by, ball bearing assemblies. The worm meshes with a 14-tooth sector attached to the top end of the pitman arm shaft. See Fig. 47-29.

In operation, a turn of the steering wheel causes the worm gear to rotate the sector — and the pitman arm shaft. This movement is transmitted to the pitman arm and throughout the steering train to the wheel spindles.

WORM AND TAPERED PEG STEERING

The manual worm and tapered peg steering gear has a three-turn worm gear at the lower end of the steering

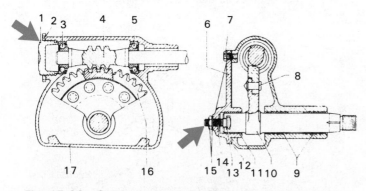

Fig. 47-29. Cross-sectional views of manual worm and sector steering gear picture assembled parts and points of adjustment (see arrows): 1—Worm bearings adjuster. 14—Gear mesh adjuster screw.

shaft supported by ball bearing assemblies. The pitman shaft has a lever end with a tapered peg that rides in the worm grooves.

When the movement of the steering wheel revolves the worm gear, it causes the tapered peg to follow the worm gear grooves. Movement of the peg moves the lever on the pitman shaft and, in turn, the pitman arm, steering linkage, etc.

WORM AND ROLLER STEERING

The manual worm and roller steering gear is used by various Japanese manufacturers. This steering gear also has a three-turn worm gear at the lower end of the steering shaft. Instead of a sector or tapered peg on the pitman arm shaft, this gearbox has a roller assembly (usually two roller teeth) that engages the worm gear.

The roller assembly is mounted on anti-friction bearings. When the roller teeth follow the worm, the rotary motion is transmitted to the pitman arm shaft, pitman arm, etc.

MANUAL STEERING GEARBOX AND LINKAGE

Except for the rack and pinion steering gear, a steering gearbox is used to house the manual steering gear assembly. The gearbox is securely attached to the frame side rail, and it is filled with a water-resistant, extreme pressure lubricant. The pitman arm shaft projects downward from the gearbox. It is splined to the pitman arm, which converts rotary motion of the shaft to lateral movement of the arm. See Fig. 47-30.

The pitman arm, generally, is connected to a relay rod which reaches across to an idler arm attached to the

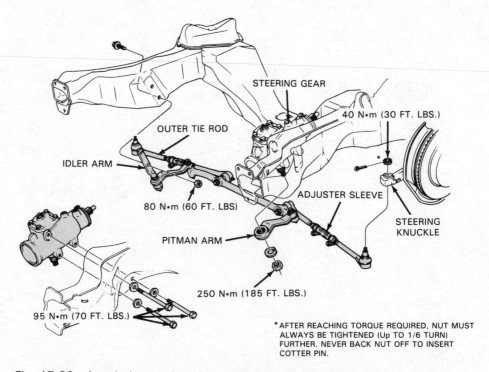

Fig. 47-30. A typical manual gearbox and steering linkage arrangement are identified. Particular emphasis is placed on torque values of fasteners. Also note gearbox mounting detail in inset at left. (Buick Motor Div., General Motors Corp.)

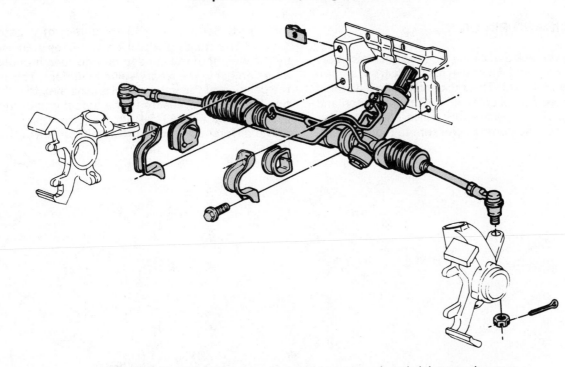

Fig. 47-31. Simplified drawing of a typical power rack and pinion steering gear assembly reveals similarity to drawing of manual assembly in Fig. 47-24. (Ford Motor Co.)

frame side rail on the opposite side. The relay rod, in turn, is connected to two adjustable tie rods that transmit lateral movement of the relay rod to the steering arms, Fig. 47-30.

The various rods and arms roughly form a parallelogram during a turn, so the arrangement is called "parallelogram" linkage. In some cars, the linkage is in front of the front wheel spindles. In others, the linkage is to the rear of the spindles.

Manual steering is considered to be entirely adequate for subcompact cars and for cars with the engine in the rear. It is light, fast, and accurate in maintaining steering control.

POWER STEERING SYSTEMS

Over the years, POWER STEERING has become a standard equipment item on many larger domestic models. With that, and the optional demand for this system, power steering is installed on over 90 percent of all domestic new car production.

Most late model passenger cars with power steering use either a POWER RACK AND PINION system, Fig. 47-31, or an INTEGRAL POWER STEERING GEAR assembly, Fig. 47-32. Generally, the rack and pinion system is installed on FWD cars. The integral power steering gear is used on many RWD cars.

All systems require a power steering pump attached to the engine and driven by a belt, a pressure hose assembly, and a return line. Also, a control valve is incorporated somewhere in the hydraulic circuit.

Automobile power steering is actually "power assisted steering." All systems are constructed so that the car can be steered manually when the engine is not running or if any failure occurs at the power source.

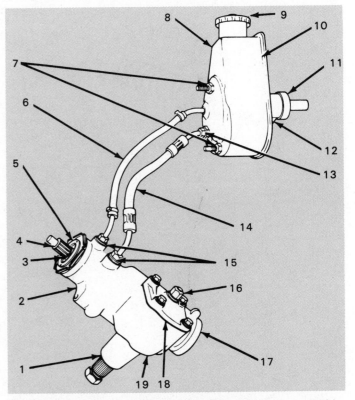

Fig. 47-32. Parts of an integral power steering gear assembly and hydraulic system include: 1—Pitman shaft. 2—Gear housing ball plug. 3—Stub shaft. 4—Torsion bar. 5—Adjuster plug. 6—Return hose. 7—Stud bolts. 8—Reservoir. 9—Cap. 10—Reservoir O-ring. 11—Pump shaft seal. 12—Pump housing. 13—Pressure port. 14—Pressure hose. 15—Pressure and return ports. 16—Adjusting screw lock nut. 17—End cover. 18—Side cover. 19—Gear housing. (American Motors Corp.)

POWER RACK AND PINION

A typical power rack and pinion steering gear assembly used on some Ford and American Motors cars is shown in Fig. 47-31 and 47-33. This rack and pinion assembly is a hydraulic-mechanical unit with an integral piston and rack assembly. An internal rotary valve directs power steering fluid flow and controls pressure to reduce steer-

ing effort. See Fig. 47-33 for details of construction.

When the steering wheel is turned, resistance created by the weight of the car and tires-to-road friction causes a torsion bar in the rotary valve to deflect. This changes the position of the valve spool and sleeve, thereby directing fluid under pressure to the proper end of the power cylinder. See Fig. 47-34.

The difference in pressure on either side of the piston

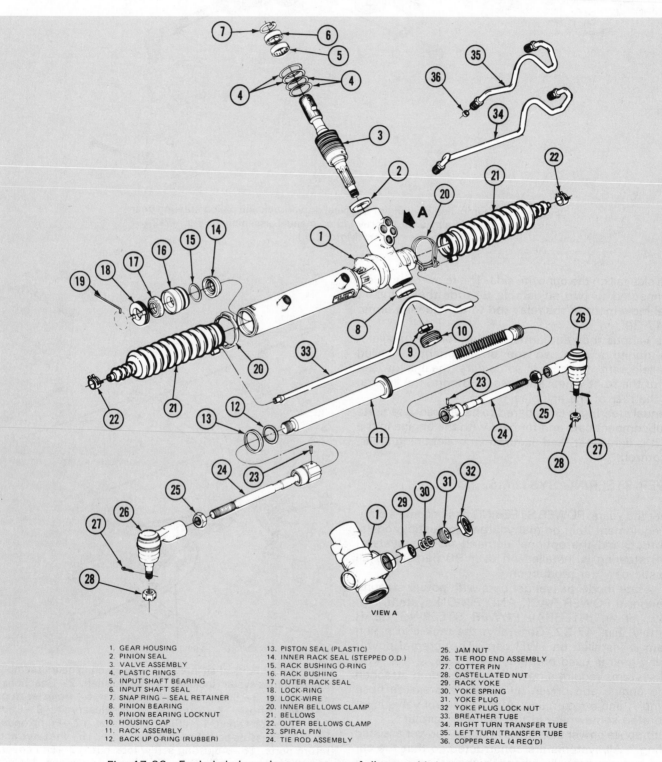

1. GEAR HOUSING	13. PISTON SEAL (PLASTIC)	25. JAM NUT
2. PINION SEAL	14. INNER RACK SEAL (STEPPED O.D.)	26. TIE ROD END ASSEMBLY
3. VALVE ASSEMBLY	15. RACK BUSHING O-RING	27. COTTER PIN
4. PLASTIC RINGS	16. RACK BUSHING	28. CASTELLATED NUT
5. INPUT SHAFT BEARING	17. OUTER RACK SEAL	29. RACK YOKE
6. INPUT SHAFT SEAL	18. LOCK-RING	30. YOKE SPRING
7. SNAP RING – SEAL RETAINER	19. LOCK-WIRE	31. YOKE PLUG
8. PINION BEARING	20. INNER BELLOWS CLAMP	32. YOKE PLUG LOCK NUT
9. PINION BEARING LOCKNUT	21. BELLOWS	33. BREATHER TUBE
10. HOUSING CAP	22. OUTER BELLOWS CLAMP	34. RIGHT TURN TRANSFER TUBE
11. RACK ASSEMBLY	23. SPIRAL PIN	35. LEFT TURN TRANSFER TUBE
12. BACK UP O-RING (RUBBER)	24. TIE ROD ASSEMBLY	36. COPPER SEAL (4 REQ'D)

Fig. 47-33. Exploded view gives sequence of disassembly/assembly of a power rack and pinion steering gear. View A shows detail of rack yoke assembly.   (Ford Motor Co.)

(attached to rack) helps move the rack to reduce turning effort. The fluid in the opposite end of the power cylinder is forced to the control valve and back to the pump reservoir.

When the steering effort stops, the control valve is centered by the twisting force of the torsion bar: pressure is equalized on both sides of the piston; the front wheels return to straight ahead position.

INTEGRAL POWER STEERING GEARS

A typical integral power steering gear used on certain General Motors RWD cars and American Motors 4WD Eagle is shown in an exploded view in Fig. 47-35. This power steering gear utilizes a recirculating ball system wherein steel balls act as rolling threads between the steering worm shaft and the rack piston.

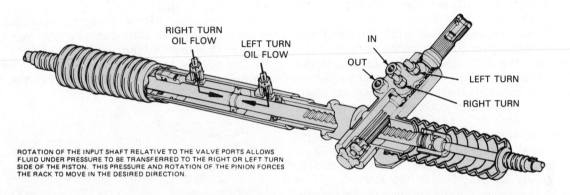

Fig. 47-34. Cutaway view and above explanation clarifies hydro-mechanical operation of power rack and pinion steering gear assembly. Note piston cutaway between large arrowheads. (Ford Motor Co.)

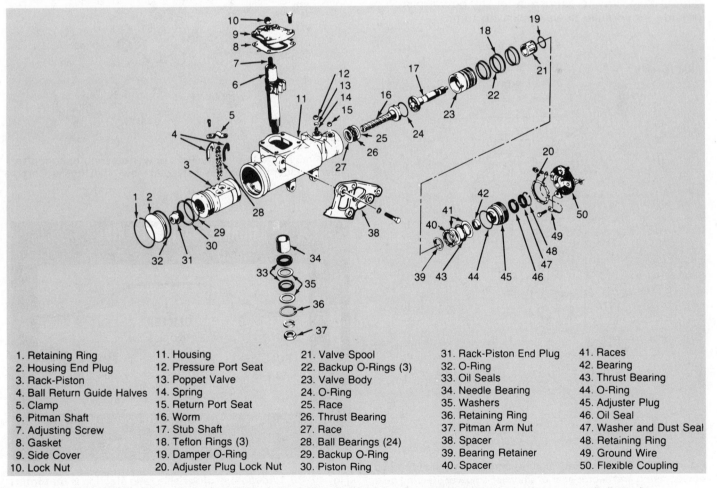

1. Retaining Ring	11. Housing	21. Valve Spool	31. Rack-Piston End Plug	41. Races
2. Housing End Plug	12. Pressure Port Seat	22. Backup O-Rings (3)	32. O-Ring	42. Bearing
3. Rack-Piston	13. Poppet Valve	23. Valve Body	33. Oil Seals	43. Thrust Bearing
4. Ball Return Guide Halves	14. Spring	24. O-Ring	34. Needle Bearing	44. O-Ring
5. Clamp	15. Return Port Seat	25. Race	35. Washers	45. Adjuster Plug
6. Pitman Shaft	16. Worm	26. Thrust Bearing	36. Retaining Ring	46. Oil Seal
7. Adjusting Screw	17. Stub Shaft	27. Race	37. Pitman Arm Nut	47. Washer and Dust Seal
8. Gasket	18. Teflon Rings (3)	28. Ball Bearings (24)	38. Spacer	48. Retaining Ring
9. Side Cover	19. Damper O-Ring	29. Backup O-Ring	39. Bearing Retainer	49. Ground Wire
10. Lock Nut	20. Adjuster Plug Lock Nut	30. Piston Ring	40. Spacer	50. Flexible Coupling

Fig. 47-35. Parts of a typical recirculating ball and rack-piston type integral power steering gear are indicated and identified. (American Motors Corp.)

Key to the operation of the integral power steering gear is a rotary valve that directs power steering fluid under pressure to either side of the rack piston. The rack piston then converts hydraulic power to mechanical force.

The rack piston moves up inside the gear when the worm shaft turns right. It moves down when the worm shaft turns left. During these actions, the steel balls recirculate within the rack piston, which is power assisted in movement by hydraulic pressure.

Force created by the movement of the rack piston is transmitted from the rack piston teeth to the sector teeth on the pitman shaft, through the shaft and pitman arm to the steering linkage.

Chrysler's power steering gear assembly used on RWD cars is contained in a gear housing at the bottom of the steering column. The gear assembly includes: a sector shaft with sector gear, Fig. 47-36; a toothed power piston that is in constant mesh with the sector shaft teeth; and a worm shaft connecting the steering wheel to the power piston.

The worm shaft is geared to the power piston through recirculating balls. A steering valve body is mounted on top of the steering gear, Fig. 47-37. This valve directs the flow of power steering fluid in the system.

In operation, movement of the steering wheel rotates the worm shaft, which actuates the power piston. Fluid supplied by the power steering pump is fed under pressure to the steering valve. The steering valve, in turn, directs fluid flow to either side of the power piston to provide a hydraulic power assist on turns.

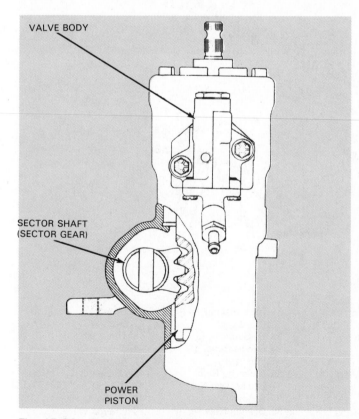

Fig. 47-36. Cutaway view pictures constant mesh of toothed power piston and sector gear of Chrysler's power steering gear assembly. Control valve in valve body directs flow of fluid to either side of power piston. (Chrysler Corp.)

VARIABLE RATIO STEERING

A major step forward in steering gear design was accomplished with the introduction of variable ratio steering. In conventional (constant ratio) steering, the degree of turn of the front wheels is always in direct proportion to the degree of turn of the steering wheel. In variable ratio steering, the ratio remains constant for approximately the first 40 deg. of steering wheel movement. Then the ratio decreases and the response of the front wheels quickens for every degree of turn of the steering wheel, Fig. 47-38.

The "variable" effect is made possible by the design of the steering gear. With constant ratio gears of the sector type, the teeth of the sector are all the same length. This causes the sector to swing the pitman arm the same number of degrees with each tooth of the sector.

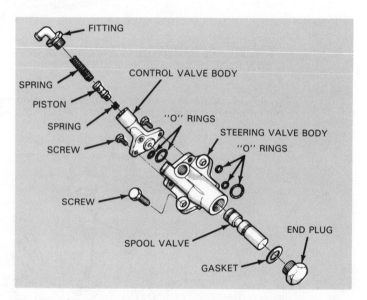

Fig. 47-37. Parts of Chrysler's power steering gear control valve are identified in this exploded view. (Chrysler Corp.)

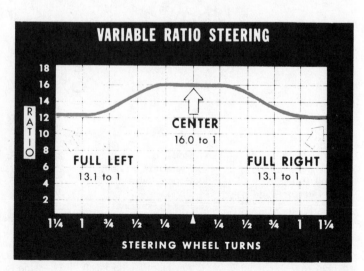

Fig. 47-38. Advantage of variable ratio steering is that front wheels respond more quickly to steering wheel movement as degree of turn increases.

With variable ratio gears, the center tooth of the sector is longer than the other teeth, which produces a slower response of the pitman arm in shallow turn situations and faster response near the extremes of steering wheel travel for sharp turns. In some applications, Fig. 47-25, a specially contoured worm gear alters the ratio.

Typically, a variable ratio steering gear will provide a ratio of about 16:1 for straight ahead driving, and about 13:1 ratio in full turns. In relation to steering wheel movement with variable ratio steering, the first quarter-turn in either direction will produce a relatively "slow" response from the front wheels. Then the response "speeds up" as the steering wheel is turned from one-half to a full turn. After that, the lowest ratio comes into effect when it is needed for parking or backing up.

PUMPS AND HOSES

Several types of power steering pumps are in use. The VANE TYPE PUMP, Fig. 47-39, incorporates a rotor with six to 10 vanes which rotate in an elliptical pump ring. Fluid trapped between the vanes is forced out under pressure as the vanes move from the long diameter of the pump ring to the short diameter.

A ROLLER TYPE PUMP operates much like the vane type. Instead of vanes, six rollers on a toothed carrier unit rotate inside of a cam insert to build up fluid pressure.

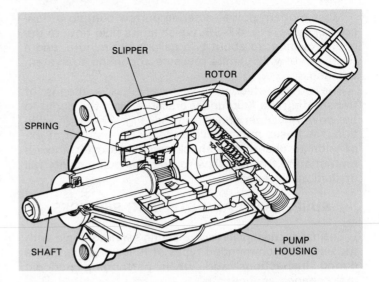

Fig. 47-40. Key operating parts of Ford's slipper type power steering pump are noted. Pumping motion of slippers in rotor grooves creates hydraulic pressure. (Ford Motor Co.)

A SLIPPER TYPE PUMP produces hydraulic pressure by means of four to 10 spring-loaded slippers in a toothed rotor rotating inside of a cam insert within the pump body. See Fig. 47-40.

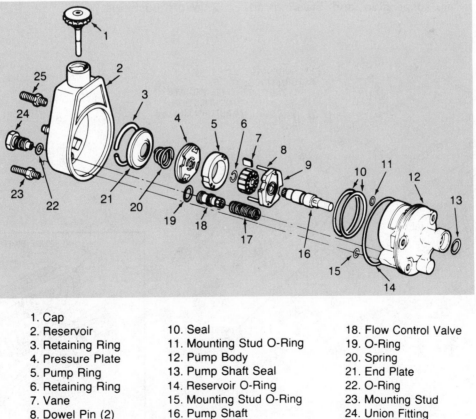

1. Cap	10. Seal	18. Flow Control Valve
2. Reservoir	11. Mounting Stud O-Ring	19. O-Ring
3. Retaining Ring	12. Pump Body	20. Spring
4. Pressure Plate	13. Pump Shaft Seal	21. End Plate
5. Pump Ring	14. Reservoir O-Ring	22. O-Ring
6. Retaining Ring	15. Mounting Stud O-Ring	23. Mounting Stud
7. Vane	16. Pump Shaft	24. Union Fitting
8. Dowel Pin (2)	17. Valve Spring	25. Mounting Stud
9. Thrust Plate		

Fig. 47-39. Typical vane type power steering pump parts are pictured in a disassembled view. (American Motors Corp.)

585

Most modern power steering pumps contain a flow control valve, Fig. 47-39, which limits fluid flow to the power cylinder to about two gallons per minute, and a relief valve which limits pressure according to system demands.

The power steering hoses serve as a means of transmitting the fluid under pressure from the pump to the power cylinder and return. See Fig. 47-41. In addition, the hoses must provide the proper amount of expansion to absorb any shock surge and offer enough restriction to the fluid flow to keep the pump cavity full of fluid at all times.

SUSPENSION AND STEERING SERVICES

Basically, suspension and steering services begin with the use of recommended types of fluids and lubricants during inspections and when performing periodic maintenance services.

Always check simpler possible causes of trouble first, such as power steering fluid level, hose routing, pump drive belt condition and tension, tire condition and inflation pressures, etc. Use special equipment and tools designed for removal and installation of coil springs, struts, bearings, and seals.

When bearings and seals are removed, they should be discarded and replaced with new complete assemblies. When prevailing torque fasteners are loosened, tightened, or removed, they should be discarded and replaced with new fasteners.

Follow the vehicle manufacturers' directions and specifications for all suspension and steering adjustments. Always consult their torque tightness specifications for suspension system and steering system fasteners.

TROUBLESHOOTING SUSPENSION

Front Wheel Shimmy
1. Worn upper ball joints.
2. Worn strut bushings.
3. Worn shock absorbers.

Front End Noise
1. Worn shock absorbers.
2. Loose or worn shock absorber mountings.
3. Worn shock struts or strut mountings.
4. Loose or worn lower control arm.
5. Worn control arm bushings.
6. Dry ball joints.

Spring Noises
1. Loose U-bolts.
2. Loose or worn spring bushings, brackets, or shackles.
3. Worn or missing spring interliners.
4. Broken spring.

Springs Bottom or Sag
1. Weak or broken springs.
2. Leaking or worn shock absorbers.

Shock Absorber Noise
1. Loose mountings.
2. Worn bushings.

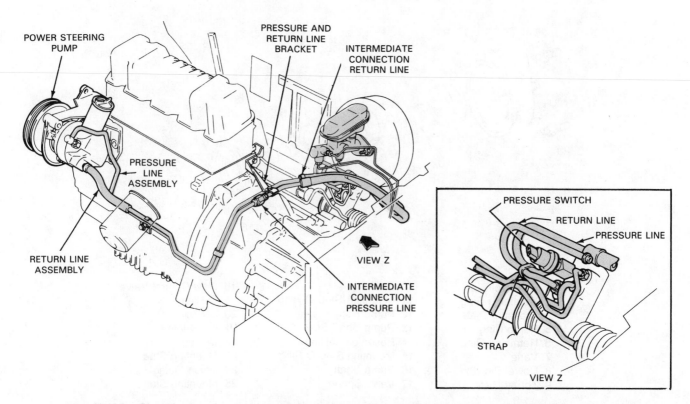

Fig. 47-41. Checking routing and bracketing of all power steering system hoses and lines are important points of inspection during any power steering service operation. (Ford Motor Co.)

Rear Wheels Do Not Track
1. Broken leaf spring.
2. Bent rear axle housing.
3. Misaligned frame.

Car Leans on Corners
1. Faulty shock absorbers.
2. Loose or worn shock absorber mountings.
3. Weak springs.
4. Broken springs.

Car Pulls to One Side
1. Mismatched or unevenly worn tires.
2. Weak springs.
3. Broken springs.
4. Loose or worn strut bushings.

Excessive Tire Wear
1. Weak springs.
2. Broken springs.
3. Faulty shock absorbers.

TROUBLESHOOTING MANUAL STEERING

Excessive Play in Steering Wheel
1. Loose or worn steering gear shaft.
2. Steering arm loose on steering gear shaft.
3. Loose or worn steering linkage.
4. Loose steering gear housing bolts.
5. Loose steering gear adjustment.
6. Loose steering arms at knuckles.
7. Loose rack and pinion mounting.
8. Maladjusted rack and pinion.
9. Loose tie rod end.
10. Loose or worn wheel bearings.

Rattle in Rack and Pinion
1. Loose mounting bracket.
2. Lack of lubricant.
3. Incorrect lubricant.
4. Loose steering gear mounting bolts.

Instability
1. Low tire pressure.
2. Uneven tire pressure.
3. Loose or worn wheel bearings.
4. Loose or worn idler arm bushing.
5. Loose or worn strut bushings.
6. Steering gear not centered.
7. Incorrect front wheel alignment.

Car Pulls to One Side
1. Uneven tire pressure.
2. Mismatched front tires.
3. Maladjusted wheel bearings.
4. Incorrect wheel alignment.

Poor Return of Steering Wheel
1. Dry ball joints or suspension joints.
2. Binding in ball joints or linkage.
3. Incorrect wheel alignment.
4. Maladjusted steering gear.
5. Low tire pressure.
6. Tight steering shaft seal.

TROUBLESHOOTING POWER STEERING

Heavy Steering Effort
1. Low on power steering fluid.
2. Loose rack piston.
3. Restricted fluid passages in gear assembly.
4. Bent or damaged rack assembly.
5. Internal fluid leakage in valve assembly.
6. External fluid leakage at pump.
7. Incorrect drive belt tension.
8. External fluid leakage at hoses.
9. Incorrect engine idle speed.
10. Weak pump flow pressure.

Hissing Noise When Parking
1. Internal leakage in steering gear.
2. Steering wheel at end of travel (normal).
3. When turning steering wheel at standstill (normal).

Growl in Steering Pump
1. Excessive pressure in hoses.
2. Worn cam ring in pump.
3. Scored thrust plates or rotor in pump.
4. Scored pressure plates.

Swish Noise in Pump
1. Defective flow control valve.

Whine in Pump
1. Air in power steering fluid.
2. Low power steering fluid level.
3. Pressure hose or line contacting other part.
4. Misaligned hose and line brackets.
5. Missing or damaged pump cover O-ring.

Rattle in Steering
1. Pressure hose contacting another part.
2. Loose pitman shaft.
3. Loose pitman arm.
4. Loose tie rod ends.
5. Loose rack and pinion mounts.
6. Loose steering gear housing bolts.
7. Loose steering gear adjustments.

Car Wanders to One Side
1. Incorrect front wheel alignment.
2. Unbalanced steering gear valve.
3. Loose tie rod ends.

Steering Wheel Surges or Jerks
1. Low power steering fluid level.
2. Loose pump drive belt.
3. Weak pump pressure.
4. Sticking flow control valve.

Excessive Play in Steering Wheel
1. Air in hydraulic system.
2. Incorrect steering gear adjustments.
3. Loose steering gear coupling.
4. Loose steering shaft universal joint.
5. Faulty rotary valve.

Increased Steering Effort on Fast Turn
1. Slipping pump drive belt.
2. Internal pump leakage.
3. Low power steering fluid level.
4. Too low engine idle speed.
5. Air in hydraulic system.
6. Weak pump output.
7. Malfunctioning steering gear.

Poor Return of Steering Wheel
1. Maladjusted steering gear.
2. Dry ball joints or linkage joints.
3. Binding ball joints or linkage joints.
4. Incorrect front wheel alignment.
5. Maladjusted wheel bearings.
6. Kinked return hoses.
7. Internal pump leakage.
8. Contaminated power steering fluid.
9. Misaligned steering gear-to-steering column.
10. Tight steering shaft bearings or bushings.
11. Bent or damaged rack.
12. Sticking or plugged spool valve.

SPECIAL SAFETY PRECAUTIONS

All general safety measures should be taken when working on suspension systems or steering systems. See Chapter 2, Auto Shop Safety. In addition, be sure to observe the following caution stressed by car manufacturers in their service manuals:

"To help avoid personal injury when a car is on a hoist, provide additional support for the car at the opposite end from which components are being removed. This will reduce the possibility of the car falling off the hoist."

Chapter 47—REVIEW QUESTIONS
SUSPENSION AND STEERING SYSTEMS

Write your answers on a separate sheet of paper. Do not write in this book.

1. Coil springs are manufactured to meet the prescribed Rated Suspension Spring _____ for the particular vehicle application.
2. This rating is designed to provide for adequate coil spring durability and vehicle stability under all _____ conditions.
3. Give two functions of a leaf spring center bolt.
4. What type of suspension system utilizes the flexibility of a steel bar or tube twisting lengthwise to provide spring action?
5. Most MacPherson struts are _____ (hydraulic or gas-filled) units.
6. Name three basic types of front suspension.
7. Independent front suspension systems utilize _____ to provide pivot points for each front wheel.
   a. Steering arms.
   b. Steering knuckles.
   c. Ball joints.
   d. Wheel spindles.

8. In the S.L.A. (short-long arm) system of front suspension, the proportionate lengths of the upper and lower control arms are designed to keep the rise and fall of each front wheel in a horizontal plane. True or False?
9. The MacPherson strut system of front suspension is used on most subcompact and compact cars with _____ (front wheel drive or rear wheel drive)?
10. Most car leveling systems are designed to automatically extend or compress the rear shock absorbers or shock struts. True or False?
11. Some collapsible steering columns are made of slotted steel mesh. Other columns are two-piece _____ type.
   a. Sleeved.
   b. Shear.
   c. Splined.
   d. Telescoping.
12. With manual rack and pinion steering, _____ (rotary or transverse) motion of the pinion is changed to _____ (rotary or transverse) movement of the rack.
13. With manual recirculating ball type steering, the balls act as a _____ between the worm shaft and the ball nut.
   a. Rolling thread.
   b. Rolling spline.
   c. Rolling sector.
   d. Rolling pinion.
14. With a manual steering gearbox, the pitman arm is splined to the pitman arm shaft. _____ motion of the shaft is converted to _____ movement of the arm.
15. All power steering systems are actually "power assisted steering." What does this mean?
16. Which of the following terms is NOT associated with power rack and pinion steering?
   a. Pitman arm.
   b. Torsion bar.
   c. Rotary valve.
   d. Power cylinder.
17. What steering gear design produces slower response of the pitman arm in shallow turn situations and faster response near the extremes of steering wheel travel on sharp turns?
18. There are three types of power steering pumps generally used in modern cars. Name two.
19. When checking out a suspension or steering complaint, always check the simpler possible causes first. Give three quick checks for power steering problems.
20. A driver of a car equipped with power steering complained that the steering wheel surges and jerks on turns. Mechanic A says the problem could be caused by weak power steering pump pressure. Mechanic B says it could be caused by a sticking flow control valve in the pump. Who is right?
   a. Mechanic A.
   b. Mechanic B.
   c. Both mechanic A and mechanic B.
   d. Neither mechanic A nor mechanic B.

Chapter 48

TIRES, TIRE SERVICE

After studying this chapter, you will be able to:
- Compare basic tire types and tire structures.
- Interpret the meaning of tire sidewall markings.
- Describe excessive and uneven treadwear patterns and possible causes.
- Outline steps for checking wheel and tire radial and lateral runout.
- Demonstrate proper techniques for using a power operated tire changer to demount and mount tires on wheels.
- State several methods for making satisfactory permanent tire repairs.

By definition, an AUTOMOBILE TIRE is a tubular corded carcass covered with rubber or synthetic rubber, mounted on a wheel and inflated to provide traction for moving the vehicle and to assist the brakes in stopping it. Properly inflated, today's tires will absorb irregularities of the road surface, and give a safe and comfortable ride while providing a reassuring grip on the road at all speeds.

TIRE TYPES AND BASIC STRUCTURE

There are two basic tire types: tubeless tires for passenger cars and light-duty trucks; and those requiring inner tubes for medium and heavy-duty trucks.

The tubeless tire is designed so that the air is sealed within the rim of the wheel and the tire casing, Fig. 48-1. When an inner tube is used in the tire casing, the air is contained within the tube, while the casing serves mainly to protect the tube and provide traction.

A TUBELESS TIRE is composed of a carcass, sidewall, and tread, Fig. 48-1. The CARCASS is the entire tire structure except sidewall and tread. The SIDEWALL is that portion of the tire between the bead and tread. The TREAD is the portion of the tire that comes in contact with the road.

The carcass of a tire is made up of layers of cord materials such as rayon, nylon, polyester, fiber glass, or steel wire strands. The CORDS are laid parallel in layers and impregnated with rubber to form plies.

The PLIES are arranged at various angles and in different combinations of layers and BELTS (plies laid circumferentially around tire). See Fig. 48-2. Then the

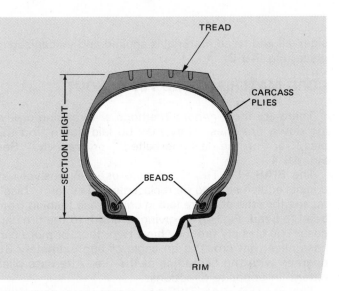

Fig. 48-1. Cross section of tubeless tire shows basic structure and air-tight fit of tire beads in bead seats of wheel.

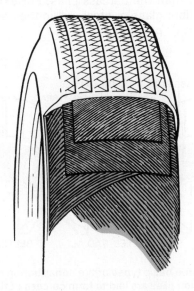

Fig. 48-2. Carcass of belted bias tire consists of plies laid diagonally and belts laid around circumference of tire.

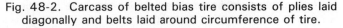

589

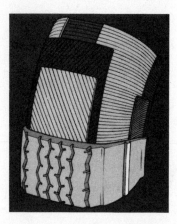

Fig. 48-3. In radial construction: carcass plies are laid radially and steel belts circle tire; sidewall and tread material is vulcanized in place.

sidewall and tread material is applied and vulcanized in place, Fig. 48-3.

CORD MATERIALS AND PLY LAYOUT

There are three general methods of arranging or laying down tire plies. They may be laid down "on the bias," or "on the bias and belted," or "radially." See Fig. 48-4.

The BIAS PLY TIRE was once used extensively as original equipment and for replacement. The term "bias" means that the plies are laid in criss-cross fashion from bead to bead, Fig. 48-4, giving strength to the tire carcass. The bias ply tire may have two, four, or more carcass plies that cross at an angle of approximately 35 degrees with the centerline of the tire. Alternate plies extend in opposite directions.

The BELTED BIAS TIRE has a carcass construction similar to the bias ply tire, but it also has two or more belts of cord that circle the tire under the tread. See Figs. 48-2 and 48-4. Often, the belts are made of a different cord material than the carcass plies. For example, the belt may be fiber glass or steel, while the carcass plies may be rayon or polyester.

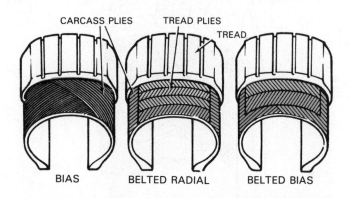

Fig. 48-4. Three basic types of tire construction can be identified by direction plies are laid to form carcass of tire. Bias and belted bias plies are diagonal; radial plies cross tire from bead to bead.

Belted tires reportedly give longer mileage than bias ply tires, and the belts make the belted bias tire much more resistant to punctures, cuts, and bruises. The belts also serve to keep the tread of the tire more firmly on the road and virtually eliminate "tire squirm."

The RADIAL TIRE has the carcass plies laid across the circumference of the tire from bead to bead, plus two or more "belts" are laid under the tread, Figs. 48-3 and 48-4. This construction gives flexibility to the sidewall and greater strength to the tread.

Radial tires are said to give longer tread life, better handling, and a softer ride at medium and high speeds than either bias or belted bias tires. However, radial tires are more likely to give a firm, almost hard, ride at low speeds.

PLY RATING

The PLY RATING of a tire is its index of tire strength. The rating does not necessarily represent the actual number of plies in the tire. Rather, ply rating is used to relate a given size tire with its load and inflation limits.

In use, a passenger car tire marked "4-ply rating/2-ply" has the same load-carrying capacity as a 4-ply tire of the same size at the same inflation pressure. When the 2-ply tire was introduced, some objections were raised with regard to cutting the conventional number of plies in half. However, cord break strength for the two plies totaled 142 lb., while four plies totaled only 104 lb.

LOAD RANGE

The ply rating system has been phased out in favor of the load range system. The term LOAD RANGE is used in conjunction with a letter, such as B, C, D, etc., to identify a given tire size with its load and inflation limits when used in a specific type of service. As load range increases, letters progress in the alphabet.

Sometimes, both ply rating and load range designations may be found on tire sidewalls. See Fig. 48-5. For example, load range B tires may be marked 4-ply rating/2-ply, or 4-ply. Load range C tires may be marked 6-ply rating/4-ply, or 6-ply. Load range D tires may be marked 8-ply rating/4-ply or 8-ply rating/6-ply or 8-ply.

A tire's load range and proper inflation pressure determine how much of a load the tire can safely carry. These important figures are marked on the sidewall of the tire, along with size designations, tire ply composition, manufacturer's name, and the letters DOT, which signify that the tire complies with Department of Transportation safety standards. In addition, tire sidewalls must be marked either "tubeless" or "tube-type" and, if a radial tire, the word "radial" must appear. See Fig. 48-5.

"Proper inflation," according to the Rubber Manufacturers Association (RMA), "is the most important rule in tire safety and tire mileage." Correct tire inflation provides better traction and braking, easier steering, better cornering, and longer, safer tire life.

The U.S. Department of Transportation (DOT) has established UNIFORM TIRE QUALITY GRADING (UTQG) for passenger car tires. The grades are molded on the sidewall of the tire. All tires are graded in accordance

Fig. 48-5. Tire sidewall markings are shown for an F78-14 tire, which replaced old size designation 7.75-14. (Rubber Manufacturers Association)

Fig. 48-6. Tread patterns are designed to improve traction, cornering, and handling. Technician is using gauge to check tread depth. (Firestone Tire & Rubber Co.)

with DOT test procedures in the areas of tread wear, traction, and temperature resistance.

The TREAD WEAR GRADING SYSTEM uses comparative ratings by the number (100, 110, 120, etc.) with regard to tests performed under controlled conditions. A tire graded 150, for example, can be expected to give 50 percent more tread life than a tire graded 100.

The TRACTION GRADE uses the symbols A, B, C, with A being the top grade based on the tire's ability to stop on wet pavement in tests made on concrete and asphalt surfaces.

The TEMPERATURE RESISTANCE GRADING SYSTEM also rates tires as A, B, or C, with A the highest grade. Grade C corresponds to the level of Federal Motor Vehicle Standard No. 109.

TREAD PATTERNS

TIRE TREADS are grooved traction surfaces around the circumference of the tire. The grooves and ribs formed during the tire manufacturing process are carefully engineered to provide good traction on wet or dry roads, control when cornering, minimum distortion at high speeds, reduced rolling resistance, and increased wear resistance. The tread and tire are designed to place the full width of the tread on the road when the tire is properly inflated.

The variety of tread patterns is very broad. Consider the fact that one publisher has produced a tread pattern identification guide that illustrates over 3000 patterns. Apparently, the number of patterns is so great because of design improvements and the manufacturers' desire for distinctive patterns of their own. See Fig. 48-6.

TREAD WEAR INDICATORS

TREAD WEAR INDICATORS molded into modern tires serve as visual proof that the tire tread is approaching worn-out condition. These 1/2 in. (12.7 mm) wide indicators are located in several positions around the circumference of the tire.

As long as the tread grooves are at least 1/16 in. (1.6 mm) deep, the grooves are unbroken. When tread depth reaches that point, the tread wear indicators will appear as solid strips across the tire, Fig. 48-7. These strips interrupt tread continuity and are clearly visible on inspection. The tire should be replaced when this condition occurs.

TIRE SIZES

In the past, tire sizes were designated only by section width and rim diameter. Then, research and development in the tire manufacturers' laboratories and at the proving grounds and test tracks triggered many major advances in tire design and construction.

TREAD STILL GOOD   TREAD WORN OUT

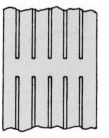

Fig. 48-7. Tire tread wear indicator appears as solid strip in tread when tread depth is reduced to 1/16 in. (1.6 mm).

When "wide oval" and "low profile" tires were introduced, the need for new tire size designations became clear. The simple, two-dimension system for specifying tire size was no longer valid because it did not take "section height" into consideration. See Fig. 48-8.

SECTION HEIGHT is the height of an inflated tire from the bottom of the bead to the top of the tread. It is an important size factor since modern tires generally are low profile in contrast to the almost round cross section of older tire designs. Section height also governs aspect ratio, and aspect ratio is a key area of identification of tires by size. See Fig. 48-9.

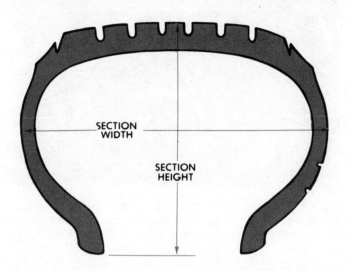

Fig. 48-8. Section height became a factor in tire size designations when tire design changed from "round" to "oval." (Oldsmobile Div., General Motors Corp.)

ASPECT RATIO

The ASPECT RATIO of a tire is the ratio of tire section height to section width. It is height divided by width. A "78 Series" tire, for example, has a section height that is 78 percent of the section width. See Fig. 48-10.

Under the old English tire size system, a tire bearing the size designation 8.25-14 will measure 8 1/4 in. from outside sidewall to outside sidewall. The 14 stands for rim diameter. The new tire size designations provide all information previously contained in the size code, plus the aspect ratio.

Under the new English tire size designation system, an F78-14 size, for example, tells three things about the tire:
1. The first letter, F, is the load carrying capacity.
2. The first set of numbers, 78, is the aspect ratio, meaning that the section height of the tire is 78 percent of the section width. The lower the ratio, the wider the tire.
3. The second set of numbers, 14, is the rim diameter. Some car manufacturers refer to this designation as the inner diameter of the tire.

Obviously, the variety of aspect ratios available has broadened tire applications for any given vehicle. In addition, other elements of tire construction have affected tire designations and applications. The Size Comparison Chart shown in Fig. 48-11 indicates tire availability by size and type.

METRIC MARKINGS

Metric tires are available in two load ranges, standard load and extra load. Most metric tire sizes do not exactly match corresponding alpha-numeric tire sizes. See Fig. 48-11. Therefore, if metric tires are replaced with other sizes, a tire dealer should be consulted to insure the closest match to the metric size tires being replaced.

An example of a popular size tire in metric is P 205/75R15, Fig. 48-12, which replaces the former

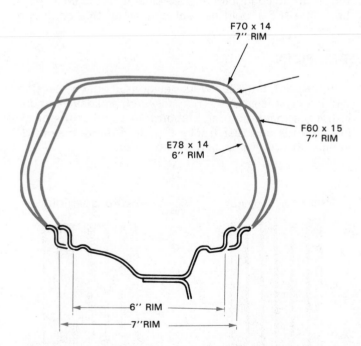

Fig. 48-9. Profile of modern tires is low and wide, resulting in aspect ratios of 78, 75, 70, 60, and 50 (section height is 50 percent of section width).

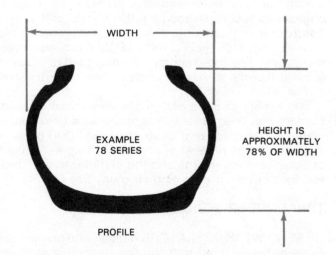

Fig. 48-10. Aspect ratio, or profile, is figured by dividing section height by section width. In this example, aspect ratio of tire is 78.

Size Comparison Chart

Interchangeability is **NOT** implied.

Interchangeability between corresponding sizes of different construction tires is not always possible due to differences in load ratings, tire dimensions, fender clearances and rim sizes, or vehicle manufacturers' recommendations.

DIAGONAL (BIAS) PLY	DIAGONAL (BIAS) AND BELTED BIAS PLY				RADIAL PLY				
	'78 Series'	'70 Series'	'60 Series'	'50 Series'	Metric	'78 Series'	'70 Series'	'60 Series'	'50 Series'
					155R13				
6.00-13					165R13				
	A78-13	A70-13	A60-13			AR78-13	AR70-13	AR60-13	
6.50-13	B78-13	B70-13	B60-13	B50-13	175R13	BR78-13	BR70-13	BR60-13	BR50-13
7.00-13	C78-13	C70-13	C60-13	C50-13	185R13	CR78-13	CR70-13		CR50-13
	D78-13	D70-13	D60-13	D50-13		DR78-13	DR70-13		
					195R13	ER78-13		ER60-13	
					155R14				
	A78-14					AR78-14		AR60-14	
6.45-14	B78-14		B60-14		165R14	BR78-14			
6.95-14	C78-14	C70-14	C60-14		175R14	CR78-14	CR70-14		
	D78-14	D70-14	D60-14			DR78-14	DR70-14		
7.35-14	E78-14	E70-14	E60-14		185R14	ER78-14	ER70-14	ER60-14	
7.75-14	F78-14	F70-14	F60-14	F50-14	195R14	FR78-14	FR70-14	FR60-14	
8.25-14	G78-14	G70-14	G60-14	G50-14	205R14	GR78-14	GR70-14	GR60-14	GR50-14
8.55-14	H78-14	H70-14	H60-14	H50-14	215R14	HR78-14	HR70-14	HR60-14	
8.85-14	J78-14	J70-14	J60-14		225R14	JR78-14	JR70-14	JR60-14	JR50-14
		L70-14	L60-14				LR70-14	LR60-14	
				M50-14					
				N50-14					
	A78-15	A70-15				AR78-15			
	B78-15		B60-15	B50-15	165R15	BR78-15	BR70-15		
6.85-15	C78-15	C70-15	C60-15		175R15	CR78-15	CR70-15		
	D78-15	D70-15				DR78-15	DR70-15		
7.35-15	E78-15	E70-15	E60-15	E50-15	185R15	ER78-15	ER70-15	ER60-15	
7.75-15	F78-15	F70-15	F60-15		195R15	FR78-15	FR70-15	FR60-15	
8.25-15	G78-15	G70-15	G60-15	G50-15	205R15	GR78-15	GR70-15	GR60-15	GR50-15
8.55-15	H78-15	H70-15	H60-15	H50-15	215R15	HR78-15	HR70-15	HR60-15	HR50-15
8.85-15	J78-15	J70-15	J60-15		225R15	JR78-15	JR70-15	JR60-15	JR50-15
9.00-15		K70-15				KR78-15	KR70-15		
9.15-15	L78-15	L70-15	L60-15	L50-15	235R15	LR78-15	LR70-15	LR60-15	LR50-15
	M78-15					MR78-15	MR70-15		
8.90-15	N78-15			N50-15		NR78-15			

Fig. 48-11. This chart compares old and new tire size designations, but interchangeability is not implied. (Rubber Manufacturers Association)

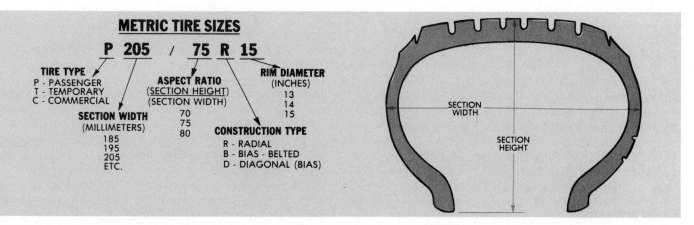

Fig. 48-12. Passenger car tire size designations are stamped in metric markings. Note P 205/75R15. Section width is 205 millimeters. (Oldsmobile Div., General Motors Corp.)

alpha-numeric size FR78-15. Each letter and number has a meaning:

P—Indicates passenger car tire.

205—Width of tire cross section in millimeters.

75—Means the tire cross section is 75 percent as high as it is wide (aspect ratio).

R—Denotes radial construction.

15—Rim diameter in inches.

If the tire is bias belted construction, the letter before the rim diameter would be ''B.'' If the body construction is bias ply, the letter would be ''D'' (for diagonal). Many tires have both metric and the alpha-numeric size designations molded in the sidewalls.

Another marking on tires is tire inflation pressure, usually printed in both metric kilopascals (kPa) and pounds per square inch (psi). A typical inflation pressure would be 207 kPa (30 psi). Air pressure gauges that measure in kilopascals are available. To convert, multiply psi by 6.9 to get kilopascals.

MAXIMUM LOAD is also given in metric and English measures. MAX LOAD typically could be 790 kilograms or 1742 pounds. Still another, more recent tire marking is a T.P.C. Spec. No. (Tire Performance Criteria Specifications Number). Replacement tires with the same T.P.C. Spec. No. should be installed.

A SPEED RATING SYMBOL is an additional sidewall making on performance tires. It is a requirement in Europe, but not in the U.S. The letter Z, V, H, T, or S is located between the aspect ratio and tire construction. For example P205/60HR15. The letters mean that the tire can sustain speeds of: Z-above 149 mph; V-above 130 mph; H-up to 130 mph; T-up to 118 mph; S-up to 112 mph.

TIRE SERVICE

Excessive or uneven TREAD WEAR results from underinflation, rapid stops, fast acceleration, misalignment, and/or unbalanced conditions. Road surface condition also affects tire life. Gravel roads and rough-finished concrete will wear tires quickly. Smooth concrete and asphalt surfaces aid in promoting maximum tire life.

Normal wear causes the tire tread to be reduced evenly and smoothly. Types of abnormal tread wear include:
1. Spotty wear.
2. Overinflation wear.
3. Underinflation wear.
4. Toe-in wear.
5. Toe-out wear.
6. Camber wear.
7. Cornering wear.

Fig. 48-13 shows a condition of spotty wear. This wear pattern usually results from a combination of conditions, including the design of the particular tire tread. Underinflation and incorrect camber are the main factors, along with excessive toe-in or toe-out.

OVERINFLATION causes tires to wear excessively at the center of the tread surface, Fig. 48-14. In addition, there usually is a little wear on the outer edges of the tire. This causes early failure at the center ribs and breaks in the tire sidewall.

Wear due to UNDERINFLATION is shown in Fig. 48-15. This is characterized by excessive wear on the

Fig. 48-13. Spotty wear results from a combination of causes, including underinflation and misalignment.

Fig. 48-14. Overinflation causes wear in center of tire tread.

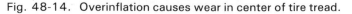

Fig. 48-15. Underinflation wear occurs at both shoulders of tire tread.

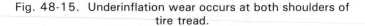

Fig. 48-16. Excessive toe-in will cause featheredging of inner edges of tread ribs. NOTE: Left front tire viewed from front.

two tread ribs adjacent to the inner and outer shoulder ribs. In many cases, underinflation also causes spotty wear, Fig. 48-13.

The amount of front wheel TOE-IN or TOE-OUT is one of the most important factors governing tire wear. Unless toe-in is correct, the tires will have a scrubbing action on the road surface, and excessive wear will result. Fig. 48-16 shows typical tread wear due to excessive toe-

Fig. 48-17. Excessive toe-out will cause featheredging of outer edges of tread ribs. NOTE: Left front tire viewed from front.

Fig. 48-18. Excessive side-of-tread wear results from incorrect camber.

in. It produces a featheredge on the inner edges of the tread ribs, which can be felt by rubbing the hand across the face of the tire.

Wear resulting from toe-out is just the reverse. The featheredge is produced on the outer edges of the tread ribs. See Fig. 48-17.

Excessive CAMBER will produce wear on one side of the tire tread, as illustrated in Fig. 48-18. If there is too much positive camber, the tread wear will be on the outer ribs. If camber is negative, the wear will occur on the inner side of the tire tread. If there is excessive wear on both inner and outer areas of the tread, it probably was caused by excessive skidding on turns.

When considering any tire tread wear condition and what caused it, remember that excessive or uneven wear usually results from a combination of conditions. Tires wear at a different rate on all four wheels due to driving conditions, weight of the vehicle, power on the driving wheels, crown of the road, alignment of wheels, overloading the vehicle, tire inflation, and probably most important of all, driving habits of the person behind the steering wheel.

Fast starts, quick stops, high speeds, and fast turns, all take their toll of tire life. Conservative driving habits promote maximum tire life and economy.

TIRE ROTATION

In order to equalize tire wear, some car manufacturers recommend that wheel and tire assemblies should be rotated from one position to another every 7500 miles (12 000 km). Other manufacturers recommend ''Service as required'' or ''Whenever uneven tire wear is noticed.'' While the generally accepted plan for rotating radial tires has been front to rear and rear to front, some manufacturers have approved the criss-cross plan, Fig. 48-19.

ACCEPTABLE ROTATION PATTERNS FOR RADIAL TIRES

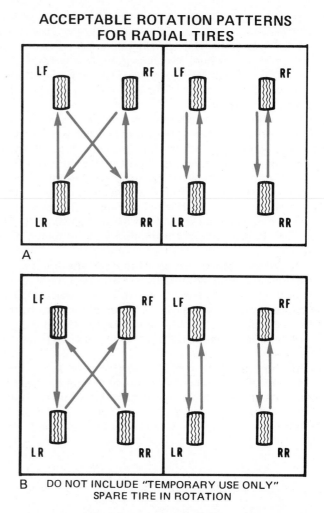

Fig. 48-19. Radial tire rotation patterns: Top. Front wheel drive models. Bottom: Rear wheel drive models. (Oldsmobile Div., General Motors Corp.)

WHEEL AND TIRE RUNOUT

Precision balanced wheel and tire assemblies are essential for a smooth, comfortable ride and for maximum tire life. See Chapter 49, WHEEL ALIGNMENT. When checking wheel balance, remember that unbalance and out-of-round are two separate conditions. A perfectly round wheel and tire assembly can be out of balance, and an annoying thump or vibration will be evident when the car is driven. An out-of-round assembly can be in balance, yet a tire thump on a smooth road will be heard and felt.

One of the major difficulties in trying to obtain smooth, vibration-free rotation of the wheel and tire assemblies is eccentricity (deviation from a circular path). The wheel and tire assembly is out-of-round, so the first step is to determine whether the runout problem is in the wheel or tire. To make the check, the wheel bearings must be properly adjusted and the tires inflated to recommended pressure. An accurate dial indicator should be used.

The correct procedure is to first check radial runout of the entire assembly as it slowly rotates through one revolution. Place the tip of the stylus of a dial indicator against the tread, rotate the assembly and see if it is running true. If radial runout of the assembly exceeds .050 in. (1.27 mm), the tire should be removed from the wheel, and the wheel checked separately for radial runout. See Fig. 48-20. Likewise, if lateral runout (wobble or waddle) exceeds .050 in., the wheel must be checked separately.

When checking a wheel for runout, it should be mounted on a hub that is free to rotate, but without end play that would give a false indicator reading. Often, a wheel balancing machine is used for this purpose, Fig. 48-21. Generally, radial runout of a steel wheel should not exceed .035 in. (0.89 mm). The lateral runout limit for a steel wheel is .045 in. (1.14 mm). Radial runout of an aluminum wheel should not exceed .030 in. (0.76 mm). The lateral runout for an aluminum wheel is also .030 in.

If the wheel checks out satisfactorily, the tire can be reinstalled in a different position (180 deg.). Of course, dust and dirt must be removed from the bead seats of the wheel, and the seats must be free of nicks or burrs. The tire beads must be clean and lubricated with a light film of rubber lubricant before the tire is reinstalled on the wheel.

With the tire on the wheel, properly inflated, and the wheel carefully installed on the drum or axle flange, the wheel nuts are tightened in an alternating sequence with uniform snugness. See Fig. 48-22. Then, using the same alternating sequence, the wheel nuts are tightened firm-

ly, and runout of the wheel and tire assembly is rechecked.

If moving the tire to different positions on the wheel does not bring lateral runout within limits, a new tire must be installed. If radial runout is excessive, the tire tread can be "trued" or "buffed." Removing rubber from the tire tread would seem to shorten the life of the tire. Actually, its life is extended since the tire will roll smoothly without thumping.

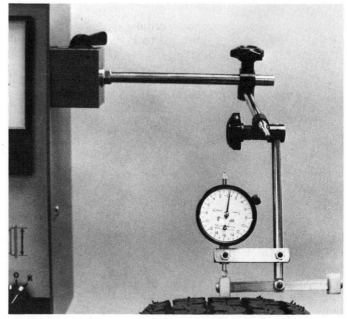

Fig. 48-21. Indicator is set up to check radial runout of a wheel and tire assembly mounted on a wheel balancing machine.

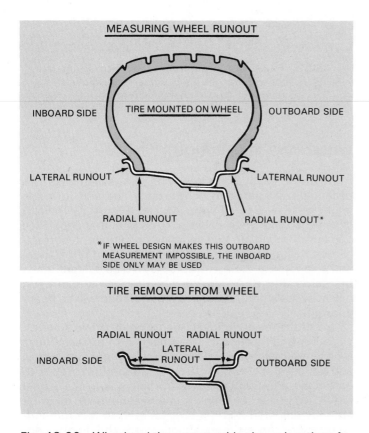

Fig. 48-20. Wheel and tire runout guide shows locations for checking radial and lateral runout of wheel and tire assembly, and of wheel alone.
(Cadillac Motor Car Div., General Motors Corp.)

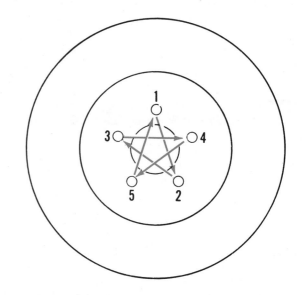

Fig. 48-22. Correct wheel nut installation involves tightening nuts in an alternating sequence to uniform snugness, then final tightening in same sequence.
(Cadillac Motor Car Div., General Motors Corp.)

Tire trueing is done by placing the out-of-round tire in a machine that shaves off only the high spots, rounding the tire. Tire buffing is done in a machine that buffs small amounts of rubber from the outer two tread rows. These methods should be followed by checking wheel and tire balance on an off-car wheel balancer, Fig. 48-23.

MANUAL TIRE DEMOUNTING AND MOUNTING

Originally, tires and wheels are match mounted. The radially stiffest part of the tire is matched to the smallest radius of the wheel. The high spot is marked with yellow paint. The low spot will be in line with the tire valve. If the paint mark is worn off, scribe a mark at the valve stem (before demounting tire) to insure remounting in the same position.

With today's low profile tires and safety wheel rims, manual demounting and mounting of tires is not recommended. In an emergency, the job can be done with smooth tire irons to avoid scoring the beads or nicking the bead seats. After breaking the bead loose from the bead seats, the tire is worked off of the wheel by taking "small bites" with the two tire irons while the beads on the opposite side are pressed into the wheel well.

To mount the tire on the wheel, a light film of rubber lubricant is applied to the beads and the tire bead is "started" on the wheel, then worked into place with the two tire irons. Again, care must be exercised to avoid damaging the beads or bead seats.

Once the tire is in place on the wheel, the tire is lifted to place the outer bead against the outer bead seat and a sudden rush of compressed air is introduced to seat the bead. Air pressure up to 40 psi (275 kPa) may be used to seat the bead, with the valve core removed. Once the beads are seated, the valve core is reinstalled and the tire is inflated to recommended pressure.

Before installing the assembly on the car, check the position of the tire in relation to the rim, making sure that it is concentric. To assist in this check, tires have a locating ring molded on the tire sidewall, Fig. 48-24. The ring should be concentric with the edge of the wheel rim. If it is not concentric, the tire and wheel assembly can be jounced on the floor until the tire is correctly mounted. Then inflate the tire to the recommended pressure.

POWER TIRE DEMOUNTING AND MOUNTING

The recommended means of demounting and mounting tires is by use of a power operated tire changer. See Fig. 48-25. Many different tires changers are available,

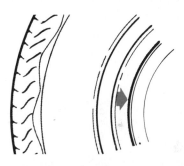

Fig. 48-24. Locating ring on tire should show equal spacing around rim flange of wheel when tire is inflated and beads are seated. (Oldsmobile Div., General Motors Corp.)

Fig. 48-23. Wheel and tire assemblies that have been serviced should be checked for "balance." This computer wheel balancer panel lights up on check spin when wheel is balanced. (Hofmann)

Fig. 48-25. Multi-purpose power tire changer handles bead-breaking and mount-demount actions on a wide range of sizes of car and light truck tires and wheels. (Ammco Tools, Inc.)

Fig. 48-26, and each is designed to do the demounting and mounting quickly and without damage to the tire or wheel.

Generally, the wheel and tire is installed on the bed of the tire changer and locked in place. Shoes of the power bead breaker are dropped in place at the point where bead and rim meet, and pressure is applied. After loosening both beads from the rim flanges, the inside of the wheel and both beads are lubricated. A special tool is used manually, or with power assistance, to remove the beads from the rim of the wheel, using the center post of the tire changer as a fulcrum.

The procedure is reversed to mount the tire on the wheel. Again, a film of lubricant is applied. Remove the valve core when preparing to inflate the tire to seat the beads in the wheel bead seats. Do not bend over or stand over the tire when inflating. The bead may break when it snaps over the safety hump of the wheel. Also, do not exceed 40 psi (275 kPa) when inflating to seat the bead of any tire, including the compact spare tire. If the bead fails to seat at 40 psi, a bead expander can be installed around the circumference of the tire. Tightening it, or inflating it, will force the tread inward and the beads outward to aid the bead-seating process.

After the tire beads are seated, check for equal spacing of the tire locating ring around the rim flange. See Fig. 48-24. Then install the valve core and inflate the tire to the specified inflation pressure. Inflate the compact spare tire to 60 psi (415 kPa).

TIRE REPAIRS

TIRE REPAIRS can be made in many different ways. Puncture holes up to 1/4 in. (6.3 mm) in diameter can be plugged and patched from the inside of the tire. Small nail hole type punctures can be repaired quickly from outside-in by inserting a plug, shooting a rubber rivet, or sealing the hole with several plies of cord type material saturated with vulcanizing cement. However, these are emergency only methods. A permanent inside-out repair must be made as soon as possible. Puncture holes in radial tires are repairable only in the tread area, as shown in Fig. 48-27.

Permanent tire repair methods include head type plug, cold patch, hot patch, and chemically or electrically vulcanized patch. Plugs and rivets are designed to stretch for easy installation into the puncture hole, then return to full molded size to seal in air and seal out dirt and moisture. Plugs and rivets can be installed by using an inserting needle, guide-and-plunger tool, or a gun. When installed, the plug top or rivet is cut off 1/16 in. above the tire tread.

Patches are cemented in place over the puncture hole by creating a bond between the underside of the patch and the inner wall of the tire. Installing filler rubber or tire repair dough in the puncture hole before the patch is installed is recommended by some repair kit manufacturers. Others have a soft, laminated patch having a layer of soft rubber that flows into the puncture hole while the car is being driven.

The cold patch and the self-vulcanizing patch are installed in the same way: The puncture hole is probed with a tool dipped in vulcanizing cement. An area twice the size of the patch is buffed and cleaned with solvent.

Fig. 48-26. Specialty power tire changer is designed to handle standard tires and wheels as well as small import wheels with no center hole. (Ammco Tools, Inc.)

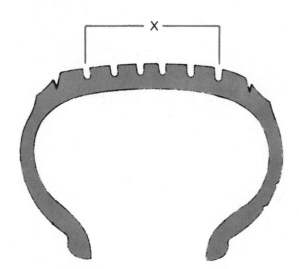

Fig. 48-27. General rule on radial tire puncture repair is to limit actual repairs to tread area shown at X. (American Motors Corp.)

Filler rubber is installed. A uniform coat of vulcanizing cement is applied to the buffed area and allowed to dry. The patch is installed over the puncture hole and stitched in place, Fig. 48-28.

The electric vulcanizing patch is snapped in place in the heating element. This assembly is centered over the puncture hole and a U-clamp is locked in place over it, Fig. 48-29. Secondary and ground wires are attached to a transformer, patch heating element, and the U-clamp. The transformer power lead is plugged into a 120 volt ac receptacle and electric vulcanization takes place automatically.

TIRE VALVES

Basically, TIRE VALVES are air checks that open under air pressure and close when pressure is removed. Details of a tire valve used in a tubeless tire are shown in Fig. 48-30. The inner valve or core acts as a check valve for the air. Positive sealing is provided by the valve cap, which contains a soft rubber washer or gasket. It is this gasket, pressed against the end of the valve stem, that seals the air in the tire. The careless practice of operating

tires without the valve cap should not be followed. Without the valve cap in place, there usually is a slow seepage of air from the tire, with the result that the tire will be operated in an underinflated condition.

Should air leaks occur around the valve base, it is necessary to install a new tire valve assembly. This is easily accomplished by means of a special lever type tool shown in Fig. 48-31.

RETREADING AND RECAPPING

The life of a tire can be materially extended by either recapping or retreading. RECAPPING means adding a top strip (called camelback) of synthetic or reclaimed rubber to the buffed and roughened surface of a worn tire. RETREADING means adding full width new rubber to the worn tire. The terms are used rather loosely and interchangeably in the tire industry, but a retread is ordinarily a better and more thorough job since new rubber is bonded to the tire from one shoulder to the other.

The experience of truck fleet operators shows that by retreading, tire life is increased from 75 to 100 percent. In general, truck tires are in need of retreading after 35,000 to 70,000 miles of service, depending on road conditions, climate, and type of service. Radial tires are said to add 12 percent more mileage to these figures.

Fig. 48-28. One recommended tire puncture repair is by buffing area around puncture, then installing a plug from inside-out and covering it with a cold patch or self-vulcanizing patch.

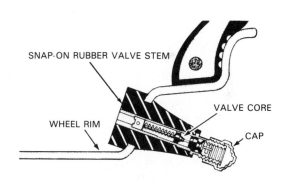

Fig. 48-30. Cross section shows location and details of tire valve in rim of tubeless tire.

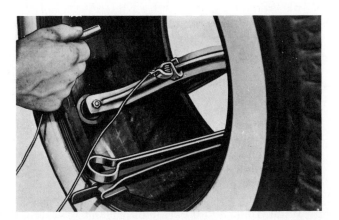

Fig. 48-29. Electric vulcanization is an effective method of tire puncture repair.

Fig. 48-31. Lever type tools are available for pushing or pulling a tire valve assembly into a wheel rim.

Tires with weak spots should not be retreaded. Most operators retread before the tread design is worn smooth.

WHEEL AND TIRE SERVICE CAUTIONS

Certain wheel and tire assembly cautions need to be observed:

1. Do not mix radial, bias ply, and belted bias tires on the same car except in emergencies.
2. Normally, install new tires in pairs on the same axle. If replacing only one tire, pair it with the tire having the most tread.
3. Always follow car manufacturer's tire inflation pressure recommendation. Radial tires appear to be underinflated in comparison with bias ply or belted tires at the same inflation pressure.
4. Generally, rotate radial tires from front to rear and from rear to front. However, certain manufacturers give optional diagonal rotation plan for radial tires. Check specifications. See Fig. 48-19.
5. Although tread designs may differ, tires built by different manufacturers with identical T.P.C. Spec. No. can be interchanged on the same car.
6. To remove "tight" wheels, tighten all lug nuts, then loosen each nut two turns. Rock car from side to side as hard as possible. Or, start engine and rock car from Drive to Reverse, allowing car to move several feet each way before applying brakes hard. Never use heat to loosen tight wheels.
7. Replace wheels if bent, dented, or if they have excessive radial or lateral runout, leak air through welds, have elongated bolt holes, or if heavily rusted.
8. Replace faulty wheels with new ones equivalent to original equipment wheels for load capacity, diameter, rim width, offset, and mounting configuration.
9. Tighten wheel nuts in sequence, Fig. 48-22, and to proper torque to avoid bending wheel or brake drum or rotor.
10. Follow equipment manufacturer's instructions for checking wheel and tire assembly balance and alignment to insure maximum tire life.

IMPROVEMENTS AND ADVANCES

Remarkable advances have been made in automobile tire design and construction over the past two decades. Tire manufacturers' research and development have led to the production of a wider range of tire sizes with much improved traction for starting, stopping, and cornering; greater durability; and less rolling resistance with the resulting reduction of tread wear and increased fuel economy.

According to a spokesperson for the Goodyear Tire & Rubber Company, proof of the impact of tire design on fuel mileage lies in the fact that "Tires have contributed 21 percent of the fuel economy improvement gained in automobiles since 1980."

Looking ahead, high technology computer techniques are creating the tire of the future. Computers are being used to design tread patterns and improve internal tire construction. Different tires for front and rear are in-work. Differences could be in size, width, construction, or tread patterns. A "thinking" or "sensor" tire is also being considered. It would receive data such as tire pressure, tread wear, spring rate, traction, and lateral friction coefficient, brake antiskid, leak and sealing rate, and tire alignment.

Chapter 48—REVIEW QUESTIONS
TIRES, TIRE SERVICE

1. Name the three major parts of a tubeless tire.
2. In tubeless tire construction, cord materials are laid _____ in layers.
3. The plies are arranged _____ in different combinations of layers and belts.
4. What are the three basic types of tire construction?
5. The ply rating of a tire is its index of tire _____.
6. Load range identifies a given tire size with its load and _____ when used in a specific type of service.
   a. Ply rating.
   b. Inflation limits.
   c. Tire construction.
   d. Tire size.
7. The U.S. Department of Transportation (DOT) has established Uniform Tire Quality Grading (UTQG) for passenger car tires. Tires are graded in all but one of the following areas. Which one is NOT graded in accordance with DOT test procedures?
   a. Tread wear.
   b. Traction.
   c. Load range.
   d. Temperature resistance.
8. When tire tread groove depth is less than 1/16 in. (1.6 mm), the tread wear indicators will appear as solid strips across the tire. True or False?
9. What is "section height" of an inflated tire?
10. _____ is the ratio of tire section height to section width.
11. Most metric tire sizes exactly match corresponding alpha-numeric tire sizes. True or False?
12. Metric tires are available in two load ranges, standard load and _____ load.
   a. Extra.
   b. Super.
   c. Heavy.
   d. Premium.
13. A speed rating symbol is an additional sidewall marking on specially designed performance tires. The speed rating appears as the letter _____ or _____ (B,D, or H,V).
14. A driver complained that front tires are wearing excessively at the center of the tread surface. Mechanic A says the wear problem is caused by underinflation. Mechanic B says the problem is caused by excessive camber. Who is right?
   a. Mechanic A.
   b. Mechanic B.
   c. Both mechanic A and mechanic B.
   d. Neither mechanic A nor mechanic B.
15. If the wheel and tire assembly is out-of-round, the first step is to determine whether the _____ problem is in the wheel or tire.

16. Generally, radial runout of a steel wheel should not exceed _____.
    a. .030 in. (0.76 mm).
    b. .035 in. (0.89 mm).
    c. .040 in. (1.02 mm).
    d. .045 in. (1.14 mm).
17. Radial and lateral runout limits of aluminum wheels are the same:
    a. .030 in. (0.76 mm).
    b. .035 in. (0.89 mm).
    c. .040 in. (1.02 mm).

d. .045 in. (1.14 mm).
18. What is the purpose of the locating ring molded in the sidewall of the tire?
19. Are puncture holes in radial tires repairable?
20. Permanent tire repair includes all but one of the following methods. Which repair is an emergency only method?
    a. Rubber rivet.
    b. Cold patch.
    c. Hot patch.
    d. Head type plug.

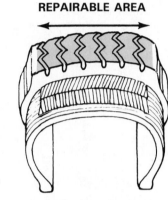

RADIAL

BIAS

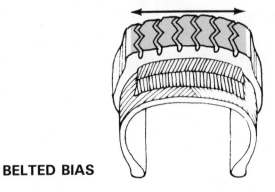

BELTED BIAS

Rubber Manufacturers Association recommends that tubeless tire puncture repairs be made in tread and shoulder area only. Also, every tire must be removed from wheel for inspection. All tread punctures, nail holes, or cuts up to 1/4 in. must be repaired by industry approved methods from inside of tire. (Rubber Manufacturers Association)

A front-end specialist prepares to align a car. This increases tire life when done at least once each year.

Chapter 49

WHEEL ALIGNMENT

After studying this chapter, you will be able to:
- Tell why four wheel alignment is necessary.
- Explain how certain elements have an influence on tire-to-road contact.
- List preliminary steps required before wheel alignment angles are set.
- Identify and describe the angles involved in front wheel alignment.

Aligning a vehicle's front wheels is the task of balancing the steering angles with the physical forces being exerted. The STEERING ANGLES are caster, camber, toe-in, steering axis inclination, and toe-out on turns. The PHYSICAL FORCES are gravity, momentum, friction, and centrifugal force.

Since so many factors are involved in front wheel alignment, it is also called front end alignment, steering alignment, steering balance, or steering geometry. Alignment, then, is more than adjusting the angularity of the front wheels. Today, with the steadily increasing production of front wheel drive vehicles with independent rear suspension, FOUR WHEEL ALIGNMENT (quadralignment) usually is required. Therefore, in addition to aligning the front wheels, you also must consider, and correct if necessary:

1. Front and rear suspension, steering, and tire condition.
2. Wheel bearing adjustment and wheel balance.
3. Car weight balance.
4. Wheelbase and tread width.
5. Thrust line and rear wheel track.
6. Suspension height.
7. Strut and shock absorber action.

STEERING BALANCE

Steering control of a vehicle in motion is maintained by keeping the vehicle's tires in close contact with the road surface. TIRE-TO-ROAD CONTACT is influenced by the condition of the tire treads, tire inflation, wheel balance, weight on the wheels, shock absorber action, spring action, and wheel angularity. A balanced condition between these elements will establish a perfect pivot point from which the front wheels can rotate with the least friction. This point on the tread of each front tire

is the target of all steering angle adjustments, Fig. 49-1.

The area of tire-to-road contact varies with tire inflation pressure and load, Fig. 49-2. Underinflation or overinflation affects the rolling characteristics of the wheels by changing the degree of friction between the tires and the road surface. If one tire is underinflated, it will hold back, and the car will steer toward the side holding back. Anything that tends to increase the area of tire tread contact with the road will increase the rolling resistance, and the car will steer to that side.

For satisfactory wheel alignment, certain conditions must be met. Ideally, both front tires will be the same brand, size, and type. Each will have the same degree of tread wear, and be inflated to the same pressure. Each will be carrying the same weight. Then, if each front wheel is properly and equally adjusted for angularity, each tire will maintain the same area of tread contact on a smooth road surface.

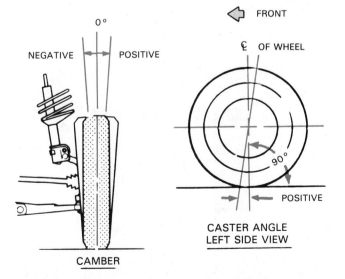

Fig. 49-1. Exaggerated alignment angles show various settings of front wheels which work together to provide smooth rolling and easy steering that extends tire life.
(Buick Motor Div., General Motors Corp.)

603

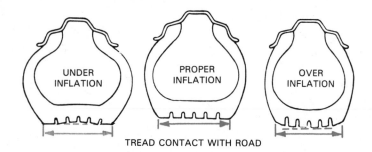

UNDER INFLATION — PROPER INFLATION — OVER INFLATION

TREAD CONTACT WITH ROAD

Fig. 49-2. Tire wear is governed by tread contact with road surface. Note area of contact under conditions of underinflation, proper inflation, and overinflation.

Obviously, though, it is impossible to maintain constant contact. The wheels bounce up and down at different times, at different rates of speed, and to varied heights. Here, the effects of momentum and inertia change the area of tread contact. Deflection of the car springs constantly changes the angles at which the steering system operates. Centrifugal force on the wheels emphasizes any lack of balance. Also, the extremely flexible characteristic of tires defeats the possibility of true and uniform steering geometry.

WHEEL BALANCE AND UNBALANCE

An important matter to be considered before alignment angles are set is checking to see that the wheel and tire assemblies are in BALANCE. Basically, STATIC BALANCE is the equal distribution of weight around the wheel and tire assembly. DYNAMIC BALANCE is the equal distribution of weight on each side of the vertical centerline of the wheel and tire assembly.

It follows, then, that UNBALANCE (imbalance) exists when there is an unequal distribution of weight around the horizontal axis of the wheel and tire assembly. See Fig. 49-3. The tires may be round and true when rotated slowly, yet give trouble on the road when they turn fast enough to get into the realm of centrifugal force. This

unbalance can exist in the tire, wheel, brake drum or rotor, or hub. Or, it may occur in any combination of these components.

When an unbalanced wheel revolves, centrifugal force acts on the heaviest portion and tends to lift the wheel off the road, then slam it down during each revolution. This results in flat spots on the tire tread and worn out ball joints, tie rod ends, steering gears, and shock absorbers.

If the unbalance lies in the plane of wheel rotation, it is known as static (or kinetic) unbalance, Fig. 49-3. If it lies on either or both sides of the plane of rotation, it is dynamic unbalance. Either condition will cause the wheels to bounce. Dynamic unbalance in the front wheels will cause them to wobble as well. Rear wheels should be kept in balance to avoid a bouncing action, which could set up a heavy vibration in the chassis and affect steering balance.

Unbalance can be detected with the aid of special equipment, Fig. 49-4, which usually indicates the proper

Fig. 49-4. This computerized wheel balancer has digital display showing amount of imbalance to 1/10th oz. (2.8 gr) on upper and lower planes. (Hunter Engineering Co.)

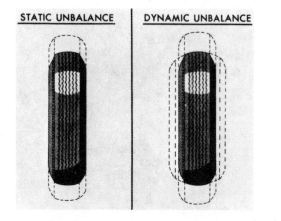

STATIC UNBALANCE — DYNAMIC UNBALANCE

Fig. 49-3. Static (kinetic) unbalance is uneven distribution of weight in tire assembly in plane of rotation. Dynamic unbalance is uneven distribution of weight to right and left of plane of rotation.

location for wheel weights to restore balance. In spite of regular maintenance, however, uneven tire wear can result from drivers' habits as their modern automobiles accelerate faster, take curves at a higher rate of speed, and stop more quickly. To counteract uneven wear that leads to unbalance, the tire industry recommends that tires should be rotated every six to eight thousand miles. See Fig. 49-5.

CAR WEIGHT BALANCE

Another preliminary step in balancing wheel alignment is to check the accuracy of attachment of the wheels to the vehicle. The frame or unitized body must be checked to see that it is square and level. The axles and wheels must be located properly in relation to the frame or body. This involves making a series of measurements to establish the parallel and right angle relationships between the frame and wheels.

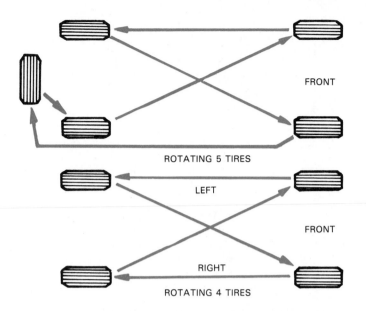

Fig. 49-5. Planned tire rotation extends tire life. Tire industry-approved patterns are shown for rotating bias, belted bias, and radial tires. (American Motors Corp.)

The essential part of this car weight balance relationship is a straight, undistorted frame, Fig. 49-6. First, an accurate centerline must be established. Then, if straight lines are drawn through the centers of both rear axles and both front spindle locations, they must be parallel to each other and form right angles with the centerline

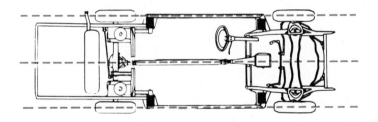

Fig. 49-6. Before making alignment checks, see that frame is straight, square, and level. Side rails must be parallel to centerline of frame.

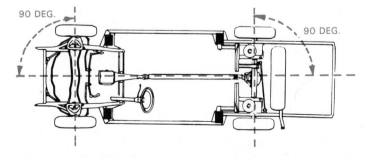

Fig. 49-7. Straight lines drawn through centers of rear axle and front spindle locations must be parallel and form right angles with centerline of frame.

of the frame, Fig. 49-7.

Then, when the wheels are attached to the front spindles and rear axles, the rear wheels should be parallel to the centerline of the frame. Likewise, the front wheels in their straight ahead position should be parallel to this line (except for slight toe-in or toe-out). This is necessary so that each wheel will roll straight and true in relation to the frame centerline.

WHEELBASE — TREAD WIDTH

Another point of importance when locating axles and spindles is the wheelbase measurement. WHEELBASE is the distance between the center of the front wheel and center of the rear wheel, Fig. 49-8. This distance (left front to left rear, right front to right rear with front wheels in "straight ahead" position) must be exactly the same on each side for proper weight balance. Correct wheelbase also contributes to the ability of the car's rear wheels to TRACK (follow directly in line with front wheels).

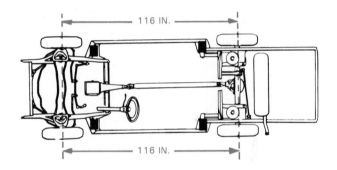

Fig. 49-8. Wheelbase, or distance between centers of front and rear wheels, must measure as specified by manufacturer and be exactly equal on each side.

Tread width is also a key measurement with respect to weight balance and rear wheel track. TREAD WIDTH is the distance between the center points of the left tire tread and right tire tread as they come in contact with the road. See Fig. 49-9. While the front and rear wheels may have different tread widths, each front wheel must be the same distance from the centerline of the frame,

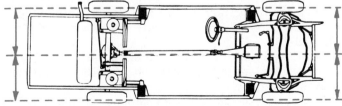

Fig. 49-9. Tread width is distance between center points of left tire tread and right tire tread. Note that measurements are total taken from frame centerline to center of each tire to establish correct frame-to-wheels relationship, left to right.

and each rear wheel must be the same distance from this centerline.

This parallel relationship between the frame centerline and wheels establishes a balance between front and rear, and between right and left. While this balance may not mean equal weight at these points, it does mean that a balanced distribution of weight and stress has been acquired for the proper setting of front wheel angles.

REAR WHEEL TRACK

As previously pointed out, the growing popularity of front wheel drive and four wheel drive vehicles has sharply increased the need for correct alignment of all four wheels. In fact, some designs require camber and toe-in adjustments on all four wheels.

The four wheel alignment ("quadralignment") procedure is required so that correct rear wheel track is established. Remember, the front wheels steer the vehicle, but the rear wheels direct it. The rear wheels determine the THRUST LINE, Fig. 49-10, which in effect is

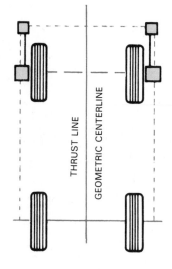

Fig. 49-11. If rear wheels are realigned so that thrust line and frame centerline agree, rear wheels will "track" front wheels. (Hunter Engineering Co.)

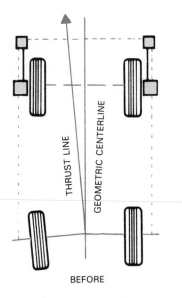

BEFORE

Fig. 49-10. If rear wheels are misaligned, front wheels must be turned to maintain straight ahead direction of travel and rear wheels will not "track." (Hunter Engineering Co.)

the REAR ROLLING DIRECTION. When the thrust line is made to agree with the vehicle frame's centerline (by aligning front and rear wheels and centering the steering wheel), correct rear wheel track will be achieved. See Fig. 49-11.

See Chapter 50 for details on making four wheel alignment checks and adjustments on a variety of vehicle makes and models.

However, if the car has been damaged in an accident, the impact may have forced the frame into a diamond shape, changing the relationship between the thrust line and the frame centerline.

An out-of-line condition not caused by an accident usually can be traced to a mechanical defect or sag due to stress in the middle or corner of the frame. In any case, a frame that is out of line must be straightened before it is possible to obtain correct steering alignment. The frame rails must be the same height from the floor on each side at the spring seats, along with the essential parallel and right angle relationships.

SPRINGS

Also vital in this matter of weight balance is the condition of the car springs. They control the up-and-down motion of the car and, therefore, the heights of the car above the road. If one or more of the springs is collapsed or broken, it causes an unbalanced distribution of weight. This unbalance creates a lopsided appearance, puts an added strain on related parts, and changes the angularity of the front wheels.

This condition also may occur when the load is distributed unequally. In fact, anything that changes the ratio of weight on the springs will have a definite bearing on the alignment angles and on the area of tire-to-road contact.

SUSPENSION HEIGHT

The heights of the car above the road must be checked (front and rear, right and left) before any steering angles are adjusted, Fig. 49-12. Although the method of checking varies with type of suspension, the measurements should be made with the car parked on a level floor with the tires equally inflated, fuel tank full, no passenger load, and no excess weight off either side.

SHOCK ABSORBER ACTION

The shock absorbers are still another factor involved in controlling the up-and-down motion of a moving vehicle. Efficient shock absorber action aids wheel alignment by furnishing a dampening effect that protects the springs from sudden overloading or unloading action. If

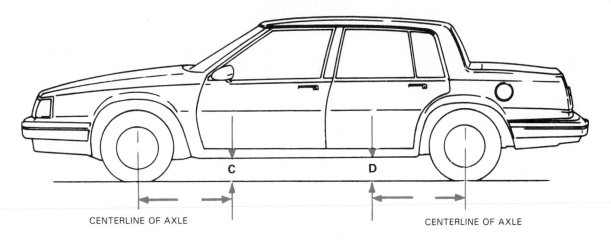

Fig. 49-12. Frame height, according to Buick, is determined by measuring heights at C and D at specified distances A and B from centerlines of axles. (Buick Motor Div., General Motors Corp.)

the shock absorbers are not operating properly, the car will bounce excessively and steering angles will change oftener and to a greater extent.

Sometimes steering angles will check out correctly on the alignment equipment, yet the car will not handle well on the road. This problem could be caused by faulty springs or shock absorbers, worn parts in the steering gear or front suspension system, driving conditions, or habits of the driver.

One other chassis control feature that merits consideration is the use of STABILIZERS or ''sway bars.'' See Fig. 49-13. Some cars require stabilizers to steady the chassis against front end roll and sway on turns. Stabilizers are designed to control this centrifugal tendency that forces a rising action on the side toward the inside of the turn.

With all of these weight balance factors to be checked out and corrected, it is obvious that wheel alignment is more than just an adjustment of the steering angles. The whole theory of wheel alignment revolves around balanced weight distribution on the wheels and proper tire tread contact with the road surface while the vehicle is in motion.

FRONT WHEEL ANGULARITY

The angles involved in front wheel alignment are caster, camber, toe-in, steering axis inclination, and toe-out on turns, Figs. 49-14 through 49-19. These angles govern the way the front wheels behave while the vehicle is in motion.

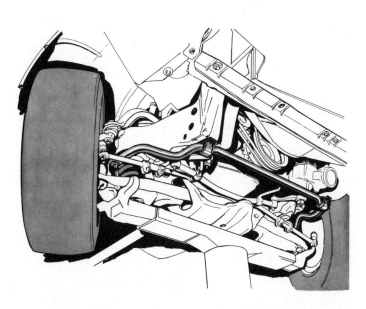

Fig. 49-13. Stabilizers provide added support for front suspension members. This 1 1/8 in. (28.6 mm) stabilizer is part of a ''handling package'' offered by car manufacturer. (Pontiac Motor Div., General Motors Corp.)

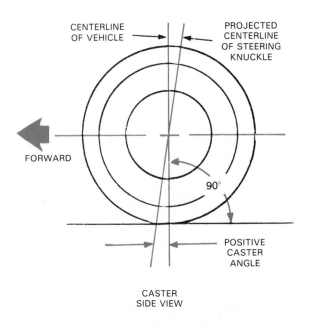

Fig. 49-14. Caster is degree of tilt of steering axis forward or backward from vertical centerline of wheel. (American Motors Corp.)

607

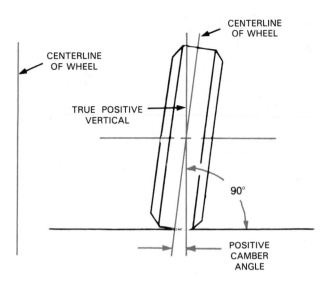

CENTERLINE
OF WHEEL

CENTERLINE
OF WHEEL

TRUE POSITIVE
VERTICAL

90°

POSITIVE
CAMBER
ANGLE

CAMBER FRONT VIEW

Fig. 49-15. Camber is amount wheel is tilted in or out at top from its vertical centerline.   (American Motors Corp.)

Actually, the alignment angles are so closely related that changing one will often change the others. In order to check and adjust them properly, it is necessary to use special equipment capable of a high degree of accuracy. In many cases, caster and camber specifications are given in minutes (fractions of a degree).

Here again, balance enters the picture. The adjustment goal becomes a balanced relationship of the steering angles, with due regard for road and load factors involved in each individual case.

CASTER

Caster is the steering angle that utilizes the weight and momentum of the car's chassis to lead the front wheels

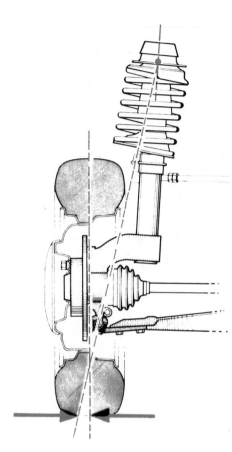

Fig. 49-17. Negative kingpin offset gives small car steering a self-centering effect.   (Volkswagen of America, Inc.)

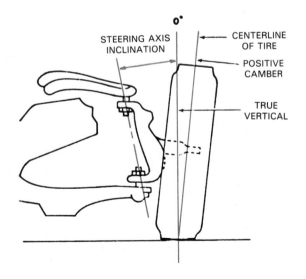

0°

STEERING AXIS
INCLINATION

CENTERLINE
OF TIRE

POSITIVE
CAMBER

TRUE
VERTICAL

LEFT HAND FRONT VIEW

Fig. 49-16. Steering axis inclination is inward tilt of steering knuckle from vertical centerline of wheel. (Oldsmobile Div., General Motors Corp.)

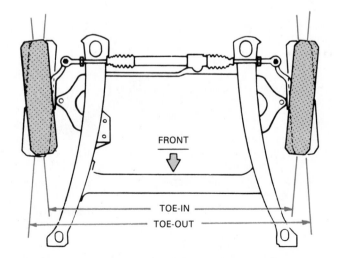

FRONT

TOE-IN
TOE-OUT

Fig. 49-18. Toe-in is amount front wheels are closer together in front than at rear at hub height. (Buick Motor Div., General Motors Corp.)

in a straight path. See Figs. 49-1 and 49-14. CASTER is the backward or forward tilt of the steering axis that tends to stabilize steering in a straight direction. It places the weight of the vehicle either ahead or behind the area of tire-to-road contact.

It would be easier to visualize the effect of the caster angle by projecting an imaginary line lengthwise through the center of the ball joints and downward to the road surface. This line, called the "steering axis," would be found to intersect the road at a point ahead of or in back of the center point of tire-to-road contact. Considering this, if the front wheels were given a generous amount of caster, they would be subjected to a leading or trailing action like a furniture caster that tends to line up and drag its wheel in the direction of movement.

POSITIVE CASTER is the angular amount that the upper ball joint is farther back than the lower joint, Fig. 49-14. NEGATIVE CASTER is the condition when the upper ball joint is farther ahead than the lower one. The CASTER ANGLE, then, is the number of degrees (or fraction of one degree) that the steering axis is tilted backward or forward from the vertical axis of the front wheels.

CAMBER — STEERING AXIS INCLINATION

CAMBER is the inward or outward tilt of the wheel at the top, Fig. 49-15. It is built into the wheel spindle by

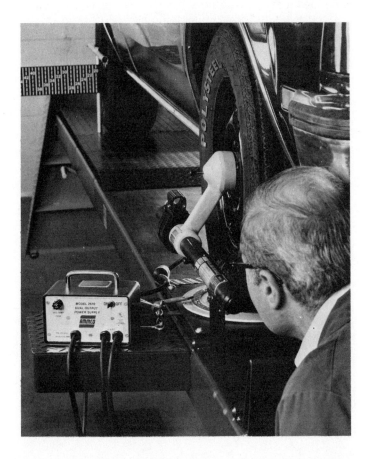

Fig. 49-19. All four wheels must be centered and "tracking" before wheel alignment correction. To check, mechanic is sighting through scope of a wheel tracking and toe gauge. (Ammco Tools, Inc.)

forming the spindle with a downward tilt to provide positive camber. STEERING AXIS INCLINCATION is the inward tilt of the steering knuckle, Fig. 49-16. It is so interrelated with camber that they share a common side (vertical axis of wheel). The combination of these two angles forms what is known as the INCLUDED ANGLE.

The purpose of this two-angle team is to place the turning point of the wheel at the center of the tire tread contact area. Originally, the front wheels were pivoted to swing in a vertical position. This difference between the pivoting centerline and the wheel centerline caused the wheels to pull or scuff on rough roads. The car manufacturers solved this problem by tilting the pivoting centerline in at the top (steering axis inclination) and tilting the wheel out at the top (camber). This created an included angle that intersected close to the center of tire tread contact and reduced the scuff area to a minimum. See Fig. 49-1.

When camber and steering axis inclination are correct, they contribute to steering ease and extended tire life. Also, by placing the tread contact area more nearly under the point of load, a "straightening up" tendency is provided.

With the steering axis tilted inward (steering axis inclination), the end of the spindle will describe an arc that is noticeably lower in the extreme turn position than in the center or straight ahead position. In normal operation, the weight of the car prevents the spindle from moving up and down. Therefore, the car is forced upward when the front wheels are turned, and the force of gravity tends to straighten the wheels.

In this way, the weight of the car helps to provide an automatic steering effect brought about by accurate adjustment of the steering angles. Additional alignment benefits become apparent when some of the troubles caused by misalignment are noted. These include hard steering, wander, pull to one side, and unequal or excessive tire wear.

Also in the area of steering axis inclination, car manufacturers have come up with "Negative Kingpin Offset," a modification of MacPherson strut design. NEGATIVE KINGPIN OFFSET refers to the fact that the steering axis of each front wheel is offset so that an imaginary line drawn along the axis would strike the ground outside the centerline of the tire, Fig. 49-17.

Most cars have a front end setup in which the steering axis is closer to vertical. In conventional design, a line drawn along the steering axis would strike the ground inside the centerline of the tire. Both designs, conventional and negative kingpin offset provide easy steering.

However, the side benefit of negative kingpin offset is a self-centering effect. Under uneven braking or rough road conditions, or if one front tire goes flat, a car with conventional geometry would pull toward the side with more resistance. With negative kingpin offset, the wheel encountering more resistance automatically turns toward the straight ahead path.

TOE-IN

Equally important with respect to steering ease is the correct setting of toe-in. TOE-IN is the term used to specify the amount (in fractions of an inch) that the front wheels are closer together in front than at the rear, when measured at hub height, Fig. 49-18. Here again, precision testing equipment and careful measurement and correction will prevent any slipping or scuffing action between the tires and road. See Fig. 49-19.

Actually, the slight amount of toe-in specified serves to keep the front wheels running parallel on the road by offsetting other forces which tend to spread the wheels apart. The major force is the backward thrust of the road against the tire tread while the car is moving forward. Other factors include compensation for unavoidable play in the tie rod assembly, and allowance for angular changes caused by wheel bounce or variations in road conditions.

If toe-in is incorrect, the tires will be dragged along the road, scuffing and featheredging the tread ribs. Changes in road or load conditions will affect more than one steering angle, and uneven tread wear patterns will result. Also in this respect, toe-in will change when other angular adjustments are made. For this reason, front wheel toe-in should be measured first and corrected last on all wheel alignment jobs.

TOE-OUT ON TURNS

It is obvious that driving conditions make it impossible to keep the front wheels parallel at all times. Regardless of how accurately the front wheels are positioned for straight ahead driving, they could be out of their correct relative positions on turns. From the mechanical standpoint, the parallel relationship between the front wheels is controlled by the tie rod (rods) and the angularity of the steering arms, Fig. 49-20. Considering that the outside wheel is approximately five feet farther away from the point about which the car is turning, it must turn at a lesser angle and travel in a greater circle than the inside wheel. See Fig. 49-21. This condition is called TOE-OUT ON TURNS, which means that

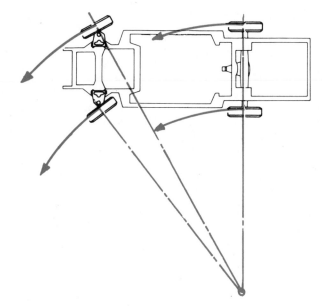

Fig. 49-21. Toe-out on turns is angular relationship between front wheels when turned to right or left.   (Ford Motor Co.)

each front wheel requires a separate turning radius to keep the inside tire from slipping and scuffing on turns.

Toe-out on turns, then, is the relationship between the front wheels which allows them to turn about a common center. To accomplish this, the steering arms are designed to angle several degrees inside of the parallel position, Fig. 49-22. The exact amount depends on the tread and wheelbase of the car and on the arrangement of the steering control linkage.

The theory of this design is that an imaginary line drawn through each steering arm will intersect near the differential. In practice, this serves to speed the action of steering arm on the inside of the turn as it moves toward the centerline of the wheel spindle. The effect on the outside steering arm is to slow it down as it moves away from the center of the wheel spindle. Therefore, the outside wheel turns at a lesser angle, and its turning circle is greater. True rolling contact is obtained.

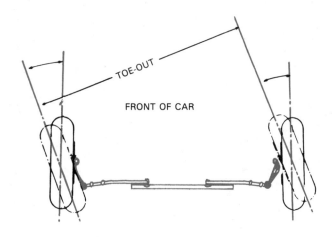

Fig. 49-20. Tie rods and steering arms control parallel relationship between front wheels, both in straight ahead driving and on turns.

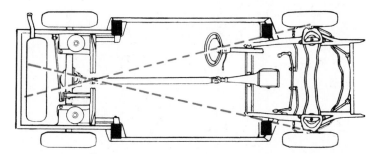

Fig. 49-22. Steering arms are angled inward to provide a separate turning radius for each front wheel.

Chapter 49—REVIEW QUESTIONS

Write your answers on a separate sheet of paper. Do not write in this book.

1. Name the five steering angles.
2. The physical forces being exerted on the front wheels when the vehicle is in motion are: gravity, momentum, friction, and _____.
3. Name five things that influence tire tread contact with the road surface.
4. The area of tire-to-road contact varies with _____ and load.
5. The extremely flexible characteristics of modern tires defeats the possibility of true and uniform steering geometry. True or False?
6. What is static balance of a wheel and tire assembly?
7. What is dynamic balance of a wheel and tire assembly?
8. Unbalance can exist in all but one of the following components:
   a. Wheel and tire assembly.
   b. Brake drum or rotor.
   c. Hub.
   d. Spindle.
9. What is the correct terminology for the distance between the center of the front wheel and the center of the rear wheel?
   a. Wheelbase.
   b. Tread width.
   c. Toe-in.
   d. Steering axis inclination.
10. What is the correct terminology for the distance between the center points of the left tire tread and the right tire tread as they come in contact with the road?
    a. Wheelbase.
    b. Tread width.
    c. Toe-in.
    d. Steering axis inclination.
11. Four wheel alignment is required so that correct _____ is established.
12. The rear wheels determine the _____, which in effect is the rear rolling direction.
13. _____ is the backward or forward tilt of the steering axis.
    a. Caster.
    b. Camber.
    c. Toe-in.
    d. Steering axis inclination.
14. If the upper ball joint is farther back than the lower ball joint, what angularity is the wheel said to have?
    a. Positive caster.
    b. Positive camber.
    c. Positive steering axis inclination.
    d. Negative steering axis inclination.
15. _____ is the inward or outward tilt of the wheel at the top.
    a. Caster.
    b. Camber.
    c. Toe-in.
    d. Steering axis inclination.
16. _____ is the inward tilt of the steering knuckle (centerline through ball joints).
17. Which two steering angles make up the included angle?
    a. Caster and camber.
    b. Caster and steering axis inclination.
    c. Camber and steering axis inclination.
    d. Camber and toe-in.
18. What is the purpose of the included angle?
    a. To reduce the tire scuff area to a minimum.
    b. To contribute to steering ease and extend tire life.
    c. To provide a "straightening up" tendency.
    d. All of the above.
19. _____ of the front wheels should be measured first and corrected last on alignment jobs.
20. When a vehicle is turning, should the front wheels toe-in or toe-out?

Certain brands of wheel alignment equipment utilize front wheel projection devices —
and rear wheel instruments — to accurately measure alignment angles projected on
calibrated charts.   (Hunter Engineering Corp.)

Chapter 50

WHEEL ALIGNMENT CORRECTION

After studying this chapter, you will be able to:
- Define the six front wheel alignment angles and the order in which they should be checked.
- List preliminary steps that are necessary before making measurements of caster, camber, and toe-in.
- Give examples of typical front wheel caster and camber adjustment methods on both rear wheel drive and front wheel drive cars.
- Describe how various front wheel toe-in adjustments are made.
- Explain the importance of "rear wheel tracking."
- Give examples of typical rear wheel camber and toe-in checks and adjustments.

Wheel alignment correction calls for a careful determination of whether or not the problem lies in misalignment, steering, suspension, or in the wheel and tire assemblies. A good alignment specialist must be able to visualize the behavior of a loaded vehicle going at high speed on the highway, while making corrective adjustments on an empty car standing on floating turntables on an alignment rack.

A thorough understanding of the principles involved and enough imagination to visualize actual operating conditions are absolutely essential in this specialized field. In addition, the service technician must have and know how to use equipment of outstanding accuracy.

As for the vehicles themselves, the need for frequent and regular wheel alignment checks has increased with technological advances. Power steering, softer springing, rubber-bushed suspension parts, more moving parts, the use of wide tread, low profile tires allow constant abuse of car suspension without forewarning the driver.

With this set of circumstances in mind, most manufacturers recommend wheel alignment checks at least once a year. Or, for another rule-of-thumb, wheel alignment should be checked at the first sign of uneven tread wear.

REAR WHEEL DRIVE/FRONT WHEEL DRIVE

In reality, front wheel alignment service procedures on the familiar engine-in-front/rear wheel drive cars has changed very little over the years. The checking and adjusting methods have remained basically the same.

However, with today's engineering and production emphasis on front wheel drive cars, front *and* rear wheel alignment procedures were found to be necessary. For example, some of these front wheel drive cars are prone to problems in the area of "tracking." It is not unusual to find that the rear axle has shifted and the rear wheels do not track (follow directly in line with) the front wheels when the steering wheel is in the straight-ahead position.

CONSIDER INTERRELATED ANGLES

Remember, front wheel alignment correction includes adjustment of all interrelated factors affecting the run-

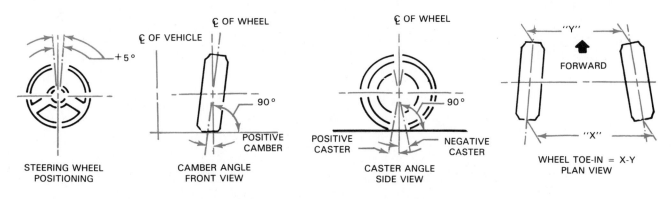

Fig. 50-1. Interrelation of alignment angles is shown in these views of centered steering wheel and camber, caster, and toe-in angularity. (Chevrolet Motor Div., General Motors Corp.)

ning and steering of the vehicle. Changing one angle will often change others, Fig. 50-1, so it is necessary to recheck all angles when one is changed.

The method of wheel alignment inspection and detection varies with type of equipment but, generally, the angles should be checked in the following order:
1. Front suspension height.
2. Caster.
3. Camber.
4. Toe-in.
5. Steering axis inclination.
6. Toe-out on turns.

PRELIMINARY CHECKS

Regardless of design of the suspension systems and the wheel alignment geometry, car manufacturers state that certain preliminary steps are necessary before making any measurements of caster, camber, and toe-in.

Ordinarily, cars should be checked for alignment at "curb height" or "trim height" and "curb weight." (Certain manufacturers specify use of alignment spacers to insure proper suspension heights.) Curb weight means the basic automobile, less passengers, with a full fuel tank and proper amounts of coolant and lubricants. The spare tire and wheel, jack and jack handle must be in design position, and the front seats should be in their rear-most position.

Then proceed as follows:
1. Place car on an alignment rack or level floor.
2. Check air pressure in all four tires. Inflate tires to manufacturer's specifications.
3. See that tire tread wear is approximately the same, and not abnormal, Fig. 50-2, and remove stones and caked mud from wheels and tires.
4. Check wheel lugs for looseness and/or improper installation.
5. Test action and rebound of shock absorbers by jouncing car an equal number of time from center of bumpers. Jounce alternately at rear, then front,

releasing at bottom of stroke. Car should rebound slowly, not bounce.
6. Test steering effort and steering wheel return from both directions. Check for inconsistent effort, harshness, noise, binding, or excessive free play. Check steering gear for excessive backlash and for "high point," with reference to steering wheel position and straight ahead position of front wheels. Ad-

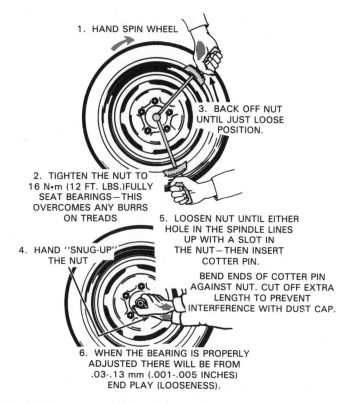

1. HAND SPIN WHEEL

2. TIGHTEN THE NUT TO 16 N•m (12 FT. LBS.) FULLY SEAT BEARINGS—THIS OVERCOMES ANY BURRS ON TREADS

3. BACK OFF NUT UNTIL JUST LOOSE POSITION.

4. HAND "SNUG-UP" THE NUT

5. LOOSEN NUT UNTIL EITHER HOLE IN THE SPINDLE LINES UP WITH A SLOT IN THE NUT—THEN INSERT COTTER PIN.

BEND ENDS OF COTTER PIN AGAINST NUT. CUT OFF EXTRA LENGTH TO PREVENT INTERFERENCE WITH DUST CAP.

6. WHEN THE BEARING IS PROPERLY ADJUSTED THERE WILL BE FROM .03-.13 mm (.001-.005 INCHES) END PLAY (LOOSENESS).

Fig. 50-3. A typical General Motors front wheel bearing adjusting procedure is pictured and described. (Chevrolet Motor Div., General Motors Corp.)

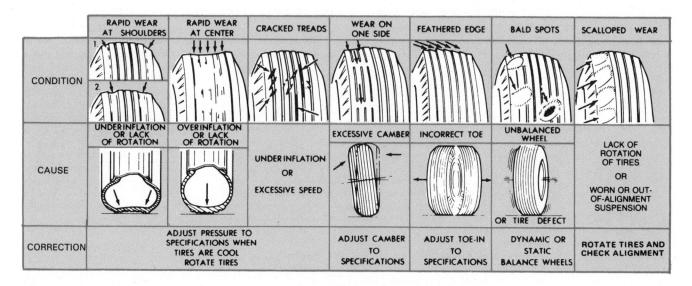

	RAPID WEAR AT SHOULDERS	RAPID WEAR AT CENTER	CRACKED TREADS	WEAR ON ONE SIDE	FEATHERED EDGE	BALD SPOTS	SCALLOPED WEAR
CONDITION							
CAUSE	UNDERINFLATION OR LACK OF ROTATION	OVERINFLATION OR LACK OF ROTATION	UNDER INFLATION OR EXCESSIVE SPEED	EXCESSIVE CAMBER	INCORRECT TOE	UNBALANCED WHEEL OR TIRE DEFECT	LACK OF ROTATION OF TIRES OR WORN OR OUT-OF-ALIGNMENT SUSPENSION
CORRECTION	ADJUST PRESSURE TO SPECIFICATIONS WHEN TIRES ARE COOL ROTATE TIRES			ADJUST CAMBER TO SPECIFICATIONS	ADJUST TOE-IN TO SPECIFICATIONS	DYNAMIC OR STATIC BALANCE WHEELS	ROTATE TIRES AND CHECK ALIGNMENT

Fig. 50-2. Condition, cause, and correction of various types of abnormal tire wear are pictured in this troubleshooting chart. (American Motors Corp.)

just steering gear, if required.

7. Raise vehicle and test front wheel bearings for looseness. Grasp tire at top and bottom and try to rock assembly on its spindle. Adjust bearings, if necessary, Fig. 50-3.

8. Use a dial indicator to check each front wheel and tire assembly for runout, Fig. 50-4, making sure that wheel is not damaged and tire beads are seated in rim of wheel. Mark point of maximum runout on tire sidewall, Fig. 50-5, then spin each front wheel and balance as required.

9. Check front end parts for looseness or wear. Inspect control arm pivot shafts or bolts, suspension ball joints, struts, stabilizer, and all mounting bolts and nuts. Visually check condition of suspension ball joints and seals.

10. Inspect all springs for sagging or breakage. Check for looseness of brake caliper attaching bolts.

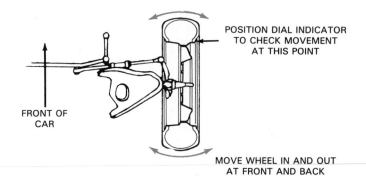

Fig. 50-6. Points of greatest wear in this steering linkage setup include tie rod ends, idler arm bushings, and relay rod-to-tie rod connections. (Oldsmobile Div., General Motors Corp.)

11. Test for looseness of steering gear attaching bolts at frame. Manually check for looseness or wear at all steering pivot points: pitman arm, relay rod, tie rod ends, and idler arm. See Fig. 50-6. Inspect for bent steering arms.

SETTING UP THE CAR

Lower the car and drive it far enough in a straight line to establish the straight ahead position of the front wheels. Then, mark the steering wheel hub and steering column collar for use as a reference point during the alignment procedure, Fig. 50-7.

At this time, rear wheel track can be checked by running the car in and out of a wet area and examining the tread marks left by the front and rear tires. Since front and rear tread widths are seldom the same, the marks may not coincide. However, there should be equal spacing between marks left by the left front and rear tires and the right front and rear tires. See Fig. 50-8.

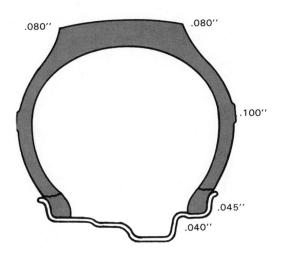

Fig. 50-4. Steel wheel and radial tire runout specifications are shown. (Chevrolet Motor Div., General Motors Corp.)

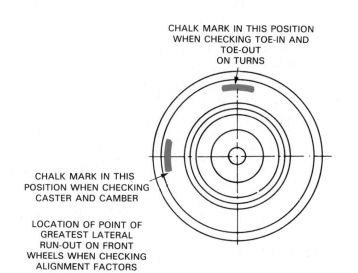

Fig. 50-5. Mark point of maximum lateral runout on front tire sidewall. Place mark to front for caster/camber checks, at top for toe-in and toe-out on turns. (Ford Motor Co.)

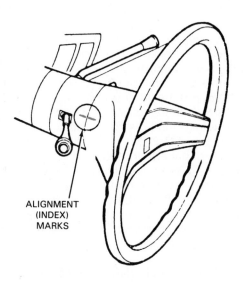

Fig. 50-7. Mark straight ahead position of front wheels on steering wheel hub and steering column collar for future reference when making alignment checks.

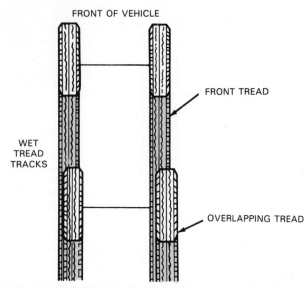

FRONT OF VEHICLE

FRONT TREAD

WET TREAD TRACKS

OVERLAPPING TREAD

IF THE WIDTH OF ONE REAR OVERLAPPING TRACK IS MORE THAN 1.50 INCHES WIDER THAN ONE FRONT TRACK, ADJUST TO CORRECT REAR TOE (DOG TRACKING).

Fig. 50-8. To check "rear wheel track," run vehicle straight through a wet area, then examine tread marks. (Ford Motor Co.)

MEASURING SUSPENSION HEIGHT

To prepare the car for a suspension height check, jounce it lightly front and rear until suspension parts equalize. If excessive friction in the suspension system is suspected, make two quick checks of bumper height and compare the difference. First lift the car manually by the bumper and let it settle slowly to normal standing height. Measure from the center of the bumper to the floor. Then push down on the bumper and release it slowly. Take this measurement and compare it with the first. If the two height measurements are not within one inch of each other, excessive suspension system friction exists.

If the above checks are within the limit, jounce the car lightly and measure front suspension height at the points specified by the car manufacturer. Then, compare the measurements with specifications. If the suspension height is below minimum requirements on cars with coil springs, replace both springs. If one side is within specifications and the other side is not, replace the weak spring. In cars equipped with torsion bars, make the necessary adjustments to obtain correct front suspension height, Fig. 50-9.

If alignment spacers are required for making certain angular checks: place car on floating turntables; raise car body and install spacers front and rear; lower car body. Generally, spacers in front are placed between suspension lower control arms and frame spring pockets. At rear, install spacers between the rear axle housing and frame.

CHECKING AND SETTING CASTER

CASTER is the angle measured between a true vertical line through the center of the wheel and the center-

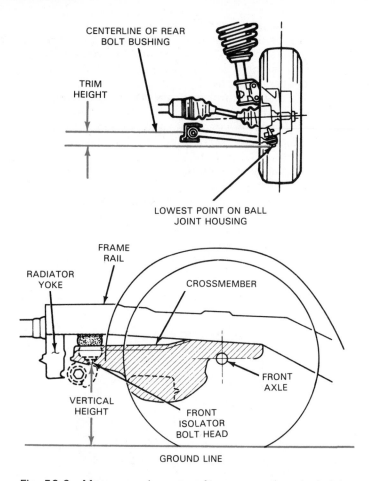

CENTERLINE OF REAR BOLT BUSHING

TRIM HEIGHT

LOWEST POINT ON BALL JOINT HOUSING

FRAME RAIL

RADIATOR YOKE

CROSSMEMBER

FRONT AXLE

VERTICAL HEIGHT

FRONT ISOLATOR BOLT HEAD

GROUND LINE

Fig. 50-9. Measure and compare front suspension trim height, left and right, to help guarantee accuracy of angular checks which follow. Top. Cadillac front wheel drive. Bottom. Chrysler front wheel drive.

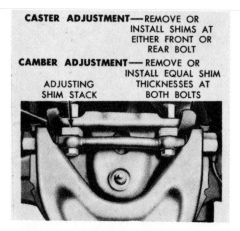

CASTER ADJUSTMENT—REMOVE OR INSTALL SHIMS AT EITHER FRONT OR REAR BOLT

CAMBER ADJUSTMENT—REMOVE OR INSTALL EQUAL SHIM THICKNESSES AT BOTH BOLTS

ADJUSTING SHIM STACK

Fig. 50-10. Shim adjustment of caster and camber provides simple means of positioning suspension control arms.

line through the upper and lower ball joints. See Fig. 50-1. To increase positive caster, move the upper ball joint to the rear or the lower ball joint to the front.

Many cars are provided with shims under the upper control arm mounting bolts, Fig. 50-10. In this design, transferring shims from under the rear bolt to the front

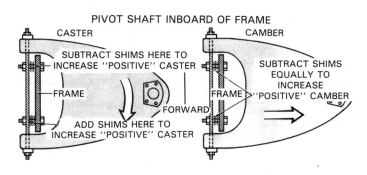

Fig. 50-11. If pivot shaft is inboard of frame bracket, adding shims will move pivot shaft farther inboard, in contrast to outboard movement in Fig. 50-10. (Buick Motor Div., General Motors Corp.)

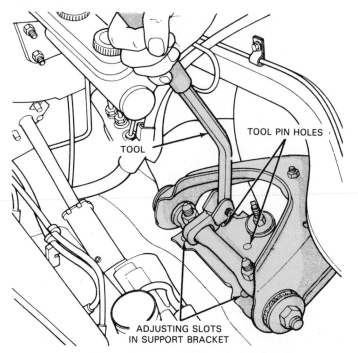

Fig. 50-13. Caster and camber on some rear wheel drive cars is adjusted by moving pivot shaft of upper control arm in or out by means of elongated bolt holes. Special tools aid in moving and holding pivot shaft. (Chrysler Corp.)

bolt increases caster. Reversing this transfer of shims decreases caster. However, if the control arm pivot shaft is located inboard of the frame bracket, then the entire shimming procedure is reversed. See Fig. 50-11.

Either of these caster adjustments affects camber, so caster and camber adjustments should be made simultaneously. Detailed charts in service manuals give exact shim changes for each misalignment situation.

Another popular caster adjustment design is the strut rod type. With this arrangement, adjustable strut rods run diagonally from the lower control arms to the frame front cross member, Fig. 50-12. To make an adjustment, loosen the lock nuts at the forward end of the struts, then shorten the rod to increase caster (this moves lower ball joint forward). Lengthening the rod by lock nut adjustment decreases caster.

Chrysler and Ford cars have used still another means of caster adjustment, Fig. 50-13. Elongated bolt holes are provided in the chassis frame where the upper control arm pivot shaft attaches. To make an adjustment, loosen the attaching bolts and move the shaft in or out

at the front or rear to tilt the steering axis forward or backward as required by the prescribed caster setting. See Fig. 50-13. Here again the same adjustment point is used for obtaining correct camber, so both angular adjustments should be made simultaneously.

Some cars have cam bolt adjustments located in the inner ends of the upper control arms, Fig. 50-14, or at the lower control arms. After loosening the lock nut, turn

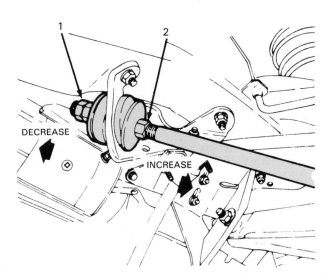

Fig. 50-12. Some cars use diagonal strut rods as a means of caster adjustment. Loosen lock nut 1, then turn adjusting nuts 2 in or out to move control arm forward or rearward. (American Motors Corp.)

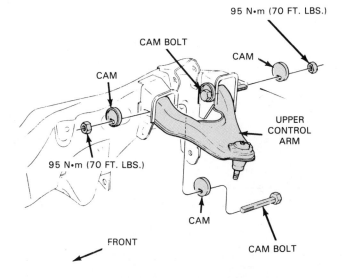

Fig. 50-14. Cam bolt adjustment at inner ends of upper control arm offers convenient way of positioning control arm to set correct caster and camber. (Oldsmobile Div., General Motors Corp.)

each cam bolt to reposition the control arm and obtain correct caster and camber settings. For least effect on camber, the correct caster setting can be obtained by turning the cams an equal amount in opposite directions.

ADJUSTING CAMBER

CAMBER is the angle formed by the true vertical centerline and the vertical centerline of the tire. See Fig. 50-1. Increase positive camber by moving the upper ball joint outward or lower ball joint inward. On cars with shims under the upper control arm pivot shaft bolts, add an equal number of shims under front and rear bolts to increase positive camber, remove an equal number of shims to decrease camber, Figs. 50-10 and 11. This adjustment must be made in conjunction with the caster adjustment to relate the angles to each other.

If the control arm pivot shaft is located inboard of the frame bracket, reverse the shimming procedure. Naturally, if the shims are located under the lower control arm pivot shaft, the opposite effects are obtained, so opposite shimming procedure must be followed.

Other types of camber adjustments that are integrated with caster settings (elongated bolt holes in chassis frame and cam bolts) must be adjusted with both caster and camber settings in mind. This means many trial-and-error settings are necessary, although several car manufacturers and equipment manufacturers provide detailed charts giving the number of shims or amount of cam bolt rotation necessary to obtain a given degree of correction.

CORRECTING TOE-IN

TOE-IN is the amount in fractions of an inch or degree that the front (or rear) wheels are closer together in front

than at the rear. It is often measured by means of a calibrated trammel bar extended at hub height between the wheel and tire assemblies with the wheels in the straight ahead position. More precise "toe" measurements can be made with the latest sophisticated alignment equipment, Fig. 50-15.

Most cars utilize two adjustable tie rods to facilitate the "toe" adjustment. See Fig. 50-16. To make the adjustment, loosen the clamp bolts on the tie rod sleeves

Fig. 50-15. Checks for toe-in and toe-out on turns are an important part of wheel alignment troubleshooting. (Ammco Tools, Inc.)

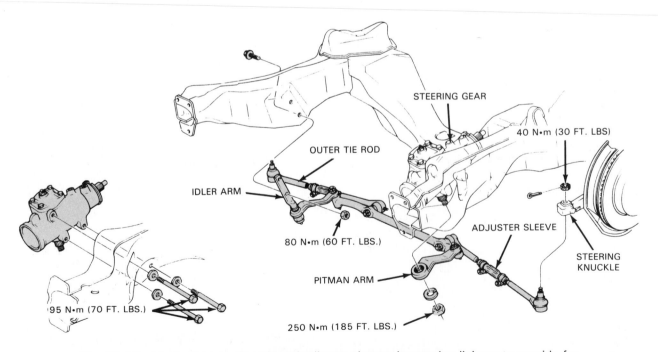

Fig. 50-16. Most cars use tie rods and adjuster sleeves in steering linkage to provide for toe-in adjustment and centering of steering wheel. (Oldsmobile Div., General Motors Corp.)

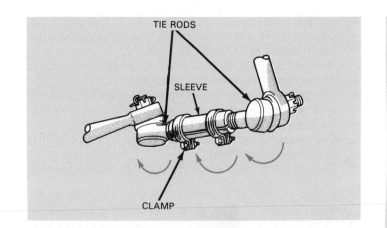

Fig. 50-17. Tie rod sleeves permit adjustment of toe-in. After making adjustment, place clamp opening away from sleeve slot and position clamp bolt at or near bottom to avoid interference. (Chrysler Corp.)

and turn the sleeves to adjust tie rod length, Fig. 50-17. A tie rod behind the front wheels must be lengthened to increase toe-in; a tie rod ahead of the front wheels must be shortened.

However, tie rod adjustment also controls the position of the steering wheel. Make the "centering" adjustment after correct toe-in has been established. Turn each tie rod adjusting sleeve to shorten or lengthen each tie rod an equal amount to center the steering wheel without disturbing the toe-in adjustment.

In some cases, alignment spacers are specified to be in place during the toe-in adjustment. In others, the spacers are removed and the car must be correct curb weight before the adjustment can be made.

CHECKING STEERING AXIS INCLINATION

STEERING AXIS INCLINATION is the angle formed by the true vertical centerline and the centerline of the upper and lower ball joints. It is created by the inward tilt of the steering knuckle and is not adjustable. If steering axis inclination is out of specifications, replace the steering knuckle and check all alignment factors.

TOE-OUT ON TURNS

TOE-OUT ON TURNS is the variation in the respective turning angles of the front wheels to avoid side slip on turns. It is built into the steering arms and is not adjustable. To get comparative readings, place the car on floating turntables, with weight of car on wheels. Set the inside wheel to a 20 deg. turn, then check the reading of the outside wheel against specifications.

Repeat this check with the wheels turned in the opposite direction. If all other angles are correct and toe-out on turns is not, replace the steering arm on the side that is out of specifications.

Straightening or welding of parts should not be attempted. Bending of parts when cold may cause stresses and cracks. Straightening by heat will destroy the original heat treatment. Welding will change the grain structure of the metal.

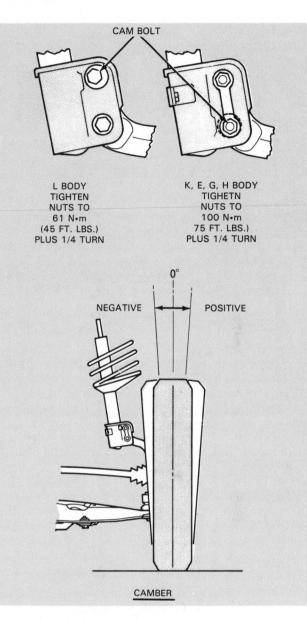

Fig. 50-18. Camber on Chrysler front wheel drive cars can be adjusted by means of a cam bolt at base of front suspension struts. Note design differences between models in upper views.

FRONT WHEEL DRIVE-ALIGNMENT

The design requirements for driving a vehicle by way of the engine, transaxle, and half shafts have resulted in certain changes in how front wheel alignment angles are adjusted. In some late model front wheel drive (FWD) cars, caster and camber are not adjustable. In others, only camber and toe-in can be adjusted.

CHRYSLER CORPORATION FWD CARS

Chrysler Corporation FWD cars, for example, feature cam bolt camber adjustment at the base of the front suspension struts. See Fig. 50-18. The caster angle cannot be adjusted. Chrysler warns that no parts should be heated or bent in order to attain alignment.

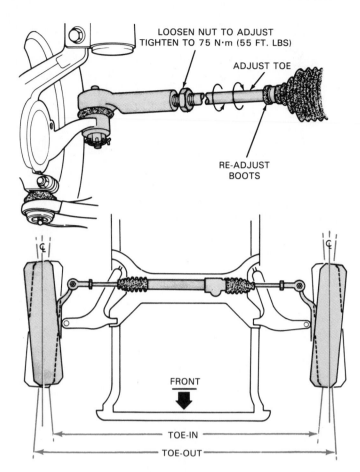

To adjust camber and toe-in:
1. Loosen cam and through bolts (each side) at strut lower housing. See Fig. 50-18.
2. Rotate cam bolt to move top of wheel in or out to obtain specified amount of camber.
3. Tighten cam and through bolts to recommend torque value.
4. Recheck camber setting.
5. Center steering wheel and hold it in place with a steering wheel clamp.
6. Loosen tie rod lock nuts, Fig. 50-19, and rotate rods to obtain specified amount of toe-in.
7. Readjust clamped end of boots if twisted during adjustment.
8. Tighten tie rod lock nuts to specified torque value.
9. Remove steering wheel clamp.

FORD MOTOR COMPANY FWD CARS

Front wheel caster and camber are not adjustable on Ford compact and subcompact front wheel drive cars. The following measuring procedure is given for diagnostic purposes only:
1. Make caster measurement on left side by turning left wheel through prescribed angle of sweep.
2. Check right side caster measurement by turning right wheel through prescribed angle of sweep.
   NOTE: If you use alignment equipment designed to measure caster on both left and right sides, turning left wheel through prescribed angle of sweep will result in an error in caster angle for right wheel.

When measuring toe-in on a front wheel drive Ford car equipped with power steering:

Fig. 50-19. Toe-in on Chrysler front wheel drive cars can be adjusted by loosening lock nuts and rotating tie rods.

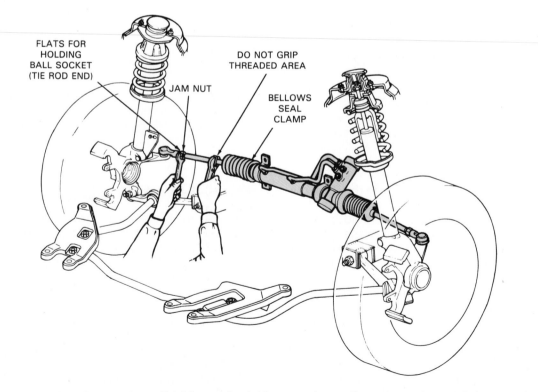

Fig. 50-20. To adjust toe-in on Ford front wheel drive cars, loosen jam nuts and rotate left and right tie rods to obtain toe-in measurements at each wheel equal to one-half of total toe-in specification.

1. Start engine.
2. Move steering wheel back and forth two or three times, then place wheel in straight ahead position.
3. Turn off engine and lock steering wheel in place, using a steering wheel holder.
4. Loosen small outer clamp on steering gear boot and slide if off of boot (to prevent boot from twisting).
5. Loosen jam nuts and adjust left and right tie rods, Fig. 50-20, until each wheel has one-half of toe-in specification.
6. Tighten jam nuts and remove steering wheel holder.

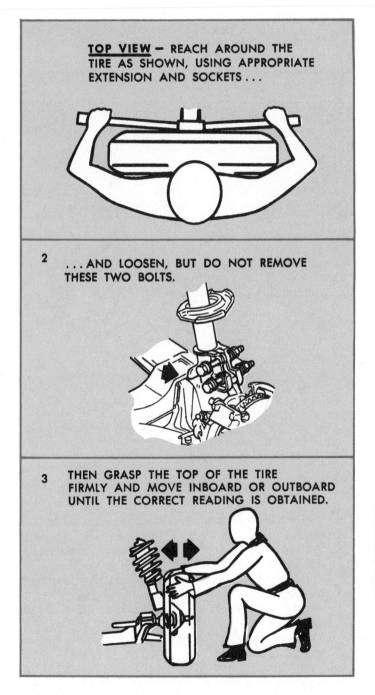

Fig. 50-21. Procedure for adjusting camber on front wheel drive Buicks is shown and described. Final step is to torque tighten bolts and nuts to manufacturer's specification to retain correct camber setting.

GENERAL MOTORS X-CARS

Only front wheel camber and toe-in are adjustable on General Motors X-cars.

To adjust camber:

1. Place vehicle on alignment equipment.
2. Reach around both sides of front wheel and tire assembly, Fig. 50-21, and loosen both strut knuckle bolts just enough to permit movement between strut and knuckle.
3. Grasp top of tire and move it in and out until correct camber reading is obtained.
4. Adjust torque of either or both strut knuckle bolts to allow slight movement between strut and knuckle yet hold correct camber reading while wheel assembly is removed.
5. Again reach around tire and tighten both bolts to specified torque, typically 140 ft. lb. (190 N·m). NOTE: If inaccessibility of bolts prevents application of full torque, remove wheel and tire assembly and apply specified torque.
6. Reinstall wheel and tire assembly.
7. Repeat this camber adjusting procedure on other front wheel.

To adjust toe-in:

1. Position car on alignment equipment and install toe-in measuring device. See Fig. 50-22.
2. Jounce front bumper three times, then clamp steering wheel in straight ahead position.
3. Loosen jam nuts on tie rods.
4. Remove clamps on tie rod boots, if so equipped.
5. Rotate tie rods to obtain specified toe-in per wheel.
6. Tighten jam nuts.
7. Adjust boots to relieve twisting, then install tie rod boot clamps.

Fig. 50-22. This alignment equipment mounts on front wheels and contains instrumentation that measures wheel angularity and transmits data to twin banks of test meters. (FMC)

Fig. 50-23. Latest total alignment equipment aligns all four wheels to a common vehicle centerline. All wheels are referenced to each other. (Hunter Engineering Corp.)

REAR WHEEL ALIGNMENT

While a basic check of "rear wheel tracking" has always been a part of the steering alignment procedure, front wheel drive and four wheel drive have put much greater emphasis on this phase of the procedure. Now, some car manufacturers furnish specifications for rear wheel camber and toe-in. In addition, and of key importance to four wheel alignment, the rear wheels MUST follow directly in line (track) with the front wheels.

Special equipment is available for checking the alignment of all four wheels. Usually, this type of test equipment uses front wheel projection and rear wheel instruments, Fig. 50-23, to measure alignment angles of each wheel relative to the vehicle thrust line.

As the alignment adjustments are made, light beams are projected on charts to guide the mechanic in making the specified settings. See Fig. 50-24. Toe-in readings, for example, are magnified five times. They are shown in both degrees and inches. As a result, angular adjustments can be made to precise settings and locked in place.

The special four wheel alignment equipment actually is a diagnostic tool. For example, it will quickly reveal the cause for abnormal rear tire wear, whether the vehicle is front wheel drive or rear wheel drive.

CHRYSLER REAR WHEEL ALIGNMENT

If special equipment is not available, Chrysler advises that the following procedure can be used to check conventional (rear wheel drive) vehicles for a bent or shifted rear axle housing.

1. Raise both rear wheels off floor, using a frame contact hoist.

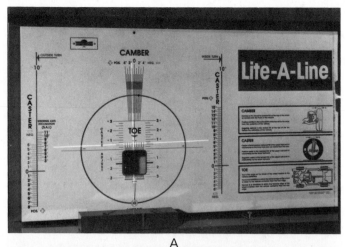

A

B

Fig. 50-24. As adjustments are made to correct alignment, results are projected on a calibrated chart A or specifications are programmed into a computer B.

2. Place a 1 in. long piece of masking tape at center of each rear tire tread as a reference marker.
3. Position tires with both reference marks pointing to front of vehicle, then measure distance between outside edges of tape.
4. Record this measurement as "front of tire reading" or (FTR).
5. Rotate rear wheels so that reference marks point to rear of vehicle.
6. Measure distance between outside edges of two pieces of tape.
7. Record measurements as "rear of tire reading (RTR)."
8. Subtract RTR from FTR to obtain "toe" of axle being checked. Chrysler specification is 1/16 in. (1.6 mm) toe-in to 3/16 in. (4.8 mm) toe-out.
9. Rotate both rear wheels so that reference marks are pointing down.

10. Measure distance between outside of two pieces of tape.
11. Record this measurement as ''bottom of tire reading'' (BTR).
12. Average sum of FTR and RTR. From this average, subtract BTR to obtain existing camber reading. Chrysler specification is 1/16 in. (1.6 mm) to in. (2.4 mm).
13. Equation is: $\dfrac{FTR + RTR}{2} - BTR = \pm$ Camber

    NOTE: If BTR is smaller than average figure, camber is positive ($+$). If BTR is larger than average figure, camber reading is negative.
14. Lower hoist.

BUICK REAR WHEEL ALIGNMENT

Buick Motor Division provides points of camber adjustment at the rear strut and knuckle assemblies. The toe-in adjustment is made by shortening or lengthening the tie rods. Both rear camber and toe adjustments are shown in Fig. 50-25.

To adjust rear wheel camber:
1. Normalize suspension by jouncing front and rear bumpers up and down several times.
2. Install alignment equipment according to equipment manufacturer's directions.
3. Loosen strut-to-knuckle mounting nuts.
4. Install camber adjusting tool, Fig. 50-25.
5. Tighten or loosen camber adjusting screw on tool as required to set camber to manufacturer's specification.
6. With camber set, tighten strut-to-knuckle nuts to correct torque tightness: typically 144 ft. lb. (195 N·m).
7. Remove camber adjusting tool.
8. Install tool on ''other'' strut and knuckle assembly and repeat camber adjusting steps 1 to 5.

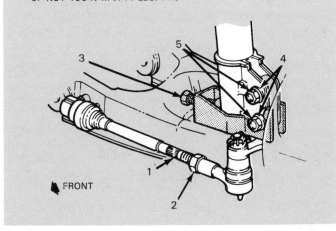

1. TURN TIE ROD TO ADJUST TOE
2. LOCK NUT, TORQUE TO 65 N·m (48 LBS. FT.)
3. J-29862
4. WASHERS
5. NUT 195 N·m (144 LBS. FT.)

FRONT

Fig. 50-25. Rear camber and toe adjusting points on certain General Motors cars. 1—Turn tie rod to adjust toe. 2—Tighten lock nut. 3—Turn camber tool adjusting screw to set camber. 4—Washers. 5—Torque tighten strut-to-knuckle nuts.

To adjust rear wheel ''toe'':
1. Loosen lock nut at both rear tie rod ends, Fig. 50-25. NOTE: Left and right side toe must be set separately ''per wheel.''
2. Adjust ''toe'' by turning inner tie rod. NOTE: Make sure boot is not twisted.
3. Adjust toe link to full toe-out position, then adjust inward to obtain correct setting.
4. Tighten lock nut on both tie rod ends to 48 ft. lb. (65 N·m).
5. Repeat toe adjusting steps 1 to 4 on ''other'' side.

ALIGNMENT TROUBLESHOOTING

Proper steering control depends on more than just the steering system. Suspension and wheel alignment contribute so much to steering that all three must be considered when troubleshooting car handling complaints.

Bear in mind that the car, load, and passengers must be balanced above the tires and springs while the vehicle is being subjected to many and varied driving conditions. This weight on the wheels moves up and down with road irregularities, tends to go sideways from the action of centrifugal force and wind pressures, and alternately shifts forward and backward under acceleration and braking. Or, there may be an unequal distribution of load because of engine torque reaction on the frame, uneven passenger loading, or uneven cargo loading.

Usually there is no quick easy remedy for a given handling problem. A series of causes and effects must be analyzed with due regard for the alignment theories involved. Often a combination of minor defects adds up to more serious trouble.

The following alignment troubleshooting checklist gives some of the more common causes of car handling problems.

Shimmy or Wheel Tramp
1. Incorrect or unequal tire pressures.
2. Cupped, eccentric, or bulged tires.
3. Unbalanced wheels.
4. Out-of-round wheel or brake drum.
5. Weak or inoperative shock absorbers.
6. Loose wheel bearing adjustment.
7. Incorrect front wheel alignment, particularly caster.
8. Loose or worn control arm bushings.
9. Loose or worn suspension ball joints.
10. Loose or worn steering linkage.
11. Loose steering gear on frame.
12. Loose steering gear adjustment.
13. Inoperative stabilizer.
14. Loose or worn strut bushings.

Hard or Rough Ride
1. High air pressure in tires.
2. Wrong type or size of tire.
3. Tight steering gear adjustment.
4. Incorrect wheel alignment, particularly caster.
5. Inoperative shock absorbers.
6. Overloaded or unevenly loaded vehicle.
7. Sagging or broken spring.
8. Lack of lubrication of front suspension or steering linkage.

Car Leads to One Side
1. Unequal tire pressures.
2. Varied tire sizes.
3. Unevenly loaded vehicle.
4. Dragging front brakes.
5. Tight front wheel bearings.
6. Bent spindle, spindle arm, or steering knuckle.
7. Incorrect or uneven front wheel alignment.
8. Loose strut bushings.
9. Sagging or broken front spring.
10. Inoperative shock absorber.
11. Broken or off-center rear spring center bolt.
12. Shifted rear axle housing.
13. Out-of-line frame or underbody.
14. Damaged rear suspension components.

Wander to Either Side
1. Incorrect or uneven tire pressures.
2. Varied tire sizes or excessive wear.
3. Unmatched tire construction.
4. Overloaded or unevenly loaded vehicle.
5. Tight front wheel bearing adjustment.
6. Bent spindle, spindle arm, or steering knuckle.
7. Incorrect front wheel alignment.
8. Tight suspension ball joints.
9. Binding control arm shafts.
10. Tight idler arm bushing.
11. Loose, worn or damaged steering linkage.
12. Loose steering gear on frame.
13. Incorrect steering gear adjustment.
14. Inoperative shock absorbers.
15. Broken rear spring center bolt.

Rear Suspension Out of Line
1. Broken or off-center rear spring canter bolt.
2. Mislocated rear spring front hanger.
3. Shifted rear axle housing.
4. Bent lower control arm.
5. Out-of-line frame or underbody.

Uneven Tire Tread Wear
1. Incorrect tire pressures.
2. Failure to rotate tires.
3. Incorrect front wheel alignment, partiacularly camber and toe-in.
4. Excessivae wheel runout.
5. Bent spindle, spindle arm, or steering knuckle.
6. Grabbing brakes.
7. Loose, worn or damaged suspension parts.
8. Excessive speed on turns.

Tire Squeal on Turns
1. Low air pressure in tires.
2. Varied tire sizes.
3. Bent spindle, spindle arm, or steering knuckle.
4. Incorrect front wheel alignment, particularly toe-in.
5. Loose or weak shock absorbers.

Tire Vibration
1. Wheel and tire assembly imbalance.
2. Wheel and tire assembly runout.
3. Incorrectly adjusted front wheel bearings.
4. Loose or worn suspension or steering components.

5. Worn or defective tires.
6. Rotor or brake drum runout.

Noise in System
1. Loose front wheel bearing adjustment.
2. Loose shock absorber mountings.
3. Loose steering gear adjustment.
4. Loose steering gear on frame.
5. Worn steering linkage.
6. Worn control arm bushings.
7. Loose suspension strut bushings.
8. Insufficient suspension ball joint lubriacation.
9. Worn idler arm bushings.
10. Loose or worn spring shackles.
11. Loose or worn stabilizer bushings.

Chapter 50—REVIEW QUESTIONS
WHEEL ALIGNMENT CORRECTIONS

Write your answers on a separate sheet of paper. Do not write in this book.

1. The need for frequent and regular wheel alignment checks has _____ (increased/decreased) with technological advances.
2. Wheel alignment should be checked at the first sign of _____ tread wear.
3. Generally, the three key wheel alignment angles should be checked in the following order:
   a. Camber, caster, and toe-in.
   b. Caster, camber, and toe-in.
   c. Toe-in, caster, and camber.
   d. Toe-in, camber, and caster.
4. With today's emphasis on front wheel drive cars, _____ and _____ wheel alignment procedures were found to be necessary.
5. Some front wheel drive cars are prone to problems in the area of _____.
   a. Shimmy or wheel tramp.
   b. Leading to one side.
   c. Wander.
   d. Tracking.
6. Ordinarily, cars should be checked for alignment at curb height or _____ height.
7. In most applications, the adjustment of front wheel roller bearings calls for end play. True or False?
8. Use a _____ to check each front wheel and tire assembly for runout.
   a. Wheel balancer.
   b. Dial indicator.
   c. Straightedge.
   d. Feeler gage.
9. Test action and rebound of _____ by jouncing car an equal number of times from center of bumpers.
10. Explain the "wet tread" test for rear wheel tracking.
11. Incorrect front suspension height can be corrected on Chrysler cars by:
    a. Installing new coil springs.
    b. Installing new shock absorbers.

c. Adjusting torsion bars.

d. Adjusting MacPherson struts.

12. Name two common caster adjusting points.

13. How is toe-in adjusted?

   a. Shortening or lengthening tie rods.

   b. Shimming control arms.

   c. Shortening or lengthening strut rods.

   d. Turning cam bolts.

14. A car was found to have shimmy or wheel tramp during a road test. Mechanic A said it could be caused by incorrect front wheel alignment, particularly caster. Mechanic B said it could be caused by unbalanced wheels. Who is right?

   a. Mechanic A.

   b. Mechanic B.

   c. Both mechanic A and mechanic B.

   d. Neither mechanic A nor mechanic B.

15. A car owner complained of a hard or rough ride. Mechanic A said it could be caused by inoperative shock absorbers. Mechanic B said it could be caused by excessive wheel runout. Who is right?

   a. Mechanic A.

   b. Mechanic B.

   c. Both mechanic A and mechanic B.

   d. Neither mechanic A nor mechanic B.

Each of the following wheel alignment procedures relates to one of the four answers given.

16. To adjust rear wheel toe-in on a front wheel drive car: Loosen lock nuts at both rear tie rod ends. Adjust toe link to full toe-out position, then adjust inward to obtain correct setting.

   a. Chrysler.

   b. Buick.

   c. Ford.

   d. GM X-cars.

17. To adjust toe-in of front wheels on a front wheel drive car: Lock steering wheel in straight-ahead position. Loosen clamp on steering gear boot. Loosen jam nuts and adjust left and right tie rods until each wheel has one-half of toe-in specification.

   a. Chrysler.

   b. Buick.

   c. Ford.

   d. GM X-cars.

18. To adjust front wheel camber on a front wheel drive car: Loosen cam and through bolts at strut lower housing. Rotate cam bolt to move top of wheel in or out to obtain correct setting.

   a. Chrysler.

   b. Buick.

   c. Ford.

   d. GM X-cars.

19. To adjust rear wheel camber on a front wheel drive car: Loosen strut-to-knuckle mounting nuts. Install camber adjusting tool. Turn adjusting screw on tool to left or right to obtain correct setting.

   a. Chrysler.

   b. Buick.

   c. Ford.

   d. GM X-cars.

20. To adjust front wheel camber on a front wheel drive car: Reach around both sides of wheel and tire assembly. Loosen both strut knuckle bolts just enough to permit movement between strut and knuckle. Grasp top of tire and move it in or out until correct setting is obtained.

   a. Chrysler.

   b. Buick.

   c. Ford.

   d. GM X-cars.

This self-contained alignment equipment attaches to front wheels and features built-in, direct reading test instruments. (Bear Automotive)

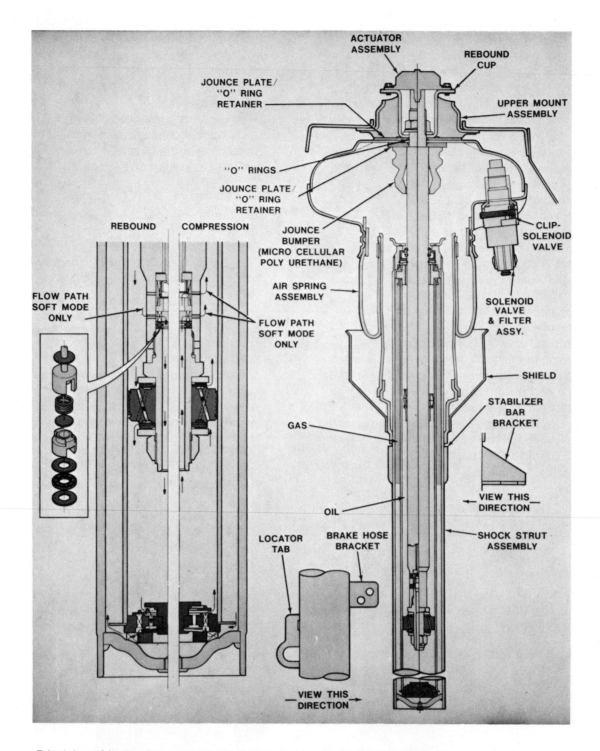

Principles of hydraulics and pneumatics are put to use in a four wheel air suspension system. Air springs and MacPherson struts are utilized. Air pressure in springs is monitored and adjusted by a microcomputer to keep car level. Shock struts are filled with oil and gas. Valves control oil flow to provide damping action.   (Ford Motor Co.)

Chapter 51

HYDRAULICS AND PNEUMATICS

After studying this chapter, you will be able to:
- Give examples of the principles of hydraulics.
- Cite the advantages of hydraulic systems.
- Define pressure and force.
- Describe various automotive applications of hydraulic principles.
- Define pneumatics.
- Name various automotive applications of pneumatic systems.
- State Boyle's Law.
- State Charles' Law.

HYDRAULICS

The study of HYDRAULICS is important to the auto mechanic because so many parts of the automotive vehicle are operated by liquids under pressure, and in motion. For example, the conventional braking system used on passenger cars is of the hydraulic type, and the automatic transmission depends on hydraulics for its operation. Hydraulics also actuate the power steering system and shock absorbers.

In the automotive service field, hydraulic jacks, lifts, presses, and various body spreading and straightening devices are in daily use.

Technically, liquids and gases are considered as fluids. They do have many characteristics in common, but differ mainly in that liquids change but slightly when they are compressed. In addition, they have a free surface. Gases, however, are compressible and will fill all parts of the containing vessel.

The science of hydraulics includes:
1. The manner in which liquids act in tanks and pipes.
2. The laws of floating bodies, and the behavior of liquids on submerged surfaces.
3. The flow of liquids under various conditions and methods of directing this flow to do useful work.

In this text, however, the study will be limited primarily to hydraulics as applied in the automotive field.

ADVANTAGES OF HYDRAULIC SYSTEMS

Among the advantages of hydraulic systems are:
1. The elimination of complicated systems of gears, cams and rods.

2. Motion can be transmitted without slack or lost motion.
3. Liquids are not subjected to wear or breakage as is the case with mechanical parts.
4. Hydraulic systems require no lubrication.
5. Applied force can be greatly multiplied and transmitted considerable distances with negligible loss.

PHYSICAL PROPERTIES OF LIQUIDS

Liquids differ from solids in that they do not have a definite form of their own. They conform to the shape of the vessel in which they are contained. Because of their shapelessness, liquids can be carried in tubing by gravity or by applying force to them.

In general, liquids may be considered as being incompressible. In fact, a force of 15 lb. (66.7 N) on a cubic inch of water will compress it only 1/20,000, and it would take a force of 32 tons to reduce it 10 percent. When pressure is removed, the liquid immediately returns to its original volume.

TRANSMISSION OF FORCES

When force is applied to a confined liquid, it will be transmitted in ALL directions. This is one of the most important characteristics of liquids, and it is known as PASCAL'S LAW.

To make this clear, consider that when a metal bar is struck on the end, the force will be transmitted the length of the bar, Fig. 51-1. The more rigid the bar, the less force lost inside the bar or transmitted at right angles to the direction of the blow.

However, when a force is applied to the end of a confined liquid, Fig. 51-1, it is transmitted straight through to the other end (same as metal bar). In addition, however, the force is transmitted equally and undiminished in every direction (forward, backward, sideward) so that the containing vessel is literally filled with pressure at right angles to the containing surfaces.

To illustrate another hydraulic principle, pressure of a liquid standing in an open vessel is dependent on the depth of the liquid. This is known as the HYDRAULIC HEAD. Pressure due to the hydraulic head is also dependent on the weight of the liquid, which is known as the

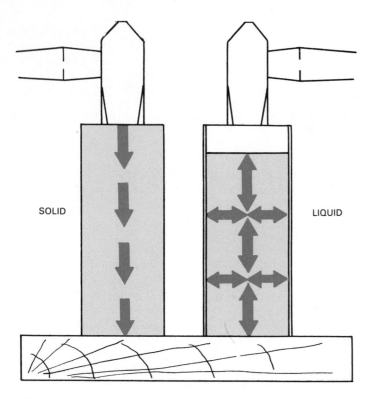

Fig. 51-1. Arrows illustrate difference in action of forces when a solid bar is struck and when a force is applied to end of confined liquid.

density of the liquid. DENSITY is the weight in pounds of a cubic inch or cubic foot of the liquid. Water weighs 62.36 lb. per cu. ft. or .036 lb. per cu. in. Heavy petroleum oil weighs .032 lb. per cu. in. and light oil .029 lb. per cu. in.

In the example illustrated in Fig. 51-2, the water would have to be 222 in. deep to exert a pressure of 8 psi (pounds per square inch). In the case of heavy oil, it would have to be 252 in. deep.

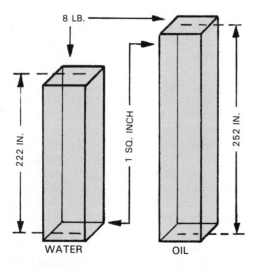

Fig. 51-2. As an illustration of affect of density on pressure, a 222 in. column of water and 252 in. column of oil produce same pressure.

SPECIFIC GRAVITY

SPECIFIC GRAVITY (sp. gr.) is a common method of comparing liquids. It is the ratio of the weight of a unit volume of that substance (its density) to the weight of 1 cu. in. of water. Since the weight may vary with temperature changes, the measurement is always made at 39.1 °F or 4 °C.

Therefore, the specific gravity of water is 1.0. The 1.0 becomes the standard for specific gravity against which all other liquids are measured. For example, the weight of a cubic inch of water is .036 lb., while the weight of a typical hydraulic brake fluid used in an automobile is .0357 lb. per cu. in. The specific gravity of the fluid is obtained by dividing .0357 by .036, which equals 0.99 sp. gr.

In automotive service work, specific gravity is used in testing antifreeze solutions to determine at what temperature the solution in the cooling system will freeze. It is also used in measuring the state of charge in a starting battery.

HYDROMETERS

To measure the specific gravity of a solution, an instrument known as a hydrometer is used, Fig. 51-3. The hydrometer consists of a glass tube that contains a calibrated float. The fluid to be measured is drawn into the glass tube by means of a rubber suction bulb. Then, the height of the float at the surface of the liquid is a mesurement of its specific gravity. See inset in Fig. 51-3.

PRESSURE AND FORCE

According to Pascal's Law, any force applied to a confined liquid is transmitted equally in all directions through the liquid regardless of the shape of the container. In Fig.

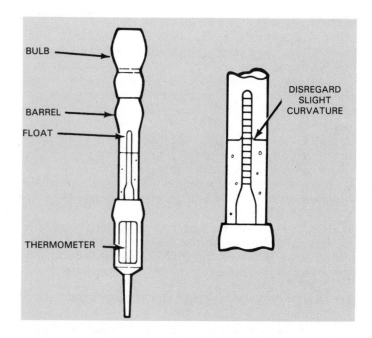

Fig. 51-3. Example of a hydrometer used to measure specific gravity of electrolyte solution in a storage battery.

51-4, when a force is applied to piston No. 1, pressure created throughout the entire system will act at right angles to all surfaces with equal strength.

FORCE is the strength or power exerted on an object. PRESSURE is defined as the force divided by the area over which it is distributed. In the case illustrated in Fig. 51-4, the force applied at piston No. 1 is 100 lb. Since the area of the piston is 10 sq. in., then the pressure is 100 divided by 10 or 10 psi.

This pressure of 10 psi is exerted over the entire system; on the sides as well as on piston No. 2, which is at the greatest distance from piston No. 1. Since the vessel containing the fluid is of uniform cross section, and both pistons have the same area, the upward force on piston No. 2 is the same as the force applied to piston No. 1. What has been done is to change the direction of the force from downward at piston No. 1 to upward at piston No. 2.

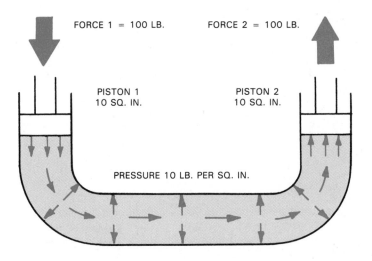

Fig. 51-4. Force applied to a fluid in a confined system is transmitted equally in all directions throughout system, regardless of its shape.

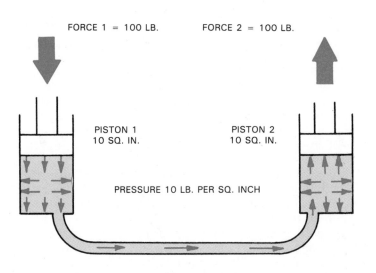

Fig. 51-5. Shape and size of connecting tube has no effect on pressure in cylinders.

Although the system shown in Fig. 51-4 has a uniform cross section, this is not a necessary requirement if you want the same force available at the output side as applied at the input side. Because of Pascal's Law, the connection between piston No. 1 and piston No. 2 can be any shape or size. This hydraulic principle is made clear in Fig. 51-5, where the connection between the two pistons is a tube of smaller diameter than the pistons.

MULTIPLYING THE FORCE

In the examples shown so far, there has been no increase in force at the output piston because it has been the same size as the input piston. However, if the output piston is larger than the input piston, the force will be increased in the same proportion as the areas of the two pistons. For example, in Fig. 51-6, piston No. 1 (input) has an area of 2 sq. in., while the area of piston No. 2 (output) is 20 sq. in.

If a force of 20 lb. is applied to piston No. 1, the pressure on the liquid will be 10 psi (20 lb. divided by 2 sq. in. equals 10 psi). Since this pressure acts equally throughout the system, there will be 10 psi acting on piston No. 2. Its area, however, is 20 sq. in., so the total force on that piston will be 200 lb. (20 sq. in. times 10 psi equals 200 lb.).

The system shown in Fig. 51-6 could also be used in a reverse manner. It could be used to reduce force rather than increase it.

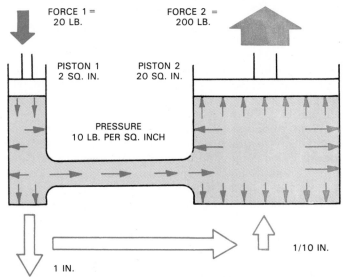

Fig. 51-6. Forces can be multiplied if output piston is larger than input piston.

MOVEMENT OF LIQUID

In the examples given in Figs. 51-4 and 51-5, the areas of the pistons are equal. Therefore, if one piston is moved down 1 in., the other piston will move up a corresponding amount. Since liquid is virtually incompressible, the liquid displaced by the first piston must have some place to go, and it can move only by displacing the second piston an equal amount.

Applying this to the system shown in Fig. 51-6, pushing piston No. 1 down 1 in., will displace 2 cu. in. of liquid. To accommodate this volume of liquid, piston No. 2 will have to move 0.10 in. The volume of fluid 2 cu. in. divided by the area of the piston 20 sq. in. equals 0.10 in. movement of the piston.

APPLICATION OF HYDRAULIC PRINCIPLES

These principles of hydraulics have wide application in the automotive industry. By proper application of these principles, heavy vehicles can be stopped with ease, and jacks are designed so that a small child can raise a heavy truck. The special application of hydraulics to automatic transmissions is discussed in the transmission chapters of this text.

HYDRAULIC BRAKES

The modern hydraulic brake system is an application of multiple outlet pistons (wheel cylinders or disc brake calipers), which distribute forces applied at the foot pedal and transmitted by the master input cylinder.

In four-wheel drum brake applications, the master cylinder in which the input piston moves is connected by tubing to a cylinder at each wheel. Generally, each of these cylinders contains two opposed pistons, and each piston operates a brake shoe. When force is applied at the brake pedal, pressure is transmitted equally throughout the fluid to each of the wheel cylinders. As a result, all of the wheel cylinders are moved outward, forcing the brake shoes against the brake drums.

If the force applied at the master cylinder is 800 lb., and the cylinder area is .8 sq. in., pressure in the brake system would be 800 x .8 or 1000 psi. Then, if the wheel cylinder piston area is .9 sq. in., the output force would be 1000 x .9 or 900 lb.

When the pressure is removed from the brake pedal, springs on the brake shoes force the shoes back to their normal released position. This movement of the shoes, in turn, forces the pistons inward, returning the fluid to the master cylinder reservoir.

This description covers the operation of a simple hydraulic brake with all wheel cylinders of the same diameter. In some instances, the wheel cylinders have stepped diameters with a large piston operating the forward shoe and a smaller piston operating the rear shoe of a single brake. This type of construction is discussed in the chapter on brakes.

The principle of operation of the floating or sliding caliper disc brake is to allow the fluid pressure to build up between the bottom of the piston and the bottom of the cylinder bore. Pressure on the piston forces the inboard shoe and lining against the inboard rotor surface. Pressure against the bottom of the bore causes the caliper to float or slide on mounting bolts or sleeves, Fig. 51-7, forcing the outboard lining against the outboard rotor surface. Then, as line pressure continues to build up, the clamping action of the friction surfaces stops the rotor and the vehicle.

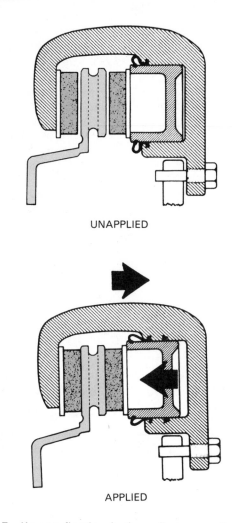

UNAPPLIED

APPLIED

Fig. 51-7. Key to floating brake caliper operation is when hydraulic pressure on bottom of cylinder bore causes caliper to float sideways and apply brake pads to rotor surfaces.

HYDRAULIC JACKS

A schematic drawing of the principle used in the operation of hydraulic jacks is shown in Fig. 51-8. In the illustration, the small piston (where force is applied) has an area of 5 sq. in. Its cylinder is connected to a large cylinder with a piston having an area of 250 sq. in. This large piston supports the platform used to raise the load.

If a force of 25 lb. is applied to the small piston, a pressure of 5 psi will be produced in the hydraulic fluid. This 5 psi will act over the entire area of the large piston with its 250 sq. in. surface. The resulting force will be 250 x 5 psi = 1250 lb. lifting force. The initial force of 25 lb. has been multiplied into a force capable of lifting more than one half ton.

Remember, however, that while the original force has been multiplied 50 times, the distance traveled is just the opposite. The large piston will travel only 1/50 as much as the small piston.

By way of explanation: if the small piston is moved 5 in., then 25 cu. in. of liquid will be displaced. Distributing this amount over 250 sq. in. of the larger piston, it will be raised 25 divided by 250 or 0.1 in. (1/50 of 5 in.)

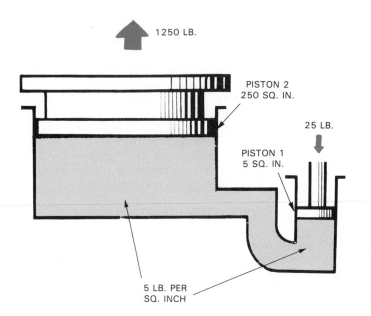

Fig. 51-8. Principle of hydraulic jack is based on multiplication of force applied at small piston.

To prevent the weight of the load on the platform from forcing the fluid back through the system, and to provide a means of lowering the load, it is necessary to include various valves in the hydraulic system, Fig. 51-9.

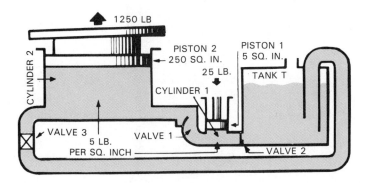

Fig. 51-9. Schematic drawing of hydraulic jack shows valving necessary to maintain load at desired height and also to permit load to be lowered when desired.

Chapter 51
REVIEW QUESTIONS—HYDRAULICS

Write your answers on a separate sheet of paper. Do not write in this book.

1. Define hydraulics.
2. Give three examples of the use of hydraulics in automotive systems.
3. Name four major advantages of a hydraulic system.
4. State Pascal's Law.
5. Liquids may be considered incompressible. True or False?
6. "Hydraulic head" is based on the principle that pressure of a liquid standing in an open vessel is dependent on the _____ of the liquid and the _____ of the liquid.
7. _____ is the weight in pounds of a cubic inch or a cubic foot of liquid.
8. _____ is the ratio of the weight of a unit volume of a substance to the weight of one cubic inch of water.
   a. Specific gravity.
   b. Hydraulic head.
   c. Hydraulic pressure.
   d. Hydraulic force.
9. In vessels containing fluid, if the output piston is larger than the input piston, the force will be _____ (increased or decreased) in the same proportion as the areas of the two pistons.
10. Define pressure as applied to a hydraulic system.
11. What automotive "assembly" depends on specific gravity for its operation?
12. In hydraulic brake operation, when force is applied at the brake pedal, pressure is transmitted _____ throughout the fluid to the wheel cylinders and caliper cylinders.
13. What is the weight of a cubic foot of water?
   a. 31.18 lb.
   b. 46.77 lb.
   c. 54.57 lb.
   d. 62.36 lb.
14. If a force of 50 lb. is applied to a piston in a hydraulic cylinder of 2 sq. in. in area, what is the pressure?
   a. 25 psi.
   b. 50 psi.
   c. 100 psi.
   d. 200 psi.
15. In hydraulic jack operation, the input piston is _____ (smaller or larger) than the output piston.
16. In a hydraulic jack, the input piston has an area of 3 sq. in. and the output piston has an area of 300 sq. in. If 30 lb. of force is applied to the input piston, what is the lifting force of the output piston?
   a. 100 lb.
   b. 300 lb.
   c. 1000 lb.
   d. 3000 lb.

PNEUMATICS

PNEUMATICS is the study of the mechanical properties of air and other gases. It has many automotive applications, particularly in the study of carburetion, tires, and vehicle leveling systems. Air brakes are a major consideration in the trucking field.

Technically, air and other gases are considered fluids. They have many of the same characteristics as liquids, but differ mainly in that they are highly compressible and completely fill any containing vessel. Gases are the same as liquids in two ways: they conform to the shape of their containers; and pressure in a gas acts equally in all directions.

PRESSURE OF AIR AT SEA LEVEL

Air and any gas has weight. Therefore, pressure is exerted by virtue of its head; that is, the depth from its upper surfaces to its lower surface. Although any small volume of any gas weighs very little, the pressure of air at sea level under normal conditions amounts to 14.7 psi. The pressure, or the head, is the weight of the air from the surface of the earth to many miles up in space.

Since air is compressed by its own weight, the same volume of air at sea level will weigh considerably more than on a mountain top. In other words, air becomes less dense as altitude or distance from the earth increases.

This natural factor is particularly important because of its affect on carburetion. As altitude increases, less air enters the carburetor. Consequently, the mixture of fuel and air becomes richer. Instruments designed to measure the pressure of the atmosphere are known as "barometers." In most applications, they are used for forecasting weather and in measuring altitudes.

As pointed out, gases are compressed by their own weight. In addition, gases expand as their temperature increases, making a volume of gas at high temperature weigh less than the same volume of gas at low temperature. This particular property of gases is why the efficiency of an automobile decreases as the temperature of the air entering the carburetor increases.

EFFECT OF ATMOSPHERIC PRESSURE

Atmospheric pressures obey Pascal's Law in the same manner as liquids, Fig. 51-10. Atmospheric pressure acting on the surface of the gas is transmitted equally to the inner walls of the container, but it is balanced by the pressure on the outer walls.

In another example, the thinnest paper suspended in the atmosphere will not be torn, in spite of the fact that air pressure of 14.7 psi is pressing on it, Fig. 51-11. It is not torn because atmospheric pressure is exerted on both sides of the sheet and the pressures are balanced.

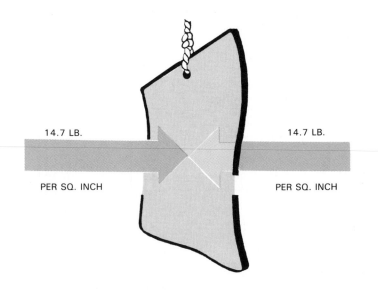

Fig. 51-11. Thin paper suspended in the atmosphere will not be torn because pressure of 14.7 psi is pressing on both sides.

In Fig. 51-12, atmospheric pressure acting on one piston is balanced by the same pressure acting on the surface of the other piston. The fact that the two pistons are of different areas makes no difference since the unit pressure (pressure per square inch) is the same on both pistons.

EFFECT OF VACUUM

Note, too, in Fig. 51-12, with equal atmospheric pressure acting on the two surfaces, the liquid will be at the same height in both sides of the U-shaped tube.

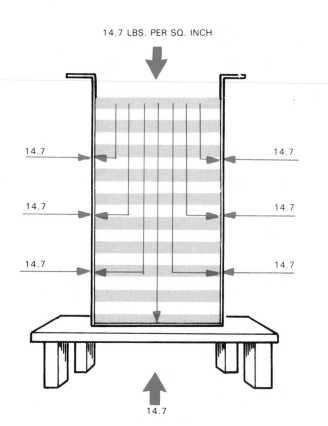

Fig. 51-10. Atmospheric pressure acting on surface of gas or liquid is transmitted equally throughout.

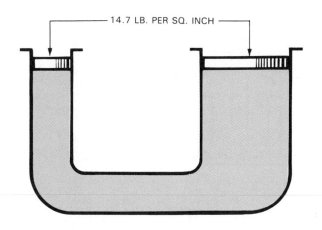

Fig. 51-12. Atmospheric pressure acting on one piston is balanced by same pressure acting on other piston.

If the pressure on one side of the tube is reduced, there will be a movement of liquid to the side of reduced pressure.

This effect can be illustrated by the familiar situation of drinking liquid through a straw, Fig. 51-13. Sucking on the straw disturbs the balance of pressures acting on the liquid. Pressure within the straw is reduced, as the result of suction, and atmospheric pressure (14.7 psi) acting on the surface of the liquid in the glass forces the liquid into the straw.

The liquid can be held at any desired level in the straw. This level will always be at a point where the pressure of the head of the liquid, Fig. 51-13, equals the difference between the pressure in the straw and that on the surface of the liquid.

Sucking on the straw has produced a partial vacuum on the surface of the liquid within the straw. A PARTIAL VACUUM is actually a pressure less than prevailing atmospheric pressure. Theoretically, the limit of this process would be a condition of zero pressure, or a complete vacuum. In actual practice, this condition is never attained.

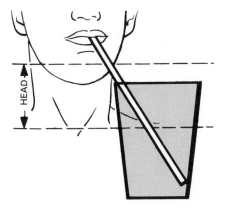

Fig. 51-13. When air pressure within straw falls below pressure of atmosphere, liquid is forced through straw.

This simple principle, illustrated by sucking liquid through a straw, is identical with that which is used in the operation of a conventional power brake, Fig. 51-14. Vacuum from the intake manifold is connected to one side of a cylinder. Atmospheric pressure on the other side causes a piston to move toward the vacuum side. This motion is used to apply the brakes.

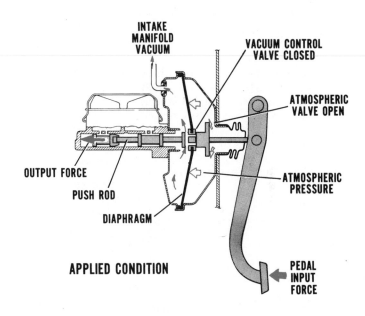

Fig. 51-14. This single diaphragm power brake booster utilizes difference in pressure between manifold vacuum and atmospheric pressure to operate master cylinder push rod and apply brakes. (Chrysler Corp.)

COMPRESSED AIR

Compressed air is air which has been forced into a smaller space than which it would ordinarily occupy in its free or atmospheric state. In the automotive field, compressed air has many uses. In addition to inflating tires, it is used for such purposes as spraying paint, blowing dirt and other foreign matter from parts, operating brakes on heavy trucks, and in powering impact tools and wrenches.

As mentioned, normal air (due to the weight of air above it) has a pressure of 14.7 psi. However, when speaking of compressed air, its initial pressure of 14.7 psi is ignored, and the pressure of the compressed air is given as the amount of pressure above atmospheric. In other words, a gauge for measuring the pressure of compressed air registers zero when connected only to the atmosphere.

By providing suitable piping, compressed air will "flow" in much the same manner as liquids flow through connecting pipes. For example, if one reservoir contains air under pressure, and another one contains air at atmospheric pressure, air will flow from the reservoir of higher pressure to that of lower pressure. This flow will continue until both reservoirs are at the same pressure.

AIR BRAKES

The application of compressed air in the operation of automotive air brakes is relatively simple. In Fig. 51-15, compressed air is admitted into a cylinder which encloses a piston. The force of the compressed air will cause the piston to move until it encounters a resistance equal to the force developed by the compressed air. For example, the piston in Fig. 51-15 has an area of 10 sq. in., while the compressed air has a pressure of 10 psi. The total force developed will be 10 x 10 or 100 psi. This is similar to the effect of hydraulic power illustrated in Figs. 51-4 and 51-6.

Remember that the quantity of air acting on the piston does not affect the force developed. The only factors involved are the air pressure and the area of the piston on which the air pressure is acting.

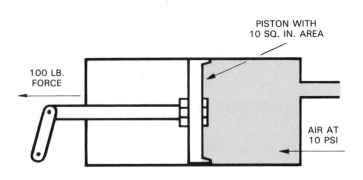

Fig. 51-15. Illustrating principle of a simple air brake.

PRINCIPLE OF THE SYPHON

Normal air pressure (atmospheric pressure) is used to do many kinds of work. For example, a syphon drains tanks by means of atmospheric pressure. In a syphon, a tube or pipe is connected to two tanks, one higher than the other. See Fig. 51-16. Once the connecting tube has been filled with liquid, it will continue to flow to the lower tank until the level of the liquid is the same in both tanks or until the upper tank is empty.

The force that causes the liquid to flow is the pressure of the atmosphere This pressure forces the liquid up the short arm of the syphon, AB. (Theoretically, water can be raised a height of 34 ft.) At higher altitudes, where air pressure is less than at sea level, the liquid would be raised a shorter distance.

The action of the syphon is interesting. The force of the atmosphere tending to push the liquid up the short arm of the syphon is opposed by downward pressure of the weight of the liquid. See AB in Fig. 51-16. Similarly, atmospheric pressure tends to drive the liquid up the long arm, CD. However, it is resisted by the weight of the liquid in CD, which is greater than in AB. So the atmospheric pressure meets greater resistance in pushing the liquid up CD than in pushing it in the opposite direction. The liquid will therefore flow up arm, AB, and continue until it reaches the lower reservoir.

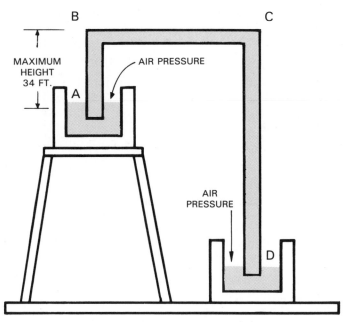

Fig. 51-16. Atmospheric pressure causes liquid in a syphon to flow from upper tank to lower tank.

VENTURI TUBE

The venturi tube is important in carburetion. A venturi is a tube with a restricted section. See Fig. 51-17. When a liquid or air is passed through a venturi tube, the speed of flow is increased at the area of restriction, and fluid pressure is decreased. The same amount or volume

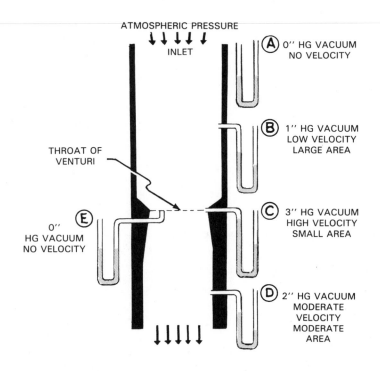

Fig. 51-17. Air moving in throat of venturi will have greatest velocity and maximum vacuum will exist, as shown at c. However, if airflow is stopped, vacuum becomes zero.

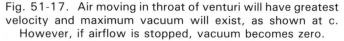

of air flows through all sections of the carburetor throat. Obviously, if the throat area decreases, the velocity must increase in order to maintain the same rate of flow. Then, when the area increases, the velocity will decrease.

This is clearly illustrated in Fig. 51-17, which shows how venturi action vacuum varies in different sections of the carburetor. Vacuum is measured in inches of mercury and designated as inches Hg (initials used in chemical symbol representing mercury). Note that vacuum and velocity of airflow are at a maximum at the point of maximum restriction. Also worth noting, vacuum is zero at the air inlet to the carburetor where air pressure is normal.

Venturi action is used in carburetors to maintain the correct air-fuel ratio throughout the range of speeds and loads of the engine.

BOYLE'S LAW

An important characteristic of air and other gases is explained in BOYLE'S LAW. It states that if the pressure on a gas in a confined space is doubled, the gas will be compressed to half its original volume, provided the temperature remains the same.

Boyle's Law is normally given as follows: If the temperature of a confined gas is kept constant, its volume will vary inversely with its pressure.

This may be expressed as follows:

$$P'V' = PV$$

P and V represent the pressure and volume of a gas before compression; P' and V' are the pressure and volume after compression.

EXAMPLE: The pressure of a quantity of gas is 50 psi, and it occupies 10 cu. ft. This air is compressed until it exerts a pressure of 75 psi while the temperature remains constant. What is the volume of the gas after compression?

$$\frac{V}{V'} = \frac{P'}{P}$$

$$\frac{75}{50} = \frac{10}{P}$$

$$75P = 500$$

$$P = 6.66 \text{ cu. ft.}$$

CHARLES' LAW

Another important law relating to the behavior of gases under different conditions is known as CHARLES' LAW. It states that under constant pressure, the volume of a gas varies directly with its absolute temperature. The absolute temperature is the temperature in °C plus 273. This law is expressed as follows:

$$\frac{V'}{V_2} = \frac{T'}{T_2}$$

V' is the volume of a gas when its absolute temperature is T' and V_2 is the volume of the same gas when its absolute temperature is T_2.

EXAMPLE: To what volume will 110 cu. ft. of gas at 15 deg. C. expand if heated at a constant pressure to 55 deg. C.?

$$T' = 15° + 273 = 288° \text{ absolute}$$
$$T_2 = 55° + 273 = 328° \text{ absolute}$$

$$\frac{110}{V_2} = \frac{288}{328}$$

$$36080 = 288V_2$$

$$V_2 = 125.3 \text{ cu. ft.}$$

An understanding of the principles of pneumatics is more important than ever to auto mechanics. Today's energy absorbing bumpers, passenger restraint systems, air pumps, vacuum door locks, and temperature control systems utilize those principles. See chapter on BUILT-IN SAFETY SYSTEMS.

Chapter 51
REVIEW QUESTIONS-PNEUMATICS

Write your answers on a separate sheet of paper. Do not write in this book.
1. Define pneumatics.
2. Technically, _____ and _____ are considered fluids.
3. What is the normal pressure of the atmosphere?
   a. 0.0
   b. 4.17 psi.
   c. 7.14 psi.
   d. 14.7 psi.
4. As altitude increases, _____ (more or less) air enters the carburetor.
5. What are the two major differences between a liquid and a gas?
6. What causes liquid to rise in a straw?
7. In a conventional power or booster brake on a passenger car, what power is used to assist the driver to apply the brakes?
8. What will a conventional gauge on a tank of compressed air register when the tank is open to the atmosphere?
   a. 0.0
   b. 4.17 psi.
   c. 7.14 psi.
   d. 14.7 psi.
9. Explain the principle of the syphon.
10. A venturi is a tube with a _____.
11. For what purpose is a venturi used in a carburetor?
12. In what area of the carburetor is airflow the fastest?
   a. At top of carburetor throat.
   b. At start of restricted section.
   c. At point of maximum restriction.
   d. At bottom of restricted section.
13. State Boyle's Law.
14. Charles' Law states that under constant pressure, the volume of a gas varies indirectly with _____.
15. Name three automotive applications of pneumatics.

Chapter 52

AUTOMOTIVE BRAKES

WARNING: BREATHING DUST CONTAINING ASBESTOS FIBERS CAN CAUSE SERIOUS BODILY HARM. ASBESTOS IS A KNOWN CARCINOGEN — A SUBSTANCE WHICH TENDS TO CAUSE CANCER. SINCE BRAKE AND CLUTCH FRICTION MATERIALS CONTAIN ASBESTOS, DO NOT CREATE AIRBORNE DUST BY GRINDING, SANDING, OR BY CLEANING THESE PARTS WITH A DRY BRUSH OR WITH COMPRESSED AIR. INSTEAD, WEAR A MASK WITH AN APPROVED FILTER AND FLUSH BRAKE AND CLUTCH PARTS WITH WATER OR USE A VACUUM SOURCE.

After studying this chapter, you will be able to:
- Explain the forces and factors involved when braking a vehicle.
- Describe brake system materials, hydraulic components, and mechanical parts.
- State how disc brakes and drum brakes operate.
- Describe how various power brake systems and anti-lock brake systems operate.
- Tell how to service brake hydraulic systems.
- Give steps of performing disc brake overhaul and drum brake overhaul.
- Solve brake troubleshooting problems.
- Give examples of power brake system and anti-lock brake system service operations.

An AUTOMOTIVE BRAKE MECHANISM is a friction device designed to change power into heat. When the brakes are applied, they convert the power of momentum of the moving vehicle (kinetic energy) into heat by means of friction. The BRAKE SYSTEM, then, is a balanced set of mechanical and hydraulic devices used to retard the motion of the vehicle by means of friction.

FRICTION

FRICTION is the resistance to relative motion between two bodies in contact. It is caused by the interlocking of projections and depressions of the two surfaces in contact. Therefore, there is less friction between polished surfaces than between rough surfaces.

Friction varies with different materials and with the condition of the materials. There is less friction between surfaces of different materials than between those of the same material. There is less friction when one surface (tire tread) rolls over the other (pavement) than when it slides.

COEFFICIENT OF FRICTION

The AMOUNT OF FRICTION created is proportional to the pressure between the two surfaces in contact. It is independent of the area of surface contact. The amount of friction developed by any two bodies in contact is said to be their COEFFICIENT OF FRICTION (C.O.F.).

The coefficient of friction is found by dividing the force required to slide the "weight" over the surface by the weight of the object. See example in Fig. 52-1. If a 60 lb. pull is required to slide a 100 lb. weight, then the C.O.F. would be 60 divided by 100 or .60. If only 35 lb. is required to slide the 100 lb. weight, then the C.O.F. would be .35.

It has been established that the coefficient of friction will change with any variation of the condition of the surfaces. Any lubricant, of course, will greatly reduce the C.O.F., which is why it is so important to keep any grease, oil, or brake fluid from brake lining. Even an extremely damp day will cause some variation in C.O.F.

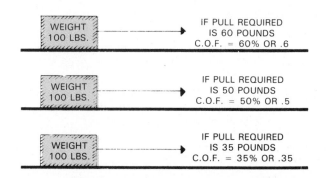

Fig. 52-1. Coefficient of friction is equal to force required to slide a body across a surface divided by weight of body.

BRAKING FORCES

Tremendous forces are involved when braking a vehicle. The vehicle must be brought to a stop in a much shorter time than is required to bring it up to speed. To better visualize this, compare horsepower required to accelerate a vehicle and horsepower needed to stop it.

A compact vehicle with a 75 hp four cylinder engine requires about 15 sec. to accelerate to 60 mph. The same vehicle is expected to be able to stop from 60 mph in not more than six sec. That is: the brakes must do the same amount of work as the engine, but 2 1/2 times faster.

EFFECT OF WEIGHT AND SPEED

The effect of weight and speed of the vehicle on braking is a big factor in heat generation in both passenger cars and trucks. If the weight of the vehicle is doubled, the energy of motion to be changed into heat energy is doubled. Also, the amount of heat to be absorbed and dissipated will be doubled. The effect of higher speeds on braking is even more serious. If the vehicle speed is doubled, four times as much stopping power must be developed. Also, the brake mechanisms must absorb and dissipate four times as much heat.

It follows that if both weight and speed of a vehicle are doubled, the stopping power must be increased eight times, and the brakes must absorb and dissipate eight times as much heat.

BRAKE TEMPERATURES

The amount of heat generated by brake applications usually is greater than the rate of heat absorption and dissipation by the brake mechanisms, and high brake temperatures result. Ordinarily, the time interval between brake applications avoids a heat buildup. If, however, repeated panic stops are made, temperatures may become high enough to damage the brake lining, Fig. 52-2, brake drums or rotors, and brake fluid. In extreme cases, the tires have been set on fire.

BRAKE AND TIRE FRICTION

When brakes are applied on a vehicle, the brake shoes and friction pads are forced into contact with the brake drums and rotors to slow the rotation of the wheels. Then, the friction between the tires and the road surface slows the speed of the vehicle.

However, friction between the shoes and drums and between the pads and rotors does not remain constant. Rather, it tends to increase with temperature. From tests, the coefficient of friction of brake lining has been found to range from 0.35 to 0.50.

The coefficient of friction of the tire on the road is approximately .02. However, this varies with the road surface. Surface contact is the determining factor. The fastest stops are obtained with the wheels rotating. As soon as the wheels become locked, there is less friction and the car will not stop as quickly or as evenly. The ANTI-LOCK BRAKING SYSTEMS work on the principle of very rapid and repeated brake applications and releases to bring the vehicle to a stop without locking or skidding.

STOPPING DISTANCE

Average stopping distance is an important consideration directly related to vehicle speed. As charted in Fig. 52-3, a vehicle that can be stopped in 45 ft. from 20 mph will require 125 ft. to stop from 40 mph. At 60 mph, the vehicle will require 272 ft. to stop; almost the length of a football field.

Note in reading the chart in Fig. 52-3, you need to consider "reaction time" in addition to the time required to make a sudden stop. It is the time you need to react to a warning of danger, move your foot, and apply the brakes. For example, when the vehicle is going 20 mph, it will travel 22 ft. before the brakes are actually applied.

EFFECT OF TEMPERATURE ON
COEFFICIENT OF FRICTION
OF BRAKE LININGS

THREE TYPES OF LININGS ON CAST IRON DRUMS
SAME FRICTION AT LOW TEMPERATURES. DIFFERENT AT HIGHER
TEMPERATURES.

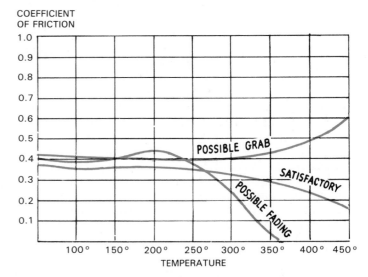

Fig. 52-2. Note how temperature affected coefficient of friction of three different brake linings.

MINIMUM STOPPING DISTANCES AT DIFFERENT SPEEDS			
MPH	REACTION TIME DISTANCE	BRAKING DISTANCE	TOTAL STOPPING DISTANCE
10	11 FEET	9 FEET	20 FEET
20	22	23	45
30	33	45	78
40	44	81	125
50	55	133	188
60	66	206	272
70	77	304	381

Based on tests made by the Bureau of Public Roads, F.H.A.

Fig. 52-3. Chart compares minimum stopping distances at different speeds on dry level concrete surfaces.

BRAKING SYSTEM OPERATION

As covered in detail in Chapter 51, Hydraulics and Pneumatics, liquids are virtually incompressible, and pressure throughout a closed hydraulic system will be the same in all directions. These principles are used to operate hydraulic service brakes on all passenger cars.

A simplified drawing of an automotive hydraulic brake system is shown in Fig. 52-4. Typically, the brake pedal is connected to a master cylinder by a push rod. The master cylinder is connected to the service brakes at each wheel by brake lines and hoses. The entire hydraulic system is filled with a special brake fluid, which is forced through the system by the movement of the master cylinder pistons.

The front brakes are "disc" type, wherein friction pads in a brake caliper are forced against machined surfaces of a rotating disc (rotor) at each wheel to slow and stop the vehicle, Fig. 52-5.

The rear brakes are "drum" type, wherein internal expanding brake shoe assemblies are forced against the machined surface of a rotating drum at each wheel to slow and stop the vehicle, Fig. 52-6.

As the brake pedal is depressed, it moves pistons within the master cylinder, forcing hydraulic brake fluid throughout the brake system and into cylinders at each wheel. The fluid under pressure causes the cylinder pistons to move which, in turn, forces the brake shoes and/or friction pads against the brake drums and/or rotors to retard their movement and stop the vehicle.

Fig. 52-7 shows how the force applied to the brake pedal is multiplied. In this instance, 800 lb. of force is applied to a master cylinder piston area of 0.8 sq. in., resulting in a pressure of 1000 psi (800 ÷ 0.8) in the hydraulic brake system.

Each front brake caliper bore has a piston area of 1.5 sq. in. Since the caliper is single piston type, a force of 1500 lb. (1000 × 1.5) is applied to the brake friction pads. Each rear wheel cylinder has a piston area of 1.0 sq. in. Since each rear wheel cylinder has two pistons, a total force of 2000 lb. (1000 × 1.0 × 2) is produced.

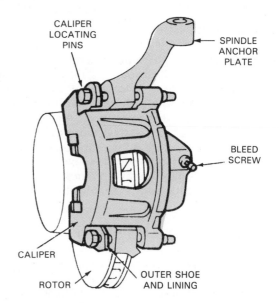

Fig. 52-5. Typical disc brake assembly uses hydraulic caliper to apply inboard and outboard brake shoes to moving rotor. (Ford Motor Co.)

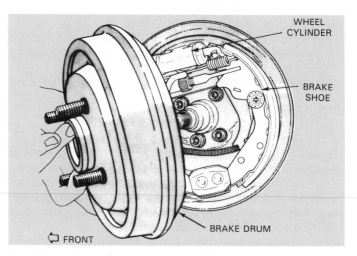

Fig. 52-6. Typical drum brake assembly uses hydraulic wheel cylinder to apply primary and secondary brake shoes to rotating drums.

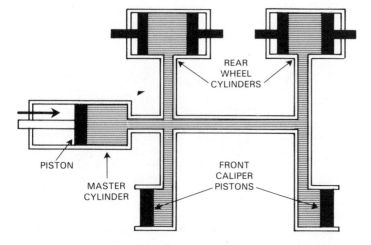

Fig. 52-4. Simplified drawing depicts major components of an automotive hydraulic brake system.

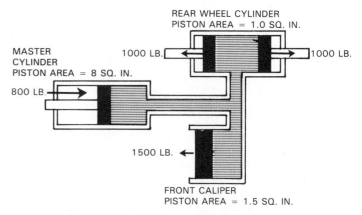

Fig. 52-7. Diagram illustrates how force applied to brake pedal is multiplied hydraulically at wheel cylinders and calipers.

BRAKE LINING MATERIALS

There are three basic types of brake lining in current original equipment use: non-asbestos organic, metallic, and semi-metallic. In the past, asbestos was used almost exclusively in the manufacture of brake lining. Then it was discovered that breathing dust containing asbestos fibers can cause serious bodily harm. (See warning on opening page of this chapter.)

Organic lining usually consists of a compound of non-asbestos friction, filler materials, and high temperature resins. These elements are thoroughly mixed, formed into shape, and placed under heat until a hard, slate-like board is formed. The material is cut and bent into individual segments and attached to drum brake shoes, or it is cut into individual "pads" and attached to disc brake shoes. See Fig. 52-8.

Metallic brake lining is made of sintered metal. It is composed of finely powdered iron or copper, graphite, and lesser amounts of inorganic fillers and friction modifiers. After thorough mixing, a lubricating oil is usually added to prevent segregation of different materials. The mixture is then put through a briquetting process and compressed into desired form.

The non-asbestos organic type brake lining or semi-metallic lining is used for conventional brake service. Under extreme braking conditions (police cars, ambulances, sports cars), the metallic type lining is used. Under severe usage, the frictional characteristics of the metallic lining are more constant than that of the organic lining.

BRAKE ROTOR AND DRUM MATERIALS

A DISC BRAKE ROTOR is defined as the parallel-faced circular rotational member of a disc brake assembly. Generally, rotors are made of cast iron with ventilating fins separating the two braking surfaces. See Fig. 52-9. Venting makes the rotors run cooler and provides quicker cool-down after a brake application.

Disc brake rotor braking surfaces are precisely machined for quality of finish, thickness, parallelism, and absence of lateral runout. Some rotors have a groove machined in the braking surfaces to help reduce brake noise.

The use of cast iron for the braking surface of BRAKE DRUMS is almost universal. The drums are either solid cast iron or steel with an inner lining of cast iron. Some

all steel drums were used in the past. However, cast iron has a higher coefficient of friction than steel so it generally is the first choice of the car manufacturers. The steel/cast iron brake drums are used on heavier vehicles because the assembly has the strength of steel and the frictional properties of cast iron.

Some brake drums are made of aluminum with a cast iron liner for the braking surface. Since aluminum has a higher conductivity of heat than cast iron, brake drums of the aluminum/cast iron construction will operate at much lower temperatures than solid cast iron drums. Regardless of the material used in brake drum construction, drums occasionally are provided with cooling fins.

DISC BRAKES

Single piston, sliding or floating caliper disc brakes have been used on the front wheels of passenger cars for many years. See Fig. 52-10. In the past, fixed

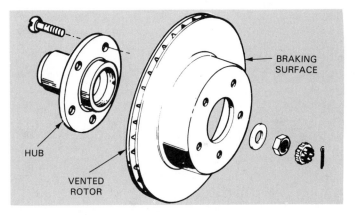

Fig. 52-9. Vented, rather than solid, rotors are commonly used on disc brakes because they run cooler. (American Motors Corp.)

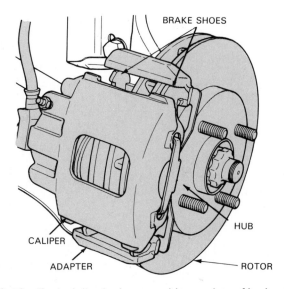

Fig. 52-10. Typical disc brake assembly consists of hydraulic caliper and brake shoes mounted on an adapter and straddling a machined rotor installed on a wheel hub. (Chrysler Corp.)

Fig. 52-8. New formula disc brake friction pads are compounded from special resins, friction modifiers, and a blend of advanced non-asbestos fibers. (Brake Systems, Inc.)

calipers with four pistons per caliper actuated the friction pads to stop the rotors and the vehicle. The two caliper housings were "fixed" in place. There was no lateral movement as with the single piston caliper.

With single piston DISC BRAKE CALIPERS, Fig. 52-11, the caliper slides or floats on mounting bolts or on sleeves on mounting bolts or pins to apply friction pads to the machined surfaces of a rotating disc. Disc brakes

are self adjusting. The caliper piston seals are designed to retract the piston enough to allow the friction pad to lightly contact the rotor without any drag.

Generally, when front wheel drive moved into prominence, some modifications of the single piston caliper became necessary. Chrysler, for example, introduced an assembly featuring a sliding caliper and adapter setup utilizing pins, bushings, and sleeves. See Fig. 52-12.

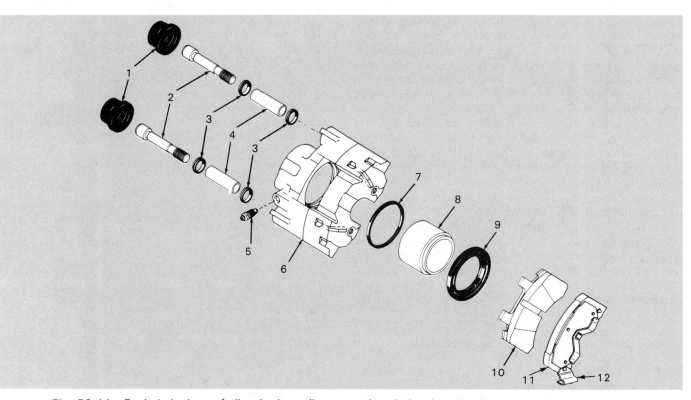

Fig. 52-11. Exploded view of disc brake caliper reveals relative locations of parts: 1—Bolt boot. 2—Mounting bolt. 3—Bushing. 4—Sleeve. 5—Bleeder valve. 6—Caliper housing. 7—Piston seal. 8—Piston. 9—Boot. 10—Inboard shoe and lining. 11—Outboard shoe and lining. 12—Wear sensor. (Cadillac Motor Car Div., General Motors Corp.)

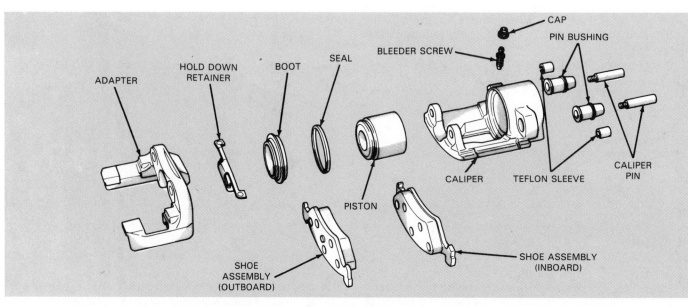

Fig. 52-12. Various parts that make up Chrysler sliding disc brake assembly are identified. (Chrysler Corp.)

GM REAR DISC BRAKES

Some General Motors cars have disc brakes front and rear. REAR DISC BRAKES, like front disc brakes, operate by means of a single piston caliper applying friction pads to a rotating disc or rotor. In addition, however, each GM rear disc brake caliper is equipped with a parking brake actuator mechanism which, in turn, is operated by a series of cables connected to the parking brake pedal.

The GM PARKING BRAKE MECHANISM on the rear caliper, Fig. 52-13, consists of a lever and screw setup whereby the screw is threaded into a nut built into the caliper piston assembly. The lever is actuated by a series of cables connected to the parking brake pedal. The parking brake pedal assembly is a ratcheting mechanism that must be pumped (up to 3 1/2 strokes) to set.

When the parking brake pedal is depressed, the lever turns the screw, moving the caliper piston outward and causing the caliper to slide inward. The resulting clamping action of the friction pads on each rear rotor locks the brakes. This action causes the rotor to reduce its speed, and therefore the car speed is reduced.

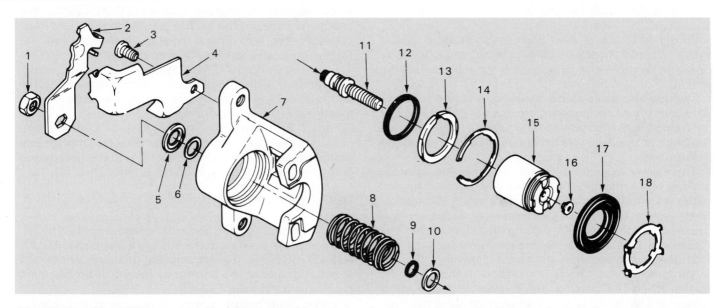

Fig. 52-13. General Motors rear disc brake assembly includes: 1—Nut. 2—Parking brake lever. 3—Bolt. 4—Bracket. 5—Seal. 6—Washer. 7—Caliper housing. 8—Balance spring and retainer. 9—Shaft seal. 10—Thrust washer. 11—Actuator screw. 12—Piston seal. 13—Piston locator. 14—Retainer. 15—Piston assembly. 16—Two-way check valve. 17—Caliper boot. 18—Shoe retainer.   (Cadillac Motor Car Div., General Motors Corp.)

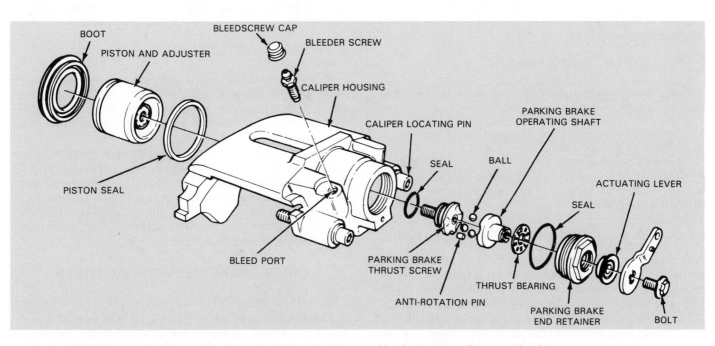

Fig. 52-14. Exploded view of Ford rear disc brake assembly shows parts disassembly of screw type parking brake mechanism.   (Ford Motor Co.)

Typically, the GM parking brake will release automatically when the transmission selector lever is placed in reverse or any drive position with the ignition ON. The automatic release system utilizes a vacuum diaphragm on the parking brake pedal assembly, a vacuum switch on the transmission range selector, and connecting vacuum hoses.

The GM parking brake system uses four separate cables. The front cable joins the intermediate cable at the adjuster screw. From there, the intermediate cable extends to the rear of the car where right and left rear cables connect by means of an equalizer.

FORD REAR DISC BRAKES

Ford's four wheel disc brake system uses a dual master cylinder, hydraulic brake booster, and a two-way pressure control valve to balance front and rear braking action.

The rear disc brake caliper assembly is similar to Ford's pin slider front brake caliper, except for the addition of a parking brake mechanism. The parking brake lever on the back of the caliper is cable operated by the parking brake pedal.

The caliper assembly consists of a housing, piston, parking brake mechanism, inboard and outboard friction pads, wear indicator, anti-rattle clip, and anchor plate. See Fig. 52-14. The caliper assembly slides on two greased locating pins (attaching bolts) between the caliper and anchor plates. Rubber insulators keep the pins from direct contact with the caliper housing.

The parking brake lever is attached to the operating shaft. When the parking brake is applied, the cable rotates the lever and shaft. Three steel balls roll between ramps formed in pockets on the opposing heads of the operating shaft and thrust screw. The steel balls force the thrust screw away from the operating shaft, forcing the friction pads against the rotor.

The parking brake is self adjusting. An automatic adjuster in the piston moves on the thrust screw to compensate for lining wear.

DRUM BRAKES

There are many factors that contribute to the effectiveness of drum brakes:

1. Radius of brake drum.
2. Radius of car wheel.
3. Area of brake lining.
4. Amount of force applied to brake shoes.
5. Coefficient of friction of braking surfaces.
6. Self-energization.
7. Servo action.
8. Coefficient of friction between tires and road surface.

Factors 1 and 2 are simply a matter of leverage. It is obvious that a small brake drum on a large wheel will require more frictional surface, or higher pressure on the surface, than a large brake drum on a small wheel.

Factor 3 presents another obvious contribution to drum brake effectiveness. Certainly the greater the area of frictional material on the brake shoes, the more effective braking action will be.

Factor 4 is important because the pressure of the brake shoes against the drums starts with the force applied to the brake pedal. Then, that force is multiplied by leverage (and usually assisted by a power brake unit) and further increased hydraulically by the size of the master cylinder bore and bore of the wheel cylinders.

Factor 5 takes into consideration the coefficient of friction of the brake lining material, its area, and the material used in the casting of the brake drums.

Factor 6 greatly multiplies the force pressing the brake shoes against the drums. SELF-ENERGIZATION is created by the tendency of the rotating drum to drag the brake lining and brake shoe along with it. The frictional force between the brake drum and lining tries to turn the brake shoe around the anchor pin. Since the drum itself prevents this, the brake shoe is "self-energized" or forced even more strongly against the drum, Fig. 52-15.

Factor 7, SERVO ACTION, is obtained by the "wedging" action of the brake shoe, which starts at the toe of the shoe and keeps increasing as the shoe tries to rotate with the brake drum.

Factor 8 involves tire-to-road surface contact, emphasizing braking to rapidly reduce wheel rotation before stopping the vehicle, rather than locking the brakes and going into a potentially dangerous skid.

DUO-SERVO ACTION

Self-energization and servo action are amplified by letting one brake shoe push the other in a move called DUO-SERVO ACTION. To accomplish this, the shoes are linked together at the bottom by means of an adjusting mechanism. See Fig. 52-15.

When the brakes are applied, the toe of the primary shoe is pulled away from the anchor pin by the revolving brake drum. The heel of the primary shoe then pushes the adjusting mechanism against the heel of the secondary shoe. This forces the toe of the secondary shoe against the anchor pin and both brake shoes are applied against the brake drum with multiplied effect.

NON-SERVO ACTION

Some front wheel drive vehicles are equipped with NON-SERVO REAR WHEEL BRAKE ASSEMBLIES. See Fig. 52-16. These non-servo systems utilize a LEADING-TRAILING SHOE DESIGN in place of the popular duo-servo design.

The non-servo brake assembly has twin anchors at the lower end of the backing plate. Since the heel end of each brake shoe contacts the anchor, there is no duo-servo action created between the shoes. Instead, the leading shoe does most of the drum-stopping action during forward motion. The trailing shoe, in turn, does most of the work during rearward motion.

DRUM BRAKE MECHANICAL PARTS

MECHANICAL PARTS of a typical single anchor automatic adjuster rear wheel drum brake assembly include: backing plate, brake shoes, shoe retracting springs, hold-down spring assemblies, self-adjusting assembly, and parking brake parts. See Fig. 52-17.

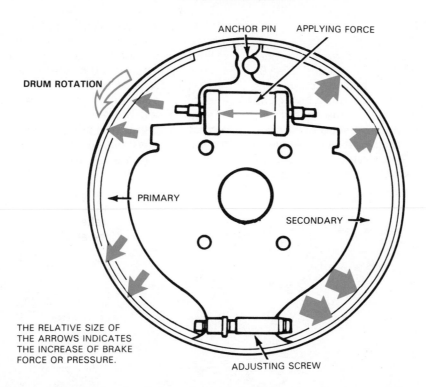

ANCHOR PIN   APPLYING FORCE

DRUM ROTATION

PRIMARY

SECONDARY

THE RELATIVE SIZE OF
THE ARROWS INDICATES
THE INCREASE OF BRAKE
FORCE OR PRESSURE.

ADJUSTING SCREW

Fig. 52-15. Drum braking action involves: self- energization of primary shoe by drum rotation; servo wedging action of primary shoe against drum; duo-servo action as primary shoe pushes secondary shoe against drum with increased force. (Ford Motor Co.)

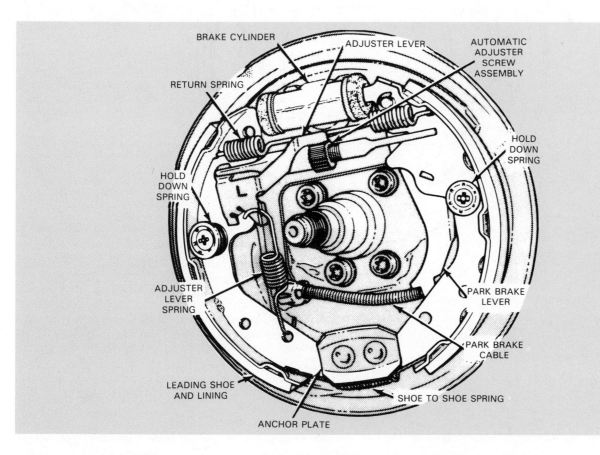

BRAKE CYLINDER   ADJUSTER LEVER   AUTOMATIC
                                                ADJUSTER
                                                SCREW
RETURN SPRING   ASSEMBLY

                                                HOLD
                                                DOWN
                                                SPRING

HOLD
DOWN
SPRING

ADJUSTER
LEVER
SPRING
                                                PARK BRAKE
                                                LEVER

                                                PARK BRAKE
                                                CABLE

LEADING SHOE
AND LINING

                        ANCHOR PLATE   SHOE TO SHOE SPRING

Fig. 52-16. Parts of Chrysler's leading-trailing type of rear wheel drum brake assembly are pointed out and identified. This non-servo design has solid anchors between heels of brake shoes.   (Chrysler Corp.)

REAR WHEEL DRIVE CARS

Most modern drum brake assemblies on rear wheel drive cars are look-alikes. See Fig. 52-18 and 52-19. The brake shoes are placed on the backing plate with the star wheel adjuster in place between the heel ends of the shoes. The toe ends seat against the anchor pin, Fig. 52-17. The primary shoe and the secondary shoe each slide on three separate raised sections of the backing plate. Each raised section is referred to as a "boss." So, there are a total of six bosses on any one backing plate.

Hold-down assemblies keep the shoes in place against lubricated bosses on the backing plate. The wheel cylinder is mounted below the anchor with the wheel cylinder links engaged in the web of each brake shoe. Hydraulic pressure at the wheel cylinder must be great enough to overcome spring pressure of the retracting springs. Once hydraulic pressure is greater than the retracting springs, the primary shoe and secondary shoe are each pushed out against the brake drum. Retracting springs hold and serve to retract the shoes after each brake application.

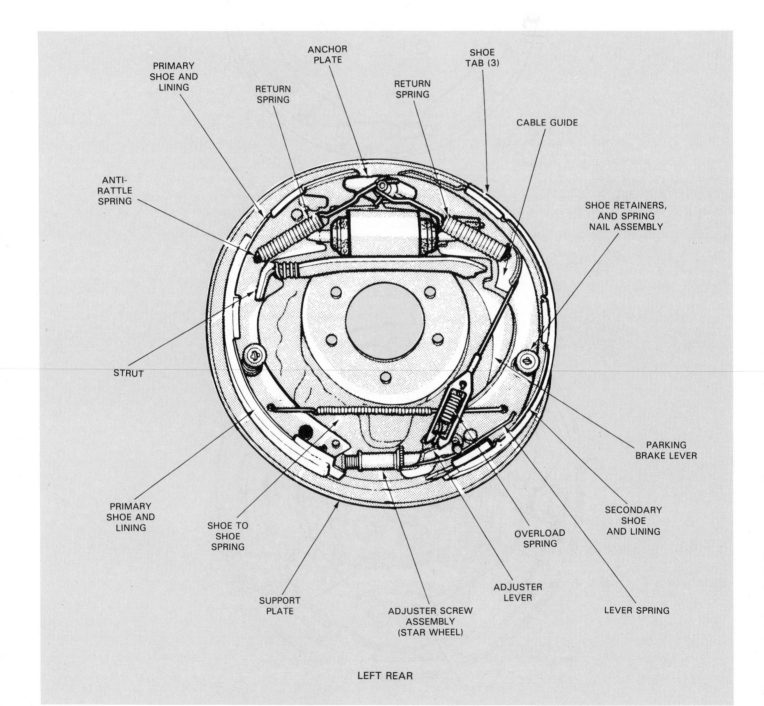

Fig. 52-17. Parts of Chrysler's single anchor duo-servo rear wheel drum brake assembly are indicated. (Chrysler Corp.)

644

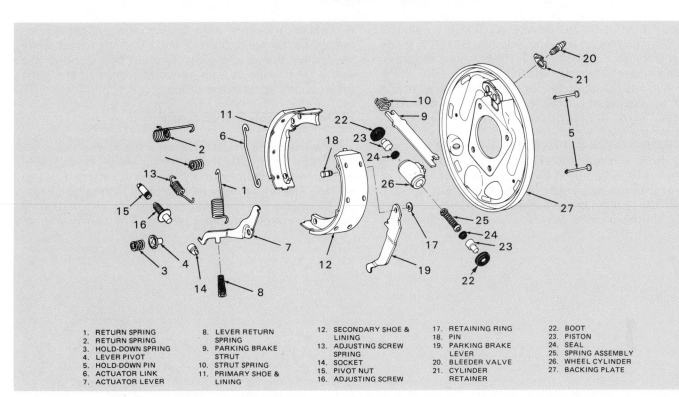

1.	RETURN SPRING	8.	LEVER RETURN	12.	SECONDARY SHOE &	17.	RETAINING RING

1. RETURN SPRING
2. RETURN SPRING
3. HOLD-DOWN SPRING
4. LEVER PIVOT
5. HOLD-DOWN PIN
6. ACTUATOR LINK
7. ACTUATOR LEVER

8. LEVER RETURN SPRING
9. PARKING BRAKE STRUT
10. STRUT SPRING
11. PRIMARY SHOE & LINING

12. SECONDARY SHOE & LINING
13. ADJUSTING SCREW SPRING
14. SOCKET
15. PIVOT NUT
16. ADJUSTING SCREW

17. RETAINING RING
18. PIN
19. PARKING BRAKE LEVER
20. BLEEDER VALVE
21. CYLINDER RETAINER

22. BOOT
23. PISTON
24. SEAL
25. SPRING ASSEMBLY
26. WHEEL CYLINDER
27. BACKING PLATE

Fig. 52-18. Exploded view shows a typical automatic adjuster rear wheel drum brake. Note parts of self-adjusting mechanism at: 6—Actuator link. 7—Actuator lever. 8—Return spring. 13—Adjusting screw spring. 14, 15, 16—Adjusting screw. (Cadillac Motor Car Div., General Motors Corp.)

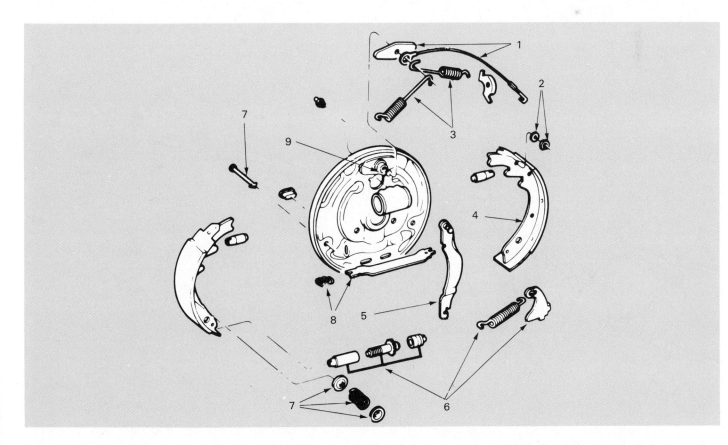

Fig. 52-19. Exploded view presents another automatic adjuster rear wheel drum brake: 1—Guide plate and adjuster cable. 2—Washer and U-clip. 3—Shoe retracting springs. 4—Secondary brake shoe. 5—Parking brake lever. 6—Adjuster screw, spring, and lever. 7—Hold-down pin and retainers. 8—Parking brake lever strut and spring. 9—Anchor pin. (American Motors Corp.)

The SELF-ADJUSTING BRAKE ASSEMBLY consists of: an actuating lever; actuator link, Fig. 52-18 or guide plate and adjuster cable, Fig. 52-19; lever return spring; adjusting screw assembly. The SELF-ADJUSTING PRINCIPLE involves actuating the lever to rotate the adjusting screw by driving the vehicle in reverse and making repeated "hard" stops with one forward brake application between each reverse stop.

The PARKING BRAKE PARTS include: a strut and strut spring; front and rear cables; and operating lever. The parking brake is actuated by means of a foot lever or hand lever in the passenger compartment, Fig. 52-20.

When the parking brake pedal (or lever) is pushed (or pulled), the front cable moves forward and carries the rear cable (or cables) with it. Since the rear cable is attached to the parking brake lever in each wheel brake assembly, the levers pivot forward and actuate the struts. The struts, in turn, move forward and apply the brake shoes against the drums.

FRONT WHEEL DRIVE CARS

On some front wheel drive cars, the rear wheel drum brake has higher placement of the wheel cylinder and a different arrangement of the mechanical parts. See Fig. 52-16. The wheel cylinder is located high on the backing plate and the toe ends of the brake shoes directly engage the wheel cylinder pistons. The star wheel ad-

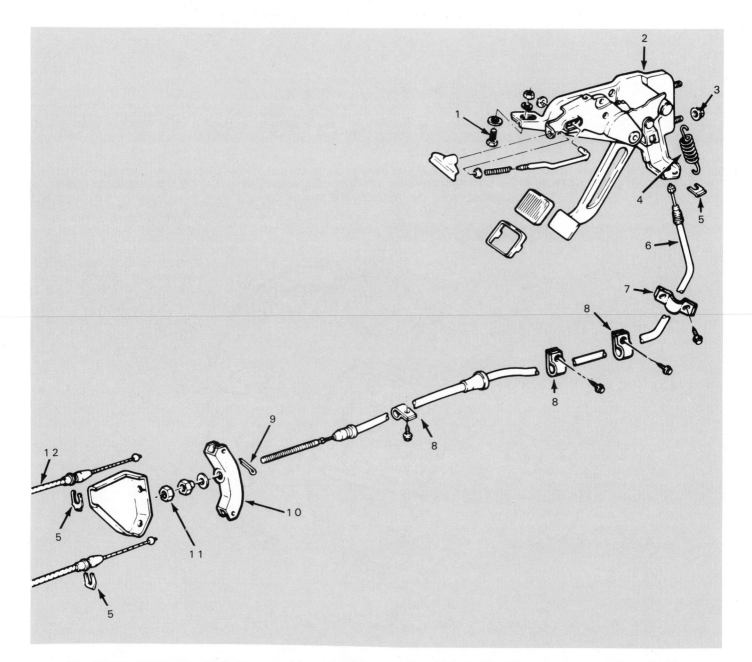

Fig. 52-20. Parking brake lever assembly and cables are pictured: 1—Mounting bolt. 2—Lever assembly. 3—Mounting stud nut. 4—Return spring. 5—Cable retaining clips. 6—Front cable. 7—Retaining clip. 8—Mounting clips. 9—Cotter pin. 10—Equalizer. 11—Cable adjuster unit and lock nut. 12—Rear cable.   (American Motors Corp.)

juster assembly fits between the shoe webs just below the wheel cylinder. The heel ends of the brake shoes seat against twin anchors behind an anchor plate.

The self-adjusting brake assembly usually consists of: an automatic adjuster lever; lever spring; automatic adjuster screw assembly. See Fig. 52-21.

The parking brake parts include: parking brake lever; rear cable and cable spring; front cable and operating lever in passenger compartment. See Fig. 52-16.

BRAKE HYDRAULIC SYSTEM

The basic BRAKE HYDRAULIC SYSTEM usually consists of a dual reservoir master cylinder, a combination valve, front disc brake calipers, rear drum brake wheel cylinders, and the connecting brake lines, hoses, and fittings.

HYDRAULIC BRAKE FLUID

To provide positive braking action under all conditions, hydraulic brake fluid must meet a lot of special requirements. The Society of Automotive Engineers has established these requirements and submitted them to the American National Standards Institute, and they are recognized as an American National Standard. With this in mind, use only brake fluids that are labeled as meeting SAE Specification J1703 (DOT-3 or DOT-4).

The SAE J1703 specification requires that brake fluids pass tests for: boiling point (not less than 401 °F or 205 °C); viscosity; pH (acidity-alkalinity) value; fluid high temperature and chemical stability; corrosion resistance; fluidity and appearance at low temperatures; evaporation; water tolerance; compatibility; resistance to oxidation; effect on rubber.

SILICONE BRAKE FLUID

SILICONE BRAKE FLUID is used in some applications, especially in high performance and commercial vehicles. It is said to be chemically stable and nonhydroscopic (will not absorb water). The manufacturers claim that silicone brake fluid serves as a lubricant between rubber-metal and plastic-metal parts, and it will not attack painted surfaces.

The Society of Automotive Engineers has established a set of minimum performance standards for silicone and other low water tolerant type brake fluids. Silicone brake fluids meeting SAE Specification J1705 (DOT-5) are functionally compatible with existing motor vehilcle brake fluids conforming to SAE Specification J1703 and with braking systems designed for such fluids.

Silicone brake fluids are said to perform uniformly over climate extremes. Brakes reportedly will not fail or fade due to fluid malfunction at temperatures as high as 550 °F (288 °C).

BRAKE FLUID VAPOR LOCK

With friction and heat governing braking action, there is always a chance of brake fluid and brake mechanisms becoming overheated.

If the brake fluid in the hydraulic system becomes hot enough to vaporize, it emits gas. A drop of brake fluid

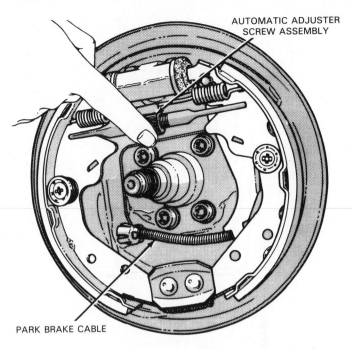

Fig. 52-21. Chrysler's leading-trailing rear brake assembly utilizes an automatic adjuster screw assembly between brake shoe webs near toes of shoes.   (Chrysler Corp.)

changed into vapor forms a gas bubble many times the volume of the liquid drop. Small quantities of bubbles produce a problem called VAPOR LOCK that could cause partial loss of braking. If vapor lock occurs in the master cylinder, the brakes could fail without warning.

Mountain driving puts an increased work load on the brakes and brake fluid. With every 2000 ft. rise in altitude, the atmospheric pressure drops approximately one pound, and the boiling point of the brake fluid drops two to three degrees. This lowered boiling point naturally increases the tendency toward vapor lock.

DUAL MASTER CYLINDER

The DUAL MASTER CYLINDER is designed to give the front and rear brakes separate hydraulic systems. Should a brake fluid leak occur in one system, the other system will still operate, making it possible to stop the car.

The dual master cylinder is provided with two separate reservoirs for storage of the brake fluid, one primary piston, and one secondary piston, Fig. 52-22. The

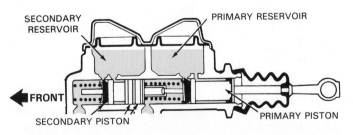

Fig. 52-22. Dual master cylinder provides two separate hydraulic brake systems to insure against brake failure if a fluid leak occurs.

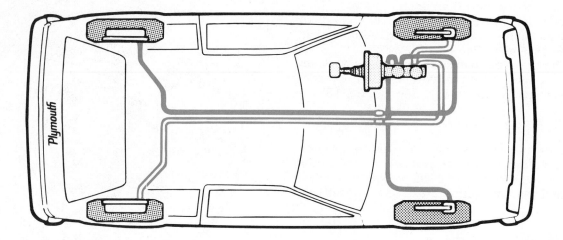

Fig. 52-23. A typical dual diagonal braking system is pictured. Primary system of master cylinder operates right front and left rear brakes. Secondary system operates left front and right rear brakes.   (Chrysler)

primary piston transfers pressure to the front brakes. The secondary piston transfers pressure to the rear brakes. This setup is a front-to-rear ''split'' system.

Most late model cars utilize a diagonal ''split'' brake hydraulic system. That is: the primary piston in the master cylinder transfers pressure to one front brake and one diagonally opposite rear brake. The secondary piston transfers pressure to the opposite front and rear brakes. See Fig. 52-23.

DUAL MASTER CYLINDER OPERATION

When the brake pedal is depressed, the push rod of the DUAL MASTER CYLINDER moves the primary piston forward in the cylinder. The hydraulic pressure created and the force of the primary piston spring move the secondary piston forward. When the forward movement of the pistons causes their primary cups to cover the bypass holes, hydraulic pressure is built up and it is transmitted to the front and rear brake assemblies.

When the brake pedal is released, hydraulic pressure in the dual master cylinder is reduced. This pressure relief allows the drum brake shoe retracting springs to retract the shoes from contact with the drums, forcing brake fluid out of the wheel cylinders and back into the master cylinder. The reduction in hydraulic pressure also allows the caliper pistons to retract by action of the piston seals, Fig. 52-24.

On fast release of the brake pedal, the retracting master cylinder pistons move faster than the returning fluid and a partial vacuum is created. Brake fluid enters the pressure chamber of the master cylinder via breather and bleeder holes in the piston heads. At the finish of release, the pistons return against retaining rings and fluid returns to the master cylinder reservoirs by way of compensating ports.

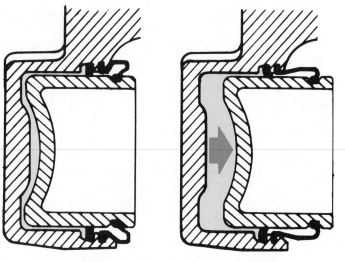

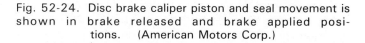
RELEASED   APPLIED

Fig. 52-24. Disc brake caliper piston and seal movement is shown in brake released and brake applied positions.   (American Motors Corp.)

MASTER CYLINDER TYPES

Earlier models and some cars having a diesel engine use a conventional CAST IRON MASTER CYLINDER with integral reservoir. A removable metal top and bail wire completes the assembly. See Fig. 52-25.

Currently, ALUMINUM MASTER CYLINDERS are used in most applications, Fig. 52-56. The aluminum body is topped by a translucent plastic reservoir. The reservoir carries minimum/maximum markings to permit visual inspection of the brake fluid level.

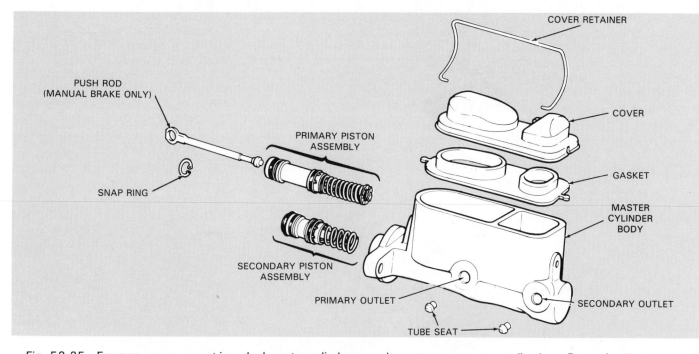

Fig. 52-25. For many years, a cast iron dual master cylinder served most passenger car applications. Parts of a disassembled cast iron unit are identified. (Ford Motor Co.)

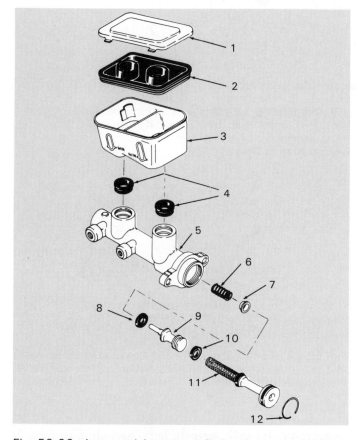

Fig. 52-26. Late model master cylinders have an aluminum body and plastic reservoir. Note arrangement of internal parts: 1—Reservoir cover. 2—Reservoir diaphragm. 3—Reservoir. 4—Grommets. 5—Cylinder body. 6—Spring retainer. 7—Secondary seal. 8—Primary seal. 9—Secondary piston. 10—Secondary seal. 11—Primary piston assembly. 12—Lock ring. (Oldsmobile Div., General Motors Corp.)

Also, in keeping with a trend toward "low drag" caliper pistons (deep-set piston seals to aid in piston retraction), a QUICK TAKE-UP MASTER CYLINDER is employed. See Fig. 52-27. The quick take-up valve is generally built into the master cylinder. It uses a spring-loaded ball check to "hold" pressure in the large rear chamber. When the brakes are first applied, movement of the rear piston causes fluid to be displaced forward past the primary piston seal and into the primary chamber which feeds the front brakes.

When hydraulic pressure reaches a predetermined pressure, the check ball unseats and allows fluid to pass from the large rear chamber into the reservoir. Meanwhile, the primary and secondary chambers supply hydraulic pressure to the front and rear brakes in the conventional manner.

When the brake pedal is released, suction created in the large chamber draws fluid from the reservoir through a small bleed hole in the ball seat and around the quick take-up lip seal. In this way, the large rear chamber is quickly refilled with fluid in readiness for the next brake application.

COMBINATION VALVES

Most brake hydraulic systems with disc brakes in front and drum brakes at rear utilize a combination valve. See Fig. 52-28. The COMBINATION VALVE usually combines a pressure differential valve, metering valve, and proportioning valve. Earlier models used similar valves, individually mounted, to accomplish specific braking effects.

The PRESSURE DIFFERENTIAL VALVE section of the combination valve is designed to sense unbalanced hydraulic pressure between the two halves of the "split" system. If the pressures are unbalanced during a brake

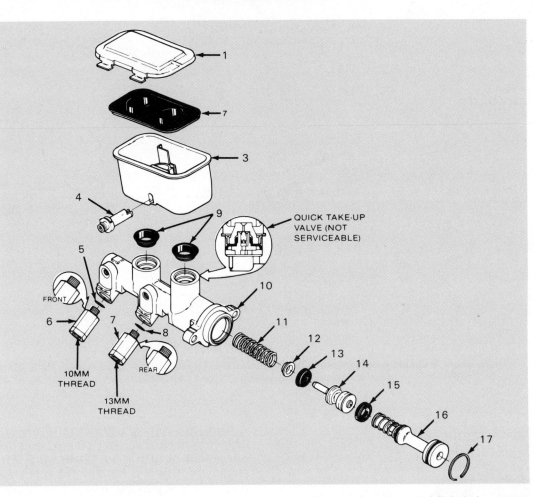

Fig. 52-27. Quick take-up valve in master cylinder provides quick recovery of fluid in large rear chamber after each brake application: 1—Reservoir cover. 2—Diaphragm. 3—Reservoir cover. 4—Fluid level switch. 5—O-ring. 6—Proportioner. 7—Proportioner. 8—O-ring. 9—Grommets. 10—Cylinder body. 11—Spring. 12—Spring retainer. 13—Primary seal. 14—Secondary piston. 15—Secondary seal. 16—Primary piston assembly. 17—Lock ring. (Cadillac Motor Car Div., General Motors Corp.)

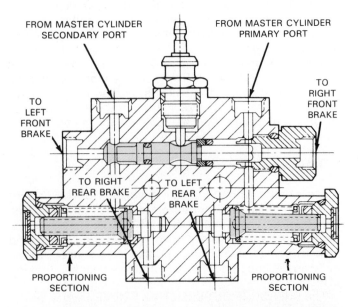

Fig. 52-28. Combination valve in brake hydraulic system utilizes three separate valves to balance pressures and braking action between front and rear brakes. (Chrysler Corp.)

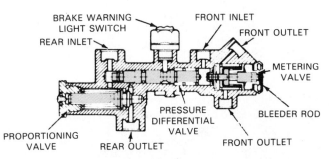

Fig. 52-29. Combination valve on cars with front disc brakes and rear drum brakes contain a pressure differential valve, metering valve, and proportioning valve. (Ford Motor Co.)

application, a brake warning lamp switch, Fig. 52-29, will activate a red light on the instrument panel.

After the brake system is serviced to correct the unbalanced pressures, the red brake warning light will shut off when the system is properly bled and the brakes are applied to center the piston in the pressure differential valve.

The METERING VALVE section of the combination valve, Fig. 52-29, limits hydraulic pressure to the front disc brakes until a predetermined front input pressure is reached. This pressure approximates the pressure required to overcome the retracting force of the rear brake shoe retracting springs.

The PROPORTIONING VALVE section of the combination valve regulates outlet pressure to the rear brakes. See Fig. 52-29. When the brake pedal is applied, the full brake fluid pressure is permitted to flow through the proportioning valve to the rear brakes. At a specific pressure point, the valve reduces the pressure to the rear brakes to create balanced braking between the front and rear wheels.

DISC BRAKE CALIPERS

As mentioned earlier, braking with disc brakes is accomplished by forcing friction pads, Fig. 52-30, against both sides of a rotating metal disc (rotor). The rotor turns with the wheel of the vehicle and is "straddled" by a housing called a CALIPER ASSEMBLY. Modern disc brakes use the SINGLE PISTON CALIPER. However, at least one manufacturer is installing TWO PISTON CALIPERS to go with thicker rotors and friction pads of greater area.

When the brake pedal is depressed, hydraulic fluid forces the caliper piston and the friction pads against the machined surfaces of the rotor. The "clamping" action of the friction pads, Fig. 52-30, creates friction and heat to slow down and stop the vehicle.

The principle of operation of a single piston caliper involves the following steps:

1. Hydraulic pressure builds up and exerts equal pressure against bottom of piston and bottom of piston bore. See Fig. 52-30 at right.
2. Pressure applied to piston is transmitted to inboard friction pad, forcing it against inboard rotor surface.
3. Pressure applied to bottom of piston bore causes caliper to "slide" or "float" inboard on mounting bolts.
4. Since caliper is one piece, its sliding action causes outboard section of caliper to apply pressure to outboard friction pad, forcing it against outboard surface of rotor.
5. As fluid pressure builds up, clamping action of friction pads stops rotor and vehicle.
6. When hydraulic pressure is released, friction pads and caliper piston move away from rotor, aided by retracting action of piston seal, Fig. 52-30.

WHEEL CYLINDERS

WHEEL CYLINDERS are used in drum brake systems to hydraulically actuate the brake shoes. A typical wheel cylinder is composed of: a single-bore cylinder casting; internal compression spring; two pistons; two rubber piston cups or seals; two rubber boots to prevent entry of dirt and water; and a bleeder screw (valve). See Fig. 52-31. In addition, wheel cylinders are generally fitted with "links" that extend from the outboard side of each piston, through the rubber boots, where they bear against the toe end of each brake shoe.

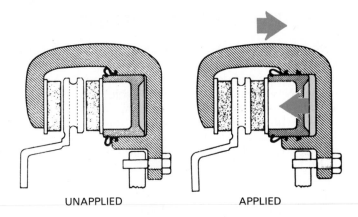

UNAPPLIED   APPLIED

Fig. 52-30. Key to floating or sliding caliper operation is when hydraulic pressure on bottom of cylinder bore causes caliper to move sideways and apply friction pads to rotor machined surfaces.

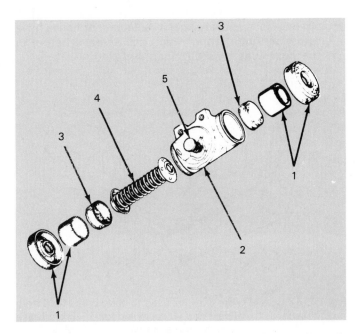

Fig. 52-31. Typical drum brake wheel cylinder consists of: 1—Boots and pistons. 2—Cylinder casting. 3—Rubber cups. 4—Spring and expanders. 5—Bleeder screw. (American Motors Corp.)

When the brake pedal is depressed, hydraulic fluid pressure produced by the master cylinder forces the wheel cylinder pistons apart and outward in the cylinder. This movement, in turn, is transmitted to the toe ends of the brake shoes, causing the shoes to contact the revolving brake drum and stop the vehicle.

When the brake pedal is released, the shoe retracting springs force the wheel cylinder pistons and cups inward. This movement pushes brake fluid back to the master cylinder reservoir. Meanwhile, outward force created by the wheel cylinder spring keeps the two sets of pistons and cups apart. This provides space between the sealing cups for brake fluid to be retained for immediate response to the next brake application.

651

BRAKE LINES, HOSES, AND FITTINGS

Double walled steel brake lines are used to safely transport the brake fluid from master cylinder to disc brake calipers and drum brake wheel cylinders. See Fig. 52-32. Never use copper tubing, which could crack or corrode and cause brake failure.

Some brake lines are "double flared" and some "bubble flared" to provide leakproof connections. Servicewise, a flaring tool must be used when a new brake line is made, Fig. 52-33. The new line must be an entire section of the same type, size, shape, and length as the line being replaced.

Flexible hydraulic brake hoses connect the steel brake lines on the rear axle housing or body to the rear wheel brake lines and to the front disc brake calipers. See Fig. 52-34. This flexibility is needed to compensate for the up and down movement of the vehicle and the turning motion of the front wheel assemblies.

A replacement flexible brake hose should be positioned to avoid contact with other chassis parts. Some original equipment hoses and equivalent replacement hoses have a lengthwise white stripe which will reveal whether or not the hose was twisted when installed.

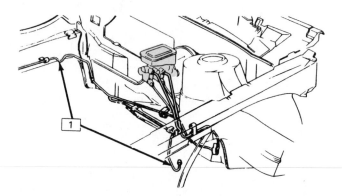

Fig. 52-32. Steel brake lines are used to carry brake fluid from master cylinder to calipers and wheel cylinders: 1—Front brake line routing is shown. (Oldsmobile Div., General Motors Corp.)

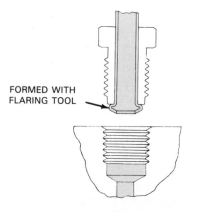

FORMED WITH FLARING TOOL

Fig. 52-33. A special flaring tool is used to form a "bubble type" flare at the end of brake line. This type flare cannot be used where a double type flare is to be used.

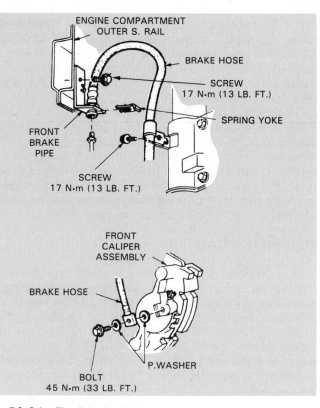

Fig. 52-34. Flexible brake hoses connect brake lines to calipers and wheel cylinders to compensate for motion of wheel assemblies. (Buick Motor Div., General Motors Corp.)

All fittings in the hydraulic brake system must be matched to the original equipment part for type and size, and tightened to the car manufacturer's torque specifications. See Chapter 1, Automotive Tools, for further details on fitting types, usage, and handling recommendations.

POWER BRAKES

Power brake units used on passenger cars are of four general types: vacuum suspended; air suspended; hydraulic booster; electro-hydraulic booster. Most power brake applications utilize vacuum suspended units.

VACUUM SUSPENDED OPERATION

In the released position, both sides of the power piston and single diaphragm of a vacuum suspended power brake unit are open to intake manifold vacuum, Fig. 52-35. As the brakes are applied, air is admitted to one side of the piston and diaphragm. Immediately, atmospheric pressure moves the diaphragm and power piston forward, causing the push rod to actuate the master cylinder pistons and apply the brakes.

Some larger vehicles are equipped with a tandem diaphragm, vacuum suspended power booster. Operation is similar to the single diaphragm unit with air being admitted to one side of each diaphragm to provide power assist.

A typical General Motors single diaphragm, vacuum suspended power booster is shown in Fig. 52-36.

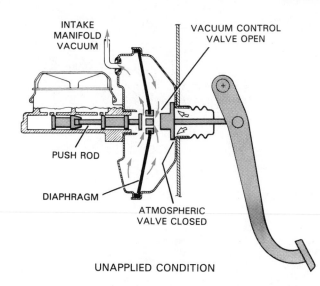

Fig. 52-35. Simplified diagram illustrates unapplied condition of a single diaphragm power brake unit. Both sides of diaphragm are open to intake manifold vacuum. In applied condition, atmosphere valve opens to permit atmospheric pressure to provide power assist to master cylinder push rod. (Chrysler Corp.)

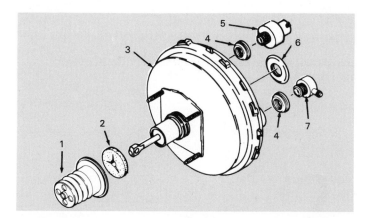

Fig. 52-36. Drawing shows exterior components of a General Motors single diaphragm power brake unit: 1—Boot. 2—Silencer. 3—Booster. 4—Grommets. 5—Vacuum switch. 6—Front housing seal. 7—Vacuum check valve. (Buick Motor Div., General Motors Corp.)

AIR SUSPENDED OPERATION

In the released position, both sides of the power piston are under atmospheric pressure. When the brakes are applied, manifold vacuum is admitted to one side of the piston. Immediately, atmospheric pressure on the other side causes the piston to move, forcing the push rod forward and actuating the master cylinder pistons to apply the brakes.

HYDRAULIC BOOSTER OPERATION

General Motors and Ford use Hydro-Boost II, a hydraulically operated power brake booster, Fig. 52-37. The power steering pump provides the hydraulic pressure to operate the power brake booster and the power steering gear.

HYDRO-BOOST II combines an open center spool valve with a hydraulic cylinder in a single housing, Fig. 52-38. This hydraulic brake booster also has a reserve system — an ACCUMULATOR — that stores power steering fluid under pressure to provide one or two power assisted brake applications in case of a pressure drop.

In the released position, fluid flows from the power steering pump through the open center spool valve in the power booster, to the power steering gear, and back to the pump reservoir.

When the brakes are applied, the open center spool valve closes the fluid return port from the booster chamber to the pump and admits fluid into the booster chamber from the pressure port, Fig. 52-38. The closing of the spool valve also restricts fluid flow to the steering gear, causing the pump to increase fluid pressure.

As hydraulic pressure in the booster chamber increases, it actuates the booster piston which, in turn, moves the master cylinder pistons forward to apply the brakes.

If there is a fluid pressure loss, foot pressure on the brake pedal causes an actuator on the spool valve to open the accumulator valve, Fig. 52-38. Pump pressure then furnishes a reserve power supply of fluid to the booster. When the supply is depleted, the system reverts to manual operation. Manual operation being a lack of power assist upon brake application; the effort to apply the brakes is increased.

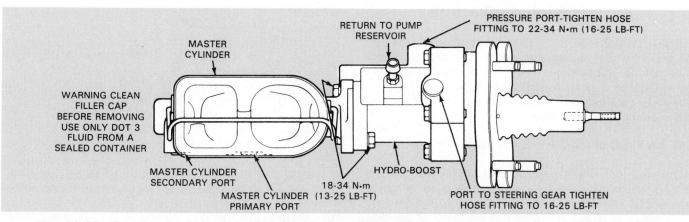

Fig. 52-37. Top view provides service technician's view of Hydro-Boost II and master cylinder. (Ford Motor Co.)

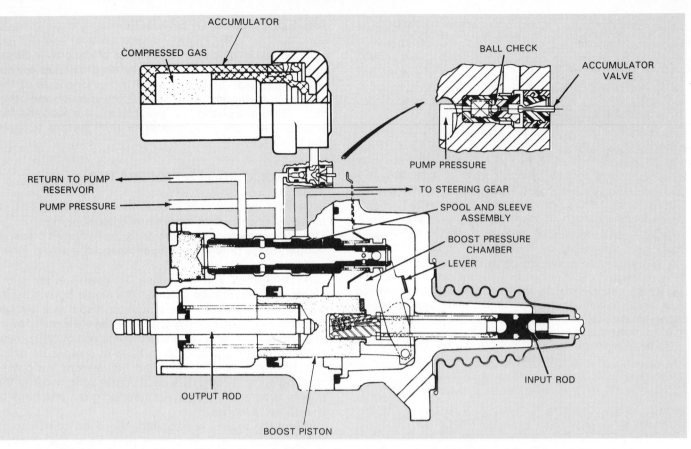

Fig. 52-38. Sectional view of Hydro-Boost II power brake unit shows internal parts and direction of flow of power steering fluid. (Ford Motor Co.)

ELECTRO-HYDRAULIC OPERATION

General Motors POWERMASTER unit is a power brake supply system featuring an electro-hydraulic pump, fluid accumulator, dual-pressure switch, and hydraulic booster with an integral dual master cylinder, Fig. 52-39.

The Powermaster pump operates between certain pressure switch limits to maintain satisfactory fluid pressure for power-boosted brake applications. When the brake pedal is depressed, fluid under pressure from the accumulator actuates the booster power piston to apply the master cylinder.

ANTI-LOCK BRAKE SYSTEMS

ANTI-LOCK BRAKE SYSTEMS, as mentioned, work on the principle of providing very rapid and repeated brake applications and releases (10-15 per second) to bring the vehicle to a stop without brake lockup or skidding. Otherwise, a panic stop could result in a four wheel skid and steering control is lost.

GM ANTI-LOCK BRAKE SYSTEMS

One anti-lock brake system used by several General Motors divisions is computer controlled to enhance steerability, stability, and stopping distance on most road surfaces. It is designed as part of the four wheel disc brake system.

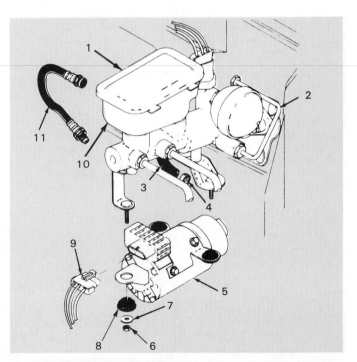

Fig. 52-39. General Motors Powermaster system includes: 1—Reservoir cover and diaphragm. 2—Tube and nut assembly. 3—Sump hose. 4—Hose clamp. 5—Electro-hydraulic pump. 6—Nut. 7—Washer. 8—Grommet. 9—Electrical connector. 10—Master cylinder and reservoir. 11—Pressure hose assembly. (Cadillac Motor Car Div., General Motors Corp.)

The GM anti-lock system, Fig. 52-40, was developed in conjunction with Alfred Teves Corp. of Germany. It consists of an electro-hydraulic booster, a speed sensor at each wheel, an electronic control unit, and associated relays and wiring harness. The booster includes an electric motor, pump, reservoir, accumulator, and valve block. See Fig. 52-41.

In operation, the speed sensors at each wheel send electronic pulsed signals to the control unit. Two microprocessors in the control unit receive and process the wheel speed and acceleration/deceleration data and produce a control signal which is sent to the hydraulic unit's valve block. If the microprocessors detect wheel slip during brake application, the computer signals the valve block to automatically adjust hydraulic pressure to each brake caliper to prevent wheel lockup.

A computerized anti-lock brake system based on the Robert Bosch ABS II design is used on late model Corvettes. See Fig. 52-42. Key elements are rotational speed sensors, an electronic control unit, and a hydraulic modulator.

In operation, the sensors "read" wheel speed and send signals to the electronic control unit. The control unit continously evaluates the signals. If they show that a wheel is about to lockup, the control unit "commands" the hydraulic modulator to decrease hydraulic pressure. As a result, magnetic valves in the modulator are designed to lower line pressure, or maintain existing pressure, or increase it based on electronic signal processing.

This anti-lock brake system also tests itself every time the vehicle is started and every time the brakes are applied. The system evaluates its own signals. If a defect is detected, the system then turns off, leaving normal braking unaffected.

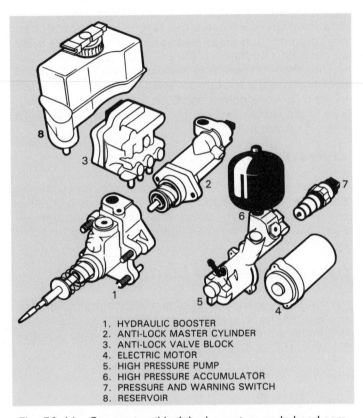

1. HYDRAULIC BOOSTER
2. ANTI-LOCK MASTER CYLINDER
3. ANTI-LOCK VALVE BLOCK
4. ELECTRIC MOTOR
5. HIGH PRESSURE PUMP
6. HIGH PRESSURE ACCUMULATOR
7. PRESSURE AND WARNING SWITCH
8. RESERVOIR

Fig. 52-41. Compact anti-lock brake system underhood components are shown in exploded view of major assemblies. (Pontiac Motor Div., General Motors Corp.)

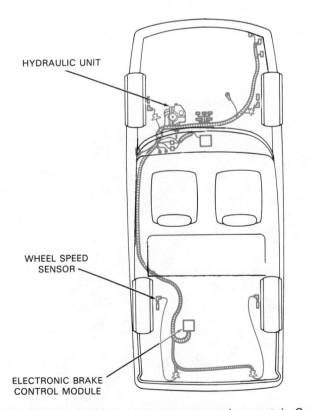

Fig. 52-40. Anti-lock brake system used on certain General Motors cars consists of a speed sensor at each wheel, electronic controller, hydraulic unit, and warning lamp at the dash. (Cadillac Motor Car Div., General Motors Corp.)

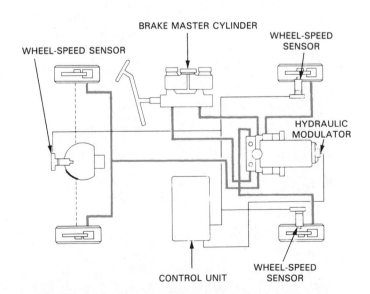

Fig. 52-42. Setup of major elements of Bosch's computerized anti-lock brake system is presented in diagrammatic form. (Robert Bosch Corp.)

FORD ANTI-LOCK BRAKES

The master cylinder in Ford's anti-lock brake system, Fig. 52-43, activates the two front disc brakes independently. The accumulator (separate from master cylinder) releases high-pressure hydraulic fluid to activate the rear brakes.

During operation, a computer monitors inputs from wheel sensors, Fig. 52-44. When a decrease in wheel rotational speed indicates that lockup is about to occur, the computer actuates solenoid valves in the valve body to modulate hydraulic pressure in the system.

The computer uses two microprocessors programmed identically. If the microprocessors detect a failure in the system, or they do not agree on a test result, the anti-lock brake system will be shut down and a warning light will signal the driver.

CHRYSLER ANTI-LOCK BRAKES

Chrysler's anti-lock brake system utilizes an electronic control unit, wheel speed sensors, a hydraulic unit, electric motor-hydraulic pump assembly, wiring relays, hydraulic tubing, and connectors. See Fig. 52-45 for details.

LUCAS GIRLING STOP CONTROL SYSTEM

Obviously, there is a lot of similarity among anti-lock brake systems. However, Lucas Girling has developed a somewhat different approach called Stop Control System, (SCS), Fig. 52-46.

The SCS is designed for use on small and medium front wheel drive cars. It has two major components termed "modulator units." These units are operated by toothed belts from the drive shafts on either side of the transmission. Each modulator is made up of an integrated sensor, pump, and the brake modulator assembly. The modulator controls the adjacent front wheel and the diagonally opposite rear wheel (through an apportioning valve).

In operation, the sensor determines when the front wheel is nearing the "lock point." Then, it signals the modulator to reduce hydraulic pressure in that particular brake circuit. When the wheel speeds up, the pump raises the pressure to resume the appropriate braking force. This alternate lowering and raising of pressure takes place many times per second to avoid wheel locking and to provide steering control and stability.

BRAKE SERVICE

WARNING: WHEN SERVICING WHEEL BRAKE PARTS, BREATHING DUST CONTAINING ASBESTOS FIBERS MAY CAUSE SERIOUS BODILY HARM. Special equipment is available to contain the asbestos particles, Fig. 52-47 and Fig. 52-48.

HYDRAULIC SYSTEM SERVICE

In order to operate satisfactorily, the various parts of the hydraulic brake system must be in good mechanical condition and the system full of clean brake fluid of the approved type. Mineral oil of any kind will swell and ruin the rubber cups and other parts of the system. Furthermore, mineral oil does not have the proper viscosity characteristics for use in an automobile.

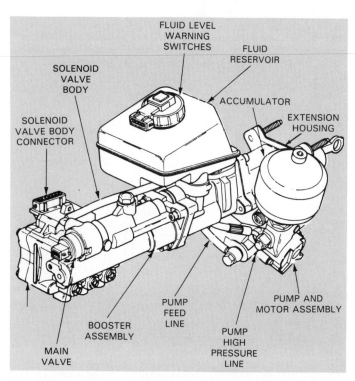

Fig. 52-43. Heart of Ford's computerized anti-lock brake system is a compact combination of assemblies including master cylinder, brake booster, and accumulator. (Ford Motor Co.)

Fig. 52-44. Toothed speed sensors at each wheel in Ford's anti-lock brake system send signals to a computer to provide advance warning of a potential brake lock up. (Ford Motor Co.)

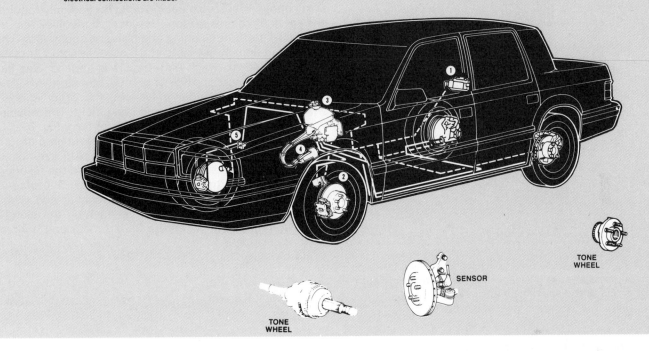

① **ELECTRONIC CONTROL UNIT (ECU):** A solid state electronic device containing a computer. The ECU controls the system valves and components based on various inputs such as wheel speed sensor signals. The ECU also has system failure detection and self-diagnostic capabilities.

② **WHEEL SPEED SENSORS:** Electro-magnetic pick-ups with toothed wheels, known as tone wheels, mounted directly to the rotating components of the drivetrain or brake system. The speed sensors supply a voltage signal to the ECU whose frequency is directly proportional to the wheel speed.

③ **HYDRAULIC UNIT:** An electro-hydraulic or electro-pneumatic device for controlling pressure to one or more of the wheel brakes. The hydraulic unit functions independently of the applied brake effort. The hydraulic unit also contains an accumulator which stores fluid and pressure for normal power assist and anti-lock function along with the sensor block through which all of the electrical connections are made.

④ **PUMP/MOTOR ASSEMBLY:** An electric motor which drives a hydraulic pump used to maintain the accumulator pressure between approximately 2,000 to 2,600 psi.

⑤ **WIRING, RELAYS, HYDRAULIC TUBING AND CONNECTORS** to attach these devices to each other, to the brake system and electrical systems of the vehicle.

TONE WHEEL

SENSOR

TONE WHEEL

Fig. 52-45. Major components of Chrysler's anti-lock brake system are coded by number to accompanying descriptive copy. (Chrysler Corp.)

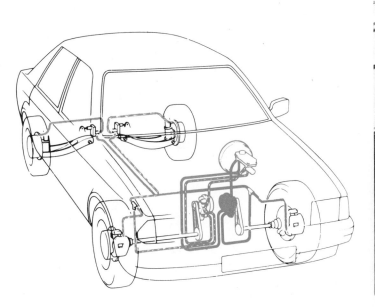

Fig. 52-46. A hydro-mechanical Stop Control System utilizes two modulator units operated by toothed belts driven by transmission drive shafts on front wheel drive cars. (Lucas Girling, Lucas Industries Inc.)

Fig. 52-47. An asbestos cleaning system has a large cleaning tank with viewing window, air gun, and air and vacuum attachments. A powerful vacuum cleaner picks up dust and asbestos fibers blasted loose by compressed air. (Nilfisk of America, Inc.)

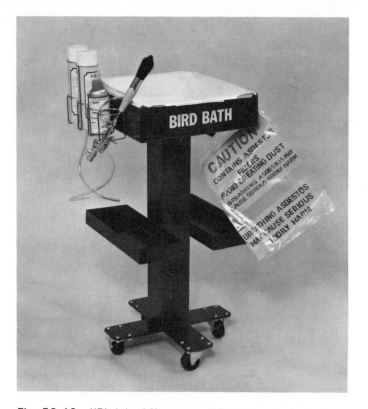

Fig. 52-48. "Bird bath" type wetting treatment controls asbestos and acts as a brake cleaner and parts washer. System uses filters and disposable bags. (U.S. Sales Co.)

The fluid MUST BE CLEAN. Dirt in the valves will cause them to leak. If there is any doubt about the condition of the old brake fluid, drain it out and flush the system. Flushing equipment and adapters are available. Flushing will avoid clogging of ports, sticking valves, leaking and scored cylinders, and erratic brake action. In addition, periodic flushing (once a year is usual recommendation) will remove any gum from the old fluid, condensed moisture, bits of scale and rubber, etc.

Before adding new fluid to the brake system, inspect the flexible hoses to make sure that they are not weakened, frayed, or swollen. All connections and fittings should be checked for leaks and to make sure that lines are securely fastened to the frame to avoid vibration and eventual breakage. Sometimes lines get kinked, dented, or worn thin from rubbing against sheet metal. If defective in any way, brake lines should be replaced.

If the master cylinder and wheel cylinders are known to be in good condition, fresh fluid can be added and the system "bled" to remove all air. If there is any air in the system, the pedal will have a "spongy" feel since hydraulic pressure is compressing the air.

SERVICING HYDRAULIC CYLINDERS

When any work must be done on either the master cylinder, calipers, or wheel cylinders, absolute cleanliness is of utmost importance. Solvents or gasoline should NOT be used to clean the boots, cups, grommets, diaphragms, or any rubber parts. Alcohol is the proper cleaning fluid.

The cylinder bore must be free of scratches, grooves, or pits. A cast iron master cylinder or wheel cylinder can be polished with a special hone made for the purpose. (NOTE: DO NOT hone aluminum master cylinders.)

BLEEDING BRAKES

There are two general methods used to bleed air from hydraulic brake systems. The manual method requires two people. Pressure bleeding is faster and only requires the services of one person. However, it involves the use of special pressure flushing and bleeding equipment. This equipment usually consists of a closed, airtight container of brake fluid to which air pressure is applied. See Fig. 52-49. With either power or manual bleeding, a hose is attached to the bleeder valve and the other end immersed in a glass jar containing brake fluid. This enables bubbles to be seen and avoids waste of fluid, Fig. 52-50.

The master cylinder fill plug opening and area around it must be thoroughly cleaned before the plug is removed. Then, the container of fluid is connected to the fill opening by suitable fittings and flexible hose. The bleeder forces fluid under pressure to each caliper and wheel cylinder. Each is bled, in turn, by opening the bleeder valve and closing it when the fluid is clear and bubbles no longer appear.

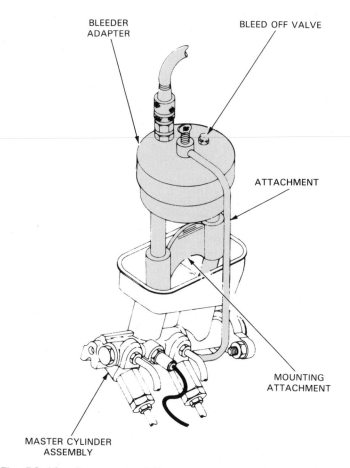

Fig. 52-49. A pressurized bleeder ball and special adapters are used to flush and/or bleed brake hydraulic system. Adapter is shown attached to master cylinder.
(Cadillac Motor Car Div., General Motors Corp.)

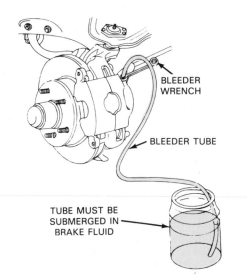

Fig. 52-50. Proper brake bleeding at calipers or wheel cylinders calls for use of bleeder tube and jar filled with brake fluid. When tube is immersed in fluid and bleeder valve is opened, bubbles indicate release of air from hydraulic system. (Cadillac Motor Car Div., General Motors Corp.)

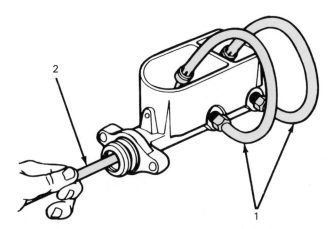

Fig. 52-51. Bench bleeding of master cylinder is done by: 1—Making two bleed tubes and installing them in outlet ports, placing other end of tubes in reservoirs. 2—With reservoirs filled with brake fluid, push rod is actuated until bubbles in fluid disappear. (American Motors Corp.)

When bleeding brakes by the manual method, it is necessary to watch the level of the fluid in the master cylinder. If it gets too low, air will be drawn into the cylinder. If possible, the master cylinder is bled first. If reconditioning on the bench, it can be bled before reinstallation as shown in Fig. 52-51.

To bleed the system manually at each wheel, generally start with right rear; next, left rear; then, right front; and left front. However, consult the manufacturer's service manual for the correct bleeding sequence for the particular vehicle being serviced.

Open the bleeder valve and have your helper slowly press the brake pedal to the floor. Close the bleeder and have your helper slowly release the pedal, then wait 15 sec. Repeat this operation until no bubbles appear in the

brake fluid in the glass jar. Then, proceed to bleed each other wheel in the recommended sequence. The 15 sec. pauses allow air to collect in large pockets that will be released more quickly and completely.

After bleeding, check the master cylinder reservoir for proper fluid level, approximately 1/4 in. from the top of the reservoir.

DISC BRAKE SERVICE

All disc brake services begin with sight, sound, and stopping tests. The feel of the brake pedal adds a check on the condition of the hydraulic brake system.

Stopping the car will indicate whether the brakes pull in one direction, stop straight, or require excessive effort to stop. Listening while stopping permits fair diagnosis of braking noises such as rattles, groans, squeals, or chatter. Some models are equipped with brake wear sensors, which contact the rotor to signal when the friction pads are worn. Take a wheel off and visually inspect the outboard shoe and lining assembly at each end of the caliper. Check the inboard lining through the hole on top of the caliper, Fig. 52-52.

A good rule-of-thumb guide to the need for lining replacement is to compare lining thickness to the thickness of the metal shoe. If the lining is not as thick as the metal shoe, it should be replaced. If the thickness of the lining is marginal, remove the caliper, carefully check the condition of the lining, and measure its thickness. Compare this measurement with manufacturer's specification. NOTE: If lining requires replacement, always replace both front wheel sets to assure equal braking action.

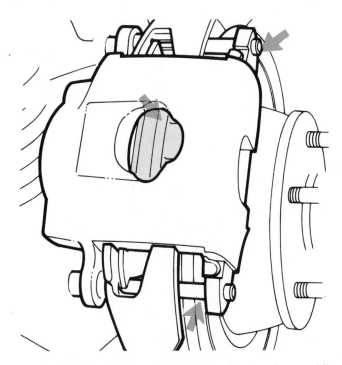

Fig. 52-52. Visual inspection of inboard brake shoe and lining assembly can be made through hole in top of caliper. Outboard shoe and lining can be viewed from end of caliper. (Buick Motor Div., General Motors Corp.)

CALIPER REMOVAL

To remove a disc brake caliper from most General Motors cars:

1. Siphon 2/3 of brake fluid from master cylinder reservoir.
2. Hoist vehicle.
3. Remove wheel and tire assembly.
4. Reinstall two lug nuts on hub to retain rotor.
5. Position adjustable pliers as shown in Fig. 52-53 and squeeze pliers to force piston to bottom of caliper bore.
6. Remove bolt holding inlet fitting.
7. Remove boots and two mounting bolts.
8. Lift caliper off mounting bracket and away from rotor.
9. Remove inboard brake shoe.
10. Use adjustable pliers to straighten bent-over shoe tab and remove outboard brake shoe.

BRAKE SHOE INSTALLATION

To install disc brake shoes (friction pads):

1. Force piston into caliper bore until it bottoms.
2. Remove sleeves and bushings from mounting bolt holes.
3. Lubricate new sleeves and bushings with silicone grease and install them in mounting bolt holes.
4. Install inboard brake shoe, Fig. 52-54.
5. Install outboard shoe with wear sensor at leading edge of shoe. See Fig. 52-55. Use a ball peen hammer to clinch shoe tab.
6. Install caliper over rotor in mounting bracket.
7. Install mounting bolts and torque to manufacturer's specifications.
8. Connect inlet fitting and torque to specifications.
9. Install tire and wheel assembly, lower car, and torque wheel lugs or nuts to specification.

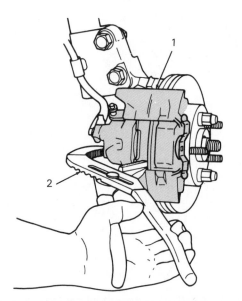

Fig. 52-53. In some disc brake applications, a pliers can be used to compress piston to bottom of caliper bore: 1—Caliper. 2—Pliers. (Oldsmobile Div., General Motors Corp.)

10. Refill master cylinder reservoir with brake fluid. Test brake pedal reserve. If pedal is spongy, bleed system.

CALIPER OVERHAUL

To overhaul a disc brake caliper:

1. Remove caliper as outlined in caliper removal procedure.
2. Place caliper assembly on clean work bench, loosen bleeder screw and drain out remaining fluid. Retighten bleeder screw.
3. Place caliper on bench. Put shop towel opposite piston and feed compressed air through inlet port until piston is forced out. See Fig. 52-56.

Fig. 52-54. Drawing illustrates how to install inboard brake shoe and lining assembly in disc brake caliper: 1—Shoe retainer spring. 2—Caliper housing. 3—Inboard shoe and lining. (Oldsmobile Div., General Motors Corp.)

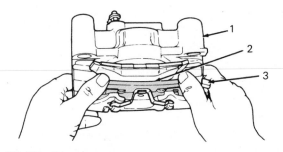
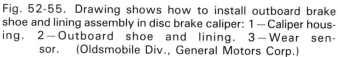

Fig. 52-55. Drawing shows how to install outboard brake shoe and lining assembly in disc brake caliper: 1—Caliper housing. 2—Outboard shoe and lining. 3—Wear sensor. (Oldsmobile Div., General Motors Corp.)

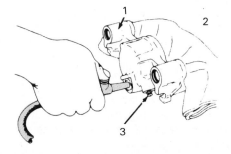

Fig. 52-56. To remove caliper piston, place shop towel opposite piston, then use air pressure to blow piston from caliper bore: 1—Caliper housing. 2—Shop towel. 3—Bleeder valve. (Oldsmobile Div., General Motors Corp.)

4. Remove dust boot from groove in caliper.

5. Use a thin-bladed plastic or wooden tool to remove piston seal from bore of caliper.

6. Clean and inspect piston for scoring, pitting, corrosion, or worn spots in plating.

7. Blow air through passageways in caliper. Inspect caliper bore for scoring, pitting, scratches, or corrosion. Use crocus cloth to clean bore, then wash bore with denatured alcohol and blow dry.

8. Use crocus cloth to clean all metal-to-metal contacts.

9. Coat caliper bore and new piston seal with brake fluid. Place seal in bore groove, making sure it is not twisted.

10. Fit new dust boot over piston with small screwdriver. Fig. 52-57.

11. Apply even pressure downward on piston until it bottoms in caliper bore.

12. Install boot in caliper housing counterbore and seat boot with suitable tool.

13. Replace sleeves and bushings and install new brake shoes as described in steps 2 - 5 in BRAKE SHOE INSTALLATION procedure.

14. Before installing caliper on rotor, check lateral runout of rotor. Tighten spindle nut to remove play from wheel bearings. Fasten a dial indicator to spindle, Fig. 52-58, or to steering linkage so that point

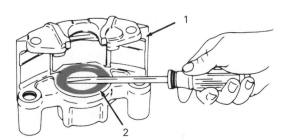

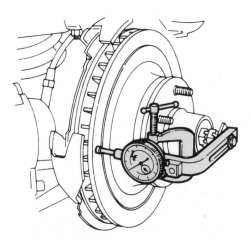

Fig. 52-57. A small screwdriver is used to install dust boot over caliper piston: 1—Caliper housing. 2—Boot. (Oldsmobile Div., General Motors Corp.)

of stylus contacts rotor face about one inch from rotor edge. Check rotor runout for one revolution and compare reading with manufacturer's specification (ranges from .002 to .005 in. or .05 to .13 mm).

Check rotor for thickness and parallelism. Use a micrometer to measure rotor thickness and thickness variation at five equidistant points from outer edge of rotor. (Thickness variation calls for maximum of .0005 in. or .013 mm).

15. Service rotor as required (clean, resurface, or replace). See Figs. 52-59 and 52-60.

Fig. 52-59. Service technician positions twin cutters independently and prepares to simultaneously cut both surfaces of rotor. (Ammco Tools, Inc.)

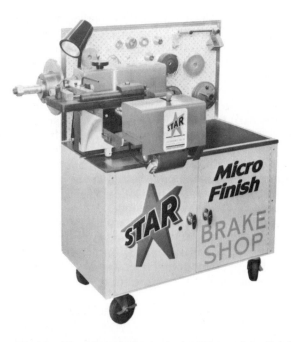

Fig. 52-60. Disc/drum lathe is designed to micro-finish disc brake rotors without grinding. Cutters machine both rotor surfaces at same time. Rotating tool plate changes disc lathe to drum turning lathe. (Star Machine and Tool Co.)

Fig. 52-58. A lateral runout check with dial indicator gives an accurate test of flatness or machined surface of rotor. (Buick Motor Div., General Motors Corp.)

16. Clean mounting bracket, especially metal-to-metal contacts.
17. Slowly slide caliper down over rotor until holes in caliper line up with holes in mounting bracket.
18. Install mounting bolts, torquing to specification.
19. Install bolt holding inlet fitting, torquing to specification.
20. Bleed system.
21. Install tire and wheel assembly and lower car.
22. Torque wheel lugs or nuts to specification.

SPECIAL PROCEDURES

Disc brake service on other-than-GM vehicles is similar to the above procedures. However, design differences and special notes and cautions are contained in the manufacturers' service manuals. Chrysler, for example, recommends ''that compressed air not be used to remove piston from rotor.'' Instead, ''with caliper removed from rotor and brake hose still attached, carefully depress brake pedal to hydraulically force piston out of bore.''

Chrysler also recommends measuring thickness of rotor at 12 points around rotor, making all measurements one inch from edge of rotor. See Fig. 52-61. Also, with piston bottomed in caliper bore, clean machined ways and lubricate adapter and guides with multipurpose lubricant.

On Ford rear wheel drive models, ''remove and discard locating pin insulators and plastic sleeves. Do not reuse these parts.'' Also on Ford models, when pressing caliper piston into bore, ''be careful not to pry directly against plastic caliper piston.''

DRUM BRAKE SERVICE

Drum brakes utilize internal expanding brake shoe assemblies to create the friction and heat required to slow and stop the rotating drums. The brake lining is a friction material attached to the near semicircular metal shoe by rivets or by bonding.

With riveting, the rivets are countersunk about two thirds of the way through the lining and exactly the same size as the rivet head for greater strength. Also, the hole in the lining is the same size as the hole in the brake shoe.

With bonding, a cement is used between the shoe and lining, and the assembly is placed in an oven for curing. With either riveting or bonding, the lining must adhere tightly to the shoe, yet with minimum resistance to the dissipation of the heat of braking.

The surface of the brake lining of newly relined shoes may not conform accurately to the surface of the brake drum. New lining has slight high and low spots. Or, if the drum has been reconditioned, it will be slightly larger in diameter and will not conform to the arc of the brake shoes.

Brake shoes should be ground with SPECIAL BRAKE SHOE-GRINDING EQUIPMENT, not only to smooth the surface, but to conform to the curvature of the brake drum. Always wear a respirator when grinding brake lining and see that the machine's exhaust system is working properly.

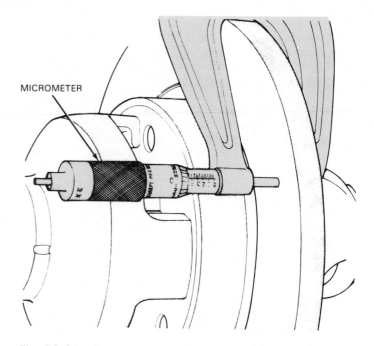

MICROMETER

Fig. 52-61. A micrometer is used to check thickness variation of disc brake rotor at 12 equidistant points on rotor surfaces on Chrysler cars.   (Chrysler Corp.)

If the brake shoes are used without grinding, the high spots of the lining will do all the braking, and much higher than normal temperatures will result. High heat will quickly heat check or completely ruin new lining.

Care must be exercised so that no grease, oil, or brake fluid reaches the brake lining. Any fluid contamination will affect the coefficient of friction and grabbing brakes will result. In this connection, always replace the grease seals when new brake lining is installed. Also, wheel cylinders should be examined to make sure they are not leaking fluid. When handling brake shoes, care must be taken to avoid ''fingerprinting'' the lining.

When lubricating the front wheel bearings, use grease specified for that purpose, and only enough to lubricate the bearing. Excess lubricant may get on the brake lining and ruin it. Or, a low melting point grease may thin out and enter the brake shoe/drum area.

BRAKE DRUMS

The surface of the brake drum must be smooth and free from galling, ridges, and heat checks. In addition, the drum must not be bell-mouthed or out-of-round. The ridges, galling, and check marks are visible, but a drum gauge should be used to check brake drum diameter, Fig. 52-62. The manner in which the brake lining is worn on the shoe will also indicate the condition of the drum. A drum that is bell-mouthed, for example, will cause the lining to wear more on one side of the shoe than on the other.

Another important reason for measuring the diameter of the drum is to note whether there is enough metal to permit reconditioning. Passenger car brake drums should not be reconditioned more than 0.060 in. (1.5 mm) oversize. If more than 0.060 in. is removed (0.030 in. per

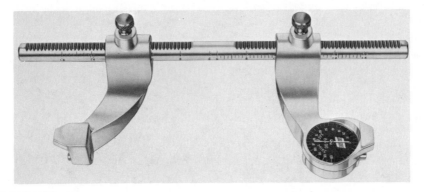

Fig.52-62. Brake drum micrometer is designed to "mike" drums on or off lathe. Instrument checks drum diameter and out-of-roundness in .005 in. increments. (Ammco Tools, Inc.)

side), it will severely weaken the drum. The drum will become oval when the brakes are applied, and, because of less metal, it will operate at much higher temperatures with attendant brake fade and short lining life.

Brake drums can be reconditioned either by turning on a lathe, Fig. 52-63, or by grinding. Both methods are used extensively. The regrinding method is used par-

ticularly in cases where the drum has hard spots.

When preparing to turn a drum on a lathe, care must be exercised that the lathe tool is sharpened correctly. Also, tool feed must be correct. If too fast, it would produce a "screw thread" surface which would cause rapid wear of the brake lining. Follow equipment manufacturer's directions, cautions, and specifications.

Fig. 52-63. Combination disc and drum brakes service center turns disc and drum at same time. Lathe automatically turns off when cuts are completed. Spindle speeds and feeds are factory set. (Hofmann Corp.)

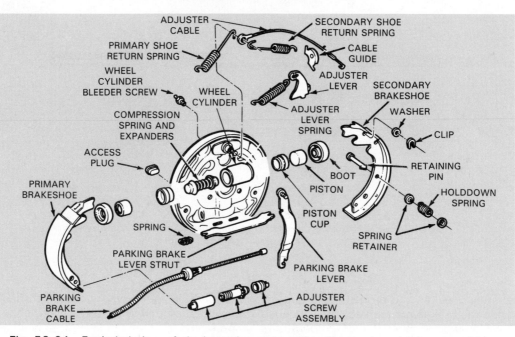

Fig. 52-64. Exploded view of single anchor automatic adjuster drum brake assembly reveals parts relationship for proper disassembly and reassembly of rear wheel drum brake.   (American Motors Corp.)

DRUM BRAKE OVERHAUL

When servicing single anchor automatic adjuster drum brake assemblies on rear wheel drive cars, Figs. 52-64 and 53-65, a typical overhaul procedure includes:

1. Raise vehicle and remove wheel and tire assembly.
2. Remove drum. If necessary, back off brake shoe adjustment. See Fig. 52-66.
3. Use special equipment to remove asbestos particles from brake assembly and backing plate.

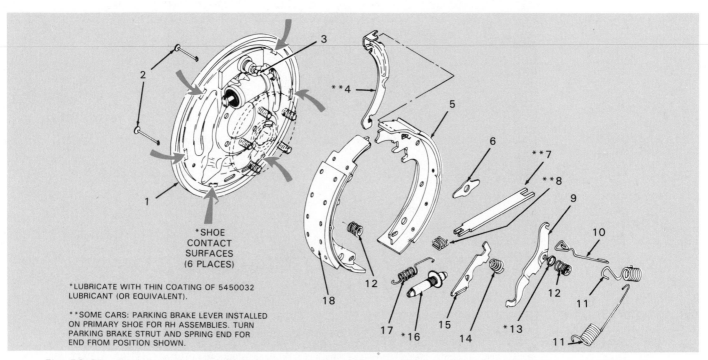

Fig. 52-65. Exploded view details makeup of single anchor automatic adjuster drum brake: 1—Backing plate. 2—Hold-down pins. 3—Anchor pin. 4—Parking brake lever. 5—Secondary shoe. 6—Shoe guide. 7—Parking brake strut. 8—Strut spring. 9—Actuator lever. 10—Actuator link. 11—Return spring. 12—Hold-down spring. 13—Lever pivot. 14—Lever return spring. 15—Pawl. 16—Adjusting screw assembly. 17—Adjusting screw spring. 18—Primary shoe.   (Oldsmobile Div., General Motors Corp.)

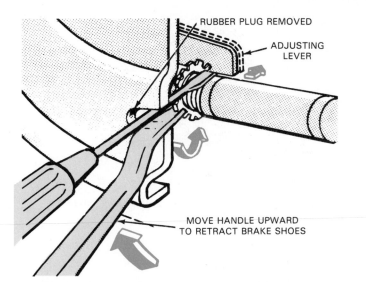

Fig. 52-66. To back off brake shoe adjustment, use screwdriver to lift adjusting lever away from star wheel, then turn star wheel with brake adjusting tool.   (Ford Motor Co.)

4. Remove return springs, adjuster cable, and anchor plate.
5. Disengage and remove adjusting lever.
6. Remove spring from pivot.
7. Pull shoes away from anchor and wheel cylinder and remove star wheel assembly.
8. Remove parking brake strut and anti-rattle spring.
9. Remove shoe hold-down assemblies.
10. Back off parking brake cable adjustment, disconnect cable, and remove lever.
11. Remove brake shoes.
12. Clean backing plate thoroughly, polish all shoe contact ledges with fine emery cloth, then coat ledges with special lubricant. See Fig. 52-65.
13. Lubricate pivot end of parking brake lever and insert lever into hole in secondary shoe from inner side of shoe web.
14. Connect parking brake cable to inside of lever.
15. Place secondary shoe against backing plate and anchor, then slide shoe web into wheel cylinder or wheel cylinder push rod.
16. Slide parking brake strut into lever slot and install anti-rattle spring in proper position on strut.
17. Slide primary shoe into position on backing plate and into wheel cylinder or wheel cylinder push rod.
18. Install anchor plate and adjuster cable.
19. Install primary shoe return spring.
20. Hold cable guide in position on secondary shoe and install return spring through guide from shoe web to anchor pin.
21. Install star wheel assembly between heels of shoes with star wheel next to secondary shoe. NOTE: Star wheels generally are stamped L and R for left and right wheel brake assemblies. Install as indicated.
22. Install adjusting lever and spring over pivot pin, then lock lever in position.
23. Install hold-down assemblies.
24. Place adjuster cable over guide and hook end of overload spring in adjusting lever.

Fig. 52-67. Computerized brake lathe has "touch" panel to control precise speeds and feeds on both finish and rough cuts on drums and rotors. Unit has safety shield, cross feed travel limiters, emergency stop button.   (Ammco Tools, Inc.)

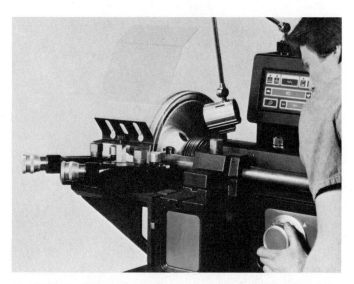

Fig. 52-68. Service techncian uses computerized brake lathe to machine brake drum. Technician positions boring bar, then sets dial for proper depth of cut.   (Ammco Tools, Inc.)

25. Inspect friction surface of drum for amount of wear and degree of scoring.
26. If necessary, resurface drum on brake drum lathe. See Figs. 52-67 and 52-68.

Fig. 52-69. To adjust brake shoes to fit drum: Left. Adjust gauge to drum diameter. Right. Adjust star wheel to fit other side of gauge. (Pontiac Motor Div., General Motors Corp.)

27. Adjust brake drum gauge to drum size, Fig. 52-69.
28. Place other side of gauge across brake shoe diameter and adjust star wheel to expand brake shoes to "fit" gauge. Proper shoe-to-drum clearance is built into gauge.
29. Install brake drum and wheel and tire assembly.
30. Lower vehicle, then adjust parking brake cables.

When servicing "leading-trailing" non-servo type rear wheel brake assemblies on front wheel drive cars, Fig. 52-70, a typical overhaul procedure includes:

1. Raise vehicle and remove wheel and tire assembly.
2. Remove hub and drum assembly. If necessary, back off brake shoe adjustment.
3. Use special equipment to remove asbestos particles from brake assembly and backing plate.
4. Install clamp over wheel cylinder pistons.
5. Remove shoe hold-down assemblies.
6. Lift entire mechanical brake assembly (shoes, springs, and adjuster) from backing plate, Fig. 52-71. Use care to avoid bending adjusting lever.

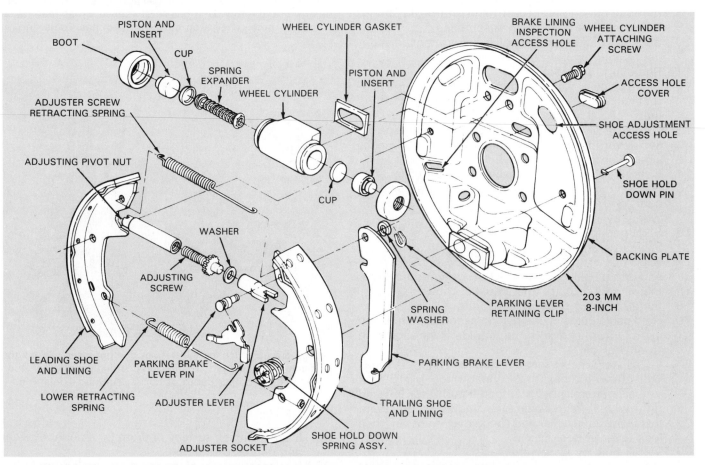

Fig. 52-70. Exploded view of leading-trailing type of drum brake assembly can aid in disassembly and reassembly operations during a brake overhaul procedure. (Ford Motor Co.)

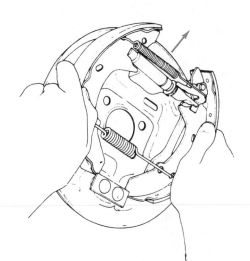

Fig. 52-71. After hold-down assemblies are removed, entire brake assembly can be lifted up and away from anchors and backing plate. (Ford Motor Co.)

TRAILING SHOE AND LINING ASSEMBLY

INSTALL ADJUSTER SCREW ASSEMBLY

PARKING BRAKE LEVER

NOTE:
SOCKET BLADE MARKED R AND L. INSTALL LETTER IN UPRIGHT POSITION FACING WHEEL CYLINDER TO INSURE PROPER SLOT ENGAGEMENT TO PARKING BRAKE LEVER

DEEP SLOT

LEFT BRAKE ASSEMBLY SHOWN
RIGHT BRAKE ASSEMBLY SYMETRICALLY OPPOSITE

Fig. 52-72. With mechanical brake assembly in place on backing plate, install adjuster screw assembly as shown and noted. (Ford Motor Co.)

7. Remove parking brake cable from parking brake lever.
8. Remove lower and upper retracting springs, freeing adjuster mechanism.
9. Remove retaining clip and spring washer, and slide lever off parking brake lever pin on trailing shoe.
10. Clean backing plate thoroughly, polish all shoe contact ledges with fine emery cloth, then coat ledges with special, high temperature lubricant.
11. Apply lubricant to adjuster screw threads and socket end of adjusting screw.
12. Install adjuster washer, Fig. 52-70, over socket end of adjusting screw, then install socket.
13. Turn adjusting screw into adjusting pivot nut to limit of threads, then back off one turn.
14. Use spring washer and new retaining clip to attach parking brake lever to trailing shoe. Crimp clip.
15. Attach parking brake cable to parking brake lever.
16. Install lower shoe retracting spring and place assembly on backing plate, sliding shoes downward inside of shoe retaining plate. See Fig. 52-70.
17. Install adjuster screw assembly between leading shoe slot and slot in trailing shoe and parking brake lever, Fig. 52-72.
18. Attach upper shoe retracting spring to leading shoe slot. Stretch other end of spring to engage notch on adjuster lever. Make sure that lever contacts star wheel.
19. Inspect friction surface of drum for amount of wear and degree of scoring.
20. If necessary, resurface drum on brake drum lathe.
21. Adjust brake drum gauge to drum size. Place other end of gauge across brake shoe diameter, hold automatic adjusting lever away from star wheel, and expand shoes to fit gauge.
22. Install brake drum and wheel and tire assembly.
23. Lubricate and adjust wheel bearings.
24. Lower vehicle and adjust parking brake cables.
25. Bleed brake system.

TROUBLESHOOTING BRAKES

Excessive Pedal Travel
1. Air in brake lines.
2. Fluid leak.
3. Faulty automatic adjusters.
4. Maladjusted master cylinder push rod.
5. Worn drum brake lining.
6. Fluid bypassing quick take-up valve to reservoir.
7. Partial brake system failure.

Excessive Pedal Effort
1. Glazed or poor quality brake lining.
2. Sticking wheel cylinder or caliper pistons.
3. Calipers binding on mounting pins.
4. Binding or damaged pedal linkage.
5. Partial brake system failure.
6. Excessively worn brake linings.
7. Clogged quick take-up valve.
8. Insufficient vacuum to power brake unit.
9. Restricted or clogged lines or hoses.
10. Contaminated brake fluid.
11. Malfunctioning master cylinder.
12. Faulty proportioning valve.
13. Leaking or loose power brake unit vacuum hose.
14. Defective power brake unit.

Pedal Spongy
1. Air in hydraulic system.
2. Bent or distorted drum brake shoes.

Pedal Pulsates
1. Out-of-round drums.
2. Excessive lateral runout of rotor.

Slow Pedal Return
1. Clogged holes in quick take-up valve.

Brake Grab

1. Grease or fluid on linings.
2. Maladjusted parking brake cables.
3. Heat-spotted or scored brake drums or rotors.
4. Maladjusted master cylinder push rod.
5. Loose caliper attaching bolts.
6. Binding brake pedal mechanism.
7. Malfunctioning power brake unit.

Brakes Drag

1. Contaminated brake fluid.
2. Maladjusted parking brake cables.
3. Faulty automatic adjusters.
4. Sticking wheel cylinders or caliper pistons.
5. Brake pedal binding at pivot.
6. Maladjusted master cylinder push rod.
7. Malfunctioning master cylinder.
8. Faulty metering valve.
9. Faulty proportioning valve.
10. Restricted lines or hoses.

Brakes Fade

1. Defective master cylinder.
2. External fluid leak.
3. Vapor lock in system.
4. Thin brake drums.
5. Crystallized brake lining.

Brakes Chatter

1. Loose or missing brake assembly attaching parts.
2. Bent or distorted brake shoes.
3. Glazed brake lining.
4. Loose caliper attaching bolts.
5. Loose front suspension parts.
6. Heat-spotted or scored brake drum or rotor.
7. Excessive lateral runout of rotor.
8. Out-of-parallel rotor.
9. Loose wheel bearings.

Brakes Pull to One Side

1. Unequal air pressure in front tires.
2. Unmatched tires on same axle.
3. Grease or fluid on brake lining.
4. Loose caliper attaching bolts.
5. Seized wheel cylinder or caliper.
6. Restricted brake lines or hoses.
7. Worn or damaged wheel bearings.
8. Loose front suspension parts.
9. Faulty combination valve.

Scraping Noise from Brakes

1. Worn out brake lining.
2. Uneven brake lining wear.
3. Contaminated brake lining.
4. Bent, broken, distorted brake shoes.
5. Loose or missing brake assembly attaching parts.
6. Incorrect wheel bearing adjustment.
7. Loose front suspension parts.
8. Interference between caliper and wheel or rotor.
9. Scored or tapered brake drum.

Brakes Squeak

1. Worn out brake lining.
2. Glazed or poor quality brake lining.
3. Contaminated brake lining.
4. Excessive brake lining dust.
5. Weak, damaged, or incorrect shoe retracting springs.
6. Heat-spotted or scored brake drum or rotor.
7. Burred or rusted caliper.
8. Rough or dry drum brake backing plate ledges.

Brake Warning Light On

1. Insufficient fluid in master cylinder reservoirs.
2. Hydraulic system failure.
3. Parking brake ON or not fully released.
4. Insufficient vacuum to power brake unit.

POWER BRAKE SYSTEM SERVICE

Generally, the same kinds of operational problems can occur on cars with either power brakes or standard brakes. Excessive pedal effort, excessive pedal travel, dragging brakes, and grabbing brakes all could be caused by a malfunction in cars with or without power brakes.

However, note in TROUBLESHOOTING BRAKES how much more prevalent the possible causes are in the mechanical and hydraulic parts of the overall brake system rather than in the power brake unit. Therefore, when brake trouble occurs, these systems should be checked out first.

GM SINGLE DIAPHRAGM UNIT

With regard to specific power brake problems:

1. Hard pedal could be caused by: a restricted air filter; vacuum failure; defective diaphragm; worn or distorted action plate or levers; cracked or broken power piston or retainer. See Fig. 52-73.
2. Failure to release could be caused by: a blocked passage in power piston; air valve stuck closed; broken piston return spring or air valve spring.
3. Dragging brakes could be caused by a piston rod (master cylinder push rod) of incorrect length. Out-of-limits push rod will cause primary cup to overlap compensating port of master cylinder.

A special disassembly and reassembly tool, Fig. 52-74, is required to unlock the two housings of the typical General Motors single or tandem diaphragm power brake unit shown in Fig. 52-73.

After disassembly, components may be inspected and replaced if defective. The power piston should not be disassembled. The inside diameter of the diaphragm lip should be lubricated and fit into the diaphragm support. A new diaphragm retainer must be installed, using a special driving tool.

The special disassembly and reassembly tool is used to lock the two housings together, Fig. 52-74. A special gauge is used to check master cylinder push rod "height" with the power unit placed in a padded vise with front housing up. See Fig. 52-75. If the push rod is out of limits, it must be replaced with an adjustable service push rod.

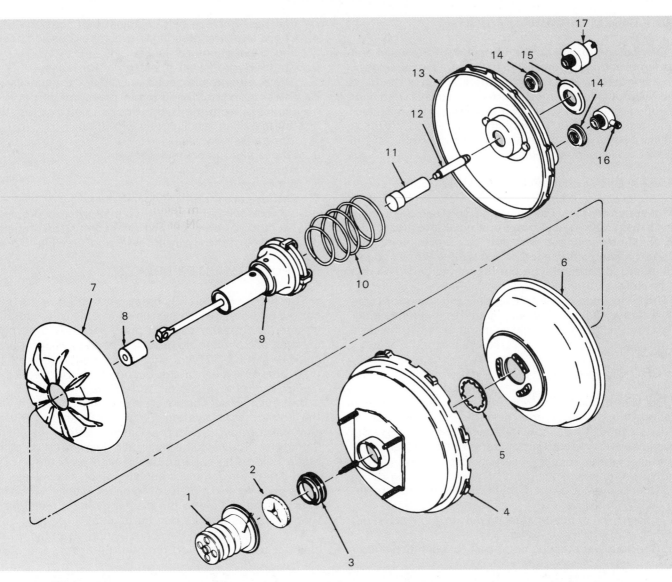

Fig. 52-73. Exploded view of General Motors single diaphragm power brake unit shows relationship of interior and exterior parts: 1—Boot. 2—Silencer. 3—Power piston bearing. 4—Rear housing. 5—Diaphragm retainer. 6—Diaphragm. 7—Diaphragm support. 8—Filter. 9—Power piston and push rod assembly. 10—Return spring. 11—Reaction retainer. 12—Piston rod. 13—Front housing. 14—Grommet. 15—Front housing seal. 16—Vacuum check valve. 17—Vacuum switch.   (Buick Motor Div., General Motors Corp.)

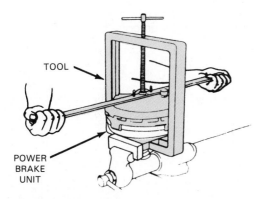

Fig. 52-74. A special holding fixture is used to apply pressure to power brake unit, then lever is turned counterclockwise to unlock front and rear housings. Lever is turned clockwise to lock housings.   (Buick Motor Div., General Motors Corp.)

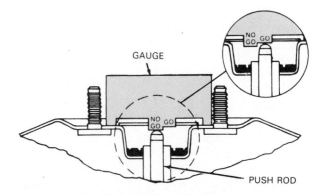

Fig. 52-75. After resssembly of General Motors single or tandem diaphragm power brake unit, a special go/no-go gauge is used to check master cylinder push rod height.   (Buick Motor Div., General Motors Corp.)

GM TANDEM DIAPHRAGM UNIT

Service operations on the General Motors single and tandem diaphragm power brake units are similar. Again, a holding fixture is needed to unlock and lock the front and rear housings. A special assembly cone is used over the push rod end of the power piston to aid in reassembling the secondary diaphragm and related parts. A special go/no-go gauge is used to check "height" of the master cylinder push rod.

BENDIX SINGLE DIAPHRAGM UNIT

American Motors, Chrysler, and Ford use the Bendix single diaphragm power brake unit on all late model cars except those equipped with anti-lock brakes. In servicing cars having a damaged or inoperative Bendix power brake unit, disassembly in not recommended. The unit is serviced as a complete assembly only.

The Bendix unit on AMC, Chrysler, and some Ford cars use a factory adjusted or nonadjustable master cylinder push rod. No attempt should be made to adjust this type of push rod.

HYDRO-BOOST II

The Hydro-Boost II power brake, Fig. 52-76, is also a part of the power steering system. Therefore, trouble in the steering system (low fluid level, low steering pump pressure, etc.) may affect operation of Hydro-Boost II.

When trouble occurs, certain preliminary checks should be made:
1. Check level of brake fluid in master cylinder reservoir. Fill, if low.
2. Check level of power steering fluid in pump reservoir. Fill, if low.
3. Check power steering pump belt for condition and/or damage. Replace belt or adjust belt tension.
4. Check all power steering lines, brake lines and hoses, and connections for leaks.
5. Check Hydro-Boost II assembly for leaks.
6. Check engine idle speed and adjust if necessary.
7. Check power steering pump pressure.

Fluid leaks from the Hydro-Boost II unit can be stopped by installing replacement seal kits:
1. Input assembly seal.
2. Power piston/accumulator seal.
3. Housing-to-housing cover seal.
4. Spool valve seal.
5. Return port fitting O-ring.

Seal replacement and correction of internal problems (faulty spool valve or piston/accumulator) requires disassembly of the Hydro-Boost II unit. See Fig. 52-76.

GM POWERMASTER BRAKES

The POWERMASTER brake assembly is a self-contained power brake system that utilizes a hydraulic booster and master cylinder pressurized by a nitrogen charged accumulator to provide a power assist for braking. See Fig. 52-77. A dual-pressure switch controls the fluid pressure level in the accumulator by turning an electro-hydraulic pump on and off as needed.

Brake fluid level checks are especially important with the Powermaster system. First and foremost, the accumulator must be depressurized before servicing. Otherwise, opening the hydraulic system could cause brake fluid to be sprayed out at high pressure.

To depressurize the accumulator, apply and release the brake pedal at about 50 lb. of force for at least 10 cycles. This will return fluid to the master cylinder reservoir so that fluid level checks can be made.

After depressurizing the accumulator, clean the master cylinder reservoir cover, remove the cover, and check

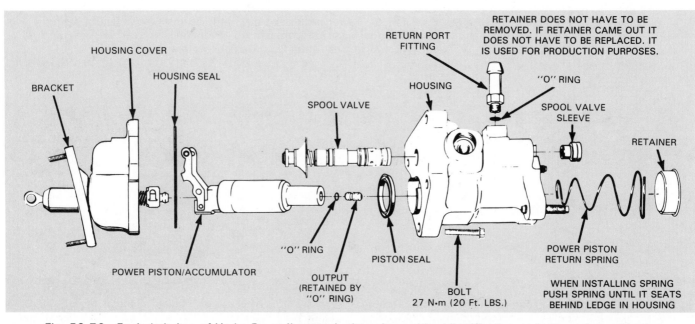

Fig. 52-76. Exploded view of Hydro-Boost II power brake unit provides identification and gives relative location of parts. Also note service cautions. (Oldsmobile Div., General Motors Corp.)

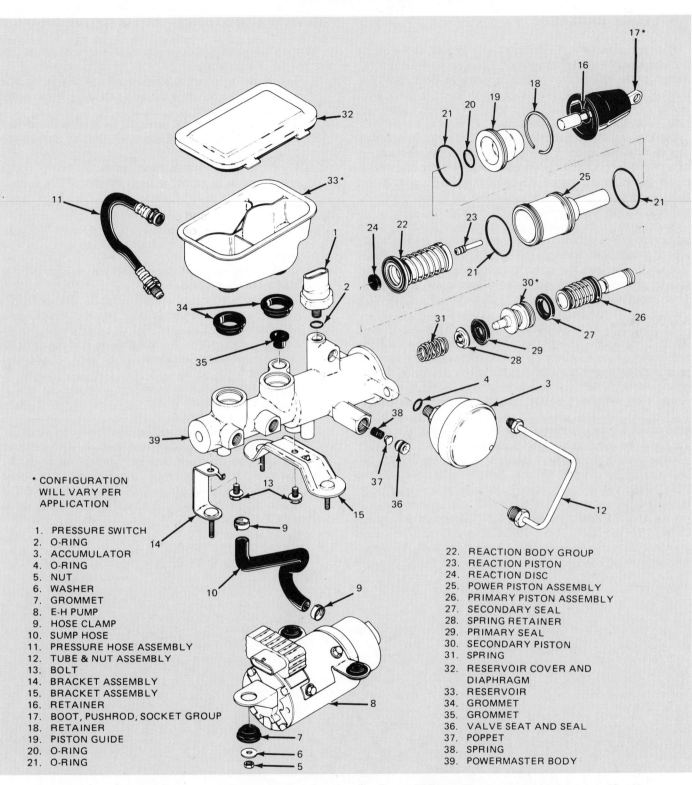

Fig. 52-77. Exploded view shows arrangement of parts of a General Motors Powermaster brake assembly. Key elements of assembly are: 1—Dual Pressure switch. 3—Accumulator. 8—Electro-hydraulic pump. 25—Power piston. (Buick Motor Div., General Motors Corp.)

* CONFIGURATION
WILL VARY PER
APPLICATION

1.   PRESSURE SWITCH
2.   O-RING
3.   ACCUMULATOR
4.   O-RING
5.   NUT
6.   WASHER
7.   GROMMET
8.   E-H PUMP
9.   HOSE CLAMP
10.   SUMP HOSE
11.   PRESSURE HOSE ASSEMBLY
12.   TUBE & NUT ASSEMBLY
13.   BOLT
14.   BRACKET ASSEMBLY
15.   BRACKET ASSEMBLY
16.   RETAINER
17.   BOOT, PUSHROD, SOCKET GROUP
18.   RETAINER
19.   PISTON GUIDE
20.   O-RING
21.   O-RING

22.   REACTION BODY GROUP
23.   REACTION PISTON
24.   REACTION DISC
25.   POWER PISTON ASSEMBLY
26.   PRIMARY PISTON ASSEMBLY
27.   SECONDARY SEAL
28.   SPRING RETAINER
29.   PRIMARY SEAL
30.   SECONDARY PISTON
31.   SPRING
32.   RESERVOIR COVER AND
        DIAPHRAGM
33.   RESERVOIR
34.   GROMMET
35.   GROMMET
36.   VALVE SEAT AND SEAL
37.   POPPET
38.   SPRING
39.   POWERMASTER BODY

the fluid levels. Markings on both sides of the reservoir indicate maximum and minimum levels.

If levels are low, fill to the marks with clean brake fluid meeting DOT-3 specifications. Replace the reservoir cover.

To bleed the booster assembly, turn on the ignition and let the pump restore pressure to the system. Turn off the ignition and pump the brakes to discharge the accumulator. Repeat this entire procedure 10 times to be sure that all air is removed from the booster.

ANTI-LOCK BRAKES

Late model GM and Ford cars use the TEVES design anti-lock brake system described earlier in this chapter. Major assemblies that make up the system are the master cylinder and hydraulic booster, electric pump and accumulator, valve body, electronic controller, reservoir, relays, and four wheel sensors.

During vehicle operation, the electronic controller monitors all electrical anti-lock braking functions. In case of a malfunction in the anti-lock brake system, the ANTI-LOCK warning lamp and/or BRAKE lamp will light. When this occurs, a quick visual check should be made of specific components. See Fig. 52-78.

Next, the problem diagnosis calls for a study of the behavior of the warning lamps. By observing when and which lamps light during a LIGHT SEQUENCE TEST PROCEDURE, the results can be compared to diagnostic charts provided in the manufacturer's service manual. Then, specific follow-up tests can be made to determine the cause of the malfunction.

The BOSCH anti-lock brake system described earlier is used in certain sports car applications. It has a high pressure hydraulic pump that runs at frequent intervals to ''charge'' the hydraulic accumulator. The four wheel sensor assemblies are connected to an electronic controller that monitors anti-lock brake system operation.

The ELECTRONIC BRAKE CONTROL MODULE (EBCM) also monitors faults in the anti-lock brake system. If an improper braking sequence is detected, the EBCM will disable the anti-lock brake system. With that, the EBCM will create a display in the DRIVER INFORMATION CENTER to warn the driver of the fault. It will also light the red brake warning lamp on the instrument panel.

Like the TEVES system, the BOSCH system uses LIGHT SEQUENCE TEST PROCEDURES and the car manufacturer provides diagnostic charts to aid in locating the source of the anti-lock brake system fault.

REVIEW QUESTIONS—AUTOMOTIVE BRAKES

Write your answers on a separate sheet of paper. Do not write in this book.

1. The brake system is a balanced set of mechanical and hydraulic devices used to halt the motion of the vehicle by means of _____.
2. The vehicle must be brought to a stop in a much shorter time than is required to bring it up to speed. True or False?
3. There are three basic types of brake lining in current original equipment use. Which of the following materials is NOT installed?
   a. Asbestos.
   b. Non-asbestos organic.
   c. Metallic.
   d. Semi-metallic.
4. Under extreme braking conditions, which type of brake lining is used?
5. Disc brake rotor braking surfaces are precisely machined for quality of finish, thickness, parallelism, and absense of _____.
6. The use of _____ for the braking surface of brake drums is almost universal.
   a. Steel.
   b. Cast iron.
   c. Aluminum.
   d. Aluminum alloy.
7. Disc brakes are self adjusting. True or False?
8. There are many factors that contribute to the effectiveness of drum brakes. Name four factors.
9. Hydraulic brake fluid must meet a lot of special requirements spelled out in SAE Specification J1703. Brake fluids meeting this specification are labeled:
   a. DOT-1 or DOT-2.
   b. DOT-3 or DOT-4.
   c. DOT-5 or DOT-6.
   d. DOT-7 or DOT-8.

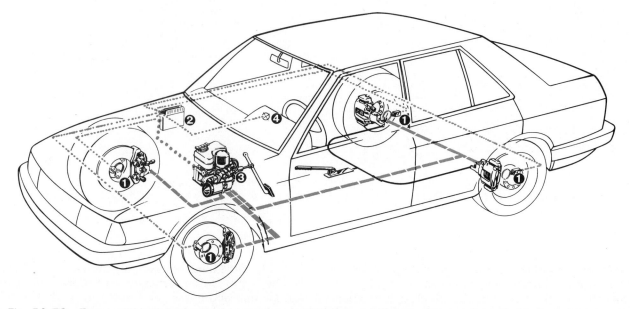

Fig. 52-78. Teves anti-lock brake system used on certain General Motors cars consists of: 1—Speed sensor at each wheel. 2—Electronic controller. 3—Hydraulic unit. 4—Warning lamp. (Alfred Teves Corp.)

10. Most late model cars utilize a _____ (front-to-rear or diagonal) split hydraulic system.

11. The hydraulic brake system combination valve usually combines three individual valves. Which of the following is not part of the combination valve?
    a. Pressure differential valve.
    b. Quick take-up valve.
    c. Proportioning valve.
    d. Metering valve.

12. Why do some original brake hoses and equivalent replacement hoses have a lengthwise white stripe?

13. Most power brake applications utilize _____ units.
    a. Vacuum suspended.
    b. Air suspended.
    c. Hydraulic booster.
    d. Electro-hydraulic booster.

14. Anti-lock brake systems provide very rapid and repeated brake applications and releases, _____ per second, to bring the vehicle to a stop without brake lock up or skidding.
    a. 5-10.
    b. 10-15.
    c. 15-20.
    d. 20-25.

15. When servicing wheel brake parts, breathing dust containing brake lining fibers may cause serious bodily harm. What type of lining is this?

16. A special hone can be used to polish the bore of a _____ master cylinder. Do not hone _____ master cylinder bores.

17. There are two general methods of bleeding air from hydraulic brake systems. What are they?

18. The complaint is a pulsating brake pedal. Mechanic A says it could be caused by an out-of-round brake drum. Mechanic B says it could be caused by excessive lateral runout of disc brake rotors. Who is right?
    a. Mechanic A.
    b. Mechanic B.
    c. Both mechanic A and mechanic B.
    d. Neither mechanic A nor mechanic B.

19. A car owner complains that the brakes drag. Mechanic A says it could be caused by an external brake fluid leak. Mechanic B says it could be caused by vapor lock in the hydraulic system. Who is right?
    a. Mechanic A.
    b. Mechanic B.
    c. Both mechanic A and mechanic B.
    d. Neither mechanic A nor mechanic B.

20. With regard to specific GM single diaphragm power brake units, hard pedal has many possible causes. Name three.

Match the question number for each of the following brake assemblies with the letter designated for each correct associated term.

21. ____ Rotor.
22. ____ Drum.
23. ____ Disc brake.
24. ____ Drum brake.
25. ____ Brake lines.
26. ____ Master cylinder.
27. ____ Parking brake.
28. ____ Power brake.
29. ____ Hydro-Boost II.
30. ____ Anti-lock brake.

A. Brake fluid.
B. Diaphragm.
C. Cable and lever.
D. Wheel sensor.
E. Friction pads.
F. Power steering fluid.
G. Caliper.
H. Primary piston.
I. Wheel cylinder.
J. Brake shoes.

Chapter 53

AUTOMOBILE AIR CONDITIONING

After studying this chapter, you will be able to:
- Describe the fundamentals of air conditioning.
- List the major parts of an air conditioning system and the purpose of each.
- Summarize the principles of air conditioning.
- Explain how the heating system works.
- Tell how an air conditioning compressor and clutch operates.
- List the different types of air conditioning systems.
- Show how-to service an air conditioning system.
- Troubleshoot an air conditioning system.

The history of automotive air conditioning, in terms of cooling by refrigeration, dates back to a few buses in the late 1930s and a few thousand Packards in the early 1940s. Now, more than three-fourths of the cars ordered each new model year are equipped with factory-installed air conditioning, and over a half-million "hang-on" units per year are installed in the field.

FUNDAMENTALS OF REFRIGERATION

AIR CONDITIONING (A/C) is the process by which surrounding air is cooled and dehumidified. In an automobile, this process is performed by a closed refrigeration system that circulates REFRIGERANT-12 under pressure. See Fig. 53-1. While making its rounds, the REFRIGERANT CYCLES FROM VAPOR TO LIQUID TO VAPOR, absorbing heat from the warm air inside the passenger compartment and discharging it to outside air, Fig. 53-2.

Changes from a liquid to a vapor are often accomplished by means of HEAT AND EVAPORATION. Heat, for example, causes water to boil and sends vapor (gas) into the air.

This same vapor can be returned to liquid form (water) by COOLING AND CONDENSATION. If a glass of cold water is placed in a warm room, the warm air collects on the outside of the glass, becomes cooler, and con-

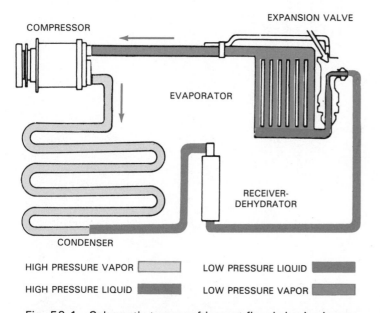

HIGH PRESSURE VAPOR ▭   LOW PRESSURE LIQUID ▭

HIGH PRESSURE LIQUID ▬   LOW PRESSURE VAPOR ▭

Fig. 53-1. Schematic traces refrigerant flow in basic air conditioning system. Refrigerant is a liquid in black high pressure area, then becomes a vapor in lighter low pressure area.

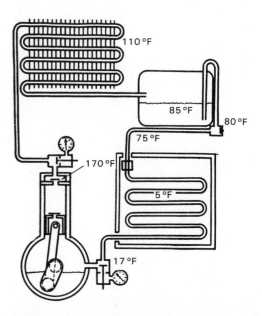

Fig. 53-2. Refrigeration process is based on thermal law that fluids absorb heat while changing from a liquid to a vapor, and they give up heat while changing from a vapor to a liquid.

denses into water.

This transformation of liquid into vapor and vapor into liquid occurs at atmospheric pressure. Higher pressures can also be used to reduce a vapor to liquid form. It is this evaporation that has a cooling effect. For example, you jump in a pool on a hot summers day. After you get out, you feel cooler. It is the water evaporating off of your body that makes you feel cooler.

Basically, automotive air conditioning systems operate on these principles of evaporation and condensation. In the passenger compartment end of the system, the liquid refrigerant is sprayed into an evaporator where it vaporizes. At the other end, refrigerant vapor is pumped into the condenser where it condenses into a liquid.

These two key steps directly relate to principles stated in this two-part thermal law:

1. A fluid will absorb heat when it changes from a liquid to a vapor. This process occurs in the EVAPORATOR, which is placed in the passenger compartment specifically for the purpose of removing heat.
2. A fluid will give off heat when it changes from a vapor to a liquid. This principle is put to use in the CONDENSER, which generally is positioned in the airstream in front of the engine cooling system radiator.

Each of these principles is utilized in automotive air conditioning by a series of major components, connected by tubing and hoses, and actuated by a belt-driven compressor that pressurizes the refrigerant.

Five major elements do the job of circulating, condensing, and vaporizing the refrigerant. These include compressor, condenser, receiver-drier (or accumulator-drier), thermostatic expansion valve (or orifice tube), and evaporator, Fig. 53-3. See CCOT PRINCIPLES.

PRINCIPLES OF A/C

Here is how a typical automotive air conditioning system works:

1. Hot refrigerant vapor (gas) is drawn into compressor, where vapor is placed under high pressure and is pumped into condenser, Fig. 53-1.
2. In condenser, a change occurs as intake air passing through core removes heat from refrigerant vapor as it changes to its liquid state.
3. Refrigerant, having done its job of discharging heat, then flows into receiver-drier where it is filtered, demoisturized, and stored for use as required to meet cooling needs.
4. As compressor continues to pressurize system, liquid refrigerant under high pressure is circulated from receiver-drier to thermostatic expansion valve.
5. Expansion valve then meters refrigerant into inlet side of evaporator.
6. Pressure drops at this point as refrigerant (suddenly released to broad area of evaporator coils) vaporizes and absorbs heat from air in passenger compartment.
7. This heat-laden, low pressure refrigerant vapor is then drawn into compressor to start another refrigeration cycle.

In operation, the refrigerant constantly recycles in the sealed system from a vapor to a liquid to a vapor. Meanwhile, heat in the passenger compartment is constantly being absorbed by the refrigerant and carried away under pressure to be given off to the atmosphere. So, in effect, the automotive air conditioning system is a HEAT

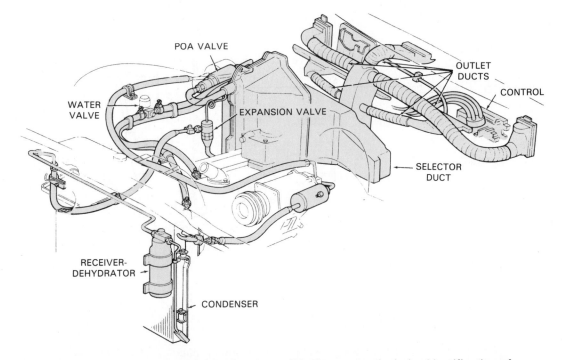

Fig. 53-3. Layout of earlier Chevrolet air conditioning system includes identification of major components, connecting hoses and metal lines, controls, ducts, and related water valve. (Chevrolet Motor Div., General Motors Corp.)

TRANSFER UNIT cooling the air by removing the heat.

However, to better understand how an air conditioner works, you need to know the nature of heat, the effect of heat and pressure on the state of matter, how heat is transferred from one object to another, and how cooling action is accomplished.

NATURE OF HEAT

Specifically, the words hot and cold are relative terms that refer to the degree of heat that is present. An object or thing is considered to be hot or cold only when it is related to something else.

If an exhaust manifold is "hot to the touch," it merely is hotter than the hand of the person touching it. If an auto shop is said to be "cold," the air within it simply contains less heat than does the air in a comfortably warm room. All these terms relate to the presence of heat. Cold refers only to the degree that heat is absent.

Actually, heat is a form of energy that has no substance. It is contained in all matter to some degree of intensity or concentration. Because of this characteristic, it is termed "sensible heat" or "temperature," which can be measured on a thermometer.

Based on the fact that heat stimulates matter, it logically follows that heat can be used to change the state of matter. Whether it is in a solid state, a liquid state, or a gaseous state, matter will change if some outside source is used to add or remove enough heat.

How fast matter will change its state, and the temperature at which it changes, depends on the makeup and movement of its molecules. Ice, for example, is matter in a solid state. It will melt at 33 °F (0.6 °C) and become water, a liquid state. Water will boil at 212 °F (100 °C) and become steam, a gaseous state.

HEAT TRANSFER

An unusual characteristic of heat is that it always flows (transfers) from hotter to cooler objects by one or more of three methods: conduction, convection, or radiation.

CONDUCTION OF HEAT is the condition when a solid object gradually heats up particle-by-particle. Metal objects heat by conduction and are considered to be good thermal conductors. Copper, for example, is used in air conditioner condensers so that the heat will readily transfer from the refrigerant, to the copper coils and fins, to the air.

CONVECTION OF HEAT occurs in liquids and gases as heated portions rise and are displaced by cooler portions, creating a convection current. Convection of heat takes place, for example, when a furnace circulates heated air within a room.

RADIATION is the transfer of heat by waves through space, such as rays of the sun. Actually, anything heated gives off radiated energy. It may be reflected (by a car painted a light color) or it may be absorbed (by a car painted a dark color).

CAR HEATING SYSTEM

Conditioning the air in the passenger compartment of an automobile involves heating, cooling, and dehumidification. Therefore, the car heating and air conditioning systems are designed to have much in common. For example, the two systems make joint use of a PLENUM CHAMBER under the dash as a means of moving conditioned air into the passenger compartment. See Fig. 53-4.

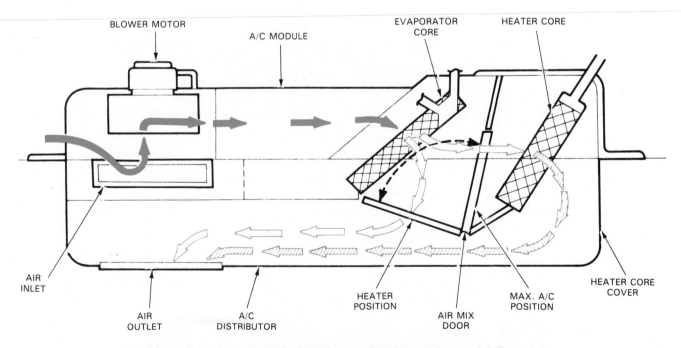

Fig. 53-4. Top view shows typical plenum chamber made up of A/C module and heater core cover. Note location of blower motor, evaporator core, and heater core. Dashed line depicts operating range of air mix door.
(Cadillac Motor Car Div., General Motors Corp.)

The heat required under cold weather conditions usually is provided by circulating hot coolant from the water pump through heater hoses and the heater core. Then, blower action forces incoming air across the tubes and fins of the heater core, and heated air is discharged at outlets in and under the dash. See Fig. 53-5.

CONDITIONED AIR

When weather conditions become uncomfortably hot, air conditioning cools and dehumidifies the passenger compartment. When A/C controls are set, the evaporator serves to absorb heat from the air passing through it. By the process of liquid refrigerant changing into a vapor, heat from the passenger compartment is absorbed and carried away by the circulating refrigerant. See PRINCIPLES OF A/C covered earlier.

The "conditioned" air enters the passenger compartment by way of various ducts and louvers. Doors in the ducts are moved mechanically, electrically, or by vacuum as directed by settings on the control panel on the dash. See Figs. 53-6 and 53-7.

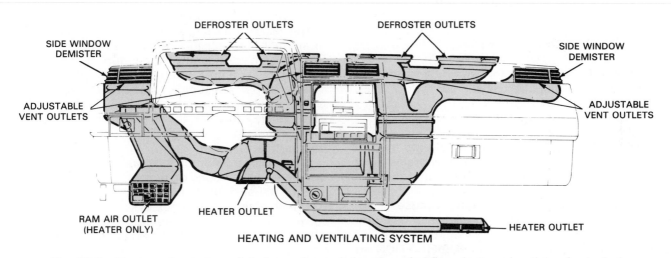

Fig. 53-5. Phantom front view of dash panel reveals location of airflow ducts and outlets of a typical car heating and ventilating system. (Chrysler Corp.)

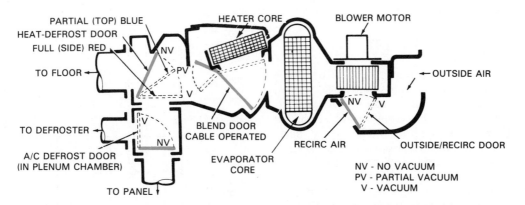

Fig. 53-6. Top view pictures another arrangement of components in plenum chamber. Vacuum-operated doors are shown in varied positions. Blend door is cable operated. (Ford Motor Co.)

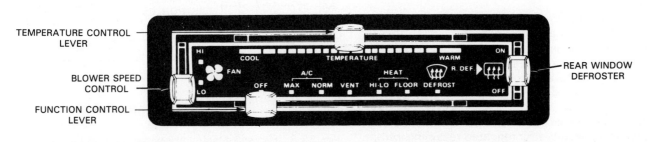

Fig. 53-7. Typical control panel for A/C and heating contains control levers and clearly indicated settings for desired temperature, blower speed, and direction of airflow. (Ford Motor Co.)

In some systems, a control lever moves an air mix door from heater position (closed to A/C airflow) to maximum A/C position (closed to heater core airflow). See Fig. 53-4. In-between settings provide a "blend" of A/C airflow and heated airflow to satisfy the driver's particular needs.

In other systems, Fig. 53-3, heated airflow is controlled by the adjustment of a WATER VALVE installed at the inlet side of the heater core. The water valve is connected by a cable to the control panel on the dash. In the HEAT position, the water valve is wide open, allowing full flow of hot coolant through the heater core. In the COOL position, the valve is closed, allowing restricted flow.

COMFORT CONSIDERATIONS

In dealing with human comfort, other things besides actual temperature must be considered:
1. Humidity control.
2. Air movement and circulation.
3. Air filtering, cleaning, and purification.

The amount of HUMIDITY in the air affects the rate of evaporation of perspiration. If the air contains much moisture, one may feel uncomfortable even if the air is relatively cool.

AIR CIRCULATION is also important because if cool, dry air is moved past a warm body, radiation of heat from the body will increase.

AIR FILTERING, CLEANING, and PURIFICATION are necessary to keep out dust, eliminate smoke and odors, and add to comfort. For these reasons, it is necessary to consider factors other than the actual temperature attained if an air conditioning system can be expected to operate efficiently and satisfactorily.

REQUIREMENTS OF REFRIGERANT

The ability to absorb and discharge heat is the prime requirement of any refrigerant. With its high boiling point, water is not suitable for use as a refrigerant. Refrigerant-12 (R-12), on the other hand, boils at −22 °F (−30 °C) and absorbs heat readily. How readily can be shown in terms of how much heat is required to cause a substance to change from one state to another without changing its temperature.

Consider that the amount of heat being applied to or being given off by any object is measured in BRITISH THERMAL UNITS (Btu). As established, one Btu is the amount of heat required to raise the temperature of a pound of water one degree Fahrenheit at sea level pressure.

The basic Btu measurement can be used to illustrate how well R-12 serves as a refrigerant:
1. In order to change water to steam at 212 °F (100 °C), each pound of water must absorb 970 Btu.
2. To change R-12 to a vapor at 5 °F (−15 °C), only 69.5 Btu per pound are needed.

The ability to change its stage easily and repeatedly, yet maintain good stability in either state, is what makes R-12 especially well suited for repeated recycling within the air conditioning system.

Another point in R-12's favor is its instantaneous reaction to pressure. An increase in pressure will raise the boiling point of a liquid, while a drop in pressure will lower the boiling point. Water at atmospheric pressure will boil at 212 °F (100 °C). Under 20 psi pressure, water will boil at 258 °F (125 °C). R-12 at atmospheric pressure will boil at −22 °F (−30 °C). Under 20 psi pressure, it will boil at 19 °F (−7 °C).

This PRESSURE-TEMPERATURE RELATIONSHIP works well with R-12 in the system, Fig. 53-8. By changing the pressure on the refrigerant, its temperature can be controlled. This, in turn, controls how much heat the refrigerant can absorb, and how readily it rids itself of the heat when the tubing carrying the refrigerant is exposed to outside air.

The value of this pressure-temperature relationship lies in the fact that pressure tests made on the "low side" will reveal the refrigerant temperature at this point in the system. For example, if the pressure reading on the low side is 30 psi, the temperature of the evaporator coils and fins will be down near the 32 °F (0 °C) mark. So you immediately know that the air conditioning system is running efficiently enough to cool the passenger compartment.

As a rule of thumb, the temperature goes up about one degree for each pound of increased pressure on the low side of the system. See Fig. 53-9.

The objective of automobile air conditioning, then, is to get the refrigerant temperature low enough so the evaporator will reach its coldest point without icing up.

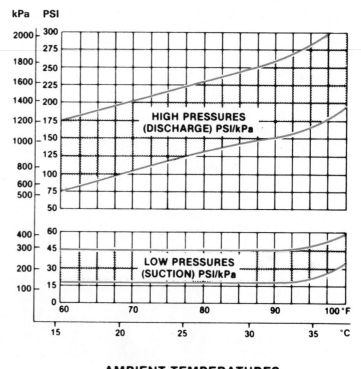

REFRIGERANT SYSTEM PRESSURES

HIGH PRESSURES (DISCHARGE) PSI/kPa

LOW PRESSURES (SUCTION) PSI/kPa

AMBIENT TEMPERATURES

Fig. 53-8. Ranges of high and low pressures at varied ambient temperatures are charted for a typical automotive refrigerating (air conditioning) system. (Ford Motor Co.)

(°F)(°C)		(PSIG)(kPa)		(°F)(°C)		(PSIG)(kPa)	
−21.7	−29.8C	0(ATMOSPHERIC PRESSURE)	0(kPa)	55	12.7C	52.0	358.5
−20	−28.8C	2.4	16.5	60	15.5C	57.7	397.8
−10	−23.3C	4.5	31.0	65	18.3C	63.7	439.2
−5	−20.5C	6.8	46.9	70	21.1C	70.1	482.7
0	−17.7C	9.2	63.4	75	23.8C	76.9	530.2
5	−15.0C	11.8	81.4	80	26.6C	84.1	579.9
10	−12.2C	14.7	101.4	85	29.4C	91.7	632.3
15	−9.4C	17.7	122.0	90	32.2C	99.6	686.7
20	−6.6C	21.1	145.5	95	35.0C	108.1	745.3
25	−3.8C	24.6	169.6	100	37.7C	116.9	806.0
30	−1.1C	28.5	196.5	105	40.5C	126.2	870.2
32	0C	30.1	207.5	110	43.3C	136.0	937.7
35	1.6C	32.6	224.8	115	46.1C	146.5	1010.1
40	4.4C	37.0	255.1	120	48.8C	157.1	1083.2
45	7.2C	41.7	287.5	125	51.6C	167.5	1154.9
50	10.0C	46.7	322.0	130	54.4C	179.0	1234.2
				140	60.0C	204.5	1410.0

Fig. 53-9. Table indicates pressure-temperature relationship of Refrigerant-12. When making manifold gauge tests: a low side reading of 30.1 psi (207.5 kPa) indicates a vaporizing temperature of 32°F (0°C), which is low enough to absorb heat from a warm passenger compartment.
(Cadillac Motor Car Div., General Motors Corp.)

WORKING PARTS OF A/C SYSTEMS

A typical automotive air conditioning system consists of five major components: COMPRESSOR, CONDENSER, RECEIVER-DRIER, THERMOSTATIC EXPANSION VALVE, AND EVAPORATOR, Fig. 53-3.

Other parts are used (suction throttling valve, evaporator pressure regulator, for example), but only to control and increase the efficiency of the system. High pressure hoses and metal lines connect the various parts and form the continuous circuit for recirculation of the refrigerant.

Each of the major components is equally important to the system. A malfunction of any one of these units will interrupt the heat transfer cycle and disrupt operation of the whole system.

COMPRESSOR

The compressor is the power unit of the A/C system. It pumps out refrigerant vapor under high pressure and high heat on the discharge side (high side of system) and sucks in low pressure vapor on the intake side (low side). See Fig. 53-1.

Pressure builds because of a restriction in the high side of the system in the form of the thermostatic expansion valve or an orifice tube. See CCOT PRINCIPLES. The small valve or metered orifice offers resistance to the flow of pressurized refrigerant to build pressure behind it.

The heat buildup is obtained when heat molecules in the low pressure refrigerant (returning from the evaporator) are concentrated by the pressurizing effect of compressor operation. This action serves to raise the temperature of the refrigerant vapor flowing to the condenser, stimulating rapid heat flow from the hot refrigerant to cooler outside air.

Remember, heat always flows from hotter objects to cooler objects.

COMPRESSOR TYPES

The basic types of air conditioning compressors are:

1. Two cylinder reciprocating piston compressors.
2. Swash (wobble) plate compressors.
3. Scotch yoke compressors.

TWO CYLINDER COMPRESSORS

Conventional RECIPROCATING PISTON COMPRESSORS usually have two cylinders arranged in a parallel "Vee." Some earlier original equipment A/C systems and most aftermarket (hang-on) installations use compressors of reciprocating piston design, powered by an engine-driven V-belt.

During operation of a typical two-stroke cycle reciprocating piston compressor, the piston creates a suction on the downstroke (intake). This draws the intake valve open and sucks refrigerant vapor into the cylinder. On the upstroke (compression), the piston pressurizes the refrigerant, forcing it past the exhaust valve and into the hoses and metal lines to the condenser. With an ambient temperature of 70° to 80°F (21 to 27°C), the hot refrigerant vapor leaves the compressor at 175 to 195 psi (1207 to 1345 kPa) to trigger system operation.

SWASH PLATE COMPRESSORS

The SWASH PLATE COMPRESSOR contains a swash (wobble) plate mounted diagonally on a straight shaft. These compressors generally have five or six cylinders. The General Motors six cylinder compressor shown in Fig. 53-10 has three sets of opposing cylinders and three double-acting pistons. The pistons are connected to the swash plate by piston balls.

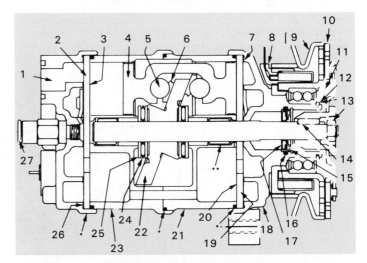

Fig. 53-10. Typical GM six cylinder swash plate compressor: 1—Suction port. 2—Rear valve plate. 3—Suction reed plate. 4—Piston and ring assembly. 5—Piston ball. 6—Shoe disc. 7—Head gasket. 8—Clutch coil assembly. 9—Pulley rotor. 10—Clutch driver. 11—Pulley bearing. 12—Bearing retainer rings. 13—Shaft nut. 14—Shaft key. 15—Seal retainer. 16—Seal O-ring. 17—Shaft seal. 18—Front head. 19—Front valve plate. 20—Suction reed plate. 21—Front cylinder. 22—Shaft and swash plate assembly. 23—Rear cylinder. 24—Thrust bearing. 25—Thrust race. 26—Head gasket. 27—Pressure relief valve. 28—Rear head. *Cylinder O-ring seals. **Shaft bearing. (Cadillac Motor Car Div., General Motors Corp.)

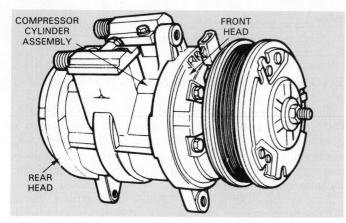

Fig. 53-11. Makeup of Ford six cylinder compressor is similar to GM compressor shown in Fig. 53-10. Swash plate actuates three double-acting pistons in a front and rear cylinder assembly. (Ford Motor Co.)

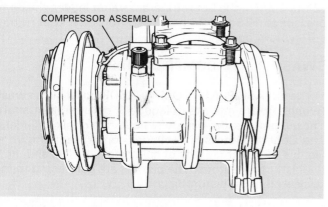

Fig. 53-12. Chrysler six cylinder compressor also utilizes a swash plate to operate double-acting pistons in sequence within three sets of opposing cylinders. (Chrysler Corp.)

As the compressor shaft rotates, the swash plate "wobbles," causing the pistons to move back and forth in the cylinders. Each cylinder has a set of reed valves for intake and exhaust. Passages from the valves are connected to one high side port and one low side port. Piston action creates high pressure at the high side port and suction at the low side port of the compressor.

Similar six cylinder swash plate compressors are used on some Ford A/C systems, Fig. 53-11. Also, Chrysler uses a six cylinder swash plate compressor in some of its A/C systems, Fig. 53-12.

Some GM A/C systems use a FIVE CYLINDER COMPRESSOR with a VARIABLE POSITION SWASH PLATE, Fig. 53-13. The swash plate is positioned by a bellows-actuated control valve that senses the demand for air conditioning under all conditions without cycling. Under high load conditions, the control valve increases the swash plate angle for greater displacement to meet the demand. During low load conditions, the valve decreases the swash plate angle to reduce displacement.

SCOTCH YOKE COMPRESSORS

The SCOTCH YOKE COMPRESSOR is a radial unit designed to change rotary motion to reciprocating motion without the use of connecting rods or piston balls. The scotch yoke design has four pistons mounted 90 deg. from each other. See Fig. 53-14. The opposed pistons are pressed into a yoke that rides on a slide block on the compressor shaft eccentric.

In operation, refrigerant enters the crankcase of the compressor from the rear. On the suction stroke, the refrigerant is drawn through reeds attached to the top of the pistons. The refrigerant is then discharged through the valve plate, and it flows out the connector block at the rear of the compressor.

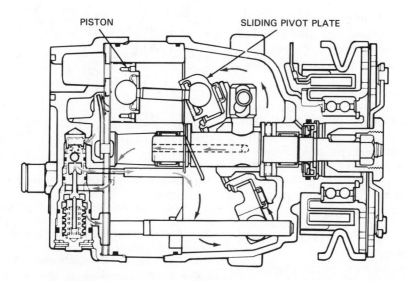

Fig. 53-13. Chevrolet variable displacement compressor: Bellows-actuated valve at lower left controls position of swash plate. Position of swash plate determines compressor displacement. Arrow code is: black, crankcase refrigerant flow; gray, suction pressure; blue, discharge. (Chevrolet Motor Div., General Motors Corp.)

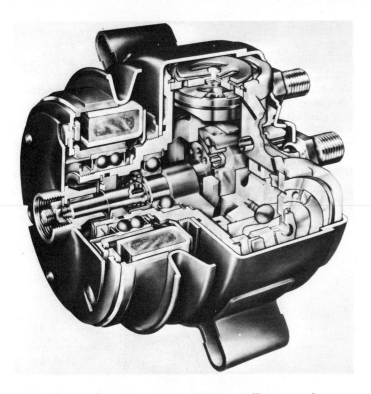

Fig. 53-14. Scotch yoke compressor utilizes a yoke type mechanism and an eccentric on compressor shaft to change rotary motion of shaft to reciprocating motion of pistons. Compressor shown in Model HR-980 used in many Ford cars and light trucks.   (Tecumseh Products Co.)

COMPRESSOR CLUTCHES

Compressors used in automobile air conditioning systems generally are equipped with an electromagnetic clutch which energizes and de-energizes to engage and disengage the compressor. Two types of clutches are in general use: the stationary field coil type, Fig. 53-15, and the once popular rotating coil type.

1. The STATIONARY CLUTCH FIELD COIL is mounted on the front end of the compressor. The pulley rotates freely on the compressor body. Electrical connections are made directly to the coil leads. When the A/C system is turned ON, the clutch field coil and compressor hub are drawn to the pulley by magnetic force, and the clutch field coil and pulley are locked together as a unit. The compressor shaft then turns the field coil and pulley-and-hub assembly for compressor operation.

2. The ROTATING COIL CLUTCH has a magnetic coil mounted in the pulley, and it rotates with the pulley. It operates electrically through connections to a stationary brush assembly and rotating slip rings. When signaled by an automatic thermostatic switch, the clutch permits the compressor to engage or disengage as required for adequate air conditioning.

The clutch, in effect, is the connecting link between the compressor pulley and the compressor. The belt-driven pulley is always in rotation while the engine is running. The compressor is in rotation and operation only when the clutch engages it to the pulley.

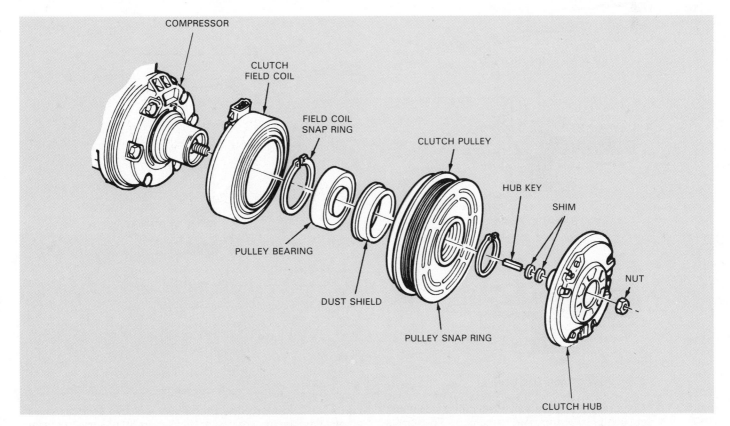

Fig. 53-15. Exploded view details sequence of parts of a typical compressor clutch assembly. With A/C OFF, pulley freewheels. With A/C ON, field coil engages pulley and compressor operates.   (Ford Motor Co.)

SERVICE VALVES AND CONNECTIONS

COMPRESSOR SERVICE VALVES are built into some systems. They serve as a point of attachment for test gauges or servicing hoses. The service valves are three-position controls: front-seated, mid-position, and back-seated. See Fig. 53-16.

Position of this double-faced valve is controlled by rotating the valve stem with a service valve wrench. Clockwise rotation will seat the front face of the valve and shut off all refrigerant flow in the system. This position will isolate the compressor from the rest of the system.

Counterclockwise rotation will unseat the valve and open the system to refrigerant flow (mid-position). Systematic checks are performed with a manifold gauge set, Fig. 53-17, with the service valve in mid-position.

Further counterclockwise rotation of the valve stem will seat the rear face of the valve. This position opens the system to the flow of refrigerant but shuts off refrigerant to the test connector. See Fig. 53-16. The service valves are used for testing pressure, for isolating the compressor for repair or replacement; and for discharging, evacuating, and charging the system.

Instead of service valves, modern compressors have "Schrader" or "Dill" SERVICE CONNECTORS or GAUGE PORT FITTINGS, Fig. 53-18. Special test hoses are available to fit these connectors, or adapters can be used with standard test hoses. The refrigerant is sealed in the system until the special hose or adapter is attached. Removal of the hose or adapter closes the system.

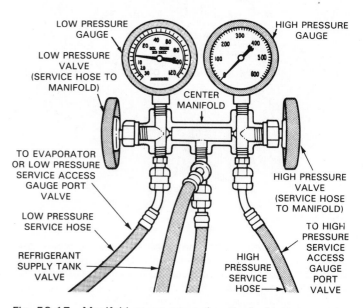

Fig. 53-17. Manifold gauge set can be attached to compressor service valves or to service gauge port valves to test, discharge, evacuate, and charge A/C system. (Ford Motor Co.)

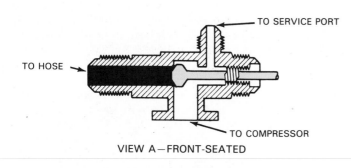

VIEW A—FRONT-SEATED

VIEW B—BACK-SEATED

VIEW C—MID POSITIONED

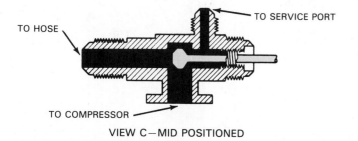

Fig. 53-16. Compressor service valve operating positions: A—For isolating compressor from A/C system. B—For normal operation of system. C—For testing, evacuating, and charging system. (Ford Motor Co.)

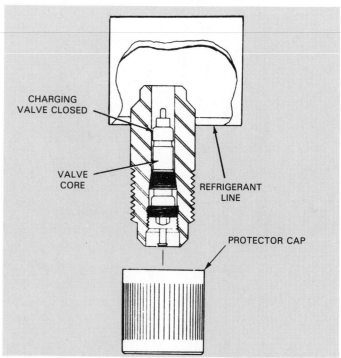

Fig. 53-18. Gauge port fittings have replaced service valves on most modern compressors. Gauge port fittings use Schrader or Dill valve cores, similar to familiar tire valves, to simplify test hose attachment. (Ford Motor Co.)

CONDENSER

The CONDENSER in the air conditioning system is a device used to change high pressure refrigerant vapor to a liquid. See Fig. 53-19. It does this by providing a means for emitting heat from the hot refrigerant to the cooler atmosphere.

The means by which the condenser performs its function is a design factor. The hot refrigerant is in contact with the inner walls of as many feet of A/C tubing as possible. This tubing is placed in the airstream to bring about a heat transfer situation. When the refrigerant vapor reaches the pressure and temperature that causes condensation, a large quantity of heat is given off and the hot refrigerant vapor changes to a warm liquid.

The condenser consists of tubing crisscrossed through thin, supporting, cooling fins. In construction, it resembles an engine radiator and usually is mounted directly in front of the radiator. This places it in the best position to receive the benefits of ram air flowing into the engine compartment while the vehicle is in motion.

When the vehicle is at rest or moving slowly, the belt-driven cooling fan draws outside air across the condenser coils and fins. Many late model cars are equipped with a thermostatically controlled electric fan, especially front wheel drive cars with transverse engine design. See Chapter 17, ENGINE COOLING SYSTEMS. In some engines in air conditioned cars, clutch-type cooling fans "engage" to permit full rpm at low vehicle speeds and "slip" at high speed when ram air cooling takes over.

Designed to achieve a similar effect is the flexible blade fan found in some air conditioned applications. The blades of this unit have a high pitch at rest and at low rotational speeds to create a strong airflow. At high speeds, the flexible blades flatten out. As the pitch of the blades decreases, so does the airflow the fan creates. Again, ram air at high speed furnishes the necessary airflow for efficient condenser operation.

In operation, refrigerant vapor under high pressure enters the condenser through an inlet at the top. Under an average heat load, the upper 1/2 or 2/3 of the condenser coils contain hot refrigerant vapor changing into a hot liquid. the lower 1/2 or 1/3 will carry the warm liquid refrigerant. This liquid, still under high pressure. flows from an outlet at the bottom of the condenser through a refrigerant line to the receiver-drier (dehydrator).

RECEIVER-DRIER

The RECEIVER-DRIER is next in line in the series of five major components that make up an automotive air conditioning system. See Fig. 53-20. The receiver-drier is the storage tank for liquid refrigerant, and it also contains a fiber and a DESICCANT (drying agent) to remove foreign particles and moisture from the circulating refrigerant.

It is necessary to have a place in the system to store the refrigerant because the demands of the evaporator vary under different operating conditions. The filter and drying agent are required to keep harmful contaminants from circulating through the system.

A SIGHT GLASS provided for viewing the condition of the refrigerant charge usually is built-into or adjacent to the top of the receiver-drier assembly, Fig. 53-20. It windows the interior of the system at a point where the charge of liquid refrigerant passing it reveals whether or not the system is fully charged.

A "clear" glass indicates that the system has a full charge of refrigerant. If bubbles appear, air has entered the system. A milky white cloudiness signals that the desiccant is escaping from the receiver-drier and is circulating through the system with the refrigerant.

The receiver-drier receives the high pressure liquid refrigerant from the condenser and delivers it through tubing to the thermostatic expansion valve.

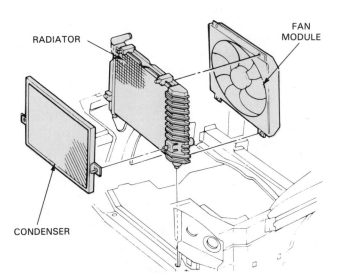

Fig. 53-19. Condenser used in A/C system is a heat exchanger. Hot refrigerant vapor enters top of condenser, cools as it passes through coils, gives up heat to surrounding air, then condenses into a liquid. (American Motors Corp.)

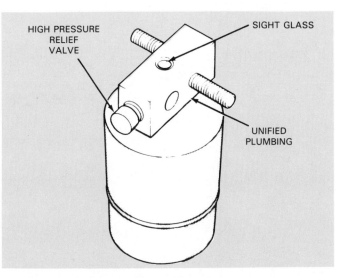

Fig. 53-20. Receiver-drier stores liquid refrigerant and removes moisture that could cause freezing in A/C system. Most units contain filters, screens, and a drying agent. (Chrysler Corp.)

THERMOSTATIC EXPANSION VALVE

The EXPANSION VALVE, Fig. 53-21, is a metering device that removes pressure from the liquid refrigerant so that it can expand and become refrigerant vapor in the evaporator. The metering action is performed by an orifice (restriction that permits compressor to build up pressure on high side of system) within the valve body. The refrigerant enters the expansion valve as a warm, high pressure liquid. It passes through the orifice and is released from the valve as a cold, low pressure, atomized liquid.

Actually, the thermostatic expansion valve has three functions: metering, modulating, and controlling. Its metered orifice, Fig. 53-21, releases the pressure on the liquid refrigerant to change it from high to low and provide a starting point for the "low side" of the air conditioning system.

Its thermostatically controlled valve opens and closes, usually on signal from a thermal bulb connected to the outlet of the evaporator. This creates a modulating effect as the valve varies the flow of liquid refrigerant to the orifice. If the outlet gets warm, the bulb signals the thermostatic valve to open and allow greater refrigerant flow. When the outlet cools, the bulb triggers the valve to close and restrict flow.

The control feature of the thermostatic expansion valve ties in with the modulating function. When the valve opens or closes, it must respond quickly to changes in heat load at the outlet of the evaporator. No liquid refrigerant must leave the evaporator and enter the compressor or damage to internal parts will result. Therefore, the thermostatic expansion valve must respond immediately to the signals sent by the thermal bulb to insure that vaporization of the R-12 is completed by the time it reaches the outlet of the evaporator. Also see CCOT PRINCIPLES.

EVAPORATOR

The EVAPORATOR is another heat exchanger in the air conditioning system, Fig. 53-22. In contrast to the condenser, however, its coils carry cold refrigerant that picks up heat from the passenger compartment to cool the interior.

The evaporator is similar to the condenser in construction. It, too, consists of coils of tubing mounted in a series of thin cooling fins. Generally, the evaporator is mounted in a housing under the cowl where warm air from the passenger compartment is blown by a fan across its coils and fins.

The evaporator receives the cold, low pressure, atomized liquid refrigerant from the thermostatic expansion valve. As this cold liquid passes through the coils of the evaporator, heat naturally moves from the warm air through the cool coils and into the cold refrigerant.

When the liquid refrigerant reaches a pressure and temperature that will cause evaporation, a large quantity of heat will move from the air into the refrigerant and the low pressure atomized liquid will change to a low pressure refrigerant vapor. This vapor returns to the inlet, or low side, of the compressor, where the whole refrigeration cycle begins again.

VALVES-IN-RECEIVER A/C SYSTEM

The five major elements of a basic automobile air conditioning system have been described. However, other elements are contained in related A/C systems. For example, General Motors introduced a system in which a VALVES-IN-RECEIVER (VIR) performs the functions of the receiver-drier, thermostatic expansion valve, sight glass, and POA (pilot operated absolute) suction throttling valve. See Figs. 53-23 and 53-24.

The VIR assembly is mounted next to the evaporator, which eliminates the need for an external equalizer line between the thermostatic expansion valve and the outlet of the POA valve. The equalizer function is accomplished by a drilled hole (equalizer port) between the two valve cavities in the VIR housing. See Fig. 53-24.

Also eliminated are the thermobulb and capillary line for the thermostatic expansion valve. The diaphragm of the VIR expansion valve is exposed to the refrigerant

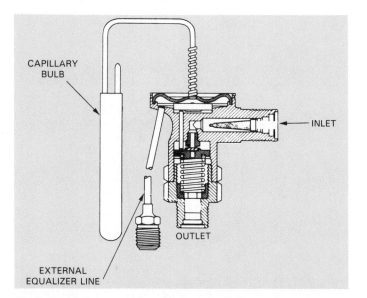

Fig. 53-21. Thermostatic expansion valve meters liquid refrigerant under high pressure into low pressure area of evaporator, as directed by a temperature sensing bulb located at evaporator outlet.

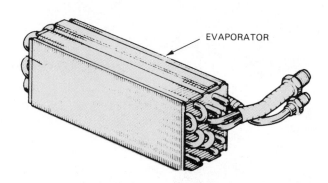

Fig. 53-22. Evaporator has coils and fins like condenser but functions in reverse. Evaporator receives atomized liquid Refrigerant-12, which vaporizes and absorbs heat from passenger compartment. (American Motors Corp.)

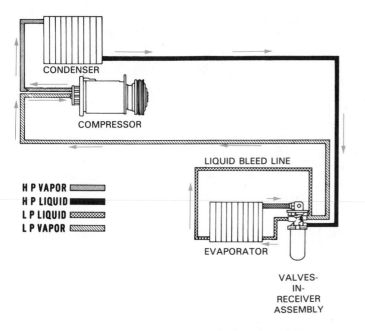

H P VAPOR
H P LIQUID
L P LIQUID
L P VAPOR

Fig. 53-23. General Motors Valves-In-Receiver A/C system features a VIR assembly that replaces three assemblies previously used: thermostatic expansion valve, receiver-drier, and POA suction throttling valve.

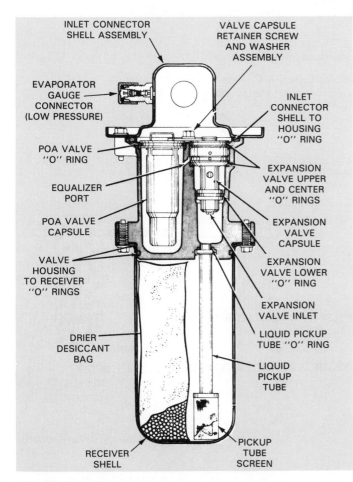

Fig. 53-24. Valves-In-Receiver unit combines two major valves, receiver-drier, and sight glass to control evaporator pressure and to regulate amount of refrigerant being metered into evaporator.

vapor entering the VIR unit from the outlet of the evaporator. The sight glass is located in the valve housing at the inlet end of the thermostatic valve cavity, where it gives a liquid indication of the refrigerant level.

The VIR thermostatic expansion valve controls the flow of refrigerant to the evaporator by sensing the temperature and pressure of the refrigerant vapor as it passes through the VIR unit on its way to the compressor. The POA suction throttling valve controls the flow of refrigerant from the evaporator to maintain a constant evaporator pressure of 30 psi. These are capsule type valves. When found to be defective, the complete valve capsule must be replaced.

The drier desiccant is contained in a bag in the receiver shell, Fig. 53-24. It is replaceable by removing the shell and old bag and installing a new bag of desiccant.

CCOT A/C SYSTEM

Many late model Ford and General Motors cars equipped with manual or automatic temperature control (ATC) air conditioning use a CYCLING CLUTCH ORIFICE TUBE (CCOT) or a FIXED ORIFICE system. See Fig. 53-25. These systems are designed to cycle the compressor ON and OFF to maintain desired passenger compartment cooling and to prevent evaporator freeze-up.

Control of the refrigeration cycle (ON and OFF) is done with a PRESSURE CYCLING SWITCH, Fig. 53-26. This switch is the freeze protection device in the system. It senses low side pressure as an indicator of evaporator temperature.

When the driver selects an air conditioning mode (MAX, NORM, etc.), voltage is supplied to the compressor clutch coil. Compressor operation reduces low side pressure; the pressure cycling switch opens and de-energizes the compressor clutch coil. Then, as the system equalizes, the pressure cycling switch contacts close, re-energizing the compressor clutch coil.

This refrigeration cycle continues as a means of maintaining evaporator discharge air at 33 °F (1 °C), with slight variation due to outside air temperature and humidity.

The CCOT refrigeration cycle begins at the compressor:

1. Refrigerant enters compressor as a low pressure, low temperature vapor, and it leaves as a high pressure, high temperature vapor. See Fig. 53-26.
2. Vapor flows to condenser where it gives up heat to cooler air passing through, and refrigerant changes to a high-pressure liquid.
3. Liquid refrigerant then passes through an orifice tube where it becomes a low pressure, low temperature liquid that is fed into evaporator.
4. Warm outside (or inside) air passes through evaporator coils where it gives up its heat and refrigerant changes to a low pressure, low temperature vapor.
5. Refrigerant vapor flows to accumulator-drier, Fig. 53-27. If any liquid refrigerant passes through evaporator, it is separated from vapor in accumulator-drier.
6. From accumulator-drier, low pressure, low temperature vapor returns to compressor and refrigeration cycle begins again.

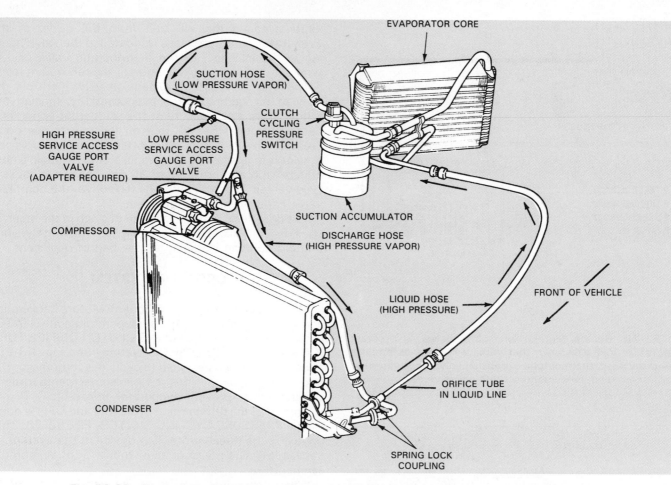

Fig. 53-25. Diagram traces refrigerant flow in Ford Fixed Orifice A/C system. Also note relative location of assemblies, especially positioning of compressor on transverse mounted engine. (Ford Motor Co.)

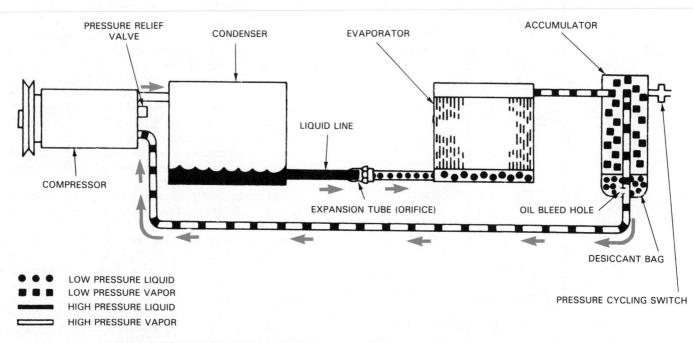

● ● ● LOW PRESSURE LIQUID
■ ■ ■ LOW PRESSURE VAPOR
▬▬▬ HIGH PRESSURE LIQUID
▭▭▭ HIGH PRESSURE VAPOR

Fig. 53-26. Diagram points out components and direction of refrigerant flow in GM Cycling Clutch Orifice Tube A/C system. Note that accumulator-drier replaces receiver-drier, and it is located at evaporator outlet rather than at condenser outlet. (Buick Motor Div., General Motors Corp.)

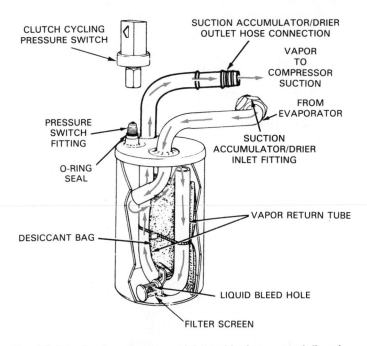

Fig. 53-27. Ford suction accumulator-drier is mounted directly to evaporator core outlet in Fixed Orifice A/C system. Desiccant bag absorbs moisture. Clutch cycling pressure switch attaches to fitting on top of canister. (Ford Motor Co.)

VDOT A/C SYSTEM

A VARIABLE DISPLACEMENT ORIFICE TUBE (VDOT) A/C system is installed on several late model General Motors vehicles. The VDOT system employs the five cylinder, variable displacement A/C compressor shown in Fig. 53-13. This compressor is designed to vary pumping displacement to match air conditioning needs. A bellows actuated control valve in the compressor senses suction pressure and varies the swash plate angle in response to heat load. Clutch cycling is not required.

The variable displacement compressor also utilizes a low pressure cut-off switch that will disengage the compressor clutch in case of system low charge due to a refrigerant leak.

SAFE WAY TO HANDLE REFRIGERANTS

Labels on REFRIGERANT-12 containers usually include a safe handling warning. R-12 is available in drums and cans, with a 15 oz. disposable can most widely used to recharge automotive air conditioning systems. Since the refrigerant in the container is under considerable pressure at ordinary temperatures, you must observe certain precautions to prevent accidents or damage to the air conditioning system:

1. Always wear goggles when working with a refrigerant. Do not allow liquid refrigerant to strike eyes (could cause blindness) or body (could cause frostbite). If an accident does occur, immediately wash eyes with dilute boric acid or another suitable eyewash solution. See a doctor immediately.
2. Open sealed air conditioning systems in a well-ventilated area having good circulation. Discharge refrigerant slowly. Fast discharge could bleed refrigerant oil from system along with refrigerant.
3. Always discharge refrigerant into service bay exhaust system. Large quantities of refrigerant vapor in a small, poorly ventilated room can cause suffocation.
4. Do not have lighted smoking materials in working area.
5. R-12 vapor passing over an open flame will give off a toxic phosgene gas. Therefore, leak testing with a Halide or propane torch, Fig. 53-28, should be done in a well-ventilated area. Also, do not weld or steam clean A/C systems.
6. Do not add anything except pure R-12 and refrigerant oil to air conditioning system. Anything else may contaminate refrigerant or cause it to become chemically unstable.
7. Handle refrigerant containers with care. Do not drop or strike containers.
8. Wear gloves when handling a damp refrigerant container; bare hands may freeze to container. If this does happen, wet container with water to thaw and free your hand from can.
9. To warm a refrigerant container, use hot water (or rags saturated with hot water) at a temperature of not more than 125 °F (52 °C). Never use a direct flame or heater.
10. When preparing a dispense refrigerant from a can, use a can valve that punctures can only after valve is installed. Also, a "safety can valve" is available that prevents refrigerant from flowing back into can from air conditioning system (which could cause an explosion).
11. Store your refrigerant containers in a cool, dry place. Never store them in direct sunlight or near a heater. If refrigerant is stored in a drum, keep drum in upright position and install a metal cap over outlet connection.

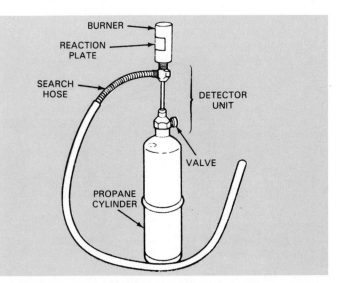

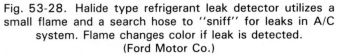

Fig. 53-28. Halide type refrigerant leak detector utilizes a small flame and a search hose to "sniff" for leaks in A/C system. Flame changes color if leak is detected. (Ford Motor Co.)

12. Use care when transporting refrigerant drums or cans. Do not carry refrigerant containers in passenger compartment of your car. If hauling containers in an open truck, use a cover to protect refrigerant from radiant heat of sun.

HOW MOISTURE AFFECTS REFRIGERANT

All top quality refrigerants recommended for use in automobile air conditioning systems are formulated to high standards of chemical purity. They are sealed in suitable containers for safe shipment and delivery.

The quality of R-12 is manufactured-in, and regardless of brand name, its purity is assured by use of the designation "12." However, if moisture, air, dirt, or some other contaminant enters the air conditioning system, the refrigerant will lose its effectiveness as a cooling agent.

Moisture, especially, is a serious refrigerant contaminant because it also causes damage to internal parts. The unwanted water reacts with R-12 to form hydrochloric acid. The more water in the refrigerant, the more concentrated the hydrochloric acid becomes. The strong acid eats holes in the evaporator and condenser coils, damages aluminum parts of the compressor, and corrodes valves and fittings. All the while the hydrochloric acid is reacting with metal parts, oxides are being given off to further contaminate the refrigerant and affect its ability to absorb and discharge heat.

Moisture usually enters the system through a break in a refrigerant line or by way of an improperly sealed connection. To combat this threat of contamination by moisture, all automotive air conditioning systems are fitted with a container of desiccant (receiver-drier or accumulator/drier). This drying agent will absorb all moisture in the system, up to its saturation point.

If an A/C system is contaminated by moisture, the best way to remove it is by using a VACUUM PUMP, Fig. 53-29, to evacuate all traces of refrigerant, air, and moisture. Once repairs have been made and a new receiver/drier or accumulator/drier is installed, the system can be evacuated and recharged with pure R-12.

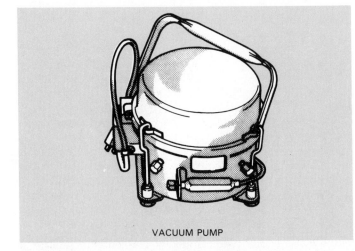

VACUUM PUMP

Fig. 53-29. Vacuum pump is mandatory equipment for servicing all A/C systems. It serves to evacuate system of R-12, air, and moisture. (Chrysler Corp.)

THE NEED FOR REFRIGERANT OIL

All automotive air conditioning systems require internal lubrication of seals, gaskets, the thermostatic expansion valve, and the moving parts of the compressor. To accomplish this, a moisture-free REFRIGERANT OIL is circulated thorough the system with the refrigerant.

Use non-foaming oil formulated specifically for use in each air conditioning system. This highly refined oil comes in several grades or viscosities for use in automotive air conditioning systems. Oils of 500 or 525 viscosity are most commonly used.

Reciprocating piston compressors usually have an oil sump and an oil dipstick. The oil level of this type of compressor should be checked every time the air conditioner is serviced. Most AXIAL PISTON COMPRESSORS must be removed from the vehicle for an oil check and refill. GM five and six cylinder swash plate compressors, for example, call for removal and oil drain. The drain oil is retained, measured, and discarded. Pure refrigerant oil of the same amount is then installed.

On certain RADIAL COMPRESSORS, the refrigerant oil can be charged through the compressor suction (low side) port. Check service manual for compressor being serviced.

Precautions in handling refrigerant oil include:
1. Replace used refrigerant oil if there is any doubt about its condition.
2. Discard used oil.
3. Use only approved refrigerant oil in air conditioning systems.
4. Buy refrigerant oil in smallest size containers consistent with immediate needs.
5. Do not transfer refrigerant oil from one container to another.
6. Make sure cap is tight on refrigerant oil container when not in use.
7. When installing refrigerant oil, make sure it is proper type and viscosity for system being serviced.

Refrigerant oils have been dewaxed, dried, and otherwise processed to keep pace with rapid advances in compressor design. These special oils are shipped in tightly capped containers to prevent contamination before use.

SERVICE TOOLS AND EQUIPMENT

Various hand and specialty tools are needed to install and service automobile air conditioners. In addition, a manifold gauge set, refrigerant leak detector, vacuum pump, thermometer, tachometer, and goggles are needed to test and service the system.

More elaborate equipment includes charging stations on two-wheel carts and mobile air conditioning system service centers, Fig. 53-30. Automatic temperature control (ATC) system analyzers are also available.

The MANIFOLD GAUGE SET, Fig. 53-17, is used to test pressure on the high and low sides of the compressor. There are usually two gauges in the set (some systems require three gauges). The gauges are mounted on a manifold assembly, complete with shutoff valves. Connections to the compressor are made at the suction and discharge service valves, or to connectors on

Fig. 53-30. Computerized A/C charging station has built-in pressure gauges, lighted pushbutton operation, audible signals, and digital readout. Station purges A/C system and pulls vacuum to 29.5 in. Hg. It charges R-12 and oil automatically. (Murray Corp.)

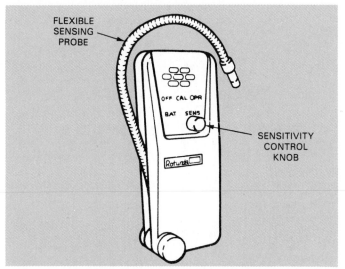

Fig. 53-31. In operation, this electronic refrigerant leak detector gives off a steady, slow "ticking." Probe is moved around system. If a leak exists, ticking will become more rapid and shrill. (Ford Motor Co.)

the compressor fitted with "Schrader" or "Dill" valves. The suction (low pressure) side of the compressor is where the hose from the evaporator attaches. The discharge (high pressure) side is where the hose to the condenser attaches.

The manifold gauge set also has a center port to which a hose can be attached to bleed excess refrigerant from the system. In addition, it can be used to discharge (purge) refrigerant from the system, evacuate air and moisture, and charge the system with Refrigerant-12.

The LEAK DETECTOR may be anything from a colored dye additive for the refrigerant, a Halide detector, or a sophisticated electronic unit, Fig. 53-31, that provides maximum sensitivity and accuracy when used according to the manufacturer's operating instructions.

The COLORED DYE LEAK DETECTOR is added to the refrigerant. Then, with the air conditioning system in operation, any discoloration at a hose connection, etc., will reveal the point of leakage.

The HALIDE DETECTOR, or propane torch, is a commonly used refrigerant leak detector, Fig. 53-28. In operation, the unit's sampling hose is moved under all parts and connections of the air conditioning system. Throughout the test, the color of the flame is observed.

A blue flame is normal; yellow indicates a slight leak; purple signals a high-quantity leak of R-12 vapor. This test should be made in a well ventilated area, because Refrigerant-12 passing over an open flame will give off a toxic phosgene gas.

The VACUUM PUMP, Fig. 53-29, is a device used to evacuate (remove air and moisture from) the air conditioning system. The pump hoses are connected to the suction and discharge ports of the compressor, then the unit is plugged into a 120 volt ac receptacle and turned on. In operation, the pump draws out air and moisture until a vacuum of 25 to 29 in. Hg. is created.

Some manufacturers place the vacuum pump on a two-wheel cart or in a mobile air conditioning service center, along with pressure gauges, automatic timers, test hoses and connectors, switches, controls, and a stock of R-12. See Fig. 53-32.

SERVICING THE SYSTEM

When an automotive air conditioner is not cooling properly, check the condition of engine cooling system components. Check the condition of the V-belts, Fig. 53-33, or serpentine (V-ribbed) belt. Inspect the fan shroud, radiator, and pressure cap. Look for signs of coolant leakage and/or refrigerant leakage. Also check the air conditioning system for loose or broken compressor mounting brackets, improper hose routing, condition of the condenser (clogged with bugs, leaves, etc.), and receiver-drier or accumulator-drier (age and appearance).

CAUTION: When performing air conditioning diagnosis on vehicles equipped with a catalytic converter, warm engine to normal operating temperature before attempting to idle engine for periods greater than five (5) minutes. Once choke is open and fast idle speed drops to normal idle, diagnosis and adjustments can be made.

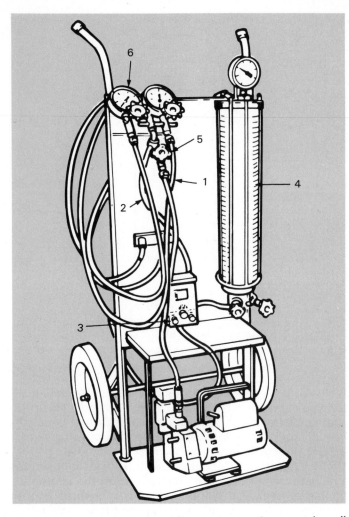

Fig. 53-32. Two-wheel mobile service station contains all equipment needed to service A/C systems: 1—High pressure hose. 2—Suction hose. 3—Vacuum pump. 4—Charging cylinder. 5—Vacuum control valve. 6—Pressure gauge. (American Motors Corp.)

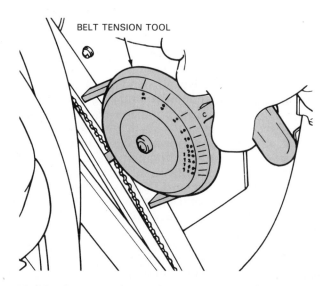

Fig. 53-33. Good condition and correct tension of compressor drive belt are required for effective A/C system operation. (Ford Motor Co.)

Then, clean or uncap the sight glass and run the engine at 1500 to 2000 rpm. Make an operational test of the air conditioner with the hood up and the doors open (unless otherwise specified by the manufacturer). Adjust the air conditioning controls for maximum cooling with the blower at high speed.

Place a large fan in front of the vehicle to substitute fan airflow for ram airflow through the condenser. Run the engine for approximately 15 minutes to stabilize all parts of the system.

Place a thermometer in an air conditioning discharge duct. Place another thermometer in engine compartment. Drop blower speed to "low." Close doors and hood.

Check the sight glass. A clear glass indicates that the system is fully charged (or empty if system fails to blow cold air). Bubbles in the glass point to a low refrigerant level. Check the thermometer reading at the air discharge duct; it should be 35 to 45 °F (2 to 7 °C). If not, shut off engine and prepare to discharge the air conditioning system.

DISCHARGING THE SYSTEM

DISCHARGING (purging) the air conditioning system is the act of releasing refrigerant from the high and low sides of the system until no pressure exists.

To discharge the system:
1. Protect your eyes with goggles. Car engine should be off and air conditioner not operating.
2. Remove compressor port caps and install manifold gauge set, Fig. 53-34.
3. Attach test hose to center connection of manifold assembly. Cover other end of hose with a shop towel.
4. Set both manifold gauge valves at maximum open position.
5. Crack open high pressure service valve and discharge refrigerant vapor from system. Check shop towel to make sure no oil is discharged. If it is, cut down on service valve opening.
6. When high pressure gauge reading falls below 50 psi, crack open low pressure service valve to obtain maximum discharge of refrigerant without loss of oil.
7. On compressors with Schrader valves, disregard steps 4, 5, and 6. Instead, crack open high pressure manifold hand valve, discharge slowly, then crack open low pressure manifold hand valve and complete discharge operation (zero on gauges), Fig. 53-34.
8. Repair cause of refrigerant leak or other problem. Also replace receiver-drier or accumulator-drier unit with a new one of good quality.

EVACUATING THE SYSTEM

EVACUATION is the process by which all air and moisture is removed from the air conditioning system. Using a heavy-duty vacuum pump, it takes at least 60 minutes to "pull down" the system to approximately 29.5 in. Hg.

To evacuate the system:
1. Connect manifold gauge set hoses to compressor low and high pressure ports, using an adapter, if necessary.

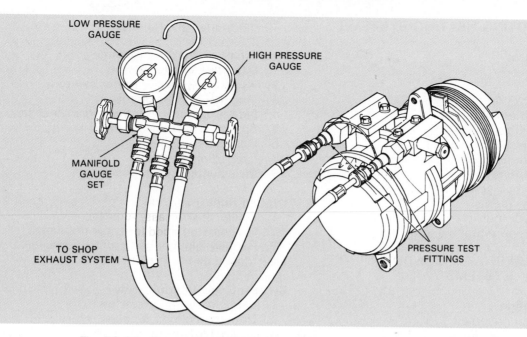

LOW PRESSURE
GAUGE

HIGH PRESSURE
GAUGE

MANIFOLD
GAUGE
SET

TO SHOP
EXHAUST SYSTEM

PRESSURE TEST
FITTINGS

Fig. 53-34. Proper installation of manifold gauge set to compressor ports is shown for discharging refrigerant. For charging A/C system, center hose is connected to refrigerant supply.   (Ford Motor Co.)

2. Connect manifold gauge set center hose to a heavy-duty vacuum pump.
3. Set both compressor service valves at mid-position, if so equipped.
4. Open manifold gauge set valves.
5. Plug vacuum pump power cord into 120 volt ac electrical receptacle and turn on pump.
6. Operate pump and watch vacuum reading on low side gauge. When gauge reading reaches at least 25 in. Hg., allow pump to run an additional 30 minutes.
7. Close both low and high side manifold gauge set valves and shut off vacuum pump.
8. Vacuum should hold at point of shut-down for 3 to 5 minutes if system is free of leaks.

CHARGING THE SYSTEM

Before disconnecting center manifold hose from vacuum pump, have sufficient cans of R-12 (or a refrigerant tank) available to charge system. Also, make use of a safety can valve to prevent high pressure from causing a backflow of refrigerant and exploding can.
To charge the system:
1. Install safety can valve in can of refrigerant.
2. Disconnect center manifold hose from vacuum pump and attach hose to can valve. See Fig. 53-34.
3. Now system is under vacuum, but hose contains trapped air. Open can valve and purge air from hose by cracking hose connector loose at manifold. Allow all air to escape, then tighten connector.
4. Hold refrigerant can upright and open low side manifold hand valve, allowing refrigerant vapor to enter system while observing gauges. NOTE: Occasionally tap refrigerant can. When it sounds empty, shut off low side manifold hand valve and can valve. Remove used can and install new can of

R-12 on can valve. Resume charging.
5. As soon as both gauge needles stop rising, close low side manifold hand valve and can valve.
6. Start engine and run at fast idle. Turn air conditioner controls for maximum cooling with blower at high speed.
7. Open can valve and low side manifold hand valve to draw additional refrigerant through low side. Check system capacity chart for amount of full charge. NOTE: Never open high side manifold hand valve when engine is running. If system does not accept enough R-12, rock can from side to side, or place refrigerant can in container of water heated to 125 °F (52 °C) to increase flow of refrigerant.
8. Observe high side gauge reading to avoid overcharging system. High side pressure should not exceed 240 psi (1656 kPa). Observe low side gauge reading; it should not exceed 60 psi (414 kPa).
9. When high and low side gauge pressures reach normal (15 to 30 psi [103 to 206 kPa] low side; 175 to 195 psi [1207 to 1345 kPa] high side), and bubbles disappear in sight glass, close low side manifold hand valve and can valve.
10. Check thermometer reading at air discharge duct nearest evaporator. Normal reading should be 35 to 45 °F (2 to 7 °C) on low blower speed.
11. Stop engine. Set both compressor service valves at maximum counterclockwise position (back seat), remove manifold gauge hoses from compressor ports and install service port caps. On compressors with Schrader valves, simply remove hoses and install port seal caps.
12. Remove refrigerant can from center manifold hose. Open safety can valve and purge remainder of refrigerant into shop exhaust system before removing can valve and disposing of refrigerant can.

TROUBLESHOOTING HEATING SYSTEMS

Insufficient or No Heat
1. Low coolant level.
2. Loose fan belt.
3. Clogged heater core.
4. Faulty engine thermostat.
5. Maladjusted control cables.
6. Collapsed or pinched vacuum hoses.
7. Leaking vacuum hose or vacuum motor.
8. Binding airflow doors.
9. Maladjusted temperature door.
10. Sluggish blower motor.
11. Defective blower motor.
12. Inoperative blower motor switch.

TROUBLESHOOTING AIR CONDITIONING SYSTEMS

No Refrigeration Action
1. Loose or broken drive belt.
2. Slipping compressor clutch.
3. Inoperative compressor.
4. Defective expansion valve.
5. Faulty fixed orifice tube.
6. Clogged screen in receiver-drier or expansion valve.
7. Clogged filter in accumulator-drier.
8. Plugged liquid refrigerant line.
9. Open clutch cycling switch.
10. Poor connection at clutch connector or clutch cycling switch.
11. Inoperative blower motor.
12. Blown fuse or defective circuit breaker.

Insufficient Cool Air
1. Low refrigerant charge.
2. Slipping compressor clutch.
3. Loose drive belt.
4. Clogged condenser.
5. Clogged evaporator.
6. Defective evaporator control valve.
7. Faulty expansion valve.
8. Faulty fixed orifice tube.
9. Clogged receiver-drier screen.
10. Clogged accumulator-drier filter.
11. Moisture or air in system.

12. Refrigerant overcharge.

Insufficient or No Air Discharge
1. Defective blower motor.
2. Inoperative blower motor switch.
3. Sluggish blower motor.
4. Blown fuse or defective circuit breaker.
5. Broken or disconnected blower motor wire.
6. Obstructed air passages.
7. Binding airflow door.
8. Maladjusted control cables.

System Runs Too Cold
1. Faulty thermostatic control.
2. Maladjusted linkage to control panel.
3. Partially plugged A/C suction line.
4. Closed clutch cycling switch.

System Cools Intermittently
1. Slipping compressor clutch.
2. Defective circuit breaker.
3. Faulty blower motor or blower motor switch.
4. Loose compressor clutch coil connection or poor ground.
5. Defective thermostatic control.
6. Stuck evaporator control valve.
7. Moisture in system, causing unit to ice up intermittently.
8. Air in system.

System Noisy
1. Refrigerant overcharge.
2. Low refrigerant charge.
3. Incorrect oil level.
4. Internal damage to compressor.
5. Loose compressor mounting.
6. Loose blower motor.
7. Loose drive belt pulley bolts.
8. Moisture in system.

AUTOMATIC TEMPERATURE CONTROL

AUTOMATIC TEMPERATURE CONTROL (ATC) is the general term for the various types of automatic air conditioning systems. See Fig. 53-35. ATC features completely automatic control of discharge air temperature.

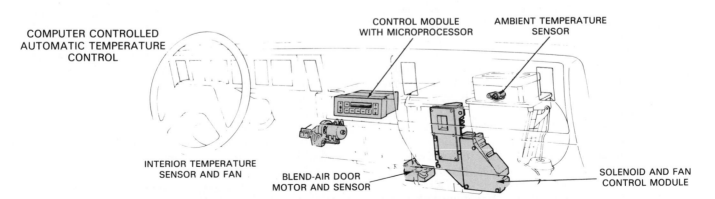

COMPUTER CONTROLLED AUTOMATIC TEMPERATURE CONTROL

CONTROL MODULE WITH MICROPROCESSOR

AMBIENT TEMPERATURE SENSOR

INTERIOR TEMPERATURE SENSOR AND FAN

BLEND-AIR DOOR MOTOR AND SENSOR

SOLENOID AND FAN CONTROL MODULE

Fig. 53-35. Microprocessor controlled ATC system regulates temperature of incoming air and makes adjustments every seven seconds to maintain desired temperature. (Chrysler Corp.)

ATC also controls the circulation and humidity of the air inside the automobile.

The only apparent difference between manual and automatic air conditioning systems is in the control panel. With ATC, the driver selects the temperature and the ATC system functions to maintain that temperature, regardless of outside temperature changes.

Many air conditioning, heating, ventilating, and defrosting systems are controlled by a COMPUTER or MICROPROCESSOR. These electronic control systems automatically adjust doors, blower speeds, and compressor cycling. See Fig. 53-36. The driver sets a particular temperature on the control panel and the system automatically adjusts various devices to obtain that temperature and airflow in the passenger compartment.

The computer uses input from various TEMPERATURE SENSORS to produce outputs for automatically controlling the ATC system. GM temperature sensors, for example, include: in-car, outside, high side, low side, and engine coolant.

Some computers also have a self-test or a self-diagnostic capability. If computer input indicates that a problem exists, the computer will send fault information to the control panel. The panel, in turn, will display a warning light or readout when the driver or service technician touches a combination of buttons or uses a jumper wire across two test terminals. A chart in the manufacturer's service manual tells what each trouble code means so that the problem area can be isolated.

ATC PRELIMINARY CHECKS

If an automatic temperature control system is not working properly, consider that these automatic system generally use the same basic "R-12 system" as the manual control model produced by the same manufacturer. See Figs. 53-26 and 53-37. Therefore, first manually inspect cooling system and A/C components to see that all are in good condition and correctly adjusted. Examine and manually check hose and line connections. Check vacuum hoses, electrical connections, fuses, control lever operation, and blower operation.

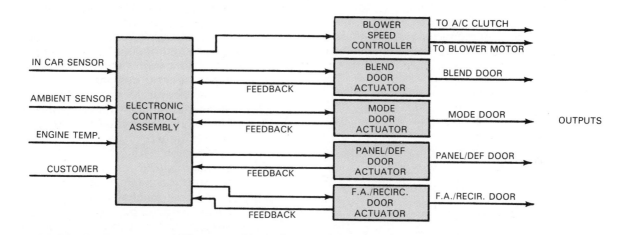

Fig. 53-36. Ford electronic ATC system block diagram shows inputs and outputs to and from electronic control assembly. A self-test feature included in control assembly lets technician utilize an "error code" to locate source of A/C problem.   (Ford Motor Co.)

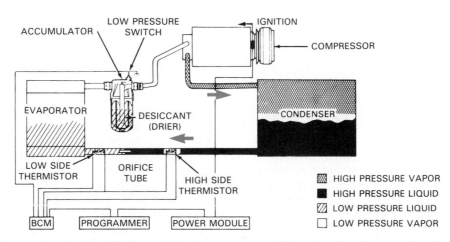

Fig. 53-37. Diagram outlines arrangement of components and direction of refrigerant flow in an Electronic Climate Control system. Basic refrigeration elements are same as manual A/C system. Automatic temperature control units, including BCM (Body Control Module), are added.   (Cadillac Motor Car Div., General Motors Corp.)

Clean debris from the condenser fins. Check the condition and tension of drive belts. Check cooling system hoses, radiator, pressure cap, cooling fan, and coolant level.

Make an operational test of the ATC system. Check the sight glass for bubbles (low on refrigerant). Test high side and low side pressures with a manifold gauge set.

Further tests of the more complicated controls and ATC system electronics (various temperature sensors, servo assemblies, control panel devices, and computer or microprocessor) call for specialized test equipment and extensive test procedures. These procedures based on manufacturer's computer diagnostics and fault code charts are beyond the scope of this text.

Chapter 53 — REVIEW QUESTIONS

Write your answers on a separate sheet of paper. Do not write in this book.

1. Air conditioning is the process by which surrounding air is _____ and _____.
2. Fluids give up heat when changing from a vapor to a liquid. True or False?
3. Heat always flows from _____ to _____ (hotter to cooler or cooler to hotter) objects.
4. A typical air conditioning and heating plenum chamber houses all but one of the following assemblies. Which one is NOT in the plenum chamber?
   a. Heater core.
   b. Evaporator.
   c. Condenser.
   d. Blower.
5. How is heat provided by the car heating system?
6. By what process is heat from the passenger compartment absorbed and carried away by the circulating refrigerant?
7. Which refrigerant is used in automotive air conditioning systems?
   a. R-11.
   b. R-12.
   c. R-20.
   d. R-500.
8. One British thermal unit (Btu) is the amount of heat required to raise the temperature of a _____ (gallon or pound) of water one degree Fahrenheit at sea level pressure.
9. Name three types of A/C compressors.
10. Which type of compressor uses a control valve to increase or decrease the swash plate angle for greater or lesser displacement?
11. The belt-driven compressor clutch pulley is always in rotation while the engine is running. True or False?
12. Compressor service valves are three-position controls: front-seated, _____, and back-seated.
13. Which of the major components of any A/C system provides a means of emitting heat from the hot refrigerant to the cooler atmosphere?
   a. Evaporator.
   b. Receiver-drier.
   c. Thermostatic expansion valve.
   d. Condenser.
14. What is indicated if bubbles appear in sight glass?
   a. System is fully charged with refrigerant.
   b. System is low on refrigerant.
   c. Refrigerant is fully discharged from system.
   d. Moisture in system.
15. Which component replaces the conventional thermostatic expansion valve in GM's CCOT A/C system?
16. Give five safety precautions to observe when working on an air conditioning system.
17. A vacuum pump is used to evaluate all traces of refrigerant, air, and _____.
18. The manifold gauge set has a center port to which a hose can be attached to perform several service operations. Which of the following is NOT a center port operation?
   a. Test pressure in system.
   b. Discharge refrigerant from system.
   c. Evacuate air and moisture.
   d. Charge system with refrigerant.
19. Using a heavy-duty vacuum pump, it takes approximately 60 minutes to ''pull down'' the A/C system to _____ in. Hg.
20. When charging A/C system, hold refrigerant can upright and open _____ (high side or low side) manifold gauge hand valve, allowing refrigerant vapor to enter system.
21. A car heater is not producing sufficient heat. Mechanic A says the coolant level may be low. Mechanic B says the heater core may be clogged. Who is right?
   a. Mechanic A.
   b. Mechanic B.
   c. Both mechanic A and mechanic B.
   d. Neither mechanic A nor mechanic B.
22. An air conditioning system has no refrigeration action. Mechanic A says the compressor clutch may be slipping. Mechanic B says the compressor clutch may have a closed cycling switch. Who is right?
   a. Mechanic A.
   b. Mechanic B.
   c. Both mechanic A and mechanic B.
   d. Neither mechanic A nor mechanic B.
23. An air conditioning system is noisy. Mechanic A says it could be caused by a refrigerant overcharge. Mechanic B says it could be caused by a low refrigerant charge. Who is right?
   a. Mechanic A.
   b. Mechanic B.
   c. Both mechanic A and mechanic B.
   d. Neither mechanic A nor mechanic B.
24. In automatic temperature control systems, the computer uses input from various temperature sensors to produce outputs for automatically controlling the ATC systems. Name four sensors.
25. Automatic temperature control systems generally use the same basic ''R-12 system'' as the manual control model produced by the same manufacturer. True or False?

Chapter 54

BUILT-IN SAFETY SYSTEMS

After studying this chapter, you will be able to:
- List dozens of major advances in automotive safety features.
- Describe current front seat lap/shoulder belt systems.
- Explain how automatic seat belt systems operate.
- Tell how air bags work.
- Compare the construction and function of the three major types of energy absorbing bumper systems.
- Describe the operation of a modern anti-lock braking system.

Safety has always been a key word for automotive engineers. First came the lights, horns, and mechanical brakes; then the emergency brakes, rear view mirrors, windshield wipers, and pneumatic tires.

Next, the car manufacturers gave us:
Safety wheel rims, Fig. 54-1, and tubeless tires.
Power brakes and power steering.
Safety glass, windshield washers and defrosters.
Dual headlamps, turn signals, and seat belts.
Warning buzzers, chimes, and indicator lights.
Neutral safety switches and steering wheel locks.
Snow tires, radial tires, and puncture-sealing tires.
Split brake systems, Fig. 54-2, and self-adjusting brakes.
Hood safety catches and coolant reserve systems.

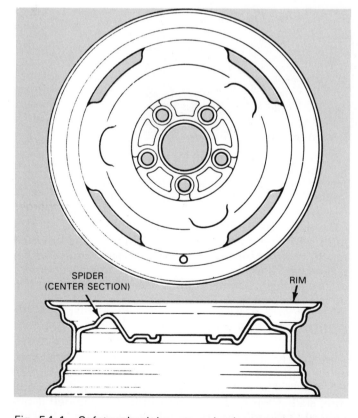

Fig. 54-1. Safety wheel rim was a simple yet major advance. In case of tire failure, raised sections around rim help hold beads of tire in position on wheel until vehicle can be brought to a safe stop. (American Motors Corp.)

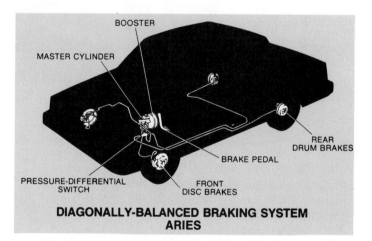

DIAGONALLY-BALANCED BRAKING SYSTEM
ARIES

Fig. 54-2. Split brake system is provided by a dual master cylinder and two separate hydraulic systems. Some have separate front and rear systems. Others have diagonally balanced systems as shown here.

Rear window wipers, defoggers, defrosters, Fig. 54-3.
Then came the government safety push for:
Collapsible steering columns and padded steering wheels.
Crash dash and recessed control knobs.
Head restraints and padded armrests and visors.

Fig. 54-3. Good rearward visibility is an important safety feature afforded by a rear window wiper and a window defogger/defroster system. (Ducellier)

54-4 and 54-5. The lap belt and shoulder belt are fixed to a connector. The lap belt usually has an automatic locking retractor, while the shoulder belt and lap/shoulder belt have an inertial-locking retractor that locks only when the vehicle stops abruptly.

Front seat belts generally incorporate a "timed" fasten seat belt reminder lamp and sound signal (buzzing). These warnings are designed to remind the driver and passengers to fasten lap and shoulder belts when the ignition key is turned to the ON position. If the driver's seat belt IS BUCKLED, the buzzer will not operate but the fasten seat belt reminder lamp will stay on for four to eight seconds. If the driver's belt IS NOT BUCKLED, the reminder lamp and sound signal will automatically shut off after the four to eight second interval.

Lap belt-to-floor pan and shoulder belt-to-roof panel or quarter panel fasteners are especially important. Failure of these attaching parts could affect the perfor-

Fig. 54-4. This automatic safety belt system meets U.S. government requirement for a passive restraint system. The system consists of two belts on retractable spools at top and bottom of door. Both belts meet at common anchor points between front seats. Operator opens door, gets seated, closes door, and spools retract spare belt material to keep belt in proper position. (Buick Motor Div., General Motors Corp.)

Positive seat anchorages and non-slip seat tracks.
Positive door locks and side-impact door beams.
Energy absorbing bumpers.
Roof crush resistance and fuel system integrity.
Reinforced panels, pillars, and floor pans in convertibles.
Dull finishes on reflective surfaces.
Voice alert systems.

Latest safety features being developed or installed include: anti-skid or anti-lock brake systems; automatic seat belts; air bags; high-mounted stop lamps; and "inner shield" (plastic-layered) windshields.

PASSENGER RESTRAINT SYSTEMS

Seat belts and shoulder belts of various types have been used in passenger cars for many years. See Figs.

mance of vital components and systems, and/or could result in major repair expenses. Fasteners must be replaced with a replacement part of the same part number or its equivalent. Correct torque values must be observed during reassembly.

FORD SEAT BELTS

Most late model Ford cars use a continuous loop, single retractor restraint system for the front seats. See Fig. 54-6. The outboard lap/shoulder belt uses a common sliding tongue. The webbing for the lap belt is anchored to the sill; the shoulder harness webbing has the other end fixed in a retractor.

The retractor for Ford's continuous loop system is designed to allow the webbing to move freely at all

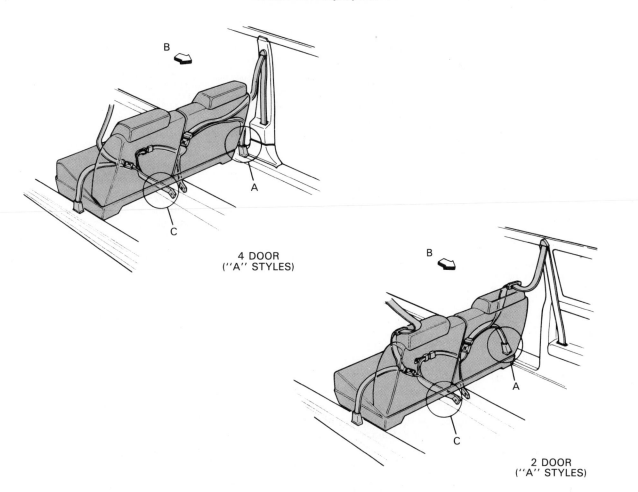

B

A

C

4 DOOR
("A" STYLES)

B

A

C

2 DOOR
("A" STYLES)

Fig. 54-5. Correct location and mounting of hardware and routing of belts is vital to convenient use and proper operation of lap/shoulder belt systems. These are typical front seat belt setups for GM cars. (Fisher body Div., General Motors Corp.)

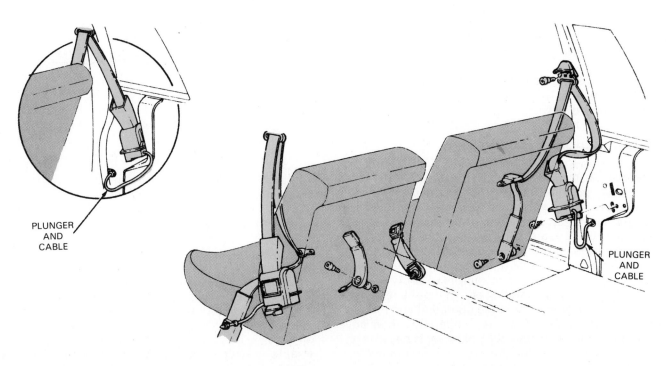

PLUNGER
AND
CABLE

PLUNGER
AND
CABLE

Fig. 54-6. Ford uses a continuous loop lap/shoulder belt system. This is a typical front seat belt arrangement for compact cars. (Ford Motor Co.)

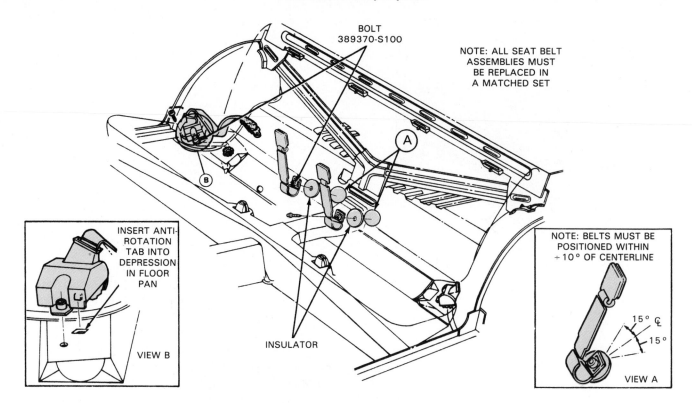

Fig. 54-7. Ford installs a two-point lap belt system for rear seat passengers. The web end of each outboard belt is attached to a retractor. (See Fig. 54-9.) (Ford Motor Co.)

times, except during vehicle deceleration when it automatically locks.

Older models used a "three-point" system for front seat belts. This system utilizes a fixed tongue on the front outboard lap/shoulder belt and two retractors. The webbing for the lap belt extends from a retractor that automatically locks when the belt is worn. This lock prevents the belt from being pulled out farther, yet the belt is free to retract and maintain a snug fit on the user.

A typical Ford rear seat lap belt setup is shown in Fig. 54-7. It is called a "two point" system because the retractor and webbing-and-tongue assembly is mounted outboard and the webbing-and-buckle assembly is mounted inboard.

OTHER PASSENGER RESTRAINTS

American Motors vehicles are also equipped with a continuous loop, single retractor restraint system in front and a two-point system at rear. Chevrolet cars utilize a similar front seat lap/shoulder belt arrangement called "single loop belt system."

Chrysler cars come equipped with front seat lap/shoulder belts as shown in Fig. 54-8. Decals are located on the lower lap belt retractors to show how to position the belt during entering or exiting of a rear seat passenger. Chrysler says that the operating and mounting of these belts should not be tampered with at any time. When removal, installation, or repair is necessary, refer to the service manual for proper system location and mounting hardware. See Fig. 54-8.

In most seat belt systems in U.S. cars, a mechanical

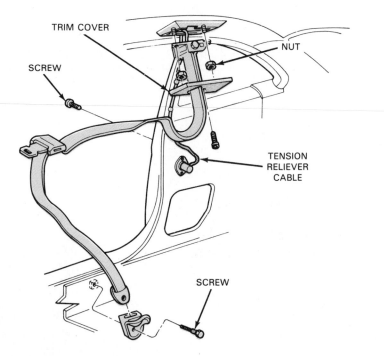

Fig. 54-8. Chrysler warns against interchanging seat belts between models. No attempt should be made to mix belt lengths. This is a typical front seat lap/shoulder belt layout. (Chrysler Corp.)

retractor is used. This type of retractor has a pendulum weight, Fig. 54-9, that locks the belt during rapid deceleration of the car. Mercedes-Benz passenger cars

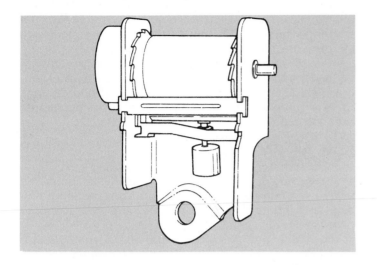

Fig. 54-9. A seat belt retractor allows belt to move in or out as wearer desires until a sudden deceleration of vehicle. Then, retractor automatically locks belt to restrain forward motion of wearer. (Ford Motor Co.)

Fig. 54-11. Automatic seat belt requires no buckling up or adjustment by driver or front seat passenger. Rider merely "gets in" and closes door. (Volkswagen of America, Inc.)

are equipped with an electronic unit, Fig. 54-10, that senses when the car is stopping abruptly. It then triggers the locking drive for the belt tightener in a matter of milliseconds.

Fig. 54-10. At collision speeds above 10 mph, this electronic unit senses sudden deceleration and signals belt tightener to restrain belted individual. (Robert Bosch Corp.)

AUTOMATIC SEAT BELTS

Most seat belt systems are "active." That is, the user must do something manually (buckle up) to make the system operable. The law regarding air bags and/or seat belts calls for "passive" (automatic) systems.

The air bag system is "passive." In order to qualify under the law effective with the introduction of the 1989 models, the seat belt system, too, must be passive. One such system is pictured in Fig. 54-11.

The "automatic" seat belt system has shoulder belts that enclose the driver and front seat passenger as they get into the car and shut their doors. This protects the

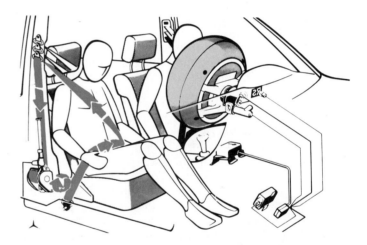

Fig. 54-12. Mercedes-Benz Supplemental Restraint System includes an air bag housing in steering wheel and knee bolster for driver. Front seat passenger is protected by a lap/shoulder belt and an emergency tensioning retractor.
(Mercedes-Benz of North America)

occupants during a crash by means of diagonal restraint across the chest.

The automatic seat belt system also has a knee restraint to prevent the occupant from sliding under the seat belt. The shoulder belt allows reasonably free movement during ordinary driving. The belt reel mechanism has a sensor which detects sudden forward movement of the occupant or abrupt deceleration of the car (as with a frontal crash). The reel locks in position, freezing belt length and preventing further forward movement of the occupant.

For post-crash purposes (or any other reason), the shoulder belt can be unfastened at the buckle on the door. Also, some automatic seat belt systems prevent restarting of the engine once it has been shut off unless both belts are again fastened in place.

AIR BAGS

AIR BAGS have been installed on certain foreign cars, Fig. 54-12, but added costs have slowed their adoption in the United States. Now, legislation demands that unless two-thirds of the U.S. population pass laws requiring the use of seat belts, either air bags or automatic wrap-around seat belts must be installed in all new cars by a specified model year.

Air bags are designed to serve as a "pillow" between front seat occupants and the vehicle's interior during the split second immediately following a frontal or front-angle crash. The air bags are built into the center of the steering wheel and, in some cases, the passenger-side instrument panel.

Current designs require a crash with an impact equivalent to hitting a wall at 12 mph or more. Then, crash sensors trigger inflators that permit nitrogen gas to fill the air bags and absorb the force of the occupants rebound.

HOW AIR BAGS WORK

The air bag protection system generally is composed of deceleration sensors, driver and front passenger air bags and inflators, knee restraints, and an instrument panel indicator lamp.

When the ignition switch is turned on, the indicator lamp lights for six to eight seconds. This pause permits a diagnostic circuit to check the operating condition of the air bag system. At the same time, a "backup" capacitor is charged (activates air bags if car's battery is destroyed on impact). When the indicator light goes out, the capacitor is fully charged and system integrity has been verified.

The air bag system also maintains a constant report of its reliability to the driver. If there is a failure in any part of the system, the indicator lamp will flash or burn steadily after the initial system check. Or, if the lamp fails to light when the ignition switch is first turned on, there is a need for service.

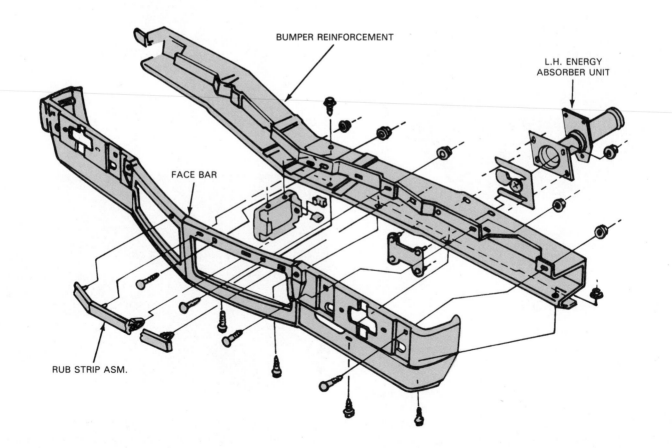

Fig. 54-13. Energy absorbers used on front and rear bumpers of most GM cars use hydraulic fluid as a dampening medium during frontal impacts. Inert gas is used to maintain unit in extended position. (Pontiac Motor Div., General Motors Corp.)

When a forceful enough impact is generated, the sudden deceleration causes the sensors to activate the inflators, which provide enough nitrogen gas to fill the air bags. As the bags inflate, they break out of their covers in the steering wheel and instrument panel and create a cushion between the occupants and the panel.

The air bags inflate in about 1/25 of a second, then actually begin deflating to minimize the force of the rebound. Air vents in the passenger's air bag aid in this deflating process. The steering wheel air bag will not deflate as quickly, but the rebound is offset by the collapsible steering column. In addition, knee restraints, shown in Fig. 54-12, are designed to keep front seat occupats from sliding under the air bags if they are not wearing seat belts.

ENERGY ABSORBING BUMPER SYSTEMS

By law, auto manufacturers are required to install bumper systems that will protect vehicle safety systems in a barrier impact of five miles per hour. The manufacturers have devised many different systems, but all are one of three major types:

1. Energy absorber somewhat like a suspension hydraulic shock absorber, but with a nitrogen gas preload that acts as a piston return after impact. See Figs. 54-13 and 54-14.
2. Energy absorber also like a shock absorber, but with a spring inside the hydraulic unit that returns the unit

and bumper to original position.
3. Plastic honeycomb pad backed by an impact bar. This pad type energy absorber, or isolator, uses no fluids or gases, but compresses on up to a five miles per hour impact, then bumper, pad, and impact bar return to original position.

HOW FLUID/GAS UNIT OPERATES

The bumper system utilizing hydraulic fluid and an inert gas consists of a piston tube assembly and a cylinder tube assembly. In extended position, Fig. 54-14, the piston tube is filled with gas and the cylinder tube is filled with hydraulic fluid.

Upon impact, the energy absorber is collapsed, Fig. 54-14, and the hydraulic fluid is forced from the cylinder tube into the piston tube through an orifice. The flow of fluid is controlled by the metering pin which, in turn, controls the energy absorbing action.

The incoming fluid displaces the floating piston, which compresses the gas in the piston tube. After impact, the pressure of the compressed gas behind the floating piston forces the hydraulic fluid back into the cylinder tube. The energy absorber unit is extended to its normal position and the bumper returns to its original position.

American Motors uses recoverable energy absorbers filled with grease and inert gas. The basic principle of operation is similar to the hydraulic fluid and inert gas

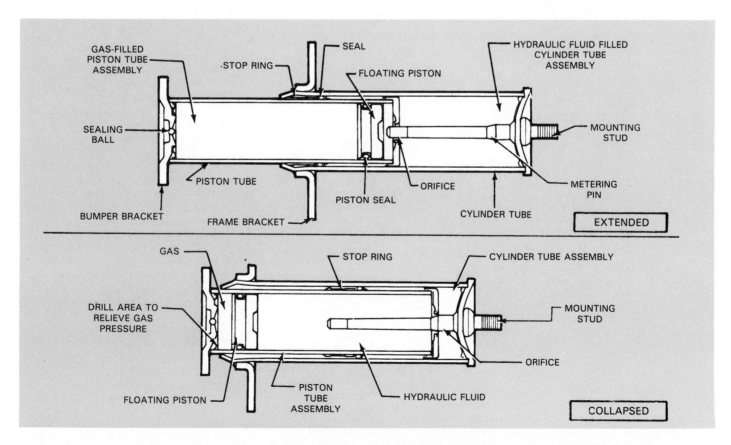

Fig. 54-14. In extended position, piston tube of energy absorber is filled with gas; cylinder tube is filled with hydraulic fluid. In collapsed position, hydraulic fluid has forced floating piston to compress gas and unit absorbs impact on bumper. (Pontiac Motor Div., General Motors Corp.)

units. The grease performs the same actions as the hydraulic fluid (displacing floating piston, etc.).

SERVICING FLUID/GAS UNITS

If an impact causes an energy absorber to leak or damages it so that it is inoperable, it should be replaced. Likewise, if the unit does not return to its original position after being compressed 3/8 in. or more, replace the defective unit.

CAUTION: Observe these precautions when handling energy absorbing devices: Do not apply heat to unit. Do not weld in area near unit. Do not work around bent sheet metal that may keep energy absorber from extending (possibility of spring-back).

If the energy absorber will not extend or if it is to be discarded, relieve the gas pressure by drilling a 1/8 in. hole in the piston tube. See Fig. 54-15. Be sure to wear approved safety glasses.

HOW FLUID/SPRING UNIT OPERATES

The hydraulic bumper system, Fig. 54-16, absorbs impact forces and dissipates impact energy. The outer cylinder of the energy absorber attaches to the frame or underbody of the car; the inner cylinder is attached to the bumper. When an impact load reaches approx-

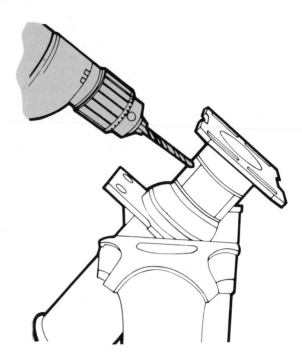

Fig. 54-15. If a gas/hydraulic fluid energy absorber is damaged, it should be relieved of gas pressure before disposal. To do this, wear safety glasses and drill a 1/8 in. hole in small cylinder.   (Chevrolet Motor Div., General Motors Corp.)

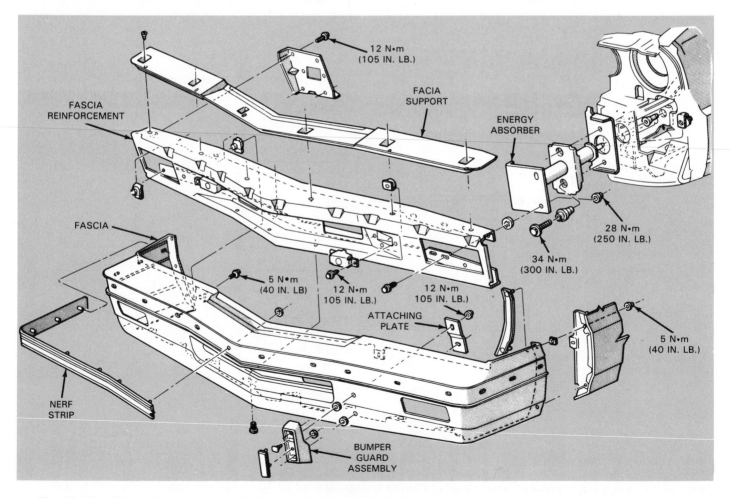

Fig. 54-16. Chrysler cars use hydraulic impact energy absorbers to mount front and rear bumpers on body frame supports. (Chrysler Corp.)

imately 8000 lb., a valve in the hydraulic unit opens and fluid is forced through a set of orifices (small openings). Impact energy is converted to heat, which is dissipated to the air and adjacent metal surfaces.

Once the impact force is removed, the heavy-duty spring inside the hydraulic unit returns the energy absorber and the bumper to their normal positions. See Fig. 54-17. These units are matched to the weight of the vehicle by the length of the stroke of the unit. The larger the vehicle: the longer the stroke.

PLASTIC PAD/IMPACT BAR UNITS

Bumper assemblies that rely on the energy absorbing characteristics of a plastic facia and plastic honeycomb pad backed by an impact bar, Fig. 54-18, have no moving parts. If damage is sustained to any of the bumper assembly elements, unit replacement is required. See Fig. 54-19.

If the honeycomb pad energy absorber must be replaced, drill out the pop rivets and install a new absorber with nuts, bolts, and lock washers.

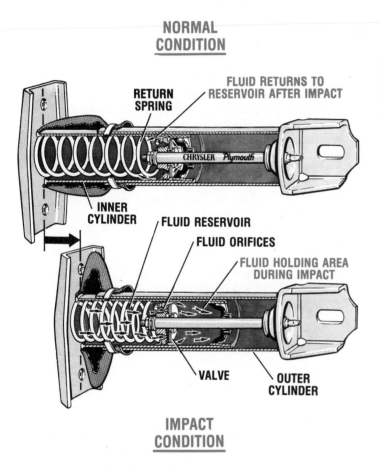

Fig. 54-17. Energy absorbers used on bumpers of Chrysler cars utilize hydraulic action and heat transfer to absorb impact. Spring returns energy absorber and bumper to normal position. (Chrysler Corp.)

SERVICING FLUID/SPRING UNITS

Hydraulic energy absorbing units that are damaged or stuck in the retracted position should be replaced. CAUTION: Units stuck in retracted position should not be drilled to relieve pressure. Drilling a hole can cause release of 8000 psi pressure, which could cause injury. If loosening attaching bolts to frame and bumper do not let energy absorber extend, discard the unit.

When installing new energy absorbers, tighten retaining nuts to hold bumper in place, then utilize adjustment allowed by slotted holes to shift bumper side-to-side and/or up-or-down to obtain correct bumper height and position. Torque-tighten attaching nuts.

Fig. 54-18. Some U.S. and foreign cars use bumper face bars made of urethane. This plastic "facia" is backed by a plastic honeycomb energy absorber and a steel impact bar. (Oldsmobile Div., General Motors Corp.)

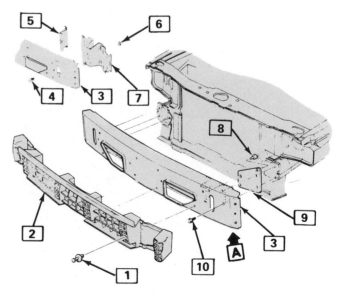

Fig. 54-19. Oldsmobile front bumper assembly (less plastic face bar): 1—Retainer. 2—Energy absorber. 3—Impact bar. 4—Bolt. 5—Reinforcement. 6—Nut. 7—Bracket. 8—Retainer. 9—Reinforcement. 10—Bolt/screw. (Oldsmobile Div., General Motors Corp.)

OTHER SAFETY FEATURES

Many innovative and reassuring types of safety features have been developed in recent years, and more of the same are being researched for incorporation in models yet to be introduced. Some of these are briefly described and pictured here.

ANTI-LOCK BRAKE SYSTEM

Certain Lincoln-Mercury models have a four-wheel anti-lock brake system, Fig. 54-20. Most unique feature of the system is that it uses brake fluid for both braking action and the hydraulic boost to the brake system.

The hydraulic brake system is divided into three circuits: left front wheel; right front wheel; both rear wheels. Major components include: master cylinder and hydraulic booster; electric pump and accumulator; valve body assembly; electronic controller; reservoir; four-wheel sensors.

Operational information and illustrations of this anti-lock brake system are contained in Chapter 52, Automotive Brakes. Failure of the system will cause the electronic controller to shut off the anti-lock system. However, normal power-assisted braking is still available.

POWER BRAKE SYSTEM

Some Oldsmobile Division cars have a power brake system that does not require vacuum to become operational. An electric pump provides hydraulic pressure to energize the system. The pump operates only when needed to maintain pressure as the brakes are applied.

Since the power brake system is independent of vacuum, it is in operation even when the engine is not running.

When the ignition is turned on, the "Powermaster" pump builds hydraulic pressure in the brake system.

The pump reportedly delivers instant response and high output for safe and reliable power braking.

"INNER SHIELD" WINDSHIELD

Certain Cadillac cars feature an anti-lacerative "Inner Shield" windshield designed "to virtually eliminate" facial cuts from broken windshields in auto accidents. This windshield is said to have superior abrasion resistance and chemical resistant properties.

The GM Inner Shield windshield has a two-part plastic layer applied to its inside surface. These layers are in addition to the construction of the "High Penetration Resistance" windshields currently in use. The HPR windshields consist of a layer of laminated plastic between two sheets of glass.

The "Inner Shield" windshield requires no special care, except that no abrasive cleaning agents or metal scraper should be used on the inner surface.

HIGH-MOUNTED STOP LAMP

Government regulations now require high-mounted stop lamps on new cars to provide an additional indica-

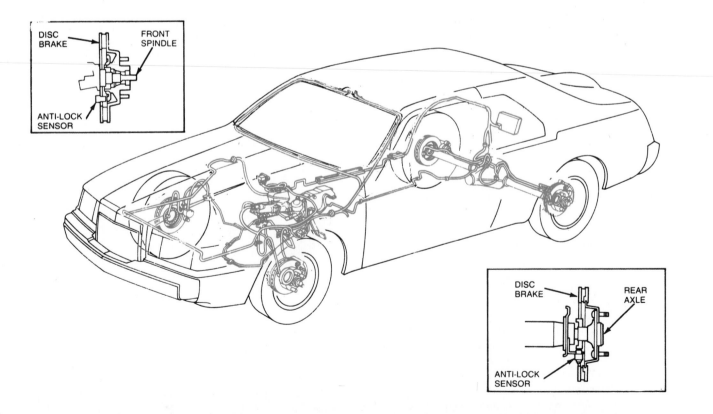

Fig. 54-20. Some Lincoln models are equipped with a four wheel anti-lock disc brake system. This system uses sensors (inset) at all four wheels to sense wheel lock conditions that will trigger anti-lock (pulsating) braking action. (Lincoln-Mercury Div., Ford Motor Co.)

tion of vehicle braking. The attention-getting feature of the high-mounted lamp is expected to help reduce the frequency and severity of rear collisions, especially in heavy traffic situations.

Cadillac's high-mounted unit, Fig. 54-21, is rectangular and measures 4 1/2 sq. in. It is mounted at the center of the rear package shelf inside the rear window.

VOICE ALERT SYSTEMS

The use of electronic "Voice Alert" systems is broadening each new model year, and the messages these systems provide are likewise being expanded. The systems basically are "voice" warnings to enhance those provided by instruments, lights, and buzzers. Voice warnings, it has been found, virtually eliminate any chance of the driver overlooking a potential problem.

One manufacturer's cars so equipped provide the following functions or voice warnings:
1. Your headlights are on.
2. Don't forget your keys.
3. Your washer fluid is low.
4. Your fuel is low.
5. Your electrical system is malfunctioning. Prompt service is required.
6. Your parking brake is on.
7. A door is ajar.
8. Please fasten your seat belts.
9. Your engine is overheating. Prompt service is required.
10. Your engine oil pressure is low. Prompt service is required.
11. All monitored systems are functioning.

INFORMATION CENTERS

Information centers provide visual displays of various kinds. Some consist of data panels on the dash or digital warnings that light up to alert the driver to certain vehicle conditions. See Fig. 54-22.

Also in the realm of driver information systems, electronics are making possible the inclusion of "message

Fig. 54-21. High-mounted stop lamp is required on all new passenger cars. It is designed to provide a more positive and additional warning to drivers of trailing vehicles. (Cadillac Motor Car Div., General Motors Corp.)

centers" on the instrument panel. The buttons can be manipulated by the driver or "navigator" to request liquid crystal displays of the condition of most all vital functions of the vehicle.

In this regard, many of the requests require in-vehicle diagnostic capability. That is: a given request for information could result in the diagnosis that the system under inquiry is about to fail. Armed with this advance warning, the driver could possibly insure his own safety by correcting the problem or having it corrected.

Chapter 54—REVIEW QUESTIONS

Write your answers on a separate sheet of paper. Do not write in this book.

1. What is the special safety feature of a safety wheel rim?

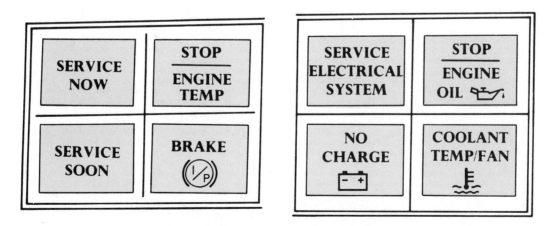

Fig. 54-22. Speedometer cluster telltale warning lights on instrument panel serve to warn driver of impending problems. (Cadillac Motor Car Div., General Motors Corp.)

a. One piece steel wheel.
b. Raised sections around rim that hold tire beads in place.
c. Drop center construction of wheel.
d. Air tight construction of wheel.

2. A typical lap/shoulder seat belt has an inertial retractor. What is the function of this type of retractor?

3. Seat belt fasteners must be replaced with a replacement part of the same _____, or its _____.

4. Most Ford cars use a _____ lap/shoulder belt system for the front seat occupants.
a. Safe restraint.
b. Positive lock.
c. Single loop.
d. Continuous loop.

5. Automatic seat belts are _____ (active or passive).

6. Air bag systems are _____ (active or passive).

7. The automatic seat belt system usually includes _____.

8. Air bags are usually built into the _____ and _____.

9. Current air bag designs require a crash with an impact equivalent to hitting a wall at _____ mph or more.
a. 5.
b. 10.
c. 12.
d. 15.

10. On an air bag equipped car, when the ignition switch is turned on, a backup _____ is charged.
a. Transistor.
b. Resistor.
c. Capacitor.
d. Diode.

11. The air bags will inflate in about _____ after a frontal or front angle collision.
a. 1/25 sec.
b. 1/5 sec.
c. 1/2 sec.
d. 1 sec.

12. Passenger car manufacturers are required to install bumper systems that will protect vehicle safety systems in a barrier impact of _____ mph.
a. 5.
b. 10.
c. 12.
d. 15.

13. Explain the operation of a hydraulic fluid/inert gas type of energy absorber.

14. If a hydraulic fluid/inert gas energy absorber will not extend or is to be discarded, what precautions should be taken?

15. What is the function of the heavy-duty spring in a hydraulic fluid/spring type of energy absorber?

16. Hydraulic fluid/spring type of energy absorbers that are damaged or stuck in the extended position should be _____.

17. These defective units should not be drilled to relieve pressure. True or False?

18. Unique feature of the Lincoln-Mercury four wheel anti-lock brake system is that it uses brake fluid for both _____ and the _____ to the brake system.

19. The hydraulic brake system of this anti-lock brake is divided into three circuits. Name them.

20. Oldsmobile has developed a power brake system that is free of _____.

Chapter 55

LAMPS, LIGHTING CIRCUITS, WIRING, AND HORNS

After studying this chapter, you will be able to:

- Explain how the complete automobile lighting circuit is divided into individual circuits and a common ground.
- State functions of electronic headlight dimming devices and headlight delay systems.
- Give service tips on headlamp and bulb replacement.
- Describe headlight aiming procedures, with and without mechanical aimers.
- Explain wire gauge numbering system.
- Select and use service manual explanatory and diagnostic information on electrical and electronic systems.
- Tell how the horn circuit operates and what tests and adjustments can be made.

Modern automobiles are loaded with lamps. A typical, fully equipped, four door sedan has more than 70 interior and exterior lamps. They range from a miniature indicator lamp of .15 candle power to a back up lamp of 32 candle power.

In current draw, automobile lighting ranges from about .27 amp for a rear window defogger switch lamp to over 5 amps for a sealed beam (unit) headlamp or composite (reflector-lens-bulb) headlamp. See Fig. 55-1.

LIGHTING CIRCUIT

The automobile lighting circuit includes the battery, frame, all the lights, and various switches that control their use. The lighting circuit is known as the SINGLE WIRE SYSTEM since it uses the car frame for the return.

The complete lighting circuit of the modern passenger car can be broken down into individual circuits, each having one or more lights and switches. See Fig. 55-2. In each separate circuit, the lights are connected in parallel, and the controlling switch is in series between the group of lights and the battery.

Fig. 55-1. Flush mounted, aerodynamic composite headlamps have a clear plastic lens bonded to a molded plastic reflector with socket and replaceable bulb. (Ford Motor Co.)

HEADLIGHTS

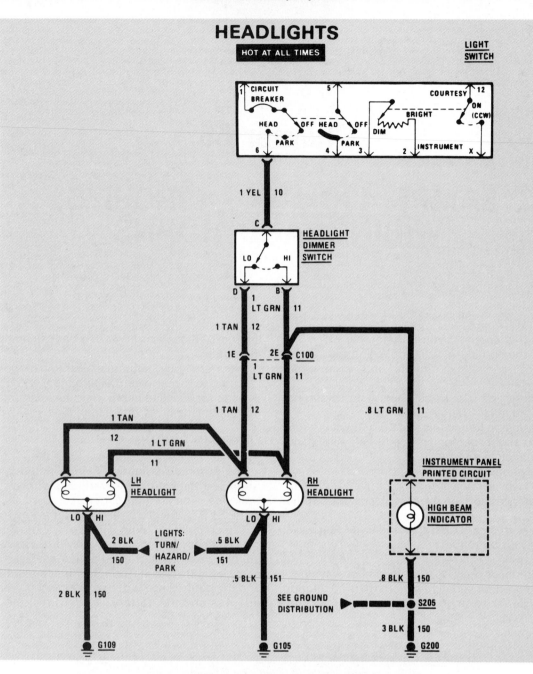

Fig. 55-2. Electrical schematic provides full details of headlight circuit from light switch to headlamps to ground. (Cadillac Motor Car Div., General Motors Corp.)

The parking lights, for example, are connected in parallel and controlled by a single switch. In some installations, one switch controls the connection to the battery while a selector switch determines which of two circuits is energized. The headlights, with their upper and lower beams, are an example of this type of circuit.

In some instances, such as the courtesy lights, several switches may be connected in parallel so that any switch may be used to turn on the lights.

MAIN LIGHTING SWITCH

The MAIN LIGHTING SWITCH (headlamp switch) is the heart of the lighting system. It controls the headlights, parking lights, side marker lights, taillights, license plate light, instrument panel lights, and interior lights. See Fig. 55-3. Individual switches are provided for special purpose lights such as directional signals, hazard warning flasher, back up lights, and courtesy lights. See Fig. 55-4.

The main lighting switch may be of either the "push-pull" or "push-pull with rotary contact" type. A typical switch will have three positions: off, parking, and headlamps. Some switches also contain a rheostat to control the brightness of the instrument panel lights. The rheostat is operated by rotating the control knob, separating it from the push-pull action of the main lighting switch.

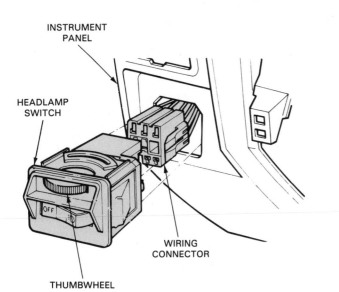

Fig. 55-3. This headlamp switch has three positions, built-in circuit breaker, and thumbwheel rheostat control of instrument panel lighting. (Ford Motor Co.)

FUSES AND CIRCUIT BREAKERS

A FUSE BLOCK, Fig. 55-5, generally is connected between the battery and the main lighting switch. Usually, the fuse block is mounted on the driver's side of the firewall.

When a short circuit or overload occurs in a circuit, the fuse burns out, Fig. 55-6, and opens that circuit so no further damage will result. Excess current will open a circuit breaker's terminals, indicating there is something wrong in that circuit. The circuit breaker will remain open until the trouble is corrected.

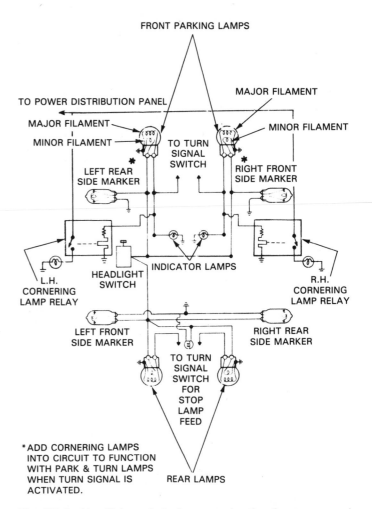

*ADD CORNERING LAMPS INTO CIRCUIT TO FUNCTION WITH PARK & TURN LAMPS WHEN TURN SIGNAL IS ACTIVATED.

Fig. 55-4. Headlight switch also controls other front, rear, and interior lighting. Turn signal lamps, indicator lamps, and cornering lamps are operated by turn signal switch. (Ford Motor Co.)

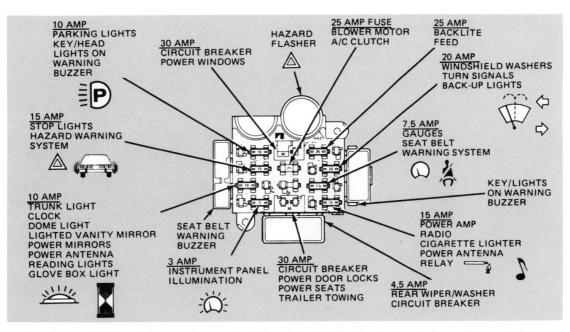

Fig. 55-5. A fuse block locates fuses, circuit breakers, and flashers on a single, easily accessible panel. (American Motors Corp.)

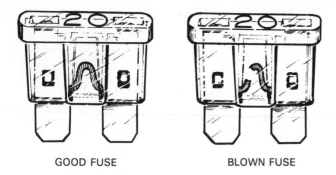

GOOD FUSE   BLOWN FUSE

Fig. 55-6. Fuse blocks on most cars contain miniaturized fuses with blade terminal design for increased circuit protection and greater reliability.   (Buick Motor Div., General Motors Corp.)

HEADLAMP TYPES

A conventional SEALED BEAM HEADLAMP incorporates one or two filaments (thread-like conductors), a reflector, and a lens in an airtight optical assembly. The filaments are correctly focused in relation to the reflector and lens at the time of manufacture.

All sealed beam headlamps are either round or rectangular. Number 1 is embossed on round sealed beam units having a single filament: 1A appears on rectangular units with a single filament. Number 2 is embossed on round units have two filaments; 2A appears on rectangular units with two filaments.

Basically:

1. Single filament sealed beam units are used in four lamp systems to provide the principle portion of the upper beam (distant illumination).
2. Two filament units are used in four lamp systems to provide the lower beam (road ahead illumination) and a secondary portion of the upper beam.
3. Two type 2 or 2A double filament sealed beam units are used in the two lamp system.

In a variation of the conventional built-in filament type of sealed beam headlamp, the HALOGEN BULB sealed beam unit was introduced. See Fig. 55-7. A tungsten-halogen inner bulb is supported by lead wires inside a sealed reflector and lens assembly.

Fig. 55-7. Small, rectangular halogen headlamp at left provides same lighting characteristics as larger lamp at right. Smaller unit allows a low, aerodynamic front end design. (Chrysler Motors)

HEADLAMP CONSTRUCTION

Headlamp construction has changed in recent years in keeping with modern vehicle exterior design and electrical power demands. Aerodynamic styling to reduce high speed drag requires flush mounted headlamps of a small vertical dimension. Therefore, rectangular low profile headlamps, Fig. 55-8, became the popular choice of design engineers.

The quest for reduced aerodynamic drag also resulted in the introduction of COMPOSITE HEADLAMPS. See Fig. 55-9. The "composite" headlamp is a reflector and lens system designed for a specific vehicle model and contoured to that vehicle's requirements. Separate replaceable halogen bulbs are used in composite headlamps. See Fig. 55-10.

Fig. 55-8. Low profile, flush mounted rectangular headlamps provide aerodynamic design that reduces car's coefficient of drag.   (Buick Motor Div., General Motors Corp.)

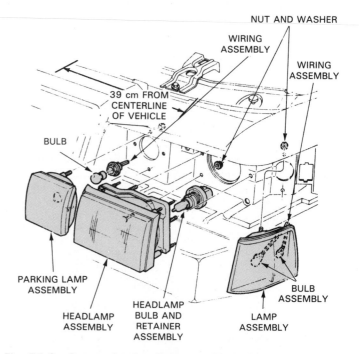

Fig. 55-9. Composite headlamps utilize reflector and lens assembly and separate bulb. Replacing bulb does not require reaiming of headlamp.   (Ford Motor Co.)

CONCEALED HEADLAMPS

A long-standing method of reducing aerodynamic drag is by means of CONCEALED HEADLAMPS. See Fig. 55-11. With this setup, the driver can operate the car at higher speeds in daylight and experience minimum drag. Movable doors that conceal the headlamps close to present flush fitting sheet metal to reduce air resistance in the headlamp area.

Most concealed headlamp doors, Fig. 55-11, are electrically operated. A single motor and gear box power two drive shafts that open and close the doors.

Some car makers installed a concealed headlamp door system powered by intake manifold vacuum. In one such system, the headlamps were fitted in a barrel housing that pivoted into position when the linkage system was actuated by power cylinder push rods. A relay valve controlled the vacuum to the power cylinders. A manual valve was provided so the doors could be opened in emergency situations.

LAMP SWITCHES

Sealed beam and composite headlamps provide the choice of driving with the help of LOW BEAMS or HIGH BEAMS. A DIMMER SWITCH, Fig. 55-12, permits selection of the required headlight beam.

When the main lighting switch completes the circuit to the headlamps, the low beam lights the way for city driving and for use when meeting oncoming traffic on the highway. When the dimmer switch is actuated, the single filament headlamps go ON, along with the high beam of the two filament headlamps. The next actuation of the dimmer switch returns the headlighting system to low beams only on the two filament lamps.

Some cars are equipped with an electronic headlight dimming device. This device automatically switches the headlights from high beam to low beam in response to light from an approaching vehicle or light from the taillight of a vehicle being overtaken.

One AUTOMATIC HEADLAMP DIMMER utilizes a sensor-amplifier unit, a high-low beam relay, a dimmer switch, a driver sensitivity control, and wiring harnesses. See Fig. 55-13. The sensor-amplifier is used to operate the high-low beam power relay for switching headlight beams. The relay has heavy-duty contacts to handle the switching actions.

The dimmer switch in the automatic headlamp dimming system is a special override type. It is located in the steering column as part of a combination dimmer, horn, and turn signal switch. The override action occurs when a slight pull toward the driver on the multi-function switch lever provides high beam headlights regardless of the amount of light on the sensor-amplifier.

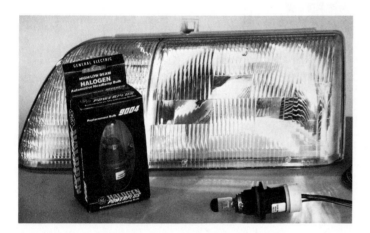

Fig. 55-10. Replacement halogen bulb and retaining ring assembly is pictured with its composite reflector and lens assembly. (General Electric Co.)

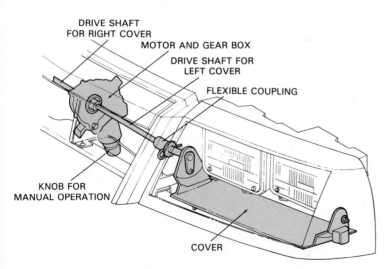

Fig. 55-11. Concealed headlamps provide better aerodynamics and improved appearance. A manual override can be used to open headlamp doors in event of an electrical failure. (Chrysler Corp.)

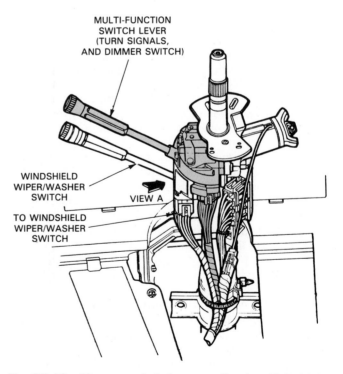

Fig. 55-12. Dimmer switch for controlling headlight high or low beam selection usually is incorporated in multi-function switch lever. (Ford Motor Co.)

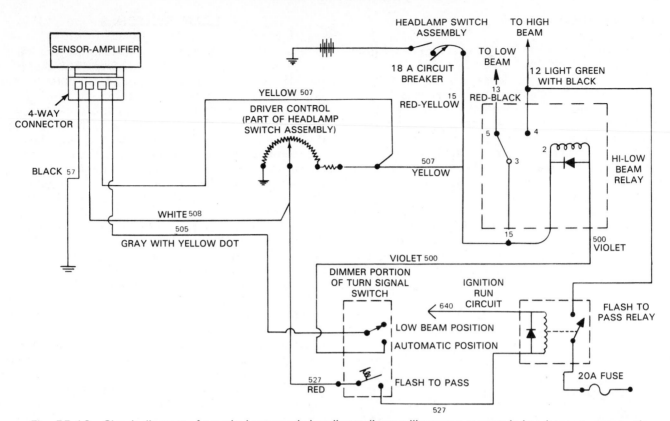

Fig. 55-13. Circuit diagram of a typical automatic headlamp dimmer illustrates system in low beam or automatic OFF position. (Ford Motor Co.)

HEADLAMP DELAY SYSTEMS

HEADLAMP DELAY SYSTEMS (Autolamp, Twilight Sentinel, etc.) automatically control headlamp ON-OFF operation after the ignition switch and main lighting switch are turned OFF. See Fig. 55-14. The system, controlled by the driver, provides a lights-on situation on a time-delay basis so that the occupants will have the convenience of headlighting when leaving the vehicle. The system automatically delays switching off the headlamps for a period of time preselected by the driver (up to 90 sec. or 4 1/2 min. depending on type of system).

In addition, the system also can be "switched" to a light sensitive, automatic ON-OFF control of the headlamps and other exterior lamps. A light sensitive photocell is mounted in an area exposed to outside light. With the main lighting switch OFF and the automatic control ON, the system will turn on the headlamps when natural outside light diminishes.

FOG LAMPS

FOG LAMPS are gaining renewed popularity, both in original equipment and aftermarket installations. See Fig. 55-15. Standard equipment lamps generally are built into the front bumper or suspended below the bumper, Fig. 55-16. Aftermarket fog lamps are available in kits that include lamps, halogen bulbs, impact resistant plastic covers, and a prewired harness with in-line fuse holder and switch.

Fig. 55-14. Convenience system automatically controls operation of exterior lights according to amount of ambient light present. Also for convenience, headlamp delay system will keep lights ON for a set time after ignition is turned OFF. (Cadillac Motor Car Div., General Motors Corp.)

Fig. 55-15. Fog lamps are factory installed on some cars, either built-in or suspended below front bumper. (Ford Motor Co.)

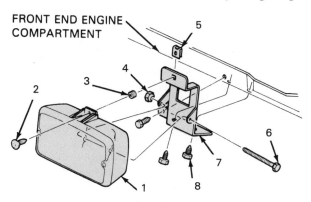

Fig. 55-16. Detail of suspended fog lamp mounting is shown. 1—Lamp assembly. 2—Screw. 3—Spring. 4/5—Nuts. 6—Screw. 7—Bracket. 8—Screw assembly. (Cadillac Motor Car Div., General Motors Corp.)

DIRECTION SIGNAL SWITCH

The DIRECTION SIGNAL SWITCH, Fig. 55-17, is installed just below the hub of the steering wheel. A manually controlled lever projecting from the switch permits the driver to signal the direction of the turn about to be made. Moving the switch handle down will light the "turn signal" lamps on the left front and left rear of the car, signaling a left turn. Moving the switch upward will light the turn signal lamps on the right (front and rear), signaling a right turn. With the switch in a position to indicate a turn, lights are alternately turned ON and OFF by a TURN SIGNAL FLASHER, Fig. 55-18.

Incorporated in the direction (turn) signal switch is the LANE CHANGE SWITCH MECHANISM. This feature provides the driver the opportunity to signal a lane change

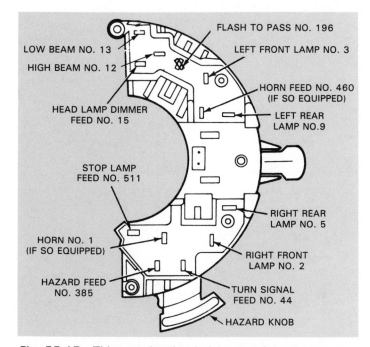

Fig. 55-17. This turn signal switch is part of a multi-function switch assembly that includes headlamp dimmer and hazard flasher switches. (Ford Motor Co.)

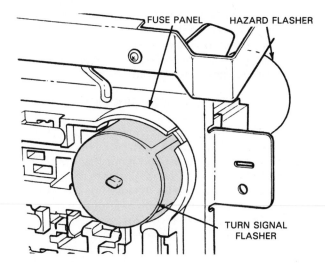

Fig. 55-18. Flasher that controls ON/OFF operation of turn signal lamps is often located in fuse panel. (Ford Motor Co.)

by holding the turn lever against a detent, then releasing it to cancel the signal immediately after the maneuver is completed.

The HAZARD WARNING FLASHER is also associated with the turn signal switch. This flasher, Fig. 55-18, actuates the hazard warning system. When the control knob is operated, all front and rear turn signal lamps light and flash simultaneously.

The hazard warning switch control knob generally is mounted on the upper portion of the steering column. The flasher usually is located under the instrument panel on or near the fuse block.

STOPLIGHT SWITCH

In order to signal a stop, a brake pedal operated STOPLIGHT SWITCH is provided to operate the vehicle's stop lamps. In addition to lighting the conventional rear lamps, the switch also operates the center high-mounted stop lamp, Fig. 55-19, that became mandatory on later models.

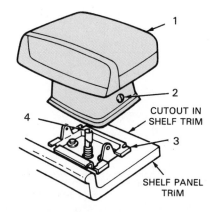

Fig. 55-19. Detail drawing shows high-mounted stop lamp in rear shelf panel trim: 1—Stop lamp assembly. 2—Attaching screw. 3—Mounting bracket. 4—Wiring harness. (Cadillac Motor Car Div., General Motors Corp.)

A typical stoplight switch and its location are shown in Fig. 55-20. Note that cruise control equipped vehicles of this make also utilize a vacuum release valve. In this case, both the vacuum release valve and the stoplight switch are actuated by movement of the brake pedal.

HEADLAMP SERVICE

Short life and frequent burning out of headlamps usually results from excessive voltage. This, in turn, may result from loose or corroded electrical connections in the battery circuit, or the charging rate may be too high.

Lighting outages in pairs (headlamps, parking lamps, tail lamps) could be caused by a defective main lighting switch. Use an ohmmeter to test the continuity of the circuit involved. Use the meter probes to check for an "open" at the switch terminals for the circuit being tested. See Fig. 55-21.

Dim lights result from low voltage, which may be caused by loose or corroded terminals in the lamp circuit. Possibly, the charging rate may be too low or the battery may be defective.

The wiring in lighting circuits should be inspected periodically for loose or corroded connections, or for chafed insulation. The connections at junction blocks and plug-in connectors should be carefully checked. Switches, bulb sockets, lamp shells, reflectors, and lenses should be inspected for loose mounting and corrosion.

In order to overcome the effects of rust, it frequently is necessary to solder a lead to a lamp socket case and ground the other end of the lead on the frame.

The voltage drop between the various lamp sockets (not the holder, reflector, or shell) and ground should be measured with a low-reading voltmeter. Each light should be turned on when making this test for high resistance at ground connections. If any reading is obtained on the voltmeter, it is an indication that there is resistance present. The shell and socket must be thoroughly cleaned to obtain a good electrical connection.

Another test that should be made is checking voltage drop between the battery and each individual lamp. To make this test, connect a long positive lead of a voltmeter to the positive battery terminal. Attach a test probe to the other lead of the voltmeter. Turn on the lights and touch the voltmeter probe to the insulated terminal of each lamp. The voltage drop should be less than 0.6 volt.

If voltage drop is greater than 0.6 volt, follow the circuit back through the switch to locate the part of the circuit in which the loss occurs. If the loss in voltage is due to a defective part, it should be replaced. Usually, the loss will be found at a terminal or plug-in connector. Cleaning and tightening will overcome the trouble.

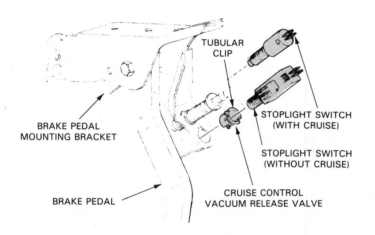
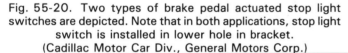

Fig. 55-20. Two types of brake pedal actuated stop light switches are depicted. Note that in both applications, stop light switch is installed in lower hole in bracket. (Cadillac Motor Car Div., General Motors Corp.)

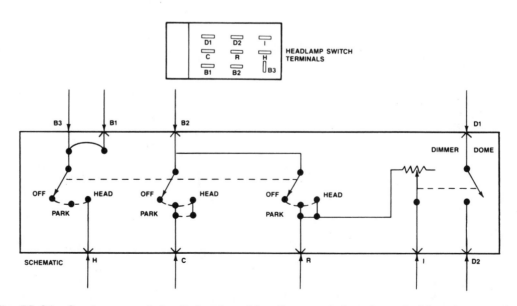

Fig. 55-21. Service manual circuit drawing of headlamp switch and terminal locations can be used as a guide for tests for open circuits: H—Headlamp. C—Chime voice alert. R—Park lamp. I—Panel lamp dimmer. D1/D2—Dome lamp dimmer. (Ford Motor Co.)

REPLACING SEALED BEAM UNITS

To replace a sealed beam headlamp:
1. Remove the screws that secure the headlamp door (bezel), then remove door. See Fig. 55-22.
2. On some models, unhook springs that hold retaining ring in position.
3. Remove screws that hold retaining ring to shell assembly (mounting ring). Do not turn adjusting screws.
4. Remove retaining ring.
5. Pull lamp forward and remove electrical connector.
6. Remove lamp.
7. Reverse procedure to install new headlamp.

REPLACING HALOGEN BULBS

When servicing composite headlamps for a halogen bulb burnout, handle the bulb by its plastic base only. CAUTION: Halogen bulbs contain gas under pressure and may shatter if mishandled or dropped. After removing the burned out bulb, immediately install a new bulb in the socket to keep contaminants from entering the headlamp body. Also, do not energize the halogen bulb until it is safely contained in the headlamp body.

To replace a halogen bulb:
1. Place main lighting switch in OFF position.
2. Remove electrical connector from bulb.
3. Unlock bulb retaining ring and remove ring and bulb from socket, Fig. 55-23.
4. Position replacement halogen bulb with flat side of plastic base up and lock retaining ring in place.
5. Install electrical connector on bulb base.
6. Turn ON main lighting switch and check headlamp operation.

REPLACING FRONT, SIDE, AND REAR BULBS

Bulb replacement, other than headlamps, is a simple operation. Some lamp assemblies require removal of the bezel and lens for access to the defective bulb (fog lamps, parking lamps, back up lamps). Others are accessible from the inside rear of the particular lamp assembly (front side marker lamps, cornering lamps, tail lamps, stop lamps). See Fig. 55-24.

Many of the front, side, and rear lamp assemblies are fitted with halogen bulbs. See Fig. 55-25. Therefore, the previously stated handling caution should be observed.

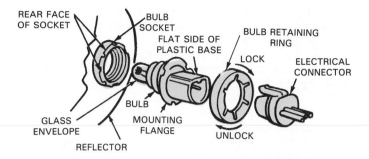

Fig. 55-23. Exploded view details order of position of composite headlamp socket, replaceable headlamp bulb, bulb retaining ring, and electrical terminal. (Ford Motor Co.)

Fig. 55-24. Many bulbs can be replaced from rear of lamp assembly, usually by means of a snap-in socket arrangement. A hinged tail lamp panel is shown. (Buick Motor Div., General Motors Corp.)

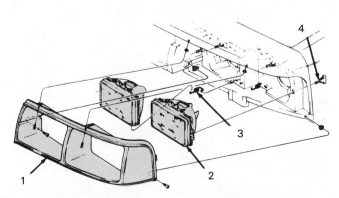

Fig. 55-22. Exploded view shows sealed beam headlamp mounting details: 1—Bezel assembly. 2—Headlamp assembly. 3—Spring. 4—Adjuster assembly. (Oldsmobile Div., General Motors Corp.)

Fig. 55-25. ''Family'' of halogen bulbs for signal lamps, back up lamps, high-mount stop lamps, etc., are pictured. (General Electric Corp.)

AIMING HEADLIGHTS

To facilitate aiming the headlights, adjusting screws are provided. In most cases, the screws for vertical aiming are at the top of the headlamp, Fig. 55-26. The horizontal aim adjusting screws are at the side. The aim adjusting screws should not be turned unless it is necessary to aim the headlights.

The three guide points formed in the front of the headlamp lens are used with MECHANICAL AIMERS. See Fig. 55-27. The equipment is provided with an accurate level, so it is not necessary for the vehicle to be on a level floor.

To check headlight aim:
1. Calibrate aimers according to equipment manufacturer's directions.
2. Install proper set of adaptors on aimers.
3. Mount headlamps so that steel inserts on adaptors contact three guide points on headlamp lens.
4. Set zero on horizontal dial.

5. Check split image and target line in viewing port, Fig. 55-28. If image is aligned, horizontal aim is correct.
6. If image is misaligned, turn adjusting screw on side of headlamp to align image on target line. Make final adjustment in clockwise direction.
7. Repeat steps 4, 5, and 6 on opposite headlamp.
8. Set zero on vertical dial. If level bubble is centered, vertical aim is correct.
9. If level bubble is off center, turn vertical adjusting screw at top of headlamp until level bubble is centered, Fig. 55-29. Finish with clockwise turn.
10. Recheck horizontal aim and readjust if necessary.
11. On four headlamp systems, repeat aiming process on other two headlamps.

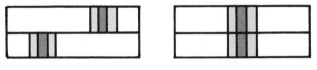

NOT ALIGNED   ALIGNED

Fig. 55-28. If split image in viewing port is not aligned, turn horizontal adjusting screw on headlamp until image aligns on target line. This will provide correct horizontal aim. (Chrysler Corp.)

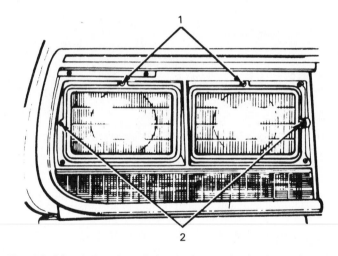

Fig. 55-26. Adjust headlight aim by turning horizontal and/or vertical adjusting screw in lamp housing: 1—Above. 2—At side of sealed beam unit. (American Motors Corp.)

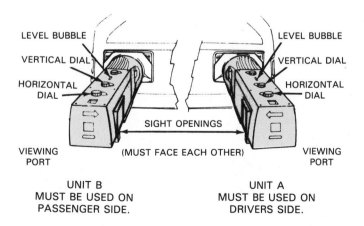

Fig. 55-27. Calibrate mechanical aimers, then position them on opposite headlamps. Sight openings must face each other. Set zero on horizontal dial. (Chrysler Corp.)

Fig. 55-29. With zero set on vertical dial, turn vertical adjusting screw on headlamp until level bulb is centered. This will provide correct vertical aim. (PPG Industries, Inc.)

AIMING BY WALL LAYOUT

Headlights also may be aimed by using a wall layout. In using this setup, the floor must be level and tires correctly inflated. Draw a line on the floor parallel to the wall and exactly 25 ft. from it. Position the car at right angles to the wall with the headlamps right over the line marked on the floor. Then, referring to Figs. 55-30 and 55-31, proceed as follows:

1. Measure height of center of headlamps from floor.
2. Transfer this measurement to wall and draw a horizontal line.
3. Measure width of windshield and rear window. Find center and mark with tape.
4. Sight through rear window, aligning tapes and establishing vertical centerline on wall layout.
5. Add line to wall layout in line with vertical centerline of left headlamp.
6. Add line to wall layout in line with vertical centerline of right headlamp.
7. Turn on headlights and check high intensity zones against those shown in Fig. 55-30 (low beam) and Fig. 55-31 (high beam).

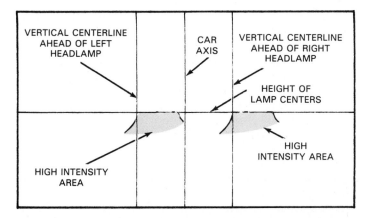

Fig. 55-30. Create wall layout as indicated. Then, with vehicle on level floor 25 ft. from wall, correct high intensity area of low beam should appear as shown. (Chrysler Corp.)

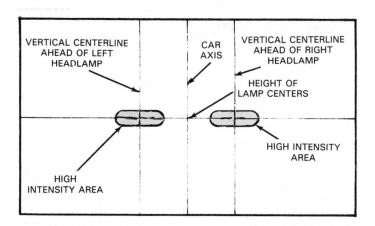

Fig. 55-31. With vehicle in place for aiming headlights by means of a wall layout, correct high intensity area of high beam should appear as shown. (Chrysler Corp.)

WIRES AND CABLES

WIRES AND CABLES are conductors of electricity. Usually made of annealed copper, they are used to carry electricity to the various electrical devices and equipment on passenger cars and trucks.

These wires and cables must be the correct size for the application and have proper insulation. If the wire or cable is too small in cross section or too long for its size, its resistance will be too great and valuable voltage will be lost. This, in turn, will result in poor operation of the electrical device in that circuit.

LIGHTING WIRE SIZES

WIRE SIZE AND LENGTH determines the resistance of the wire. Wire and cable sizes are expressed by a GAUGE NUMBER, which indicates the cross-sectional area of the conductor. Note in the Wire Gauge Table in Fig. 55-32 that the cross-sectional area of the wires is given in metric size (mm²) and in circular mils. The diameter is given in decimals of an inch. A CIRCULAR MIL is a unit of area equal to the area of a circle one mil in diameter. A MIL is a unit of length equal to .001 in. Also note in the table that the larger the diameter of the wire or cable, the smaller the gauge size number.

Cables are made up of a number of strands of wire. The cross-sectional area of a cable is equal to the circular mil area of a single strand times the number of strands. Special gauges are available for measuring the gauge size of wires and cables. See Fig. 55-33. Many multi-purpose electrician's pliers feature wire size holes for stripping, cutting, and crimping operations.

Remember, the resistance of a length of wire or cable decreases as its cross section increases. Therefore, it is advisable to use wire of relatively large cross section. In general, nothing smaller than No. 16 gauge wire should be used for lights of low candle power. For headlights and back up lights, and other lights of high candle power, wire of still larger gauge is required.

CONDUCTORS			
SAE Wire Size (gauge)	Metric Wire Size (mm²)	Minimum Cross-sectional Area (circular mils)	Diameter (in.)
20	0.5	1072	.032
18	0.8	1537	.040
16	1.0	2336	.051
14	2.0	3702	.064
12	3.0	5833	.081
10	5.0	9343	.102
8	8.0	14810	.129
6	13.0	25910	.162
4	19.0	37360	.204
2	32.0	62450	.258
1	40.0	77790	.289
0	50.0	98980	.325

Fig. 55-32. Wire and cable size is given in gauge number, metric area, circular mils, and diameter in decimals of an inch.

Fig. 55-33. A typical wire gauge is pictured. Wire being checked is placed in various gauge openings until "proper fit" is obtained. Openings are coded in wire gauge sizes. (L.S.Starrett Co.)

When comparing cables, consider that the external diameter of the insulated wire or cable has nothing to do with its current-carrying capacity. Thick insulation will make a small gauge wire look much larger. It is important that only the size of the metal conductors are compared.

LOW TENSION PRIMARY CABLES

BATTERY CABLES connect the battery to the rest of the starting and charging circuits. Because a starting motor cranking an engine will draw approximately 200 amps of current, the battery cables must be of sufficient size to carry such heavy current.

Battery-to-starter and battery-to-ground cables range from gauge size No. 6 through No. 4/0. See Fig. 55-34. Passenger car battery cables usually are No. 1 or No. 2 gauge. The insulation may be thermoplastic, synthetic rubber, or cross-linked polyurethane.

Because the cables are close to the battery and could corrode, it is important that the cables make good electrical contact with the cable clamps. Likewise, clamps

BATTERY CABLES			
SAE Wire Size (gauge)	Metric Wire Size (mm²)	Minimum Cross-sectional Area (circular mils)	Diameter (in.)
6	13.0	25910	.162
4	19.0	37360	.204
2	32.0	62450	.258
1	40.0	77790	.289
0	50.0	98980	.325
2/0	62.0	125100	.365
3/0	81.0	158600	.410
4/0	103.0	205500	.460

Fig. 55-34. Battery cables, necessarily, are heavy gauge size. Chart covers wire gauge sizes from No. 6 through No. 4/0. Passenger cars generally use No. 1 or No. 2.

must make good electrical contact with the battery posts. Any looseness or corrosion between the cable and its clamp, or between cable clamp and battery, will result in high resistance and consequent voltage drop.

High resistance between cables and terminals can be checked easily by means of a voltmeter. With a current of approximately 20 amps flowing, connect one lead of a voltmeter to the cable. Connect the other lead to the other cable terminal. Voltage drop in the starter-to-ground circuit should not be more than 0.1 volt.

LOW TENSION PRIMARY CABLES other than battery cables, range from gauge size No. 20 through No.4. See Fig. 55-32. Low tension primary cable insulation could be thermoplastic, thermoplastic with a braided cover, synthetic rubber, or cross-linked polyurethane.

RESISTOR IGNITION CABLE

To reduce interference with radio and TV reception, automotive ignition systems are provided with resistance in the secondary circuit. Resistor spark plugs or special resistor type ignition cable may be used. In order to work efficiently in modern ignition systems, it is essential that the resistor ignition cable is capable of producing a specified designed resistance. Currently, SAE (Society of Automotive Engineers) specifications for resistor ignition cable call for 3000 to 7000 ohms per foot for low resistance (LR) cable and 6000 to 12,000 ohms per foot for high resistance (HR) cable.

In addition, resistor cables must be covered with ample insulation that will withstand heat, cold, moisture, oil, grease, chafing, and corona. CORONA is an electrical phenomenon not readily visible, but it rapidly deteriorates rubber. The passage of high tension electricity through a cable builds up a surrounding electrical field. The electrical field liberates oxygen in the surrounding air to form ozone, which will attack the rubber insulation if it is not properly protected. Ozone causes the rubber to deteriorate and lose its insulating qualities. Electrical losses result which, in turn, will seriously weaken the spark at the plug gap.

Service-wise, never pull on the resistor ignition cable and rubber boot when disconnecting the cable from the terminal of a spark plug. Rather grasp, twist, and lift the boot (and cable) from the plug. Also, never puncture the insulation of a resistor ignition cable when making a connection for timing an engine. The puncture probably would sever the conductor, and eventual failure would result.

When checking the condition of resistor ignition cables, carefully examine both the insulation and the terminals. Bend the cable to form a small circle, then note if any cracks appear in the insulation. Replace the set of cables if the insulation is cracked, dried out, brittle, or fails to meet resistance tests by ohmmeter. Resistor ignition cable is available in custom lengths designed for installation on specific makes and models of engines.

Before replacing resistor ignition cables, thoroughly clean each distributor cap socket. When installing the cables, be sure to push them to the bottom of the cap sockets. If not, the spark will jump the air gap and cause corrosion and burned contacts. Press the boots firmly in place over the towers of the distributor cap.

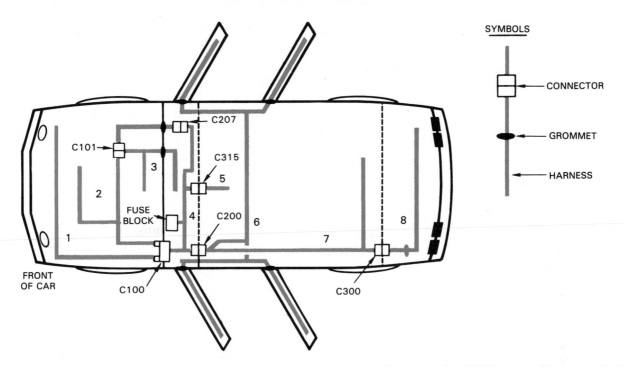

Fig. 55-35. Diagram illustrates typical electrical harness routing system and connectors (C100, etc.). Harnesses include: 1—Forward lamp. 2—Engine. 3—Air conditioning. 4—Instrument panel. 5—Console. 6—Cross body. 7—Body front. 8—Body rear. (Cadillac Motor Car Div., General Motors Corp.)

Care must be taken when replacing high tension ignition cables to install them in their original position. Not only must they be connected to the correct spark plug, but they also must be placed in the correct slot in their respective brackets. If this is not done, cross firing will result and maximum power will not be attained.

Basically, the wires should be located in their brackets so that the cables for cylinders next in firing order are as far apart as possible. For example: if the firing order is 1-5-4-2-6-3-7-8, the cables for cylinders No. 4 and No. 2 should be separated as much as possible since cylinder No. 2 fires immediately after cylinder No. 4.

WIRING HARNESSES AND CONNECTORS

The car manufacturers have made significant improvements in the durability and serviceability of engine and chassis electrical systems. They have designed and produced modular instrument panels or instrument clusters. They have installed halogen headlamps for 25 to 50 percent more light output. They made lamp sockets more durable, lamps longer lasting, and wire and cable insulation less affected by contaminants. They have made greater use of plastics to avoid rusting. They have provided multi-function switch levers for safety and convenience.

The car manufacturers have upgraded electrical wiring harnesses, harness routing systems, bulkhead connectors, and in-line connectors. The harnesses and harness routing system used on many General Motors cars is shown in Fig. 55-35. Typical harnesses include: engine, power distribution, air conditioning, body and chassis, front and rear lighting, instrument panel and interior lighting.

To complement the electrical wiring harnesses, the car manufacturers have devised systems of multi-pin bulkhead connectors and in-line connectors that interconnect the major wiring harnesses. See Fig. 55-36. Each connector can be disconnected to simplify testing and diagnosis.

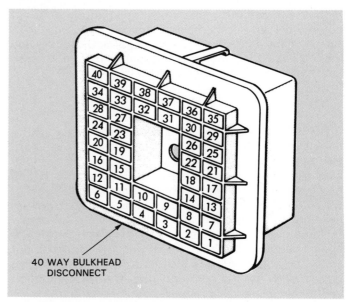

Fig. 55-36. Car manufacturers' service manuals identify bulkhead connector cavities by number, circuit, and wire color codes. For example: 13—Left turn signal. 14—Right turn signal. 25—Parking lamps. 29—Headlamp low beam. 30—Headlamp high beam. (Chrysler Corp.)

719

COMPUTERS, DIAGNOSTIC DISPLAYS

Add to these electrical system advances, increased use of on-board computers. Units such as Electronic Control Modules (ECM) accept inputs from various sensors, switches, and relays and provide outputs that control many electrical and electronic systems. Computers also supply information for instrument panel diagnostic displays. Full coverage of these complicated systems is beyond the scope of this text.

To aid service personnel in understanding these systems, the car manufacturers provide hundreds of extra service manual pages of explanatory and diagnostic information:

1. ELECTRICAL SCHEMATICS, Fig. 55-2, picture electrical current paths when the system is in proper operation.
2. COMPONENT LOCATION LISTS give specific locations of parts of the circuit.
3. SYSTEM CHECKS tell how the circuit should be operated and what should occur when the system is in operation.
4. TROUBLESHOOTING HINTS provide tests and give suggested shortcuts for solving problems in a given circuit.
5. SYSTEM DIAGNOSIS lists a step-by-step procedure designed to pin point the cause of a malfunction in a circuit.
6. CIRCUIT OPERATION describes circuit components and how the circuit works.
7. HARNESS CONNECTOR FACES show the cavity or terminal locations and wiring color codes and terminals to help locate test points.
8. HARNESS ROUTING VIEWS show the routing of major wiring harnesses and the location of connectors. See Fig. 55-35.

With modern technology shaping the design, construction, and operation of today's passenger cars, service technicians need to make a continuing study of latest automotive developments and service procedures. With this in mind, consider the car manufacturers' service manuals as "specialty tools" needed to meet and reach your automotive occupational goals.

HORNS

HORNS on passenger cars provide the driver with a means of sounding an audible warning signal. The horn electrical circuit generally includes: battery, fuse or fusible link, horn relay, horn(s), steering column wiring harness, horn switch, and body sheet metal. See Fig. 55-37. Often, a cadmium plated screw is used to ground the horn to the body of the vehicle.

Horns usually are located in the forward part of the engine compartment, Fig. 55-38, or in the front fender well. The horn switch is built into the steering wheel, Fig. 55-39, or incorporated into the multi-function switch lever (also turn signals, dimmer switch).

HORN RELAY AND FUSIBLE LINK

Horns on passenger cars use an electromagnetically actuated diaphragm to produce a resonating air column

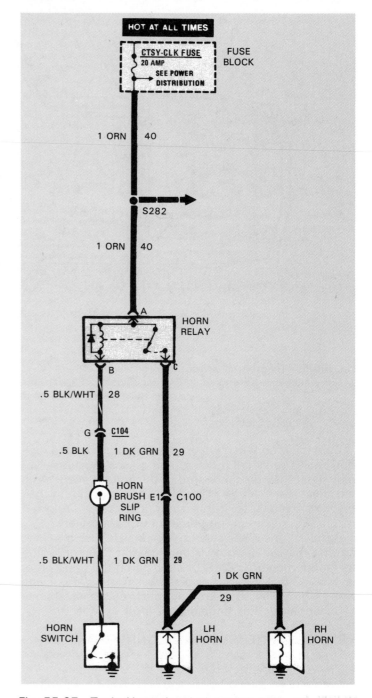

Fig. 55-37. Typical horn electrical circuit is fed by "hot" lead from fuse block. Pressing horn switch completes ground circuit to horn relay, where contacts close and current flows to horn. (Pontiac Motor Div., General Motors Corp.)

(sound) in the horn projector. Horn operation requires fairly high current (4.5 amps minimum), so a horn relay is used to make a more direct connection between the horn and battery. In that way, voltage drop is lessened and higher voltage is available for operating the horn diaphragm. Often, the horn circuit is fused.

In some cases, a FUSIBLE LINK is used in the main wiring harness just ahead of the horn relay. The fusible link is a protective device that consists of a smaller gauge wire that will "blow" if the horn circuit is grounded or

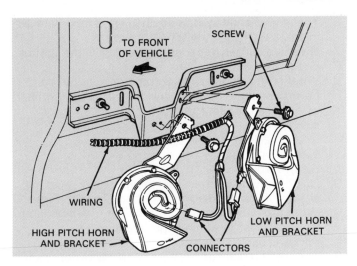

Fig. 55-38. Horns are located up front, usually in pairs and grounded to frame or body sheet metal. (Ford Motor Co.)

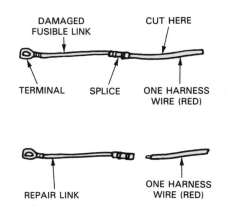

Fig. 55-40. To replace fusible link: Cut off damaged link beyond splice; strip wire; install repair link, crimping splice in two places. (Cadillac Motor Car Div., General Motors Corp.)

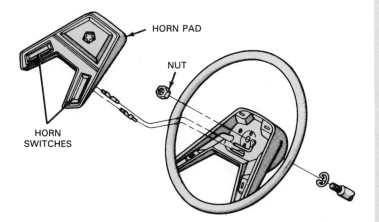

Fig. 55-39. Some horn switches are built into a horn pad mounted on steering wheel. Pressing horn pad completes horn circuit to ground. (Chrysler Corp.)

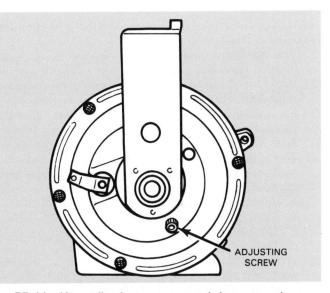

Fig. 55-41. Horn adjusting screw controls horn operation two ways, amperage draw and horn tone.
(Cadillac Motor Car Div., General Motors Corp.)

overloaded. New links generally must be crimped or soldered in place, Fig. 55-40.

HORN TROUBLESHOOTING

If a horn fails to sound when the switch is depressed, check the condition of the fuse or fusible link. Next, connect a jumper wire from the battery positive terminal to the horn terminal. If the horn still does not operate, provide a good ground for the horn. If the horn operates, the existing ground connection is at fault. Correct by removing the ground wire and establishing a good electrical connection to clean and shiny sheet metal. If necessary, replace the used screw with a cadmium plated screw.

If the horn operated when the jumper wire was placed between the battery terminal and the horn terminal, perform the following procedure:

1. Connect a voltmeter and an ammeter to horn and battery.

2. If current reading is 20 amps or more, a short is indicated. Replace horn.
3. If current reads zero amps, turn horn adjusting screw, Fig. 55-41, counterclockwise until ammeter reads 4.5 to 5.5 amps at 11.5 to 12.5 volts. NOTE: Turn adjusting screw only 1/10 of a turn at a time while observing changes in ammeter readings.
4. Clinch horn housing metal against adjusting screw to lock it in place.
5. If minimum amps adjustment cannot be reached, replace horn.
6. If specified amps adjustment can be made but horn fails to operate, replace horn.
7. Also check all mounting bolts and electrical connections to see that they are tight and inspect condition of horn circuit wiring.
8. If horn fails to operate after taking preceding steps, substitute a known good horn relay for old one and/or check condition of horn switch.

If the horn sounds continuously, disconnect horn relay wire and wires from horn terminals. The usual cause for horn blowing without depressing the horn switch is a grounded wire to the horn switch or a grounded switch. Another possibility is a faulty horn relay. Use an ohmmeter to test horn relay continuity. Voltage is applied to the relay at all times. Closing the horn switch grounds the relay coil, contacts close, and current flows to the horn. Therefore, there should be no current flow through the relay until the horn switch is depressed. If the ohmmeter shows current flow through the relay at all times, replace the relay.

If the horn sounds intermittently on turns, the horn brush slip ring under the steering wheel is defective.

If the tone and character of the horn signal is weak, try turning the horn adjusting screw in short moves until the tone indicates best point of adjustment.

Chapter 55—REVIEW QUESTIONS

Write your answers on a separate sheet of paper. Do not write in this book.

1. The lighting circuit is known as the _____ since it uses the car frame for the return.
2. What is the purpose of the rheostat used on some main lighting switches?
3. For identification, number 1A appears on rectangular sealed beam units with a single filament. True or False?
4. The _____ headlamp is a reflector and lens system designed for a specific vehicle model and contoured to that vehicle's requirements.
   a. Aerodynamic.
   b. Concealed.
   c. Composite.
   d. Halogen.
5. An electronic headlamp _____ device switches the headlights from high beam to low beam in response to light from an approaching vehicle.
   a. Delay.
   b. Dimming.
   c. Light sensitive.
   d. Sentinel.

6. The lane change switch mechanism is incorporated in the _____ switch.
7. Give two causes of excessive voltage in the lighting circuit.
8. What is the permissible voltage drop between the battery positive terminal and the insulated terminal of each lamp being tested?
   a. .06 volt.
   b. 0.1 volt.
   c. 0.3 volt.
   d. 0.6 volt.
9. Halogen bulbs contain gas under pressure and may shatter if mishandled or dropped. True or False?
10. What provision is made in the front of a headlamp lens to assist in aiming the headlights?
11. Wire and cable sizes are expressed by a _____.
12. The resistance of a length of wire or cable decreases as its cross section _____ (increases or decreases).
13. Why are automotive ignition systems provided with resistance in the secondary circuit?
14. Bulkhead connectors and in-line connectors that interconnect major wiring harnesses can be disconnected to simplify _____.

Match the question number for each of the following service manual categories with the letter designated for each correct associated phrase.

15. ___ Circuit operation.
16. ___ System diagnosis.
17. ___ Electrical schematics.
18. ___ System checks.
19. ___ Troubleshooting hints.
20. ___ Harness connector faces.

A. Tell how circuit should be operated and what should occur.
B. Provides tests and gives shortcuts for solving problems.
C. Show cavity or terminal locations.
D. Lists step-by-step procedure to pinpoint cause of malfunction.
E. Describes circuit components and how circuit works.
F. Picture electrical current paths.

Chapter 56

WINDSHIELD WIPERS AND WASHERS

After studying this chapter, you will be able to:
- Summarize the principles of a DC motor.
- List the different types of motor construction.
- Explain the difference between a depressed and non-depressed system.
- Describe how the washer system works.

PRINCIPLES OF A DIRECT CURRENT (DC) MOTOR

To understand how the speed of a wiper motor is controlled, there are two principles that must be understood. The first, the stronger the magnetic field or the more windings in an armature, the slower the motor turns. The second, the slower the armature turns, the more current the motor draws while increasing its torque.

WIPER MOTOR CONSTRUCTION

There are three different types of motors that can be used for windshield wipers, Fig. 56-1. The permanent magnet motor does not use field windings. This design has two ceramic magnets, Fig. 56-2, that are cemented to the field frame. Also, this type needs less energy than the other types of motor design. However, the switch must be wired in series. This can create many areas of resistance. The shunt wound motor provides a consistent speed, but does not provide much torque upon starting. The compound motor has a strong starting torque and provides a consistent speed, but is the most expensive.

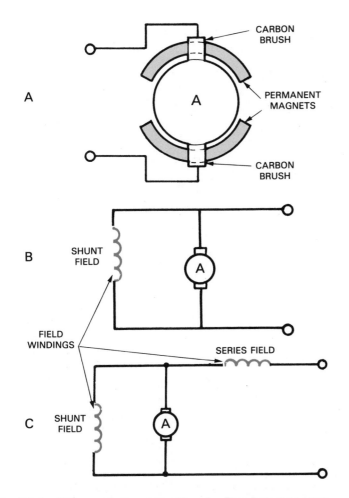

Fig. 56-1. Wiper motor construction. A—Permanent magnet type motor. B—Shunt wound motor has field winding parallel with armature. C—Compound motor has field windings parallel to and in series with the armature.

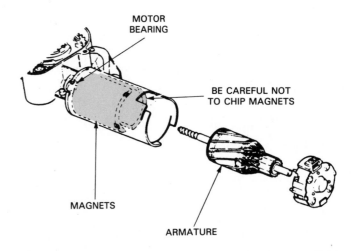

Fig. 56-2. A permanent magnet motor contains no field windings. (Oldsmobile)

Most cars also have an intermittent wiper system, Figs. 56-3 and 56-4. This permits the driver to select a delayed wipe that operates only every three to thirty seconds in this mode.

GM WIPERS

A typical wiper/washer unit is the wiper assembly shown in Fig. 56-5. It incorporates a depressed park system that places the wiper blades below the hood line in the parked position.

The relay control consists of a relay coil, relay armature, and switch assembly. It controls starting and stopping of the wiper through a latching mechanism. An electric washer pump is mounted on the gear box section of the wiper. It is driven by the wiper unit gear assembly, Fig. 56-5.

FORD WIPERS

Two types of motors are used, the depressed park type and the non-depressed park type. A view of a motor used is shown in Fig. 56-6.

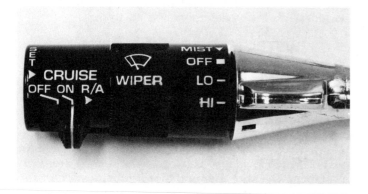

Fig. 56-3. Some wiper controls are mounted at the end of the turn signal lever. Note that the cruise control selector is also located there. (Chevrolet)

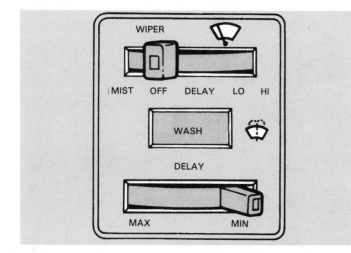

Fig. 56-4. Other wiper controls are mounted on the dash.

CHRYSLER WIPERS

Chrysler cars either have a two speed or three speed wiper system that uses an electric washer pump. On cars with the non-depressed park system, the wiper blades park in the lowest portion of the wiper pattern. On cars with the depressed park system, the blades automatically park in the depressed position.

The two speed wiper motor has a permanent magnet field, controlled by feeding current to different brushes for low and high speeds. The low speed circuit uses a torque limiting resistor.

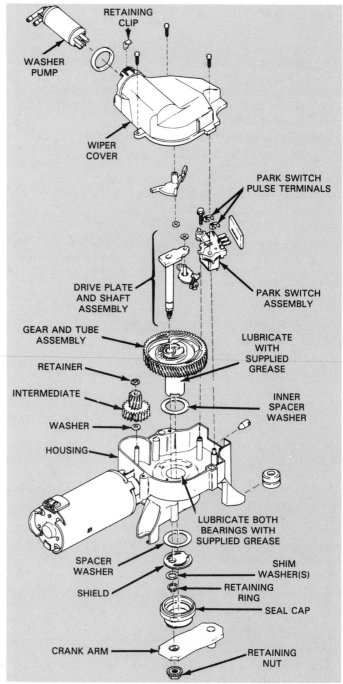

Fig. 56-5. A wiper motor combined with a washer pump. (Oldsmobile)

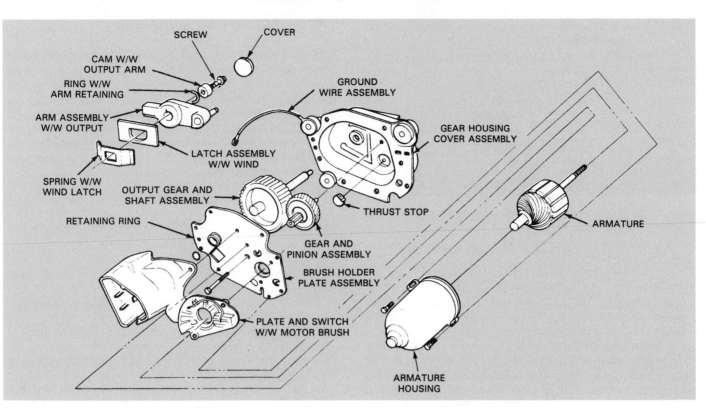

Fig. 56-6. Construction of a Ford wiper motor.

Chrysler's three speed wiper motors all have the depressed park feature. It is accomplished by means of an eccentric motor shaft and by reversing the direction of motor rotation. When the switch is turned off, the inner shaft of the motor stops, while the outer shaft rotates 180 deg. This changes the length of the drive link/crank to park the wiper blades in the depressed position, Fig. 56-7. All Chrysler windshield wiper systems use a circuit breaker with the wiper switch to protect the circuitry of the wiper system and the car.

TROUBLESHOOTING

For any electric windshield wiper to work trouble free, it is essential that the motor, linkage, and drive pivots do not bind. The wiper system may be noisy, slow, balky, or inoperative.

Noisy operation of electric wipers is sometimes caused by too much end play of the armature. The amount of end play varies with different makes. Noise will also be caused by incorrect relation between the motor and the linkage and pivot shaft assemblies. Reducing friction in the drive mechanism should reduce noise and binding.

Failure to operate can be caused by a blown fuse, open circuit, loose wiring harness connector, wiper motor not grounded, or a bad wiper switch, or motor.

WINDSHIELD WASHERS

All cars use an electric pump-operated windshield washer. A positive displacement washer pump is used. On some, the motor is placed in the washer reservoir. On others, it is driven by the wiper motor, Fig. 56-5.

When the pump is attached to the wiper motor, the four lobe cam actuates a spring-loaded follower. However, the pump does not operate all the time that the wiper motor is running. This is because the pumping mechanism is locked out and no pumping action occurs.

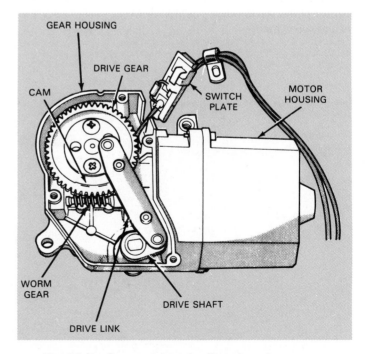

Fig. 56-7. Construction of a Chrysler wiper motor.

725

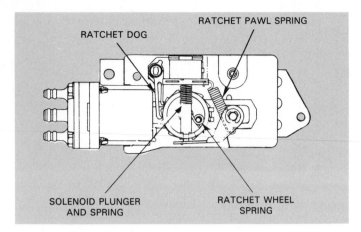

Fig. 57-8. Control section of a GM washer pump.

In this design, Fig. 56-8, the solenoid plunger is pulled toward the coil, allowing the ratchet pawl to engage the ratchet wheel. It then starts to rotate, one tooth at a time. Each lobe of the cam actuates the follower. The follower, in turn, moves the piston actuator plate and piston away from the valve assembly and compresses the piston spring. This creates a vacuum in the pump cylinder through the intake valve, Fig. 56-9. As the high point of each cam lobe passes the follower, the piston spring expands. This forces the piston toward the valves, pressurizing the washer solution so it flows out the exhaust valves to the spray nozzles.

Intake and exhaust strokes occur four times for each revolution of the wiper motor output gear. The pumping cycle is completed automatically when the ratchet wheel has been rotated through 360 deg., Fig. 56-8. Then, the spring-loaded plunger pushes through an opening in the rim of the ratchet wheel, pushing the pawl away from the ratchet teeth. At this point, the ratchet wheel has moved to a position where it is holding the piston actuator plate in a lockout position until the washer switch is pressed again.

TROUBLESHOOTING WASHERS

When troubleshooting washer pumps, check the following:

Washer Inoperative
1. Not enough washer solution.
2. Hoses damaged, loose, or kinked.
3. Plugged screen at end of reservoir hose.
4. Wiper switch bad.
5. Pump valve bad.
6. Plugged washer nozzles.
7. Loose electrical connection to washer pump or wiper switch.
8. Open circuit in feed wire to pump solenoid coil.
9. Pump solenoid coil bad.
10. Missing ratchet wheel tooth.
11. Missing ratchet pawl spring.

Washer Pumps Continuously While Wiper Is Operating
1. Wiper switch is bad.
2. Grounded wire from pump solenoid to switch.
3. Missing ratchet wheel tooth.
4. Ratchet wheel pawl or dog not contracting ratchet wheel teeth.
5. Lock-out tang broken or bent on piston actuator plate.

Chapter 56—REVIEW QUESTIONS

Write your answers on a separate sheet of paper. Do not write in this book.
1. A shunt wound motor has:
   a. Permanent magnets.
   b. A field winding parallel with the armature.
   c. A field winding parallel to and in series with the armature.
   d. A field winding in series with the armature.
2. A compound motor has:
   a. Permanet magnets.
   b. A field winding parallel with the armature.

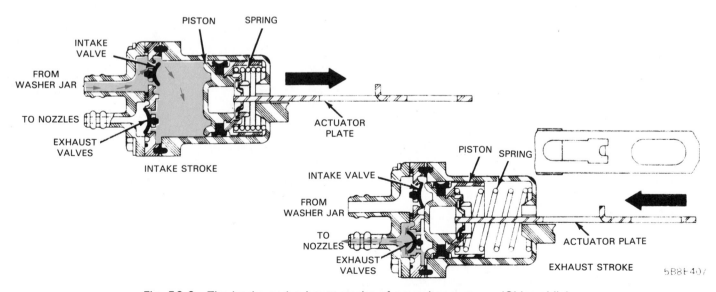

Fig. 56-9. The intake and exhaust stroke of a washer pump.   (Oldsmobile)

   c. A field winding parallel to and in series with the armature.

   d. A field winding in series with the armature.

   e. None of the above.

3. What is meant by a depressed park system?

4. What is meant by a non-depressed park system?

5. What are the two principles of a direct current motor?

6. Friction in the drive system of the wipers causes:

   a. Noise.

   b. Binding.

   c. Both a and b.

   d. None of the above.

7. Some GM wipers have the selector switch on the turn signal lever. True or False?

8. Some washer pumps are mounted:

   a. On the wiper motor.

   b. In the washer reservoir.

   c. Both a and b.

   d. None of the above.

9. If the washer pumps all of the time while the wipers operate, the No. 1 cause is:

   a. Blown fuse.

   b. Open in the circuit.

   c. Wiper switch needs to be changed.

Chapter 57

SPEEDOMETERS

After studying this chapter, you will be able to:
- Explain how an analog speedometer operates.
- Describe how a digital speedometer operates.
- List the different types of digital display.
- Troubleshoot an analog speedometer/odometer, including the cable.

ANALOG SPEEDOMETERS

The analog speedometer used on cars indicates the speed of the car and records distance traveled, Fig. 57-1.

A speedometer is driven by a flexible cable connected to the speedometer pinion within the transmission.

Speedometers are calibrated in miles per hour and/or in kilometers. When the instrument also records the distance traveled, it is recorded in miles or kilometers. That portion of the instrument is known as the odometer, Fig. 57-1. Most odometers record the total distance traveled. Some also record the distance of individual trips. These can be reset to zero, Fig. 57-2.

To measure the speed of the car and the distance traveled, many internal parts are needed.

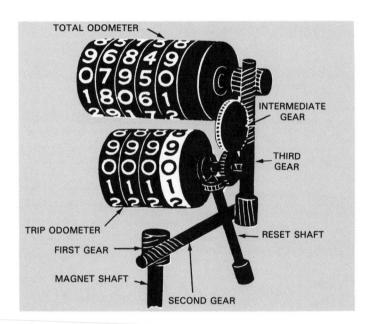

Fig. 57-2. Speedometer gear train from magnet shaft.

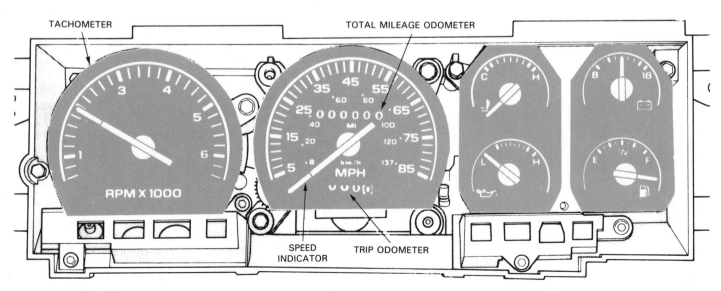

Fig. 57-1. A typical analog speedometer. Note that there is a trip and total mileage odometer. The trip odometer can be reset. (Chrysler)

728

SPEEDOMETER OPERATION

The speedometer and odometer are driven by a cable housed in a casing, Fig. 57-3. The cable is connected to a gear at the transmission. This gear is designed for a specific model, tire size, and rear axle ratio.

In most cases, the speedometer is designed to convert 1,001 revolutions of the drive cable into one mile on the odometer. In other words, 1,001 cable revolutions in a minute, will result in a speed indication of 60 mph.

SPEED INDICATION

The speed indication of an analog speedometer works on the magnetic principle. It includes a revolving permanent magnet driven by the cable connected to the transmission. Around this permanent magnet is a stationary field plate. Between the magnet and field plate is a nonmagnetic movable speed cup on a spindle. The magnet revolves within the speed cup, Fig. 57-4.

The revolving magnet sets up a rotating magnetic field which exerts a pull on the speed cup, making it revolve in the same direction. The movement of the speed cup is retarded and held steady by a hairspring attached to the speed cup spindle. The speed cup comes to rest at a point where the magnetic drag is just balanced by the retarding force created by the hairspring. An additional function of the hairspring is to pull the pointer of the instrument back to zero when the magnet stops rotating.

There is no mechanical connection between the revolving magnet and the speed cup. As the speed of the magnet increases, due to the movement of the car, the magnet drag on the speed cup also increses and pulls the speed cup further around. In that way, a faster speed is indicated by the pointer on the face of the dial.

The magnetic field is constant, and the amount of movement of the speed cup is (at all times) proportional to the speed at which the magnet is being rotated. Temperature effect on the magnet is compensated for by a special alloy attached to the magnet. This applies to all magnetically driven speedometers, including disc and indicating cylinder types.

SPEEDOMETER ACCURACY

The accuracy of a speedometer and odometer is affected by the size of the tires, the rear axle ratio, and the gears used to drive the speedometer. Changing tire size or rear axle ratio alters the accuracy of the speedometer and odometer.

To provide accuracy of the instrument, car manufacturers provide many drive pinions for their speedometers. Some speedometers drive pinions may be interchanged because of the pinion adapter, Fig. 57-5.

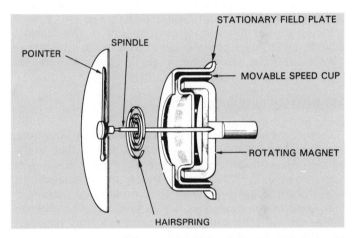

Fig. 57-4. The speed cup, magnet, field plate, hairspring, and pointer of an analog speedometer.

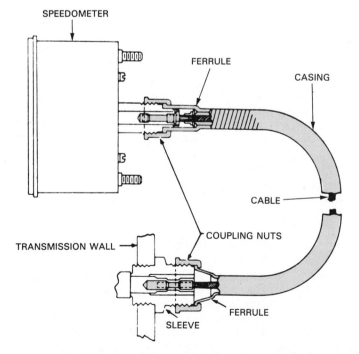

Fig. 57-3. Speedometer cable from transmission to speedometer head.

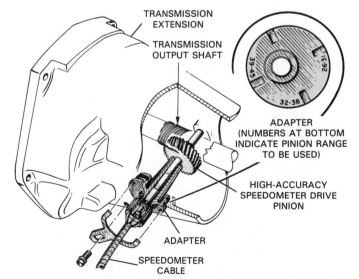

Fig. 57-5. Speedometer drive pinion and adapter. The adapter must be positioned in relation to the number of teeth indicated on the pinion, or indicated speed will be incorrect.   (Dodge)

INSPECTION/LUBRICATION

To test the speedometer for a tight mechanism, insert a test cable and turn. No binding or tightness should be felt. The test cable is the drive end of a short length of speedometer cable. A fast spin of the test cable should swing the pointer of the instrument from zero to about half scale. From half scale, the pointer should quickly return to zero. This indicates that the hairspring and magnet are in good working order. The same basic test also applies to the drum or indicator cylinder type of speedometer. The indicator cylinder should advance to at least 30 mph, then quickly return to zero.

To test the speedometer for calibration, place the unit in a test stand and run at various speeds. Compare readings of speedometer and test stand pointer movement.

Operate speedometer long enough to record two to three miles. All figure wheels should be lined up evenly, except those wheels which may be operating. If too much grease is present in the speedometer head, the cable and casing should be cleaned.

When lubricating a speedometer cable, the special lubricant should be applied lightly. Too much lubrication may result in the lubricant working up the cable and into the speedometer head.

SPEEDOMETER CABLE

Speedometer cables break as the result of age, lack of lubrication, or because the cable casing has sharp bends. To correct the problem of sharp bends, the clamps holding the casing must be relocated to straighten the casing. When the bends have damaged the inside of the casing, it will be necessary to replace the assembly. The rough spots tend to cause binding, friction, and rapid wear of the cable.

Another cause of frequent breakage of the speedometer cable is too much friction in the speedometer head. The test for this condition has been described. Withdraw the cable, spread a thin coat of speedometer cable grease evenly over the lower two-thirds of the cable. Do not apply grease to the entire cable as that would result in the lubricant working up the cable into the speedometer head and causing damage.

After applying the lubricant to the cable, insert the cable into the upper end of the casing, lower end first. This will spread the grease evenly over the entire length of the cable.

Connect the upper end of the casing to the speedometer case, making sure that the cable tip engages in the speedometer drive member. Tighten the ferrule nut, finger tight. Then, twist the lower end of the cable with your fingers to make sure it turns freely. A sharp twist of the cable should cause the speedometer needle to register. Then, connect the lower end of the casing to the transmission fitting, making sure that the cable fits in the speedometer driven gear.

TROUBLESHOOTING

Most problems in the speedometers start in the drive cable. The cable may be broken, kinked, frayed, or in need of lubrication. If the speedometer pointer fluctuates, the problem may be caused by a kinked cable. Or, the trouble may be in the speedometer head. The kinked cable rubs in its housing and winds up, slowing down the pointer. The cable then unwinds suddenly and the pointer jumps.

To check a cable for kinks, remove it from the casing and lay it on a flat surface. Then, rotate one end of the cable with the fingers. If the cable turns smoothly, it is not kinked. But if part of the cable turns suddenly, it is kinked and should be replaced.

Another method of testing a cable for kinks is to hold each end in your hands with the cable looped down in front of you. Then rotate the ends of the cable slowly with your fingers. If the cable is kinked it will "flop" and not turn smoothly, Fig. 57-6.

Cables should be inspected for fraying and wear. Cable fraying indicates sharp turns or a bad casing. If needed, replace cable and casing, then reroute assembly removing sharp turns. Visually check cable tips for straightness. A cable that lacks stiffness should be replaced. Other troubles and possible causes include the following:

POINTER FLUCTUATES: Defective cable or casing. Worn or dirty spindle bearings. Excessive end play in magnet shaft. Dirt or grease on magnet or speed cup. Speed cup assembly rusted at spindle ends. Worn main frame magnet shaft bearing (shaft side play should not exceed .003 in.). Bent speed cup spindle. Field plate not positioned correctly. Worn first, second, or third gears.

POINTER DOES NOT RETURN TO ZERO: Weak, broken, or improperly adjusted hairspring. Pointer improperly set. Front jewel too tight. Dirt or grease in mechanism.

INCORRECT SPEED INDICATION: Dirty or grease-filled mechanism. Out of calibration. Out of balance pointer. NOTE: Pointer balance may be checked by turning speedometer clockwise to different positions while it is running at a set speed. Indicated speed variation means that the pointer or speed cup is out of balance.

INCORRECT SPEED OVER HALF OF SCALE: Hairspring coils touching. Field plate eccentric with speed cup. Indicator drum out of balance.

EXCESSIVE NOISE: Too much end play in magnet shaft. Worn frame bearings. Worn gears.

INOPERATIVE ODOMETER: First gear stripped. Excessive end play in second gear. Second and third gears stripped, warped, or worn. Damaged idler gears.

ODOMETER READINGS INCORRECT: Worn second or third worm gears. Wrong transmission drive gear. Stripped transmission drive gear. Wrong tire size. Wrong rear axle ratio.

DIGITAL SPEEDOMETERS

Unlike an analog speedometer, the digital speedometer, Fig. 57-7, is operated by a vehicle speed sensor, Fig. 57-8. It produces electrical pulses that are processed by the computer. The computer, then, turns on segments of a display to form numbers, which is the speed of the car. The display types can be Light Emitting Diode (LED), Liquid Crystal Display (LCD), Vacuum Fluorescent Display (VFD), or Cathode Ray Tube (CRT).

	CAUSE	PROCEDURE
	LOOSE FERRULE AT SPEEDO HEAD.	PUSH FERRULE AGAINST SPEEDO HEAD AND RECHECK FOR NOISE.
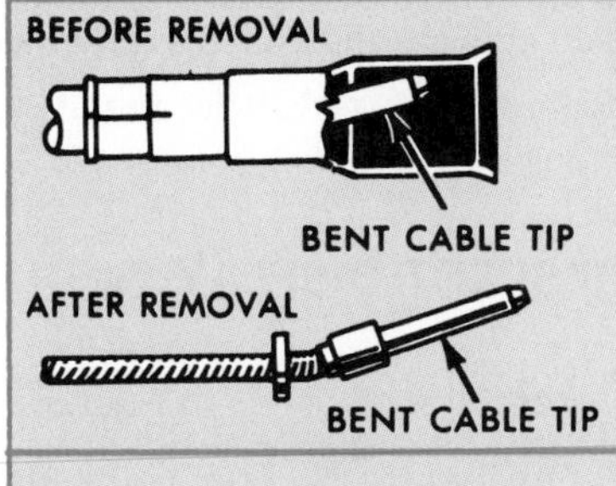 **BEFORE REMOVAL** **BENT CABLE TIP** **AFTER REMOVAL** **BENT CABLE TIP**	BEND CABLE TIP AT SPEEDO HEAD.	REPLACE (LUBRICATE ENTIRE LENGTH OF CABLE WITH A THIN COAT OF SPEEDOMETER CABLE LUBRICANT.)
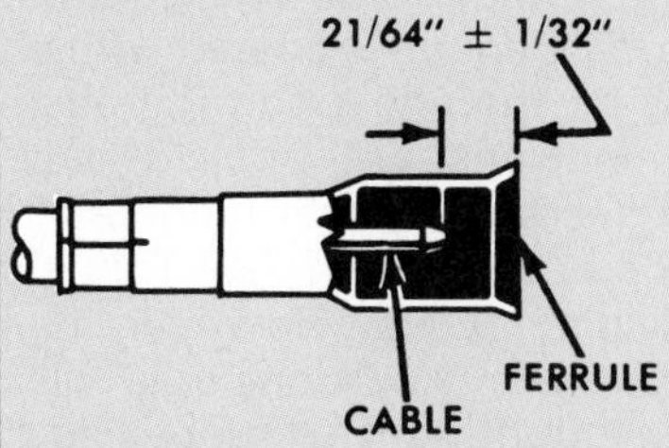 $21/64'' \pm 1/32''$ **FERRULE** **CABLE**	CABLE EXTENDS TOO FAR INTO TRANSMISSION.	DISCONNECT FERRULE AT SPEEDO HEAD WITH LOWER END STILL CONNECTED. PUSH CABLE INTO SHAFT UNTIL IT BOTTOMS. THE CABLE MUST BE RECESSED $21/64'' \pm 1/32''$ FROM THE END OF THE FERRULE. IF TOO LONG OR TOO SHORT, REPLACE CABLE AND RECHECK FOR NOISE. NOTE: DO NOT CUT OFF CABLE
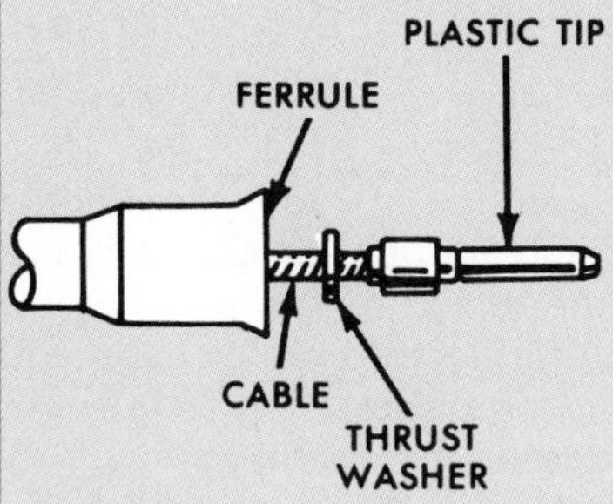 **PLASTIC TIP** **FERRULE** **CABLE** **THRUST WASHER**	DOUBLE OR MISSING THRUST WASHER ON CABLE AT SPEEDO HEAD.	ONLY ONE THRUST WASHER IF USED BEHIND THE PLASTIC TIP. IF WASHER IS MISSING (MAKE SURE IT IS NOT STUCK INSIDE THE FERRULE), REMOVE CABLE, ADD PROPER THICKNESS WASHER, INSTALL CABLE IN CASING, AND RECHECK FOR NOISE. IF TWO WASHERS ARE PRESENT (MAKE SURE ONE IS NOT STUCK INSIDE FERRULE), REMOVE ONE OF THEM, INSTALL CABLE IN CASING, AND RECHECK FOR NOISE.
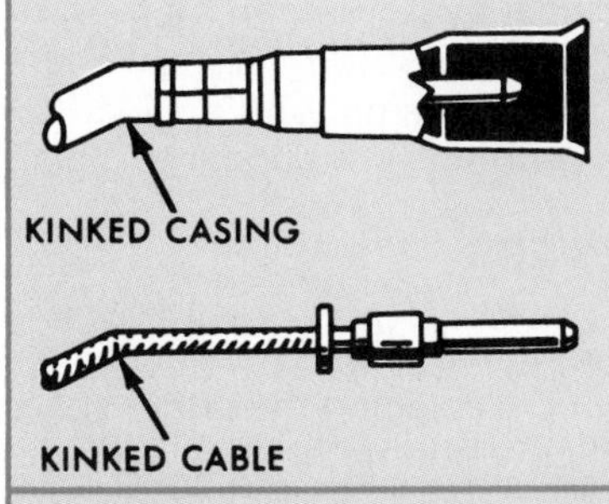 **KINKED CASING** **KINKED CABLE**	CABLE AND/OR CASING IS KINKED.	DISCONNECT FERRULE FROM SPEEDO HEAD AND PULL OUT CABLE. IF CABLE HANGS UP DURING REMOVAL, CABLE AND CASING MAY BE KINKED. INSPECT CABLE, AND IF IT IS KINKED, REPLACE. RECHECK FOR NOISE. IF CABLE REMOVAL IS NORMAL, INSPECT IT FOR KINKING. IF IT IS KINKED, REPLACE AND RECHECK FOR NOISE. (LUBRICATE ENTIRE LENGTH OF CABLE WITH THIN COAT OF SPEEDOMETER CABLE LUBRICANT.)
	CABLE IS NOT PROPERLY LUBRICATED.	APPLY A THIN COAT OF SPEEDOMETER CABLE LUBRICANT ALONG ENTIRE LENGTH OF CABLE, INSTALL IN CASING AND RECHECK FOR NOISE.
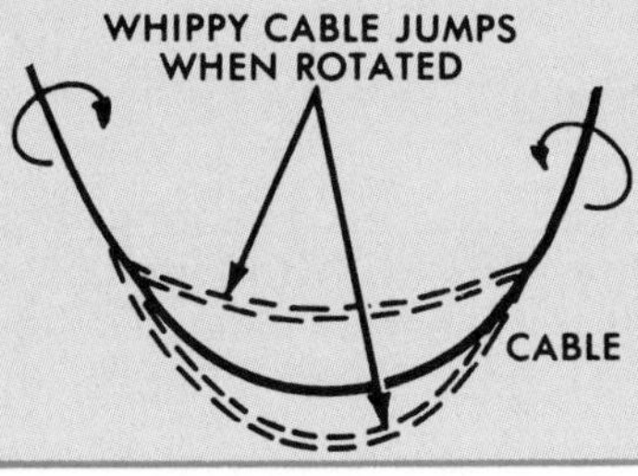 **WHIPPY CABLE JUMPS WHEN ROTATED** **CABLE**	CABLE IS "WHIPPY."	HOLD CABLE IN POSITION SHOWN AND ROTATE. A "WHIPPY" CABLE DOES NOT TURN SMOOTHLY, BUT JUMPS. IF THIS CONDITION EXISTS, REPLACE WITH A NEW PROPERLY LUBRICATED CABLE AND RECHECK FOR NOISE.

Fig. 57-6. Causes and cures for noisy speedometer operation. (Cadillac)

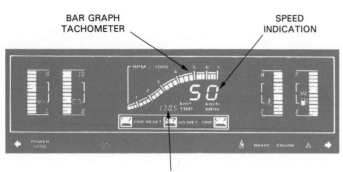

Fig. 57-7. A digital display dash is sometimes referred to as an electronic dash. (Chrysler)

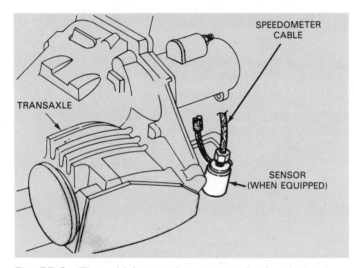

Fig. 57-8. The vehicle speed sensor sends electrical pulses to the computer. (Chrysler)

LIGHT EMITTING DIODE (LED)

The LED is a semiconductor diode. When light is introduced at its junction, light can be seen at the one end with the naked eye. The color of the light, most of the time, is red. This is due to the type of semiconductor that is used, which in this case is gallium arsenide. The display is composed of many segments that are turned off and on to form numbers, Fig. 57-9. When a segment is turned on, light is allowed through a specific diode. The problem with the LED digital dash is that it cannot be seen in bright sunlight.

LIQUID CRYSTAL DISPLAY (LCD)

The LCD has voltage applied to its crystal. This causes the crystal's molecules to be aligned as to form a straight line. When outside light enters the section that has voltage applied to it, it turns black to form numbers, Fig. 57-9. The section of crystal that has voltage applied to it is determined by the computer. The problem with the LCD digital dash is that it must be illuminated so that it can be seen at night. Also, the LCD does not work well in extreme cold weather.

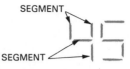

Fig. 57-9. Segments are turned off and on by the computer to form numbers, which indicate the speed and/or mileage of the car.

VACUUM FLUORESCENT DISPLAY (VFD)

The VFD uses a special resistance wire heated by passing current through it. A coating on the filament, when heated, produces electrons. The electrons are attracted to an anode. The anode is coated with phosphor. When the electrons hit the phosphor, it emits a bluish-green light. The electrons are applied only to the segments that are needed to form numbers, which is determined by the computer, Fig. 57-9. This is the most common of the display types. However, it must be mounted and isolated from vibrations or it will fail. This is accomplished by mounting it to rubber bushings.

CATHODE RAY TUBE (CRT)

The CRT is the same as a television. However, numbers are displayed instead of pictures. The cathode emits electrons. The anode attracts the electrons. The electrons pass through the anode and strike a coating of phosphorus on the inside of the screen to form the numbers. The computer decides which segments will be turned on to form the numbers, Fig. 57-9.

By touching the screen at certain points, a menu will appear and the driver will select the desired display, whether it is the speed of the car or the diagnostic mode. In the diagnostic mode, the powertrain, brakes, air conditioning, and electrical systems can be monitored. An "OK" will be next to the listed system if there are no problems. If there are problems with a specific system, a logical sequence of screens will appear to aid diagnosis.

DIGITAL ODOMETERS

The digital odometer chip, Fig. 57-10, can be replaced if it is defective without replacing the entire speedometer cluster. However, a new odometer chip will register zero mileage. On the other hand, if the cluster has to be replaced, the old odometer chip can be transferred to the new cluster, Fig. 57-11. With this procedure, the new cluster will display the current mileage, as the chip retains the mileage in its memory.

TROUBLESHOOTING

To verify if the speed sensor is operating properly, turn the drive wheels by hand with the ignition turned to the ON position. If no speed is indicated, replace the sensor with a known good sensor. Repeat the test. If there is still no indication of speed, the electronic dash will have to be tested. The electronic dash has self-diagnostic capabilities. Consult the individual service manuals for test procedures.

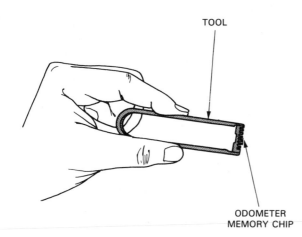

Fig. 57-10. An odometer chip retains the mileage in its memory. (Chrsysler)

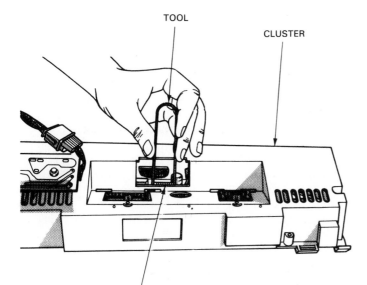

Fig. 57-11. The odometer chip is serviced separately from the digital dash. (Chrysler)

Chapter 57—REVIEW QUESTIONS

Write your answers on a separate sheet of paper. Do not write in this book.

1. How is an analog speedometer driven?
2. The speedometer shows only the speed of the car. True or False?
3. On what principle does the speed indicating portion of an analog speedometer operate?
   a. Electronic.
   b. Mechanical.
   c. Magnetic.
   d. Electrical.
4. What is used to control the pull on the speed cup?
   a. Hairspring.
   b. Mechanical brake.
   c. Magnetic brake.
5. Describe the analog speedometer operation.
6. What does an odometer record?
7. How is an analog odometer driven?
8. How many revolutions of the drive cable will register one mile on the meter?
   a. 101 revolutions.
   b. 1001 revolutions.
   c. 3.77 revolutions.
   d. 4.01 revolutions.
9. Where do most troubles in a speedometer start?
10. Describe the procedure for checking a speedometer cable for kinks.
11. Describe a method of checking an analog speedometer to see if there is any binding present.
12. What is the result of too much friction in the speed cup bearing?
    a. Speedometer indicates higher than normal speed.
    b. Speedometer indicates lower than normal speed.
    c. Incorrect odometer readings.
13. Give two common causes why a speedometer cable becomes frayed.
14. Will too much end play in the magnet shaft cause the speedometer pointer to flucturate? Yes or No?
15. A digital speedometer operates the same as an analog speedometer. True or False?
16. What is the most common type of display found with a digital speedometer?
17. Describe how a digital speedometer operates.

Chapter 58

SPEED CONTROL SYSTEMS

After studying this chapter, you will be able to:
- Explain how the cruise control servo operates.
- List the components of a cruise control system.
- Describe the different cruise control systems.

SPEED CONTROL

Speed control systems installed by the car manufacturers vary in makeup and controls, but all are designed to automatically regulate the car speed set by the driver.

This speed will be maintained until a new rate of speed is set, the brake pedal is depressed, or the system is turned off by the driver.

SERVO OPERATION

While some servos use a governor to maintain the speed setting, Fig. 58-1, others use a variable inductance position sensor, Fig. 58-2. Both are vented to manifold vacuum and atmospheric pressure.

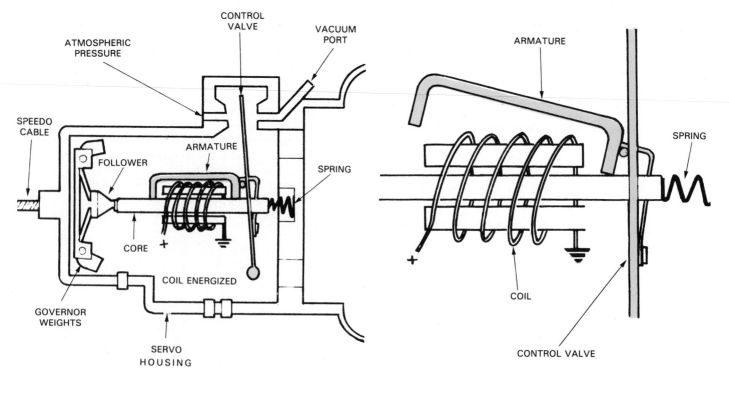

A

B

Fig. 58-1. Governor type cruise control servo. A—When the system has been engaged, the armature locks the control valve to the core. On a level road, with the system engaged, the control valve will be between the vacuum port and the atmospheric pressure port. B—The armature in a de-energized position. Note that the armature is attached to the control valve.   (Chrysler)

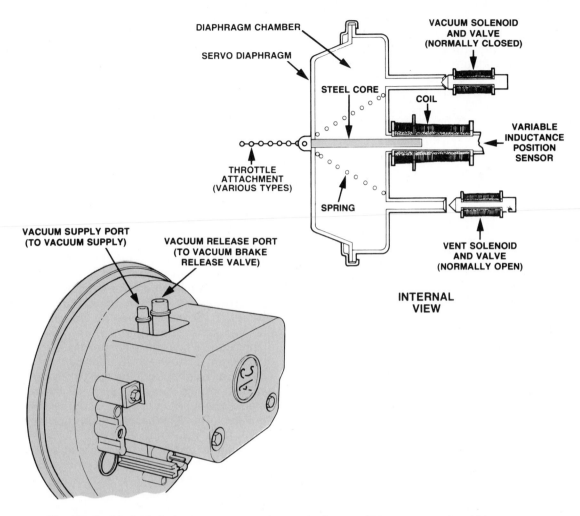

Fig. 58-2. Variable inductance type cruise control servo. The vacuum solenoid is energized by an electronic module during periods of low vacuum while the cruise control is engaged. The low vacuum condition is determined by the position of the steel core in the coil.   (AC Spark Plug)

GOVERNOR TYPE

Manifold vacuum entering the servo housing, Fig. 58-3, is controlled by the control valve. The control valve position is determined by the governor, Fig. 58-1, which is driven by the speedometer cable. As car speed is increased, the governor weights are thrown outward, which pushes on the follower. The follower, then, pushes on the core. When the locking coil is energized, the armature locks the core to the control valve, thereby connecting the two. So, when the armature is energized and the core moves, the control valve is adjusted.

When the car is on a level road, the desired speed is maintained when the control valve is between the air bleed and the manifold vacuum port, Fig. 58-1. If the car speed is reduced by going up a steep grade, the vent to atmospheric pressure, Fig. 58-3 is closed off by the control valve. This maintains the set speed, as the vacuum can then act on the diaphragm. When a car descends a steep grade, the governor pushes the control valve against the vacuum port, Fig. 58-4, to prevent the engine from overspeeding.

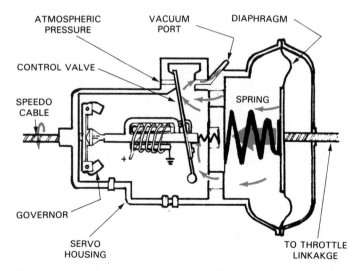

Fig. 58-3. Vacuum pulls on diaphragm against spring pressure. A cable is attached to the diaphragm and moves in the same direction. This cable is attached to the throttle linkage, which pulls and holds the throttle linkage. This action maintains a set speed.   (Chrysler)

When the brakes are applied, the brake release valve is energized, Fig. 58-4, and the vacuum is dumped through the port. The control valve blocks the vacuum port to prevent any vacuum from entering while the brake release valve is energized. The cruise control system is then disengaged until the driver depresses the RESUME or SET button. This forces the brake release valve against its seat, blocking atmospheric pressure from entering the servo housing.

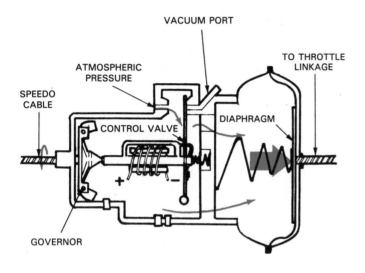

A

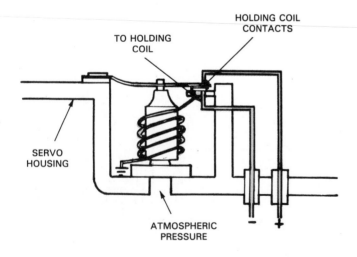

B

Fig. 58-4. Servo operation that prevents the engine from overspeeding. A—When descending a steep grade, the governor pushes the control valve against the vacuum port. During braking, the control valve also blocks vacuum from acting on the diaphragm. B—When the brakes are applied, the brake release valve opens allowing atmospheric pressure to act on the diaphragm. The brake release valve will not close until the RESUME or SET button is depressed.   (Chrysler)

VARIABLE INDUCTANCE TYPE

The servo, Fig. 58-2, is controlled by an electronic module. The position of the steel core in the coil creates a specific voltage signal that is sent to the module. If the steel core deviates from its original position while the cruise control is energized, a different voltage signal is sent to the module. The module then energizes or de-energizes the vacuum or vent solenoid. This closes or opens the respective valves.

During a cruise condition on a level road, with the cruise control turned ON, the vent and vacuum solenoid are both de-energized. This causes each valve to be closed. Since vacuum is supplied to the diaphragm in the servo, the vacuum pulls the diaphragm against spring pressure. Since the diaphragm is attached to the throttle linkage through a bead chain, it pulls on the throttle linkage and then keeps it at a specified position.

If a load is placed on the engine, such as a car going up a steep grade, the vacuum in the chamber is reduced. The spring pressure, inside the chamber, is greater than the vacuum. The spring then pushes out on the diaphragm. Since the steel core is also attached to the diaphragm, it moves in the direction of the diaphragm. The voltage signal from the coil to the module is changed because of the new position of the steel core. The module, then, energizes the vacuum solenoid, and opens the valve. This exposes the diaphragm to more vacuum, which pulls the diaphragm and the steel core back to their original position. The vacuum solenoid is then de-energized. The vent solenoid remains de-energized during the process.

However, if the car is going down a steep grade, vacuum will remain high and pull on the diaphragm. This pushes the steel core further into the coil, and changes the voltage signal sent to the module. The module, then, energizes the vent solenoid. This will open the vent valve exhausting the vacuum in the chamber. The diaphragm and steel core then return to their original position. The vacuum solenoid remains de-energized during the process.

When the brake pedal is depressed, the vent solenoid is energized and the valve is opened. The vacuum solenoid and valve remain closed. Also, an extra vacuum release port is opened during this time to speed up the dumping of the vacuum from the chamber upon brake application. The cruise control system then disengages until the driver presses the RESUME or SET button.

CHRYSLER SPEED CONTROL

The speed control system used on Chrysler cars is electrically actuated and vacuum operated. A slide switch mounted on the turn signal lever has three positions: OFF, ON, and RESUME SPEED, Fig. 58-5. The SET SPEED button is located in the end of the lever.

To engage the Chrysler system, the driver moves the slide switch to the ON position, accelerates the car to the desired rate of speed, then presses and releases the SET SPEED button. This sets the speed memory of the system and engages it to hold the car speed at that rate.

To disengage the speed control system, the driver makes a light or normal brake application. This

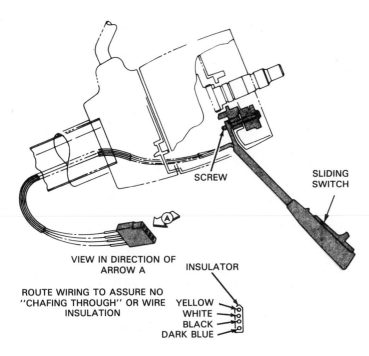

Fig. 58-5. Control system uses a sliding switch in the turn signal lever.

adjusted, Fig. 58-8. The lock-in screw is turned counterclosewise 1/4 turn for each one mph decrease in speed. However, the lock-in screw is turned clockwise 1/4 turn for each one mph increase in speed. The lock-in screw can be turned *only* two turns in either direction. Any more will damage the servo.

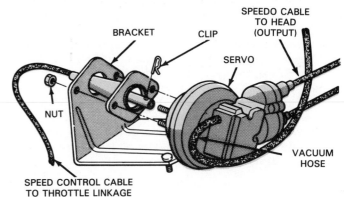

Fig. 58-6. Speed control servo, control cable, and speedometer cable connections. (Chrysler)

disengages the control unit without erasing the speed memory. If the driver moves the slide switch to OFF, or turns off the ignition switch, the system is disengaged and the speed memory is erased.

The RESUME position of the slide switch is used after the driver has applied the brake pedal. As mentioned, braking disengages the control unit without erasing the speed memory. Pressing the RESUME button, then, allows the car to return to the last memorized speed.

To increase the speed, the driver accelerates the car to the higher rate of speed, then depresses and releases the SPEED SET button. Or, to increase the rate of speed by small degrees, tap the SPEED SET button while the speed control unit is engaged and the car's speed will rise slightly.

To decrease speed, the driver taps the brake pedal slightly to disengage the speed control system. When the car decelerates to the new speed, the SPEED SET button is depressed and then released.

As with other speed control systems, Chrysler's system permits the driver to accelerate at any time. When the greater speed is no longer needed, the driver releases the accelerator pedal and the speed control is resumed.

In addition to the sliding switch, Chrysler's speed control system uses a servo unit, Fig. 58-6, throttle cable assembly, and stop lamp switch, which is located at the brake pedal, Fig. 58-7.

SPEED INCREASE/DECREASE

If the speed of the car increases or decreases upon activating the speed control system, and: (1) Engine is properly tuned, (2) Engine is not pulling a load, (3) Throttle cable is properly adjusted, then the servo should be

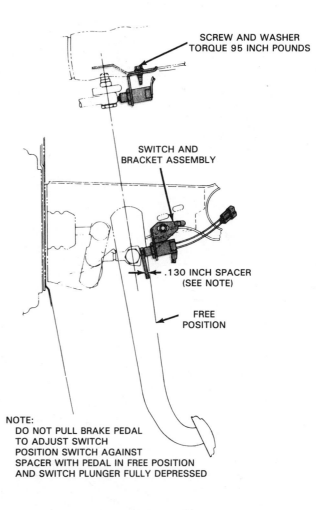

NOTE:
DO NOT PULL BRAKE PEDAL
TO ADJUST SWITCH
POSITION SWITCH AGAINST
SPACER WITH PEDAL IN FREE POSITION
AND SWITCH PLUNGER FULLY DEPRESSED

Fig. 58-7. Stop lamp switch also energizes brake release valve in servo housing.

FORD'S SPEED CONTROL

The speed control system used on Ford cars includes: an OFF-ON switch, SET-ACCEL and COAST switches, servo (throttle actuator) assembly, speed control sensor, amplifier assembly, check valve assembly, vacuum reserve tank, vacuum connections, wiring, and linkage.

The switches are located in the steering wheel spokes, Fig. 58-9. To use Ford's speed control system, the engine must be running and the car traveling at from 30 to 80 mph. Then, by actuating the on/off switch in the steering wheel, the system is ready to accept a set speed signal.

Once the car is at a designated speed, the driver presses, then releases, the SET-ACCEL button. This speed will be maintained until: a new rate of speed is set by the driver, the brake pedal is depressed, or the system is turned off by the driver.

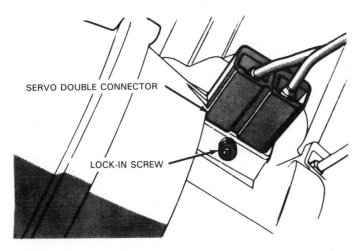

SERVO DOUBLE CONNECTOR

LOCK-IN SCREW

Fig. 58-8. Lock-in screw can be adjusted to compensate for speed increase or decrease. Do not adjust more than two turns in either direction.

If a reduced speed is desired, the driver can tap the brakes, and set the new speed by pressing the SET-ACCEL button. Or, the driver can apply the brakes, press the COAST switch and allow the car to coast down to the new speed. Then, upon releasing the COAST switch, the new speed is set. However, if the car speed drops below 30 mph, the driver must accelerate and reset it.

If an increased speed is desired, the driver can depress the accelerator until the higher rate of speed is reached. The SET-ACCEL button is depressed, then released, and the car maintains the new set speed.

GM'S CRUISE CONTROL

General Motor's cruise control system allows the drive to ''set a desired rate of speed (over 30, 35, or 40 mph, depending on car application), which the system will automatically maintain.

GM speed control systems include:
1. Engagement switch, located on end of turn signal lever, Fig. 58-10.
2. Servo unit, mounted at left inner front fender and connected by a cable to throttle linkage.
3. Brake release switch, mounted on brake pedal bracket. It energizes the brake release valve when brake pedal is depressed.

As with other speed control systems, the driver of a GM car accelerates it to the cruising speed desired. Next, the SET button is depressed and then released. This allows the cruise system to take over throttle control and maintain this speed in spite of changes in terrain.

The GM system automatically disengages whenever the brake pedal is depressed. To resume ''cruise control,'' the driver presses the RESUME. The driver can adjust the speed upward by accelerating to the new rate of speed, then depress the SET button. To override the system at any time, the driver depresses the accelerator (to pass another car, for example). Release of the accelerator pedal will return the car to the previous constant cruising speed.

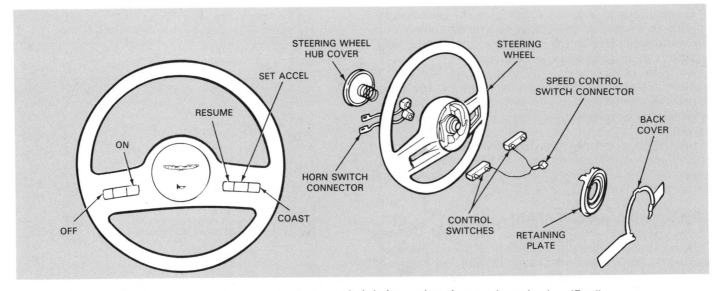

Fig. 58-9. The cruise control selector switch is located at the steering wheel. (Ford)

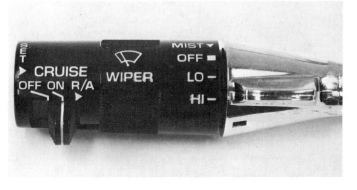

Fig. 58-10. The cruise control selector switch is combined with the windshield wiper selector at the turn signal lever. (Chevrolet)

Chapter 58 — REVIEW QUESTIONS

Write your answers on a separate sheet of paper. Do not write in this book.

1. The components of a cruise control system are:
   a. Servo.
   b. Selection control.
   c. Brake disengagement switch.
   d. All of the above.
   e. None of the above.

2. Mechanic A states that manifold vacuum can enter the servo (either type) housing.
   Mechanic B states that atmospheric pressure can enter the servo (either type) housing.
   Who is right?
   a. Mechanic A.
   b. Mechanic B.
   c. Both Mechanics A and B.
   d. Neither Mechanic A nor B.

3. The core is directly connected to the control valve of the governor type system. True or False?

4. The amount of atmospheric pressure or vacuum that enters the servo (either type) is regulated. True or False?

5. Mechanic A states that during a low vacuum condition with the cruise control energized, the control valve closes or blocks off the atmospheric port in the servo (governor type) housing.

Mechanic B states that during periods of high vacuum with the cruise control energized, the control valve blocks or closes the vacuum port in the servo (governor type) housing.
Who is right?
   a. Mechanic A.
   b. Mechanic B.
   c. Mechanics A and B.
   d. Neither Mechanic A nor B.

6. With the cruise control energzied (governor type), the control valve is between the atmospheric and vacuum ports when on a level road. True or False?

7. During braking, atmospheric pressure enters the servo (either type) housing. True or False?

8. Vacuum is supplied to the servo (either type) housing. True or False?

9. Explain what must be done for the cruise control to regain control of the throttle after the brakes have been applied? After accelerating to pass another car?

10. The control module energzies the vent and vacuum solenoid on the variable inductance type servo. True or False?

11. Mechanic A states that on a variable inductance type servo, the vacuum and vent valves are open during a cruise condition on a level road with the cruise control energized.
Mechanic B states that on a variable inductance type servo, under low vacuum conditions and the cruise control energized, the vent valve is opened.
Who is right?
   a. Mechanic A.
   b. Mechanic B.
   c. Mechanics A and B.
   d. Neither Mechanic A nor B.

12. Mechanic A states that the position of the steel core in the coil (variable inductance type) determines which valve is opened.
Mechanic B states that to prevent overspeeding of the engine, when the car is going down a steep grade, the vent valve is opened (variable inductance type) while the vacuum valve remains closed.
Who is right?
   a. Mechanic A.
   b. Mechanic B.
   c. Mechanics A and B.
   d. Neither Mechanic A nor B.

Chapter 59

BODY REPAIRING AND REFINISHING

After studying this chapter, you will be able to:
- Describe how to straighten structural components.
- Show the proper sanding methods.
- Give examples of how to repair dents.
- Tell how to mask the entire car.
- Demonstrate how to weld and cut sheet metal.
- Explain the proper painting method.

BODY WORK

No matter how badly a body panel or fender has been damaged, it can be straightened. Special tools and equipment are needed, plus skill on the mechanic's part. However, in cases of severe damage, it may be quicker and cheaper to replace the part than to repair it.

Straightening sheet metal is much easier than it appears to be. With modern equipment and tools, the work proceeds at a fast pace. The needed skill can be attained in a short time by practicing on junked fenders, doors, or panels.

The ease and speed with which sheet metal can be straightened is largely dependent on starting the repair work in the right way. When done correctly, the amount of "dinging" is reduced, Fig. 59-1. Also, stretching of the sheet metal will be kept to a minimum, and the amount of hand filing and sanding will be reduced.

When straightening a wrinkled panel, the damage should be removed in the reverse order in which it was made. When a collision occurs, there will be a major depression in the panel, followed by a buckled area, and then by a series of ridges.

Without proper instruction, a mechanic will apply pressure at the spot where the panel was struck first and where it is depressed the most. The correct method is to apply pressure at the ridge farthest from the point where the body was struck first. When this is done, the entire damage will spring back into its original position.

To make the procedure clear, assume that the original form of the panel is shown at A in Fig. 59-1. Point B is where it was struck, and C is a ridge formed last. As indicated, start at point C. Place a spoon, Fig. 59-2, on top of the ridge and strike it with a mallet or hammer. Follow the ridge with the spoon and mallet, and you will find that as the ridge is removed, the major depression at B will also spring back and conform very closely with

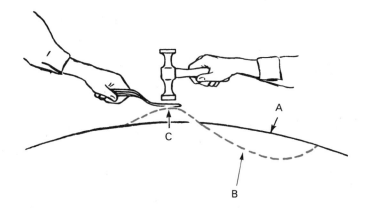

Fig. 59-1. Apply pressure first at the ridge farthest from where the panel was struck.

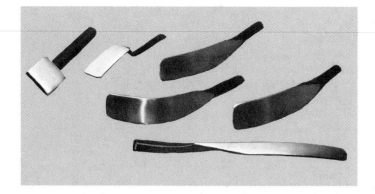

Fig. 59-2. Spoons are used to restore sheet metal to original shape. (Snap-on Tools)

the original contour of the panel.

The few remaining dents are then removed with a dolly block, Fig. 59-3, and hammer. Select a dolly block with a face of the same curvature as the panel. Hold it under the panel and strike the high point of the dents with a dinging hammer. In this way, the dolly blocks acts as an anvil. The blows tend to stretch the metal by making it thinner.

740

Fig. 59-3. Assortment of dolly blocks. Above. Heel, utility, and mushroom dollies. Below. Wedge, toe, and general purpose dollies.

REQUIRED TOOLS

Hand fender-straightening tools
Bench for straightening panels and doors
Bolt cutters
Car stands
C-clamps
Center punches and drifts
Cold chisels
Air compressor
Creepers
Drill sets
Bolt extractors
Fender covers
Fire extinguishers
Bench grinder
Hammers
Hand jacks
Lift
Metal shears
Pliers
Pry bars
Hacksaws
Hole saws

Power saws
Screwdrivers
Power sheet metal saw
Seat covers
Steel rule
Headlight testers
Complete wrench sets, pull rods
Electric drills (1/4, 1/2 and 3/4 in.)
Trouble light and extension cords
Paint sprayer, striping brushes
Spray booth, drying lamps
Welding equipment and accessories
Sander and polisher, glass cutting, and grinding outfit
Panel-clamping repair units
Frame straightener, body straightening jacks
Wheel alignment equipment, wheel balancer
Wheel pullers, wheel straightener
Workbench, bench vise, arbor press
Ventilating fan and exhaust hoses

HAMMERS AND DOLLY BLOCKS

All that is needed of the hammer is to press the sheet metal back into position. Therefore, a lot of light hammer blows should be used rather than a few heavy ones. If the metal is stretched, a large bulge will result which will need shrinking.

The hammer blows should be at the rate of 60 per minute. Try to "pull" the hammer so it strikes the surface of the sheet metal with a sliding or glancing blow.

Note, too, that when the dent rises above the surface of the dolly block, the hammer should strike the center of the dent. But if the dent is below the surface of the metal and toward the dolly, place the dolly against the head of the dent and direct the hammer blows against the edge of the dent. Hold the hammer loosely with the thumb along the top of the handle for better control of the bounce.

There are many designs of hammers, Fig. 59-4. They come in many faces (square faces, round faces, serrated faces) and varying length shanks (pointed shanks, roughing hammers, etc.), each designed for a specific type of work.

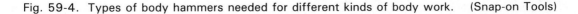

Fig. 59-4. Types of body hammers needed for different kinds of body work.   (Snap-on Tools)

These hammers are not to be used to strike against other hardened objects. They are to be used only for striking car type sheet metal.

A short shank hammer is needed where there is not much space to work. The long shank type is needed when working in a deep contour. The serrated face hammer is for shrinking metal; the tapered shank type is for working on molding, etc. All should be included in a body worker's kit.

There are a large variety of spoons, Fig. 59-2, and dolly blocks, Fig. 59-3. Each is shaped and sized to make certain though jobs easy. The spoons are used on polished surfaces. That is, the spoon is placed against the finished surface of a panel and is struck with the hammer. Spoons can be used as a dolly, if space prevents the use of a regular dolly. They are also used for prying a bulge in a door or trunk lid back into place.

Dollies vary in weight, shape, and contour so that they will conform to the curve of the panel and can be used in cramped quarters. Some provide grooves for working beads and molding. Skill in using these tools can be quickly attained by working on junk panels and fenders. The point is to have a wide selection of spoons, dollies, and hammers so that all types of body work can be handled.

As the dent in the body panel is being removed, rub your hand over the surface. This will help determine those spots which need more straightening. Then, when that method fails to show any high or low spots, use the body file, Figs. 59-5 and 59-6. Only light cuts should be made. Remember that the purpose is not to remove metal, but to show the areas that need further attention— with the dolly and hammer. Use a sander to locate the few irregularities. This will remove any roughness that cannot be removed with the dolly. Sometimes the hammer and dolly method cannot be used due to structural interference. When this occurs, pull rods or slide hammers must be used.

USING PULLRODS/SLIDE HAMMER

When removing dents and creases from body panels, a great deal of time is needed to remove inside trim. Also, the work is complicated when the damage is located in doors and rear trunk lids. In these areas, metal braces and other structural members make it hard to use the dolly and hammer method.

On many jobs, the use of pull rods and/or slide hammer makes it unnecessary to remove inside trim since the work is done entirely from the outside of the damaged panel. The procedure is to drill a series of 9/64 in. (3 mm) holes in the deepest part of the crease. These holes should be about 1/4 in. (6 mm) apart. The crease is then worked by inserting the hooked ends of the pull rods in the holes and pulling on the handles, Fig. 59-7. Or, by screwing the slide hammer into each hole and slamming the sliding weight rearward, Fig. 59-7. Start at the front and work to the rear. Light reflection is a big help in locating high and low spots.

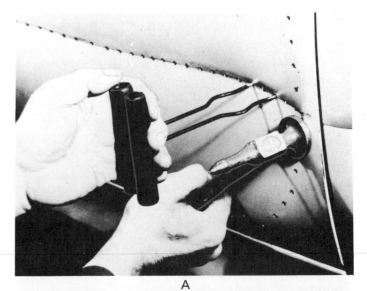

A

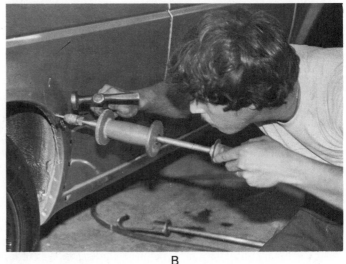

B

Fig. 59-7. Drill a series of 9/64 in. holes in deepest part of dent. A—Dent is then pulled out with rods. B—Or, with slide hammer until panel is aligned with original contour.
(Chilton's Motor/Age)

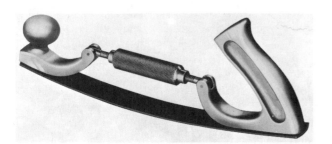

Fig. 59-5. Holder for flexible mill tooth file.

Fig. 59-6. Flexible mill tooth file.

BODY FILLER

After the dent has been lifted to the original contour, as much as possible, and the paint has been removed from the dent and surrounding area, body filler is then applied. First, etch the bare metal where the filler will be applied. This will remove any dirt, grease, and rust from the surface. Mix the filler with correct amount of hardener until it becomes one color, Fig. 59-8. Apply the mixture to the panel using a plastic spreader, Fig. 59-9. Make sure that the car has been at room temperature (70 °F) 24 hours prior to applying the filler. An infrared lamp should also be used on humid days. Direct the lamp toward the panel at a distance of three feet. After the filler has dried, shape to the contour of the body, Figs. 59-10 and 59-11.

Fig. 59-10. Using special file to shape body filler after it has dried. (Marson Corp.)

Fig. 59-8. Mixing plastic body filler with hardener on a nonporous pallet. A golf ball size of filler needs about a 1 in. ribbon of hardener. Mix thoroughly. (Oatey Co.)

A

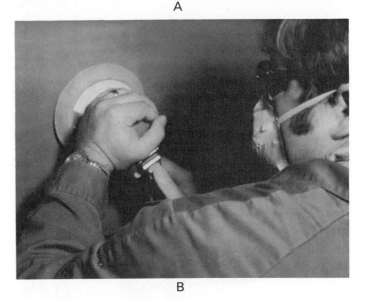

B

Fig. 59-9. Apply filler evenly to dented portion. Filler should not be thicker than 1/8 in. or it will crack when dry. (Marson Corp.)

Fig. 59-11. Sand filler smooth after roughing it to shape. A—Hand sanding. B—Sanding with orbital sander. (Marson Corp. and 3M Co.)

POWER STRAIGHTENING

While the hand dolly and dinging hammer are used most of the time, there is a trend toward the use of power dinging equipment. Power tools of this type are available from a number of manufacturers. Electric and pneumatic types are available. On panels where they can be used, a lot of time can be saved. Also, power tools will not stretch the metal as much as a dolly and hammer.

It is awkward to use power dinging hammers on car tops and other large areas where damage is more than 18 or 20 in. from the edge of the panel. Power equipment works well where damage is close to the edge.

Another piece of equipment for straightening bodies is the hydraulic jack or pump and ram. This type of repair kit has fittings designed to remove dents and to push or pull damaged panels and parts back into position, Figs. 59-12 to 59-17.

Hydraulic rams have many other uses. Applications include: straightening diamond-shaped door and window frames; squaring bodies; correcting door curvature; frame and bumper work. See Figs. 59-18 to 59-23.

When using hydraulic equipment to take a dent out of a panel, the same method used with hand dollies should be followed. Apply pressure first at the outer edge of the dent, then work around the dent. Gradually work toward the center. Complete the work with a hand dolly.

Before starting to straighten a panel, clean all the dirt from both sides. This can be done by scraping or by heating it lightly with a torch. Remove any undercoating from the fenders and panels. Mud and grit that stick to the panels will mar the surface of the straightening tools. Undercoating will make the job harder.

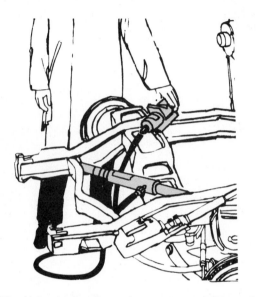

Fig. 59-12. Using hydraulic equipment to straighten a frame. (Blackhawk)

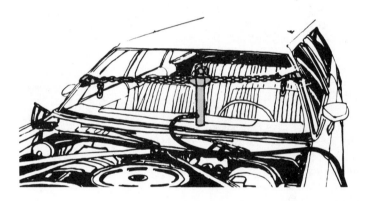

Fig. 59-14. Straightening a window opening.   (Blackhawk)

Fig. 59-13. Using a hydraulic pump, extension tubing, and chain to pull a door post into alignment.   (Blackhawk)

Fig. 59-15. Hydraulic pump, base plate, and extension tube are used to push door opening into alignment.

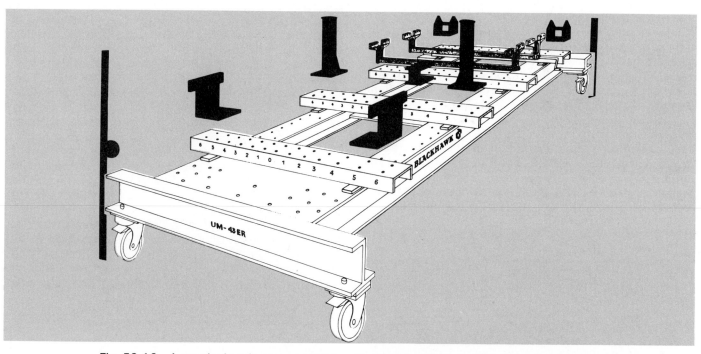

Fig. 59-16. A wrecked car is strapped to this rolling bench. It is then rolled to the straightening area of the shop. (Blackhawk)

UNITIZED BODIES

Heat and the use of heavy-duty jacks must be controlled when straightening unitized bodies. Care must be taken because of the difference in the gauge of the metal in the subframe of the body and at the stress points. It is possible to pull damaged areas back into place and in alignment by means of lightweight jacks and hydraulic equipment without the use of heat.

However, many body shops find that repairs can be made faster if special equipment is used. With certain types of equipment, the damaged car is first secured to a "bench" (floor or rack type), Figs. 59-16 and 59-17. Then, corrective pulls and/or pushes are made at several points at the same time. Dimensional drawings of the car are needed when working on a unitized body.

Fig. 59-17. A unitized body is secured to bench and steel members in floor. Pressure is then applied at several places on the frame at the same time. (Blackhawk)

Fig. 59-18. Spreading engine compartment opening with hydraulic equipment. (Hein-Werner)

When checking a unitized body for misalignment, measurements are taken between reference points on the car against those on the drawings. These measurements are indicated not only in the horizontal plane, but also vertically from the floor or from the bench to which the car has been secured. These dimensions are held to 1/16 in. (1.6 mm) limits.

Damaged areas should be roughed out before taking any measurements for squaring up the body. In severe cases, reinforcement brackets and other inner construction may have to be removed before restoration of the outer shell and pillars. This will avoid excessive strain on the parts. Always straighten, install, and secure such parts in place before attempting to align the unitized body.

Fig. 59-21. Using a hydraulic pump and extension tube to push windshield post into alignment with door. (Hein-Werner)

Fig. 59-19. Straightening front end damage. (Hein-Werner)

Fig. 59-22. Removing dent in deck lid with hydraulic spreader. (Blackhawk)

Fig. 59-20. Spreading fenders to align hood opening. (Hein-Werner)

Fig. 59-23. A hydraulic pump, ram, and extension tube to realign opening with trunk lid. (Hein-Werner)

FILING

After the sheet metal has been made as smooth as possible by means of a hammer and dolly, file or sand the surface to remove any tool marks or other dents that are too small to remove by the hammer and dolly. Also, it is necessary to sand back (feather) the paint, Fig. 59-24, surrounding the edges of the straightened area of sheet metal. This is important because a smooth surface is needed for the filler, primer, and other coats of refinishing material.

Special files, sanding materials, and equipment designed for auto body work are available.

A body file is flexible and made to fit a special holder, Fig. 59-7. The holder can be adjusted to arch the file to conform to the curve of the body panel. The teeth of the file are curved and designed to cut fast and not load up when used on the sheet metal of the body.

The surface is filed first in one direction, then at a right angle. On the return stroke, the file should be lifted from the surface being filed. This will not only produce a smoother surface but will also prolong the life of the file. Dragging the file along the surface of the metal on the return stroke will tend to dull the teeth. It is important to note that special body files can be resharpened.

SANDING

Because a sanding disk is flexible, it will follow the larger indentations in a body. For that reason, a power sander is used to locate the high and low spots when the straightening process has been nearly completed. Of course, its main function is for the final finishing of the metal surface. A sander can also be used to remove paint or other refinishing material that surrounds the damaged area. This is known as featheredging.

Before sanding a panel, select the disk having the correct abrasive for that surface. Many shops use three different grits to prepare the surface for repainting. They first use a 16 grit disk to remove rust and loose paint and for cutting down solder spots. This is followed with a 24 grit disk for surfacing the metal restoring contours, and for cutting down welds. Then, for an excellent final finish, a 50 grit disk is used.

Instead of three different grits, some body workers prefer to use a 24 grit disk as an all-purpose sander. However, one manufacturer of sanding disks claims that on the same type of job, the three-disk method will take 11.7 minutes to complete the work while 15 to 18 minutes will be needed for the single abrasive method.

For sharply curved surfaces, which cannot be reached by normal sanders, special cone-type sanders are needed. These sanders will reach curved surfaces around headlights, fender joints, back deck panels, etc.

The surface of the panel must be sanded. The edges surrounding the area of the straightened panel must also be sanded. Some body workers use a disk-type sander, Fig. 59-24. In disk featheredging, a 100 grit disk is recommended. An 80 grit disk is used in the sander and for hand sanding too, with 220 grit being used for finished featheredging.

When disk sanding, hold the disk grinding machine at an angle of 20 degrees to work, Figs. 59-25 and 59-26.

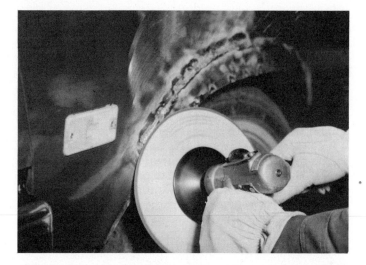

Fig. 59-24. Grinding sheet metal. Note feathered edges. (3M Co.)

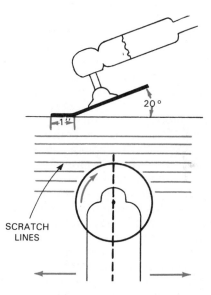

Fig. 59-25. Hold disk sander 20 deg. to the surface of panel.

Fig. 59-26. Note the angle of grinder and that only about 1 in. of grinder is flat against sheet metal. (3M Co.)

Apply enough pressure so that about 1 inch of the disk is bent and is in contact with the surface being sanded. The disk sander should never be operated so the entire area of the disk is flat against the surface of the work, nor at an extreme angle.

Also, the disk grinder should not be swung in an arc. It should always be moved so that it is perpendicular to the scratch lines. By sanding in this fashion, less conditioning is needed to prepare the metal for priming.

A sander should be operated so that the scratch lines will be parallel. Hand sanding should produce the same effect. There are many types and grits of sanding disks. Follow the manufacturers' instructions for their use.

REMOVING SAND SCRATCHES

Sand scratches have ruined many jobs which otherwise would have been perfect. These scratches do not show up until after the finish coat has been sprayed.

Unless the person repairing and smoothing the metal does a good job, it will be impossible for the painter to fill the scratches so that they will not show. Careless filing or bearing too hard on a coarse disk leaves scratches, gouges, and furrows that are hard to fill.

Many body workers use a coarse disk for roughing and cutting down weld spots. Then, the major part of the sanding is done with a No. 24 disk and final finishing of the metal with a disk of No. 50 or 80 grit. Even with such care, some sand scratches may occur because of small burrs or fins of torn metal along the edges of the sand scratches. It pays to follow up the heavy power sanding with a little hand sanding, using No. 150 paper.

While primers have been improved in their ability to fill and cover a surface, they cannot be depended on to do a job with a single coat. Apply several coats of primer and allow ample time for each coat to dry. This is better than applying a single heavy coat, since it is hard to tell when the heavy coat has dried all the way through.

Use fine paper when sanding priming coats. No. 220 or 240 paper will produce scratches that show through the first coats. In some cases, this paper can be used for the first sanding of primers, but bodymen advise the use of No. 320 or 360, then final finish sanding with No. 400 paper.

When lacquer is used to finish a car, the lacquer thinner penetrates the undercoat and causes swelling where the undercoat is heaviest. The swelling will be greater if the lacquer is sanded and polished before all the thinner has evaporated. A good practice is to first spray a light fog coat of lacquer. This will reduce the possibility of sand scratch swelling, which spoils the appearance.

Scratches can also be caused in the final polishing of the finish coat if care is not used in the selection of the rubbing compound. The finer the abrasive in the rubbing coat, the less change there is of scratches.

When doing spot painting, featheredge the spot. Give the area and edge a final sanding with No. 360 or No. 400 paper to remove any scratches. If rubbing compound is used, clean the area with a good wax and grease remover. Many rubbing compounds contain a lubricant.

Exercise care with synthetic enamel. While there are no strong solvents, the high lustre of the enamel will magnify any scratches that may be present.

Fig. 59-27. After grinding the rusted surface, a sheet of fiberglass that has been soaked in a special solution is placed over the hole.

PATCHING RUSTED AREAS

When body panels have become rusted through, Fig. 59-27, many body workers repair the damage by one of the methods developed for this purpose. This method consists of using sheets of special "fabric" such as fiberglass. First, sand the surface to remove all traces of rust, paint, and other foreign material. Then, fill it with resin-soaked fiberglass patches, cutting the final patch large enough to lap over the surrounding undamaged surfaces.

After the fiberglass patches dry, grind them as smooth as possible. Then, apply body filler over the fiberglass patches, Figs. 59-8 to 59-11. This allows the filler to be shaped. This is done because the fiberglass is too hard to shape to the contour of the body when it is dry.

WARNING: Use special care — and goggles — when adding hardener (catalyst) to fiberglass resin. If one drop of hardener gets in your eye, it will progressively destroy eye tissue and result in blindness. The hardener MUST be washed from the eye within four seconds after the accident.

REPLACING PANELS

Instead of straightening a badly damaged area, time can be saved by installing a new panel or part (complete door or trunk lid). In case of a damaged body panel, cut out the damaged area and weld in a section of a new panel. Replacement panels are available. The entire panel can be replaced, or only a portion, depending on the size of the damaged area.

In replacing the panel, proceed as follows:

Rough out and shape the damaged area, making sure that the undamaged portion is in correct contour and not sprung out of alignment. Measure the piece of metal to be replaced, Fig. 59-28. Take these measurements from the edge of the panel, the molding, or beading. This is important since these points are to be transferred to the replacement.

Next, scribe a line around the area to be cut from the service panel, then cut along the scribed line. The method of cutting will vary with the type of equipment: electric arc, gas, or mechanical cutters can be used.

Straighten the edges of this portion of new panel and position the new section over the damaged area. Scribe a line around its outer edge, and use this line as a guide in cutting out the damaged area, Fig. 59-29.

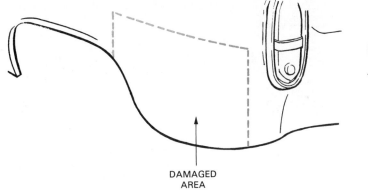

Fig. 59-28. Outline damage area of fender as shown.

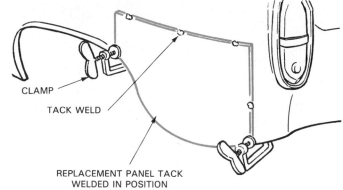

Fig. 59-30. Secure new section of fender in place with C-clamps, and then weld in place.

Fig. 59-29. Cut damaged area from fender with electric torch.

After straightening the cut edge of the fender on the car, fit the new section in position and hold it by means of C-clamps, Fig. 59-30. Tack well the section in place, starting the welds at the top center. Work out to the sides, then down the sides. Make a continuous weld, doing a length about 6 in. long at a time. To reduce distortion, stagger the welds.

With a grooved dolly, hammer the weld so it is about 1/16 in. below the surface of the surrounding panel, Fig. 59-31. Sand the area around the weld with a power sander or file the surface to produce the correct contour. Next, fill the groove with solder. Then, sand the surface to prepare it for painting. If the damaged area to be replaced is at a pillar post or at a spot-welded seam, split the seam by driving a thin sharp chisel between the two pieces.

MASKING

In order to protect surfaces and panels while adjacent areas are being painted. the car should be covered with paper secured in position with tape. The paper is called masking paper, and the tape is known as masking tape.

Manufacturers of masking tape and paper have gone to great expense to improve their products. Their research in this field has produced special tape and paper dispensers, Fig. 59-32, as well as shortcut methods of masking.

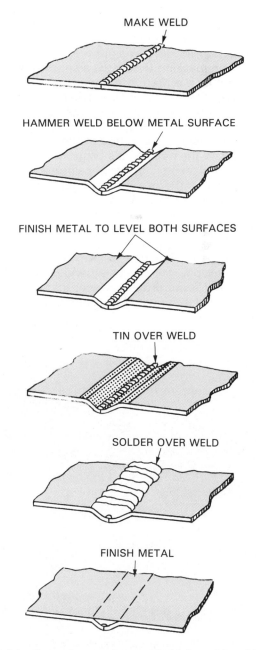

Fig. 59-31. Steps in covering welded joint with solder.

Fig. 59-32. Dispenser for masking paper and tape.

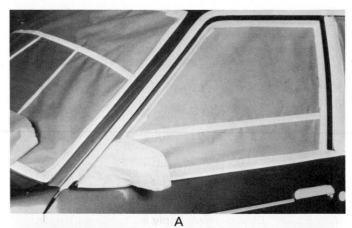

A

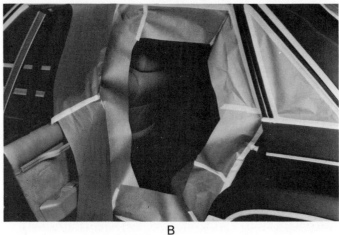

B

Fig. 59-34. Masking operation. A—Masked window, trim, and side mirror. B—Also, mask the inside to protect upholstery from paint spray seeping through. (3M Co.)

Good masking paper will not permit paint to seep through to the panel it is protecting. It should be tough, but flexible enough not to scratch the paint.

The tape must adhere easily to painted and unpainted surfaces, chrome, and other materials. It must have a strong texture so that it will not tear readily while being applied. The masking tape must also retain its adhering qualities when it is drenched during wet sanding operations. Flexibility or stretch is another necessary quality This is important when applyng the tape to curves.

One method has the tape applied along the edge of the masking paper so that half of the width of tape extends beyond the edge of the paper. When the paper is positioned on the car, the exposed area of the tape is pressed against the panel or trim to hold the masking paper in place.

FRONT END MASKING

Masking a car with large areas of chrome on the front end can be done fast by using wide paper. Each car presents a different problem. A car that has been properly masked is shown in Fig. 59-33. There are many methods of masking a window, Fig. 59-34. The first piece of paper is applied along the upper edge. The second goes along a portion of the bottom edge.

Hang masking paper from the top of the tire, Fig. 59-35. This protects wheel and tire from overspray.

Fig. 59-33. A car properly masked will look like this. (3M Co.)

Fig. 59-35. Protect the tire from overspray with masking paper. (3M Co.)

When masking a windshield, one method is to use 3/4 in. tape on 12 in. wide masking paper, Fig. 59-36. Next, lay the paper on the windshield from bottom to top, securing the tape to the window's botton edge. Curve the overlapping ends up the two side edges.

After the 12 in. mask is in place, lay a 6 in. mask along the windshield's top edge, allowing the paper to overlap the surface of the first covering. When both the 6 in. and 12 in. masks are in place, finish the job by applying a 3/4 in. strip of tape over the seam formed by the overhanging mask. For very large windshields, use 12 in. masks on both the lower portion and upper portion of the window.

Before masking a front door, first mask off all chrome fittings and molding. Then, apply a 12 in. width of masking paper over the lower portion of the window, and place a 6 in. wide mask over the upper portion. Next, apply a 12 in. wide mask from the door's rear edge, back over the rear window and side panel area. Finally, install a 6 in. wide mask from the front fender to the rear fender along the door's bottom edge.

Some manufacturers warn that masking tape should never be pulled or stretched during application. The proper method is to lay it down easily as it comes from the roll. In this way, pulling it back during painting is prevented. By not stretching the tape's backing, it is permitted to expand and contract without pulling away when the solvents are applied. For inside curves, narrow moldings and tabbing, 1/4 in. or 1/2 in. tapes are used. For wider moldings, 3/4 in. and 1 in. are more satisfactory.

When masking emblems, Fig. 59-37, 3/4 in. tape will do a good job. First, apply the tape along the edges of the emblem to form a sharp separation line. At sharp outside curves, lay the tape over the sharpest point of the curve and draw the loose ends back along the edge of the emblem. After all the edges have been masked, finish by filling the open areas with short strips.

WELDING

Skill in using welding equipment is not hard to develop. In gas welding, practice, adjustment of the flame, and the selection of the correct tip for a given job are the main concerns. When welding or cutting with electricity, correct current is the most important concern.

Before starting any gas welding or cutting job, the oxygen and acetylene cylinders must be chained either to a post or placed in a cylinder truck, Fig. 59-38. This prevents them from being tipped over. Before attaching the regulators, Fig. 59-39, each valve should be opened slightly to blow any dirt from the valve seat.

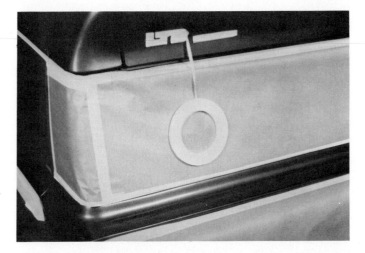

Fig. 59-37. Masking emblems is also needed. Note that taillight lens is masked, too. (3M Co.)

Fig. 59-38. Oxygen and acetylene tanks chained to a truck.

Fig. 59-36. With wiper arms removed, mask the windshield and also antenna mast, if so equipped. (3M Co.)

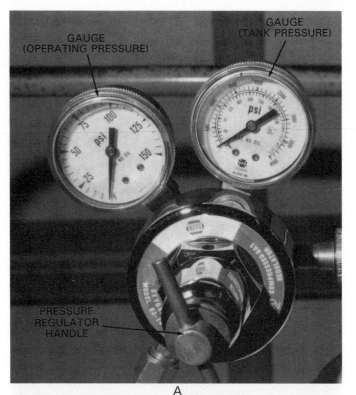

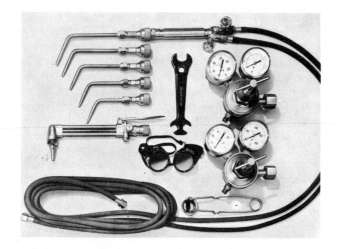

Fig. 59-40. Welding tips, cutting torch, gauges, welding goggles, wrenches, and igniter.

Fig. 59-39. Pressure regulators and gauges. A—For oxygen. B—For acetylene.

To avoid danger of fire, be sure there is no flame (or sparks) close to the acetylene cylinder. Always be certain that fire extinguishers are nearby. Acetylene connections have left-hand threads, and the hoses are red. Oxygen hoses are green and have right hand threaded connections.

Install the oxygen regulator and open the handwheel. The lower gauge will register the pressure in the tank. Attach the acetylene regulator and open the acetylene valve about 1/2 turn.

Connect the welding hoses to their regulators, welding head (tip) and torch, Fig. 59-40, to the other end of the hoses. The size tip selected will depend on the type of welding or cutting to be done. The size varies with manufacturers. The smallest tip is used when welding body sheet metal. If body sheet metal is to be cut, a small tip is preferred. Larger size tips are needed to weld or cut heavy sections, such as frames.

Different pressures are needed for welding and cutting different thicknesses of metal. For welding sheet metal: acetylene pressure should be 5 psi; oxygen pressure should be 10 psi. For cutting sheet metal: the pressure of the oxygen should be 10—25 psi, and acetylene 3—5 psi.

To light the flame, first open the oxygen valve 1/4 turn. Then, open the acetylene valve one full turn, and light the gas at the tip with a friction-type lighter. Never use matches. When lighting the gas, have the tip of the torch turned down and away from any person.

Adjust the flame by opening the oxygen valve slowly. The flame will change from a yellow acetylene flame to a blue flame, which is called a reducing flame. Start with an excess acetylene flame. Then, adjust to a neutral flame by closing the acetylene valve until the acetylene "feather" around the tip of the inner cone of the flame disappears, Fig. 59-41.

To obtain an oxidizing flame, increase the oxygen or decrease the acetylene until the inner cone of the flame is about 2/10 shorter. If the flame is yellow or backfires, readjust the acetylene to 10 psi, and open the torch needle valve more. If this does not correct the problem, the torch needs cleaning.

To weld sheet metal, a neutral flame should be used. Skill can be attained by practicing on strips of sheet metal. At first, do not attempt to weld two pieces of sheet steel together, but move the flame across the surface of the sheet metal, carrying the "puddle" along the surface, Fig. 59-42. Do not use any welding rod.

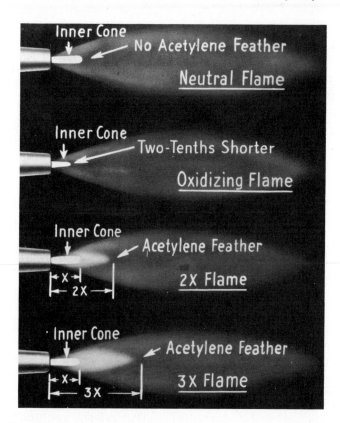

Fig. 59-41. Adjust to a neutral flame by increasing acetylene or reducing oxygen, until desired acetylene feather is obtained.

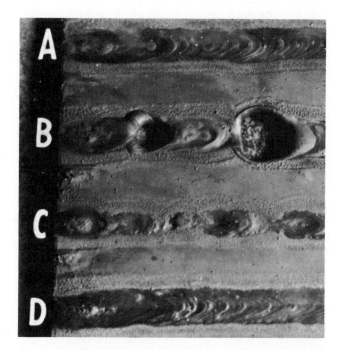

Fig. 59-42. Results of a practice piece. A and D show good results. B—Too much heat was used. C—Not enough heat was used.   (Linde Div. of Union Carbide)

The purpose of this is to obtain skill in carrying a puddle across the surface of the sheet. The torch should be held so that the flame points in the same direction that

Fig. 59-43. Good and poor welds. A and D—Satisfactory. B—Too much heat. C—Not enough heat. (Linde Div. of Union Carbide)

the weld will be made, and at an angle of about 45 deg. The inner cone of the flame should be about 1/8 in. away from the surface of the sheet.

Hold the torch in this position until a pool of molten metal about 3/16 to 1/4 in. in diameter is formed. Then, move the torch slowly to move the puddle in the desired direction to obtain an even ripple effect. Swing the torch from side to side in a small arc. If you move the torch too slowly, holes may be burned through the sheet metal. If you move it too quickly, the needed melting and overlapping of the puddles will not be obtained.

After skill is attained without using a welding rod, repeat the exercise using a welding rod, Fig. 59-43. The addition of the welding rod will produce a slight ridge of metal above the surface of the sheet.

When using a welding rod, hold the rod in about the same position as the welding torch. Hold it in the left hand and at an angle of slightly more than 45 deg. Try to bring the spot on the sheet and the tip of the welding rod to the melting temperature at the same time. The best position for the end of the welding rod is just inside the outer end of the flame. The flame is concentrated on the spot at the start of the weld.

After having practiced with a welding rod, place the edges of two pieces of sheet metal 1/16 in. apart and weld them together. In this case, make sure that the welding action penetrates through to the underside of the sheet so that the weld will have enough strength.

During the welding action, control the welding puddle so it will not fall through the gap. However, the metal added from the rod must be fused with the base metal on both sides of the joint for the entire thickness of the sheet. Once skill has been attained in welding small pieces of sheet metal together, try welding a fender or body panel.

CUTTING BODY PANELS

With the type of car body used today, many shops use the policy of replacing sections of panels rather than straightening. In cases of severe damage, this saves time and enables the shop to turn out more jobs per day. Replacement panels are available from car dealers and parts jobbers.

Cutting out panels for replacement is simple with modern equipment: the oxyacetylene cutting torch, Fig.

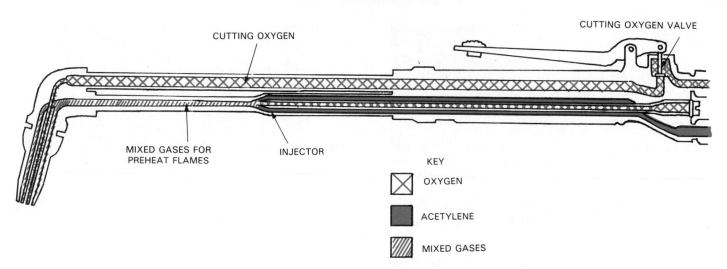

Fig. 59-44. Sectional view of oxyacetylene cutting torch.

CUTTING OXYGEN

CUTTING OXYGEN VALVE

MIXED GASES FOR PREHEAT FLAMES

INJECTOR

KEY

OXYGEN

ACETYLENE

MIXED GASES

59-44, the electric torch, Fig. 59-45, and various types of power-driven cutters, Fig. 59-46.

A special torch is needed to cut sheet metal with oxyacetylene, Fig. 59-44. It differs from the one used for welding. A cutting torch provides a stream of pure oxygen which does the cutting after the starting point of the cut has been heated to a cherry red by small oxyacetylene flames.

In the cutting torch, the oxyacetylene flames are produced at a series of openings in the tip. These openings surround the central opening or jet from which the oxygen passes. Details of construction vary with manufacturers.

Cutting is accomplished when the sheet metal is heated red hot, then exposed to the oxygen. Not only is the oxide that is formed melted, but some of the unoxidized steel is heated enough so that it, too, is melted.

The direction of the cut can be changed because the cutting nozzles are made with a ring of openings, which surround the oxygen orifice. In this way, several smaller flames of oxyacetylene are supplied that permit change in direction of the cut.

The cutting torch has three valves: two to regulate the amount of oxygen and acetylene that are mixed for the preheat flame; a third vlave, operated by a lever, to control the stream of oxygen.

When using a cutting torch, follow the same safety precautions for welding. Fire extinguishers should be

nearby. It is unsafe to feed oxygen into a confined space, since it will cause oil, wood, clothing, or sound deadening material to burn with great intensity, once it ignites.

When cutting out a body panel, mark the line with chalk where the cut is to be made. Make allowance for the width of the metal that will be melted, keeping the chalk mark 1/2 in. from the line. Remove any upholstery or other material from the other side of the body panel.

Use both hands when cutting metal with a torch, one to control the flow of oxygen and the other to steady the torch. Hold the torch nozzle at a right angle to the surface of the work and in the same spot until the metal is bright red. Open the oxygen valve. As soon as the flame starts cutting, there will be a shower of sparks from the metal. Then, move the torch slowly, but steadily, in the desired directions.

If you move the torch too slowly, heat from the preheating flames will tend to melt the edges of the cut and produce a ragged appearance. If you move it too fast, the cutting jet will fail to go through the metal. Should this occur, close the oxygen valve and reheat the point where the cut stopped. Then, reopen the oxygen valve to start the cut again.

Cutting is also done with an electric arc, Fig. 59-45. While any electric arc welder can be used for cutting, the use of large, high-capacity units results in too wide a cut and wastage of metal. Smaller, low-amperage units are preferred for cutting and welding body sheet metal.

Fig. 59-45. Electric cutting and welding equipment.

Fig. 59-46. Power cutter used on body panels.

Hand shears can be used, but most bodymen prefer special cutters driven by electric or pneumatic drills, Fig. 59-46. These cutters can cut curves with radii as small as 1 in., and they will cut sheet metal up to .040 in. They do not bend or stretch the metal.

PAINTING

The following procedure is for preparing a surface for touch-up and for refinishing individual panels. It is also used for the entire car if the original paint is in poor shape.

Before painting begins, it is essential that you prepare the surface for the paint by removing all traces of wax, grease, oil, and dirt. If the paint on the car or truck is of poor quality, remove it.

In this final preparation of the body before applying paint, you have many methods to choose from. The method you select depends on the condition of the existing paint, and the available equipment.

If the paint on the car is in good condition (good adherence and without surface defects), go over the surface with a disk sander. An open coated disk of No. 16 to 24 grit is needed. Hold the disk at a slight angle to the surface and work it forward and backward. This will remove most of the old finish down to the metal. Follow with a No. 50 close coated disk to remove scratches.

If the paint is being removed from only a portion of the panel, taper the sanded area into the old paint to produce a featheredge. Follow up with a 150 grit paper in a block sander, and complete the featheredge by water sanding with wet or dry paper of 280 or 320 grit. Some manufacturers of abrasive paper advise different grits with variations of the above procedure. Follow the instructions of the manufacturer.

For removing paint from the entire car, many shops prefer sandblasting, hot caustic strippers, or paint removers. When using paint removers, follow the manufacturer's instructions. The procedure is to apply the remover to the surface with a paintbrush or sponge. Then, after the proper time interval, scrape the paint from the surface with a putty knife or flush it from the surface with a strong stream of water or steam. Because of fumes created by the paint remover, the room should be well ventilated.

Removing paint by sandblasting is favored by many shops. In the city, specialists limit their work to removing paint by this method. Among the advantages claimed for the sandblasting method are speed and low cost. The surface that results promotes good paint adherence.

After removing the old paint, prepare the surface for repainting by using special cleaners to remove any rust, wax, or oil film. This is needed to obtain good paint adherence.

Apply the primer coats as soon as possible after the paint is removed. This is important when the surface has been sandblasted, because the metal surface is almost in the raw state and quickly starts rusting.

CLEAN THE SURFACE

The life and appearance of a paint job depends on the condition of the surface to which the finish coats are applied. So, do a good job of straightening the sheet metal, and make sure that the rest of the surface of the car is in good shape. The surface must be clean, free from rust, dirt, wax, oil, or other foreign matter. The old paint must have good adherence to the base metal.

So, before starting a refinish job, there are two points which have to be checked before any spraying is done. First, see that any original paint has good adhesion. Second, make sure the surface is clean. To check for adhesion, sand a small spot through to the base metal and feather the edges. If the thin edge does not break or crumble, there is good adhesion. The other point in preparing a surface for paint is that the surface must be clean. Old wax, rust, oil film, and other foreign material must be removed. The best method is to use one of the special cleaners that are available. Gasoline is not good, since it will not dissolve wax.

Use the special cleaner before and after the final sanding. Directions that come with the cleaner should be followed. When wiping the surface, do not use the normal shop cloths, because they retain a certain amount of grease or other chemicals from the laundry. If air is used to blow off dust, the compressor supplying the air must be fitted with a water trap so the air is free of oil and moisture. Another point to remember is not to touch the clean surface with your hands. Natural oil from the skin will cause poor adhesion and the finish will peel.

AIR REQUIREMENTS

The first step in setting up a paint department is to make sure there is enough air to handle the spray guns and other equipment. Also, the air compressor must be in good shape and delivering its rated capacity. Many shops install a separate compressor for paint work. This avoids overloading the shop air compressor. The extra equipment can be cut into the shop line in case of emergency.

To estimate compressed air needs of the shop and the load on the compressor, you must know the amount of air used by the pneumatic equipment in the shop. The method of calculating total needs is given in Fig. 59-47.

Note columns A, B, C, D, E, and F. Column D is for equipment in average use. Column E is for use where specialized departments are maintained. For example, a paint department where many air tools may be used by one person. Column F is for the use by large shops where there may be many hammers, paint guns, or other equipment needing a steady supply of air.

In using this form, obtain the needed CFM of the tools in your shop. When column C is filled out, multiply each figure in the column by the factor given in column D, E, of F, whichever applies to your shop. Place the answer in that column.

When these figures have all been totaled, you will have the minimum CFM needed for a compressor. To have a safe working margin for busy periods, and to handle extra tools or equipment, add 25 percent to the total.

Totaling the CFM demands of the pieces of equipment in the shop does not furnish the capacity of the air compressor needed. Some tools and equipment are used for only a short period and at irregular intervals; others are used almost constantly. To obtain the capacity of the compressor needed to operate the shop's equipment, follow the instructions in the table, Fig. 59-47.

AIR OPERATED EQUIPMENT	ESTIMATED AVERAGE C.F.M. AIR CONSUMPTION	A NO. OF UNITS OF EACH TYPE	B C.F.M. PER UNIT	C TOTAL C.F.M.	D TOTAL C.F.M. TIMES 100	E TOTAL C.F.M. TIMES 300	F TOTAL C.F.M. TIMES 500
Air filter cleaner							
Dusting gun							
Car lift							
Drill							
Engine cleaner							
Fender hammer							
Garage door opener							
Grease gun							
Spray gun (touch-up)							
Spray gun (production)							
Sander							
Spark plug cleaner							
Tire inflator							
Tire changer							
Undercoat gun							
Vacuum cleaner							
Wrench							
					Total D	Total E	Total F

1. Add D, E, F together. Place a decimal point before the last three figures. This will give the minimum C.F.M. required of the compressor.
2. Add on 1/4 of the above as a safety factor.
3. Add the above two for recommended minimum rating of the compressor required.

Transfer Total Here →

Transfer Above Total Here →

Fig. 59-47. Estimating needs for compressed air.

To get the best performance and long life from any air compressor, it must be serviced and inspected at regular intervals. A compressor and its water trap need more care if clean air is to be supplied.

Follow the manufacturer's service instructions. If instructions are not nearby, change the oil in the compressor every 60 to 90 days. Clean the air filter each month. Drain the water trap every morning. In extremely humid weather, this should be done many times each day.

If the equipment has a separate receiver with a pop valve, check it to make sure that it is operating. Otherwise, check the pressure gauges and switches, noting the time to cut-in and cut-out. This time interval, compared to the specified time, will serve as a warning for many air supply system troubles.

Check all lines for leaks. When installing a new system, be sure to select pipe of proper size to carry the needed amount of air. Also, when installing the piping see that it drains back to the receiver, rather than forward to the air hose.

Air hose, too, must be of proper size to keep air pressure drop at a minimum, Fig. 59-48. common sizes of spray gun air hose are 1/4 in., 5/16 in., and 3/8 in. The smaller the diameter, the greater loss in pressure. The 3/8 in. diameter hose is preferred.

SPRAY GUN

The condition of the spray gun and the way in which it is used determines the quality of the paint job. It is impossible to do a good job of spray painting with a gun that has not been cleaned or is otherwise bad.

The compressed air used for spraying must be free of moisture, oil, and dirt. Pressures must be regulated. The

Size of Air Hose	5 ft. length	10 ft. length	15 ft. length	20 ft. length	25 ft. length
AIR PRESSURE DROP AT SPRAY GUN					
1/4 in.					
at 40 lbs. pres.	6.0 lbs.	8.0 lbs.	9.5 lbs.	11.0 lbs.	12.7 lbs.
at 50 lbs. pres.	7.5 lbs.	10.0 lbs.	12.0 lbs.	14.0 lbs.	16.0 lbs.
at 60 lbs. pres.	9.0 lbs.	12.5 lbs.	14.5 lbs.	16.7 lbs.	19.0 lbs.
5/16 in.					
at 40 lbs. pres.	2.2 lbs.	2.7 lbs.	3.2 lbs.	3.5 lbs.	4.0 lbs.
at 50 lbs. pres.	3.0 lbs.	3.5 lbs.	4.0 lbs.	4.5 lbs.	5.0 lbs.
at 60 lbs. pres.	3.7 lbs.	4.5 lbs.	5.0 lbs.	5.5 lbs.	6.0 lbs.

Fig. 59-48. Air pressure drop at spray gun.

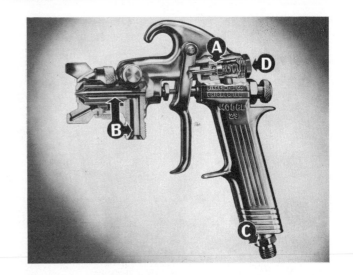

Fig. 59-50. Sectional view of paint spray gun. A—Cartridge type air valve. B—Passage for paint. C—Compressed air fitting. D—Alternate air entrance. (Binks Mfg. Co.)

compressor must be equipped with pressure regulator, Fig. 59-49, which provides clean, filtered air for painting.

Be sure to follow the instructions when taking care of a spray gun. Thorough cleaning each time the gun is used, lubrication of bearing surfaces, and packing at regular intervals is a must. A typical spray gun is shown in Fig. 59-50.

Use thinner to clean the gun, but never immerse the gun in the solution, since thinner will destroy the lubricant in the packing. Never use caustic acid solutions for cleaning. They will corrode the aluminum alloy portions of the gun.

The gun and cup should be cleaned as soon as spraying is completed. Empty all lacquer or enamel from the cup. Rinse the cup with thinner. Then, put a small amount of thinner in the cup and spray it through the gun. This will clean all the passages in the gun. Then, dry the parts with air. The gun and cup are ready for the next job.

Lubricate the air valve stem daily with a few drops of light oil. All packing should be kept soft and pliant by oiling. To insure that the compressed air used for spray painting is clean and free from oil or moisture, the air compressor must have a water trap. These units are designed not only to trap oil and water vapor and prevent them from reaching the gun, but also to supply air to specified pressures for different types of spray paint.

Water traps come in different sizes so that one or more spray guns can be used from a single unit. For large departments, pressure feed paint tanks are available. These are designed for large amounts of finishing material to the spray guns, under constant and accurate control.

When setting up a paint spray booth, enough air must be available. Many shops, therefore, use a separate compressor, Fig. 59-51. The size needed will depend on the

Fig. 59-49. Pressure regulator combined with water trap. Water trap holds moisture from compressed air that has condensed. Water trap should be drained daily by opening a valve at bottom of trap. (DeVilbiss Co.)

Fig. 59-51. A typical air compressor and tank. (DeVilbiss)

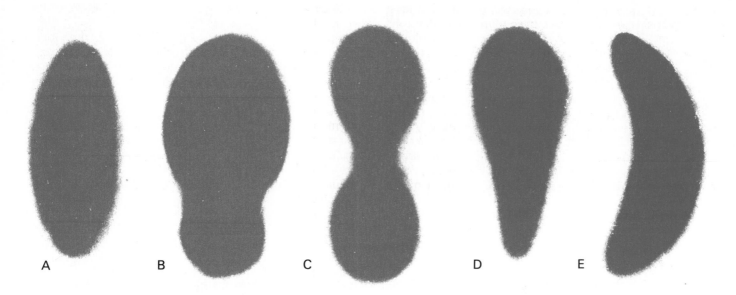

Fig. 59-52. Proper and improper spray patterns. A—Correct spray pattern. B—Not enough air pressure. C—Air pressure too high. This can also be corrected by increasing the width of spray pattern. D—Fluid has dried around the tip of nozzle causing this pattern. E—This pattern caused by a clogged wing port.

type and number of paint spray guns, and the refinishing material to be sprayed. Compressor units capable of handling any number of guns are available.

Spray guns have two adjustments. One controls the amount of fluid being sprayed. The other governs spray shape, so that a round or fan-shaped spray can be obtained. The various patterns obtained from a spray gun are shown in Fig. 59-52.

TIPS ON SPRAYING

Anyone can spray paint. But to do a job that will dry smooth with lustre (no sag or ripple) takes know-how that can be attained with practice.

The gun used for refinishing cars is of the syphon cup type, Fig. 59-53. With this gun, the trigger controls both the air and the paint. Spray guns for first-class work have many tips, needles, and spray cups which will adapt the gun for use with any type material and any size job. Most shops have several guns, one each for primer, lacquer, synthetic enamel, and acrylic enamel. In this way, there is no danger of mixing different types of paints, which results in a poor paint job.

One of the "musts" in spray painting is that the paint should have the correct viscosity. This can be determined by following the instructions on the paint can. Too many painters determine the viscosity by the rate at which the paint runs from the stirring rod. This can lead to trouble, since only a slight change in viscosity can spoil a good job. This happens because the amount of thinner only determines the thickness of the coat. It also affects the evaporation rate between the time the material leaves the gun and the time it contacts the panel.

High viscosities result in sag and orange peel. Low viscosities produce improper flow-out and waste of thinner. To avoid these problems, measure the thinner and lacquer or enamel in a graduated measuring cup.

The temperature at which the spraying is done is also a factor in turning out a good job. This applies not only to the temperature of the shop, but to the temperature of the car or truck as well. The shop should be maintained at 70°F. Try to bring the car into the shop well in advance of spraying time so that it becomes the same temperature as the shop. Spraying lacquer on a surface that is too cold, or too hot from being in the sun, will upset the flowing time of the material and will cause orange peel and poor adherence to the surface.

Another factor in doing a good paint job is the thickness of the paint film on the surface. A thick film takes longer to dry than a thin one. As a result, the paint will sag, ripple, or orange peel. If enamels are used, blistering may result.

Fig. 59-53. Spray guns of the syphon cup type are used for refinishing cars.

You should produce a coat that will remain wet long enough for proper flow-out, but no longer. The amount of material you spray on a surface with one stroke of a gun will depend on the width of the fan, the distance of the gun from the sprayed surface, the air pressure, and the amount of thinner used.

The speed of the spray stroke will also affect the thickness of the coat. The best method is to adjust the gun to obtain a wet film which will remain wet only long enough for good flow-out. Get the final finish thickness by spraying another coat after the first one has dried.

Standard spray guns are designed to give best performance when held at a distance of 8 to 12 in. from the surface to be sprayed. When the gun is held too close, the air pressure tends to ripple the wet film if the film is too thick. If the distance is too great, a large percent of the thinner will evaporate in the spraying operation. Orange peel or a dry film will result, because the spray droplets will not have time to flow together.

Hold the spray gun at the specified distance from the work. Do not tilt it or hold it at an angle. Also, never swing the gun in an arc, but move it parallel to the work. The only time it is allowed to fan the gun is when you want the paint to thin out over the edges of a small spot. The effects of incorrect handling of the spray gun are shown in Fig. 59-54.

The spray gun with an attached cup is good enough for most jobs. Many bodies have undercut surfaces where it is necessary to hold the gun at such an angle that a gun with attached cup cannot be used. A gun with a remote or separate cup is needed.

Guns with special spray heads have been developed to properly atomize acrylic paints. A pressure of 40 to 45 psi is enough to produce the needed shade, maximum amount of leveling, and high gloss. Higher pressure causes orange peel and a lighter shade with iridescent colors. So, there are many variables that affect the outcome of a paint job.

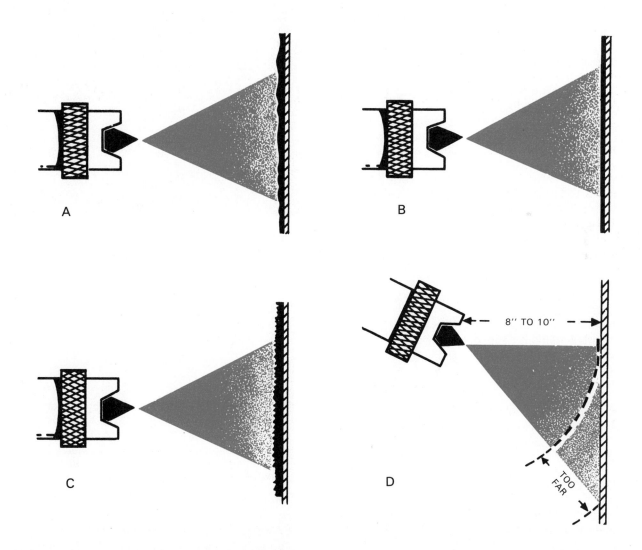

Fig. 59-54. Cause and effect of proper and improper paint application. A—Heavy coat of paint produces a ripple or orange peel. This may be caused by a dirty nozzle, spray gun too close to surface, paint too thin, low air pressure, spray gun movement too slow, or too much overlap. B—Good flow out is obtained when paint is thinned properly, air pressure is correct, movement of gun at correct speed, and 50 percent overlap. C—Thin paint coat is rough, dry, and without lustre. This may be caused by using wrong type air nozzle, holding gun too far from surface, moving gun too fast, or not enough overlap. D—Thickness of paint will vary if gun is fanned or held at an angle.

SURFACES/REFINISHING

Poorly prepared surfaces are shown in Figs. 59-55 through 59-68. You must determine whether the original finish is lacquer or enamel. To make a quick check, moisten a finger with lacquer thinner and rub a small area. If the finish is lacquer, it will dissolve. To distinguish between nitrocellulose lacquer and acrylic lacquer, rub a small area with silicone polish remover. Acrylic lacquer will rub off while nitrocellulose lacquer will not be affected.

On lacquer jobs which are to be refinished with lacquer, you have to prevent swelling of the old coat. Swelling occurs when sanding has been done, and unless you can keep the new solvents from reaching the old finish, no amount of care will prevent the old scratches from showing.

Swelling of the old coat does not occur on the unmarred or scratched surface of the lacquer, which is covered with an insoluble outer layer. It does occur when the new lacquer contacts freshly exposed surfaces in the scratches. After all the solvents have evaporated, and the new finish shrinks, small furrows following the scratches will result.

So, it is necessary to use a "sealer" on lacquer repaint jobs where much of the old refinishing material remains. Apply the sealer after sanding and treating the bare metal. Sealer has good adhesion to the old finish and will prevent penetration of the new lacquer and prevent swelling. If it is necessary to use any primer surfacer for filling rough spots, apply this first. Then, after sanding, apply the sealer.

Enamel finishes must be sanded. Make sure that the abrasive is not too coarse, and sand the old finish to produce a good surface for the new finish. A surfacer is not needed if the enamel is in good condition. If the old enamel is badly worn and pitted, use a surfacer or primer for better adhesion and appearance.

Modern primers, glazing putties, fabric patches, and body filler will fill almost any rough surface. However, the surface should be as smooth as possible before any of these are applied.

After the primer and/or other surfacing material is applied, thorough sanding is needed. Many painters recommend three or four grades of paper, ranging from coarse to fine. For example, use a No. 16 open coated paper first, followed by No. 50 close coated, and final sanding with No. 150 paper.

Modern surfacing and refinishing materials have made auto painting simple. However, good appearance and long life of the finish depends on the care taken in preparing the surface for the final coats.

Lacquer Over Old Finishes

1. Remove old wax or silicone polish with special remover. Water sand the old finish, using a No. 320 paper.
2. Using clean air, blow out all cracks.
3. Clean the surface with special grease, rust, and wax remover.
4. Spray surfacer on bare metal spots. If needed, use spot putty or equivalent.

Fig. 59-55. Lifting. A puckering and wrinkled effect results in applying material carrying strong solvents to a partially oxidized surface. It could also be caused by surface not being cleaned properly. REMEDY: Sand and refinish.

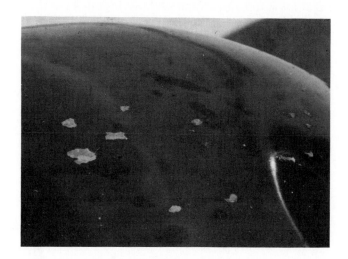

Fig. 59-56. Chipping caused by stones, etc., striking surface. REMEDY: Sand and refinish.

Fig. 59-57. Peeling over solder that is noticed a few weeks after refinishing. REMEDY: Wash surface with a solution of equal parts of ammonia, alcohol, and water.

5. Water sand undercoats with No. 320 paper. If any spots are sanded through to base metal, spray again with surfacer and water sand.
6. Seal scratches with special sealer if car was finished with lacquer.
7. Blow out cracks with clean air.
8. Again clean surface with special cleaner.

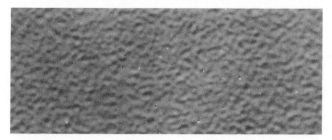

Fig. 59-58. Orange peel may be caused by improper air pressure, not enough reduction, poor selection of solvent, use of a thinner that dries too quickly, or lacquer sprayed on a hot surface. REMEDY: Check thinner, air pressure, and make sure surface is 70 °F.

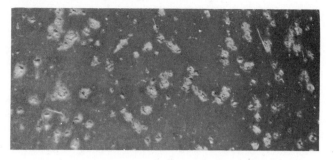

Fig. 59-62. Rust spots under finish appear as raised sections or blistering. Problem is caused by poor penetration and cleaning of surface. REMEDY: Sand off surface, treat surface with rust remover, and refinish.

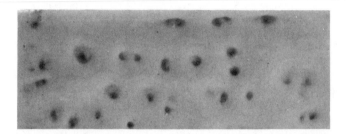

Fig. 59-59. Fish eyes may be caused by failure to remove silicone polish. REMEDY: Sand and refinish surface.

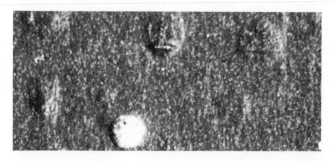

Fig. 59-63. Pitting is caused by oil or moisture escaping through air line. REMEDY: Sand and refinish surface. Also, rebuild compressor and replace water trap.

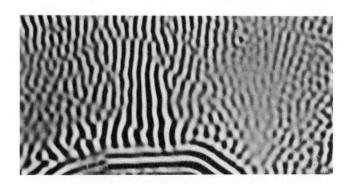

Fig. 59-60. Wrinkling is found only in synthetic enamel finish. Results from application of a heavy coat that is made worse by high temperatures. REMEDY: Apply thinner coats.

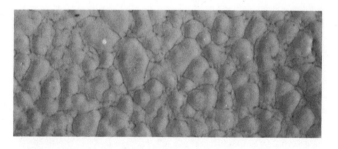

Fig. 59-64. Blistering is caused by rust, moisture, oil, grease, wrong thinner, or other foreign material working in between coats and causing them to separate. Oil or water in air lines, high temperatures, or high humidity may be the cause. REMEDY: Sand to bare metal and then refinish.

Fig. 59-61. Water spotting is caused by washing car in bright sunlight. REMEDY: Use paste cleaner and refinish.

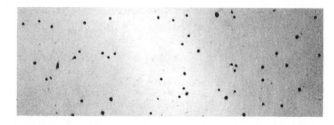

Fig. 59-65. Pinpoint blistering is often confused with pitting because small broken blisters have appearance of pits that range from a pinhead to a point. REMEDY: Sand to bare metal and then refinish.

Fig. 59-66. Mottled appearance is if paint is applied on surface which has been polished with silicone. REMEDY: All traces of polish must be removed from surface before refinishing.

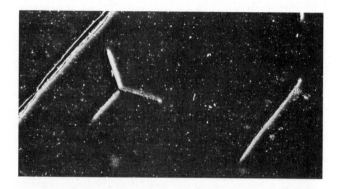

Fig. 59-67. Cracking and checking extends to the metal, or may go only as far as undercoating. Applying a second coat before first is dry, poor paint mixing, flexing of panels, or temperature stress may be the cause. REMEDY: Sand to bare metal and then refinish.

Fig. 59-68. Chalking is due to weathering and sunlight, which causes a dull powdery surface. REMEDY: Use paste cleaner and then polish. It may be necessary to refinish the entire car if severe.

9. Apply lacquer color coats. Three double coats are recommended.
10. Water sand with No. 400 paper.
11. Polish.

Enamel Over Old Finishes

1. Remove all the wax and silicone polish with special cleaner.

2. Wet sand old finish with No. 320 paper.
3. Clean surface with a special wax, grease, and rust remover.
4. Spray on undercoats.
5. Sand undercoats with No. 280 paper.
6. Respray if sanding has gone to base metal.
7. Resand undercoat.
8. Blow out all cracks with clean air.
9. Clean surface with special cleaner to remove any hand marks.
10. Wipe surface with tack rag to remove lint and dust.
11. Spray a light coat of enamel over all cracks.
12. Apply a tack coat and follow immediately with a full coat of enamel. If drying lights are not available, allow to dry at least 12 hours in dust-free room.

PAINT/MATERIALS

Acrylic lacquer, acrylic enamel, urethane enamel, and synthetic enamel are now being used in refinishing. Thinners, primers, surfacers, reducers, solvents, sealers, and metal conditioners are needed as well. Also used for exterior finish are wood grained overlay and vinyl.

ACRYLIC LACQUER: This material dries by evaporation of volatile solvents. Since is remains more or less soluble, the new coat of acrylic lacquer will bond with the original coat.

ACRYLIC ENAMEL: A solvent blend of binder and pigment materials, acrylic enamel dries in two stages. The first stage is oxidation of the solvent. The second is oxidation of the binder. No polishing is needed.

URETHANE ENAMEL: Used in the refinishing of cars, urethane provides a hard, tile-like finish. It has high gloss, improved flow and appearance, good adhesion, and flexibility. Urethane enamel dries slower than acrylic enamel.

SYNTHETIC ENAMEL: Not soluble in most solvents, synthetic enamel is currently used for refinishing cars. Refinishing shops prefer acrylic enamel or acrylic lacquer.

COMPARISON OF COSTS: Acrylic lacquer is more easily applied than acrylic enamel. However, the lacquer needs several coats and, therefore, more time is needed for application. This is an important cost factor.

PRIMER SURFACERS: These are designed to improved adhesion to the metal and to fill slight surface imperfections. After drying, the primer surfacer is sanded smooth. Two types are available. One is used under acrylic enamels. Another is used under acrylic lacquers.

PRIMERS: For adhesion to special surfaces, manufacturers provide primers. These are different from primer surfacers. Primers are widely used when painting aluminum or galvanized surfaces. If the surface also needs filling, a primer surfacer is applied over the primer.

SEALERS: These are used for sealing sanding scratches made when preparing to paint over an acrylic surface. Special bleeder sealer is used over a red or maroon surface.

METALLICS: When metallic flakes (aluminum) are added to lacquers and enamels, a luminous quality is given to the surface. This is a popular finishing material, but presents a problem in matching colors.

THINNERS AND REDUCERS: These are solvents used to thin or reduce paints to the desired viscosity (thickness). Thinners are used for acrylic products.

Reducers are used for synthetic base materials.

PUTTY: Made of the same material as the primer surfacer, putty is used for filling deep nicks and scratches.

WAX AND POLISH REMOVERS: Traces of wax, polish, or grease must be removed from the surface before applying paint. Removers are used to do this job, or flaking will result.

METAL CONDITIONERS: These compounds are applied to metal after all paint has been removed to prevent rusting.

TACK RAG: This is a specially treated cheese cloth. It has been dipped in a thin nondrying varnish. Used to wipe the surface of the car before painting, it removes all traces of dust.

RUBBING COMPOUNDS: Mildly abrasive, these pastes or liquids are used to polish acrylic lacquer surfaces. They bring a higher polish to the surface.

SELECTING PAINT

When refinishing a car, use of proper materials is important. Fewer troubles arise if the same material is used for refinishing as was originally used.

Today, most cars are refinished in acrylic enamel or acrylic lacquer. Nitrocellulose lacquer is used only when there is little drying time. This material may also be used for retouching small scratches.

Acrylic lacquer is used for all cars originally finished in nitrocellulose lacquer. If acrylic lacquer is used over enamel, a sealer should first be applied over the enamel. Complete panels, never portions, should be sprayed. Less trouble in matching colors is the result.

When spraying acrylic lacquer, a surface in good condition need not be sanded before applying the finish coat. The surface must be thoroughly cleaned. If acrylic lacquer is applied over synthetic enamel, the surface must be sanded to make the new paint stick. When repairing or refinishing over acrylic enamels, the surface must be cleaned and sanded to provide both good adhesion and resistance to peeling and chipping.

Synthetic enamels are often used in repainting cars originally finished with enamel. Complete panels should be refinished when enamel is used for repair because it is hard to spot paint a small area without leaving a ring around the spot.

Some painters prefer acrylic enamel because compounding is not needed. Others will use synthetic enamel because of lower costs. When a striking appearance is wanted, many shops prefer urethane enamels. Desirable qualities of acrylic enamel and acrylic lacquer include durability, gloss retention, and hardness.

MATCHING COLORS

Even though ready-mixed paints for standard car colors are available, the number is so great that no jobber carries a complete line. The painter is often faced with the mixing of colors.

Matching colors is not easy. Since cars are being turned out with more shades and tones, painters are finding their work harder. The problem of fading hinders the situation. Many manufacturers provide instructions, specialized equipment, and basic colors that help solve the color matching problem. One type of equipment designed to prepare paint of a certain color, Fig. 59-69.

The most important part in mixing colors is that the painter must have good color perception. Many color mixing aids are available, including thirty basic colors, mixing containers, stirring paddles, test panels, and color mixing equipment.

Another point related to color matching is that every color has what is known as a "mass-tone" and a "tint-tone." The mass-tone can be judged from the color as it appears on the painted panel or in the can. The tint-tone of a color is the shade resulting from mixing a small amount of the color with a large amount of white.

A dark green mass-tone, for example, will have a blue tint-tone, and most maroons have a violet or purple tint-tone. It is impossible to add white to a dark green to get a light green, or add white to a maroon to get a light red. Small additions of color will tint according to its tint-tone. Large amounts will affect others according to mass-tone. Black darkens a color and white lightens it. Black tends to dull a shade. Addition of white dilutes the tint.

Clean equipment is a must when matching colors. Dust, old paint, or other material will spoil the effect. Thoroughly stir each basic color or mixture. Do your color matching in sunlight. Artificial light changes tints and tones. Tightly close cans of paint not in use to reduce evaporation of the solvents.

Since almost all shades darken on drying, wait until the color is dry before making comparisons. When matching a color on a car, remove all waxes and polish because they tend to change the color. Also, when making comparisons, the larger the surface, the lighter the color will appear because of light reflection. Always compare areas of equal size.

You can save a lot of material by mixing small amounts and using predominating colors first. If a formula is being followed, start with the major shade, adding the minor amounts according to volume.

The larger proportion of the formula will provide the depth of color. Further toning will be needed to produce the shade being matched. Only a very small amount of

Fig. 59-69. Equipment designed to prepare a desired shade of color.

color is needed for toning. For example, a touch of red may mean a small amount on the tip of a spatula added to a quart batch. Add this touch last. Mix colors full strength for matching, then dilute them to spraying consistency.

White or opalescent is the base of almost all colors. Exceptions are reds, maroons, dark greens, dark browns, and dark blues. Red, blue, yellow, and green will give brightness to a mixture.

SOFT BODY PARTS

Many parts on modern cars are made of synthetic materials. See Fig. 59-70. These parts need special treatment when being restored after damage.

Minor tears, splits, and cracks can be repaired by first cleaning with naptha solvent. Next, apply a thin coating of special adhesive on the edges or sides to be bonded. Then, position the torn, split or cracked surfaces so they come together in their original position. Apply firm hand pressure to the bonded area for about one minute. Follow all instructions for use of the particular adhesive.

If repainting is needed, first sand the entire area with No. 400 grit sandpaper. Be careful not to sand through the enamel on the surrounding area, and never sand through the existing primer. Next, clean the area with naptha. Then, apply color coat of special paint in accordance with instructions of the paint manufacturer. Follow this by applying a clear coat of special color paint.

To repair minor gouges and holes in synthetic material, first roughen the damaged area with coarse sandpaper of about 36 grit. Flame treat the exposed surface with a propane torch with about a 1 in. (2.5 cm) blue flame. Move the flame back and forth over the exposed surface two or three times. Be sure to keep the flame moving.

Then, apply special adhesive. Follow the instructions with the material, paying attention to the mixing process. Be sure to slightly overfill the area so that it protrudes over the surrounding area. If a hole is being filled, masking or aluminum tape should be applied to the under surface to lend support to the filler material.

If a heat curing system is being used, heat to 190 °F (88 °C) for 20 minutes with a heat lamp placed 4 to 5 ft. (1.2 to 1.5 m) away.

If the air dry system is being used, wait one to three hours at room temperature for curing before sanding. When the area is cured, sand with No. 240 fine cut paper to bring the surface to the proper contour. Then, finish sand with No. 400 paper. If needed, apply a second coating of filler paste. The surface can then be primed with special primer designed for synthetic surfaces.

To repaint replacement parts and spot repairs, use color coat designed for use on synthetic materials. This special paint can be used on parts such as flexible bumpers, fender extensions, stone, or gravel shields. These parts are supplied primed and ready for installation.

PLASTIC PARTS

It is important to know what kind of plastic is used on the car. This is so the proper painting materials and procedures can be used. There are three different types of plastic. They are ABS, polypropylene, and vinyl.

To determine which plastic is used, cut a small piece from the back side of a panel. Holding the piece of plastic with a pair of needle nose pliers, hold a lit match to the piece of plastic. If the smoke becomes black, Fig. 59-71, the plastic is ABS. If there is very little smoke, the plastic is polypropylene, Fig. 59-71. To test if the plastic is vinyl, heat a piece of copper wire and touch the backside of a panel. Next, hold this piece of copper wire with the melted plastic in a flame. If the flame becomes bluish-green, the plastic is vinyl, Fig. 59-71.

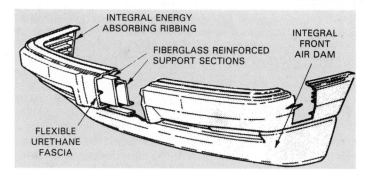

Fig. 59-70. Front bumper is made of synthetic parts to reduce weight of car. (PPG Industries)

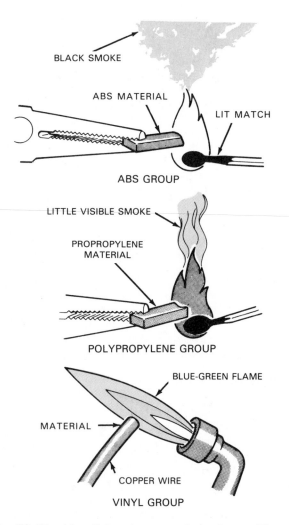

Fig. 59-71. Identifying the type of plastics. (Chrysler)

PAINTING POLYPROPYLENE

Painting polypropylene parts involves the use of a special primer. Since polypropylene is a hard plastic, it can be color coated and primed with a normal acrylic lacquer. Failure to use the needed primer will result in color coat lifting or peeling off of the panel. Allow primer to dry at least one minute, and no longer than 10 minutes. This is known as the flash time. Then, apply acrylic lacquer color as needed. Applying the paint during this time provides the best adhesion.

PAINTING ABS PLASTICS

ABS plastic needs no primer. Prep the surface with Acryli-Clean or the equivalent. Apply normal acrylic lacquer.

PAINTING VINYL PLASTIC/FLEXIBLE ABS PLASTIC

The paint for vinyl and flexible ABS plastic involves the use of an interior vinyl color and a clear vinyl top coat, Fig. 59-72. No primer or primer sealer is needed. Prep the surface with a solvent and wipe dry with a lint free cloth. Apply several coats, but allow a flash time between coats. Apply one coat of vinyl clear coat with proper gloss level to match adjoining parts. The clear coat prevents the color coat from rubbing off after drying.

WATER/DUST LEAKS

Leaks often result from the dislocation of weatherstripping. These are easy to locate and repair. In other cases, special effort and procedures are needed to locate, then repair the problem. If the exact location of the source of a leak is not known, first inspect the area of the leak for watermarks, rust, or dust trails. Then trace these marks back to the source.

If there are no marks to follow, you will need to use a water hose to help find the trouble spot. Sit in the car while your partner sprays water over the outside of the suspected leak area. Watch for water trickling in, and try to locate the exact point of entry. You may have to remove head lining or other trim to locate the source of the leak.

Another method of locating leaks is to fill a syringe with powdered chalk, water, or a mixture of the two. Syringes can be purchased at any drugstore and powdered chalk is available at most hardward stores. Spray the suspected seam with the contents of the syringe. The dust formed by this operation will quickly show the point of entry of the rain and dust.

A variety of materials are used for correcting water and dust leaks, including:

Black caulk and sealer
Gray caulking cord
Auto body sealer
Rubber cement
Metallic caulk and sealer
Pressure gun for applying caulk
Sponge rubber stripping

Before attempting to repair any leaks around doors or deck lids, make sure that the doors and lids are correctly fitted. Poor fits always result in water and dust leaks.

The easiest method of checking the fit of doors and deck lids is to note whether the edges of the door or lid are the same distance from the surrounding body panel. When that has been corrected, slide a feeler gauge (.005 in.) or a dollar bill along the weather strip with the door or deck lid closed. If no resistance is noticed to the passage of the feeler gauge, or a dollar bill, leakage will occur at that point. Repair leaks by installing new weather stripping, cementing it in place with sealer.

Leaks around the windshield can be repaired by means of the pressure gun filled with black caulk and sealer. Slide the nozzle of the pressure gun between the rubber and the glass, and force the compound as shown in Fig. 59-73. The area in which to apply sealer, when leaks occur, is between the windshield weather strip and the body flange. In some cases of leaks around the windshield or rear window, you must remove the glass, then replace it, using ample sealing compound. Areas where leaks may occur are shown in Fig. 59-74.

Plastic Type	Examples	Painting Procedure
Rigid Vinyl	Bumper Fillers	Flex Agent Required
RIM Urethane (Reaction Injection Moulding)	Fascias	Flex Agent Required
TPU (Thermoplastic Urethane)	End Caps Soft (Same as RIM)	Flex Agent Required
TPO (Thermoplastic Olefin)	Bumper Fillers	Flex Agent Required
FRP (Fiberglass Reinforced Polyester)	Nose Cones (Hard)	Same as Steel
Phenolic	Ash Trays	Same as Steel
Nylon	Spoilers, Louvers	Same as Steel
ABS (Acrylo-nitrile/Butadiene/Styrene	Louvers	No Flex Agent
Polypropylene	Hard Seat Back, Garnish Moulding	No Flex Agent
Flexible ABS	Dash	No Flex Agent

Fig. 59-72. Some plastics need a flex agent added to the paint. (Chrysler)

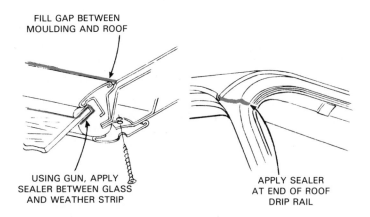

FILL GAP BETWEEN MOULDING AND ROOF

USING GUN, APPLY SEALER BETWEEN GLASS AND WEATHER STRIP

APPLY SEALER AT END OF ROOF DRIP RAIL

Fig. 59-73. Areas of windshield that may develop a leak.

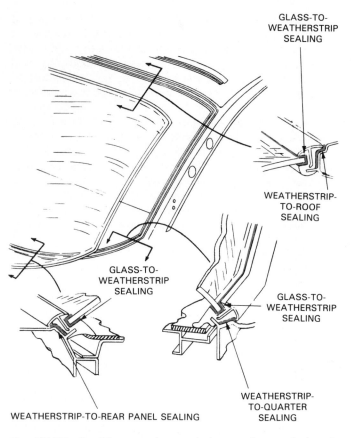

GLASS-TO-WEATHERSTRIP SEALING

WEATHERSTRIP-TO-ROOF SEALING

GLASS-TO-WEATHERSTRIP SEALING

GLASS-TO-WEATHERSTRIP SEALING

WEATHERSTRIP-TO-QUARTER SEALING

WEATHERSTRIP-TO-REAR PANEL SEALING

Fig. 59-74 Caulking may be needed around rear window to overcome leaks.

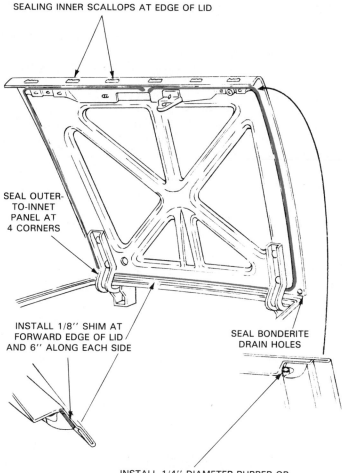

SEALING INNER SCALLOPS AT EDGE OF LID

SEAL OUTER-TO-INNER PANEL AT 4 CORNERS

INSTALL 1/8″ SHIM AT FORWARD EDGE OF LID AND 6″ ALONG EACH SIDE

SEAL BONDERITE DRAIN HOLES

INSTALL 1/4″ DIAMETER RUBBER OR WINDSHIELD WIPER HOSE ON EACH REAR CORNER AND 12″ BOTH WAYS FROM CORNER.

Fig. 59-75. Rear deck lid may leak in these areas.

Leaks may also occur through bolt and nut holes used to attach chrome trim to the body panels. This can be overcome by applying special sealer to each of the clips and nut ends.

Fig. 59-75 shows the location of the weather stripping of a deck lid. In some cases, build up the weather stripping by means of 1/8 in. thick weather strip rubber. Leakage may also occur around deck lid locks. To solve the problem, install a small rubber washer on the lock cover shaft, between the lock housing and spring.

When water leaks into the passenger compartment around the doors and cowl hinge pillar, make sure that all drain holes on the bottom of each door are open. Also, remove the door trim panel and inspect the bottom edge of the water shield. A good seal to the door must be maintained around the shield. Check by pouring water into the door at the belt line, to make sure that none of it will splash past the shield. Leaks at the cowl hinge pillar may be corrected by installing a drain tube inside each hinge pillar.

DRAIN LOCATIONS

Car bodies are designed for draining water that enters certain areas. The location of the drain holes are shown in Fig. 59-76. These drain holes must be clean to insure proper drainage. Each door has at least two drain holes. In some cases, the holes are covered by a sealing strip which prevents dust entry into the body. A drain hole is located in the rocker inner panel beneath the rear

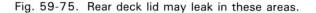

DOOR

QUARTER PANEL

Fig. 59-76. Drain holes prevent body from rusting. Make sure to keep holes open so that water can escape.

quarter window area, and another located behind the rear wheel housing panel. Deck lids have drain holes on either side to provide drainage for any moisture that may collect in the inner lid. Convertible models have a drain hole to the rear of each door. A short drain hose prevents the entrance of dust.

Chapter 59—REVIEW QUESTIONS

Write your answers on a separate sheet of paper. Do not write in this book.

1. When straightening a wrinkled panel, the damage should be removed:
   a. In same manner it was made.
   b. In reverse manner it was made.
2. If a dent rises above the surface of a dolly block, the hammer should strike:
   a. Center of dent.
   b. Edge of dent.
3. What is the purpose of a body file?
4. Describe what is meant by the term featheredging.
5. For what purpose is body filler used?
6. Describe the procedure for replacing a portion of a body panel.
7. What is the purpose of masking?
8. Describe the procedure for masking a head lamp.
9. The reason for chaining oxygen and acetylene tanks to a post is:
   a. To prevent theft.
   b. To prevent tipping over.
10. Before attaching a regulator to the oxygen and acetylene tanks, why should the valve first be opened for an instant?
11. The connections of acetylene tanks have:
    a. Right-hand threads
    b. Left-hand threads.
    c. Both a and b.
12. Oxygen hoses are:
    a. Red.
    b. White.
    c. Blue.
    d. Green.
13. If the flame at the torch is yellow or backfires, what should be done to correct the condition?
14. Before applying any paint, what should be done to the surface of the panel?
15. Why should primer coats be applied just after the paint has been removed.
16. Describe the procedure for taking care of a paint spray gun.
17. What is wrong if the spray pattern of a spray gun is heavy at the ends and light at the center?
18. How far should a spray gun be held from the surface of the work?
19. What is the material to use when repairing surface of a body painted with acrylic lacquer?
20. ABS plastic gives off little smoke. True or False?

Electrical Systems Technician for auto manufacturer uses a microprocessor to test operation of vehicle's electrical systems. (Ford Motor Co.)

Development Engineer runs a final emissions test on a 1.8 liter overhead cam, electronic fuel injected four cylinder engine (Pontiac Motor Div., General Motors Corp.)

"Quality Operators" get a full week of analytical troubleshooting training. Included is a complete tear-down and rebuilding of an engine to familiarize Production Employees with engine parts and functions. (Cadillac Motor Car Div., General Motors Corp.)

Chapter 60

CAREER OPPORTUNITIES IN THE AUTOMOTIVE FIELD

After studying this chapter, you will be able to:
- Identify careers directly involved with automotive service.
- Describe duties of various levels of Service Technicians.
- Explain why Specialty Service Technicians are necessary.
- Describe duties of supervisory and management level personnel in a car manufacturer's dealership.
- Name career opportunities in automotive service-related businesses.

The automotive field offers almost unlimited career opportunities. In the service area alone, typical job classifications include: Apprentice Auto Service Technician, Fig. 60-1; General Service Technician; Master Technician; Specialty Technician; Truck Service Technician; Auto Body and Paint Technician; Auto Service Advisor/Writer; Shop Supervisor; Service Manager; Service Training Instructor; Factory Service Representative; Vocational Teacher or Auto Technology Instructor, Fig. 60-2.

Consider, too, that Specialty Technicians are trained

Fig. 60-1. Apprentice Auto Service Technicians receive three or four years of well-rounded instruction and on-the-job experience. (FMC Corp.)

Fig. 60-2. Vocational Teachers not only teach auto technology, they also attend classes sponsored by parts and equipment manufacturers. This helps them keep current with latest technological advances and service procedures. (Deere & Co.)

in a specific phase of repair work. They spend full time servicing vehicles having problems in their area of expertise (expert skill or knowledge).

The National Institute for Automotive Service Excellence (ASE) recognizes the following service specialties: Engine Repair; Engine Performance; Automatic Transmission/Transaxle; Manual Drive Train and Axles; Electrical Systems; Heating and Air Conditioning; Brakes; Suspension and Steering.

A GROWING FIELD

With the ongoing and predicted advances being made by the car manufacturers' research and development engineers, service technicians are meeting new challenges each new model year. At the same time, the need is being created for new kinds of ''specialists'' in the areas of Electronic Engine Control, Carburetion and Fuel Injection, Emission Control, Front Wheel Drive/Four Wheel Drive, Automatic Temperature Control.

There is a shortage of trained auto service technicians, and the ever increasing complexity of modern vehicles only serves to worsen the shortage and heighten the need for ''specialists.''

To meet the need for trained service technicians, car manufacturers—both domestic (U.S.) and foreign—are expanding their training facilities. They are presenting their ''Opportunities in Automotive Service'' programs at high school and community college ''Career Days.'' They are assisting automotive programs at these schools by donating engines, transmissions, and other major assemblies for hands-on training.

Car manufacturers' dealers also are involved in cooperative vocational education programs in the automotive field. These programs combine classroom instruction with supervised, part-time employment planned to contribute to a student's overall education and employability.

The students' schedule, basically, is balanced between academic subjects required for graduation and employment in an automotive service establishment. The cooperative vocational education program is designed to bridge the gap between school and full-time employment in the automotive service industry.

THE JOB MARKET

Mechanically inclined students and recent graduates who have had some training in automotive service and repair work should consider these facts about motor vehicles and the nation's work force.

According to the Motor Vehicle Manufacturers Association of the United States, Inc.:

1. Nearly 162 million cars, trucks, and buses are registered in the United States.
2. About 585,000 automotive-related businesses are in operation in the U.S.
3. Over 12.4 million persons are employed in the manufacture, distribution, maintenance, and commercial use of motor vehicles. About one out of every six private, non-agriculture workers in the U.S. is employed in an automotive-related occupation. See Figs. 60-3 and 60-4.

Fig. 60-3. Suppliers of automotive parts and assemblies play a major role in overall success of wide-ranging automotive field. This Subassembler is carefully assembling a series of hydraulic control valves. (United Technologies Automotive Group)

Fig. 60-4. Engineering Technician for original equipment manufacturer assembles a breadboard microprocessor base circuit for an advanced anti-lock braking system. (Allied Automotive)

These facts and figures are a good indication of the tremendous breadth of the automotive field. With these facts in mind, those mechanically inclined job seekers may take a different view of the career opportunities available in this field.

JOB DESCRIPTIONS

The following brief job descriptions are designed to familiarize you with some of the many areas of opportunity that exist in the automotive industry. While the usual first step for the job seeker is to investigate the role of the trainee or apprentice, you should also view this first job opportunity as a stepping stone toward a higher position and greater earnings.

APPRENTICE SERVICE TECHNICIAN

Apprentice Auto Service Technicians divide their work time between the ''classroom'' and the shop, Fig. 60-1. They learn the trade by studying principles of operation in a structured apprenticeship training program, and by applying service techniques taught on the job by experienced technicians. During the three or four year training program, the apprentices are regularly tested and studies continue for the duration of the program.

During the course of apprenticeship training, the apprentices receive periodic raises in pay until they reach the journeyman status at the end of the program. Even as General Service Technicians, however, the study of new developments and latest servicing techniques goes on.

GENERAL SERVICE TECHNICIAN

A General Auto Service Technician's job assignments call for a broad range of both light and heavy repair, Fig. 60-5. General Technicians must know how to diagnose trouble and maintain all systems of automotive vehicles in good working order by applying recommended service procedures.

The technician's skill depends upon sound education in the principles of automotive service, on-the-job experience in service and repair, and constant upgrading of know-how to keep abreast of technological changes in the field. Small wonder, then, that good service technicians are well paid, and their work is always in demand.

With the current trend toward specialization in automotive service and repair, General Auto Service Technicians are becoming more involved with troubleshooting and diagnosis. They pinpoint the problem area through a study of symptoms and the results of road tests and various tests with diagnostic equipment. Once the problem area is established, a specialty technician takes over the service and repair assignment.

SPECIALTY SERVICE TECHNICIANS

Speciality Service Technicians, or Specialists, concentrate on a single phase of repair work. They choose a specialty they feel they are well qualified to perform. Then, they further improve efficiency and proficiency through daily involvement with jobs of a similar nature.

Examples of specialties from among the many areas that make up the ''general'' total are the following:

1. Front End Service Technicians who align and balance wheels, repair steering mechanisms and suspension systems. With the current trend toward compact front wheel drive vehicles, the Front End Technician has much more complicated techniques to master.
2. Brake Service Technicians troubleshoot and correct brake system problems. They service disc brakes, drum brakes, brake boosters or power brake units, parking brakes, and anti-skid systems. In many specialty shops, they turn (machine) drums and rotors on lathes designed for the purpose, Fig. 60-6.

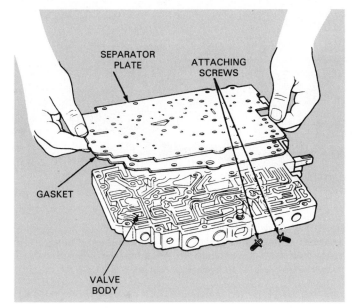

Fig. 60-5. A General Service Technician must be able to repair small, complex, precision fit parts. The valve body in an automatic transmission is just one example.   (Ford)

Fig. 60-6. Specialty Service Technicians master a specific area of automotive service work and devote full time to performing their specialty. This specialist is servicing a brake caliper.   (Star Machine & Tool Co.)

3. Auto Electrical Technicians analyze problems with starting, charging, ignition, and lighting systems. They perform tests on electrical components and circuits, and make necessary repairs or unit replacements. Auto Electrical Technicians trained and qualified to do so, diagnose engine electronic control systems problems by means of on-board computers or sophisticated test equipment.

4. Auto Radiator Service Technicians clean radiators in special tanks filled with caustic solutions. They locate leaks and make repairs. They install new radiator cores, heater cores, A/C condensers, A/C evaporators, automatic transmission oil coolers and, in some specialty shops, they repair or replace fuel tanks and replace glass.

5. Air Conditioning Service Technicians install and service automotive A/C systems. They troubleshoot cooling problems and make necessary repairs that usually require evacuation of the refrigerant and recharging and retesting after the repair is made. Automatic temperature control systems require the services of trained specialists in shops having special instrumentation to test the electronic controls involved.

6. Automatic Transmission Service Technicians, Fig. 60-7, diagnose problems of slippage, shifting, and noise. They road test the vehicle, make on-car inspections, oil pressure tests, air pressure tests, and a stall test before removing the transmission, if necessary, for major internal repairs. On-car repairs involve shift linkage adjustments, band adjustments, fluid changes, seal replacement, control valve body cleaning and parts replacements.

TRUCK SERVICE TECHNICIAN

A Truck Service Technician needs service know-how, plus special skills and strength to handle heavy parts and assemblies, both manually and with the aid of various heavy duty jacks, cranes or chain hoists, wheel dollies, and hydraulic presses. While tolerances, in general, are greater and "fits" are less critical, service techniques remain basically the same as passenger car work. However, some areas require special training such as double reduction axles, full floating axles, air brakes, etc.

In establishing Certification Tests for Master Heavy-Duty Truck Technician, the National Institute for Automotive Service Excellence breaks down the truck service specialities into Gasoline Engines, Diesel Engines, Drive Train, Brakes, Suspension and Steering, and Electrical Systems.

MASTER SERVICE TECHNICIAN

The Master Technician inherits the particularly troublesome service assignments—repeat comebacks, unusual symptoms, mysterious noises, etc. See Fig. 60-8. The Master Technician also: helps get work back on schedule by filling in for absent technicians; authorizes repairs when unexpected defects are found; oversees the apprenticeship training program; and generally represents the dealership at the car manufacturer's service school.

Fig. 60-8. This Master Service Technician is using a special troubleshooting chart coded to built-in diagnostic plug to find cause and cure for problem in computerized engine control system. (Pontiac Motor Div., General Motors Corp.)

Fig. 60-7. This automatic transmission specialist positions a jack especially designed to lower and raise an automatic transmission from the car.

AUTO BODY AND PAINT TECHNICIANS

Body and Paint Technicians perform auto body and chassis repair and realignment, along with carefully controlled refinishing procedures. In the process, they operate various setups of pulling and straightening equipment and install replacement panels and structural parts. Their collision repair work and paint spraying requires separate facilities. New equipment operation must be mastered. Latest repair and refinishing techniques must be learned and applied. See Fig. 60-9.

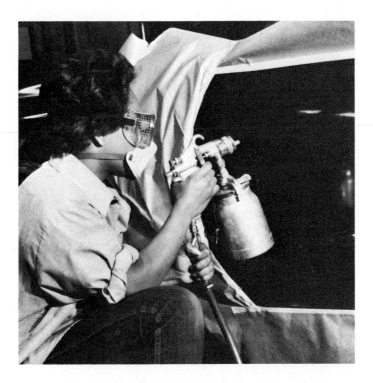

Fig. 60-9. Auto Body and Paint Technicians are also specialists, often to a point of specializing either in body repair or paint spraying. This particular technician specializes in refinishing only.

AUTO SERVICE ADVISOR/WRITER

The Service Writer greets customers and writes repair orders based on symptoms described by the car owner, Fig. 60-10. The repair orders must clearly and concisely state the problems and possible solutions. Service Writers generally have a background in troubleshooting and diagnosis. They also must be familiar with the content of current factory service bulletins covering complaints from the field.

SHOP SUPERVISOR

The Shop Supervisor is directly in charge of the Service Technicians: directing, routing, and scheduling service and repair work. The Supervisor helps hire, transfer, promote, and discharge technicians to meet the needs of the service department. The Supervisor also instructs and oversees the technicians in their work procedures, inspects finished repairs, and is responsible for quality service and satisfactory shop operation.

DRIVEABILITY QUESTIONNAIRE

Please complete the form as **accurately** as possible to provide our technicians with the best opportunity to **FIX-IT-RIGHT**. Check the areas that correspond with your particular problem. Blanks have been provided in specific areas for your use, if additional comments are required.

Customer Name ________ Vehicle Year and Type ________

MAJOR SYMPTOM

- Hard Starting*
- Starts and Dies
- Idle Rough*
- Idle Speed too High
- Idle Speed too Lo
- Dies at Idle*
- Poor … Had Problem
- … ew
- … roblem Began After Vehicle Accumulated ______ Miles

- Surge*
- … Driven 2 Mi…
- After Driven 10 Miles o…
- Wet Weather, Rain/Snow
- Damp Weather, Fog
- On Acceleration
- On Deceleration
- At Constant Speeds
- During Braking
- While Turning Corners

- Engine … ccessories
- F…

Fuel Tank Level During Occurrence:

- ¼ or Less
- ½
- ¾ or More
- All Levels

CUSTOMER DRIVING HABITS

DO YOU?

- Start Cold Engine and Drive Immediately
- Start Cold Engine Allow Warm-Up Period
- Use Mainly on Highways
- Use Mainly within City

Average Distance of Miles Driven Daily: ________

FUEL USED?

- No Lead, Regular
- No Lead, Premium
- Regular Leaded
- Blends of Gasohol

Brand of Fuel Used: ________

* Defined on reverse side

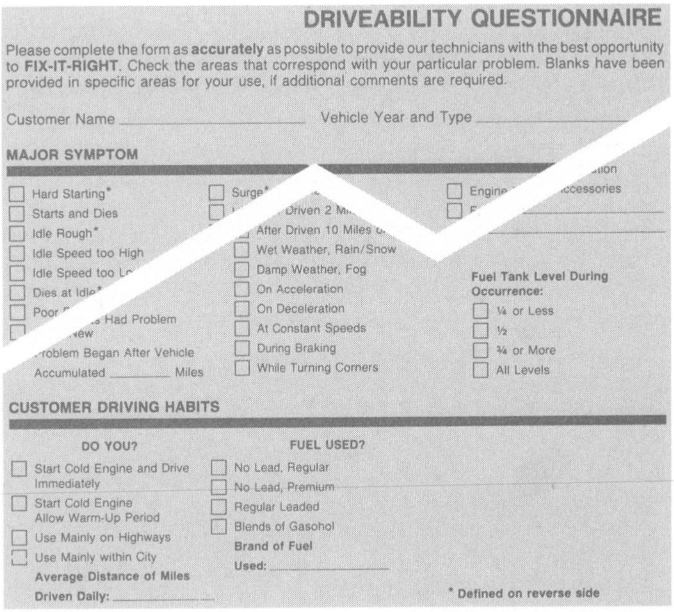

Fig. 60-10. A GOOD service advisor uses a check sheet like this when questioning a customer about performance problems. This eliminates or reduces diagnostic time for the technician that works on the car.

SERVICE MANAGER

The Service Manager is the department head in charge of planning, supervising, and coordinating the activities of all shop employees. Primarily responsible for hiring, transferring, promoting, and discharging workers, the Service Manager oversees scheduling of appointments for service and repair work, training of apprentices, and familiarizing technicians with new service procedures. The Service Manager also reviews records of operation to plan cost control measures, improve shop practices, and raise work standards. Other duties include investigation of complaints, assignment of responsibility for service errors, and adjustments of bills or charges. In addition, the Service Manager must try to build business for the service department with advertising and sales promotion activities.

MOTOR VEHICLE SALESPERSON

Motor Vehicle Sales is the job for you if you enjoy selling. Experience in the service department will give you an excellent background for sales work. If you know the mechanics of a vehicle, you can do a much better job of explaining the mechanical and electronic features of a car or truck to a potential customer, then demonstrating it and comparing the vehicle with competing makes.

SALES MANAGER

A Sales Manager has charge of the entire selling activity of the dealership. This is one of the top positions in the retail automotive field. It usually is held by someone who has made a success of selling over a period of years and one who has managerial ability. The

Sales Manager must spearhead the sales and service operations, and therefore must work closely with the owners, Service Manager, Parts Manager, and Shop Supervisor.

PARTS MANAGER

The Parts Manager for a car or truck dealership has an important job of ordering, stocking, and selling replace-

Fig. 60-11. Parts Manager keeps Service Technicians supplied with correct replacement parts and assemblies. Other service outlets and do-it-yourselfers are also served by Parts Department. (Federal-Mogul Corp.)

ment parts and accessories. The Parts Manager supplies the dealership shop needs and sells parts and accessories at wholesale to independent garages, service stations, and specialty shops in the community. Training in service work and a vast knowledge of part numbers and part locations are necessary. Also required is the ability to maintain an adequate stock—yet not an overstock—of parts. See Fig. 60-11.

JOBBER SALESPERSON

Jobber Sales is a job in the parts and accessories field that should appeal to a sales-minded young person with some automotive service training. A Jobber Salesperson, representing a wholesale parts house, travels over a certain territory selling the products of several manufacturers to automotive repair and supply shops.

Closely related is the Counter Sales Specialist who not only sells replacement parts and accessories over the jobber's counter, but also offers installation advice to do-it-yourselfers.

CAR MANUFACTURERS REPRESENTATIVES

Employment with car manufacturers often attracts individuals with Service Technician's training and other customer relations-oriented qualifications. Positions include: Factory District Manager; Factory Supervisor, Fig. 60-12; Factory Service Representative; Factory Parts Manager; Factory Service Instructor; and Research Laboratory Technician.

CAR FACTORY/SUPPLIER EMPLOYEES

Employees in car manufacturers' factories or with original equipment suppliers also make good use of training in jobs such as: Subassembly; Final Assembly, Fig.

Fig. 60-12. Supervisor for auto manufacturer conducts Employee Involvement Session to discuss job-related problems and how to solve them. (Ford Motor Co.)

Fig. 60-13. Final Assembly Worker in car manufacturer's engine plant loads 1.8 liter four cylinder engine on "line" in preparation for 100 percent "loaded" hot test. (Pontiac Motor Div., General Motors Corp.)

Fig. 60-14. Quality Control Technicians study results of final tests of electronic engine control systems. Assembly line computer is attached to diagnostic connector inside car to obtain printout of system operation. (Pontiac Motor Div., General Motors Corp.)

60-13; Assembly Quality Control, Fig. 60-14; Dynamometer Testing, Experimental Driver; Driver Technician; Engineering Garage Technician.

VOCATIONAL TEACHER OR AUTO TECHNOLOGY INSTRUCTOR

Teaching is an interesting and rewarding career. If you obtain experience in automotive service work, have a good knowledge of automotive construction and principles of operation, and have teaching ability, you may qualify for one of many careers in this field. You might be employed by a car manufacturer or parts/equipment supplier to train service personnel in new technological advances. Or, you might want to teach automotive service classes in a public school, trade school, or a private vocational school. See Fig. 60-2. Still another teaching opportunity presents itself with replacement parts manufacturers, conducting service clinics or symposiums.

TRUCK AND BUS DRIVERS

Truck and Bus Drivers are part of a workforce of nine million men and women employed in the trucking industry. Many operators of large fleets of trucks or buses prefer that their drivers have automotive service training. Drivers so qualified take better care of their vehicles and can make repairs in certain emergency situations.

INSURANCE ADJUSTER AND CLAIM EXAMINER

Insurance Adjuster and Claim Examiner are jobs that insurance companies like to fill with young people who, in addition to other academic qualifications, have automotive service training. Knowledge of auto body work, refinishing, and replacement parts pricing is vital.

REPRESENTATIVES

Sales and Service Representatives work for companies that supply parts and/or equipment to the automotive industry. They frequently are aggressive, high-caliber people who began their careers in automotive service stations, independent shops, or department store automotive facilities.

OWNERS OF SERVICE STATIONS OR SPECIALTY REPAIR SHOPS

Owners and lessees of service stations usually got their start in the business as Pump Attendant or Technician's Helper in the station service bays. Owners and Franchisees of Specialty Repair Shops (muffler shops, tire dealerships, fast oil change and lube chains, brake service centers, transmission service outlets, etc.) probably learned the business from the "bottom up."

AUTOMOTIVE DEALERS

Automotive Dealers who operate their own business— and frequently are leaders in their communities—often started out as employees of the dealership.

AUTOMOTIVE CAREERS

From these job descriptions, you can see that training in the automotive service field could be your key to any one of a number of interesting and rewarding careers. You can see that automotive service is a big, broad, opportunity-filled field of endeavor.

Today, many dedicated young men and young women are entering the automotive field to face the challenge of change. The catchword is "electronics" and those who can meet and keep up with the challenge will be tomorrow's well-respected Master Electronics Technicians. It is an established fact that, in 1976, Cadillac cars had one electronic function — fuel injection. Today, Cadillac cars have 40 or more electronic functions.

ENTREPRENEURSHIP

An ENTREPRENEUR is one who undertakes ownership of a business or enterprise. ENTREPRENEURSHIP is that person's ability to organize, manage, and assume the risks of operating the business.

Owning your own business is the goal of some auto technicians. This requires a certain type of person. Not everyone is suited to owning a business. Besides your technical skills, business skills and schooling are needed. As an owner, you must have good public relation skills and be a leader at work as well as in the community. Most of all, you must be fair and honest with your customers and employees. At times this can be a real juggling act and can be a cause of great stress and pressure. There are disadvantages and advantages of having your own business.

DISADVANTAGES

There are more disadvantages of having your own business than advantages. First, about 80 to 85 percent of small business firms fail in the first year. If you make it past the first year, you may spend from 16 to 20 hours a day at work. You will have to work weekends to do all of the required paper work. You will not be able to take time off for a vacation for two to three years after starting the business. Most important, you must find good people that can be trusted to work for your firm.

ADVANTAGES

The most common reason people want to own a business is to be their own boss. The only person you will have to answer to is the customer. The financial return is another reason some start their own business. Some entrepreneurs have become millionaires overnight. However, most of the time it can take from three to four years before showing a profit.

Once the business is established, you can set your own hours. On the other hand, if you spend too much time away from the business, it more than likely will fail unless you have a good manager that can be trusted.

SUCCESS

A good owner has to have many qualities. You must be aggressive and take the initiative. This is the sign of a leader. You must set good examples for your employees by being on time, dependable, fair, honest, and responsible. You must be able to get along with people.

Communication is another essential element of business management. You must be able to instruct your employees. They must be comfortable with you so that they will ask questions when they do not know the answer, Fig. 60-15.

You must set high goals for yourself and the business, then see them through. You must be a good manager so that your expenses do not exceed your income. You must be innovative or creative as to how you will meet the competition. Sounds hard, but it is rewarding when things go right.

Fig. 60-15. An entrepreneur must be able to teach as well as manage the business.

TYPES OF OWNERSHIP

There are several types of ownership possible. You may own the business entirely yourself. This is called a SOLE PROPRIETORSHIP. It means you assume all the profits as well as the losses.

A PARTNERSHIP is another form of ownership. At least two people are jointly responsible for the profits and losses. However, one person may own a greater percentage of the business than the other. There may even be a silent partner. A silent partner supplies the needed funds and receives his or her share of the profits without being involved in the day-to-day operation of the business.

The business may also be turned into a CORPORATION, which is a business association endowed by law with the rights and liabilities of an individual. There are certain advantages and disadvantages of turning a business into a corporation. The primary advantage is that if the business is sued, none of the stockholders can be sued. A stockholder "buys" a small percentage of the business, hoping that the value of the stock will increase over the original purchase price. Most of the time the person who operates the business has controlling interest — at least 51 percent of the available stock.

The disadvantage of incorporation is that there are government regulations that must be met and a charter created that is approved by the state. Any changes must be approved by the state. A charter must be drawn up or amended by a lawyer.

THE THREE A's

There are many expenses involved in running a business. Attorneys, accountants, and advertising are three big expenses in addition to paying rent for the building.

Attorneys are needed to draw up legal documents, read contracts before you sign, and represent you in the event of any legal conflicts.

Accountants are needed to keep your books and prepare your taxes. There are so many tax laws that it is not possible for the average person to know all of them and run a business.

Advertising is a must. Without advertising, people will not know you are in business. Also, they will not know your prices and services to compare to the competition. All of this takes money.

LOANS

There are many ways to secure money to meet your expenses. Banks and credit unions may loan you money. However, they may ask for collateral or that you sign over material items to them in the event you default or go out of business.

Certain types of life insurance policies let you borrow against the amount of money that you have paid in over the years, at interest rates lower than that of a bank or credit union. In the event you should die before repaying the loan, the amount borrowed is deducted from the agreed amount that the beneficiary is to receive.

Another way to secure the needed funds is to borrow the money from a friend or family member. However, this may cause a great amount of strain on the relationship if the business should fail and you are not able to repay the loan.

Some people who cannot obtain a loan by the ordinary means go to a person who is referred to as a "loan shark." A loan shark will loan just about anybody money. However, the interest rates are higher than those allowed by the law. This person should be avoided at all costs.

Chapter 61

OWNER'S/SERVICE MANUALS

After studying this chapter, you will be able to:
- List what type of information can be found in the owner's manual.
- Explain what type of information can be found in a service/repair manual.
- Determine the difference between a service and repair manual.
- Demonstrate how to use a flat rate manual.

OWNER'S MANUAL

The owner's manual is normally kept in the glove box of the car. It contains *nontechnical* information for the proper operation of the car. It also contains data on when maintenance items should be checked, Fig. 61-1. Also, the *specifications on the various fluids* that are to be used are described. Other items covered include:

1. How to start the engine under different conditions. Starting a car with electronic fuel injection (EFI) is different than a carbureted engine. Also, starting a flooded engine needs a different procedure than starting it if it were not flooded.
2. Towing. The maximum weight limit that a specific car can tow behind it, like a trailer, camper, etc. Also, any related service procedures are discussed. Also,

information on how the car should be towed, if it is disabled. A short or long distance means different procedures.
3. Components, gauges, and accessories. This includes what each of the dash gauges are for and where located. Also, how to set the radio, clock, cruise control, air conditioning, and other accessories are discussed.
4. Service assistance. If you are having problems in getting your car repaired, most car makers have a zone office in every major city in the U.S. The telephone and addresses for these offices are listed in the back of the owner's manual. Make sure that you have the following information when calling:
   a. Vehicle Identification Number (VIN). This is located on the car, Fig. 61-2, and the warranty papers, which should be in the glove box.
   b. In-service date (when the car was bought). This is entered on the warranty papers.
   c. Current mileage.
   d. Keep a copy of all warranty repair orders, after the work has been done. If there is a recurring problem and the car goes out of warranty, the car maker will more than likely take care of the problem, at no expense to you, if it is documented

EMISSION CONTROL SYSTEM MAINTENANCE	SERVICE INTERVALS		MILEAGE IN THOUSANDS	7.5	15	22.5	30	37.5	45
			KILOMETERS IN THOUSANDS	12	24	36	48	60	72
ENGINE OIL CHANGE EVERY 12 MONTHS		OR		X	X	X	X	X	X
ENGINE OIL FILTER-REPLACE AT EVERY SECOND OIL CHANGE (1)		OR			X		X		X
REPLACE CARBURETOR AIR FILTER (225 cu. in. California Engine, or 225 cu. in. Engine equipped with O^2 Feedback carburetor)		AT					X		
APPLY SOLVENT AND CHECK FOR FREEDOM OF OPERATION OF CHOKE SHAFT FAST IDLE CAM, AND PIVOT PIN EVERY 12 MONTHS		OR					X		
REPLACE SPARK PLUGS (WITH CAT. CONVERTER)		AT					X		
REPLACE SPARK PLUGS (WITHOUT CAT. CONVERTER)		AT			X		X		X
INSPECT AND ADJUST TENSION ON DRIVE BELTS; REPLACE AS NECESSARY		AT			X(2)		X		X(2)

Fig. 61-1. Inspection and/or replacement of maintenance items at prescribed intervals can be found in the owner's manual. (Chrysler)

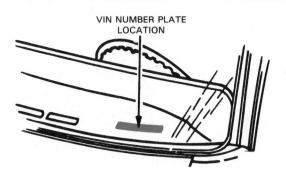

Fig. 61-2. The VIN has 17 digits and is located at the upper left-hand corner of the dash. It can be seen through the windshield. (Cadillac)

with the warranty repair order. Also, if the problem is intermittent, make sure to have this documented. If the problem manifests after the warranty expires and it is documented, the car maker may take care of the problem, at no cost to you.

CONSUMER LAWS

Most owner's manuals do not discuss "lemon laws." However, some states today have such laws. A lemon law means that the car is a certified "lemon" if:

1. Four attempts have been made to correct a problem and it still exists; or
2. Car is in the dealership for more than 30 consecutive days having repairs made or waiting for parts.

If the consumer proves these points and the complaint is valid, the state can order the factory and/or the dealer to repurchase the car from the owner, at no cost to the owner. However, this law applies only to new cars. As long as the problem occurs while the car is under warranty, the car is eligible for the lemon law. Contact the state's attorney for details. In Texas, contact the Texas Motor Vehicle Commission (TMVC) in Austin.

SERVICE/REPAIR MANUALS

These manuals contain very specific *technical* information. It is needed by the technician to make the proper repairs. A service manual is published by the car maker for every different model every year.

A repair manual is published by a company other than that of the car maker. It contains a limited amount of technical information. It covers most all domestic models for a seven year period. However, some are more detailed, as they contain data on all domestic models for one model year only.

Service manuals contain very detailed step-by-step procedures for disassembly, inspection, repair, and reassembly of the many parts of the car. Also, troubleshooting procedures, Fig. 61-3, and specifications, Fig. 61-4, are included. New car dealerships use service manuals.

Independent repair shops use repair manuals because of the wide variety of cars they service. However, most independent repair shops do not have the needed test equipment for all makes of cars, so service is limited.

TABLE OF CONTENTS

GENERAL INFORMATION		**0.**
OA.	**General Information**	
OB.	**Maintenance and Lubrication**	
CLIMATE CONTROL		**1.**
1C.	**Electronic Climate Control**	
1D1.	**R-4 Compressor**	
BODY, FRAME, AND BUMPERS		**2.**
2A.	**Frame and Body Mounts**	
2B.	**Bumpers**	
2C.	**Chassis Sheet Metal**	
STEERING, SUSPENSION WHEELS AND TIRES		**3.**
3.	**Diagnosis**	
3A.	**Wheel Alignment**	
3B5.	**Steering Wheels and Colums**	
3B6.	**Steering Linkage**	
3B7.	**Power Steering Gear and Pump**	
3C.	**Front Suspension**	
3D.	**Rear Suspension**	
3E.	**Wheels and Tires**	
DRIVE AXLE AND SHAFT		**4.**
4A.	**Propeller Shaft**	
4B.	**Rear Axle**	
BRAKES		**5.**
5.	**Brakes**	
5A3.	**Master Cylinder**	
5B1.	**Disc Brakes**	
5C1.	**Drum Brakes**	
5D2.	**Power Booster**	
5F.	**Specifications**	
ENGINE - 5.0L V-8 VIN Y		**6.**
6.	**Diagnosis**	
6A.	**Mechanical**	
6B.	**Cooling**	
6C.	**Fuel System**	
6C1.	**Carburetor**	
6D.	**Electrical**	
6E.	**Driveability and Emissions**	
6F.	**Exhaust**	
TRANSMISSION		**7.**
7A.	**General Information**	
7A2.	**On Car Service**	
HDS.	**Hydraulic Diagnosis**	
200-4R	**Transmission**	
ELECTRICAL		**8.**
8A.	**Electrical Diagnosis**	
8B.	**Chassis Electrical**	
8C.	**Instrument Panel and Gages**	
8E.	**Windshield Wiper/Washers**	
ACCESSORIES		**9.**
9A.	**Radio and Antenna**	
9B.	**Cruise Control**	
9C.	**Dimming/Twilight Sentinel and Automatic Day/Night Mirror**	
9D.	**Theft Deterrent and Garage Door Opener**	
INDEX		**11.**

Fig. 61-3A. Service manuals can be used for troubleshooting. Trouble codes for this car are found in Chapter 6, section E under Driveability and Emissions. (Cadillac)

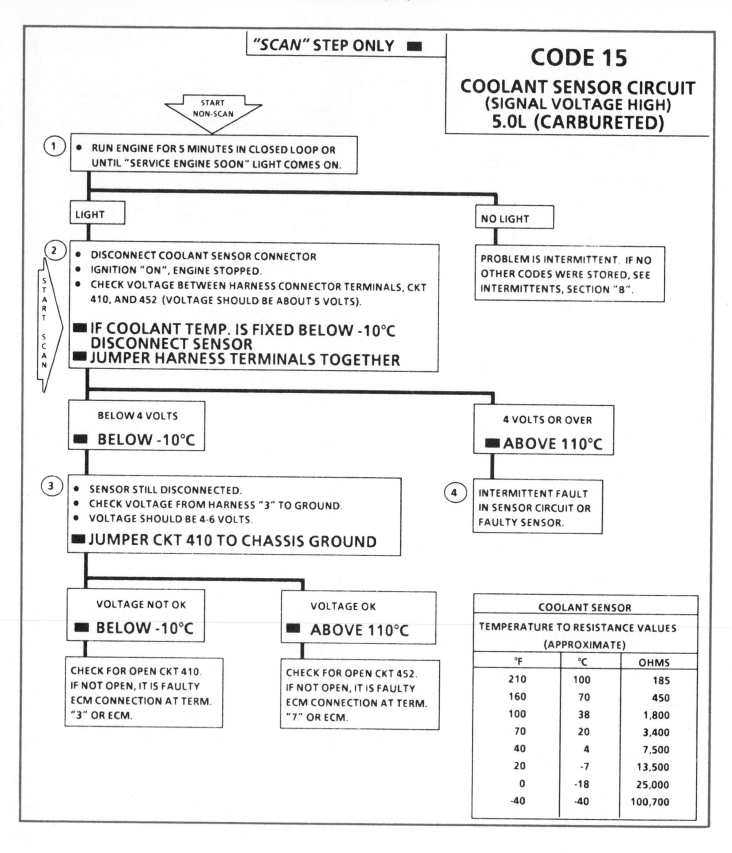

"SCAN" STEP ONLY ■

CODE 15
COOLANT SENSOR CIRCUIT
(SIGNAL VOLTAGE HIGH)
5.0L (CARBURETED)

START NON-SCAN

1
- RUN ENGINE FOR 5 MINUTES IN CLOSED LOOP OR UNTIL "SERVICE ENGINE SOON" LIGHT COMES ON.

LIGHT

NO LIGHT

2
- DISCONNECT COOLANT SENSOR CONNECTOR
- IGNITION "ON", ENGINE STOPPED.
- CHECK VOLTAGE BETWEEN HARNESS CONNECTOR TERMINALS, CKT 410, AND 452 (VOLTAGE SHOULD BE ABOUT 5 VOLTS).

■ IF COOLANT TEMP. IS FIXED BELOW -10°C DISCONNECT SENSOR
■ JUMPER HARNESS TERMINALS TOGETHER

PROBLEM IS INTERMITTENT. IF NO OTHER CODES WERE STORED, SEE INTERMITTENTS, SECTION "B".

START SCAN

BELOW 4 VOLTS

■ BELOW -10°C

4 VOLTS OR OVER

■ ABOVE 110°C

3
- SENSOR STILL DISCONNECTED.
- CHECK VOLTAGE FROM HARNESS "3" TO GROUND.
- VOLTAGE SHOULD BE 4-6 VOLTS.

■ JUMPER CKT 410 TO CHASSIS GROUND

4
INTERMITTENT FAULT IN SENSOR CIRCUIT OR FAULTY SENSOR.

VOLTAGE NOT OK

■ BELOW -10°C

VOLTAGE OK

■ ABOVE 110°C

CHECK FOR OPEN CKT 410. IF NOT OPEN, IT IS FAULTY ECM CONNECTION AT TERM. "3" OR ECM.

CHECK FOR OPEN CKT 452. IF NOT OPEN, IT IS FAULTY ECM CONNECTION AT TERM. "7" OR ECM.

COOLANT SENSOR		
TEMPERATURE TO RESISTANCE VALUES (APPROXIMATE)		
°F	°C	OHMS
210	100	185
160	70	450
100	38	1,800
70	20	3,400
40	4	7,500
20	-7	13,500
0	-18	25,000
-40	-40	100,700

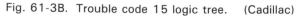

Fig. 61-3B. Trouble code 15 logic tree. (Cadillac)

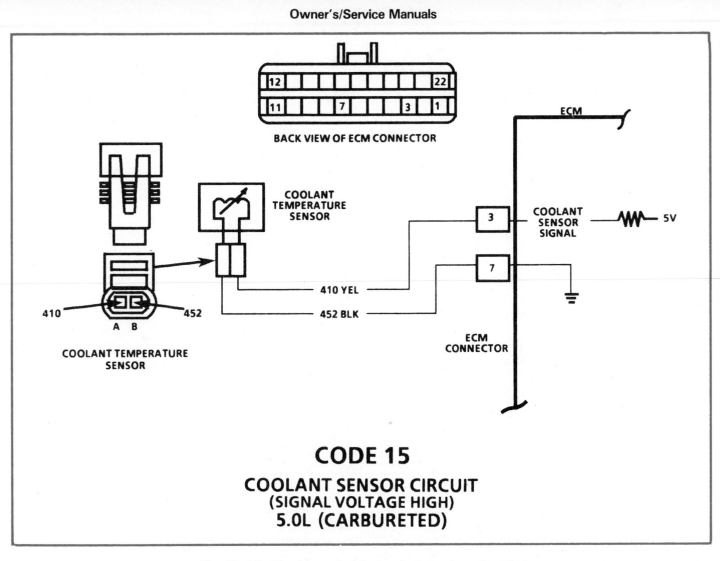

CODE 15
COOLANT SENSOR CIRCUIT
(SIGNAL VOLTAGE HIGH)
5.0L (CARBURETED)

Fig. 61-3C. Trouble code 15 electrical circuit. (Cadillac)

To make sure that you have the correct service manual for the year of the car that you are working on, check the VIN. The VIN is a 17-digit number that is coded. It contains the year of the car, Fig. 61-5, as well as the model and other data.

TECHNICAL SERVICE BULLETINS (TSB)

TSBs are another source of technical information for the technician. The TSB makes it easy for the technician to diagnose certain problems. It contains symptoms of a problem, and outlines the needed fix. The TSBs are distributed to new car dealership technicians by the factory. This is because most TSBs cover only new car models. However, the TSB can be requested by *anybody* through the local zone office of the car maker. At the end of each new car model year, all TSBs are compiled into book form and are available for purchase.

FLAT RATE MANUAL

A flat rate manual is used to determine how much to charge the customer for the needed repairs. For example, the flat rate manual may list that a tune-up will take 1.8 hrs. on a 1988 Dodge V-6 engine. The 1.8 is multiplied by the hourly rate charged by the shop. If this rate is $40.00/hr., then the labor for the tune-up would cost $72.00. The cost for parts has to be added to the labor. This amount of time is charged whether the technician takes one hour or three hours to complete the job.

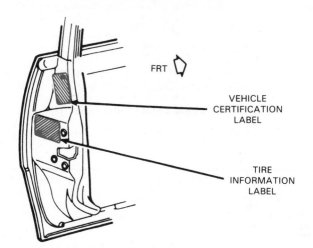

Fig. 61-4A. Specifications can be found in service manual. Service manual shows location of decal is on driver's door. (Cadillac)

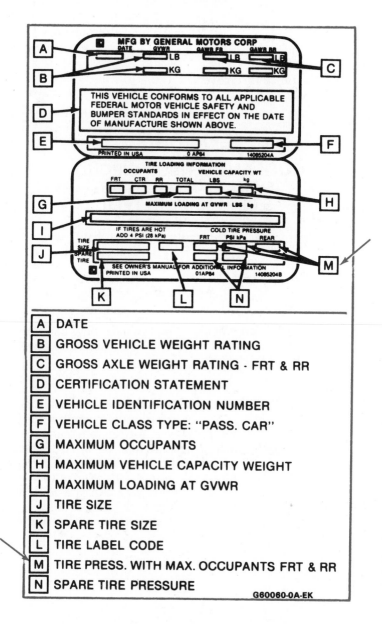

A	DATE
B	GROSS VEHICLE WEIGHT RATING
C	GROSS AXLE WEIGHT RATING - FRT & RR
D	CERTIFICATION STATEMENT
E	VEHICLE IDENTIFICATION NUMBER
F	VEHICLE CLASS TYPE: "PASS. CAR"
G	MAXIMUM OCCUPANTS
H	MAXIMUM VEHICLE CAPACITY WEIGHT
I	MAXIMUM LOADING AT GVWR
J	TIRE SIZE
K	SPARE TIRE SIZE
L	TIRE LABEL CODE
M	TIRE PRESS. WITH MAX. OCCUPANTS FRT & RR
N	SPARE TIRE PRESSURE

G60060-0A-EK

Fig. 61-4B. Decal has recommended tire pressure. (Cadillac)

Cylinder Block

Bore Diameter	96.5 mm (3.800")
Bore Out-of-Round-Max.	.0381 mm (.0015")
Bore Taper-Max.	.0381 mm (.0015")
Runout-Rear Face of Block to Crankshaft Centerline	.203 mm (.008")

Piston

Clearance in Bore	.019 - .044 mm (.00075" - .00175")
Piston Diameter (Nominal Outside)	96.5 mm (3.800")
Weight Less Pin & Rings (All)	(596g + 2g)
Skirt Taper (Larger at Bottom)	.076 - .0431 mm (.003" - .0017")
Piston Pin Offset to Thrust Side	1.397 - 1.657 mm (.055" - .065")
Ring Grove Width-Both compression	2.052 - 2.029 mm (.0808" - .0798")
Ring Grove Width-Oil	4.803 - 4.777 mm (.1891" - .1881")

Piston Rings

Compression Ring Width (2)	1.9812 - 1.9558 mm (.0780" - .0770")
Compression Ring Gap Both	.2286 - .4826 mm (.009" - .019")
Compression Ring Side Clearance in Grove	.0457 - .0965 (.0018" - .0038")
Oil Ring Width	.5969 - .640 mm (.0235" - .0252")
Oil Ring Gap	.381 - 1.397 mm (.015" - .055")
Oil Ring Side Clearance in Grove	.03 - .13 mm (.001" - .005")

Piston Pin

Diameter	24.90 - 24.906 mm (.98035" - .98055")
Pin Clearance, Check @ 21°C (70°F)	
Pin to Piston	.0076 - .0127 mm (.0003" - .0005")
Pin to Rod	.0038 - .024 mm (.00015" - .00095")

Crankshaft and Connecting Rod

Main Bearing Journal	
Diameter	
(2, 3, 4 & 5)	63.4619 - 63.4873 mm - (2.4985" - 2.4995")
(1)	63.4695 - 63.4949 mm (2.4988" - 2.4998")
Width – Main, Thrust Bearing Journal (No. 3)	
Including Fillets	30.441 - 30.518 mm (1.1985 - 1.2015")
Out-of-Round-Max.	.013 mm (.0005")

Fig. 61-4C. Specifications for engine rebuilding are at the end of Chapter 6 of this specific service manual. (Cadillac)

VEHICLE IDENTIFICATION NUMBER

Each 1987 Cadillac carries a 17 digit Vehicle Identification Number used for license and insurance identification and in general reference to the automobile. The number is located on a plate riveted to the windshield lower frame at the driver's side of the car where it is visible through the windshield. The 1987 Cadillac Vehicle Identification is decoded as follows:

1 G 6 CD 5 1 8 X H 4 200001

NATION OF ORIGIN — 1 = USA

MANUFACTURER — G = GENERAL MOTORS

MAKE
6 = CADILLAC

CARLINE/SERIES
CB = FLEETWOOD D'ELEGANCE
CD = DEVILLE
CH = LIMOUSINE
CS = FLEETWOOD SIXTY SPECIAL
DW = BROUGHAM
EL = ELDORADO
JG = CIMARRON
KS = SEVILLE
VR = ALLANTE

VIN BODY CODE = BODY TYPE
1 = 47 — COUPE 2 DOOR NOTCHBACK
1 = 57 — COUPE 2 DOOR NOTCHBACK
3 = 67 — COUPE 2 DOOR CONVERTIBLE
5 = 19 — SEDAN 4 DOOR
            6 WINDOW NOTCHBACK
5 = 23 — SEDAN 4 DOOR LIMOUSINE
5 = 33 — SEDAN 4 DOOR LIMOUSINE
            WITH CENTER PARTITION
5 = 69 — SEDAN 4 DOOR NOTCHBACK

PRODUCTION SEQUENCE NUMBER
100001 — ALLANTE
200001 — DEVILLE
500001 — CIMARRON
600001 — ELDORADO
700001 — BROUGHAM
800001 — SEVILLE

ASSEMBLY PLANT
4 = LAKE ORION, MICHIGAN
9 = DETROIT, MICHIGAN
J = JANESVILLE, WISCONSIN
U = HAMTRAMCK, MICHIGAN

MODEL YEAR — H = 1987

CHECK DIGIT

ENGINE CODE — SEE BELOW

RESTRAINT SYSTEM
1 = MANUAL BELTS

FWD-C COMMERCIAL BODY/CHASSIS
VIN IS AS FOLLOWS:
IGEDZ908XH4200001

A

B

Fig. 61-5. Interpreting the digits of the VIN. A—The position of the ''H'' indicates a 1987 car model. B—This information is found in the service manual.   (Cadillac)

APPENDIX

CONVERSION TABLES

LINEAR:

Millimeters	×	.0394	=	Inches
Inches	×	25.400	=	Millimeters
Centimeters	×	.394	=	Inches
Inches	×	2.54	=	Centimeters
Meters	×	3.2809	=	Feet
Feet	×	.3048	=	Meters
Kilometers	×	.6214	=	Miles
Miles	×	1.6093	=	Kilometers

AREA:

Square centimeters	×	.1550	=	Square inches
Square inches	×	6.4515	=	Square centimeters
Square meters	×	10.7641	=	Square feet
Square feet	×	.0929	=	Square meters
Square kilometers	×	247.1098	=	Acres
Acres	×	.0041	=	Square kilometers
Hectares	×	2.471	=	Acres
Acres	×	.4047	=	Hectares

VOLUME:

Cubic centimeters	×	.0610	=	Cubic inches
Cubic inches	×	16.3866	=	Cubic centimeters
Cubic meters	×	35.3156	=	Cubic feet
Cubic feet	×	.0283	=	Cubic meters
Quarts	×	0.9465	=	Liters
Liters	×	1.0565	=	Quarts
Liters	×	61.023	=	Cubic inches
Cubic inches	×	.0164	=	Liters
Liters	×	.2652	=	U.S. Gallons
U.S. Gallons	×	3.7854	=	Liters

MASS:

Grams	×	15.4324	=	Grains
Grains	×	.0648	=	Grams
Grams	×	.0353	=	Ounces, avoirdupois
Ounces, avoirdupois	×	28.3495	=	Grams
Kilograms	×	2.2046	=	Pounds
Pounds	×	.4536	=	Kilograms
Metric tons (1 000 kilograms)	×	1.1023	=	Tons (2000 pounds)
Tons (2000 pounds)	×	.9072	=	Metric tons

Continued.

PRESSURE:				
Kilopascals	×	.145	=	Pounds per square inch
Pounds per square inch	×	6.895	=	Kilopascals

TORQUE:				
Newton-meters	×	.7376	=	Pound feet
Pound feet	×	1.3558	=	Newton-meters
Pound-inch	×	0.11298	=	Newton-meters

POWER:				
Kilowatts	×	1.3405	=	Horsepower
Horsepower	×	.746	=	Kilowatts

FORCE:				
Pounds	×	4.45	=	Newtons
Newtons	×	.225	=	Pounds
Kilograms	×	9.8	=	Newtons
Newtons	×	.102	=	Kilograms

VELOCITY:				
Mph	×	1.6093	=	Km/h
Km/h	×	.621	=	Mph

TEMPERATURE:				
(°F − 32)	÷	1.8	=	°C
(1.8 × °C)	+	32	=	°F

DETERMINING SPEED/DISTANCE TRAVELED:

To find the distance a car travels in one foot each second, and the speed (mph) is known:

Indicated speed (mph) × 1.47 = ft./seconds.

However, if the distance (ft.) and time (seconds) is known, and the speed (mph) is unknown, then:

1. Distance (ft) ÷ time (seconds) = ft./sec.; then
2. Ft./sec. ÷ 1.47 = speed (mph)

DECIMAL AND METRIC EQUIVALENTS

Fractions	Decimal In.	Metric MM.	Fractions	Decimal In.	Metric MM.
1/64	.015625	.39688	33/64	.515625	13.09687
1/32	.03125	.79375	17/32	.53125	13.49375
3/64	.046875	1.19062	35/64	.546875	13.89062
1/16	.0625	1.58750	9/16	.5625	14.28750
5/64	.078125	1.98437	37/64	.578125	14.68437
3/32	.09375	2.38125	19/32	.59375	15.08125
7/64	.109375	2.77812	39/64	.609375	15.47812
1/8	.125	3.1750	5/8	.625	15.87500
9/64	.140625	3.57187	41/64	.640625	16.27187
5/32	.15625	3.96875	21/32	.65625	16.66875
11/64	.171875	4.36562	43/64	.671875	17.06562
3/16	.1875	4.76250	11/16	.6875	17.46250
13/64	.203125	5.15937	45/64	.703125	17.85937
7/32	.21875	5.55625	23/32	.71875	18.25625
15/64	.234375	5.95312	47/64	.734375	18.65312
1/4	.250	6.35000	3/4	.750	19.05000
17/64	.265625	6.74687	49/64	.765625	19.44687
9/32	.28125	7.14375	25/32	.78125	19.84375
19/64	.296875	7.54062	51/64	.796875	20.24062
5/16	.3125	7.93750	13/16	.8125	20.63750
21/64	.328125	8.33437	53/64	.828125	21.03437
11/32	.34375	8.73125	27/32	.84375	21.43125
23/64	.359375	9.12812	55/64	.859375	21.82812
3/8	.375	9.52500	7/8	.875	22.22500
25/64	.390625	9.92187	57/64	.890625	22.62187
13/32	.40625	10.31875	29/32	.90625	23.01875
27/64	.421875	10.71562	59/64	.921875	23.41562
7/16	.4375	11.11250	15/16	.9375	23.81250
29/64	.453125	11.50937	61/64	.953125	24.20937
15/32	.46875	11.90625	31/32	.96875	24.60625
31/64	.484375	12.30312	63/64	.984375	25.00312
1/2	.500	12.70000	1	1.00	25.40000

AUTOMOTIVE ABBREVIATIONS

AMP. - AMPERE(S)
A/C - AIR CONDITIONING
ACC - AUTOMATIC CLIMATE
    CONTROL
ADJ. - ADJUST
A/F - AIR/FUEL (AS IN AIR/FUEL RATIO)
AIR - AIR INJECTION REACTION
    SYSTEM
ALC - AUTOMATIC LEVEL CONTROL
ALCL - ASSEMBLY LINE
    COMMUNICATIONS LINK
ALT. - ALTITUDE
APT - ADJUSTABLE PART THROTTLE
AT - AUTOMATIC TRANSMISSION
ATC - AUTOMATIC TEMPERATURE
    CONTROL
ATDC - AFTER TOP DEAD CENTER

BARO - BAROMETRIC ABSOLUTE
    PRESSURE SENSOR
BAT. - BATTERY
BAT. + - POSITIVE TERMINAL
BBL. - BARREL
BHP - BRAKE HORSEPOWER
BP - BACK PRESSURE
BTDC - BEFORE TOP DEAD CENTER

CAT. CONV. - CATALYTIC CONVERTER
CB - CITIZENS BAND (RADIO)
CC - CATALYTIC CONVERTER
    CUBIC CENTIMETER
    CONVERTER CLUTCH
CCC - COMPUTER COMMAND
    CONTROL
CCDIC - CLIMATE CONTROL DRIVER
    INFORMATION CENTER
CCOT - CYCLING CLUTCH (ORIFICE)
    TUBE
CCP - CONTROLLED CANISTER PURGE
C.E. - CHECK ENGINE
CEAB - COLD ENGINE AIRBLEED
CEMF - COUNTER ELECTROMOTIVE
    FORCE
CID - CUBIC INCH DISPLACEMENT
CL - CLOSED LOOP
CLCC - CLOSED LOOP CARBURETOR
    CONTROL
CLTBI - CLOSED LOOP THROTTLE
    BODY INJECTION
CONV. - CONVERTER
CP - CANISTER PURGE
CU. IN. - CUBIC INCH
CV - CONSTANT VELOCITY
CYL. - CYLINDER(S)

DBB - DUAL BED BEAD
DBM - DUAL BED MONOLITH
DEFI - DIGITAL ELECTRONIC FUEL
    INJECTION
DFI - DIGITAL FUEL INJECTION
DIFF. - DIFFERENTIAL
DIST. - DISTRIBUTOR

EAC - ELECTRONIC AIR CONTROL
    VALVE
EAS - ELECTRONIC AIR SWITCHING
    VALVE
ECC - ELECTRONIC COMFORT
    CONTROL

ECM - ELECTRONIC CONTROL
    MODULE
ECS - EMISSION CONTROL SYSTEM
ECU - ENGINE CALIBRATION UNIT
EEC - EVAPORATIVE EMISSION
    CONTROL
EFE - EARLY FUEL EVAPORATION
EFI - ELECTRONIC FUEL INJECTION
EGR - EXHAUST GAS RECIRCULATION
ELC - ELECTRONIC LEVEL CONTROL
EMF - ELECTROMOTIVE FORCE
EMR - ELECTRONIC MODULE RETARD
EOS - EXHAUST OXYGEN SENSOR
ESC - ELECTRONIC SPARK CONTROL
EST - ELECTRONIC SPARK TIMING
ETC - ELECTRONIC TEMPERATURE
    CONTROL
ETCC - ELECTRONIC TOUCH
    COMFORT CONTROL
ETR - ELECTRONICALLY TUNED
    RECEIVER
EXH. - EXHAUST

FMVSS - FEDERAL MOTOR VEHICLE
    SAFETY STANDARDS
FT. LB. - FOOT POUNDS (TORQUE)
FWD - FRONT WHEEL DRIVE

HD - HEAVY DUTY
HEI - HIGH ENERGY IGNITION
HG. - MERCURY
HI. ALT. - HIGH ALTITUDE
HVAC - HEATER-VENT-AIR
    CONDITIONING
HVACM - HEATER-VENT-AIR
    CONDITIONING MODULE
HVM - HEATER-VENT-MODULE

IAC - IDLE AIR CONTROL
IC - INTEGRATED CIRCUIT
ID - IDENTIFICATION
    - INSIDE DIAMETER
ILC - IDLE LOAD COMPENSATOR
IP - INSTRUMENT PANEL
ISC - IDLE SPEED CONTROL

km - KILOMETER
km/h - KILOMETER PER HOUR
KV - KILOVOLTS (THOUSANDS OF
    VOLTS)
km/L - KILOMETERS/LITER (mpg)
kPa - KILOPASCALS

L - LITER
LF - LEFT FRONT
LR - LEFT REAR

MAN. VAC. - MANIFOLD VACUUM
MAF - MASS AIR FLOW
MAP - MANIFOLD ABSOLUTE
    PRESSURE
MAT - MANIFOLD AIR TEMPERATURE
    SENSOR
M/C - MIXTURE CONTROL
MPG - MILES PER GALLON
MPH - MILES PER HOUR
MT - MANUAL TRANSMISSION

N·m - NEWTON METERS (TORQUE)

OD - OUTSIDE DIAMETER
OL - OPEN LOOP
OSM - OUTPUT SWITCHING MODULE
O_2 - OXYGEN

PAIR - PULSE AIR INJECTION
    REACTION SYSTEM
P/B - POWER BRAKES
PCV - POSITIVE CRANKCASE
    VENTILATION
PECV - POWER ENRICHMENT
    CONTROL VALVE
P/N - PARK, NEUTRAL
PROM - PROGRAMMABLE, READ ONLY
    MEMORY
P/S - POWER STEERING
PSI - POUNDS PER SQUARE INCH
PT. - PINT

QT. - QUART

R - RESISTANCE
R-4 - RADIAL FOUR CYL. A/C
    COMPRESSOR
RF - RIGHT FRONT
RPM - REVOLUTIONS PER MINUTE
RR - RIGHT REAR
RTV - ROOM TEMPERATURE
    VULCANIZING (SEALER)
RVR - RESPONSE VACUUM REDUCER

SAE - SOCIETY OF AUTOMOTIVE
    ENGINEERS
SI - SYSTEM INTERNATIONAL
SOL. - SOLENOID

TAC - THERMOSTATIC AIR CLEANER
TACH - TACHOMETER
TBI -THROTTLE BODY INJECTION
TCC - TRANSMISSION CONVERTER
    CLUTCH
TCS - TRANSMISSION CONTROLLED
    SPARK
TDC - TOP DEAD CENTER
TPS - THROTTLE POSITION SENSOR
TV - THROTTLE VALVE
TVRS - TELEVISION & RADIO
    SUPPRESSION
TVS - THERMAL VACUUM SWITCH

U-JOINT - UNIVERSAL JOINT

V - VOLT(S)
V-8 - EIGHT CYLINDER ENGINE -
    ARRANGED IN A ''V''
VAC. - VACUUM
VATS - VEHICLE ANTI-THEFT SYSTEM
VIN - VEHICLE IDENTIFICATION
    NUMBER
VMV - VACUUM MODULATOR VALVE
VSS - VEHICLE SPEED SENSOR

W/ - WITH
W/B - WHEEL BASE
W/O - WITHOUT
WOT - WIDE OPEN THROTTLE

PHYSICAL PROPERTIES OF CERTAIN METALS

METAL	MELTING POINT (F)	BOILING POINT (F)	COMMENTS
Aluminum	1,215	4,100	1. Does not return to original shape after being overheated. 2. Oxidizes (becomes dull) with heat. 3. Good conductor of electricity and heat. 4. Resists corrosion. 5. Exists in the ore corundum and bauxite; must be separated from the ore. 6. Malleable and ductile metal. 7. Very reflective. 8. A nonferrous metal.
Antimony	1,167	2,516	1. Expands while cooling. 2. Brittle metal.
Cadmium	609	1,409	1. Poisonous. 2. Ductile and malleable metal.
Chrome	3,407	4,829	1. Hard metal and wear resistant. 2. Resists rusting. 3. Used in alloys and electroplating.
Cobalt	2,728	5,250	1. Remains hard up to 1,800 °F. 2. A ferrous metal. 3. Occurs in nature combined with iron and nickel.
Copper	1,981	4,217	1. Excellent conductor of heat and electricity. 2. Ductile and malleable metal.
Gold	1,945	4,586	1. Excellent conductor of heat and electricity. 2. Resists rust and tarnishing. 3. Ductile and malleable metal. 4. Very expensive.
Iron (steel)	2,790	5,400	1. Will return to its original shape after being overheated. 2. Heavy, but ductile and malleable metal. 3. A ferrous metal. 4. Rusts very easily.
Lead	620	2,950	1. Resists corrosion. 2. Radiation cannot penetrate through it. 3. Heavy (dense), but a very soft malleable and ductile metal.
Lithium	357	12,426	1. Lightest known metal. 2. Used in nuclear reactions.
Magnesium	1,203	2,030	1. 30% lighter than aluminum. 2. Shavings are easy to catch on fire; use sand to put out a magnesium fire. 3. Malleable and ductile metal. 4. Produces an intense white light while burning.
Manganese	2,273	3,900	1. Wear resistant. 2. Strengthens steel by remvoing oxides and sulfur. 3. A hard and brittle metal. 4. A nonferrous metal.
Mercury	−102	675	1. A liquid at normal temperatures. 2. A poisonous metal. 3. Used in thermometers and barometers. 4. Also referred to as quick silver.
Molybdenum	4,730	10,000	1. A hard metal, but softer than chrome. 2. When alloyed with steel, it allows steel to keep it's cutting edge when heated.
Nickel	2,651	6,110	1. Controls thermal expansion of metal. 2. Hard metal; used basically in alloys and electroplating. 3. Malleable and ductile metal. 4. Resists corrosion.
Platinum	3,220	7,770	1. Used as a catalyst. 2. Very expensive. 3. Heavy, but ductile and malleable metal. 4. Does not corrode.
Palladium	2,826	7,200	1. Used as a catalyst. 2. Malleable and ductile metal.

PHYSICAL PROPERTIES OF CERTAIN METALS

METAL	MELTING POINT (F)	BOILING POINT (F)	COMMENTS
Silver	1,761	3,551	1. Excellent conductor of electricity and heat. 2. Very expensive. 3. Ductile and a very malleable metal.
Sodium	208	1,638	1. Explosive reaction when mixed with water.
Tin	450	4,118	1. A flash coating on other metals provides excellent lubrication properties. 2. A soft, malleable, and ductile metal at ordinary temperatures.
Titanium	3,035	5,900	1. Strong as steel, but 45% lighter. 2. 60% heavier than aluminum, but twice as strong.
Tungsten	6,170	10,706	1. Metal with the highest melting/boiling point. 2. Resists acids. 3. Resists abrasions. 4. Heavy, hard, and ductile metal. 5. Also called wolfram.
Vanadium	3,110	5,432	1. Adds tensile strength to steel. 2. Malleable and ductile metal.
Zinc	786	1,661	1. Prevents rust. 2. Ductile in its pure form, but brittle in its commercial form.

METAL ALLOYS

ALLOY	METALS INVOLVED:
Brass	Copper and zinc
Bronze	Copper and tin
Nichrome	Nickel and chrome
Stainless steel	Chrome, steel, and nickel
Stellite	Cobalt, tungsten, and chrome
White gold	Gold and palladium

TYPES OF ELASTOMERS

NATURAL RUBBER

Provides high resilience and tensile strength. Also, its resistance to wear and flexibility is good at low temperatures. Temperature range is from −55 to +90 °C. However, it does not wear well when exposed to petroleum products, sunlight, ozone, or oxygen.

NEOPRENE

Provides good resistance to weather, petroleum products, water, and heat. Also, it provides resilience and flexibility.

NITRILE

Provides excellent resistance to petroleum products and acids. However, it is not compatible with synthetic oil. Temperature range is from −53 to +121 °C.

EPDM

Provides excellent resistance to the weather and heat. Temperature range is from −50 to +150 °C. It also provides excellent dielectric qualities and its cost is low. However, it should not be exposed to petroleum products and is not as resilient and strong as natural rubber.

HYPALON

Provides excellent resistance to the weather, ozone, acids, heat, petroleum products, and abrasions.

SILICONE

Provides excellent high and low temperature qualities. Temperature range is from −60 to +200 °C. Also, it provides good resistance to the weather, petroleum products, flexing, and fatigue.

VITON

Provides excellent resistance to petroleum products at high and low temperatures. Also, it provides good resistance to chemical action and low compression set, while providing strength and resilience. Temperature range is from −40 to +204 °C.

TEFLON

Provides a material that is inert with all chemicals. It also provides a nonstick (slippery) surface.

DICTIONARY OF
AUTOMOTIVE TERMS

AAA: American Automobile Association.

ABRASION: Wearing or rubbing away.

ABS: Anti-lock Brake System.

A/C: Air conditioning.

ACCELERATOR: A pedal for regulating speed of an engine.

ACCELERATOR PUMP: Small pump in carburetor, operated by accelerator pedal linkage, which supplies additional fuel needed for acceleration of vehicle.

ACETYLENE OR OXY-ACETYLENE WELDING: Utilization of an acetylene flame to heat metal to fusion or melting point when uniting it.

ACKERMAN PRINCIPLE: Design having wheel spindles mounted on axle ends to permit spindles to be turned at an angle to axle for steering purposes.

ACRYLIC: A surface finish, made from synthetic polymers, which dries by solvent evaporation.

ACTIVE MATERIAL: In a storage battery, peroxide of lead (brown) in positive plates and metallic lead (gray) in negative plates upon which sulphuric acid acts.

ACTUATOR: An output device controlled by the computer.

ADAPTOR CARBURETOR: A device attached to a gasoline carburetor which permits an internal combustion engine to run either on gasoline or liquefied petroleum gas (LP-Gas).

ADDITIVE: In automotive oils, material added to oil to give it certain properties. Example: to lessen its tendency to thicken at low temperature.

ADS: Association of Diesel Specialists.

AEA: Automotive Electronic Association.

AERA: Automotive Engine Rebuilders Association.

AIR: A gas containing approximately 4/5 nitrogen, 1/5 oxygen, and some carbonic gas. Also, abbreviation for Air Injection Reaction system.

AIR BAG: Protective device designed to serve as a "pillow" between front seat occupants and vehicle interior immediately following a frontal or front-angle crash.

AIR CLEANER: A device for filtering, cleaning, and removing dust from intake air to an engine, air compressor, etc.

AIR CONDITIONING: Process by which surrounding air is cooled and dehumidified.

AIR-FUEL RATIO: Ratio by weight of fuel compared to air in carburetor mixture.

AIR GAP: Space between spark plug electrodes, starting motor and generator armatures, field shoes, etc.

AIR HORN: Air inlet of carburetor to which air cleaner is ordinarily attached.

AIR INJECTION SYSTEM: Means of injecting fresh air into hot gases in exhaust manifold to reduce emissions.

AIR-LOCK: A bubble of air trapped in a fluid circuit which interferes with normal circulation of fluid.

AIR SPRING: An air-filled bag or device that is pressurized to provide spring action.

AIRFLOW METER: Measures rate at which air enters engine.

ALCL: Assembly Line Communications Link. Diagnostic connector.

ALIGNMENT: An adjustment to bring related components into a line.

ALL WHEEL DRIVE: Four wheel drive capability with automatic shifts.

ALLEN WRENCH: A hexagonal wrench, which is "L" shaped, fits into a recessed hexagonal hole.

ALLOY: A mixture of different metals. Example: solder is an alloy of lead and tin.

ALTERNATING CURRENT: An electric current alternating back and forth in direction of flow.

ALTERNATOR: Generator in which alternating current is changed to direct current by means of rectifiers (diodes).

ALUMINUM: A metal, noted for its lightness, often alloyed with small quantities of other metals.

AMBIENT: Surrounding on all sides.

AMMETER: An instrument for measuring flow of electric current.

AMPERE: Unit of measurement for flow of electric current.

AMPERE-HOUR CAPACITY: A term used to indicate capacity of a storage battery. Example: delivery of a certain number of amperes for a certain number of hours.

ANALOG COMPUTER: Imitates signal it receives and adjusts actuators proportionately.

ANNEALING: A process of softening metal. Example: heating and slow cooling of a piece of iron.

ANNULAR BALL BEARING: A ball bearing with a nonadjustable inner and outer race or races.

ANNULUS: In planetary gear system, an internal ring gear that operates in conjunction with a sun gear, pinion gears, and pinion carrier. See RING GEAR.

ANODE: A positive pole of an electric current.

ANTIFREEZE: A material, such as ethylene glycol, added to water to lower its freezing point.

ANTIFRICTION BEARING: A bearing constructed with balls or rollers between journal and bearing surface to provide rolling instead of sliding friction.

ANTI-LOCK BRAKE SYSTEM: Provides rapid and repeated brake applications and releases to bring vehicle to a stop without brake lockup or SKIDDING.

ANTISMOG DEVICE: A special part or system designed to reduce or eliminate emission of noxious gases from exhaust of engine. See EXHAUST EMISSIONS.

APERTURE: An opening, hole, or port.

API: American Petroleum Institute.

ARC WELDING: A method of utilizing an electric current jumping an air gap to provide heat for welding metal.

ARCING: Electricity bridging gap between two electrodes.

ARMATURE: Part of an electrical device which includes main, current-carrying winding.

ARTICULATED MOUNTING: A term used where parts are connected by links and links are anchored to provide a double hinging action.

ASBESTOS: A natural fibrous mineral with a great heat resisting ability.

ASE: National Institute for Automotive Service Excellence.

ASIA: Automotive Service Industry Association.

ASME: American Society of Mechanical Engineers.

ASPECT RATIO: Ratio of tire section height to section width.

ATA: American Trucking Association.

ATF: Automatic Transmission Fluid.

ATMOSPHERIC PRESSURE: Weight of air at sea level, about 14.7 psi.

ATOM: Smallest distinct chemical unit of a substance, composed of electrons, neutrons, and protons.

AUTOMATIC LEVEL CONTROL: Front and rear load leveling by means of four rubber or plastic air springs or air adjustable shock absorbers or shock struts.

AUTOMATIC RIDE CONTROL: Electronically operated soft or firm ride as required.

AUTOMATIC STEERING EFFECT: Built-in tendency of an automobile to resume travel in a straight line when released from a turn.

AXLE: Shaft or shafts of a vehicle upon which wheels are mounted.

B & S GAUGE: Brown and Sharpe gauge, which is a standard measure of wire size. Smaller the number, larger the wire.

BACKFIRE: Clearance or "play" be-manifold by flame from a cylinder.

BACKLASH: Clearance or "play" between the teeth of two gears.

BACK PRESSURE: A resistance to free flow, such as a restriction in the exhaust system.

BAFFLE OR BAFFLE PLATE: An obstruction for checking or deflecting flow of gases or sound.

BALK RING: A friction-regulated pawl or plunger used to facilitate engagement of gears.

BALL BEARING: An antifriction bearing consisting of a hardened inner and outer race with hardened steel balls interposed between two races.

BATTERY: Any number of complete electrical cells assembled in one housing or case.

BATTERY CAPACITY: Amount of current battery will deliver.

BATTERY PLATE: Component made of special active materials contained in cast grids.

BATTERY RATINGS: Standards of power-delivering capability of batteries as established by Battery Council International.

BCI: Battery Council International.

BCM: Body Computer Module.

BDC: Bottom dead center.

BEAD: Part of tire shaped to fit the rim.

BEARING: A part in which a journal, shaft, or pivot turns or moves.

BELL HOUSING: Covering around flywheel and clutch or torque converter.

BELTED BIAS TIRES: Carcass construction has ply cords that extend diagonally from bead to bead at alternate angles plus two or more belts of cord that circle tire under tread.

BENDIX GEAR OR BENDIX DRIVE: A gear mounted on a screw shaft attached to starting motor armature, which automatically engages and disengages electric starting motor.

BENZOL: A by-product of manufacture of coke. Sometimes it is used as an engine fuel.

BEZEL: A grooved ring in which a transparent instrument cover is placed.

BHP: Brake horsepower is a measurement of power developed by an engine in actual operation.

BIAS PLY: Pneumatic tire structure in which ply cords extend diagonally from bead to bead, laid at alternate angles.

BLEED: To remove air from hydraulic brake system while fluid in system is under pressure. Also, slowly reducing pressure in an air conditioning sytem by releasing liquid refrigerant or vapor.

BLOW-BY: A leakage or loss of pressure, often used with reference to leakage of compression past piston ring between piston and cylinder.

BODY COMPUTER MODULE: Key element of self-diagnostic system used to control vehicle functions based on monitored inputs.

BOILING POINT: Temperature at atmospheric pressure at which bubbles or vapors rise to surface and escape.

BONDED LINING: Brake lining cemented to shoes or bands which eliminates need for rivets.

BOOSTER: A mechanical or hydraulic device attached to brake or steering system to increase power or effectiveness.

BORE: Diameter of a cylinder. Also, to enlarge a hole as distinguished from making a hole with a drill.

BORING BAR: A stiff bar equipped with multiple cutting bits used to machine a series of bearing bores in proper alignment with each other.

BOSS: An extension or strengthened section, such as projections within a piston which support piston pin or piston pin bushings.

BOTTLED GAS: Liquefied petroleum gas compressed and contained in portable cylinders.

BOUNCE: Applied to engine valves, a condition where valve is not held tightly to its seat when cam is not lifting it. Also, a condition where breaker points make and break contact when they should remain closed.

BRAKE: An energy conversion mechanism used to retard, stop, or hold a vehicle.

BRAKE ANCHOR: Pivot pin or brake backing plate against which the brake shoe bears.

BRAKE BAND: A band within a brake drum, to which lining is attached.

BRAKE BLEEDING: Procedure for removing air from the lines of a hydraulic system.

BRAKE CYLINDER: A cylinder in which a movable piston converts pressure to mechanical force to move brake shoes against braking surface of the drum or the rotor.

BRAKE DISC: Parallel-faced circular plate against which brake lining is forced to retard vehicle. Also ROTOR.

BRAKE DRUM: A metal cylinder attached to wheel and acted upon by friction material.

BRAKE "FADE": A condition where repeated severe applications of brakes cause expansion of brake drum or loss of frictional ability or both, which results in impaired braking efficiency.

BRAKE FLUID: A compounded liquid for use in hydraulic brake systems, which must meet exacting conditions (impervious to heat, freezing, thickening, bubbling, etc.).

BRAKE FLUSHING: A procedure for removing fluid from a brake system and washing out sediment.

BRAKE HORSEPOWER: Actual horsepower delivered by crankshaft, measured by means of a dynamometer or prony brake.

BRAKE HOSE: A flexible conductor for transmission of fluid under pressure in brake system.

BRAKE LINING: A material having a suitable coefficient of friction, which is attached to brake shoe and which contacts brake drum to retard vehicle.

BRAKE SHOE: Carrier to which brake lining is attached, used to force lining in contact with brake drum or rotor.

BRAKE SHOE HEEL: Generally, end of brake shoe opposite anchor pin.

BRAKE SHOE TOE: Generally, end of brake shoe nearest anchor pin.

BRAZE: To join two pieces of metal with use of a comparatively high melting point material. Example: join two pieces of steel by using brass or bronze as a solder.

BREAKER ARM: Movable part of a pair

of contact points in an ignition distributor.

BREAKER POINTS: Two separable points, usually faced with silver, platinum, or tungsten, which interrupt primary circuit in distributor for purpose of inducing a high tension current in ignition system.

BREAK-IN: Process of wearing into a desirable fit between surfaces of two new or reconditioned parts.

BRINELL HARDNESS: A scale for designating degree of hardness possessed by a substance.

BROACH: To finish surface of metal by pushing or pulling a multiple edge cutting tool over or through it.

BRUSHES: Bars of carbon or other conducting material which contact commutator of an electric motor or generator.

BTU (British Thermal Unit): A measurement of amount of heat required to raise temperature of 1 lb. of water 1 °F.

BURNISH: to smooth or polish by use of a sliding tool under pressure.

BUSHING: A removable liner for a bearing.

BUTANE: A petroleum hydrocarbon compound which has a boiling point of about 32 °F, which is used as engine fuel. Loosely referred to as Liquefied Petroleum Gas and often combined with Propane.

BYPASS: An alternate path for a flowing substance.

CALIBRATE: To determine or adjust graduation or scale of any instrument giving quantitative measurements.

CALIBRATION: A precise factory setting, make to produce a given output or effect.

CALIPER: Non-rotational components of disc brake that straddles disc and contains hydraulic components.

CALIPERS: An adjustable tool for determining inside or outside diameter by contact and retaining dimension for measurement or comparison.

CALORIFIC VALUE: A measure of heating value of fuel.

CALORIMETER: An instrument to measure amount of heat given off by a substance when burned.

CALORY: Metric measurement of amount of heat required to raise 1 gram of water from 0 ° to 1 ° Celsius.

CAM OR BREAKER CAM: Multi-lobed cam rotating in ingition distributor, which serves to interrupt primary circuit to induce a high tension spark for ignition.

CAM ANGLE: Number of degrees of rotation of distributor shaft during which contact points are closed.

CAMBER: In wheel alignment, outward or inward tilt of wheel at top.

CAM GROUND PISTON: A piston ground to a slightly oval shape which, under heat of operation, becomes round.

CAMSHAFT: Shaft containing lobes or cams which operate engine valves.

CANISTER: Reservoir of evaporative emission control system, usually containing activated charcoal granules for absorbing fuel vapors.

CAPE CHISEL: A metal cutting chisel shaped to cut or work in channels or grooves.

CARBON: A common, nonmetallic element that is an excellent conductor of electricity. It also forms in combustion chamber of an engine during burning of fuel and lubricating oil.

CARBON DIOXIDE: Compressed into solid form, this material is known as ''dry ice'' and remains at a temperature of $-109 °F$. It goes directly from a solid to a vapor state.

CARBON MONOXIDE: Gas formed by incomplete combustion. Colorless, odorless, poisonous.

CARBONIZE: Process of carbon formation within an engine. Examples: deposits on spark plugs and within combustion chamber.

CARBURETOR: A device for automatically mixing fuel in proper proportion with air to produce a combustible gas.

CARBURETOR ''ICING'': A term used to describe formation of ice on a carburetor throttle plate during certain atmospheric conditions.

CARCASS: Tire structure except for sidewall and tread.

CARDAN JOINT: A universal joint with corresponding yokes at right angle with each other.

CAS: Cleaner Air System.

CASE-HARDEN: To harden the surface of steel.

CASTELLATE: Formed to resemble a castle battlement. Example: a castellated nut.

CASTER: In wheel alignment, backward or forward tilt of steering axis.

CATALYTIC CONVERTER: Emission control device in exhaust stream that chemically treats exhaust gases after combustion to oxidize noxious emissions.

CATHODE: Negative pole of an electric current.

CCC: Computer Command Control.

CCEC: Constant Current Electronic Circuit.

CCOT: Cycling Clutch Orifice Tube air conditioning system.

CCS: Controlled Combustion System.

CEC: Combination Emission Control.

CELL: Unit of a battery containing a group of positive and negative plates along with electrolyte.

CELSIUS: A scale of temperature measurement on which, under standard atmospheric pressure, water freezes at 0 ° and boils at 100 °.

CENTER OF GRAVITY: Point of a body from which it could be suspended, or

on which it could be supported, and be in balance. Example: center of gravity of a wheel is center of wheel hub.

CENTRIGRADE: See CELSIUS.

CENTRIFUGAL FORCE: A force which tends to move a body away from its center of rotation. Example: a whirling weight attached to a string.

CENTRIFUSE BRAKE DRUMS: To combine strength of steel with desirable friction characteristics of cast iron, a lining of cast iron is sprayed on inside of a steel drum. Both metals are handled while hot to encourage fusing of two metals.

CFI: Central Fuel Injection.

CHAMFER: A bevel or taper at edge of a hole.

CHARGE (or Recharge): Passing an electrical current through a battery to restore it to activity. Also, filling and pressurizing an air conditioning system with refrigerant.

CHASE: To straighten up or repair damaged threads.

CHASSIS: Framework of a vehicle without a body and fenders.

CHASSIS DYNAMOMETER: A machine for measuring amount of power delivered to drive wheels of a vehicle.

CHECK VALVE: A gate or valve which allows passage of gas or fluid in one direction only.

CHEMICAL COMPOUND: Combination of two or more chemical elements, which can be a gas, a liquid, or a solid.

CHEMICAL ELEMENT: Gaseous, liquid, or solid matter which cannot be divided into simpler form.

CHILLED IRON: Cast iron with hardened surface.

CHIP: To cut with a chisel.

CHOKE: A reduced passage. Example: valve in carburetor air inlet to cut down volume of air admitted.

CHROMIUM STEEL: An alloy of steel with a small amount of chromium to produce a metal which is highly resistant to oxidation and corrosion.

CIRCUIT: Path of electric current, fluids, or gases. Examples: for electricity, a wire; for fluids and gases, a pipe.

CIRCUIT BREAKER: A device for interrupting an electrical circuit; often automatic and also known as contact breaker, interrupter, cut-out, or relay.

CIRCULAR MIL: Unit of area equal to area of a circle one mil in diameter.

CLEARANCE: Space allowed between two parts. Example: space between a journal and a bearing.

CLOCKWISE ROTATION: Rotation in same direction as hands of a clock.

CLUTCH: Friction device used to connect and disconnect a driving force from a driven member.

CO: Carbon monoxide.

COEFFICIENT OF FRICTION: Amount of friction developed between two surfaces pressed together and moved one on the other.

COIL: Ignition transformer designed to increase primary voltage.

COIL SPRING: Spiral-shaped, coiled steel or steel alloy, compression type suspension device.

"COLD" MANIFOLD: An intake manifold not heated by exhaust gas.

COMBINATION VALVE: Brake system hydraulic control device includes a pressure differential valve, metering valve, and proportioning valve.

COMBUSTION: Process of burning.

COMBUSTION CHAMBER: Volume of cylinder above piston with piston on top center.

COMMUTATOR: A ring of adjacent copper bars, insulated from each other, to which wires of armature or winding are attached.

COMPENSATING PORT: An opening in a brake master cylinder to permit fluid return to reservoir.

COMPOSITE HEADLAMPS: Reflector and lens system designed for specific vehicle model.

COMPOUND: A mixture of two or more ingredients.

COMPOUND WINDING: Two electric windings: one in series, other in shunt or parallel with other electric units or equipment. Applied to electric motors or generators: one winding is shunted across armatrue; other is in series with armature.

COMPRESSION: Reduction in volume of a gas. Also, condition when coil spring is squeezed together. Opposite of tension.

COMPRESSION RATIO: volume of cylinder and combustion chamber with piston at bottom center as compared with volume of chamber at end of compression stroke.

COMPRESSOR: Engine-driven unit that circulates and pressurizes refrigerant in air conditioning system. Also, unit that pressures air in truck air brake system. Also, component of a turbocharger that pumps air into engine.

COMPUTER CONTROLLED COIL IGNITION: System that incorporates no distributor.

CONCEALED HEADLAMPS: Headlamp doors close to present flush fitting sheet metal to reduce air resistance in headlamp area.

CONCENTRIC: Two circles having same center but different diameters.

CONDENSATION: Process of a vapor becoming a liquid. Reverse of evaporation.

CONDENSER: Device for turning refrigerant vapor into liquid, causing heat to be discharged from refrigerant. Also, a device for temporarily collecting and storing a surge of electrical current for later discharge.

CONDUCTANCE: Current-carrying ability of a wire or electrical component.

CONDUCTOR: A material along or through which electricity will flow with slight resistance. Silver, copper, and carbon are good conductors.

CONNECTING ROD: Rod that connects piston to crankshaft.

CONSTANT MESH TRANSMISSION: An arrangement of gearing where gears remain in mesh instead of sliding in and out of engagement.

CONSTANT VELOCITY: Double universal joint that cancels out vibrations caused by driving power being transmitted through an angle.

CONTACT POINTS: See BREAKER POINTS.

CONTRACTION: A reduction in mass or dimension. Opposite of expansion.

CONTROL MODULE: Used in electronic ignition systems to switch current on and off in primary circuit.

CONVECTION: A transfer of heat by circulating heated air.

CONVERTER: Applied to liquefied petroleum gas: a device which converts or changes LP-Gas from liquid to vapor for use in engine.

COOLANT: Liquid circulated through cooling system of a "water-cooled" engine, usually a mixture of about 50 percent ethylene glycol and 50 percent water.

COOLANT SENSOR: Measures temperature of coolant and sends signal to computer.

CORD: Textile, steel wire strands, etc., forming plies of a tire.

CORE HOLE PLUG: See FREEZE PLUG.

CORPORATION: Business association endowed by law with the rights and liabilities of an individual.

CORRODE: To eat away gradually as if by gnawing, especially by rust.

COUNTERBORE: To enlarge a hole to a given depth.

COUNTERCLOCKWISE ROTATION: Rotating opposite direction of hands on a clock.

COUNTERSHAFT: Intermediate shaft in transmission that transfers motion from one shaft to another.

COUNTERSINK: To cut or form a depression to allow head of a screw to go below surface.

COUPLING: A connecting means for transferring movement from one part to another. May be mechanical, hydraulic, or electrical.

COWL: Portion of body between engine compartment and driver, which ordinarily contains instruments used by operator.

CRANKCASE: Housing within which crankshaft operates.

CRANKCASE DILUTION: Under certain conditions of operation, unburned portions of fuel get past piston rings into crankcase where they "thin" engine lubricating oil.

CRANKING CIRCUIT: Battery, starting motor, ignition switch, and related electrical wiring.

CRANKSHAFT: Main shaft of an engine which, in conjunction with connecting rods, changes reciprocating motion of pistons into rotary motion.

CRANKSHAFT COUNTERBALANCE: Series of weights attached to or forged integrally with crankshaft and placed to offset reciprocating weight of each piston and rod assembly.

CROSSMEMBER: Crosswise structural component of vehicle frame or unitized body.

CRT: Cathode ray tube.

CRUDE OIL: Liquid oil as it comes from the ground.

C^{3}I: Computer Controlled Coil Ignition.

CTO: Coolant Temperature Override.

CU. IN.: Cubic inch.

CURB WEIGHT: Weight of a vehicle, (without driver or load), including fuel, coolant, oil, and all standard equipment items.

CURRENT: Flow of electricity.

CUT-OUT: A valve used to divert exhaust gases directly to atmosphere instead of through muffler.

CVT: Continuously Variable Transmission.

CYCLE: A series of events which are repeated. Example: intake, compression, power, and exhaust strokes of an internal combustion engine.

CYLINDER: A round hole having some depth bored to receive a piston. Also referred to as "bore."

CYLINDER BLOCK: Largest single part of an engine. Basic or main mass of metal in which cylinders are bored or placed.

CYLINDER HEAD: A detachable portion of an engine fastened securely to cylinder block which contains all or a portion of combustion chamber.

CYLINDER HEAD GASKET: Seal between engine block and cylinder head.

CYLINDER SLEEVE: A liner or tube interposed between piston and cylinder wall or cylinder block to provide a readily renewable wearing surface for cylinder.

DASH: Also known as firewall. A partition between engine and operator.

DASHPOT: A device consisting of a piston and cylinder with a restricted opening used to slow down or delay operation of some moving part.

DC: Direct current.

DEAD CENTER: Extreme upper or lower postion of crankshaft throw at which point piston is not moving in either direction.

DEAD REAR AXLE: A rear axle that does not turn. Example: rear axle of front wheel drive car.

DEGREE: Abbreviated deg. or indicated by a small ° placed alongside of a figure. May be used to designate temperature readings or angularity (one degree is 1/360 part of a circle).

DEMAGNETIZE: To remove magnetization of a pole which has previously been magnetized.

DENATURED ALCOHOL: Ethyl alcohol to which a denaturant has been added.

DENSITY: Compactness: relative mass of matter in a given volume.

DEPOLARIZE: To remove polarity. Example: to demagnetize a permanent magnet.

DESICCANT: Drying agent used in air conditioning system to remove excess moisture.

DETERGENT: A compound of a soap-like nature used in engine oil to remove engine deposits and hold them in suspension in oil.

DETONATION: An engine sound that indicates a too rapid burning or explosion of air-fuel mixture in engine cylinders. It becomes audible through a vibration of combustion chamber walls.

DIAGNOSIS: Refers to use of instruments to determine cause of improper function of parts or systems of a vehicle.

DIAGNOSTIC CODE: Code displayed on instrument panel which can be used to determine area in system where malfunction may be located.

DIAL GAUGE: A type of test instrument which indicates precise readings on a dial.

DIAPHRAGM: A flexible partition or wall separating two cavities.

DIE: One of a pair of hardened metal blocks for forming metal into a desired shape. Also, a device for cutting external threads.

DIE CASTING: An accurate and smooth casting made by pouring molten metal or composition into a metal mold or die under pressure.

DIESEL ENGINE: Named after its developer, Dr. Rudolph Diesel, engine ignites fuel in cylinder from heat generated by compression. Fuel is an oil rather than gasoline and no spark plug or carburetor is required.

DIESELING: Engine tends to keep running after ignition key is turned off.

DIFFERENTIAL: Gear system which permits one drive wheel to turn faster than other.

DIGITAL COMPUTER: An ON-OFF computer that turns actuator on, or it remains in OFF position.

DILUTION: See CRANKCASE DILUTION.

DIMMER SWITCH: Permits selection of headlamp low beams or high beams.

DIODE: An electronic device that permits current to flow through it in one direction only.

DIRECT CURRENT: Electric current which flows continuously in one direction. Example: current from a storage battery.

DIRECT DRIVE: In automobile transmissions: refers to direct engagement between engine and drive shaft where engine crankshaft and drive shaft turn at same rpm.

DIRECT IGNITION SYSTEM: Distributorless system which carries high voltage from ignition coils to spark plugs.

DIRECTION SIGNAL SWITCH: Permits driver to signal direction of turn.

DISC BRAKE: Brake system utilizing rotors to which frictional forces are applied to retard motion of vehicle.

DISCHARGE: Flow of electric current from a battery. Also, to bleed some or all refrigerant from an air conditioning system. Opposite of charge.

DISPLACEMENT: See ENGINE DISPLACEMENT.

DISTORTION: A warpage or change in form from original shape.

DISTRIBUTOR ROTOR: Designed to rotate and distribute high tension current to towers of distributor cap.

DISTRIBUTORS: A valve, often rotary in design, which conducts a vapor or fluid to a number of outlets. Example: diesel engine oil distributors. See IGNITION DISTRIBUTOR.

DOMAINS: Groups of atoms that have same magnetic polarity.

DOUBLE REDUCTION AXLE: A drive axle construction in which two sets of reduction gears are used for extreme reduction of gear ratio.

DOWEL PIN: A pin inserted in matching holes in two parts to maintain those parts in fixed relation to each other.

DOWN-DRAFT: Carburetor in which mixture flows downward to engine.

DOWNSHIFT: Forcing a shift to a lower gear.

DRAG LINK: Connecting rod or link between steering gear pitman arm and steering control linkage.

DRAW: To form by a stretching process, or to soften hard metal.

DRAW-FILING: File is drawn across work at right angles.

DRIER: A device containing a desiccant in liquid refrigerant line to absorb moisture in an air conditioning system.

DRILL: A tool for making a hole, or to sink a hole with a pointed cutting tool rotated under pressure.

DRIVE-FIT: Term used when shaft is slightly larger than hole and must be forced in place.

DRIVELINE: Universal joints, drive shaft, and other parts connecting transmission with driving axles.

DRIVE SHAFT: Shaft connecting transmission ouptut shaft to differential drive pinion shaft.

DRIVE TRAIN: All parts that generate power and transmit it to driving wheels.

DRIVING AXLES: Used to hold, align, and drive rear wheels and support weight of vehicle on rear wheel drive cars. Or, half shafts on front wheel drive cars that provide torque force to front wheels.

DROP FORGING: A piece of steel shaped between dies while hot.

DRY CHARGED BATTERY: A complete battery unit which does not contain liquid electrolyte.

DRY SLEEVE: A metal barrel or sleeve which is pressed into an oversize cylinder bore.

DUAL FUEL ENGINE: An engine equipped to operate on two different fuels such as gasoline and LP-Gas.

DUAL MASTER CYLINDER: Primary unit consisting of two sections for displacing fluid under pressure in a split hydraulic brake system.

DUAL REDUCTION AXLE: A drive axle construction with two sets of pinions and gears, either of which can be used.

DURASPARK SYSTEM: Ford electronic ignition system.

DWELL METER: An instrument for measuring cam angle.

DWELL PERIOD: See CAM ANGLE.

DYNAMO: A generator of electricity.

DYNAMOMETER: A machine for measuring power produced by an internal combustion engine.

ECC: Electronic Climate Control.

ECCENTRIC: One circle within another circle not having same center.

ECM: Electronic Control Module.

ECONOMIZER: A device installed in a carburetor to control amount of fuel used under certain conditions.

ECU: Electronic Control Unit. Also, Engine Calibration Unit or ''Prom.''

EEC: Evaporative Emission Controls. Or, Electronic Engine Control.

EECS: Evaporative Emissions Control System.

EFE: Early Fuel Evaporation system.

EFI: Electronic Fuel Injection.

EGR: Exhaust Gas Recirculation.

ELC: Electronic Level Control.

ELECTRIC WELDING: Welding by using an electric current to melt both metal (work) and welding rod, or electrode.

ELECTRODE: Refers to insulated center rod and rod attached to shell of spark plug. Also, welding rod.

ELECTROLYTE: A mixture of sulphuric acid and distilled water used in storage batteries.

ELECTROMAGNET: A coil of insulated wire wound around an iron rod (or series of rods) will magnetize it when an electric current is passed through wire. Example: a solenoid magnet.

ELECTROMAGNETIC INDUCTION: Voltage is induced in a coil of wire by moving coil through a magnetic field or by keeping coil stationary and moving magnetic field.

ELECTRON: That portion of an atom which carries a negative charge of electricity.

ELECTRONIC IGNITION: A system that

electronically controls current flow in primary circuit.

ELEMENT: One set of positive battery plates and one set of negative plates, complete with separators and assembled together.

ELLIOTT STEERING KNUCKLE: Type of axle in which ends of axle beam straddle spindle.

EMF: Electromotive force, or voltage.

EMISSIONS: Harmful components of exhaust gas, fuel vapors, and crankcase fumes released to atmosphere.

EMULSION: A milk-like viscous mixture of two liquids.

ENAMEL: A combination of varnish and coloring pigment, sometimes heated during or after application to provide a hard surface.

EN-BLOC: Refers to cylinder block of an engine cast in one section.

END PLAY: Amount of lengthwise clearance between parts.

ENERGY: Prime source of power generated to propel a vehicle.

ENERGY ABSORBING BUMPER: System designed to protect vehicle safety systems during impact at low speed.

ENGINE: Prime source of power generated to propel a vehicle.

ENGINE DISPLACEMENT: Sum of piston displacement of all engine cyliders. See PISTON DISPLACEMENT.

ENGINE TORQUE: Amount of twisting effort exerted by crankshaft of engine.

ENGINE TUNE-UP: Service operation designed to restore engine's best level of performance while maintaining good fuel economy and minimum exhaust emissions.

ENTREPRENEUR: One who undertakes ownership of a business or enterprise.

ENTREPRENEURSHIP: A person's ability to organize, manage, and assume risks of operating a business.

EPA: Environmental Protection Agency.

ESC: Electronic Spark Control.

EST: Electronic Spark Timing.

ETHYL GASOLINE: Gasoline to which a compound of tetraethyl lead, ethylene dibromide and ethylene dichloride has been added.

ETHYLENE GLYCOL: Liquid chemical mixed with water to form low-freezing-point coolant.

EVACUATE: To create a vacuum in an air conditioning system to remove all traces of air and moisture.

EVRV: Electronic Vacuum Regulator Valve.

EXHAUST BACK PRESSURE: Pressure exerted in exhaust system in reverse direction.

EXHAUST EMISSIONS: Products of combustion that are discharged through exhaust system of vehicle.

EXHAUST GAS ANALYZER: An instrument for determining efficiency with which an engine is burning fuel.

EXHAUST PIPE: Pipe connecting engine to muffler to conduct spent gases away from engine.

EXPANSION: An increase in size. Example: when a metal rod is heated, it increases in length and diameter. Opposite of contraction.

EXPANSION PLUG: See FREEZE PLUG.

EXPANSION VALVE: See THERMOSTATIC EXPANSION VALVE.

EXTREME PRESSURE LUBRICANTS (E.P.): A lubricant to which an ingredient has been added to increase lubricant's ability to withstand high pressures between gear teeth, etc.

FAHRENHEIT (F): A scale of temperature measurement on which, under standard atmospheric pressure, water freezes at 32° and boils at 212°.

FEEDBACK: System of air-fuel mixture control utilizing a computer controlled stepper motor.

FEELER GAUGE: A metal strip or blade, finished accurately with regard to thickness, used for measuring clearance between two parts.

FERROUS METAL: Metals which contain iron or steel, enabling them to be magnetized.

F-HEAD ENGINE: An engine designed with one valve in cylinder block at side of piston and other valve in cylinder head above piston.

FIELD: Area in which magnetic flow occurs in a generator or starting motor.

FIELD COIL: A coil of insulated wire surrounding field pole.

FILE: To finish or trim with a hardened metal tool with cutting ridges.

FILLET: A rounded filling between two parts joined at an angle.

FILTER: A device designed to remove suspended impurities or particles of foreign matter from intake air, fuel system, or lubricating system.

FIREWALL: Insulated partition between engine and vehicle occupants.

FIRING ORDER: Sequence in which combustible mixture is ignited in cyclinders of engine.

FIT: Satisfactory contact between two machined surfaces.

FLANGE: A projecting rim or collar on an object for keeping it in place.

FLARE: A flange or a cone-shaped end applied to a piece of tubing to provide a means of sealing two similarly angled areas formed in fitting body and the nut.

FLASH POINT: Temperature at which an oil will flash and burn.

FLOAT: A hollow part which is lighter than fuel or fluid in which it rests, and ordinarily used to operate a valve controlling entrance of fuel or fluid.

FLOATING PISTON PIN: A piston pin which is free to turn or oscillate in both connecting rod and piston.

FLOAT LEVEL: Predetermined setting of float to control height of fuel in carburetor bowl, usually regulated by means of a suitable valve.

FLOODING: Too much fuel for operating conditions. Also, too much liquid refrigerant being metered into evaporator of an air conditioning system.

FLUID: A liquid, gas, or vapor.

FLUID COUPLING: A hydraulic clutch used to transmit engine torque to transmission gears. See FLUID DRIVE.

FLUID DRIVE: A pair of vaned rotating elements held close to each other without touching. Rotation is imparted to driven member by driving member through resistance of a body of oil.

FLUTTER: See BOUNCE.

FLUX: Electric or magnetic lines of force passing or flowing in a magnetic field. Also, material used to cause joining metal to adhere to both parts to be joined.

FLYWHEEL: A heavy wheel in which energy is absorbed and stored by means of momentum.

FOOT POUND (or lb. ft.): A measure of amount of energy or work required to lift 1 lb. 1 ft.

FORCE: The amount of push or pull exerted on an object.

FORCE-FIT: See DRIVE FIT.

FORGE: To shape metal while hot and plastic by hammering.

FORWARD BIAS: Conductive condition that exists when current flows through a diode.

FOUR CYCLE ENGINE: Engine in which an explosion occurs every other revolution of crankshaft. A cycle, also known as Otto cycle, is considered 1/2 revolution of crankshaft. Strokes are: suction, compression, power, exhaust.

FOUR-GAS ANALYZER: Equipment for testing exhaust gas for hydrocarbons, carbon monoxide, carbon dioxide, and oxygen.

FOUR WHEEL DRIVE: Power transfer system that permits a vehicle to be driven by all four wheels.

FREE-WHEELING: A mechanical device in which driving member imparts motion to a driven member in one direction but not other.

FREEZE PLUG: A disc or cup-shaped metal device inserted in a hole in a casting through which core was removed when casting was formed.

FREEZING POINT: Temperature at which coolant starts to freeze, based on mixture percentages and pressure.

FREON: A particular brand of refrigerant.

FRICTION: Resistance to relative motion between two bodies in contact.

FUEL: Substance that will burn and release heat.

FUEL KNOCK: See DETONATION.

FULCRUM: A support, often wedge-shaped, on which a lever pivots when it lifts an object.

FULL-FLOATING AXLE: Drive axle construction where axle driving shaft does not carry vehicle weight.

FUSE: A piece of wire which will carry a limited amount of current only, then melt and open electrical circuit as a safety measure to avoid damage from excessive current flow.

FUSIBLE LINK: Special length of smaller gauge wire designed to ''blow'' if heavy current flows in circuit.

GAL: Gallon.

GALVANIZE: To coat with a molten alloy of lead and tin to prevent rusting.

GALVANOMETER: An instrument used for location, measurement, and direction of an electric current.

GAS: A substance which can be changed in volume and shape according to temperature and pressure applied to it. Example: air can be compressed into smaller volume or expanded by application of heat.

GASSING: Bubbling of battery electrolyte which occurs during process of charging a battery.

GASKET: Anything used as a packing, such as a substance placed between two metal surfaces to act as a seal.

GEAR RATIO: Number of revolutions made by a driving gear as compared to number of revolutions made by a driven gear of different size. Example: if one gear makes three revolutions while other gear makes one revolution, gear ratio is 3 to 1.

GENERATOR: A device consisting of an armature, field coils, and other parts which, when rotated, will generate electricity.

GLAZE: An extremely smooth or glossy engine cylinder surface polished over a long period of time by friction of piston rings.

GLAZE BREAKER: A tool for removing glossy surface finish in an engine cylinder.

GOVERNOR: A device to control and regulate speed. May be mechanical, hydraulic, or electrical.

GRAM: A unit of measure of weight or mass equal to 0.03527 oz.

GRID: Metal framework of an individual battery plate in which active material is placed.

GRIND: To finish or polish a surface by means of an abrasive wheel.

GROOVE: Space between two adjacent tire tread ribs.

GROSS HORSEPOWER: Brake horsepower of an engine with optimum ignition setting and without allowing for power losses caused by engine's accessory units.

GROSS TORQUE: Maximum torque developed by crankshaft of engine without allowing for power absorbed by engine's accessory units.

GROUND: Terminal of battery connected to frame of vehicle to serve as ''return wire'' to complete electrical circuit.

GROUP: A set of battery plates, either positive or negative, joined together but not assembled with separators.

GROWLER: An electrical device for testing electric motor armatures.

GUM: Oxidized petroleum products that accumulate in fuel system, carburetor, or engine parts.

HALOGEN HEADLAMPS: Tungsten-halogen bulb used in sealed beam unit or as separate bulb in composite headlamp.

HARD PEDAL: A loss in braking efficiency so that an excessive amount of pressure is needed to actuate brakes.

HARD SOLDER: Uniting two pieces of metal with a material having a melting point higher than ''soft'' solder. Example: silver soldering.

HARMONIC BALANCER: A device designed to reduce torsional or twisting vibration which occurs along length of crankshaft used in multiple cylinder engines.

HAZARD WARNING FLASHER: Actuates warning system of flashing front and rear turn signal lamps.

HC: Hydrocarbons.

HEADER: Special exhaust pipes, used on high performance engines to reduce back pressure.

HEADLAMP DELAY SYSTEM: Automatically controls headlamp ON-OFF operation after ignition and main lighting switch are turned OFF.

HEAT EXCHANGER: A device that utilizes exhaust system heat to aid in fuel vaporization.

HEAT RISER: Passage between exhaust and intake manifolds.

HEAT SINK: Metal bracket in end frame of alternator that contains and absorbs heat from diodes.

HEAT TREATMENT: A combination of heating and cooling operations timed and applied to a metal in a solid state in a way that will produce desired properties.

HEEL: Outside or larger half of gear tooth. Also, end of brake shoe not against anchor.

HEI: High Energy Ignition.

HELICAL: Shaped like a coil of wire or a screw thread.

HELICAL GEAR: A gear design where gear teeth are cut at an angle to shaft.

HEMI: Hemispherical or dome-shaped combustion chamber in some engines.

HERRINGBONE GEAR: A pair of helical gears designed to operate together in form of a V.

HIGH TENSION: Secondary or induced high voltage electrical current. Circuit includes wiring from ignition distributor cap to coil and to each spark plug.

Hg: Chemical symbol for mercury.

HIGH SIDE: High pressure portion of an air conditioning system.

HOLE THEORY: Assumption that move-ment of a free electron from atom to atom leaves a hole in atom it left, which is filled by another free electron.

HONE: An abrasive tool for correcting small irregularities or differences in diameter in an engine cylinder, brake cylinder, etc.

HORN: Provides driver with means of sounding an audible warning signal.

HORSEPOWER: Energy required to lift 550 lb. 1 ft. in 1 sec.

HOTCHKISS DRIVE: A driving axle design in which axle torque is absorbed by chassis springs or control arms.

HP: Horsepower: energy required to lift 550 lb. 1 ft. in 1 second is 1 hp.

HYDRAULIC: Pertains to fluids in motion, such as hydraulically operated brakes, hydraulic torque converters, power steering, etc.

HYDRAULIC BRAKE SYSTEM: System in which brake operation and control utilizes hydraulic brake fluid.

HYDROCARBON: Any compound composed entirely of carbon and hydrogen.

HYDROMETER: An instrument for determining state of charge in a battery by measuring specific gravity of electrolyte.

HYDROSTATIC GAUGE: Used in referring to gauges, such as a gasoline tank gauge, where depth of gasoline in tank controls air in connecting line to instrument which registers depth on a scale or dial.

HYPOID GEARS: A design of pinion and ring gear where centerline of pinion is offset from centerline of ring gear.

ID: Inside diameter.

IDLE SPEED: The rpm of a spark ignition engine with closed throttle opening at manufacturer's recommended speed.

IGNITION COIL: Electrical device used to step up battery voltage to a level high enough to fire spark plugs.

IGNITION DISTRIBUTOR: An electrical device usually containing circuit breaker for primary circuit and providing a means for conveying secondary or high tension current to spark plug wires as required.

IGNITION SYSTEM: Means for igniting fuel in cylinders. Includes spark plugs, wiring, distributor, ignition coil, and source of electrical current.

IGNITION TIMING: Synchronization of distributor to engine so ignition takes place in each cylinder at proper time.

IHP: Indicated horsepower developed by an engine and a measure of pressure of explosion within cylinder expressed in pounds per square inch.

IMCO: Inproved Combustion.

IN: Inch.

INCLUDED ANGLE: Combined angles of camber and steering axis inclination.

INDEPENDENT SUSPENSION: A construction in which wheel on one side of vehicle may rise or fall independently of wheel on other side.

INDUCTION: Influence of magnetic fields of different strength not electrically connected to one another.

INDUCTION COIL: Essentially a transformer which, through induction, creates a high tension current by means of an increase in voltage.

INDUCTION HARDENING: Method of heating cast iron (valve seats, for example) to about 1700°F, which hardens it to a depth of .05 to .08 in.

INERTIA: A physical law that tends to keep a motionless body at rest or keep a moving body in motion. Effort is required to start a mass moving or to retard it once it is in motion.

INFORMATION CENTERS: Visual displays which alert driver to certain vehicle conditions.

INHIBITOR: A material to restrain or hinder some unwanted action. Example: a rust inhibitor added to cooling systems to retard formation of rust.

INJECTOR: A pump that injects a fluid or gas into a cylinder or chamber. Also, fuel injection system electrical solenoid which, when energized, allows fuel to enter combustion chamber.

INLET VALVE: See INTAKE VALVE.

INPUT SHAFT: Transmission shaft which receives power from engine and transmits it to transmission gears.

INPUTS: Information from various sensors that tells electronic control module how engine is performing.

INSULATION: Any material, which does not conduct electricity, used to prevent leakage of current from a conductor. Also, a material which does not readily conduct heat.

INSULATOR: A nonconducting material or shield covering an electrical conductor.

INTAKE MANIFOLD OR INLET PIPE: Tube or housing used to conduct air-fuel mixture from carburetor to engine cylinders.

INTAKE VALVE: A valve which permits a fluid or gas to enter a chamber and seals against exit.

INTEGRAL: Formed as a unit with another part.

INTENSIFY: To increase or concentrate. Example: increase voltage of an electrical current.

INTERCELL CONNECTORS: Battery element terminal posts.

INTERMEDIATE GEAR: Transmission gear or gears between low and high.

INTERMITTENT: Motion or action that occurs at intervals.

INTERNAL COMBUSTION: Burning of a fuel within an enclosed space.

JOURNAL: That part of a shaft or axle in actual contact with bearing.

JUMP SPARK: A high tension electrical current which jumps through the air from one terminal to another.

JUMP START: Use of jumper cables to trasnfer power from a good battery to a discharged battery.

KEY: A small block inserted between shaft and hub to prevent circumferential movement.

KEYWAY OR KEYSEAT: A groove or slot cut to permit insertion of a key.

KICKDOWN SWITCH: An electrical switch used to cause a transmission to downshift from a higher to a lower gear ratio.

KILOMETER: A metric measurement of distance which is equivalent to approximately 5/8 of a mile.

KILOWATT: A measure of electrical energy consisting of 1000 watts or 1 1/3 horsepower.

KINGPIN: Shaft around which steering spindle of a truck front wheel turns.

KINGPIN INCLINATION: Angle at which kingpin is inclined inward from true vertical centerline.

KNOCK: Term used to describe various noises in an engine made by loose or worn mechanical parts, preignition, detonation, etc.

KNOCK SENSORS: Designed to eliminate knock associated with detonation or preignition.

KNURL: To indent or roughen a finished surface.

LACQUER: In automotive painting, a solution of solids in solvents that evaporate with great rapidity.

LAMINATE: To build up or construct out of a number of thin sheets. Example: laminated core in an electric motor or generator.

LAND: Metal portion separating the grooves that rings ride against.

LAPPING: Process of fitting one surface to another by rubbing them together with an abrasive material between two surfaces.

LATERAL RUNOUT: Amount of side movement of a rotating wheel, tire, or rotor from the vertical.

LATHE: Machine on which a piece of solid material is spun on a horizontal axis and shaped by a fixed cutting or abrading tool.

LB: Pound.

LEAD BURNING: Joining two pieces of lead by melting or fusing the metal.

LEFT HAND RULE: To determine direction of lines of force, grasp conductor with left hand thumb extended in direction of current flow. Fingers indicate direction of lines of force.

L-HEAD ENGINE: An engine design in which both valves are located on one side of engine cylinder.

LIFT: Maximum distance valve head is raised off its seat.

LIMITED SLIP DIFFERENTIAL: Directs power flow to axle of wheel having best traction.

LIMITER: Device placed on carburetor idle mixture adjustment screw so that richness of mixture can be made only within predetermined limits.

LINER: Usually a thin section placed between two parts. Example: a replaceable cylinder liner in an engine.

LINKAGE: Any series of rods, yokes, and levers, etc., used to transmit motion from one unit to another.

LIQUID: Neither a gas nor a solid. Any substance which assumes shape of vessel in which it is placed without changing volume.

LIQUID WITHDRAWAL SYSTEM: A method of piping where liquid is taken from bottom of an LP-Gas tank and converted into gas by a vaporizer.

LITER: A measure of volume equal to 61.027 cu. in.

LIVE: Electrical parts connected to insulated side of electrical system. Example: an insulated wire connected to battery.

LIVE AXLE: Shaft through which power travels from drive axle gears to driving wheels.

LOAD RANGE: Tire designation, with a letter (A, B, C, etc.), used to identify a given size tire with its load and inflation limits. Replaces term PLY RATING.

LOCK WASHER: A form of washer designed to prevent attaching nut from working loose.

LOCKUP TORQUE CONVERTER: Converter with internal mechanism that locks turbine to impeller in direct drive.

LONGITUDINAL: Lengthwise.

LOST MOTION: See BACKLASH.

LOUVER OR LOUVRE: Openings or vents in hood or body, usually intended for ventilation.

LOW PEDAL: A condition where excessive clearance at some point in braking system causes full pedal movement for application of brakes.

LOW SIDE: Low pressure portion of an air conditioning system.

LOW SPEED: Gearing provided in an automobile which causes greatest number of revolutions of engine as compared to driving wheels.

LP-GAS: LIQUEFIED PETROLEUM GAS: Made usable as a fuel for internal combustion engines by compressing volatile petroleum gases to liquid form. LP-Gas must be kept under pressure or at low temperature in order to remain in liquid form.

LUG: Extension of battery plate grid for connecting plate to strap.

LUGGING: Reduction in speed due to increased load.

MACPHERSON STRUT: Long, telescopic shock absorber strut surrounded by a coil spring.

MAGNET (Permanent): A piece of hard steel often bent into a "U" shape to create and retain opposite poles when charged with magnetic power.

MAGNETIC FIELD: Flow of magnetic

force or magnetism between opposite poles of a magnet.

MAGNETISM: Invisible force that attracts certain materials such as steel.

MAGNETO: An electrical device which generates alternating current when rotated by an outside source of power. Device used to generate either low tension or high tension current.

MALFUNCTION: Problem in system that affects normal operation.

MALLEABLE CASTING: A casting which has been toughened by annealing.

MANGANESE BRONZE: An alloy of copper, zinc, and manganese.

MANIFOLD: A pipe with multiple openings used to connect various cylinders to one inlet or outlet.

MANIFOLD GAUGE SET: Instrument used to test pressures on high and low sides of compressor. Also, can be used to discharge refrigerant, evacuate air and moisture, and charge air conditioning system with refrigerant.

MANIFOLD HEAT CONTROL VALVE: Thermostatically controlled valve that diverts hot exhaust gases around intake manifold during cold engine starting.

MANIFOLD VACUUM: Source of vacuum in manifold below carburetor throttle plate.

MANOMETER: A device for measuring a vacuum, consisting of a "U" shaped tube partially filled with fluid. One end of tube is open to air, other is connected to chamber in which vacuum is to be measured. A column of mercury 30 in. high equals 14.7 psi, which is atmospheric pressure at sea level. Readings are given in inches of mercury (Hg).

MANUAL: Pertaining to or done with the hands. Also, requiring or using physical skill or energy.

MAP SENSOR: Manifold Absolute Pressure sensor tells computer how much pressure is in the intake manifold.

MASTER CYLINDER: Single or dual primary unit for displacing hydraulic fluid under pressure in brake system.

MCU: Microprocessor Control Unit.

MCV: Manifold Control Valve.

MECHANICAL EFFICIENCY: Ratio between indicated horsepower and brake horsepower of an engine.

MELTING POINT: Temperature at which solid material becomes liquid.

MEMA: Motor and Equipment Manufacturers Association.

MERCURY COLUMN: A reference term used in connection with a manometer.

METER: A measure of length equal to 39.37 in.

METERING: Passage of liquid or gas through a fixed orifice or nozzle, diameter of which determines volume of flow.

METERING VALVE: Limits hydraulic pressure to front disc brakes until predetermined front input pressure is reached.

METHANOL OR WOOD ALCOHOL: A poisonous alcohol made synthetically or from distillation of wood.

MEWA: Motor and Equipment Wholesalers Association.

MICRO FINISH: Degree of surface roughness, measured with a profilometer.

MICROMETER: A measuring instrument for either external or internal measurement in thousandths and sometimes tenths of thousandths of inches.

MIL: Unit of length equal to .001 in.

MILL: To cut or machine with rotating tooth cutters.

MILLIMETER (mm): One millimeter is metric equivalent of .039370 of an inch. One inch is equivalent to 25.4 mm.

MISFIRING: Failure of an explosion to occur in one or more cylinders while engine is running. This may be a continuous or intermittent failure.

MODE: A particular state of operation.

MODULATOR: A pressure regulating device used in automatic transmissions.

MONEL METAL: Corrosion resistant alloy of nickel, copper, iron, and manganese.

MONITORING: Maintaining a continuous control of an operation or function, varying control as required by specific conditions.

MONO-BLOCK: All cylinders of an engine are contained in one casting. Same as en-bloc or in-block.

MOTOR: Principally, a machine which converts electrical energy to mechanical energy.

MPH: Miles per hour.

MUFFLER: A chamber attached to exhaust pipe which allows exhaust gases to expand and cool. It is usually fitted with baffles or porous plates and serves to reduce noise created by exhaust.

MULTIPLE DISC: A clutch having a number of driving and driven discs as compared to a single plate clutch.

MVMA: Motor Vehicle Manufacturers Association.

NADA: National Automobile Dealers Association.

NAPA: National Automotive Parts Association.

NC: Normally Closed.

NEEDLE BEARING: An antifriction bearing using many rollers of small diameter in relation to their length.

NEGATIVE POLE: Point from which an electrical current flows as it passes through circuit. Designated by a minus sign ($-$).

NET HORSEPOWER: Brake horsepower remaining at flywheel of engine to do useful work after power required by engine accessories has been provided.

NET TORQUE: Torque available at flywheel of engine after power required by engine's accesories has been provided.

NEUTRAL SAFETY SWITCH: Eliminates possiblity of starting engine when transmission selector lever is in position to drive car.

NEUTRON: Portion of an atom which carries no electrical charge and, with protons, form central core of atom about which electrons rotate.

NICKEL STEEL: Nickel is alloyed with steel to form a heat and corrosion resistant metal.

NITROGEN OXIDES: See OXIDES OF NITROGEN.

NO: Normally Open.

NOBLE METAL: Rare or precious metals used as catalyst agent in catalytic converters.

NONFERROUS METALS: Metals which contain no iron or very little iron, and not subject to rusting.

NORTH POLE: Pole of a magnet from which lines of force start. Opposite of south pole.

NOx: Nitrogen oxides.

NPN: Three-element transistor made of two types of semiconductor materials.

OCTANE NUMBER: A unit of measurement on a scale intended to indicate tendency of a fuel to knock.

OD: Outside diameter.

ODOMETER: A device for measuring and registering number of miles traveled.

OHM: A measurement of resistance to flow of an electrical current through a conductor.

OHMMETER: An instrument for measuring resistance in ohms.

OHM'S LAW: Mathematical relationship between voltage, resistance, and amount of currnet in an electrical circuit. It states: $E = I \times R$; $I = E \div R$; $R = E \div I$.

OIL COOLER: Device incorporated into design of radiator on automatic transmission-equipped cars to keep transmission fluid at a lower temperature.

ONE-WAY CLUTCH: See FREE-WHEELING.

OPEN CIRCUIT: An incomplete electrical circuit.

ORIFICE: Small opening in a tube, pipe, or valve.

ORIFICE TUBE: Tube with calibrated opening, used in place of expansion valve in some air conditioning systems.

OSAC: Orifice Spark Advance Control.

OSCILLATE: To swing back and forth like a pendulum.

OSCILLOSCOPE: An electronic device used to observe and measure instantaneous voltage in an electrical circuit.

OSHA: Occupational Safety and Health

Administration.

OTTO CYCLE: Four stroke cycle named after man who adopted principle of four stroke operation in an engine cylinder. They are: suction, compression, power, and exhaust.

OUT-OF-ROUND: Condition where engine cylinder bore has greater wear at one diameter than another.

OUTPUT: Functions controlled by electronic control unit.

OUTPUT SHAFT: Shaft which receives power from transmission and transmits it to vehicle drive shaft.

OVERDRIVE: Any arrangement of gearing which produces more revolutions of driven shaft than driving shaft.

OVERHEAD VALVE OR VALVE-IN-HEAD ENGINE (OHV): An engine design having valves located in cylinder head directly above pistons.

OVERRUNNING CLUTCH OR COUPLING: See FREE-WHEELING.

OXIDES OF NITROGEN: Compounds of nitric oxides and nitrogen dioxide produced by combustion process, especially at high temperatures.

OXIDIZE: To combine an element with oxygen or convert into its oxide. Examples: when carbon burns, it combines with oxygen to form carbon dioxide or carbon monoxide; iron combines with oxygen in air to form an oxide of iron, or rust.

OXYGEN SENSOR: Exhaust device that detects amount of oxygen (O_2) in exhaust stream and sends information to electronic control module.

PAD: Disc brake friction material generally molded to metal backing, or shoe.

PANCAKE ENGINE: A design where cylinders are laid horizontal to obtain a minimum of height.

PARALLEL CIRCUIT: An electrical circuit having more than one path.

PARKING BRAKE: Brake system used to hold one or more brakes continuously in applied position.

PARTICULATES: Minute solid particles emitted from vehicle's exhaust.

PARTNERSHIP: Business owned by at least two people.

PAWL: A pivoted bar adapted to engage with teeth of a ratchet to prevent or impart motion.

PCV: Positive crankcase ventilation.

PEAK INVERSE VOLTAGE: Amount of voltage a diode can take in reverse direction without being damaged.

PEEN: To stretch over by pounding with rounded end of a hammer.

PERIPHERY: Circumference of a circle. Example: tread of a tire.

PETCOCK: A small valve placed in a fluid circuit for draining purposes.

PETROLEUM: A group of liquid and gaseous compounds composed of carbon and hydrogen.

PHILLIPS SCREW OR SCREWDRIVER: A type of screwhead having a "cross" instead of a "slot" for a corresponding type of screwdriver.

PHOSPHOR-BRONZE: An alloy consisting of copper, tin, and lead sometimes used in heavy-duty bearings.

PILOT SHAFT: Tool used temporarily to align parts of a mechanism being assembled.

PILOT VALVE: A small valve used to control action of a larger valve.

PINGING: Sound produced when either preignition or detonation occurs.

PINION: A small gear which engages a larger gear.

PINION CARRIER: Mounting or bracket which retains bearings supporting a pinion shaft.

PISTON: A cylindrical part, closed at one end, which is connected to the crankshaft by a connecting rod. Force of explosion in cylinder is exerted against closed end of piston causing connecting rod to move crankshaft.

PISTON COLLAPSE: A condition describing a sudden reduction in diameter of piston skirt due to heat or stress.

PISTON DISPLACEMENT: Volume of air moved or displaced by moving piston from one end of its stroke to other.

PISTON HEAD: Part of piston above the rings.

PISTON LANDS: Parts of piston between piston rings.

PISTON PIN: Journal for bearing in small end of an engine connecting rod which also passes through piston walls.

PISTON RING: An expanding ring placed in grooves of piston to provide a seal to prevent passage of fluid or gas past piston.

PISTON RING EXPANDER: A spring placed behind piston ring in groove to increase pressure of ring against cylinder wall.

PISTON RING GAP: Clearance between ends of piston ring.

PISTON RING GROOVE: Slots in piston in which piston rings are placed.

PISTON SKIRT: Part of piston below the rings.

PISTON SKIRT EXPANDER: A spring or other device inserted in piston skirt to compensate for collapse or decrease in diameter.

PITMAN ARM: Lever extending from steering gear to which steering linkage is attached.

PITOT TUBE: An instrument for measuring fluid velocity by means of difference in pressure between tip and side openings.

PIVOT: A pin or short shaft upon which another part rests or turns, or about which another part rotates or oscillates.

PLANETARY GEARS: A system of gearing which is modeled after solar system. A pinion is surrounded by an internal ring gear with planet gears in mesh between ring gear and pinion.

PLANET CARRIER: Carrier or bracket in a planetary system which contains shafts upon which pinions or planet gears turn.

PLANET GEARS: Gears interposed between ring gear and sun gear and meshing with both in a planetary system.

PLATINUM: An expensive metal having an extremely high melting point and good electrical conductivity.

PLUG-IN DIAGNOSIS: On-board computer provides means for special test equipment to be plugged in for making a series of programmed tests to check condition of various units and systems on car.

PLY: Layer of rubber-coated parallel cords forming tire body, or carcass.

PLY RATING: See LOAD RANGE.

PNEUMATIC: Pertaining to air. Example: a device operated by air pressure is a pneumatic device.

PNP: Three-element transistor made of two layers of semiconductor materials.

POA: Pilot Operated Absolute valve in some air conditioning systems.

POLARITY: Refers to positive or negative terminal of a battery of an electric circuit; also north or south pole of a magnet.

POPPET VALVE: A valve structure consisting of a circular head with an elongated stem attached in center. It is designed to open and close a circular hole or port.

PORCELAIN: General term applied to material or element used for insulating center electrode of a spark plug.

PORT: An opening in cylinder head or engine block for intake air-fuel mixture or exhaust gas flow. Also, to smooth and enlarge passageways to intake valves.

PORTED VACUUM: Source of vacuum in carburetor above closed throttle plate.

POSITIVE CRANKCASE VENTILATION: System for clearing engine crankcase of blowby gases.

POSITIVE CRANKCASE VENTILATION VALVE: Device that regulates amount of airflow through crankcase.

POSITIVE POLE: Point to which current returns after passing through a circuit. Designated by plus sign (+).

POST: Heavy, circular part to which a group of battery plates is attached, and which extends through cell cover to provide a means of attachment to adjacent cell or battery cable.

POTENTIAL: An indication of amount of energy available.

POTENTIAL DIFFERENCE: A difference of electrical pressure that sets up a flow of electric current.

POTENTIAL DROP: A loss of electrical pressure due to resistance of leakage.

POWER BRAKES: Hydraulic, vacuum, air, or electrohydraulic boost.

POWER STEERING: Application of hydraulic or mechanical power in addition to manual power in steering of an automobile.

POWER TAKE-OFF: A device, usually mounted on side of transmission or transfer case, used to transmit engine power to wheels.

POWER TRAIN: Group of components used to transmit power to wheels—clutch, transmission, universal joints, drive shaft, and rear axle.

PPM: Parts Per Million.

PREHEATING: Application of heat as a preliminary step to some further thermal or mechanical treatment.

PREIGNITION: Ignition occurring earlier than intended. Example: explosive mixture being fired in a cylinder by a flake of incandescent carbon before electric spark occurs.

PRELOADING: To adjust a small amount of pressure on an antifriction bearing to eliminate any looseness.

PRESS-FIT: See DRIVE FIT.

PRESSURE: Force per unit of area.

PRESSURE DIFFERENTIAL VALVE: Senses unbalanced hydraulic pressure between two halves of the split brake system.

PRESSURE-VACUUM CAP: Fuel tank filler cap designed to prevent loss of fuel or vapor from tank.

PRIMARY BRAKE SHOE: Brake shoe in a set which initiates the self-energizing action.

PRIMARY CIRCUIT: A low voltage circuit energized by battery to begin ignition circuit.

PRIMARY WINDING: A wire which conducts low tension current to be transformed by induction into high tension current in secondary winding of ignition coil.

PRIMARY WIRES: Wiring circuit used for conducting low tension or primary current to points where it is used.

PROM: Programmable Read Only Memory. Engine calibration unit.

PROPORTIONING VALVE: Regulates outlet pressure to rear brakes.

PROTON: Portion of an atom which carries a positive charge of electricity.

PRONY BRAKE: A machine for testing power of an engine while running against a friction brake.

PROPANE: A petroleum hydrocarbon compound which has a boiling point about $-44\,°F$. It is used as an engine fuel and is loosely referred to as LP-Gas. It is often combined with butane.

PROPELLER SHAFT: Drive shaft connecting transmission with rear axle.

PROPORTIONING VALVE: Device used to improve braking balance during heavy brake application.

PSI: Pounds per square inch.

PULSE AIR SYSTEM: An exhaust emission control system that uses exhaust pulse in a pipe to permit air to be drawn into exhaust system.

PURGE: To remove air and moisture from an air conditioning system or component by flushing with a dry gas refrigerant.

PUSH ROD: A connecting link in an operating mechanism. Example: rod between valve lifter and rocker arm on an overhead valve engine.

QUADRANT: Designates gearshift or transmission control lever selector mounting.

QUENCHING: A process of rapid cooling of hot metal by contact with liquids, gases, or solids.

QUICK TEST: A functional diagnostic test of Ford's EEC system that displays test results as a series of service codes.

RACE: A finished inner and outer surface in which or on which ball bearings or roller bearings operate.

RACE CAM: A type of camshaft for race car engines which increases lift of valve, speed of valve opening and closing, length of time valve is held open, etc. Also known as Full, Three-quarter, or Semi-race cams, depending upon design.

RADIAL PLY: Pneumatic tire structure in which ply cords extend from bead to bead at right angles to centerline of tire.

RADIAL RUNOUT: Variation in diameter of a wheel, tire, or rotor from a specified amount.

RADIATION: Transfer of heat by rays. Example: heat from sun.

RADIUS RODS: Rods attached to axle and to frame to maintain correct horizontal position of axle, yet permit vertical motion.

RAM AIR: Air forced through a condenser or radiator, or into a carburetor air cleaner snorkel, by movement of a vehicle.

RATIO: Relation or proportion that one number bears to another.

REAM: To finish a hole accurately with a rotating fluted tool.

RECAP: Adding top strip of synthetic or reclaimed rubber to buffed and roughened surface of a worn tire.

RECEIVER-DRIER: Storage tank and filter for liquid refrigerant and containing a drying agent to remove moisture from circulating refrigerant. Also called ''receiver-dehydrator.''

RECIPROCATING: A back and forth movement. Example: action of a piston in a cylinder.

RECTIFIER: An electrical device for transforming or changing alternating current into direct current.

REFRIGERANT: A substance used in an air conditioning system which absorbs and gives up heat as it changes from a liquid to a vapor to a liquid.

REGULATOR: An automatic pressure reducing valve.

RELATIVE HUMIDITY: Actual moisture content in air in relation to total moisture that air can hold at a given temperature.

RELAY: Switching device operated by a low current circuit that controls opening and closing of another circuit of higher current capacity.

RELIEF: Amount one surface is set below or above another surface.

RELIEVING: Removal of some metal from around racing engine valves and between cylinder and valves to facilitate flow of gases.

RESISTANCE: Opposition to flow of current in an electrical component or circuit.

RESISTOR: A current-consuming piece of metal wire or carbon inserted into circuit to decrease flow of electricity.

RETARD: To cause spark to occur at a later time in cycle of engine operation. Opposite of spark advance.

RETREAD: Used tire with new rubber bonded to worn surface from shoulder to shoulder.

REVERSE BIAS: Nonconductive condition that exists when current flow is blocked by a diode.

REVERSE ELLIOT STEERING KNUCKLE: Type of axle construction in which steering spindle straddles ends of axle beam.

RHEOSTAT: A variable resistor. Example, the switch that dims the dash lights.

RIM: Metal support for tire or tire and tube assembly on wheel.

RING GEAR: Outer gear within which other gears revolve in a planetary system. Also, driven gear which mates with drive pinion in a differential assembly.

RIVET: To attach with rivets or to batter or upset end of a pin.

RMA: Rubber Manufacturers Association.

ROCKER ARM: A lever located on a fulcrum or shaft, one end bearing on valve stem, other on push rod.

ROCKWELL HARDNESS: A scale for designating degrees of hardness possessed by a substance.

ROLLER BEARING: An inner and outer race upon which hardened steel rollers operate.

ROTARY ENGINE: Wankel type internal combustion engine causes cycle of intake, compression, expansion, and exhaust by rotation of a triangular rotor in a housing shaped roughly like a figure 8. Air-fuel mixture enters and burned gases are ejected through ports covered and uncovered by movement of rotor.

ROTARY VALVE: A valve construction in which ported holes come into and out of register with each other to allow entrance and exist of fluids or gases.

ROTOR: Parallel-faced circular plate

against which brake lining is forced to retard vehicle. Also, a rotating part of an electrical or mechanical device.

ROTOR RUNOUT: Lateral movement of rotor friction surface as it rotates past a fixed point.

RPM: Revolutions per minute.

R-12: Refrigerant-12 commonly used in automobile air conditioning systems.

RUBBER: An elastic vibration-absorbing material of natural or synthetic origin.

RUNNING FIT: Where sufficient clearance has been allowed between shaft and journal to allow free running without overheating.

RUN-ON: See DIESELING.

RUNOUT: Out-of-round condition of a rotating part.

SAE: Society of Automotive Engineers.

SAE STEELS: A numerical index used to identify composition of SAE steel.

SAE THREAD: A table of threads set up by Society of Automotive Engineers and determines number of threads per inch. Example: a quarter inch diameter rod with an SAE thread would have 28 threads per inch.

SAFETY FACTOR: Degree of strength above normal requirements which serves as insurance against failure.

SAFETY RELIEF VALVE: A spring-loaded valve designed to open and relieve excessive pressure in a device when it exceeds a predetermined safe point.

SANDBLAST: To clean a surface by means of sand propelled by compressed air.

SAYBOLT TEST: A method of measuring viscosity of oil with use of a viscosimeter.

SCALE: A flaky deposit occurring on steel or iron. Ordinarily used to describe accumulation of minerals and metals accumulating in an automobile cooling system.

SCORE: A scratch, ridge, or groove marring a finished surface.

SCR: Silicon controlled rectifier.

SEALED BEAM LAMPS: Lamp construction with reflector, lens, and filament hermetically sealed in one unit.

SEAT: A surface, usually machined, upon which another part rests or seats. Example: surface upon which a valve face rests.

SEAT BELT: Passenger restraint system, usually consisting of a lap belt and a shoulder belt.

SECONDARY BRAKE SHOE: Brake shoe in a set which is energized by primary shoe and increases servo, or self-energizing, action of brake.

SECONDARY CIRCUIT: Electrical circuit designed to produce and deliver high voltage to spark plugs.

SECONDARY WINDING: A wire in which a secondary or high tension current is created by induction due to interruption of current in adjacent primary winding of an ignition coil.

SECTION HEIGHT: Height of an inflated tire from bottom of the bead to the top of the tread.

SECTION WIDTH: Width between exteriors of sidewalls of an inflated tire at its widest point.

SEDIMENT: Active material of battery plates that is gradually shed and accumulates below the plates.

SEIZE: When a surface moving upon another sticks, it is said to seize. For example: a piston seizes in a cylinder due to a lack of lubrication or overexpansion due to excessive heat.

SELECTIVE TRANSMISSION: Arrangement of gearing and shifting device in which it is possible to go directly from neutral position into any desired pair of gears.

SELF-ENERGIZATION: Placing of brake shoes so that drum tends to drag lining along with it, resulting in a wedging action between anchor and drum.

SELF TEST: A part of functional diagnostic test procedure that verifies operation of sensors and actuators, detects hard faults, and stores information for later retrieval.

SEMICONDUCTOR: Manufactured material somewhere between range of conductors and nonconductors.

SEMI-DIESEL: A semi-diesel engine operates on comparatively high compression and utilizes solid injection of fuel. However, it does use an electrical ignition system rather than depend solely upon heat generated by compression to furnish ignition.

SEMI-FLOATING AXLE: A drive axle construction in which axle shafts support weight of car.

SENSOR: A device which mechanically, electrically, or thermally senses a state of change and activates a mechanism to compensate for change.

SEPARATORS: Sheets of rubber or wood inserted between positive and negative battery plates of a cell to prevent contact with each other.

SERIES CIRCUIT: An electrical circuit having only one path.

SERIES PARALLEL CIRCUIT: An electrical circuit having some devices connected in series and others in parallel.

SERIES WINDING: An electric winding or coil of wire in series with other electrical equipment.

SERPENTINE BELT: Single belt that drives all accessories. It is a combination of a V-ribbed belt and a flat back belt.

SERVICE CODES: A series of two digit numbers that represent results of a self test.

SERVICE PORT: A fitting on service valve for attachment of a gauge.

SERVO: Automatic transmission hydraulic piston and cylinder assembly used to control drum bands.

SERVO ACTION: A brake construction in which a primary shoe pushes a secondary shoe to generate self-energization.

SHACKLE BOLT: A link for connecting one end of a chassis spring to frame which allows spring end to oscillate laterally.

SHEAR: To cut between two blades.

SHIM: Thin sheets used as spacers between two parts. Example: shims between control arm pivot shaft and frame serve to adjust caster and camber.

SHIMMY: In automobile steering, a wobbling or shaking of front wheels.

SHOCK ABSORBER: A device to provide hydraulic friction to control excessive deflection of automobile springs.

SHORT CIRCUIT: To provide a shorter electrical path. Often used to indicate an accidental ground in an electrical device or conductor.

SHRINK FIT: An exceptionally tight fit. Example: if shaft or part is slightly larger than hole in which it is to be inserted, outer part is heated above its normal operating temperature or inner part chilled below its normal operating temperature, or both, and assembled in this condition. Upon cooling, a shrink fit is obtained.

SHUNT: To bypass or turn aside. Also, an alternate path for current in electrical apparatus.

SHUNT WINDING: An electric winding or coil of wire which forms a bypass or alternate path for electric current. Example: in certain electric generators or motors, each end of field winding is connected to an armature brush.

SHUTTLE VALVE: A valve for diverting pressure from one channel to another.

SIDEWALL: Portion of tire between tread and bead.

SILENCER: See MUFFLERS.

SILICON: A nonmetallic element, often alloyed with steel.

SILICON CONTROLLED RECTIFIER: Semiconductor having an anode, cathode, and gate.

SILICON STEEL: An alloy of silicon and chromium with steel, often used for exhaust valves.

SILICONE: Any of a group of semi-organic polymers, used in lubricants, adhesives, and protective coverings.

SILVER SOLDERING: See HARD SOLDER.

SINGLE WIRE SYSTEM: Lighting circuit which uses car frame for return.

SLEEVE VALVE: A reciprocating sleeve or sleeves with ported openings placed between piston and cylinders of an engine to serve as valves.

SLIDING FIT: Where sufficient clearance has been allowed between shaft and journal to allow free running without overheating.

SLIP-IN BEARING: A liner, made to extremely accurate measurements, which can be used for replacement purposes without additional fitting.

SLIP RINGS: Insulated metal rings mounted on alternator rotor shaft on which brushes make continuous sliding contact.

SLUDGE: A pasty composition of oxidized petroleum products and an emulsion formed by a mixture of engine oil and water that clogs oil lines and passages.

SMOG: Unburned hydrocarbons combined with oxides of nitrogen and acted upon by sunlight.

SMOKE: Matter in exhaust emissions that obscures transmission of light.

SOLDER: An alloy of lead and tin used to unite two metal parts.

SOLDERING: To unite two pieces of metal with a material having a comparatively low melting point.

SOLE PROPRIETORSHIP: Business owned entirely by one person.

SOLENOID: An iron core, surrounded by a coil of wire, which moves due to magnetic attraction when electric current is fed to coil. Often used to actuate mechanisms by electrical means.

SOLID INJECTION: System used in full diesel and semi-diesel, where fuel in fluid state is injected into cylinder rather than a mixture of air and fuel drawn from a carburetor.

SOLID STATE: Electronic device or assembly with no moving parts.

SOLVENT: A solution which dissolves some other material. Example: water is a solvent for sugar.

SOUTH POLE: Pole of a magnet to which lines of force flow. Opposite of north pole.

SPACER, SPACER WASHER: A sheet of metal or other material placed between two surfaces to reduce clearance or to provide a better thrust surface for a fastener.

SPARK: An electric current possessing sufficient voltage to jump through air from one conductor to another.

SPARK ADVANCE: To cause spark to occur at an earlier time in cycle of engine operation. Opposite of retard.

SPARK GAP: Space between electrodes of a spark plug which spark jumps.

SPARK PLUG: A device, inserted in combustion chamber of an engine, containing a side electrode and insulated center electrode spaced to provide a gap for firing an electrical spark to ignite air-fuel mixture.

SPECIFIC GRAVITY: Relative weight of a substance compared to water. Example: if a cubic inch of acid weighs twice as much as a cubic inch of water, specific gravity is 2.0.

SPEED CONTROL: Accessory system designed to maintain rate of speed of vehicle desired by driver.

SPEEDOMETER: A device for measuring and indicating speed of a vehicle in miles per hour and/or kilometers per hour.

SPINDLE: Machined steel shaft that supports wheel bearings that bear a portion of weight of vehicle. Shaft upon which wheels are mounted and rotate.

SPIRAL BEVEL GEAR: A ring gear and pinion in which the mating teeth are curved.

SPLAYED SPRING: A design in which leaf springs are placed at other than a 90 degree angle to axle.

SPLINE: A long keyway.

SPLINE JOINT: Two mating parts each with a series of splines around their circumference, one inner and one outer to provide a longitudinally movable joint without any circumferential motion.

SPLIT HYDRAULIC BRAKE SYSTEM: Service brake system with two separate hydraulic circuits to provide braking action in one circuit if other one fails.

SPONGY BRAKE PEDAL: Air in hydraulic lines, distortion or stretching of connecting parts or swelling of hydraulic hose may allow pedal to be spongy or springy instead of solid.

SPOT WELD: To attach in spots by localized fusion of metal parts with aid of an electric current.

SPRINGS: Suspension devices including leaf, coil, air type, or torsion bars.

SPRUNG WEIGHT: A term used to describe all parts of an automobile that are supported by car springs. Example: frame, engine, body, payload, etc.

SPUR GEAR: A gear in which teeth are cut parallel to shaft.

SPURT-HOLE: A hole drilled through a connecting rod and bearing that allows oil under pressure to be squirted out of bearing for additinal lubrication of cylinder walls.

SQ. FT.: Square feet.

SQ. IN.: Square inch.

SSI: Solid State Ignition.

STARTING MOTOR: An electromagnetic device that converts electrical energy into mechanical energy.

STATIC ELECTRICITY: Atmospheric electricity as distinguished from electricity produced by mechanical means.

STATOR: A wheel having curved blades interposed between torque converter pump and turbine elements. Also, a metal frame of alternator with three stationary windings that give overlapping pulses of alternating current.

STEEL CASTING: Cast iron to which varying amounts of scrap steel have been added.

STEERING AXIS INCLINATION: Angle formed by centerline of suspension ball joints and true vertical centerline.

STEERING GEAR: Gears in steering unit. Also, assembly of parts and units required to control angularity of wheels to body of a vehicle.

STEERING GEOMETRY: See TOE-OUT ON TURNS.

STEERING KNUCKLE: Part about which front wheel pivots when turning.

STEERING POST OR COLUMN: Shaft connecting steering gear unit with steering wheel.

STEERING SPINDLE: A journal or shaft upon which steerable wheels of a vehicle are mounted.

STELLITE: An alloy of cobalt, chrome, and tungsten often used for exhaust valve seat inserts. It has a high melting point, good corrosion resistance, and unusual hardness when hot.

STOPLIGHT SWITCH: Brake pedal operated switch which completes circuit to vehicle's stop lamps.

STRAP: A lead section to which battery plates of a group are joined.

STRESS: Force or strain to which a material is subjected.

STROBOSCOPE: A term applied to an ignition timing light which, connected to distributor points, gives effect of making a mark on a rapidly rotating pulley or harmonic balancer which appears to stand still for observation.

STROKE: Distance traveled by a piston from BDC to TDC.

STROKING: Remachining crankshaft throws "off center" to alter stroke.

STUD: A rod that threads on both ends.

SUCTION: Suction exists in a vessel when pressure is lower than atmospheric pressure. See VACUUM. mospheric pressure. See VACUUM.

SULFATED: When a battery is improperly charged, or allowed to remain in a discharged condition for some length of time, plates will be coated with an abnormal amount of lead sulfate.

SUMP: Fluid reservoir.

SUN GEAR: Central gear around which other gears revolve.

SUPERCHARGER: A blower or pump which forces air into cylinders at higher than atmospheric pressure, enabling more gasoline to be burned and more power to be produced.

SUSPENSION: Use of front and rear springs to suspend a vehicle's frame, body or unitized body, engine and power train above wheels.

SWEAT: To join metal pieces by clamping them together with solder in between, then applying heat.

SYNCHROMESH: A device used in transmission gearing to facilitate meshing of two gears by causing speed of both gears to coincide.

SYNCHRONIZE: To cause two events to occur in unison or at same time.

TAC: Thermostatically Controlled Air Cleaner.

TACHOMETER: A device for measuring and indicating speed of an engine.

TAP: To cut threads in a hole with a tapered, fluted, threaded tool.

TAPER: Condition where cylinder is worn more at top of bore than at bottom.

TAPPET: Adjusting screw for varying clearance between valve stem and cam. May be built into valve lifter in L-head engine or installed in rocker arm on an overhead valve engine.

TBI: Throttle Body Injection.

TCS: Transmission Controlled Spark.

TDC: Top dead center.

TEMPER: To change characteristics of metal by application of heat.

TEMPERATURE: Heat intensity measured on a thermometer.

TENSION: Effort that is devoted toward elongation or ''stretching'' of a material.

TERMINAL: A junction point where electrical connections are made.

TFI: Thick Film Ignition.

T-HEAD ENGINE: An engine design in which inlet valves are placed on one side of the cylinder and exhaust valves placed on other.

THERMAC: GM's thermostatically controlled air cleaner system.

THERMACTOR: Ford air pump type exhaust emission control system.

THERMAL EFFICIENCY: A gallon of fuel contains potential energy in form of heat when burned in combustion chamber. Some heat is lost and some is converted into power. Thermal efficiency is ratio of work accomplished compared to total quantity of heat contained in fuel.

THERMAL REACTOR: Emission control device that accepts raw exhaust gases from engine and subjects them to extremely high temperatures to oxidize noxious emissions.

THERMISTOR: Resistor that changes its resistance inversely with temperature.

THERMOSTAT: A heat-controlled valve used in cooling system of engine to regulate flow of water between cylinder block and radiator. Also, a valve used in modern air cleaners in which inlet air temperature is regulated.

THERMOSTATIC EXPANSION VALVE: Metering device that removes presure from liquid refrigerant, permitting it to expand and vaporize in evaporator.

THERMOSTATIC VACUUM SWITCH: A temperature sensitive switch which allows spark advance when engine idles for long periods.

THERMO-SYPHON: A method of cooling an engine which utilizes difference in specific gravity of hot and cold water. No pump is used, but water passages are larger than in pump type circulation system.

THREE WAY CATALYST: Dual catalytic converter that controls HC, CO, and NOx.

THROTTLE STOP SOLENOID: A device that maintains engine at a speed over curb idle.

THROW: Distance from center of crankshaft main bearing to center of connecting rod journal.

TIE ROD: Metal rod connecting steering spindle arms on opposite side of vehicle.

TIMING CHAIN: Chain used to drive camshaft of an engine.

TIMING GEARS: Any group of gears driven from engine crankshaft to cause valves, ignition, and other engine-driven apparatus to operate at desired time during engine cycle.

TIRE: A tubular corded carcass covered with rubber or synthetic rubber, mounted on a wheel and inflated to provide traction for moving and stopping the vehicle.

TIRE VALVE: Air check that opens under air pressure and closes when pressure is removed.

TOE: Inside half of a gear tooth. Also, end of brake shoe against anchor.

TOE-OUT ON TURNS: Related angles assumed by front wheels of vehicle when turning.

TOLERANCE: A permissible variation between two extremes of a specification of dimensions.

TORQUE: Effort devoted toward twisting or turning.

TORQUE CONVERTER: Assembly of rotating elements in a fluid-filled housing used to multiply engine torque to geartrain of automatic transmission.

TORQUE WRENCH: A special wrench with a built-in indicator to measure applied force.

TORSION BAR: Rod with built-in twist to provide spring action.

TORUS: An oil-filled member of a torque converter.

TRAMP: An oscillating motion and heavy vibration when wheels are turning.

TRANSAXLE: Transmission and differential combined in one unit.

TRANSDUCER: An electrically activated vacuum regulator.

TRANSFER CASE: Power takeoff to drive both axles on four wheel drive vehicle.

TRANSFORMER: An electrical device, such as a high tension coil, which transforms or changes characteristics of an electrical current.

TRANSISTOR: In electronics, a miniature amplifying or switching device.

TRANSISTOR IGNITION: Ignition system utilizing transistors, a special coil, and conventional breaker points.

TRANSMISSION: A system of trading speed for power, or vice versa, through gearing or torque conversion. It includes various devices and combinations for changing ratio between engine revolutions and driving wheel revolutions.

TRANSMISSION CONTROLLED SPARK ADVANCE: A system used to control ignition spark advance by means of transmission gear selection.

TRANSVERSE: Crosswise.

TREAD: Portion of tire that comes in contact with road. Also, distance between center of tires at points where they contact road surface.

TREAD WEAR INDICATORS: Crosswise strips molded into tire to signal need for tire replacement when tread is worn.

TROUBLE CODE: Engine self diagnosis. Electronic control module questions sensor reading and stores code for which circuit trouble is located.

TROUBLESHOOTING: A process of diagnosing possible sources of trouble by observation and testing.

TUNE-UP: A process of accurate and careful adjustments and parts replacements to obtain utmost in engine performance.

TURBINE: A series of blades on a wheel, situated at an angle to the shaft, against which fluids or gases are impelled to impart rotary motion to shaft.

TURBOCHARGER: A device which utilizes pressure of exhaust gases to drive a supercharger which, in turn, forces more air into cylinders.

TURBULENCE: A disturbed, irregular motion of fluids or gases.

TURNING RADIUS: Diameter of a circle which a vehicle can be turned around.

TVS: Thermostatic Vacuum Switch.

TWC: Three Way Catalyst.

TWO CYCLE ENGINE: An engine design permitting a power stroke once for each revolution of the crankshaft.

UIC: Universal Integrated Circuit.

UNDERCOATING: Spraying insulating material on exposed undersections of an automobile to retard corrosion and deaden noise.

UNIBODY: Design which incorporates body and frame of vehicle in a single structure.

UNIVERSAL JOINT: A connection for transmitting power from a driving to a driven shaft through an angle.

UNLEADED GASOLINE: Motor fuel containing no tetraethyl lead additive.

UNSPRUNG WEIGHT: Weight that includes wheels, axles, etc., that are not supported by car springs.

UPDRAFT: A carburetor in which mixture flows upward to engine.

UPPER CYLINDER LUBRICATION: A method of introducing a lubricant into fuel or intake manifold in order to permit lubrication of upper cylinder, valve guides, etc.

UPSET: To compress at ends, causing an increase in diameter.

VACUUM: A pressure less than atmospheric pressure (14.7 psi at sea level).

VACUUM ADVANCE: Advancing ignition spark timing by applying or increasing vacuum to distributor vacuum unit.

VACUUM CONTROL: A diaphragm attached to ignition distributor spark advance which is controlled by changing of vacuum in intake manifold.

VACUUM GAUGE: An instrument designed to measure degree of vacuum existing in a chamber.

VACUUM POWER UNIT (MOTOR): A device for use in opening doors in heating and air conditioning systems.

VACUUM PUMP: Used to remove air and moisture from air conditioning system.

VALVE: A device for opening and sealing an aperture.

VALVE CLEARANCE: Gap allowed between end of valve stem and valve lifter or rocker arm to compensate for expansion due to heat.

VALVE FACE: Part of valve which mates with and rests upon a seating surface.

VALVE GRINDING: A process of mating valve seat and valve face.

VALVE HEAD: Portion of a valve upon which valve face is machined.

VALVE-IN-HEAD ENGINE (OHV): See OVERHEAD VALVE ENGINE.

VALVE KEY OR VALVE LOCK: Key, keeper, washer, or other device which holds valve spring cup or washer in place on valve stem.

VALVE LIFTER: Solid part or hydraulic plunger placed between cam and valve on an engine.

VALVE MARGIN: Space or rim on a poppet valve between surface of head and surface of valve face.

VALVE OVERLAP: An interval expressed in degrees where both valves of an automobile engine cylinder are open at same time.

VALVE SEAT: Mating surface upon which valve face rests.

VALVE SPRING: A spring attached to a valve to return it to seat after lift is released.

VALVE STEM: Portion of valve which rests within a guide.

VALVE STEM GUIDE: A bushing or hole for valve stem.

VALVE TIMING: Indicates relative position of valve (open or closed) to piston in its travel, in crankshaft degrees.

VALVE TRAIN: Mechanism or linkage used to transmit motion of engine cam to valve stem, causing valve to open.

VANES: Any plate or blade attached to an axis and moved by or in air or a liquid.

VAPORIZE: Transforming or helping to transform a liquid into a vapor.

VAPOR LOCK: A condition in which fuel boils in fuel system, forming bubbles which retard or stop flow of fuel to carburetor.

VAPOR PRESSURE: Pressure developed over a liquid in a closed vessel, depending upon liquid and temperature.

VAPOR WITHDRAWAL: A system of piping and connections to operate an engine directly on vapor taken from top of an LP-Gas tank.

V-BELT: Drives accessory by wedging action in a pulley groove.

VDOT: Variable Displacement Orifice Tube air conditioning system.

VENTURI: Two tapering streamlined tubes joined at their small ends to reduce internal diameter.

VIBRATION DAMPER: See HARMONIC BALANCER.

VIN: Vehicle Identification Number.

VIR: Valve In Receiver. Found in some air conditioning systems.

VISCOSIMETER: An instrument for determining viscosity of an oil by passing a certain quantity at a definite temperature through a standard size orifice or port. Time required for oil to pass through, expressed in seconds, gives viscosity.

VISCOSITY: Considered to be internal friction of a fluid. Also, resistance to flow, or adhesiveness characteristics, of an oil.

VOICE ALERT SYSTEM: Audible warnings to enhance those provided by instruments, lights, and buzzers.

VOLATILITY: Tendency of fluid to evaporate rapidly. Example: gasoline is more volatile than kerosene, since it evaporates at lower temperature.

VOLT: A unit of electrical force that will cause a current of one ampere to flow through a resistance of one ohm.

VOLTAGE: Electromotive force which causes current to flow in a circuit.

VOLTAGE DROP: Decrease in voltage as current passes through a resistance.

VOLTAGE REGULATOR: An electrical device for regulating voltage output.

VOLTMETER: An instrument for measuring voltage in an electrical circuit.

VOLUME: Measure of space expressed as cubic inches or cubic centimeters.

VOLUMETRIC EFFICIENCY: A combination between ideal and actual efficiency of an internal combustion engine. If engine completely filled each cylinder on each induction stroke, volumetric efficiency of engine would be 100 percent. In actual operation, however, volumetric efficiency is lowered by inertia of the gases, friction between gases and manifolds, temperature of gases, and pressure of air entering carburetor. Volumetric efficiency is ordinarily increased by use of large valves, ports, and manifolds and can be further increased with aid of a supercharger.

VORTEX: A whirling movement or mass of liquid or air.

WANDERING: A condition in which front wheels of an automobile tend to turn slowly in first one direction, then the other, interfering with directional control or stability.

WANKEL ENGINE: A rotary type internal combustion engine.

WATER COLUMN: A reference term used in connection with a manometer.

WATT: A measuring unit of electrical power. It is obtained by multiplying amperes by volts.

WEDGE BLOCK: Combustion chamber design in which top of piston and surface of block form an angle.

WEIGHT TRANSFER EFFECT: Since center of gravity of vehicle is located above centers of wheel rotation, a sudden stoppage of vehicle tends to cause center of gravity to move forward, thus throwing more weight on front wheels and less on rear wheels.

WELDING: To join two pieces of metal by heating them to their melting point.

WET SLEEVE: A metal barrel or sleeve which is inserted in an engine cylinder in contact with coolant.

WHEEL CYLINDER: Unit for converting hydraulic fluid pressure to mechanical force for actuation of brake shoes and lining against brake drum.

WHEELBASE: Distance between centerlines of front and rear axles.

WHITE METAL: An alloy of tin, lead, and antimony having a low melting point and a low coefficient of friction.

WIRE HARNESS: Wires grouped together in a sleeve and interconnecting electrical components of vehicle.

WIRING DIAGRAM: A detailed drawing of all wiring, connections, and units that are connected together in an electrical circuit.

WORM GEAR: A shaft having an extremely coarse thread which is designed to operate in engagement with a toothed wheel, as a pair of gears.

WOT: Wide Open Throttle.

WRINGING-FIT: A fit with less clearance than for a running or sliding fit. Shaft will enter hole by means of twisting and pushing by hand.

WRIST PIN: See PISTON PIN.

INDEX